Racial and Cultural Minorities

REVISED EDITION

HARPER'S SOCIAL SCIENCE SERIES

Under the Editorship of

F. Stuart Chapin

Racial and Cultural Minorities

AN ANALYSIS OF PREJUDICE AND DISCRIMINATION

REVISED EDITION

George Eaton Simpson

AND

J. Milton Yinger

OBERLIN COLLEGE

Harper & Brothers

PUBLISHERS   NEW YORK

TO

E. B. S.

AND

W. M. Y.

CONTENTS

Part III. Prejudice, Discrimination, and
Democratic Values

PREFACE TO THE
—— FIRST EDITION ——

Books, monographs, and articles dealing with prejudice and discrimination and with the place of racial and cultural minorities in a social structure are now very numerous. Many of them are of excellent quality, and the scope of their coverage is so wide that no one volume can hope even to indicate the range of materials. It was with some hesitance, therefore, that the writers undertook the present study that might seem simply to add one more title to an already unmanageable bibliography.

Two important questions, however, have encouraged us to believe that another analysis of minority groups might be of value. First, the very quantity of present studies increases the problem of synthesis—of relating the various analyses to each other and to a systematic group of principles that underlie them all. Many of the studies are highly specialized, with reference both to the groups which they examine and to the concepts and explanatory principles which they employ. Only by bringing them into a common framework of analysis can the valid observations be separated from the errors and exaggerations and the omissions be pointed up. This volume certainly makes no claim to having examined all the minorities for whom analyses are available and significant; its materials refer largely, although not entirely (references to Europe, Asia, and Africa are made at many points), to the United States; and, when a choice has had to be made for sake of brevity, it refers to the Negro group—the largest minority in the United States and that for which the most extensive studies are available. There is a fairly intensive analysis, however, of the Jewish minority, and references to American Indians and Americans of Mexican, Italian, Japanese, and Chinese descent, among others, occur frequently. It is our hope, moreover, that a larger share of the principles involved in majority-minority relations and in the development of prejudice and discrimination have been brought into our analysis. If this hope is realized, the reader interested in an intensive study of a minority-majority situation not dealt with in this volume will have been furnished some guiding concepts for his own work. He may be less likely to adopt an oversimplified, one-factor view and less likely to study one situation in isolation from the total society of which it is a part.

The second question that seems to us to demand further attention in the literature on majority-minority relations is the connection between studies in this field and the whole area of the sciences of human behavior. Valid analyses of prejudice and discrimination must rest squarely on broader principles of human behavior. We have consistently tried to write from the point of view that the material we were discussing was simply one manifestation of the total complex of human life, not to be understood as an isolated or unique phenomenon. Every proposition concerning intergroup relations should be harmonious with, in fact a part of, the general principles being developed in social science. If we have succeeded in any measure in achieving this aim, the careful student should gain from this volume, not only some understanding of prejudice and of the place of minorities in the social structure, but also a grasp of the nature of personality, the types of social interaction, the functions of institutions, and the meaning of culture. It is also our hope that he will be alerted to some of the problems of methodology faced by social scientists today. A fairly large share of the writings in the field of majority-minority relations are quite uncritical of the sources of their material—the objectivity of the reporting, the extent to which it is typical, the usefulness of the concepts employed, and the kinds of causal inference that are justified. To take account of these methodological and logical problems requires more tentative statements, the addition of qualifying phrases, the recognition of the need for more carefully controlled studies on which one can place more reliance. This caution makes the analysis less clear-cut and sharp; but to fail to take into account methodological problems is to give an impression of finality that no science, and particularly no science of human behavior, can accept.

Our indebtedness to the hundreds of scholars and action leaders in majority-minority relations is partially indicated by the Bibliography. The authors are also indebted, in informal but no less important ways, to many teachers, students, and friends, of many races and groups, who have given stimulation, encouragement, and insights which may find some imperfect expression in this book.

Oberlin College
January, 1953

GEORGE E. SIMPSON
J. MILTON YINGER

PREFACE TO THE
— REVISED EDITION —

Events have moved swiftly in racial and cultural relations in the last several years. In almost every area of the world, existing patterns of intergroup relations are being challenged. And the flood of events has been matched by an increasing amount of study and research by social scientists.

In preparing this revision, the authors have concentrated both on recent theoretical developments, experimental studies and empirical research, and also on the dramatic changes in majority-minority affairs. They have given special attention to studies of the causes of prejudice, to desegregation in education, to the place of minorities in the economic, political, and legal processes in the United States, and to the efforts to reduce prejudice and discrimination. About half the chapters have been extensively revised, with slight revisions in each of the others.

In the five years since the appearance of the first edition, the authors have profited not only from the large amount of new published material, but from many letters and conversations with persons who have used the book. Once again they have been made aware of how thoroughly a work of this kind is the product of the collaborative efforts of many persons.

Oberlin
January, 1958

GEORGE E. SIMPSON
J. MILTON YINGER

PART I

The Causes and Consequences

of Prejudice and Discrimination

CHAPTER I

Types of Majority-Minority Situations

Wherever one looks in these dramatic times, the puzzling phenomena of intergroup relations leap to attention. Civil rights, prejudice, desegregation, discrimination, cultural pluralism, apartheid, genocide—these are terms the student of contemporary life must learn to use. England, with a steady migration of persons from Africa and the West Indies, finds herself faced with problems of a color bar; France, struggling with an enormously difficult question in Algiers, which she can neither hold nor relinquish, is caught in part by the antipathies between Algerians of French and of African descent; Indonesians cheer the expulsion of the Dutch, only to find themselves dominated by internal groups scarcely less "imperialistic"; the South African government boldly proclaims a policy of apartheid but keeps stumbling over the problem of economic interdependence; the United States, rapidly becoming a thoroughly urbanized society, discovers that desegregation is a national question; Russia, faced with difficult problems at home and a vast restlessness among her satellites, reverts again to anti-Semitism. How shall we seek to understand these developments? To what system of concepts shall we turn?

Throughout the course of his existence, man has been struggling to understand the world, to predict the sequence of events, and to achieve some control over the forces that operate in the world around him. In the last few centuries, the method of inquiry that we call science has occupied a more and more important place in this struggle. Slowly we have begun to grasp the meaning of some of the complicated interactions of the natural world. Only recently, however, have the efforts to understand through science been turned toward man himself. Other methods of inquiry, to be sure, have contributed, and continue to contribute, to our understanding of man. Some of these methods are not sharply distinct from science. They often involve careful observation and an acute understanding of the variables influencing a given situation. The work of the historian, the philosopher, the artist demands our careful attention. The particular role of the scientist is to contribute to our knowledge by isolating, one by one, each of the many variables that are involved in every situation and then studying the effects of their interaction. Either through laboratory manipulation or by the analysis of comparative situations, the scientist measures the influence of each factor alone and in interaction with other variables.

This book is an attempt to study one aspect of man's behavior from the point of view of contemporary science—particularly from the point of view of sociology, anthropology, and social psychology. For decades men have been studying and observing the puzzling phenomena of intergroup relations; but recently these studies have begun to turn from description to analysis, from isolated observation to controlled observation that begins to place the study of intergroup relations within the framework of the social sciences. Good will and a high interest are no longer sufficient to understand the complicated problems of "race relations" (as this area of human behavior is frequently called). We must keep ourselves thoroughly in touch with the methods of science and the total body of information that makes up the emerging knowledge of the sciences of man.

One needs to make no lengthy defense of the great significance of the study of intergroup relations—the study of prejudice and discrimination with their causes and consequences. Its importance is a matter of daily observation. Pick up the daily paper or read the record of an international debate or watch the actions of a crowd: prejudice is there, sometimes unrecognized, but more often today defended or attacked— for we are becoming self-conscious about our prejudices.

Will Christians stand up and be counted for adherence to the DIVINE RULE OF SEGREGATION, ordained by the Creator in His Creation, or will they yield to the guile of the (arch) enemy, atheistic Communism, and blaspheme and defy Him?

SUMTER L. LOWRY, in his candidacy for governor, dedicates himself to the maintenance in Florida of the Creator's divine law of SEGREGATION, and vows that if elected to join our State with the others of the South and fight to the bitter end the forces of atheistic Communism now plotting our disruption and destruction.

IN CONCLUSION: Besides working for Christian civic righteousness, the writer sells real estate in the fast developing area west of Coral Gables. . . .[1]

There is no Arab in his right mind who believes that there can be peace,

[1] A political advertisement in the Miami Herald, May 3, 1956; quoted by H. D. Price, *The Negro and Southern Politics. A Chapter of Florida History*, New York University Press, 1957, p. 85.

stability and security in the Middle East, until Israel is wiped off the face of the map of the region, and Palestine is returned without reservation to its former status. No one in the Arab World disputes the fact that the Arab nations are in a state of war with Israel and with World Jewry. This state of war will be maintained until justice is restored in spite of the artificial agreements of the armistice which have been imposed upon us.[2]

The Los Angeles Times, 1942: "A viper is nonetheless a viper wherever the egg is hatched. . . . So, a Japanese American born of Japanese parents, nurtured upon Japanese traditions, living in a transplanted Japanese atmosphere and thoroughly inoculated with Japanese . . . ideals, notwithstanding his nominal brand of accidental citizenship almost inevitably and with the rarest exceptions grows up to be a Japanese, and not an American in his . . . ideas, and is . . . menacing . . . unless . . . hamstrung. Thus, while it might cause injustice to a few to treat them all as potential enemies . . . I cannot escape the conclusion . . . that such treatment . . . should be accorded to each and all of them while we are at war with their race."[3]

In Nürnberg's warm, well-lighted courtroom, the lawyers tried to get the point across—these Nazis had killed 6,000,000 Jews. . . . This was no report from a refugee agency. Here it was, right out of the Nazi files. The Gestapo chief Jew catcher, Adolf Eichmann said that 4,000,000 died in concentration camps and 2,000,000 were killed by extermination squads. Fat, brutal Hans Frank counted 3,500,000 Jews in western Poland in 1941, "perhaps 100,000" in 1944. If the untellable crime could ever be told, Nürnberg's evidence, as clear and specific as last week's robbery, had told it. But its immense inhumanity made it almost immune to translation into human terms.[4]

In Humphreys County [Mississippi] Negroes were not even permitted to pay their poll tax until 1953. When seventeen Negroes finally brought suit against the sheriff, a Federal court ordered him to end this practice, and in 1953, 485 Negroes succeeded in paying their poll tax. But these 485 soon found themselves the victims of a campaign of pressure and intimidation, and only two hundred of them actually registered. A year later the number was down to 126. The newly formed Citizens' Council began circulating lists of the registrants and still more withdrew. As the 1955 gubernatorial primary approached, Negro registration dropped to ninety-two. These few held firm until the shotguns came out.

On May 7, 1955, one of the county's Negro leaders, the Reverend George W. Lee, was shot in the face by a shotgun fired from a car passing close to the one he was driving. His murderers were never apprehended. The sheriff said that Lee probably had had a heart attack and was killed in the

[2] An editorial in the Jordanian newspaper, El Jihad, 1955, quoted by Arnold Forster and Benjamin R. Epstein, Cross-Currents, Doubleday & Company, Inc., 1956, p. 363.

[3] Quoted by Alexander Leighton, The Governing of Men, Princeton University Press, 1945, pp. 17–18.

[4] Time, December 24, 1945, p. 29.

crash that followed, and that the lead pellets in his face were probably fillings from his teeth. . . .

No Negroes vote in Humphreys County today.[5]

The national president of Alpha Xi Delta sorority, commenting on the pledging of a Negro girl by the University of Vermont chapter, 1946: "Life is selective, and maybe it's just as well to learn it while we're young. . . . I'm sorry this happened both for [Crystal's] sake and for ours. But I expect the girls up there thought she was an exotic and interesting person— the way you would think of someone from a foreign country. . . . When other fraternities decide to [admit Negroes] we probably will too. We don't try to be different."[6]

Thus the stories range, from "polite" exclusion to vicious mass murders. Our task is to try to understand such phenomena as these. Do they have anything in common? What are the factors in individual personality and group conflict that account for these expressions of prejudice and discrimination? What various forms do prejudice and discrimination take?

It would be a mistake to assume from the incidents quoted above that prejudice is universal or that there is no evidence on the other side. There are many variations in time and space; opposition to discrimination and the absence of categorizing prejudices are also newsworthy items in the contemporary scene.

A Negro educator who became the first of his race to defeat a white man at the polls here [Atlanta, Georgia] in this century said today his victory means Southerners are "far ahead of what some people think."

Dr. Rufus E. Clement, president of Atlanta University, defeated J. H. Landers for a place on the Board of Education Landers had held 25 years. . . . Clement defeated Landers by 22,595 votes to 13,936 in the city-wide election. The Negro figures that less than half of his total votes were cast by members of his race. . . .

The last time a Negro was elected over a white man here was in 1871 during the reconstruction period.[7]

"The only way to sell homes in the same project to both Negroes and whites is to believe in it. I live in my own project. So does my sales manager."

That's how Morris Milgram built a 158-home project in a Philadelphia suburb and sold it to 55% whites and 45% Negroes. . . .

"No one has moved out because they didn't like their neighbors. Since completion of the first home in the spring of 1955, we've had three homes resold. Two owners took jobs in other cities. One inherited a lot of money and left the area," he said.[8]

[5] Edward Gamarekian, "A Report from the South on the Negro Voter," *The Reporter*, June 27, 1957, p. 9.
[6] Quoted in *Time*, May 6, 1946, p. 90.
[7] *Arkansas Gazette* (Little Rock), May 14, 1953.
[8] *The Cleveland Press*, May 10, 1957.

Today, education is perhaps the most important function of state and local governments. . . . It is the very foundation of good citizenship. To-day, it is a principal instrument in awakening the child to cultural values, in preparing him for later professional training, and in helping him to ad-just normally to his environment. . . .

Does segregation of children in public schools solely on the basis of race, even though the physical facilities and other "tangible" factors may be equal, deprive the children of the minority group of equal educational op-portunities? We believe that it does. . . . To separate them from others of similar age and qualifications solely because of their race generates a feel-ing of inferiority as to their status in the community that may affect their hearts and minds in a way unlikely ever to be undone. . . .

We conclude that in the field of public education the doctrine of "sep-arate but equal" has no place. Separate educational facilities are inherently unequal. Therefore, we hold that the plaintiffs and others similarly situated for whom the actions have been brought are, by reason of the segregation complained of, deprived of the equal protection of the laws guaranteed by the Fourteenth Amendment.[9]

A report on race relations in Bahia, Brazil: "Today one finds at Bahia a freely competitive order in which individuals compete for position largely on the basis of personal merit and favorable family circumstances. Individual competence tends to overbalance ethnic origin as a determinant of social status.

"However, the darker portion of the population . . . have had to contend with the serious handicap that their parents or grandparents or other im-mediate ancestors began on the bottom as propertyless slaves of the white ruling class and now bear constantly with them, by reason of color and other physical characteristics, indelible badges of this slave ancestry, ineradi-cable symbols of low status. It is not surprising, therefore, to find that the relatively unmixed blacks are still concentrated in the low-pay, low-status employments and that they gradually disappear as one ascends the occupa-tional scale, until in the upper levels they are seldom to be found. . . .

"But it is just these few individuals who indicate most clearly the actual racial situation in Bahia. The Negroes began at the bottom. The acceptance, then, of an occasional black, a few dark mulattoes as well as numerous light mixed-bloods into the upper circles points conclusively to the fact that if a person has ability and general competence, the handicap of color can be, and is constantly being, overcome."[10]

The Rapidly Changing Contemporary Scene

The student of race relations is confronted with a rapidly changing situation, both as to the facts of prejudice and discrimination and as to our knowledge of the meaning of those facts. In the enormous inter-national struggles of our time, with their power and ideological aspects,

[9] Supreme Court of the United States, May 17, 1954.
[10] Donald Pierson, *Negroes in Brazil*, University of Chicago Press, 1942, pp. 177, 204.

the role of minority groups inevitably became tremendously important. How maintain national unity? How win or preserve the coöperation of colonial or former colonial peoples? How adjust to the rising literacy, power, and demands of minority groups everywhere? How preserve and extend a democratic ideology in the face of its obvious violations in almost every land? Such questions might, perhaps, have been treated casually a generation ago; they have leaped, now, to the forefront of international attention and cannot be disregarded. The result is a ferment in minority-majority relations of greater importance than the modern world has witnessed before.

In the United States, the national compromise over the "Negro question" that lasted for two generations has been broken by changes in the nature of American society and is being intensely reëxamined. Crucial Supreme Court decisions, changes in the practices of labor unions, the migration and industrialization of an important part of the Negro labor force, the demands made by our position on the international scene—these and many other factors are forcing us to work out a new and more effective adjustment among the races.

More than 500 groups are working to reduce discrimination in the United States. At least 16 states and 36 cities have fair employment practices laws. The industrialization of the South has been enormously speeded up since 1940. Tens of thousands of new industrial concerns have been added to its economy, increasing its income by several billions, shifting its population toward the cities, breaking the status patterns of Jim Crow that rested heavily upon the social structure of the plantation. The North and West have had a rapid increase in the size of their Negro populations. Sharp disputes and conflicts as well as gains have accompanied these changes. But as Blumer says: ". . . Race relations cannot avoid being incorporated to the full in the unsettling and dynamic changes that are part and parcel of the industrialized and urbanized mass society that is emerging in the world today."[11]

Important political changes (1,400,000 Negroes voted in the South in 1956), international changes (the violation of human rights, not only in Hungary and South Africa but in the United States, is a subject of great interest in the United Nations), educational changes (between 1954 and 1957, schools enrolling one-third of a million Negroes and one and three-quarter million whites shifted from a segregated to an integrated basis), religious changes (the virtual disregard of the problems of minorities by most churches is slowly giving way to official pronouncements deploring prejudice and discrimination and to some action programs)—these are illustrative of the changing patterns of

[11] Herbert Blumer in A. W. Lind (ed.), *Race Relations in World Perspective*, University of Hawaii Press, 1955, p. 17.

Negro-white relations in the United States.[12] We shall examine these trends in detail in later chapters.

The status of other minorities and the conceptions of how best to deal with the diverse peoples in this country are also changing. During World War I many people were made aware of the problem of minorities by the discovery here, in time of crisis, of partially assimilated national groups. They were shocked at the failure of the "melting-pot" idea. One reaction was antiforeignism, a demand for tightened immigration restrictions. Some few, however, began to wonder whether the melting-pot idea might not itself be inadequate, demanding, as it did, Americanization on quite narrow terms. Many of our immigrants, as Randolph Bourne points out, are not simply those who missed the *Mayflower* and came over on a later boat; when they did come they took a *Maiblume*, a *Fleur de Mai*, a *Fior di Maggio*, or a *Majblomst*. There were national, cultural, religious, and lingual differences to be accommodated. In a world of international tension and publicity, insistent "Americanization" of our national minorities, with the strong implication that their ways of doing things are queer, foolish, and unacceptable, is unlikely to be a successful procedure. Myrdal says that ". . . the Negro problem is not only America's greatest failure but also America's incomparably great opportunity for the future."[13] And in the same vein, Bourne declares: "To seek no other goal than the weary old nationalism, belligerent, exclusive, inbreeding . . . is to make patriotism a hollow sham. . . . The failure of the melting-pot, far from closing the great American democratic experiment, means that it has only just begun. . . . In a world which has dreamed of internationalism, we find that we have all unawares been building up the first international nation."[14]

Other facets of majority-minority relations are appearing rapidly in the contemporary world. Imperialistic domination of "native" peoples is running into self-contradictions and costs that have greatly weakened it. The 400-year period of colonial domination, at least by the West, is passing. (Russian domination of eastern Europe and parts of Asia, involving the more open use of force, more frequent manipulation of local political movements, and exploitation of an international ideology, shares some aspects of the old pattern. It adds, however, surveillance and control over the total life of the people that makes it in important ways a new phenomenon. Its survival seems to rest upon the possibility of a continuing monopolization of power.) The western nations have

[12] See Carey McWilliams, *Brothers Under the Skin*, Little, Brown & Company, rev. ed., 1951, pp. 3–58.

[13] Gunnar Myrdal, *An American Dilemma*, Harper & Brothers, 1944, p. 1021.

[14] Quoted in Alain Locke and B. J. Stern (eds.), *When Peoples Meet*, Hinds, Hayden and Eldredge, Inc., 1946, pp. 730–731.

found that the practical advantages of colonialism have sharply declined just at the time when the costs of maintaining the old pattern have vastly increased. Native labor is no longer so cheap and tractable; local political movements can be stopped only by costly suppression; the defense of colonies against rivals is difficult and expensive. During the period of domination there has been a diffusion of western ideas of nationalism, democracy, and freedom that have armed the colonies against their overlords. Meanwhile, the growth of democratic movements in the mother countries themselves has weakened the colonial system. Many people have come to the conviction that lack of democracy anywhere endangers world peace.[15]

These forces, and others, are bringing important changes to the colonial world. Japan's effort to extend her imperial domination has been completely broken. China has freed herself from the extraterritorial privileges that many western nations demanded and held. (Protests against these privileges may be one of the factors in the rise of contemporary counterimperialism in China; she may have learned her lessons from the West too well.) India, Pakistan, Burma, and Ghana have won dominion status in the British Commonwealth, and a large part of the East Indies has achieved a similar relationship with the Netherlands. The Philippines have become independent of the United States; Puerto Rico has been granted a larger measure of self-government; and the United States, through her Good Neighbor Policy, has modified the dominating aspects of her relationship to Central and South America. Many of the new and renewed nations of the world are inhabited primarily by colored persons. Thus "race relations" increasingly takes on the pattern of contact between sovereign peoples. This shift is important, not only in international affairs, but in the internal processes of many nations.

These examples are simply illustrative of what has taken place in the status of colonial "minorities" in the last few years. Discontent is high in eastern Europe, in the Near East, in Africa; and we can expect significant developments in the next few years. All of this does not mean that domination across national boundaries is on the decrease, but only that the pattern is changing. Communist-style imperialism has greatly increased in the last few decades. Nor does it indicate the growth of democracy, for the decline of imperialism is not necessarily a gain for the majority of human beings; it may represent only a shift in power from an external to an internal ruling class. Iran nationalizes oil in the name of the welfare of her peasants; Egypt abrogates a treaty with Great Britain concerning control of the Suez Canal on the same grounds; but the patterns of domination within these nations are scarcely changed.

[15] Raymond Kennedy, "The Colonial Crisis and the Future," in Ralph Linton (ed.), *The Science of Man in the World Crisis*, Columbia University Press, 1945, pp. 338–346.

J. H. Boeke describes this situation well: ". . . There is abundant evidence that often new national governments, behind the screen of nationalism, fight colonialism by taking over its policy. But it is no longer colonialism since foreign capitalists have been eliminated. The small villager and the poor consumer who are the victims of this game of puss in the corner have every reason to remember the Dutch proverb that it is all the same whether one is bitten by a she-cat or a he-cat."[16]

Policies concerning industrialization, landholding, imports, granting of credit, and the like, may be primarily in the interests of the new internal elite, as Boeke points out, the masses being paid in slogans of nationalism and anticolonialism. One must be alert to the domination factor even in the decisions of the United Nations, for they represent, to some degree, the coercive power of strong nations over weaker ones. This coercion seems to the authors to be far more mindful of common interests, far more responsive to the rights of smaller nations, than any previous international arrangement. But one must not overlook the power element that remains.

We cannot at this point describe other aspects of the contemporary scene in minority-majority relations. Eastern Europe is going through a new phase in its struggles with the question of the dozens of national and cultural minorities living there. The Zionist movement and the founding of the nation of Israel have added a new dimension to the question of the status of Jews in many lands. Wherever we look, new adjustments to the age-old problems of group interaction are being tried. Such a time of change can yield valued insights into the nature of the subject with which we are concerned in this book. Fixed notions of causes and cures are obviously inadequate for the student today. Equipped with tentativeness and modesty we can, with the knowledge available, begin to grasp the basic nature of intergroup relations, of prejudice and discrimination, of hierarchies of power within and between societies.

The Changing Scientific View of Intergroup Relations

The speed with which majority-minority relations are changing in the contemporary world is matched by the development of scientific theories in the field. The concepts and beliefs of competent scholars only a few decades ago are now looked upon as entirely inadequate; and the writings of many of the men who were most widely read are seen today as scarcely more than elaborate rationalizations for existing stereotypes and prejudices. (This fact of rapid change in our conceptions of the nature of intergroup relations should encourage us to hold present hypotheses and theories—including those advanced in this book—

---

[16] A. W. Lind (ed.), *op. cit.*, p. 73.

tentatively. They may prove to be inadequate to account for the evidence of tomorrow.)

We shall not undertake here a history of "race" theories; but a brief statement may indicate the recency of scientific views and help to show the relationship between theories in this field and the total intellectual and power aspects of the environment. There is no clear line between the writers who were propagandists for the belief in "white" supremacy and more objective scholars who were led into error by inadequate theories and insufficient evidence. One can, however, make a rough distinction between the two on the basis of the way they handle evidence and by studying the change, or absence of change, in the theories of their successors. The followers of the propagandists express the same faith, repeat the same arguments, for they "know" the answers; those who build upon the work of scholars revise, discard, and seek to correct as well as to supplement the work of their predecessors. At various points in the chapters that follow we shall refer to the work of such well-known propagandists as Count de Gobineau, Houston Stewart Chamberlain, Lothrop Stoddard, and Madison Grant. For two or three generations their type of analysis of "race relations" was widely circulated among the literate group and helped to reinforce the traditional views of millions who had never heard of these authors. The work of such writers was intellectually respectable only a few decades ago. Their contemporary successors, however, have no such standing. Even the "popular" intellectual supports to prejudice are crumbling.

Meanwhile, professional students of human behavior have also been struggling with the questions of majority-minority relations, and their various concepts have reflected their general theoretical and value orientations. Lester F. Ward, often thought of as the founder of American sociology, was an environmentalist and a firm believer in the value of social science in directing social change. Consequently he minimized the biological factors in race differences and did not believe that the existing patterns of race relations were inevitably fixed in the mores. He doubtless underestimated the tenacity of prejudice, but many of his conceptions, although inadequately supported by evidence, seem quite sound today. A more influential writer at the turn of the century, however, emphasized very strongly the rigidity of the pattern of intergroup relations. William Graham Sumner adopted a fatalistic attitude toward social change that was widely accepted: race relations are fixed in the mores; scientific knowledge, legislation, reform efforts can have little effect. Only recently has the reduced applicability of this conception of rigid mores to modern urban industrial society been adequately emphasized. Sumner developed his theories largely by the analysis of relatively stable primitive societies. Their overly simplified transference to modern societies continues, even today, to block a thorough understanding of the nature of minority-majority relations.

In 1910, a man who became a highly respected scholar in the field, by keeping up with the evidence and the changing theories, took a position that was very inadequate. As Franklin Frazier says: "When one views today the opinions expressed in the book [*Social and Mental Traits of the Negro*], it is clear that they reflect not only outmoded conceptions concerning primitive people but all the current popular prejudices concerning the Negro." At the same time another man who was to become a well-known scholar, in *Sociology and Modern Social Problems* ". . . assumed that the Negro has a 'racial' temperament and that his 'shiftlessness and sensuality' are partly due to heredity and that he is inferior in his adaptiveness to a complex civilization. The infiltration of white blood is responsible for ambition and superiority on the one hand and vice and immorality on the other."[17]

During the First World War and for a few years thereafter some of the psychologists working with intelligence test scores were so convinced of their validity—as measures of inherited intelligence, unaffected by experience—that they accepted them as definite proof of racial differences. Negroes made much lower scores on these tests on the average; so did American Indians, Mexicans, Italians, and other groups. We shall discuss the validity of intelligence test scores in the next chapter; we need to say here only that virtually all psychologists today insist that comparisons are meaningless except within a group that has very similar background, experience, and status.

Scarcely more than three decades ago the authors of one of the most important textbooks in sociology wrote: "It is evident that there is in race prejudice, as distinguished from class and caste prejudice, an instinctive factor based on the fear of the unfamiliar and uncomprehended."[18]

Alongside such inadequate conceptions as these, more valid ideas began to appear, occasionally before the First World War and more often since that time. W. I. Thomas and Robert E. Park, although in error at many points, related the study of race relations to general questions of social structure and social process. More recently, other dimensions of social scientific analysis—particularly the social psychological—have been added by the work of many researchers. The cumulative effect of the contributions of Charles S. Johnson, Louis Wirth, John Dollard, E. B. Reuter, R. M. MacIver, Gordon Allport, Otto Klineberg, Gunnar Mydral, Kurt Lewin, Carey McWilliams, Donald Young, E. Franklin Frazier, W. Lloyd Warner, and many others is to furnish us with a rich fund of theoretical and descriptive work on which to base

[17] E. Franklin Frazier, "Sociological Theory and Race Relations," *American Sociological Review*, June, 1947, p. 267. See also E. B. Reuter, "Racial Theory," *American Journal of Sociology*, May, 1945, pp. 452–461.
[18] Robert Park and Ernest Burgess, *Introduction to the Science of Sociology*, University of Chicago Press, 2nd ed., 1924, p. 578.

our attempts to understand the important phenomena with which we are concerned. The work of many of these men will appear frequently in the pages of this book. If we cannot speak yet of a mature science of intergroup relations, thoroughly integrated with a systematic science of man, we do have the fundamental parts of such a discipline and can profit greatly by studying them with care.

What Is Prejudice?

Many writers have tried to define the key concepts involved in the study of intergroup relations. Sharp disagreements have frequently resulted from differences in definition, partly because of a misunderstanding of the nature of definitions. Definitions do not reveal what the data in question "really are." The phenomena of the world are not divided into neat, mutually exclusive types which, if we study hard enough, we can discover. They flow endlessly one into another, by minute gradations, and any definition which tries to draw a sharp line is bound to be arbitrary to some degree. The phenomena included within the definition are not exactly alike, but only more or less alike; some phenomena excluded are also alike—but presumably less rather than more. In defining relations as complicated as those with which we are dealing in this study, with so many variables involved, one is bound to run into disagreement over what is more and what is less.

Yet definitions are necessary for communication. We must remember simply that they are "constructs of convenience," as George Lundberg calls them, and to some degree empirically arbitrary.

For our purposes, we shall define prejudice as an emotional, rigid attitude (a predisposition to respond to a certain stimulus in a certain way) toward a group of people. They may be a group only in the mind of the prejudiced person; that is, he categorizes them together, although they may have little similarity or interaction. Prejudices are thus attitudes, but not all attitudes are prejudices. They both contain the element of prejudgment, but prejudiced attitudes have an affective or emotional quality that not all attitudes possess. This aspect has been emphasized by a number of writers. W. F. Ogburn stressed the way prejudice selects some facts for emphasis, completely blinds one to other facts. Walter Lippmann, in his famous analysis of stereotypes, made a similar point. He showed how prejudice causes one to look upon all members of a "group" as if they were alike. New experiences are fitted into the old categories by selecting only those cues which harmonize with the prejudgment or stereotype. Prejudiced attitudes, because of their emotional quality, have a relative unmodifiability that is not characteristic of all attitudes. Many people have attitudes toward various kinds of automobiles (predispositions to respond favorably or

(no)

unfavorably to their conceptions of certain types of cars). These may be defended with a good deal of emotion, but far more often they are subject to change. An unfavorable attitude toward a given make of automobile may shift quite readily when one has a series of favorable experiences—or a gift from one's father-in-law—that bring new facts into the situation.

Are all attitudes that are heavily laden with emotion, then, to be considered prejudices? Is belief in democracy or the value of the scientific method a prejudice? Certainly they involve predispositions to respond to these stimuli in a particular way. Something is to be gained by seeing the similarities between value stands and tastes and what we are calling prejudices. There are sufficient differences, however, to make it seem wise to the present writers to classify such attitudes in a different category. By prejudice we shall mean a rigid, emotional attitude toward a human group.

Prejudice involves not only prejudgment but, as Vickery and Opler point out, misjudgment as well. It is categorical thinking that systematically misinterprets the facts. Again, not all misjudgment is prejudice. Prejudice is misjudgment of the members of a supposed human group; it is socially oriented action. One may misjudge the speed of an approaching car, but one is anxious to correct the error. Prejudice is a misjudgment that one defends.[19] Gordon Allport takes a similar view in stating that when a preëxisting attitude is so strong and inflexible that it seriously distorts perception and judgment, one has a prejudice.

The limitation of the meaning of the term "prejudice" to human interaction has some etymological justification. As Kimball Young points out, the word comes from the Latin *prejudicum*—a preceding judgment. "It took on a more special meaning when it came to refer to a judicial examination in Rome held before a trial as a means of determining the status of the would-be litigants. This status-defining function of prejudice has never been lost."[20] Prejudice puts an individual "in his place."

Many writers have worked on refinements of the term in order to isolate what seems to be a more homogeneous group of phenomena for inclusion. Communication is made more accurate by limiting a term to homogeneous elements. If I say, "Will you bring me that piece of furniture from the next room," I may get anything from a footstool to a grand piano. If I ask for a small chair, I'm quite likely to get what I want. Prejudice is a "furniture" kind of word. As it is normally used, it includes a wide variety of phenomena. Efforts to make it more

[19] See William Vickery and Morris Opler, "A Redefinition of Prejudice for Purposes of Social Science Research," *Human Relations*, 1948, vol. 1, pp. 419–428.
[20] Kimball Young, *Social Psychology*, Appleton-Century-Crofts, 2nd ed., 1944, p. 258.

precise are very useful, provided their arbitrary quality is recognized and one does not quarrel with a person who makes a different limitation based on different criteria.

In isolating homogeneous phenomena, one can either talk about types of prejudice ($prejudice_1$, $prejudice_2$, $prejudice_3$) or find different terms to assign to the related, yet different, phenomena (prejudice for one type, intolerance for another, stereotypy for a third, for example).

Robin Williams, Jr., distinguishes between prejudices based on functional differences in the social order or real differences in value, on the one hand, and those that emphasize stereotypes centered on some symbol, such as skin color, that has no functional significance, on the other. Thus for a democrat to be prejudiced against communists or fascists is different from his being prejudiced against Japanese—not entirely different, to be sure, but sufficiently so to require separation in our vocabularies ($prejudice_1$ and $prejudice_2$). It is the latter type that is the subject of this book.

Even in this narrower meaning prejudice is a blanket concept, covering a variety of concrete phenomena. The prejudice may be mild or violent. There is a contrast between prejudice manifested against groups with whom one has had no personal contact, and against those with whom contact is intensive and continuous. There is the prejudice of the provincial—to anything strange, different, "foreign"—and the rather different prejudice of the dweller in cosmopolitan centers. . . . There is prejudice based on conformity to the social customs of a group as against the prejudice, anchored in deep aggressive needs in the personality, which may persist even in the face of group pressure. There is the prejudice of economic or political opportunism, often calculating and impersonal, in contrast to the fanaticism of the religious or cultural zealot. There is the prejudice manifest in a specific idée fixe concerning a particular group, on the one hand, and the prejudice expressive of generalized antipathy to out-groups, on the other. Even the prejudice which arises primarily out of individual psychological needs appears in many forms; it may serve, for example, as a projection of repressed hatreds and other "antisocial" urges of the individual, a prop for ego-level or sense of self-esteem, a defense against repressed sexual drives, or a method of winning group approval.[21]

Most of the distinctions that Williams draws are based on analysis of the causes and functions of prejudice—a subject with which we shall be concerned in several chapters. Recognition of the diversity of the phenomena with which we are dealing, in terms of causes and functions, is essential to understanding and control. Our analysis and our vocabulary must reflect that diversity.

Some writers prefer to distinguish among the varieties of related phenomena by using different terms, rather than by describing types

[21] Robin Williams, Jr., *The Reduction of Intergroup Tensions*, Social Science Research Council, 1947, pp. 37–38.

and degrees of "prejudice." Ackerman and Jahoda, for example, distinguish between prejudice and stereotypy:

> Prejudice . . . is a term applied to categorical generalizations based on inadequate data and without sufficient regard for individual differences. . . . But inherent in the process of forming prejudgments is the danger of stereotyped thinking. The stereotype is distinguished from the prejudgment only by a greater degree of rigidity. Prejudgment occurs where facts are not available. But stereotypy is a process which shows little concern for facts even when they are available.
> Prejudice in its narrowest sense is distinct from prejudgment and stereotypy. It is a sub-category of prejudgment and it uses stereotypy but it is not identical with either. In the psychological context . . . , *prejudice is a pattern of hostility in interpersonal relations which is directed against an entire group, or against its individual members; it fulfills a specific irrational function for its bearer.*[22]

It is the last phrase of this quotation that requires attention. It limits the term "prejudice" more sharply than most definitions—to irrational personality factors. This is quite legitimate, provided other terms are indicated for *closely related* phenomena. Ackerman and Jahoda, in the study from which this definition is taken, are concerned primarily with anti-Semitism. They write:

> If a person alleges that Jews are economically powerful, he is employing stereotyped thinking. He may be right or wrong; if sufficient facts are presented to him, he may change the content of his stereotype to saying: Jews are not powerful economically. But neither of these two statements is in itself a sufficient indication of prejudice. Only when there is evidence that his stereotypes are used as rationalizations for an irrational hostility rooted in his own personality are we talking of prejudice. That anti-Semitism in the cases here investigated is a prejudice in the sense of this definition, and not just a prejudgment or a manifestation of stereotyped thinking, is the main hypothesis of this investigation.[23]

This statement shows an awareness of the arbitrary quality of a definition; but it also reflects a belief on the part of the authors, shown throughout their book, that they are analyzing the "basic" or "fundamental" cause of anti-Semitism when they study personality factors. If their definition of prejudice is used, one must be alert to the other forces causing anti-Semitism. It is prejudice—plus. The fact that they have taken over what is doubtless the primary term—prejudice—to refer to the phenomena with which they are mainly concerned seems to reflect a theoretical limitation.

The tendency for definitions to reflect theoretical positions is shown

[22] Nathan Ackerman and Marie Jahoda, *Anti-Semitism and Emotional Disorder,* Harper & Brothers, 1950, pp. 3–4.
[23] *Ibid.,* p. 4.

clearly by the very different interpretation of the relationship between prejudice and anti-Semitism that Oliver Cox makes. He believes that economic forces are the fundamental ones in determining the patterns of intergroup relations that we are discussing. He is also concerned primarily with race relations. He therefore uses the basic term "prejudice" to refer to attitudes that facilitate economic exploitation of racial minorities. Unlike Ackerman and Jahoda, Cox declares that anti-Semitism is not prejudice, but intolerance:

Anti-Semitism, to begin with, is clearly a form of social intolerance, which attitude may be defined as an unwillingness on the part of a dominant group to tolerate the beliefs or practices of a subordinate group because it considers these beliefs and practices to be either inimical to group solidarity or a threat to the continuity of the status quo. Race prejudice, on the other hand, is a social attitude propagated among the public by an exploiting class for the purpose of stigmatizing some group as inferior so that the exploitation of either the group itself or its resources or both may be justified. Persecution and exploitation are the behavior aspects of intolerance and race prejudice respectively. In other words, race prejudice is the socio-attitudinal facilitation of a particular type of labor exploitation, while social intolerance is a reactionary attitude supporting the action of a society in purging itself of contrary cultural groups.[24]

That economic exploitation is importantly involved in majority-minority relations no one can doubt. That the term "prejudice" may be used to refer only to the attitudes that facilitate economic exploitation is also legitimate. But Cox, in his enthusiasm for the economic interpretation of human behavior, obscures the similarities between the various types of majority-minority relations and oversimplifies the causal complex. Thus he is led to such inaccurate and oversimplified statements as these:

Anti-Semitism is an attitude directed against the Jews because they are Jews, while race prejudice is an attitude directed against Negroes because they want to be something other than Negroes.
Probably the clearest distinction between intolerance and race prejudice is that the intolerant group welcomes conversion and assimilation, while the race-prejudiced group is antagonized by attempts to assimilate. . . .
Religious persecution and racial domination are categorically different social facts.[25]

It is wise to emphasize the variety of types of majority-minority relations, to isolate separate causes, and to develop a terminology based on these distinctions. But if this procedure leads to the claim that related phenomena are "categorically different social facts," it will block our ability to see interconnections. Science must search not only for dif-

[24] Oliver C. Cox, Caste, Class and Race, Doubleday & Company, Inc., 1948, p. 393.
[25] Ibid., pp. 394, 481.

ferences that lie behind superficial similarities, but also for similarities that may be disguised by superficial differences.

It is the contention of the present authors that the causes of antipathy between groups are *cumulative* and *interactive*. They prefer, in order to emphasize this relatedness, to use the term "prejudice" to refer to the total complex involved in the rigid prejudgment and misjudgment of groups. The discussion, then, must give full attention to the differences in types and variations in degree of prejudice. We shall be concerned with that problem in Chapters 3, 4, and 5.

The Relation of Discrimination to Prejudice

Prejudice is an attitude, a *tendency* to respond or a symbolic response. It may never involve overt action toward members of the minority group, either because no situation presents itself or, in situations where one might show antipathy, because other attitudes inhibit open expressions of hostility. You may have a strong prejudice against the residents of southwest Euthanasia, but since you have never met one of them, you have had no opportunity to express your attitude. A colored man may have a vigorous prejudice against white men, but in a large proportion of situations he disguises his feelings or gives them very indirect expression.

Thus prejudice must not be equated with discrimination. Yet they are closely related. Discrimination is "the differential treatment of individuals considered to belong to a particular social group."[26] One might discriminate against a member of a minority without feeling any prejudice; but almost certainly it would be because he believes other persons hold a prejudice. A businessman, for example, might refuse to accept clients from a minority group, despite his own lack of prejudice, because he thinks that their presence would injure his business. Ordinarily, however, discrimination is the overt expression of prejudice; it is the categorical treatment of a member of a group because he is a member of that group, and supposedly, therefore, of a particular type. Williams points out that it also involves some violation of an important institutional standard in a society: "Thus, except for the probable deviations around such social norms, it is expected in our society that occupational opportunity will be available on the basis of merit or ability, that all citizens are entitled to specified legal rights, that economic transactions will be carried out according to the rules of the market. Discrimination may be said to exist to the degree that individuals of a given group who are otherwise formally qualified are not treated in conformity with these nominally universal institutionalized codes."[27]

The word "discrimination" has a strange double meaning—one favor-

---

[26] Robin Williams, *op. cit.*, p. 39.
[27] *Ibid.*

able, the other unfavorable—in our society that sometimes blocks understanding. In 1947 the president of the National Interfraternity Conference (which refused to take action against discrimination in fraternities)
defended the refusal in these words: "I love the discriminating tongue,
the discriminating eye, and the discriminating ear, and, above all, the
discriminating mind and soul. The person for whom I can find no love
and respect is the indiscriminate person. To be indiscriminate is to be
common, to be vulgar."[28] He uses one meaning of the term to justify
the other. He makes it impossible to see that the kind of discrimination most fraternities show renders their members incapable of being
the kind of discriminating person he is acclaiming. It is precisely because fraternities treat all Chinese or Negroes or Jews as if they were
alike (discrimination$_1$) that they cannot see distinctions between
undesirable and desirable, attractive and unattractive, intelligent and
unintelligent members of minority groups (discrimination$_2$).

The distinction between tendency to act and overt action, between
prejudice and discrimination, has been emphasized strongly by a number
of writers in recent years. It has played a particularly important part in
the analyses of those who are working to reduce intergroup hostility.
They have pointed out that it is frequently possible to prevent discrimination—by making it unprofitable, painful, or simply unusual—
without reducing prejudice directly. We shall examine this problem in
Part III.

Analysis of the relationship between prejudice and discrimination can
also prevent an easy assumption of a particular causal connection between them. Behind many of the studies of "the prejudiced personality"
is the hypothesis that personal needs and insecurities, expressing themselves in prejudices, are the primary cause of discrimination. (It would
follow that any important reduction in discrimination requires large-
scale reduction of personal insecurity.) There is good evidence, however, that prejudice is in part the *result* of discrimination—a way of
rationalizing and getting rid of guilt feelings that arise when one has
treated an individual unfairly, according to one's own definition. By
emphasizing that conflicts over power and gain and traditional factors,
as well as personal insecurities, are involved in prejudice, we can more
readily understand the interaction between prejudice and discrimination.

McWilliams believes that our understanding of minority-majority
relations is being reduced by excessive attention to prejudice:

Race relations are not based on prejudice; prejudice is a by-product of
race relations—as influenced by other factors. Current psychological theories
of race relations, however, are almost exclusively concerned with prejudice,
which is discussed as though it were the cause of discrimination. . . . To
make a theory of the function of prejudice in the psychic economy of the

[28] Quoted by Carey McWilliams, *op. cit.*, p. 54.

individual do double duty as a theory of group discrimination is to confuse different, if related, levels of meaning. Case histories of every German would have failed to explain what happened to the Jews in Germany between 1918 and 1939. The clearest delineation of the personality types most susceptible to anti-Semitism will not explain why Jewish dentists find it almost impossible to practice dentistry in certain Western states. In the same way, concepts of social psychology are relevant to an understanding of race relations, but they do not explain the strategies by which certain groups maintain their dominance over other groups.[29]

The strong emphasis, in recent studies, on psychological explanations of prejudice, with consequent disregard of "power" factors, reflects, in McWilliams' judgment, our inability to study our society objectively in this time of crisis and conflict. It is safer to study individual personalities than the strategies of privileged social groups. Our only quarrel with McWilliams concerns his failure to emphasize the *interactive* aspects of the several causes of prejudice and discrimination. Why do some people, in the struggle for income or power, use group discrimination instead of some other weapon? Partly, no doubt, because they are equipped with prejudices that make discrimination seem reasonable.

Thus no one expression of the relationship between prejudice and discrimination is adequate:
1. There can be prejudice without discrimination.
2. There can be discrimination without prejudice.
3. Discrimination can be among the causes of prejudice.
4. Prejudice can be among the causes of discrimination.
5. Probably most frequently they are mutually reinforcing.

The need is for careful analysis of the conditions under which these various relationships prevail.

Prejudice and discrimination are the aspects of intergroup relations most frequently studied. Williams distinguishes a third dimension— group conflict. "Although often closely connected in life situations, these elements have a considerable range of independent variation."[30] There can be a great deal of prejudice and discrimination—for example, in a caste system—with relatively little open conflict. Attempts to reduce discrimination, on the other hand, may lead, at least in the short run, to *increased* conflict; and efforts to avoid conflict may take the form of accepting patterns of discrimination. On the whole, however, group conflict is an outgrowth of widespread prejudice and discrimination. It is particularly likely to occur in an open-class society, where the suppressed group have some hope of improving their status and the dominant group has some fear that the minorities may advance (and perhaps ambivalent feelings that they ought to advance).

---

[29] *Ibid.*, pp. 315–317; see also Arnold M. Rose, "Intergroup Relations vs. Prejudice," *Social Problems*, October, 1956, pp. 173–176.
[30] Robin Williams, *op. cit.*, p. 36.

In our discussion we must be alert both to the distinctions among prejudice, discrimination, and conflict and to their important interconnections. We shall sometimes use the term "prejudice" alone as an abbreviated reference to the whole pattern of intergroup antipathy when we are referring to situations where several forms occur together.

Types of Minorities

In some counties of Mississippi there are three times as many colored persons as white. Negroes make up an even higher proportion of the population of South Africa. For two centuries a handful of British dominated hundreds of millions of Indians. Yet we frequently refer to these situations as majority-minority situations—clearly meaning a pattern of relationship, the distribution of power, and not numbers. According to Louis Wirth: "We may define a minority as a group of people who, because of their physical or cultural characteristics, are singled out from the others in the society in which they live for differential and unequal treatment, and who therefore regard themselves as objects of collective discrimination. The existence of a minority in a society implies the existence of a corresponding dominant group with higher social status and greater privileges. Minority status carries with it the exclusion from full participation in the life of the society."[31]

From the perspective of the individual minority-group member, his status is characterized primarily by its categorical nature; he cannot resign or escape by merit. Whatever his unique characteristics, he is treated simply as one unit of a group by those of dominant status.

Minorities, however, are not all alike. They differ in the symbols which set them apart, in the nature of their relationship to the dominant group, and in their reactions to the situation. It was once thought that the difference in symbols was most important—that the study of racial minorities was different from the study of groups set apart by religion, nationality, or culture. While recognizing that symbolic differences do affect the nature of the interaction, we must see that it is the pattern of relationship that is crucial. Several variables affect that pattern, as Wirth points out. A situation in which there is only one minority will be different from one in which there are several. A single minority has to absorb all the anxieties and frustration of the dominant group and become the object of all its power manipulations. Where there are several minorities, as in the United States, some may escape relatively easily; a hierarchy develops among them. The majority will play one minority off against another—and this maneuver will affect the way minorities respond to one another.

The degree of difference in culture, language, and race is another

---

[31] Louis Wirth, in Ralph Linton (ed.), *op. cit.*, p. 347.

variable that affects the nature of majority-minority relations. The sharper the differences, the more the status pattern tends to persist.

Analysis of majority-minority interaction must also pay attention to the different effects of various types of social structure. The master-slave relationship, the exploiter-exploited pattern, a caste system, an extralegal system of suppression—each requires some measure of separate analysis.[32]

Perhaps the most useful classification of minority situations is on the basis of the ultimate objectives of the minorities. Wirth distinguishes four types:

1. Pluralistic: a minority desiring peaceful existence side by side with the majority and other minorities. Pluralism is often a precondition of a dynamic civilization, for it allows mutual exchange and stimulation. It usually takes the form of a desire for basic political and economic unity along with toleration of cultural, lingual, and religious diversity. The awakening of the ethnic minorities of eastern Europe in the late eighteenth century was first of all a cultural renaissance, a change from feelings of inferiority to pride in their distinctness. Where economic and political equality have been achieved or granted, this awakening has continued to be pluralistic. When cultural diversity has been suppressed, the minorities have tended to become secessionistic.

The concept of pluralism varies from setting to setting. In some societies it implies toleration among cultural groups, but little active coöperation; political and economic unity, but little exchange and common participation in other matters. This pattern has often been the dominant one in eastern Europe. Cultural pluralism may imply, however, a more active kind of unity among diverse groups, a reaching out toward common goals, a sharing of their different heritages. This has frequently been the response of ethnic groups in the United States. After they have become thoroughly established in this country, pride in their cultural heritage becomes less defensive and protective. The last shreds of secessionism are gone, but a desire to contribute to the full range of American life out of their earlier experience remains.[33]

2. Assimilationist: a minority desiring absorption into the dominant group. Assimilation is likely to occur only when the majority accepts the idea. It was widely accepted in the United States, as reflected in the concept of the "melting pot," with the major exception of the Negro and perhaps other racial minorities. A rise in economic conflict and the fact of sharper cultural differences between newer immigrants and "old" Americans have modified this idea somewhat in recent decades. Minorities themselves are sometimes split over the relative desira-

---

[32] *Ibid.*, pp. 353–354.
[33] See Horace M. Kallen, *Cultural Pluralism and the American Idea*, University of Pennsylvania Press, 1956.

bility of pluralism and assimilationism. Jews whose families have been in the United States for several generations, for example, are more likely to be assimilationists; more recent Jewish immigrants are likely to be pluralistic. Negroes are almost all assimilationists, desirous of full participation in American society, thinking of themselves as sharing the common culture.

3. Secessionist: a minority that seeks both cultural and political independence. When a friendly plural existence or assimilation is frustrated, a minority may develop a movement dedicated to complete independence. They become discontented with cultural pluralism and antagonistic to assimilation. Such a movement most often occurs among a minority who has once had political independence—for example, Zionism. There may be some tendencies in this direction among other minorities, however, as illustrated in a minor way by the Garveyite movement for a separate nation among American Negroes.

4. Militant: a minority that goes beyond the desire for equality to a desire for domination—the total reversal of statuses. It becomes convinced of its own superiority. When Hitler overran Czechoslovakia, the Sudeten Germans sought domination over the Czechs and Slovaks. When Britain withdrew from Palestine, both Arabs and Jews attempted to establish a dominant status.[34]

Oliver Cox, in a similar analysis, also points out the need for distinguishing among the many different kinds of situations which characterize majority-minority relations. He is primarily interested in racial minorities, for which he describes seven situations:

1. Situations in which the colored person is a stranger in a white society, such as a Hindu in the United States or a Negro in many parts of Canada and in Argentina—we shall call this the stranger situation.

2. Situations of original white contact where the culture of the colored group is very simple, such as the conquistadors and Indians in the West Indies, and the Dutch and Hottentots in South Africa—the original-contact situation.

3. Situations of colored enslavement in which a small aristocracy of whites exploits large quantities of natural resources, mainly agricultural, with forced colored labor, raised or purchased like capital in a slave market, such as the pre-Civil War South and in Jamaica before 1834—the slavery situation.

4. Situations in which a small minority of whites in a colored society is bent upon maintaining a ruling-class status, such as the British in the West Indies or the Dutch in the East Indies—the ruling-class situation.

5. Situations in which there are large proportions of both colored and white persons seeking to live in the same area, with whites insisting that the society is a "white man's country," as in the United States and South Africa—the bipartite situation.

6. Situations in which colored-and-white amalgamation is far advanced

[34] Louis Wirth, op. cit., pp. 354–363.

and in which a white ruling class is not established, as in Brazil—the amalgamative situation.

7. Situations in which a minority of whites has been subdued by a dominantly colored population, as that which occurred in Haiti during the turn of the eighteenth century, or the expulsion of the whites from Japan in 1638—the nationalistic situation.[35]

Several variables are involved in this classification: the proportionate size of the minority, the nature of the original contact, the degree of cultural contrast, and others. It is clear that we cannot talk about majority-minority relations without careful attention to the many influences that condition them.

How do minorities arise? There are unique elements in the history of every minority situation, but a few general principles are involved. Since a minority is a group of people that can be distinguished by physical or social characteristics, it follows that anything which makes a population more heterogeneous may create a minority situation. The kind of heterogeneity that will be noticed, of course, depends upon national, cultural, religious, and racial ideologies—in other words, on the characteristics of the majority, those with the greatest power and highest status. Migration, culture contact, conquering armies bring diverse peoples together. This process has doubtless been accelerated by modern technology and transportation. "The genesis of minorities must therefore be sought in the fact that territory, political authority, people, and culture rarely coincide."[36] Whether or not a minority situation would develop in a stable, isolated society starting from an original homogeneity one can only guess. It is possible that the internal struggle for the values of that society would result in some categorical system of rights and privileges. The evidence of anthropology, however, seems to show that homogeneous societies have little group prejudice. There are conflict and hostility (in widely varying amounts) but they are focused on individuals, not on supposed categories of people. It is the modern, mobile, heterogeneous society that is most likely to face a minority situation.

Types of Majority Policies

Majority-minority situations must be understood not only with reference to the ultimate objectives of the minorities, but also by study of the interacting aims of the majority. These may range all the way from peaceful assimilation to complete extinction of the minority people. C. A. Macartney shows how the various majority policies are illustrated

---

[35] Oliver C. Cox, op. cit., pp. 353–354; see also E. K. Francis, "Variables in the Formation of So-Called 'Minority Groups,'" *American Journal of Sociology*, July, 1954, pp. 6–14; and E. Franklin Frazier, *Race and Culture Contacts in the Modern World*, Alfred A. Knopf, Inc., 1957.

[36] Louis Wirth, op. cit., p. 365.

in the history of Europe. There are cultural and "national" minorities in almost every part of Europe, from Great Britain, with her "Irish question," to the Soviet Union, with her complex mixture of racial and cultural groups. Minorities arose when expanding tribes or nations came into conflict with each other. Subjugation of one by the other was often the result.

The Roman Empire brought scores of separate groups under one military and political rule. At the height of her power, the Empire maintained a policy of gradual or indirect assimilation; conquered groups were allowed to keep their culture and language. But the natural result of centralized administration, culture contact, and the superior technical powers of Rome was the Romanization of many of the peoples. After the fall of Rome, the assimilation process within what were to become the major nations began. Geographical and economic conditions, and the nature of their contact with other groups, made this a more rapid process in some nations than in others. France and England developed a strong unity, with only minor regional differences remaining. In other areas—Germany, Spain, Italy, and particularly eastern Europe—because of different conditions, the broader national unity developed much more slowly. The differences that remained were kept somewhat in check during the medieval period because of the atomization of political power under feudalism and, oppositely, because of the unity that was brought by the church, with its universal language and ideology.

With the coming of the era of nationalism, however, with the Renaissance, the rise of trade, and increasing secularization, the problem of minorities became very important. Merchants and kings were demanding national unity at the same time that minorities were becoming more self-conscious. The theories of national sovereignty and the divine right of kings were manufactured to fill the need for opposing the universalist claims of the papacy on the one hand and the decentralization of power of feudalism on the other. In the process of national centralization, institutions were modeled after those of the majority, and the minorities were required, with varying degrees of rigidity, to bring their customs into line. When nationalism began to come to the more diverse peoples of central and eastern Europe, with their histories of imperial domination, the cultural minorities had a strong feeling of unity that resisted the larger nationalism. As Macartney points out, the Serb had never been a true part of the Ottoman Empire, but he knew that he was a Serb. Centuries of domination had produced a secessionist feeling that would not easily be worn away.[37]

Along with the growth of nationalism, new minority problems were

---

[37] See C. A. Macartney, National States and National Minorities, Oxford University Press, 1934.

developing as a result of imperialism and a fresh wave of conquests. Even greater diversity—of culture, of religion, of race—was brought into one political framework by the expansion of European power. The dominant groups were faced with new questions of policy with regard to minority groups. Extermination, subjugation, toleration, assimilation— each of these was tried at various times and places, as "external" minorities (the "colonies") were added to "internal" minorities (those within the mother country). England had scarcely worked out a peaceful *modus vivendi* with Scotland and Wales and was still fighting bitterly with Ireland when she was faced with the problems of policy in dealing with American Indians, Asiatic Indians, Arabs, Africans, Malayans, and a host of other peoples. Czarist Russia crossed mountains and plains, rather than oceans, but she absorbed an equally diverse group of minorities, as did many other nations.

With this brief sketch of the rise of internal and external minorities in mind, we may ask: What major types of policies have the dominant groups developed? Six varieties may be seen, sometimes paralleling, sometimes opposing the aims of minorities:

1. Assimilation.
   a. Forced.
   b. Permitted.
2. Pluralism.
3. Legal protection of minorities.
4. Population transfer.
   a. Peaceful transfer.
   b. Forced migration.
5. Continued subjugation.
6. Extermination.

A brief discussion of these types of policies will indicate the wide range of responses that dominant groups may make to majority-minority situations.

1. ASSIMILATION

One way to "solve" the problem is to eliminate the minority—as a minority. We have noted that this is the aim of some minorities, but their approach to assimilation is often very different. Dominant groups have frequently adopted an extreme ethnocentrism that refused minorities the right to practice their own religion, speak their own language, follow their own customs. The czarist regime went through periods of vigorous Russification during which the only alternatives available to minorities who wished to preserve their identity—who resisted assimilation on Great Russian terms—were rigid segregation, expulsion, or extermination. Perhaps the most extreme manifestation of forced assimilation was the Nazi regime, with its ideology of a monocultural, monolingual, monoracial people ruled by an authoritarian state. The Nazi policy went beyond forced assimilation, of course, for its doctrine of race superiority claimed that some groups were unassimilable. For them, forced population transfers and extermination were the policies adopted.

Oscar Janowsky points out that the basis of Nazi policy lies in the old conception that the best nation is a homogeneous one:

> The savagery of Nazism does not derive exclusively from the distorted mind of a Hitler or a Goebbels. The deliberate and cold-blooded manner in which several million Jews, Poles, Russians, and others have been done to death in Nazi extermination camps, like Maidanek, near Lublin, must not be ascribed solely to the frenzy of the hooligans, maddened by the prospect of defeat. The roots of that depravity lie deeply imbedded in the teachings of respectable *Junkers* like Bismarck and von Bülow. It stems from the belief that "members of different nationalities, with different languages and customs," cannot possibly live side by side in one and the same state; that when fate has cast two peoples upon the same territory, one must inevitably be "the hammer and the other the anvil"; that the suppression of the language and culture of the weaker nationality is a legitimate state policy: in a word, that the relentless pursuit of national-cultural uniformity is a law of historical development.[38]

Thus forced assimilation is an extreme manifestation of ethnocentrism developed into an active policy for the supposed benefit of a national state.

Peaceful assimilation is in marked contrast. It is a long-run policy of cultural and sometimes racial unity; but it permits minorities to absorb the dominant patterns in their own way and at their own speed, and it envisages reciprocal assimilation, a blending of the diverse group, not a one-way adjustment. Brazil has an ideology that looks with favor on the eventual blending of diverse racial types into a Brazilian stock. Gunnar Myrdal declares that the assimilation of many of her minorities is part of the value creed of the United States, although the creed does not have a strong reciprocal emphasis (minorities are to give up their differences) and it excludes racial minorities. The supposed unassimilability of the Negro and other racial groups in the United States adds a dimension that must be taken into account in any analysis of American policy.

2. PLURALISM

Parallel to the pluralistic aim of some minorities is the willingness on the part of some dominant groups to permit cultural variability within the range still consonant with national unity and security. This is frequently the immediate policy of an ultimate assimilationist approach. The Soviet Union sought, and apparently won, the support of scores

[38] Oscar Janowsky, *Nationalities and National Minorities*, The Macmillan Company, 1945, pp. 30–31.

of cultural and national minorities who had bitterly resented the czarist policy of suppression. In 1917 the communists appealed to the various minorities by defending the right of cultural autonomy: "Mohammedans of Russia . . . Tartars of the Volga and Crimea; Kirghiz and Sartes of Siberia and Turkestan; Turks and Tartars of Transcaucasia, your beliefs and customs, your national institutions and culture, are hereafter free and inviolable."[39] Stalin, himself a member of a small nationality, was made People's Commissar for Nationalities and was important in the policy that separated statehood from cultural nationality and race. Native languages and arts were not only permitted but encouraged, and the political organization of the Soviet Union reflects, to some degree, cultural units of the population. The Soviet policy was not, however, thoroughly pluralistic, and it has become less so. It opposed the extraterritorial pluralism of the Zionists; religious autonomy was systematically undermined by antireligious propaganda; vigorous insistence upon political and economic orthodoxy reduced the significance of cultural autonomy; and, since the beginning of World War II, a resurgent Russian nationalism has brought some return of the Russification policy of the czars. During that war, some Soviet minorities were forcefully broken up and dispersed; Jews and others have in recent years been attacked for being "cosmopolites"; and the theory of the Great Russian as the "elder brother" of the other groups in the Soviet Union implies at best an Orwellian equality, the Russian being "more equal than others."[40]

Janowsky, referring to the nations of east central Europe—all of which are complex mixtures of many culture types and religions—believes that pluralism is the only way to reduce the internal dissension that has characterized those nations:

The core of the minorities problem, as envisaged in this book, can be grasped in a few sentences. The states of east-central Europe are not homogeneous in language or culture. A considerable proportion of the citizens of a state speak distinctive languages and cherish diverse historical memories or usages. Therefore national uniformity, which is symbolized by a single countrywide language and a single national culture, is unattainable except through the suppression or elimination of the minorities. Such efforts inevitably engender strife which in turn endangers the peace of the world. If oppression and conflict are to give way to harmony and contentment, the way must be found to recognize cultural differences within a framework of political and economic unity. The multi-national state provides the principle for sanctioning differences, and national federalism furnishes the means of integrating minorities, along with their institutions and customs in the life of the larger community.[41]

[39] Quoted by Sidney Webb and Beatrice Webb, in Alain Locke and B. J. Stern (eds.), op. cit., p. 673.
[40] See W. J. Kolarz in A. W. Lind (ed.), op. cit., chap. 9.
[41] Oscar Janowsky, op. cit., p. xiii.

Switzerland is probably the outstanding example of a thoroughgoing use of the policy of pluralism. For several centuries the French and Italian Swiss have not been minorities, in our sense of the term, nor have they given up lingual and cultural differences from the German Swiss, who make up three-fourths of the population. A strong political and economic unity overrides the cultural differences. Geographical location, the presence nearby of large supporting nations for each of the three major groups in the Swiss confederation, a democratic ideology, and other factors have contributed to this development. Canada has been less successful in her policy of pluralism. The United States has followed this pattern to some degree in her treatment of religious differences, in the recent policy toward American Indians, and in her "hands-off" policy toward the private associations, foreign-language newspapers, and private schools of many immigrant groups. There is enough accumulated experience throughout the world to make it clear that heterogeneous populations do not have to be faced with the problems of prejudice and intergroup discrimination. Their effective development, however, requires the elimination of the concept of the national state, with its monocultural ideal. The majority must give up its claim to cultural dominance and superiority; the minorities must give up their hope of political and economic separation and "freedom." In many parts of the world, cultural pluralism can only follow, probably after many years, the reduction of tension and discrimination and the development of an international situation filled with less anxiety and conflict.

3. LEGAL PROTECTION OF MINORITIES

Closely related to pluralism, or a subdivision of it, is the policy of protecting minorities by legal, constitutional, and diplomatic means. This is often official pluralism, but the emphasis on legal protection implies that there are important groups in the populations involved that do not accept the pattern. After the First World War, for example, the constitutions of Bulgaria and Turkey guaranteed rights of autonomy for minorities. The Thirteenth, Fourteenth, and Fifteenth Amendments to the United States Constitution, although not pluralistic in aim, sought to protect the equal rights of minorities, primarily Negroes, in a situation that had been unfavorable to that aim. Recent fair employment practices legislation in several states has similar objectives.

Another variety of legal protection of minorities involves international action. This again implies that there are important groups who do not accept the principle of equal rights for minorities and that therefore some coercive legal force is necessary. The Genocide Convention of the United Nations is perhaps more moral than legal in its implications, but it seeks to establish a clear-cut international law against the kind of mass extermination of peoples that was part of Nazi policy.

The Versailles Treaty was also concerned with the problems of minorities—particularly the minorities in the countries of the old Austro-Hungarian Empire, where so many conflicts had originated. One "solution," involved in Woodrow Wilson's famous Fourteen Points, was the "self-determination of peoples." Had this been carried out it would have eliminated "national" minorities within the nations involved by making each minority into a nation, if it so chose. It was based on the assumption that a monocultural, monolingual state was most likely to be successful; but it minimized the important economic forces that demanded multigroup unity. It tended to encourage small cultural group self-consciousness rather than large multigroup coöperation. Moreover, it was virtually impossible to carry out, without enormous migrations, for many of the minorities were scattered in small "islands" throughout the area. Nevertheless, it represented a significant change in peacemaking when the rights of minorities were given careful consideration. And when the "self-determination" principle was disregarded, as it often was, an additional treaty provision for pluralism within nations was invoked.

It must be reiterated that never before in the history of peacemaking was so much attention given to the principle of nationality. The attempt was made to draw frontiers along "ethnic" or nationality lines, and where conflicting claims were encountered, the plebiscite was freely resorted to. Yet, because of the composite character of the population, national minorities remained in every new or enlarged state of east-central Europe. . . . In numerous states it proved utterly impossible to disentangle mixed populations, while in a number of instances economic and strategic considerations were allowed to determine the final territorial decision.

Once they were convinced that minorities would remain, the leaders of the Paris Peace Conference proceeded to draft the minimum guarantees necessary for their protection. With the exception of Czechoslovakia, whose spokesman was Eduard Beneš, the states containing minorities resisted vigorously. But the "Big Three" stood their ground, overriding all opposition and compelling every new and enlarged state—except Italy—to assume international obligations to protect minorities. Poland, Czechoslovakia, Rumania, Jugoslavia and Greece, each was obliged to sign a special Minorities Treaty; appropriate articles were incorporated in the general treaties with the defeated states, except Germany; and the Baltic States, as also Albania, made Declarations accepting League supervision of their treatment of minorities.[42]

Civil and religious liberties, the right of citizenship, language rights, and special attention to the rights of Jews—who had been the most disadvantaged minority in most of these nations—were among the provisions in the treaties.

The United Nations has not followed the lead of the League of Nations in regard to the minorities question, for a number of reasons.

[42] *Ibid.*, pp. 110–112.

The League had applied legal protection clauses mainly to the defeated nations and new nations of eastern Europe. The United Nations, with more attention to world-wide problems, inevitably becomes entangled with questions of diplomacy and international conflict. The United States, eager to hold the support of Latin-American countries, has emphasized nonintervention in internal affairs by the United Nations, and thus can scarcely support strenuous international efforts to protect minorities within a state. The Soviet Union, the dominant power in the eastern European area, will not accept international surveillance over states that she wants under her control. Nations which found that some members of their national minorities had been disloyal during World War II—Czechoslovakia, for example—are entirely unwilling to think in terms of their international protection. If the spotlight shifts to South Africa and her treatment of Indian and Bantu groups, she virtually withdraws from the United Nations. Nor do the Soviet Union and the United States respond favorably to debate in the United Nations concerning their minority policies. The result of such forces as these has been a deinternationalization of the minorities problem since the days of the League of Nations.[43]

This does not mean that the United Nations is unconcerned with problems of minorities. There has been a shift in emphasis toward human rights—the rights of all individuals as individuals, not as members of groups. And as we shall see below, the United Nations has given attention to the process of population transfer. Active efforts to protect minorities by international legal means, following the pattern of the League of Nations, have, however, been weak.

The effectiveness of legal action as a way of protecting minorities is a subject of great complexity that we shall not discuss here. Some aspects of this question will be dealt with in Part III. Certainly the policy established in the Versailles Treaty was not carried out with great success, except perhaps in Czechoslovakia. But how much of this weakness was a reflection of the general weakness of the League of Nations and the sharp conflicts of the period between the wars and how much was a reflection of the inability to protect minorities by international legal action can scarcely be decided on the basis of this limited experience. The United Nations, through many of its agencies, is interested in the question of minorities and may well develop more effective techniques (indirect approaches that reduce the causes of discrimination).

4. POPULATION TRANSFER

Majorities have sometimes adopted a policy of population transfer to attempt to reduce minorities problems. This matches the secessionist

[43] See Inis L. Claude, Jr., *National Minorities*, Harvard University Press, 1955.

aim of some minorities—both hoping for a reduction of tension through physical separation. In a few instances population transfer has been a peaceful process, with some concern for the rights and desires of individual minority-group members and a general interest in improving their situation. More often it has been a thoroughly discriminatory policy aimed at "solving" the problem by driving minority-group members out of an area.

In the early 1920's a fairly successful exchange was made among Greece, Turkey, and Bulgaria. There are many obstacles, however, to the widespread use of this policy. When the transfer is on an exchange basis, many will not want to move. Are they to be compelled to? The minorities may be of unequal size and trained for different occupations. Can they, under such conditions, be absorbed into the new lands? The basic difficulty is that this policy assumes that a homogeneous population will be a more peaceful one, although transfer of minorities does little to reduce the primary causes of conflict. These causes will be discussed in later chapters.

Some Americans have felt that the way to solve the "Negro problem" was to recolonize Negroes in Africa or segregate them in a "forty-ninth state." Many thousands of Negroes did, in fact, return to Africa during the nineteenth century. The forty-ninth-state idea is often the manifestation of a vigorous prejudice, as in the support given to it by the late Senator Bilbo. It is sometimes, paradoxically, part of the communist policy. And it is sometimes given well-meaning support by persons of relatively mild prejudice mixed with good intentions. When Paul Robeson was graduated from college, wealthy alumni of his school proposed that he coöperate with them, as a leader, in helping to establish a separate geographical area for Negroes in the United States. The response of Robeson and of most Negroes to such a suggestion— few have the secessionist minority aim—is one of strong disagreement. Why, they ask, should we any more than other group of individuals be separated from the total community? Most Negroes are very old Americans; they are thoroughly identified with America's society.

If population transfer sometimes has good intentions, it far more often expresses only hostility and discrimination as a policy of the majority. The transfer can be of two types—direct and indirect. In the former, the minority involved is specifically required and forced to leave. Many nations and cities drove out Jews in the late medieval period; the United States drove the Indians out of area after area; the British kept the Irish beyond the Pale; and Nazi Germany followed a relentless policy that sought for a homogeneous nation by forcibly transferring large numbers of persons of many minorities. The indirect policy is to make life so unbearable for members of the minority that they "choose" to migrate. Thus czarist Russia drove out millions of Jews. This was also part of Germany's policy.

After the Second World War, efforts to reduce minority problems in Europe by population transfer received a great deal of support. During the war, some German groups had been brought back to the *Vaterland*; and after the war, others were expelled. The desire in eastern Europe to drive out a "disloyal minority" showed a great deal of categorical prejudice, because there was little effort to distinguish between loyal and disloyal members of the national minorities. (This was paralleled in some measure in the United States, where those of Japanese ancestry, the vast majority of whom were loyal to the United States, were "driven out" of the West into relocation camps.)

Population transfer may be effective in a few marginal cases, but in the modern world it can scarcely solve, or in most cases even reduce, the minorities problems. It is based on the monocultural ideal, which in a day of mobility and international communication is progressively less meaningful. To be effective, it would have to block later population movement, despite labor demands or other economic changes, an action that contradicts the growing internationalization of the economy. Even when carried out in a humane way, it violates many of the most basic rights of individuals.[44]

5. CONTINUED SUBJUGATION

The policies just discussed have sought either to incorporate the minorities into a society (on an assimilated or pluralistic basis) or to drive them out. Often, however, the dominant group wants neither of these results; it wants the minority groups around, but it wants them kept "in their place," subservient and exploitable. There may be some ultimate promise of equality, but often not even that. The average white South African cannot conceive of the time when the black man will be his equal. Yet he would be dismayed at the thought of a nation without the Negro. Who would do all the hard work?

Many persons in the United States have supported large-scale immigration in the expectancy that it would bring cheap labor. Today it is difficult to enforce laws regarding the migration of Mexicans into the United States because many powerful people in the Southwest and elsewhere want an exploitable minority. Were the "wetbacks" not a subjugated minority, were they able to command wages equal to those of American citizens, it would be far less difficult to enforce immigration laws.

Persons in the South who have a deep prejudice against Negroes occasionally express sentiments in favor of their leaving; but when the matron loses her servant and the plantation manager loses his field hand, they complain bitterly about the labor agents from the North or the draft calls of the army that are taking "their Negroes." Much of

[44] See *ibid.*, especially chaps. 8, 10.

this volume will be concerned with the subjugation policy employed by majorities.

6. EXTERMINATION

Conflict between groups sometimes becomes so severe that physical destruction of one by the other becomes an accepted goal. This may have been true of some ancient tribal contacts; modern history gives many definite examples. The United States destroyed perhaps two-thirds of the Indian population before her policy changed. The small Tasmanian population was completely wiped out by the British (and by the civilized diseases that they brought to the island). The Boers of South Africa looked upon the Hottentots as scarcely more than animals of the jungle and hunted them ruthlessly. And Germany, between 1933 and 1945, murdered six million people.

These six policies of dominant groups are not, of course, mutually exclusive; many may be practiced simultaneously. Some are conscious long-run plans; some are ad hoc adjustments to specific situations; some are the by-products (perhaps unintended) of other policies. In some instances they are the official actions of majority-group leaders; in others they are the day-by-day responses of individual members of the dominant group. In this book we shall see many of the policies in operation—from complete acceptance, to toleration, to subjugation, to extermination.

Conclusion

This chapter has been primarily concerned with some of the terms that are basic to the analysis of intergroup relations: prejudice, discrimination, and minority. We have seen that they can be defined in many ways, but we have tried to develop a meaning that will be useful in the study of the relationships with which we are concerned. One term, "race," is of such importance that it will be dealt with separately in the next chapter. This book is not limited to the study of "race relations"; but because that phrase is so frequently used to refer to the larger field of majority-minority relations, and because "race" is used so broadly and vaguely by many people, we need to develop clear-cut definitions.

It is the thesis of this book that relations among races have a great deal in common with relations among groups that think of themselves as different on other grounds—culture, nationality, religion. Race differences are primarily important for what people believe them to be. Some writers object to this approach. They declare that race prejudice, or religious prejudice, or some other variety, is fundamentally different. In sofar as they are pointing out that there are unique elements in the employment of any symbol, that each has some historically distinct roots, the present writers agree. But insofar as they obscure the similarities that underlie the use of different symbols of group differentiation, disregarding the common pattern of causes and functions, we disagree.

The study of "race" alone will yield little understanding of the nature of prejudice and discrimination. But seeing race as a symbol that is *used* to set people apart for differential treatment will cause our understanding to grow. This analysis needs also to be enlarged to include the use of other symbols by means of which "minorities" are designated, which expansion will lead to the study of all phases of majority-minority relations, the search for patterns of relationship, for causes and functions, for trends. Even this, however, does not complete our task. If our analysis is to be valid, it must rest upon the foundation of contemporary social science. Prejudice and discrimination can be understood only as manifestations of larger situations, not as isolated phenomena. We must understand the nature of individual and group behavior. Our analysis of majority-minority relations must be thoroughly in harmony with the broader principles of all human relations. It must draw its fundamental concepts from the sciences of man.

Our approach might be charted as shown in Figure 1.1. Our primary

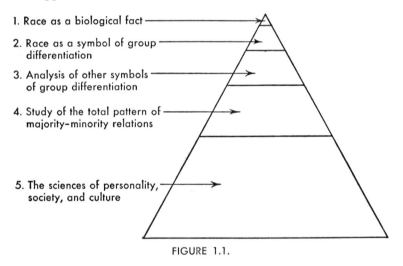

1. Race as a biological fact

2. Race as a symbol of group differentiation

3. Analysis of other symbols of group differentiation

4. Study of the total pattern of majority-minority relations

5. The sciences of personality, society, and culture

FIGURE 1.1.

concern will be with levels 1 to 4 of this pyramid, but we shall draw continually on principles that derive from level 5—from the sciences of sociology, cultural anthropology, and social psychology particularly.

Let us turn now to an analysis of race.

CHAPTER 2

Three Approaches to Race:
The Mystical, the Administrative,
and the Biological

Race is one of the most misunderstood concepts in modern vocabularies. Formal and informal definitions of this word run into the thousands, but we shall consider three broad approaches to this term.

The Mystical Conception of Race

The first conception we shall label "mystical," although it would be almost as appropriate to call it "romantic," or "literary," or "political." This viewpoint on race has been the stock in trade in the chicanery of rabble rousers, fanatics, demagogues, adventurers, and charlatans (rational or psychopathic). It has been a convenient rationalization for conservatives and reactionaries in opposing social change. It has provided a crutch for lesser artists in the stereotyping of characters in their mediocre products. And it has been immeasurably useful to the mass populations of the modern world whose members are largely unaware of the nature of prejudices, their sources and their functions.

During the Middle Ages and for centuries later, the nobility of Europe considered itself of better ancestry than the common people. In France, for example, Count de Boulainvilliers declared that there were two races: the nobles, who were descended from the Germanic conquerors, and the masses, who were the descendants of the subject Celts and Romans. In this manner he sought to defend the privileges of the nobles. After the French Revolution Count de Gobineau brought out his famous *Essay on the Inequality of the Human Races*. Gobineau hated democracy and admitted that his purpose in writing was to strike at liberal ideas. His racial theory, a new version of the old defense of feudalism, was popular among the slaveowners of the Old South in the years preceding the Civil War.

H. S. Chamberlain, an Englishman who took a German wife and became a Germanophile (or Teutonophile), utilized a "racial" approach in his influential work, *The Foundations of the Nineteenth Century.* According to Chamberlain: "Whoever reveals himself German by his acts, whatever his genealogical tree, is a German." T. L. Stoddard's *Rising Tide of Color* included the thesis that there are higher races and lower races, that intermixture produces a race which reverts to the lower type, and that the downfall of the great civilizations has been due to the crossing of higher and lower races. Madison Grant's *The Passing of a Great Race* developed the theme that the United States was founded by Anglo-Saxon Protestants with democratic ideals and that this country should be reserved for their kind.

Perhaps the most repercussive racial dogma was set forth by Adolf Hitler in *Mein Kampf,* in which the author stated: "If we divide the human race into three categories—founders, maintainers, and destroyers of culture—the Aryan stock alone can be considered as representing the first category."

About thirty years ago a southern statesman declared,

"No statutory law, no organic law, no military law, supersedes the law of racial necessity and social identity.

"Why apologize or evade? We have been very careful to obey the letter of the Federal Constitution—but we have been very diligent and astute in violating the spirit of such amendments and such statutes as would lead the Negro to believe himself the equal of a white man. And we shall continue to conduct ourselves in that way."[1]

The same idea was expressed more recently by a somewhat less reputable but equally frank spokesman for white supremacy:

"Grand Dragon Dr. Samuel J. Green of the Ku Klux Klan gave an interview for *The Nation* to Negro Journalist Roi Ottley, who told Green that scientific thought and world opinion ran counter to the theory of Negro inferiority. Insisted Green: 'I'm still livin' in Georgia, no matter what the world and science thinks.' "[2]

The Administrative Conception of Race

The administrative conception of race is frequently closely related to mystical viewpoints. It is an official conception and has far-reaching consequences in the lives of large numbers of human beings. Either by

---

[1] *Liberty Magazine,* April 21, 1928, p. 10.
[2] *Time,* July 11, 1949, p. 38.

legislative act or by bureaucratic ruling, certain "racial" categories are established and governmental actions are based on them. Examples of such conceptions include the Nazi dichotomy of Aryan and non-Aryan, the United States Bureau of the Census definition of Negro, and the distinction between "native" and "colored" in South Africa. In Hitler's Germany it was a tragedy to be classified as "non-Aryan." To be so singled out meant dismissal from civil service and university positions, severe restrictions in the practice of medicine, law, dentistry, and journalism, special schools for one's children, special identity cards, the adoption of Jewish first names for all Jews, business and property restrictions and confiscations, deprivation of the rights of citizenship, and the prohibition of marriage to an "Aryan."

According to the United States Census Bureau, a person who has any Negro ancestry is recorded as "Negro," even though he is indistinguishable in appearance from "white" Americans. The practical consequences of such a definition on the part of the federal, state, and local governments ramify into church membership, schools and colleges attended south of the Mason-Dixon line (with some exceptions in recent years), marriage, voting and officeholding, certain aspects of the administration of criminal justice, and the administration of relief. The census defines as "Indian" anyone who is regarded by the community in which he lives as "Indian." Although the effects of this definition are not as marked as in the case previously cited, some official policies are laid down on this "racial" line, notably school attendance and marriage.

The distinction between "native" and "colored" in the Union of South Africa has meant certain advantages in the past for members of the latter (mixed) group in such matters as labor-union membership, wage differentials, voting, and the holding of government positions.

Biological Viewpoints on Race

The third broad approach to race does not present a united front on the part of the physical anthropologists and the biologists. Neither does it show complete disagreement. Rather there are several schools of thought at present, with differing terminologies, techniques, and emphases. We shall try to show, underlying these differences, the substantial agreement on the meaning of race from a biological standpoint.

THE TRADITIONAL PHYSICAL ANTHROPOLOGICAL APPROACH TO RACE

First consideration goes to the traditional physical anthropological attack on race. Endeavors along this line began with more or less crude observations of obvious physical differences, followed later by careful measurement of external physical traits and broadened in recent years to take account of several physiological tests. Among the most widely used characteristics are skin color, nasal index, hair texture, head form, lip form, hair and eye color, facial index, and stature. Brief reference will be made to each of these traits.

Skin color has been called the most obvious racial feature; certainly it is sociologically the most important one. However, it is one of the most unreliable traits if taken singly, because of the great variation within the major divisions of mankind, because of the overlapping from one group to another, and because of environmental influences. Extreme types can, of course, be identified by inspection without the use of refined techniques. Thus the ordinary person has no difficulty in distinguishing a Swede from a north Chinese or a Bantu, or, to add two other "colors," a Crow Indian from a Samoan. But man's great proclivities for travel and interbreeding have mixed human genes to such an extent that it is by no means easy to tell the racial background of many of the earth's inhabitants by glancing at skin surfaces. The color-top method of rating skin color by adjusting color proportions of the top and spinning it on the upper arm was an improvement over the quick look, but it is none too satisfactory. The new technique of spectrophotometry permits accurate and more objective measurement of skin colors. As Hooton points out, the sources of skin color are five pigments, the main ones being melanin and carotene, and an effect known as scattering.[3]

By nasal index is meant the relationship between the width of the nose, measured between the wings, and the length of the nose from the juncture of the nasal bones and the frontal bone to the juncture of the septum with the upper lip. If the percentage of the width relative to the length is less than 70, the index is called leptorrhine (narrow-nosed); if it is 84 or over, the indexes are known as platyrrhine or chamaerrhine (broad-nosed); intermediate indexes are mesorrhine (medium-nosed). Generally speaking, these nasal forms are characteristic of Caucasoids, Negroids, and Mongoloids respectively.

Hair form, one of the most reliable criteria of race, falls into three main categories: ulotrichy (oval, tightly curled strands), leiotrichy (straight, round in cross section), and cymotrichy (wavy, intermediate in cross-section shape). Typically, these three types of hair form are found in Negroes, Mongoloids, and whites.

One of the most widely known racial indexes is head form, although it is less useful in racial classification, except in the establishment of subracial categories, than a number of other physical traits. The cephalic index is obtained by dividing the maximum transverse head breadth by the maximum glabello-occipital length. A percentage of less than 75

[3] E. A. Hooton, Up from the Ape, The Macmillan Company, rev. ed., 1946, p. 456.

indicates dolichocephaly (long-headedness), one of 75–80 mesocephaly (medium-headedness), and over 80 brachycephaly (broad-headedness or short-headedness).

Lip form refers to lip thickness, which ranges from the thin, inverted, anthropoidal lips of Caucasoids through the intermediate structures of Mongoloids to the wide, everted, highly evolved Negroid lips. According to Hooton, lip form is significant in racial classification chiefly when there is a Negro strain in the group under study.

Hair color and eye color in human beings is an exceedingly complex and technical subject, and details concerning it cannot be presented here. Hooton states that "the commonest hair pigment is granular, brown or black pigment identical with that in the skin" although "a diffuse and soluble red-gold pigment is sometimes present in the hair." Eye color is determined mainly by the pigment in the iris, and seems to be due more to quantitative than to qualitative differences in pigment. An overwhelming majority of the world's population has black hair. Blonds are numerically insignificant. When eyes are classified on the basis of primary or background color and secondary detailed hue, there are four main types: "light," "pale mixed," "mixed," and "dark." In general, light and dark coloration in hair and eyes are associated, although there are differences in these associations between the sexes, and dark hair-blue eye combinations occur frequently where there has been a crossing of ethnic stocks.[4]

Even less useful in racial classification than the cephalic index is the facial index. This criterion is obtained by dividing the length of the face from the root of the nose to the bottom of the chin by the maximum breadth across the malars. When the percentages are 88 or over the index is called leptoprosopic or narrow-faced; indexes of less than 84 are euryprosopic or broad-faced; and those between 85 and 88 are mesoprosopic or medium-faced. Broad-headed persons usually have broad faces and narrow-headed individuals are usually narrow-faced, although notable exceptions include some unmixed Negroes who have long heads and broad faces and some Armenoids with relatively broad heads and narrow faces. Pronounced prognathism (protrusion of the jaws) is found mainly among Australoids and Negroids, but, according to Hooton, facial protrusion tends to be recessive and so most Negro-white mixtures in the United States have little prognathism.[5]

Coon's comments on facial contours, which are not susceptible of exact measurement, are interesting. He refers to the "extreme cragginess and ruggedness" of the facial features, including the forehead,

---

[4] For full discussions of hair and eye color, see ibid., especially pp. 469, 477–478, 480.

[5] Ibid., pp. 506–507.

the brow ridges, the cheekbones, the jaws, and the nose, associated with the "western marginal fringe area (of Europe), and especially with the region of largest heads and maximum Palaeolithic survival." Nordics and Mediterraneans are said to display a maximum of facial relief without the appearance of bony massiveness. "Facial flatness" typifies the Mongoloids but is also characteristic of eastern Europe, Poland, Finland, and Hungary. The "maximum nasality" of Near-Eastern peoples is accompanied by a convexity of the nose as a whole, the depression of the tip of the nose, and eyebrows over the nose.[6]

Stature or bodily height is one of the least satisfactory criteria of race because of the great range found within each major human grouping. There is also the question of the extent to which stature may be regarded as a heredity character. Numerous studies have attempted to show that height is affected by such environmental factors as diet, sickness, occupation, and social class.

Data concerning such physiological differences as basal metabolism, pulse, temperature, and respiration in racial groups are inconclusive. There is some evidence that all of these phenomena tend to be higher in whites than in the other races, but it is insufficient and somewhat inconsistent. Also, sex differences and environmental factors must be taken into consideration in these matters. Further investigation may reveal significant differences, but generalizations are not in order at present. Blood groups, taste, vision, and pathologies related to race are reserved for discussion in connection with genetic theory.

It must not be thought that the traits considered here are the only sorting criteria used in the traditional anthropological approach to race, or that all of these characteristics are utilized by every classifier. In racial classification much depends on the selection of criteria and how the characteristics are defined. There is, of course, much variation with respect to a single trait within a given race, but the classifications are based on combinations of three or more characteristics. Once the measurements have been taken on the selected racial traits, the physical anthropologist proceeds to find averages for a given group. From the averages hypothetical "ideal types" are established, although it is clear that no individual will exemplify in himself the precise set of averages for the racial type. Races, then, in this procedure become statistical abstractions, artificial mental constructs to be used as measuring sticks in identifying the world's peoples. It is recognized that subjectivism cannot be entirely avoided in such classifications even though measurements are carefully taken and complicated statistical techniques are employed. As Kroeber says, some opinions are supported by masses of coherent evidence, others by fragmentary and selected data; and where conclusive proof is not possible, the problem is to "discriminate be-

[6] Carleton S. Coon, *The Races of Europe*, The Macmillan Company, 1939, p. 279.

tween better and worse judgments and better and worse evidence."[7]

There are no absolutely "pure" races, and the less isolated and the more mobile a particular group has been the greater the problem of classifying it. In fact, as Boas points out, the differences between family lines are much greater than the differences between races. According to him, "It may happen that members of one family line, extreme in form and function, are quite different from those of a family line of the opposite extreme, although both belong to the same race; while it may be very difficult to find individuals or family lines in one racial type that may not be duplicated in a neighboring type."[8]

With these qualifications in mind, we shall turn to some of the principal attempts at racial classification. One of the first, made by Linnaeus in 1738, divided mankind into four categories: *Americanus rufus* (American Indians), *Europaeus albus*, *Asiaticus luridus*, and *Afer niger*. Blumenbach's list of 1775 included Caucasian, Mongolian, Ethiopian, American, and Malayan, and for more than a century this breakdown in color terms was taught in grade-school geography courses in many countries. Deniker's elaborate analysis of 1889, based on hair form, skin color, and nose shape, identified six major divisions, seventeen subdivisions, and twenty-nine races and is remarkably similar to some of the most highly regarded recent classifications. In 1933 von Eickstedt set up three basic subspecies (Europid, Negrid, Mongolid), divided into thirteen "series" and thirty-eight races.

Actually there is less disagreement among physical anthropologists than some people have maintained. Regardless of the terminology used for the main physical groupings (divisions, stocks, races, subspecies) and for the smaller physical sections (subraces, sub-subraces, breed, ethnic groups, etc.), there is an impressive underlying consensus. For most discussions of the physical anthropological aspects of race, the classification by Kroeber shown in Table 2.1 is quite satisfactory.

As an example of the more elaborate classifications, Hooton's revision is summarized.

SUMMARY OF E. A. HOOTON'S RACIAL CLASSIFICATION OF MODERN MAN[9]

Primary Races

I. Caucasoid Race
    1. Mediterranean (basic long-headed brunets)
        a. Upper Palaeolithic survivors or Atlanto-Mediterranean (mainly in Ireland, Scotland, Wales)

[7] A. L. Kroeber, *Anthropology*, Harcourt, Brace & Company, rev. ed., 1948, p. 148.
[8] Franz Boas, *Anthropology and Modern Life*, W. W. Norton & Company, Inc., 1928, p. 50.
[9] E. A. Hooton, *op. cit.*, pp. 575–643.

b. Iranian Plateau or Irano-Afghan (principally in Iraq or Iran)
c. Classic Mediterranean
  (1) Reduced derivative of Upper Palaeolithic subrace (straight-nosed type in Near East and Mediterranean basin and in parts of eastern, central, and northwestern Europe)
  (2) Reduced derivative of Iranian Plateau subrace (convex-nosed type in Arabia and Near East among Arabs and Jews)
2. Ainu (northern Japan)
3. Keltic (light-eyed, dark- or red-haired long-heads, chiefly in British Isles)
4. Nordic (pure-blond or near-blond long-heads of Scandinavia, but also found around the Baltic, in British Isles, in United States, and in British colonies)
5. Alpine (basic brunet round-heads with medium broad noses of central Europe, southern Norway, Denmark, northern Italy, Balkans, and sporadically in Near East)
6. East Baltic (blond round-heads with medium broad noses, chiefly in Finland, Russia, Baltic states, Poland, north Germany)
7. Armenoid (stabilized blend of Classic Mediterranean, Alpine, and Iranian Plateau; brunet, hook-nosed, acrocephalic round-heads concentrated in Turkey, Syria, Palestine, but common in Iraq, Iran, Balkan countries, and in urban populations of eastern and central Europe)
8. Dinaric (stabilized blend of Upper Palaeolithic, Alpine, Armenoid, and Nordic concentrated in Dinaric Alps region of Yugoslavia, Austrian Tyrol, sporadic in central Europe)
9. Nordic-Alpine (interbreeds intermediate between Nordic and Alpine subraces)
10. Nordic-Mediterranean (long-headed interbreeds with darkish pigmentation)

II. Negroid Race
  1. African or Forest Negro
  2. Nilotic Negro (probably with a small degree of "Hamitic" Mediterranean ancestry); upper waters of White Nile and upper course of Blue Nile
  3. Negrito
    a. Infantile type of Congo forest area, Andaman Islands, Malay Peninsula, Philippines, and probably interior of New Guinea
    b. Adultiform of Congo forest area, probably also in Malay Peninsula and interior of New Guinea

III. Mongoloid Race
  1. Classic Mongoloid
  2. Arctic Mongoloid or Eskimoid

Composite Races

A. Composite, predominantly white
  1. Australian (stabilized blend of Archaic White, Tasmanian, and recent minor fraction of Melanesian-Papuan)
    a. Murrian (chiefly in southeastern Australia)

TABLE 2.1. A. L. Kroeber's Outline Racial Classification of Mankind[10]

Primary Stocks and Races	Texture of Hair of Head	Hair of Body and Face	Head	Nose	Prognathism	Skin Color	Stature	Remarks
Caucasian or "white"								
Nordic	Wavy	Abundant	Narrow	Narrow	Slight	Very fair	Tall	Often blond, eyes light
Alpine	Wavy	Abundant	Broad	Narrow	Slight	Fair	Above average	Hair brown, eyes brown
Mediterranean	Wavy	Abundant	Narrow	Narrow	Slight	Dark white	Medium	"Regular features," graceful
Hindu	Wavy	Abundant	Narrow	Variable	Moderate	Brown	Above average	Dark admixture especially in south
Mongoloid or "yellow"								
Mongolian	Straight	Slight	Broad	Medium	Medium	Light brown	Below average	Broad face, Mongolian eye
Malaysian	Straight	Slight	Broad	Medium	Medium	Brown	Below average	Broad face
American Indian	Straight	Slight	Variable	Medium	Medium	Brown	Tall to medium	
Negroid or "black"								
Negro	Woolly	Slight	Narrow	Broad	Strong	Dark brown	Tall	Everted lips
Melanesian	Woolly	Slight	Narrow	Broad	Strong	Dark brown	Medium	Some aquiline noses
Pygmy black	Woolly	Slight	Broadish	Broad	Strong	Dark brown	Very short	
Bushman	Peppercorn	Slight	Narrow	Broad	Slight	Yellowish	Very short	Wrinkles, steatopygy, thin lips, Mongolian eye
Of doubtful classification								
Australoid	Wavy	Abundant	Narrow	Broad	Strong	Dark brown	Medium	Negroid traits preponderate, some Caucasian resemblance
Veddoid (Indo-Austral.)	Wavy	Moderate	Narrow	Broad	Medium	Brown	Short	Generalized proto-Caucasian, some Australoid resemblance
Polynesian	Wavy	Moderate	Variable	Medium	Medium	Brown	Tall	Mongoloid and Caucasian traits, with local Negroid admixture
Ainu	Wavy	Abundant	Narrow	Medium	Medium	Light brown	Medium	Probably generalized Caucasian

Hair and eyes are "black" unless otherwise stated.

[10] A. L. Kroeber, Anthropology, Harcourt, Brace & Company, Inc., rev. ed., 1948, p. 132.

   b. Carpentarian (Melanesian-Papuan increment; northern Australia)
   c. Tasmanoid (refuge areas of Queensland)
2. Indo-Dravidian (stabilized blend of Classic Mediterranean, Australoid, Negrito, and minor fractions of Iranian Plateau or Armenoid,
   Nordic, Mediterranean of India and Ceylon)
   a. Classic Indo-Dravidian (approaches the Classic Mediterranean;
      northern India)
   b. Armenoid-Iranian Plateau (western littoral and Bengal)
   c. Indo-Nordic (northwestern Himalayan tribes)
   d. Australoid or Veddoid (central and southern India)
   e. Negritoid (southern India)
3. Polynesian (stabilized blend of Brunet White, Mongoloid, and
   Melanesian-Papuan of Polynesian Islands: Hawaii, New Zealand,
   Samoa, etc.
B. Composite, predominantly Negroid
   1. Tasmanian (Negrito and Australian; now extinct, but formerly Tas-
      mania and probably most parts of Australian continent)
   2. Melanesian-Papuan or Oceanic Negroid (stabilized blend of Negrito,
      Australoid, convex-nosed Mediterranean, plus minor fractions of Ma-
      lay and Polynesian)
      a. Papuan (New Guinea and other islands of Melanesia)
      b. Melanesian (more widely distributed in Melanesia than the Papuan
         subrace; nasal index higher and head form oftener mesocephalic
         or brachycephalic than in Papuans)
   3. Bushman-Hottentot (Negrito, Palaeolithic Boskop of South Africa,
      and minor fractions of Bantu Negro and Hamitic Mediterranean in
      Hottentots)
      a. Bushman (Kalahari Desert, South Africa)
      b. Hottentot (Southwest Africa)
C. Composite, predominantly Mongoloid
   1. Indonesian-Mongoloid or Indonesian-Malay (Mongoloid, Mediter-
      ranean, Ainu, and Negrito mixture)
      a. Malay-Mongoloid (Indo-China, Thailand, Burma, Malay Penin-
         sula, Dutch East Indies, Philippines, etc. Includes most Japanese)
      b. Indonesian (pre-Mongoloid groups in southern China, Indo-
         China, Burma, Thailand, and many interior tribes of Malay
         Archipelago)
      c. American Indian (Mongoloid, Iranian Plateau, Australoid, and
         very small Negritoid element)
         (1) Brachycephals (cephalic index of 80 or over; hawk-nosed and
             snub-nosed subtypes. Hawk-nosed brachycephals the most
             common type in North America)
         (2) Dolichocephals (cephalic index under 80; hawk-nosed and
             snub-nosed subtypes. Hawk-nosed dolichocephals mostly in
             eastern woodlands area of United States and Canada)

   It is impossible to draw hard and fast lines which divide the European population into Nordic, Alpine, Mediterranean, and other racial
areas. As Dahlberg says: "There is no reason whatever for presuming

that there ever was in Scandinavia a pure Nordic race subsequently contaminated in this way [i.e., blended by migrations of tribes, nations, individuals]. According to an examination of army recruits undertaken in the years 1897–98 to analyze the racial make-up of the Swedish people, only 10% of them were classified as examples of the pure Nordic type."[11] This problem is met in part by the trait maps which Coon and others have prepared showing "degrees of Nordicism," "degrees of Alpinism," and so forth.[12]

GENETIC THEORY PROPOSALS CONCERNING RACE[13]

Modern genetics is based upon the remarkable work of a Moravian monk, Gregor Mendel, in the years 1857 to 1865. Mendel discovered the units of heredity, the genes, from the way in which the characters of the parent plants reappeared in their offspring. His observations were made on garden peas and he learned that contrasting traits did not blend when plants were crossed, but that each trait retained its identity through many generations. When a purple-flowered plant was crossed with a white-flowered plant, the offspring in the first generation were invariably purple-flowered. A character such as purple color which seemed to submerge white color was called "dominant" over the covered-up "recessive" trait. Mendel also found that when two of the purple-flowered hybrids were mated, the offspring appeared in a definite and constant proportion generation after generation. The ratio was three purple to one white, two of the three purple plants being hybrids and one pure. Thus, ". . . it has been shown that the genes contributed to the hybrids by the parents do not mix but are segregated into the different sex cells of the hybrid, so that in the progeny of hybrids a character of the parent will reappear uncontaminated by its passage through the hybrid."[14] This principle of heredity is called the law of segregation.

When Mendel traced two or more characters simultaneously by breeding together double hybrids, he discovered that all possible combinations appeared in the offspring by pure chance.[15] This hereditary principle is known as the law of independent assortment. Every additional pair of "independent character differences which show domi-

[11] Gunnar Dahlberg, Race, Reason and Rubbish, Columbia University Press, 1942, p. 202.

[12] See A. L. Kroeber, op. cit., pp. 145–147.

[13] This summary is based on L. C. Dunn and T. Dobzhansky, Heredity, Race, and Society, Penguin Books, Inc., 1946, pp. 37–108.

[14] Ibid., p. 37.

[15] For example: ". . . In the second generation from the cross of yellow round by green wrinkled the color of the seeds was quite independent of the seed shape. Of the ¾ yellows, ¾ were round and ¼ were wrinkled, and of the ¼ of greens ¾ were round and ¼ were wrinkled; in other words, ¾ of ¾ or 9/16 were yellow round, ¼ of ¾ or 3/16 were yellow wrinkled; ¾ of ¼ or 3/16 were green round, and ¼ of ¼ or 1/16 were green wrinkled." Ibid., p. 41.

nance doubles the number of combinations." Dunn and Dobzhansky use such differences in a human family as (1) taster or taste-blind, (2) dark or light eyes, (3) short-fingered or normal to illustrate this law. With three independent characters there are eight possible combinations.

The discovery of these laws does not mean that the problems of human heredity have been solved. No one suggests that there is only one gene for each of the thousands of human traits, or that a given gene may not affect more than one part or process. In fact, there is most certainly interaction between genes, although one of the effects of a particular gene may be more apparent than the others.

The point, then, genetically, is that heredity is not a matter of mixing the blood of parents but rather of transmitting discrete genes according to the laws of segregation, independent assortment, and interaction. Geneticists make the further point that there is much hereditary diversity in any group, small or large, and that "races can be defined as populations which differ in the frequencies of some gene or genes."[16]

One possibility of applying genetic principles to human races lies in the blood groups. While every human group includes individuals of each of the four human blood groups (O, A, B, AB), the races differ in the proportion of persons in each group. Hooton points out that peoples who are physically very different have almost exactly the same blood-group distribution (Eskimos and Australoids; Negrito pygmies, Russians, and Iranians; South African and Melanesian Negroids, California and Tunisian whites; etc.).[17] Likewise, groups from the same racial populations have very dissimilar blood-group frequencies. However, further advances in serology will undoubtedly make important contributions to physical anthropology.

The ability or lack of ability to taste phenyl-thio-carbamide seems to be inherited. Each country has its characteristic proportion of tasters and taste-blinds (in the United States the percentages are 70 and 30 respectively). The genes for color blindness, for blood characters other than the four blood groups, and for certain hereditary defects (some deafness, some blindness, some epilepsy, some mental defectiveness, some minor malformations of organs of the body) appear also to have different frequencies from country to country.

The conclusions which some geneticists have reached are as follows: (1) The distribution of genes which determines the racial traits of the world's population is very complex; (2) genes are not blended but are segregated in the sex cells of the hybrid; (3) the different genes are transmitted independently; (4) many races exist even though it is difficult to define them; and (5) more knowledge of gene distribution will

[16] Ibid., p. 108.
[17] E. A. Hooton, op. cit., p. 557.

permit the elaboration of racial classifications which are more adequate than those produced to date.

Kroeber regards as pure wish fulfillment the proposal to replace the usual physical anthropological methods of classifying races with the genetic approach.

We know hundreds of actual bodily traits or phenotype "appearances" for every known genetic unit character of heredity. In fact, the "laws" of heredity are every year themselves proving to be more ramified, even when we operate on problems simplified by breeding fruit flies in the laboratory. For man, on whom we cannot experiment, whom we have to take as he comes, the genetic situation is now almost as complex as the bodily zygotic one, but its data are fewer. What evidence we have on human heredity to date that can be reduced to formulas, besides the A-B-AB-O blood types, is a few other blood groupings and a limited series of abnormalities. . . . For attacking the total problem of races and their origins and histories, these few present scraps of definite knowledge of human heredity are pitifully inadequate.[18]

Nevertheless, Boyd has presented a tentative classification of six races based on gene frequencies, including blood-group genes, the genes for tasting phenyl-thio-carbamide and related compounds, and the "secreting gene." His classification is as follows:

1. Early European (hypothetical). Represented today by their modern descendants, the Basques.
2. European (Caucasoid) group.
3. African (Negroid) group.
4. Asiatic (Mongoloid) group. "It is possible that the inhabitants of India will prove to belong to an Asiatic subrace, or even a separate race, serologically, but information is still sadly lacking.")
5. American Indian group.
6. Australoid group.

Of his classification Boyd says: "It will be noted that our proposed racial calssification, although it is based upon gene frequencies . . . does not really differ in any very startling way, in so far as the ultimate categories are concerned, from some of the older classifications based on skin color, hair form, etc."[19]

THE ETHNIC GROUPS VIEWPOINT

One group of physical anthropologists (Montagu, Hogben, Huxley, Haddon) have proposed that the term "ethnic group" replace what they consider to be the outmoded concept of "race." This suggestion

[18] A. L. Kroeber, op. cit., p. 162.
[19] William C. Boyd, Genetics and the Races of Man, Little, Brown & Company, 1950, pp. 268–269. A table giving the approximate gene frequencies in the six genetically defined races is shown on p. 269.

would not eliminate consideration of physical characters, but these would be analyzed further in terms of the frequency distributions of human genes in the world's populations. Three main points are stressed in connection with this viewpoint. (1) Local populations are so mixed that they can never be genetically purified (broken down to earlier states of their ancestral groups—no assumption is made concerning preëxisting "pure races"); (2) "race" is likely to be thought of as fixed; and (3) "race" is often associated with mental and cultural factors. Montagu speaks of the process of averaging the characters of a given group in racial classifying as omelette-making and says that "the omelette called 'race' has no existence outside the statistical frying pan in which it has been reduced by the heat of the anthropological imagination."[20]

While awaiting definitive studies along genetic lines, these scientists suggest that anthropologists look at the four great "divisions" of mankind (Negroid, Mongoloid, Caucasoid, and Australoid) strictly in the biological or ecological context and that sociologists study group differences in the cultural reference in terms of "caste" and social problems. In this division of labor, an ethnic group would be defined as representing "one of a number of populations, which together comprise the species Homo sapiens, but individually maintain their differences, physical and cultural, by means of isolating mechanisms such as geographic and social barriers."[21] This definition is supplemented by the remark that where these barriers are of low power, neighboring ethnic groups will hybridize with one another; where they are of high power, the groups will remain more or less distinct or replace each other geographically.

Montagu's classification of the divisions and ethnic groups of man follows:

THE DIVISIONS AND ETHNIC GROUPS OF MAN[22]

Division: Mongoloid
    Classical Mongoloids
    Ethnic Group: a. An undetermined number of ethnic groups in the older populations of Tibet, Mongolia, China, Korea, Japan, and Siberia, including such tribes as the Buriats east and west of Lake Baikal, the Koryak of northern Siberia, the Gilyak of northernmost Sakhalin and the mainland north of the Amur estuary (who appear to have mixed with the Ainu), and the Goldi on the lower Amur and Ussuri.

[20] M. F. Ashley Montagu, *Man's Most Dangerous Myth: The Fallacy of Race,* Columbia University Press, 2nd ed., 1945, p. 31.
[21] *Ibid.,* p. 72.
[22] M. F. Ashley Montagu, *Statement on Race,* Henry Schuman, Inc., 1951, pp. 79–82.

THE DIVISIONS AND ETHNIC GROUPS OF MAN (*Continued*)

Arctic Mongoloids

Ethnic Group: a. Eskimo, extreme northeast of Asia, arctic coast of North America, Greenland. The type includes the Reindeer and coastal Chukchee of northeastern Siberia.

b. Evenki or true Tungus, Mongolia, Siberia, Asiatic highlands north of the Himalayas.

c. Kamtchadales, Kamchatka.

d. Samoyedes, Kola Peninsula, White Sea and Yenisei regions.

e. Aleuts, Aleutian Islands.

American Indians

Ethnic Group: a. An undetermined number of ethnic groups of North, Middle, Central and South America.

Indo-Malay

Ethnic Group: a. Indonesian, Southern China, Indo-China, Burma, Thailand, interior of Malay Archipelago.

b. Malay, in addition to Indonesian distribution, Malay Peninsula, Dutch East Indies, Philippines, Okinawa, and adjacent islands.

Division: Negroid

African Negroes

Ethnic Group: a. The True Negro, West Africa, Cameroons and Congo.

b. The Half-Hamites, East Africa and East Central Africa.

c. Forest Negro, Equatorial and Tropical Africa.

d. "Bantu-speaking Negroids," Central and Southern Africa.

e. Nilotic Negro, Eastern Sudan and Upper Nile Valley.

f. Bushman-Hottentot, South Africa.

Oceanic Negroids

Ethnic Group: a. Papuan, New Guinea.

b. Melanesian, Melanesia.

African Pygmies or Nigrillos

Ethnic Group: a. African Pygmies or Negrillos, Equatorial Africa.

Asiatic Pygmies or Negritos

Ethnic Group: a. Andamanese, Andaman Islands.

b. Semang, Central region of Malay Peninsula, and East Sumatra.

c. Aeta, Philippine Islands.

Oceanic Pygmies or Negritos

Ethnic Group: a. New Guinea Pygmies, New Guinea.

THE DIVISIONS AND ETHNIC GROUPS OF MAN (Continued)
Division: Caucasoid
  Ethnic Group: a. Basic Mediterranean, Borderlands of the Mediter-
                     ranean Basin.
                  b. "Nordic," Central Europe, Scandinavia and neigh-
                     boring regions.
                  c. East Baltic, East Baltic regions.
                  d. Lapp, Northern Scandinavia, Kola Peninsula.
                  e. Alpine, France along the Alps and Carpathians to
                     Russia.
                  f. "Dinaric," Eastern Alps from Switzerland to Al-
                     bania, Asia Minor and Syria.
                  g. "Armenoid," Asia Minor.
                  h. Indo-Dravidian, India and Ceylon.
                  i. Polynesian, Polynesia.
                  j. Australian, Australia.
                  k. Veddah, Ceylon.
                  l. Pre-Dravidian, India.
                  m. Ainu, Japan, Hokkaido.

Montagu believes that discarding the term "race" and substituting
"ethnic group" would clarify the conceptual approach to the problem of
the world's populations. Others are not convinced of the desirability or
the efficacy of such a change. As Dunn and Dobzhansky say, " 'Ethnic
group prejudice' is easily exchangeable for 'race prejudice'; and one can
hate 'ethnic groups' just as venomously as real or imaginary races."

Regardless of these different viewpoints, it should be emphasized that
there is general agreement today among the students of the physical
aspects of race that racial groups are not clearly defined entities.[23] The
biogenetic groups which are called "stocks" or "races" are plastic and
are always in process of change.[24]

The Causes of Racial Differentiation

A detailed treatment of the factors responsible for racial differentiation is beyond the scope of the present work. Homo sapiens does not
go back much more than 25,000 years. All of the earlier precursors of
modern men from Pithecanthropus erectus to Homo neanderthalensis
belonged to other genuses, or at least to other species. Cro-Magnon
men and related groups lived in Europe until about 15,000 years ago.
The present four grand divisions of mankind have developed since the
decline of Upper Paleolithic men (Cro-Magnon and others). Racial dif-

[23] See S. M. Garn and C. S. Coon, "On the Number of Races of Mankind,"
American Anthropologist, October, 1955, pp. 996–1001, for a distinction between
geographical races (four to six) and local races (thirty to forty).
[24] W. M. Krogman, "The Concept of Race," in Ralph Linton (ed.), The Science
of Man in the World Crisis, Columbia University Press, 1945, p. 59.

ferentiation is not fully understood, but it certainly cannot be explained in terms of any one "cause." Among the most frequently mentioned reasons for the appearance of the major physical differences which characterize the main divisions are recombination of genes, mutation, survival selection, social selection, self-domestication, endocrine relations, and adaptation to environment.

Recombination, which comes about through the principle of gene segregation previously mentioned, juggles existing genes and may produce new effects on characters. Mutation, the exact causes of which are not yet understood, alters the nature of the genes and occasions changes in characters which are inheritable.[25] In small, isolated groups, inbreeding tends to fix any mutations which appear.

Recombination and mutation have provided the raw material for natural selection in the world of living things since the beginning of organic time, but it seems doubtful if any of the four major living races are equipped with physical characters of significant survival value. The main possible exception to this statement is skin color.

Social selection may have played some part in racial history, although, as Coon points out, this type of selection must have worked slowly in most groups because in any society except an industrial, civilized one there are few unmarried persons. Linton suggests that the ablest or richest men in primitive civilization get what are regarded as the most desirable women, and that their children have better survival chances than do the children of poorer providers. In some cases social selection has been so vigorous that infants showing undesired traits have been put to death. An example of this form of social selection is found in the Red and Black clans among the Tanala of Madagascar. In the Red clan, babies who are regarded as too dark in skin color are put to death. Light children in the Black clan are disposed of.[26] We have no way of knowing how frequent this kind of social selection has been in the human drama.

Man's self-domestication has some bearing on the differentiation of physical types. The most important characteristics of domesticated life, both for humans and for nonhumans, are artificial control of food supply, the modification of food consumed, and artificial protection against enemies. As a result of his self-domestication, man shares with domesticated animals a great variability of bodily traits as compared with the greater uniformity in the features of wild animals. Both blondness and blackness of hair are rare among wild animals, the hair of wild animals is almost always straight, and the hair of no wild species reaches the length it does in man. The great differences in size found both in

---

[25] See Julian Huxley, *Evolution, The Modern Synthesis*, Harper & Brothers, 1942, p. 21.

[26] Ralph Linton, *The Study of Man*, Appleton-Century-Crofts, 1936, p. 30.

man and in domesticated animals are not encountered among wild animals. According to Boas, "The elongation of the Negro face forward and the reduction of the European face find their parallels in breeds of dogs, horses, and pigs. Variations in the relative length of limbs as compared to length of the body, and concomitant variations in the form of shoulder girdle and pelvis are common."[27]

Some scholars have suggested that endocrine balance may be related to racial origins. Underfunctioning of the thyroid gland results in poorly developed nose and hair and a flat face, the adrenals affect the color of the skin, and other glands influence other physical features and the rapidity of development. The determination of the role, if any, of the endocrines in racial differentiation will have to await further research. Even if it could be shown that these glands had affected racial development, there would still be the question of what caused the changes in the behavior of the glands.

The question of environmental effects, other than those of natural selection, upon racial types is complex and controversial. The study of plants reveals that certain species show a great increase in the number of mutants produced when they are introduced into a new environment, but until recently there have been no satisfactory investigations along this line in the human field. Two studies[28] have yielded highly interesting data. Shapiro established three groups: sedentes (natives and still resident in Japan), immigrants (born in Japan and since 1884 migrants to Hawaii), Hawaiian-born (born in Hawaii of Japanese-born parents). Numerous measurements, indexes, and observations were made on 2500 men, women, and children. Krogman gives the following summary of this study:

"The amazing fact emerges that between sedentes and immigrants there was a significant difference in about 75% of all measurements and indices; correspondingly, between immigrants and Hawaiian-born the percentage was nearer 50. But that isn't all: the changes in the first group compared were disproportionate, those in the second group proportinate. In other words, the immigrant type tended to differ in kind from the sedentes, whereas the Hawaiian-born tended to differ in degree from the immigrants. Or, to put it another way, the trend once established tended to perpetuate itself."[29]

[27] Franz Boas, in Boas et al., General Anthropology, D. C. Heath and Company, 1938, p. 110.
[28] H. L. Shapiro, Migration and Environment, Oxford University Press, 1939; M. L. Goldstein, Demographic and Bodily Changes, University of Texas Press, 1943.
[29] W. M. Krogman, op. cit., p. 59. For a comprehensive summary and evaluation of twenty-five studies of the relationship between environment and human plasticity, see Bernice Kaplan, "Environment and Human Plasticity," American Anthropologist, October, 1954, pp. 780–800. See also Clyde Kluckhohn, "Physical Anthropology," American Anthropologist, December, 1955, pp. 1280–1295.

The Biological Effects of Race Mixture

Much emotion has been generated over the question of race mixture. Rationalizations are constantly developed to justify opposition to interbreeding; legislation and terrorism are employed to discourage it; and the offspring of racial crosses are often stigmatized. We shall give some of the impressive evidence which has accumulated concerning the biological effects of race crossing.[30]

The descendants of nine mutineers from the English warship *Bounty* and Tahitian women are vigorous, long-lived, and alert people. Members of this group have interbred for five generations, and, according to Shapiro, they equal or exceed in physical exuberance either parent stock. In Hawaii there has been much crossing between Polynesians, whites of many nationalities, Filipinos, Japanese, Chinese, Koreans, and others. The mixed population produced by these crosses seems to be made up of very satisfactory physical and mental types. Further evidence of successful race crossing in Polynesia is found in New Zealand where Maori-white mixture has produced unusually healthy and capable hybrids.

The thesis that the crossing of quite different racial stocks results more frequently in physical disharmonies than is normally the case has been sharply questioned in recent years. If such results were to be expected anywhere, the most logical place would be South Africa. Fischer's study of the descendants of Hottentots and Boers in South-West Africa does not reveal a disproportionate number of disharmonious types. These hybrids, known as Bastaards, are taller than their parental stocks, show a high vitality, and are very fertile.

Negro-white crossing in the United States has produced a group of hybrids which has survived, increased, and prospered in spite of tremendous social and economic obstacles.

A number of studies of Indian-white mixture in the United States, Canada, and Mexico show that the mixed offspring have the usual hybrid vigor, and that they are taller and more fertile than the original parental stocks.

Mongoloid-white crosses have not been studied extensively, but there is one interesting report concerning Dutch soldiers and the women of Kisar, an island in the Indo-Malayan Archipelago. Rodenwald found that the hybrids born of these unions were quite satisfactory physical types.

Although social conditions have been most unfavorable for the hybrids resulting from the matings of whites and Australian aborigines, the offspring are said to be excellent physical specimens. Their repro-

[30] See M. F. Ashley Montagu, *Man's Most Dangerous Myth: The Fallacy of Race*, pp. 100–133.

ductive and survival rates are probably higher than for whites, and in other respects they compare favorably with whites of comparable socioeconomic backgrounds.

The weight of present opinion seems to be on the side that regards race mixture as biologically advantageous. The older viewpoints concerning physical disharmonies, defectiveness, and constitutional unbalance are not supported by recent investigations. Unfavorable characteristics in hybrids are no longer thought to be the results of crossing per se, but are considered due to defective genes carried recessively by particular individuals. In fact, it is now thought that the chances are greater for matching such genes within a group than in matings between members of different groups. On this point Montagu says:

> . . . It must be remembered that gene distributions are not so much a matter of the distribution of the genes of individuals as of the distribution of genes within populations. It is not, therefore, a matter of speaking in terms of two individuals who, characterized by either a superior or a mediocre assortment of genes, transmit them to their offspring, but of the continuous interchange and shuffling and reshuffling of every kind of gene within a population to yield a very large number of gene combinations. Some of these will be superior to others; in fact, there will be every possible form of variation within the limits set by the genetic equipment of the population. This is true of all populations. No population has a monopoly of good genes, and no population has a monopoly of bad genes; normal and defective genes are found in all populations of all human beings. Furthermore, it is most unlikely that the kind of defective genes distributed in one population will be found to occur in anything like as great a frequency, if at all, in another population or ethnic group.[31]

The dire claims and the dismal forecasts of those who oppose race mixing on biological grounds are not supported by the achievements of nations where crossing has occurred. The ancient Egyptians were a mixture of Mediterranean, Negroid, Armenoid, and possibly other elements. The ancient Greeks were hybridized people of Mediterranean, Armenoid, Alpine, Nordic, and possibly other lines of descent. The ancient Romans were by no means a "pure" race. The great civilizational developments in recent times have been centered in western Europe and the United States where "mongrelization" has been exceedingly common. Geographical position, historical events, natural resources, contacts with neighbors and strangers, and other factors, as well as hybridization, must be taken into consideration in explaining "the blossoming of culture," but it cannot be demonstrated that race mixture per se causes cultural blight. In fact, the hybrid members of racial minorities have frequently showed capacities for leadership in many lines of endeavor, probably not so much because of biological factors as such

[31] *Ibid.*, pp. 129–130.

(although there is some evidence that mixed offspring are biologically superior to both parent stocks) as because of stimulating culture contact situations and the influences of marginal social status.

The biological consequences of race mixture may be summed up in these statements:

1. Race mixture does not produce biologically or mentally inferior offspring.

2. Race mixture tends to produce offspring which exceed their parental groups in vitality, stature, and fertility.

3. Radical crosses between races in the United States, and in certain places outside this country, occasion serious personal problems for parents and children in the 1950's. The hybrid is frequently treated as an outcast and discriminated against in matters which are crucial to happiness and success. Race mixture has its sociological disadvantages, and these will be discussed later, but the evidence does not indicate that it is biologically inadvisable.

Do the Jews Constitute a Race?

The answer to this question depends upon the existence of a combination of physical traits which would distinguish Jews from others. No such grouping of traits has been discovered by a reputable scientist. In every country Jews tend to approximate the local gentile type because of the intermixture which has invariably occurred. Usually a considerable part of a given Jewish population is physically indistinguishable from the Christian or Moslem inhabitants of the area.

Whether there is a quality of "looking Jewish" is a controversial matter. Carleton Coon maintains that this quality is undeniable, although he states that the deciding factor may not be so much physical as social and psychological. According to Coon, "It is possible that the feature which confirms the tentative identification of a person as a Jew, aside from clothing, speech, and other external cultural phenomina, is a characteristic facial expression centered about the eyes, nose, and mouth; this seems to be a socially induced element of behavior. . . . Not all Jews . . . have it. . . . The Jewish look may be seen occasionally upon members of other ethnic groups. . . ."[32] Kroeber writes that there is certainly no single crude index by means of which distinguishable Jews can be identified. "What is most characteristic of the so-called Jewish nose is not its total profile—which can be abundantly matched in many Gentile populations—but its 'nostrility,' a little accentuation of the curl of the nostril where it joins the face. This is a trait that was

[32] Carleton S. Coon, *op. cit.*, p. 441. See also Coon's "Have the Jews a Racial Identity?" in Isacque Graeber and S. H. Britt (eds.), *Jews in a Gentile World*, The Macmillan Company, 1942, pp. 20–37; and Melville Jacobs, "Jewish Blood and Culture," in *ibid.*, pp. 38–55.

first noted by a Jewish observer, and which is on the border line between an organic 'feature' and a functional 'expression.' "[33]

Herskovits points out that "nasality" was regarded for many years as
an identifying trait of the Jew, but that Fishberg's analysis (1905) of
Topinard's conception of the "hooked," or aquiline, nose as Jewish
showed the following percentages for nasal profile in Jews of European
origin living in New York City:

	Males (Percent)	Females (Percent)
Straight	58	59
Hooked, aquiline	14	13
Retroussé (snub)	22	14
Flat and broad	6	14

Herskovits adds, "The aspects of the trait that figure in the stereotype
may, of course, be other than profile—Fishberg himself felt that it might
be a matter of 'nostrility.' But to date no device for measuring this
exists, so that, on the basis of other studies, and until data to the contrary are presented, it can be regarded as a stereotypical rather than typical 'Jewish' characteristic."[34] On the question of the "Jewish look"
Herskovits remarks:

Is the "Jewish look" contained in the gestures the Jew employs when he
talks? That Jews "talk with their hands" is a fundamental element in the
Jewish stereotype, and one that is not easily susceptible of objective analysis.
The study made by Efron (1941) does, however, throw considerable light
on the matter. With the aid of an artist and using motion pictures, he
analyzed the gestures of Italians and Jews, dividing each group into "assimilated" and "traditional" categories. The findings demonstrate how little
validity there is in the assumption that the Jewish type is to be described
in terms of patterns of gesturing. Both from the standpoint of number of
people gesturing and of frequency and manner of gesticulation in those
people who do gesture, the assimilated Eastern Jews and the assimilated
Southern Italians in New York City (a) appear to differ greatly from their
respective traditional group, and (b) appear to resemble each other.

The quality of "looking Jewish" was further tested in an ingenious study,
instituted by the late Franz Boas two decades ago and carried on with the
co-operation of various universities over the country. Its purpose was to
discover how far racial or national origin could be determined through inspection. Freshmen, grouped in sections of large classes, were asked during
the first week of sessions, before they knew one another, to indicate on forms
provided for the purpose their places of birth, that of their parents and
grandparents, the language they spoke at home, their "race"—however they
might wish to define this term—and its characteristics as they conceived
them. Then each student, in turn, called by number only, stood before the

[33] A. L. Kroeber, op. cit., p. 144.
[34] M. J. Herskovits, "Who Are the Jews?" in Louis Finkelstein (ed.), *The Jews,
Their History, Culture, and Religion*, Harper & Brothers, 1949, vol. 2, p. 1167.

class while his fellows wrote what they thought his origin to be, their degree of certainty in drawing this judgment, and why they classified him as they did.

The results of this study were never published, but in conversation Professor Boas stated that at one of the New York colleges, forty per cent of the Italians were taken to be Jews, and the same percentage of Jews were adjudged Italians. This would seem to argue that if there is a "Jewish look" it is also in a large number of cases an "Italian look"—quite possible, since Southern Italians, like stereotyped Jews, are of Mediterranean stock. . . .[35]

The conclusion of the present writers is that the Jews are a mixed people derived originally from Caucasoid stocks in the eastern Mediterranean area. Insofar as the original stock remains the basis of their inheritance, they can sometimes be identified as eastern Mediterranean peoples but not as Jews. Since there are very few eastern Mediterranean peoples in the United States except Jews, their identification with this wider stock is not usually made.[36]

Five Unproved Racial Beliefs

Among the commonly held notions about race are the following: Some races are mentally superior to others; race and temperament are closely related; definite relationships exist between race and biological endowment; race and culture are correlated; some races outrank others in morality.

1. THE DOCTRINE OF MENTALLY SUPERIOR AND MENTALLY INFERIOR RACES

The belief that some groups have greater innate intellectual capacity than others goes back at least as far as Aristotle, who justified slavery on the ground that nature intends some men to rule and some to serve. We have referred earlier to the dogmas of Boulainvilliers, Gobineau, Chamberlain, Stoddard, Grant, and Hitler. Like these writers in contributing to the perpetuation of a false idea, but unlike them because he is a scholar, is Lucien Lévy-Bruhl. This sociologist contended that the primitive mind is prelogical. According to Lévy-Bruhl, primitives are unable to separate ideas or objects from the sentiments and emotions engendered by them. Primitives were adjudged by him to be emotional and mystical in contrast to civilized men, who are supposedly logical. This viewpoint is unacceptable in scientific circles today. In *The Mind of Primitive Man*, Boas has shown that the reasoning processes of nonliterate peoples are perfectly logical. The fact that such peoples, lacking the storehouse of modern knowledge, start from different premises and arrive at different conclusions has nothing to do with their basic intellectual processes. The Italian sociologist Vilfredo Pareto has

[35] *Ibid.,* pp. 1167–1168.
[36] On this point, see M. F. Ashley Montagu, *Statement on Race,* p. 65.

amply demonstrated the importance of nonlogical behavior in recent and contemporary civilized affairs. C. S. Myers, professor of experimental psychology at the University of Cambridge, concluded after many years' study of local populations in Australia and Africa "that the mental features of the rural populations in Europe correspond essentially to those observed in primitive peoples, and that differences, where they occur, must be ascribed to environmental influences."

The development of mental testing seemed to many to offer possibilities for determining the relative abilities of racial groups. Numerous mental measurements were taken on United States racial and cultural groups in the period 1915 to 1935, and, while the conclusions of the testers vary, "the results show that groups like the English, Scotch, Germans, Jews, Chinese, and Japanese [test] close to the norm (white American); and American Negroes, Indians, Italians, Portuguese, and Mexicans [test] definitely below the norm."[37]

A number of questions arise in connection with the interpretation of intelligence testing of racial and cultural groups. One of the most important problems is *sampling*, that is, finding test groups which are truly representative of the total groups. Different studies have shown considerable differences in median I.Q. for groups within the same race. An example is the comparison of southern Negroes and northern Negroes during World War I. In the army study of nearly 15,000 southern Negroes and 8000 northern Negroes in 1918, the northern Negroes were clearly superior to the southern Negroes. This study also revealed the interesting fact that although northern Negroes ranked below northern whites, the median I.Q.'s for Negroes from Ohio, Illinois, New York, and Pennsylvania were higher than the median I.Q.'s for whites from Mississippi, Kentucky, Arkansas, and Georgia. A later study by Peterson and Lanier showed white children in Nashville markedly superior to Nashville Negro children, Chicago whites slightly superior to the Chicago Negroes (only three ingenuity tests were used in this part of the study), but no significant differences in New York City. These authors suggest that their results may be due to (1) a highly selected group of Negro children in the New York sample, (2) the superior environmental opportunities of these subjects, and (3) the possibility that the white group was an inferior sample. Klineberg points out that the third suggestion is inapplicable when the scores are compared with norms obtained by Yerkes. His own investigation of selective migration creates great doubt concerning the first interpretation of Peterson and Lanier. Klineberg examined the school marks obtained by the northern migrants as compared with the nonmigrants and investigated school records in Birmingham, Nashville, and Charleston. There was no evidence

---

[37] Otto Klineberg (ed.), *Characteristics of the American Negro*, Harper & Brothers, 1944, p. 35.

in the 562 cases studied to indicate that the migrants constituted a superior group. In further studies Klineberg found that the lowest average
scores in a sample of Harlem school children were made by the groups
which had arrived most recently from the South,[38] thus showing the
effects of opportunity on I.Q.

Another factor which merits consideration in racial testing is *socioeconomic background*. An investigation of this factor by Arlitt showed
that when the Stanford-Binet was administered to 341 native white,
Negro, and Italian children in the primary grades, each of a single
school, the variation in results was greater in groups separated according
to Taussig's classification of social classes than when the comparison was
made on the basis of race. When *all* the native white children were
compared with *all* the Italian and *all* the Negro children, the I.Q. averages were 106.5, 85, and 83.4; but when lower-class native whites were
compared with lower-class Italian and Negro children, the results were
92, 85, and 83.4. The undifferentiated figure measures class more than
race. By controlling one variable, the investigator eliminated two-thirds
of the difference. In H. G. Canady's study of West Virginia State College freshmen the rank order by occupational groups of median scores
on the American Council Psychological Examination was professional,
commercial, artisan, skilled labor, and unskilled labor. Similar results
have been found in comparable studies of white students. Obviously
the task of matching individuals of two or more racial or cultural
groups socioeconomically is an extremely difficult one.

The importance of *the language factor* has been demonstrated in
many studies of European immigrant groups, Chinese, Japanese, American Indians, and Mexicans. In all of these cases the average I.Q. obtained on performance tests is higher than that obtained on tests calling
for language facility. Klineberg points out that the language handicap
of the American Negro is more indirect than in the other cases. It is
obvious that the Negro, particularly the southern Negro, does not have
the same language facility as the average white, and this difference may
have some influence on the scores made on linguistic tests.

Perhaps the most important factor in racial testing is *schooling*.
While intelligence tests were designed originally to measure innate ability, evidence has accumulated to show that results are affected by educational opportunities. This factor is particularly important in the case
of Negro-white testing since Negro schools, especially in the South,
have often been substandard. Only when educational conditions have
been equalized can racial testing be taken seriously, and even then other
factors influencing scores must be carefully scrutinized.

[38] See *ibid.*, Part II, chaps. 1–3, and, also by Klineberg, *Negro Intelligence and Selective Migration*, Columbia University Press, 1935, and *Race Differences*, Harper &
Brothers, 1935, chaps. 8–9.

Other factors to be considered in this type of testing are *motivation, rapport,* and *speed.* It cannot be assumed that all racial and cultural groups are equally interested in making the best possible showing in the tests. In this connection Dahlberg's remark is pertinent: "The Negro comes into the world with a skin which darkens quickly after birth, and with a brain which soon blackens before the realization that he must abandon all hope." Many testers have reported that their Negro subjects were indifferent, inattentive, or suspicious as to the value of the test. Investigators who have worked with American Indian children report cultural factors which are tied up with motivation, including the interesting refusal of Hopi children to compete against one another.[39] Rapport, or the relation between the investigator and the subject, may be a significant factor in test scores. That distrust, embarrassment, and uneasiness may enter into the results has been shown by studies like those of Canady. This investigator found a variation of six points in the I.Q., both for Negro and for white college students, when the students were tested on different occasions by a Negro and a white psychologist. The attitude toward speed needs to be taken into account, even in tests like the Binet where speed is less important than in some other tests. In the tests used by Peterson, Lanier, and Walker in a study of ingenuity and speed in white and Negro children where speed and accuracy were measured separately, the accuracy scores showed little or no difference between the two groups. Other investigations of Negro children, of American Indian children, and of Australian subjects have revealed a relative indifference to speed.

Another problem which arises in racial testing is *race mixture.* This factor is especially important in the mixed American Negro population, where an estimated three-fourths have some white ancestry. The results of tests administered to Negro samples, subdivided according to amount of white ancestry by means of general impression, anthropometric measurements, and genealogies, are inconclusive. G. O. Ferguson, Jr., found, in his study both of Virginia school children and of Negro recruits at Camp Lee, Virginia, during World War I, that lighter Negroes were superior to darker Negroes. M. J. Herskovits found no statistically significant correlations between four separate physical measurements (width of nose, thickness of lips, black element in skin color, white element in skin color) and scores on intelligence tests made by 539 adult male Negroes at Howard University. Peterson and Lanier correlated test scores with four anthropometric traits separately and with a composite of the four traits on seventy-five New York subjects. Klineberg correlated three traits separately with intelligence test scores in a study of 139 Negro boys in rural West Virginia. The latter two

[39] On this point, as well as others mentioned in this section, see Otto Klineberg, *Characteristics of the American Negro,* Part II, chap. 3.

studies produced results similar to those obtained by Herskovits. Studies of this type have not been numerous, and in most of them the number of subjects has been small. In no case has the investigator shown that the parent groups which have entered into the mixture are not either relatively superior or relatively inferior and therefore not representative samples of the total populations. Even if it could be shown that those with a higher percentage of white ancestry in groups such as the American Negro or the American Indian did stand higher on the intelligence tests, it would be necessary to determine whether differentials in educational and socioeconomic opportunities existed on the basis of amount of intermixture.

In the light of present evidence there is no justification for concluding that one racial or cultural group is better endowed mentally than others. Testing programs will have to be more successful than they have been thus far in obtaining representative samples, and in controlling such factors as schooling, motivation, rapport, speed, socioeconomic background, the language factor, and degree of race mixture, before any defensible conclusions can be reached.[40]

2 .THE BELIEF THAT RACES ARE TEMPERAMENTALLY DIFFERENT

Folk beliefs concerning innate racial and national temperaments have persisted through the centuries and provide the basis for widely held stereotypes. Dozens of scientific studies have been made in attempts to

---

[40] In view of the widely publicized contention of F. C. J. McGurk (*U.S. News & World Report*, September 21, 1956) that intelligence tests prove that "Negroes are below whites in capacity for education" and that "improvement of Negroes' social and economic status does not reduce this difference," the statements of four groups of scientists are cited. The Society for the Psychological Study of Social Issues and the American Anthropological Association went on record against the position that race is a determiner of innate psychological characteristics. Both organizations stated that such a relationship had never been scientifically demonstrated. In July, 1950, a group of distinguished experts on race from the fields of biology, anthropology, psychology, and sociology issued a "Statement on Race" which included this section:

"Whatever classification the anthropologist makes of man, he never includes mental characteristics as part of those classifications. It is now generally recognized that intelligence tests do not in themselves enable us to differentiate safely between what is due to innate capacities and what is the result of environmental influences, training and education. Wherever it has been possible to make allowances for differences in environmental opportunities, the tests have shown essential similarity in mental characters among all human groups. In short, given similar degrees of cultural opportunity to realize the potentialities, the average achievement of the members of each ethnic group is about the same." Ashley Montagu, *Statement on Race*, p. 14.

In 1952, a statement submitted by thirty-five social scientists to the Supreme Court as an appendix to appellants' briefs in the school segregation cases contained this passage: "The available scientific evidence indicates that much, perhaps all, of the observable differences among various racial and national groups may be adequately explained in terms of environmental differences. . . . It seems clear, therefore, that fears based on the assumption of innate racial differences in intelligence are not well founded." *Social Problems*, April, 1955, p. 231.

verify or refute these popular beliefs, but they have yielded few definite conclusions.[41] According to Klineberg, there is a suggestion, from the use of the Bernreuter Personality Inventory and the Rorschach test, of greater extroversion in Negroes. Also, Negroes seem more suggestible, but the problem of the relation of subject to investigator has not been adequately explored. Tests of Negro musical ability appear to indicate that the Negro is inferior except in rhythm, but the tests and their interpretation are under criticism. Results on handwriting tests are negative, and color preference tests have produced no significant conclusions. Work habits are said to show no special Negro characteristics, and gesture seems to be a matter of response to cultural environment. Studies of play habits show that Negro children play school more. This may be compensatory activity in view of the smaller success of Negroes in school and the fact that schools and learning are symbols of prestige and power. Until more adequate tests of temperamental characteristics have been constructed and the groups studied are equated on the basis of class and other background factors, no objective generalizations can be made on the question of race and temperament.

3. The Notion of Biologically Superior and Biologically Inferior Races

Proof of the biological inferiority of nonwhite peoples in the United States has been seen by some in certain differential mortality and morbidity rates. The mortality rate from tuberculosis is at least three and one-half times as high for Negroes as for whites, the disease begins actively at an earlier age, and the annual decline of the tuberculosis mortality is slower than among whites. The mortality rate for syphilis is eight times as high among Negroes as among whites. The infant mortality rate for Negroes greatly exceeds that for whites, as can be seen in the report of the U.S. Census for 1950. Seventy-three out of every thousand live Negro infants failed to reach age one, as compared to forty-three white babies out of every thousand born, and it is thought that more accurate reports would show a greater differential. According to Lewis, Negroes are less susceptible to diphtheria, yellow fever, and cancer and more susceptible than whites to lobar pneumonia and nephritis. Also, the incidence of peptic ulcers, gallstones, appendicitis, trachoma, and caries appears to be less for Negroes than for whites, but the incidence of uterine fibroid (benign) tumors is higher.[42] Sickle-cell anemia is fairly common among Negroes, but whites seem to be immune to it. Hemophilia is extremely rare among Negroes. In some skin

[41] Otto Klineberg, *Characteristics of the American Negro*, Part III, chap. 3.
[42] See J. H. Lewis, *The Biology of the Negro*, University of Chicago Press, 1942. A summary of this work is given in E. A. Hooton, *op. cit.*, pp. 563–567. See also Gunnar Myrdal, *An American Dilemma*, Harper & Brothers, 1944, pp. 142, 162, 173.

diseases the differences in incidence may be racial—psoriasis is rare among Negroes; ainhum is limited almost entirely to Negroes.

From the standpoint of the question of innate racial vitality, the most meaningful pathologies would seem to be tuberculosis, syphilis, infant mortality, heart disease, and cancer. The higher mortality rates from tuberculosis for American Negroes and American Indians as compared with whites are due in part to differences in housing, sanitation, and nutrition. Another factor is medical care, both early diagnosis and adequate treatment. It is interesting to note that the Negro mortality rate for tuberculosis is now lower than the white rate was fifty years ago. The differences in the syphilis mortality rates are partly explainable in terms of differences in living conditions, knowledge of the disease, and medical treatment. It is believed that the longer exposure of whites to these two diseases has resulted in the development of relative immunities to them. The differentials in infant mortality would seem to be due mainly to greater lacks in diet, knowledge of child care, and medical attention on the part of Negroes and Indians. Both cancer and heart disease are more prevalent among whites than among Negroes or Indians, but this difference may be attributed in part to the higher proportion of whites that survives into old age.

At the end of the last century some scholars thought the Negro would eventually disappear in this country because of general biological inferiority. He was not considered rugged enough to survive the fast tempo of life in a temperate climate. The record of the past six decades shows how mistaken these views were. As Donald Young has said: ". . . Such immunities and susceptibilities as may exist between the peoples of the earth—and there is little agreement as to either their nature or extent—have already been rendered so ineffective whenever the full force of our scientific knowledge of health has been applied that we may be assured that the health record of any American minority could be so controlled as to approximate that of the old American stock."[43]

THE MYTH OF RACIAL CULTURES

There is no correlation between race and culture. One looks in vain for a "Negro" culture, or a "Mongoloid" or a "Caucasoid" culture. There is considerable variation in government, family institutions, religious beliefs, economic practices, artistic traditions, and other aspects of culture from one section of Africa to another and even from tribe to tribe in the same area. The same is true for pre-Columbian America, and for Europe, Asia, and Oceania. Before the age of discovery and exploration, a number of inventions were made independently by racially unlike and geographically remote peoples. Since the development of rapid means of communication and transportation, the inventions

[43] Donald Young, *American Minority Peoples*, Harper & Brothers, 1932, p. 341.

and beliefs of diverse peoples have been transplanted to all habit-
able regions of the earth. The young children of any race have no difficulty absorbing any set of cultural norms provided they are constantly
exposed to it. One of the best examples of the lack of relationship between race and culture is seen in the American Negro population.
Very few African cultural traits have been retained in the United States.
Close and continuous contact has given Caucasoids and Negroids the
same basic western European type of culture. Such differences in
behavior as are observed between individual whites and Negroes in this
country seem to be attributable to (1) class, educational, occupational,
and other nonracial factors and (2) the somewhat different "social
world" in which the Negro lives because of racial segregation and discrimination.

5. The Dogma of Racial Morality

A widespread belief exists that there are strong connections between
skin color (and other physical characteristics) and ethical standards.
Deviations from genteel middle- or upper-class norms on the part of
members of racial or cultural minorities are often credited to the "wild
blood" of the recently domesticated savages or to the "low-grade blood"
of peasant hordes. Back of these explanations is the notion that nonliterate peoples are untamed men controlled by personal whim and
feeling rather than by self-restraint and laws for the general good. This
idea is worthy of somewhat more careful examination.

The practices usually cited to show the brutality and undeveloped
moral sense of nonwhite, nonwestern Europeans include infanticide,
the abandonment of disabled kin, cannibalism, polygyny, incest, and
premarital sexual intercourse. All of these customs occur in specific
cultural contexts. They are not random forms of behavior, nor are they
race-linked. Infanticide is found under special conditions such as poverty
or a belief that twins or triplets will bring misfortune. Moreover, this
practice is not unknown to Caucasoid populations, as, for example, in
ancient Sparta, ancient Egypt, and ancient Rome. Abandonment of
disabled kin is not brutal, callous behavior since it is often initiated by
the sick, crippled, or aged person himself and may involve a return for
the deserted one if the hunting party succeeds in replenishing its supplies.
Cannibalism seems not to have been widespread in primitive society. It
occurs for different reasons, including magical beliefs, revenge, and near-
starvation, and cannot be attributed to group bestiality. Polygyny can
seldom, if ever, be explained on the basis of masculine lechery. A long
period of lactation, running to two or three years in certain societies,
during which marital intercourse is prohibited seems to have been a
factor in the emergence of polygyny in some groups. In others, polygyny
appears to have been a consequence of an unbalanced sex ratio. Elsewhere, several wives have been desired because of their economic and

prestige values. Polygyny has had social approval in a number of Caucasian groups, including the ancient Egyptians, the ancient Babylonians, the ancient Hebrews, the early followers of Mohammed in Arabia, the ancient Slavs, Teutons, and Irish. Every human society has rules against incest, although the definition of incest varies. According to Malinowski, premarital freedom in nonliterate societies tends to reduce the importance of the erotic element in courtship, thus allowing nonsexual considerations to exert more influence on matrimonial choice.

Western civilization is notable mainly for technological and economic developments and the corresponding growth of order. As Hobhouse, Wheeler, and Ginsburg point out, economic development "does not imply greater considerateness or a keener sense of justice, and may in some ways be held even adverse to them." When comparative morality is under discussion, it is well to keep in mind current crime and delinquency rates, divorce rates, gangsterism, political corruption, lynchings, race riots, unemployment, mental disease, and atomic warfare in the United States.

Regardless of ever present discrepancies between ideals and performances, the basic morality of literate and nonliterate groups is much the same. Lowie says, ". . . Notwithstanding undeniable differences in outward manifestations, savagery and civilization display the same sentiments with reference to the basic human relations. Not unbridled self-indulgence, but restraint; not brutality, but kindness; not neglect of one's neighbors, but regard for them, are prescribed as proper goals of social conduct. What differs is essentially the extent of the group to which these sentiments are applied."[44]

Summary and Conclusion

In spite of (1) the lack of full genetic data on human beings, (2) a great amount of race mixture, (3) semantic problems, (4) the modifiability of races, and (5) the many difficulties of racial classification, race is not just a figment of the imagination. Scientists can identify major categories of mankind and there is fairly general agreement on smaller groupings.

Students of intergroup relations need to acquaint themselves with the techniques and problems of race from the standpoint of physical anthropology. They may choose from among four schools of thought on the biology of race:

1. Genetic theory. (Example: Dunn and Dobzhansky; Boyd)
2. The taking of more and more measurements and more accurate

[44] R. H. Lowie, "Intellectual and Cultural Achievements of Human Races," in H. S. Jennings et al., *Scientific Aspects of the Race Problem*, Longmans, Green & Co., Inc., 1941, p. 233.

measurements, plus the use of whatever genetic data are available. (Example: Hooton)
3. Traditional physical anthropological classifications, plus trait maps, combined with a skepticism about the usefulness of genetic theory for racial classification. (Example: Kroeber)
4. The investigation of mixed ethnic groups. (Examples: Ashley Montagu; Huxley and Haddon)

Regardless of the viewpoint favored, students have much to gain from a careful examination of physical anthropology. If there are no final answers as to what constitutes a race, the physical anthropologist can at least dispel common misconceptions about human physical differences. Physical anthropology has value for the study of race relations, even if the value is largely negative.

The student of intergroup relations cannot stop with physical anthropology. It is only the beginning for him because he has to deal with the attitudes and behaviors of the scientifically uninitiated. He must operate primarily in the fields of sociology and social psychology for the simple reason that, while most people use the term "race" inaccurately, it means something definite to them and they have strong feelings about it. The man in the street can see that men differ in physical appearance and he is certain that the differences are more than skin deep. Sociologically, race is a real thing to him. He "knows" that physical traits are linked with intelligence, temperament, character, morality, and so forth. He knows that Jews constitute a "race," and he is convinced of racial superiorities and inferiorities. To him races differ inwardly as well as outwardly, and he proceeds to treat those who differ from himself in special ways. He behaves "as if" men with other traits were a different species of the animal kingdom. This book is mainly concerned with the special conceptions which the members of one racial or cultural group have of other groups, and the believed-to-be-proper treatment of the others in certain historical associations.[45]

[45] In A. W. Lind (ed.), *Race Relations in World Perspective*, University of Hawaii Press, 1955, a social conception of race as a group of people who are regarded and who regard themselves as a race is followed. A number of recent studies have emphasized a shift from racial to class distinctions: Ralph Beals, "Indian-Mestizo-White Relations in Spanish America," chap. 18 in *ibid.*; Donald Pierson, "Race Relations in Portuguese America," chap. 19 in *ibid.*; Charles Wagley (ed.), *Race and Class in Brazil*, UNESCO, 1952. In a Mexican community, Lasker found that "practically the whole range of physical types occurs both in individuals whose parents are described as Indians and in those whose parents are considered to be Mestizos or Spanish. It is clear therefore that the physical appearance of the people cannot enter appreciably into their categorization of themselves. This supplements direct evidence that the ethnic identification is considered a cultural and linguistic matter and eliminates the possibility that considerations based on biological race significantly enter into the judgments." Gabriel W. Lasker, "Ethnic Identification in an Indian Mestizo Community," *Phylon*, Second Quarter, 1953, p. 190.

C H A P T E R 3

The Personality Functions of Prejudice

A Theory of Prejudice

In the early studies of prejudice and majority-minority relations two elements blocked an adequate explanation: prejudice was seen as a distinct and separate item of behavior, to be studied by itself; and its explanation was sought in some simple, one-factor analysis. In contemporary studies the explanations for prejudice are sought in the general body of systematic sociological and psychological theory about human behavior. One cannot be a student of majority-minority relations without at the same time being a student of personality and of the whole pattern of intergroup adjustments. In the development of our knowledge in this field the relationship has been reciprocal; the study of prejudice has been a fruitful approach to many problems of general sociology and social psychology. At the same time, the advances in the sciences of human behavior have made possible, and imperative, the reformulation of our explanations of prejudice. One-factor explanations clearly could not survive such a shift in approach. To say simply that there is an "instinct" or natural tendency toward prejudice, or that there is an inevitable "dislike of the unlike," or that so-called prejudice against minority groups is a natural reaction to their factual inferiority—explanations that abound in the early literature—is to fail to bring the study of prejudice into the framework of contemporary theory of human behavior.

An effective way to begin the search for the explanations of prejudice is to ask ourselves a group of questions:

Do groups differ in the direction and amount of prejudice which they exhibit? If so, why?

Do individuals differ in the direction and amount of prejudice which they exhibit? If so, why?

Is there change, through time and space, in the groups, and kinds of groups, toward which prejudice is directed?

What is the process by which an individual acquires prejudice?

What forces, in the life of individuals and of groups, operate to sustain, and to reduce, prejudice?

To answer such questions as these we must turn to a social science that deals adequately both with the process of individual personality development and with the dynamics of group interaction.

While studies of prejudice still stress a large number of separate forces—and there are many specialists who try to reduce the explanation to what they call the one "ultimate" or basic cause—a comprehensive theory is developing around three highly interactive but analytically distinct factors, each the convergence of several lines of theory and evidence.

Prejudice may be partly understood as a manifestation of the "needs" of individual personalities—needs that are an amalgam of constitutional and learned forces, that are to some degree unique but in part shared by fellow group members. On this level we need give little attention to the characteristics of the groups against whom prejudice and discrimination are directed; the attention, rather, must be given to the prejudiced person himself, the process by which he was "socialized," the values instilled in him by his society, and the degree to which he is able to satisfy those values. We need to be especially alert to any factors that help to differentiate the more prejudiced from the less prejudiced, because these factors may well be important in helping to explain the origins of prejudice.

The second level of explanation of prejudice looks for evidence not in the individual personality, but in the structure of society. It is particularly concerned with the power arrangements. It seeks to find out who makes the key economic, political, educational, and religious decisions in a society, and to what degree they employ prejudice against minority groups in order to make those decisions as favorable to themselves as possible. Such use of prejudice is seldom rational and conscious; it is hidden, as we shall see, by many protective beliefs. The task of the social scientist is to uncover the power relationships that are thus disguised, to show how prejudice is, in part, simply one manifestation of intergroup conflict and competition. This is an area where one-factor explanations abound. It is easy to say that prejudice is nothing but a way of getting an economic advantage, that it is forced on the great majority by the propaganda of a small ruling group who profit mightily from it. The exaggerations of the proponents of such a view, however, must not blind us to the accumulated evidence that prejudice *is* an economic and political weapon. We shall examine that evidence in Chapter 4.

The distinction between the personal and the social factors in prejudice is, of course, an analytic one. Since Cooley, it has been impossible for the careful student to reify society as separate from individual members; also—what is perhaps more often forgotten—it is impossible to interpret individual behavior adequately without careful attention to the social dimension. The behaving individual will carry within his personality the social norms and processes which permit the use of prejudice as a power device; and, oppositely, the individual personality, with its "need" for prejudice, will to some degree influence and interpret the social processes and norms to which it has been socialized. However, bearing carefully in mind the nature of our abstraction, we can analyze prejudice more effectively by seeing it as a manifestation both of the "needs" of individual personalities and of group conflicts.

The third basic cause of prejudice is culture itself. In almost every society, if not in all, each new generation is taught appropriate beliefs and practices regarding other groups. Prejudices are, in part, simply a portion of the cultural heritage; they are among the folkways. We learn these cultural responses in the same way that we acquire other attitudes and behavior patterns. Belief in the superiority of the Caucasian race is as natural to the average white American as belief in monogamy or knowledge of the "correct" way to dress. The speech and action of those around him, his observation of status differentials among the races, the jokes he hears, the histories he reads, the rewards and punishments he receives for various actions toward members of minority groups all teach him the correct behavior as it is defined by his society. He does not have to have any individual experience with members of minority groups; he will often be equipped with ready-made responses in advance of any such experience, or even in the complete absence of contact.

On this level of explanation we need not refer to personality needs or to group conflicts. A person can be prejudiced even when he has a minimum of the frustrations for which prejudice is an outlet and even when his economic or political interests, far from being served by the discriminatory attitude, are actually injured by it as we shall see later. To be sure, the prejudice may not be so deeply rooted when it is acquired simply as a culture norm and is unsustained by personality and group needs. But for purposes of scientific understanding of the causes of prejudice and for any kind of effective action in its reduction, if that be one's aim, the analytic separation of the cultural factor from the others is very important. This "culture norm" theory does not explain the origin of a prejudice as part of a group's culture. One can understand how an attitude toward minority groups can be passed along as tradition, but to explain the origin of that tradition, and perhaps its continuing vitality, one must refer to the personality and group functions. Similarly, one can understand the "need" for prejudice without seeing why specific groups should be used for the supposed satisfaction of that need. The selection of certain groups as targets can be understood only by analysis of the traditions of the society in which the prejudice operates. Thus the three factors interact. Any specific individual, in his pattern of prejudice, almost certainly reflects all of the causes. The importance of the various causes, however, will vary from person to person. Prejudice will be most intense, and least subject to change, when all three factors are concentrated in the same individual. A person brought up in a culture that is rich with traditions of prejudice, who identifies himself with groups which stand to gain, or think they do, from discriminatory actions, and who is insecure and frustrated will have a high probability for prejudice.

We can say that the *probability* is high that such a person will have a deep prejudice, but not that he positively will have it. Several closely related factors require this qualification. Other influences doubtless tend to produce prejudice that are unmentioned and unmeasured; since they are unmeasured, we cannot know to what degree they act upon this individual. Moreover, every person is influenced also by many unique experiences which make him something different from a perfectly typical representative of the groups to which he belongs. One may be a member of a group that believes it profits from an exclusionist policy; but he may have had experiences that cause him to doubt or deny this. Finally, a culture that is rich in traditions of prejudice may also be rich—or at least not lacking—in traditions of nonprejudice. If one has experienced this aspect of his culture in more than normal amount, the traditions of prejudice may be offset or counteracted.

Thus in its attempt to predict the likelihood of prejudice by study and measurement of its causes, social science must speak in terms of probabilities. So it must in every other phase of its work, and so must science in general, to the degree that it is not dealing with homogeneous units, and to the degree that it does not control or measure the effects of all the variables influencing a given interaction. Our belief is that the systematic study of these three clusters of factors, with the refinements in observation and measurement that are being made, will yield scientifically useful results. This picture of the roots of prejudice is tentative, of course. It will have to be refined both by the breakdown of these major factors into analytically more precise elements and by the isolation of new variables as yet unaccounted for.

Gordon Allport has developed a similar theory of prejudice that deserves careful study. He speaks of six levels of causation (separating some factors that we have classified together) that every researcher should be alert to, regardless of the special causal problem he is studying:

1. The stimulus approach—study of the objects of prejudice. Are they "living inkblots" who can be interpreted almost any way by a prejudiced person depending upon *his* tendencies, not upon theirs;

or are persons against whom prejudice is directed significantly different, on the average?

2. The phenomenological approach—study of the prejudiced individual's definition of the situation he finds himself in. This is in part a function of the total situation, but in part a function of his personal hypotheses. Analysis of this level alone will not explain prejudicial behavior, because it will not tell what determined the individual's definitions of a situation.

3. The approach through personality dynamics and structure—study of the functions of prejudice for the individual. Does it help to satisfy needs—excuse failure, maintain self-esteem, improve competitive position, or give a sense of belonging? ". . . Prejudiced attitudes may serve as a psychological crutch for persons crippled in their encounters with life."

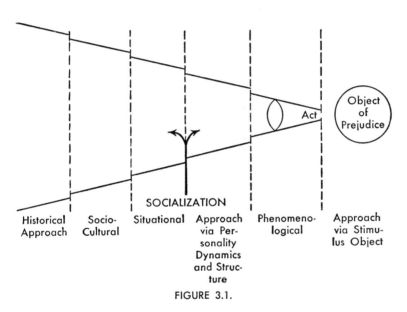

FIGURE 3.1.

4. The situational approach. How does the situation in which the minority-group member is encountered affect prejudice? The effects of contact with persons of equal status, of contact in a group with democratic or autocratic atmosphere, of contact through some verbal test (a questionnaire or interview *about* one's prejudices) must be measured carefully.

5. The approach through analysis of cultures and subcultures. Degrees and kinds of prejudices vary widely not only among individuals, but among cultures. Group prejudice is most likely in highly differentiated societies, particularly those with a great deal of social mobility where many people are hoping and trying to improve their status.

Virtually all the hostility in some simpler societies is directed against specific individuals, not against categories of people.

6. The historical approach. The analysis of the history of contact between Negroes and whites in the United States, for example, is important in understanding the contemporary scene.[1]

Allport's analysis of the levels of causation of prejudice is charted in Figure 3.1.[2]

This emphasis on different levels of causation is essential to an adequate theory of prejudice. Complete understanding of specific acts of prejudice requires the analysis of each of many causes and close attention to their interaction.

A Theory of Personality

In recent years, evidence from cultural anthropology, psychiatry, psychology, social psychology, and sociology has made possible the emergence of a theory of personality that is of great value in the analysis of prejudice. In this study we can only sketch its major outlines, while urging the reader to refresh and extend his information in the field by reference to the extensive literature available.[3] The theory is new and tentative, and only part of it has direct application to the study of prejudice and minority-majority relations. Its key concepts must be stated, however, for they furnish the context in which our analysis of the personality functions of prejudice is carried on.

An adequate theory of personality has been slow in developing for reasons that it is well to know if we are to avoid oversimplifying our problem. As Kluckhohn, Murray, and Schneider have pointed out, great difficulties come from the fact that many of the workings of personality are hidden, their forms only to be inferred from manifestations in word and action. Personality is a process; it will not stop to be examined. Many of the forces that operate are unconscious, and they operate through time, so that one may have to wait for hours, days, or years to see the effects. Personality must, to some degree, be studied as a

---

[1] See Gordon Allport, "Prejudice: A Problem in Psychological and Social Causation," *Journal of Social Issues*, Supplement Series, November, 1950.

[2] *Ibid.*, p. 7.

[3] These are among the books that are of value in the field: J. F. Brown, *Psychology and the Social Order*, McGraw-Hill Book Company, 1936; Norman Cameron, *Psychology of Behavior Disorders, A Bio-Social Interpretation*, Houghton Mifflin Company, 1947; Walter Coutu, *Emergent Human Nature*, Alfred A. Knopf, Inc., 1949; Abram Kardiner, *Psychological Frontiers of Society*, Columbia University Press, 1945; Clyde Kluckhohn, H. A. Murray, and David Schneider, *Personality in Nature, Culture, and Society*, Alfred A. Knopf, Inc., rev. ed., 1953; Kurt Lewin, *A Dynamic Theory of Personality*, McGraw-Hill Book Company, 1935; Ralph Linton, *The Cultural Background of Personality*, Appleton-Century-Crofts, 1945; Gardner Murphy, *Personality*, Harper & Brothers, 1947.

totality, and even as part of a larger situation or field, for it exhibits some degree of wholeness in its functions and is interactive with its environment. Add to these difficulties the blind spots and inadequacies of the scientists themselves as personalities, and the obstacles thrown in the way of research by society—both strongly operative in the study of prejudice—and it is easy to understand the delay in the development of an integrated science of personality.

Despite these difficulties, important steps have been taken toward a theory of personality that is of great value for the student of prejudice. It is too early to speak of a unified theory, combining the several levels of analysis on which various students have worked. There is, however, a growing awareness of the need for taking a series of factors into account. The heredity versus environment controversy has been dismissed as meaningless. The effort now is to find out what the range of biological potentialities is, and then to study which of those potentialities result from a particular series of experiences in the physical, social, and cultural environments. One of the most important ideas is that personality is best conceived as process, not as a collection of fixed traits. As process, it can be understood only by analysis of the flow of behavior that comes from the interaction of the individual with the situation. An individual does not exist or behave in a vacuum, but always in some situation. Which tendencies—from among the numerous and often contradictory tendencies of which we all are capable—will be set in motion cannot be predicted from knowledge of the individual alone. With what "reference groups" is he most closely identified at the moment? Which of his various potentialities are being encouraged by the existing situation, which are being blocked? How do the structured aspects of his "role" channel his behavior? Role is a social concept designating the expected behavior of a person in a given social relationship. The process of carrying out the functions of "shop steward" in a union, "superintendent of schools," or "courteous customer" does not allow full individual variation to come into play. The roles themselves have some compulsions that influence which of various tendencies the individual will express. Thus personality thought of as process is "field" determined.

This does not mean that we can disregard individual differences. Knowledge of the groups within which one develops and within which behavior occurs is vital. Frequently knowledge of group values and role requirements alone will yield good predictive power concerning individual behavior. Under other circumstances, however, such knowledge is inadequate. The individual is never completely socialized. Innate motivations may to some degree contradict his socialized motives, the unique elements in his genetic make-up and in his experience give him some unique needs, and every cluster of group experiences develops some mutually contradictory needs.

An adequate theory of personality, therefore, whether used with reference to prejudice or to some other aspect of life, must be concerned with the study both of tendencies and of the situations in which they are expressed.[4] In this chapter we shall describe some of the processes involved in the generation of hostile tendencies, but will also note the way in which their expression is affected by the situation.

Prejudice as a Product of Frustration

One of the most frequent applications of modern social psychological theory to prejudice is found in the frustration-aggression hypothesis and a group of concepts related to it. Every person is a cluster of propelling forces—original organic forces that have been shaped, coerced, and heavily supplemented by sociocultural forces—pointed toward goals. But no human being moves smoothly toward all the goals that have become part of him. Major and minor frustrations are a continuing part of everyone's life. Achievement of these goals may be blocked by other people, by natural forces (illness, for example), by one's own lack of skill or some other personal tendency. We may have mutually contradictory goals, one of which inevitably must be denied.

There is much evidence to indicate that the blocking of goal-directed behavior frequently creates hostile impulses in the individual. In many instances this hostility cannot be directed toward the source of the frustration; there may be no human agent, or the agent may be unknown, or too powerful to strike. A pattern of beliefs may define the agent as an in-group member, a friend, a protector, so that it is impossible to recognize him, consciously, as a source of frustration. One may be tied to him in an ambivalent relationship of both love and hostility—as is the child to the parent. The hostility under such circumstances may be stored up, or it may be directed toward oneself or toward some substitute target that is more accessible or less able to strike back. In other words, a "free-floating," undirected hostility may result from frustration when the actual frustrating agent cannot be attacked; and the social context often favors displacement of this hostility onto minority-group members.

The newly directed attack does not take place, however, without some emotional and intellectual strains; the irrationality and injustice of such hostility, from the point of view of the prejudiced person himself, cannot be completely ignored, although it may not be consciously recognized. The substitute target is, after all, a substitute. In order to make himself seem reasonable and moral, according to his own standards, the person who has shown prejudice or discrimination toward a scapegoat looks for justifications. He creates or accepts convincing reasons for

[4] See Walter Coutu, *op. cit.*; and Gardner Murphy, *op. cit.*, pp. 866–902.

hating or discriminating against members of the minority group. He discovers and believes many kinds of evidence that "prove" that the members of that group thoroughly deserve the treatment he gives them. In a strange, but common, perversion of the facts he even projects onto the scapegoat some of the evil traits (again according to his own definition) which characterize his own behavior, in an attempt to get rid of the feeling of guilt that is too heavy for his ego to bear.

Do my fantasies wander a bit in lascivious direction? I should not feel sinful, for I ponder (and gossip about) the moral laxity of others. Does my conscience plague me for the low wages that I pay my Negro employees? I can be at rest, for *they* would only grow "biggety" if they had more money. After all, what a small thing my own greed is, for the Jew will skin you alive if he gets a chance. In the catalogue of indictments drawn by the nazis against the Jews we find a faithful listing of the nazi's own monstrous sins.[5]

Finally, to get rid of any sense of doubt and to give an absolute quality to his beliefs, the prejudiced person categorizes all the various individual members of the minority group by means of stereotypes, usually furnished by society, which help him to rationalize his prejudice toward the whole group, despite the variations which characterize any human group.[6]

In this process, the theory goes on to state, the prejudiced person is not wholly successful in reducing his feelings of hostility. Attacks on a scapegoat, after all, are of little use in reducing the actual source of frustrations. They may, in fact, protect the frustrating agent, because attention is diverted in the wrong direction, permitting the person or the social situation which is causing the frustration to continue its activities or even to intensify them. Thus, for example, if the true cause of the frustrations of unemployment of an industrial worker is a group of attitudes held by management and/or his fellow workers, but he thinks that he is unemployed because of competition from colored workmen, he may displace his hostility onto the colored man while the true cause of his frustrations continues unaffected. There is another reason for the ineffectiveness of this frustration-hostility-displacement cycle in reducing hostility. The displacement of hostility on a substitute may well be accompanied by some doubts concerning its effectiveness and justice; and projection of one's own failings onto others almost certainly leaves, at least unconsciously, a sense of guilt and a fear of retaliation. These doubts and feelings of guilt create further anxiety and hostility—the more so because they cannot be consciously recognized—and lead to even further displacement and projection. The whole

[5] Gordon Allport, "The Bigot in Our Midst," *Commonweal*, October 6, 1944.
[6] Cf. Bohdan Zawadski, "Limitations of the Scapegoat Theory of Prejudice," *Journal of Abnormal and Social Psychology*, April, 1948, pp. 127–141.

procedure "can lead to apparently reasonless hostile behavior toward those who are guilty only of being the objects of our hostility."[7] Such a vicious circle helps to explain the tenacity with which prejudice, once started, survives attempts to reduce it by appeal to reason.

It is clear that this theory of prejudice owes much to Freudian doctrines. Some of the writers who support it continue to interpret the process in "classic" Freudian terms. Almost any social norm is looked upon as a frustrating restriction of the "natural" organic man. Frustration and hostility are thus not only widespread and inevitable but basic to the very process of socialization. Non-Freudians contend that the needs of the socialized human being are scarcely to be understood solely by reference to original tendencies. The channeling of behavior by culture is not necessarily the inhibiting of behavior, for learned patterns are just as natural as biological needs, and they may be much more urgent. Whatever the balance between innate and acquired needs—the present authors incline toward an emphasis of the latter—it is clear that we all face frustrations of those needs. What is the relationship of those frustrations to prejudice? The evidence is by no means definitive, and there are contradictory views, but it is worth examining.

In a study by Miller and Bugelski, boys at a camp were compelled, as part of a testing program, to take a long, dull exam composed of questions which were, on the whole, too difficult for them to answer. At first relatively unaware of what was in store for them, the boys presently realized that the tests were running overtime and that they would be unable to attend bank night at the local theater—an event to which they looked forward all week. The authors used this situation to give the boys brief attitude tests before and after the examination with its attendant frustrations. Before the exam, half were asked to rate Japanese and half were asked to rate Mexicans; afterward, those who had rated the Japanese rated the Mexicans, and vice versa. In both instances unfavorable attitudes increased.[8] Whether the increase in prejudice was a temporary verbal response or a more lasting attitude would be important to know. If we grant that the boys were more prejudice-prone after the exam, did the fact that they were furnished groups upon whom to displace their hostility at just that time help to fixate an attitude toward those groups? The study does not provide an answer to this question.

The authors of *Frustration and Aggression* connect the many frustrations of the Germans from 1914 to 1933 with the ease with which they adopted overt anti-Semitism. Defeated in war after an exhausting effort, their prestige destroyed, forced to accept the Treaty of Versailles

---

[7] John Dollard, "Hostility and Fear in Social Life," *Social Forces*, October, 1938, p. 18.

[8] See John Dollard, Neal Miller, Leonard Doob, et al., *Frustration and Aggression*, Yale University Press, 1939, pp. 43–44.

and to relinquish their colonies and other territory, they came to the peace only to face depression, a ruinous inflation (which virtually destroyed a middle class that had sought security through frugality), and finally a world-wide economic collapse that deepened their own depression. Direct aggression against the Allies was impossible, but various kinds of displaced aggression appeared. Many joined the Social Democratic and Communist parties to fight the old order, some joined youth movements, and an increasingly large number gave support to Hitler's anti-Semitism and other aggressive moves.[9]

Allport and Kramer, in a study of college undergraduates, sought to find out if those who felt themselves to be the victims of prejudice, and thus presumably experiencing frustration, were more likely to be prejudiced themselves. Of 110 Catholics, 78 percent of those who felt more victimized than the average were among the students who showed more prejudice toward the Negro. But among the Catholics who felt that they had themselves been the victims of prejudice in less than an average amount, 62 percent fell in that half of all the students who showed more prejudice toward the Negro. No adequate statistical test of significance is possible with these data, but the little weight that they do carry supports the hypothesis that frustration encourages prejudice. Allport and Kramer also discovered that the Jews who felt themselves more victimized were also the more anti-Semitic. Perhaps out of fear of reprisals from the dominant group, they turn on their own group. The evidence of these authors, however, does not all support this hypothesis; they also discovered that persecuted minorities may develop sympathies for other minorities. A U-shaped curve seems to describe the data. The Jews who felt more victimized (of the 63 who were studied) had more individuals among those most friendly to the Negro than did the Jews who felt less victimized, the latter tending to take an intermediate position:

Among 63 Jewish Students	First Quartile (Least Anti-Negro)	Second Quartile	Third and Fourth Quartiles
More victimized	29%	44%	27%
Less victimized	10%	72%	17%

Moreover, it was found in this study that Jews were the least prejudiced, although they are often victims of prejudice; thus the frustrations produced by persecution do not necessarily lead to prejudice.[10] Here the need for taking account of many other variables is clear.

Frenkel-Brunswik measured the explicit ethnic prejudices of 250 sixth- to eighth-grade pupils, and then found, by sociometric tests, that

[9] Ibid., pp. 153–156.
[10] Gordon Allport and B. M. Kramer, "Some Roots of Prejudice," Journal of Psychology, July, 1946, pp. 9–39.

the more highly prejudiced tended to be less often mentioned as best friends, were less popular, more seeking of attention, more unwilling to be bossed, more frustrated and complaining, less trustworthy and helpful.[11] We must carefully avoid assuming that such a study, even if its measurements are considered reliable and valid, proves that the observed personality tendencies cause the prejudice, that, perhaps, the prejudice is an attempt to get rid of hostility. It may be simply that the kinds of experiences—family training, for example—that produce untrustworthy, attention-seeking, frustrated individuals are also the kinds of experiences that are likely to furnish them prejudices. The causal sequence may even be the opposite from that inferred. Children who are taught to be prejudiced may thereby be trained in rigidity of mind, lack of ability to adjust to reality, and other tendencies which produce the inclinations the study found. It is perhaps most likely that all of these possibilities are involved in a complicated interaction.

PREJUDICE AND PROJECTION

Closely associated with the hypothesis that free-floating hostility may be important in prejudice through the process of displacement is the conception that prejudice may be an attempt to help individuals accept the rigid inhibitions that culture imposes on them or to rationalize violations of those inhibitions when they do occur. This idea has been suggested at various points above but now needs explicit formulation. The "reasoning" of the prejudiced person might be stated briefly in this way: "I must not do that" (show uninhibited aggressive or sexual acts, for example), "but there is no great loss—only inferior people do that anyway." Or "I should not have done that" (joined in mob violence against a member of a minority group or violated the sex code), "but these people are inferior, so I have not really done anything bad." John Dollard formulates this idea clearly in his article, "Hostility and Fear in Social Life." Society, he says, is a unity, maintained by interdependence, by the suppression of in-group aggressions, and by defensive-aggressive actions against out-groups. Hostility toward the in-group is generated in the process of transmitting its patterns of behavior to each member, but society suppresses such hostility by many sanctions and rewards. For the most part, individuals find that such hostile moves are either useless or dangerous and abandon them as overt responses. No one is perfectly socialized, however; each is the record of a battle in which frustration, hostility, and fear have played roles. The hostility toward in-group members and norms that is built up in the process of socialization and that continues as a result of the controls on adult behavior is often underestimated, says Dollard. Control over it is

[11] Else Frenkel-Brunswik, "Studies of Social Discrimination in Children," *American Psychologist*, October, 1946, p. 456.

one of the chief problems of social life. No society requires the complete renunciation of in-group aggression, of course. There are standardized, culturally defined channels for aggression. In modern American society, economic competition and sports, for example, may serve this function. Moreover, aggression can be suppressed to some degree—one of man's most useful capacities from the point of view of adjustment to society. Seldom, however, does a society rechannel aggressions effectively enough or permit sufficient aggression to drain off all hostility. In-group members live in a constant state of readiness for aggressive responses.[12]

As was stated earlier, the degree to which frustration and hostility are the *inevitable* result of *any* socialization (the position of the doctrinaire Freudian) is a question on which the evidence is as yet incomplete. Anthropological evidence seems to indicate that human beings can be socialized to widely different cultural standards, including some highly restrictive practices, without having their hostility raised to the point where social cohesion is endangered. Doubtless it is a matter in part of the restrictiveness of the cultural norms and in part of the way in which those norms are transferred to the maturing individual. More hostility may be aroused by the inhibitions imposed on the aspiring middle-class American or the maturing boy among the Manus of New Guinea than results from socialization in a Latin-American culture or in aboriginal Samoa. But more serious hostility arises when cultural norms, whatever they are, are brought to conscious attention and scrutiny by culture contact, by social and technological change. Then the weight of the inhibitions imposed by society begins to be felt. As Alexander Goldenweiser put it: "A weight one is not aware of is only half a weight."[13]

Whatever the degree of truth in the Freudian contention that social norms inevitably lead to hostility, it is clear that many societies, including modern American society, do have individuals who carry within themselves both propelling needs and inhibitions against the satisfaction of those needs. Such individuals must block overt response to these tendencies in order to avoid social pressure and guilt feelings (to the degree that they have taken the cultural standards into their own personalities); but the tendencies continue to work on them. This situation is favorable to the development of prejudice. The inhibition seems more bearable if it is only inferior people who behave that way anyway; or the violation of a norm is less of a blow at one's self-respect and conscience if the violation has been aimed at a member of a "lower" group. Here the familiar process of projection comes into use. Many studies have shown, for example, that a ruling group which has exhibited violent aggression against a racial minority and has exploited it sexually

---

[12] See John Dollard, *op. cit.*
[13] Alexander Goldenweiser, *Anthropology*, Appleton-Century-Crofts, 1937, p. 416.

is likely to be firmly convinced that members of the racial minority are uniformly violent and sexually unrestrained. MacCrone states that the sexual life of the "natives" has a perennial fascination for the South African whites. There is a widespread belief that native men are more potent sexually and native women more voluptuous. This is combined with morbid fear of miscegenation and great emotional fear of rape[14]— a strange combination of beliefs in light of the fact that virtually all sexual contact has been initiated by white men, despite intense social disapproval. This prejudice against the natives—we have described only a part of the whole cluster of attitudes that defines the native as inferior and evil—seems to be a clear case of projection. The picture of the natives as vicious and violent can be interpreted in the same way, since the whites have often been ruthless in their use of violent suppression. Having ignored their own standards regarding the use of violence and the control of the sex impulse, the ruling whites find the strains on their consciences too heavy to bear. They attempt to reduce the tension by projecting the traits of violence and sexuality onto the native group. As already noted, this attempt to reduce strain may not work, for it may be accompanied by a sense of guilt, which leads to further anxiety, more hostility, the need for even more projection—and thus a vicious circle which can be broken only by a change of action or of conscience on the part of the projecting person.

Dollard describes much the same combination of beliefs and actions in "Southerntown." Most of the sex contacts between Negroes and whites are initiated by white men, most of the violence is used by whites against the Negroes; yet there is an emotionally vivid belief in the violent and sexually aggressive nature of the Negro. This belief is needed not only to rid many white people of a sense of guilt for having violated their own standards, but to help them resist the impulses toward violation. The Negro, a designated inferior group, symbolizes the repressed impulses that one must not admit are still motivating him. In "Southerntown" the white male is torn by a group of contradictory desires and accompanying beliefs: to maintain "race purity," to live up to the dominant moral code with regard to sex, and yet to take advantage of the relatively defenseless status of the colored population for wider sexual contact. He sees that preventing contact of Negroes with whites will help to satisfy the first desire; but he forgets that if whites initiate such contacts, the results are not different. His belief in the inferiority of the Negro helps him to satisfy the second desire or to rationalize its violation: if the inferior Negro is sexually promiscuous, I must not be; or if I make advances toward a Negro woman, it isn't really a violation of the code. This same concept of the inferiority of the Negro and

[14] See I. D. MacCrone, *Race Attitudes in South Africa*, Oxford University Press, 1937, pp. 294–310.

belief in the strong sex urges and easy virtue of Negro women help him to satisfy the third desire. Race prejudice is a natural outcome of such a complex of mutually contradictory desires, feelings of guilt, and repressions.[15] There are many other factors operating too, of course; they will be studied in later chapters.

In *Color Blind* Margaret Halsey states in an interesting way the ease with which many people believe stories that involve the issues of race and sex:

> One of the most monotonous aspects of race relations in the United States is the blind acceptance—by otherwise sensible people—of any wild, half-baked, fragmentary, unsubstantiated or even patently absurd cock-and-bull story that comes along, provided it has to do with Negroes and sex. People who balance their checkbooks, tot up the slips from the grocery, count over the laundry when it comes back, and in many other ways behave with cool, hard-headed realism will turn out to be the suckers of the world when it comes to Negro sexuality. Nobody on God's green footstool could sell these people stock in a phony gold mine, but when the issue is sex and Negroes, they sit with their mouths open like fledgling birds and swallow whatever is dropped in. If white Americans conducted the rest of their careers with the same childlike gullibility they bring to bear on stories about Negroes and sex, a staggering percentage of our Caucasian population would spend its life in receivership.[16]

This whole matter of repression, guilt, and projection is illustrated, in a complicated way, by the question: "Would you want your sister, or daughter, to marry a colored man?" On the surface it seems to be a demand for complete separation of the races for fear that Negro men, if they had the opportunity, would promptly ask white women to marry them. But marriage is a voluntary affair, for the most part, in our society. There seems in this question to be a hidden fear, not only that the Negro men will ask, but that the white women will accept. Why should white men have this fear? A number of factors may be involved, related to the way our society handles the question of sex and to the race-sex problem. Our society tends to inhibit sex impulses and yet at the same time to exalt sex experience as highly desirable. Having, for reasons noted above, pictured the Negro as highly sexual, the white man cannot thoroughly get rid of the notion that he may therefore be highly desirable. Dollard suggests that in "Southerntown" white women to some degree, unconsciously, do find Negro men attractive—both as embodiment of their own repressed impulses and perhaps in a hidden desire to strike back at their own men who have not been entirely faithful. The white men, having taken Negro women, fear unconsciously

[15] Cf. John Dollard, *Caste and Class in a Southern Town*, Yale University Press, 1937, pp. 363–388.

[16] Margaret Halsey, *Color Blind*, Simon and Schuster, Inc., 1946, pp. 36–37.

that the white women may have similar, unknown desires.[17] Such a phrase as "the rising tide of color," says MacCrone, may have more than rhetorical significance. Color, the uninhibited and unrepressed native, may symbolize one's own repressions; the rising tide is within oneself. All of this is very tenuous, of course. Even were it a well-established theory, it would be only one part of the explanation of prejudice. But there seems to be some evidence in its support and it harmonizes with the developing theory of personality.

One need not assume, in this discussion, that the claims of prejudiced persons that "inferior" groups are violent and sexually uninhibited are entirely false. Such characteristics are not uncommon among groups discriminated against—the American Negro in the South, for example. The partial truth of the stereotype of the minority group upon whom a dominant group has projected its faults helps to reinforce the prejudice, to make it seem reasonable. The personality functions served by the prejudice are thereby carried on more effectively, unmindful of several complications: actual errors in the picture of the minority group, with gross exaggeration of most other traits; assumption that the traits are innate; categorization of the whole group, without attention to wide individual variations; and an emotional defense of the total picture which shows how important it is to the prejudiced person that the issue not be examined.

We must be careful to note that this scapegoat theory of prejudice is by no means adequate by itself. There seems to be good evidence that frustration does not always lead to aggression and hostile acts. The theory does not explain how the hostile *impulses* become transformed into hostile *attitudes*—persistent, patterned hostility toward an individual or a group—rather than selecting some new and unique target each time.[18] And it does not explain why this patterning takes the form of prejudice against specific groups. One may say correctly that frustration may well make a person more susceptible to prejudice, that it is one of the forces found where prejudice is most common; but the many other factors involved must be taken into account. Persons in whom the frustrations and guilt feelings we have discussed are at a minimum are, nevertheless, often prejudiced because of the other factors that we shall discuss later. Although the scapegoat theory helps to explain some of the force behind prejudice, the "need" for it, it does not explain the direction that prejudice takes.

We shall be concerned with that question in Chapter 5, but a brief comment here will help us to avoid misunderstanding. Zawadski holds that extreme proponents of the scapegoat theory are reacting against

---

[17] John Dollard, *Caste and Class in a Southern Town*, pp. 166–170.
[18] Cf. Theodore M. Newcomb, "Autistic Hostility and Social Reality," *Human Relations*, 1947, vol. 1, pp. 69–86.

the earlier racist doctrines which explained prejudice simply by reference to the supposed traits of the minority groups: We are prejudiced against them only because of their "well-earned reputation" for evil acts and inferior abilities. Such an explanation pays attention only to the groups against which prejudice is directed; but the scapegoat theory pays attention only to the tendencies of the prejudiced persons. It is not adequate to explain why a given group, or groups, have been selected for the role of scapegoats. Part of the explanation, says Zawadski, may lie in the characteristics of the minority groups themselves that make them particularly vulnerable. In the process of disproving that the traits which typify a group are not innate or inevitable, contemporary students have sometimes denied the possibility of distinguishing at all among groups on the basis of average differences in tendencies toward certain kinds of behavior. This error is perhaps as likely to prevent an adequate social psychology of prejudice as the error which it supplants. It would be remarkable indeed if the members of minority groups, experiencing as they do significantly different influences throughout the course of their lives, did not develop some personality tendencies by which, to some degree, they can be distinguished. Having said that, one must then, in any complete theory of prejudice, seek to isolate such distinctive tendencies, measure them, and explain them. Here the interaction of the various factors in prejudice becomes clear, because one of the key explanations of these minority-group characteristics lies in prejudice and discrimination themselves. To begin with, the tendencies are responses, at least in large measure, to the treatment received from the majority.[19] But within a specific interacting field they are, however caused, among the forces to be studied. Thus we must state again that the study of prejudice from the point of view of analysis of prejudiced persons is a scientific abstraction—necessary for research, but eventually requiring synthesis with the total interacting field.

Prejudice and Personality Needs

In many instances writers who have explained prejudice by examining the personality of the prejudiced individual have limited themselves to the discussion of frustration, repression, and closely related topics. There are, however, a number of other "needs," which in only a very general sense can be brought into this kind of explanation, that are also important in helping us to understand how prejudice reflects the personality.[20] Prejudice may be an attempt to bring meaning into a confusing and ambiguous crisis situation. Few of us like the feeling that we do not

[19] Cf. Bohdan Zawadski, op. cit.
[20] Cf. David Krech and Richard Crutchfield, Theory and Problems of Social Psychology, McGraw-Hill Book Company, 1948, pp. 443–498.

understand an important situation close to us; yet there are many situations that we cannot understand. If the content of our culture includes prejudices, or if, in a new situation, the media of communication offer prejudices, we may adopt them to "explain" the crisis. If a businessman or worker is suddenly confronted with an economic crisis, his vague ideas and beliefs about the economy of the country may not be able to explain the depression and his personal problems. If there is available the "explanation" of the international Jew, with monopoly power and shady business practices, he may adopt it. On this level, prejudice is an attempt to find meaning, to explain; it may be the search for a reason, not an alibi.[21] Seldom, if ever, would such a factor in prejudice be the only one operative in a given situation, but in a society as complex as our own it may play an important part. Lacking true explanations, we rely on comforting pseudo explanations.

Prejudice may be an attempt to enhance one's self-esteem or to remove a threat to self-esteem. In a culture that stresses the opportunities each person has for success but prevents success (by its own definition) for a great number, it is not surprising to find a great many people creating a shadowy image of success by placing themselves, categorically, above all members of "inferior" groups. Success may be blocked by personal incapacity or ill fortune, by membership in a disadvantaged group, or simply by the fact that, by definition, only a few can attain success. Whatever the cause, many will feel failure as a blow to self-esteem. The white "failure" may get some small comfort from the belief that he is better than Ralph Bunche, Richard Wright, and Willie Mays all rolled into one. The sense of failure may be temporary —a result, perhaps, of loss of job. If the prejudice is available, one may then accept the belief that unscrupulous Jews caused the loss of job. "His pride has been saved, but an anti-Semite has been created."[22]

A "genteel" kind of prejudice may be sustained simply by the need for social acceptance in one's group. "Nice" people have no social contact with Negroes. They wish them no harm; there is little projection or displacement involved; the individuals are well adjusted. Nevertheless, prejudice directs their activities, and the polite "gentlemen's agreements" of various kinds furnish the context in which more vigorous prejudices thrive.

Prejudice is apparently a functioning part of the system of beliefs of some persons who are mentally ill. Sadists and paranoiacs, for example, may use prejudice to rationalize and "explain" their deviant behavior. There is a bit of evidence in the study by Frenkel-Brunswik and Sanford that persons scoring high in anti-Semitism have more paranoid tendencies. They agree significantly more often to the statement: "To a

[21] Ibid., pp. 454–455.
[22] Ibid., p. 456.

greater extent than most people realize, our lives are governed by plots hatched in secret by politicians."[23] Although strongly conventional in their attitudes toward sex, they seem to exhibit a repressed striving that sometimes takes on sadistic connotations—a great willingness, for example, to agree with the statement that persons who commit sex crimes deserve not mere punishment, but a public whipping. The tensions of the mentally ill often have no specific referent. In a given culture, they may have learned, as many normal people have, that some racial or other minority group is an appropriate object for attack. The paranoiac, who lives in a world of groundless suspicions (groundless from the point of view of the outsider), who attributes sinister motives to every act, may feel that his own actions are explained and justified by his "information" about a minority group. Such persons are doubtless few in number; but if the intensity of their prejudice is high, they may become the leaders of antiracial mobs or movements, drawing in others who are less highly motivated to act in a discriminatory way. Their propelling need for aggression may be so strong that they seek out and create incidents, rather than merely waiting for them.[24]

In a recent study Nathan Ackerman and Marie Jahoda explored the relationship between anti-Semitism and emotional disorder. Their data are drawn from intensive analyses of patients who had sought the help of psychoanalysts in solving their emotional problems. The difficulties of the patients ranged from fairly mild personality disturbances to serious mental illness—degrees of disorder that require some separate analysis. We may see among the patients, however, certain common problems that frequently were associated, in a functional way, with anti-Semitism:

Each of these individuals is plagued by pervasive anxiety. Deeply confused in his own self-image, he derives no strength from his personal identity with which to face a menacing world. His personal relationships are shallow and unsatisfying. His group relations are characterized by an exaggerated surface conformity, beneath which lurks a primitive, untamed hostility. Within his group the slightest indication of nonconformity appears as a threat. Outside his group, differences are exaggerated. Lacking a basis of genuine identification, he tends in a compensatory way to define his group status by reference to qualities he does not actually possess. He achieves only a partial adaptation to reality, and is unable to develop spontaneous and genuine personal relationships. His conscience is underdeveloped and unreliable, his repressions incomplete and inefficient, thereby necessitating recourse to the laborious tasks of conscious suppression.[25]

[23] Else Frenkel-Brunswik and R. N. Sanford, "Some Personality Factors in Anti-Semitism," *Journal of Psychology*, October, 1945, p. 283.
[24] See David Krech and Richard Crutchfield, *op. cit.*, pp. 448–449.
[25] Nathan Ackerman and Marie Jahoda, *Anti-Semitism and Emotional Disorder*, Harper & Brothers, 1950, pp. 39–40.

The authors then relate this kind of personality instability to the life experiences of the patients and to anti-Semitism as a mechanism of "adjustment." For example:

Common to every case of anti-Semitism collected for this study is the strikingly similar psychological atmosphere into which the patient was born. There is not a single example of a permanently well-adjusted marital relationship between the parents. . . .

Generally a sharp contrast characterized the parents as individuals. They were at cross-purposes on every possible occasion. In temperament, ethical values, sexual attitudes, and social interests, father and mother seemed to represent different worlds. Even where such basic differences were not understood by the children, the fundamental hostility between the parents was inescapable fact. . . .

Both open rejection and narcissistic exploitation damage considerably the self-esteem and self-confidence of the child, who, consequently, feels unwanted, unloved, and unworthy. . . . To find a semblance of balance in spite of their frustrations, they mobilize against their anxiety and self-hate a variety of defense mechanisms. In the interlocking pattern of these defenses anti-Semitism seems to fulfill a functionally well-defined role. It represents an effort to displace the self-destroying trends in the personality. At the psychic level, anti-Semitic hostility can be viewed as a profound though irrational and futile defensive effort to restore a crippled self. At the social level, it can be regarded as a device for achieving secondary emotional and material gain.[26]

Evidence of the kind represented by this study scarcely permits one to say that emotional disorder "causes" prejudice in general or anti-Semitism in particular. The data concern a relatively small number of people in the New York area who had sought help from psychoanalysts and whose cases, in turn, had been arbitrarily selected as offering insights by the psychoanalysts who were willing to coöperate in the study. The problems of sampling and the chances for bias are clear. Nor can we assume that even for the type of person studied a clear causal sequence is indicated. As Ackerman and Jahoda point out: "The syndrome of emotional predispositions and character tendencies that we have described cannot of course be considered unique in the anti-Semite. It exists in many persons and there is no reason to believe that all who share such characteristics will necessarily manifest anti-Semitic attitudes."[27] Many people are prejudiced, moreover, who are not troubled with emotional disorder. And one major type of personality disturbance, depression, was not found among the cases. The sample is too small for statistical test, but probably the guilt and self-destructive features of a depression psychosis are incompatible with the tendency to blame outside forces for all of one's difficulties that characterizes prejudice.

[26] *Ibid.*, pp. 43–55.
[27] *Ibid.*, p. 55.

Nevertheless, the study demonstrates in a valuable way the manner in which anti-Semitism may be used, in a society which furnishes this prejudice, by some persons suffering from emotional disorder.

Is There a Prejudiced "Personality Type"?

Some of the research in the field of the social psychology of prejudice has sought to discover the degree to which an attitude of prejudice should be interpreted as a more or less independent personality tendency and the degree to which it should be seen as simply one manifestation of a total personality. The question might be put in this way: Are there certain kinds of total personality integrations that have prejudice as a natural expression, or is prejudice a specific response to specific stimuli, likely to be associated with almost any kind of personality? This problem is closely related to our discussion of personality "needs," but can profitably be given separate attention. Social psychology has gone through a long controversy over the question of the generality and the specificity of personality attributes—a controversy that has not yet been closed by the evidence. There have been rather drastic swings from the position that supposed "traits," such as intelligence or honesty, were general—expressed themselves in any situation where they applied—to the opposite position that personality was simply a loosely joined bundle of specific responses to specific stimuli. We need not examine that controversy here, except to note the contemporary point of view: Neither extreme should be asserted in a doctrinaire way; specific studies should attempt to measure the degree of generality or specificity; and tendencies should be studied in the context of the situations with which they interact.

For us the question becomes: Is there a "prejudiced personality" that is different from the unprejudiced in major ways, or is prejudice a specific response to a specific stimulus? In recent years the impact of psychiatry and cultural anthropology has encouraged greatly increased attention to the matter of personality integration. In the process of acquiring the responses characteristic of his culture, particularly in the intimate contacts within the family during his earliest years, the individual has built a basic "ego structure." This is a fundamental attitude toward himself and toward others which, once established, reacts upon objective experiences and strongly influences their meaning for the individual. A person, for example, who in his earliest experiences acquires an attitude of superiority and a tendency toward domination may continue to hold that attitude when the objective situation contradicts it. He may fail in a certain endeavor according to the judgments of others, but he can find for himself reasons that prove that he did not "really" fail; luck was against him, or the other party was dishonest or had some undue advantage, or the referee was blind—at least he won a moral victory.

The Authoritarian Personality

In the last decade there has been a great deal of research which has sought to test the hypothesis that prejudice is part of a complicated personality "syndrome." According to this thesis, prejudice is one manifestation of a basically insecure person, one who is "ego alien"—that is, has repressed many of his own impulses—one who looks upon life as capricious and threatening, and one who looks upon all human relationships in competitive power terms. Prejudice, moreover, is tied in a functional way to many other personality trends, to particular styles of politics, religion, and sex behavior. The authors of *The Authoritarian Personality* write:

The most crucial result of the present study, as it seems to the authors, is the demonstration of close correspondence in the type of approach and outlook a subject is likely to have in a great variety of areas, ranging from the most intimate features of family and sex adjustment through relationships to other people in general, to religion and to social and political philosophy. Thus a basically hierarchical, authoritarian, exploitive parent-child relationship is apt to carry over into a power-oriented, exploitively dependent attitude toward one's sex partner and one's God and may well culminate in a political philosophy and social outlook which has no room for anything but a desperate clinging to what appears to be strong and a disdainful rejection of whatever is relegated to the bottom.[28]

In one of the studies that preceded and led up to *The Authoritarian Personality*, Frenkel-Brunswik and Sanford analyzed the deep-seated personality functions of prejudice. The authors applied an anonymous scale on anti-Semitism to twenty-four University of California men and seventy-six women. The scale measured the tendency to accept or reject anti-Semitic statements and attitudes, allowing several steps for agreement or disagreement. There were also questions on politics, group membership, and public issues, to see if anti-Semitism was part of a complex of attitudes. There were "projective" items to find the subjects' goals, fears, identifications: Whom do you most admire? If you had six months to live, and could do what you wished, what would you do? The eight women who scored highest in anti-Semitism and the eight who scored lowest were then interviewed at length and given Rorschach and Thematic Apperception Tests. With this evidence, the questionnaire was revised, with added items on conventionality, aggression, superstition, attitudes toward family, and others; and the revised scale was given to 140 University of California women.

The girls who were high in anti-Semitism were, on the average, well groomed, of higher than average income, greatly interested in social

28 T. W. Adorno, Else Frenkel-Brunswik, D. J. Levinson, and R. N. Sanford, *The Authoritarian Personality*, Harper & Brothers, 1950, p. 971.

standing, conservative, from socially mobile families, ethnocentric. All of them said they liked their parents and subscribed to statements that indicate obedience to authority. The girls low in anti-Semitism were more nondescript in appearance, less at ease socially, more willing to talk about themselves and to make critical appraisals of their parents. An analysis of responses to the pictures in the Thematic Apperception Tests indicates, moreover, some other differences. Girls high in anti-Semitism responded to one picture with ideas of violence, death, murder, and aggression. The same picture shown to the girls low in anti-Semitism elicited little aggression and no reference to death. One picture showed an older woman with a younger one; violence and suspicion came out in the responses of the girls high in anti-Semitism. "The mother starts a racket," says one; "the mother has the daughter mingle with the rich and sort of act as bait. . . . The mother is a very clever woman and always manages to have all her schemes work."[29] The girls low in anti-Semitism saw little conflict between the young and the old woman. The pattern of human relations as seen by the "highs" is fundamentally a struggle between dominance and submission. They interpret a picture of a hypnotist as a story of the misuse of "superhuman" powers for evil or queer deeds. The "lows" describe it as an "experiment," a "demonstration in class."

Those high on the anti-Semitic scale show a great deal of "social anxiety." They draw a sharp line between nice people and bad people. They are more prone to think in terms of fate. Among the 140 who took the revised questionnaire, the one-fourth at the top of the anti-Semitic scale were much more likely to agree with the following statement than the one-fourth at the bottom: "Although many people may scoff, it may yet be shown that astrology can explain a lot of things."[30] The difference between the two groups was statistically significant, with a critical ratio of 4.4.[31] The "highs" deny overtly what the tests reveal to be strong covert tendencies. They praise self-sacrifice and kindness but have many underlying aggressive feelings; they are reluctant to express such strong drives as aggression and sex but project them onto out-groups. "Inferior" and "lower" people are seen as aggressive and uninhibited sexually.

---

[29] Else Frenkel-Brunswik and R. N. Sanford, op. cit., p. 283.

[30] Ibid., p. 278.

[31] Occasionally in this book we shall refer to such statistical terms as "critical ratio," "significant difference," "standard error," and "level of significance." For those unfamiliar with these terms, this brief explanation may be of value. A significant difference (as, in this case, between the acceptance of a statement by girls high on an anti-Semitic test and its acceptance by those low on the test) is a difference too large to be accounted for by chance, by the accidents of sampling. The difference may be stated in terms of critical ratio or standard error (3.0 or more being regarded as significant) or percent level of significance (measures that differ at the 1 percent level being regarded as significantly different).

There is no implication in this study that the persons low in anti-Semitism are in any way more "normal" than those with high scores, nor is the middle group more "normal." The scale was applied to a group of patients in a mental hospital, and the scores were in the middle range. The point is that somehow those in one group seem to use anti-Semitism in their attempt to adjust to the problems they face. The repressions and rigidities that characterize them seem to make a congenial home for anti-Semitic ideas. Both the "highs" and the "lows" come mainly from the middle class; but the highs have a conformist, rigid attitude toward middle-class standards. There are fears of losing status—not so much fear of economic loss as fear that with respectability gone they may be tempted to release their impulses, to act in the uninhibited way that they imagine Jews do. Thus anti-Semitism helps them to maintain their identity with the middle class and to ward off anxiety.[32]

These tendencies cannot be understood, of course, except in the light of the social and cultural situations in which these persons developed. The authors note that insecure times cause the parents anxiety and encourage the excessively rigid teaching of standards in the attempt to cling to status.

In a study of social attitudes, Hartley throws a great deal of light on the way in which prejudice is related to a whole complex of personal tendencies. He asked several groups of college students to mark, on a standard social-distance scale, their attitudes toward a large number of racial, religious, national, and economic groups. The scale permitted a differentiation of response ranging from "Would admit to close kinship by marriage" to "Would exclude from my country," with five intervening steps at least roughly scalable. Among the thirty-five groups, Hartley included the names of three nonexistent groups—Danireans, Pireneans, and Wallonians. Some students may have associated the names with some existent groups—thinking the Pireneans to be people who live in the Pyrenees, for example—but they almost certainly knew nothing about these groups, even when thus identified; and the very fact that they tended to find an existent group for the label in order to express an attitude, is itself significant. Since in reality there are no such groups, one can explain the attributes assigned to them only by studying the individual who makes the judgment. If his response to the nonexistent groups is very similar to his response to the existent and partially known groups, one is perhaps justified in speaking in terms of generalized prejudice or nonprejudice. "Our hypothesis is that such tolerance represents to a significant extent a function of the persons responding rather than of the groups responded to."[33] To test this hypothesis,

[32] Cf. Else Frenkel-Brunswik and R. N. Sanford, *op. cit.*, pp. 271–291.
[33] Eugene Hartley, *Problems in Prejudice*, King's Crown Press, 1946, p. 26.

Hartley correlated the average tolerance for the thirty-two existing groups with the expressed attitude toward the three "nonesuch" groups. The Pearsonian product-moment coefficients of correlation, computed separately for the students from the five schools who took the test, ranged from .78 to .85, a strong confirmation of the hypothesis.

On the basis of this study, Hartley makes the following summary description of the relatively tolerant and relatively intolerant personality:

The *relatively tolerant personality* in this type of collegiate sample is likely to exhibit some combination of the following characteristics: a strong desire for personal autonomy associated with a lack of need for dominance, a strong need for friendliness, along with a personal seclusiveness, fear of competition, a tendency to placate others along with lack of general conformity to the mores. He is likely to be fairly serious, to be interested in current events, to have ideas about bettering society, to be a member of a political group and to have great need for personal achievement in the vocational area. He is likely to be an accepting personality, disliking violence, able to appreciate the contributions of others, conscious of feeling that people tend to be more or less alike and adopting a nurturant rather than a dominant attitude toward those younger than he. He is conscious of conflicts concerning loyalties and duties, and thinks very seriously about moral questions. His interests center about what are commonly called the social studies, reading and journalism. Although personally seclusive, he has a great need to be socially useful.

The *relatively intolerant personality* might be expected to combine in varying degrees the following characteristics: unwillingness to accept responsibility, acceptance of conventional mores, a rejection of "serious" groups, rejection of political interests and desire for groups formed for purely social purposes, absorption with pleasure activities, a conscious conflict between play and work, emotionality rather than rationality, extreme egocentrism, interest in physical activity, the body, health. He is likely to dislike agitators, radicals, pessimists. He is relatively uncreative, apparently unable to deal with anxieties except by fleeing from them. Often his physical activity has in it a compulsive component; it may be that this compulsion to be on the move, that is constantly occupied with sports, motoring, traveling, etc., serves for him the same function that study and activities with social significance serve in the case of the individual with high tolerance. Both the tolerant and intolerant individuals have anxieties, but there seems to be a distinct difference in the way in which they work them out.

Such characteristics as projectivity, distrust of people, feelings of inferiority, feelings of not belonging, and personal seclusiveness, seem to break across these tolerance categories.[34]

This picture of the relatively intolerant personality corresponds rather closely to the description of the anti-Semite given by Frenkel-Brunswik and Sanford in the study discussed previously. This study and

[34] *Ibid.*, pp. 62–63.

the others that form the basis of *The Authoritarian Personality* give a great deal of supporting evidence to the hypothesis that prejudice is frequently a symptom of a basic personality organization, and not simply an isolated and independent attitude. There is not just one type of prejudiced personality, to be sure (Adorno identifies six types from the evidence in these studies);[35] but many tendencies seem to occur frequently among all the varieties. On the basis of interview materials, Frenkel-Brunswik states that those with high scores on prejudice tests exhibit, among other tendencies, rigidity of outlook (inaccessibility to new experience), intolerance of ambiguity (they want to know *the* answers), pseudoscientific or antiscientific attitudes (more superstition, reliance on accidents as explanations, attribution of behavior to heredity), suggestibility and gullibility, and autistic thinking in goal behavior (unrealistic views of what will achieve the desired goals). Those low in prejudice, on the other hand, show more flexibility of judgment, greater tolerance of ambiguity, a more scientific-naturalistic explanation of events, greater autonomy and self-reliance, and realistic thinking about goal behavior.[36]

Several other studies have produced evidence that seems to support these hypotheses. Allport and Kramer discovered that prejudice is associated with one's general outlook or "philosophy of life," and thus perhaps can be understood in part by study of the total mental context. More prejudiced individuals were significantly (at the 1 percent level) more in agreement with the belief that the world is a hazardous place in which men are basically evil and dangerous.[37] Although there is a tendency to give specific rationalizations or "explanations" for particular beliefs, they can often be understood only with reference to a more general belief. Allport and Kramer found, for example, that 11 percent of the students they tested were opposed to the Fair Employment Practices Commission, giving such "reasons" as: it will only make matters worse; you cannot legislate good behavior. But 87 percent of those who took this position were in the more prejudiced half of the total group, indicating that the reasons given for opposing FEPC were a cover for the basic fact that they were more prejudiced.[38] That is not to say that the reasons may not be objectively valid. Unless one assumes, however, that the prejudiced persons are better social scientists than the nonprejudiced (and therefore know more thoroughly what the actual effects of the FEPC would be), there is no reason to expect that more than half of those opposed to the FEPC would come from the prejudiced group.

[35] See T. W. Adorno, Else Frenkel-Brunswik, D. J. Levinson, and R. N. Sanford, *op. cit.*, pp. 753 ff.

[36] See *ibid.*, p. 461.

[37] Gordon Allport and B. M. Kramer, *op. cit.*, pp. 32–33.

[38] *Ibid.*, p. 34.

Scores of studies in the last ten years have sought to test and refine, and more recently to qualify, the thesis that prejudice is to an important degree the expression of an insecure personality. They converge on such concepts as self-rejection, repression, a strong concern for power in human relationships, a general "threat orientation," as Newcomb calls it.[39] Many of these studies have introduced new variables and some, as we shall see in the next section, have required extensive modifications of the thesis of *The Authoritarian Personality*. Those that are concerned with general descriptions of individuals high in prejudice substantially agree with this summary of the studies by Gough: "anti-intellectuality, a pervading sense of pessimism and lack of hope and confidence in the future; feelings of cynicism, distrust, doubt, and suspicion; a diffuse misanthropy and querulousness; a hostile and bitter outlook which verged on destructiveness; a grumbling and discontented evaluation of their current status; a rigid, somewhat dogmatic style of thinking; a lack of poise and self-assurance; and an underlying perplexity related to a feeling that something dreadful is about to happen."[40]

A Critique of "The Authoritarian Personality." The scales developed in the Berkeley studies of the authoritarian personality were immediately put to use in replications and modifications of the original research. The methodology and theoretical perspective of the book have been carefully analyzed. A brief examination of this process of testing and criticism can be of value as a lesson in the way in which science grows, as well as a source of knowledge concerning the personality factors in prejudice.

Broadly speaking, there have been three types of commentary and interpretation: comments on the methodology of the original study,

[39] See, for example, Bernard M. Bass, "Authoritarianism or Acquiescence," *Journal of Abnormal and Social Psychology*, November, 1955, pp. 616–623; Roger W. Brown, "A Determinant of the Relationship Between Rigidity and Authoritarianism," *Journal of Abnormal and Social Psychology*, October, 1953, pp. 469–476; Loren J. Chapman and Donald T. Campbell, "Response Set in the F Scale," *Journal of Abnormal and Social Psychology*, January, 1957, pp. 129–132; Harrison G. Gough, "Studies of Social Intolerance," *Journal of Social Psychology*, May, 1951, pp. 237–269; Jerome Himelhoch, "Tolerance and Personality Needs; A Study of the Liberalization of Ethnic Attitudes Among Minority Group College Students," *American Sociological Review*, February, 1950, pp. 79–88; Nathan Kogan, "Authoritarianism and Repression," *Journal of Abnormal and Social Psychology*, July, 1956, pp. 34–37; William J. MacKinnon and Richard Centers, "Authoritarianism and Urban Stratification," *American Journal of Sociology*, May, 1956, pp. 610–620; Marian Radke-Yarrow and Bernard Lande, "Personality Correlates of Differential Reaction to Minority Group Belonging," *Journal of Social Psychology*, November, 1953, pp. 253–272; Patrick L. Sullivan and Joseph Adelson, "Ethnocentrism and Misanthropy," *Journal of Abnormal and Social Psychology*, April, 1954, pp. 246–250; W. D. Wells, Gene Chiaravallo, and Seymour Goldman, "Brothers Under the Skin: A Validity Test of the F-Scale," *Journal of Social Psychology*, February, 1957, pp. 35–40.

[40] Richard Christie, in Richard Christie and Marie Jahoda (eds.), *Studies in the Scope and Method of "The Authoritarian Personality,"* The Free Press, 1954, p. 159.

further research that has sought to refine the measurement of the variables used and to discover other variables that affect the extent of prejudice, and discussion of the adequacy of the theoretical assumptions. These approaches cannot be sharply distinguished, but they can be discussed separately.

Confidence in the findings of *The Authoritarian Personality* is increased by the wide variety of research instruments used by the authors. The effort to measure several different levels of personality also strengthens the study. There were, however, serious methodological weaknesses. The authors paid little attention to questions of sampling; hence the extent to which their findings could be generalized to a wider group was unknown. Memories of childhood, which they obtained from many interviewees, are not necessarily accurate records of past events. Failure to control such variables as education and group membership sometimes led to unwarranted interpretations of the findings. If a person high on a scale of prejudice (ethnocentrism) admires generals and political figures and one low in prejudice admires scientists and writers, this is not necessarily evidence of a different outlook on life. If the prejudice scale is negatively correlated with education (as many studies have shown), the difference in selection of admired persons may be a function of the educational differences, not of the attitudes toward minorities. The study also faced serious problems in coding qualitative material. One respondent said: "Very, very fine man—intelligent, and understanding, excellent father, in every way." Is this to be classed as "conventionalized idealization" or "positive affect"?[41]

These methodological problems do not, in the judgment of most observers, refute the contention that prejudice is part of certain personality configurations. They do, however, indicate the need for further research with more careful controls. A sampling of the studies that have been made will indicate the way in which new variables have been introduced and the analysis of others refined. Taking twenty-nine items from the Berkeley prejudice scales, Sullivan and Adelson rewrote them to refer to "people" or "most people," instead of to Jews, Negroes, or other specific groups. Thus, "Jews seem to prefer the most luxurious, extravagant, and sensual way of living," becomes "People seem to prefer the most luxurious, extravagant, and sensual way of living." Two hundred and twenty-one students at a midwestern university were given this revised M (for misanthropy) scale, along with a 20-item E (ethnocentrism) scale. There was a correlation of .53 between the two. Thus prejudice is correlated, in these data, with a general misanthropy. It appears that for the antidemocratic person ". . . there may be no in-group other than the self."[42] How far this finding applies

[41] On this and other questions of methodology, see *ibid.*, especially the chapter by H. H. Hyman and P. B. Sheatsley.

[42] Patrick L. Sullivan and Joseph Adelson, *op. cit.*

to persons other than the college students involved is not yet known, but the study suggests a need for further exploration.

Several writers have suggested that "response set" or a tendency toward acquiescence, not authoritarianism, can account for what appears to be a strong relationship between an authoritarian outlook on life and prejudice. In the original F scale, all items were "agree" items. To get a low "authoritarian" score on an item, one needed to disagree with the statement. Bass reversed 28 statements on the original F scale to make what he labeled a G scale. Thus, "People can be divided into two distinct classes, the weak and the strong," became, "People cannot be divided into two distinct classes, the weak and the strong." Half of the F items and half of the G were then put into one test, and the remainder into another. Sixty-three students were given form 1, then form 2 two weeks later. Twenty-one students were given form 2 first and then form 1. By factor analysis, Bass found that three-fourths of the variance of the F scale could be accounted for by acquiescence, only one-fourth by authoritarianism. That is, the tendency to accept a positively stated item (however that tendency may be explained) accounted for a larger part of the score than authoritarian attitudes.[43]

One of the presumed characteristics of the prejudiced person is a general mental rigidity, an inflexibility of mind. In a well-known study closely associated with the Authoritarian Personality research, Rokeach tried to discover if the tendency toward ethnocentrism (categorical judgments in favor of one's own group) was associated with a general rigidity of mind. Having separated a group of University of California students into high and low ethnocentric groups on the basis of a standardized test, he asked them to do a series of "puzzles," in order to determine the degree to which they would rigidly pursue a complicated method that had been used in illustration, rather than adopt a simple solution. The puzzles were of the familiar variety: If you have 3 jars which hold, respectively, 31, 61, and 4 quarts, how can you measure out 22 quarts? Some of the puzzles could be solved only by a fairly complicated method, others could be solved by a simple procedure. When puzzles requiring complicated solutions were followed by several that could be done simply, Rokeach found that ethnocentric persons tended rigidly to continue to use the complicated method. The difference between those high and those low in ethnocentrism was statistically significant, seeming to demonstrate that ethnocentric individuals are more rigid in their approach to nonsocial as well as to social problems.[44]

Several recent studies, however, have shown that the relationship be-

[43] See Bernard M. Bass, op. cit.; see also Loren D. Chapman and Donald T. Campbell, op. cit.

[44] Milton Rokeach, "Generalized Mental Rigidity as a Factor in Ethnocentrism," Journal of Abnormal and Social Psychology, July, 1948, pp. 259–278.

tween rigidity and ethnocentrism is not a simple one. Jackson, Messick, and Solley found that rigidity in the jar test was correlated with score on a reverse-F as well as on the original F scale (and also that there was a correlation of .35 between scores on the F and reverse-F scales). This study is not strictly comparable with Rokeach's, for the latter employed the E scale of the California research, but it indicates the need for studying "response set" and "acquiescence," as well as authoritarian tendencies, as variables related to rigidity. A person who gets a high reverse-F score is presumably low in authoritarianism. If he rigidly pursues complicated methods of solving the jar tests, this cannot be part of a syndrome which includes authoritarianism (in which he scores low), but shows a tendency to persist in an established way of doing things.[45]

Not finding the same relationship between rigidity and authoritarianism described by Rokeach, Brown looked for refinements in the meaning of rigid. With hundreds of subjects he had always failed to get a significant correlation between rigidity and authoritarianism (as measured by the California F scale). Were the differences in results due to differences in the atmosphere of the testing situation? Rokeach had made his test in a large lecture class; problems were given as a "test" in bluebooks. Brown had made his measurements in small laboratory groups. He suspected that the former situation created a strong ego-involving atmosphere and that the rigidity was ". . . a defensive, situationally dependent rigidity . . . ," not a generalized trait. To test this possibility, Brown gave the jar test to two matched groups. For the first group he created an ego-involving atmosphere, stressing the test as a measure of intelligence and motivation, cautioning the subjects repeatedly against looking at the test ahead of time. The experimenter was aloof; he dressed quite formally. The subjects wrote their names before they took the test. For the second group the experimenter created a relaxed atmosphere. He was dressed in sports clothes, treated the test casually, showed little interest in the results, and asked for the names of the subjects only at the end. The results confirmed his hypothesis. The correlation between the F scale (authoritarian) score and the jar test score was significantly higher for the ego-involved group than for the casual group. This does not indicate a lack of difference in rigidity between those high and those low in authoritarianism. But it does indicate the need for careful definition of rigidity and the recognition that results are affected by the situation, not simply by the personalities involved. Rokeach had defined rigidity as ". . . inability to restructure a field in which there are alternative solutions to a problem in order to solve the problem more efficiently." Brown prefers this definition,

[45] D. N. Jackson, S. J. Messick, and C. M. Solley, "How 'Rigid' Is the 'Authoritarian,'" *Journal of Abnormal and Social Psychology*, January, 1957, pp. 137–140.

". . . inability to restructure a field when a familiar structuring is perceived as warding off personal failure." Rigidity is not sluggishness of the nervous system; it is very sensitive to situational factors. When the authoritarian is in a relaxed setting, he solves the problems as easily as the equalitarian; when he senses a threat, he clings to security.[46]

These modifications of our conceptions of the mental rigidity of prejudiced persons illustrate the gradual refinement of our knowledge of one of the factors in their style of life. Srole extends our knowledge by suggesting a new factor, one that was implied in earlier studies of the highly prejudiced person but required explicit study. Drawing on a long interest in sociology in the concept of "anomie" or the sense of isolation from others, he hypothesized that this might well be related to the tendency toward prejudice and the rejection of out-groups. There is a vast literature relating this sense of isolation to political movements, of both right and left, to many of the developments in modern religions—in fact to almost every aspect of life today. Many different responses may be seen as functionally alternative ways of attempting to deal with "the breakdown of the individual's sense of attachment to society" (to use MacIver's phrase). May not our knowledge of prejudice be increased by studying it in this same context? A sample of 401 white, native-born adults in an eastern city were interviewed and asked questions from three different scales. Five questions and their spontaneous comments measured the degree of racial and religious prejudice; five questions, in revised form, were drawn from the Berkeley F scale to measure authoritarian tendencies; and five questions were devised to measure feelings of anomie or isolation from others. The degree of anomie was measured by asking respondents the extent to which they agreed with such statements as these: "There's little use writing to public officials because often they aren't really interested in the problems of the average man." "These days a person doesn't really know whom he can count on." There was a significant correlation between both authoritarianism and anomie and the scores on the prejudice scale. By means of partial correlation, Srole was able to discover the degree to which each of the former was *independently* correlated with the prejudice score, that is, the degree to which authoritarianism was correlated with prejudice when the effect of anomie was held constant, and the degree to which anomie was correlated with prejudice when the effect of authoritarianism was held constant. The partial correlation of anomie and prejudice was .35; that of authoritarianism and preju-

---

[46] See Roger W. Brown, *op. cit.*; see also E. E. Levitt and S. L. Zelen, "The Validity of the Einstellung Test as a Measure of Rigidity," *Journal of Abnormal and Social Psychology*, October, 1953, pp. 573–580; and Nora C. Forster, W. E. Vinacke, and J. M. Digman, "Flexibility and Rigidity in a Variety of Problem Situations," *Journal of Abnormal and Social Psychology*, March, 1955, pp. 211–216.

dice, .12. For the sample studied and with the scales used, it appears that the sense of isolation was more closely associated with antiminority views than was authoritarianism.[47]

Using the same five-item anomie and authoritarianism scales and a ten-item ethnocentrism scale from the Berkeley studies, Roberts and Rokeach obtained somewhat different results than Srole did. With a sample of 86 adults, they found a correlation of .53 between authoritarianism and ethnocentrism when anomie was held constant, and a correlation of .37 between anomie and ethnocentrism when authoritarianism was held constant. Since this study is not an exact replication of Srole's, we cannot know the degree to which differences in samples, in the scales used, in the scoring methods, or other factors affected the results. Nevertheless together they establish the tentative thesis that the prejudiced person is likely to be one who feels isolated and alone.[48]

The methodological criticisms and follow-up studies of *The Authoritarian Personality* have tended to qualify its thesis but not to deny its essential accuracy. There has also been substantial criticism of its basic theory, however. This more thoroughgoing questioning of the concept of a prejudiced personality type has not usually dismissed this line of approach to the analysis of prejudice. It has instead emphasized the need for studying the personality dimension in context with other factors. A brief examination of this question of theoretical perspective can help us to grasp the complexity of the roots of prejudice.

Three related ideas may help us to see the range of theoretical criticism. (1) Overly zealous students of the personality factors in prejudice would benefit from using the concept of "functional alternatives." (2) They are insufficiently aware of subcultural and group factors in prejudice. (3) They fail to give adequate attention to situational influences. These weaknesses stem from what, in our view, is an inadequate theory of personality—a theory that emphasizes traits, not process and interaction, a theory that isolates the individual as the unit of analysis, when what is needed is a series of concepts that functionally interrelate the individual and the situation of which he is a part.

The person who is "ego alien," insecure, suffering from feelings of anomie and powerlessness may, as the authors of *The Authoritarian Personality* indicate, express hostility and prejudice toward minority groups and support fascistic types of totalitarian political movements. They may, however, express their insecurities and seek to resolve their doubts in other ways. What the functional alternatives are for a given

[47] See Leo Srole, "Social Integration and Certain Corollaries: An Exploratory Study," *American Sociological Review*, December, 1956, pp. 709–716.
[48] See A. H. Roberts and Milton Rokeach, "Anomie, Authoritarianism, and Prejudice: A Replication," *American Journal of Sociology*, January, 1956, pp. 355–358; see also letters to the editor by Srole and Rokeach, indicating differences of interpretation, *American Journal of Sociology*, July, 1956, pp. 63–67.

individual depends upon his total situation.[49] Shils has well argued that in certain circumstances the "authoritarian" may support the "radical left" not the "reactionary right"—indeed, the whole picture of a simple right-left continuum is inadequate, for the two extremes share a great deal in common. The fascist who says that Jews control everything and the communist who contends that big business has absolute power express views that are concretely very different. "Yet looked at from another point of view, they are strikingly similar. Both aver that a small group has with doubtful legitimacy concentrated the power of the country in their hands."[50] They may also share an extreme hostility toward out-groups, submissiveness in in-groups, the tendency toward all-or-none judgments, the vision of the world as a realm of conflict.[51] Some religious movements may be interpreted in part in these same terms. Even some aspects of anti-authoritarian sentiments and organizations can be interpreted as manifestations of hostility and ego alienation. Which expressions of the inner insecurity will be made depends upon the whole range of values and motives of the individual and on the surrounding social situation.

Before one can explain antiminority feelings in terms of a harsh, capricious, and unloving childhood, he needs to be aware of group structure and of variation in values among the "subcultures" of a society. We shall examine the social and cultural aspects of prejudice in detail in the next two chapters, but a brief statement here may help us to see more accurately the way in which personality tendencies interact with other influences. If residents of Mississippi have a higher anti-Negro score than those of Minnesota, this does not prove that they are more "authoritarian"—more intolerant of ambiguity, more cynical, more rigid, less self-accepting. It may be that they simply express different cultural influences. Differences in agreement with the idea that there are two kinds of people in the world, the weak and the strong, may simply indicate differences in actual experience. As Christie says:

> Anyone familiar with lower socio-economic groupings can scarcely be unaware of the fact that there is realistic justification for their view that the world is indeed jungle-like and capricious. They have no relatives or friends with the power to intercede successfully when they are rightly or wrongly accused of legal offenses. . . . The acceptance of an item referring to people prying into personal affairs may reflect paranoid tendencies among middle-class respondents; it may be reality based among lower-class individuals who are the first to be questioned by police, social workers, and other functionaries of the social structure.[52]

[49] For a discussion of the concept of functional alternatives, see J. Milton Yinger, *Religion, Society, and the Individual*, The Macmillan Company, 1957, pp. 118–124.

[50] E. A. Shils, in Richard Christie and Marie Jahoda (eds.), *op. cit.*, p. 32.

[51] See *ibid.*, pp. 24–49; and Eric Hoffer, *The True Believer*, Harper & Brothers, 1951.

[52] Richard Christie in Richard Christie and Marie Jahoda (eds.), *op. cit.*, p. 175.

Before one draws personality conclusions from the tendency of one person to select General MacArthur as a hero, another to choose Bertrand Russell, he should be aware of any educational differences in the respondents. MacKinnon and Centers found that authoritarianism varied with age, with social status, with income, with education.[53] Differences in the realities of the situation, in cultural values, in role, in the ways different groups use language and respond to the testing process, and other variables are involved. All of this is not to say that deep-lying personal insecurity, frustration, guilt, and diffuse hostility are not involved in the origins of prejudice. It is to say that before the extent of these personality factors can be measured, other variables must be controlled. To disregard group membership is to permit all sorts of spurious factors to obscure the actual relationships on the personality level. One might sketch the research needs in an overly simplified way, using only a few variables and dichotomizing those for purposes of brevity; such a scheme is shown in the accompanying tabulation. With

A								B							
Those with ego-crushing experiences								Those with ego-supporting experiences							
I				II				I				II			
Residents of a sub-culture low in anti-minority folkways				Residents of a subculture high in antiminority folkways											
a		b		a		b		a		b		a		b	
Persons of low socio-economic status		Persons of high socio-economic status													
1	2	1	2	1	2	1	2	1	2	1	2	1	2	1	2
Persons of low education	Persons of high education														

this scheme the research task would be to compare the eight subgroups under A with their matching subgroups under B. Since they would be "alike" in subculture, socioeconomic status, and educational level, any differences that continued between A and B could more confidently (but not, of course, in this limited design, with great confidence) be attributed to the personality-forming conditions that were the focus of the study. Lacking this, we must hold tentatively to any generalizations concerning personality factors in prejudice.

Situational Factors in Prejudice and Discrimination. In addition to the concept of functional alternatives and the emphasis on group mem-

---

[53] See William J. MacKinnon and Richard Centers, op. cit.

bership, we can bring the analysis of the personality factors in prejudice into a larger theory by examining the influence of situational influences on behavior. Thinking of personality as process, not as a fixed essence, we are concerned with the way in which it unfolds. Here again the self-other relationships are vital to a theory of personality and an understanding of prejudice.

In part, we are concerned with reëmphasizing here the distinction between prejudice and discrimination. How a person will behave cannot be understood solely with reference to his internal attitudes, his verbal expressions of prejudice or nonprejudice. In part, however, we are insisting that even on the personality level, when one is concerned with the prejudices of the individual, situational factors must be taken into account. There is now widespread if not universal agreement that collective behavior in intergroup relations cannot be explained by what is "in" individuals. Men are role-playing creatures; they act in structured situations; to an important degree they behave in terms of their obligations and group-defined interests. As Shils emphasizes, only by ability to inhibit many tendencies can men live in societies. We shall cite some of the evidence for this point of view below. There is less agreement—yet we think the point is vital—that personality itself may be thought of in interactional terms. A person "is" what he "does." To hypothesize some "essence" previous to the doing is to complicate analysis and make prediction of behavior more difficult.

This point of view does not make the individual a wholly malleable agent of the situation. It is equally inappropriate to hypothesize some fixed structure for the situation (patterns of roles, norms, group interests) as the determining factor in behavior. Situations must also be defined "in process."

Some of these problems are illustrated in this statement by Adorno and his associates:

Although personality is a product of the social environment of the past, it is not, once it has developed, a mere object of the contemporary environment. What has developed is a *structure* within the individual, something which is capable of self-initiated action upon the social environment and of selection with respect to varied impinging stimuli, something which though always modifiable is frequently very resistant to fundamental change. This conception is necessary to explain consistency of behavior in widely varying situations, to explain the persistence of ideological trends in the face of contradicting facts and radically altered social conditions, to explain why people in the same sociological situation have different or even conflicting views on social issues, and why it is that people whose behavior has been changed through psychological manipulation lapse into their old ways as soon as the agencies of manipulation are removed.[54]

[54] *The Authoritarian Personality*, p. 6.

Insofar as this statement emphasizes the need for taking account of personal tendency, it is helpful. It fails to note, however, that we must explain inconsistency as well as consistency (being tolerant of Negroes in one's union but not in one's neighborhood); that an adequate theory must account for changes in ideological trends as well as persistence (many navy officers dedicated to segregation have reversed their judgment on an integrated ship); that one must note that persons in the same sociological situation often do have similar views (and what appears to be the "same" situation often proves, on close study, to be different constellations of group influences); and finally, that people do not always lapse into their old ways when influencing agencies are removed, and if they do, it may well be because they return to the old pattern of situations.

In our use of the concept, personality is what personality does; and the doing varies with how a situation is defined, the reference group with which one identifies at the moment, the sanctions and rewards in a given setting, the roles into which one is cast, and the range of tendencies brought by the individual. Lohman and Reitzes report how a group of industrial workers supported and applauded a racially integrated union but lived in a segregated neighborhood which they defended against "invasion."[55] In a study of 800 Jewish displaced persons in a camp in Italy, Fensterheim and Birch describe the way in which group patterns shape and channel attitudes. The initial behavior of most of the people in the camp was a vast personal aggressiveness toward almost everything and everybody. Gradually a group structure appeared. One group of 80 members and another of 90, although alike in age distribution and sex ratio and composed of individuals much alike in background experience, responded very differently to the camp situation. The first was right-wing Zionist and militarist; among them aggressiveness continued, although it was more disciplined; leadership was hierarchical. The other group was less antagonistic to the camp situation; its members favored a socialist Palestine; leadership was democratic. Although these differences might have been the result of self-selection, the authors believe this to be an inadequate explanation, because at first the groups were similar; little was known about their ideologies, yet few individuals changed groups. It is more likely that group ideology and structure shaped individual responses in important ways.[56]

An interesting test of situational influences on prejudice and dis-

---

[55] J. D. Lohman and D. C. Reitzes, "Note on Race Relations in Mass Society," *American Journal of Sociology*, November, 1952, pp. 240–246; J. D. Lohman and D. C. Reitzes, "Deliberately Organized Groups and Racial Behavior," *American Sociological Review*, June, 1954, pp. 342–344; see also Lewis M. Killian, "The Effects of Southern White Workers on Race Relations in Northern Plants," *American Sociological Review*, June, 1952, pp. 327–331.

[56] Herbert Fensterheim and H. G. Birch, "A Case Study of Group Ideology and Individual Adjustment," *Journal of Abnormal and Social Psychology*, October, 1950, pp. 710–720.

crimination was made in a fashionable suburb in the Northeast. Two white young women went into a restaurant and were seated; a Negro young woman then entered, asked for her party, and was seated. This was repeated in ten different places and in each instance they were all served without incident. In two places the party attracted some attention. Two weeks later, the management of each restaurant was sent a letter requesting a reservation for an interracial party. In seventeen days not one of the letters was answered. The managers were then phoned, with a variety of results. Eight denied having received the letter; five finally gave tentative approval to the party, although each acceptance was qualified in some way. The next day each restaurant was called to request reservations without any mention of the race issue. Ten accepted the reservation and the eleventh indicated that no reservation was necessary.[57] Here we have a series of responses to interracial situations: acceptance (the original situation), avoidance (no responses to the letter), and a variety of improvisations (to the telephone call). Which represent the "true" attitudes? They all do; they all represent potentialities of the individuals involved in certain kinds of situations with a variety of influences at work. Sometimes it is assumed that the "true" attitudes, somehow unaffected by a situation, are expressed in paper-and-pencil tests or interview situations in which persons are asked to express their feelings toward minority groups. If behavior in another setting deviates from the verbal description, it is often assumed that the "true" attitude has been blocked and that the individual will "return to normal" under more usual circumstances. We prefer to state that the verbalized attitudes are also behavior in a situation—the situation of a paper-and-pencil test or an interview. They express the tendencies of the person that are set in motion in that particular set of conditions. Other sets of conditions facilitate the expression of different tendencies. They all are part of the personality, they all can be understood only by studying process, by searching for "the conditions under which" an individual acts in various ways.

Are Americans Prejudice-Prone?

At several points in the preceding discussion it was suggested that societies differ in the amount of frustration they impose on the average member and in the amount and kinds of repressions demanded in the

---

[57] See Bernard Kutner, Carol Wilkins, and P. R. Yarrow, "Verbal Attitudes and Overt Behavior Involving Racial Prejudice," *Journal of Abnormal and Social Psychology*, July, 1952, pp. 649–652. For further examination of situational influences, see Muzafer Sherif and Carolyn Sherif, *Groups in Harmony and Tension*, Harper & Brothers, 1953; Wilbur Brookover and John Holland, "An Inquiry into the Meaning of Minority Group Attitude Expressions," *American Sociological Review*, April, 1952, pp. 196–202; Alvin Winder, "White Attitudes Toward Negro-White Interaction in a Number of Community Situations," *Journal of Social Psychology*, August, 1956, pp. 15–32.

socialization process. They also vary in the amount of group differentiation and in the degree of competitive striving for improved status that are encouraged. They differ, therefore, in the extent to which they create conditions that nurture prejudice.

It may be well to ask where contemporary America stands in this regard. Some factors seem to indicate an environment unfavorable to prejudice. Members of the dominant white group have, perhaps, a somewhat better chance of improving their status than do majority-group members in many other societies. There are fewer basic physical privations than in almost any other society. A strong tradition of democracy permits one to gain a feeling of belonging, security, and social rewards, to some degree, by beliefs and actions of nonprejudice. (This factor is easy to exaggerate, because in specific local situations it often does not hold true.)

There seem to be more forces in the contemporary American environment, however, that make it a favorable place for prejudice to thrive, from the point of view of the social psychological forces we have been discussing. In a society that is socially mobile and competitive, there is always the anxiety that one will fail to climb, that he will fall behind. His closest associates are often his closest competitors, so that a feeling of identification and security is difficult to achieve. There has been a "progressive alienation from the satisfaction of work," not only for the worker on the assembly line but for many professional and business people who have come to judge their occupational roles not by what is done but by how much is made out of them.[58]

Numerous segments of our population have rather strict child-training methods, in a society that simultaneously bombards the child with stimuli encouraging noninhibited behavior and that, with its great diversity of norms, frequently fails to back up the parent. Oppositely, an uninhibited childhood, with few restraints and responsibilities, may lead to lack of the self-discipline necessary for maximum satisfactions. Literacy and formal education have advanced rapidly in the modern world, but probably not as rapidly as the breakdown of old systems of belief. The result is a gap in our "explanations" which prejudices often fill.

Karen Horney, in her well-known book *The Neurotic Personality of Our Time*, describes the contradictions in contemporary American culture that make anxiety and frustration particularly widespread. We are taught that every man can get ahead; but there is categorical limitation on the advance of millions of minority-group members and scarcely less rigid limitation on the advance of millions in the "dominant" group who are caught in a vicious circle of poverty, ill health, poor education, and low status. We are encouraged to desire, and perhaps to need, a large number of material things; but great numbers of people are kept

[58] See Nathan Ackerman and Marie Jahoda, *op. cit.*, p. 90.

near the subsistence level. We are taught that brotherly love should rule our lives but that competition, every man for himself, is what makes our land great. One set of influences gives us a fairly strict "Victorian" sex code; but another set plays upon sex attraction as the most highly desirable and exciting thing in the world.[59]

Robin Williams points out that "the tension level of any social grouping is in part a function of the relative emphasis in that group's culture upon participation in common values as over against individual or group acquisition of scarce 'goods.' " In every society there are some values that can be shared by everyone (religious salvation and national prestige, for example); but other values are scarce—to the degree that one person has these values, others tend to lack them (power, individual prestige, and income are the principal types). "It seems to be generally agreed among serious students of American society that our culture places a rather extraordinary stress upon competition for distributive values. The 'competitive' motif is not merely a matter of such competition being permitted; rather, the striving for 'success' is positively enjoined to such an extent that in many areas and classes it approaches the status of a culturally obligatory pattern."[60] At the same time, American society shows a rather weak development of the shared, integrating values. This situation may be associated with a high level of anomie, a concept we have discussed above. Although precise comparisons are lacking, there is wide agreement that a mobile urban society contributes to the isolation of "the lonely crowd," in contrast to the closer identity with community that one feels in more stable societies.

Altogether it seems fair to say that from the point of view of the social psychological factors involved, modern American society is characterized by influences that tend to produce a fairly large amount of prejudice.

Conclusion

Gradually emerging out of the type of material discussed above is a theory of the personality functions of prejudice that is in harmony with contemporary social psychology. The interpretation is still too eclectic— it puts separate concepts side by side in a mechanical way—because we lack a truly integrated theory of personality. But the latter is being built by the combined efforts of several social sciences, and with it the scattered and sometimes contradictory concepts relating to prejudice can be coördinated. Much of our knowledge, however, is still on the de-

[59] See Karen Horney, *The Neurotic Personality of Our Time*, W. W. Norton & Company, Inc., 1937, pp. 281–290. See also Ruth Benedict, "Continuities and Discontinuities in Cultural Conditioning," *Psychiatry*, 1938, vol. 1, pp. 161–167.

[60] Robin Williams, Jr., *The Reduction of Intergroup Tensions*, Social Science Research Council, 1947, pp. 55–56.

scriptive level. We can expect systematic effort in the years ahead to explain the meaning of several relationships that have been observed but not yet adequately explained. In our society, for example, women seem to have less prejudice than men. Careful examination of *why* this should be true can tell us a great deal about the personality functions of prejudice. Such an explanation depends upon adequate knowledge of the different social roles of men and women in our society, the differences in their socialization, and—in connection with other functions of prejudice—their different relationships to power centers. It can, in turn, contribute to our knowledge of these questions. Several studies have observed that prejudiced persons tend to be more conventionally religious. There is, however, no study of the religious influence when other variables have been controlled, so that only tentative hypotheses can be based on this observation. There is always the grave danger, when research is on the descriptive level, that the careless student will take the observed relationship as "proof" of some theory. In the case of religious influence, this error is easily avoided because other data indicate that persons with very *little* prejudice sometimes show a strong religious influence. In the study by Allport and Kramer, 28 percent of the students indicated a marked influence of religious training, 41 percent reported a moderate influence; and this 69 percent was more prejudiced than the 31 percent who reported little or no religious influence. The difference was significant at the 1 percent level. Sixty-two percent of the Protestants, 71 percent of the Catholics, but only 22 percent of the Jews and 27 percent of those with no religious affiliation were in the "more anti-Negro" half.[61] Frenkel-Brunswik and Sanford also found that the more anti-Semitic girls were more conventionally religious. Both studies discovered, however, that many of the persons who were least prejudiced also reported a strong religious interest—an interest, to be sure, that was less often tied to traditional forms. Bettleheim and Janowitz, in a study of 150 veterans, asked their interviewees, among other questions dealing with army experiences: "How did the fellows feel about religion?" In the discussion that followed, it was revealed that veterans who stressed ". . . the acceptance and importance of religion in the army were significantly more tolerant than the rest of the sample. . . . Intolerance, however, was concentrated in the group whose answers indicated their indifference to religion by statements to the effect that 'most soldiers followed their own habits' or 'everybody has his own opinions.' "[62]

---

[61] See Gordon Allport and B. M. Kramer, *op. cit.*, pp. 25–27; see also Charles T. O'Reilly and Edward J. O'Reilly, "Religious Beliefs of Catholic College Students and Their Attitudes Toward Minorities," *Journal of Abnormal and Social Psychology*, July, 1954, pp. 378–380.

[62] See Bruno Bettleheim and Morris Janowitz, *Dynamics of Prejudice. A Psychological and Sociological Study of Veterans*, Harper & Brothers, 1950, pp. 51–52.

The need is for an analysis of the kind of religious training a person has received, a study of why and how he is religious. Thus it is not to religion *per se*, if such an influence could be isolated, but to the interaction between religious training and the total personality context that we must look for an understanding of the question of religion and prejudice. Religion may have nothing to do with it at all. Middle-class people seem to be more anti-Semitic in our society than lower-class people; they are better educated; they are more likely to attend church and to be "religious"; but they are also in more direct economic competition with Jews. To say that middle-class people are more anti-Semitic *because* they have received more education or *because* they go to church more often, when other variables have not been controlled, is clearly unwarranted. Nor can we assume that this might not be true. To make the issue absurdly clear—or perhaps just absurd—middle-class people are fatter than lower-class people, and also more anti-Semitic; therefore, corpulence leads to prejudice. In the next chapter we shall try to see the degree to which the economic competition factor, with which religion and education in this instance are correlated, must be taken into account. Descriptive studies can be of use in science only when they are related to a general theory which prevents one-sided surface "explanations."

The study of personality during the last several decades has undoubtedly added a great deal to our understanding of prejudice. The evidence seems to indicate clearly that certain types of personality are prejudice-prone; that a wide variety of needs may, in appropriate social settings, be served by prejudice; that a person's relationships with those around him may strongly influence his attitudes and behavior toward the members of minority groups. These explanations must come into any total theory of prejudice. We must be alert, however, to the weaknesses of this approach. There has been a tendency on the part of many writers to interpret prejudice as if it served *only* the need for ridding oneself of fear, guilt, and hostility. We require a more systematic study of the use of prejudice in the service of other needs—for "explaining" a complex situation, making it seem simple, and for giving one a sense of belonging, for example. Some authors have assumed not only that frustration can lead to prejudice, but that frustration is always present when there is prejudice. The authors of *Frustration and Aggression* declare: "For race prejudice to occur, *not only must there be frustration and ensuing aggression*, not only must there be permission to be aggressive but there must also be a way of identifying the people to be hated."[63] They do not hold that frustration is a sufficient cause of prejudice but do contend that it is a necessary cause, a force

---

[63] John Dollard, Neal Miller, Leonard Doob, *et al., op. cit.*, pp. 152–153. Italics ours.

that is always present where prejudice is found. There seems to be little evidence for this, unless one defines frustration so broadly that the term is meaningless.

Writers who have been strongly influenced by psychoanalysis tend to assume, in advance of the evidence, that the "basic" cause of prejudice, as of virtually all other aspects of personality, is reaction to the coercions of early training. Other forces may be used in the total explanation, but in a secondary way. Scudder Mekeel, for example, takes the position that the anxieties and hostilities that arise from the way we are socialized, especially in our culture, "are deeper and more fundamental" than those aroused by "external conditions." "Economic scarcity and lack of job opportunities are not by any means causes of race prejudices, as the Marxists would have us believe. Economic factors are a stimulant to the expression of prejudice."[64] If this is simply a caution that economic factors alone can never explain a given prejudice (for they cannot explain why prejudice should be the adjustment or why a specific prejudice should be the one selected), we can only welcome this criticism of a one-factor theory. If the effect, however, is simply to reduce the explanation of prejudice to another "fundamental" cause, the statement is inadequate. Prejudice is a complicated phenomenon compounded of social and cultural elements as well as individual personality elements. The various specialties in research, while abstracting one influence from the total, must avoid the error of reductionism— explaining the total by the abstracted part. Keeping in mind the important evidence concerning the personality factors involved in prejudice, we now turn to a study of the social and cultural influences.

[64] Scudder Mekeel, "Race Relations. Cultural Aids to Constructive Race Relations," *Mental Hygiene*, April, 1945, p. 185.

CHAPTER 4

Prejudice as a Weapon in Group Conflict

It is gradually becoming established, among students of human behavior, that when human beings come together in groups a new influence on their behavior begins to operate that cannot be explained by analysis of their separate personalities. There is, of course, no independent group mind or personality, but emergent influences in the group situation arise from the *interaction* of individuals, influences which do not occur except when individuals come into communication with one another. The situation is analogous to that in chemistry where the most complete analysis of the properties of the gases hydrogen and oxygen cannot explain the properties of the liquid water, which is a result of their interaction. This distinction between individual and group influences is analytic, of course; there is continuous mutual conditioning of one by the other. The way an individual will respond to group influences is in part a function of his personality, and the nature of his personality is in part a result of the group influences he has experienced. The understanding of any given situation will require the examination of both sets of influences. For purposes of scientific analysis, however, they must be studied separately.

The study of the influences on behavior that arise from groups, from human interaction, is usually considered to be the heart of the science of sociology. Like all other abstract sciences, its explanations are of the "if and when" variety: If certain kinds of individual personalities are involved, and when certain group influences are operative, then the results of a given interaction can be predicted. The explanation of any existing situation, in contrast with the explanation of abstract situations where variables have been controlled, requires the examination of all

111

the "ifs and whens" that may be involved. In terms of our problem, the analysis of the group influences in prejudice will be insufficient to explain existing manifestations of prejudice until the kind of forces examined in Chapter 3 are also taken into account. Similarly, analysis of the personality functions of prejudice is not sufficient to explain actual cases of prejudice, for they almost certainly involve group influences as well.

Keeping in mind this distinction between empirical and abstract explanations of human behavior, we can profitably make a strictly sociological approach to prejudice. In what way is prejudice a manifestation of group processes? When human beings come together, they tend both to unite for common purposes and to oppose each other. There is coöperation and accommodation, but there is also competition and conflict; and the coöperating members of one group are often united for purposes of opposition toward another group. Thus the two processes of association and dissociation are opposite sides of the same interaction. The study of prejudice can perhaps best be made from the side of dissociation—of conflict and competition. Many of the things that human beings desire—prestige, power, income—come in scarce quantity; and much of the social process, both of association and of dissociation, can be understood as an attempt to hold on to or to increase one's share of these scarce values. We coöperate with some in order to compete more effectively with others.

One of the widespread and probably universal results of this process is the stratification of human societies into many ranks, sharing differently in the distribution of prestige, power, and income. These ranks may be defined in the folkways, buttressed by tradition, and are often maintained by force. But the distribution of values is not permanent; human beings are constantly widening or narrowing their claims. Technological change, culture contact, and new systems of belief continually bring new forces into the "moving equilibrium" that makes up a social order. The entrance of these factors is obviously more rapid in some situations than in others, but they can scarcely be entirely lacking in any human society. To protect their established position or to improve upon it, human groups are quick to invent or to accept systems of belief and attitudes that justify and explain what they are trying to do. The explanation may be "religious"—the infidel, the barbarian, the pagan deserves no better—or cultural, or national, or based on class distinctions. In our time it is frequently racial, or pseudoracial. In the following pages we shall examine some attempts to use these distinctions as bases for maintaining or improving a group's position in the struggle for prestige, power, and income.

One must avoid exaggerating, as many writers have done, the role of conflict and competition in human life. There are those who think of conflict as "the father of all things" and those who, especially since

Darwin's day (despite Darwin, one might add), think of it in moral terms—conflict is good, and without it life would lack both zest and progress. Our position here is simply that conflict and competition are important social processes, natural to human society (as is coöperation) and probably inevitable. That is *not* to say, however, that any specific mode of conflict is inevitable or that any particular group alignment is natural. History is filled with evidence of the shifting pattern of groups among whom conflict occurs and of the wide range of modes of conflict, from violence to rational argument, that characterize human interaction.

The scientific study of social stratification and of the struggle for power has been one of the key jobs of social scientists for a century. But its full import for the understanding of human behavior, including such specific manifestations of behavior as prejudice, has been recognized very slowly by the average American and by a number of the scientists themselves. Many of the facts of American life, particularly in its early years, and almost all of the beliefs and traditions with which Americans interpret their society have prevented an adequate study and understanding of the role of power and of group conflict as expressions of human interaction. It is commonly thought that the United States has no class structure, no ruling class, for such concepts violate our ideas of individualism and democracy. To be sure, our behavior—particularly that of the middle and upper classes—is not so lacking in realism. As Charles A. Beard once said: "We talk like Thomas Jefferson and act like Alexander Hamilton." Our beliefs may, in fact, serve the function, among other things, of obscuring the class alignment and the pattern of conflict. However that may be, Americans have been slow to understand the facts of social stratification and the nature of group conflict. This circumstance has left a gap in our explanation of prejudice. We shall now turn to the evidence for the theory that prejudice is, in part, a manifestation of group conflict and a rationalization for discrimination.

Prejudice in the Struggle for Power, Prestige, and Income

Qualified statements and even exaggerated assertions of the role of economic factors in prejudice are not difficult to find, but well-tested evidence is less common. In this field, even more than in the material discussed in Chapter 3, the theory of prejudice is based on observation of historical relationships, not of controlled experimental situations, so that the precise role of political and economic factors, analytically separate from other factors, is not easy to demonstrate. Nevertheless, the great fund of evidence indicates clearly, if not with precision, the importance of group prejudice in the struggles within and between societies.

The fundamental attitude underlying the use of prejudice as a group weapon is ethnocentrism—belief in the unique value and "rightness" of one's own group. This widespread and perhaps universal tendency of human beings to consider their own society the best society was explained at first by the theory that there was a natural aversion to difference. Having been socialized to the patterns of behavior and belief of his own society, seeing them as "natural," each individual inevitably judged other patterns of behavior and belief as unnatural. The very standards by which one judges the value or desirability of any action are part of the culture which the growing individual absorbs; therefore he cannot avoid ethnocentrism. While this explanation is still regarded as valid, another element has been added to the explanation of ethnocentrism which relates it to the topic of this chapter. Ethnocentrism is functional; it serves the group in its struggles for power and wealth. (We noted in Chapter 3 that it also serves the individual in his attempt to find personal security.) It flourishes best in conflict situations. In the eighteenth century an East Indian, traveling in England, was received as an honored guest; there was also a general admiration for the Chinese. With the growth of conflicts of power between Britain and the East, however, this attitude faded; there was a loss of appreciation for the civilizations of the eastern lands; ethnocentrism and prejudice grew.[1]

If ethnocentrism is functional in group conflict, as well as a result of the limitations in perspective that come from the process of socialization, it is an expression of the "needs" of the powerful people as a ruling group, not simply a reflection of the frustrations of powerless individuals. This is also true of group prejudices within a society; the designation of inferior groups comes from those on top—an expression of their right to rule—as well as from frustrated persons, often near the bottom, as an expression of their need for security. In the former case, those in power may use prejudice in a "rational" and objective way without necessarily sharing the attitude; in the latter case, one could not possibly use prejudice without believing it, at least on the conscious level. In the one case, prejudice is used to manipulate other persons, and hence can be outside oneself; but in the other case, prejudice is an attempt to govern oneself—to reduce tensions and hostilities —hence must be believed, to be effective. This is an analytic distinction, of course. Usually the "outside" and "inside" uses of prejudice would be blended and mutually reinforcing.

Sherif has stated clearly the theory that prejudice is functional in the power struggle:

The scale of hierarchy of prejudice in settled and stable times, flows from the politically, economically, and socially strong and eminent down to lower

[1] See Arnold J. Toynbee, A Study of History, Oxford University Press, 1934, vol. 1.

hierarchies of the established order. The time to look for the greatest and most impregnable hierarchies of social distance is in the mightiest periods of the empires. A glance at the Greek, Roman, Turkish, British, or French empire, for example, shows convincingly that the periods of highly observed social distances and their psychological correlates were the "golden ages" of those empires. The caste system in India, which is disintegrating now, was not the idea of the ignorant and frustrated "untouchables." It was the philosophical Brahmins and the British masters of the local Indian princes and rulers who were interested in keeping these delineations intact. . . . The most elaborate "race" superiority doctrines are products of already existing organizations of superiority-inferiority relationships and exploitations. The superiority doctrines have been the deliberate or unconscious standardizations of the powerful and prosperous groups at the top and not the ideas of the frustrated and deprived majority at the bottom.[2]

In examining the evidence to discover the usefulness of this theory in helping us to account for prejudice, we must be careful not to limit the study to prejudices with which we happen to be familiar. Although race prejudice, for example, is doubtless most important in our time, it has not always been, nor will it necessarily continue to be. A few centuries ago it was easier to designate "inferior" groups by religious than by racial lines of division. In Europe there was relatively little contact with the members of non-Caucasian races, for instance. Differences in religious belief, however, frequently reflected different status positions; social changes and conflicts were accompanied by religious differentiation. At a time when the religious view of life was extremely powerful, it was easy to believe that a religiously different group was inferior.

Subsidiary beliefs (subsidiary from the point of view of a theory of prejudice) helped to account for the use of *religious* prejudice in *secular* group conflicts. The medieval world believed that life on earth was a brief second, that eternal salvation was the most important thing. Was it not common humanity to kill any Antichrist who might lead thousands to eternal damnation?[3] An examination of the setting in which this religious prejudice flourished, however, shows that a strictly "religious" explanation of the conflict is insufficient. Involved in the Inquisition of the thirteenth century, for example, were many power gains for the inquisitor—confiscation of property, political gains, weakening the hold of emerging new ruling groups, avoiding attention to the role of the church in the secular power structure. "Heresy hunting was profitable, and all those who sought riches and power eagerly took advantage of the opportunity, masking their satisfactions behind the

---

[2] Muzafer Sherif, *An Outline of Social Psychology*, Harper & Brothers, 1948, p. 343.
[3] See Ruth Benedict, *Race: Science and Politics*, Modern Age Books, 1940, pp. 220–223 ff.

dogma that the heretics were guilty of treason against the Almighty."[4]

A clear example of the use of religious heresy for economic and political purposes is the attack on the Albigenses in southern France. The Albigenses were an ascetic medieval cult which was distinguished from the dominant church not only by a number of "heretical" religious beliefs and practices but also by several important secular traits. The new sect was followed especially by the rising burgher class in the towns—a class whose economic power was based on functions quite distinct from the functions of the medieval ruling class and therefore a threat to that class. Moreover, the Albigenses prospered in Provence, an area that was politically free from the authority of the French king, whose power, in turn, was closely related to the power of the papacy. The cities of Provence were among the richest in France. To make them even more vulnerable to "religious" attack, the Albigenses, for both religious and economic reasons, made vigorous protests against the corruption of the contemporary clergy. "The Papacy ordered the faithful clergy of northern France to preach a campaign of extermination against heretical Provence, and the crusade became one of the most implacable of religious wars. Its conclusion established the Capetian kings of northern France as monarchs in Provence after mass executions had decimated the independent burghers of the cities and had destroyed the civilization that had flourished in southern France. The burning of heretics continued for a hundred years, and at last the cult was exterminated."[5]

Such "religious" conflicts persisted, in one form and another, for several centuries. In the sixteenth and seventeenth centuries many of the rising middle class, the bourgeoisie, joined the Huguenots (French Protestants) partly, at least, because the Catholic Church was so well accommodated to medieval society that it was very slow in making room in its system of economic morality for the activities of the middle class. The Huguenots opposed the concentration of power in the king, who was a key figure in the whole medieval power structure which blocked their advance. The bloody religious wars of the late sixteenth century masked a political and economic conflict. For several decades the Edict of Nantes reduced the amount of open violence, but by the time of Louis XIV the Huguenots were again actively persecuted. The Edict of Nantes was revoked, and hundreds of thousands of Protestants were killed or driven from the country. New needs and new economic opportunities had appeared with the age of discoveries, with expanding world trade, with emerging industrialization. New groups had arisen to exploit these opportunities, and they had often found sectarian reli-

---

[4] *Ibid.*, p. 225.

[5] *Ibid.*, p. 227. For another discussion of the use of religion in secular conflicts, see J. Milton Yinger, *Religion in the Struggle for Power*, Duke University Press, 1946.

gious beliefs congenial because these beliefs also stood against an important aspect of the old order—its religious justification. But the new power groups, with their new religious justification, were met with confiscation of property, persecution, and death by the ruling powers of the old society.[6] All this was done in the name of religion, but the economic and political aspects of the struggle are unmistakable.

FROM RELIGIOUS TO RACIAL PREJUDICE

In our time, religious lines of demarcation are less useful in group conflict. Religious cleavages coincide less well with political and economic divisions. If there had been as many Huguenots among the landed aristocracy and among the peasantry of France as there were among the middle class, it would have been impossible for the government of Louis XIV to attack the growing power of the bourgeoisie under the claim of religious heresy. To be sure, there is one cleavage in modern society where religious differentiation and political economic differentiation coincide, with something of the same results as were found in the "religious wars" of medieval Europe. Most communists are antireligious as well as being opposed to the political and economic structure of capitalism. Those who fight communists, therefore, can oppose them for their irreligion as well as their secular ideas—and it is not always easy to know when or to what degree the opposition is on religious grounds and when it is on secular grounds. Possibly, for example, the opposition of the Catholic Church to communism in Hungary is in part related to the fact that under the communist regime the landholdings of the church have fallen from 42 percent of the land of Hungary to less than 5 percent, just as the opposition of the aristocrats of eighteenth-century France—and of their church—to French Protestantism was related to the threatening economic and political power of the middle classes.

Strictly religious differentiation, however, is less often used for group conflict in modern society because the religious frame of reference is less crucial today. In a large measure, racial differentiation, or supposed racial differentiation, has come to take its place. We now fight our economic and political opponents not by claiming that they believe the wrong things in religion but by claiming that they are natively inferior. Even modern anti-Semitism, as we shall see, is in only a small measure dependent upon symbols of religious differentiation for its "justification." Prejudice against the Jews has been assimilated into the standard "racial" frame of reference.

It was not difficult to make the transition from the religious to the racial line of demarcation. Europe's first extensive contacts with the Negroes of Africa and the Orientals occurred at a time when religious

[6] Ruth Benedict, *op. cit.*, pp. 228–230.

differences were still regarded as vitally important. The relative reign of tolerance in religious matters had not yet developed. The members of other races were, in most cases, not only racially different but also religiously different. If, at first, the white European did not condemn the Negro because he was a Negro, he could condemn him because he was a pagan. But what if the black pagan were converted to Christianity? When there were only a few such persons, the adjustment was not difficult; they could be given a higher status or even admitted to the dominant group. MacCrone states that the earliest practice in South Africa was to free slaves who had been baptized. But in time this threatened to become a costly economic burden and a challenge to the whole status structure. "When, in 1792, the question was explicitly raised by the Church Council of Stellenbosch, whether owners who permitted or encouraged their slaves to be baptized would be obliged to emancipate them, the matter was referred to the Church Council of Capetown for its opinion. That body replied that neither the law of the land nor the law of the church prohibited the retention of baptized persons in slavery, while local custom strongly supported the practice. . . ."[7] Thus the line of cleavage, originally symbolized by religion, had come to be symbolized by race.

Racial reasons for persecution are convenient in modern life, as Benedict has pointed out, because of the greatly increased contact among the members of different races and because of the racial heterogeneity of many societies. Emerging science, with its efforts to measure physical differences and its studies of racial origins, drew attention to race, and its data were distorted to justify the use of race differences in economic conflict. The racial line of cleavage had the additional advantage, as a weapon, of relative permanence. Poverty, or occupation, or language, or religion can set a group apart as sharply as skin color or head shape, but the line of distinction may be more difficult for the dominant group to maintain.[8] George Bernard Shaw has caricatured this difficulty in *Pygmalion* by having a speech expert transform a servant girl into a "duchess" by giving her an Oxford accent. The transformation was not complete, to be sure, for it proved harder to control what she said than to change how she said it. After six months of training she seldom slipped back into cockney accent when she said "the rain in Spain falls mainly in the plain"; but it was a bit disconcerting to her teacher to see how often the weather conditions of southwest Europe came into her conversation. Nevertheless she could "pass" relatively successfully. Had her skin been black, the most perfect Oxford accent and all the appropriate ideas to go with it would not have sufficed. It

[7] I. D. MacCrone, *Race Attitudes in South Africa*, Oxford University Press, 1937, p. 135.

[8] Cf. Ruth Benedict, *op. cit.*, pp. 233–236.

might be well to add that even the racial line is far from permanent, for wherever races have come into contact, miscegenation has produced a mixed group. The "line" between the dominant and subordinate races may then be drawn at one of several places, depending on the power needs of the dominant group.

In the study of this shift from a religious to a racial mark of distinction, it is apparent that to understand race conflict in the modern world one must understand conflict, not race.

Persecution was an old, old story before racism was thought of. Social change is inevitable, and it is always fought by those whose ties are to the old order. . . . Those who have these ties will consciously or unconsciously ferret out reasons for believing that their group is supremely valuable and that the new claimants threaten the achievements of civilization. They will raise a cry of rights of inheritance or divine right of kings or religious orthodoxy or racial purity or manifest destiny. These cries reflect the temporary conditions of the moment, and all the efforts of the slogan-makers need not convince us that any one of them is based on eternal verities.[9]

Once race differences had become established as symbols of superiority-inferiority, they were used as weapons in many group conflicts. Until the French Revolution there had been little racial prejudice; but by that time the slave trade had become a big business. The nominally Christian slave trader found belief in the inferiority and even non-human nature of the Negro a very convenient idea. When the British first established economic interests in India, they encouraged intermarriage with the native population. When, however, the mixed-bloods threatened to outnumber the whites and began to offer competition for positions—particularly minor managerial and administrative jobs—the racial policy changed and a pattern of acute racial discrimination appeared. As Charles Johnson said: "The Indians and mixed bloods were relegated to a fixed economic subordination, and their consequent poverty and degradation were used to justify the judgment of an inherent degeneracy and shiftlessness and unfitness for the society of the English."[10]

Race prejudice was not only a weapon of imperialism, as in Africa and India, but a weapon of class conflict within many nations. In the eighteenth century the Count de Boulainvilliers, an admirer of feudalism, tried to oppose not only the peasantry but Louis XIV as well by claiming that the nobles, who were losing their autonomous power to the absolute monarch, were of superior "Teuton" blood. To attack their power was to destroy the racial leadership of France. It was not until the nineteenth century, however, that this idea was widely used.

[9] Ibid., pp. 230–231.
[10] Charles S. Johnson, "Race Relations and Social Change," in E. T. Thompson (ed.), Race Relations and the Race Problem, Duke University Press, 1939, pp. 275–276.

In *The Inequality of Human Races*, de Gobineau declared that the hope of the world was the fair-haired Teutons—"Aryans." All the countries of Europe had been swamped by "Gallo-Romans" while the racial aristocrats were being destroyed. The revolutionary movements of 1848 were, to de Gobineau, an uprising of racial trash. Since the masses were innately inferior, the democracy and liberalism for which they fought were impossible. Thus he fought a class battle with racism.[11]

Anti-Semitism will be studied in detail in Chapters 9 and 10, but here we must indicate that out of the political and economic struggles of Europe in the latter half of the nineteenth century there emerged an anti-Semitic program which demonstrates clearly the role of prejudice in group conflict. Overt expressions of anti-Semitism had gradually subsided in western Europe during the eighteenth and first half of the nineteenth centuries. The merchant and industrial middle class had fought its way to power under the banner of democracy and liberalism; it had sought, and won, the support of many Jews in its struggles. Legal and political discriminations against Jews were generally abolished. By the middle of the nineteenth century, however, the central political-economic battle was no longer between the new middle class and the old feudal aristocracy but had become a struggle between the now powerful middle class and a rising proletarian movement (of many types). Whereas democracy and liberalism had been appropriate ideologies for the earlier struggle, they were embarrassing and difficult concepts for the middle class to use in its conflicts with the proletariat. In this setting anti-Semitism began to revive. In Germany, where the conflicts were sharpest, there was no time between 1870 and 1945 when there was not a frankly anti-Semitic political party. Bismarck, although probably personally disdainful of the intellectual "supports" to anti-Semitism, nevertheless began to use it to fight the liberal movement. Since several Jews or persons of Jewish parentage had been prominent in his government, it was not religious or cultural difference which led to the new attacks, but the usefulness of Jews as symbols. "It was a political maneuver which found the Jews useful ammunition, but had no interest in them as Jews."[12] Finding it difficult to get a positive political program behind which they could unite a sufficiently large following, the conservatives discovered that they could achieve a kind of negative unity by the use of anti-Semitism.

> It mattered nothing to the conservatives that the reason for Stoecker's [leader of the Christian Socialists] semi-socialistic antisemitism was that the Jews were capitalists, for Stoecker himself sat in Parliament with the conservatives; and it did not disturb Stoecker that the conservatives supported

---

[11] See Arthur de Gobineau, *The Inequality of Human Races*, G. P. Putnam's Sons, 1915; see also Ruth Benedict, *op. cit.*, pp. 173–179.

[12] James W. Parkes, *An Enemy of the People: Antisemitism*, Penguin Books, Inc., 1946, p. 10.

him because they felt that his tepid socialism would be an insurance against the more violent or "Jewish" form of the disease, represented by Marx and Lassalle. It was an adequate bond of union to regard Jews as the enemy. Antisemitism also helped to bring the second group whose support Bismarck desired to cultivate, the Roman Catholic center, into alliance with the Protestant conservatives. For the Kulturkampf could now be represented as the work of Jewish-led liberal secularists. . . . It was altogether a most curious alliance. . . . Its real point of union was hostility not to Jewry but to the progressive ideas of liberalism; it mattered little to Bismarck from which gun-site the enemy was discomfited.[13]

Since the 1870's many other struggles between the political left and right, including some in the United States, as we shall see later, have involved the use of anti-Semitism. Gradually, during this period, the attacks on Jews shifted from a religious and cultural base to a "racial" one. As late as 1899 Chamberlain, in his *Foundations of the Nineteenth Century*, declared that Jews were enemies, not because of biological differences but because of their special ways of thinking and acting. "One can very soon become a Jew." By the time of Hitler, however, anti-Semitism had become thoroughly biologized. Jews were held to be innately inferior and vicious, the destroyers of civilization. Throughout this period anti-Semitism, whether rationalized on cultural or "racial" grounds, was a clear example of the use of prejudice for political and economic purposes.

Interlaced with the use of race prejudice in class conflict was its employment for national purposes. If you can condemn your economic opponent on the grounds that he is racially inferior, why not condemn your national enemy for his biological inferiority? We shall not try to examine here[14] the rather extensive literature upholding this policy. It is only necessary to state that the attempt to define a nation as a homogeneous racial group, to "prove" the superiority of that group over others, and to explain history in terms of inherited differences does such violence to the facts that it can be understood only as a weapon in a conflict situation. Hitler and his "intelligentsia" made the issue clear by the extremes to which they went. Only the "Aryan" can be a leader, a builder of civilization (although some other "racial" groups may be sustainers). Wherever genius has been shown, there the presence of Aryan blood has been proved. Leonardo da Vinci and Dante become Aryans; the Japanese share in the biological guarantee of leadership (were they not allies of the Germans?) because of a small admixture of Aryan blood. But their leadership is precarious; it would be bound to fade if they lost contact with the creative Aryan peoples. Said Hitler: ". . . If, starting today, all further Aryan influence upon Japan should stop . . . , Japan's present advance in science and technology could

[13] *Ibid.*, pp. 10–11.
[14] See Ruth Benedict, *op. cit.*, pp. 199–218.

take place for a little while longer, but in the time of a few years the source would dry out, Japanese life would gain, but its culture would stiffen and fall back into the sleep out of which it was startled seven decades ago by the Aryan wave of culture."[15]

Such racism stems from politics, not science. It is not only Germans who have used it thus. Before the First World War Carlyle claimed that the German tribes were ancestors of the British, but by 1914 many British discovered that Germans were the barbarians who had fought their ancestors and had destroyed Roman civilization. Germans were the Huns and Mongols. Since the use of racism in this manner stems from political needs, it can be expected to change widely and rapidly. These changes can be understood only by study of the functions which such prejudice serves.[16]

Prejudice as a Weapon in the United States

Most of the preceding material has referred to the use of prejudice as a weapon in the economic and political struggles of Europe. No less convincing a demonstration of the role of prejudice in group conflict can be found in the history of the United States. Our country was being settled at the very time that racial lines of cleavage were beginning to be drawn. Several factors in American history encouraged the use and elaboration of race prejudice. As the colonists became numerous and began to press deeper into the lands controlled by the Indians, sharp conflicts inevitably arose. Few of the settlers seriously considered that the Indians might have some rights to the land. It was easier to develop a picture of the lying, thieving, murdering savage, pagan in religion, racially stupid except for a kind of animal cunning. Such a person has no rights; the only good Indian is a dead Indian. This picture of the aborigines was frequently not held by the trappers and traders who moved individually among the Indians. They gained by friendly contact and therefore tended to judge the Indian differently. But the prejudice of the farmer-settler prevailed. There were qualifications and exceptions and ambivalent feelings of course. These were never strong enough, however, to prevent the continuing seizure of Indian lands with a minimum of compensation, the decimation of the Indian population to scarcely more than one-third its original size, and the development of a rationalizing prejudice that moved with the white man across the continent. In recent decades categorical race prejudice against the Indian has sharply declined—and so has the economic function which that prejudice formerly served.

The development and entrenchment of prejudice against the Negro

---

[15] Adolf Hitler, *Mein Kampf*, Reynal and Hitchcock, 1940, p. 399.
[16] See Ruth Benedict, *op. cit.*, pp. 215–218.

are also made more meaningful by an examination of the economic situation in which it throve. The situation before the American Revolution had potentialities for several different attitudes, and economic factors were important in helping to select the one that finally became dominant. Many of the Negroes who came to America first were indentured servants, not slaves; there were also white indentured servants. From this situation it was possible that both Negro and white bondsmen would move toward freedom as the settlements became more stable, or that both would sink into a permanent status of inferiority (whether of slavery or some other legal form), or that one group would break out of servitude while the other was kept in. Before the Revolution the first possibility seemed most likely. In the seventeenth century a Virginia court had upheld the right of one Negro to claim the perpetual service of another Negro—showing that no categorical race line had yet been drawn. With the failure of tobacco, rice, and indigo to support the plantation economy, the settlers became lukewarm toward slavery.

In Granville County, North Carolina, a full-blooded Negro, John Chavis, educated at Princeton, conducted a private school for white children, and was a licentiate under the local Presbytery, preaching to white congregations in the state. One of his pupils became Governor of North Carolina, another was the state's Whig Senator. Two were sons of the Chief Justice of North Carolina. He was not stopped until the Denmark Vesey uprising in South Carolina (the first state to show promise of economic prosperity through the cotton industry) threatened the whole structure of slavery.[17]

Myrdal states that in the first two decades of the nineteenth century the abolitionist movement was as strong in the South as in the North, if not stronger.[18]

Into this setting came some new factors. The invention of the cotton gin and other mechanical devices for the processing of cotton cloth began to make cotton agriculture profitable. In 1793, 500,000 pounds of cotton were exported to Europe. The cotton gin was patented in 1794, and the next year six million pounds were exported. By a decade later, 1805, the amount had grown to forty million pounds, and by 1850 to over a billion pounds.[19] The effects of this increase were soon felt. The price of cotton rose, the value of slaves doubled, and land values increased sharply; "and with every increase in value the difficulty of breaking the status of Negro slavery increased."[20] The belief in slavery, which had been on the decline for a century or more, began to revive in the South. After 1830 an extensive literature to justify slavery ap-

[17] Charles S. Johnson, *op. cit.*, pp. 280–281.
[18] Gunnar Myrdal, *An American Dilemma*, Harper & Brothers, 1944, p. 86.
[19] W. D. Weatherford and Charles S. Johnson, *Race Relations*, D. C. Heath and Company, 1934, p. 136.
[20] C. S. Johnson, *op. cit.*, p. 282.

peared. It attempted to show that slavery was contrary neither to nature nor to religion, and that since the Negro was inferior and subhuman, it was even harmonious with democracy. Occasionally a writer would recognize the economic foundation of these beliefs. In *Sociology for the South*, 1854, George Fitzhugh wrote, "Our Southern patriots, at the time of the Revolution, finding Negroes expensive and useless, became warm antislavery men. We, their wiser sons, having learned to make cotton and sugar, find slavery very useful and profitable, and think it a most excellent institution. We of the South advocate slavery, no doubt, from just as selfish motives as induce the Yankees and English to deprecate it."[21] But Fitzhugh hastened to add, "We have, however, almost all human and divine authority on our side of the argument. The Bible nowhere condemns, and throughout recognizes slavery."[22]

That racial distinctions by themselves are unimportant in explaining the use of prejudice in group conflict is shown in a study of the changing attitude toward immigrants and immigration in the United States. Since many of the same arguments and beliefs are involved in the treatment of white and of colored immigrants, one must conclude that something other than "race difference" lies behind the situation. This conclusion is also supported by the fact that an immigrant group that is accepted and even welcomed in one circumstance, despite a racial difference, may be condemned and attacked in another situation "because" of its race. It is obviously impossible to explain the changing amount of prejudice by the racial constant.

The belief is rather widespread that there was no "immigrant problem," no prejudice against the newcomers to America, until the late nineteenth century. A careful study of our early history will show this to be false. It is easy today to assume that the early immigrants were readily accepted because of their passion for liberty, their thrift, their industry. Their contemporaries, however, were as likely to complain of the immigrants' foreign ways, criminality, and filth. The agitation of the Know-Nothing Order was directed against the Irish and Germans. The supposed contrast between the "new" immigration (from south and east Europe) and the "old" immigration (from north Europe) that was drawn so sharply by many writers in the early twentieth century is interestingly paralleled by a writer comparing the "new" and the "old" of 1835: "Then our accessions of immigration were real accessions of strength from the ranks of the learned and the good, from the enlightened mechanic and artisan and intelligent husbandman. Now, immigration is the accession of weakness, from the ignorant and vicious, or the priest ridden slaves of Ireland and Germany, or the outcast tenants of the poorhouses and prisons of Europe."[23] Compare that

---

[21] Quoted by Gunnar Myrdal, *op. cit.*, p. 1188.
[22] *Ibid.*
[23] Quoted by Isaac A. Hourwich, *Immigration and Labor*, G. P. Putnam's Sons, 1912.

with the writers of 1910–1920 who were exalting the quality of the early immigrants in order to condemn the newcomers. Lothrop Stoddard writes:

. . . The white race divides into three main sub-species—the Nordics, the Alpines, and the Mediterraneans. All three are good stocks, ranking in genetic worth well above the various colored races. However, there seems to be no question that the Nordic is far and away the most valuable type. . . . Our country, originally settled almost exclusively by Nordics, was toward the close of the nineteenth century invaded by hordes of immigrant Alpines and Mediterraneans, not to mention Asiatic elements like Levantines and Jews. As a result, the Nordic native American has been crowded out with amazing rapidity by these swarming, prolific aliens. . . .[24]

It is easy to see from such statements that things are not as good as they used to be—and perhaps they never were.

Our interest here is not to discover the truth or falsity of the various opinions about immigrant groups but to see if the attitudes toward immigration—both the constant and the changing attitudes—can be understood in part by use of a theory of group conflict. Racial differences or supposed differences, national, religious, cultural differences, or simply a general "inferiority" are the reasons ordinarily given to explain opposition to immigrants. Do these "explanations" hide, perhaps even from the person who uses them, economic and political conflicts which are the more basic causes of the attitude toward the alien groups? Two cautions are necessary before we examine this question. One does not need to assume that all opposition to immigration is a result of prejudice, as we are using that term. We have not called the defense of values prejudice, unless that defense is tied up categorically with attitudes toward whole groups of people. If one says that he is opposed to immigration because it leads to a higher rate of criminality or because it makes more difficult the functioning of a political democracy, he has not necessarily expressed a prejudice; he may be giving a judgment on the consequences of cultural heterogeneity. The social scientist asks at this point: Is this judgment correct? Does immigration lead to greater criminality or a weakened political democracy? What are the other effects on social structure and process? These are complicated questions which we shall not deal with here. When, however, one says that he is opposed to immigration because it leads to more crime and weakens democracy, and this is true because of the categorical inferiority of the immigrant group, he has then taken a value stand of that special type which we have called group prejudice.

The second caution is that we must not assume all categorical opposition to immigrants to be a result of economic and political interests. Part of it is simply a matter of tradition, as we shall see in the next

[24] Lothrop Stoddard, *The Rising Tide of Color Against White World-Supremacy*, Charles Scribner's Sons, 1920, pp. 162–165.

chapter. Many people are opposed to alien groups in this country not because they have, or think they have, any economic interest in such opposition but simply because they have been taught that "America for the Americans" is a proper attitude if they are to feel at home in their group. It is also clear that opposition to immigrants may serve all the personality functions dealt with in the preceding chapter. Newcomers to a country, because they can be easily identified by their differences and because they are relatively powerless, are convenient targets for random aggressions.

Nevertheless, the evidence seems to indicate clearly a tradition of opposition to immigrants, who are accepted targets for aggression partly because of economic and political conflicts. There seems to be a direct correlation between the peaks of "nativist" activity and the valleys of economic depression. The Native American party of the 1830's, the Know-Nothing Order of the 1850's, the American Protective Association in the last two decades of the nineteenth century, and the scores of anti-alien, one-hundred-per-cent-American groups in the 1930's— these all show the tendency to try to bolster a shaky economic situation by prejudice against recent immigrant groups.[25] This correlation between prejudice and economic insecurity is low because many other variables influence the strength of prejudice, and they may operate strongly in different circumstances from those that encourage the use of prejudice as an economic weapon. Anti-Semitic activities may increase in the United States because of political factors in Germany which have reverberations here. Such activities may have no direct relation to economic stresses in the United States except as those stresses create a favorable setting for the borrowing of the German pattern. It should also be noted that economic forces may encourage prejudice in "good times" (and among the economically powerful), hope of gain rather than fear of loss being the underlying motive. In a multiple-factor situation, such as prejudice, it is important not to assume that because the course of events does not follow the pattern indicated by one factor (economic crisis, for example) the factor in question isn't operative. Its influence may simply be canceled out by other factors which obscure its effects.

ANTI-IMMIGRATION LEGISLATION

The most convincing evidence that anti-immigrant prejudice reflects economic forces in part is the story of federal legislation that gradually controlled and restricted immigration after 1882. Many people joined in support of this legislation who had no economic interest—probably, in fact, in opposition to their long-run economic interest. But some of

[25] See Donald Young, *Research Memorandum on Minority Groups in the Depression*, Social Science Research Council, 1937.

the strongest proponents of restriction were groups who could see some immediate economic advantage in weakening or getting rid of immigrant competitors. The arguments used were partly racial or biological —continued immigration means "blood pollution" or "mongrelization"; they were partly religious and cultural—"our capacity to maintain our cherished institutions stands diluted by a stream of alien blood." But the economic factor was occasionally stated in undisguised fashion: "The Chinaman is here because his presence pays, and he will remain and continue to increase so long as there is money in him. When the time comes that he is no longer profitable *that* generation will take care of him and will send him back."[26]

Vigorous exclusionist sentiments developed first on the west coast, where a visible racial minority with a unifying cultural tradition came into economic competition with some of the "native" whites, who in their efforts to seize and exploit the resources of a new area were accustomed to a conflict pattern and a vigilante tradition. When unskilled workers were needed in large numbers to build railroads and to begin the development of the resources of the West, many Chinese were imported and welcomed. "Race relations between the whites and the Chinese were characterized by great tolerance. Their different background was accepted for its difference, and admired. When, however, the economic emergency passed and the large numbers menaced the security of the native workers of the West, antagonisms developed and stereotypes were created, which eventually resulted in Chinese exclusion."[27] Agitation against the Chinese began, perhaps, in the 1860's. During this decade the Central Pacific Railroad was completed, so that competition for jobs among the unskilled was intensified. The gold boom began to fade and unemployment to rise. Serious economic crises in the 1870's, accompanied by extensive migration of unemployed from the East, brought sharper and sharper demands from the white workers that the continuing Chinese immigration be stopped. In 1876 both major parties in California had anti-Chinese planks in their platforms, and a state-wide vote in 1879 was overwhelmingly for exclusion.[28]

The changing economic situation was accompanied by a shifting stereotype of the Chinese. From worthy, industrious, sober, law-abiding citizens they rather suddenly developed into unassimilable, deceitful, servile people smuggling opium. "There were no new personal experiences to account for the contrast. There was no increase in native aggressiveness on the part of the White group. There was no heightening of an instinctive consciousness of kind. There was, however, a change in the economic conditions in California which made it to the advan-

---

[26] Quoted from the Sacramento *Record Union*, January 10, 1879, by Oliver C. Cox, *Caste, Class and Race*, Doubleday & Company, Inc., 1948, p. 413.

[27] W. D. Weatherford and Charles S. Johnson, *op. cit.*, pp. 54–55.

[28] See B. Schreike, *Alien Americans*, The Viking Press, Inc., 1936, pp. 3–22.

tage of the Whites to eliminate the Chinese as a factor in competition, and the attitude toward them was an effect of this situation."[29]

In 1882 Congress passed a law that suspended all immigration of skilled or unskilled Chinese labor for ten years. The legislation was renewed from time to time and in 1904 the time limit was removed. Since 1882 there has been virtually no immigration from China. The act of 1924 stopped it completely by assigning Asiatic countries no quota from the total amount of immigration to be permitted. Even the alien wives of citizens of Oriental ancestry were barred by the clause which stated that "no alien ineligible for citizenship shall be admitted to the United States." That this final complete exclusion of all Chinese and other Asiatics was an expression of a purely traditional race prejudice, by 1924 almost completely independent of its economic origins, seems clear from the fact that, had China been assigned a quota according to the formula contained in the act of 1924, she would have been granted approximately 100 immigrants per year. During World War II, in fact, the United States made this gesture to her Chinese ally by giving her a quota. Permanent immigration of Chinese into the United States may now total 105 per year.

The exclusion of Japanese immigrants followed much the same pattern. At first they were welcomed.

Their farming methods, evolved through centuries of intensive farming, supported an efficiency of production which won the admiration of the country. However, this very efficiency became a serious threat to their less accomplished white neighbors, who could not successfully compete with them. Moreover, the Japanese were rapidly changing as a nation to a basis of international rivalry, and the self-protective interest of the American group soon dictated exclusion. Here again "racial instincts" followed economics rather than the original nature of either race.[30]

By 1900 there were demands that the Japanese be excluded, and these grew more and more insistent. On March 1, 1905, the California legislature, by a vote of 28–0 and 70–0 in the two houses, passed a resolution urging Congress to exclude Japanese from the country.[31] In 1906 the San Francisco school board passed a resolution that barred Japanese children from white schools. This was repealed, under pressure from the federal government, but continued agitation finally led to the "gentlemen's agreement" of 1907 in which the Japanese government agreed to issue no more passports to skilled or unskilled workers, except those who had previously resided in the United States or their wives or their children under twenty-one years of age. The immigration of women to

[29] Otto Klineberg, *Social Psychology*, Henry Holt & Company, Inc., 1940, pp. 385–386.

[30] W. D. Weatherford and Charles S. Johnson, *op. cit.*, p. 55.

[31] Carey McWilliams, *Prejudice—Japanese-Americans: Symbol of Racial Intolerance*, Little, Brown & Company, 1944, p. 19.

become the wives of Japanese already in the United States was permitted until 1920, when Japan agreed to refuse emigration to the "picture brides." The act of 1924 stopped all immigration from Japan.

Anti-Japanese activity had not stopped with the virtual cutting off of immigration by the gentlemen's agreement. Newspaper headlines and editorials, nativist organizations such as the Native Sons of the Golden West, mob action, political oratory, and legal enactments all continued to show the extent of the prejudice, particularly in California. Gradually the federal government became involved after having tried for several decades to restrain California's anti-Japanese expressions because of the difficulties they created in international diplomacy. By the Immigration Act of 1924, and by the resettlement policy of 1942, the federal government expressed agreement with the racial sentiments involved.

It is our concern to ask at this point: Who profited, or thought they profited, from such moves? Perhaps the most tangible and continuous gains accrued to men running for office or in office, who, by striking out at the Japanese, could create in-group feeling, could sponsor a cause, could exploit the tensions of the average voter, and could avoid reference to any of the critical issues which might have two opposing sides that were difficult to occupy simultaneously. Many California politicians since 1900 have made use of prejudice against the Japanese to win an election. If the existing fund of prejudice was not enough to make the tactic effective, their supporting newspapers could manufacture enough to help. Before World War II there was a strong correlation between the waves of anti-Japanese agitation and election years. Since the Japanese group was small and politically and economically weak, candidates could attack it almost without fear of reprisals; it was as politically safe to be against the Japanese as to be against sin. Even Woodrow Wilson, speaking in California during the presidential election of 1912, declared: "The whole question is one of assimilation of diverse races. We cannot make a homogeneous population of a people who do not blend with the Caucasian race." McWilliams reports that the Democratic party distributed over 100,000 copies of this relatively innocuous statement around the state.[32] State politicians used the issue more vigorously:

United States Senator James D. Phelan, a Democrat seeking re-election when every sign pointed to a Republican landslide, premised his entire campaign upon the issue of White Supremacy. Writing in the Grizzly Bear [publication of the Native Sons of the Golden West, of which he was a member] for February, 1920, he said: "Imagine a Japanese seeking the hand of an American woman in marriage. . . . If you knew," he said in the same article, "how these people raise their garden truck, you would never let a bite of it pass your lips." To aid the sorely pressed Senator, his colleagues

[32] Ibid., p. 39.

arranged for the Committee on Immigration and Naturalization to hold hearings in California during the summer of 1920. The hearings were opened on July 12, 1920, by Senator Phelan himself. He testified that the "Japanese people are an immoral people"; proceeded to confuse Buddhism and Shintoism; charged that California was headed toward "mongrelization and degeneracy"; claimed that mysterious threats had been made upon his life; and urged that the Japanese be ousted to save the state from the threat of Bolshevism! A man of great wealth, Senator Phelan financed the Anti-Asiatic League and the Oriental Exclusion League, both of which organizations were integral parts of his political machine.[33]

Sometimes anti-Japanese feeling has been used to obscure an embarrassing situation. The resolution of the San Francisco school board that barred Japanese students from white schools was issued in 1906 just on the eve of the indictment of Mayor Eugene Schmitz and political leader Abe Ruef on several charges of graft, as well as just before an election. The resolution ordered all Oriental children to attend a segregated school in Chinatown. There were only 93 Japanese students out of a total of 25,000 in the city; and there was no record of any protest from white parents over the presence of the Japanese in various schools. "The conclusion is inescapable that the school board, which was completely dominated by Ruef and Schmitz, acted at this time to divert public attention from the graft scandals."[34]

There were doubtless economic as well as political motives involved in the anti-Japanese activities on the west coast after 1900. At various times trade unions and small landowners took part in these agitations, but organized opposition stemmed most directly from the owners of the huge estates which characterize parts of California. These men certainly did not fear the competition of the few Japanese farmers with their relatively small holdings. What they did fear was the opposition of the small white landowners who found it difficult to compete with the estates, the struggles for improvement of their own very badly paid field hands, the traditions in favor of family-sized farms and homesteads, and federal legislation that prevented them from monopolizing the water supplied through governmentally sponsored irrigation projects. If they could divert attention from their own control of the land by attacking the Japanese farmer as the cause of everybody's difficulties, they might funnel off some of the hostility to which they were vulnerable and get political support for laws favorable to them.

This explanation may help to make understandable their support of the nativist associations and their backing of alien land laws which in actuality had little effect on the control of the land—but which made many people *think* that the land problem was solved. If the farm laborers, working at low wages and often under very poor working con-

[33] *Ibid.*, pp. 58–59.
[34] *Ibid.*, p. 26.

ditions, could be persuaded that the Japanese farmers were the cause of their difficulties, they might show less hostility toward the owners of the large estates. Out of this situation came the Alien Land Acts of 1913 and 1920 in California, and similar bills in other states. The 1920 act was passed as an initiative measure, and approved by a majority of three to one. These two bills did not change the actual landholding situation much, for they could not dispossess alien Japanese of land they already held nor could they apply to the increasing number of second-generation Japanese who were American citizens. To be sure, by 1940 the acreage controlled by Japanese had fallen to 226,094 from 361,275 in 1920 (a tiny fraction of the agricultural land in the state in either year), and the average farm had been reduced from 80.1 acres to 44 in 1940. But the total value of the produce from these farms increased during the period. It seems likely that few people were interested in enforcing the law anyway, for Japanese "managers" rather than "tenants" appeared, and title to land was transferred to American- or Hawaiian-born Japanese—with little objection from officials.[35] The chief gains to economic and political groups came not from the provisions of the bill, but from the controversy, the pseudoconflict situation, that was built up in the process of passing the bill. Actually, most of those who voted for the 1920 act, insofar as it was effective at all, suffered from the legislation—the landowner by lower rentals (he had been able to charge the Japanese tenant high rents) and the consumer by higher prices. But the powerful few found the anti-Japanese agitation very useful in their diversionary tactics.

The economic motives involved in prejudice are almost always alloyed with other motives and may be explicitly denied. Lothrop Stoddard, writing during the anti-immigration period at the close of the First World War, built his attack against immigration around a "racial purity" argument; he criticized those who supported immigration on economic grounds: "There is no more damning indictment of our lopsided, materialistic civilization than the way in which, throughout the nineteenth century, immigration was almost universally regarded, not from the social, but from the material point of view, the immigrant being viewed not as a creator of race-values, but as a mere vocal tool for the production of material wealth."[36] Yet a few pages later in the book he writes that the Asiatic ". . . is perfectly justified in trying to win broader opportunities in white lands. But we whites are equally justified in keeping these opportunities for ourselves and our children. The hard facts are that there is not enough for both; that when the enormous outward thrust of colored population-pressure bursts into a white land *it cannot let live*, but automatically crushes the white man

[35] See *ibid.*, pp. 64–65.
[36] Lothrop Stoddard, *op. cit.*, p. 252.

out—first the white laborer, then the white merchant, lastly the white aristocrat; until every vestige of white has gone from that land forever."[37] This is a straight appeal to power and income desires, not to the race-purity myth that occupies the superficially important place in Stoddard's book.

Economic factors in the prejudice against the Japanese continued to operate in the period of their "relocation" from the west coast during the Second World War. After Pearl Harbor the groups that had long agitated against the Japanese lost no time in telling Washington that the presence of 110,000 Japanese on the west coast, including about 40,000 "enemy aliens" (those born in Japan were ineligible for citizenship), was a grave threat to the safety of the country. There were many motives involved in the evacuation order, of course, but the climate of opinion which had been built up by those who saw economic and political gain in anti-Japanese agitation was important in the complex of causes. The Japanese who might have been a military danger were already known to the FBI and were taken into custody within a few days. That all the rest, including 70,000 American citizens, should be treated as military threats was an act of unprecedented official racism in the United States.

Judgments differ concerning the importance of various influences that led to the relocation order. The direct pressure of interested economic groups was probably relatively unimportant as an immediate fact. Their influence had been to help create the atmosphere in which such an order was accepted with little protest. TenBroek, Barnhart, and Matson argue cogently that the direct responsibility must be shared by many groups—the general public, particularly in the West; the military leaders; President Roosevelt and his staff, who concurred with the military decision; the Congress, which reinforced the process with legislation; and finally the courts, especially the Supreme Court, which gave the relocation order what now seems to many students a dubious constitutional sanction. All of these acted out of fear and, in our opinion, bad judgment. But behind the fear and the error stood prejudice, distorting the ability to deal rationally with the situation. Definitive support for the relocation came from the Supreme Court:

The Japanese American cases—*Hirabayashi, Korematsu,* and *Endo*— . . . represent a constitutional yielding to the awe inspired in all men by total war and the new weapons of warfare. They disclose a judicial unwillingness to interfere with—or even to look upon—the actions of the military taken in time of global war, even to the extent of determining whether those actions are substantially or somehow connected with the prosecution of the war. . . . In these cases, the historically established balance between the military and the civil—constitutionally sanctified in the United States by the classic

[37] *Ibid.,* p. 274.

majority opinion in *Ex parte Milligan*—has been shifted dangerously to the side of the military by the known and unknown terrors of total war and by a quiescent and irresolute judiciary. In them, the *Milligan* rule of subordination of the military to the Constitution except in battlefield conditions is abandoned. Instead, the national war powers, though explicitly conferred by the Constitution and not exempted from its limitations, are founded on and circumscribed by a military estimate of military necessity. Citizens, on a mass basis, were allowed to be uprooted, removed and imprisoned by the military without trial, without attribution of guilt, without the institutional or individual procedural guarantees of Article Three and Amendments Five and Six, and without regard to the individual guarantees of Amendments One, Four, Five, and others.[38]

Whatever the role of economic factors in causing the evacuation of Americans of Japanese descent from the west coast, the economic results were clear-cut and severe for the people involved. They suffered a loss variously estimated from 350 to 500 million dollars, with losses averaging nearly $10,000 per family.[39] Some of this loss resulted in no gain for anyone else; property deterioration, inefficient and incomplete use of skills, costs of property transfer and storage, etc., profited no one. Some of the losses to the Japanese-Americans, however, were direct gains to others; property sold in desperation at a fraction of its worth or abandoned completely, vandalism of goods that had to be stored for several years, further monopolization of job and business opportunities by whites—these gave economic incentive to prejudice, to the few who thus profited. The costs to the whole nation were scarcely noticed.

This brief reference to the wartime relocation of Americans of Japanese descent would be incomplete without some mention of the current situation. Gradually, from 1943 on, residents of the relocation centers were allowed to leave, to attend college, to accept jobs, and to enter the armed services, where they achieved outstanding records. After the war, 80 percent of the Japanese-Americans returned to the west coast, with three-fourths of these going to California. Slowly their claims for property losses received legislative and judicial attention. With the help of the Japanese-American Citizens League and other groups, 24,000 claims totaling 130 million dollars have been filed. Congress has passed legislation permitting claims up to $100,000 to be set-

---

[38] Jacobus tenBroek, Edward N. Barnhart, and Floyd W. Matson, *Prejudice, War, and the Constitution*, University of California Press, 1954. Of the extensive literature on the relocation question, see also Leonard Bloom and Ruth Riemer, *Removal and Return: The Socio-Economic Effects of the War on Japanese Americans*, University of California Press, 1949; Morton Grodzins, *Americans Betrayed*, University of Chicago Press, 1949; Alexander Leighton, *The Governing of Men*, Princeton University Press, 1945; Carey McWilliams, *op. cit.*; Dorothy S. Thomas, *The Salvage*, University of California Press, 1952; and Dorothy S. Thomas and Richard S. Nishimoto, *The Spoilage*, University of California Press, 1946.

[39] See Leonard Bloom and Ruth Riemer, *op. cit.*, chap. 5; see also E. V. Rostow, "Our Worst Wartime Mistake," *Harper's Magazine*, September, 1945, pp. 193–201.

tled administratively, without court litigation.[40] It is not yet clear what proportion of the actual losses may ultimately be recovered; it will doubtless be a small fraction, but some restitution at least is under way. The Japanese-Americans who did not return to the west coast have been absorbed into many cities with relatively little prejudice and at fairly high job levels.[41] The Walter-McCarran Act of 1952 brought Japan into our immigration quota system (185 Japanese are now permitted to migrate to the United States per year, in addition to spouses of American citizens and unmarried minor children) and made foreign-born Japanese eligible for citizenship. Over 6000 Japanese have been naturalized since 1952. These developments all represent a substantial change from the prewar and wartime situation.

RECENT TRENDS IN IMMIGRATION

We shall not undertake an analysis of the political and economic setting out of which American immigration policy has grown. There is general agreement that the Quota Act of 1924, the culmination of decades of agitation to restrict immigration, was partly the product of economic and political forces related to the closing of our frontier, the ideological and power aspects of "manifest destiny" imperialism at the turn of the century, and the postwar tensions and economic difficulties of the early 1920's. In a rather strange combination of forces, industrialists, unionists, and farmers, exuberant nationalists, racists, and many intellectuals, combined to produce the pressure for legislation. The 1924 law not only restricted the number, to approximately 150,-000 a year, but sought to determine the national origin of future immigrants. Immigration from Asiatic countries was barred—they were given no quota; no quantitative restrictions were placed on migration from the western hemisphere; and the 150,000 was divided among other nations in proportion to their supposed representation in our population in 1920. The result was to assign 68.9 percent of the quota to Great Britain, Ireland, and Germany. Immigration from southern and eastern Europe was drastically curtailed.

There is no doubt that immigration from the countries affected has been sharply reduced. Migration from the countries under the quota averaged well over 500,000 a year during the first quarter of the twentieth century; in the second quarter of the century the average was scarcely 100,000 per year. Great Britain, with over 40 percent of the quota, seldom has used more than a fraction of her assignment, whereas

[40] New York *Times*, August 12, 1956, p. 38.

[41] See William Caudill and George DeVos, "Achievement, Culture and Personality: The Case of the Japanese Americans," *American Anthropologist*, December, 1956, pp. 1102–1126; and Alan Jacobson and Lee Rainwater, "A Study of Management Representative Evaluations of Nisei Workers," *Social Forces*, October, 1953, pp. 35–41.

many countries with small quotas have waiting lists for years to come.

In 1952, our immigration legislation was slightly revised by the Walter-McCarran Immigration and Naturalization Act. The quota system and the quantitative limit were essentially retained, except that Asiatic countries were now assigned their "appropriate" quota. In most instances, this has meant the minimum number of 100 per year. The total number was raised to approximately 155,000; and resident aliens from the Orient, formerly ineligible for citizenship, were granted naturalization rights. Racial distinctions continue to be drawn, however, not only by the differences in quotas, but by the mode of defining country of origin. A person of German descent, born and living in Brazil, for example, is Brazilian; but a person of Chinese descent, born and living in Brazil, is Chinese. He could immigrate to the United States only by obtaining one of the 105 places annually allotted to the Chinese.

The changes in the law slightly reduced the national and racist prejudices it contains—but only slightly. The whole quota system makes sense only if one assumes that there are racial and national differences in desirability, that is, that desirability can be determined by one's race and national origin, not by individual characteristics. The Italian quota under the 1952 legislation is 5800 per year; the German is over four times that. There is no waiting list for Germans, but the Italian list is oversubscribed for years to come. By the irrelevant use of nationality an Arturo Toscanini, a Fiorello La Guardia, an Enrico Fermi, or a Joe DiMaggio might be barred.

Dedication of the United States to the "national origins" approach to immigration has been scarcely modified by the crises of the last twenty-five years. A very large proportion of international migrants during this period have been refugees from political, economic, and religious oppression. The movement across national lines during this period has been characterized by the extreme cruelty of the propelling forces, the difficulty in escaping, the reluctance of many nations to grant asylum, the creation of a great deal of statelessness.[42] Brewton Berry estimates that there have been at least 40 million uprooted persons since the First World War.[43]

From Hitler's rise to power in 1933 until the end of World War II, the United States officially did almost nothing to aid refugees; in fact, by her tight administrative policy, she kept immigration down. Net immigration during this period was less than one-fifth of the quota. A bill to admit 20,000 refugee children in 1939 was defeated. A total of 982 (children in a refugee camp maintained in this country during the war) were admitted outside the quota.[44]

[42] See Maurice R. Davie, *Refugees in America*, Harper & Brothers, 1947.
[43] Address to the Ohio Valley Sociological Society, April, 1955.
[44] Maurice R. Davie, *op. cit.*

At the end of the war, although the United States took a major part in such aid programs as UNRRA, she admitted few newcomers to her own shores. The 1948 Displaced Persons Act stayed fully within the quota system, simply allowing nations to "mortgage" the future up to a limit of one-half of their quota for any number of years ahead. Some nations are now mortgaged for decades ahead, but some 400,000 displaced persons were admitted during the application of the bill. The 1953 Refugee Relief Act authorized the admission of 214,000 persons beyond the quota limits within the next three years. It was so hedged about with restrictions, however, and so tightly administered, that fewer than 100,000 had been admitted by the expiration date.

The abrupt reduction of immigration in 1924 had a number of unanticipated effects. It produced serious diplomatic strains, particularly with the nations of the East. Many economists hold that it sped the approach of the depression of the 1930's and made it worse. It increased the northward migration of white and Negro workers from the South (thereby probably speeding desegregation). And it greatly increased the number of migrants from the western hemisphere. Mexico has been the chief source of immigration for the last thirty years. There are now about two and a half million persons of Mexican descent in this country, most of them having migrated since the act of 1924 was passed. Their experience has matched that of earlier migrants: economic exploitation, political powerlessness, educational handicaps, the sting of prejudice and of stereotypes.

Some of the Mexican-American immigration is illegal. Migrant workers—wetbacks—cross the Rio Grande to fill the tremendous demand for temporary workers to harvest the crops. Conflicting interests in the United States make their status very uncertain. They are deported or allowed to stay—until the crops are in—depending upon a delicate balance of forces in American politics. Some desire low-paid, tractable laborers; others try to keep out "undesirables" or workers who depress the wage scale. In either event, the migrant feels the full weight of discrimination and prejudice.

Native Americans of Mexican descent and permanent immigrants from Mexico share many of these burdens. Broom and Shevky have pointed out how their low status is reinforced by a series of interacting factors. Many of them work in homogeneous gangs, with few contacts with non-Mexicans; the kind of casual labor which they usually find means migration, unemployment, isolation in labor camps; the language barrier reinforces the other problems; the cleavage between generations means that Mexican youth have inadequate adult models, a problem that is often associated with the formation of gangs which block integration further.[45]

[45] Leonard Broom and Eshref Shevky, "Mexicans in the United States, A Problem in Social Differentiation," *Sociology and Social Research*, January–February, 1952, pp. 150–158.

Prejudice and segregation have helped to keep the Mexican-American on the bottom rungs of the ladder, but there are important signs of improving status. Their segregation in schools has sharply diminished; contract conditions and distribution centers for migrant workers have been improved, partly under government pressure from both Mexico and the United States; more are finding industrial jobs, although still largely at the unskilled and semiskilled levels, and are getting the support of labor unions; at least 250,000 have served in the armed forces, thus breaking the patterns of isolation; and defense organizations such as the Alianza Hispano-Americana are beginning to fight discrimination.[46]

Restriction of European immigration is also involved in the increased number of Puerto Ricans entering this country. This is not, strictly speaking, immigration, since Puerto Ricans are American citizens. But they have shared in the prejudice and discrimination so frequently directed toward the newcomer. Between 1945 and 1954 there was a net migration of over 400,000 persons from Puerto Rico, most of them staying in New York; and by 1956 a total of 750,000 were residents of the United States. The migration has been welcomed and aided by employers. The total experience of the newcomers, however, has been difficult. Their jobs are largely at the lowest skill levels, they live in the least desirable sections of the cities, landlords and sharks exploit them, their crimes become "crime waves," and they are caught, quite unprepared, in "the Negro problem," for many of them who are "white" in Puerto Rico are "colored" by mainland standards. In general, as Senior puts it, all sorts of conditions "of which the newcomer is a victim are laid at his door."[47]

The Puerto Rican migrant may experience a somewhat briefer period of exploitation and prejudice than have some earlier groups. The fact that he is a citizen, the greater appreciation today of the nature of culture contact and conflict, the serious efforts being made in New York City and elsewhere to strengthen education for Puerto Ricans, and other factors are hopeful aspects of the situation.

Economic and Political Beliefs in Support of Prejudice

The situations we have described give credence to the theory that prejudice is often used, consciously or unconsciously, to help a group win or maintain a larger share of life's values. Whether or not prejudice

[46] See J. Milton Yinger and George E. Simpson, "The Integration of Americans of Mexican, Puerto Rican, and Oriental Descent," *Annals of the American Academy of Political and Social Science*, March, 1956, pp. 124–131; see also John H. Burma, *Spanish-Speaking Groups in the United States*, Duke University Press, 1954.

[47] Clarence Senior, in Joseph Gittler (ed.), *Understanding Minority Groups*, John Wiley & Sons, Inc., 1956, p. 110; see also J. Milton Yinger and George E. Simpson, *op. cit.*; and C. W. Mills, Clarence Senior, and R. K. Goldsen, *The Puerto Rican Journey*, Harper & Brothers, 1950.

is an effective weapon for this purpose we shall discuss in Chapter 8; but it is often so used. The power function of prejudice is seldom explicitly recognized, however, for the American tradition—and that of many other lands—does not allow the open use of inequality and discrimination as legitimate economic and political weapons. Most Americans are quite heavily saturated, on the speech-reaction level, with democratic and Christian ideals which can be reconciled with the constant factual contradictions in the treatment of minorities only by a group of rationalizing beliefs. The nature and functions of stereotypes will be taken up in the next chapter, but it may be well at this point to indicate some of the specifically economic beliefs that make it easier for the American to use prejudice as an economic weapon. That there may be some truth in these beliefs should not cause us to lose sight of their function. This function is especially difficult to recognize when it is formulated into an institutional pattern, into law and custom, because then the individual can place all responsibility on the institution.

In *Religion and the Rise of Capitalism*, R. H. Tawney has pointed out the ease with which the wealthy classes accepted the idea of predestination. They were naturally disposed, he said, to regard the poor as damned in the next world, because that was a fine justification for making their life a hell in this world. Similarly, belief in the "predestined" inferiority or viciousness of minority groups makes discriminatory treatment of them seem reasonable, or, as Dollard says, at least inevitable. If the American Negro is shiftless, lazy, unable to master the skills necessary for handling modern machinery, and especially if these traits are innate, then it is not prejudice that limits him to the most tedious, least desirable unskilled work; it is his own lack of capacity. Interestingly enough, with regard to the widespread belief that the Negro is naturally unable to acquire mechanical skills, one of the most vigorous protests against him in the decades following the Civil War was precisely that he monopolized the skilled crafts, because of the protected training he had received under slavery. Rationalizing beliefs for conflict situations do not need to be mutually consistent; they are *ad hoc* creations for specific battles. Slaveowners did not find it difficult to believe that slaves were inferior, unable to absorb civilization, suitable only for menial tasks, and yet at the same time to train them to do most of the skilled work around the plantation. The picture of the Jew as an international banker and simultaneously as a communist organizer doesn't strain the logical capacity of many people.

One of the most elaborate rationalizations of a power position has been built up around the dominations of modern empires. The European nations, we discover, are in Africa or the East Indies to rescue the natives from barbarism, to convert them to Christianity, to bring them the benefits of civilization. It is unfortunate that the natives are incapable of self-government, not yet ready for independence, unable to manage the machinery of modern technology—they are the white man's burden. We do not mean to imply that no other motives than economic and political are involved in the relations between modern states and their empires. We are simply indicating that the power motives, while very important, are seldom explicitly stated. Even in the recent instances in which powerful nations have "voluntarily freed" a subject people, economic and political considerations have not been unimportant. American sugar interests, for example, wanted Philippine sugar outside the tariff walls, and Britain knew that the balance of shipments which for over a century before 1931 had sent more goods from India to Britain than from Britain to India had since 1931 been continuously the other way around. A large part of the white man's burden has been the burden of carrying Indian cotton and steel, Javanese rubber and tin, and Philippine sugar and gold back to the empires' homelands. That some benefits have been carried in the other direction and that the difference between what he receives and what he gives is obscured for the white man by his comforting beliefs are testimony to the fact that the dominators have a conscience which cannot be completely disregarded. They are also evidence of the presence of some bargaining power in the hands of the colonists.

Rationalizing economic beliefs may originate in a group who profit by the situation which they disguise, but they may be accepted by people who have nothing to gain—and perhaps much to lose—from that situation. They may be accepted even by persons who do not *believe* they profit from the situation. This circumstance should prevent us from making an oversimplified economic interpretation of these beliefs. Many people on the west coast have believed that the Japanese farmer was a menace to "the American standard of living," that the long hours he worked and the degree to which the Japanese father used his own family as cheap labor made it impossible for the white farmer to compete. The white man's income was lowered, his ability to buy goods from other producers (who in turn were injured) was curtailed, and thus out went the injury in an ever widening circle until the whole economy, presumably including the original Japanese farmer, was harmed. This type of reasoning was popular over a century ago when Henry Clay fought political battles with his "American system." That most economists think it false has not prevented it from becoming a part of the system of economic beliefs of a great many Americans. The economist is more likely to say: The Japanese farmer, by his efficiency, forces other farmers to be more efficient, and by the lower prices which he makes possible he leaves extra dollars in the purses of west coast housewives. Those extra dollars, in turn, permit them to buy other goods, which they otherwise would not have been able to afford, make other businesses more prosperous, put more wages in circulation, so that further production is encouraged, until, presumably, even the white farmer who was immediately injured by the competition of the Japanese farmer may in part be compensated. We are not trying to argue the economics of the case but to indicate that people often hold economic beliefs which qualified experts consider false. The function of those beliefs is not changed; a gun that backfires is still intended to shoot the other way.

Economic Conflict and the Origins of Jim Crow

We have surveyed some of the evidence for the theory that prejudice can be understood partly as an expression of the economic, political, and other interests of groups. In their attempts to maintain or increase their share of income, prestige, and power, groups find it easy to invent or accept the idea that other groups are inferior and thus less deserving of life's values. The idea can be put briefly. Prejudice exists because someone gains by it. Some writers lean upon this interpretation so heavily that they make it *the* theory of prejudice. Just as the doctrinaire Freudian insists that the "fundamental" cause of prejudice is the frustrations and anxieties of individuals, so the doctrinaire Marxian insists that the "fundamental" cause of prejudice is class conflict. Some people contend that racial stereotypes are consciously created by the ruling class as weapons to fight minority groups and the lower classes of their own race.

Race prejudice in the United States is the socio-attitudinal matrix supporting a calculated and determined effort of a white ruling class to keep some people or peoples of color and their resources exploitable.[48]

The Negro people are oppressed because the rulers of our society find it highly profitable to oppress them. In terms of fundamental motivations, the explanation of the Negro question is as simple as that. . . . If there is anything which the history and contemporary life of America clearly reveal about the Negro question, it is the stark material, profit-seeking core from which all of the varied forms of anti-Negro discrimination and oppression emerge.[49]

This theory of prejudice has received especially intense examination in the last few years because of the publication, in 1944, of Gunnar Myrdal's well-known study, *An American Dilemma*. Because it is not only a descriptive account of the American Negro but attempts also a theoretical explanation of the prejudice against the Negro, this research has stimulated a great deal of further study. Myrdal develops a multiple-factor theory of prejudice in which he gives a relatively unimportant place to the economic and political forces discussed above. His formulations have been accepted widely (and sometimes uncritically), but they have also been sharply attacked by some writers.

[48] Oliver C. Cox, *op. cit.*, p. 475.
[49] Doxey Wilkerson, in the introduction to Herbert Aptheker, *The Negro People in America*, International Publishers, 1946, pp. 8–10.

We can perhaps approach an understanding of the actual role of the forces of group conflict in prejudice by examining this controversy. Compare, for example, the very different interpretations of the factors involved in the continued subjugation of the Negro in the United States after 1865. There is general agreement that after the Civil War anti-Negro prejudice continued to serve—or seemed to serve—functions for several groups of whites. There is a great deal of dispute, however, regarding the roles of the various classes of whites in reaffirming the inferior status of the Negro that had been legally broken by emancipation. Left-wing writers claim, and not without some historical evidence in their favor, that the poor whites and Negroes recognized their common problems even before the war to some degree, but very explicitly afterward, and set about, in 1865, to establish a political and economic structure that would serve the majority. The Reconstruction legislatures of several of the southern states had written, by 1875, some of the most liberal state constitutions in the country—constitutions which, if put into effect even today, would radically change economic, political, and educational practices in the South.[50] These legislatures were composed largely of "poor whites" (not from the former slave-holding group), Negroes, and abolitionists and carpetbaggers from the North. The contention is that the breaking, for the moment, of the dominance of the planter class, their demoralization and loss of prestige, allowed the poor whites and Negroes to see their common economic and political interests and to act upon them together. Here the economic force was working in the direction of nonprejudice. This theory goes on to state, however, that the confusions of the postwar period, the continued economic power of the planters through their control of the land, and the clumsiness, if not the outright collusion, of the federal government permitted the old southern aristocracy to come back into power. By 1900 most of the new constitutions had been repealed or rewritten; the Negroes' claim for equality was pushed farther and farther back by disfranchisement, segregation statutes (passed in every southern state by 1907), and economic barriers.

It was not difficult for the ruling group to draw the masses of white workers back into the circle of prejudice. One of the first places where economic conflict occurred was among the artisan group. Many of the former slaves were skilled carpenters, bricklayers, and blacksmiths. Under slavery they were protected from direct attack of the white workers who felt that their economic opportunities were blocked by the work of the artisan slaves. After 1865, however, there was nothing to prevent the white worker from striking out at his black competitor. Each successive census shows the decline in proportion of skilled workers who

[50] Cf. James S. Allen, *Reconstruction, the Battle for Democracy*, International Publishers, 1937; and John Hope Franklin, *From Slavery to Freedom*, Alfred A. Knopf, Inc., 1947, pp. 293–338.

are Negro. Between 1910 and 1940 the proportion of Negroes in seven skilled crafts fell, in the South, from 26.3 percent to 15.2 percent, and in the nation from 4.3 to 3.8 percent.[51] Among the carpenters and painters—the two largest crafts—the proportion of Negroes rose, in the nation as a whole, between 1890 and 1940, from 3.6 percent and 2.0 percent respectively to 3.9 and 3.8 percent. But in the South the percentages fell from 25.6 and 22.2 to 13.7 and 14.5 during the half-century. "In the Atlanta riot of 1906 one of the chief incitements to violence was the circulation of cards showing Negro carpenters and bricklayers building houses, thus menacing the economic security of white men. . . ."[52]

Even the poorest of whites was convinced rather easily that he had more to gain by keeping the Negro down than by uniting with him in common cause against the upper-class whites. His own deprivations were made somewhat more bearable by the continuous sight of even more serious deprivations among the Negroes. Though he was actually injured by a system which rested upon the exploitation of cheap labor, he was not perceptive enough to recognize the true source of his difficulty. Moreover, as Dollard has shown, he received some prestige and sexual gains over the Negro which made it easier for him to acquiesce in the system. The more doctrinaire Marxists assume that the upper-class whites understood all this and by conscious decision "used" prejudice as a weapon, implanting it in the poor whites by propaganda, by control over the schools, churches, and newspapers, as well as by control of job opportunities. The process was doubtless far less rational than this assumption would have it appear; prejudice simply seemed "right" to the upper class, for it is always easy to believe that which harmonizes with one's class interest. And it also seemed right to the lower-class white because he did not understand the true causes of his economic difficulties. On the surface the Negro was obviously his direct competitor, and the white worker felt that he received some gains from restricting active competitors for jobs. In any event he was highly frustrated and in need of easily accessible outlets for his hostility.

It should not be forgotten, however, that *there were some tendencies for the lower-class white to join with the Negro in political and economic action.* They would doubtless have been stronger but for the systematic opposition to that development from the upper class. Even the powerful interests of the North, after having finished a war against the southern planters, found it to be in their interest to permit the South to develop its own pattern of race relations. Attempts to interpret the Fourteenth and Fifteenth Amendments in radical equalitarian fashion were blocked by the Supreme Court. Northern banking, indus-

---

[51] Herbert Northrup, *Organized Labor and the Negro,* Harper & Brothers, 1944, pp. 18–19.
[52] Charles S. Johnson, *op. cit.,* p. 286.

trial, and insurance interests, with large holdings in the South, found the cheap labor system to their liking. Even when the Republican party, strictly a northern party, was at the height of its power, there was virtually no attempt to achieve full civil rights for the Negro—one of the aims for which, presumably, they had led the North during the Civil War. The coöperation of northern and southern upper classes is a political commonplace even today, although it is complicated by the pull of other forces in their respective environments.

In a recent book, Woodward reminds us of the "forgotten alternatives" which were being debated in the South between 1865 and 1895. His account of the ways in which all of these alternatives were pushed aside one by one, except for the victorious pattern of segregation and discrimination against the Negro, indicates well the way in which economic and political factors were involved. Before the doctrines of the extreme racists were adopted, conservatives, liberals, and radical populists also sought to establish their points of view. "All three of these alternative philosophies rejected the doctrines of extreme racism and all three were indigenously and thoroughly Southern in origin."[53] The period during which these alternatives contested for supremacy was not, of course, a peaceful period in race relations. Lynching and violent intimidation of Negroes were at their worst in the 1880's and 1890's. Yet in 1897, a Charleston, South Carolina, newspaper wrote: "The common sense and proper arrangement, in our opinion, is to provide first-class cars for first-class passengers, white and colored. . . . To speak plainly, we need, as everybody knows, separate cars or apartments for rowdy or drunken white passengers far more than Jim Crow cars for colored passengers."[54]

The liberal alternative was probably least well represented during this period. Yet a few, such as George Washington Cable, spoke for equality in every sphere of life and fought discrimination and segregation. The conservatives thought in terms of a stratified society, with Negroes in a subordinate role; but they opposed the idea that Negroes should be segregated and humiliated. Radical populism sought to join with the freed Negroes to achieve agrarian reform. Over a period of a generation of debate, however, these alternatives failed. The pattern of extreme segregation and discrimination that was to prevail for half a century won out. What political and economic forces were involved in this outcome? Woodward discusses a number of interacting factors.

Beginning with the compromise of 1877, northern liberal opinion progressively disregarded the race issue and left the South to its own pattern. This was in part due to the fact that sectional reconciliation, healing the wounds of the Civil War, was a clear liberal cause. Since

[53] C. Vann Woodward, *The Strange Career of Jim Crow*, Oxford University Press, 1955, p. 27.
[54] Quoted in *ibid.*, pp. 30–31.

many persons in the North shared the racial attitudes of most South-erners, sectional reconciliation was easily put ahead of racial equality. The Supreme Court reflected, if it did not lead, this development by a series of decisions between 1873 and 1896 that progressively limited the privileges and immunities of Negroes and sanctioned discrimina-tion. Then into this scene came America's imperialist adventures in the Caribbean and the Pacific. In view of the white supremacy mys-tique with which European and American imperialism was being jus-tified, racial arguments in the South could not be answered. "Senator Ben Tillman, the most impudent racist in the South, could now gloat over his Republican colleagues from the Yankee North and defy them to do anything about the Counterrevolution then taking place in the South."[55]

While the North was relaxing its opposition to extreme racism, southern restraints also were greatly weakened, primarily as a result of the economic and political struggles going on. The conservative forces had at first joined with the anti-Negro whites to win power from the carpetbaggers. Then, as Woodward shows, they sought to conciliate the Negro freedman by opposing the extremists and offering him small po-litical plums. This stage, however, was a casualty of the political weak-ness of the conservatives. Their sympathy with the political and eco-nomic views of northern conservatives was in sharp opposition to the money policies and agrarian reforms supported by poorer Southerners. To save themselves politically in face of the challenge of the populists, they turned to the anti-Negro views that had helped them defeat the carpetbaggers. "The same means of fraud, intimidation, bribery, vio-lence, and terror were used against the one that had been used against the other. 'I told them to go to it, boys, count them out,' admitted the conservative Governor William C. Oates of Alabama. 'We had to do it. Unfortunately, I say it was a necessity. We could not help our-selves.' "[56]

Thus Negroes were "counted out" by the conservatives. This tactic helped to split the populists, who had continued their precarious ef-fort to unify white and Negro voters. Weakened by the serious depres-sions of the 1890's, seeing some of their members pulled away by the racist views of the opposition, receiving "permissions to hate" from the Supreme Court and northern intellectuals, the populists saw their bi-racial policy "dissolve in frustration and bitterness."

Having served as the national scapegoat in the reconciliation and reunion of North and South, the Negro was now pressed into service as a sectional scapegoat in the reconciliation of estranged white classes and the reunion of

---

[55] William G. Carleton, in the introduction to H. D. Price, *The Negro and South-ern Politics. A Chapter of Florida History*, New York University Press, 1957, p. xii.
[56] C. Vann Woodward, *op. cit.*, p. 61.

the Solid South. . . . The only formula powerful enough to accomplish that was the magical formula of white supremacy, applied without stint and without any of the old conservative reservations of paternalism, without deference to any lingering resistance to Northern liberalism, or any fear of further check from a defunct Southern Populism.[57]

Thus economic and political conflicts played a vital role in determining which of the various alternative ways of dealing with the freedmen would predominate. By the end of the nineteenth century, disfranchisement, segregation, and relegation to second-class citizenship had won out.

There are also alternatives on the race relations scene today. Which ones will be forgotten in half a century is not clear. Some are stridently racist, continuing to use prejudice as a weapon to protect or win economic and political advantages. Economic coercion and political pressure are also being used in an effort to prevent desegregation. There are other alternatives, however; and if in a day of White Citizens' Councils and court litigation they seem obscured, they may nevertheless be the ones likely to win out. There are now powerful economic, political, and other forces supporting desegregation and the full enfranchisement of Negro Americans. Throughout Part II of this volume we will give the evidence that leads us to the conclusion that this time segregation will be the "forgotten alternative."

Conclusion

The interpretation holding that the continued subjection of Negroes after emancipation was to an important degree the result of economic and political conflict among whites is sharply challenged by Myrdal and others. They contend that the upper-class white man in the South, far from being one of the key sources of prejudice and the segregation system, is the Negroes' best friend. Louis Wirth writes: "It has been repeatedly found by students of Negro-White relations in the South that the so-called white aristocracy shows less racial prejudice than do the 'poor whites' whose own position is relatively insecure and who must compete with Negroes for jobs, for property, for social position, and for power. Only those who themselves are insecure feel impelled to press their claims for superiority over others. . . ."[58] Myrdal contends that it was impossible that the Negro and lower-class white should have joined hands after 1865 to get land reform. When the feedbox is empty, says a Swedish proverb, the horses will bite each other. Lower classes are not naturally radical, or even liberal; they do not readily take a favorable attitude toward disadvantaged groups.

[57] Ibid., pp. 65–66.
[58] Louis Wirth, "Race and Public Policy," Scientific Monthly, April, 1944, p. 304.

Our hypothesis is that in a society where there are broad social classes, and in addition, more minute distinctions and splits in the lower strata, *the lower class groups will, to a great extent, take care of keeping each other subdued*, thus relieving, to that extent, the higher classes of this otherwise painful task necessary to the monopolization of the power and the advantages.

It will be observed that this hypothesis is contrary to the Marxian theory of class society. . . . The Marxian scheme assumes that there is an actual solidarity between the several lower class groups against the higher classes, or, in any case, a potential solidarity which as a matter of natural development is bound to emerge. . . .

A solidarity between poor whites and Negroes has been said to be "natural" and the conflicts to be due to "illusions.". . . Everything we know about human frustration and aggression, and the displacement of aggression speaks against it. For an individual to feel interest with a group assumes his psychological identification with the group. This identification must be of considerable strength, as the very meaning of solidarity is that he is prepared to set aside and even sacrifice his own short-range private interests for the long-range interests of his group. Every vertical split within the lower class aggregate will stand as an obstacle to the feeling of solidarity. Even within the white working class itself, as within the entire American nation, the feeling of solidarity and loyalty is relatively low.[59]

Myrdal has made two mistakes in this statement which render his conflict with the "Marxian" interpretation unnecessarily sharp. When he says that "everything we know about human frustration and aggression" points to vigorous conflict between various divisions within the lower class, he overlooks the fact that some, and in some instances much, of the aggression of lower-class people is directed against the upper classes. As we shall see in Chapter 7, the *apparent* nonaggressiveness of Negroes toward the dominant whites hides a great deal of subtle attack. His second error is in dismissing completely the fact that to some degree the lower-class Negroes and whites *did* join forces after the Civil War and are joining forces today to a greater degree. This situation shows two forces at work that give opposite encouragement to prejudice and discrimination. Myrdal has emphasized one, and left-wing writers such as Cox and Aptheker have emphasized the other. Each has then been quick to point up the errors of his opponent without seeing his own omissions. Myrdal is right in noting that a great deal (not all) of the frustrations of the lower-class white and Negro tend to keep them apart, to encourage prejudice between them. Not all the hostility is displaced, however. Lower-class whites often feel a bitter resentment against upper-class whites, and in some instances this is accompanied by a feeling of common fate with lower-class Negroes— even though there is a simultaneous attitude of prejudice. Leonard Doob reports that in Southerntown, Negroes are viewed somewhat

[59] Gunnar Myrdal, *op. cit.*, p. 68.

neutrally by lower-class whites. To be sure, they verbalize the stereo-types of their culture; but their prejudice is not strong.[60] Horowitz care-fully reviewed all the available studies that sought to discover whether there was a correlation between income and prejudice toward the Ne-gro, and concluded that no relationship could be established. "With respect to the problem of the relation between variations in individual economic position and variations in attitudes toward Negroes, the studies available suggest that there is no systematic relationship be-tween these two variables."[61]

One must be careful, moreover, not to use data about the distribu-tion of prejudice against one minority to generalize about attitudes to-ward other minorities. Members of the lower class may verbalize more prejudice against one minority, and middle- or upper-class members may express more prejudice against another. We need also to keep in mind the distinction between discrimination and prejudice. It is one thing to note that lower-class whites get a higher prejudice score against Negroes on verbal tests. It is another to discover what class of whites is most discriminatory. Middle- and upper-class people may have more skillful rationalizations and verbal disguises. They may re-cite the American creed more spontaneously. They may have a greater need to seem reasonable and tolerant. Hence their prejudice score may be low. These tendencies, however, could be accompanied by vigorous discrimination against minority-group members—low wages paid to them, high rents charged for slum dwellings, cheating them at the plantation store. If it is true that the powerful, upper-class whites are the chief defenders—not without exceptions, of course—of the whole institutional structure by which the minority group is exploited, then their more polite verbal behavior is of relatively little importance.

It is also well to note that the economic interests of the upper classes are not always served by discrimination. As employers, they would profit from free choice among all members of the labor force on the basis of skill.

Many Negroes *believe* that upper-class whites are less prejudiced. This conviction may indicate that prejudice is defined in terms of day-to-day contacts, not on the basis of the underlying discriminatory pat-tern that the upper classes may be most important in defending. It may show also that Negroes share the status values—belief in the marks of superiority—that define the upper classes. It reflects in part, of course, the effects of the leadership that some upper-class whites furnish to movements for the improvement of the Negro's position.

Some Negroes, particularly those in the middle class, contend that

[60] In John Dollard, *Caste and Class in a Southern Town*, Yale University Press, 1937, pp. 470–471.

[61] In Otto Klineberg (ed.), *Characteristics of the American Negro*, Harper & Brothers, 1944, p. 223.

middle-class whites are their chief opponents. Dollard reports that in Southerntown many of his informants believed that the upper classes are too secure to need much prejudice and the lower-class whites feel some sympathy for Negroes because of similar difficulties, whereas the middle classes, not certain of their status and anxious to improve it, draw a sharp line of prejudice. Negroes often call them "strainers," a term that corresponds well with the position of the middle class.[62]

Altogether it seems clear that we dare not assume, as Myrdal tends to do, a clear-cut relationship between class position and the likelihood of prejudice.

The Marxian theory is correct in pointing out that prejudice brings more gains to the upper classes of the dominant group than to the lower, that sometimes the ruling class consciously manipulates prejudice as a power device, that in some situations lower-class whites will turn away from race prejudice in order to work together with a minority group against the upper class. The theory is one-sided, however, in failing to note that some of the forces encourage nonprejudice among the upper class (greater personal security, a feeling of *noblesse oblige*, and probably their long-run economic interests). Oppositely, the theory is weak in failing to indicate the forces that encourage prejudice among lower-class whites (greater personal insecurity, a richer tradition with regard to violence and aggression, and direct immediate economic competition with minority-group members). The Marxian analysis is too rationalistic; the dominant group does not often create and exploit prejudice to its own advantage. It simply finds an attitude that justifies its position very easy to accept.

Many contradictory forces are at work in any given expression of prejudice. Which one will predominate depends upon their relative strength and the setting in which they work. The "economic" element in prejudice is *least* likely to predominate where traditional definitions of roles are most stable, where economic classes are least self-conscious and organized, where the "intellectual climate" encourages the interpretation of individual frustrations in terms of personal opponents. The "economic" element in prejudice is *most* likely to predominate where traditional definitions of roles are being challenged, where large-scale organizations along class lines are most highly developed, and where group differentiation tends to correspond with differences in economic functions. The careful student will not accept a blanket statement of the *general* role of group conflict in prejudice, whether it be a statement that stresses or one that minimizes that role. He will rather seek to find the role of group conflict in *specific* situations as it interacts with the other forces at work in those situations. Group conflict from one point of view, moreover, works in favor of nonprejudice, for it

[62] See John Dollard, *op. cit.*, pp. 77–78.

establishes attitudes favorable to members of the in-group with which one has identified himself. A white union member may feel more solidarity with fellow members, of whatever race, than with the white race. He may, of course, seek to maintain solidarity with both the union and the white race by a segregated union. Contemporary experiences are demonstrating, however, that when other factors combine to make a segregated union impossible or undesirable, race prejudice, or at least discrimination, among the members of highly integrated unions drops rapidly. In other words, though prejudice may be one of the manifestations of group conflict, a particular kind of prejudice is not inevitable. Racial or religious prejudice may be used as an economic weapon; but in another setting the racial and religious lines may be obscured and the class line emphasized. The degree to which group conflict is involved in prejudice and the targets of that prejudice both vary widely.

Finally, it should not be forgotten that an attitude of prejudice, once launched, becomes in some measure a force on its own, able to continue, at least for a time, without the supports of group conflict or personal insecurity. The discussion of this phase of prejudice will occupy the next chapter.

CHAPTER 5

The Cultural Factor in Prejudice

The last two chapters have shown how prejudice can be understood in part as an attempt to satisfy certain individual and group needs; it is functional in the life of the individual and of the group and must be studied as part of the dynamic process of human interaction. Even the most complete analysis of the personality and socioeconomic functions of prejudice, however, does not explain why any particular group should be selected as the object of prejudice. Nor does it explain why prejudice should continue even among individuals and groups who are in virtually no way served by it. There is nothing intrinsic about group conflict or personality insecurity that requires that certain specific groups should be the objects of hostility. A group must be socially visible, recognizably distinct from the majority, to be subject to discrimination; but visibility is a function of attention. Blond hair could be as useful as brown skin in setting a person apart for prejudicial treatment. Why has modern America selected the latter? And why will a stable and secure person exhibit prejudice against the brown skin when he has a very low amount of hostility, has never known a Negro, and has no conceivable economic or political interest to be served by that prejudice? In this chapter we shall attempt to answer these two related questions. We shall see that, in addition to the functions of prejudice already discussed, other sociological and historical factors are involved that must be taken into account in any complete analysis of prejudice.

An attitude toward a minority group can be seen, from one point of view, as simply one of the folkways, one of the learned ways of responding that have been acquired as part of the standard cultural equipment. A person is taught to be prejudiced against certain groups just as he is taught to dislike certain foods that people in other societies consider great delicacies. He may be equipped with a number of culturally learned responses to minority groups that he is never called upon to use. These responses can scarcely be called functional, except in the general sense of representing the cohesiveness of a culture group. They survive, however, as group-patterned ways of thinking, ready to influence one's responses if an occasion arises. Other aspects of the folkways of prejudice are also a constant part of the interaction between members of the dominant group and members of culturally defined minority groups. A brief statement concerning the origin and nature of cultural definitions may be of help in the study of this cultural root of prejudice.

Many, perhaps most, of the ways of behaving that are agreed upon by members of a society had their origin in an attempt to meet a specific need. The attempt was not necessarily rational or objectively valid, though it may have been, but somehow it came to be accepted as the appropriate way to meet a certain situation. Individuals could not possibly bear the strain that would come from trying to decide, for each of the hundreds of actions they perform each day, what the best response might be. For this and other reasons they accept the cultural norm. Not to do so not only would put them in the intolerable position of having constantly to make decisions but would also tend to cut them off from the groups with which they identify—thus producing a sense of isolation that few human beings can accept. Some of these folkways designated by culture perform their functions as well as any alternative form would, for the action is symbolic. So long as everybody accepts the symbol it "works," even though its meaning may have changed. Shaking hands may originally have been a way of saying: "See, my hand is not on my sword; it is outstretched; I am a friend." Having lost some of its original meaning, it can still serve as the symbol of greeting. Other folkways, however, are not symbolic, but adjustments to actual circumstances. If they are used outside the situation in which they developed, therefore, they may serve the functions for which they are intended very badly. Wearing a coat of mail may help one survive the thrusts of the spear of an enemy, but its modern survival, the stiff shirt of formal clothing for men, is hardly adequate to protect one against the barbed remarks or the arrows of love that he may encounter in gatherings to which the dress suit is appropriate.

The things that are important about cultural norms, from our point of view, are their tendency to continue beyond the situation in which they were devised and their coercive power over individuals. These traits were probably overemphasized by the early students of culture, who drew much of their material from primitive, isolated societies and tried to apply their conclusions unmodified to a complex, mobile, urban society. Critics of Sumner's famous work *Folkways* are doubtless correct in noting that his theories were influenced, in part, by his conservative political ideas, by his desire to prove that society cannot be manipulated very effectively by rational action—therefore laissez faire.

This exaggeration should not cause us, however, to go to the opposite extreme that overemphasizes the speed with which new patterns of thought and behavior are created in the modern world. It is reported that George III of England suffered from a goiter which he felt was disfiguring. His tailor came up with the brilliant thought one day that the goiter could be hid by a piece of brightly colored silk wrapped around the king's neck. The men of the court, anxious to show the king that they admired his taste, were soon copying the pattern. So today uncomfortable males in many lands wear ties because King George III had a goiter.

Folkways change, of course, and in modern society they doubtless change more rapidly than they did formerly; but in varying degrees they continue to coerce individual behavior and to furnish guides to thought and action. They may have outlived their original meaning, they may even bring pain and discomfort to those who follow them, they may seem absurd to the outsider, but they seldom die out abruptly. To contradict the folkways of one's group is to set oneself apart, to subject oneself to the charges of heresy and eccentricity with which the group tries to maintain its unity. It may be that each member of a group, as an individual, would gladly dispense with a given pattern of behavior, but none can take the first step. How long have language requirements for the Ph.D. degree persisted in American universities, past the time when most of the candidates actually knew and used the languages, because few schools have been willing to subject themselves to the charge of "lowering standards" (standards which really have been lowered long since by the nature of the examinations themselves)?

If this view of one aspect of culture is correct, it may help us to understand prejudice. Attitudes toward minority groups have been started by various circumstances doubtless related to the personality and group conflict functions, have become fixed as part of the culture—embodied in its lore, developed in its literature, built into its institutions—and have continued even when the original circumstances were drastically changed. The institutional formulation of the folkways of prejudice is especially effective in preserving them for a number of reasons. The basic institutions are so important in the socialization of the individual that they can build into him the very standards by which they themselves are judged. Institutions are the chief symbol of group cohesion; they are surrounded with ritual and an elaborate system of protective beliefs. And the functionaries of institutions, and others who profit most from their pattern of control, are diligent in defense of the institutional framework.

To some degree, the reasons for the development of prejudice in a culture are unique for each minority; but to some degree they are generic. Once members of a different race, for example, have been set apart by a given group of historical circumstances as legitimate objects of discrimination, it is likely that other minority races will also be set apart, even though the particular sociological and historical forces involved are different. We cannot analyze the reasons for the selection of all, even of the largest, American minorities. We can only suggest some kinds of factors, particularly those that are common to a group of minorities, and encourage the reader to look for the specific elements in other minorities in whom he is interested.

Early theorists tried to explain the origin of a tradition of prejudice by reference to a supposed natural tendency to "dislike the unlike." Giddings coined the famous phrase "consciousness of kind" to describe what he thought of as the basis of unity in a group. Some writers have added a kind of narcissism to the explanation—we admire ourselves and dislike the different. This theory suffers from two weaknesses. It does not take sufficient account of the fact that most people are interested in the novel, as well as the familiar, and desire new experience as well as repetition of the old. Nor does it explain why certain differences are emphasized while others are completely disregarded in drawing the line between in-group and out-group. It is not difference per se that is related to prejudice, but certain kinds of differences which, in a given situation, prove to be useful to the individual or group making the distinction. That is why small children don't have the prejudices proper for their group—they have to be taught which differences are supposed to place others beyond the pale. Middle-class children, for example, may be tempted at first to admire the aggressive youngster who has the nerve to strike back at inhibiting adults or to lead them in excitingly forbidden activities; or they may admire the junkman because of all the fascinating objects he carries on his truck. It is only after some little effort that the parents are able to teach the child whom it is proper for him to admire and whom he should dislike or shun. Finally, if the process of socialization is carried on with reasonable skill, the child will be equipped with the appropriate prejudices. That "dislike of the unlike" is not a very useful theory by itself is also shown by the fact that what is considered sufficiently "unlike" to justify prejudice varies in time and place, as we have seen in Chapter 4. Day before yesterday many Americans liked the Japanese because "they are the most Western of all Oriental peoples." Yesterday we disliked them because of their "Asiatic mentality." Today we like them again "because" they share many traits in common with us. The Japanese haven't changed with such speed, but the usefulness of certain lines of distinction can vary rapidly.

We are not trying to say that group differences are not involved in the establishment of traditions of prejudice—for a group has to be different, has to be set apart some way in order to be discriminated against—but only that the kinds of differences chosen are accidental by-products of a given situation, not intrinsically important in themselves. In each situation the question is: Why were these particular differences seized upon as legitimate ones for marking a group off as inferior? There are two basic factors that help to answer this question. First, those differences will be used which help to distinguish a group whose exploitation will be profitable (in terms of all the gains discussed in Chapters 3 and 4) for the dominant group. Second, each group has a hierarchy of values, a system of beliefs which it carries into conflict situations. It will most readily set apart another group which differs from it in a high-order value. As the system of values and standardized beliefs changes, so will the pattern of prejudice tend to change.

We have already analyzed some of the factors involved in setting in motion the tradition of anti-Negro prejudice. At the time of first continuous contact between Negro and white, religious symbols had a high place in the hierarchy of values, making it relatively easy for the whites to differentiate the Negro as heathen. This combined with the felt "need" for seizing the Negroes' land and its resources or for seizing the African himself, to transport him to the New World to use his muscles and skill to develop a plantation economy. In time, slavery itself became part of the traditional pattern. Contemporary whites still react to the Negro in a given way, to a certain extent because he once was a slave. Attitudes were then formed which have become part of the culture, to some degree living an independent and autonomous life and to some degree continually reinforced by the actual present status of the Negro, which is partly a result of those very attitudes.

Where this historical background was different a different pattern of relationship has become fixed in the traditions and passed on to contemporary people. The differences between attitudes toward race lines in North and South America, for example, have been explained by Frank Tannenbaum as a result of legal differences which were involved in the early contact. Gilberto Freyre believes that the relative lack of race prejudice in Brazil can be understood in a measure by analysis of the earlier contacts between Portuguese and Moors, by the nature of the early migration to Brazil (a large proportion of unattached men), and by the fact that slavery was abolished without a war to cause resentment. Similarly, Romanzo Adams accounts for the attitude toward Orientals in Hawaii, as contrasted with California, by reference to the nature of the earliest contacts between white and nonwhite. Some of the white men who served as advisers to the court of the king of Hawaii were honored by permission to marry ladies of the king's court. As Klineberg remarks, "This set a pattern of racial friendliness which was later extended to other racial groups as well. It soon became impossible to set up any hard and fast racial line since for so many white families it had become a sign of honor to have intermarried with members of a nonwhite group. In this case historical factors can be shown to have had an effect which continues long after the situation has changed;

without knowledge of this history, adequate understanding of this difference in attitudes between Hawaii and California is not possible."[1]

The American Pattern of Social Distance

We have given only a sketchy outline of some of the possible origins of attitudes toward other races. The point here is that *however started and to some degree independent* of contemporary functions, such attitudes continue to affect behavior by persistence in tradition. Individuals for whom prejudice is highly functional today will doubtless be more likely to express a tradition of prejudice or to act in a discriminatory way. One of the factors involved in the prejudice of a great many people, however, is the traditional way of looking at things that most members of a group absorb.

The evidence for this theory is the similar pattern of prejudice, as measured by social-distance scales, that is found across the country. This pattern varies to some degree with income, region, occupation, and education. Yet even minority groups accept it—rejecting only that part of it that applies to them, and partially accepting even that. There is little or no correlation between the amount and type of prejudice and the degree of contact with members of a minority group or extent of information about them. A large number of studies in the last twenty-five years have tried to describe the American pattern of prejudice. Before indicating the major conclusions of these studies, we must state an important caution: Almost all of the evidence has been in the form of verbal responses to paper-and-pencil tests. Insofar as these tests are valid, they show that most Americans share a verbal tradition. They do not indicate, for the most part, the degree to which this verbal behavior might be correlated with other behavior, nor do they indicate whether there are important differences among individuals in the ease with which the verbal behavior might be changed. If the analysis in the preceding two chapters is correct, individuals who express similar verbal opinions about a minority group may vary widely in the extent to which their prejudice reaches into the core of their personalities, in the degree to which the prejudice functions for them. One person may express the "proper" opinions, may sincerely "believe" them, but may act in a way that shows the prejudices have little functional significance for him. Another person may have not only the same traditional prejudices, but a strong contemporary need for their defense. This will influence the vigor with which he holds to his attitudes and acts upon them. When LaPiere traveled 10,000 miles around the country with a Chinese student and his wife, his party was refused service only once out of 250

[1] Otto Klineberg, *Tensions Affecting International Understanding*, Social Science Research Council, 1950, p. 192.

visits to restaurants, hotels, and tourist camps. Yet when he sent these same places a questionnaire asking if they would accept members of the Chinese race as guests, 93 percent of the eating places and 92 percent of the lodging places said no. When he sent the same questionnaires to over 100 establishments that he had not visited, he received almost identical answers.[2]

The Importance of Traditional Prejudices

The existence of such wide contrasts between verbal behavior and nonsymbolic behavior should make us cautious in our study of the role of tradition in a theory of prejudice. Frequently the contrast will be the other way around—a person will verbally deny that he is prejudiced, while confirming the existence of prejudice by his actions. A study of intergroup hostility that limited itself to the traditional verbalizations, unmindful of the contemporary personality and group functions involved, would certainly be inadequate. Equally inadequate, however, would be dismissal of the traditional element in prejudice as a "mere survival." It is very much a part of the contemporary process. A traditional prejudice can produce complacence, acquiescence, and a fertile area for the cultivation, by interested groups, of more vigorous prejudices. Even the relatively innocuous statement or acceptance of a verbal tradition of prejudice can set in motion a chain of events that is highly significant in the relationship between majority- and minority-group members.

1. Acceptance of the tradition by those who are only mildly served by it helps to reinforce the prejudice of those who use it to satisfy more fundamental needs. It is easy to say, "I can scarcely be accused of being prejudiced because of self-interest when those people who obviously have no self-interest express the same prejudice." In other words, anyone who accepts a tradition of prejudice helps to sharpen the sword for those who want to use it.

2. The mild verbal prejudice may govern a person's actions in one of those either-or decisions which have a watershed effect on many subsequent events. Shall the community accept or oppose a segregated school that is gradually appearing because of housing shifts? One with the traditional prejudice may easily assume that segregation is pretty normal and natural. He has nothing in particular to gain or lose by it, but it seems right. Once fixed as a pattern, however, the segregated school has a long sequence of effects on the personalities of the colored and white students, on comparative educational and economic opportunities, on the extent and nature of interracial contacts, on the whole life of the community. An action which came about as the logical result

---

[2] See R. T. LaPiere, "Attitudes vs. Actions," *Social Forces*, December, 1934, pp. 230–237.

of a mild, verbal, traditional prejudice may have effects as significant in race relations as actions which result from more deeply rooted prejudice.

3. Finally, traditional attitudes keep alive a mind-set which, when crisis situations arrive, will be strengthened and attached to contemporary needs. Having survived as tradition, the prejudice takes on renewed life as a weapon. Had the traditional prejudice not been available, some other adjustment to the situation might have occurred—an adjustment conceivably more in harmony with the realities of the situation and thus more in the interest of the prejudiced person as well as the target of his hostility. For long periods, anti-Semitism has lingered as tradition, functional in the lives of only a small proportion of those who believed it. But when conflict situations and frustrations have arisen, it has been asserted with a renewed force, blocking adjustments that were more in line with the actual problems.

For these reasons the social scientist must study the traditional factor in prejudice. The fact that it is "only verbal," "skin-deep," and relatively nonfunctional should not be allowed to obscure the basic role it often plays. In any complete analysis of prejudice one cannot ignore the casual, verbal, "proper" prejudices of the average person, for they are involved in this important interactional way with the other factors in prejudice. They are not simply survivals or cultural lags that are gradually disappearing and meanwhile have little significance for social interaction. They are part of the total process by which prejudice is sustained and through which it functions.

DESCRIPTIONS OF THE AMERICAN PATTERN OF PREJUDICE

Many studies have sought to describe the pattern of prejudice in the United States and have come out with similar results. In a pioneer study Bogardus devised a "social-distance scale" with which he secured the responses of nearly 2000 Americans to forty racial, national, and religious groups. The respondents were asked to which step on the following scale they would admit the members of each group:

1. To close kinship by marriage.
2. To my club as personal chums.
3. To my street as neighbors.
4. To employment in my occupation.
5. To citizenship in my country.
6. As visitors only to my country.
7. Would exclude from my country.

These steps were assumed to be on a quantitative scale that ranged from most favorable to least favorable. It is unlikely that all the respondents would regard the questions in this way or would agree entirely on the amount of social distance expressed by each question, but the instrument is certainly of sufficient precision to give an approximate preference ranking of the forty groups. Near the top are British, native white Americans, and Canadians; then come French, Germans, Norwegians, Swedes, and other north Europeans; then Spaniards, Italians, south and east Europeans, and Jews; and near the bottom Negroes, Japanese, Chinese, Hindus, and Turks.[3]

This pattern appeared, with only minor fluctuations, in several studies. Compare the rankings obtained when Bogardus asked 110 businessmen and schoolteachers on the west coast the degree of social intimacy to which they were willing to admit various ethnic groups with the rankings that Thurstone found in studying the likes and dislikes of 239 midwestern college students. (The two studies used different measuring devices, and we have omitted groups that did not appear in both studies.)[4]

West Coast Businessmen and Schoolteachers	Midwestern College Students
1. English	1. English
2. Scotch	2. Scotch
3. Irish	3. Irish
4. French	4. French
5. Swede	5. German
6. German	6. Swede
7. Spanish	7. Italian
8. Italian	8. Spanish
9. Pole	9. Jew
10. Russian	10. Russian
11. Armenian	11. Pole
12. Jew	12. Greek
13. Greek	13. Armenian
14. Mexican	14. Japanese
15. Chinese	15. Mexican
16. Japanese	16. Chinese
17. Negro	17. Hindu
18. Hindu	18. Turk
19. Turk	19. Negro

Five of these groups have identical ranking; nine differ by only one rank; four by two ranks; the largest disagreement is three ranks, which occurs only once.

In 1928 Guilford found that the students in seven widely separated colleges had the same pattern of prejudice. Those from New York University, which has a high proportion of students from minority groups,

[3] See Emory S. Bogardus, *Immigration and Race Attitudes*, D. C. Heath and Company, 1928, pp. 13–29 ff.

[4] See Theodore M. Newcomb and E. L. Hartley (eds.), *Readings in Social Psychology*, Henry Holt & Company, Inc., 1947, p. 204.

showed correlations ranging from .84 to .89 with the rankings of the
other schools; the correlations among the other six universities ranged
from .975 to .99.[5] Hartley discovered that the girls in Bennington College, Vermont, had the same attitudes toward minority groups as did
the Negro students of Howard University, Washington, D.C. In general he found the same pattern in 1946 that Bogardus had found in
1928, and concluded that ". . . this pattern of prejudice is practically
an American institution."[6]

Minority groups themselves tend to share this tradition, although
with some variations. Zeligs and Hendrickson found a correlation of .87
between the rankings of Jewish and non-Jewish children.[7] Compare the
rankings that Bogardus obtained from 202 American Negroes and 178
native-born Jews with those of the businessmen and schoolteachers
listed above. (We have eliminated groups that were not found in all
three studies, so the comparisons should be taken as a rough indication
of the degree of similarity in attitudes.)[8]

Native White Businessmen and Schoolteachers	American Negroes	Native-Born Jews
1. English	1. Negro	1. Jew
2. French	2. French	2. English
3. German	3. Spanish	3. French
4. Spanish	4. English	4. German
5. Italian	5. Mexican	5. Spanish
6. Jew	6. Hindu	6. Italian
7. Greek	7. Japanese	7. Mexican
8. Mexican	8. German	8. Japanese
9. Chinese	9. Italian	9. Turk
10. Japanese	10. Chinese	10. Greek
11. Negro	11. Jew	11. Chinese
12. Hindu	12. Greek	12. Hindu
13. Turk	13. Turk	13. Negro

It is well to remember that these are the rankings of particular times
and places. Although there is stability in traditions of social distance,
there is also change. In a study of Negro college students, for example,
Prothro and Jensen found that the tendency to share the ratings of
whites which had been found in most prewar studies was not duplicated in the postwar situation. In this study, Negroes rated whites no
higher than whites rated Negroes. Both rated Jews higher than most

[5] J. P. Guilford, "Racial Preferences of a Thousand American University Students," *Journal of Social Psychology,* May, 1931, pp. 179–204.
[6] See Eugene Hartley, *Problems in Prejudice,* King's Crown Press, 1946.
[7] R. Zeligs and G. Hendrickson, "Racial Attitudes of 200 Six-Grade Children,"
Sociology and Social Research, September–October, 1933, pp. 26–36.
[8] Adapted from Emory S. Bogardus, *op. cit.*

prewar studies had shown, again indicating that patterns of social distance change.[9]

Cultural forces tell us not only whom to like and dislike but why we have these attitudes. Katz and Braly asked twenty-five students to list all the traits they thought typical of Germans, Italians, Irish, English, Negroes, Jews, Americans, Chinese, Japanese, Turks. This list was supplemented by other traits commonly found in the literature. One hundred Princeton students were then asked to select, from the eighty-four characteristics listed, the five traits that were typical of each of the ten groups. If there had been no patterning in the pictures that the students had of these groups, forty-two (half) of the traits would have received 50 percent of the votes. Oppositely, if the students had agreed perfectly on the five traits that were typical of a group, 2.5 traits would have received 50 percent of the votes. The degree of uniformity in attitude is shown by the fact that only 4.6 traits were needed to include half of all selections referring to Negroes; only 5.0 to include half the selection of traits referring to Germans; and for the Turks, about whom there was least agreement, only 15.9 traits were required, compared with the 42 that would have occurred on a chance basis. With eighty-four characteristics to select among, over half the designations were to only five that supposedly typify the Negro: He is superstitious, lazy, happy-go-lucky, ignorant, and musical. Just half of all the traits listed for Germans were selected from five: They are scientifically-minded, industrious, stolid, intelligent, and methodical. Over half of all listings for Jews were chosen from six traits: They are shrewd, mercenary, industrious, grasping, intelligent, and ambitious.[10] When it is seen that even these few traits are often virtual synonyms (superstitious and ignorant, scientifically-minded and intelligent, mercenary and grasping), the limited picture that the students had of these groups is emphasized. The pictures can scarcely be a description of reality, for the students had had relatively little contact with some of these groups, and probably no contact with a few. That did not prevent them from "knowing" what they were like, for they were the heirs of a tradition that informed them.

In 1941 Bayton discovered that 100 Negro students at the Virginia State College had nearly the same picture of the Negro that the Princeton students had, although they added a few more favorable traits (e.g., progressive) to the list.[11]

[9] E. T. Prothro and J. A. Jensen, "Comparison of Some Ethnic and Religious Attitudes of Negro and White College Students in the Deep South," *Social Forces*, May, 1952, pp. 426–428.

[10] See David Katz and Kenneth Braly, "Racial Stereotypes of One Hundred College Students," *Journal of Abnormal and Social Psychology*, October–December, 1933, pp. 280–290.

[11] J. A. Bayton, "The Racial Stereotypes of Negro College Students," *Journal of Abnormal and Social Psychology*, January, 1941, pp. 97–102.

In a follow-up study, Gilbert found that Princeton students in 1950 checked many of the same "traits" that Katz and Braly had measured in 1932. There were, however, some important differences, indicating again the fact that the traditional element in prejudice is not static. There was more resistance to stereotyping in 1950; although the traits put at the top for various national and racial groups tended to be the same, they were checked by fewer persons. In the following list, the first figure indicates the percentage who, in 1932, checked an adjective as applying to Negroes; the figure that follows in parentheses indicates the percentage who checked that adjective in 1950: superstitious, 84 (41); lazy, 75 (31); happy-go-lucky, 38 (17); ignorant, 38 (24); and musical, 26 (33). The number of characteristics necessary to get half of the votes, out of the 84 adjectives listed, was substantially increased for most groups between 1932 and 1950: from 4.6 to 12.0 for Negroes, from 5.0 to 6.3 for Germans, from 5.5 to 10.6 for Jews, from 6.9 to 11.3 for Italians. These data indicate less agreement on the supposed characteristics of various groups in 1950 than in 1932, although there is still a large amount of agreement. Why the change? Gilbert suggests that it may reflect in part a change in the student body (more persons from the lower classes), the growing influence of social science, a reduction in stereotypes in the entertainment media, or perhaps only changing verbal conventions—because in both years there was knowledge of what the various groups were supposed to be like.[12]

Studies of the changes in shared pictures of minority groups qualify, but by no means refute, the idea that the presence or absence of prejudice is partly a result of group membership. One gets his prejudices just as he gets other values and loyalties, and there need be little or no experience of his own. As Horowitz says: ". . . Attitudes toward Negroes are now chiefly determined not by contacts with Negroes, but by contact with the prevalent attitude toward Negroes."[13]

In the literature on "social distance" too little attention has been given to subcultural variations. Although there is substantial similarity among groups, some differences have been observed that should not be overlooked. Shared attitudes within a group may also be traditional, taught to the members as part of the subculture. Educational, regional, and class differences have been measured.[14] Westie measured the differ-

---

[12] See G. M. Gilbert, "Stereotype Persistence and Change Among College Students," *Journal of Abnormal and Social Psychology*, April, 1951, pp. 245–254.

[13] Eugene L. Horowitz, "Development of Attitude Toward Negroes," *Archives of Psychology*, No. 194, 1936, pp. 34–35.

[14] See Richard Christie and John Garcia, "Subcultural Variation in Authoritarian Personality," *Journal of Abnormal and Social Psychology*, October, 1951, pp. 457–469; E. T. Prothro and O. K. Miles, "Comparison of Ethnic Attitudes of College Students and Middle Class Adults from the Same State," *Journal of Social Psychology*, August, 1952, pp. 53–58; Frank R. Westie, "Negro-White Status Differentials and Social Distance," *American Sociological Review*, October, 1952, pp. 550–558;

ences in response of white persons to Negroes in various occupations. Sixty lower-class, 56 middle-class, and 58 upper-class whites, chosen by random sample blocks in Indianapolis, were interviewed in their homes. The degree of "social distance" which they felt toward Negroes was measured by a series of four scales which referred to various kinds of interpersonal contact. Lower-class whites made very little distinction among Negroes in various occupations, whether the Negroes were doctors, bankers, machine operators, or ditch diggers. With a score of 24 representing the maximum social distance, lower-class whites averaged from 14.03 to 15.10 for the eight occupations listed in the study, a range of only 1.07 scale points. The scores of the middle-class whites were from 10.91 to 13.09, indicating both less social distance and the willingness to distinguish more sharply among Negroes in various occupational groups. The range for upper-class whites was from 9.38 to 12.52, again indicating a lower amount of social distance and a greater willingness to differentiate among Negroes of different occupations.[15] Since the white respondents were not classified by education, region of birth, or other variables, we cannot know how much their class standing per se influenced the results. But the study indicates the need for measuring the variations in social distance as well as the nationally shared traditions.[16]

The traditional prejudices, whether cultural or subcultural, are not static, of course. In the United States, prejudice against many of the immigrant groups disappeared in the course of two or three generations, because some of the forces in the American environment were working to reduce prejudice, because more "visible" groups came in to take their place, and because it is more difficult to fix in tradition a prejudice against a group that is rapidly losing its physical, psychological, and sociological differentia. The impact of new economic and political situations is especially destructive of traditional prejudices. The attitudes associated with the Indian caste system, for example, will probably not survive the effects of the urban and industrial society which is gradually appearing. It would be a mistake, however, to forget the tenacity of cultural norms. How rapidly they change depends on many factors in the situation where they exist. But the mental inertia characteristic of most human beings, the efforts of groups who stand to gain by continuation of the tradition, the need for ready-made responses to most

Charles U. Smith and James W. Prothro, "Ethnic Differences in Authoritarian Personality," Social Forces, May, 1957, pp. 334–338; T. F. Pettigrew, "Desegregation and Its Chances for Success: Northern and Southern Views," Social Forces, May, 1957, pp. 339–344.

[15] See Frank R. Westie, op. cit.

[16] For extensive summaries of studies of social distance, see Eugene L. Horowitz in Otto Klineberg (ed.), Characteristics of the American Negro, Harper & Brothers, 1944, pp. 139–247; Eugene Hartley, op. cit.; and Muzafer Sherif, An Outline of Social Psychology, Harper & Brothers, 1948, pp. 339–363.

situations in life, and the desire to be a good group member, to share the values of one's group—these and other forces give rigidity to the traditions of prejudice.[17]

Within every society there are some individuals who for a number of reasons turn out to be atypical. They may have acquired a system of beliefs and values from some other frame of reference (a different culture, a thoroughgoing belief in science, or the teachings of religion taken seriously), or they may be simply maladjusted as individuals, with no integrated system of beliefs. From the point of view of the majority, they are heretics, radicals, and eccentrics. They do not share the dominant values of the society, and they frequently do not share its prejudices. No statement of the traditional factors in prejudice should disregard these exceptions. An analysis of their relationships to the group is helpful in understanding the roots of prejudice. Murphy and Likert found that acceptance of the traditional scale of social distance was negatively correlated with radicalism; those who were dissatisfied with the social scene were also dissatisfied with its prejudices. Horowitz found that the children of a group of communists showed markedly less prejudice against the Negro than did other children of the same age.

There are, of course, traditions of nonprejudice as well; for example, what Myrdal calls the American creed contains traditions of democracy and equality. One cannot say, therefore, that the reduction of the hold of tradition on an individual will, other things being equal, make him less prejudiced. We need to know further whether or not the atypical person has experienced an emotional reaction against all cultural norms; we need to know why he is atypical; we need to know what part of the culture he does accept. The Nazis, while building upon many traditional ideas, were at the same time flaunters of tradition. Further study along these lines is necessary before we can make an adequate statement of the relationship between atypicality and prejudice.

Finally, it must be remembered that each society has its own scale of social distances, its own traditions of prejudice, reflecting its past experiences and the present social structure. Our analysis has been concerned with the American pattern. It is well known that race is considered to be a relatively unimportant line of cleavage in Brazil and Hawaii, that France shows little prejudice against the Negro, that many colored American soldiers were reluctant to leave Italy because they found so little discrimination there. For a long time before Hitler, anti-Semitism had been part of the traditional equipment of almost every German; and it is unlikely that war, defeat, and the virtual elimination of the Jewish population of Germany have destroyed that tradition. Race prejudice is a fundamental part of the culture of the white people of South Africa (and probably also, reciprocally, of the colored people),

[17] See Muzafer Sherif, op. cit., pp. 356–358.

no more easily to be escaped by the great majority of the population than belief in other major aspects of the culture.[18]

Stereotypes as the Embodiment of a Tradition of Prejudice

In the preceding section we noted that a tradition of prejudice not only tells the members of a group what the proper scale of social distance is but assigns to each group a list of characteristics which are supposed to typify it. These characteristics are not wholly imaginary, as we shall see, but they are such a compound of error, exaggeration, omission, and half-truth that they tell more about the people who believe them, the needs of the group in which they circulate, than about the group to which they are supposed to refer. One of the most important aspects of a tradition of prejudice is the stereotyped pictures it contains. These are to some degree explicitly functional, as we have seen in Chapters 3 and 4, but to some degree simply traditional, part of the mental equipment that an individual receives as a member of a culture. Once fixed in the culture, they react back upon it, guiding the interaction of the groups involved.

Stereotypes are found in the folk thought of a dominant group; they are found in its humor, its superstitions, its aphorisms. We sometimes categorize a whole nation by a stereotype. The story is told of the professor in a cosmopolitan university who asked his class to write an essay on "The Elephant." The Englishman wrote, "The Elephant and How to Hunt Him." The Frenchman wrote, "The Strange Love Life of the Elephant." The German student prepared a paper on "Is the Elephant Aryan?" The American's was titled "Business Opportunities in the Elephant Trade." The Pole wrote on "The Elephant and the Polish Question." And the Russian, writing in red ink, studied "The Elephant as a Bourgeois Tool for the Exploitation of the Masses."

Stereotypes of the majority group also abound in the thinking of minorities, so that interaction is, in part, not among individuals as they are but among individuals as they are thought to be. The beliefs about the majority are perhaps less important to the student of prejudice for two reasons. Minority-group members are frequently in a better position to know the true characteristics of the majority than the other way around; a servant knows his master better than a master knows his servant. The servant may be more highly motivated to know what the master is really like, for he can scarcely afford the luxury of the errors involved in a stereotype. In spite of oversimplification and distortion in the picture of the dominant group held by the dominated, it contains a larger share of truth. Secondly, even though there are many errors in

---

[18] For a discussion of the many different meanings and uses of stereotyping, see Joshua A. Fishman, "An Examination of the Process and Function of Social Stereotyping," *Journal of Social Psychology*, February, 1956, pp. 27–64.

the stereotypes held by the minority, the consequences of these errors are less important, because the minority group does not have as much power to make reality out of its beliefs.

Stereotypes are most readily observed today in literature and in the characterization of minority groups in movies, radio, and television. This topic will be treated in more detail in Chapter 21, so we shall make only a brief reference to it here. In 1944, the Writers' War Board and its Committee to Combat Race Hatred asked the Bureau of Applied Social Research at Columbia University to study contemporary fictional characterizations. One hundred and eighty-five short stories were examined in eight widely circulated magazines, 1937–1943. Most of the attention in these stories was given to "Anglo-Saxons." They were the nice people, seldom the undesirable characters. Minority-group members were not treated so flatteringly: "The behavior of these fictional characters could easily be used to 'prove' that the Negroes are lazy, the Jews wily, the Irish superstitious and the Italians criminal."[19] Characterizations in the theater have more variety, but even there we find the Uncle Toms, the quarrelsome Jewish businessman type, the stage Irishman. Of 100 movies that pictured Negroes, the study found that 75 percent were stereotyped or disparaging, 13 percent neutral or unobjectionable, and 12 percent favorable. Most radio heroes are white Protestant Anglo-Saxons; the Negro is a comic, "addicted to drink, dice, wenching, and razors."[20]

Literature is not without attempts to describe the Negro and other minority groups with realism, bringing in the complexity of types that characterizes any human group. Nor are the stereotypes always disparaging. The Negro is sometimes pictured as a shrewd judge of human nature, a witty philosopher, a loyal friend to his "white folks," highly gifted in music and sense of rhythm, a born actor and orator.[21] Movies, television, and radio occasionally portray a Negro or other minority-group member in a sympathetic or realistic role. It seems likely, in fact, that the trend in the mass media is away from the more obvious minority-group casting. Yet much stereotyping remains. Moviegoers have a picture of the American Indian which is scarcely less stereotyped than the statement: All Indians walk in single file—at least the one I saw did.

Johnson has summarized the major elements in the American stereotype of the Negro:

One might compile a catalogue of "What Every White Man Thinks He Knows about Negroes." Its main themes would be as follows: The Negro is

[19] David Krech and Richard Crutchfield, *Theory and Problems of Social Psychology*, McGraw-Hill Book Company, 1948, p. 472.
[20] See *ibid.*, pp. 471–473.
[21] Guy B. Johnson, in Otto Klineberg (ed.), *Characteristics of the American Negro*, p. 4.

lazy. He will not work if he can get out of it. He cannot manage complicated machinery because he cannot give it sustained attention and will fall asleep. He is dirty, "smelly," careless of his personal appearance. He is fond of loud colors and flashy clothing. He is less inhibited than the white man, is more given to loud laughter and boisterous talk. He is a natural-born clown and mimic. He is endowed with an inordinate sexual passion which overrides all considerations of modesty, chastity, and marital fidelity. He has no sense of time, never gets anywhere on time. He does not know the value of a dollar and will spend his money on "foolishness" and then beg for the necessities of life. Even when he acquires property, he cannot take care of it. He is very gullible and is a great "joiner." He will join anything which promises a good time or a big noise or gives him a chance to "show off." He is naturally religious, but his religion is all feeling, emotion, and superstition. He believes in ghosts, spirits, voodoo charms, and magic formulae. His mind works like a child's mind. His thoughts are shallow, his associations flimsy and superficial. His emotions are powerful but fickle. He is given to high criminality because he has no respect for life or property or morality and cannot control his impulses. He is incapable of appreciating the deeper values of white civilization, is incapable of self-government, and therefore must have the supervision and guidance of the white man.[22]

Such stereotypes as these are easy ways of explaining things. They take less effort and give an appearance of order without the difficult work that understanding the true order of things demands. They are a way of classifying, which in itself is a necessary process for any kind of thinking. The word "chair" is an abstraction that leaves out a large number of specific traits of specific chairs in favor of general characteristics. A scientific abstraction, however, differs from a stereotype in including all important traits, and in selecting those traits on purely rational grounds. The traits assigned to a stereotype are selected for their ability to produce some desired effect or on the basis of an emotional predisposition. Classification and typing are justified, and necessary, even in the study of human beings; but science insists that the process follow all the rules of logic and be based on all possible evidence.

There is doubtless some truth in many stereotypes, but the commonplace application of them as descriptive of the behavior of all the members of a group is in error in several ways:

1. The stereotype gives a highly exaggerated picture of the importance of some few characteristics—whether they be favorable or unfavorable.

2. It invents some supposed traits out of whole cloth, making them seem reasonable by association with other tendencies that may have a kernel of truth.

3. In a negative stereotype, personality tendencies that are favorable,

[22] *Ibid.*, p. 3.

that would have to be mentioned to give a complete picture, are either omitted entirely or insufficiently stressed.

4. The stereotype fails to show how the majority, or other groups, share the same tendencies or have other undesirable characteristics.

5. It fails to give any attention to the cause of the tendencies of the minority group—particularly to the place of the majority itself, and its stereotypes, in creating the very characteristics being condemned. They are thought of rather as intrinsic or even self-willed traits of the minority.

6. It leaves little room for change; there is a lag in keeping up with the tendencies which actually typify many members of a group.

7. It leaves no room for individual variation, which is always wide in human groups. One does not deal with a group average, but with specific individuals. One of the functions of stereotypes is shown by this failure to adjust to individual differences—to do so would be to destroy the discriminatory value of the stereotype. We shall see shortly how easy it is for the human mind to overlook completely or to treat as unimportant exceptions the evidence which contradicts a well-established belief.

These logical and factual weaknesses of the stereotype do not prevent it from occupying an important role in the pattern of prejudice. One does not readily challenge the definitions passed on to him by his culture. Moreover, they are useful; they are effective weapons. We seldom see them in that light, but our actions may reveal an unconscious appreciation of their functional importance.

The stereotyped pictures of the minority groups held by members of dominant groups are not all alike. They differ both because of the various historical circumstances out of which they grew and also because they are related to different kinds of conflict situations. But even stereotypes can be classified. One often can discern a great similarity between the stereotyped pictures of two minority groups who are related in about the same way to a dominant group. One group of stereotypes seems aimed especially at *keeping* a group down, another at *pushing* a group down that has achieved some degree of competitive power. Thus the picture of the American Negro as lazy, shiftless, irresponsible, unable to acquire a skill, and unable to appreciate a higher standard of living is matched by the stereotype of similarly disadvantaged groups in other settings. ". . . One could not distinguish the stereotype of the Polish worker which developed in Germany in the latter part of the last century from the stereotype of the Negro which exists in the United States today."[23] The same picture was drawn of the migrants to California from Oklahoma and Arkansas during the 1930's, despite the

---

[23] Carey McWilliams, A Mask for Privilege: Anti-Semitism in America, Little, Brown & Company, 1948, p. 163.

fact that they were overwhelmingly white Protestant Anglo-Saxons.[24]

There is another pattern to the stereotypes of groups which have been somewhat more successful in competing with the dominant group. It would be too great a distortion of the fact to label them lazy or unintelligent, so they are pictured as too ambitious, and with a crafty kind of self-interested intelligence. In various settings this picture has arisen in connection with Jews, Greeks, Syrians, Armenians, the American Japanese, Chinese in the Philippines, and other groups. Such stereotypes indicate the skill that human beings have in interpreting almost any phenomenon so that it reinforces their established beliefs. The stereotype of "the Jew" shows particularly clearly that it is not what the out-group does or fails to do that causes prejudice. "Superficial appearances notwithstanding, prejudice and discrimination aimed at the out-group are not a result of what the out-group does, but are rooted deep in the structure of our society and the social psychology of its members."[25] It is a simple matter for most of us to make what we consider virtues in ourselves into vices when they are found in the behavior of a minority-group member. Merton puts the matter sharply:

. . . The very same behavior undergoes a complete change of evaluation in its transition from the in-group Abe Lincoln to the out-group Abe Cohen or Abe Kurokawa. . . . Did Lincoln work far into the night? This testifies that he was industrious, resolute, perseverant, and eager to realize his capacities to the full. Do the out-group Jews or Japanese keep these same hours? This only bears witness to their sweatshop mentality, their ruthless undercutting of American standards, their unfair competitive practices. Is the in-group hero frugal, thrifty, and sparing? Then the out-group villain is stingy, miserly, and penny-pinching. All honor is due the in-group Abe for his having been smart, shrewd, and intelligent, and, by the same token, all contempt is owing the out-group Abes for their being sharp, cunning, crafty, and too clever by far. Did the indomitable Lincoln refuse to remain content with a life of work with the hands? Did he prefer to make use of his brain? Then, all praise for his plucky climb up the shaky ladder of opportunity. But, of course, the eschewing of manual work for brain work among the merchants and lawyers of the out-group deserves nothing but censure for a parasitic way of life. Was Abe Lincoln eager to learn the accumulated wisdom of the ages by unending study? The trouble with the Jew is that he's a greasy grind, with his head always in a book, while decent people are going to a show or a ball game. Was the resolute Lincoln unwilling to limit his standards to those of his provincial community? That is what we should expect from a man of vision. And if the out-groupers criticize the vulnerable areas in our society, then send 'em back where they came from. Did Lincoln, rising high above his origins, never forget the rights of the common man and applaud the right of workers to strike? This testifies only, that like real

[24] See *ibid.*
[25] Robert K. Merton, *Social Theory and Social Structure*, The Free Press, 1949, p. 185.

Americans, this greatest of Americans was deathlessly devoted to the cause of freedom. But, as you examine the recent statistics on strikes, remember that these un-American practices are the result of out-groupers pursuing their evil agitation among otherwise contented workers.[26]

Whether we are dealing with a stereotype which attacks a minority group for failing to be like the majority or with one that accuses the minority group of having virtues—but in excess—the important thing to keep in mind is that these categorical judgments are part of the stream of culture. They are transferred to children in the process of socialization. They are not dormant traditional items but active ingredients in human interaction, helping to shape experience, to color observations, and finally, as we shall see in the next section, to create the very tendencies with which they were in the first instance justified.

"Facts" as the Embodiment and Support of a Tradition of Prejudice

Having noted the important place of essentially false stereotypes in our judgments of minority groups, must we conclude that there are no important differences among human groups? Are our observations so completely distorted by the "pictures in our heads" that reality disappears? Apparently when majority-group members look around for confirmation of the "inferiority" of minority groups, they do not look entirely in vain. This point needs careful study, for it has been the subject of much misunderstanding. We have noted several times that man, at least in our society, likes to think of himself as a rational animal. He would probably not accept a tradition of prejudice as readily as he does if he could not, in his daily experiences, find support—or what seems to be support—for the validity (granted certain premises) of the tradition. Stereotypes, as we have seen, lend a kind of support; the beliefs and verbalizations of other people, the definitions of roles found in the culture—these are taken by most people as "evidence" of the inferiority of some groups. And for many people this is all the evidence they ever have, for they lack contact with the minority groups themselves.

Some majority-group members, however, see for themselves. And what do they see? Negroes, on the average, for example, live in poorer houses than whites; they perform more menial tasks; they are more often illiterate and poorly educated; their sexual behavior more often violates the dominant mores; they probably break the letter of the law more often. Are these signs of inferiority? The scientist makes no such judgment, for his job is to describe, not to evaluate. When we have said "poorer houses," "more menial tasks," "poorly educated," we have taken, for purposes of understanding their prejudice, the value position

[26] *Ibid.*, pp. 186–187.

of the dominant group and, to a large degree, the value position of the minority groups as well. *To them*, these are signs of inferiority. It would be equally possible from a different value premise to find inferiority in much education (it spoils one for hard, useful labor), in expensive houses (one has to cheat a lot of people to be able to afford them), or in restricted sexual behavior (it makes for frustration and hostility). From this value stand, people with a great deal of education who live in costly houses and sharply inhibit their sexual activity are inferior. Hereafter when we state that minority groups are inferior, we refer to the fact that they can frequently be differentiated from the majority group in terms of the dominant standards of a society. From this value stand, the characteristics of minorities can be made to seem a confirmation of the tradition of prejudice; minority-group members are given an inferior status because that is the only one they deserve or can fill. In other words, these "facts" are the basis of a theory of prejudice. The traits of a minority group are the cause of its low status, not the result of that status.

That this is an inadequate theory our whole discussion to this point should demonstrate. The word "cause," however, is a slippery concept. Many scientists and philosophers have stopped using it entirely because of the misunderstandings that result from its naïve application. Only the use of the concept of many "levels of causation" can prevent the attempt to explain a phenomenon by one surface relationship. Behind each cause is another cause, and behind that another, and the third may, in turn, affect the first. Science is not interested in finding the "ultimate" cause but in describing the total group of interacting forces which occur in connection with the phenomenon being studied. Some forces, to be sure, may be more important than others. This is determined by a simple criterion: How consistently does the force occur in connection with the phenomenon, when other forces are controlled? How well can one predict the occurrence of the phenomenon by analysis of the "cause"?

From this point of view, the attempt to explain prejudice as a result of the inferiority of minority-group members is very inadequate. There can be inferiority without prejudice; and there can be prejudice without inferiority. Even when the two occur together the likelihood is that the majority group assumes a *post hoc, ergo propter hoc* relationship which is not justified. It is reported that during the London blitz rescue workers were tunneling into a demolished house when they discovered a frightened but unhurt old man sitting in a bathtub. He was shaking his head, looking very puzzled, and mumbling: "I can't understand it! I can't understand it! I pulled out the plug and the house blew up." Majority-group members are less modest. They declare: "We do understand it. We grew up observing the factual inferiority of the Negro, and our attitudes toward him are simply a result of that fact." Our analogy here is not perfect, for presumably the bathtub plug was not a booby trap; it was completely uninvolved in the cycle of forces that led to the demolition of the house. The "inferiority" of the Negro, however, is a booby trap; it helps to explode discriminatory activities. To be sure, that inferiority is in part the product of prejudice and discrimination in the first place; but *once established*, it becomes a part of the cycle of interaction. This is the interaction that Myrdal has described as "the vicious circle," or, if one's value premises are different, "the beneficent circle." If a group of forces (associated with slavery, for example) have created an inferior status for a minority, there will appear, both as rationalization of the discrimination shown and as a result of the fact of observation of that inferior status, an attitude of prejudice toward the minority group. Such prejudice will block members of the "inferior" group from the life chances necessary to advancement. By limiting the opportunities of a minority group, by segregating it, by putting it at every competitive disadvantage, the prejudice helps to create the very inferiority by which it seems "justified" in the minds of the dominant group. Start out by saying that the colored man is inferior; use this as the reason for giving him poor schools, poor jobs, poor opportunities for advancement; and one soon proves himself correct by creating and enforcing that very inferiority. This, in turn, will deepen the prejudice, which, again, will further restrict the opportunities of the colored person.[27]

MacIver and Merton have shown how the idea of the "vicious circle" in race relations can be seen as one manifestation of a general principle, "the self-fulfilling prophecy."[28] Men respond not only to the objective features of a situation, but to their own definition of that situation—to the meaning it has for them. Even though the original definition of the situation is false, it may, by becoming part of the interacting forces, help to make itself true. A rumor (a false definition) spreads that the local bank is insolvent; a run on the bank starts; and, since no bank can immediately honor all claims upon it, the bank has to close. "The rumor is self-confirming." This self-fulfilling postulate is not completely circular, since the original state does not recur, but it illustrates how a belief—and actions based upon it—can produce the very situation with which it is supposed to have started. In other situations the interaction is circular. ". . . The process of international armament may run as follows:

> armament in country A→fear in country B→armament in country B→fear in country A→armament in country A, and so on *ad infinitum*—or *ad bellum*."[29]

---

[27] See Gunnar Myrdal, *An American Dilemma*, Harper & Brothers, 1944, pp. 75–78.

[28] R. M. MacIver, *The More Perfect Union*, The Macmillan Company, 1948, pp. 52–81; and Robert K. Merton, *op. cit.*, pp. 179–195.

[29] R. M. MacIver, *op. cit.*, p. 63.

This kind of sequence in race relations would move from discrimination to conditions confirmed or imposed by discrimination back to discrimination.

"In symbolic form the circle proceeds:

$$D^1 \rightarrow C^1 \rightarrow D^2 \rightarrow C^2 \rightarrow D^3 \rightarrow C^3 \text{ etc.,}$$

where D stands for discrimination and C for the sequent conditions relevant to it. The situation here symbolized is one of progressive discrimination. Where discrimination is established and relatively constant, we have a circle in a stricter sense, as follows:

$$D \rightarrow C \rightarrow D \rightarrow C \rightarrow D \rightarrow C \text{ etc.}"[30]$$

If we may accept this approach that the characteristics of the members of minority groups are involved in the process of prejudice (note again that they are a "cause" of prejudice in only the most superficial sense), what "traits" are used to make the discrimination possible? Krech and Crutchfield have observed that there are physical, psychological, and sociological "cues" for designating the "inferior" groups. Racial differences may furnish a fairly clear line of demarcation physically; the dominant group defines its particular combination of physical traits as good or beautiful, whereas the traits of the minority race are bad or ugly. In some instances the minority will accept the dominant standards, will try to match the physical appearance of the ruling group, and perhaps will itself be internally stratified partly on the basis of the differences in approaching those standards. This practice has, to some degree, been characteristic of the American Negro. On the other hand, a highly integrated minority, more anxious to be independent of the ruling group than to be assimilated, may counter with its own standards of beauty, and thus differentiate itself from the majority. For the American Indian, "pale face," "flop ears," and "crooked feet" were terms of contempt for the ugly appearance of the white man.

Obviously physical cues alone are not sufficient to designate the inferior group. They are too unpredictable and, in most societies where race mixture has been fairly common, too vague to draw a sharp line. Psychological cues are universally used as an explanation for discriminatory behavior: We are not prejudiced against them but are simply assigning them to the status which they deserve owing to lack of intelligence or certain personality traits. Is there any evidence to support this conception of group differences? In Chapter 2 we examined the question of differences in average native intelligence among racial groups. Although one must speak cautiously, because of the great difficulty in equating the variables involved, it is certainly accurate to say that there is a great deal of overlapping in the distribution of native capacity among the races. And the fact that the more the cultural variables are controlled the smaller become the differences in group averages points

[30] *Ibid.,* p. 67.

in the direction of the theory that native capacity is distributed in pretty much the same way through all races. The wide differences in opportunity, however, make for significant differences in average intellectual *ability* among human groups—at least according to the standards of intelligence as defined by the dominant group. Most persons do not make a scientific interpretation of those differences but take them as evidence of inherited differences, as facts which prove that their attitude toward the members of the minority group is not a prejudice.

The "facts" concerning other differences in personality are subject to the same interpretation. They are also used to support a tradition of prejudice, to make it seem reasonable. The next chapter will examine in detail some of the consequences of discrimination for those who experience it. We need only say at this point that groups are probably distinguished to some degree by personality differences. These are almost entirely, if not entirely, due to different experiences. The Negro, seeing little to be achieved by effort, may, on the average, be less responsible than the white; the Jew, having been barred from association with others on the basis of individual choice, may, on the average, be more "clannish." To the naïve observer these are simply "facts" that make the traditional prejudices he has been taught seem to be based on experience.

Often correlated with these physical and psychological cues which point out the "inferior" persons are a large number of sociological cues which are learned by the member of the dominant group as he is growing up, simply as facts of the environment. The minority group is segregated—in places of residence, in churches, in schools, in jobs, in labor unions, in the armed forces. Its share of the values associated with these things is almost always inferior, as we shall see in detail in later chapters. If one starts with a prejudice, these again are confirming facts of the inferiority of the members of the group involved. Sociological distinctions are most likely to be used to support a tradition of prejudice against a group that is already in a disadvantaged position and is to be *kept* there—for contrast will be sharpest with them. Psychological distinctions are more likely to be used to support a tradition of prejudice against a group that the ruling group is trying to *push* down. Altogether, the sociological facts are probably the most persistent support to prejudice because they are easiest to perceive and least ambiguous. They are often built into our legal, religious, educational, and military institutions, thus being given, for many people, a cultural sanction that makes them acceptable. Moreover, in our society at least, one's occupation, residence, and class are considered especially important, carrying definite implications concerning one's ability, character, and personality.[31]

These physical, psychological, and sociological differences among

[31] See David Krech and Richard Crutchfield, *op. cit.*, pp. 464–467.

groups mean that a tradition of prejudice is constantly being reinforced by reference to observed facts. It is thus made far more complicated (and far more difficult to uproot) than it would be if it were based completely on error and bias. To be sure, the causal sequence may be very different from what most persons believe, but pragmatically the prejudice "works," it explains, and not many are interested in testing the scientific logic involved in the explanation. Partial observation and crude logic satisfy most of us, particularly if the resulting conclusion is useful for our individual and group needs. A primitive medicine man may cure an infection by hiding a stone in his mouth, sucking on the wound, and then pulling the stone out of his mouth with the statement that it was causing the infection. It is unlikely that in a stable society where this practice was used a person would have much success in getting the people to drop it by appeal to John Stuart Mill's second canon of causation. Their belief in the practice would be based on some observation: Most infections treated in this way cleared up; and perhaps even more cleared up under this treatment than under other known practices. As long as it works, why doubt it, why take a chance? It explains things pretty well to everybody but the doubter who wants to control a few variables—and there are not many such. You could even silence some of them, if you could show that 95 percent of all infections treated in this way were healed, whereas only 90 percent of those treated solely by dancing and incantation were healed. Here is evidence, facts. Who is left to say that the stone had nothing to do with the infection, that it was the sucking, the greater blood circulation, the opening up of the wound that was the true "cause" of the cure?

Prejudice too is based on facts. That these facts happen simply to correlate with other phenomena (including the prejudice itself) and are not the true cause of the prejudice is a sophisticated observation that most of us are not able—or willing—to make. MacIver says:

Prejudice is not a simple thing. It is not a mere expression of human blindness and bias. Prejudice, so to speak, is not altogether prejudice. It has a rational element combined with an irrational one. The irrational element is often sustained by a response to observed behavior that might be accounted fair and proper if the observation were not so selective or if the observed behavior were the whole evidence. The proportion of the two ingredients, the rational and the irrational, will vary according to the kind and degree of prejudice.[32]

In studying the way in which a culture transmits attitudes of prejudice, therefore, we must take into account the support given the tradition by the facts of group differences. Many theories in recent years have failed to consider this relationship, probably because of equali-

[32] R. M. MacIver, op. cit., p. 77.

tarian and democratic value premises. The present authors happen to share those premises, but they also believe that such values will best be served by a scientifically adequate theory of prejudice, a theory that does not avoid a body of evidence because, on the surface, it seems to be "undemocratic." The theory of the vicious circle is, to be sure, only one part of a complex explanation of prejudice. To borrow a couple of terms from Hitler, the vicious circle is a "sustainer" of prejudice, not a "creator." That the support of "facts" is not essential to prejudice is shown by the elaborate cultural equipment for prejudice that most Americans share even when they know no facts, when they have had no contact with the people to whom the prejudice refers. Nor could appeal to the "facts" justify the categorical nature of prejudice—for the facts are very uncategorical; Negroes may have lower I.Q.'s on the average than whites, but there are Negroes with I.Q.'s of 200. The "facts" help to sustain prejudice only because of man's capacity for partial observations, rigid ideas, and poor logic.

It should be stated again that, in saying the facts of group differences support prejudice, we have taken the point of view of the prejudiced person: to *him* they are a proof of the reasonableness of his attitudes. That he is in error, from the point of view of the scientist, does not prevent his attitude from being a factor in prejudice. We have already noted some of the errors involved in the reasoning that uses the facts of group differences to support prejudice, but it may be well to summarize them.

1. The minority groups are not inferior in any absolute sense, but only relative to the standards of the dominant group. The "proof" that the prejudice is justified, therefore, is convincing only to a person who accepts the values of the dominant group as absolutely valid.

2. Reality is taken *as is* by the prejudiced person. He is scarcely interested in *why* minority groups are "inferior"; or his explanation is likely to be very simple—it is their nature. MacIver calls this the vicious-circle argument:

Its peculiar property is that it takes the existence of one link in the circle as independently given, as a fact of nature or even as ordained by God, and concludes from that premise that the next link, the behavior predicated on the earlier link, is not prejudicial or discriminatory but a rational and proper response to the inferior capacities or qualities of the group subjected to it. Those who put forward the argument wilfully or blindly ignore the sector of the circle that lies on the other side of the evidences to which they appeal. They refuse to recognize that the conditions on which they base their argument arise out of, or are themselves sustained by, a prior process of discrimination.[33]

This kind of "logic" or use of evidence is doubtless encouraged by

[33] *Ibid.*, p. 65.

the fact that it comes out with the "right" answer—the answer which profits the individual or group using it or corresponds to their established notions. It may be due in part, however, to a cultural pattern of thought. We are gradually discovering that the forms of logic and the kinds of evidences that one will accept are to some degree cultural. The kind of thinking which "explains" prejudice by the "nature" of minority groups is the *substantive mode of mentality*, ". . . the tendency to account for or describe events (social and otherwise) in terms of the 'essence' of things instead of in terms of related processes."[34] This is an easy kind of thinking; it gives the answer by an examination of surface relationships without concern for the complicated chain of events which preceded those relationships. Why are the roles and statuses of men and women different in the United States? Because they are different by nature. Very simple, isn't it? And very inadequate; for we know that the roles and statuses of men and women vary widely in time and space, whereas their "natures" presumably are quite constant.

More and more people are accepting the *process mode of mentality*[35] in dealing with the physical world. If something goes wrong with one's car, he is not likely to say that it is the "nature" of cars to behave that way; he looks, or has an expert look, for a disturbance in the usual process. Gradually that way of looking at things is being applied to human behavior. It is less commonly said today than formerly that children behave in a particular way "because it is the nature of children." We are beginning to be interested in the sequence of events that leads to certain behavior. At least a few people are beginning to study criminal behavior and abnormal behavior in the same way. To say that a person commits a crime because he is criminal by nature is as useless a statement as to say that a person or group is in an inferior status because he or it is inferior by nature. To some degree, this kind of explanation is simply part of our cultural equipment; but there seems to be a trend—however slow in its reference to human behavior—toward the process mode of mentality. Meanwhile "facts" support prejudice.

3. Another error in the assumption that prejudice is simply a description of reality is the use of incomplete and distorted pictures of reality. The truth, the whole truth, and nothing but the truth would support prejudice far less effectively than the part-truth, the half-truth, and error with the truth. Human events are almost always ambiguous, and our preconceived notions assign them the proper interpretation. What is thrifty, businesslike behavior in our gentile neighbor may be stingy, unfair competition from our Jewish competitor. Under such circumstances it is difficult to know what "facts" are justifying prejudice. The "sampling errors of experience" give us only a one-sided view

---

[34] Muzafer Sherif, *op. cit.*, p. 361.
[35] See *ibid.*, pp. 359–361.

of the "facts." We know the Negro janitor, but not the Negro author; the Mexican field hand, but not the Mexican doctor.[36]

Thus the facts of group differences are a reinforcement to prejudice only for the superficial and biased observer. Since a high proportion of us are superficial and biased observers, however, an adequate theory of prejudice must take account of this factor.

How Does the Individual Acquire the Traditions of Prejudice?

We have discussed the traditional element in prejudice—its place as part of culture, embodied in stereotypes and supported by selective observation of facts. Now comes the question: How is this tradition transferred to the maturing individuals of a new generation? One of the most important areas of modern sociology is the study of *how* an individual is inducted into his social groups, how he learns—or fails to learn—their values, how he acquires his various roles. This is the study of the process of socialization. Reference to it can help us understand the mechanisms by which a tradition of prejudice is passed on.

It is now universally agreed among scientists that there are no innate antipathies toward the members of different racial, national, religious, or other groups. We have to learn whom to dislike just as we learn other group norms. The baby is an iconoclast, with no respect for even the most cherished beliefs of his elders. He is dependent, however, on adults for the satisfaction of most of his needs; they are likely to reward and punish according to his orthodoxy. Sometimes a child will take quite a bit of punishment before he acquires the proper prejudices. Negro and white boys, for example, may have a common interest in a game or sport that for some time brings enough pleasure, is a strong enough drive, to outweigh the requests, threats, or punishments that the white parents bring upon their children. Prejudice is usually acquired less painfully than that. The very acquisition of language may start a child off with a mind-set favorable to the absorption of the traditions of prejudice. Some things are "white and clean," others are "dirty and black." He will hear his parents say: "That is white of you," or "He tried to jew me down." He will hear the older boys laugh uproariously about the behavior of "Rastus"; and then in some of his earliest stories and movies he will see Rastus come to life. The more serious conversations of adults that he overhears may refer to the inferiority or undesirable traits of several minority groups. They will be associated with observations of the social segregation of those groups, which, to the child, seems a confirmation of their inferiority.

These influences will be joined, even in the young child, with several of the needs discussed in Chapter 3. The need for "belonging," for

[36] See David Krech and Richard Crutchfield, *op. cit.*, pp. 466–467.

feeling secure in relation to the groups with which one is most closely identified, will be served by accepting the values of those groups. The need for aggression is strong in most children. It arises from conflict with parental discipline, with sibling rivalry, with the clashes on the playground. This, of course, does not directly produce prejudice, for the child may strike back at the parent, sibling, or playmate. If these channels are blocked, however, as they frequently are, both by the outside forces and from within (by the felt need for belonging), and the child has simultaneously learned that Negroes are inferior or that he is not to play with the children of the immigrant Italian family across the street, and that aggressions against these children are less severely punished, he easily learns to accept prejudice.

The development of prejudice begins very early. Horowitz found that most of the boys in a kindergarten, children barely five years of age, had acquired anti-Negro attitudes. In one test he asked them to select from a group of pictures the ones they liked best; in another test he asked them to show him the pictures of the boys they would like to sit next to on the streetcar, or play ball with, or swim with; and in a third test he asked them to select from pictures of various social situations (some containing only white boys, others containing both white and Negro boys) which ones they would like to join. The tests produced somewhat different results, but they all revealed a prejudice among the five-year-olds, and an increasing prejudice to the age of fourteen, which was the oldest age group studied.[37]

Using a different technique from Horowitz's, Moreno came to the conclusion that personal antipathy toward the members of other races did not begin until children were about ten years of age. Moreno, the leader of the sociometric approach to the study of human behavior, asked children what one or two other children they would most like to sit beside in class. Racial prejudice was involved in only a few cases until the fifth grade.[38] Criswell used the same technique to discover the prejudices of children in a school where 75 percent of the pupils were Negroes. She found that the white children did not begin to withdraw from the Negroes until the fourth grade and did not think of themselves as a group until the fifth. Even in the eighth grade there were many associations across the race line. It is interesting to note that the Negro children began withdrawing from the whites somewhat earlier than the white children withdrew from the Negroes, in terms of their responses to this test.[39]

[37] See Eugene L. Horowitz, in T. M. Newcomb and E. L. Hartley (eds.), op. cit., pp. 507–517.
[38] See J. L. Moreno, *Who Shall Survive?* The Beacon Press, 1934.
[39] See Joan H. Criswell, "Racial Cleavage in Negro-White Groups," *Sociometry*, 1937, vol. 1, pp. 81–89.

The differences in age at which prejudice appeared, in the studies of Horowitz and those of Moreno and Criswell, probably reflect in part the difference in measuring techniques. In one case prejudice must be defined as a response to pictures involving interracial situations; in the other case it must be defined as response to the idea of sitting next to a member of a different race. The differences may also be a result of the fact that different communities were being studied. We cannot, with the evidence at hand, state that prejudice begins precisely at age five, or six, or ten; but it is clear that after a few years of training in intergroup attitudes most children have acquired some measure of the prejudice characteristic of their group.

A person is not likely to be aware of his own categorical prejudice at an early age. Allport and Kramer asked their respondents to estimate the time when they became prejudiced. The average estimate was 12.6 years for anti-Negro and 13.7 for anti-Jewish attitudes. The great majority estimated that their prejudice began in elementary or junior high school, especially the latter; and there were some new recruits even to age twenty-two.[40] These estimates doubtless reflect the stronger and stronger pressures toward prejudice that are brought to bear on children as they grow older. With the approach of adolescence and the beginning of "dating" the line between proper and improper associates is likely to be drawn sharply and categorically by the adult society, whereas a somewhat more tolerant attitude is usually shown toward interracial or other intergroup activity of small children.

The prejudice of small children is likely to be "inconsistent"—the hierarchy of attitudes has not become well established, so that one cannot predict which value will come to the fore in a specific instance. A small child may have been taught to dislike Negroes but to like curly hair. She may then show an "inconsistency" in her prejudice by expressing liking for a curly-haired Negro.[41] Gradually the child learns which kinds of attitudes take precedence in his social group. At first he will explain his negative responses on the basis of differences between himself and the disliked person. The older child, however, will increasingly recognize the role of social pressures. If asked why he dislikes the members of a minority group, he will recite the reasons taught him by his culture, by the adults around him—always assuming, of course, that they are strictly his own reasons and that they are the true reasons. He has forgotten the punishment, the threats, the stories and jokes that have given him the prejudice. The cultural norm is now his norm; he is socialized.

[40] See Gordon Allport and B. M. Kramer, "Some Roots of Prejudice," *Journal of Psychology*, July, 1946, pp. 21–22.

[41] See Ruth Horowitz, "Racial Aspects of Self-Identification in Nursery School Children," *Journal of Psychology*, January, 1939, pp. 91–99.

Conclusion

In this chapter we have examined the role of tradition in sustaining and passing along a prejudice. The analysis of personality needs and group conflicts can go a long way toward answering the question, "Why prejudice?" but it cannot explain "Why prejudice toward this group?" The choice of a target for group hostility frequently rests upon historical conflicts that have been fixed in tradition. There can also be traditions of nonprejudice, of course, that emerge out of one group of circumstances but survive to affect others. Part of what Myrdal calls "the American creed" is a product of the French and American revolutions—times when concepts of equality were effective weapons for rallying the support of the masses to the middle class. Equality was a useful idea then. Once lodged in the democratic societies, it became fixed in tradition, supported by some institutional structures, and passed on to later generations. Many have found it an embarrassing idea that runs counter to their group or individual interests. Yet they cannot escape all of its influence over them. Some of the most extreme prejudices—belief in the subhuman nature of another race, for example—are in part a sign of an equalitarian tradition that the persons involved are having a difficult time forgetting. Such traditions are likely to be largely verbal in their influence if they are not sustained by contemporary functions, but they have some power to react back upon the society that carries them.

We have used the term "functional" to describe the sustaining force of prejudice in group conflict situations and in the service of personality needs. The term "traditional," on the other hand, carries the connotation of lacking in contemporary functions. That implication is not strictly true, for the traditional is certainly functional in the general sense of contributing to group solidarity; and it is functional for the individual to accept and act upon a tradition that will help him to identify with his group. Tradition cannot be regarded as an unimportant and powerless survival from the past, for it is thoroughly involved in the interactions of the present. One might say that personality and group needs furnish the motive power of prejudice, and that tradition is the steering wheel. But tradition is even more important than that; it is in part a motor. It may sustain prejudice as a mode of adjustment when its absence might have permitted a more satisfactory adjustment to be made.

In examining the three clusters of factors involved in prejudice, we have noted that the distinctions drawn were analytic. In virtually every case the several elements are interactive and mutually reinforcing. The use of prejudice as an economic weapon strengthens the tradition, and the presence of the tradition makes it easier to employ prejudice in

economic conflict. A stereotype facilitates projection; and having projected one's faults onto a minority group, one's belief in the stereotype
is strengthened. Moreover, every prejudicial activity tends to affect the
members of the minority group involved in such a way as to create
superficial justification for the original activity. The often baffling tenacity of prejudice, in the face of emotional and rational appeals, moral
arguments, and proof that it is against obvious self-interest, can be understood only by an appreciation of the interaction of the many forces
involved and their consequent strength. Myrdal exaggerates the ease
with which prejudice can be changed when he says that a change in any
one segment of the interacting circle will have effects on all other segments. The impulse toward change may be temporary and local; it may
be submerged by the cumulative force of the continuing factors in
prejudice. A wartime labor shortage, for example, may temporarily obscure the economic element in discrimination against minority groups
in industry, but it will not necessarily produce a long-run reduction in
prejudice. An organism is not killed by one wound; and unless the
blow that produced the wound is dealt over and over again, the organism will not be any weaker after recovery. The mutually interlocking
and sustaining forces of prejudice give it power of recovery. We do not
mean that prejudice as a cultural element cannot be reduced, but only
that it has a strength that one-factor analyses are likely to minimize.

Hence we must revise the proposition that an upward change anywhere in
the lower caste complex will tend to raise all the other conditions within it.
Instead we should say that a favorable change in any one of the distinctive
conditions will, if it can be held constant long enough, tend to raise the other
conditions and to bring about a readjustment of the whole system in conformity with the favorable change. By "long enough" we denote the period
within which the requisite habituations and reconditionings, the responses
of the group to the altered condition, are formed and established. Thus the
receipt of high wages must last long enough to be translated into a higher
standard of living and to evoke the attitudes and expectations congenial to
it. When we say that the advance must be "held constant" we mean that the
forces that brought it into being must continue in operation, aided by whatever new forces the change may evoke, in sufficient strength to resist the
assaults of resurgent opposing forces. Such assaults are indirect as well as
direct. If, for example, a new statute against discrimination has been set up
there is the danger that it will be evaded or even nullified even though it is
most unlikely that it will be actually repealed.[42]

In the light of the evidence cited in this chapter, MacIver's last point
needs careful attention. A person may experience a vigorous attack on
his prejudice—a scientific course of study or close acquaintance with
atypical (from his point of view) members of a minority group. A slight
reshuffling of some of the surface manifestations of his prejudice may

[42] R. M. MacIver, op. cit., p. 71.

be required, some new rationalizations, the granting of a few more "exceptions"; but these very changes may be a way of protecting the core of the prejudice unaltered.

Prejudice is a deep-rooted part of American culture, a vital part of the adjustment systems of most individuals, a weapon in economic and political conflict, a significant part of the stream of tradition that brings the influences of the past into the present and puts them to use in contemporary conflicts. As we turn to the study of the manifestations of prejudice, its effects, we must keep steadily in mind the complex and interlocked forces that sustain it.

The next three chapters will examine some of the consequences of prejudice, first for those against whom it is directed and then for those who use it. It is too simple to designate these consequences as effects only, with the factors we have discussed being regarded as the causes. Once established, these consequences become part of the total interaction by which prejudice is sustained, part of the total causal complex.

CHAPTER 6

The Consequences of Prejudice: The
Responses of Minority-Group Members

At several points in the preceding chapters we have noted the impossibility of distinguishing sharply between the "causes" of prejudice and discriminatory activity and the "effects" that follow from them. In a complicated interactive process an "effect," once started, may significantly influence the situation in which it is found. However, there are also differences among the various factors in the primacy of their influence. One would weaken both his scientific understanding and his moral effectiveness if he failed to see that certain behavioral aspects of prejudice and discrimination are primarily consequences, and only secondarily causes. This distinction is especially true of the behavior of minority-group members, but the same can be said for majority-group members as well, as we shall see in Chapter 8. In this chapter and the next two, therefore, we shall deal with the aspects of behavior that are primarily the results of having received, or having used, prejudice and discrimination. It must be kept clearly in mind, of course, that these responses, once set in motion, become a part of the total interaction, in an important way affecting the maintenance, the increase, or the decrease of the original "causes."

There are two closely related but distinguishable consequences of prejudice for minority-group members: the effects on the personality tendencies of the individuals involved and the effects on the structures and processes of the groups that are formed as a result of the prejudice. Our concern here is not directly with the details of the social institutions and groups which have grown up to serve minority-group members; these will receive a great deal of attention in Part II. We shall be largely concerned in this chapter and the next with the general principles of personality formation and to a small degree with the group processes and structures that underlie the specific economic, political, familial, educational, religious, and aesthetic patterns of minority groups.

Does Minority Status Affect Personality?

It is a matter of common observation that members of minority groups exhibit ways of behaving that are somewhat different from those of majority-group members. The differences are often exaggerated by the dominant group; it is assumed that they mark the minority group as inferior, and they are usually explained, if at all, by very inadequate concepts. These errors should not, however, obscure the significant differences in personality that are bound to result from the important differences in experience. It would be surprising indeed if the whole range of influences at work on the individual who is identified as a member of an "inferior" group did not produce significantly different personality tendencies from those that result from majority-group membership. It must be added, of course, that minority-group members almost always share with the other members of the society of which they are a part a great number of societal and cultural influences. Minority and majority are likely to have many more values and aspirations and behavioral tendencies in common than differences which separate them. But in a study of prejudice it is primarily the differences that count.

Members of the dominant group are likely to take these differences thoroughly for granted, assuming them to be the inevitable signs of superiority-inferiority rankings. If they offer any explanation, it is usually in terms of "natural" or "innate" factors that are simply being reflected in social differentiation. The task of an adequate sociology and social psychology dealing with this problem is to try to answer four questions.

1. What, specifically, are the differences in personality tendencies? This question cannot be answered by studying the partial and biased stereotypes that are so frequently used for "evidence." Common-sense observation may say, for example, that the Negro is more criminal. The scientific observer, however, points out the vast differentiation among Negroes (the Negro is as useless a concept as the white). In studying criminality he compares not all Negroes with all whites, but Negroes with whites of similar economic, educational, religious, and familial backgrounds (to mention only a few factors). He also asks: Does criminality mean the same thing with reference to the two groups? Does it mean the number of crimes of each type committed, or the number of arrests, or of convictions, or the number in prison? If it refers to any of the last three, is there equal chance of arrest, conviction, and serving a

full term in prison for Negro and for white? Until one knows the answers to these questions, he can scarcely speak of "personality differences." The gradually accumulating evidence permits us to speak tentatively, but with some confidence, about the personality consequences of membership in a minority group, paying full attention to the wide range of subgroupings that differentiate experience. We shall discuss that evidence later.

2. What personality tendencies of minority-group members are the result of factors that happen simply to be correlated with minority-group status but are not the direct product of that status? It would clearly be a mistake to try to explain all aspects of the behavior of Negroes, for example, by reference to the prejudice and discrimination they experience. In part their behavior tendencies are the result of influences which act upon all members of the society, thus reflecting the general pattern of social organization and disorganization. To some degree the personalities of Negroes reflect the background of rural society in which about half of them live and from which a large proportion of the other half has recently migrated. The effects of urbanization, entirely apart from prejudice, would have to be examined in order to give an accurate picture of many Negro personalities. Personality tendencies of Jews will have to be explained partly as a result of the sharing of a common tradition (which itself has been influenced by, but not created by, prejudice), partly by occupational and residential factors and other influences, *along with* the direct and indirect effects of prejudice.

Many aspects of behavior are the consequences of class status, not simply of prejudice. They are shared with fellow class members of other races and groups. Lower-class Negroes, for example, often exhibit a low degree of motivation for education; but that this is not simply a product of their race status but in part a result of their class status is shown by the similar pattern of motivation found among lower-class white children.[1] Prejudice doubtless increases the likelihood that a Negro will be a member of the lower class, and thus lies behind this personality tendency; but the class factor *per se* must also be considered. Thus, in our analysis of the personality tendencies of minority-group members we must not rest the whole explanation on prejudice and discrimination.

3. What value stands are stated or implied in the study of personality? This is an important question, because not only do the members of the dominant group assume that the behavior of the minority group is inferior but most scientific studies, while maintaining objectivity in the explanation of causes of behavior, assume the value stand of the dominant group in evaluating the results. It is almost universally assumed that to be thrifty, ambitious for job improvement, interested in

[1] See A. B. Hollingshead, *Elmtown's Youth*, John Wiley & Sons, Inc., 1949.

formal education, etc., is good, that to lack such attitudes or tendencies is bad. Such a value stand is legitimate, even for the scientist, provided it is made entirely explicit. The danger is that it will be used implicitly as "proof" of the general "inferiority" of minority-group members.

4. The fourth question is the basic one. What are the causes of observed differences in personality tendencies between members of majority and minority groups? We cannot be content with observing them or taking them for granted. In Chapter 2 we saw that a racial-biological explanation of behavioral differences was virtually useless. Not that biological factors are unimportant in personality differences, but they do not vary in any important way with race. For any differences in behavior that vary from group to group we must look to differences in experience. Explanations that rely on "natural" differences seem fairly good in a stable environment, but under conditions of mobility and culture contact they are seen to be inadequate. Under such conditions the "traits" that are supposed to characterize the members of a given group undergo a great deal of change; the "naturally lazy and ignorant" Negro peasant may become, in a city where he is given the opportunity, a typical occupationally ambitious and thrifty member of the middle class.

We have avoided the term "trait" in our discussion of personality. Unless carefully defined, it is likely to carry the connotation of a fixed and rigid aspect of personality, perhaps of an innate origin and not varying with the situation in which the person is behaving. The attempt to explain an individual's behavior by an analysis of his "traits" fails to give sufficient attention to the fact that what a person "is" cannot be defined independently of the whole situation with which he is interacting. Each person has a great many potentialities for behavior. Which ones will appear depends upon the situation, but none can appear for which there is no potentiality. As Gardner Murphy puts it: "We cannot define the situation operationally except in reference to the specific organism which is involved; we cannot define the organism operationally, in such a way as to obtain predictive power for behavior, except in reference to the situation."[2]

Such a social psychological concept may seem to be far removed from the study of prejudice, but the present authors contend that minority-majority relations can be understood only within the framework of a thoroughly adequate science of human behavior. If we look for the "traits" of members of dominant and minority groups, even accounting for them by reference to their differing experiences, we shall add a rigidity to our observations that will block understanding. Hereafter, in using the term "trait" we shall mean by it a more or less

[2] Gardner Murphy, *Personality*, Harper & Brothers, 1947, p. 891.

consistent behavior tendency manifesting itself in a more or less highly repetitive situation.

Keeping these four questions in mind, we can turn to the study of the personality consequences of prejudice and discrimination. The pioneer work of William James, James M. Baldwin, John Dewey, Jean Piaget, Charles H. Cooley, and George H. Mead has given us a great deal of insight into the way a child acquires basic attitudes toward himself, toward the norms of the groups of which he is a member and the norms of the larger society, and toward those in authority over him. These aspects of personality are the results of his experiences with others, the ways they define his roles for him, the ways in which they encourage him (by their behavior toward him) to look at himself—all conditioned, of course, by his particular inherited tendencies and previous experiences. Even the way one looks upon himself is a product of his social experiences. In Cooley's classic phrase, we have a "looking-glass self," compounded of others' reactions to us, our interpretation of those reactions, and a response to the interpretation. Or, as George Herbert Mead put it, we know ourselves only by "taking the role of the other," by reacting to ourselves as we imagine others react toward us. In time we learn to take the role of the "generalized other"—the norms of society and the groups with which we are associated. We come to see ourselves in the light of these norms.

It is clear that such a process is significantly different for the members of a minority group from what it is for members of a dominant group. In American society a high proportion of non-Caucasian children come to see themselves, at an early age, as somehow different from white children—unable to do certain things, to go certain places, rebuffed by words and violence. From early childhood to death minority-group members are likely to experience a long series of events, from exclusion from play groups and cliques to violence and the threat of violence, that are far less likely to be experienced by the average member of the majority group. Not all of the experiences of the low-status person are necessarily "bad" or unfortunate from the point of view of generally accepted values. He may have a more permissive and relaxed play environment or, in some situations, less sharply competitive group associations. Moreover, his difficulties may lead to achievement, to a kind of "challenge-response" situation, to use Arnold Toynbee's phrase. Some of the notable contributions of minority-group members, to art, to religion, to science, may have been achieved because of their difficulties, not simply in spite of them. The artistry of a Marian Anderson, the insight of a Richard Wright, the brilliance of an Albert Einstein can partially be explained in this way. A marginal role can lead to understanding; suffering can produce personal warmth and regard for others. Such results, however, are probably not the most common and most important. The great weight of prejudice and discrimination often cramps and distorts the personality development of the minority-group member. Many of his experiences, varying with several factors that we shall note, put him into disorganizing conflict situations and cause him, to an important degree, to be at odds with himself.

Richard Wright puts the matter sharply:

William James, in discussing the way in which the "social self" of man exists in society says, ". . . a man has as many social selves as there are individuals who recognize him and carry an image of him in their minds." Then, in speculating upon what a man would feel if he were completely socially excluded, he says, "No more fiendish punishment could be devised, were such a thing physically possible, than that one should be turned loose in society and remain absolutely unnoticed by all the members thereof. If no one turned round when we entered, answered when we spoke, or minded what we did, but if every person we met 'cut us dead,' and acted as if we were non-existent things, a kind of rage and impotent despair would ere long well up in us, from which the cruelest bodily tortures would be a relief; for these would make us feel that, however bad might be our plight, we had not sunk to such a depth as to be unworthy of attention at all."

There can be, of course, no such thing as *complete* rejection of anybody by society; for, even in rejecting him, society must notice him. But the American Negro has come as near being the victim of complete rejection as our society has been able to work out, for the dehumanized image of the Negro which white Americans carry in their minds, the anti-Negro epithets continuously on their lips, exclude the contemporary Negro as truly as though he were kept in a steel prison, and doom even those Negroes who are as yet unborn.[3]

This statement does not give sufficient attention to the crucial importance, for personality formation, of the small groups within which so much of one's activities takes place, but it points to a major difference in experience between Negro and white in American society.

Variables That Affect the Responses of Minority-Group Members

Before turning to specific personality consequences of prejudice and discrimination, we must make careful note of the many variables which affect the nature of the experience for a minority-group member. We shall draw chiefly upon studies of the American Negro, for the evidence is more extensive than for perhaps any other minority; but the same need for subclassifying, on the basis of several factors, applies to any minority group. Both the amount and type of prejudice and discrimination and the *meaning* of them for members of the minority groups will vary according to such factors as these: nature of parental advice

[3] From the introduction to *Black Metropolis* by St. Clair Drake and Horace Cayton, Harcourt, Brace & Company, 1945, pp. xxxii–xxxiii.

and training with regard to the dominant group; level of education; income; occupational status; temperament of the individual; amount of minority-group cohesiveness and solidarity; nature of the minority-majority contact (contrast the experience of the north European immigrant, for example, with that of the American Indian in terms of the kinds of contact they had with the dominant group); region of the country; nature of surrounding group support or opposition to prejudice; age; extent of experience with other intergroup patterns (for example, the Jamaican-born Negro in Harlem will see the situation very differently from the way the native-born New Yorker sees it, and to both it will look different from the way the migrant from Georgia sees it); color variations *within* the minority group (there is ample evidence that a light-skinned Negro and a dark-skinned Negro have, in many ways, significantly different experiences).

In our discussion of personality consequences of prejudice we must keep constantly in mind the ways in which these variables, and others, affect the nature of the experience of the minority-group member. We cannot, of course, discuss every possible combination, for even with subdivision on the basis of only five or six variables there would be hundreds of subgroups. Warner, Junker, and Adams, in a study of the effects of minority-group status on the personality development of Negro youth in Chicago, distinguished their group on the basis of three criteria only—yet they had to examine thirty-two "types." Their basic hypothesis was that systematic subordination of Negroes to whites has a definite effect on the development of the personalities of the Negroes. But corollary hypotheses were that the effect was different for men and for women; that the evaluation of color and other physical traits made by Negroes themselves conditioned the effect; and that social-class position and occupational status in Negro society affect the nature of the influence. Having differentiated four social-class positions and four color categories, they had thirty-two types for analysis:[4]

Men	Women
I. Upper class	I. Upper class
1. Passable	5. Passable
2. Lightskin	6. Lightskin
3. Brownskin	7. Brownskin
4. Darkskin	8. Darkskin
II. Upper middle class	II. Upper middle class
9. Passable	13. Passable
10. Lightskin	14. Lightskin
11. Brownskin	15. Brownskin
12. Darkskin	16. Darkskin

[4] See W. Lloyd Warner, B. H. Junker, and W. A. Adams, *Color and Human Nature, Negro Personality Development in a Northern City*, American Council on Education, 1941, p. 26.

Men	Women
III. Lower middle class	III. Lower middle class
17. Passable	21. Passable
18. Lightskin	22. Lightskin
19. Brownskin	23. Brownskin
20. Darkskin	24. Darkskin
IV. Lower class	IV. Lower class
25. Passable	29. Passable
26. Lightskin	30. Lightskin
27. Brownskin	31. Brownskin
28. Darkskin	32. Darkskin

Within these types informal refinements were made on the basis of other characteristics—education, birthplace, number of years in Chicago, and others. As Warner, Junker, and Adams explain the process:

> Our hypothetical types served as a set of sieves, the purpose of which was to bring together for analysis those individuals who are similar in social experience and to distinguish them from other individuals of different background. Using a sieve of fine mesh, a type based on numerous characteristics, we could compare two individuals of almost identical social personality for individual psychological differences. At the same time it was thought desirable to use the coarser mesh of fewer criteria so as to bring together a larger number of individuals under one classification and develop generalizations of wider reference and greater meaning for the problem with which we began. . . .
>
> In general . . . social position carries with it certain experiences, attitudes, and activities not shared by people at other levels, which do modify self-evaluation and general outlook on life. Within social position, furthermore, experiences will differ for men and women and for individuals of different skin color. It therefore seems valid and useful to talk of a person's social personality; meaning that part of his make-up which is contributed by the society in which he lives and moves and which he shares in large measure with all other persons living under the same conditions. This social personality is obviously different from his personal temperament or psychological individuality, which is developed by another set of factors entirely.[5]

Although we shall not, in our discussion, develop a system of "social personality types," we shall make frequent reference to the different effects of prejudice on persons who play different social roles. The following questions will be raised: What are the effects of prejudice in encouraging members of minority groups to accept the dominant pattern of motivation and morality? How does prejudice affect attitudes toward oneself and one's own group? What are the various kinds of responses that can be made to a situation filled with prejudice and discrimination? These questions can best be examined against the background of some illustrative experiences.

[5] *Ibid.*, pp. 25–27.

Richard Wright, in the autobiography of his boyhood, describes his feelings as he goes to work as a servant in a white household in Mississippi:

What would happen now that I would be among white people for hours at a stretch? Would they hit me? Curse me? If they did, I would leave at once. In all my wishing for a job I had not thought of how I would be treated, and now it loomed important, decisive, sweeping down beneath every other consideration. I would be polite, humble, saying yes sir and no sir, yes ma'am and no ma'am, but I would draw a line over which they must not step. Oh, maybe I'm just thinking up trouble, I told myself. They might like me. . . .

The next morning I chopped wood for the cook stove, lugged in scuttles of coal for the grates, washed the front porch and swept the back porch, swept the kitchen, helped wait on the table, and washed the dishes. I was sweating. I swept the front walk and ran to the store to shop. When I returned the woman said:

"Your breakfast is in the kitchen."

"Thank you, ma'am."

I saw a plate of thick, black molasses and a hunk of white bread on the table. Would I get no more than this? They had had eggs, bacon, coffee. . . . I picked up the bread and tried to break it; it was stale and hard. Well, I would drink the molasses. I lifted the plate and brought it to my lips and saw floating on the surface of the black liquid green and white bits of mold. Goddam . . . I can't eat this, I told myself. The food was not even clean. The woman came into the kitchen as I was putting on my coat.

"You didn't eat," she said.

"No, ma'am," I said. "I'm not hungry."

"You'll eat at home?" she asked hopefully.

"Well, I just wasn't hungry this morning, ma'am," I lied.

"You don't like molasses and bread," she said dramatically.

"Oh, yes, ma'am, I do," I defended myself quickly, not wanting her to think that I dared criticize what she had given me.

"I don't know what's happening to you niggers nowadays," she sighed, wagging her head. She looked closely at the molasses, "It's a sin to throw out molasses like that. I'll put it up for you this evening."

"Yes, ma'am," I said heartily.

Neatly she covered the plate of molasses with another plate, then felt the bread and dumped it into the garbage. She turned to me, her face lit with an idea.

"What grade are you in school?"

"Seventh, ma'am."

"Then why are you going to school?" she asked in surprise.

"Well, I want to be a writer," I mumbled, unsure of myself; I had not planned to tell her that, but she had made me feel so utterly wrong and of no account that I needed to bolster myself.

"A what?" she demanded.

"A writer," I mumbled.

"For what?"

"To write stories," I mumbled defensively.

"You'll never be a writer," she said. "Who on earth put such ideas into your nigger head?"

"Nobody," I said.

"I didn't think anybody ever would," she declared indignantly.

As I walked around her house to the street, I knew that I would not go back. The woman had assaulted my ego; she had assumed that she knew my place in life, what I felt, what I ought to be, and I resented it with all my heart. Perhaps she was right; perhaps I would never be a writer; but I did not want her to say so.[6]

In another incident Richard Wright illustrates the violence which is a part of the pattern of life that many Negroes experience at the hands of whites. The situation demonstrates some of the functions of prejudice for members of the dominant group as well as some of the personality consequences for the object of their attack. Wright has applied for a job at a small firm that manufactures optical instruments. The owner is a native of Illinois who has migrated to Mississippi.

Mr. Crane called me to his desk and questioned me closely about my schooling, about how much mathematics I had had. He seemed pleased when I told him that I had had two years of algebra.

"How would you like to learn this trade?" he asked.

"I'd like it fine, sir. I'd like nothing better," I said.

He told me that he wanted to train a Negro boy in the optical trade; he wanted to help him, guide him. I tried to answer in a way that would let him know that I would try to be worthy of what he was doing. He took me to the stenographer and said:

"This is Richard. He's going to be with us."

He then led me into the rear room of the office, which turned out to be a tiny factory filled with many strange machines smeared with red dust.

"Reynolds," he said to a young white man, "this is Richard."

"What you saying there, boy!" Reynolds grinned and boomed at me.

Mr. Crane took me to the older man.

Pease looked at me and nodded. Mr. Crane then held forth to the two white men about my duties; he told them to break me in gradually to the workings of the shop, to instruct me in the mechanics of grinding and polishing lenses. They nodded their assent.

"Now, boy, let's see how clean you can get this place," Mr. Crane said.

"Yes, sir."

I swept, mopped, dusted, and soon had the office and the shop clean. In the afternoons, when I had caught up with my work, I ran errands. In an idle moment I would stand and watch the two white men grinding lenses on the machines. They said nothing to me and I said nothing to them. The first day passed, the second, the third, a week passed and I received my five dollars. A month passed. But I was not learning anything and nobody had

[6] Reprinted from *Black Boy* by Richard Wright, pp. 128–129, by permission of Harper & Brothers. Copyright 1937 by Harper & Brothers.

volunteered to help me. One afternoon I walked up to Reynolds and asked him to tell me about the work.

"What are you trying to do, get smart, nigger?" he asked me.

"No, sir," I said.

I was baffled. Perhaps he just did not want to help me. I went to Pease, reminding him that the boss had said that I was to be given a chance to learn the trade.

"Nigger, you think you're white, don't you?"

"No, sir."

"You're acting mighty like it," he said.

"I was only doing what the boss told me to do," I said.

Pease shook his fist in my face.

"This is a white man's work around here," he said.

From then on they changed toward me; they said good morning no more. When I was just a bit slow in performing some duty, I was called a lazy black sonofabitch. I kept silent, striving to offer no excuse for worsening of relations. But one day Reynolds called me to his machine.

"Nigger, you think you'll ever amount to anything?" he asked in a slow, sadistic voice.

"I don't know, sir," I answered, turning my head away.

"What do niggers think about?" he asked.

"I don't know, sir," I said, my head still averted.

"If I was a nigger, I'd kill myself," he said.

I said nothing. I was angry.

"You know why?" he asked.

I still said nothing.

"But I don't reckon niggers mind being niggers," he said suddenly and laughed.

I ignored him. Mr. Pease was watching me closely; then I saw them exchange glances. My job was not leading to what Mr. Crane had said it would. I had been humble, and now I was reaping the wages of humility.

"Come here, boy," Pease said.

I walked to his bench.

"You didn't like what Reynolds just said, did you?" he asked.

"Oh, it's all right," I said smiling.

"You didn't like it. I could see it on your face," he said.

I stared at him and backed away.

"Did you ever get into any trouble?" he asked.

"No, sir."

"What would you do if you got into trouble?"

"I don't know, sir."

"Well, watch yourself and don't get into trouble," he warned.

I wanted to report these clashes to Mr. Crane, but the thought of what Pease or Reynolds would do to me if they learned that I had "snitched" stopped me. I worked through the days and tried to hide my resentment under a nervous, cryptic smile.

The climax came at noon one summer day. Pease called me to his workbench; to get to him I had to go between two narrow benches and stand with my back against a wall,

"Richard, I want to ask you something," Pease began pleasantly, not looking up from his work.

"Yes, sir."

Reynolds came over and stood blocking the narrow passage between the benches; he folded his arms and stared at me solemnly. I looked from one to the other, sensing trouble. Pease looked up and spoke slowly so there would be no possibility of my not understanding.

"Richard, Reynolds here tells me that you called me Pease," he said.

I stiffened. A void opened up in me. I knew that this was the showdown. He meant that I had failed to call him Mr. Pease. I looked at Reynolds; he was gripping a steel bar in his hand. I opened my mouth to speak, to protest, to assure Pease that I had never called him simply Pease, and that I had never had any intention of doing so, when Reynolds grabbed me by the collar, ramming my head against a wall.

"Now, be careful, nigger," snarled Reynolds, baring his teeth. "I heard you call 'im Pease. And if you say you didn't you're calling me a liar, see?" He waved the steel bar threateningly.

If I had said: No, sir, Mr. Pease, I never called you Pease, I would by inference have been calling Reynolds a liar; and if I had said: Yes, sir, Mr. Pease, I called you Pease, I would have been pleading guilty to the worst insult that a Negro can offer to a southern white man. I stood trying to think of a neutral course that would resolve this quickly risen nightmare, but my tongue would not move.

"Richard, I asked you a question!" Pease said. Anger was creeping into his voice.

"I don't remember calling you Pease, Mr. Pease," I said cautiously. "And if I did, I sure didn't mean . . ."

"You black sonofabitch! You called me Pease, then!" he spat, rising and slapping me till I bent sideways over a bench.

Reynolds was up on top of me demanding:

"Didn't you call him Pease? If you say you didn't, I'll rip your gut string loose with this f-k-g bar, you black granny dodger! You can't call a white man a liar and get away with it!"

I wilted. I begged them not to hit me. I knew what they wanted. They wanted me to leave the job.

"I'll leave," I promised. "I'll leave right now!"

They gave me a minute to get out of the factory, and warned me not to show up again or tell the boss. Reynolds loosened his hand on my collar and I ducked out of the room. . . .

For weeks after that I could not believe in my feelings. My personality was numb, reduced to a lumpish, loose, dissolved state. I was a non-man, something that knew vaguely that it was human but felt that it was not. As time separated me from the experience, I could feel no hate for the men who had driven me from the job. They did not seem to be individual men, but part of a huge, implacable, elemental design toward which hate was futile. What I did feel was a longing to attack. But how? And because I knew of no way to grapple with this thing, I felt doubly cast out.

I went to bed tired and got up tired, though I was having no physical exercise. During the day I overreacted to each event, my banked emotions spilling around it. I refused to talk to anyone about my affairs, because I knew that I would only hear a justification of the ways of the white folks and I did not want to hear it. I lived carrying a huge wound, tender, festering, and I shrank when I came near anything that I thought would touch it.[7]

Such clear-cut cases of discrimination are perhaps more the exception than the rule. Much more common is the continuous flow of small incidents, the segregation, the closed doors and blocked opportunities that give the person to understand that he belongs to an "inferior" group. As Fineberg says, the man who had the capacity to become an excellent surgeon, but instead spends his life in a butcher shop because of anti-Jewish quotas in colleges and medical schools, "has been injured economically, socially, and psychically immeasurably more than he could have been by anything less than a paralyzing beating. . . . The most seriously injured victim of intolerance is not necessarily the one who has been reviled by bigots or buffeted by a gang of bullies. The most criminal injuries are inflicted on Victimians who daily travel a thornier path, whose hourly lot is much harder, whose opportunities for a happy and satisfying life are sharply reduced because prejudice has clamped a yoke on their necks—has, indeed, determined their fate and their status before their birth."[8]

Margaret Halsey reports one of the "run-of-the-mill" experiences that are part of the life of every minority-group member. She is describing an incident at the New York Stagedoor Canteen during World War II: "One of the Junior Hostesses on my shift was a very light Negro girl, just out of college, who had an ethereal, Madonna-like beauty and a character to match. She was, and still is, one of the sweetest and most rewarding human beings I have ever known. One night a white serviceman asked her to dance, and when he got her out on the floor, where the light was stronger, he said, 'My God, a nigger!' and walked away, leaving her standing alone among the dancers."[9]

The world of the minority-group member is shaped not only by such individual experiences but also by group responses that are passed along in the stream of culture. The experiences of one's parents and grandparents are built into their personalities, shaping their responses to their children and affecting the kinds of advice or unconsciously chosen influences they furnish to the growing generation. Fear and insecurity and hostility are thus to some degree cumulative. A terrifying experience for one Negro affects many others, in different times and places. The personality tendencies of contemporary Jews are affected to some degree by the accumulated experiences of preceding generations.

---

[7] Reprinted from *Black Boy* by Richard Wright, pp. 163–170, by permission of Harper & Brothers. Copyright 1937 by Harper & Brothers.

[8] S. A. Fineberg, *Punishment Without Crime*, Doubleday & Company, Inc., 1949, p. 56.

[9] Margaret Halsey, *Color Blind*, Simon and Schuster, Inc., 1946, p. 115.

Responding to the Culture of the Dominant Group

How do such circumstances affect the likelihood that a member of a minority group will become thoroughly assimilated to the dominant culture? Will he take on the pattern of motivation and morality that the majority group considers right? We have seen that prejudiced persons often justify their attitudes and actions by reference to the inferior behavior and ideals of the members of the minority group. Is that inferiority—in terms of the standards of the dominant group—in a significant way the very product of prejudice and discrimination? Sutherland points out that there are many minority-group members who have never experienced "the American dream." They have never known a society composed largely of respectable, law-abiding, industrious families whose ambition and self-discipline were rewarded by a comfortable house, improved status, or a better job. A child is responsive to the rewards and punishments of his immediate environment, his family, his clique, his community. Behavior patterns which bring social approval and satisfaction from these groups are adopted very early. Only slightly does one strive for patterns of action that are approved by "society in general."

Ambition is not an automatic yearning for improvement; it is a social product. Youth who are responsive to the middle-class requirements for ambitious striving in their occupation, for conventional morality in family relations, and for the other sorts of behavior commonly attributed to middle-class culture, follow these patterns only if their first efforts to do so have brought approval, and if contrary conduct has brought disapproval or punishment. The Negro youth who has acquired what the established community considers the "better ways of living" has done so because he has been permitted to share . . . in the rewards for such conduct.[10]

Many white children and youth, of course, are also blocked from effective understanding or sharing of "the American dream"—with many of the same personality results. There are areas in our large cities where jackrolling and shoplifting are far more normal than school attendance and Boy Scouts. Children respond to the patterns of behavior and motivations of their immediate surroundings. The restrictions and barriers to social interaction between members of different classes help to maintain fairly well-defined subcultures, with important behavioral differences among them. It is well to remember that many of the personality tendencies of minority-group members are the product of their class status, and not specifically of their racial or national status. Prejudice, of course, is often involved in determining a person's class status,

[10] Robert L. Sutherland, *Color, Class, and Personality*, American Council on Education, 1942, pp. 22–23.

be it prejudice against one's race, nationality, religion, or even against the class status of one's parents, as this has affected the style of life, the motivations, the mode of speech, the appearance, etc., of the children.

CLASS AND PERSONALITY

We cannot undertake here a systematic analysis of the relationship between class and personality; but a brief statement will help in understanding many tendencies of minority-group members who, because of prejudice, make up a significantly high proportion of the lower class. Even a quick survey of social classes as learning environments will show that what is rewarding to the middle-class child may not be at all rewarding to the child brought up in a lower-class environment. What the two children fear, crave, work for, and fight for will vary significantly, despite their common membership in a larger society. "The usual parent in each social class is preparing his child for the kind of life (the types of manners, of work, of sexual controls, and of education) which is approved and desired by that social class."[11] The middle-class parent will begin early to develop a respect for cleanliness, for property, for sexual control, for achievement. Aggressive behavior on the part of the middle-class child is sharply curtailed. His daily schedule is more rigidly supervised, and his training is more systematic and complex—to equip him for the more highly skilled and complex world into which he will go. He is given an anxiety to achieve—an anxiety which motivates him but which, if transferred clumsily, can disorganize and confuse him.

In workingclass families, however, the child learns to seek other pleasures and to want other types of prestige. Growing up in the street-culture of blighted areas, living in tenements and kitchenettes, the children of our white and colored slums learn a characteristic pattern of ambitions, of pleasures, and habits. From their earliest days, as contrasted with middle-class infants, they usually gain more organic pleasure from life. First, they are not severely restricted to a schedule of nursings, as is the middleclass baby. They stand less chance, therefore, of going hungry. Second, they usually are nursed at the breast, and therefore have a closer, more indulgent relation to the mother. Third, they usually have the run of the house, and are not punished for marring the furniture. Fourth, their organic needs for micturition and defecation are brought under control more slowly and leniently. Thus, the child in workingclass families is allowed a *deeper physical enjoyment of his body* during his first three or four years than is the middleclass child.

Not only is his organic life expressed more directly. His basic *psychological* responses are also less frustrated. He is allowed to fight when he is angry, and to laugh when he is triumphant. Frequently he fights even his brothers and

[11] Allison W. Davis and Robert J. Havighurst, *Father of the Man. How Your Child Gets His Personality*, Houghton Mifflin Company, 1947, p. 24.

sisters (he does not have to accept the "false peace" between brothers which middleclass parents severely impose). Physical aggression is regarded as normal. Because fighting is common both in his family and in his neighborhood, he learns to take a blow and to give one.

His parents themselves believe that whippings are the normal way of controlling a child (or a wife). Thus he gets his thrashings regularly and learns not to fear them. Because his punishment is chiefly *physical*, he is spared the constant attacks of prolonged guilt, and the fears of losing parental love, which middleclass parents continually seek to arouse, and to maintain over long periods, in training their children. The poor workingclass child also has his share of fear and worry, however. His family is more often struck by disease and by separation. Their chronic poverty breeds fear of eviction, and of homelessness, and the most constant of all his fears, that of starvation. On the other hand, his family and his gang teach him not to be afraid of a fight, not to be intimidated by the teachers and the police, and not to fear injury or death as keenly as your child. The child in workingclass families, that is, is less stimulated *by his culture to be fearful and guilty.*[12]

This statement properly emphasizes the differences between the experiences of a child brought up in one class environment and those of a child brought up in another. It needs to be qualified, however, in several ways. Other variables may offset or enhance the class factor in personality. Moreover, individual families within each class will vary widely from the patterns described. It should be pointed out also that much of the literature dealing with the subject of class influences on personality carries, usually implicitly, one or the other of two very different value positions. The first is a middle-class bias. The author may treat sympathetically the causes of the personality tendencies of lower-class people but hold them to be, nevertheless, unfortunate or bad. The lack of personal ambition, of a sense of property, of motivation for education, etc., is in this view the mark of an inferior person. The other bias, illustrated fairly clearly by the quotation from Davis and Havighurst, is basically Freudian. The writers who take this view assume that scheduling, inhibitions on the activities of the child, particularly the infant, the restriction of aggression, and the like may well lead to disorganizing tensions. The assumption that an uninhibited, easygoing socialization process, as contrasted with a child-training procedure that emphasizes schedules and discipline, produces less anxiety and lower feelings of aggression is far from established as a theory. The task of the scientist in dealing with this issue is to draw a clear distinction between the question of values and the problem of causes. He then can say: If

---

[12] *Ibid.*, pp. 25–26; see also Martha C. Ericson, "Child-Rearing and Social Status," *American Journal of Sociology*, November, 1946, pp. 190–192; Bernard C. Rosen, "The Achievement Syndrome," *American Sociological Review*, April, 1956, pp. 203–211; and Louis Schneider and Sverre Lysgaard, "The Deferred Gratification Pattern," *American Sociological Review*, April, 1953, pp. 142–149.

this is the value, the personality tendency that you want to produce, these are the ways most likely to achieve it.

This discussion of the relation between class status and personality is important for the understanding of the consequences of prejudice because, as we have indicated, prejudice is a significant factor in the determination of class status. While noting the valuational and theoretical biases in studying this problem, we should not fail to see the widespread agreement on the importance of the class structure in creating significantly different learning environments for children in different class locations. If a Negro from the rural peasantry or the city slums is, from the point of view of the dominant society, careless, without ambition, immoral, or criminal, the causes are to be sought in the personality-forming conditions which he has experienced.

In the customs governing sex behavior, the isolation of Negroes from the general culture is easily observable. It is one thing to know what the accepted standards are and then to violate them—such infringements are not uncommon in any class—but it is quite another thing to have no conception of such standards. In a group of ten boys in Chicago, all separated from their own parents and living a foot-loose existence, the investigator found an almost complete absence of inhibition in their reporting of sex relations. These boys were not "naturally" immoral because they were Negroes, as white judgments so often indicate, they merely had never known other standards. They reported their sex behavior, which a middle-class schoolteacher would condemn as immoral, as freely and unemotionally as they did their employment records or their love of swimming. With them some forms of sex behavior were taboo, and they had received some warnings and instructions from friends, but their sex behavior would indicate that they were thoroughly isolated from accepted middle-class standards.[13]

To "explain" or judge the behavior of the adult without a thorough understanding of the experiences of the child is clearly to miss the basic causes. If the dominant elements in American society—or any other society—isolate a segment of the people from contact with the prevailing norms and prevent them from sharing in any of the rewards which may follow from abiding by those norms, they should not be surprised at the appearance of a subculture with very different standards of conduct and motivations.

BARRIERS TO THE AMERICAN DREAM

It would be a mistake, of course, to exaggerate the extent of "isolation from the American dream." Charles Johnson found among Negroes in the black belt high occupational ambitions, frequent desire to escape the drudgery of sharecropping, dreams of migration. Most of the

[13] Robert L. Sutherland, *op. cit.*, pp. 36–37.

occupational desires were escape "fantasies," considering the realities of their status, but they represent some penetration of the dominant American ideas of social mobility. Johnson also noted that peasant Negroes were not without ambition for education: "The results of our study indicate that the presumed practical values of education have become a motivating force for both parents and children to a remarkable degree, even in the plantation areas."[14] Literacy, they realize, may help to protect them against fraud and is regarded as a means of escape from an unpleasant job.

It is also pointed out by Frazier that some Negro families—mostly early "free Negro" families—have accepted the sex mores of the dominant group. He calls them "The Black Puritans." The growing numbers of middle-class Negroes also hold to standard middle-class values. A great many Negroes, however, have not shared thoroughly in the predominant ideas of sexual morality. Slavery, Reconstruction, mobility, low socioeconomic status, residence in urban slums, etc., have been factors in a significantly different experience, with inevitable differences in standards and behavior.[15]

A somewhat different cluster of personality tendencies is seen among minority-group members who are less isolated from the dominant culture. Although some Negroes have scarcely encountered the "American dream," many more have come in contact with it in school, in church, in movies and magazines. Its promises, however, have little relationship to their own lives, with consequent disillusionment and frustration. This sharp contrast between promise and fulfillment is a highly important factor in the development of personality tendencies of minority-group members (as, indeed, it is to a lesser degree in the development of the great majority of dominant-group members, who are taught to aspire to goals that few will reach). Examine the experience of Harry X, a Negro boy discussed by Sutherland. While in school in a small northern town he felt the friendship of the leading citizens. His home life was limited by low income, but it was similar to the pattern found generally in the town. When Harry finished high school, however, he found no job as clerk in a store, or bookkeeper, or on the town paper. He was limited to the role of bootblack or janitor. His high aspirations, which had been encouraged by the honors he received in high school, had to be toned down sharply. He began to grow embittered, to develop compensatory tendencies in his behavior. Instead of going on to higher education, which was open to him, he assumed that the world was against him, and developed skills in excusing himself from any responsibility. He became distrustful of all whites, including his former friends, and reacted strongly to any criticism as proof of race

[14] Charles S. Johnson, Growing Up in the Black Belt, American Council on Education, 1941, pp. 114–115.

[15] See E. Franklin Frazier, The Negro Family in the United States, The Citadel Press, rev. ed., 1948.

prejudice. To make a living he engaged in many illegal activities wholly out of line with his former life.[16]

It is exceedingly unlikely that one would find the patterns of behavior and motivation of the dominant community in the personality of a person thus torn by promise and hope and then frustration. A person could scarcely escape confusion when a service club would help him to complete his high-school course—and then its members would refuse to give him a job after his schooling was over. Harry A. Overstreet, in commenting on this story, says:

I doubt . . . that any white person would be presumptuous enough to cast the first advice by telling Harry how he might gracefully have turned the other cheek to the community's slap-in-the-face and become a docile bootblack or janitor; or to indicate to him that, while "from bootblack to president" is the possible route for the white boy, "from high school gradu- ate to bootblack" is the justifiable direction for the colored boy.

Or the objection might be made that this Northern community should never, in the first place, have made Harry aware of the promises contained in the American Dream. The school should not have urged him, hand on heart, to recite: "With liberty and justice for all." It should, in all caution, have provided a revised version: "With liberty and justice for all except Negroes and other colored folk."[17]

Harry X and his thousands of counterparts throughout the "liberal North" are likely to be seen by the adult white community not as products of these frustrating and discriminatory experiences, but sim- ply for what they are—with little or no analysis of causes, no time di- mension in their understanding, no conception of the fact that the child is father to the man.

"To all appearances he is irresponsible; 'uppity'; ugly of temper; with- out ambition; always shifting the blame for his failures on someone else; engaged in illegal activities. The white man sees him thus; sees the surface manifestations of him; and the white man says: 'Bad nig- ger!' . . . The white man finds all the traditional stereotypes fulfilled in Harry's behavior. 'It only goes to show,' he probably says. 'Give these niggers education and it only makes them worse!' "[18]

Were members of the white community to examine the whole case of Harry X, they would find that their own behavior and the structure of race relations which they help to maintain were important factors in his behavior. A white man making a thorough study of Harry's person- ality ". . . would see him as a deeply wounded Negro boy unable to make his recovery among alien people who, strange to say, are not even aware that he has been wounded. He would see him building compen- satory defenses for himself, precisely as would any other person, white

[16] See Robert L. Sutherland, op. cit., pp. 32–33.
[17] Harry A. Overstreet, "Racial Attitudes of the 'Liberal' North," Saturday Review of Literature, March 31, 1945, p. 8.
[18] Ibid.

or black, who had been shocked into a neurosis. He might even be astonished at the tough, defiant resiliency of the boy."[19]

Members of a dominant group frequently charge that minority-group members are lacking in any sense of responsibility, any ability to look ahead, to make the temporary sacrifices necessary for later success. (As we shall see later, the charges against minority groups whose activities obviously contradict this picture—for example, the Jews—are of a different order.) Aside from the categorical nature of the charge, it probably represents a partially correct, if superficial, observation. "It can hardly be denied that the prospect of eventually securing a job that is both enjoyable and remunerative supplies a tremendous motive for putting forth effort and developing personality traits that will enhance one's chances in the pursuit of a career. Conversely, lack of any real hope may easily result in careless indifference. When the cards seem stacked against one, there is all the more incentive for him to get what he can out of the passing moment."[20] A child is not nearly so likely to be impressed by a general ideology that "anybody who really wants to can get ahead in America" as he is by the circumstances of people with whom he has direct contact. America is witnessing a slowly increasing Negro middle class. The results of this growth—if the objective situation continues to permit it—will be cumulative, for each person who is able to change his class status will be an illustration, to many more, of the specific gains to be made from the effort and discipline that a more skilled job requires.

When Boyd matched 25 Negro and white children in Portland, Oregon, for I.Q., economic status of parents, and age, and tested them for "level of aspiration," he found that the Negro children had the higher scores. They were given arithmetic and target tests, then asked to state their expected scores on the next tests. The Negro children anticipated larger gains. They also had somewhat higher occupational hopes and wanted more foreign travel; when asked to select the "greatest person in the world" and "the person to be like," 24 out of the 28 mentioned by Negro children were Negroes.[21] Thus when backgrounds are similar, the differences between Negro and white children in hope and pride disappear, or are even reversed. There are still, however, far too many illustrations of blocked roads, of unrewarded effort, of promise followed by frustration, as in the case of Harry X, to allow us to expect a rapid adoption of middle-class motivational patterns by suppressed minorities.

[19] *Ibid.*

[20] D. W. Wyatt, in J. H. Atwood, D. W. Wyatt, V. J. Davis, and I. D. Walker, *Thus Be Their Destiny*, American Council on Education, 1941, p. 13.

[21] George F. Boyd, "The Levels of Aspiration of White and Negro Children in a Non-Segregated Elementary School," *Journal of Social Psychology*, November, 1952, pp. 191–196.

One of the consequences of knowing and sharing but being blocked from full participation in the "American dream" is the ambivalent attitudes that oppressed persons get toward the nation and its laws. It is impossible for them to give full allegiance to a society which itself has not fully accepted them. When Americans of Japanese ancestry were forcibly evacuated from the west coast in 1942, doubts were inevitably raised in their minds about the sincerity of America's democracy. The Issei (those born in Japan, and therefore unable to become citizens) were particularly disillusioned and frustrated. Leighton says of those who came to Poston (one of the relocation camps): "The Isseis came to Poston with feelings of a life's work wasted, bitterness, apathy, and fear, shot through with the conviction that there was no future in America for the Japanese. As for democratic principles and form of government, they thought that had proved a failure."[22] One would scarcely expect the Issei to show unalloyed enthusiasm for a nation which refused them citizenship and discriminated against them so drastically. (Despite their resentment, the great majority of Japanese-Americans supported the United States, and the Nisei, who are citizens, gave the nation unflinching support.)

The responses of Japanese-Americans to relocation illustrate again not only some of the personality-forming conditions for minority-group members, but the general social psychological theory that personality is a function of situations and tendencies in interaction, not of fixed "traits." The evacuation meant financial disaster to most of the Japanese-Americans; self-government in the camps was limited; salary schedules ranged from $12 to $19 a month; the first-generation Japanese were defined as enemy aliens. In this context, in January, 1943, all residents of the relocation centers over sixteen years of age were required to declare their loyalty or disloyalty to the United States. Six thousand Japanese-Americans answered "no" to the loyalty question. Grodzins indicates very clearly the ways in which discrimination affected these results. A declaration of disloyalty was a protest: "We have citizenship and still we are . . . treated just like aliens. So what's the use of talking about citizenship and being loyal citizens?" It was also an indication of family loyalty, an expression of the identity of the Nisei with their alien parents who were not permitted to become citizens and had suffered great economic loss. A declaration of disloyalty was an attempt to find security in a situation that was very threatening.[23] It is important to note that there were great differences in the percentage of people in

[22] Alexander Leighton, The Governing of Men, Princeton University Press, 1945, p. 71.
[23] For a discussion of these and other factors involved in the declarations of disloyalty, see Morton Grodzins, "Making Un-Americans," American Journal of Sociology, May, 1955, pp. 570–582; and for a general treatise on the meaning of loyalty, see his The Loyal and the Disloyal, University of Chicago Press, 1956.

the ten relocation centers who declared themselves disloyal (ranging from 8 to 52 percent of adult males). This range reflects the differences in social situations in the centers—residential conditions, the frequency of change of administration, location of the center, attitudes of governing officials, types of leadership among the Japanese-Americans, etc. Grodzins summarizes the situation well:

Loyalties change as social situation changes and individuals assess previous experience, present plight, and future promise. Loyalty to his nation comes easily if an individual's job and career are secure, if he participates amiably in work and play with colleagues and friends, if he feels accepted and secure, if his relationship to the larger community is not strained. Destroy his career, disrupt his work and play groups, isolate him, persecute him, show your disdain for him, and you plant the seeds of his disaffection. His allegiance will withstand maltreatment. But the multiplication of abuses will weaken his loyalty; and, as abuse continues, loyalty to nation erodes away—the more completely and rapidly if he believes that the government is directly responsible for his difficulties. Loyalty does not thereby disappear. It is transferred to another cause, another group, perhaps another nation.[24]

Discrimination may encourage ambivalence in matters of lawfulness on the part of those who have experienced only inadequate protection by the law. Richard Wright describes his feelings when, as a ticket taker in a theater, he tries to decide whether to join the ticket seller and an accomplice in cheating the theater owner by reselling some of the tickets. The owner has pointed out that if Wright, as ticket taker, is honest, the others cannot steal; and he asks his coöperation. Richard Wright says: "I gave him a pledge of my honesty, feeling absolutely no qualms about what I intended to do. He was white, and I could never do to him what he and his kind had done to me. Therefore, I reasoned, stealing was not a violation of my ethics, but of his; I felt that things were rigged in his favor and any action I took to circumvent his scheme of life was justified. Yet I had not convinced myself. . . . I knew that if I were caught I would go to the chain gang. But was not my life already a kind of chain gang? What, really, did I have to lose?"[25] Wright had been trying to save enough money to move to the North. He had always felt that his industry and intelligence would suffice to solve the problem, but the accumulation was so exasperatingly slow that he began to entertain the idea of stealing.

I had never stolen a penny from anyone. Even hunger had never driven me to appropriate what was not my own. The mere idea of stealing had been repugnant. I had not been honest from deliberate motives, but being dishonest had simply never occurred to me.

Yet, all about me, Negroes were stealing. More than once I had been

[24] Morton Grodzins, "Making Un-Americans," p. 582.
[25] Richard Wright, *op. cit.*, pp. 177–179.

called a "dumb nigger" by black boys who discovered that I had not availed myself of a chance to snatch some petty piece of white property that had been carelessly left within my reach.

"How in hell you gonna git ahead?" I had been asked when I had said that one ought not steal.

I knew that the boys in the hotel filched whatever they could. I knew that Griggs, my friend who worked in the Capitol Street Jewelry store, was stealing regularly and successfully. I knew that a black neighbor of mine was stealing bags of grain from a wholesale house where he worked, though he was a stanch deacon in his church, and prayed and sang on Sundays. I knew that the black girls who worked in white homes stole food daily to supplement their scanty wages. And I knew that the very nature of black and white relations bred this constant thievery.

No Negroes in my environment had ever thought of organizing, no matter in how orderly a fashion, and petitioning their white employers for higher wages. The very thought would have been terrifying to them, and they knew that the whites would have retaliated with swift brutality. So, pretending to conform to the laws of the whites, grinning, bowing, they let their fingers stick to what they could touch. And the whites seemed to like it.

But I, who stole nothing, who wanted to look them straight in the face, who wanted to talk and act like a man, inspired fear in them. The southern whites would rather have had Negroes who stole, work for them than Negroes who knew, however dimly, the worth of their own humanity. Hence, whites placed a premium upon black deceit; they encouraged irresponsibility; and their rewards were bestowed upon us blacks in the degree that we could make them feel safe and superior.[26]

In a society where legal controls are notoriously weak one must be cautious not to assume that the response of Richard Wright is simply an expression of a minority-group member. There seems to be evidence, however, that the pressures of an inferior status predispose one to certain forms of illegality. It is known, for example, that some kinds of gambling, particularly the policy or numbers racket, are widespread forms of lawbreaking among the disadvantaged Negro slum dwellers. This situation can be understood as the result of a total experience that promises much but gives little. The numbers game has the attraction of large possible returns: one cent brings five dollars. Few win, of course (not more than one in a thousand); but in a large community like Harlem no day passes without somebody's winning—and many hear of it and are encouraged to live in hope. It could probably be shown that chance-taking and gambling are quite congruent with many aspects of our culture, and thus occur among a far wider range of people than minority-group members. Among the latter, however, there is the additional stimulus to gambling that results from losing hope of achieving

[26] *Ibid.*, pp. 174–175; see also Earl R. Moses, "Differentials in Crime Rates Between Negroes and Whites, Based on Comparisons of Four Socio-Economically Equated Areas," *American Sociological Review*, August, 1947, pp. 411–420.

even a modest success by the more stable methods of hard work and thrift. The prejudice and discrimination that they see all around them cause them to doubt the rewards of "virtue." They turn, rather, to a kind of magic (just as men seem to do everywhere when the odds are heavily against them) in their search for success.

In his well-known essay, "Social Structure and Anomie,"[27] Robert Merton discusses the consequences for behavior of a society that places strong emphasis on the desirability of specific goals without a corresponding emphasis upon institutionalized procedures. One type of adjustment that people make to such a situation is to strive for the goals they have been taught to desire with little regard for the legitimacy of the means used. Recent analyses of "white-collar crime" show this adjustment to be not uncommon among members of the dominant group; but the pressures toward deviation are probably greater on those who have least opportunity for success by legitimate means.

It would be a mistake, of course, to assume from this discussion that a different pattern of motivation and regard for law are the inevitable results of minority-group status in a society or, conversely, that membership in the dominant group is a promise of high motivation and complete honesty. It is a matter for careful study that many Negroes, despite the obstacles, continue to strive for improved status and, notwithstanding the unequal protection of the law and resentment against discriminations, are reliable and honest in their relationships with others. The differences in motivation and morality should not be exaggerated, but insofar as they do exist, they can be accounted for by the differential sharing in the rewards and encouragement of society.

The Marginal Man and Cultural Participation

There is an extensive literature dealing with the concept of "the marginal man" that offers a number of valuable hypotheses for the study of the personality development of minority-group members. In our society most members of minority groups are marginal. They share the dominant culture to a significant degree, they absorb its aspirations, yet they are blocked from full participation. The personality consequences of marginality are not limited to minority-group members, of course, for in a rapidly changing society the lack of a stable, continuous, unchallenged set of life definitions makes virtually everyone, to a greater or lesser degree, marginal and likely to exhibit the tendencies characteristic of that condition. But inability to participate fully in the life of society according to one's individual interests and talents complicates this experience for those in low status. Most discussions of the marginal man are somewhat impressionistic, so generalizations must be highly tentative. The consequences vary, moreover, with the height of the

[27] See Robert K. Merton, *Social Theory and Social Structure*, The Free Press, 1949, pp. 125–149.

barriers to full participation, with the presence or absence of a minority culture to which the marginal man feels attached, and with the degree to which an individual is self-conscious of his status between two groups —part of both, yet belonging to neither.

Keeping these qualifications in mind, we can note some of the personality tendencies that seem to be associated with marginal status. There is an ambivalence, a strain of roles, that heightens self-consciousness and attention to oneself. This may take the form of self-hatred (see the discussion of self-attitudes below) and an inferiority complex, or it may express itself in egocentrism, withdrawal, and/or "aggressiveness," a tendency, as Stonequist remarks, that is supposed to characterize Jews and northern Negroes (this claim is often made by those on top who resent the efforts of those below to push themselves "out of their place").[28]

Some writers have emphasized the influence of a marginal role in encouraging a rational instead of a traditional view of life. Robert Park wrote in the introduction to Stonequist's study, "The fate which condemns him to live, at the same time, in two worlds is the same which compels him to assume, in relation to the worlds in which he lives, the role of a cosmopolitan and a stranger. Inevitably he becomes, relatively to his cultural milieu, the individual with the wider horizon, the keener intelligence, the more detached and rational viewpoint."[29] If thinking comes from perplexity and doubt, from problems posed but not solved by established traditional answers, then indeed the marginal man may take a more rational view of life.

Other authors emphasize the personal instability that they believe is likely to characterize persons who lack a strong feeling of identification with one group. It is well established that personality integration is, to an important degree, a function of group experiences. Personal stability is greatly aided by a sense of security in group identifications, by a feeling of belongingness. The minority-group member who feels torn between his association with the group in which he is categorically placed by prejudice and his feelings of identification with the dominant society may well lack some of the security that comes from stable and acceptable group relationships. This generalization must be used with care, however, for, as Wirth and Goldhamer point out, one is very likely to "read into" the behavior of the minority-group member (they were referring specifically to the mulatto) the tendencies that supposedly characterize the marginal man.[30]

The personality consequences of the marginal role vary greatly from

[28] See Everett V. Stonequist, The Marginal Man. A Study in Personality and Culture Conflict, Charles Scribner's Sons, 1937, pp. 139–158.

[29] Ibid., pp. xvii–xviii.

[30] See Louis Wirth and Herbert Goldhamer, "The Hybrid and the Problem of Miscegenation," in Otto Klineberg (ed), Characteristics of the American Negro, Harper & Brothers, 1944, Part V.

group to group, and the interested student will need to explore carefully the differential effects on the American Indian (this in itself being a highly differentiated group, varying with the type of contact with the dominant white society and the nature of the aboriginal culture), the first-generation immigrant, the second-generation immigrant, etc. Feelings that one's status as a minority-group member is permanent and unchangeable, regardless of one's individual beliefs or behavior, produce different influences than knowledge or belief that one can in time become a member of the majority group. For example, the Issei (Japanese immigrants to the United States), faced before 1952 with the legal impossibility of becoming citizens, were probably more protective of their original culture and less likely to be enthusiastic American nationals than were immigrants who were faced with lower barriers to assimilation.

We can develop only a few illustrations of the ways in which marginal status affects personality development, but these may help us to see the principles involved. It is, of course, a mistake to attribute all of the consequences of marginal position to prejudice. Individuals who stand between two cultural worlds, influenced by two sets of values, often exhibit strong personality effects even when no prejudice is involved. Frequently, however, the marginal man is not only bicultural but the recipient of prejudice as well. These two factors interlock and increase the impact of his position.

Studies of the American Indian furnish a great deal of information on the personality consequences of culture contact. As the white man came into contact with the Indians, he usually treated them with harshness and prejudice. He looked upon the native cultures as inferior and demanded either rapid assimilation or segregation. The Indian leaders, often subjected to the authority of the white stranger, lost the respect and confidence of their people. They felt themselves to be in a cultural vacuum, without incentives or objectives. The native religions were generally condemned and efforts were made to force their replacement by Christianity; but faith in the original beliefs was lost long before Christianity was adopted, with resulting personal and social disorganization. This loss of an integrated value system helps to account for the brutality that many settlers claimed was embedded in the very nature of the Indians. The tribes of the Iroquois League, for example, were much less warlike before the white settlers began to seize their lands and undermine their culture. Then the decline of cultural cohesion expressed itself in increased personal aggressiveness and organized violence.

Nonliterate peoples, experiencing the process of the destruction of their cultures while still clinging to many of the old values, often lose incentive, become lazy and indolent, "die of boredom." As Goldenweiser says:

Racial prejudice or its twin, social snobbishness, bars the way to their adequate participation in the culture of the White intruders. Their own culture, on the other hand, no longer offers them any objectives worthy of effort or sacrifice. They find themselves in a cultural vacuum, serving the white master for whatever little favours or emoluments may fall to their share, wasting their lives and their substance in dissipation, an existence not so much immoral, perhaps, as amoral, for a cultural in-between has no morality.

, . . When Rivers mournfully refers to the Melanesians as "dying from boredom," when we hear about the native migrants of Siberia that they are losing their zest for life, when the American Indians, especially the men, are represented by government officials as lazy, indolent parasites devoid of all stamina and ambition, these are merely different formulae for the same fundamental fact that life in a cultural void is no life at all for man, and this is precisely the tragic setting bestowed upon the natives by the intrusion of White man and his civilization.[31]

MacGregor has described the disorganizing effects on the American Indians of the reservation policies to which they were subjected in the latter part of the nineteenth century:

Excerpts from the statement of the educational policy for all Indian children at this time are enlightening. The policy was "to civilize," "to humanize," and "to put the children in boarding school where they will learn English" and "not relapse into their former moral and mental stupor." In connection with this statement, the federal superintendent of Indian Schools in 1885 makes one remark which is highly significant in light of this study. "The Indian is the strangest compound of individualism and socialism run to seed. It is this being that we endeavor to make a member of a new social order. . . . To do this we must recreate him, MAKE A NEW PERSONALITY."

Children were virtually kidnaped to force them into government schools, their hair was cut, and their Indian clothes thrown away. They were forbidden to speak in their own language. Life in the school was under military discipline, and rules were enforced by corporal punishment. Those who persisted in clinging to their old ways and those who ran away and were recaptured were thrown into jail. Parents who objected were also jailed. Where possible, children were kept in school year after year to avoid the influence of their families.[32]

This particular expression of the white man's burden continues to have important effects on the personality development of Indian children today. MacGregor found among the Dakota Indian children an anxiety that arises from not knowing "how to behave." "Rebuffed in their contacts with others and unable to find inner satisfactions, they withdraw further into themselves and lack warm and emotional respon-

---

[31] Alexander Goldenweiser, Anthropology, Appleton-Century-Crofts, 1937, pp. 429–430.

[32] Gordon MacGregor, Warriors Without Weapons, University of Chicago Press, 1946, p. 36.

siveness and vigor."[33] Stories and fantasies that were given in Thematic Apperception Tests indicated that the Dakota children thought of the world as a dangerous and hostile place. "Characters in the children's stories often have too little to eat and few of the other material things which make life comfortable. Hence they feel deprived and dissatisfied. In their uncomfortable surroundings they often become tired or sick. . . . The characters in the stories, with whom the children identify themselves, are uncertain and suffer many accidents and lose what little security they have."[34] These stories express the confusion and pain of children caught between two cultures.

There are, of course, many different responses possible to the intrusion of a dominant society, varying with the nature of the aboriginal culture and with the types of contact. Earliest contacts between the Puyallup Indians in Washington and white settlers were friendly. Many legal intermarriages took place and Indians and whites frequently worked side by side, so that assimilation was rapid. This pattern was broken, however, by several changes. The white settlers began to show more social discrimination against the Indians, and the sale of Indian lands had a devastating effect on their patterns of life. They received a good deal of ready cash, for which they had no pattern of use, and lost the need for steady work. The result was a sharp rise in personal disorganization; idleness, drunkenness, and murder increased.

The Fox Indians of Iowa have shown another pattern of adjustment, having successfully maintained group solidarity. They had a long period of rather slight contact, which permitted a gradual adjustment. There has been no abrupt loss of their means of subsistence. While accepting much of the new technology, they have shown a high degree of resistance to changes in language, religion, and social organization.[35]

This same kind of analysis is useful in understanding the problems often faced by immigrants and the children of immigrants in American society. Thomas and Znaniecki, in their classic study, *The Polish Peasant in Europe and America*, describe the demoralizing effects of the transfer from the stable, closely knit agricultural village in Poland to the rapidly changing, complex American industrial city. The immigrants' disorganization is increased by the prejudice shown against them. Some of the immigrants and their children were able to make the adjustment without major difficulties, but many others exhibited

---

[33] *Ibid.*, p. 204.

[34] *Ibid.*, p. 205.

[35] See Ralph Linton (ed.), *Acculturation in Seven American Indian Tribes*, Appleton-Century-Crofts, 1940. For two excellent accounts of variation in the extent of acculturation among Indians and differences in personality types, see Evon Z. Vogt, "The Acculturation of American Indians," *Annals of the American Academy of Political and Social Science*, May, 1957, pp. 137–146; and George D. Spindler and Louise S. Spindler, "American Indian Personality Types and Their Sociocultural Roots," *Annals*, May, 1957, pp. 147–157.

several forms of demoralization. Thomas and Znaniecki illustrate at length the increase, among adults, of economic dependency, of divorce and desertion, and of murder. They describe the increase of vagabondage and delinquency in boys and sexual immorality among girls.[36]

Since 1924, the communities of European immigrants in America have been shrinking, although they have by no means disappeared. There has been, for many of them, a gradual reduction of "cultural shock" and disorganization. Their place is being taken, however, to a degree unrecognized by most Americans, by a continuing flow of new migrants, primarily from the rural South (both white and colored), from Mexico, and from the West Indies. The same pattern of disorganization and of self-contradictory marginal statuses has developed, frequently intensified by race prejudice and rigid demands for segregation on the part of the dominant group.

"It is a staple article of belief throughout the Southwest that the Mexican immigrant was the 'lowest' of any group to enter this country. It is a belief shared not only by the exploiters of Mexican labor, to whom it might be expected to come naturally, but by educators, clergymen, social workers—the friendly and sympathetic as well as the inalterably prejudiced."[37] Such is the context, with all that it means for personality development—feelings of marginality, attitudes toward oneself and toward the dominant society—in which the Mexican immigrant was, and to a substantial degree is being, absorbed into American society. Tuck well describes the feelings of the Mexican in the United States:

There was one thing which impressed Juan and his *compadres* as they talked, in bunk houses, around picking fires, or in the cheap cafes of El Paso's poor districts. The life they had led before was valueless to them here. No American was interested in it; no one considered it anything but "low" or "savage" or "funny"; manifestations of another culture were likely to be met with reactions ranging from aversion to ridicule to incarceration. Juan had not enjoyed high status in his own country; he had known both exploitation and injustice; but he had been able to feel a certain sureness in his way of life. The little pattern of Los Conejos was part of the big pattern of Mexico; it had its place, its validity, and its worth. But in the United States it had no worth; he began to feel powerful pressures on him to make him into something he was not prepared to be, a person he hardly understood— the man who was "just like everybody else." He could refuse, he could hang back, or he could fail. The penalties would not be obvious. He would not be sent to prison or deprived, openly, of his few possessions. He would just be pushed into a half-world, a place reserved for the "foreigner" and the half-assimilated, where advantage, opportunity, and recognition were

---

[36] See W. I. Thomas and Florian Znaniecki, *The Polish Peasant in Europe and America*, Alfred A. Knopf, Inc., 1927, vol. 2, pp. 1647–1827.

[37] Ruth D. Tuck, *Not with the Fist*, Harcourt, Brace & Company, 1946, p. 61.

sharply limited. He would be hung between his old world and the new, with no place except among other dwellers in the half-world.[38]

The United States, with her prejudices, with her patterns of segregation, with her tendencies to permit assimilation of culturally diverse peoples only on the terms of the dominant group, continues to increase the shock of culture transfer. That shock is large, at best, in a society where even the privileged groups are confused by the lack of an integrating system of values. For the "marginal man" it may be severe; and personal demoralization, loss of incentive, feelings of resentment continue to be among the consequences. Louis Adamic illustrates the problem through the comments of a young American of Japanese ancestry:

That winter—1934–35—can't be laughed off easily. "*Nothin' doin'!* . . . *Don't hire Japs!* . . . *Sorry, we don't take on any Japanese!* . . . *I couldn't use you if you was a white man!* . . ." My feet still hurt when I think of all the walking I did up and down the hills of San Francisco. I was really frightened. Didn't I belong here at all? But, damnit, I was an American! If not, what was I? I was no "Jap"! This was my country. I *did* belong! . . . Then there were times when my brain and feelings went numb. Occasionally a flash would come through the numbness: I've got to fight this thing out! But I could not shake off the dead mood. The only thing that shook it off for me was a visit to my home, although I did not begin to call it that again for some time. . . .

When I entered college, I had no definite plan. I was too young and green to try to blueprint my future; also too self-conscious and lacerated by my job-seeking adventures and resentful of my process of adjustment as a houseboy.

I did not quite admit this to myself, but somewhere in me I knew that the world in which I was living was a mess so far as I was concerned, but no more so than I was a mess within myself. Very early in my sociology class I came upon the phrase "marginal man," which described me fully. I was neither here nor there; an orphan who was not an orphan, a "Jap" who was not a "Jap," an American who was not really an American. When this occurred to me, I told myself it was funny and laughed, but it also cut into me.[39]

The Effects of Prejudice and Discrimination on Self-Attitudes

Prejudice and discrimination affect not only the attitudes and behavior of minority-group members toward the standards set by the dominant society but also their responses to themselves and their groups. We have noted that self-regarding attitudes are as much a product of one's social experience as are attitudes toward other persons and toward social norms. The nature of that experience effectively condi-

[38] *Ibid.*, pp. 89–90.
[39] Louis Adamic, *From Many Lands*, Harper & Brothers, 1939, pp. 203–205.

tions the basic ego structure, the central core of personality. At an early age Negro children develop an awareness of themselves as different, particularly with regard to skin color. This awareness varies with their color and with the social definitions of color differences given by the Negro and white communities (important class, regional, and other variables are involved). It is, however, a very widespread experience, embedded even in language—"that was white of you," or "black as the devil."

Our analysis will be built largely around the experience of learning that one is of an "inferior" color, but this should be seen as illustrative of the whole experience of learning that one belongs to an "inferior" group, that one can never be completely himself but must act according to the demands of a "specifically limiting minority role."[40] Lillian Smith reports her conversation with the young secretary of the president of a Negro college in the South.

She was a lovely thing to look at, quiet, poised, and I found her face more interesting than buildings and spacious gardens. We walked near the entrance that led to the street and stood, watching a streetcar pass by toward the "white" section of town. And then we turned back toward the library. I said, "It is beautiful in here, peaceful, quiet. I find it hard to remember the world out there that I will go back to tomorrow." She did not answer for a moment, then she said softly, "I wish I never had to go out there, even to shop. I would like never to go. In here, one forgets; you can believe you are real, a person. You go out there and they tear it off of you, your belief in yourself as something good, they tear it off in five minutes. It doesn't take much, a word you hear a man say, a glance, some one draws aside, that is all; a clerk in a store asks you your first name as if she cannot otherwise sell you a pair of shoes. Little things. . . . And suddenly you are an untouchable. In here . . . sometimes for a month I do not remember those people, outside."[41]

It is in the context of slights, rebuffs, forbidden opportunities, restraints, and often violence that the minority-group member shapes that fundamental aspect of personality—a sense of oneself and his place in the total scheme of things.

The Clarks, in a study of 253 Negro children aged three to seven, some from a segregated southern school and some from a mixed school in the North, found that a high proportion of the children (over 90

---

[40] See R. L. Cooper, "The Frustrations of Being a Member of a Minority Group: What Does It Do to the Individual and to His Relationships with Other People," *Mental Hygiene*, April, 1945, pp. 189–195.

[41] Lillian Smith, *Killers of the Dream*, W. W. Norton & Company, Inc., 1949, pp. 218–219. We would not be doing full justice to Miss Smith's point if we did not add her next sentence—a value judgment that the present authors share: "I wonder which of those liberals who say they believe it could tell her that segregation is 'best' for her and her people, that it is 'here to stay' and no one should 'try to change it.'"

percent) were aware of racial differences. Even at these ages, however, there were important differences. When asked to choose, between a white and a colored doll, "the doll that looks like you," only 20 percent of the light-colored children selected the colored doll, whereas 73 percent of the medium and 81 percent of the dark children identified with the Negro doll. When asked to give their preferences, a majority of the Negro children preferred the white doll:[42]

	Colored Doll %	White Doll %	Don't Know or No Answer %
Give me the doll that you like to play with	32	67	1
Give me the doll that is a nice doll	38	59	3
Give me the doll that looks bad	59	17	24
Give me the doll that is a nice color	38	60	2

There are significant differences in the answers when they are analyzed by age groups. A higher proportion of the three-year-old Negro children selected the colored doll to play with or as the one that was a nice doll (still, however, a minority) than did the four-, five-, and six-year-olds. The four-year-olds rejected the colored doll most often (about three-quarters selected the white, in answer to the first two questions), the seven-year-olds again approximated the proportion of the three-year-olds (about 60 percent). The third question showed an irregular variation, with the seven-year-olds least often indicating that the colored doll "looks bad"; but even they selected the colored doll over twice as frequently as the white doll. In answer to the fourth question, the four- and five-year-olds definitely preferred the "nice color" of the white doll (3–1), but preferences of the six- and seven-year-olds turned toward the colored doll, with just half of the older age group selecting that as the one with the "nice color."[43]

These data suggest that the valuations of the dominant society are known and shared by three-year-old Negro children, that four- and five-year-olds have an even stronger rejection of their own color, and that the six- and seven-year-olds have begun to acquire a group identification to counter the self-devaluating beliefs they had absorbed. This change may not eliminate the earlier beliefs but may represent a greater verbal skill on the part of the older children in disguising feelings that seem, by that time, to be inappropriate. Thus an ambivalence toward oneself is indicated that will continue to have important personality consequences. This is revealed to a degree in the rationalizations that some

[42] See Kenneth B. Clark and Mamie P. Clark, "Racial Identification and Preference in Negro Children," in Theodore M. Newcomb and E. L. Hartley (eds.), *Readings in Social Psychology*, Henry Holt & Company, Inc., 1947, p. 175.
[43] See *ibid.*, pp. 169–178.

of the older children felt obliged to offer: "A northern medium six-year-old justified his rejection of the brown doll by stating that 'he looks bad 'cause he hasn't got a eyelash.' A seven-year-old medium northern child justified his choice of the white doll as the doll with a 'nice color' because 'his feet, hands, ears, elbows, knees, and hair are clean.' "[44] Differences between northern and southern Negro children were not statistically significant, but there was consistently a somewhat higher preference for the white doll among the northern children.

The evaluations of one's own color are affected both by what he is taught in his own group and by the attitudes of the dominant group. White people in the United States have generally and consistently shown a preference for the lighter shades of brown, insofar as they have made any distinctions among Negroes. This has also been true among Negroes, as indicated by the Clarks' study, but not without some important countercurrents that create a strong ambivalence of feeling in many Negroes. In recent years, as self-confidence and group identification have increased among Negroes, there have been some forces to encourage them to take pride in their racial identity and, in a few instances, to assert it as a mark of superiority. Negro parents are less likely, either intentionally or unintentionally, to teach their children that white is superior; and there has been a slow reduction, in many communities, of actions on the part of the dominant whites that convey this racial preference. Johnson found that northern Negro youth showed less self-devaluation than southern youth, reflecting a less discriminatory environment and the influence of a closer acquaintanceship with a racial ideology.[45] The continuing force of a reciprocal prejudice, and often a hatred, against whites that is the natural product of the experiences of the Negro is also among the factors working against self-devaluation.

"The greatest task in growing up consists of coming to terms with oneself, of learning to know who one is, what one can do, and how one stands in relation to others."[46] It is almost universally agreed among social scientists that this "coming to terms" is made difficult for Negro children by segregation and prejudice. Perhaps too little attention has been paid to the fact that for some Negro children the first five or six years of life may be a period of warm and rewarding family experience, leading to a good start in developing a healthy self-regard. Later stress situations may then be handled with less crushing impact. A sound "ego" can develop a kind of external response system to the outer world

[44] *Ibid.*, p. 178; see also Mary Ellen Goodman, *Race Awareness in Young Children*, Addison-Wesley Press, 1952.

[45] See Charles S. Johnson, *op. cit.*

[46] Group for the Advancement of Psychiatry, *Psychiatric Aspects of School Desegregation*, Report No. 37, 1957, p. 32.

of conflict. As Milner points out, the psychologically vulnerable Negro, the person with a heavy load of self-doubt, cannot thus isolate the stresses of the world when they hit him. They enhance and confirm his inner insecurities.[47] Insofar as discrimination and segregation invade the personality-forming family situation by the creation of poverty, ill health, frustration of many kinds, they indirectly increase the weak ego defenses that later must deal with a harsh experience. Yet it is wise to recognize, with Milner, the variety of family influences. There has often been a disregard of the families of minority groups as "intervening variables" that influence the meaning of prejudice. In favorable circumstances they furnish a child strong defenses.

The stronger forces are still, however, on the other side. The Negro, as a member of the American society, tends to take on the culture of that society, including its prejudices. He sees that most Negroes are "inferior" in occupation, in education, and in general status. "He unconsciously comes to feel that by rejecting Negroes and 'Negro ways' he can escape being a Negro and all the handicaps that involves."[48] Displacement onto oneself and one's group is also involved in the self-attitude of a minority-group member. "When one is abused or insulted and forces oneself to react passively, the hatred that would normally be directed toward the abusing or insulting person is instead turned inward."[49]

Displacement is related to another response that can be understood only against the background of partial belief in one's own inferiority and also great frustration. This response is envy of fellow minority-group members who improve their status, an unwillingness to assist in, or even to accept, their advance. Even within a family, differences in color can give rise to problems of favoritism, resentment, and invidious comparisons. A protest is frequently heard, usually from Negro business and professional people, that Negroes don't "stick together," don't support members of their "own group." This protest is in part an attempt by the middle classes to get a protected position, free from the competition of white business and professional people. But it is also in part descriptive of the attitudes that Negroes have toward their more successful fellow group members.

A Negro actress who traveled with an otherwise white Northern company throughout the South reported that several Southern Negroes were viciously envious of her escape from Jim Crow and tried to force her back into the segregated patterns.

[47] See Esther Milner, "Some Hypotheses Concerning the Influence of Segregation on Negro Personality Development," *Psychiatry*, August, 1953, pp. 291–297.
[48] Arnold M. Rose, *The Negro's Morale*, University of Minnesota Press, 1949, p. 89.
[49] *Ibid.*

"In Texas, a colored man told me I was on the wrong side of the station. 'You belong over here with me. Why try to highhat somebody? I know you are colored.' When I didn't move over to the Jim Crow side he protested to the station master."[50]

A middle class Negro in North Carolina declared: "Negroes hate to see one another get ahead. Any time anybody starts getting anything everybody tries to pull him down. These [local] Negroes just won't work together, and they hate to see Negroes get anywhere. They will let white people use them against their own race.[51]

Many white people take these expressions of lack of solidarity among Negroes as another sign of their inferiority, instead of seeing them as a natural personality consequence in the members of a suppressed group struggling to work out some adjustment to the hostile environment. They seldom wonder about the obvious lack of solidarity among white people under many circumstances. Self-hatred and feelings of inferiority are not, of course, rational or effective responses, but they are among the natural results of the pressures acting upon a minority group. The suffering which discrimination causes, as Oliver Cox says, "may be aggravated by a consciousness of incurability and even blameworthiness, a self-reproaching which tends to leave the individual still more aware of his loneliness and unwantedness. . . . The dominant sociopsychological pressure of color prejudice seems to produce a collapsing effect upon the individual's self-respect—to render him ashamed of his existence. It is intended to reduce him to a condition of no social consequence, and to a lesser or greater extent he commonly accepts the definition."[52]

Seldom are feelings of inferiority or self-hatred expressed in an unambiguous way. They are more likely to take the form of an ambivalent attitude which shows both antipathy toward and solidarity with one's group. This is shown in a study of 837 Negro boys and 1377 Negro girls in the South that sought to discover their attitudes toward skin color. They were asked to check the color of the most stupid boy (or girl), the most handsome, the smartest, the one most disliked, and the one most liked of all the persons they knew. "Considering the southern rural Negro youth as a whole, our results show a decided tendency to classify as black a disproportionately large number of negative judgments."[53] There was also a tendency to be negative toward "yellow" persons and "white"—in the sense both of Negroes who look white and of members of the white race. The results can be summarized

[50] *Ibid.*, pp. 90–91.

[51] D. W. Wyatt, *op. cit.*, p. 55.

[52] Oliver C. Cox, *Caste, Class and Race*, Doubleday & Company, Inc., 1948, pp. 382–383.

[53] Charles S. Johnson, *op. cit.*, p. 258.

briefly by reference to answers to the question on "The worst color to be":[54]

Worst Color	Percentage Checking
Black	34.9
Dark-brown	1.9
Brown	1.4
Light-brown	1.4
Yellow	28.2
White	32.1

An interesting aspect of this tendency for southern Negro youth to disparage black, both aesthetically and morally, is the way in which they consistently rated their own color a shade or more lighter than they appeared to be to the researchers. The boys in 7.5 percent of the cases and the girls in 2.4 percent rated themselves black, whereas the testers estimated that 28.1 percent of the boys and 23.3 percent of the girls were in that category. Oppositely, 35.8 percent of the boys and 40.2 percent of the girls estimated that their complexions were light brown, but the testers thought that 6.5 percent and 9.9 percent belonged in that group.

When 833 Negro boys and 1402 Negro girls in the South were asked to check their attitudes toward Negroes, these were among the results:

Statement	Percentage Responding "True"	
	Boys	Girls
Negro doctors are just about as good as other doctors.	92.0	94.0
Only a few Negroes become famous, but a large number would if given a chance.	85.0	84.6
Negroes are always fighting and cutting each other up.	83.2	79.3
Negroes drink too much.	71.1	70.7
It's harder to work for a Negro than for anyone else.	62.9	60.5
Negroes are the meanest people in the world.	12.5	11.8

There is an interesting inconsistency in these responses. On the one hand, there is criticism of the disorderly behavior of the lower-class Negro, particularly with respect to fighting and drinking. There is also strong indication of preference for white over Negro employers. On the other hand, there is recognition of the barriers to distinction, and there is confidence in the ability of Negro doctors. In this respect Negro youth are more liberal in their judgment than older rural Negroes, who have not yet developed full confidence in Negro doctors.[55]

The attitudes of middle- and upper-class Negroes toward themselves, and especially toward lower-class colored persons, cannot be understood

[54] Ibid., p. 263.
[55] Ibid., p. 247; see also Melvin Seeman, "Skin Color Values in Three All-Negro School Classes," American Sociological Review, June, 1946, pp. 315–321.

wholly as a result of their acceptance of the standards of the dominant group, or as a consequence of projection. These attitudes reflect, in part, a simple class difference. Middle- and upper-class whites express the same attitudes toward lower-class whites. There are important differences in values and behavior among the classes, and, granted the premises of a given class (whether Negro or white), their attitudes toward the other classes inevitably follow.

The ambivalence of feeling of minority-group members toward themselves sometimes takes the form of extreme expressions of "race pride" or chauvinistic claims. It would be a mistake to interpret these as unambiguous signs of feelings of equality or superiority. As Rose says:

> Still another phenomenon that is psychologically related to Negro self-hatred, although it appears to be just the opposite, is the blatant, nationalistic claim to the cultural achievements of Negroes with whom there is no cultural contact. For American Negroes to be proud of the achievements of Alexander Dumas, who had some Negro ancestry but whose culture was entirely French, indicates an unconscious assumption on the part of Negroes that race is important for achievement (which they usually consciously, and correctly, deny), and a feeling that they are inferior and must hunt far afield for something to be proud of.
>
> This phenomenon is not unimportant. The whole tendency of the Negro History movement—not as history but as propaganda—is to encourage the average Negro to escape the realities—the actual achievements and the actual failures—of the present. Although the movement consciously tends to build race pride, it may also cause Negroes unconsciously to recognize that group pride is built partly on delusion, and therefore may result in a devaluation of themselves for being forced to resort to self-deception.[56]

THE PREJUDICES OF MINORITY-GROUP MEMBERS

Related to minority-group chauvinism are the various prejudices that are often found among those in low status—expressed partly toward other minority groups and partly toward the dominant group. Guy Johnson has described the extreme vigor with which the Croatan Indians in North Carolina try to distinguish themselves from the Negroes of the area. The whites tend to class Indians and Negroes together in a lower caste, but the Indians strive for a separate status. The large amount of admixture of Negro blood among the Indians has produced sharp internal cleavages based largely on the amount of Negro ancestry. The ultimate insult to a Croatan is to be mistaken for a "Negro"—a classification somewhat difficult to establish, since many of the Indians clearly have Negro blood. The darker Indians are particularly likely to show this prejudice in an attempt to free themselves from the caste stigma to which their color makes them especially susceptible. "So intense is the feeling on this subject that one can only conclude that

[56] Arnold M. Rose, *op. cit.*, pp. 92–93.

there is present in many persons a certain 'sense of guilt' which arises from the observed reality and which calls for constant denial of the reality."[57]

Negro anti-Semitism, not uncommon among urban Negroes, is partly a displaced prejudice, using another minority group as a substitute target for the hostilities felt toward the more powerful white gentiles, and partly a reciprocal prejudice against whites directed at Jews as a group of whites with whom urban Negroes have fairly frequent contact. As Ottley points out, the northern Negro comes in contact with discriminatory white men at four vital points—as fellow worker, as landlord, as merchant, as employer. In the latter three particularly, the white man with whom he deals is likely to be a Jew. The anti-Semitism of the Negro can be understood partly, therefore, as simply an expression of antiwhite feeling.[58]

> . . . A large proportion of the white merchants who solicited Negro trade and set up shop in Negro slums were Jews; many of the housewives who hired Negro servants in Northern cities were Jews; and many of the property owners who were willing to sell or rent to Negroes were Jews.
>
> Negro hatred for the merchants was based partly on the relatively high prices a small merchant—a large part of whose business is credit—must charge; partly on the inferior quality of the goods sold to a customer who demands "the cheapest"; and partly on the failure of the merchants—who often staffed their small stores with members of their families—to hire Negro clerks. Since the Jewish storekeepers were located in Negro areas, they were subjected to strong retaliation in the Northern cities, especially in the "don't buy where you can't work" campaigns and on the part of the nationalist racketeers who required storekeepers to pay for "protection."
>
> Negro businessmen find anti-Semitism a major weapon in the struggle for customers.[59]

Thus Negro anti-Semitism has many facets. It is partly a sign that Negroes share an attitude that is quite prevalent in our culture. It is partly an attempt by Negroes to make their own status seem better by expressing prejudice against another minority group. It is partly an expression of the general prejudice toward whites directed specifically at a group of whites with whom they have quite a bit of contact. (It should be noted, on the other hand, that many Negroes realize that Jews are probably, on the average, less prejudiced against them than are other whites; that they are more often willing to trade with them, hire them, rent to them; that they give a great deal of support to organiza-

---

[57] See Guy B. Johnson, "Personality in a White-Indian-Negro Community," *American Sociological Review*, August, 1939, pp. 516–523.

[58] See Roi Ottley, *New World A-Coming*, Houghton Mifflin Company, 1943, pp. 122–136.

[59] Arnold M. Rose, *op. cit.*, p. 129.

tions dedicated to reducing discrimination against all minorities.)[60]

The reciprocal prejudices of minority-group members toward the dominant group sometimes become as rigid and stereotyped as the attitudes of the majority. This is an important result of prejudice and, in turn, may become a cause of the continuation of prejudice. In a useful study, MacCrone describes the attitudes of a group of educated Bantu in South Africa. They were persons with very different backgrounds, but most of them were teachers, taking training in social work at Johannesburg, and all were quite highly "Europeanized." Their reactions to domination were hostility, hatred, suspicion, and "counterdomination," expressed particularly against the "Boers," the Afrikaansspeaking "Dutch." Despite their differences in background and despite the complexity of the race situation, these educated Bantu had converged on this attitude of hatred for the "Boer." Such a polarization has put other groups—for example, the British—in a more favorable light than the facts might indicate. The lesser of two evils has become a positive good. South Africans of English descent have, in fact, shown less hostility in the past and are more favorably inclined toward the African today; but to many of the Bantu the difference is almost an innate one between the English and the Dutch.

MacCrone believes that the subjects of his study show a "Boerphobia," not a simple case of resentment against discrimination. The Boer is used as a scapegoat, unrealistically, for displacement, projection, and compensation in a kind of mass neurosis that is unseen because it is so widespread in the group. There is, of course, a great deal of real provocation in the highly discriminatory treatment that the Bantu experience. But a scapegoat is a standing temptation to use autistic thinking and to overlook one's own faults. Out of this situation has come a caricature of the Boer—a quarrelsome, stubborn, brutal person—that is as one-sided and inaccurate as other caricatures. The students resisted MacCrone's suggestion that their picture of the Boer was a caricature, for it was so convenient a vehicle for hostility and an important rallying ground for their unity against a common enemy— two very common functions of scapegoats. Altogether, the frustrations of their drives for equal status have had many devastating effects on the personalities of these Bantu, manifest in pathological states of aggressiveness and sensitivity.[61]

The various prejudices of the minority-group member—toward him-

[60] See *ibid.*, pp. 129–139; and E. T. Prothro and J. A. Jensen, "Comparison of Some Ethnic and Religious Attitudes of Negro and White College Students in the Deep South," *Social Forces*, May, 1952, pp. 426–428.

[61] See I. D. MacCrone, "Reactions to Domination in a Colour-Caste Society: A Preliminary Study of the Race Attitudes of a Dominated Group," *Journal of Social Psychology*, August, 1947, pp. 69–98.

self, toward other minorities, and toward the dominant group—are among the most important results of the discriminatory pattern.

Minority-Group Solidarity

The feelings of inferiority, the self-hatred, and the reciprocal prejudices that may be the product of membership in a group which is the object of prejudice and discrimination are not, however, the only attitudes produced by such experiences. There is a lack of group solidarity, but there is also a group cohesiveness and even an interest in the problems of other minority groups. There are strong tendencies toward self-devaluation but also genuine feelings of pride and self-confidence that come from achievements made in the face of severe handicaps. One aspect of this response is the development of protest groups and social movements which tend to bind the group together, whether for attacks against their status or for escape. A sense of group identification is, in fact, to a greater or lesser degree an almost universal result of discrimination. Locke and Stern use this concept of group consciousness, forced by the treatment received as members of the group, as the core of their definition of minority group: "A minority group, irrespective of size or constituency, is thus best characterized as a social group whose solidarity is primarily determined by external pressure, which forces it to live in terms of opposition and ostracism."[62]

In other words, Negroes would not think of themselves as Negroes first, but as lower-, middle-, or upper-class persons, as Methodists, Baptists, or Catholics, as farmers, factory workers, or teachers, as Southerners or Northerners, and so on, were they not identified by most members of the dominant community *primarily* as Negroes. There is nothing intrinsically important about sharing the trait of race in common that binds people together into a group. The same principle applies to other minority groups. Jews, for example, are a heterogeneous people with a vast range in income, occupation, education, interests of various kinds, and, of course, even religion. In a friendly environment they begin to stop thinking of themselves as Jews *first*. (They do not, of course, necessarily stop thinking of themselves as Jews at all, although that is the result with some. Episcopalians think of themselves as Episcopalians, but usually they think of themselves first as Americans, or lawyers, or New Yorkers, or identify themselves primarily by some group association other than religious.)

Group solidarity or morale, as Arnold Rose calls it, is thus one of the consequences of prejudice. A feeling of common fate and shared problems exists alongside intragroup conflict and jealousy. Which of the two will predominate in a given situation depends upon the extent and

[62] Alain Locke and B. J. Stern (eds.), *When Peoples Meet*, Hinds, Hayden and Eldredge, Inc., 1946, p. 465.

the nature of the prejudice, cultural aspects of the minority group (for example, its family and community patterns), the resources of the group, and the nature of its leadership. In general, a relatively weak group, with disorganized institutions and wide internal differences, will tend toward intragroup conflict and a lack of solidarity in its dealings with the dominant group. A minority with greater resources in income, education, and skill, however, and with well-organized family and community life, is likely to have a strong feeling of group cohesion and identification, at least in the situations that involve contact with the dominant group. Americans of Japanese ancestry represent a group with rather high morale or solidarity. Negro Americans, who for a generation or more after the Civil War were greatly lacking in any sense of group cohesion, have, since the early years of the twentieth century, been moving toward greater and greater solidarity. This is shown both in the organized protests against discrimination and in the growth of group pride.[63]

The sense of cohesion that comes from sharing the burdens of minority-group status may extend to other minority groups. (This does not, of course, prevent the opposite tendency, projection of one's hostility onto other low-status groups. The two reactions can exist side by side, even in the same individual in different situations.) Jews are among the most vigorous and numerous workers for equality of status for all minorities in the United States—a fact that is sometimes noticed, with complaint, by those who oppose equality of status.

The response of many Negroes to the Italian attack on Ethiopia showed that they identified their problems with those of other colored people. During the latter years of India's struggle for independence the Pittsburgh *Courier* and the Chicago *Defender* had regular columnists in India "who wrote mainly of the struggles of the colored people of Asia." The Negro press gave relatively more space than white papers to the conflict between the Dutch and Indonesia, virtually all of it sympathetic to the colonial peoples.[64]

In a study of 183 Negro public-school and college students, Grossack suggests a typology of responses among Negroes that may have more general applicability. He distinguishes among the respondents who showed "Non-defensive group pride," Ethnocentric group pride," "Ambivalence," "Defensive reaction," and "Hostility to own group."[65] This list is paralleled in many ways by Antonovsky's comparison of six types of Jewish orientation, which is also based to a large degree on the extent of identification with one's group. He lists these types: "Active Jewish," "Passive Jewish," "Ambivalent," "Dual," "Passive General,"

[63] See Arnold M. Rose, *op. cit.*, pp. 3–6.
[64] *Ibid.*, p. 125.
[65] Martin M. Grossack, "Group Belongingness Among Negroes," *Journal of Social Psychology*, February, 1956, pp. 167–180.

"Active General."[66] The task of further research is to describe and measure the variables—in personality tendencies, in group structures, and in the total situation—that determine the extent of group solidarity and group withdrawal.

Other Personality Differences That Are Affected by Minority Status

There is scarcely an aspect of personality that has not been held to vary with race or to be differentially associated with various groups. General intelligence; specialized capacities (e.g., music, athletic prowess); tendencies toward aggressiveness, criminal behavior, mental illness; interest and potency in sexual behavior; temperament—all these and other aspects of personality are thought by some to differ from group to group. We saw in Chapter 2 that biological explanations of differences in group averages, with reference to such attributes as those mentioned here, are unlikely. Not that there are no personality differences, but they must be explained by differences in experience. The experiences we are particularly concerned with here are those that grow out of minority-group status, that reflect the impact of prejudice and discrimination on personality development. In this field there is a lack of carefully controlled studies of an experimental nature. Dozens of paper-and-pencil and performance tests of various kinds have compared the personality tendencies or behavior of Negroes, or other racial groups, with those of whites. Few of them, however, have even approximately solved the complicated methodological problems involved in such studies, and we must therefore be very careful in evaluating the results. Many of the studies assume that they are trying to measure a racial difference per se. To do this, the influence of all other factors would have to be eliminated by matching the groups compared—an almost impossible task in a society where the members of minority races are almost universally the objects of prejudice and discrimination. To discover, for example, whether the single fact of being a Negro or a white (independent of any experience or training) is related to the degree of suggestibility, the "power of inhibition," or intelligence, one would have to compare Negroes and whites who were entirely alike in class status, education, reaction to test situation, motivation, cultural values and goals, and many other factors. Where can one find Negro and white groups whose general experiences have been so similar in all regards that any observed differences in personality can be attributed to the racial difference?

In some of the earlier attempts to study the personality tendencies of

[66] Aaron Antonovsky, "Toward a Refinement of the 'Marginal Man' Concept," *Social Forces*, October, 1956, pp. 57–62.

minority-group members the difficulty of controlling the many variables that affect personality and the dangers of bias greatly hampered the achievement of valid results. These two problems are shown in an extreme way in a study by A. L. Crane.[67] The bias of the author is shown in the way he posed the problem: "What is the psychological explanation of the impulsiveness, improvidence, and immorality which the Negro everywhere manifests?" He looks for an answer by studying the degree of "inhibition" in Negroes and whites, "inhibition" being measured by a little "guillotine" which allowed a weight to drop toward the subject's hand. The weight was stopped only a short distance above his hand, while at the same time a slight electric shock was administered. There were 100 Negroes and 100 whites, equally divided between the sexes, in the experiment. Klineberg gives an excellent critique of the procedures and conclusions:

Crane states that he attempted to choose his subjects from a variety of social groups. It is clear, however, that there is a marked socioeconomic difference between the Negro and white samples. For example, among the 50 white men 36 were either skilled laborers or in a superior category, and only 14 in the unskilled group; among the colored men 47 out of 50 were unskilled laborers. The two groups therefore can hardly be regarded as comparable. As far as the relationship of the investigator to the subject is concerned, it does not seem that Crane was particularly successful. He reports that "threats, cajolery, flattery, bribery and every other conceivable ruse within the bound of reason and the law were resorted to in order to bring the number of [Negro] subjects up to the desired hundred." Bribery was resorted to, but even at that there were cases in which the subjects ran away in fright from the laboratory at the last moment. The rapport with the white subjects was clearly superior, and the difficulty of obtaining their cooperation was not nearly so great.

The results with the guillotine test did not show any clear differences between the "races," since both groups gave an almost equal number of withdrawals. The bias of the investigator again appears in his explanation of this finding as "due to the fact that both the drive and the volitional factors in the case of the Negro were operating on lower planes than in the case of the white,—the two factors being lowered to almost functionally equal degrees, with the result that these differences tended to offset each other so far as the withdrawal score is concerned." An interpretation of the same score in two diametrically opposite ways hardly suggests an impartial attitude. . . .

This study has received so much attention that it has seemed worth while to summarize it in some detail. It illustrates an approach characteristic of what might be termed the "precritical" stage of research on "racial" differences. The bias of the investigator, the lack of comparability of the two groups tested, the doubtful rapport with the Negro subjects, and the very

[67] *Archives of Psychology*, No. 63, 1923.

questionable interpretation of the results rob the study of any real significance.[68]

Klineberg's criticism of this study seems entirely justified and very
restrained. Research that can *assume*, without any evidence, that the
"drive and the volitional factors" cancel each other out, and thus, conveniently, that the original hypothesis is "proved," must be looked
upon as scarcely more than a scientific disguise for prejudice. The weaknesses of such studies, however, should not lead one to assume that
there are no personality differences. Other studies of differences among
racial groups start from the premise that racial difference, unaffected by
experience, is unimportant (or at least unmeasurable at the present
time), and seek rather to measure the differences that are the result of
differing experience. This is safer scientific ground. The question of
perfect matching of the groups is far less important in these studies,
for the task is to measure the personality consequences precisely when
important factors do vary. The chief methodological problem in such
studies is to know how widely the results may be generalized. How typical is the sample studied? Negro college students are an accessible
group for study—but how much may one know of other Negro groups
from study of this one? Case studies, interviews, and general observations—many of which we have drawn on in this chapter—are far more
common research techniques in this area than are more objective "experimental" devices. Whatever the technique used, we must continually
ask: How widely does this result apply?

Illustrative of research of this type is the attempt to discover whether
there are differences in types and amounts of mental illness and
whether prejudice and discrimination are among the factors that affect
the development of personality disorder. It is difficult to give an adequate appraisal of this question because the data on the incidence of
mental illness are seldom comparable. How mental illness is defined
and the amount of hospitalization vary greatly from time to time and
in different places. In comparing the rates for minority and majority
groups there is the additional hazard of assuming that differences are
caused by different biological tendencies, without regard to the many
differences in experience and pattern of life that make that assumption
impossible. Keeping these difficulties in mind, we may note that contemporary explanations of the causes of mental illness would lead us
to expect a higher incidence, at least for many varieties of illness, among
an oppressed group. For example, according to the data on Negroes in
New York State given by Malzberg (these cannot be generalized to
include Negroes in other situations; data with regard to mental illness
among Negroes in the South, for instance, are very inadequate), when

[68] Otto Klineberg (ed.), *op. cit.*, pp. 120–121.

standardized for age differences, first admissions to all hospitals in New York State, 1929–1931, showed a ratio of 2.3 for Negroes to 1 for whites. When the comparison is made between Negroes and several groups of foreign-born whites, the Negroes still have the higher rates, in a ratio of 1.9 to 1.[69]

These ratios vary with particular diseases. Without citing the data for the various types, we may note that differences in experience account for the variations in rates. For example, Negroes in New York State, 1929–1931, had a rate for general paresis (caused by syphilis) 4.1 times the white rate. The differences in family pattern and sex mores resulting from slavery and the contemporary problem of slums in which many live, and the great difference in availability of medical facilities explain the difference. In summarizing his study of mental disease among Negroes Malzberg says:

We have shown that fundamental qualitative differences with respect to mental disease do not exist as between Negroes and whites. There is not a type of mental disorder among whites which is not to be found among Negroes. Contrariwise, Negroes suffer from no mental disorder that does not find its counterpart among whites. It is clear, however, that there is a fundamental difference with respect to the incidence of mental disease, which is much more frequent among Negroes.

To what is this difference due? Is it the result of some "racial" qualities which make the Negro more susceptible to a mental and nervous breakdown? Of this there is no evidence. True, there are Negro families in which mental disease appears with unusual frequency, but this must be attributed to a familial and not to a "racial" basis, precisely as in the case of white populations.

We turn therefore to a consideration of environmental factors and here we find ample explanation of the high rates of mental disease among Negroes. These rates are due to the direct and indirect influences of conditions of life over which the Negro has as yet little control. Since the doors of economic opportunity are largely closed to him, he is compelled to pursue the heaviest, least desirable, and least remunerative occupations. His low income subjects him to correspondingly low levels of living—homes in vicious and undesirable neighborhoods, unhygienic surroundings, overcrowding, undernourishment, together with the moral handicaps associated with such conditions of life. Surely, if mental life is an adaptation to environment, then the Negro is burdened, indeed.[70]

We cannot state categorically that there are no purely racial differences in the amount or types of mental illness, but the evidence indicates strongly that the differences in rates are the result of different ex-

---

[69] See Benjamin Malzberg, "Mental Disease Among American Negroes: A Statistical Analysis," in Otto Klineberg (ed.), *op. cit.*, pp. 382–383.

[70] *Ibid.*, p. 394.

periences, that prejudice and discrimination help to create environmental influences which significantly increase the likelihood of mental illness.[71]

The study of the incidence and the causes of mental illness among minority-group members has received relatively little direct attention. The ground is being laid for important advances, however, by the current work in the field of "social psychiatry," which seeks to isolate the social and cultural factors involved in personality disorder.[72]

In Chapter 2 we discussed the evidence regarding differences in group averages in intelligence test scores. There is no need to repeat that account here, but only to state that some minority groups do exhibit consistently lower scores on intelligence tests, that these differences in group averages become progressively smaller as life conditions (income, residence, education, occupation, etc.) become more nearly similar, and that it seems correct at the present time to hold that native intellectual capacity is substantially equal among human groups. Thus, although members of some minority groups do exhibit lower average scores in the abilities that intelligence tests measure, these must be looked upon as personality consequences of their status and not as biological causes of an inferior status.

Such, then, are the consequences of minority status. The pressures at work on those who are the targets for prejudice and discrimination require that they develop some mechanisms of adjustment and response. These may be looked upon as further personality consequences of the experiences that come from an inferior position. They are the subject matter of the next chapter.

[71] See ibid., pp. 373–399; see also Henry J. Myers and Leon Yochelson, "Color Denial in the Negro," Psychiatry, February, 1948, pp. 39–46, for a study of the place of self-hatred and denial of race in the development of psychoses among Negroes.

[72] See, for example, Abram Kardiner and Lionel Ovesey, The Mark of Oppression, W. W. Norton & Company, Inc., 1951, for a psychoanalytic approach. For recent work in social psychiatry, see Morris K. Opler, Culture, Psychiatry and Human Values, Charles C. Thomas, Publisher, 1956; and Arnold M. Rose (ed.), Mental Health and Mental Disorder. A Sociological Approach, W. W. Norton & Company, Inc., 1955.

CHAPTER 7

The Consequences of Prejudice: Types of Adjustment to Prejudice and Discrimination

Probably no two persons respond in exactly the same way to the problems they face as members of a minority group. It is possible, however, to classify the patterns of adjustment into broad types, for purposes of analysis, and to point out the kinds of persons who are most likely to adopt each type as the primary mode of response to prejudice and discrimination. Response to the dominant world is not simply a matter of individual trial and error, for the culture of a minority group contains traditional adjustment techniques that are passed on, intentionally and unintentionally, to the oncoming generation. These techniques will vary from group to group; the responses of Jews will be different from those of Japanese-Americans, and both, in turn, different from those of Negroes. There will be many variations, moreover, within each group. As Charles S. Johnson points out with respect to Negroes, the response to prejudice varies with the regional and cultural setting, the social status of the person involved, the specific situational factors in a given response, and the basic personality type of the individuals, among other factors.[1] Somewhat the same classification could be used for Jews. Adjustments to the problems they face in the American environment vary greatly, for example, among an immigrant from the

[1] See Charles S. Johnson, *Patterns of Negro Segregation*, Harper & Brothers, 1943, p. 231.

Ukraine, a refugee from Nazi Germany, and a member of an old-American Jewish family.

How one learns the nature of his status as a minority-group member and acquires modes of adjustment to that status ranges all the way from systematic training by parents to entirely informal and accidental picking up of points of view from small incidents or major crises. Some parents feel it necessary to give their children explicit attitudes with regard to the nature of their relationship to the dominant world—whether they be attitudes of acceptance or rejection of that relationship. Some may try to teach specific ways of avoiding trouble, or of facing trouble if it comes. Other parents, however, make no conscious effort to equip their children with attitudes or techniques. These are then acquired informally by observation, by the learning of traditional modes of behavior, by the use of peer-group folkways, and by on-the-spot adjustments to members of the dominant group.

What, then, are the basic types of response to prejudice and discrimination? There are three fundamental varieties:

> Avoidance.
> Aggression.
> Acceptance.

These types of response represent a special application of the outline of types of social interaction employed in sociological analysis: association (acceptance), dissociation (aggression), and the absence of communication (avoidance). Few individuals follow one of these patterns at all times, and few adjustments are purely of one type or another. It is useful, however, for analytic purposes, to distinguish among the three varieties, for they represent important different personality consequences of prejudice and discrimination.

Alexander Leighton, in his study of the reactions of Americans of Japanese ancestry to the relocation camps in which they were held during World War II, found a pattern of response that closely resembles the three types suggested above. At the Poston camp some of the internees were aggressive, attacking many of the decisions of the authorities and protesting against the inadequacies of the facilities; others were coöperative, accepting the relocation move and working with the camp administration; but the largest number were passive, avoiding contact wherever possible and withdrawing from the life of the camp.

"Fear, frustration and anger were the basic emotions and they pervaded all the Japanese, both alien and American. In some, as typified by members of the Japanese American Citizen's League, these feelings resulted in efforts to prove their loyalty and to insure their future by all-out collaboration with the Government. Others reacted by becoming apathetic, submissive and withdrawn from any initiative or spontaneous action. Still others brought their anger to the surface and were ever ready to complain and attack, at least in words."[2]

Each of these three responses to discrimination can be expressed in numerous ways, so we shall need to examine them in some detail.

Avoiding Prejudicial or Discriminatory Situations

If a member of a minority group cannot abolish the status restrictions under which he lives, he can, at least under many circumstances, avoid situations where he must experience prejudice, or he can avoid some aspects of situations and thus reduce their painful and disagreeable impact. The avoidance can be permanent (passing or assimilation) or temporary and partial (simply crossing to the other side of the street to avoid contact, or reticence in speaking to a member of the dominant group). Many motives encourage avoidance: the desire to preserve self-respect, to escape the need for conforming to the role of an "inferior," to gain status, power, and income *within* the minority group, to protect personal safety, etc. Avoidance is an adjustment device more frequently found in and more readily available to middle- and upper-class members of a minority group, but it is used to some degree among all classes.

TYPES OF AVOIDANCE

1. The most complete form of avoidance, clearly, is to withdraw entirely from the minority group. Where the color line is drawn as sharply as it is in the United States, this adjustment is open to only a small proportion of mixed-bloods among the racial minorities. Estimates of the extent of Negro "passing," which of necessity are very rough, range from a few thousands to tens of thousands per year in the United States. Even in the case of national or religious minorities, passing into the dominant group is often restricted by the presence of identifying characteristics; language accents, names, cultural differences, or knowledge, by the dominant community, of the family background can inhibit passing. Obviously these are much less categorical and permanent differences. Mass assimilation, after three or four generations, has been the rule for national and cultural minorities in the United States and in many other societies.

In some situations, for example in eastern Europe, where cultural and national minorities have not wanted to be assimilated into the dominant group but have worked and fought for cultural and/or national independence, this process has, of course, not taken place. Under such circumstances relatively few members of a minority group have sought to avoid the penalties of that status by joining the majority.

[2] Alexander Leighton, *The Governing of Men*, Princeton University Press, 1945, p. 45.

They have, far more often, joined with their fellow minority-group members to try to win independence or at least a protected position within the larger society for the continuation of their group as a distinct cultural-national population. Having felt the repressions of a long series of outside imperialisms—Turkish, Austro-Hungarian, German, Russian—most eastern European minorities have had their group self-consciousness and cohesiveness sharply accentuated. It seems not unreasonable to suppose that the present Russian domination of this area, as well as the highly centralized national domination within the eastern European countries, will face the same kind of group resistance already witnessed, in both external and internal affairs, in Yugoslavia.

The Jewish minority in the United States has had, as we shall see in some detail in Chapter 9, a somewhat different experience from that of other immigrant groups. Jewish history, class status, and to some degree religious beliefs have created a different pattern of interaction between Jews and the dominant group than has been the case, for example, with the successive waves of Irish, German, and Italian immigrants.

Racial passing particularly and assimilation on an individual basis (e.g., a Jew who gives up his religion and leaves the Jewish Community) as well are not guaranteed to permit the individual to avoid all the consequences of minority-group status. There is the danger of "discovery," which might destroy the whole pattern of adjustment that the individual had achieved. There is the problem of relationship to one's old friends and community. To break contact completely is a painful experience. Sutherland cites the case of a Negro brother and sister who passed, but who were deeply upset when their mother became ill, and later died, and they were unable to visit her for fear of revealing their identity.[3] Some persons who pass develop a sense of guilt that they have deserted "their group." They cannot completely break off identification with it. Some members of their former community may look with approval and encouragement at their decision (happy that they are avoiding some of the hardships of their former status or glad that they are putting something over on the whites). Others, however, may strongly disapprove of their action, and so give those who pass a sense of fear or guilt. Passing is largely limited to urban communities, where one's former status can more readily be hidden.

Despite these difficulties, passing is for a few members of minority groups a decisive way to avoid some of the penalties of their status. Doubtless many more use it temporarily for specific purposes, than attempt to cross permanently into the dominant group.

2. Upper-class members of a minority are able to avoid some of the

[3] See Robert L. Sutherland, *Color, Class, and Personality*, American Council on Education, 1942, p. 43.

prejudice and discrimination directed against their group by sealing themselves off from contact with lower-class members of their group as much as possible, and insulating themselves from their struggles and problems. They are able to afford well-ordered lives free from contact with the dominant group in large measure, and free from dependence upon it. Under these circumstances, some upper-class persons develop a complacency about "race problems." Having achieved a satisfactory adjustment, they see no reason to endanger it by allowing themselves to be identified with the minority group as a whole. (Many upper-class persons, of course, refuse to make this adjustment and instead become aggressive leaders of the minority.) Those who choose this kind of avoidance do not find the tactic wholly successful. Even those who have most successfully reduced the necessity for contact with the dominant group run into rigid barriers, especially with regard to finding a good place to live and in economic matters. Some have feelings of guilt in connection with their disregard of the problems of the whole group with which the majority identifies them, making their "complacency" in the matter somewhat less than whole-hearted.[4]

An interesting aspect of the desire to avoid economic dependence and involvement with the dominant community, found particularly among middle- and upper-class business and professional people—and useful mainly to them—is the effort to persuade the members of a minority group to patronize only business and professional people from their own group. Some leaders have developed this into an ideology of a "separate economy" or a "nation within a nation." This ideology, largely found among Negroes in our society, is closely related to the growth of Negro "nationalism." Its appeal has not been large for the great bulk of Negro people. For a small minority, however, who see in it a mode of adjustment, it has often led to support of segregation. It is an attempt to derive "advantages from the disadvantages." Some businessmen have appealed to "race pride" to reduce or eliminate competition with white businessmen. A few Negro teachers have said: If we are going to be discriminated against in securing employment in mixed schools, why not encourage the development of segregated schools in which all the jobs will be opened to us? The effects of lack of competition in the first example or of segregation on the personalities of white and Negro pupils in the second are given little or no attention by those who take such a stand.

3. The avoidance response to prejudice is made by a few in the development of communities composed only of minority-group persons—for example, the all-Negro town of Mound Bayou, Mississippi. Far more common are the segregated areas in our cities which are largely

---

[4] See *ibid.*, pp. 44–46.

forced upon the minority group but to some degree are encouraged by the desire to find an island partly free from the prejudice and discrimination of the dominant group. The people of Harlem, a major city in its own right, with a population of well over half a million, are able to avoid some of the daily and even hourly symbols and experiences of "inferiority." The great majority of the residents of Harlem cannot, however, avoid the fact that the very existence of Harlem as a separate community is largely a result of prejudice. They are still largely dependent upon white employers and white landlords. And even the *internal* structure and the processes of daily interaction within the segregated community are strongly influenced by the fact that it is a segregated area. This fact is always in the background, conditioning the internal status structure, influencing the nature of its leadership, affecting the cohesiveness of the community. Segregated communities have a decided tendency to split into factions—partly because of the intensified internal struggle for status, partly because of disagreements over the best way to deal with the dominant group. They often generate an ultranationalism among some of the members, a movement that is likely to increase the prejudice of the majority.

Thus a forced segregated community is an inadequate device for avoiding the consequences of prejudice and discrimination. Immigrant communities, faced with the additional problems of a language barrier and the question of cultural assimilation, are not to be understood simply as devices for avoiding the pressures of the dominant group. On the one hand, they serve as stepping stones to the new society; on the other, they serve to slow down the transition by acting as a center for the old culture—with native-language papers, schools and churches in the native tongue, and a general emphasis on the common background. The balance of these two tendencies varies from community to community, depending upon the size and type of the immigrant group and the attitudes of the larger society. Until about 1924 these communities were often kept intact by the constant influx of newcomers from abroad; but in the second and third generations there has been a progressive loss of functions, including the function of avoiding prejudice, as individual members were absorbed into the general community.

Jewish communities, again, are not entirely similar to those of other immigrant groups. The desire to avoid the continuous pressure of prejudice is important in their survival, although they are in part also a direct product of enforced segregation. As Louis Wirth points out, an individual Jew, having been successful in his field and having developed normal associations with a narrow circle outside Jewry, will come to think that prejudice does not apply to him; he relaxes, his personality expands. Then his hopes are shattered by a strong personal experience of prejudice or a significant rise in anti-Semitism as a movement. Few can face the hostility; they prefer to return to the community where they are accepted and where at least the daily contact with prejudiced persons can be reduced.[5]

4. The desire to escape a highly discriminatory situation has often been a powerful motive in the migration of persons of low status. Religious prejudice was one of the factors in the migration of some of the early settlers to America; discrimination against socialist workers encouraged a great many of them to leave Bismarck's Germany; discrimination and violence in Poland and Russia, particularly after 1880, and in Germany after 1933, caused millions of Jews to seek avoidance by emigration to western Europe, South America, Palestine, and the United States; and one of the propelling forces behind the migration of Negroes from South to North has been the hope of escaping from their position of low status. The success of such moves has varied greatly, depending on many factors: existing prejudices in the new situation; the ease with which the newcomers could be absorbed economically; the size of the migrating group; the degree to which the migrants desired assimilation or a separate, protected status, etc. One aspect of this kind of avoidance is the belief—based partly on known facts, partly on fervent hope—that the new land is the promised land, where the great problems of discrimination are solved. This has been the attitude of many southern Negroes toward the North.

5. For most people the rather intensive avoidance techniques which we have discussed are either impossible or held to be undesirable. Most members of minority groups have to face the fact of frequent contact with prejudiced members of the dominant group. They may try to reduce these by ordering goods from a catalogue or making reservations by telephone or patronizing the business and professional people of their own group. Charles S. Johnson reports the remarks of a Negro laborer who had severed his relations with several white insurance companies:

"I used to belong to two or three white insurance companies, but they have been dropped because they did not do right by me. I belong to a Negro company now, and I think I will remain with them and let the whites go their way. The Negroes need some help anyway. We have to do something to show these peckerwoods that they ought to respect us."

Another informant, a domestic servant living in the same area, goes fifty miles to Memphis to consult a Negro doctor because the local white doctors show so little concern and respect.[6]

These actions are largely motivated by the desire to maintain self-respect. In some situations, particularly in the rural South, Negroes try to avoid contact with whites for fear some violation, or supposed violation, of the etiquette of race relations may endanger their personal

[5] See Louis Wirth, *The Ghetto*, University of Chicago Press, 1928, pp. 263–281.
[6] Charles S. Johnson, *op. cit.*, p. 275.

safety. "The inability of Negroes to achieve reasonable protection through the courts against the danger of injury to person and property is a source of deep-lying and permanent feelings of insecurity. Situations holding such dangers are, therefore, consistently avoided."[7]

No matter how intensive the efforts to avoid contact with prejudiced persons, however, members of minority groups, particularly those of the lower classes, because of their economic dependence are almost certain to have frequent associations with persons of high status. Their efforts under these circumstances are directed toward avoiding some of the unwanted aspects of the contacts—the blows to self-respect or the dangers to personal safety.

"The small Negro professional or businessman is more likely to employ an avoidance device, which neither offends the white by behavior that would be interpreted as impudent, such as keeping his hat on, nor offends his own dignity too greatly, as would be the case if he removed his hat. He may not wear a hat at all, or he may remove it before meeting a white person, or wipe his brow to suggest that his head is too warm with a hat on."[8]

Johnson also tells of a lower-class Negro who drove his old car, with defective brakes, into a new and expensive car carrying a white man and three white women, badly denting the new car and slightly injuring one of the women. He avoided what might have been very painful consequences of this contact by the diversionary tactics of assuming a humble and caricatured role. He abused his old car for its bad sense in bumping into a white man's pretty automobile.

He pointed to the damage it had done to the new car and to the passengers; stroked the crushed fenders and side with his hat; elaborated on the stubborn and sinful recklessness of his "no-count" vehicle; threatened to take an ax and beat it into scrap iron. An upper-class Negro chanced to be passing shortly after the crash; and when he saw the cars in difficulty, stopped his car a short distance away and walked back to see if he could be of any assistance. In the midst of the tirade against his "ole fool of a nothin'," the old Negro without shifting the tempo of his speech signaled frantically to the other one to go back. Misunderstanding the signal, the upper-class Negro came closer, and without looking directly at him the other whispered, "Man, go on out of the way befo' you get me in trouble." The upper-class Negro withdrew to a distance and observed the remainder of the drama. In the end the white owner of the wrecked car helped the Negro push his old wreck off the highway, and the incident was closed.[9]

6. Frazier has recently described a somewhat different type of avoidance response. This is an effort not to avoid punishing or humiliating contact with the dominant group, but to escape the feelings of inferi-

[7] *Ibid.*, p. 272.
[8] *Ibid.*, pp. 261–262.
[9] *Ibid.*, pp. 283–284.

ority and futility that the discriminations of the dominant group have forced into one's own self-image. Some aspects of this process may have happy results, as judged by the dominant values, whereas other results are unfortunate. There may be strong efforts at self-improvement and an emphasis on education. There may develop, however, a "world of make-believe," as Frazier calls it, in which the members of a minority group struggle with their feelings of inferiority in wholly unrealistic terms. Frazier describes the exaggerations in the Negro press of the economic and cultural achievements of Negroes and the emphasis on Negro "society" as part of this world of make-believe. More particularly, he describes the search for excitement, glamour, and entertainment among the "black bourgeoisie," the new Negro middle class. "Their escape into a world of make-believe with its sham 'society' leaves them with a feeling of emptiness and futility which causes them to constantly seek an escape in new delusions. . . . However, the majority of the black bourgeoisie who seek an escape from their frustrations in delusions seemingly have not been able to find it in the delusion of wealth or power. They have found it in magic or chance, and in sex and alcohol."[10]

These escape devices doubtless indicate to an important degree "the mark of oppression," inadequate and self-defeating efforts to avoid a world that denies one the basis of self-respect. Before we conclude that such responses are wholly the result of prejudice and discrimination, however, we need to measure the extent to which similar patterns are found among "the white bourgeoisie." Negroes certainly have no monopoly on the world of make-believe. In a complex and rapidly changing society, most people carry some feelings of inadequacy and inferiority, and many develop awkward ways of responding to those feelings— chauvinism, perhaps, or prejudice; alcoholism or mental illness. Here again the concept of "functional alternatives" can be helpful, for widely different types of response can partly be understood as alternative ways of dealing with the same situation. Thus "the return to religion" in some may be matched in others by peer-group identification and "other-directedness," in Riesman's phrase. In *Blackways of Kent*, Hylan Lewis interprets a wide variety of different responses—aggression, heavy drinking, loitering, some aspects of religion—as alternative ways of struggling with a very difficult situation for Negroes in a small southern town. Studies of low-status whites in the same community indicate that they make many of the same responses.[11] The research task is to discover the conditions under which the various alternative responses to the sense of inferiority occur, and to describe the similarities and differences between members of the majority and minority groups in types of response.

[10] E. Franklin Frazier, *Black Bourgeoisie*, The Free Press, 1957, pp. 213, 231.
[11] Hylan Lewis, *Blackways of Kent*, University of North Carolina Press, 1955.

In sum, we see that avoidance, as a means of adjusting to prejudice and discrimination, varies all the way from complete withdrawal to playing a role in a specific incident. The behavior patterns it represents are largely *responses*—the results of the attitudes and behavior of the dominant group; but they also become part of the interaction which affects the dominant group. Seldom is a given action a pure case of avoidance; it more often contains also elements of aggression and protest, and perhaps also of acceptance.

VARIABLES AFFECTING TYPES AND EXTENT OF AVOIDANCE

At several points we have referred to the fact that avoidance, as an adjustment to prejudice, is not equally available to all members of a minority group. Those least dependent on the majority for jobs, housing, protection in the courts, etc., are most able to avoid painful contact. Segregation therefore does little to aid avoidance, because it is most often found precisely in those regions where minorities are most dependent on the dominant group. Other things being equal, the higher the income and occupational status of a minority-group member, the more successfully can he avoid direct contact with prejudice. Avoidance, in fact, may become part of the culture of upper-class members of a minority, as is the case among American Negroes. Even wealthy members of a low-status group, however, cannot avoid all contacts with prejudice and discrimination and cannot insulate their children completely from the dominant group.

Besides the occasional, though important, firsthand contacts which they must have with whites they are constantly brought into contact with the white world through books, newspapers, magazines, the movies, and the radio. Whenever through these various agencies of communication children of upper-class families hear or read things which are derogatory to the Negro, their parents are quick to combat such influences with ideas of their own and build up a conception of Negroes more suitable to their hearts' desire. Thus, the youth in the upper-class families acquire "ideal" defenses for their egos which become the fabric of their conventional selves. For the investigator it often proves an almost insuperable task to pierce these defenses and discover the real attitudes and feelings of upper-class youth in regard to their status as Negroes. These "ideal" defenses which protect their egos are often responsible for the contradictions between their actual behavior and their verbal explanation of their attitudes.

Thus, while one may say that children of upper-class Negro families are more sophisticated in their attitudes and responses toward their status as Negroes, it should be noted that much of this sophistication represents rationalizations and verbalizations which serve as protective covering for their inner feelings.[12]

---

[12] E. Franklin Frazier, *Negro Youth at the Crossways*, American Council on Education, 1940, pp. 63–64.

For lower-class members of a minority group, daily contacts with members of the dominant group in their roles of employer, landlord, merchant, police, etc., are almost inevitable. They are much less likely to use avoidance as a mode of adjustment, therefore; and when they do use it, the application is of the temporary and partial variety.

Aggression: Striking Back Against Prejudice and Discrimination

From the point of view of a contemporary science of personality, it seems unlikely that members of minority groups could experience the frustrations, the fears, and the tensions that come from their contact with prejudice and discrimination without feeling a large amount of hostility, of desire to strike back, to attack the source of their frustration or a substitute target. The nature of this aggression varies greatly from person to person and from group to group. Much of it will be unconscious—unrecognized as hostility either by the person using it or by the majority. A great deal of aggression will be directed away from the primary source of frustration because of the dangers or difficulties in attacking members of the dominant group. Underlying this diversity of expression, however, will be a common personality function. As we shall see, some writers go so far as to interpret almost all responses of minority-group members, no matter how unagressive they may seem on the surface, in terms of hostility. It does not seem possible, at our present level of knowledge, to accept this hypothesis with complete assurance. It is doubtless a mistake to try to bring all personality responses of minority-group members into this framework. But the evidence does point to the need for seeing the relationship between outward, more or less obvious acts of aggression and internal or covert modes of adjustment which seem very different but which, from the point of view of the person using them, serve the same social psychological functions. Majority-group members frequently fail to see the similarity in these different ways of behaving, and consequently seriously misunderstand the meaning of the behavior of minority-group members with whom they come in contact. In fact, the more completely the modes of aggression have to be disguised—in areas where overt hostility would be most vigorously suppressed and most violently punished by the dominant group—the more likely are people of high status to misinterpret the behavior of people of low status. It is precisely in these areas that the claim "to know" the minority group is most frequently asserted, because outward behavior is usually more uniform and predictable there. A deeper knowledge of personality, however, knowledge of the feelings, the desires, the motives of the persons of low status, will probably be lacking under these conditions.

In a valuable essay Hortense Powdermaker notes how modes of aggression change with varying conditions.[13] Even the faithful slave and the "meek, unaggressive" Negro that followed him after the Civil War were not, she asserts, lacking in hostility but were simply forced by circumstances, and taught by their culture, to express their hostility mainly in indirect and hidden ways. The nature of their religion, their internal relationships, even the strong tendency to identify with the master can be interpreted, in part, as modes of aggression. The slave was dependent upon the white man. His security and the avoidance of pain demanded the white man's good will, so that much of the hatred the Negro felt had to be repressed. There were, of course, direct expressions of hostility. Thousands ran away; others committed crimes against whites despite brutal punishment; there were slave revolts. The great majority, however, were "loyal," and expressed their hostility indirectly.

Powdermaker interprets even the meekness and deference to whites exhibited by the slave and the freedman, not as a lack of aggression but as a form of adaptation containing a great deal of aggression, an aggression whose mode of expression was appropriate to the personalities of those involved and the nature of the cultural surroundings. It was somewhat analogous, she says, to the behavior of the masochist, who gets pleasure from self-inflicted pain because of unconscious guilt feelings. There are basic differences, of course. The Negro's suffering was not unconsciously self-inflicted, as is the masochist's, but came from the cultural surroundings. The meekness, nevertheless, served some of the same personality functions as the masochist's self-inflicted pain. Following the sharply modified Freudian view of Theodore Reik, Powdermaker interprets the self-effacing humbleness of most slaves and the freedmen as an attempt to rescue victory from defeat—one's suffering is only a prelude to ultimate victory and reward; one gets power from his suffering. Meek Negroes, moreover, have feelings of guilt because of their hostile feelings toward the whites. They have taken the Christian injunctions against hatred seriously, yet they are continuously faced with situations that produce hatred. The meekness is a way of appeasing their own guilt feelings. A feeling of superiority is also a part of the pleasure of the "meek" Negro. He gets a sense of Christian virtue and also a feeling that he is fooling the whites—they don't know his true thoughts.

The nature of this "aggressive meekness" is perhaps best seen in the types of religious expression which have been important in the lives of many Negroes. Christian missionaries of pre-Civil War days emphasized the rewards for humbleness and the glories of the future life. This emphasis stemmed partly from their own doctrines and partly from the insistence of planters that they preach only that kind of religion. In any event it harmonized, considering the status they were caught in, with

---

[13] Hortense Powdermaker, "The Channeling of Negro Aggression by the Cultural Process," *American Journal of Sociology*, May, 1943, pp. 750–758.

the needs of the Negroes. The meek shall inherit the earth; the suffering shall be rewarded; and ultimate victory shall be given to the faithful, not the powerful. Not all the rewards were to be postponed to "the sweet by-and-by," but there was a strong other-worldly emphasis. It is also possible to interpret such religious beliefs as a kind of "vicarious avoidance" or escape; they help one to avoid the penalties of low status by devaluing this life, thus making one's sufferings here less important. Almost all of the responses we are discussing represent a combination of two, or all three, of the basic adjustment patterns.

Powdermaker points out that this type of adjustment has probably diminished. There has been a decline in religious faith, a less sincere belief in the rewards in heaven, and thus a deeper feeling of injury at the deprivations on earth. The reduction of illiteracy has brought more independence to the Negro. Migration to the cities has created a situation in which the meek adjustment is less likely to be successful. Most Negro leaders and institutions are stressing other ways of adaptation and protest. Altogether, more overt modes of aggression have increased and can be expected to increase further as the goals of Negroes become more and more like those of whites and as the rewards for the humble, unaggressive response decline.

Keeping in mind this concept of the hostility functions of many seemingly unaggressive acts, we can turn to a listing and brief discussion of some of the many ways in which minority-group members express their resentment against their status and attempt to strike back against their oppressors. These vary with the personalities of the people involved and with the environment. The response that is permitted, or likely to be effective, in one place might be dangerous or ineffective in another.

TYPES OF AGGRESSION

1. Some individuals become active and aggressive group leaders, professionally championing the claims of the whole group by editing papers, leading protest groups, organizing boycotts, trying to persuade friends among the dominant group to support them economically and politically. (To a few, this furnishes middle- and upper-class status and thus simultaneously aids them in avoiding some of the hardships of the group whom they defend.)

A few members of subservient groups express their aggression by proclaiming a racial patriotism or a strong group chauvinism. We shall discuss this in a later section on social movements among minority groups, but it needs some mention here in terms of the personality tendencies of the individuals involved. One small phase of the Negro protest movement in the United States is the assertion of the superiority of all things black, best shown in the doctrines of Marcus Garvey. This phenomenon reaches beyond the normal range of ethnocentrism in an attempt to turn what seems to be a handicap (because of the social situation) into an advantage. "I want to be black," some Negroes declare (including many who are most clearly Negro in physical type). This is in part a reflexive prejudice and in part an overcompensation for a strong desire to "be white"—that is, to have the advantages of being white.[14] There is some evidence that both the origin and the survival of the Jewish concept of a "chosen people" are in a measure products of the oppressions the Jews have experienced as a group. Japanese propaganda in the Far East before and during World War II to some degree exploited the feelings of resentment that Asiatics felt toward the race prejudice of the white man by developing a doctrine of the superiority of the darker peoples.

2. Direct physical aggression against one's oppressors is not unusual, especially among children but also among adults in some classes and areas. From the days of slavery some Negroes have expressed their resentment by furtive, individual acts of violence. Organized hostility has been very uncommon, largely, perhaps, because of a feeling of inevitable failure, partly because of the lack of internal solidarity among the oppressed group, particularly with regard to agreement on the appropriate means of dealing with the white man. The police and the courts are especially likely to side with a member of the dominant group in a case of physical aggression (see Chapter 14). Dollard cites the case of a white farmer who constantly allowed his horses to trample the corn of a Negro neighbor. When the Negro farmer finally, in desperation, threatened the white man with a gun, a lynching was barely averted, because the white neighbors reacted on "principle," not on the merits of the case.[15] The direct expression of aggression by violence is a larger part of the culture, or at least more readily permitted, in the lower than in the higher classes. It is also more likely, as we shall see, to be directed toward substitute targets near at hand—and less able to retaliate with a full arsenal of sanctions—than against a member of the dominant group.

3. Some counterassertion or aggression is more appropriately seen as against the whole status system than against specific individuals or situations. Efforts on the part of a member of a minority group to climb the economic ladder, and to demonstrate that climb by purchases appropriate to his new status, are usually interpreted as aggression by the dominant group. Dollard points out that in Southerntown a Negro's "place" is in the fields. When he becomes a skilled worker, seeks the frills of education, acquires more than a small parcel of land, or simply appears on the streets in good clothing on weekdays, he has shown an unwillingness to accept his "place," and his acts are interpreted as aggression. Since members of the dominant group will probably see

[14] See Robert L. Sutherland, op. cit., pp. 47–49.
[15] John Dollard, Caste and Class in a Southern Town, Yale University Press, 1937, pp. 291–292.

economic advance in this light, the minority-group member who has made economic gain may take them "at their word" and be encouraged to attack his status by ostentatious display and conspicuous consumption. For a Negro of moderate income to drive a high-priced automobile is, in effect, to say: This is my mark of equality. He attacks the status pattern not only by economic advance but by exaggerating his economic advance. (This is, of course, a phenomenon found widely among majority-group members as well. As *The New Yorker* would have Mrs. Smith say to Mrs. Jones: "You mean to say that all the while we have been trying to keep up with you, you have been trying to keep up with us?")

Ostentation is not to be interpreted solely as a means of aggression against a confining definition of economic "place." In part it is a mode of self-expression that may become exaggerated under conditions which prevent other modes of self-expression from being used. Thus it is likely to be exaggerated among minority-group members who have made some advancement, particularly in income, but whose activities are blocked from many channels. It should also be noted that the dominant group's interpretation of efforts to climb the economic and occupational ladder as aggression may be reason to hide and disguise, not display, any success in this regard, in order to avoid retaliation from the majority. In Southerntown, one Negro who owned and competently ran a large farm refrained from buying more land, which he could have afforded, in order to reduce the chance of attack. Another Negro owned several small parcels of land, hoping to avoid being too obviously in violation of the accepted role.[16]

4. Under some circumstances members of a minority group can express their hostility by withdrawing trade from the businesses of the dominant group, or from those individuals in the group who show the most prejudice and discrimination. This is partly an avoidance device, as we have seen, but it is also a sign of aggression. Where there is legal protection, this way of expressing resentment may take the form of organized boycotts, of "don't buy where you can't work" movements. The device is effective only where the minority group has substantial purchasing power and is important to the success of specific individuals in the dominant group.

In St. Louis, for example, when a white-owned chain store which did business almost exclusively with Negroes refused to employ Negro help, the local Urban League organized a boycott. Later, this campaign extended to the employment of Negroes in trucking companies and bakeries, and to motion-picture operators in houses that catered to Negroes. A Negro Housewives' League was formed by the Pittsburgh *Courier* to demonstrate the buying power of Negro customers to white advertisers. When one large dairy

[16] See *ibid.*, pp. 297–299.

company, which served Negroes, refused to hire them, the Housewives' League launched a boycott that caused the company's sales to drop alarmingly.[17]

In some plantation situations the mode of wage payment to the field hands is devised to keep them buying, on credit, at the plantation or company store. Any expression of resentment at the kind of treatment they receive or the prices they have to pay can be made, under these circumstances, only by risking the loss of a large part, or all, of a year's wages. With the development of an urban economy, however, with its regular wage payments and increased purchasing power, the situation changes. The successful bus boycott by Negroes in Montgomery, Alabama, in 1955–1956, is testimony not only of skilled leadership, but of the economic strength of Negroes in that city.

5. A form of aggression available to, and often used by, even the most powerless member of an oppressed group is to work slowly and awkwardly, or to leave a job entirely if the treatment is too offensive. Inefficient, lazy—and therefore costly—work is a source of a great deal of complaint from members of the dominant group. They usually assume it to be a proof of inferiority, failing to see that, whether by conscious intent or by lack of motivation, it is an expression of hostility and primarily a result of the low ceiling on opportunities which they impose on the minority group. Irresponsible or awkward work is a natural personality consequence of the situation. A Negro field hand or unskilled factory worker or janitor may not dare to stop work entirely, but he can be careless with the white man's time and goods. And, as Dollard indicates, the white man's resentment shows that he recognizes in this response an act of aggression. The situation is somewhat similar to the low efficiency and low motivation usually characteristic of "buck privates" in their nonfighting jobs in the Army. They too are caught in a status that many of them resent; they feel hostility that cannot be expressed openly against those who give them orders; their response is to "soldier" on the job, to do only what they are told to do, and that only to the barest minimum.[18] The same principle applies, in fact, to any work situation in which lack of confidence in the employers and lack of hope for advancement lead to low morale. Only slowly are many employers learn-

[17] Roi Ottley, *New World A-Coming*, Houghton Mifflin Company, 1943, pp. 113–114.
[18] The authors of *The American Soldier* found that the Army situation produced among white soldiers many of the same protests that Negroes had long used in reference to their treatment. "When white soldiers wrote about authoritarian practices in the Army, 'They treat us like dogs,' or 'This is supposed to be a democracy,' or 'Why don't they treat us like men?' the phrases have a familiar ring to those acquainted with Negro protests." See Samuel Stouffer, Edward Suchman, Leland DeVinney, Shirley Star, and Robin Williams, Jr., *The American Soldier: Adjustment During Army Life*, Princeton University Press, 1949, pp. 502–503.

ing that attention to the hopes and aspirations of their workers is essential for efficient production.

High labor turnover can be a similar expression of resentment. It may not be an effective method of hostility, but it brings some satisfaction as a sign of independence. The alarm that whites show in the South during times of heavy Negro emigration indicates the potential power of this weapon. In many situations the unreliability of servants is a source of much complaint but is little understood as an expression of aggression against inferior status. The Negro cook who leaves her job without warning must look upon her action as a form of aggression, and she therefore fears to reveal her intention in advance. By leaving an unpleasant situation she says, "I may be inferior and you may have many advantages over me, but at least you do not own my body."[19]

6. Aggression may be expressed under some circumstances by the withdrawal of the forms of deference and etiquette, by the loss of earlier feelings of affection and the development of feelings of distrust and suspicion. Dollard reports that in Southerntown the failure to follow the prescribed pattern of etiquette is immediately sensed by the whites as an act of aggression. This realization explains their insistence upon the established prestige forms. Their enforcement of this demand, even in some instances to the extreme of lynching, makes most Negroes in the South disguise their feelings of distrust and resentment and abide, overtly, by the enforced pattern of etiquette.[20] In the North, where the deference forms are largely lacking, Negroes far more frequently express their resentment by vigorous verbal attack. Johnson cites the case of an accomplished Negro woman lawyer in Chicago:

On one occasion she went to shop in a fashionable district. First, the elevator girl refused to take her upstairs, and then after she got upstairs nobody waited on her. When a man finally came to order her out, the lawyer attacked him verbally with great violence. She reported the story in part:

"I really shouted then. I was pointing my finger in his face and I said, 'If you touch me again (the man had touched her hand while she rang for the elevator), even my little finger, I'll have you arrested, and I've practiced in the courts long enough to have just enough influence to do it. Why,' I said, 'I kick your kind around every day in court. You've been used to Negroes who tuck their heads and run when you scowl. Well, let me tell you, this is a new kind of Negro and there are plenty more like me, so you'd better watch out. If I were a man I'd knock you down.' "[21]

Persons of different temperament, or in different areas, who have the same feelings of hostility that this woman had may feel the need to

[19] John Dollard, *op. cit.*, p. 301.
[20] See *ibid.*, pp. 301–307.
[21] Charles S. Johnson, *op. cit.*, p. 311.

inhibit their direct expression. We shall seriously misunderstand them, however, if we fail to see that these feelings will strongly affect their behavior in other ways.

7. Aggressive feelings may be embodied in literature—an articulate voice for the deep-seated but unexpressed hostilities of large numbers of people. This may take the form of folk tales and myths or of written literature. Among the American Indians, for example, many of the original myths have gradually taken on a content that helps them express their resentment against the white conquerors, giving support to Malinowski's remark: ". . . Myth . . . is not an idle rhapsody, not an aimless outpouring of vain imaginings, but a hard-working, extremely important cultural force."[22] One myth among the Iroquois Indians described the struggles between two brothers, one thought of as the Good Spirit, the other as the Evil Spirit. Among contemporary Oneidas, a branch of the Iroquois, the struggles between the brothers are often described in terms of a battle between Jesus and the Devil and also have been transmuted in an interesting way into a conflict between the Indian and the white man. One Oneida resident calls the good spirit Uncle Sam; in his version of the myth, as in others, the good spirit kills the evil one: "After Dawis-da got killed, Uncle Sam stayed on a big mountain. He slept there. . . . He said when he really wakes up he is going to chase the white people out. . . . Uncle Sam wanted to chase the white people out because they're steppin' on our necks."[23] In another version of the myth, the person telling the story, after describing a victory of "the great spirit or Jesus," says, ". . . He came back to where the Oneidas live and talked with them, he told them he was going west. . . . He said not to do away with your ways and customs. When I come back, show yourself by having a large feather in your head, so I will know which is Indians and whites. . . . I am going to wipe the whites into the ocean when I come back."[24]

These stories show the way in which myths become repositories for the new influences at work in a culture, and the bearers of the hopes and wishes of the people. The desires of the Oneidas (for freedom from abuses from white people) have been brought into their folklore, wherein they receive mystical sanction—a sanction not achieved in actual relations.

Written literature may contain a much more explicit aggressive theme in protest against prejudice and discrimination. Claude McKay writes:

> If we must die, let it not be like hogs
> Hunted and penned in an inglorious spot

---

[22] Bronislaw Malinowski, *Myth in Primitive Psychology*, W. W. Norton & Company, Inc., 1926, p. 12.
[23] From an unpublished manuscript by J. Milton Yinger.
[24] *Ibid.*

While round us bark the mad and hungry dogs,
Making their mock at our accursed lot.
If we must die, Oh let us nobly die,
So that our precious blood may not be shed
In vain; then even the monsters we defy
Shall be constrained to honor us though dead!

Oh, kinsmen! we must meet the common foe!
Though far outnumbered let us show us brave,
And for their thousand blows deal one death-blow!
What though before us lies the open grave?
Like men we'll face the murderous cowardly pack
Pressed to the wall, dying, but fighting back![25]

8. An almost universal way of expressing aggression is humor. Members of a dominant group are sometimes surprised to learn that their stereotyped jokes about minority-group members are matched in number and barbed sharpness by the jokes which the "inferior" people tell about them. As Myrdal says, "The main 'function' of the joke is thus to create a collective surreptitious approbation for something which cannot be approved explicitly because of moral inhibitions. To the whites the Negro jokes further serve the function of 'proving' the inferiority of the Negro. To the Negroes the function of the anti-white jokes is partly to pose the whites in a ridiculous light, which to them is a compensation. Partly it is a mechanism of psychological adjustment; they 'laugh off' their misfortunes, their faults, their inferiority."[26]

That humor is found in most conflict situations gives point to Myrdal's remark that it is a mode of adjustment. It may be used as a means of social control, to prevent individuals from following a disapproved course of action or to stop the action. It may, however, have no effect on the objective situation but serve rather to make one's own role in that situation seem more desirable, or to make the whole situation seem less important—and therefore one's own disadvantaged role of less consequence. Burma cites a number of authors who hold that the conflict element is essential to humor: "Jowett has said that every amusing story must of necessity be unkind, untrue, or immoral. Thomas Hobbes believed that humor arises from a conception of superiority in ourselves by comparison with the inferiority of others. Crothers has called it the 'frank enjoyment of the imperfect,' and more recently James L. Ford has said that humor 'is founded on the deathless principle of seeing someone get the worst of it.' "[27]

Some jokes require simply the addition of color to the persons in-

[25] From *Harlem Shadows* by Claude McKay, copyright, 1922, by Harcourt, Brace & Company.

[26] Gunnar Myrdal, *An American Dilemma*, Harper & Brothers, 1944, pp. 38–39.

[27] John H. Burma, "Humor as a Technique in Race Conflict," *American Sociological Review*, December, 1946, p. 710.

volved to express race conflict: ". . . When a *colored* boy could not do his geometry, his *white* teacher says he should be ashamed, for when George Washington was his age he was a surveyor. To which the Negro youth replies, 'Yes, and when he was your age he was President.' "[28] A joke may cut two ways, revealing both the Negro's plight and the white man's meanness or susceptibility to flattery: "A Negro drives through a red light in a Mississippi town. The sheriff yells, 'Hey, boy, where you think you going?' The Negro thinks fast and answers: 'Well, boss, when I see that green light come on an' all them white folks' cars goin' through, I says to myself, "That's the white folks' light!" So I don' move. Then when that ol' red light comes on, I jus' steps on the gas. I says, "That mus' be us niggers' light!" ' The sheriff replies, 'You're a good boy, Sam, but next time you kin go on the white folks' light.' "[29] Negroes have jokes that help them to laugh at Jim Crow incidents or the commands of whites. Two Negro maids are comparing notes: "At my place I have a terrible time; all day it's 'Yes, Ma'am,' 'Yes, Ma'am,' 'Yes, Ma'am.' " "Me, too," says the other, "but with me it's 'No, Sir,' 'No, Sir,' 'No, Sir.' "[30]

DISPLACED AGGRESSION

In Chapter 6 we discussed some of the attitudes that members of minority groups develop with regard to their fellow group members. We also noted that much of the aggression that might be expected to be directed against the dominant group is redirected, instead, against one's fellows or other substitute targets. These two ideas need now to be combined briefly in order to observe the hostility and tensions that characterize the interaction *within* a minority group. Two cautions are necessary at this point. Along with the forces making for conflict within these groups there are, as we have seen, a number of other forces that encourage cohesion and group solidarity, the balance varying with many factors. Secondly, it should not be supposed that all of the aggression within a minority group is displaced from the dominant group, which is the real target and cause of the hostility. Some of it is simply a product of the normal interaction *within* the group, the prejudice of the majority being, at most, an indirect factor.

Despite these qualifications, it seems apparent that some of the violence and hostility that, for example, Negroes show toward other Negroes is to be explained by displaced aggression and is properly included in this discussion of the aggressive response to prejudice and discrimination. Not knowing the true source of one's difficulties, or being unable

[28] *Ibid.*, p. 711.
[29] St. Clair Drake and Horace Cayton, *Black Metropolis*, Harcourt, Brace & Company, 1945, p. 723.
[30] John H. Burma, *op. cit.*, p. 712.

to attack what one believes is the true source because of its power, one turns upon an easily accessible and relatively powerless fellow group member. This person then receives not only the hostility which his own acts might have caused, but all the pent-up and blocked hostility that the accumulated experiences with the dominant group have caused. A higher level of conflict within a minority group is to be seen, then, not as a sign of a different nature, but as a product of prejudice.

The displacement may be not only toward one's immediate associates but also toward other minorities with whom one happens to be in contact. (Again, a feeling of solidarity *with* other minorities may also be a product of prejudice.) Negroes are sometimes susceptible, as we have seen, to anti-Semitism, beyond their hostility to other whites. Mexicans in the United States often show a strong anti-Negro feeling, partly in an effort to dissociate themselves, in their own minds and in the minds of the dominant whites, from identification with Negroes and partly as a form of displaced aggression. The hostility may be between subgroups of a minority—between Negroes from the West Indies and those born in the United States, between German Jews and those from eastern Europe.

Not all of the tendencies toward aggression—direct and displaced— of minority-group members are to be explained, of course, by prejudice and discrimination. Hostile feelings and impulses are part of the equipment of all human beings because of the gap between what they have learned to want or their innate desires and what they are permitted to attain. Physical laws of the universe, social rules, the competing desires of other persons, and the mutually contradictory desires within each person all combine to frustrate to some degree even the best-satisfied individual. It is not necessarily true that a person of inferior status will have more aggressive tendencies than the one who is dominant over him, because there are so many sources of aggression, prejudice being only one. Moreover, a member of a minority group may make an avoidance or an acceptance adjustment instead. On the other hand, the tendencies for aggression in the minority-group member may be stronger than can be explained by the prejudice he has experienced. Personal maladjustment or failures that are the result of other causes may be blamed on discrimination. A Negro, for example, as Sutherland points out, may be sensitive not only to real racial barriers but to imagined ones, every act of a white person being interpreted in racial terms, every criticism being an expression of prejudice, any failure to advance a sign of a categorical barrier. If such a person were white, he would find some other reason than race prejudice to explain his failure. In both instances, the causes are to be sought in the total personality-forming conditions.[31]

[31] See Robert L. Sutherland, *op. cit.*, p. 54.

VARIABLES AFFECTING TYPES AND EXTENT OF AGGRESSION

In the last several pages we have seen that minority-group members can express their hostility toward the dominant group in a number of ways, ranging all the way from direct and overt aggression to humor. It is important not to mistake the absence of overt aggression for a lack of feelings of hostility or for a lack of effects. If these effects are covert or heavily disguised, if they are obscured by external gestures of acceptance of an inferior status, they are nevertheless exceedingly important in the analysis of the personality tendencies of minority-group members. The powerful underlying feelings may be revealed overtly only in unusual circumstances—when anger overcomes fear, or a mob situation reduces the usual inhibitions. But the feelings are there at all times, influencing action and the whole pattern of intergroup relations.

There are important class, locality, and other group differences in expressing aggression, because of different personality tendencies, different traditional modes of expression of a particular minority group, different attitudes and culture patterns in the dominant group, different chances of success, and the chance factors of a specific situation. "The weapons employed by lower-class Negroes in expressing hostility covertly may take the form of petty sabotage, unexplained quitting of jobs, gossip, pseudo-ignorant malingering. Middle-class Negroes are in a better position to use the economic weapon of controlled purchasing power. Upper-class Negroes may use this also, but in addition they find it effective to use the method of indirect attack on the offending institutions by arousing outside public opinion."[32]

Because opportunities for successful direct aggression are much more limited for low-status members of a minority group than for those of middle or upper status, they are more likely to employ displaced aggression, to express their pent-up hostility against fellow group members. They probably do not conceive of their problems as a result of a generalized prejudice and are therefore more likely to attack the persons immediately around them. Fighting and physical violence have a more important place in the culture of lower classes, so that both direct and displaced aggression will take this form in the behavior of low-status persons more often. Their feelings of hostility may also be more intense. "Because of the large amount of family disorganization among lower-class Negroes, the child fails to enjoy the security, affectional as well as economic, which children in the middle and upper class enjoy. The child not only sees violence, but is also the object of the violent behavior of his parents."[33]

There are important regional differences in the types and extent of aggression, because of class differences, different chances of success, and

[32] Charles S. Johnson, op. cit., p. 302.
[33] E. Franklin Frazier, Negro Youth at the Crossways, p. 52.

different personality tendencies that result from varying processes of socialization. Lower-class Negro parents in border states, for example, are more likely to instruct their children to strike back when attacked by whites than are parents in the South. Negroes in the two areas experience prejudice in different ways. As Frazier says:

> Rather than being at least subconsciously made to be chronically afraid, the border Negro is ignored and treated with indifference or frank contempt. I believe that the commonplace Negroes fare more ill in personality in this atmosphere than do they under the distance-fixing etiquette and caste-distinguishing system of taboos of the southern regions. I believe that there are far more contented Negroes there, despite the lower basic scale of living, the seasonal hardships, and other undesirable conditions. Gifted youth in the South comes early to suffer the limitations in educational opportunities. Gifted Negroes in both areas come all too soon to recognize the limitation in opportunity to exercise their talents. Neither area is conducive of mental health for those well above the average in endowment.
>
> The border Negro struggles with rage where the southern Negro suffers from fear. The unconstructive wish fulfilling fantasies that are evoked by these states are respectively malevolent and escapist.[34]

Altogether, it is important to see the wide variety of ways aggressive feelings may be expressed and to keep carefully in mind the many influences which affect the extent and types of aggressive response to prejudice and discrimination.

Acceptance of Status as a Form of Adjustment

Contemporary sociology and cultural anthropology have shown that people can learn to adjust to, and even accept, extremely diverse circumstances that seem strange, painful, or evil to those who have received different training. Standards of value by which the desirability of a given status is judged, as well as the status itself, are a product of society. A whole group may accept what to others seems to be an inferior role, because it seems perfectly normal to them; it is taken for granted. Only contact with other standards of value, the acquisition of levels of aspiration that are blocked in the old status, may destroy acceptance of that status.

TYPES OF ACCEPTANCE

1. Whole-hearted. Under some circumstances members of a minority may fairly whole-heartedly accept an inferior position. This pattern of adjustment was fairly common, several decades ago, among American Negroes. It has frequently been said that Gandhi's biggest task was to persuade the outcastes of India to protest against their status. In both situations, acceptance of an inferior position is now far less common.

[34] *Ibid.*, p. 232.

Among Negroes in the United States it is limited almost entirely to what Johnson calls the "folk Negro," found in isolated rural areas, and to a few family servants who find their position acceptable because they identify closely with their employers.

2. Specific. Far more common than this acceptance of the whole status pattern is acceptance of some specific situation or some phase of a relationship that implies inferiority, either out of belief or out of desire to escape some unwanted aspect of the relationship. In the latter case, the acceptance borders closely on avoidance in terms of its social psychological function in the personality of the individual.

3. Unconscious. There is also a measure of acceptance in the attitude toward oneself and one's group that we have discussed in the preceding chapter. Even those members of a minority group who have come in closest contact with the values and aspirations of the dominant society, and thus are least willing to accept a categorical position of inferiority, often acquire, by that very contact, attitudes toward themselves and their group which characterize the majority. Thus we find feelings of inferiority and even of self-hatred, often deeply unconscious or disguised by assertions to the contrary, in many members of minority groups who have come to see themselves from the point of view of the majority.

It is clearly necessary to distinguish carefully among these three varieties of acceptance, for they have very different consequences for the behavior of persons who exhibit them. Complete acceptance is closely correlated with resignation and passivity. It becomes the dominant factor in the life of the individual who follows this pattern. Acceptance of some specific situation that requires an inferior role is far more likely to be a conscious or even a rational decision. It tells little about the total personality of the individual involved, for were he faced by a different situation he would make another mode of adjustment. Members of the dominant group may well misinterpret this kind of acceptance, mistaking it for passivity and a *general* willingness to abide by the requirements of inferior status. The unconscious adoption of feelings of inferiority and self-hatred produces ambivalence and tension in the individual that are important in his behavior. It may arouse an extraordinary amount of striving and even of aggressiveness, in order to overcome the feelings of inferiority. It may, however, be related to a disorganizing ambivalence, a tendency that is often found among "marginal men." Stonequist refers to the dual self-consciousness and identification of the marginal man, the fluctuating and contradictory opinions, the irrational, moody, and "temperamental" behavior, the "inferiority complexes" accompanied, in overcompensation, by "superiority complexes."[35]

[35] See Everett V. Stonequist, *The Marginal Man*, Charles Scribner's Sons, 1937, pp. 144–156.

Such personality tendencies as these may come from an unconscious acceptance of inferiority alongside contrary feelings and hopes of equality.

The whole-hearted acceptance of inferiority is characteristically a product of isolation—physical and/or social. There are few points of contact between the lower-class rural Negro and the white social world, for example, so that the segregation and discrimination involved are often not questioned.

The "folk Negro" is not, except in cases of helpless conflict with the white world, consciously aware of racial segregation and accepts it unemotionally as a part of his social world. The mobility of members of this group is within a narrow radius; they do not read and thus cannot make comparisons between their status and that of other Negroes elsewhere. For them the racial situation is not, as a rule, generalized but is conceived in terms of their personal relationships with good or bad landlords. The "white folks" are the ones who record their ages, see that they get "advances" for living, get them out of trouble, and get attention for them when they are sick. They know their world and have worked out sufficient satisfactions within it to permit life to go on without complaint, except as to "physical ailments," poor crops, church standing, and occasionally the wild behavior of those of their children who get dangerous notions in their heads about how they ought to act toward white people. Some folk Negroes do not consider the question of relations with white people important enough to discuss, or perhaps safe to discuss. The answer is usually, "We git 'long fine with our white folks— 'course them po' whites (or peckerwoods) make a lot of trouble."

The increased mobility of rural Negroes and the beginnings of a new education for their children are having their effect upon the "Negro folk society" as it continues to emerge from the cultural isolation of the plantation; but the basic folk patterns of life persist in some areas and in some individuals transferred from this setting to an urban environment.[36]

Acceptance may be based on a role that, despite the inferiority implied, brings security and a reflected glory. A Negro servant may feel rewarded by the friendly atmosphere, by the economic and personal security his job brings him, and by a sense of pride when appreciation is shown for his work. He can, in addition, have a feeling of identification with his employers, thus sharing their prestige and position.

Acceptance may be based on a genuine belief in the inferiority of one's own group—a result of accepting the standards of the dominant group. Johnson cites the case of a Birmingham millworker who felt far more comfortable when he was following the etiquette of race relations than when he was not and accepted his role as a natural result of his inferiority. With regard to voting, for example, he declared:

[36] Charles S. Johnson, op. cit., p. 245.

"I can't read and write, so I don't need to be voting just to be doing something. Ain't much need of these Negroes getting in that voting business anyhow. The white folks running the country, and he can't do no good. That's the way it looks like it is to me."

In spite of full acceptance of the Negro status and belief in his own inadequacy, there is a tinge of self-pity and even resentment in his estimate of this disparity. "Sambo," he said with an exaggerated gesture of emphasis, "sho' has a hard time. He got to make it easy for everybody else."[37]

Even in this instance the entering wedge of conflict is apparent. The number of persons in the United States and, one may say with confidence, around the world who are willing to accept whole-heartedly an inferior status and find themselves well adjusted to that role is declining sharply. The picture of the "folk Negro" is important, not so much because that is a common type as because it is an important part of the background out of which the other two types of acceptance are emerging. Belief in inferiority may be gone, but one may still accept his status to hold a job, to gain a favor, or simply to avoid trouble: "There is an insistent urge to conform to the pattern of expected behavior in the desire for personal security; and the resultant acceptance behavior may conceal varying degrees of resentment, hostility, or sheer fatalistic resignation."[38]

Having lost belief in the doctrines of inferiority which justify discrimination, and feeling at odds with oneself for accepting an inferior position, one may feel obliged to rationalize the acceptance or develop a protective ignorance about the situation.

"A Negro real-estate man in Atlanta, who has a fairly large business bringing him in frequent contact with the institutions of the white community said:

" 'At the Court House they have a colored elevator, but that don't bother me. *It runs like the rest of them.*'

"Regarding the matter of voting, he said:

" 'I'm a Republican and in Georgia they don't have primaries. They have a convention. *I never go, but I could if I wanted to. . . .*' "[39]

A Negro dentist in Houston declared that he knew of nothing special that a Negro was expected to do. He noted that when there were meetings that included white and colored dentists, there was never any eating; and this was a sore spot with him. Yet he said, "It may be we could eat if we tried," without indicating who would try or suggesting that the subject was taboo. A helpful ignorance protected him, at least on the surface, against the injury involved in this taboo.[40]

[37] *Ibid.,* p. 256.
[38] *Ibid.,* pp. 256–257.
[39] *Ibid.,* p. 264.
[40] See *ibid.,* pp. 264–265.

VARIABLES AFFECTING TYPES AND EXTENT OF ACCEPTANCE

In acceptance, as in avoidance and aggression, one cannot speak of the reaction of "the" Negro, or "the" colonial, or "the" Jew. In each instance there are variations among classes, age groups, regions, and many other types of groups. There are also variations in individual experience and temperament that affect the nature of the response. We cannot discuss all of the possible variables but for illustrative purposes will refer to the differences in amount of acceptance of status found among Negroes of different ages. Powdermaker contends that the older Negroes, those born into the Reconstruction or even the pre-Civil War pattern, are far more likely to share belief in their own inferiority. They look to the whites for help and advice and acknowledge their superiority.

Middle-aged Negroes less often believe whites are superior but often act as if they do. They have grown up to less dependence upon the whites, have more education, are no longer helplessly illiterate. They have heard about democracy, and have seen some of their contemporaries succeed in climbing the occupational and income ladders. Oppositely, they have seen white men suffer economically and politically. Thus they have come quietly to the conclusion that the white man is not different. They keep these attitudes to themselves as much as possible, however, to avoid arousing the white man's fears and prejudices, and counsel their children to avoid open protests.

Younger Negroes agree with their parents in holding themselves equal but frequently disagree on the proper response to prejudice. They are better educated, are more completely in contact with the total American culture, are more mobile. They are far more likely to express open resentment against the imposition of an inferior status. The gap between their aspirations and their achievements is too wide for them to accept the situation quietly.[41] Before World War II a great many movements of protest and assertion swept the ranks of urban Negroes, particularly in the North. And the war, with the ideology it emphasized and the sacrifices it demanded, greatly stimulated these movements. Insofar as there is acceptance, the type that is most frequently found among younger Negroes in our cities is the third type discussed above: the unconscious feeling of inferiority drilled into them by the power of the dominant community. Such acceptance does not result in a lack of protests. The ambivalence it creates, however, affects the nature of the protests, making them more emotional and probably less effective.

The difference in degree of acceptance among age groups is highly complicated, of course, by other variables. An upper-class older Negro will react differently from an isolated rural older Negro. Age itself is probably not the important variable. It happens simply to be correlated

[41] See Hortense Powdermaker, *After Freedom. A Cultural Study in the Deep South*, The Viking Press, Inc., 1939, pp. 325–333.

with education, degree of urbanness, knowledge of "the American dream," and availability of contact with social movements and ideas, both Negro and white, which expose and oppose the old status patterns.[42]

It is well to recall again that seldom will a response be purely of an acceptance, aggressive, or avoidance variety. In studying acceptance one must particularly avoid mistaking surface accommodation for a thoroughgoing willingness to stay in one's "place." Oppositely, one must not assume that overt expressions of hostility and aggression against his status position prove that a minority-group member in no way accepts the majority definition of his role. It is probably true that most southern Negroes have much stronger feelings of aggression than their accommodating behavior indicates; and northern Negroes have more unconscious feelings of acceptance ("self-hatred") than their avoidance or aggressive behavior indicates. Frazier writes:

> As indicated by their overt behavior, the youth in lower-class families included in our investigation were, on the whole, accommodated to the inferior status of the Negro in the community. But the outward accommodations often concealed latent conflicts between their wishes and conceptions of themselves on the one hand, and the status assigned them by the white community on the other. These conflicts were revealed in their expressions of resentment toward subordination to whites, in their sporadic outbursts of aggression, and in their sullen and "mean" dispositions, which reflected their humiliations and frustrations.
>
> The attitudes of the youth are undoubtedly influenced by the resentment which their parents, though accommodated to their inferior status, often expressed within the security of the family.[43]

The student of the personality consequences of prejudice must look for the combination of responses on all levels of personality, and must be particularly alert to the many variables that produce that combination.

Organized Protests and Social Movements Among Minority Groups

One of the consequences of prejudice and discrimination for minority groups is the development of a wide variety of social movements and

[42] Banks has found, in fact, in a recent study in Columbus, Ohio, that there were few differences among age groups in sensitivity to discrimination. Migrants from the South were most sensitive to discrimination, perhaps because their earliest experiences had made them alert to the problems of low status. Thus Powdermaker's data may apply only to a limited time and place, but they indicate the need for studying the differentiating factors involved in the determination of responses to discrimination. See W. S. M. Banks, II, "The Rank Order of Sensitivity to Discrimination of Negroes in Columbus, Ohio," *American Sociological Review*, August, 1950, pp. 529–534.

[43] E. Franklin Frazier, *Negro Youth at the Crossways*, p. 41.

organized group pressures to escape from or to improve their status. These range from highly emotional religious or nationalistic mass movements to the carefully planned use of legal, political, and economic weapons. They stem from the individual personality tendencies we have discussed above; but as these tendencies come to focus in organized groups and mass movements, they take on an analytically distinct new element—that of collective behavior. They cannot be understood simply by studying the needs and tendencies of isolated individuals because the interactional aspects of group phenomena require additional analysis.

We shall not at this point make a detailed study of such group effects, for they will be involved in a number of places in the analysis of social structure, and those that are especially concerned with social change will be discussed in Part III. Here, however, a brief statement of the general principles underlying such groups is necessary to relate them to the theme of this chapter.

Some of the social movements among minority groups are primarily attempts to escape or avoid the difficulties of their status; some are primarily aggressive protests against their lot; some, which on the surface may seem to be escape devices, are tangentially or indirectly attacks upon the dominant group. Insofar as it becomes concentrated in protest organizations, the sense of group solidarity discussed earlier tends to lead to attacks on the distribution of power and prestige. All over the world in the twentieth century, minority groups have organized for more effective opposition to their status. The group factor has focused their individual feelings of frustration, has given them some measure of common objectives, has intensified, by the reciprocal exchange involved, their antagonism to specific situations. The Congress party in India, over a period of more than half a century, has helped the Indians to bridge many internal differences that split them; it has focused their resentment, making it more effective. South Africa is witnessing a rising Bantu nationalism. American Negroes are participants in a wide variety of protest and/or escape movements—religious, political, and economic. In later chapters we shall study in some detail such diverse organizations as the National Association for the Advancement of Colored People, the Urban League, Negro nationalism, the followers of Marcus Garvey, the cult of Father Divine, etc. They represent many different kinds of attempts to change or adjust to the situation in which American Negroes find themselves. They are among the consequences of prejudice and discrimination. One can understand them only by analyzing the personality tendencies of the individuals involved and by studying the emergent new forces that result from more or less formalized group structure. The resentment of individual Negroes toward legal inequality is one thing; the same resentment focused through the organized legal activity of the National Association for the Advancement of Colored People is another; and both need analysis.

Most group responses to prejudice are of two varieties, not three; they are active aggressive protests against low status, or they are escapist avoidance devices. Seldom do they represent organized acceptance. The appeal of a Marcus Garvey, with at one time an estimated two million dues-paying members among American Negroes, is the attack appeal: Take advantage of one's difficulties; develop a reciprocal black national- ism (there was, of course, also escapism in the "back to Africa" slogan). Although this may, on the whole, have been an ineffective response, changing few of the forces that submerged American Negroes, it did give some a feeling of dignity and worth that was lacking in many other forms of adjustment. The appeal of Father Divine, on the other hand, is largely an escapist one; race disappears, problems of poverty and discrimination are not solved but devalued.

The analysis of group responses to prejudice must take account of such widely varying movements as the Ghost Dance religious cult among the Sioux Indians, Zionism among Jews, the pan-Asian movement spon- sored by Japan before and during World War II. The need is to interpret the combination of attack and escape represented by each development. The systematic study of organized protests and social movements is an important part of the analysis of the consequences of prejudice.

CHAPTER 8

The Consequences of Prejudice: Effects on Prejudiced Persons and Dominant Groups

We have seen in the preceding two chapters that prejudice and discrimination have important consequences for the personality development of minority-group members and important influences on the nature of social movements among them. The consequences for the dominant group are no less significant. Again it is difficult to separate causes from effects in this highly interactive situation. Once set in motion, many "consequences" become, in their turn, "causes" of further prejudice and discrimination. Feelings of guilt in the prejudiced person (effect) may be allayed by projection—by further prejudicial activity— and thus be the immediate "cause" of that activity. Or discrimination in the form of segregated schools (usually an effect of prejudice) may, because it proves to be an expensive luxury for a community, set in motion a host of other events which increase prejudice. The effect thus becomes a cause: The cost of duplicating facilities will lower the quality of schools for the children of the dominant group and cause resentment; segregation will minimize the kind of friendly, equal-status contact that reduces prejudice; blinding stereotypes will be perpetuated.

Before indicating some of the consequences of prejudice for members of the dominant group, we must also point out that they are almost always discussed in terms of some value stand, implicit, or explicitly stated. One can speak, for example, of the gains and the costs of prejudice. These may be gains and costs in terms of the values of the prejudiced person himself, or according to some scheme of "generally agreed-upon values," or in light of the premises of the person making the judgment. Often these three value schemes will coincide, but they may not. There are conflicts of value within a society and particularly there are differences in the ranking of values. "Freedom from contact with the members of a minority group" may in itself become a value, high in the ranking of some persons, of lower importance for others, and completely lacking for others.

The present authors do not see how the indication of value stands can be avoided in this discussion; nor do they see any reason to avoid them. The only requisite of a scientific approach in this regard is that the premises be made explicit. As we discuss the gains and the costs of prejudice and discrimination, we shall try to make clear to whom the particular consequence is a gain or a cost. If the reader has a different value stand or a different order in his hierarchy of values, he will, of course, make a different judgment. Description and analysis of the effects themselves, however, will, if they are valid, be agreed upon by all.

We must distinguish the gains or losses to individuals from those to groups—the community, nation, or world. We must remember that what is a gain to one member of the dominant group (granted his value hierarchy) would be a loss to another member of the dominant group with different preferences. And we must discriminate carefully between short-run and long-run consequences, for they may be very different— if not, indeed, opposites.

The Gains from Prejudice and Discrimination

It seems unlikely that man would show the enormous capacity for prejudice and discrimination which he frequently exhibits were it not for the gains he seems to acquire. To be sure, these may be primarily short-run individual gains, tied inextricably with serious long-run losses. Most of us, however, prefer a bird in the hand (the immediate gains from prejudice) to two in the bush (the gains to the whole society in the long run from abolishing prejudice), particularly if the concerted community action necessary for the long-run gains seems to be lacking. Moreover, the complicated interaction that makes prejudice costly in the long run is difficult to understand. The international consequences of my discriminatory treatment of Mexican migrant workers is far less apparent to me than the desirability of getting my crops picked as inexpensively as possible. If the latter course means gross underpayment, unsanitary living quarters, and great insecurity for the workers, a rationalizing prejudice will help me to justify the situation or see it as inevitable.

In *Caste and Class in a Southern Town*, John Dollard describes the three primary gains made by white people in terms of economic, sexual, and prestige advantages, all closely related (and, it should be noted again, all tied to disadvantages).

1. Economic gains are almost entirely limited to middle- and upper-class whites. They avoid the heavy manual and monotonous types of work that our society considers most undesirable. (Dollard points out that this has a boomerang effect. In a society where the whites are not so completely assured of a monopoly on the more favorable jobs by the automatic workings of the status system they are motivated to work for them, with gains in achievement. Oppositely, because Negroes in Southerntown cannot obtain such jobs even when they do strive, they too tend to be lacking in motivation.) White people are able, in a much higher proportion, not only to avoid the hardest work but also to escape the poorest-paid jobs. Many can take advantage of the Negro's helplessness to get cheap help. One informant told Dollard how she loved to ring the bell at her bedside at three o'clock in the morning to have her maid bring her ice water. She gave the maid a cabin, her food, and $2.50 a week (better than average wages in the 1930's), in return for which the maid did all the cooking, the laundry, and acted as baby sitter seven nights a week.[1]

The apparent economic gains are often reduced by the inefficiency of workers with low morale and the "pseudo-ignorant malingering" which we discussed in the preceding chapter, as well as by the long-run social costs we shall discuss later; but there remains a residue of economic advantage for those able to command the labor of minority-group members or otherwise take advantage of their relative powerlessness. When one rents a house to a person of low status, he often is able to charge a rent considerably higher than he could get from a member of the dominant group, because of the limited opportunities for housing the "inferior" person has. In a society characterized by job insecurity and the threat of unemployment it may be an immediate gain to an individual to reduce his competition for jobs by branding minority groups "inferior," keeping them out of his union, his social clubs (where jobs are often found), his medical association (for this is not simply a practice of the lower classes), or limiting their chances for vocational and professional training. The short-run, individual economic gains that come from prejudice are the opposite side of the same coin that we discussed at length in Chapter 4.

2. Often, in the relationships between a dominant and an oppressed group, a pattern of sexual contact between the men of the majority and the women of the minority group develops which allows some of the men of the dominant group to gain an immediate sexual advantage. The total effects of this pattern are, of course, distinct from the immediate physical gratification. Sexual contacts between "superior" and "inferior" influence in many important ways the nature of the relation-

---

[1] See John Dollard, *Caste and Class in a Southern Town*, Yale University Press, 1937, pp. 78–133.

ship between the dominant men and women, the family patterns of the majority and minority groups, the feelings and frustrations of the men of the oppressed group, the status position of the mixed offspring who may result, etc. Some of the disadvantages and costs of the sexual gain—the price paid—we shall discuss in the next section. This advantage will be seen as actually part of a vicious circle (vicious in terms of the total values of the dominant men themselves) and thus very costly.

Dollard discusses the sexual gains available to white men in Southerntown. The frequency of contact has perhaps declined considerably in recent decades, but the attitudes involved continue to prevail and to affect relationships between Negroes and whites. Many white men, of course, avoided and opposed sexual contact with Negro women because they could not accept the dual morality involved, or because the dominant moral code prevented full enjoyment, or for other reasons. Even they, however, have been affected by the attitudes and beliefs which have arisen to legitimatize the practice—that "the" Negro woman is aggressively sexual and easily accessible, that because she is "inferior" violation of the code of the dominant society is of little importance.

Why, in a situation where prejudice is strong, should Negro women seem sexually attractive to some white men? It may be that, precisely because the white men think them inferior, the men have less burden of guilt with regard to sex—a burden that is related to the way our society handles the question of sex. It may be aggression against Negro men. It may be a way of escaping the tight cultural controls on sex activity. Negro women are relatively "unprotected," and one of the functions of racial etiquette and the whole status pattern is perhaps to keep them unprotected and therefore accessible. It may be that Negro women on the average, because of the lack of other gratifications, are relatively more responsive, particularly when compared with white women who have been taught to fear sex—partly by the very situation we are describing. It is also important to ask why some Negro women permit white men, who relegate them to an inferior status, to achieve this gain. These are among the reasons mentioned by Dollard: the prestige that comes from being attractive to a white man (a rapidly declining factor as race consciousness has grown); an element of revenge on white women and on white men, by pulling them down from their own proclaimed values; the economic gain; the looseness, in many instances, of Negro marriage ties; and perhaps the greater desire, in an underprivileged group, for the immediate, transitory gratification of sexual pleasure.[2]

3. Most normal people enjoy the feeling that they are not just average members of society but are to some degree special and important. The enthusiastic way with which most of us identify with a winning baseball

[2] On this whole question see *ibid.*, pp. 134–172.

team or a glamorous and successful movie star indicates our appetite for prestige, vicarious as well as real. If my school is best, my community most attractive, and my nation all-powerful and all-wise, I somehow have gained in significance. If a whole group of fellow human beings can be kept in an inferior position and especially if they can be made to give daily signs of deference and humility—and if I can persuade myself by a system of beliefs that they really are inferior—I can get a comforting feeling of prestige that my own individual achievements might not command. Compare, says Dollard, the feeling one gets from having a bag carried by a porter in New York City with the feeling that comes from the work of a porter in the deep South: "In the Grand Central the Negro is a mechanism for moving weight from one point to another on the earth's surface; in the South he is this, and something more. The southern porter is extremely nice about it to boot and does various things that are flattering and exhilarating. If the traveler approaches the experience as an average individual rather than as a moral philosopher, he is bound to find it a pleasant contrast."[3] The constant show of deference from the minority group gives one "an expansive feeling of being something special and valuable," a sense of mastery.

The prestige gain of belonging to a "superior" group is seldom unambiguous; there are often self-doubts and doubts over the whole-hearted acceptance of his status by the minority-group member—doubts which lead to an almost compulsive need for reassurance in some instances, and thus to a rigid insistence that all the deference forms be followed to the letter.[4] The long-run total consequences, moreover, may add up to losses that far exceed the prestige gain, as we shall see. From the point of view of day-to-day adjustments, however, the feeling of mastery and importance may seem to be a real gain. It also assists in achieving the economic and sexual advantages. And, particularly for those of the dominant group who are most frustrated and least successful, it may have an adjustment value that prevents their lot from seeming unbearable. In a society where the "success pattern" is stressed but in which the technically open-class system imposes obstacles to success on a great many, egos are constantly being convicted of inferiority. The pseudo success of prejudice may allay the fear and sense of failure (even while it contributes to the likelihood of failure).

Therapists who fail to see this prestige gain, and the other gains as well, may attempt a head-on attack on prejudice instead of trying to create a situation in which prejudice is relatively useless. Where individuals are given some chance at economic security and advancement, where sexual contacts within the approved cultural framework are free of anxieties, rigidities, and internal contradictions, where members of

---

[3] *Ibid.*, p. 173.

[4] See *ibid.*, pp. 173–187; and Bertram Doyle, *The Etiquette of Race Relations in the South*, University of Chicago Press, 1937.

the dominant group have genuine opportunities for achievement, how-ever small, that will give them a feeling of self-confidence and worthi-ness—under these conditions prejudice will progressively decline and may come to be seen as a costly and inefficient way of achieving human values.

4. The nature of human society and culture makes one gain of preju-dice a peculiarly difficult one to reduce rapidly. Once established as a value, the sheer maintenance of a status system—even in the face of obvious costs—is considered desirable, an end in itself. The pattern of superiority-inferiority comes to be looked upon as good and right. To violate it is bad, an attack on one's sense of selfhood and feelings of solidarity with the community. A completely effective demonstration that prejudice and discrimination are costly in terms of a person's desires will not persuade him to abandon them, at least in a hurry, if he thinks they are essentially right. Few of us choose our course of action only after weighing the costs. Many a white South African, for example, might be shown that his pattern of discrimination against the Negroes of the area costs him money, produces a schizophrenic morality and religion, confuses the political life of the nation, and weakens its inter-national position, but he would continue to insist, probably into the second and third generation after the demonstration, that segregation and discrimination are right, are good in themselves—in spite of the cost. Such beliefs may have been, in the first place, rationalizations to justify other gains, but after being built into the whole fabric of a society, they tend to take on an independent existence. This assertion does not mean that they cannot be changed (see Part III of this volume), but it does mean that there will be a lag in the lives of some people between the reduction of the functions of prejudice and the reduction of prejudice itself. Many of us are capable of saying: That which is, is good—even if it's bad.

The Personality Costs of Prejudice

Our discussion of the gains that come from prejudice and discrimina-tion was continually qualified by the need for referring to the concomi-tant losses. Seldom are the gains achieved without cost to the individual and to the group. The evidence indicates, in fact, that in almost all instances the costs greatly outweigh the gains in terms of the values of prejudiced persons themselves. The great *interdependence* of all people within a society, and today of all the people in the world, makes it impossible for a dominant group to inflict penalties on minority groups without being penalized itself. In the eloquent words of John Donne, "No man is an *Iland*, intire of it selfe; every man is a peece of the *Continent*, a part of the *maine*; if a *Clod* bee washed away by the *Sea*, Europe is the lesse, as well as if a *Promontorie* were, as well as if a Mannor of thy friends or of thine owne were; any man's death diminishes me, because I am involved in Mankinde; And therefore never send to know for whom the bell tolls; It tolls for thee."[5] Booker T. Washington expressed something of the same idea when he said that the white man could not keep the colored man in the ditch without getting down there with him. Or we might put the notion of interdependence in the no less vivid terms of The New Yorker cartoon: Three mountain climbers are tied together as they climb a steep canyon wall. The woman at the top begins to slip and the man in the middle calls to the man below him, "There she goes!" "What do you mean," comes the reply, " 'There she goes'?" In a very real sense, the death of or the confining discrimination against any person "diminishes me."

We cannot write with great confidence of the personality costs of prejudice, because of the lack of well-controlled studies and the difficulty of separating cause from effect. In such a situation, implicit value judgments are particularly likely to slip into the discussion and interfere with objective analysis. (With the present authors, these would take the form of tendencies to exaggerate the personality damage that results from prejudice.) Keeping this danger in mind, we think that the evidence, nevertheless, indicates rather clearly that prejudice is an expensive luxury in terms of the prejudiced person's own total interests and values. The personality costs of prejudice will differ, of course, from individual to individual and from situation to situation. It is necessary to distinguish, for example, between the consequences of a prejudice that is taught to a child as a normal part of his culture and of one that is seized upon by an insecure person as an attempted adjustment pattern. The former prejudice may create guilt, tension, and tendencies toward projection in a person who is simultaneously taught democratic ideas of nonprejudice; but it may not pervade the whole personality in such a way as to affect most aspects of his behavior. The latter prejudice, however, may result not only in guilt, tension, and projection, but in a rigidity of mind and a compulsiveness in adjustment that block a realistic appraisal of one's problems. We cannot, in this brief discussion of the personality costs of prejudice, make a refined analysis in terms of types of individuals and types of situations involved. We shall speak in terms of some of the general consequences, only noting that the degree to which each consequence is applicable to a particular situation and the combination of consequences found there will vary widely.

THE COSTS OF IGNORANCE

By definition, prejudice is a categorical prejudgment of an individual because he is classified as a member of a particular group. One of the

---

[5] From *Devotions upon Emergent Occasions*, Cambridge University Press, 1923, p. 98.

inevitable effects of such judgment-before-the-fact, applying to a greater or less degree, is a loss of contact with reality. Rationality is held in high esteem in our society. It is contradicted by prejudice, which furnishes a greatly oversimplified or completely inaccurate "explanation" of one's difficulties and often also a program of action that is supposed to solve them. Because it is blind to the real causes, this program of action is unable to effect a real cure. Keeping the Negro "in his place" will somehow reduce our tensions, improve our economic position, and boost our shaky feelings of self-esteem. But what if this protection of our place in the status system actually has very little to do with our tensions, our economic insecurity, or our lack of self-confidence; what if, in fact, it is one of the *causes* of our difficulties (as we shall see below)? Then our prejudice blocks us from a realistic appraisal of the problems we face. Its program of action is a modern form of magic that manipulates symbols and follows rituals but knows nothing of the true course of events. When a great many Germans came to believe that most of their difficulties were caused by Jews, when they adopted a program of action dominated by anti-Semitism, they were blinded to the true causes of their problems. They were led then to accept leadership that was equally lacking (or uninterested) in understanding the basic forces at work, with the result that they soon faced the overwhelmingly greater problems of war. One pays a penalty for ignorance in interhuman relations as he does for ignorance of the physical world.

Myrdal speaks of "the convenience of ignorance." He refers to the almost studied lack of information and the misinformation with which the white American tries to protect the status system and make it seem reasonable and moral:

> One need not be a trained student of the race problem to learn a lot in a couple of days about the Negroes in a community which is not known by even its otherwise enlightened white residents. To an extent this ignorance is not simply "natural" but is part of the opportunistic escape reaction.
>
> It thus happens that not only the man in the street, but also the professional man, shows ignorance in his own field of work. One meets physicians who hold absurd ideas about the anatomical characteristics of the Negro people or about the frequency of disease among the Negroes in their own community; educators who have succeeded in keeping wholly unaware of the results of modern intelligence research; lawyers who believe that practically all the lynchings are caused by rape; ministers of the gospel who know practically nothing about Negro churches in their own town. In the North, particularly in such groups where contacts with Negroes are lacking or scarce, the knowledge might not be greater, but the number of erroneous conceptions seems much smaller. The important thing and the reason for suspecting this ignorance to be part of the escape apparatus is that knowledge is constantly twisted in one direction—toward classifying the Negro low and the white high.

The ignorance about the Negro is the more striking as the Southerner is himself convinced that he "knows the Negro," while the Yankee is supposedly ignorant on the subject. The insistence on the part of the Southern whites that they have reliable and intimate knowledge about the Negro problem is one of the most pathetic stereotypes in the South. In fact, the average Southerner "knows" the Negro and the interracial problem as the patient "knows" the toothache—in the sense that he feels a concern—not as the diagnosing dentist knows his own or his patient's trouble. He further "knows" the Negro in the sense that he is brought up to use a social technique in dealing with Negroes by which he is able to get them into submissive patterns of behavior. . . .

The ignorance about the Negro is not, it must be stressed, just a random lack of interest and knowledge. It is a tense and highstrung restriction and distortion of knowledge, and it indicates much deeper dislocations within the minds of the Southern whites. The blind spots are clearly visible in stereotyped opinions. The "function" of those stereotypes is, in fact, to serve as intellectual blinds. Thinking and talking in terms of stereotypes appear to be more common in the Negro problem than in other issues and more dominant in the regions of America where the race problem is prominent.

The stereotypes are ideological fragments which have been coined and sanctioned. They are abstract and unqualified, as popular thinking always tends to be. They express a belief that "all niggers" are thus and so. But, in addition, they are loaded with pretention to deep insight. It is because of this emotional charge that they can serve to block accurate observation in everyday living and detached thinking. They are treated as magical formulas. It is amazing to see the stern look of even educated people when they repeat these trite and worn banalities, inherited through the generations, as if they were pointing out something new and tremendously important, and also to watch their consternation and confusion when one tries to disturb their conventional thoughtways by "outlandish" questions.[6]

Myrdal might as aptly have entitled this observation "the inconvenience of ignorance," for one must point out not only the lack of information and the functions of that lack in serving the interests of the dominant group, but also the serious problems that result from faulty knowledge and attempts to make magical cures. When energies are directed by misinformation into activities that cannot possibly produce the desired result, the prejudice which helps to create that misinformation becomes a heavy cost.

Many Americans are also "conveniently ignorant" about Jews, vastly exaggerating their economic power and their group solidarity and holding a stereotyped view of their personality tendencies. This ignorance helps them rationalize anti-Semitic attitudes or behavior. The loss of contact with reality, however, which this ignorance entails reduces their ability to understand and to deal effectively with the real problems they face.

[6] Reprinted from *An American Dilemma* by Gunnar Myrdal, pp. 40–42, by permission of Harper & Brothers. Copyright 1944 by Harper & Brothers.

The Cost of Moral Ambivalence

Another personality consequence of prejudice is the development of seriously ambivalent, mutually contradictory views of life which cause one to be at odds with himself. What are the effects on the white child of being taught a democratic and Christian ideology and then also being taught, by words and actions, the contrary ideology of intergroup prejudice? The prejudice encourages him to displace his hostilities onto members of the socially designated "inferior" groups, but his democratic and Christian training prevents him from being quite sure of himself. There is a burden of guilt which will not, for the most part, be consciously recognized (although some of it may be revealed in the nature of the religion which a person accepts) but will be projected onto the minority group, with further feelings of hostility, more aggression, and intensified feelings of guilt. This vicious circle wastes one's resources and diverts his energies into ineffective actions. Myrdal considers this moral ambivalence the most important factor in race relations in the United States.

Though our study includes economic, social, and political race relations, at bottom our problem is the moral dilemma of the American—the conflict between his moral valuations on various levels of consciousness and generality. The "American Dilemma," referred to in the title of this book, is the ever-raging conflict between, on the one hand, the valuations preserved on the general plane which we shall call the "American Creed," where the American thinks, talks, and acts under the influence of high national and Christian precepts, and, on the other hand, the valuations on specific planes of individual and group living, where personal and local interests; economic, social, and sexual jealousies; considerations of community prestige and conformity; group prejudice against particular persons or types of people; and all sorts of miscellaneous wants, impulses, and habits dominate his outlook.[7]

The moral ambivalence produced by prejudice is illustrated in an important way by the tensions and the sustaining beliefs that are created by sexual activity between majority- and minority-group members. Lillian Smith, in *Killers of the Dream*, has given an insightful account of the costs to white men and women of the race-sex situation in the South. Although the pattern of relationship has changed a great deal in the last several decades, many of the beliefs and attitudes of earlier days survive to affect significantly the personality development of those who share them. The effects of contact between the races were sharply influenced by the religious and moral teachings which white children received: God was a God of love, and yet of wrath. "We were told that He loved us, and then we were told that He would burn us in everlasting flames of hell if we displeased Him."[8] They were taught that their

---

[7] *Ibid.*, p. xliii.

[8] Lillian Smith, *Killers of the Dream*, W. W. Norton & Company, Inc., 1949, p. 79.

bodies were things of shame and mystery, and yet that their white skin was a thing of glory, a source of strength and pride. They were taught that the black person was inferior and evil, yet many of their warmest relationships were with a colored nurse, and in adult life many white men found sexual pleasure with Negro women.

What a strange ugly trap the white race made for itself! Because these slaveholders were "Christian," they felt compelled to justify the holding of slaves by denying these slaves a soul, and denying them a place in the human family. Because they were puritan, they succeeded in developing a frigidity in their white women that precluded the possibility of mutual satisfaction. Lonely and baffled and frustrated by the state of affairs they had set up in their own homes and hearts, they could not resist the vigor and kindliness and gaiety of these slaves. And succumbing to desire, they mated with these dark women whom they had dehumanized in their minds, and fathered by them children who, according to their race philosophy, were "without souls" —a strange exotic new kind of creature, whom they made slaves of and sometimes sold on the auction block. The white man's roles as slaveholder and Christian and puritan were exacting far more than the strength of his mind could sustain. Each time he found the back-yard temptation irresistible his conscience split more deeply from his acts and his mind from things as they are.

The race-sex-sin spiral had begun. The more trails the white man made to back-yard cabins, the higher he raised his white wife on her pedestal when he returned to the big house. The higher the pedestal, the less he enjoyed her whom he had put there, for statues after all are only nice things to look at. More and more numerous became the little trails of escape from the statuary and more and more intricately they began to weave in and out of southern life. Guilt, shame, fear, lust spiralled each other. Then a time came, though it was decades later, when man's suspicion of white woman began to pull the spiral higher and higher. It was of course inevitable for him to suspect her of the sins he had committed so pleasantly and often. What if, he whispered, and the words were never finished. What if. . . . Too often white woman could only smile bleakly in reply to the unasked question. But white man mistook this empty smile for one of cryptic satisfaction and in jealous panic began to project his own sins on to the Negro male.[9]

Thus the white man confronted himself with guilts and fears that it took a great deal of emotional energy to try to dispel—the fear of "mongrelization" (which he projected onto the black man); guilt over the rejection of some of his own children; confusion in trying to free himself from a deep-seated childhood affection for a colored nurse, a second mother; fear "lest their sons, and especially their daughters, should feel the same attraction they felt and should perhaps continue the blending of races to which they and their forefathers had made such lavish contributions. And because they feared this, knowing the strength of temptation, they blocked their children's way by erecting

[9] *Ibid.*, pp. 116–117.

as many barriers as possible, extracting energy from their own guilt to build fortifications of law and custom against what they considered an 'irresistible sin.' "[10]

In this setting, a combination of circumstances set in motion a vicious circle. Rigid religious training, particularly with regard to the sinfulness of sex; the subtle or direct teaching of doctrines of race superiority; but along with these a warm and satisfying relationship to a colored nurse who was often more permissive and satisfying to the infant and the child than was his own mother—these had helped to shape an individual's personality when, in adult life, he sought for a satisfying physical relationship.

In the old days, a white child who had loved his colored nurse, his "mammy" with that passionate devotion which only small children feel, who had grown used to dark velvety skin, warm deep breast, rich soothing voice and the ease of a personality whose religion was centered in heaven not hell, who had felt when mind is tender the touch of a spirit almost free of sex anxiety, found it natural to seek in adolescence and adulthood a return of this profoundly pleasing experience. His memory was full of echoes . . . he could not rid himself of them. And he followed these echoes to back-yard cabins, to colored town, hoping to find there the substance of shadowy memories. Sometimes he found what he sought and formed a tender and passionate and deeply satisfying relation which he was often faithful to, despite cultural barriers. But always it was a relationship without honor in his own mind and region, and the source of profound anxiety which seeped like poison through his personality. Yet with it was always the old longing, the old desire for something that he could not find in his white wife.

Stifled, sometimes forced into the unconscious, though betrayed ingenuously by the bathos of the "my old mammy" theme, this ambivalent and tragic relationship of childhood—the white child and his colored nurse—has powerfully influenced the character of many southerners of the dominant class.[11]

This total combination of circumstances was shared directly by only a small minority perhaps, but a minority particularly important in affecting the nature of the society and the culture of the southern region. Others shared many of the traditional attitudes which grew up in this situation and participated, by identification, in its support. Although the elements in this pattern have all been modified, they survive with sufficient strength in fact and in tradition to be a primary factor in the personality development of many whites. The energy with which segregation is defended, the feeling that one has asked the really profound question when he asks, "Would you want your daughter to marry a colored man?" represent a deep separation in the personality of the white man.

[10] *Ibid.*, pp. 121–122.
[11] *Ibid.*, pp. 123–124.

Because white mother has always set up right and wrong, has with authority established the "do" and the "don't" of behavior, his conscience, as it grows in him, ties its allegiance to her and to the white culture and authority which she and his father represent. But to colored mother, persuasive in her relaxed ministrations, generous with her petting, he ties his pleasure feelings. . . . Part of him stays more and more in the world he "belongs" in; part of him stays forever in the world he dare not acknowledge. . . .

His "white" conscience, now, is hacking at his early love life, splitting it off more and more sharply into acceptable and unacceptable. . . .

He has almost completed the cheapening of this tender profound relationship that his culture insists upon. The segregation of his first love feelings is nearly perfected, but not quite; not ever is it quite finished. Deep down in him, he often reserves his play, his "real" pleasure, his relaxed enjoyment of sex activities, and his fantasy, for women as much like his nurse (they may or may not have colored skin) as his later life can discover.[12]

Not only the white men, of course, but also the white women were strongly influenced by this whole pattern. There was a strong tendency for the cultural taboos surrounding sex to be referred primarily to white women; the repressed sex feelings were directed, whether in action or fantasy, toward Negroes. "Sacred" white womanhood came to symbolize not just a barrier to Negro males but part of the ambivalent attitude toward sex of white men as well. White women who were taught that sex was to be shunned, and at the same time often experienced the loss of their own men (whose sex interest could not find complete expression with the women they themselves had designated as sacred), came to feel that sex was indeed largely an evil that split their homes. Their sexual unresponsiveness then encouraged their men to direct more of their sexual interest and to project more of their ideas of sexual vitality onto colored people, which further enhanced the dogma of sacred white womanhood, which in turn further frustrated the white women and blocked them from a normal warm relationship with their husbands.

This vicious circle was (and to a lesser degree is) costly to the white men and women involved. A few women fought against it by trying to adopt a masculine role. In recent years, more have fought against it by organizing to resist some elements in the whole pattern of relationship. "They would not have used the word 'sex' aloud, but their questions and answers told them that all a woman can expect from lingering on exalted heights is a hard chill afterward; that indeed, white women had not profited in the least from the psychosexual profit system which segregation in the South supported so lavishly. . . ."[13] Such thoughts at first were spontaneous individual protests—a conversation between a mother and a daughter, or indeed between a mistress and a maid. In

[12] *Ibid.*, pp. 128–130.
[13] *Ibid.*, p. 139.

time they took the form of an Association of Southern Women for the Prevention of Lynching and the support of other groups that were protesting some aspects of the pattern of discrimination. "They primly called themselves church women but churches were forgotten by everybody when they spoke their revolutionary words. They said calmly that they were not afraid of being raped; as for their sacredness, they could take care of it themselves; they did not need the chivalry of a lynching to protect them and they did not want it."[14]

Such protests, however, were from a minority. The majority tried to fill the gaps which their social role left in their lives by piety, by mastery of an elaborate social etiquette, by loving care of a garden—"planting and transplanting little secret dreams, making them live in an azalea, a rose, a camellia, when they could not live in their own arid lives."[15] "Culturally stunted by a region that still pays nice rewards to simple-mindedness in females, they had no defenses against blandishment. They listened to the round words of men's tribute to Sacred Womanhood and believed, thinking no doubt that if they were not sacred then what under God's heaven was the matter with them! Once hoisted up by the old colonels' oratory, they stayed on lonely pedestals and rigidly played 'statue' while their men went about more important affairs elsewhere."[16]

The women thus affected did not escape feelings of resentment, some of which were expressed in the form of rigid and repressive control over their own families. Having been among the victims of a tradition that repressed them and tried to make of them "psychic children," they became the vigilant guardians of that tradition.

Many a man went into politics, or joined the KKK, had a nervous breakdown or forged checks, got drunk or built a great industry, because he could no longer bear the police-state set up in his own home. But this would have been a hard thing for these good mothers and wives to believe, and for the men also. . . . With a rigid training they armored their children against their fantasies and sex feelings, preparing them for human relations as if for a cruel medieval battle. Thus they segregated sex from love and tenderness and obligations, and did not see how inevitably it would slip into secret back-door union with hate and guilt.[17]

Our discussion of some of the personality consequences of prejudice has been only illustrative. It has shown that in a society where rationality is prized and where the values of democracy and sexual fidelity are widely held, prejudice is a costly item. Further personality conse-

---

[14] *Ibid.*, p. 142.
[15] *Ibid.*, p. 138.
[16] *Ibid.*, p. 137.
[17] *Ibid.*, p. 147.

quences could be discussed. Most people would believe that a realistic appraisal of one's own worth and a lack of arrogance were to be prized. These are blocked by prejudice. Dominant individuals in a society characterized by discrimination bear an often overwhelming burden of fear and insecurity. White South Africans sometimes show an almost obsessive fear of revolt and violence from the repressed black men. The small southern town in the United States is characterized by locked doors and incidental firearms to a greater extent than an equivalent town in the North which lacks a minority group. Thus a pattern of discrimination is supported only at the cost of much irrationality, moral confusion, arrogance, and fear.

The Economic Costs of Prejudice

It is of course impossible to designate in precise dollar figures how much it "costs" to maintain a pattern of prejudice and discrimination, although there have been guesses by economists that the bill may be as high as thirty billion dollars a year in the United States. We can, however, indicate some of the ways in which specific groups among the dominant members of society are injured economically and in related ways by prejudice, and how society as a whole suffers.

Prejudice prevents the training and the use of man power at the highest possible skill. "When an aviation company turns away excellent aviators—former fliers of Uncle Sam—because their skins are the wrong color or they don't worship in the right church, and when the company's officials put into the pilots' seats men less competent but with a more correct ancestry, the lives of all passengers are endangered. . . . Who loses when should-be clerks are made executive heads and should-be executives are turned into delivery boys?"[18] John E. O'Gara, vice-president and general manager of Macy's Department Store, speaking to the Annual Conference of the American Management Association, declared that employment of Negroes in jobs demanding their highest skills would add six billions of dollars to the nation's buying power. Oppositely, the failure to do so makes them "a soft spot for subversive penetration" and forces a larger share of Negroes to be an economic burden on the community.[19]

In many areas of the country during the last several years, there has been a shortage of skilled carpenters, bricklayers, plumbers, and other craftsmen. Yet thousands of Negroes, veterans who worked as carpenters during World War II, are unable to practice their trade because of

[18] S. A. Fineberg, *Punishment Without Crime*, Doubleday & Company, Inc., 1949, pp. 60–61.
[19] Cited in *The Nation*, October 29, 1949, p. 407.

rulings from the building-trades unions that construction is almost entirely a white man's job.[20]

Prejudice that takes the form of segregated areas in housing and severe limitations on the economic opportunities of minority-group members is an important factor in the development and continuation of slums. Beyond the loss of skills and the loss of purchasing power that such a situation creates, there is the direct financial cost of large expenditures for public health, for fire protection, for police and courts, and for relief. These costs are much higher per capita in slum areas than in other parts of a community. Discriminatory limitation on the supply of housing for minority groups means that owners of the houses that are obtainable have less incentive to maintain their property in decent condition—they can rent anyway. This deterioration lowers the value of the bordering property of white persons and injures the whole community through the total costs of slums.[21]

In recent years, opposition to desegregation and the tensions over race relations that have characterized some parts of the South have prevented a number of industries from moving to the South. In 1956, a representative of the Fantus Factory Locating Service in New York stated that "at least 20 corporation moving projects" on which his firm was working were being reconsidered in light of the conditions in the South.[22] White employees of these firms do not want to move into an area threatened by conflict and dissension; furthermore, more and more companies have Negro personnel to consider.

The economic costs of prejudice are to be seen in South Africa, where the dominant white group is thoroughly dedicated to apartheid.

> The Government's objectives are to maximise profit as well as apartheid; indeed, profit is a major incentive for apartheid. Insofar as they are compatible, there is no problem for the Government. . . . However, difficulties in reconciling apartheid and profit arise in the industrial field . . . there is already industrial pressure to open up more semi-skilled and skilled occupations to the nonwhites, to employ workers in terms of their value to the organisation rather than on the basis of race, and to rationalise industry by the impersonal criterion of efficiency.[23]

These considerations have led the South African government to delay full application of apartheid to industry. They indicate the contradictions between the development of a full-scale modern economy, with

[20] See Elmo Roper in R. M. MacIver (ed.), *Discrimination and National Welfare*, Institute for Religious and Social Studies (distributed by Harper & Brothers), 1949, pp. 21–22.

[21] See *ibid.*, pp. 25–35.

[22] Reported in the column by Sylvia Porter, Cleveland *Plain Dealer*, March 3, 1956, p. 53.

[23] Leo Kuper, "The Control of Social Change: A South African Experiment," *Social Forces*, October, 1954, p. 26.

its demands for mobility, skilled workers, and rational organization, and a segregation pattern. South Africa may nevertheless cling to apartheid or, as Kuper suggests, may try to swing back from secondary industry to mining (especially with the growing importance of uranium), where segregation is more easily maintained. But this will be at the expense of full freedom in economic development.

Contemporary studies of modern industry are yielding abundant evidence that failure to pay attention to the workers' need for being treated with respect, for feeling that their judgments are considered in decisions that affect the job situation, leads to lower productivity, higher labor turnover, and, in the last analysis, higher costs. Workers from minority groups are particularly likely to lack the sense of being treated with full respect; hence this factor in the loss of efficiency applies especially to them. In Chapter 7 we noted that a partially intentional, partially unconscious inefficiency on the job was one of the aggressive responses to prejudice. It can be seen in the present context as one of the costs of prejudice.

The economic costs of segregated schools and other facilities must be measured not only in terms of duplicated expenditures but also in terms of the long-run expense of inadequate education and less efficient services. It is a case of buying a poorer product with more money. And in a society where millions of persons live outside the regions of their birth, poor schools in one area vastly affect the life of every other area as well as its own. It is well to recognize, however, that despite the long-run economic costs of segregated schools, the immediate fact is that in some communities desegregation will be very costly. This is true in communities with a high proportion of Negro pupils, if, as is often true, the expenditure per Negro child has been much less than the expenditure per white child. Desegregated schools that tried to maintain the standards set for white children would be more costly. The standards for Negro children have of course been very low in many areas and vastly need raising, and the long-run gains would be extensive; but it is unwise to forget the immediate fact that desegregation in some areas will be expensive.[24]

It is sometimes supposed that, although the upper classes—the employers and professional people—pay an economic price for prejudice in the loss of consumers and less choice among workers, the working classes—those who would face the most immediate competition from the labor of minority-group members—profit from a system that protects their advantages in the job market. We have seen that this is sometimes true for certain individuals, if one disregards the costs they carry as members of the general community. For many more, however,

[24] See Ernst W. Swanson and John A. Griffin (eds.), *Public Education in the South Today and Tomorrow*, University of North Carolina Press, 1955, especially chap. 7.

prejudice has proved to be a great economic burden. It has made it possible for some employers to pay them less—making up the difference in the currency of racial superiority. Racial, religious, and national prejudices have often stood in the way of union organization, whether through the conscious manipulation of the employer or the unintended effect of divided feeling. Recognition of this experience stands behind the vigorous attempts on the part of some labor unions to eliminate prejudice from their ranks.

A prejudice that has permitted a minority of the dominant whites in the South to exploit Negro labor is one of the key factors in the poverty of many of the *white* people of the region. Johnson noted that this situation goes back to the time of slavery:

> The plantation system did not require whites in any large numbers, and the lack of industries limited the growth both of a middle class and of white-collar workers. The "tarheelers" and "sand hillers" of the Carolinas, the "crackers" of Georgia, the "red necks" of Alabama, the "wool-hats" of Mississippi, the "piney woods folks," the "swamp dwellers" of Louisiana, together with others of the lower middle and lower classes, felt the brunt of the slave system. While the planters lived in the rich river bottoms, the poorer whites lived in the hills, nursing their illusion of a common destiny by virtue of a common color. The two classes seldom came into contact where dangerous economic contrasts could be made. The interclass struggle, hatred, and antagonism of the poorer whites were mitigated both by this geographical segregation and by the consoling rationalization of a superiority to the black labor that was controlled by the planters.[25]

Large numbers of "poor whites" continue to suffer economically from a system that tries to get a large share of its labor from a suppressed group. The adverse effects for the whole nation are heightened in an economy based on specialization and the division of labor, where the functional interrelatedness makes each individual highly dependent on others. As John Dollard says, barriers to the freely competitive location of each person in the economy are "technologically out of date."

Eric Johnston, former president of the United States Chamber of Commerce, stresses the interdependence that characterizes our economy:

> The withholding of jobs and business opportunities from some people does not make more jobs and business opportunities for others. Such a policy merely tends to drag down the whole economic level. You can't sell an electric refrigerator to a family that can't afford electricity. Perpetuating poverty for some merely guarantees stagnation for all. True economic progress demands that the whole nation move forward at the same time. It demands that all artificial barriers erected by ignorance and intolerance be removed. To put it in the simplest terms, we are all in business together. Intolerance is a species of boycott and any business or job boycott is a

[25] Charles S. Johnson, *Patterns of Negro Segregation*, Harper & Brothers, 1943, p. 79.

cancer in the economic body of the nation. I repeat, intolerance is destructive; prejudice produces no wealth; discrimination is a fool's economy.[26]

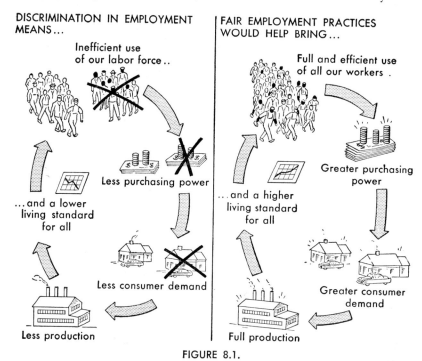

DISCRIMINATION IN EMPLOYMENT MEANS...

Inefficient use of our labor force..

Less purchasing power

...and a lower living standard for all

Less consumer demand

Less production

FAIR EMPLOYMENT PRACTICES WOULD HELP BRING...

Full and efficient use of all our workers .

Greater purchasing power

...and a higher living standard for all

Greater consumer demand

Full production

FIGURE 8.1.

The Report of the President's Committee on Civil Rights gives a graphic description of economic interdependence (see Figure 8.1).

Prejudice and the National Welfare: Politics

It is generally held in the United States that a nation unified by common purposes and a shared allegiance is greatly to be desired. Virtually everybody also defends a political system in which differences of interest are resolved or compromised in a process of free discussion and by the action of democratically elected representatives. It is a truism to say that prejudice and discrimination attack these values; but some of the precise ways in which they injure the democratic process should be noted. Not everybody, of course, shares these values or gives them top priority. Some people have political power or hold office precisely because of prejudice and tend, therefore, to look upon the results that we mention below not as costs but as gains. A reader who takes this position

[26] Quoted in the report of the President's Committee on Civil Rights, *To Secure These Rights*, Simon and Schuster, Inc., 1947, pp. 142–143. Figure 8.1 is from this report.

will want to reverse the value orientation of the following discussion but will concur, if the analysis is accurate, on what the effects are.

In the South, one important political concomitant of prejudice has been the long series of devices, used since the days of Reconstruction, for keeping the Negro disfranchised. We are not interested at this point in describing the role of minority groups in the political process (see Chapters 14 and 15), but simply in noting some of the costs of this situation for the majority. Not only has the Negro been prevented until recently from achieving the gains that he might make by using the political instrument, but the great majority of white people of all classes have been injured. The lower-class whites have been made politically ineffective by the prevailing system; all the people of the southern region, even those who technically manage the governmental machinery, have been affected by the limitation on issues that come to the fore in a political situation geared to protecting a status system; and the nation as a whole is vitally influenced in a federal system in which the votes of representatives from each area determine policies that affect citizens in every area. Let us examine each of these situations briefly.

1. Some of the laws that have been devised to disfranchise the Negro have a similar effect on many of the whites. If the poll tax in five states is an economic barrier to colored citizens, it is scarcely less so to an even larger number of whites. The poorer whites are also affected to a minor degree by educational and property requirements in some states. Actual disfranchisement, however, is far less significant than a general political ineffectiveness. Approximately 25 percent of eligible voters go to the polls in a typical election in the South, compared with about 50 percent in the North. This reflects not only inability to vote but also a lack of interest in government. The lower classes have little power in party circles, except for the few who actively enter politics. (This is an important avenue of vertical social mobility for some, but seldom do they stand as representatives of the lower classes.)

A political system whose key function, at least on the surface, has been to keep the Negro from political power puts a sharp limitation on the kinds of issues that will be discussed. There is a tendency for all candidates to center their claims around their enthusiasm for, and their ability to enforce, the status system. "Personalities" thus tend to be the "issues" of the campaign. In a one-party system—the product of a desire not only to disfranchise the Negro but to control the average white citizen—significant local, national, and international issues are obscured even more than they are in the usual dual-party or multiparty campaign. When all candidates must try to prove that they are the "true" representatives of the party, they inevitably tie themselves to old slogans and tradition.

Not only do the masses of whites in the South find themselves, because of their desire to keep the Negro down, faced by a political system that obscures the central political issues; they also put themselves more largely under the influence of demagogues. With one-party politics enforcing a kind of unnatural political unity on white men, they are reduced to a negative least common denominator of solidarity—white supremacy. The person seeking political power is encouraged to appeal to this common emotion. A candidate who tried to make a rational analysis of an issue would divide the electorate, but one manipulating the theme of white supremacy could count on a vigorous emotional agreement from the great majority. "Men hungry for political and economic power could not resist exploiting this terrifying complex of guilt, anxiety, sex jealousy, and loneliness. By pumping from this vast reservoir—which had accumulated during long periods of stress—the mass hysteria they need to irrigate their political and economic crops, they kept them green. And they are still green today, cultivated by the same system."[27] That important changes are occurring in this situation we shall see in Chapters 14 and 15; but for decades past, and even now to an important degree, the great majority of white Southerners pay for prejudice by political ineffectiveness.

2. It is usually assumed that even if the Negro and the poorer whites suffer from an oligarchic political situation, at least the small group of dominant whites profit by the one-party system, the small electorate, and their own controlling position in political activity. Even this assumption is not entirely correct. They too suffer from a political system that easily gives power to men who play upon hate, fear, and prejudice. They suffer from the support this gives to all the other costs discussed above. And although it is not eliminated, the power they might have in national political circles is reduced. It is not by accident that no American President since the Civil War has come from the South. (Woodrow Wilson may be looked upon as a partial exception, since he was born in Virginia; but he was elected from New Jersey.) Until recently, the Democratic party has largely been able to count on the southern vote and thus has been able to give its major rewards to other sections. (We shall see shortly that some other factors increase the national power of southern political leaders.) Middle- and upper-class persons who are part of the rapidly expanding urban South are less effective politically because the race issue is the central problem of southern politics. Even more than in the rest of the country, rural areas are over represented in southern legislatures. So long as the race theme dominates political discussion, urban leaders are in a poorer position to work for policies much more important to their interest than segregation.

3. The political costs to the whole nation of a political system that rests in an important measure on race prejudice must also be noted. Each legislator in Congress, no matter how elected, represents every

[27] Lillian Smith, op. cit., p. 118.

citizen in the country; he sets policies and votes on laws that affect everybody. A senator from Mississippi elected by 3 or 4 percent of the adult population represents every citizen of Maine and South Dakota. Because of the one-party system and the small electorate, politicians in the South tend to have a longer tenure of office than those in the North. Thus, owing to the seniority system in Congress, southern representatives have a large number of committee chairmanships when the Democratic party is in power. They have the additional advantage of experience, which increases their power.

4. The political effects of prejudice in the North are somewhat different from those in the South but are also costly to people who start from a democratic value premise. There is little actual disfranchisement of Negroes or other minority-group members. By crowding them into slums, however, by limiting their economic opportunities and their educational incentives, the North helps to encourage bossism (a vote may seem to be a cheap price for a relief check or a Thanksgiving basket), political corruption, and apathy. And the whole community is affected by the political machine thus sustained. Democratic representation is also sometimes blocked in the North by gerrymandering—determining the boundaries of election districts in such a way that the vote of a minority group is cut into small segments, each too small to elect a candidate. This maneuver is reinforced by the failure to redistrict election areas when population changes. People may flow into an urban district and find themselves with the same representation as a rural area having perhaps only one-tenth the population. This problem does not apply only to minority groups; but as Myrdal points out with respect to Negroes, they are more seriously affected, even if there is no prejudicial intent, because they are moving to cities, which are underrepresented, because they live in the most crowded areas of the cities, which are most poorly represented, and because they are recent migrants.[28]

5. A final political cost of prejudice to the majority has not yet loomed large in the United States but under some circumstances grows in importance. This is the appeal to minority groups of political movements and ideologies that the dominant community considers subversive and dangerous. Every imperialist nation in recent years has carried the burden of arms, and often of battle against nationalist uprisings, as a price for its discriminatory treatment of colonial peoples. Where discrimination has been strongest, the national protests have taken the form of a reflexive prejudice that has reduced the chances for peaceful and coöperative interchange. Thus the relations of the nations of the West with the emerging nations of the Far East are complicated not simply by the desire for freedom, but by the suspicion and the prejudice that many of the people of the East have for the nations of the West.

[28] See Gunnar Myrdal, *op. cit.*, pp. 492–493.

The situation within the United States is not entirely different, although it has not developed very far. Negroes in northern cities, for example, have become communists in insignificant numbers (although perhaps in somewhat higher proportion than have whites), despite intensive efforts by the Communist party to win them. Many of them find it difficult, however, to give an unqualified allegiance to a nation that makes them second-class citizens. They were far less willing in World War II than in World War I to postpone their demands for equal rights. In the 1920's and 1930's a million or more gave some support to the chauvinistic Garvey movement. Many worked with the communists or admired some of their work, even if they did not join them. Drake and Cayton say of this question in Chicago:

With the Depression, "the Reds" emerged as leaders—fighting against evictions, leading demonstrations for more adequate relief, campaigning to free the Scottsboro Boys. Their reservoir of good will was filled to overflowing, with even the *Defender* writing an editorial on "Why We Cannot Hate Reds."

There has been much loose talk about Negroes going Red. A few hundred Negroes in Midwest Metropolis did "join the Party," some of them becoming prominent officials in the American Communist movement. They studied Marxism and became ideologically committed to the extension of World Socialism. But the Negro masses who "could not hate Reds" were not Marxian Socialists dreaming of a Socialist society—they were hungry, frustrated, angry people looking for a program of action. And the Reds had a plan. So Negroes joined the parades, attended the picnics, and fought bailiffs and policemen. As they did so they found white men marching and fighting beside them. . . . Hundreds, too, voted for Foster and Ford, Browder and Ford, for what other party since Reconstruction days had ever run a Negro for vice president of the United States? . . .

"The Reds" won the admiration of the Negro masses by default. They were the only white people who seemed to really care what happened to the Negro. Yet few Negro sympathizers were without reservations. Some thought Communists were "using Negroes." Others felt that "if they ever gain power they'll be just like the other crackers." Many regarded the interracial picnics and dances as "bait." But Negroes are realists. They take "friends" and allies where they can find them.[29]

If America has not yet faced the problem of a thoroughly restive political minority in her midst it is partly because of the inarticulateness of the masses of minority-group members, the compelling hope of the American dream, the progress toward equality that has been made in the last fifty years, and the lack until recently, in the world outside, of a powerful and successful competing system. If these conditions change,

[29] St. Clair Drake and Horace Cayton, *Black Metropolis*, Harcourt, Brace & Company, 1945, pp. 735–736; see also Wilson Record, *The Negro and the Communist Party*, University of North Carolina Press, 1951; and chaps. 14 and 15, below.

as the first and last have already changed, one can look for sharper internal conflicts, with the costs they entail. As the President's Committee on Civil Rights declared: "No nation can afford to have its component groups hostile toward one another without feeling the stress. People who live in a state of tension and suspicion cannot use their energy constructively."[30]

Prejudice and the National Welfare: International Relations

Closely related to the consequences of prejudice discussed in the preceding section are the effects on the relationships among nations of different race or religion. In times of international tension these become a particularly heavy cost and command the careful attention of policy makers. It has been widely noted that American treatment of minority groups receives world-wide attention. During World War II the forced relocation of Americans of Japanese ancestry and the discrimination and brutality shown toward Negroes in the United States were thoroughly exploited by Japan as propaganda among the colored peoples of the world. Even Germany, whose basic philosophy and practice were thoroughly discriminatory, played upon the theme of American hypocrisy. The propaganda was often exaggerated or distorted, but there were many instances of violence and injustice upon which to build, so that enemies of the United States had only to cite our own papers, or accounts in the press of our allies or of neutrals, to get evidence. A riot, a lynching, or a case of legal injustice in the United States was, and is, a subject of great interest in London, in Oslo, in Tokyo, in Moscow.

In the current conflicts between the Soviet Union and the United States, communist policy makers and propagandists are given a genuine advantage by past history and present incidents in American race relations. Both the imperialism and the color prejudice of many of the western powers have been of great advantage to the communists in winning the support of large numbers of colored people in the Far East. Winning the war was complicated for the United States by the mistrust and often hostility of colored allies who had heard of and experienced so much of the white man's prejudice. And now the even more important problem of finding a road to international coöperation under law is confused by the barriers of prejudice. Negroes have petitioned the United Nations for an investigation of their treatment in the United States—an indication of the fact that our prejudice is even less of a local issue than it used to be. In a world which has become so thoroughly interdependent white people dare not disregard the growing power and population of predominantly colored nations. For decades and probably centuries to come, white people will become a progressively smaller part

---

[30] President's Committee on Civil Rights, *op. cit.*

of the world's population. If they wait until colored people have achieved great power before they "grant" them equality, they may well face a reciprocal prejudice which will not be content simply with equality. As Myrdal says, "Their race pride and race prejudice is still mostly a defensive mental device, a secondary reaction built up to meet the humiliations of white supremacy. . . . It should be apparent that the time to come to an understanding on the basis of equality is rapidly running out. When colored nations have once acquired power but still sense the scorn of white superiority and racial discrimination, they are likely to become indoctrinated by a race prejudice much more akin to that of the whites—a race prejudice which can be satisfied only by the whites' humiliation and subjugation."[31] If, on the other hand, Myrdal goes on to say, America now moves toward a fuller realization of her own creed, if she takes the lead in abolishing color prejudice, she will gain immensely in prestige and power around the world. "In this sense the Negro problem is not only America's greatest failure but also America's incomparably great opportunity for the future."[32] A continuing shift toward equality for all on the part of the United States, in attitude and action, would probably not directly affect our relationship with the communist world, but it would deprive the communists of a powerful instrument and greatly reduce their attraction to the colored peoples.

Some of the precise ways in which prejudice and discrimination have been costly to the United States need to be indicated. The attitudes of the people of the Far East, one of the critical areas of the world today, have been greatly influenced by American action. Beginning with the Chinese Exclusion Act of 1882 and coming to a climax in the comprehensive immigration law of 1924, we have proclaimed to the Asiatic people that they were unfit for citizenship, that they were racially unqualified to associate with us. From the very beginning, this attitude affected international relations. Carey McWilliams points out that in 1882 an active anti-Semitic movement was being organized in Germany and that it immediately used the anti-Oriental laws and activities in the United States as an example to prepare German public opinion to favor exclusion of Jews.[33] In the Far East there were many reverberations of our "yellow peril" agitations; the Boxer Rebellion in China and the rise of militarism in Japan both drew power from American prejudice. Particularly after the passage of the Immigration Act of 1924 (which explicitly barred further Japanese immigration to the United States despite the fact that a "gentlemen's agreement" of almost two decades' standing had effectively achieved the same result with less resentment), nationalists in Japan began to exploit antiwhite sentiments. The act was

---

[31] Gunnar Myrdal, op. cit., p. 1018.
[32] Ibid., p. 1021.
[33] Carey McWilliams, A Mask for Privilege, Little, Brown & Company, 1948, p. 16.

very important in the defeat of Japanese liberals and in the rise of militarists to political power. Our prejudice was used ". . . as a means of inflaming Japanese public opinion against America; as the excuse for ever-increasing military and naval appropriations; as an excellent issue to exploit for domestic political purposes inside Japan; as a *quid pro quo* in dealings with the United States; and as a means of diverting widespread social discontent in Japan into chauvinistic channels."[34] People of the Orient are acquainted with the restrictive covenants in America, with laws that prohibit, in many states, the marriage of a white and an Oriental, with the economic barriers that many Asiatics face. Roger Baldwin writes: "In Japan in 1947 I heard repeated statements from high Japanese authorities, and former ambassadors to the United States, that the 1924 act did more than any other single factor to break the bonds of friendship with the American people and to set Japan on the road to anti-Americanism."[35] We do not imply that American prejudice completely explains or justifies Japanese activity; but it does indicate an important factor, and a heavy cost, in America's international relations. Between 1945 and 1952, modifications were made in our immigration laws to allow the entry of a few persons from each of the countries of the Far East (the quota being 100 per year for most of them), to permit the immigration of wives of American citizens from those lands, and to make it possible for legal entrants to become citizens. This belated and small recognition of some of the international consequences of our prejudice is perhaps significant.

Discrimination is also an expensive luxury for the United States in Central and South America. Our treatment of the two and a half million people of Mexican descent is a continuing problem between the United States and a nation whose friendship is of great importance to both the security and the economic interests of Americans. Particularly in the Southwest, along the extensive boundary that divides the two countries, people on both sides are continually asking favors that depend upon good will. "Interruption of this cooperative attitude would cost literally millions of dollars to individuals, businessmen, and local governments along the border. . . . You can almost measure the tempo of American relations with Mexico by the kindliness and non-discrimination—or its absence—in Texas."[36]

The Good Neighbor Policy, which has been such an important part of the foreign policy of the United States in recent years, is vitally affected by prejudice and discrimination. Our protestations of friendship sound less than sincere to the nations of the south when they are followed by expressions of race prejudice, either against them, against the

---

[34] Carey McWilliams, *Prejudice. Japanese-Americans: Symbol of Racial Intolerance*, Little, Brown & Company, 1944, p. 8.
[35] In R. M. MacIver, *op. cit.*, p. 87.
[36] Adolf Berle, Jr. in *ibid.*, p. 95.

citizens of other nations, or against residents of the United States itself who have migrated from these lands. Most of the Central and South American countries are complicated mixtures of Indian-Negro-white stock. Race lines are relatively unimportant and race prejudice is looked upon as an affront not only to the individual but to the nation as well.

An Inter-American conference was called last year to meet at Biloxi, Mississippi. The duly accredited diplomatic delegate of one of the invited countries was excluded from the hotel in which the conference was being held. During World War II, the Allied forces drove Mussolini's invading troops out of Abyssinia, whose reconstructed government the United States promptly recognized. Envoys from Abyssinia reached Washington, and, until the State Department got to work, were denied admission to any first-rate living quarters. Not long after, the wife of the Governor of a great French territory on an official visit to the United States was refused admission to a diner car on her trip North to be entertained at the White House. A relative of the President of a neighboring republic went into a cocktail lounge in Florida; the management undertook to throw him out; in the ensuing fray he was killed. One could multiply these stories.

. . . It is no exaggeration, I think, to say that the habit of race discrimination practiced in considerable parts of the United States is the greatest single danger to the foreign relations of the United States, and conceivably may become a real threat to American security.[37]

Berle points out that there is a strictly military as well as a diplomatic aspect to race relations in the western hemisphere. We have a ring of bases in the Caribbean area and in Panama that require the coöperation of the surrounding people, particularly because it is the stated United States policy that these bases are for hemispheric defense, not for nationalistic purposes. The race attitudes of military commanders and personnel are thus of great importance. If they show prejudice, they create ill will among the people and establish a focal point for propaganda against the United States and against the very existence of the base. "The 'Jim Crow' principle applied in the Caribbean area is a direct, continuing, and standing insult to the mass of population immediately surrounding the vital military establishments."[38]

The "Jim Crow" policies of the American armed forces themselves have been (and to a significantly smaller degree, owing to recent changes, are today) a threat to American security. Apart from the lowering of morale of minority-group members and the propaganda weapon it furnishes opponents, discrimination in the armed services makes for inefficiency. When the President's Committee on Equality of Treatment and Opportunity in the Armed Services began its study, they found that until recently all three military services had held that Negroes did not have the education and skills for the more technical military occupa-

[37] *Ibid.*, pp. 91–92.
[38] *Ibid.*, p. 97.

tions and that, because of precedent and custom, they had to be used in segregated units. For example, as of August, 1949, the Army had 490 active occupational specialties. In 198 of these specialties there were no authorizations for Negroes, despite the fact that ". . . the Army was seriously under strength in a great many of the specialties which had no Negro authorizations."[39] In its report to the President the committee, by reason and evidence, indicated the costliness and error in this situation:

> Meeting the military on its own premises and considering these questions strictly from the viewpoint of military efficiency, the Committee had serious doubts as to the reasoning by which the military had traditionally arrived at its policies of limited utilization and racial segregation. . . .
>
> The Committee, conscious of the handicaps under which many Negroes live and their lack of full educational advantages, did not question the contention that the Negro population as a whole did not parallel the white population as a whole in technical skills or education. . . .
>
> What the Committee questioned were the conclusions which some military officials drew from it. Conceding the differential in skill and ability between the white and Negro elements in the services, did this group difference justify denying to the individual Negro—solely on the ground of race—the opportunity to qualify for, and serve in, any job whatsoever? To put racial restrictions upon job opportunities seemed to the Committee to ignore completely the essential factor of individual differences. And insofar as a service refused to a single Negro the technical training and job for which he was qualified, by just so much did the service waste potential skills and impair its own effectiveness. Quite apart from the question of equal opportunity, the Committee did not believe the country or the military services could afford this human wastage.
>
> Furthermore, in considering the question of the Negro unit, it seemed to the Committee that segregation merely aggravated this waste and multiplied the inefficiency. Because of the group differential in skill and education, it seemed obvious that Negro units could not be created which would perform the complete range of functions required of white units, and Negro units therefore could not provide the opportunity for the same diversity of individual skills as white units. Yet a policy of segregation made mandatory the assignment of highly qualified Negroes to racial units where there might be no opening for their skills.[40]

When the committee asked the further question: Was it not better to suffer these losses than to face the loss of efficiency that might come from impaired morale in mixed units? they turned to the evidence from the few already existing mixed units and found an *improvement* in morale. Even the officers who had opposed the President's Executive Order directing the armed services to eliminate any barriers to equality

[39] President's Committee on Equality of Treatment and Opportunity in the Armed Services, *Freedom to Serve*, Government Printing Office, 1950, p. 58.
[40] *Ibid.*, pp. 12–13.

of treatment and opportunity on the basis of race, religion, or national origin agreed that the new program improved the services and caused less trouble.[41] America is beginning to learn the costliness of discrimination in her armed forces.

Summary

We have examined only a few of the costs and consequences of prejudice for members of the dominant group. Although there may be some gains, there are, from the point of view of the interests and values of the prejudiced person himself, far more losses in the long run. One could scarcely expect otherwise among a people who proclaim a democratic ideology with great fervor and in a highly interactive world of many races and religions. For those who rank "race purity" and segregation as in themselves among the most desirable of values this assertion is, of course, not true. But for those who give such values a low ranking or even a negative position, the costs of prejudice are demonstrably great. Many people agree with MacIver that the greatest cost of discrimination is the loss of purpose and solidarity that are the strength of a people. This statement may well sum up the whole question: "Whatever is distinctive about this country, its spiritual heritage, comes from the recognition and the liberation of the universal in man, transcending division and harmonizing differences. It is this heritage, exalting the rights and the liberties of men, that more than anything else America must stand for if it stands for anything. It cannot stand on alien traditions but on this thing that is peculiar to its own being. Without that, we are spiritually impoverished, voiceless, and inarticulate before the world."[42]

[41] See *ibid.*, p. 42; a more extensive analysis of changes in the armed services will be found in chap. 15.
[42] R. M. MacIver, *op. cit.*, p. 6.

CHAPTER 9

Anti-Semitism—A Case Study in Prejudice: The Sociology of Anti-Semitism

In the preceding six chapters we examined the major factors involved in prejudice and the consequences of prejudice for both the dominator and the dominated. Our primary concern has been with general principles, not with the analysis of prejudice as it refers to any particular group. Throughout the rest of the book we shall continue to approach the question topically, not by the study of particular minorities. In this chapter and the next, however, our aim is to use the principles already discussed to analyze the prejudice against a specific group. By a detailed study of one minority, the usefulness of the concepts we have employed may be tested and a more unified picture of the complex interactions involved may be observed.

Anti-Semitism is in many ways the "classic" prejudice. Through the course of centuries it has illustrated all of the intricately related forces at work. It has ranged all the way from "polite" social exclusion to vicious pogroms. Insecure persons have found the Jews a convenient scapegoat—available in almost every land, relatively powerless, distinguishable by religion and in some instances by culture, and approved by tradition as a target for hostility. In almost every major economic or political conflict in the last several centuries one of the opposing forces, or both, has employed anti-Semitism as a weapon. Millions of people who have never known a Jew are equipped with a ready-made picture of his supposed physical appearance and personal characteristics.

Hasty observers—including many Americans—are likely to say "there must be something to it" if a prejudice has existed so long and expressed itself in so many different settings. They completely misunderstand the self-perpetuating nature of a deep-seated prejudice, once it has become thoroughly established. Nowhere is the cumulative force of several factors more clearly shown than in the discriminations directed against Jews. A careful study of anti-Semitism is a magnifying glass of great value in the examination of prejudice. There are unique elements, of course, for no two cases of prejudice are exactly alike. But the uniqueness consists largely in the particular combination of forces in the history of anti-Semitism. Most of the forces involved are also found in other cases of prejudice, which will, therefore, be better understood by the analysis of anti-Semitism.

The term "anti-Semitism" was first used by a German journalist, Wilhelm Marr, in 1873, to express and to encourage opposition to Jews. Anti-Semitism may be defined as any activity that tends to force into or to hold Jews in an inferior position and to limit their economic, political, and social rights. It is not simply opposition to Jews because they are different, although that has sometimes been the explanation. It is more often, at least in the modern world, opposition to Jews because they are not different, i.e., because they have become effective competitors for the values being pursued by the prejudiced person.

The term "anti-Semitism" called attention to the Semitic origin of (many) Jews in order to identify them as a "race," and thus make use of feelings of race prejudice against them. In Chapter 2 we noted the errors involved in designating the Jews as a race; we need only repeat here that they are a very mixed group, by no means purely Semitic, that there are many Semites who are not Jews and many Jews who are not Semites, that Semites are simply a branch of the Caucasian race, and that even were the Jews a distinct race the fact would create no consequences of importance for human behavior.

The Origins of Anti-Semitism

Although the term "anti-Semitism" is comparatively new, opposition to Jews is very old. Its recent manifestations can be understood only by an account of the historical conditions out of which they emerged. Historical analysis cannot reveal the contemporary forces that sustain this attitude. It can, however, reveal the traditional source of the prejudice and help in understanding its functions and dysfunctions. Although the circumstances which set going the chain of events leading to modern anti-Semitism are probably impossible to discover, they are doubtless related to the conflicts between the Jewish people and their neighbors in the ancient world. Located at a strategically important point in the Near East, the land of the Jews was under almost constant pressure from the succession of empires in ancient times (and pressure on that area continues down to the present). Out of the conflicts of this early period the Jews developed a strongly unified religion-culture. Their unity, more intense than that of other people, was doubtless at first a reflection of the continuous threats and attacks which their geographical position encouraged. But, once established, that unity, with its ethnocentrism, reacted upon the situation, making them more vulnerable to attack. Their land was invaded and many of the Jews were driven into other areas.

There were three major dispersals of Jews during antiquity: the Babylonian captivity of the sixth century B.C., the dispersals of the Hellenic period, especially under Alexander the Great in the late fourth century B.C., and the migrations caused by the Roman conquests, particularly in the first century A.D. This last dispersal saw Jews following the Romans into Italy, Spain, and France. Many crossed the Rhine into what is now Germany, and that was the home of a large proportion of European Jews during the Middle Ages. Not until the first Crusade (A.D. 1096) did this group begin to move east of the Rhine valley.[1]

Conflicts accompanied these migrations and contacts. There was no anti-Semitism as we know it today, for the conflicts were probably similar to other national and imperial struggles of the time; but owing to the constantly repeated pressures on the Jews, and their reciprocal intense group cohesion, the opposition gradually became traditional. There was opposition between the ancient Greeks and the Jews because the national, economic, and religious interests of the two nations frequently collided. But this was scarcely anti-Semitism; there was also strong opposition between Greek and Persian, Greek and Roman, and finally Greek and Greek. While the Roman Empire dominated the land of the Jews, it was relatively tolerant of religious and cultural differences if they did not obstruct political allegiance. Not until Christianity became the dominant force in Europe did opposition to the Jews begin to develop into categorical anti-Semitism. This fact has led many people to suppose that religious conflict is the "ultimate" cause of anti-Semitism. It is more likely that several causes were involved from the beginning. Although religious symbols were often used to describe the conflict, this can be understood only against the earlier conflicts of empire and the dispersals.

One of the most puzzling problems in the story of the origins of anti-Semitism is that the Jews survived at all as a distinct group, rather than disappearing into the ranks of the dominant society or changing too much to be recognizable. No other ancient cultural-national group has survived with such distinctness. It is tempting, in trying to explain this continued identity of the Jews as a people, to rely on some simple one-factor theory. Many authors believe that religion is the basic cause of their survival. Car Mayer says:

[1] See R. H. Lowie, The German People, Farrar and Rinehart, 1945, p. 87.

I contend that the *prima causa* of their survival is *religion*. The term "religion" must be understood here not in any narrow theoretical or abstract way but in the meaning it has to the Jewish people, inextricably interwoven as it is with the whole social and political texture. . . . The pure idea of monotheism is the first powerful factor for the preservation of the Jews. The second reason for their survival is to be found in the Messianic idea with its accompanying idea of the kingdom of God on earth, for it has provided the Jews with the supreme certainty that the kingdom of God on earth will eventually be realized if only they remain faithful and true to the one God. Another potent factor in the situation is the idea of the special mission that the Jews as the chosen people have to fulfill. This gave them a rare confidence in themselves which proved of tremendous survival value. Finally, there is the ritual whose importance in the survival of the Jews as a people can hardly be exaggerated.[2]

These four characteristics of Judaism are doubtless involved in the complex of factors which have preserved the identity of the Jews. We would add only that these elements themselves have to be explained. Judaism was not carved in all of its complexity on the tablets of Mount Sinai, but is itself one of the adjustments of a people to the circumstances of their history. If we replace the idea of religion as the *prima causa* with the concept that religion is one of a complex series of interacting causes, then an analysis of the elements in Judaism that give it survival power is valuable. Mayer himself describes some of the other elements in the interaction that resulted in the continued identity of the Jews as a people (only, it must be added, he sees them as working in the opposite direction): "They persist despite all temptations and threats to merge which they have encountered in their history. They persist in the face of pressure, hardship, hatred, and persecution which have constantly been their lot. They persist despite their loss of statehood, despite dispersion and exile, and despite their precarious existence everywhere."[3] Threats, persecution, loss of statehood, dispersal, and a precarious existence, in the total setting within which they functioned, actually brought cohesion to the Jews. As Hertzler says:

This sentiment of solidarity, exclusiveness, and superiority was not created by the Jews themselves. Originally they were a conglomeration of tribes, distracted by internal dissensions between families, classes, tribes, and the major cleavage between Israel and Judah. Extraneous pressure and a common protective need forced them so closely together that there was no room for intranational fighting and they were forced to think in terms of unity and act in effective concert. The Jews, in brief, were crushed into the cohesion of an invincible national cultural solidarity. In no other people is this common cultural consciousness so emphatic and so enduring.[4]

[2] In Isacque Graeber and S. H. Britt (eds.), *Jews in a Gentile World*, The Macmillan Company, 1942, pp. 316–317.
[3] *Ibid.*, p. 315.
[4] J. O. Hertzler, in *ibid.*, p. 71.

Keeping in mind the concept of interacting causes, we can profitably examine the role of religious differences in anti-Semitism. These differences alone would probably not have produced the observed results, but they intensified and sustained them. In A.D. 313 Christianity became the official religion of Rome. By the fifth century full citizenship rights became dependent upon religion—as contrasted with the relatively tolerant view of the early empire. Jews were forbidden to try to convert Christians; intermarriage became a crime, as did the acceptance of Judaism. These developments occurred, significantly, at a time when the Roman Empire was torn by conflict and dissension. Christians were no longer available as targets for hostility, a role they had filled in earlier conflicts not perhaps so much for their religious difference as for their lack of enthusiasm for the secular power of Rome. The Emperor Tertullian declared: "If the Tiber rose to the walls of the city, if the inundations of the Nile failed to give the fields enough water, if the heavens did not send rain, if an earthquake occurred, if famine threatened, if pestilence raged, the cry resounded: 'Throw the Christians to the lions.'"

Now the Jews, easily distinguished as a religiously different group at a time when religious beliefs were of great importance, began to fill the same role.

There was especially sharp conflict between Christianity and Judaism because of the nature of their relationship. The Christian inevitably felt an ambivalent feeling toward the Jew. Both shared belief in the Old Testament but interpreted it differently. Jesus was a Jew, but he was accepted only as a prophet or rejected entirely by those who clung to the older religion. The strength of the antipathy toward Jews was in part a result of the very fact that Christianity was in such an important measure of Jewish origin. Christians got rid of their doubts and ambivalent feelings on this score by projecting exaggerated hostility onto the Jews. An "intolerant minority under an intolerant majority" produced a sharp line of cleavage. Once politically disfranchised and religiously condemned, the Jew was subjected to a long chain of pressures which made hostility toward him progressively easier. He was not to be an employer of labor, a physician, an artisan with a Christian apprentice —on the basis of the fact that he was not a believer, and was therefore a dangerous person.

It would be a mistake to assume that these religious differences were not involved in the complex of forces which produced anti-Semitism, just as it is a mistake to assume that they are the basic cause. They help to explain why the Jews were selected as a target for hostility but do not explain the need for that hostility. Judaism was the only non-Christian religion found to any important extent in Europe. Owing to the background we have discussed, it was an especially ethnocentric religion; the Jews' god was the only god, their customs were the divinely revealed and therefore true way of life. This attitude is characteristic of all people, but, perhaps as a compensation for the sufferings they had experienced, Jews gave it special emphasis. They turned suffering and persecution into a kind of religious victory; their pains "were actually a matter of congratulation, pride, and self-glorification, because they were to result eventually in historic vindication."[5] Their very emphasis on religion, in the midst of a dynamically expanding Christianity, made the Jews particularly vulnerable to attack. And they clung to their religion with a rigid conservatism—it seemed to be their one dependable source of security—that made it at many points out of place in a changing civilization.[6]

The idea that they were God's "chosen people" was doubtless an attempt to compensate for the fact that they had obviously not been "chosen" by all the forces in their history to lead a life of security and power on earth. To the medieval Christian, however, this arrogant belief was just a fact. His own life had not always been comfortable, and here were those who challenged the verity of his religion—one of the few things that brought, or at least promised, him comfort. So the Jews became the "Christ killers." Fantastic beliefs about Jews circulated freely—they had tails; they had a special odor "over and above the all-pervading unwashed odor of medieval humanity." They were supposed to sacrifice Christian children, using their blood in Passover rites. (Jews actually had a religious injunction against the consumption of any blood; they required special meat.) It was believed that they sometimes got hold of sacred bread and tortured it until it bled. This myth was the precipitating cause of thousands of deaths. In 1243, scores of Jews at Beelitz near Berlin were burned at the stake on this charge, and in 1420 the whole Jewish community of Vienna was exterminated on the same allegation.[7] Such violence created an ever more intense need for anti-Semitism to justify it. It is very difficult not to hate someone whom you have harmed.

One of the aspects of this cumulative and self-sustaining process was the segregation of Jews in ghettos. At first segregation was voluntary, if not actually a right demanded by the Jews for services rendered the rulers of a city. Within the ghetto they could more readily protect their way of life from the invasions of the surrounding culture and they could protect themselves more easily. This self-imposed segregation, however, encouraged the very differences by which anti-Semitism justified itself. There was a transition from voluntary to compulsory segregation. By the time of the Crusades, the church was restricting contact, for fear that the alien beliefs of the Jews would weaken the faith of Christians. "The Lateran Council of 1179 definitely forbade true be-

[5] *Ibid.*, p. 70.
[6] See *ibid.*, pp. 67–70.
[7] See Louis Golding, *The Jewish Problem*, Penguin Books, Inc., 1938.

lievers to lodge among the infidels, lest they be contaminated by false beliefs. The Counter Reformation perfected this system and made it universal as far as Catholic Europe was concerned. Pope Paul IV in 1555 decreed that Jews were henceforth to be segregated strictly in their own quarter, which was to be surrounded by a high wall and provided with gates, closed at night."[8]

The religious terms in which opposition to Jews was phrased disguised, even in earliest times, but more and more from the time of the Crusades, an equally fundamental economic conflict. Before the tenth century, Jews were the chief merchants of Europe; many of them were international traders, bringing together the mutually hostile Christians and Mohammedans. Probably only a fraction of the Jewish population of Europe were traders; some of the Jewish communities on the Rhine had the longest record of continuous European settlement to be found; there were many agriculturists and artisans. Nevertheless, their loss of citizenship after the fifth century and their isolation in the midst of a civic-religious society forced a relatively higher proportion of them into marginal economic activities.

Beginning about the tenth century, trading became less marginal. Cities grew; there was an increase in business and in prosperity. More and more Christians turned to trade and soon outnumbered the Jews. As citizens, the Christians had a great competitive advantage over their rivals.

They formed themselves into municipal corporations and trade guilds for competitive purposes. Using their commercial resources to increase their political power, and joining with the prelates in their agitations against the Jews, they presently had the Jews limited in their property-owning and industrial activities by various restrictions. Being unable to compete with their Jewish rivals, who were both more experienced and better connected with coreligionists in distant commercial cities, the Christian businessmen urged the actual exclusion of Jews from trading. In this they were soon successful.[9]

The growth of cities in Italy in the tenth century and in Germany in the eleventh brought with it a strong increase in the practice of and demand for a money economy. The church prohibited the lending of money at interest, but the canon law allowed Jews to lend to non-Jews. Being gradually forced out of the large-scale trading ventures, many Jews turned to usury. This established a complicated series of relationships with the emerging commercial and industrial economy. The lending of money was an important contribution in the transition from a barter to a money economy; but while making the contribution, Jews made themselves targets for a many-sided attack—from merchants who

---

[8] J. O. Hertzler, in Isacque Graeber and S. H. Britt (eds.), *op. cit.*, p. 72.
[9] *Ibid.*, p. 87.

wanted to borrow from them but at the same time to fight them as competitors, from the church which condemned their usury, from the nobility who used them as tax collectors and bankers but wanted at the same time to exploit them as much as possible, and a little later from Christian bankers and usurers who wanted to drive them out. It was not that they were traders and bankers that made the Jews subject to attack in the emerging new commercial world, for they had occupied those roles in the early medieval world with much less prejudice shown them. Anti-Semitism grew rapidly after the tenth century because Jews were traders and bankers in a setting which made these occupations increasingly attractive and profitable and therefore led to their being invaded by Christians in large numbers.

The church's condemnation of usury made sense in the relatively self-sufficient, largely barter economy in which a large proportion of the population lived, even down to the eighteenth century. Under those circumstances, a person borrows money only when he has suffered some unusual loss—long illness of the breadwinner, loss of crops, a destructive fire. To charge interest in such a situation is to kick a man when he is down. To the great majority of people, this continued to be the perspective on interest-taking: it was robbery; money was unproductive and yet one had to pay for its use. Since Jews were identified as the usurers, they were hated for this injustice. There was a great deal of stereotyping in this judgment, of course. Not all Jews (in fact, only a small minority of them) were usurers nor were all usurers Jews. "The statement that one constantly meets that 'all usurers were Jews, because the church forbad usury' is as true as that all adulterers were Mohammedans because the church forbad adultery."[10] But at first there were more Jewish moneylenders, especially of the pawnbroking variety with which the average man might have dealings; Christian moneylenders were likely to work in secret, for their activities were condemned. Thus the stereotypes held by the masses of medieval citizenry were reinforced.

Prejudice and discrimination against Jews by the Christian merchants themselves had a different motivation. "Those who speak of the 'Shylocks' in medieval ghettos seldom ask themselves: What were the rest of the townspeople doing? How could they have borrowed, had they not been earning enough to meet a high interest on loans?"[11] The tradition-minded peasantry may have opposed the Jewish merchant and moneylender because his activities were bad according to their standards, but the Christian townspeople attacked the Jew because his activities were good—i.e., profitable. Having found trading a profitable venture, many Christians, by the thirteenth century, had turned to banking. The church's condemnation of usury was not enforced or it was circumvented

[10] James W. Parkes, *An Enemy of the People: Antisemitism*, Penguin Books, Inc., 1946, p. 64.
[11] Miriam Beard in Isacque Graeber and S. H. Britt (eds.), *op. cit.*, p. 379.

by accommodating formulas. Anti-Semitism, involving both projection (the Christian bankers were perhaps not without some guilt feelings) and economic conflict, was a natural product of this situation.

A third group was related in an ambivalent way to the Jews during this period of an emerging modern economic and political life. The Jew, lacking citizenship, was permitted to reside in a city only at the will of its prince. The prince exchanged protection for certain economic services. "The royal method of collecting a substantial proportion of their revenue was to license their Jewish serfs to lend money to their Christian subjects, and then collect the profits."[12] It was in the interests of many of these princes to keep their Jewish subjects as dependent as possible, and yet they found them of great assistance in financial undertakings such as the purchase of war supplies. Only when Christian bankers became so powerful that the Jews no longer were indispensable for major loans did the princes join in open opposition.

The medieval church was involved in the discrimination against Jews not only because it regarded the religious difference as dangerous but also because it was an enormous secular power, particularly in Italy and southern Germany. One of the important supports to the Reformation in northern Europe was the effort of the emerging industrial and merchant class to free itself from domination by Italian financial houses. This secular aspect of the church involved it in discrimination not only against Jews, who could be robbed under the pretext of their disbelief, but also against the Albigenses, as we saw in Chapter 4, and against the whole heretical Protestant movement.[13]

Opposition to Jews was not the only significant conflict of the period. There is good evidence that much of the stereotype of the medieval Jewish "Shylock" is a result of the selective memory of modern historical accounts, and it tells as much about contemporary anti-Semitism as about the anti-Semitism of medieval Europe. Such works as Sombart's *The Jews and Modern Capitalism* try to show that the Jews were primarily responsible for the first stages of capitalist development. Extensive commercial activity was carried on by gentiles in Italian cities as early as the tenth century, however, and the inevitable strains connected with the emergence of a new society led to their condemnation as well as to dislike of Jews. Miriam Beard writes:

The medieval mind did not, in fact, regard the Jew as the financial master of Europe. On the contrary, it recognized the far more dangerous threat to feudal economy emanating from Gentile Italians, in particular the papal bankers of Florence. . . . The grasping extortioners who are seen writhing on the burning sands of Dante's Hell, expiating their usurious crimes, are all

---

[12] James W. Parkes, op. cit., p. 65.
[13] See Miriam Beard, in Isacque Graeber and S. H. Britt (eds.), op. cit., pp. 382–383.

excellent Christians of the best Italian families. One of the worst "Shylocks" of medieval France was the stepson of Dante's adored Beatrice. . . . The Jews had been accused on occasion of "ritual murder," and similar charges were leveled at the Templars; . . . the Christian bankers were said to have roasted their own illegitimate children and smeared their idols with the fat thereof. Not only were high leaders of the Order tortured and tried on such charges, but at last, in 1314, some of them were burned alive in Paris. Undoubtedly the monks were innocent of the more hideous of these crimes, but nothing saved them from the wrath of a desperate royal creditor. . . .

The myth of Shylock, then, has persisted largely because we lack two important histories: (1) we have no complete story of the *friendly* relations between Jews and Christians and (2) we have no history of the *popular animosity toward Gentile bankers and monopolists* through the Middle Ages and Renaissance.[14]

These observations should help us to keep the anti-Semitism of medieval Europe in perspective. They do not, however, eliminate the long story of discrimination, expulsion, and bloody violence that characterized European treatment of the Jews from the time of the Crusades on. ". . . In north European lands, Ashkenazim Jews were no sooner forced to make debtors of nobles and neighbors than they enlarged the risks of being discriminated against. . . . Those who owed him money at a high rate of interest were only too easily tempted by the incitements of fanatics and demagogues."[15] The course of some of the Crusades could be traced by the trail of violence against Jews which they left. In 1290 the Jews were expelled from England, in 1306 from France, and during the fourteenth and fifteenth centuries from many of the cities in Germany and Austria. In 1298, 146 Jewish communities in Germany were utterly destroyed on a charge of ritual murder in one of them. During the middle of the fourteenth century, a quarter to a third of the population of Europe was wiped out by the Black Death. The suffering and fear were enormous. Greatly in need of an "explanation" to allay its fears and a scapegoat upon whom to thrust its hostilities, community after community turned on the Jews. Owing to religiously prescribed diet and cleanliness, Jews were struck down less often by the disease. They were in league with the devil; they had poisoned the wells. Driven by this myth, many towns did not wait for the plague to hit them but attacked the Jews as potential well-poisoners. "Within two years nearly three hundred and fifty Jewish communities were exterminated."[16]

In 1492 the Jews were expelled from Spain. The push to the northeast which began with the Crusades was given another impetus. In earlier centuries the Sephardic Jews of Spain and Portugal, who had not been

[14] *Ibid.*, pp. 380–384.
[15] J. O. Hertzler, in Isacque Graeber and S. H. Britt (eds.), *op. cit.*, pp. 87–88.
[16] *Ibid.*, p. 95.

forced into moneylending, had been an accepted part of the population. But by the late fourteenth century they were caught by the conflicts of the Inquisition and a century later were driven out of the Iberian Peninsula. Year by year, from the Crusades on, western Europe forced its Jewish population back. When Russia threw up a barrier on the east by prohibiting Jewish migration into her lands, the waves of refugees settled in the ancient kingdom of Poland. Here, until the twentieth century, resided the largest Jewish population of the world. And here the vicious attacks on Jews that had characterized western Europe were repeated. Hundreds of Jewish communities were exterminated in repeated pogroms from the sixteenth to eighteenth centuries. ". . . The outbreak of the Ukrainian Cossacks against Polish misrule in the seventeenth century was accompanied by a series of onslaughts on the Jews. The toll of Jewish lives between 1648 and 1658 may be reckoned at 100,000. A hundred years later, bands of 'Haidamack' rebels rose again in the Ukraine, perpetrating atrocities which at least rivalled these."[17]

Anti-Semitism in Czarist Russia

By the nineteenth century, Russia had become the center of anti-Semitic violence. Although she had excluded Jews from her territory, her own imperial expansion, both into Poland and into the Black Sea area, had brought millions of Jews under her domination. They were not to be absorbed into the mass of citizenry, however. A series of decrees and edicts limited their rights, restricted their mobility, and severely discriminated against them. An edict of Nicholas I in 1827 regulated military service. Although Jews received none of the privileges of citizenship, they were forced to give a double share of military service, twenty-five years, often at great distance from their homes. During this period every effort was made to force them to accept Christianity—their food was confined to pork for long periods or they were compelled, under threat of severe military discipline, to perform some Christian rite.[18] Almost complete segregation of Jews was the rule in Russia.

Down to the end of Tsardom she remained determined to exclude this unwanted mass from penetration into the old provinces of Russia. A new kind of ghetto was created in the form of a series of provinces along the western frontier in which the Jews were compelled to live, and even within these provinces their rights of settlement and choice of occupation were severely restricted. Outside of these provinces selected categories of Jews might reside, visit certain fairs, and, provided they did not exceed a small

[17] Louis Golding, op. cit., quoted in Alain Locke and B. J. Stern (eds.), *When Peoples Meet*, Hinds, Hayden and Eldredge, Inc., 1946, p. 269.
[18] See James W. Parkes, *The Jewish Problem in the Modern World*, Thornton Butterworth, 1939, pp. 82–83.

proportion of the total enrollment, study at the universities. The area of settlement was known as the Pale, and it contained more than a half of the Jewish population of the world.[19]

Anti-Semitism in czarist Russia was not simply an official policy. Time after time it took the form of a mass movement. The complete destruction of Jewish communities, with the same pattern of murder and looting that had characterized the earlier anti-Semitism of western Europe, was common. The government was indifferent to these attacks or, more probably, actively interested in funneling off hostility onto the Jews. Russia had been least affected by the economic and political changes of the nineteenth century. Her standard of living was very low, her government highly oligarchic and inefficient.

Alexander II, to be sure, was somewhat liberally inclined. During his rule educated and wealthy Jews gained a few rights—to live ouside the prescribed area, for example—and the military inquisition was replaced by universal military service. More Jewish students attended Russian schools and universities. The great masses of Jewish people, however, remained culturally isolated and outside the protection of the law. And when, in 1881, Czar Alexander was murdered—a symbol of the great discontent in the land—renewed waves of anti-Semitism began. The government virtually invited the masses to riot on Easter to punish the Jews (no Jew had been among the murderers). There followed two weeks of pogroms which the government explained as the incitements of revolutionary parties. Further rioting occurred that summer and during the spring of 1882, followed by new decrees (the "Temporary Rules"— which lasted for thirty-five years) that even more sharply limited the freedom of Jews. (During these years millions of Jews fled from Russia and Poland, a majority of them to the United States.)

Anti-Semitism in Russia, particularly after 1881, was closely related to the problems associated with rising revolutionary pressure against the czarist regime. It is not that Jews were the primary leaders in the revolutionary movement. The repressive measures, to be sure, made radicals of many Jewish youth. The protests, however, went far beyond them. The rulers sought, by attacking Jews, to make "the struggle for liberty appear detestable to the people by representing it to be the work of the Jews."[20] Alexander III showed some personal dismay at the pogroms; he wrote in the margins of the government reports on the pogroms such remarks as "extremely sad and perplexing." But it did not occur to him that his own anti-Semitism—he and his son Nicholas II had the traditional stereotyped views of the Jew as a parasite and extortioner—and

[19] Ibid., p. 80.
[20] Hugo Valentin, Anti-Semitism Historically and Critically Examined (trans. from the Swedish by A. G. Chater), The Viking Press, Inc., 1936, p. 81.

the activities of his own officials were important causes of the violence.

The attempt to use anti-Semitism to fight liberal ideas is shown in a leaflet published in 1905 by the League of the Russian People, an anti-revolutionary group: "The cry of 'Down with the autocracy!' comes from the bloodsuckers who are commonly known as Jews, Armenians and Poles. Beware of the Jews! They are the root of all evil, the sole cause of our misfortunes. The glorious moment is already approaching when there will be an end of all Jews in Russia. Down with the traitors! Down with constitutions!"[21]

Not all of the Russian ruling class looked with favor on anti-Semitism as a weapon against reform or revolutionary activity. In speaking against the severely repressive "Temporary Rules" that Count Ignatyev, Minister of Interior, was seeking to apply against the Jews, Count Reutern declared, "The governmental authorities remain inactive in the face of obvious Jew-baiting. . . . Today they hunt and rob Jews, tomorrow they will go after so-called kulaks, who morally are the same as Jews only of the Orthodox Christian faith, then merchants and landowners may be next. In a word, in the face of such inactivity on the part of the authorities, we may expect in a not distant future the development of the most horrible socialism. . . ."[22] Count Reutern was not demonstrating a personal lack of anti-Semitism or a liberal view but was pointing to the inefficiencies of hatred as a weapon.

Events seem to have proved him correct. Political anti-Semitism continued to grow (there were 100 openly anti-Semitic members in the second Duma and more in the third), and pogroms continued; but they did nothing to slow down the demands for drastic changes. The short-lived Kerensky republic brought complete emancipation to the Jews. The Bolshevik revolution, however, and the civil war that followed caught them between the opposing forces. The aristocracy identified Bolshevism with Jews, the Bolsheviks identified the Jews with wealth and power, whereas in fact the great majority of Jews had supported the liberal and social-democratic movements.

Thus the great final struggle between the Bolsheviks and their opponents in 1919–20 brought upon Russian Jewry a catastrophe of dimensions previously unknown. The desperate Bolshevist troops and robber bands, who looked on the Jews as hated bourgeois and, moreover, were themselves by no means free from anti-Jewish feelings, often started pogroms, which, however, were punished as far as possible by their leaders. But the White generals deliberately handed over the Jewish communites to the mercy of their soldiery. The orthodox Jewish masses of the Ukraine, to whom Bolshevism was a godless abomination, were put to the sword as—Bolsheviks.[23]

[21] Quoted in *ibid.*, pp. 86–87.
[22] Quoted by Mark Vishniak from the diary of E. A. Peretz, in K. S. Pinson (ed.), *Essays on Antisemitism*, Conference on Jewish Relations, 1946, p. 134.
[23] Hugo Valentin, *op. cit.*, pp. 93–94.

The Revival of Anti-Semitism in Modern Europe

The violent attacks and discriminations against Jews in czarist Russia might be called the last expression of medieval anti-Semitism. Russia was still to a large extent a feudal society, and the complex causes operating there were quite similar to those in western Europe centuries earlier. The fall of the czarist regime, however, by no means brought an end to anti-Semitism. That cycle was completed, but another was already under way. As early as the middle of the nineteenth century in western Europe a new wave of anti-Semitism, based on the old antipathies which had been carried along as tradition, but with new factors added, began to rise. For a hundred years or more, economic improvement, the Enlightenment, and the growth of traditions of religious liberty and political democracy had brought more and more freedom to the Jews. Almost everywhere the rising middle classes in their fight for power, looking for support in all quarters, encouraged and won the active support of Jews. Slogans of liberty and individualism, so appropriate to their battle against the feudal society, did not harmonize with the surviving restrictions on Jewish life. Jews, for their part, saw in the emerging new society the possibilities of far greater freedom. In 1791 the National Assembly declared that all Jews in France were full-fledged citizens. The Edict of Toleration, issued by Emperor Joseph II in 1781, removed some of the restrictions imposed on Jews in Austria. One by one the German states granted civic equality to Jews. By 1870 virtually all of the legal restrictions on their economic, political, and religious activities had been abolished in the nations of western Europe.

This freedom had scarcely been accomplished, however, before a new revolutionary struggle began to shake the foundations of the European social structure. Unemployment and economic distress brought new frustrations to the masses. And the ruling groups found themselves faced with strong revolutionary pressures. It was soon apparent that the traditions of anti-Semitism were still strong and that many of the economic causes of antipathy toward Jews were still operative despite the legal changes of the nineteenth century. By 1870 anti-Semitism was surging up with renewed vigor as a manifestation of the tensions and conflicts of the time. There was a strong resurgence in Germany, where the most diverse groups found anti-Semitism a common rallying ground or, equally, an effective weapon with which to fight each other. The last third of the nineteenth century brought to Germany, more rapidly than to almost any other country, the social strains that everywhere accompanied the industrial revolution—threatened loss of power for the old landed aristocracy; insecurity for the lower middle class; the emergence of a large class of toolless proletariat, subject to the vicissitudes of the economic market; and a peasantry that found its accommodations continually upset by the new society. Granted a tradition of anti-Semitism, the Jews could be made to seem responsible for the troubles of these widely differing groups. To many of the peasants they were the symbol of urbanism; to the urban middle class they were direct competitors and symbols of "big business"; to the old aristocracy they were leaders of the new radicalism; and to some of the proletariat they were powerful industrial and financial leaders. One of the key factors in Germany's tragic history since 1870 is that these groups, whose accommodation somehow had to be worked out, directed much of their energy into attacking their opponents with the weapon of anti-Semitism while disregarding the real issues that were ripping the social fabric. Each group could, to be sure, find evidence to support its stereotype of the Jew. He was largely urban middle class. Having been forced into cities by earlier restrictions, he was in a favorable position to take part in the growth of urban industrial society. German Jews were not only "town-dwellers in the first century of an almost entirely urban civilization, but they were most numerous in just those groups which were rapidly rising through prominence to the control of political and national life."[24] They were merchants and financiers and, as the educational system was opened to them, lawyers, doctors, journalists. Jews not only were urban but had an international cosmopolitanism which was of great advantage as they joined in the expansion of trade throughout the world during the nineteenth century.

Besides being deeply involved, *although as a small minority*, in the development of the urban industrial society, Jews oppositely occupied an important place in economic and political movements which carried direct and indirect threats to the power of the ruling group of that very society.

The nineteenth century was the century of constitutional radicalism, of liberalism and individualism—all the movements in which Jews found themselves most at home. It was natural that they should play their part in these parties, for it was to the great ideas of the French Revolution and the idealism which preceded it that they owed their emancipation; it was to liberalism and "the Manchester School" that they owed the removal of the bars to their economic advancement; and in the new spirit of social reform, and the new demands of social justice, they found a field of practical activity for which the deepest principles of their rabbinic inheritance had admirably prepared them.[25]

Thus Jews had a part in almost every phase of the development of industrial society. There were Jews among the proletariat, among the lower and upper middle classes, and among the wealthy financiers. There

[24] James W. Parkes, *The Jewish Problem in the Modern World*, p. 39.
[25] *Ibid.*, pp. 39–40.

were conservative Jews, stanch supporters of Bismarck, who defended nineteenth-century capitalism, and others who were important in the growth of social democracy and communism. Such a variety of roles cannot explain anti-Semitism, but it helps to describe the supports to the traditional prejudice which the various groups were able to find in the environment around them. Start with this tradition that reaches back for more than a thousand years, add intense economic and political conflict with all the personal insecurities and frustrations that accompanied it, and you have the background for the revival of anti-Semitism in Germany after it had receded for a century or more.

The tradition of anti-Semitism had survived most completely among the isolated peasantry and "among the more obstinate of those who stood to lose from the developments of the century—the old landowning aristocrats, and the clericals anxious to retain the privileged position of the churches. They hated the entry of the Jews into their 'Christian' society; they hated the democratic, urban, commercial and secular civilization in which the emancipated Jews found themselves at home."[26] This latter group soon discovered that the tradition of anti-Semitism was still widespread and could be used effectively to confuse political issues, to unite otherwise divergent groups—all of those who, for widely different reasons, disliked the nineteenth century—and to fight the rising liberal and radical movements. We showed in Chapter 4 how Bismarck, despite the important roles that several Jews had occupied in his government, used anti-Semitism to hold together the alliance upon which his power rested. Needing the support of the Catholic center parties, whom he had offended by his earlier Kulturkampf with its anti-Catholic and secular elements, he could represent the Kulturkampf as a Jewish-led secular movement. Hoping to kill the attraction of radical socialism, the conservatives gave some support to the mild reform program of Adolf Stoecker, founder of the Christian Social Workers' party and leader of the Antisemitic League. By using or at least accepting anti-Semitism, Bismarck hoped to split this group sharply from any feeling of identity with left-wing socialism, which was continuously identified as a Jewish product.

Stoecker at first had also hoped, with his Christian Social Workers' party, to keep the workers from social-democratic leanings. During the early years anti-Semitism was unimportant in his pronouncements, and demands for social reform for the workingman were important in his program. Stoecker failed, however, to appeal to the workers. His group became more and more of lower-middle-class composition, and in 1881 it officially dropped the word "Workers'" from its name. Beginning in 1879, anti-Semitism occupied a much more important place. Stoecker became the leader of the "Berlin Movement"—a group of diverse forces

[26] James W. Parkes, *An Enemy of the People: Antisemitism*, p. 4.

united in opposition to liberalism and clearly anti-Semitic "in the fight for God, Kaiser and Reich."

The anti-Semitism of the conservative forces was to some degree limited by traditions of western civilization and by religious symbols. By 1890 there were signs that it would lose out to an anticonservative anti-Semitism appealing more thoroughly to mass frustration and confusion. "When in November, 1892, against all expectations, more than twice as many votes were cast for the anti-Conservative anti-Semite Ahlwardt as for the Conservative candidate, the *Kreuzzeitung* emphatically called the event to the party's attention: 'Anti-Semitism which once in the Berlin Movement was the bridge for crossing over from the Liberal to the Conservative Party,' could again serve Conservative interests if the party took the lead in the battle against Jewry."[27] It was becoming apparent that the use of anti-Semitism in the political battles of the time could not be limited to the relatively conscious manipulations of the conservatives. Equipped for anti-Semitism by tradition, made ready for scapegoatism by the frustrations growing from a deeply rifted society, encouraged to hate the Jews by a ruling group that wanted to control them, and aroused to passion by rabble rousers, a small proportion of lower- and middle-class Germans were intense anti-Semites. They supported political parties whose main platform was anti-Semitism. This group was never large before World War I; its political representation, at least on the national level, was tiny. But it foreshadowed the developments of later years when defeat in war, a ruinous inflation, an ever sharper class conflict were to combine to increase its numbers enormously.

This extreme anti-Semitism was in itself a complex phenomenon, drawing together individuals of widely differing tendencies. One branch was composed largely of small-town people and was justified, by a perverted interpretation of Christianity, by religious symbols. Some of its leaders were drawn from the clergy who had links with the political anti-Semitism of the upper class, but many of the followers were from the traditional-minded lower middle class. Another branch, which later was to prove to be the dominant type, was anti-Christian as well as anti-Jewish. It opposed the Junkers and the big industrialists and, on the surface at least, supported the radical political tendencies of the time. This was a very unstable support, however, for the movement was essentially negativistic, drawing far more from personal frustration than from organized economic interest. Its members came from the most unstable elements of the middle class, who mixed their anti-Semitism with other panaceas—"body-building, vegetarianism, soul-breathing, monetary re-

---

[27] Paul W. Massing, *Rehearsal for Destruction. A Study of Political Anti-Semitism in Imperial Germany*, Harper & Brothers, 1949, p. 65.

form."[28] In the last analysis it was not the peasantry or the landed aristocracy but the urban lower middle class who formed the core of the anti-Semitic movement. Not clerical power but deep-seated antireligious sentiments furnished much of the motive force.

The Beginning of "Racial" Anti-Semitism

At the end of the nineteenth century an anti-Semitism based on a traditional economic-religious conflict and on a contemporary political-economic struggle was being complicated by the addition of the passion of the "racial purity" myth. Perhaps more than any other one factor, this myth permitted modern anti-Semitism to become the focal point for the most diverse hostilities and frustrations. The tying together of individuals with enormously varying needs and desires inevitably made anti-Semitism a thoroughly nihilistic movement. The one common denominator was made up of fear, frustration, and hostility. If the various segments of the anti-Semitic movement had been guided by their differing economic, political, and religious beliefs and interests they would have attacked each other or some part of the social structure. But the times were too confused and insecurity was too great for them to know where to strike. Here was the answer, supported by tradition, reinforced by the cumulative effects of the allegiance of differing groups, and now made utterly definitive by an absolute racial ideology. Until the end of World War I there were relatively few converts or at least few active supporters for this myth; but it was elaborated and perfected in heavy tomes and propagandistic pamphlets and was ready at hand as an all-embracing explanatory principle when the enormous frustrations of the postwar period descended upon Germany.

The earlier anti-Semitism of the nineteenth century was rarely based on the supposed racial difference and inferiority of Jews. The historian Treitschke, for example, based his opposition to Jews on cultural grounds: "If it were possible to get our Jewish fellow citizens to feel themselves solely as German citizens of Israelitic faith, many a one-sidedness in the German character might find its salutary complement in Judaism. But only a part of the German Jews have so completely fused with our culture. . . ."[29] Even Houston Stewart Chamberlain, a British-born German citizen who became the intellectual leader of the "Aryan cult," did not rationalize his prejudice against the Jews in bio-logical-racial terms. He used the term "race" in a very ambiguous way. It was not something entirely innate; non-Aryans might acquire the Aryan "spirit," and an Aryan might lose it. Nevertheless, Chamberlain developed a sharp contrast between the supposed traits of the Semite

[28] Carey McWilliams, A Mask for Privilege, Little, Brown & Company, 1948, p. 98.
[29] Quoted by R. H. Lowie, op. cit., p. 96.

and of the Aryan and made the conflict between the two a leading principle of history. If anything was good, it was Aryan; if it was bad, it was
Semitic. This distinction led to complications, because followers of the
Aryan-Semitic conflict myth often did not agree on what was good and
what was bad. "Thus to Chamberlain himself Goethe was so perfect an
example of the purest Aryan that he quoted him in his *Foundations* no
less than 127 times (according to the index). But another writer of the
same school, Lenz, calls Goethe a 'Teutonic-Western-Asiatic cross-
breed,' and proves it by an examination of the poet's mentality; while
yet a third, Otto Hauser, proves his mongrel nature by the fact that in
Faust there are 'hundreds of quite pitifully bad verses.' "[30]

Other writers, however, anticipated the extreme racial anti-Semitism
of Hitler by declaring that the supposed inferiority of Jews was entirely
innate. In 1886 George von Schönerer, an Austrian politician, proposed
an immigration ban on Jews (modeled after the American anti-Oriental
legislation) and special laws for native-born Jews. Religious differences
were unimportant, he declared; it was the racial characteristics of the
Jews that mattered. We shall see how this became the central item in
the Nazi world mythology.

The Dreyfus Affair

Having discussed in some detail the revival of anti-Semitism in late-
nineteenth-century Germany, we cannot undertake an analysis of the
use of the prejudice in other countries. A brief statement concerning
the famous Dreyfus case, however, will indicate that the political and
social conflicts in Germany were matched by similar (not identical)
struggles elsewhere. Massing gives an interesting interpretation of the
differences in social structure—and therefore differences in conflict patterns—in Germany, France, and England.

In Germany, the forces that bred and used anti-Semitism were stronger
and resistance to them weaker than in England or France. Politically speaking, conservative-clerical France, the France of the anti-Dreyfusards, had
been beaten in 1789 and ever since had been engaged in a difficult comeback
fight. Its counterpart in Germany had never lost its paramount position in
state and society. In England and France, a national ideology had been
developed by the middle classes which regarded themselves as the backbone
of the modern state. In Germany conservatism took the national ideology
away from the middle classes, its erstwhile herald, infused it with conservative-clerical values, and monopolized it to the exclusion of all other groups.
By the end of the century Germany had become a leading industrial nation
but its astounding industrial transformation was grafted upon a preindustrial
political structure. Groups victimized by industrialization saw the villain in
"liberalism," in those forces which made for the socioeconomic transformation of the nation but did not have the power or will to account also for its

[30] James W. Parkes, *An Enemy of the People: Antisemitism*, pp. 49–50.

political life. In Germany, anti-Semitism thus found allies it could not have found at all or not in such strength in nations where the industrial revolution was accompanied by one in politics. In France and England the same social groups suffered from the advance of capitalism which in Germany registered their protest through anti-Semitism and antiliberalism. But in these countries they found no semifeudal, semiabsolutistic forces in power with which to align themselves against the upper bourgeoisie. They had to fend for themselves but they also had the opportunity to participate in forming the political will of the nation.[31]

The French Revolution had indeed produced a different distribution of power from that in Germany, but it had not created a liberal, democratic state. After 1870 the chief political conflict concerned the desirability of a lay state, with lay education, as opposed to a state and educational system tied closely to the church. French Jews were among the anticlericals and were therefore opposed by the old aristocracy.

The Dreyfus affair pointed up this conflict. In September, 1894, it became known to the French general staff that the German military attaché in Paris had received secret military information from a French officer. Captain Alfred Dreyfus, the only Jew on the general staff, was accused, tried in an atmosphere of national tension, and sentenced to life imprisonment. The French conservative press and aristocracy made full use of the conviction to attack the Third Republic as a corrupt "Jew Republic," and for a time the conservatives made political gains from the controversy.

Gradually, however, the facts came to light. In 1896 Major Picquart, new chief of the Intelligence Department, learned that the papers on the basis of which Dreyfus was convicted were the forgeries of a Major Esterhazy. Major Picquart was thereupon transferred to Tunis by the general staff—in the hope of silencing him. In 1898, however, further forgeries by a Colonel Henry were exposed (Henry had been among the leaders of those who had accused Dreyfus), strengthening the hand of those who, like Clemenceau and Zola, were demanding a new trial. Colonel Henry committed suicide, and shortly thereafter Esterhazy was convicted of embezzlement and dishonorably discharged. He fled to England where he confessed his part in the forgeries. But even this did not settle the affair. The opponents of the Republic were not willing to give up the powerful weapon of anti-Semitism with which they had made some gains. The affair was an important issue in election campaigns, and the forces backing the anti-Dreyfusards were so strong that in the new trial in 1899, despite the evidence, Dreyfus was not acquitted. His sentence was reduced to ten years for "treason in extenuating circumstances," and then he was pardoned. In 1903 he appealed for a retrial; but this was not granted until 1906, when Clemenceau had

[31] Paul W. Massing, *op. cit.*, pp. 80–81.

become prime minister. Dreyfus was then acquitted and reinstated in the army with the rank of major. The issue was formally closed.[32]

This case is a very interesting example of the way anti-Semitism has become involved in the political struggles of modern nations. By playing on the insecurities and patriotic sentiments of the masses, the conservative and clerical forces were able to win some support from them. That Dreyfus was a wealthy man whose family had fled from Alsace to Paris when the Germans had taken over the province, that he was a fervent French patriot and hater of the Germans, that he was among the Jews who had assimilated to the French upper class to the point, in some instances, of adopting anti-Semitism—these facts did not prevent the conservatives from manipulating the trial to their own advantage for a time. In the long run, the forgeries boomeranged, and the political use of anti-Semitism was largely stopped in France until the confusing days of the Vichy regime during World War II.

The fact that many Jews had been assimilated rather thoroughly into the French upper class did not prevent the conservatives from using anti-Semitism.

This adjustment to the French aristocracy had one inevitable result: the Jews tried to launch their sons upon the same high military careers as were pursued by those of their new-found friends. It was here that the first cause of friction arose. The acceptance of the Jews into high society had been relatively peaceful. The upper classes, despite their dreams of a restored monarchy, were a politically spineless lot and did not bother themselves unduly either one way or the other. But when the Jews began seeking equality in the army, they came face to face with the determined opposition of the Jesuits who were not prepared to tolerate the existence of officers immune to the influence of the confessional. Moreover, they came up against an inveterate caste-spirit, which the easy atmosphere of the salons had led them to forget, a caste-spirit which already strengthened by tradition and calling was still further fortified by uncompromising hostility to the Third Republic and to the civil administration.[33]

During the early years of the Dreyfus affair, even some of the socialists —vigorous opponents of the conservatives and clericals—were convinced of Dreyfus' guilt. They could not believe that such a wealthy man would be given an unfair trial. They looked upon the struggle as nothing but a conflict between two bourgeois groups. Jaurès, the leader of the socialists, took this view at first and was only gradually persuaded by the course of events—and by Clemenceau—that a victory for the anti-Dreyfusards would be a victory for a conservative-clerical state and against the Republic.

[32] See the analysis of the Dreyfus affair by Hannah Arendt, in K. S. Pinson (ed.), op. cit., pp. 173–217.
[33] Ibid., pp. 191–192.

Thus the Dreyfus forgeries did not "work." They did not succeed in assuring aristocratic control of the army or in destroying the Republic. But they were sufficiently powerful to keep France in political turmoil for years and to obscure basic political issues. It remained for the same kind of claims, repeated a hundred times in a defeated and confused postwar Germany, to occur in an environment more favorable to their success—with what results we are all too well aware.

Anti-Semitism in Germany After World War I

We have sketched some of the background against which one can begin to understand the most extreme and violent expression of anti-Semitism in history. In the 1890's, when the use of anti-Semitism as a political device was common in Germany and even more common in Austria, a young Austrian came to Vienna. There he saw a frankly anti-Semitic party win two-thirds of the seats on the city council and witnessed the political manipulations of anti-Semitism by Karl Lueger, who for fourteen years was burgomaster of the city. Lueger's anti-Semitism ". . . was an open anti-liberal platform device. His pupil really set out to destroy physically those whom his master so constantly taught him to regard as the most dangerous enemies of the German people."[34] We shall not undertake to analyze the personality basis for Hitler's anti-Semitism. Apparently he had an overpowering need for a prejudice that would allow him to thrust off his frustrations and would "explain" a complex conflict situation. His personal frustrations were matched by the frustrated nationalism of an Austrian-German. It may well be that a rigid, authoritarian upbringing had created in him a self-splitting need for the contradictory feelings of dependency and domination described by Eric Fromm in *Escape from Freedom*. The important thing about Nazi anti-Semitism is not the personality of Hitler but the millions of times these same personality needs were repeated, for whatever reasons, in other Germans (and in people of many other lands), and the tremendous impetus given to the growth of those needs by the utter disorganization of the postwar period. That, combined with a long tradition of anti-Semitism and its immediate use as a political-economic weapon in the generation just preceding, is the major element in the rise of Nazism. The defeat, after four years of bitter war, the loss of colonies and homeland territory, the Versailles Treaty with its "guilt clause," the political conflict of the left and right (with the Weimar Republic, in between, being torn to pieces), and the utter confusion of the inflation so enlarged the group of the hopeless, cynical, and confused that the basis was laid for the development of a strong anti-Semitic movement.

[34] James W. Parkes, *An Enemy of the People: Antisemitism*, p. 18.

The active core of the Nazi party was at first drawn largely from the demobilized soldiers. Intensely nationalistic, embittered by defeat, unable to find a stable place in a shattered economy, accustomed to violence, they turned to a party that promised once again to exalt their nation above all others, that gave them a sense of power to overcome the feelings of hopelessness and a political philosophy that explained all their problems in simple terms: The Jews are to blame.

There is no way of knowing how large a proportion of the German people were stanch Nazis, even during the time of the party's greatest success. During the 1920's any slight improvement in the political-economic situation, as during the Locarno period, brought a reduction in members. By 1930, however, the Nazis were a major force in German political life. At least five groups of Germans could be distinguished then, and later during the period of Nazi rule, according to their attitude toward the party: There was 'the fervent group of active members. 2 There was a larger group who agreed with many of the things for which Nazism stood or were persuaded by its propaganda, though they may have disliked some aspects of the movement. They voted the National Socialist ticket and supported its growth while not taking an active role in the party or its related groups. Its nationalism, its anti-Semitism, anti-communism, antidemocracy took their generalized, vague fears and insecurities and focused them, thus seeming to bring them under control. It "explained" things. A third group supported Nazism for rather conscious political-economic reasons—it could be used to defeat communism. By 1930 a world-wide depression was compounding Germany's internal economic problems; both the Communist and the Nazi parties began to get more votes; the balance of power in the German cabinet shifted to the right. In 1932, however, the Nazis lost a few votes while the Communists continued to gain. At that point Hitler was invited to become premier, a position he assumed in January, 1933. Fear of communism on the part of the military and industrial rulers of Germany was an important factor in this legal coup.

4 .The fourth group of German citizens were opposed to the Nazi movement generally but were unwilling or unable to take an active stand against it. The enormous risks to themselves and their families, or the feelings of helplessness, prevented them from open resistance. Another factor which reduced their opposition, however, was their partial sharing of the beliefs of Nazism. We are describing here a continuum, not sharply separate groups, and to some degree a high proportion of Germans were appealed to by the anti-Semitism and ultranationalism of Hitler. These were not the dominant beliefs of this fourth group, but their feelings were sufficiently ambivalent to make them helpless and ineffective in the conflict. The party propaganda machine skillfully played on these underlying attitudes in order to keep this group con-

fused and helpless. The fifth group was composed of active and convinced anti-Nazis. Some fled the country to escape domination by the Nazi regime or to fight it from abroad (not all who fled were anti-Nazi). Others opposed it from within the country; and a large number of Germans, Christians as well as Jews, faced the firing squad or were sent to concentration camps, beginning as early as 1934.

Whatever the relative proportions of these various groups, it is clear that a large number of Germans, by about 1935, supported or tolerated the Nazi movement. And in its growth to power anti-Semitism was the central coördinating belief. It was a theory of history, a source for a scapegoat, and a weapon for fighting both communism and democracy all rolled into one. The Jews made up less than 1 percent of the population of Germany, so they could hardly strike back. Yet they were sufficiently prominent, owing to geographical and occupational concentration (itself in part a result of anti-Semitism) for adroit propaganda to show, to the person ready to believe, how they "dominated" certain occupations. Before 1933 the leaders of the Weimar Republic, thoroughly insecure and on the defensive, were unwilling to endanger their shaky position by defense of the Jews,[35] whereas large numbers of Germans were entirely ready, because of tradition and frustration, to accept just such an "explanation" of their woes as the Nazi anti-Semitic doctrine provided. Perhaps the most skillful use of anti-Semitism by Hitler was the way he won the support—or at least held off the opposition—of some of the most powerful industrial and military figures of Germany by making communism seem to be a Jewish product. This idea also appealed to many of the middle class, who identified themselves with the old regime in opposition to the urban proletariat. A traditional prejudice can be played upon in such a way that judgment is thoroughly lost, when the will to believe is strong. Only one out of eighty-nine Communist members of the 1932 Reichstag was a Jew; there were only 600,000 Jews in Germany, but the Communists received almost six million votes—yet Nazi propaganda was able to link the Jews with communism in many people's minds.

In *Mein Kampf* Hitler develops a theory of history that solves, at one blow, all the complicated problems with which modern social science works. Success and failure, the good and bad are all to be explained by race:

"Everything that today we admire on this earth—science and art, technique and inventions—is only the creative product of a few peoples and perhaps originally of one race. On them now depends also the existence of this entire culture. If they perish, then the beauty of this earth sinks into the grave with them.

[35] See *ibid.*, pp. 46–47.

"The blood-mixing . . . is the sole cause of the dying-off of old cultures."[36]

Starting from this premise that race is the most important thing in the world, Hitler develops his conception of the Jews and their role in Germany's problems. He distinguishes three types of races: the culture-founders, the culture-bearers, and the culture-destroyers. Only "Aryans" are culture-founders; some other "races" are culture-bearers, although their role is precarious, depending upon contact with the superior Aryans; but Jews, says Hitler, are culture-destroyers. He pictures them simultaneously as weak and cowardly yet enormously powerful and dangerous, giving his followers a sense of fear, but then a way to escape their fear—if they will follow him. He exploits the individual feelings of powerlessness and terror in the modern world of confusion by describing the supposed plots and strength of the Jews, then gives his followers a sense of collective strength by making the Jews out to be cringing weaklings and by encouraging attacks against them. The mutually contradictory qualities in these sterotypes are no obstacle for those ready to believe and needing a security-giving formula.

If the Jews were alone in this world, they would suffocate as much in dirt and filth, as they would carry on a detestable struggle to cheat and ruin each other, although the complete lack of the will to sacrifice, expressed in their cowardice, would also in this instance make the fight a comedy.

. . . The Jew is led by nothing but pure egoism on the part of the individual. . . .

Slowly the fear of the Marxist weapon of Jewry sinks into the brains and souls of decent people like a nightmare.

One begins to tremble before the terrible enemy, and thus one has become his final victim.

If we let all the causes of the German collapse pass before our eyes, there remains as the ultimate and decisive cause the nonrecognition of the race problem and especially of the Jewish danger.[37]

Using that kind of doctrine as rationalization, the Nazis launched the most extensive and bloody campaign against the Jews that the world has ever seen. We cannot undertake to list here in any detail the legal and economic discriminations, the systematic expulsion from almost every phase of German life, and the violence that characterized it. A few items will illustrate the cumulative attack on the very existence of the Jews. In 1933 a new civil service law dismissed all "non-Aryan" officials, excepting ex-servicemen or those who held their jobs before August 1, 1914. This affected teachers, university professors, judges, public prosecutors, as well as the staffs of government bureaus. Non-Aryan lawyers were debarred and non-Aryan doctors deprived of their panel practice,

[36] Adolf Hitler, *Mein Kampf*, Reynal and Hitchcock, 1940, pp. 396, 406.
[37] *Ibid.*, p. 416, 447, 451. See especially chap. 9, "Nation and Race."

with the same exceptions. In 1934 the "Aryan clause" was adopted by the army. In 1935 the Nuremberg laws deprived all Jews of citizenship and therefore eliminated all exceptions to the employment of Jewish officials that previous decrees had allowed. In 1936 the expropriation of Jewish-owned firms without compensation began. On November 10, 1938, an anti-Jewish pogrom started simultaneously in all German towns; all Jewish stores were demolished and thousands of Jews arrested. Jews were then required to repair all the damage; they forfeited any insurance claims to the government and were fined, collectively, about 400 million dollars (one billion marks). On February 25, 1939, the Jewish community of Berlin was given orders to produce daily the names of one hundred persons who were to receive two weeks' notice to leave the country.[38]

That is only a very partial list of the cumulative development of Nazi anti-Semitism. Both before and after Hitler's rise to power, threats and violence were part of the plan. After the outbreak of World War II and the extension of German domination over most of Europe, any restraints that still protected the Jews of Europe were abandoned. The Nazis systematically overworked, starved, and murdered the Jews in every land they occupied. The outside world could scarcely believe the reports of the slaughter until German records, brought into the Nuremberg trials after the war, gave conclusive evidence. By 1945 the Nazis had killed six million Jews. Before the war there were over three million Jews in Poland; today there are only twenty-five to fifty thousand. At the end of the war scarcely ten thousand of the Jewish population of Germany remained. To the personal violence of the Crusades and the planned violence of the czarist regime the Nazis added a technological violence that virtually destroyed the Jewish population of Europe outside of Russia. Perhaps a million escaped (to Russia, Palestine, the United States, Latin America, and elsewhere); perhaps a million are yet alive in Europe; but six million were killed.

Anti-Semitism has not disappeared from Europe, although the present period is one when its political use is not prominent. In the summer of 1949 the voters of West Germany held their first free election since 1933. Parties that were rather frankly ultranationalistic, pro-Nazi, and anti-Semitic received a vote variously estimated at from three to six millions, out of a total of twenty-five million votes. There is good evidence that anti-Semitism has been involved in political conflicts in eastern Europe and the Soviet Union in recent years, as for example, in the purge of Rudolph Slansky in Czechoslovakia. After the purge, Premier Antonin Zapotocky declared: "We shall not tolerate any foreign influence in our affairs whether from Washington or London or Rome

---

[38] For a much more complete listing of decrees, see "Twentieth Century Ghetto" in *Living Age*, April, 1939, pp. 154–160.

or Jerusalem," and added that this was not the first time that "Jewish and other capitalists" had tried to interfere in Czechoslovakia."[39] We may not have seen the end of anti-Semitism, even the organized and political type, in Europe.

Anti-Semitism in the United States

Some Americans assume that anti-Semitism is a characteristically European phenomenon with no hold in the United States. Others, stirred to action by the rise of Nazism in Germany, have perhaps over-estimated the strength of anti-Semitism in this country. Our task is to examine the evidence to discover, as nearly as possible, its actual strength.

Overt manifestations of anti-Semitism were rare in the early period of American history. From the establishing of the federal government, Jews had complete legal and political equality, and it has never been lost. This is an important part of the total interacting pattern, for we have seen how the picture of the Jew as a noncitizen helped to shape the attitudes and actions of Europeans. Most Americans were Euro-peans, of course, and they brought much of their culture—including their prejudices—with them. The liberalizing influence of the American Revolution, however, and the vast opportunities available in the new land did not encourage the growth of anti-Semitism. The relatively small number of Jewish colonists and early immigrants, largely from Spain, Germany, and the countries of western Europe, was absorbed without a great deal of discrimination against them. The number grew slowly during the first century of the nation's history, and by 1880 there were 230,000 Jews in the United States.

At about that time several forces converged to stimulate the growth of anti-Semitism in America. "The second American Revolution," as Charles Beard calls it, was being won by large-scale business and indus-trial enterprise. The earlier pattern of small competitive firms was being broken by the rise to dominance of large oligopolistic concerns; and that shift demanded a whole chain of other adjustments. "Once triumphant, the industrial tycoons discovered that they could not function within the framework of the social and political ideals of the early Republic."[40] An open-class structure with rapid social mobility and free competition (and not simply free "enterprise") would be a serious obstacle to their power. Most of the men in this group of industrialists and financiers

---

[39] See the New York *Times*, December 23, 1951; Claire Sterling, "Anti-Semitism in the Satellites: The Wave of Fear Advances," *The Reporter*, April 14, 1953, pp. 17–20; and Arnold Forster and Benjamin R. Epstein, *Cross-Currents*, Doubleday & Company, Inc., 1956.

[40] Carey McWilliams, *op. cit.*, p. 9.

were of north European ancestry. Perhaps the most important challenge to their dominance came from the German Jews who had climbed with great speed to positions of power in middle-western and western cities.

Among the first expressions of open anti-Semitism in the United States were the social restrictions imposed on upper-class Jews by upper-class gentiles. At Saratoga Springs in 1877, Joseph Seligman, the New York banker, was refused accommodations at the Grand Union Hotel —perhaps the beginning of explicit segregation. The social exclusion of Jews spread rapidly, justified on the grounds that a person has a right to pick his social companions but ignoring the important place that clubs and other "prestige organizations" have in economic power struggles. They ". . . help to maintain higher and lower ranking in the community; . . . they function as a mechanism for placing people in the class hierarchy; and . . . they serve to impede movement out of the middle class into the upper class. In short, they organize and regulate upward social mobility. . . . Institutions of this character are not based on the innate congeniality of like-minded persons, but rather on the strategical consideration of consolidating a power relationship. Social power is organized by exclusion."[41]

The existence of a political democracy and the important role that many Jews played in the civic life of many American cities prevented a direct attack on their economic and political rights. The American upper class adopted a different approach, much less characteristic even of fairly intense anti-Semitism in Europe, that of blocking Jewish entry into the "social" life of the upper class and thereby restricting Jewish ability to compete.[42]

The rise of anti-Semitism in America after 1875 was not simply an expression of upper-class economic conflict. Other forces began to operate at about this same time to encourage its development. We have traced the growth of political anti-Semitism in Europe after 1870. This inevitably had effects, both direct and indirect, across the Atlantic. Cultures exchange their prejudices as well as other practices. In the 1880's an Austrian politician modeled his anti-Jewish legislation after the pattern of the anti-Chinese acts in the United States. Similarly, the rising tide of anti-Semitism abroad gave impetus to it in America.

One of the important effects of European anti-Semitism on the United States was the tremendous force it gave to immigration, especially after the Russian pogroms of 1881–1882. From 1881 to 1914 nearly two million Jews, mostly from Russia and Poland, fled from the brutalities and discriminations to which they were subjected in eastern Europe. This influx did not contribute immediately to an increase in anti-

[41] Ibid., p. 116. See also W. Lloyd Warner and Paul S. Lunt, The Social Life of a Modern Community, Yale University Press, 1941, pp. 112 ff.
[42] See Carey McWilliams, op. cit., pp. 18–22.

Semitism in the United States. The Jewish immigrants came in, for the most part, on the lowest levels of our economy. The economy was still expanding rapidly so that, except during years of depression, it absorbed the newcomers with relative ease. Most of the powerful groups in America still encouraged immigration as a source of unskilled, and cheap, labor; and the native workers had not yet come to identify the fact of immigration as a major cause of their troubles—most of them were too close to the immigrant role themselves. By the turn of the century, however, America began to feel the effects of the closing up of the frontier; her economy took on a rigidity, a "stickiness," that it had not known before. Workers from abroad were not so readily absorbed, and agitation for their exclusion, which had already begun with the Chinese, grew in strength.

Meanwhile, many of the new Jewish immigrants, a majority of them skilled laborers to begin with, exhibited some of the same ability to improve their status that their western European predecessors had shown. They climbed in class status just when the "native" middle class was feeling strongly the effects of the increasing rigidity of the economy. The middle class was hard hit by the recurring depressions. And those in small businesses were being progressively weakened by the growing power of the larger concerns. The hostilities of the middle class were readily directed against the Jews because they, more than any other recent immigrant group, were in open competition with it. Moreover, the Jewish immigrants continued to be a distinguishable group into the second and third generations. This characteristic was partly due to the already existing tradition of anti-Semitism in the United States, but it was perhaps due more to the strong cultural cohesiveness that Jews had developed through centuries of conflict in the European environment. Cultural differences did not of themselves, of course, cause prejudice. They simply assisted the revival of a tradition of anti-Semitism. As middle-class groups felt more competition from the Jews, they found the prejudice ready at hand and a fairly distinct group against whom to direct it.

The cultural contrasts not only separated the Jewish immigrants from the "native" population but also divided the Jews from Germany and west Europe from those who fled from the persecutions in Russia and east Europe after 1881. This distinction had a number of consequences, reflected in the relationships between Jews. The recent immigrants had been affected very differently by the growing nationalism of the period. "The older members of the western Jewish communities had become citizens before nationalism had become a dominant disease. They, therefore, when they became nationalists, became patriotic Englishmen, Frenchmen, Germans, or others. But these new arrivals had become nationalists while they were still living as Jews in an environment which did not desire to assimilate them. Their nationalism, therefore, was

Jewish; and this division led to a violent, and still enduring conflict within the Jewish community."[43]

Gordon has pointed out that in Minneapolis, as in most other communities, east European Jews settled in separate residential areas (after the pattern of many other immigrant groups).

Variations in religious practices, though minor, were often regarded as of the utmost importance by the Jews of the community. Memories associated with the "old home" required that persons who knew of the places of which the immigrant spoke should be at hand or easily available. The reason for this self-segregation appear to be (1) the similarity of language and custom, (2) the greater opportunity to observe religious practices and duties in the company of like-minded individuals, (3) the characteristic inability to pay high rentals for homes, (4) the refusal of native residents to rent other than the poorest homes to immigrants, and (5) the convenient location of the new residences from the point of view of distance to work. . . . The German-Jewish community had been able to avoid establishment of a voluntary ghetto because it possessed superior financial means and the ability to speak English.[44]

This pattern of segregation helped to accentuate the feelings of difference that, in the context of nationalism, economic insecurity, and personal frustration, gave impetus to the rise of anti-Semitism.

World War I strengthened many of these trends, and the immediate postwar period witnessed a number of overt anti-Semitic developments in the United States. The forgery of the *Protocols of the Elders of Zion* (purported to be the plot of "international Jewry" to overthrow governments and conquer the world) was circulated. Part of the "red scare" was in the form of claims that communism was a Jewish product. The Ku Klux Klan, with its violent anti-Semitism, took on renewed vigor. In May, 1920, Henry Ford began a series of anti-Semitic articles in the Dearborn *Independent*, a paper with a circulation of 700,000, and in four pamphlet reprints from the articles. Ford gave wide currency to the *Protocols* and other anti-Semitic ideas, continuing his campaign, with various interruptions, until 1926. In 1927 he became convinced that the *Protocols* was a forgery and—after a threatened libel suit, it might be added—publicly apologized.

Some of the anti-immigrant agitation of the postwar years involved opposition to the further entry of Jews into the United States. The laws of 1921 and 1924 were so drawn as to reduce the Jewish immigration to a small fraction of what it had been.

Overt anti-Semitism receded after 1927, only to come to the fore with renewed force in 1933. A deep depression, a slight rise in revolutionary sentiment (tempting reactionary forces to use the rusty weapon of anti-

[43] James W. Parkes, *An Enemy of the People: Antisemitism*, p. 74.
[44] Albert I. Gordon, *Jews in Transition*, University of Minnesota Press, 1949, pp. 19–20.

Semitism), opposition to changes brought about by the New Deal, and the coming to power of Nazism in Germany were among the factors contributing to its growth.[45] Strong records the founding of 5 anti-Semitic organizations in the United States between 1915 and 1932, 9 in 1933, and 105 between 1934 and 1939—a clear indication of the rapid increase in organized prejudice during the 1930's.

During this period political anti-Semitism made its first significant appearance here. At no time did it reach a position of important political influence or become the central rallying point of a political party; but it appeared often enough in political debate to show that the United States is not immune, under certain conditions, to the growth of organized anti-Semitism. An occasional congressman (e.g., Representative Louis T. McFadden, Senator Theodore Bilbo) attacked Jews. "In a speech in the fall of 1935, the manager of the Coughlin-Lemke third party charged that 'the trouble with this country now is due to the money powers and Jewish politicians. . . . The American people must shake off their shoulders the Jewish politicians.' "[46]

The statewide campaign in 1938 in which Harold Stassen undertook to wrest the governorship from Elmer Benson was in large measure built around the issue of a "Jew-controlled state capitol." At first in a whispering campaign, then in the form of the never-to-be-forgotten pamphlet entitled "Are They Communists or Are They Catspaws?" each Jew who had worked in the state capitol under Governors Floyd Olson and Elmer Benson was singled out for attack and by indirection made to appear as a Communist. Just before the election the Minneapolis *Journal* (the predecessor of the Minneapolis *Star*, then owned by other interests) devoted a page of its rotogravure section to photographs of the men who surrounded Governor Olson. Most of those whose pictures were used were Jews, though they represented only a small fraction of the governor's intimates. . . .

So vicious did the attack become that several Jewish Republicans visited Harold Stassen and urged him to make a public repudiation of those people who used the anti-Semitic argument during the campaign. In his concluding radio address, delivered the night before election day, Stassen declared that he did not wish to identify himself with those responsible for the attack.[47]

More important than such scattered political efforts were the activities of the 121 or more frankly anti-Semitic organizations that sought, by agitation, propaganda, and marginal political efforts, to arouse and exploit hatred of Jews. We cannot undertake here an analysis of these groups, but they occupy an important place in American anti-Semitic agitation in the 1930's. Since 1941 such organizations, although they were perhaps more numerous in the immediate postwar years than at

---

[45] See Donald S. Strong, *Organized Anti-Semitism in America*, American Council on Public Affairs, 1941, p. 15.

[46] Carey McWilliams, *op. cit.*, p. 42.

[47] Albert I. Gordon, *op. cit.*, pp. 51–52.

any other time, have been insignificant, in terms of influence, in the United States.[48]

Throughout the administration of Franklin Roosevelt anti-Semites sought to attack his policies by identifying them with Jews. Though their ideas were recorded in dozens of pamphlets and periodicals, they won little hearing even during the sharp controversy over isolationism before the Second World War. The same type of attack has been directed against President Eisenhower, as illustrated by the following statement:

> . . . The election of Eisenhower means that Baruch and his gang of powerful international Jews have captured the White House again . . . This vicious international Jew machine . . . is as powerful among Republicans as it is among Democrats. . . .
>
> The first step of Baruch and his ruthless ilk of international manipulators . . . will be to complete conscription of all human beings from 17 to 70. Their second gesture of tyranny will be to repeal the McCarran Immigration Act so that 20 million Jews and colored will be dumped on American shores. They propose to see to it that never again will the great white Christian population of America be able to express majority power. . . .[49]

Ugh!

Agitational groups appealed to only a small minority of the American people, however, even in a time of depression. "Politer" kinds of economic, social, and educational discrimination are much more widespread. They reflect the transition of many Jews from the insecurities of immigrant status to effective competition for middle-class positions and show also the economic and personal insecurities of large numbers of people in our society.

Severson found no discrimination against Jews reflected in the want-ad columns from 1872 to 1911. Beginning in the latter year, however, ads requesting "Christians only" or "Gentiles only" appeared at the rate of 0.3 percent per 1000, rose to 4 percent in 1921, to 8.8 percent in 1923, to 13.3 percent in 1926; averaged 11 percent from 1927 to 1931; dropped to 4.8 percent in 1931; and then rose to 9.4 percent in 1937. Most of the discriminatory ads were for female office employees indicating that the second-generation girls were beginning to seek white-collar employment. . . . The decisive factor was the appearance, on the clerical labor market, of a new group of competitors who could be identified for purposes of dis-

---

[48] See, in addition to the works of McWilliams and of Strong, Leo Lowenthal and Norbert Guterman, *Prophets of Deceit. A Study in the Techniques of the American Agitator*, Harper & Brothers, 1949; and John Roy Carlson, *Under Cover*, E. P. Dutton & Co., Inc., 1943. Using a somewhat different listing from Strong (who, they say, included moribund as well as active hate groups for his prewar estimate), the Anti-Defamation League listed the following totals for anti-Semitic organizations in the United States: 1940, 60; 1941, 73; 1942, 69; 1943, 73; 1944, 91; 1945, 112; 1946, 130; 1947, 115; 1948, 78; 1949, 66. See Arnold Forster, *A Measure of Freedom* (an Anti-Defamation League report), Doubleday & Company, Inc., 1950, p. 81.

[49] From the newsletter of Gerald Smith, quoted by Arnold Forster and Benjamin R. Epstein, *op. cit.*, pp. 61–62.

crimination. The moment this happened, the doors to clerical and white-collar jobs began to be slammed in the face of Jewish applicants much in the same manner that the doors of the Grand Union Hotel had been slammed in the face of Joseph Seligman.[50]

In 1922 an employment office reported that 67 percent of requests for employees indicated that Jews were not wanted. A survey of middle-western teachers' agencies in 1925 revealed that 95 to 98 percent of vacancies were to be filled by "Protestants only."[51] In 1947, representatives of the American Jewish Congress called 121 white-collar employment agencies in New York City. Without identifying themselves, they requested white Protestant applicants for secretaries. Of the 121 agencies, 107 expressed a readiness to coöperate in this discrimination, although it violates a statute of the state of New York.[52] They apparently accepted as normal the exclusion of all but "white Protestants" from white-collar jobs.

In Chapter 19 we shall analyze in detail the attitudes and policies toward Jews in American education. Suffice it to say here that since World War I, quotas and restrictions on the admission of Jewish students have spread widely among both undergraduate and professional schools. Only in the last eight or ten years have laws against discrimination in education (in New York and Massachusetts, for example) and various public protests, informed by the data from the report of the President's Commission on Higher Education, begun to offset this trend.

How Widespread Is Anti-Semitism in the United States?

It is easy to play up the activities of a few violent agitators, a handful of politicians, a tiny number of desecrators of synagogues. But it is also easy to overlook the receptivity that many Americans might show to anti-Semitism under conditions of prolonged depression or hardship. The United States government almost without exception (the immigration laws of 1924 and 1952 may be an exception) has consistently opposed anti-Semitism.[53] Many individual citizens, however, have shown by word and action that they are not free from it. Most studies that seek to discover the amount of this prejudice measure willingness to accept certain anti-Semitic statements. This technique may yield very different results from attempts to measure participation in stated kinds of anti-Semitic activities (joining "hate groups," attacking Jews, discriminating against them in employment or education, etc.). Polls tell little about

[50] Carey McWilliams, op. cit., pp. 28–29.
[51] Ibid., p. 37.
[52] See New Republic, December 15, 1947, p. 22.
[53] See Cyrus Adler and Aaron M. Margolith, With Firmness in the Right, American Diplomatic Action Affecting Jews, 1840–1945, American Jewish Committee, 1945.

intensity of feeling or readiness to act. Often people who verbalize the traditional attitudes of prejudice will not take part, at least at the present time, in discriminatory acts. Knowledge of attitudes, however, may help to describe potential hostile acts if conditions change.

Most polls have shown that about 10 percent of the respondents will make spontaneous anti-Semitic statements. Another group, ranging from 30 to 60 percent in various studies, will agree with anti-Semitic statements or will offer them when questioned directly about Jews. In February, 1946, the *Fortune* poll, in a cross-section study of American adults, found that 8.8 percent were anti-Semitic in the sense that they responded "The Jews," to one or both of the following questions: "Are there any organizations or groups of people in this country who you feel might be harmful to the future of the country unless they are curbed?" "Are there any groups of people you think are trying to get ahead at the expense of people like you?"[54] In October, 1947, the *Fortune* poll, listing the major religious groups, asked, "Do you think any of these groups are getting more economic power anywhere in the United States than is good for the country?" Over a third answered "The Jews." Nearly a quarter specified the Jews in response to a similar question regarding political power.

Such data are difficult to interpret because they classify together persons of very different intensities of feeling and with widely varying readiness to act. They do indicate, however, the extensive sharing of verbal stereotypes and point out, to some degree, the potential followers of an anti-Semitic movement if the level of anxiety and confusion is raised. Ten percent of the American people might, under highly disorganized conditions, be direct supporters of such a movement, and perhaps half of the remainder would be sufficiently vulnerable to its appeal to give it some support or fail to resist it. Americans who oppose prejudice and discrimination cannot afford to be indifferent to this possibility.

[54] Elmo Roper, *Fortune*, February, 1946, p. 257.

CHAPTER 10

Anti-Semitism—A Case Study in Prejudice: The Social Psychology of Anti-Semitism

In the preceding chapter some aspects of the history of anti-Semitism in a few societies were described. That analysis was largely concerned with the conflict and traditional factors that caused and renewed the prejudice. We turn now to an examination of some of the personality factors in anti-Semitism. What experiences and tendencies are most likely to predispose a person to accept and act upon antipathy toward Jews? This problem, as applied to prejudice in general, was the theme of Chapter 3; hence we may be brief in our examination of it here, needing only to refer it specifically to prejudice against Jews. In the next section we shall ask: What are the personality consequences of anti-Semitism for Jews?

What Types of Persons and Groups Are Likely to Be Anti-Semitic?

There have been many attempts to discover whether certain occupational groups, classes, regions, or personality types are likely to be more anti-Semitic than others. References to this problem were made in Chapter 9, but we need now to direct our attention specifically to it, in terms of the interaction of all the basic factors in prejudice. Not all individuals or groups are equally susceptible to anti-Semitic beliefs or actions. The results of studies seeking to isolate the factors that predispose an individual to acceptance of this prejudice are somewhat contradictory, but it is well to examine them to discover the degree of agreement and to make clear that any easy explanation is impossible.

They point to the need for distinguishing carefully among the various kinds of anti-Semitism (from sharing the verbal stereotypes to active discrimination) and for continuing analysis of the many different roots of anti-Semitism.

Harlan asked 502 college students (from three southern and one northern school) to check their degree of agreement or disagreement with twelve brief stories that described pro- or anti-Jewish behavior. He found, as most studies do, that women were less prejudiced than men. Students whose home residences were in larger communities were more prejudiced than those from smaller communities. Students whose parents were engaged in business or professional occupations were more prejudiced than those from the homes of skilled workers, farmers, or clerical workers. Prejudice varied directly with income; the higher the income of the family, the more the prejudice. It also varied directly with frequency of contact with Jews, even when two groups were compared that had been matched for region, size of home community, income, sex ratio, and number of Jewish friends. And finally, it varied inversely with the number of intimate Jewish friends; those without them were most prejudiced. (There is no indication whether this attribute is cause or effect.) Each of these differences is statistically significant at the 1 percent level; that is, the probability that differences as large as those found, for example, between high and low income groups could be due simply to chance is less than one in a hundred.[1]

These data would seem to indicate that persons likely to be in most direct competition with Jews and those who are most likely to oppose social change (because they receive high rewards in the existing situation) are most anti-Semitic, as measured by Harlan's type of scale. The *Fortune* poll of February, 1946, had similar results. Roper found that rich, upper middle class, and lower middle class made up 71.4 percent of United States adults but contributed 81.9 percent of the anti-Semites. The data also indicate a greater willingness to make anti-Semitic statements among people in the Northeast and Middle West than among those from the South and Far West and found more prejudice among the residents of large cities tham among farmers and small-town residents.[2]

It is important to recognize the limitations and weakness of this kind of measurement. Anti-Semitism must be defined, in this context, as willingness to make the verbal responses that have been designated as anti-Semitic by the poll taker. Response to different questions often indicates different results. For example, a *Fortune* poll in October, 1947, using a secret ballot, found, contrary to the data above, that a larger proportion of farmers and residents of small towns than residents

---

[1] See Howard H. Harlan, "Some Factors Affecting Attitude Toward Jews," *American Sociological Review*, December, 1942, pp. 816–827.

[2] Elmo Roper, "The Fortune Poll," *Fortune*, February, 1946, pp. 257–260.

of cities thought Jews had "too much say in government." This result must be qualified, however, by the fact that the city vote contained a much higher proportion of Jewish respondents. It may also measure simply the response to a stereotype, not readiness to engage in overt anti-Semitic activity; or, more specifically, it may measure a stereotype only in the field of politics.

Another difference in the results of various measures of anti-Semitism is shown in the data on regional variation. As we have seen, Roper found from a sample of adults that respondents in the Northeast and Middle West made or accepted more anti-Semitic statements than those from the South and West. Harlan found the same thing in his college sample; students from the North showed more prejudice than those from the South. In 1949, however, Roper interviewed a cross section of 1000 freshmen and 1000 seniors on fifty different campuses and found southern students to be the most anti-Semitic.[3] Owing to the greater adequacy of his sampling procedure, Roper's measure of prejudice among students must be accepted as the more reliable; but the differences indicate the need for caution in our judgments.

A study made for the Jewish Labor Committee by the Institute of Social Research of Columbia University raises some doubts also about the occupational and class distribution of anti-Semitic attitudes. Interviews with 600 industrial workers in five cities revealed that about 20 percent were strongly anti-Semitic, another 20 percent were fully tolerant, the rest were intermediate or inconsistent. This distribution is similar to that found in studies of the general population. Attitudes did not vary significantly with length of union membership or type of union to which one belonged. The stereotype of "the" Jew was primarily that of the small businessman.[4]

It is well to note again that this was a study of attitudes and did not measure salience or readiness to participate in overt anti-Semitic activities of various kinds. It may well be that the traditional factor in this prejudice—the willingness to share the verbal stereotypes—varies little from group to group within the boundaries of a society, but that participation in active anti-Semitic movements varies with the personality and conflict factors. Evidence from both the United States and Germany seems to support this hypothesis. If we take account of only one factor, our data are bound to seem contradictory or inexplicable. If we assume, for example, that economic status is the sole determinant of attitudes, we will be surprised to find persons of different status sharing the same attitude, or persons of similar status having different attitudes.

[3] See Arnold Forster, *A Measure of Freedom*, Doubleday & Company, Inc., 1950, pp. 157–160.
[4] See Herbert Northrup, in R. M. MacIver (ed.), *Discrimination and National Welfare*, Institute for Religious and Social Studies, 1949, pp. 73–74.

The authors of *The Authoritarian Personality* discovered that the working-class men in their sample did not differ significantly from service-club (middle-class) men in attitudes of prejudice toward Jews. This study sought to isolate the personality factors in prejudice, not the total tendency to engage in discrimination, and the evidence indicated that the tendency toward an "authoritarian character structure" did not vary between these two classes. This result is not surprising in view of the many factors at work. To interpret this finding, however, requires that we distinguish between an authoritarian outlook that is rooted in day-by-day experience (the world *is* more authoritarian to the lower-class member) and one derived from ego-alien insecurity.

Similarly, one expects to find shared opinions among the members of occupational, religious, fraternal, and other groups; but there will be variation and exceptions because of other factors. "There is reason to believe that individuals, out of their needs to conform and to belong and to believe and through such devices as imitation and conditioning, often take over more or less ready-made the opinions, attitudes, and values that are characteristic of the groups in which they have membership. To the extent that the ideas which prevail in such a group are implicitly or explicitly antidemocratic, the individual group member might be expected to be receptive to propaganda having the same general direction."[5] We must distinguish, of course, between cases in which the individual is conditioned by the group and those in which he joins the group because he already agrees with the ideas for which it stands. In either event we must be alert to variation within the group, because of different personality needs and because of different combinations of group membership.

With these qualifications in mind, it will be useful to explore in more detail the personality and group factors that seem to be associated with anti-Semitism. A recent intensive study of 150 veterans in Chicago has revealed a number of significant relationships between personal and group characteristics and anti-Semitism in this largely lower-middle-class group. On the basis of exploratory interviews with a small group of veterans not included in the final sample, Bettleheim and Janowitz developed a classification of four types of veterans according to their attitudes toward Jews:

1. The *intensely anti-Semitic* veteran was spontaneously outspoken in expressing a preference for restrictive action against the Jews even before the subject was raised. For example, he might have advocated Hitler's solution to the Jewish problem here in America, when asked whether there were any groups of people trying to get ahead at his expense. When questioned directly about the Jews, he maintained his outspoken preference for restric-

[5] T. W. Adorno, Else Frenkel-Brunswik, D. J. Levinson, and R. N. Sanford, *The Authoritarian Personality*, Harper & Brothers, 1950, p. 9.

tive action. For example, he might have objected to having Jews as next-door neighbors, to working on the same job with them, or he might have advocated prevention of intermarriage with Jews. Finally he also displayed a wide range of unfavorable stereotyped opinions about the Jews.

2. The *outspokenly anti-Semitic* veteran revealed no spontaneous preference for restrictive action against the Jews. Instead, outspoken hostility toward the Jews emerged only toward the end of the interview when he was questioned directly. As in the case of the intensely anti-Semitic veteran, his thinking contained a wide range of unfavorable stereotypes.

3. The *stereotyped anti-Semitic* veteran expressed no preference for hostile, or restrictive action against the Jews, either spontaneously or when questioned directly. Instead, he merely expressed a variety of stereotyped notions about the Jews, including some which were not necessarily unfavorable from his point of view. For example, he might have thought Jews clannish, or that they are people who engage in shrewd business methods. But he felt, for any number of reasons, that these characteristics did not justify aggressive action against the Jews, by the government or by society at large.

4. The *tolerant* veteran revealed no elaborate stereotyped beliefs about the Jews although even the most tolerant veterans expressed isolated stereotypes from time to time. Moreover, neither spontaneously nor when questioned directly, did he advocate restrictive action against the Jews. In fact, on policy questions, the tolerant person either denied any just grounds for differentiating between Jews and non-Jews, or affirmed his lack of concern about such differences.[6]

When the 150 men in the study were classified on the basis of these types, the following distribution resulted:[7]

	Distribution of Anti-Semitism		Distribution of Anti-Negro Attitudes	
	Number	Percentage	Number	Percentage
Tolerant	61	41	12	8
Stereotyped	42	28	40	27
Outspoken	41	27	74	49
Intense	6	4	24	16
Total	150	100	150	100

For purposes of comparison, attitudes toward the Negro, based on the same classification, are also given. For the most part, as intolerance toward the Jew increased, even greater intolerance toward the Negro was exhibited. There was only one case in which tolerance toward the Negro was accompanied by outspoken anti-Semitism.

By what personal and group characteristics were the tolerant veterans distinguished from the intolerant? An answer to this question helps to reveal the causes of anti-Semitism. The authors thought that the children of European immigrants might show more prejudice than those

[6] Bruno Bettleheim and Morris Janowitz, *Dynamics of Prejudice. A Psychological and Sociological Study of Veterans*, Harper & Brothers, 1950, pp. 12–13.

[7] See *ibid.*, pp. 16, 26.

of native-born parents, since anti-Semitism had been so strong in parts of Europe. This assumption did not prove to be true. There was a difference, too small to be statistically significant, between children of mixed parentage (one parent foreign-born) and those whose parents were both native or both foreign-born. Subjects who had one native and one foreign-born parent were somewhat more intolerant of both Jews and Negroes. It is a tenable hypothesis—only suggested, not substantiated by this study—that persons brought up in mixed families felt less family cohesion and therefore experienced a greater insecurity that led to aggression.

Bettleheim and Janowitz, seeking to test the hypothesis that social mobility was related to anti-Semitism, were able to get precise data on the social mobility of 130 of the 150 veterans. They found a significantly greater number of aggressive attitudes among the downwardly mobile group than among those who had advanced in social status since the period of their last civilian employment. Those who had experienced no mobility were in between. It seems, from this study, that the level of status is not related to anti-Semitism but that the direction of change of satus is important.[8]

Anti-Semitism and Social Mobility

	Downward Mobility		No Mobility		Upward Mobility		Total	
	No.	%	No.	%	No.	%	No.	%
Tolerant	2	11	25	37	22	50	49	38
Stereotyped	3	17	26	38	8	18	37	28
Outspoken and intense	13	72	17	25	14	32	44	34
Total	18		68		44		130	

These data cannot be taken without qualification. Twenty of the original 150 veterans could not be classified according to social mobility with the data in hand. Twelve of the twenty were in the tolerant group and five in the stereotyped. If a large proportion of these were in the downward mobility group, the hypothesis would not be substantiated. This situation is unlikely, but the possibility should not be overlooked; it is conceivable that lack of data is precisely a sign of downward mobility.

A more serious qualification demands that we not assume a causal relationship. This study does not prove that several of the veterans are outspokenly and intensely anti-Semitic because they are downwardly mobile. The causation may run another way. Persons who are frustrated, aggressive, rigid-minded (and therefore anti-Semitic) are unable to do the kind of work (or get along with the boss) that allows upward social mobility. Only carefully controlled observation can reveal which

[8] *Ibid.*, p. 59.

of these time sequences, or what other, most accurately explains the relationship. An interactional pattern may be involved. Bettleheim and Janowitz cite evidence from the German situation that points in the direction of a time sequence running from downward mobility to intense anti-Semitism:

The socially and economically downward-moving lower middle class groups (frequently referred to as the "squeezed-out group") were the followers of Hitler, while the "respectable," relatively secure, and static middle classes (those who had not yet experienced downward mobility) held apart from this extreme form of nationalism (and anti-Semitism). Before Hitler, they were the followers of the Stahlhelm, of the conservative parties who embraced "stereotyped" anti-Semitism without being outspokenly intolerant. All this changed with the advent of Hitler. Then anti-Semitism became not only respectable, but the social norm. Moreover, these middle classes which had formerly enjoyed relative security now themselves became part of the squeezed-out group, squeezed first by the new ruling group of National Socialists and then by the war mobilization economy. At this point, most of them became intensely hostile to the Jews, both because they were again following the accepted and successful pattern and also because they needed more violent outlets for the hostility aroused by sudden and severe frustration.[9]

This study revealed other interesting relationships. The veterans who had had longer or more arduous army careers, those who had suffered more deprivations, were not more intolerant than those who had had fewer deprivations. There was, however, a significant correlation between the *belief* that one had received a bad break in the army and anti-Semitism. Those who had subjectively experienced army life as full of deprivation were more intolerant. Similarly, when asked how "things in general" would turn out, the tolerant veterans were significantly more optimistic, the anti-Semitic veterans more pessimistic. The tolerant respondents were more likely to have recollections of affectionate parents, the intolerant to remember a lack of parental love.

In interpreting each of these relationships and the many others described in *Dynamics of Prejudice*, we must remember that the correlations are frequently small, even though statistically significant, and that the causal sequence is by no means clear. Are persons who have experienced a lack of parental love more likely to be anti-Semitic and otherwise prejudiced, or are those who develop intolerant attitudes for some other reason likely to take a dim view of the world and therefore have less happy memories of relationships with parents? Although such questions as these are not thoroughly answered in the study, the analysis does contribute to our understanding of the group and personal factors associated with intolerance.

[9] *Ibid.*, p. 60; see also Hans H. Gerth, "The Nazi Party: Its Leadership and Composition," *American Journal of Sociology*, January, 1940, pp. 517–541.

Is There an Anti-Semitic Personality?

In Chapter 3 we examined the evidence for the hypothesis that prejudice was not simply a specific attitude but part of a total personality configuration in many instances. This hypothesis is based on the observation that prejudices tend to come in clusters and that, moreover, they are associated with other personality tendencies—rigidity of mind, high anxiety, ambivalence (outward submissiveness and conventionality but an unconscious hostility and desire to break free from social inhibitions). According to this conception, one understands prejudice by examining the personality needs of the prejudiced individual. If we avoid the danger of assuming that this is the only explanatory principle, that all prejudice is to be explained by the presence of unconscious hostility and ambivalence, the hypothesis can be of great help in understanding anti-Semitism. The evidence of many studies indicates that the most extreme opposition to Jews, at any rate, cannot be explained simply by analyzing economic competition and traditional factors. Anti-Semitism seems to be highly correlated with a "character structure" that contains the following tendencies:

a. *Conventionalism.* Rigid adherence to conventional, middle-class values.
b. *Authoritarian submission.* Submissive, uncritical attitude toward idealized moral authorities of the ingroup.
c. *Authoritarian aggression.* Tendency to be on the lookout for, and to condemn, reject, and punish people who violate conventional values.
d. *Anti-intraception.* Opposition to the subjective, the imaginative, the tender-minded.
e. *Superstition and stereotypy.* The belief in mystical determinants of the individual's fate; the disposition to think in rigid categories.
f. *Power and "toughness."* Preoccupation with the dominance-submission, strong-weak, leader-follower dimension; identification with power figures; overemphasis upon the conventionalized attributes of the ego; exaggerated assertion of strength and toughness.
g. *Destructiveness and cynicism.* Generalized hostility, vilification of the human.
h. *Projectivity.* The disposition to believe that wild and dangerous things go on in the world; the projection outwards of unconscious emotional impulses.
i. *Sex.* Exaggerated concern with sexual "goings-on."

These variables were thought of as going together to form a single syndrome, a more or less enduring structure in the person that renders him receptive to antidemocratic propaganda.[10]

Many persons object to the idea that one can think of anti-Semitism as a unidimensional tendency, ranging from the acceptance of verbal stereotypes to active participation in violence against Jews. Samuel

[10] T. W. Adorno, *et al., op. cit.,* p. 228.

contends, as we shall see, that the basic factor in intense anti-Semitism is hatred of Christianity—a hatred that cannot be openly acknowledged and is therefore projected onto Jews. When this factor enters, according to Samuel, an essentially unique phenomenon, not just another prejudice, is created. Similarly, Ackerman and Jahoda draw a distinction between dislike of Jews as a prejudice and anti-Semitism as an emotional disorder based on unconscious hostilities that are involved in the total personality configuration of the individual. The former is ". . . based on nothing but erroneous prejudgment or stereotyped thought process."[11] The latter is rooted in a fundamental personal insecurity. This kind of analysis is right insofar as it emphasizes that when the deeply irrational and unconscious forces of self-conflict and ambivalence become involved in anti-Semitism, it takes on a rigidity, an intense motivational energy, and a complexity that give it a highly important place in the total personality of the individual and make explosive and vicious social movements more likely. Such an analysis is in error, however, in failing to see that most anti-Semitic individuals suffer, to some degree, from emotional disturbance or from a desire to throw off the restraints of religious teaching, so that there is no sharp break between those who have an anti-Jewish prejudice and those who exhibit the more intensive anti-Semitism. The analysis is in error, also, in failing to describe the interaction among the many causes of anti-Semitism. Political, economic, and cultural factors are not ranged on one side, producing anti-Jewish sentiments, while personal confusion and hostility, on the other, create the more intense anti-Semitism. There are numerous ways in which a person could "adjust" to the frustrations of an authoritarian upbringing or to the confusions of modern life. That anti-Semitism is often chosen in some societies cannot be understood by even the most intensive analysis of the personality unless that analysis is accompanied by a study of the cultural and conflict factors in the environment of the person involved. Some persons make a different "adjustment"; and in some societies, where anti-Semitism is unknown, all unstable and confused persons make a different response.

In sum, there can, from our point of view, be anti-Semitism without serious personality disturbance, and there can be serious personality disturbance without anti-Semitism. This prejudice is most likely to occur among emotionally disturbed individuals in a society where a traditional anti-Jewish prejudice is available, and under circumstances in which political and economic conflicts encourage the attitude and give the disturbed individual "good" reasons for thinking his anxiety will be reduced by attacks against the Jews.

[11] Nathan Ackerman and Marie Jahoda, *Anti-Semitism and Emotional Disorder*, Harper & Brothers, 1950, p. 6.

The Effects of Anti-Semitism on Jews

In Chapters 6 and 7 we discussed the influence that prejudice and discrimination have on the personalities of minority-group members. It is well now to raise this question specifically with reference to Jews. Many people "justify" their anti-Semitism by pointing to the supposed characteristics of Jews. Is there any evidence that Jews have, on the average, a greater tendency for this or that characteristic than other groups with whom they may be compared? If so, is there any way in which these differences may be looked upon as a "cause" of prejudice?

Evidence on this subject is highly inadequate. Assertions range all the way from the belief that Jews are fundamentally different (innately so, many anti-Semites would say) to the claim that there are no differences in group averages, that Jews have the same range and distribution of personality tendencies as other groups (a proposition resting upon a democratic ideology, but not always fully informed). Although our evidence is incomplete, based almost entirely on uncontrolled observation, not on controlled study, these statements seem to be in harmony with present knowledge of the nature of personality:

1. There are no inherited behavioral differences between Jew and non-Jew.

2. Differences in experience (including discrimination) have produced some differences in personality tendency between some Jews and members of the dominant group.

3. These differences are frequently exaggerated and misinterpreted by anti-Semites and others (sometimes including Jews). They are often assumed to apply universally, without regard to individual variation; the anti-Semite pays attention only to what he regards as unfavorable differences; his selective perception distorts the picture enormously; and he has an entirely inadequate idea of why there are differences.

It would be surprising indeed if Jews, having experienced the kinds of discrimination that we have described in the preceding chapter, had not developed some personality tendencies different (in degree, not kind) from those of persons with very different experiences. Among the most important consequences of prejudice and discrimination, for example, are the attitudes toward oneself and one's group. Many Jews have had sufficiently stable early experiences to be able to adjust on a "reality" level to the discriminations they meet. Others, being unable, in a social context that defines them as inferior or obnoxious, to develop a satisfying sense of selfhood, react by overemphasizing their Jewishness or by trying to hide it. Neither of these extremes is likely to be an effective adjustment from the individual's own point of view. Overemphasis on one's status as a Jew (with consequent underemphasis of one's statuses in a given occupational role, educational level, community, nation, and other group associations) requires that one identify himself closely with a group which the majority treats with prejudice. Minimization of one's role in the Jewish group, on the other hand, or an attempt to break completely one's identification with Jews, requires the denial of a strong sense of community and often leads to a feeling of guilt that one has deserted his group. In either event, anxiety and feelings of unworthiness are likely to follow. Kurt Lewin says, with regard to the adjustment of Jewish students to the discriminatory aspects of college life, that many show a well-adapted and balanced behavior. "There are, however, a large number of Jewish students who show decided lack of adjustment. To one who has come to America from pre-Hitler Germany it is quite impressive to find such typical signs of Jewish maladjustment as over-tension, loudness, over-aggressiveness, excessively hard work—sometimes to an even higher degree here than over there."[12]

A study of 159 Jewish students at the University of Minnesota (May, 1942) reveals some of the feelings of frustration felt by this group. All but six were born in the United States; half had attended a Hebrew or religious school; three-fourths came from families of moderate income. Among the answers they gave to questions seeking to determine the degree to which they felt they were deprived of equal opportunities were these:[13]

	Agree	Disagree
I believe that being born a Jew means that you have two strikes against you	30.1	69.9
I am convinced that anti-Semitism is likely to interfere with my search for personal success or happiness	40.2	59.8
I often feel a great personal insecurity because of existing discriminations	45.9	54.1
I find life as a Jew unsatisfactory because of existing discriminations	11.3	88.7
I feel that my opportunity for getting the job I would really like is seriously restricted because I am a Jew	33.9	66.1
I feel that at any moment my feelings may be hurt because I am a Jew	22.6	77.4

Sklare and Vosk asked a sample of the Jews in an industrial city of 130,000 population whether they had experienced any anti-Semitism. Seventy-five percent of the adults and 86 percent of the adolescents said yes. Their experiences, doubtless ranging from imagined slights to serious discrimination, are part of the setting in which Jewish personality development takes place.[14]

[12] Kurt Lewin, *Resolving Social Conflicts*, Harper & Brothers, 1948, p. 170.
[13] See Albert I. Gordon, *Jews in Transition*, University of Minnesota Press, 1949, pp. 59–60.
[14] Marshall Sklare and Marc Vosk, *The Riverton Study. How Jews Look at Themselves and Their Neighbors*, American Jewish Committee, 1957, p. 45.

Jewish Anti-Semitism

In Chapter 6 we referred to the phenomenon of self-hatred, particularly among Negroes. It is a tendency found also among Jews, among some second-generation immigrant groups, and among others who feel caught in a status that is defined as inferior by the dominant group. The self-hatred is seldom an open and uncomplicated reaction. It is more often indirect, even unconscious, and accompanied by ambivalent feelings of superiority and chauvinism. Self-hatred is the product of three interacting factors. Those of high status define one's group as inferior; one experiences discrimination because of group membership, yet the attitudes of the majority prevent one from leaving the group. Those who try to solve this problem by accepting the definitions of the dominant group are caught in a difficult situation so long as prejudice continues.

A person for whom the balance is negative will move as far away from the center of Jewish life as the outside majority permits. He will stay on this barrier and be in a constant state of frustration. Actually, he will be more frustrated than those members of the minority who keep psychologically well inside the group. We know from experimental psychology and psychopathology that such frustration leads to an all-around state of high tension with a generalized tendency to aggression. The aggression should, logically, be directed against the majority, which is what hinders the minority member from leaving his group. However, the majority has, in the eyes of these persons, higher status. And besides, the majority is much too powerful to be attacked.[15]

Under these circumstances one attacks himself (feelings of unworthiness and blame) or one's group ("negative chauvinism") or some part of one's group (an "inferior" part which endangers one's security because the majority draws no distinctions) or one's family (the cause of one's group location). This Jewish anti-Semitism is a psychologically somewhat different phenomenon from the anti-Semitism of non-Jews. Both expressions represent an attempt to achieve a satisfying sense of self by identifying with the dominant group. This is more difficult for the Jew, for he must deny more of himself. In the study of a group of emotionally disordered persons Ackerman and Jahoda found two differences between Jewish and gentile anti-Semitism.

First, in examining the content of the anti-Semitic projections of Jewish anti-Semites, the absence of "good" qualities is conspicuous. Here, there are no conscious claims that Jews are intelligent, powerful, successful, sexually potent, or ethical. The reason for this probably lies in the precarious illusion of not belonging to the Jewish group, the even greater ambivalence stemming from a dread of discovery, and even more, "conversion" to their

[15] Kurt Lewin, *op. cit.*, p. 193.

Jewishness. Their anti-Semitism seems better fortified by denying the "good" elements of the cultural stereotype. Knowing deep down that they are Jews —and failures, to boot—they cannot reconcile the culturally favorable aspects of the Jewish stereotype with their own state of being.

Second, it appears that while most Gentiles in our case material hate not only Jews but also other groups as well, the Jewish need for hatred is more exclusively directed against Jews. None of the Jewish patients and clients manifested significantly any other form of prejudice.[16]

Negative chauvinism and self-hatred seem particularly strange in view of the undoubted achievements of many Jews. They are well represented in numerous lines of endeavor that are held in high regard in modern society—in science and art, in business and the professions. In Germany, for example, thirteen of the thirty-eight who won Nobel prizes before 1933 were Jews. The cultural traditions of Judaism, the community solidarity (in important measure a result of discrimination), high individual desire for achievement (again in part a result of discrimination), the intellectual alertness which comes from the marginal position of membership in two cultures—these and other factors have encouraged high achievement.

In a context of prejudice, however, even notable contributions become a source of embarrassment, not of pride. What is a virtue in the dominant group becomes a vice in the minority group. Episcopalians or Texans or Americans of Swedish descent may boast of the number of their members who have become important businessmen, scientists, doctors, musicians. But Jews and the opponents of anti-Semitism spend a great deal of energy to prove that the Jews have *not* made extraordinary contributions, whereas anti-Semites document the "dominance" (contributions) of Jews to many lines of endeavor. Merton describes the situation well.

In a society where, as a recent survey by the National Opinion Research Center has shown, the profession of medicine ranks higher in social prestige than any other of ninety occupations (save that of United States Supreme Court Justice), we find Jewish spokesmen manoeuvred by the attacking in-group into the fantastic position of announcing their "deep concern" over the number of Jews in medical practice, which is "disproportionate to the number of Jews in other occupations." In a nation suffering from a notorious undersupply of physicians, the Jewish doctor becomes a deplorable occasion for deep concern, rather than receiving applause for his hardwon acquisition of knowledge and skills and for his social utility. Only when the New York Yankees publicly announce deep concern over their eleven [seventeen, 1957!] World Series titles, so disproportionate to the number of triumphs achieved by other major league teams, will this self-abnegation seem part of the normal order of things.[17]

---

[16] Nathan Ackerman and Marie Jahoda, *op. cit.*, pp. 79–80.
[17] Robert K. Merton, *Social Theory and Social Structure*, The Free Press, 1949, pp. 190–191.

The opposite side of this self-abnegation is the claim by many anti-Semites that Jews are highly gifted, "of admirable endurance and resilience." This approach was formulated by Wilhelm Marr in his pamphlet, *Sieg des Judentums über das Germanentum*, 1873, in which he tried to prove that the Jews were not weak and inferior but talented and strong, "the first major power in the West."

It must not be assumed that Jewish efforts to minimize their own achievements are necessarily signs of self-hatred. They may be simply a strategy (very ineffective in the writers' judgment) to reduce hostility. But they shade off into doubt over the accomplishments of one's group and into feelings of antipathy.

OTHER PERSONALITY EFFECTS OF PREJUDICE

The effort to minimize achievements or to escape identification with the group and the tendency even to hate oneself or one's group are not the only personality consequences of anti-Semitism. To some degree, Jews exhibit compensatory feelings of superiority (illustrated by the orthodox religious conception of the "chosen people"), of individual aggressiveness, and of incomplete identification with the dominant society.[18] During the centuries in which they were deprived of citizenship, limited in occupational and residential choice, and liable to physical attack, Jews inevitably developed modes of response that involved individual aggressiveness and group cohesiveness. Periods of tolerance have encouraged assimilation, but they have seldom lasted long enough to get rid of the fear and the sense of doubt that centuries of discrimination have encouraged. In Germany, for example, during the greater part of the nineteenth century and the first two decades of the twentieth, Jews were assimilated more and more into the dominant pattern. Intermarriage was quite common. There were periods of political anti-Semitism, as we have seen, but a mass following was not achieved. With the devasting conditions of the twenties and thirties, however, came virulent attacks on Jews. Their fears were confirmed; the liberal, democratic dream faded; and the conviction that only in their own community could they find strength and freedom from anxiety was encouraged. The effects were felt in America; a renewed interest in Judaism, a revived sense of Jewish community, an increased opposition to intermarriage were among the results. Jews in the United States have one of the lowest rates of intermarriage of any "immigrant" group.

The pull toward assimilation and the internal splits within the Jewish group are still strongly operative in the United States, of course. But the period of Nazi anti-Semitism revived the feelings of biculturality.

[18] See A. P. Sperling, "A Comparison Between Jews and Non-Jews with Respect to Several Traits of Personality," *Journal of Applied Psychology*, December, 1942, pp. 828–840; see also Keith Sward and Meyer Friedman, "Jewish Temperament," *Journal of Applied Psychology*, February, 1935, pp. 70–84.

"To the children the vacillation of the thirties is particularly trying. One year a Christmas tree is legitimate; the next it is anathema. One day it is legitimate to eat milk and meat together; the next it is proscribed. Or it is legitimate when grandmother is not visiting, proscribed when she is there. Little children become intensely conscious of their biculturality."[19]

An insecure assimilation and recurring attacks on Jews lie behind the remark of Rabbi Stephen S. Wise: "I may have been an American for sixty-four years, but I have been a Jew for four thousand years." They lie behind the conception that Judaism is not simply a religion but a nation or the unifying center of a "people." They have been the sustaining force of the Zionist movement, whose founder developed his ideas in the context of the Dreyfus affair in France. "The dominant motive which goaded Theodor Herzl on in the last decade of the nineteenth century was not Judaism, with its attendant age-old allegiance to culture and 'race,' but persistent anti-Semitism with its intolerable contemporary realities."[20] The fervor with which the idea of Zionism has been embraced can be understood only against the background of Nazi persecution and mass exterminations. As Kurt Lewin says:

I remember how, as an adolescent, I was deeply disturbed by the idea that the accusation against Jews as being incapable of constructive work might be true. I know that many Jewish adolescents growing up in an atmosphere of prejudice felt similarly. Today, a Jewish youth who has watched Palestine grow is in an infinitely better situation. Whatever one's opinion about Zionism as a political program may be, no one who has observed closely the German Jews during the fateful first weeks after Hitler's rise to power will deny that thousands of German Jews were saved from suicide only by the famous article of the *Judische Rundschau*, with its headlines "Jasagen zum Judentum" ("Saying Yes to Being a Jew"). The ideas expressed there were the rallying point and the source of strength for Zionist and non-Zionist alike.[21]

Most American Jews support Zionism, of course, not for themselves, but for the remnants of central and eastern European Jewry who survived the Nazi genocide machine. The great majority of the Jews of the world now live in the United States and the Soviet Union. The degree and direction of their biculturality will be *primarily* determined by their experiences in these two countries. Persecution anywhere in the world, however, will affect their identification with Judaism.

Zionism as a political movement can be understood and evaluated only by reference to the problems and rights of the Arabian masses in Palestine, the strategic conflicts of the major powers, the interests of

[19] Jessie Bernard, in Isacque Graeber and S. H. Britt, (eds.), *Jews in a Gentile World*, The Macmillan Company, 1942, p. 282.
[20] J. O. Hertzler, in *ibid.*, p. 85.
[21] Kurt Lewin, *op. cit.*, p. 198.

the Arabian ruling class, as well as the claims and rights of the Jews. But from the point of view of the social psychology of Jews, it is strongly affected by anti-Semitism, with the attendant encouragement to the sense of separate "nationality."

Among American Jews in recent years there has been a decline of "self-hatred," on the one hand, and of biculturism, on the other. This is partly a repetition of the experience of other immigrant groups who have felt the burden of discrimination and some loss of self-confidence, and then have gradually won their way to full participation in the larger society. There is a difference, however, in the somewhat stronger sense of distinctiveness among Jews, despite their rapid climb in status, than among other "ethnic" groups. This distinctiveness is rooted in the long religious and cultural tradition interacting with the recent currents of anti-Semitism in the world. But it is also a product of the fact that with the loss of "foreignness" through the years, and with America's tradition of religious liberty, it is easier to accept one's Jewishness without anxiety or overcompensation. At the same time, in a society in which the sense of anomie is strong, there is a powerful desire to know "who I am," to have a "brand name," as Herberg put it. Thus, although Judaism has been greatly "Americanized" in many ways, there are no signs of diminution in feelings of identity with it among American Jews.[22]

Are Jewish "Traits" the Cause of Anti-Semitism?

If the above discussion is correct, prejudice and discrimination against Jews (as against other groups) have created some differences in individual and group behavior. They have been among the factors causing a high level of individual achievement but have also caused self-doubt, frustration, and hostility. They have encouraged solidarity but also intragroup conflict and barriers to adjustment with the dominant groups in society. To the anti-Semite, these differences are the causes of his attitudes. Basically he is wrong. He exaggerates the differences enormously, he forgets differences favorable to the minority group, and he has a thoroughly inadequate idea of the cause of the differences. Selective and adroit use of the facts can, however, give a superficial support to his prejudices. In the study of anti-Semitism as in the study of other prejudices, failure to examine the whole process of the vicious circle that we discussed in Chapter 5 will lead to an incomplete under-

[22] See Marshall Sklare, *Conservative Judaism: An American Religious Movement*, The Free Press, 1955; Will Herberg, *Protestant-Catholic-Jew*, Doubleday & Company, Inc., 1955; H. J. Gans, "American Jewry: Present and Future," *Commentary*, May, 1956, pp. 422–430, and "The Future of American Jewry," *Commentary*, June, 1956, pp. 555–563; Nathan Glazer, "The Jewish Revival in America," *Commentary*, December, 1955, pp. 493–499, and January, 1956, pp. 17–24; and J. Milton Yinger, *Religion, Society, and the Individual*, The Macmillan Company, 1957, pp. 288–293.

standing of the roots of prejudice and an underestimation of the tenacity with which it resists direct, rational attack.

The Interacting Causes of Anti-Semitism

To get a more unified picture of the complicated spiral of forces that have created and support anti-Semitism, it might be well to draw together, in summary, the many factors we have traced above. Some of these factors have already been discussed, and so will only be listed here; others that have been disregarded until now will need fuller treatment. It is especially important to keep in mind that these forces are interactive, mutually reinforcing, and to an important degree self-perpetuating. Once a group has been set apart as a target for hostility, it is chosen more readily for that role the next time, because tradition suggests it, guilt feelings demand it, and perhaps the responses of the minority group, having differentiated the group more sharply, encourage it. These are among the interactive forces:

1. In the pre-Christian era, the Jewish people, living astride important trade routes and in a strategically vital area of the ancient world, were caught up in conflict with many nations. The conflicts were so continuous that traditions of antipathy were given root. They helped to develop a strong Jewish ethnocentrism which at the same time reinforced the antipathy.

2. With the domination of Europe by the Christian Church, Jews stood out as the only large minority religious group at a time when religious symbols were of enormous importance. The conflict between Christianity and Judaism was more than usually sharp because of the ambivalent relationships between the two—the Jews denied Christ, yet he was a Jew.

3. By the fifth century, Jews had been deprived of their citizenship. This action may have begun as religious intolerance, but it led to many social and economic consequences. Jews had no role in the gradual development of the nation-state system that was to predominate in Europe; they had no legal rights or powers until the end of the eighteenth century. Thus their differentiation from the rest of the "body politic" was increased.

4. Having no legal rights in the medieval world, Jews were permitted to reside in the cities only at the pleasure of the princes. The princes used them as revenue officers and "royal usurers." The royal treasuries seemed always to be empty, so Jews were continually forced to demand payment from the unwilling citizenry. While being drawn into these "banking" activities, Jews were, oppositely, driven from many other occupations, forbidden to own land, and excluded from the artisan guilds. Thus their economic differentiation increased.

5. The rapid growth of cities and the development of commerce

from the tenth century on encouraged more and more Christians to come into the formerly marginal occupations associated with trade. They used their advantages as citizens and members of the dominant religion to fight their Jewish competitors, even succeeding in driving them out of most of the nations and cities of western Europe.

6. In eastern Europe, to which most of the Jews fled, they were still barred from citizenship, and the violent attacks which they had experienced at least since the days of the Crusades were repeated. This treatment kept in motion the forces of anti-Semitism.

7. Inevitably the lack of citizenship, economic discrimination, and personal violence to which the Jews were subjected intensified their cohesiveness as a cultural-religious group. Their ethnocentrism was maintained. The Jewish community seemed to be their only protection against the hostilities they continuously experienced. They were bicultural and binational; they could scarcely give full allegiance to the nation or culture in which they resided because of the interaction between the discrimination against them and their own ethnocentrism. They were blocked from the full participation which would have led in time to assimilation in the societies where they lived, and then were accused of being different. They could see no advantage in deserting a rich cultural heritage for a precarious position in the dominant society. Just how precarious that position might be has been shown again by the destruction of German Jewry, one of the most "assimilated" groups in the world. Biculturality has been an important part of the vicious circle that has kept anti-Semitism alive. Being different, Jews were more easily selected for hostile treatment; they were forced back upon their own group and its traditions, thus maintaining its differences. In earlier days, this vicious circle revolved mainly around religious symbols. Only with the decline of feudalism and the rise of nations, often with relatively distinct cultures, did the position of Jews as "foreigners" become vital. Having evolved painfully into unified nations, the European countries found the Jewish aliens (whom they themselves had kept alien and had prevented from participating in their evolution into statehood) in their midst. It is doubtless significant that there is a high (but not perfect) correlation between the areas where independent statehood was achieved with great difficulty and the areas where anti-Semitism has been most prevalent. Compare England and France with Germany and Poland. There is also a social psychological aspect to the emphasis on nationalism. As Parsons says:

It is a striking fact that the extreme kind of nationalistic sentiment is often found in groups where frustration of the sort described above is likely to be most severe; as for instance, in the lower middle class. The pattern of sentiments seems to be somewhat as follows: "I may not be a successful person, able to live in luxury the way others do; but there is one thing you can't deny—I am just as much an American (or German or Englishman) as anybody." Part of the intensity of national sentiment may undoubtedly be interpreted as "compensation" for frustration elsewhere. National identification allows the individual to participate in the glory of the achievements of his nation and relieves him of the blame for lack of *personal* achievements. Patriotism is very much of a social and economic leveler, and a very appropriate way in which to appease one's own uneasy conscience (usually on an unconscious level) and to "run down" the superior achievements or good fortune of others. The fact that the Jews form a suitable symbol in both these contexts is important in understanding the concentration of aggression on them.[23]

In an era when nationalism has loomed large, Jews have been simultaneously more provincial (with stanch loyalty to the Jewish community) and more international (with a sense of identification with the Jewish culture in every part of the world and frequently with friends and relatives residing in many different lands).

8. With anti-Semitism established by the factors listed above, it became fixed in tradition and passed on to each new generation in the socialization process. Once used, a pattern of prejudice is more likely to be used again than is a new pattern, for the old has acquired reinforcements. It has the sanction of tradition; it has helped to create some of the very differences by which it was at first justified; and the minority group has absorbed some of the projections of the dominant group—to admit that the prejudice was not "justified" would then require of the dominant group that they reëxamine the projected evils which they have thrust from themselves. Since this is too painful an experience for most individuals, they maintain the old prejudice. Many Germans today have strong unconscious guilt feelings about the anti-Semitism of the Nazi regime, whether they participated in it or simply failed to oppose it. Those very guilt feelings may well *increase* their anti-Semitism. And in some individuals at least, the stronger the guilt, the stronger must be the prejudice to try to allay the tensions. Here is another important factor in the vicious circle of anti-Semitism.

9. Part of the tradition of prejudice is the stream of stories, jokes, and stereotypes that carries the culturally established attitude on to the next generation. Millions of people who have scarcely ever seen a Jew "know" why a joke is funny when it shows a "typical" Jewish trait or has a Jew acting in a way completely unfitting to the stereotype. By laughing at the joke we share a bond of common "knowledge" with our associates, we get a feeling of superiority, and by acknowledging its humor we get a twisted kind of proof that our original attitude was correct. Literature contains a number of stereotyped and hostile pictures of Jews, beginning with the medieval miracle plays and the later morality plays—indicating their connection with the popular forms of

---

[23] Talcott Parsons, in Isacque Graeber and S. H. Britt (eds.), *op. cit.*, p. 117.

medieval Christian teachings. Chaucer's "Prioress's Tale," Marlowe's *The Jew of Malta*, and Shakespeare's *The Merchant of Venice* have helped to reinforce attitudes toward the Jew. Of themselves, they would not create a prejudice; it is the reader, more than the writer, who makes them reinforce a belief already established. In a different context they would have a wholly different effect.

It mattered little in the ultimate anti-Semitic effects that Shakespeare's Shylock is presented with great imaginative penetration. The name became in time the popular designation for all Jews, and the subtler humanity of the great dramatist's character remained unknown to the vast majority who have since its creation used the name Shylock as synonymous with Jew. . . . Most would agree that it is invidious and incompetent criticism which stresses anti-Semitism as such in creative literature like Shakespeare's. As Dickens once said in reply to Jewish criticisms of his character Fagin in *Oliver Twist*, "All the rest of the wicked dramatis personae are Christians."[24]

Even great literature, however, read from the perspective of an already established prejudice, can be made into stereotypes.

The stereotype of the Jew is subject to all the errors we discussed in Chapter 5. The myth of the "wandering Jew" has flourished among the descendants of the restless Vikings, the traveling New England Yankees, the British and Germans who wandered over the face of the earth in search for gain, whereas the Jews have often clung to their homes in the face of bitterest persecution. "It occurred to none to call the Jew a 'wanderer' until modern times. Only after he was expelled by force from European centers, in the seventeenth century did the myth of the 'Wandering Jew' arise."[25] Such errors in a stereotype, however, are easily obscured by the willing believer.

10. Anti-Semitism has been sustained to some degree by the wide dispersion of Jews around the world. When a gentile moved from one nation to another, his pattern of prejudice was not broken, for in the new land he was likely to find Jews. International contacts did not challenge the traditional prejudice against the Jew. ". . . Because he is a continuous minority in all the communicating lands of the Western world, the apprehensions regarding him as a minority were transferable, interchangeable, and even cumulative to a degree."[26]

11. Some of the interactive forces that sustain anti-Semitism are particularly prominent in the modern world. They have given it a force and a tenacity unmatched even by medieval pogroms. Freud (and many others following him) contended that anti-Semitism is in part simply a way of attacking Christianity itself. The anti-Semitic person is protesting against Christ as a symbol of brotherhood, peace, and

[24] Joseph W. Cohen, in *ibid.*, pp. 354–355.
[25] Miriam Beard, in *ibid.*, p. 375.
[26] J. O. Hertzler, in *ibid.*, p. 82.

equalitarianism; he is protesting against the demands on his behavior that Christian teachings make. A song of the Hitler Youth declared: "Pope and Rabbi shall be gone. We want to be pagans once again. No more creep to churches." And another said: "We are the joyous Hitler Youth. We do not need any Christian virtue. Our leader, Adolf Hitler is our Saviour.[27] "No more creep to churches"—an important phrase of self-revelation. Anti-Semitism thrives among those who feel Christianity as repression. They attack Jews not as Christ killers but as Christ givers. This hostility may break into the open, as in the case of the Hitler Youth, or it may be unconscious displacement, as with the more traditionally religious Americans. The unconscious hostility that the latter feel toward Christian authority over their lives is displaced onto the Jews. Maurice Samuel insists that this is *the* cause of anti-Semitism. He draws a sharp line between anti-Jewish sentiment and anti-Semitic hallucination: "Anti-Jewish sentiment (a dislike of Jews based on contact, direct or indirect, with some Jews) is in fact the ordinary variety of racial, religious and economic bitterness, overflowing in ordinary human abuse. Anti-Semitic hallucination is a unique phenomenon (the word unique must be taken quite literally here) in modern group relations."[28]

That anti-Semitism, like all other prejudices, has some unique aspects, and that the desire to attack Christianity obliquely is one of them seem to be highly probable. (We do not need to share Samuel's enthusiasm for this as the only explanation, or assume, as he does, that those who disagree with him are obstinate, naïve, or themselves anti-Semitic.) This aspect of anti-Semitism has become increasingly important in recent years, particularly in Nazism, which was thoroughly antithetical to Christianity as well as to Judaism, but also in many other movements and in many individuals.[29]

12. Having discussed the personality factors in prejudice at length above, we need only mention them here to bring them into the list of interacting forces. The loss of an integrating system of values, the "freedom" that is felt as loneliness and confusion, the alienation from satisfaction with one's work, the gap between achievement and one's desires—these and the other aspects of modern society that have contributed to insecurity have made a great many of us particularly susceptible to prejudice.

13. Akin to the theory that modern anti-Semitism rests in part on a reaction against Christianity is the theory that it is a disguised attack on liberal democracy as it has developed since the eighteenth century. This source of opposition to Jews is often a consciously chosen weapon in political-economic conflict. Anti-Semitism can obscure basic prob-

---

[27] Quoted by Carl J. Friedrich, in *ibid.*, p. 8.

[28] Maurice Samuel, *The Great Hatred*, Alfred A. Knopf, Inc., 1940, p. 10.

[29] See, in addition to Samuel, Jacques Maritain, *A Christian Looks at the Jewish Question*, Longmans, Green & Co., Inc., 1939.

lems, can divert the hostility of the masses, can cloak an attack on democracy as "necessary" for protection against the dangerous Jews. "The history of anti-Semitism, in both its classical and modern form, shows that it is profoundly symptomatic of political, economic, and institutional change."[30] In periods of rapid change, with their attendant frustrations, a nation with a tradition of anti-Semitism can be led away from democracy and liberalism by the manipulation of hostility toward the Jews.

14. One of the forces involved in modern anti-Semitism implied above is explicit propaganda and the work of organized groups. Propaganda and "hate groups" are a "cause" of anti-Semitism only when there is already a favorable attitude toward their message. In such a situation they can increase and intensify the prejudice. Propaganda to whip up hatred of the Jews was carried on systematically by the Nazis and has been used extensively by "hate groups" in the United States.

15. Modern anti-Semitism has been sustained not only by the attacks on Christianity and democracy that characterize some aspects of our society, but also by the increasing importance of commerce and industry. The Jews, having been forced into the cities and into commercial occupations by the process which we have discussed, naturally took an important part (although one that is often exaggerated by anti-Semites) in the development of modern economy. They became competitors of the increasingly powerful middle class, while at the same time representing to those who were suffering from the new order the essence of the society they opposed. This latter group included the old ruling class, who often identified Jews as the key factors in the new economy; and it included the masses of people in many situations. As trade developed in eastern Europe, Jews in high proportion took over the "marginal" job of buying and selling cattle. "Since a cattle dealer is never a popular figure in agricultural communities, the only living contact between the precapitalist peasant masses of central and eastern Europe and the market economy of modern industrial society was the Jew."[31]

16. Oppositely, Jews have been used as symbols of communism— sometimes, as in the case of Hitler, by the same person who identifies them as the epitome of capitalism. Jews have, of course, participated in the growth of communism and other left-wing developments in the last century. It scarcely matters, for a theory of anti-Semitism, whether they have furnished more or less than a proportionate number of left-wingers, for prejudice can create the necessary observation.

17. Jews have been important in the rise of the trade-union movement. Since trade unionism has been able to get increasing recognition and rewards for workers in all industrialized nations, employers and

---

[30] Carey McWilliams, *A Mask for Privilege*, Little, Brown & Company, 1948, p. 108.

[31] Carl J. Friedrich, in Isacque Graeber and S. H. Britt (eds.), *op. cit.*, p. 5.

others have often fought it vigorously. Those who already had a prejudice against Jews could easily convince themselves that unionism was a Jewish product.

Modern urban industrial society is thus not only prejudice-prone, as we saw in Chapter 3, but peculiarly prone to anti-Jewish prejudice. The Jews, who occupy places on almost every status level of society, are more apt scapegoats for more diverse groups than is a minority that is concentrated primarily in lower status levels. Jews are importantly involved in most of the sharply conflicting developments of modern life. The prejudices of various groups are thus mutually reinforced. The long history of violence against Jews has created such deep-going guilt feelings that many people dare not admit—their ego involvements being so intricately related to the question—that their hostility to Jews is a categorical prejudice. Thus economic conflict, personal insecurity, traditional stereotypes, cultural disorganization, and propagandistic distortion have come together to create and sustain the blinding prejudice of anti-Semitism.

The Future of Anti-Semitism

In Part III we shall examine the question of techniques in the reduction of prejudice and discrimination. That analysis will apply to anti-Semitism as well as to other kinds of categorical group judgments. At this point we wish simply to comment briefly on the kinds of conditions likely to increase and those likely to decrease anti-Semitism. Many writers take the position that there will be anti-Semitism so long as Jews continue as an identifiable religious or cultural group. J. F. Brown declares that the prejudice will be overcome only ". . . by immediate cultural and final racial assimilation." He thinks that Jewish leaders should encourage a wider distribution of Jews into all occupations.[32] (The pattern of occupational distribution is to a large degree the result of prejudice.) I. S. Wechsler takes the same position: "The only condition on which it can be eliminated, the Jew is neither willing nor able to meet. For antisemitism to disappear the Jew must cease to be; but this is precisely what he cannot do and the price he is unwilling to pay."[33] J. O. Hertzler says, even more strongly, that

. . . to cease to be a cultural irritant the Jew must be completely assimilated. Any old sense of allegiance to his "chosen people" idea will have to disappear; he must consciously remove characteristics of behavior which are recognizably Jewish; he must deliberately mold himself and his life on Gentile patterns. . . . He will have to be completely absorbed ethnically. . . . He will have to give up all pride in his group and his people's history and

[32] See *ibid.*, pp. 143–146.
[33] In K. S. Pinson (ed.), *Essays on Antisemitism*, Conference on Jewish Relations, 1946, p. 39.

denationalize himself as a Jew. Paradoxically he will have to individualize himself completely so far as a Jewish nation is concerned, and become a 100 percent conformist so far as the nation of his sojourn is concerned. . . . He will have to thrust himself into the background in his economic activities and never allow himself to be numerous or conspicuously successful as a competitor in any occupation, profession, or other economic pursuit. . . .[34]

It is not surprising that these authors take a pessimistic view of the chances of eliminating anti-Semitism. Strong in-group feelings among Jews, some feeling of identification with an international Jewish community, religious differentiation, and an occupation distribution that varies from that of most other groups are, to an important degree, the result of prejudice. To ask that these be changed before the prejudice can be reduced is to ask that an effect eliminate a cause. If the prejudice were not there, members of the majority would not be concerned with the cultural, religious, or occupational differences between themselves and Jews. Few Americans are disturbed over the fact that Episcopalians have had more than "their share" of occupants of the White House, or that Baptists insist upon immersion.

If Jews were to disappear completely as identifiable individuals, anti-Semitism, to be sure, would disappear. But that this is in no way useful as an approach to the reduction of anti-Semitism is indicated by two simple facts. So long as there is prejudice, the dominant group will not let them disappear (German Jews were among the most assimilated, but Hitler created the idea that one Jewish grandparent makes a Jew); and so long as there is prejudice, Jews will not want to disappear (they look upon their own community and religion as a source of strength and solace). Such a "solution" is certainly not in the American tradition. The complex pattern of national, religious, racial, and cultural groups in the United States rests upon the thesis that there can be unity in diversity.

The future of anti-Semitism is not conditioned upon the self-liquidation of Jews as a distinct group. Virtual disappearance as a group may, after some centuries, be a result of the elimination of prejudice, but it can scarcely be the cause. Anti-Semitism will be reduced when and if the causes that we have discussed in several of the preceding chapters are reduced. The reduction of personal insecurity; the growth of an integrated set of values; an increase in economic security; encouragement of political processes based on free discussion, on acceptance of majority rule, and on conciliation of differences; education that reveals the cultural roots of prejudice, that exposes stereotypes, that reduces the learned and unlearned ignorances about other groups that most of us share—these and additional changes can attack the foundation of anti-Semitism and other prejudices and can simultaneously free man's energies for the solution of other problems.

[34] In Isacque Graeber and S. H. Britt (eds.), op. cit., pp. 98–99.

PART II

Minorities in the Social Structure: The Institutional Patterns of Intergroup Relations

---

CHAPTER 11

Majority-Minority Relations and Social Stratification

The Meaning of Social Structure

Social structure may be regarded as a system of ideal or expected patterns of action within which individuals occupy certain positions.[1] Social positions are thought of here as of two types, statuses and offices, although no absolutely sharp line of demarcation can be drawn between these concepts. A status implies a more generalized kind of standing and one which is more likely to be ascribed by birth than achieved by personal effort. This characteristic tends to give more permanence to statuses as compared with offices. As a rule there is more emphasis on sentiments and less on specific actions in a status than in an office.[2]

Characteristics associated with social positions may include age, sex, race, nationality, family background, income, wealth, occupation, religion, education, political affiliation, place of residence, circle of intimate friends, clubs, manners, speech, general appearance, and behavior. Examples of statuses would be such positions as aristocrat, peasant, slave, scientist, hoodlum, radical, mother, Italian, youth, and Caucasian. Typical offices are army captain, professor of English, member of school board, newspaper editor, superintendent of Sunday school, factory foreman, chairman of Republican county committee, and labor-union president.

The sum total of a person's statuses and offices at a given time constitutes his station in life. Thus a hypothetical individual might occupy

[1] Ralph Linton, *The Study of Man*, Appleton-Century-Crofts, 1936, p. 253.
[2] For a conceptual analysis of stratification, see the article with this title by Kingsley Davis, *American Sociological Review*, June, 1942, pp. 309–321.

such statuses as male, Negro, young adult, British subject, college graduate, middle-class urbanite, Protestant, socialist, athlete, husband; and such offices as United Nations official, special lecturer at New York University, lay reader at St. Mark's Episcopal Church, tennis club president, secretary of parent-teacher association, and correspondent for *The Gleaner.*

Every society, and every group within a society, is structured in the sense that power and prestige are unevenly distributed among its members. Lines of influence and amounts of social esteem may be temporary or more or less permanent, clear-cut or imperfectly defined. The qualities deemed worthy of recognition or adoration vary with time and place, as do the mechanics of acquiring, retaining, and losing rank.

Social Stratification

Although sociologists and anthropologists readily agree on social differentiation in terms of the unequal distribution of property, power, and honor in every society and in every social group except amorphous, temporary social gatherings, the question of social stratification is controversial. If social strata are thought of as layers in a pyramid with individuals of about the same station in life on each level, there is little or no disagreement in referring to an estate system as stratification. The same is true of the caste system of India, but the concept of caste is challenged by some students when it is applied outside of India. Problems have arisen in connection with the use of social class because of the difficulty of finding objective criteria which distinguish one social class from another. In the sections which follow we shall examine caste, estate, and social class in an attempt to relate the concept of social stratification to majority-minority relations.

THE CASTE SYSTEM OF INDIA

In the caste system of India the subcaste rather than the caste is the unit of social organization that is important to the individual.[3] The subcaste is organized and it is endogamous; the caste is neither unless it has no subcastes. Nevertheless, as Weber points out, a strong unity exists in the caste as well as in the subcaste. Sanctions against marriage and commensalism outside the caste are stronger than those enforced against members of subcastes within a caste, and caste barriers are maintained with much greater perseverance than are the barriers between subcastes.[4]

[3] For discussions of the Indian caste system see Hans H. Gerth and C. W. Mills, *From Max Weber: Essays in Sociology,* Oxford University Press, 1946, chap. 16; Oliver C. Cox, *Caste, Class and Race,* Doubleday & Company, Inc., 1948, pp. 6–118; and J. W. Bennett and M. M. Tumin, *Social Life: Structure and Function,* Alfred A. Knopf, Inc., 1948, chap. 24.
[4] Hans H. Gerth and C. W. Mills, *op. cit.,* p. 411.

Among the most important characteristics which distinguish castes are eating habits, marriage, and occupation.[5] Eating is a ritual which affects a man's social standing and the welfare of his soul. A meal may be polluted if a lower-caste person looks upon it. Food may be contaminated if at mealtime an upper-caste person looks at certain lower-caste people or at a dog. The kind of food, as well as one's table companions, is of great concern. Although upper-caste Hindus are vegetarians, many castes do eat meat, but only the very lowest eat beef. Generally speaking, only those who may intermarry are allowed to eat together, but the prohibition on interdining is somewhat less strict than that on intermarriage. The taboo on intermarriage has nothing to do with protecting the purity of the biological stock of the castes but is intended rather to prevent the disruption of the community's ordered way of life. Endogamy protects the sacred style of life, the dharma, of a caste and thus preserves the caste from cultural defilement. Child marriage is highly functional in the caste system because it keeps the community intact. Romantic marriages would disrupt the closed system.

Each caste is believed to have a sacred duty, yet its many subcastes may have different occupations. It is the subcaste that strives to maintain its occupational integrity. Normally the individual follows the occupation of his father. When a change in occupation is made—and this is not frequent—it is initiated by the subcaste rather than by the individual. If circumstances make it impossible for a caste to live by its hereditary work, the caste is permitted to find other employment. In such a case, a caste may not take up the vocations of superior castes but only those of castes inferior to itself.

Max Weber refers to certain categories of castes in the two to three thousand, or even more, contemporary castes ranked by the Census of India (1901). At the top stand the Brahmans, and following them the two other "twice-born" castes: the Kshatriya and the Vaisya. The third group consists of the Satsudra, the "clean Sudra" of classical theory. Next are the Sudra, and finally the castes considered ritually unclean. All temples are closed to the members of unclean castes, and no Brahman and no barber will serve them. They are compelled to live outside the villages, and they infect members of other castes both by touch and by their presence. Further gradations of caste rank can be made within these groupings, but such gradations would include varied characteristics.

. . . Among the upper castes the criterion would be the correctness of life practices with regard to sib organization, endogamy, child marriage,

---

[5] According to Max Weber, commensality is usually attached to the caste; "connubium is almost always attached to the sub-caste; whereas usually, although with exceptions, the services by priests and wage-workers are attached to commensality." *Ibid.*, p. 409. On deviation from parental occupations, as well as some evidence that the taboos on intercaste marriage and eating are being softened, see Noel P. Gist, "Caste in Transition: South India," *Phylon*, Second Quarter, 1954, pp. 155–164.

widow celibacy, cremation of the dead, ancestral sacrifice, foods and drink, and social intercourse with unclean castes. Among the lower castes one would have to differentiate according to the rank of the Brahmans who are still ready to serve them or who will no longer do so, and according to whether or not castes other than Brahmans accept water from them. In all these cases, it is by no means rare that castes of lower rank raise stricter demands than castes who otherwise are considered to have a higher standing. . . . The acceptance or avoidance of meat, at least of beef, is decisive for caste rank, and is therefore a symptom of it, but an uncertain one. The kinds of occupation and income, which entail the most far-reaching consequences for connubium, commensalism, and ritual rank, are decisive in the case of all castes.[6]

There is constant rivalry among the castes to maintain their respective positions in the hierarchy as they are defined by tradition and public opinion. Occasionally a subcaste makes a collective advance in the system, but since such advancement is a threat to the caste order, ordinarily each caste is on the alert to prevent the castes nearest to it from moving upward. Position in the caste hierarchy is not determined by physical differences of groups, by wealth, by religion. Rank among castes seems to be a matter of caste dharma, or the way of life of the caste. Among the factors influencing caste mobility Risley mentions that ". . . the status of certain castes has been raised by their taking to infant-marriage or abandoning the remarriage of widows; . . . [that] the status of some castes has been lowered by their living in a particular locality; . . . [that] the status of others has been modified by their pursuing some occupation in a special or peculiar way."[7]

The rightness of the caste regime goes unquestioned because of the underlying sanction provided for it by the doctrines of karma and transmigration of souls. According to the karma doctrine, all human acts have moral significance. After death, judgment on one's behavior determines whether he will have a favorable or an unfavorable rebirth. If his deeds in a former life have been good, that is, if he has lived up to the obligations of his caste, he will be reborn into a higher caste. Theoretically the Hindu admits caste mobility of the individual only through rebirth. Actually, caste membership involves initiation as well as direct blood relationship, and the caste (subcaste) may exclude or include a person regardless of birth outside the caste. It should be emphasized that individual mobility is rare and that conscious striving for social advancement is taboo. However, certain rajahs have been known to raise men to higher ranks, some Sudras have advanced to high-ranking castes, and under certain conditions women may marry upward (hypergamy). Falling in rank is a frequent occurrence, and a number of castes are willing

[6] Hans H. Gerth and C. W. Mills, op. cit., p. 410. For additional comments on the ranking of castes see ibid., pp. 410–411.
[7] Quoted in Oliver C. Cox, op. cit., p. 13.

to admit outsiders of higher standing. An individual does not voluntarily slip in the caste system, but if he has been expelled from his own caste he may prefer to belong to a lower caste rather than to live without any caste at all.

Since the caste order is not based on color or any other physical characteristics, it is possible for two or more castes to combine or for one caste to divide without disrupting the system. Separation is more common than fusion, and is due mainly to migration, change of occupation, the adoption of new religious practices, and internal group dissension.

The general status of all members of a caste is somewhat equal when compared with the members of another caste. However, within castes there are considerable differences in standing. "The caste is not a unity of colorless, undifferentiated individuals. Indeed, the very nature of its organization entails internal differentiation. Castes of any size always have their superior and privileged families. Individuals within the caste may differ in wealth, in occupational efficiency, in physical attainments, in choice of vocation among those to which the caste is limited, in political position, in number of Vedas read, or in number of knots in the sacred cord and so on."[8]

The spirit of the caste system of India is clearly seen in the idea of impurity. Social distance between groups is scrupulously maintained to prevent spiritual and bodily defilement. A state of impurity, which is a ceremonial rather than a hygienic matter, may exist between the members of the same caste, between those who belong to different castes, or even between human beings and other objects. The degree of pollution depends upon the distance one man is below another in the caste hierarchy.

It should be pointed out that this rather rigid and relatively static type of social stratification is characterized by mutual expectations and mutual protections, and that it does not necessarily mean that one caste dominates another. Position in the system and the way of life which goes with his caste are willingly accepted by the individual because of the explanations and justifications provided by the religious principles of karma, metempsychosis, and purity.

Finally, it should not be thought that cultural change was absent in the caste system prior to the impact of western culture.[9] Reference has been made to the possibility that a group within a caste will form a subcaste and perhaps eventually become a new caste, or that a subcaste will climb up or slide down a short distance in the hierarchy. In the case of rising in status a new genealogy has to be invented in order to main-

---

[8] *Ibid.*, p. 10.
[9] For discussions of modifications in the Indian caste system due to industry and urban life, see Hans H. Gerth and C. W. Mills, *op. cit.*, pp. 413–415, and J. W. Bennett and M. M. Tumin, *op. cit.*, pp. 464–465.

tain the principle of the immutability of the social order. Support from the Brahmans is essential to gaining general recognition for the higher standing in the face of the opposition of rival castes.

CASTES IN PRIMITIVE SOCIETIES

It is not uncommon for cultural anthropologists to use the concept of caste in describing the marked social stratification of certain nonliterate societies. Lowie criticizes Rivers for restricting the term "caste" to India after giving the four criteria of caste as endogamy, hereditary occupation, hierarchical grading, and rules of avoidance between grades. He points out that in India hypergamy modifies endogamy; occupations do not coincide exactly with castes; ranking differs from locality to locality; and the rules of avoidance vary locally. Furthermore, in his view, all the criteria are found in other societies, sometimes all of them together. The Masai tribe of East Africa, where the blacksmiths constitute an endogamous pariah caste, is cited as an example of a primitive caste system. The Polynesians are said to have a "castelike" system, and the Ruanda system of East Africa is called a borderline case with elements of a caste system. Japanese social stratification prior to the middle of the nineteenth century is regarded by Lowie as a rigid class system with two pariah classes at the bottom.[10]

A number of primitive groups, including the Eskimos, Andaman Islanders, Australians, Semangs, Veddas, Great Basin Shoshones, Fuegians, African Bushmen, many hunting societies of North and South America, certain Indonesian societies outside the areas of strong Hindu influence, and some Melanesian peoples, are classless. Among primitives having class systems Hoebel lists some of the Plains Indians, tribes of the northwest coast of North America, the Aztecs, the Natchez of Mississippi, and some Melanesian groups. The Kingdom of Ankole in Uganda is given as an example of a formal caste system, the basic caste division being between the pastoral Bahima and the gardening Bairu.[11] Caste is seen by Hoebel as "the result of intensification of the class principle . . . the freezing of social classes by means of endogamy and hereditarily ascribed status" so that the dominant group may attempt "to perpetuate and guarantee unto itself and its descendants a special and favored position in life."

Chapple and Coon refer to caste systems in India, among the Fula in the western Sudan of Africa, in southern Arabia, and in Hawaii,

[10] R. H. Lowie, Social Organization, Rinehart & Co., 1948, pp. 273–274, 276–277. For an interesting account of the Eta, a Japanese caste of three million persons who are indistinguishable physically and linguistically from the general population, see H. H. Smythe, "The Eta: A Marginal Caste," American Journal of Sociology, September, 1952, pp. 194–196.
[11] E. D. Hoebel, Man in the Primitive World, McGraw-Hill Book Company, 1949, pp. 323–325.

Samoa, and some of the other more complexly organized islands in Polynesia.[12]

Two castes are reported by Gillin in eastern Guatemala. The Ladinos and the Indians constitute distinct strata, with the former occupying the superordinate place in the social structure.[13]

CASTES IN THE UNITED STATES

American sociologists and cultural anthropologists are divided on the applicability of the term "caste" to the United States. The Warner group considers the Negro and white populations two castes. Caste is defined as

. . . a theoretical arrangement of the people of a given group in an order in which the privileges, duties, obligations, opportunities, etc., are unequally distributed between the groups which are considered to be higher and lower. There are social sanctions which tend to maintain this unequal distribution. Such a definition also describes class. A caste organization, however, can be further defined as one where marriage between the two groups is not sanctioned and where there is no opportunity for members of the lower group to rise into the upper group or for members of the upper to fall into the lower one.[14]

This conception is adopted in Dollard, *Caste and Class in a Southern Town*; Davis, Gardner, and Gardner, *Deep South*; and Davis and Dollard, *Children of Bondage*. The following remark appears in the latter work: "The most important fact about society in the South is that it consists of a dual system: there is a system of white and of Negro castes, and also a system of social classes within each caste, further stratifying groups and defining privileges."[15]

This viewpoint was modified somewhat in a study of race and personality formation in the Chicago Negro community. Here the authors state that "the situation must be described as at least a castelike system."[16] A qualified stand is also taken by Warner in his comments on *Black Metropolis*:

This evidence strongly supports the hypothesis that, while there is a noticeable difference between *Deep South* and *Black Metropolis*, a great improvement in the status of the Negro, and an increasing assurance that

[12] E. A. Chapple and C. S. Coon, *Principles of Anthropology*, Henry Holt and Company, 1942, pp. 435–437.

[13] John Gillin, *The Ways of Men*, Appleton-Century-Crofts, 1948, p. 355.

[14] W. Lloyd Warner, "American Caste and Class," *American Journal of Sociology*, September, 1936, p. 234. See also W. Lloyd Warner and A. Davis, "A Comparative Study of American Caste," in E. T. Thompson (ed.), *Race Relations and the Race Problem*, Duke University Press, 1939, chap. 8.

[15] Allison W. Davis and John Dollard, *Children of Bondage*, American Council on Education, 1940, pp. 12–13.

[16] W. Lloyd Warner, B. H. Junker, and W. A. Adams, *Color and Human Nature*, American Council on Education, 1941, p.12.

he will continue to advance, nevertheless the *type* of status relations controlling Negroes and whites remains the same and continues to keep the Negro in an inferior and restricted position. He cannot climb into the higher group although he can climb higher in his own group. Legally, he is permitted to marry across the color line but there is very little intermarriage. The children of such marriages are always Negro and suffer, as do their parents, the "restrictions" and deprivations of the Negro caste. The rewards and punishments, the rights and duties, knowledges and advantages are unequally distributed. In short, there is still a status system of the caste type. It is of small consequence what we call it if we remember that it is a status system which organizes and controls the lives of our people and "educates" the oncoming generation to learn its ways and conform to its precepts.[17]

The caste concept is also adopted by Myrdal in his study, *An American Dilemma*. Here caste, as distinguished from class, consists ". . . of such drastic restrictions of free competition in the various spheres of life that the individual in a lower caste cannot, by any means, change his status, except by a secret and illegitimate 'passing,' which is possible only to the few who have the physical appearance of members of the upper caste."[18]

Among the cultural anthropologists who apply the caste concept to Negroes and whites in the United States are Lowie,[19] Gillin,[20] and Hoebel.[21]

Kroeber regards the Jews as "a social quasi-caste based originally and mainly on a religion that of course is voluntary, not enforced. Their social segregation is markedly stronger than their cultural distinctness, though the latter is not absolutely lacking."[22]

We do not favor the application of the term "caste" to the race relations situation in the United States, especially in the North. While there are resemblances between the caste system of India and the race system of the South, there are also great differences. Although some churches give tacit support to the separation of the races, we lack a set of religious principles justifying a rigid system of social stratification and causing it to be willingly accepted by those at all levels. In fact, the exact opposite is the case here, as Myrdal has pointed out so vividly in *An American Dilemma*. Our basic moral principles are phrased in terms of the dignity of man, the sacredness of human personality, equality of opportunity for all men, equal protection of the law, and the right of all to vote. There are great discrepancies between our ideals and our

---

[17] W. Lloyd Warner, "A Methodological Note," in St. Clair Drake and Horace Cayton, *Black Metropolis*, Harcourt, Brace & Company, 1945, pp. 781–782.

[18] Gunnar Myrdal, *An American Dilemma*, Harper & Brothers, 1944, pp. 674–675.

[19] R. H. Lowie, *op. cit.*, pp. 274–275.

[20] John Gillin, *op. cit.*, p. 355.

[21] E. A. Hoebel, *op. cit.*, p. 325.

[22] A. L. Kroeber, *Anthropology*, Harcourt, Brace & Company, rev. ed., 1948, p. 279. R. H. Lowie (*op. cit.*, p. 276) says that the Jews under Hitler became a "degraded caste" comparable to the untouchables of India.

practices, but considerable socioeconomic mobility is possible for Negroes. Even in the South the grandson of a slave or the son of a Negro sharecropper may aspire to and achieve a position as physician, college professor, or business administrator within the limits of the segregated community. Also, as Bennett and Tumin point out, Negroes and white workers in industrial areas often compete for the same jobs. While Negro-white marriages are prohibited by law in twenty-seven states, they are legal in the other states. Outside the South, especially in urban communities, interdining and other kinds of "social" activities are not uncommon.

A cogent point was made by Charles Johnson in his objection to applying the term "caste" to the South, namely, the Southerner's lack of faith in traditional sanctions to preserve the *status quo*. In a caste system legal restrictions are unnecessary, as is the expenditure of enormous amounts of energy to maintain the system. The instability of the southern race system is apparent in the overt fight carried on by the superordinate whites to prevent the struggling Negro from changing his subordinate status.[23]

In the debate on the question of whether or not there are castes in the United States it is well to remember that caste and class are not realities, essences, but concepts. Relationships among prestige groups fall along a continuum ranging from highly flexible to highly rigid. The system of stratification in the United States has some rigidity, some endogamy, some acceptance of the system by the members of the society. At the same time it lacks a set of religious principles to justify a rigid system of stratification; social class lines are often vague and contradictory; most Negroes and many white persons do not accept the *status quo*; and many institutional forms are contrary to it. As Bennett and Tumin point out, "The American system at the present time, although predominantly a class system, contains some features of the other two," i.e., the caste system and estates.[24]

ESTATES

Intermediate conceptually between caste and social class is the estate. Estate systems have included such categories as the nobility, clergy, bourgeoisie, tradesmen, craftsmen, workers, and peasants. Estate systems of stratification, exemplified best in feudal Europe, show less rigidity than do caste systems. Religious criteria, though present, are much less important than in caste. In India each caste constitutes a religious cult; in estates an official church serves all members of the society. The legal aspects of estates—taxation, citizenship, freedom of movement, and so on—are more highly developed than in a caste sys-

[23] Charles S. Johnson, *Growing Up in the Black Belt*, American Council on Education, 1941, pp. 325–327.
[24] J. W. Bennett and M. M. Tumin, *op. cit.*, p. 574.

tem. There is greater variation of occupation, wealth, and cultural characteristics within the estate system, and it is possible to move up, and to move up legally, within the system. Intermarriage is not prohibited, as in a caste, but is usually confined to the marriage of persons of adjacent estates. The underlying religious sanctions of the Indian caste system caused a general acceptance of its features, but the estate system of feudal Europe was notable for its instability—workers' rebellions, conflicts between king and nobility, and clashes between nobility and clergy.[25]

The transition of feudalism into capitalism resulted in a decline of the estate system in many parts of the world and its replacement by the social-class system or an estate-class mixture. The French Revolution represented the climax in the struggle of individualism, capitalism, and urbanism against ruralism and estatism. Cox presents an interesting diagram to show the impingement of the social-class system upon feudalism at about the end of the seventeenth century (see Figure 11.1),[26]

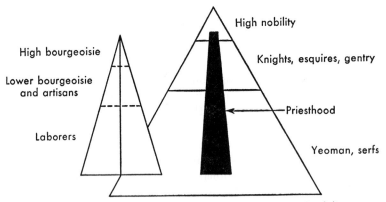

FIGURE 11.1. Impingement of Social-Class System upon Feudalism.

and Tomašić shows the nature of an estate-class mixture in his diagram of the structure of Balkan society (see Figure 11.2).[27]

Bennett and Tumin point out that estatelike tendencies are present in the stratification system of the United States in three forms.

First, the growing rigidity of the top may result in the formation of attitudes of privilege and hereditary prerogative. Such attitudes are more typical of an estate than a class system. Second, the tendency toward inherited wealth and the freezing over of the top of the system may result in informal legal distinctions between the members of different classes. Some

[25] See *ibid.*, pp. 466–470.
[26] From Oliver C. Cox, *Caste, Class and Race*, Doubleday & Company, Inc., 1948, p. 146.
[27] From D. Tomašić, "The Structure of Balkan Society," *American Journal of Sociology*, September, 1946, p. 135.

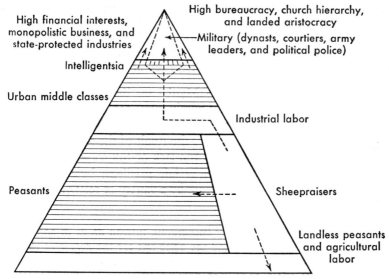

FIGURE 11.2. The Structure of Balkan Society.

of these exist to an unknown extent at the present time in the form of relatively light sentences and fines for upper-class persons for minor infringements of the law. Third, the possible formation of a powerful labor movement may result in a "class-conscious" lower-class worker's group with its own status system and with its closed privileges.[28]

Social Classes

Three Conceptions of Social Class. Although the social-class system has long been a subject for investigation in Europe, its study has been neglected by social scientists in the United States until comparatively recent years. This neglect is perhaps not surprising in a country where free land, an abundance of natural resources, the absence of hampering traditions, and a strong spirit of individualism played important roles in the first century and a half of national life. The study of social classes in the United States has been undertaken seriously since 1935, but there is a lack of consensus on the most reliable criteria of social class and the most satisfactory number of social classes for analytical purposes.

Three conceptions of social classes stand out in the recent literature. These definitions are given by the Warner group:

By class is meant two or more orders of people who are believed to be, and are accordingly ranked by the members of the community, in socially superior and inferior positions.[29]

[28] J. W. Bennett and M. M. Tumin, op. cit., p. 583.
[29] W. Lloyd Warner and Paul S. Lunt, *The Social Life of a Modern Community*, Yale University Press, 1941, p. 82.

A social class is to be thought of as the largest group of people whose members have intimate social access to one another. A class is composed of families and cliques. The interrelationships between these families and cliques, in such informal activities as visiting, dances, receptions, teas, and larger informal affairs, constitute the structure of a social class.[30]

This viewpoint is criticized by Myrdal on the ground that it puts too much emphasis on the role of purely social contacts and not enough on the importance of other criteria. His approach is that "classes and class differences in America are . . . the result of the restrictions of free competition and, consequently, of the lack of full social integration."[31] He sees the upper classes enjoying certain privileges because the lower classes are restricted in their activities by a variety of relative or absolute social monopolies.

Attaching importance to family background instead of, or in addition to, merit is one type of monopoly and the basic one for the degree of closeness and rigidity of a class system. The ownership of wealth and income and, in America, national origin or religion become other causes of monopolies, if education is not absolutely democratic and if positions in the occupational hierarchy are not filled with regard to merit only. In view of the inequality of opportunity in getting an occupation, and since occupational positions carry incomes roughly in proportion to their status associations, it is possible, in an approximate way, to determine social class by considering income or occupation as the chief index of social monopoly.[32]

Thus while Myrdal makes income and occupation the main criteria for social class, the Warner group think of social class in terms of "common participation of individuals in noneconomic groups" and of an "economic group" as a large informal group whose members behave similarly with respect to economic traits, namely, money, property, and occupation.[33]

Cox asserts that there is "no such thing as an objective social class" which can be physically circumscribed and that therefore there is not a recognizable social-class hierarchy in class systems of western civilization. He thinks of estates and castes as stratified social-class systems but regards social classes as a nonstratified social-status system. This system is a social-status continuum or gradient along which the atomized status-bearing objects are arranged. The Warner group's definition of class as "the largest group of people whose members have intimate access

---

[30] Allison W. Davis and John Dollard, op. cit., p. 13.

[31] Gunnar Myrdal, op. cit., pp. 673–674.

[32] Ibid., p. 674.

[33] Allison W. Davis, B. B. Gardner, and M. R. Gardner, Deep South, University of Chicago Press, 1941, p. 237. For recent examinations of the social-class structure in the United States, see Joseph A. Kahl, The American Class Structure, Rinehart & Co., 1957; and John F. Cuber and William F. Kenkel, Social Stratification in the United States, Appleton-Century-Crofts, 1954.

to one another" is called "incomprehensible" by Cox. According to him it would be just as fruitful to try to determine where the sky begins as to go out with such a definition to locate social classes in a city like Chicago. To Cox it is not useful for analysis and comprehension to go beyond a "broad, workable idea of what is meant by the upper, middle, and lower class."

It is interesting to note that Cox considers the social class "a conceptual stratum of status-bearing entities" and not a form of social organization, whereas West says that the class system of Plainville might well be called a "superorganization. . . . It provides for every person living there a master pattern for arranging according to relative rank every other individual, and every family, clique, lodge, club, church, and other organization or association in the Plainville society."[34] In the same vein, the authors of *Deep South* state that "social classes are essentially participation groups" and they add that "the members of a social class themselves recognize that the fundamental test of their class status is their ability to participate regularly in the social life of certain other persons."[35] Of a mill town in South Carolina where Negroes constitute about one-third of the population, Lewis says:

> If a class-organized society is one in which there is a well-defined system of ranking that distinguishes cohesive, self-conscious segments marked by differences in social honor and power, then Kent Negro society of today is not organized on a class basis. A clear-cut system of social ranking and basis of association or intimate access was not discovered. This does not mean that there is not level consciousness; it does not mean there is not a status pattern marked by different measure of prestige and privilege. . . . Rather it suggests . . . that the people themselves do not in behavior or verbalizations make references to or relate themselves to such prestige collectivities. . . . Insofar as there are status differences and insofar as the society is changing and becoming more differentiated, one might say that class is incipient, rather than full blown.[36]

Some Studies of Social Classes in the United States.   Before dealing specifically with the subject of racial and cultural groups in the social structure, we call attention to three studies which treat the social-class system as a whole.

One of the most comprehensive and influential studies of social classes in the United States is the Warner investigation of "Yankee City." Six social classes were delineated in this New England city of 17,000 by the interview and other techniques. The upper-upper class

See definition

---

[34] James West, *Plainville, U.S.A.*, Columbia University Press, 1945, p. 115.

[35] Allison W. Davis, B. B. Gardner, and M. R. Gardner, *op. cit.*, p. 238.

[36] Hylan Lewis, *Blackways of Kent*, University of North Carolina Press, 1955, pp. 223–224. According to Lewis, the most significant cleavage from the viewpoint of the Negroes of Kent is the line between the "respectables" and the "nonrespectables." *Ibid.*, p. 233.

is made up of Yankees who marry late and have the smallest percentage of children and the largest proportion of persons over sixty years of age. An overwhelming majority of the people in this class (83 percent) are found in the professional and proprietary positions. A large percentage of the upper-uppers live in large houses in the best residential areas. They belong in significant numbers to so-called social clubs and to associations organized for charity. Most of the members of this class belong to the Unitarian and Episcopal churches, and most of the children attend private schools. The social power of the upper-upper-class members protects their adolescents from the police, "while the subordinate position of the lower classes leaves their families more vulnerable to the sanctions of the rest of the community." There are significant differences in the reading habits, as regards both books and magazines and newspapers, of this class as compared with classes which are lower in the social scale. The characteristics of the lower-upper class resemble fairly closely those of the upper-upper group except that most of its members either are newly arrived persons from outside the geographical

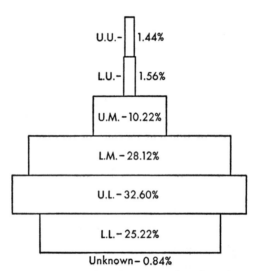

FIGURE 11.3. The Class Hierarchy of Yankee City.

limits of Yankee City or are recently arrived from a lower position in the social scale. For the social characteristics of the other four classes the reader is referred to Warner and Lunt, *The Social Life of a Modern Community.* The class hierarchy of Yankee City is given in Figure 11.3.[37]

[37] From W. Lloyd Warner and Paul S. Lunt, *The Social Life of a Modern Community,* Yale University Press, 1941, p. 88.

Another important study of social classes is Hollingshead's analysis of Elmtown, a middle-western community of some 10,000 population. Five classes are distinguished, but no labels except Roman numerals are attached to them. Class II is of interest because of the leadership it provides in the community. Its members control the associations which wield power in Elmtown's affairs—the Chamber of Commerce, the luncheon clubs, Masons, country club, and major political parties. From Class II to Class V there are steady increases in size of family, percentage of wives employed outside the home, amounts received in charity, family disorganization, and contact with law-enforcing agencies; and constant decreases in age at marriage, size of income, amount of education, home ownership, savings, residence in the most highly desired sections, participation in community activities, and church membership. Hollingshead concluded that each of the five strata has a distinct subculture.[38]

West's research in Plainville, a middle-western village of sixty-five homes and a population of 275 in a trade area of some 300 household units, resulted in the social-class diagram shown in Figure 11.4.[39] The criteria of class for "country people" in this study include type of land where farm families live, technological patterns of agriculture, lineage, wealth, "morals," and "manners." "Town people" belong to one or another of the social classes according to the latter four traits.

It is worth noting that while students of social classes have used from two to seven categories, most of the classifications represent some variation of the upper-middle-lower pattern. Regardless of the number of social classes utilized for a particular purpose, there is always overlapping.

It should of course be emphasized that the four classes are not rigidly set off from one another. Being open classes, they shade off into each other. In much the same way, the categories of age (childhood, adolescence, maturity, and old age) are distinguishable and useful to refer to differences in the age range.[40]

Social classes overlap in their membership, therefore, because there are always individuals who participate intimately with two classes. These mobile individuals are men of two social worlds. Frequently they are the children of mixed-class marriages whose parents subject them to conflicting types of class training. In American society, white or Negro, there is a relatively large number of socially mobile persons, "who look both up and down" in the class system.[41]

We emphasize again that social classes are not entities but constructs

[38] A. B. Hollingshead, "Selected Characteristics of Classes in a Middle Western Community," *American Sociological Review*, August, 1947, pp. 385-395.
[39] From James West, *Plainville, U.S.A.*, Columbia University Press, 1945, p. 117.
[40] W. Lloyd Warner, B. H. Junker, and W. A. Adams, *op. cit.*, p. 20.
[41] Allison W. Davis and John Dollard, *op. cit.*, p. 14.

or tools which are useful in sociological analysis. As Bennett and Tumin remark, ". . . There is a continual danger of confusing an analytic or diagrammatic presentation with some real order of social relationships.

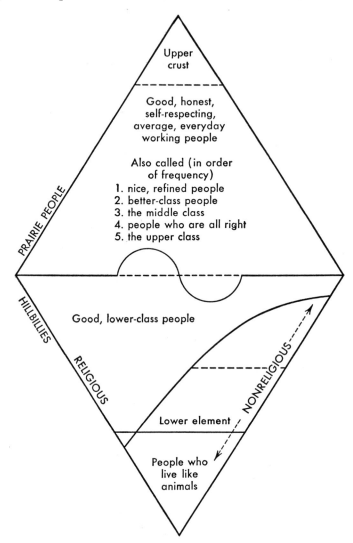

FIGURE 11.4. Plainville Social Classes.

The 'layer cake' of stratification is a most useful but also most illusory concept."[42]

The Concept of Social Class in This Book. It is advantageous analytically to distinguish "class," in the sheerly economic sense, from "social class," in the sense of prestige, and from "party," in the sense of

[42] J. W. Bennett and M. M. Tumin, op. cit., p. 491.

the acquisition of social power. In our discussion of stratification, social class refers to the prestige group, that is, to a group of people who have about the same station in life in a hierarchical ranking.[43]

We shall show that members of prestige groups, both in the majority and in minorities, are status-conscious, and that social class is related to "life chances" (jobs open to the individual, whom one may marry, the security that may be looked forward to, the chances of improving one's general status, etc.).

Social Classes in the Ante-Bellum South. An appropriate starting point for understanding the relationships between racial and cultural groups and the social structure of the United States is the slavery system. The first Africans to arrive in the colonies were brought to Virginia in 1619, and for three decades Negroes there had the status of indentured servants.

There can be little doubt that the earliest Negroes in Virginia occupied a position similar to that of the white servants in the colony. They were listed as servants in the census enumerations of 1623 and 1624; and as late as 1651 some Negroes whose period of service had expired were being assigned land in much the same way that it was being done for white servants. The records of Virginia contain many indentures of Negro servants during the forty-year period following their introduction; and during the same period there are records of free Negroes in the colony.[44]

Laws were passed gradually which recognized the presence of slaves and these Virginia statutes became the model for neighboring colonies.[45] These codes defined their status both as persons and as property. Economic forces soon settled the fate of the Negro for many generations.

[43] Max Weber defined "classes" as "groups of people who . . . have the same economic position." In his "status-group" (social class), "status" is "a quality of social honor or a lack of it, and is in the main conditioned as well as expressed through a specific style of life." Parties, in Weber's usage, are "oriented toward the acquisition of social power,' that is to say, toward influencing a communal action no matter what its content may be." Hans H. Gerth and C. W. Mills, op. cit., p. 405. For critical discussions of social-class concepts and studies, see the following articles: Arthur Kornhauser, "Public Opinion and Social Class," *American Journal of Sociology,* January, 1950, pp. 333–345; Harold W. Pfautz and O. D. Duncan, "A Critical Evaluation of Warner's Work in Community Stratification," *American Sociological Review,* April, 1950; pp. 205–215; Paul K. Hatt, "Stratification in the Mass Society," *ibid.,* pp. 216–222; Oliver C. Cox, "Max Weber on Social Stratification: A Critique," *ibid.,* pp. 223–227; Walter Goldschmidt, "Social Class in America—A Critical Review," *American Anthropologist,* October–December, 1950, pp. 483–498; Llewellyn Gross, "The Use of Class Concepts in Sociological Research," *American Journal of Sociology,* March, 1949, pp. 409–421; Milton M. Gordon, "Social Class in American Sociology," *ibid.,* November, 1949, pp. 262–268; and the bibliography in Philip M. Hauser, "The Labor Force as a Field of Interest for the Sociologist," *American Sociological Review,* August, 1951, p. 535 n.

[44] John Hope Franklin, *From Slavery to Freedom,* Alfred A. Knopf, Inc., 1948, p. 70.

[45] U. B. Phillips, "Slavery—United States," *Encyclopædia of the Social Sciences,* The Macmillan Company, 1934, vol. 14, p. 84.

As Frazier points out, tobacco had become indispensable to the economic life of the colonies by the end of the seventeenth century, and Negro slaves had proved to be more profitable than white servants. Tobacco declined in importance at the end of the eighteenth century, but slavery increased rather than decreased at that time by virtue of the invention of the cotton gin.[46]

One justification of the slave trade by Christian slave traders and slaveholders was phrased in terms of "just wars." This principle was more applicable to the enslavement of Indians than of Negroes since the colonists had had no opportunity of fighting "just wars" against them. The argument had to be applied indirectly in justification of the original enslavement of Negroes in Africa. Another defense was that those purchased as slaves were already slaves, an argument not wholly true in the case of some traders. One of the favorite early rationalizations was the "heathenism" of the Africans. In rescuing men and women from the "dark Continent" a noble service was rendered to the former heathen and to God. After a time these rationalizations seemed insufficient and were rather generally replaced by the racialist theory, that is, the belief in the inherent inferiority of Negroid peoples.[47] This angle made slavery foolproof from the standpoint of logic. If it could be shown that Negroes constituted a lesser breed of mankind, then not too much could be expected of them. Slavery could be pictured as a beneficial institution perpetuated by benevolent men of a superior race. One of the most interesting defenses of slavery was George Fitzhugh's identification of slavery with socialism. "He defined socialism as a system of thought that would abolish free competition, protect and support the laboring classes, bring about a qualified community of property and the association of labor. These purposes, he insisted, were fully and perfectly attained by slavery."[48]

Legislators, judges, ministers, physicians, and "scientists" hastened to seek evidence of Negro inferiority. They found what they were looking for. The decision prepared by Chief Justice Taney of the United States Supreme Court in the Dred Scott case in 1857 stated that Negroes had been regarded for more than a century as "beings of an inferior order, and altogether unfit to associate with the white race, either in social or political relations; and so far inferior, that they had no rights which the white man was bound to respect; and that the negro might justly and lawfully be reduced to slavery for his benefit." The doctrine of the inherent inferiority of the Negro reached a high point in 1861 with the

[46] E. Franklin Frazier, "The Negro in the American Social Order," *Journal of Negro Education*, July, 1935, p. 294.

[47] W. E. Moore, "Slave Law and the Social Structure," *Journal of Negro History* April, 1941, pp. 172–184.

[48] Harvey Wish, "George Fitzhugh, Conservative of the Old South," *Southern Sketches*, No. 11, 1st series, 1938, p. 15.

publication by J. H. Van Evrie, M.D., of a work entitled *Negroes and Negro Slavery: The First an Inferior Race: The Latter Its Normal Condition*. Van Evrie "showed" that the Negro is incapable of standing upright, that the beard of the Caucasian is indicative of superiority, that no Negro can speak the language of the white man correctly, that in mere (brain) volume, "and therefore in the sum total of mental power, the Negro is vastly inferior to the white man."

The ante-bellum South did not consist solely of large plantations worked by multitudes of slaves. About two-thirds of the farmers were nonslaveholders,[49] and according to Phillips, "at all times in the South as a whole perhaps half of the slaves were owned or hired in units of twenty or less . . . and perhaps half of this half were on mere farms or in town employment, rather as 'help' than as a distinct laboring force."[50] The large planters, then as later, tended to dominate the economic, social, and political life of their counties. There was little need for a middle class in the rural areas of the ante-bellum social order.

> The plantation largely markets its own crops; it procures supplies, directly or indirectly, for its entire population; hence the trader class is small and usually dependent upon the estate. Economic groups outside the plantation are also decidedly limited. The professional class is not numerous. Most of the population bears some relation to the plantation and falls into one or the other of the categories into which its people are divided. Furthermore the plantation tends, precisely as in the old plantation system of the southern United States, to prevent the development of a middle class farming population, in that it crowds out the small agricultural holding.[51]

Social stratification in plantation society, then, had something like the following layers: (1) large planters; (2) business and professional classes; (3) small planters, independent nonslaveholding yeomen, artisans; (4) impoverished farmers; (5) slaves.[52]

Not only was plantation society structured in a given area, but each plantation had its hierarchy of rank, privilege, and esteem. On the large

---

[49] T. J. Woofter, Jr., *Landlord and Tenant on the Cotton Plantation*, Works Progress Administration, 1936, p. xviii. According to Spero and Harris, "Southern society at the outbreak of the Civil War was made up not of two classes, white masters and Negro slaves, but of four classes. These were: first, the slave-holding families, about 350,000 in number, representing about 1,750,000 individuals; second, the Negro slaves, nearly 4,000,000 in number; third, the free Negroes who numbered about 500,000 throughout the whole country and about 260,000 in the South; and fourth, the 'poor white' small farmers, artisans, laborers, and tradesmen, who numbered more than 5,250,000." S. D. Spero and A. L. Harris, *The Black Worker*, Columbia University Press, 1931, p. 3.

[50] U. B. Phillips, *Life and Labor in the Old South*, Little, Brown & Company, 1939, p. 207. T. J. Woofter, Jr. (*op. cit.*) states that "50% of the slaveholders owned less than five slaves."

[51] G. M. McBride, "Plantation," *Encyclopædia of the Social Sciences*, The Macmillan Company, 1934, vol. 12, p. 152.

[52] See W. E. Moore and R. M. Williams, "Stratification in the Ante-Bellum South," *American Sociological Review*, June, 1942, pp. 343–351.

plantation the master and his family occupied an exalted place, with the overseers beneath them and the house servants (often mulattoes), skilled workers, and field hands following in that order.

An absent master wrote: "I wish to be remembered to all the servants, distinguishing Andrew as the head man and Katy as the mother of the tribe. Not forgetting Charlotte as the head of the culinary department nor Marcus as the Tubal Cain of the community, hoping that they will continue to set a good example and that the young ones will walk in their footsteps." The foreman, the miller and the smith were men of position and pride. The butler, the maid and the children's nurse were in continuous contact with the white household, enjoying the best opportunity to acquire its manners along with its discarded clothing. The field hands were at the foot of the scale, with a minimum of white contact and privileged only to plod, so to say, as the brethren to the ox.[53]

Slaves identified themselves with their masters, and those who belonged to prominent families tended to have a higher status than those who were owned by less distinguished whites.[54] Of course, on the numerous small plantations the slaves were in more or less close contact with their masters, and their experiences were of a more personal and intimate nature than were those of slaves living on the large plantations.[55]

Approximately one-tenth of the Negro population of the United States consisted of free persons at the time of the Emancipation Proclamation, but free Negroes had been an inconspicuous part of the population where the plantation system flourished. The free Negro population was concentrated in the tidewater region of Virginia and Maryland; the Piedmont region of North Carolina and Virginia; the seaboard cities of Charleston, Mobile, and New Orleans; northern cities, especially Boston, New York, Philadelphia, Baltimore, Chicago, Cincinnati, and Washington; parts of the Northwest Territory; isolated communities of Negroes mixed with Indians; and the Seminole area of Florida.[56] A high percentage of the free Negroes were mixed-bloods who had had economic, social, and educational advantages not enjoyed by the majority of unmixed slaves. Social stratification existed in all of the free Negro communities, but it was most highly developed in Charleston, South Carolina, and New Orleans. The upper class among the free Negroes included families that held considerable property and could claim aristocratic white ancestry or the absence of a tradition of slavery. Unskilled free Negroes with small income constituted the lower class, and a large class of artisans with moderate incomes and stable family life made up

---

[53] U. B. Phillips, *Life and Labor in the Old South*, pp. 206–207.

[54] E. Franklin Frazier, *The Negro in the United States*, The Macmillan Company, 1949, p. 275.

[55] E. T. Thompson, "The Plantation: The Physical Basis of Traditional Race Relations," in E. T. Thompson (ed.), *op. cit.*, p. 205.

[56] E. Franklin Frazier, *The Negro in the United States*, p. 63.

the middle class.[57] After emancipation there was a marked cleavage between Negroes of free ancestry and the former slaves. Both the mulatto aristocrats and the less prosperous skilled artisans tended to withdraw into their small circles of relatives and friends and to exclude the emancipated blacks. Some families moved to other parts of the country where they could join upper-class mulatto groups or merge with the white population.[58]

Social Stratification in the Rural South After the Civil War. With the passing of time the distinction between free ancestry and color has become less important in the rural South. Frazier distinguishes two general social classes among rural Negroes in the plantation areas of the South where the majority are tenants: "the more prosperous farmers who maintain stable family life and support the churches and lodges" and "the poorer sharecroppers with unstable and uncertain family relations." The same writer finds more differentiation in Virginia and North Carolina where three social classes are discernible: well-to-do landowners with family traditions; small landowners and tenants with stable family life; and the unstable farm laborers and turpentine mill laborers.[59]

In a study of eight selected counties in five southern states, Charles Johnson found that the rural Negro population could be divided into an upper class (6 percent), a middle class (12 percent), and a lower class (82 percent) "on the basis of occupation, income, education, family organization, relationship to property, and general community recognition of standing."[60] The lower class is subdivided into lower-lower and upper-lower classes to distinguish those with the very lowest standard of living, little or no education, and the least skill, from the rank and file of the rural Negro population who are not much better off economically and educationally but who are concerned with " 'staying out of trouble,' getting some education for their children, and advancing into the next highest classification."

The investigation of "Old City" and "Old County" in the heart of the rural South revealed the "people (white) at all levels were thinking in terms of, and often referring to three broad social classes—'upper,' 'middle,' and 'lower.' " Closer study convinced the researchers that subclasses existed within each of these larger groups, and the result is a sixfold classification which is identical with that used in the Yankee City study. Class differentiation is much less highly developed in the Negro "caste," but they found that upper-class Negroes thought of three social classes within the Negro group. Particularly interesting is their conclusion concerning the development of new class standards.

[57] *Ibid.*, p. 276.
[58] *Ibid.*, pp. 277–278.
[59] *Ibid.*, p. 279.
[60] Charles S. Johnson, *op. cit.*, p. 77.

Most of the members of the upper class today are brown in color, and very few of them have white types of hair. Membership in the learned professions has become a more powerful positive sanction than light color. Today, the questions tacitly asked about a person who is "pushing" into the upper class are these: (1) What has been his education? (2) Has he professional or semiprofessional status? (3) Are his language, manners, and dress "polished"? (4) Is he black? (5) In the case of women, have they had sexual relations with white men? The approved answer to these last two questions must be negative.[61]

Social Classes in the Negro Communities of Southern and Border Cities. In their study of the personality development of Negro youth in the urban South, Davis and Dollard use a modification of the Warner categorization of social classes by omitting the lower-upper division. The viewpoint of these authors is that "the people of any community ask only one question to determine an individual's class position, namely, 'Whom does he associate with?' . . . In the colored society of New Orleans and Natchez, the best way to identify the members of the various social classes is (1) to attend the large Negro dances, receptions, chili suppers, barbecues, and picnics, and (2) to secure the membership lists of the large social clubs."[62]

Frazier finds less social stratification in the Negro populations of southern cities than in border cities. The greater complexity in the social structure of the Negro communities of Baltimore, Washington, and St. Louis as compared with Birmingham, Memphis, and New Orleans is attributed mainly to more occupational differentiation in the border cities. Since the professional and clerical groups are much smaller in the southern cities, they have a smaller upper class based upon income and occupation. In both groups of cities Frazier identifies Negro upper, middle, and lower classes. The Washington Negro community, regarded by Frazier as typical of the border cities, is described as follows:

1. Lower Class.
   The lower class has a larger proportion of dark or black Negroes than the middle or upper class. Many of them are recent migrants from the rural South. Among this class there is considerable family disorganization. The lower class includes laborers, many service workers (barbers, charwomen, porters, janitors, etc.), many domestic workers, and semi-skilled workers. The group is characterized by a high rate of illiteracy, low incomes and poverty. The social life of the more stable elements revolves about the Church and the lodge. The less stable elements account for the high degree of criminality in the Negro community.
2. Middle Class.
   The middle class includes a larger proportion of Negroes of lighter complexion who have had a longer residence in the city. Unlike the lower

[61] Allison W. Davis, B. B. Gardner, and M. R. Gardner, op. cit., p. 246.
[62] Allison W. Davis and John Dollard, op. cit., p. 260.

class, with whom they are anxious not to be identified, the middle class exhibits considerable "race pride" and strives to be respectable. Members of this class maintain a stable family life and place considerable value upon conventional sex behavior. For a livelihood middle-class families depend upon wage earners in skilled and semi-skilled occupations, domestic service and the service occupations. The more ambitious of the middle-class families in the Negro community seek through education, the professions, or business to make themselves eligible for upper-class status. They may even disown their families if identification with them would prove a handicap because of their occupation, color, or morals. And since the upper class is often of fair complexion, the associates whom they seek in friendship and in marriage will most likely be of fair complexion. In such selections, they are not simply seeking to identify themselves with a group because of its light skin complexion but mainly because they wish to improve their status.

3. The Upper Class.

The upper class in the Negro community has long had a reputation for snobbishness toward dark or pure-blooded Negroes. To a stranger in the Negro community it might appear that a fair complexion alone determined admission to this class. But, in fact, such factors as family and general culture, occupation and income, and personal achievement and morals help to determine membership in this class. The majority of those of fair complexion will possess a good family background, will be of professional and business standing, and enjoy good incomes as well as a reputation for respectability. Among the women of fair complexion there will be a few of middle or even lower-class origin, who because of education or personal qualities have married men who could give them upper-class status. Among the men there will be a larger proportion of men of brown or dark complexion. Many of these men represent elements in the middle class who moved up in social status. At the present time, a growing race consciousness and the rise of members of the darker middle and lower classes have tended to neutralize the snobbishness of the light upper class. If light-skinned Negroes feel an antipathy toward the darker members of the community, they usually conceal it and only confess it among intimates.

Among the upper class there is still much talk about "culture," but it generally turns out that "culture" is restricted to the social amenities, since it is difficult to find among this group many who read good books or have a genuine appreciation of literature or art or music. Rather it is in the matter of conspicuous consumption that the upper class expresses most explicitly its position and role in the social stratification of the Negro community. A teacher or physician is not simply a professional worker, but generally regards himself as a member of an aristocracy which requires certain standards of consumption. High standards of consumption are often made possible by the fact that upper-class married women in the border cities, unlike those in the South, engage in professional and clerical occupations. Thus fine homes, expensive clothes, and automobiles give an appearance of wealth which is one of the chief values of this class. In order to maintain these standards some families live beyond their means, or, as one investigator found some years ago, the head of the family engages in so-called "sundown" occupations. But it also happens that the wife with a secure and fairly large income from teaching is the main support of the family, while her husband, doctor or businessman with low income, presents a "social front" for the family. Though the upper class is relatively small in numbers, it is important in the Negro community because it provides the standards and values, and symbolizes the aspirations of the Negro community.[63]

Of the new Negro middle class of the urban South, Hylan Lewis writes: "Although there is still unfavorable white-Negro disparity in the labor force of the South at job levels above service and unskilled labor, and although few changes have been made in the rigid racial employment pattern in southern industry, the absolute and relative gains in job mobility and income have fermented a disproportionate social mobility within the Negro community itself."[64] For the lower-class Negro in a southern city, "a precarious and marginal existence, and the isolation and proscription of class compounded by race, an added emphasis and what may appear to be distorted meaning are given to mere getting along and survival, the inviolability of the ego, and religious salvation."[65]

Lewis concludes that Negroes in the South today are developing a new sense of group pride and group solidarity.

Negroes as a whole today are developing a new sense of personal dignity and group pride that is more akin to the pride of an integrating cultural minority than to pride in race as such. This group solidarity derives not only from changes in conditions and expectations, but also from the consolidating effects of the mass media of communication which see a constant stream of news, features and picture stories of Negro achievements (and setbacks) in sports, politics, the armed forces, education and the market places. Extremely effective in this connection is a new postwar journalism (*Ebony, Jet, Our World, Tan Confessions*, and the magazine sections of Negro weeklies) that uses mass circulation techniques. They employ the *Time-Life-Look-Quick-American Weekly* styles and formats to feature news, pictures, and advertisements (with a modal-type brownskin model), achievements and success stories, human interest features. They are circulating and idealizing tastes and images that are middle class and only incidentally brown-skinned slices of conventional America and the world. And then there is network television, usually, emanating from outside the South, with its images of Negroes in sports and entertainment; and the daily Southern press with an increasing quota of news indicating direct and oblique recognition of the Negro as a person and as a new kind of issue or problem. South-

[63] Reprinted from *Negro Youth at the Crossways* by E. Franklin Frazier, pp. 24–28, by permission of the American Council on Education. Copyright 1940 by the American Council on Education. See also E. Franklin Frazier, *The Negro in the United States*, pp. 286–289.

[64] Hylan Lewis, "Innovations and Trends in the Contemporary Southern Negro Community," *Journal of Social Issues*, 1954, vol. 10, No. 1, pp. 22–23.

[65] *Ibid.*, pp. 23–24.

ern Negroes have traveled in the last fifteen years and are now traveling in unprecedented numbers in this country and abroad. These developments which were recently innovations are quickly entering the phase of being taken for granted. The new experiences and the revamped expectations that flowed from them are quickly given mass circulation and become the bases for a new kind of group solidarity.[66]

Social Classes in the Negro Communities of the Urban North.

Four main social classes in the Negro community of Chicago are distinguished in a study of color and personality, namely, the upper class, the upper-middle class, the lower-middle class, and the lower class.

Negroes of the upper class are found in the professions, in the civil service, and in prosperous businesses. In many cases they have had the advantage of higher education. As a rule the women in this group do not work outside the home, although some of them are teachers or social workers. The income of this class is frequently above $250 a month, and members can afford to live in good apartment houses and maintain summer homes. These people strive for refinement and deplore the behavior of lower-class Negroes. Membership on the boards of such organizations as the Y.M.C.A. and Y.W.C.A. is restricted to the upper class, and this group likewise supports the National Association for the Advancement of Colored People. In general, they belong to Episcopal, Congregational, or Presbyterian churches. The women of this class are usually passable, light, or fair in complexion but a larger proportion of the men are dark. Though most Negroes in this group are economically independent of the white community, many of them participate actively in interracial philanthropic and civic activities.

Included in the upper class are many "shady" individuals whose economic position sets them off from the rest of the Negro community. Except in cases of conflict with their business interests, these people emulate the behavior of upper-class whites. Often they are seen at highly publicized civic affairs, cabarets, race tracks, and prize fights. Some of the women try to purchase respectability for themselves and their children by contributing large amounts to philanthropy. In some instances, the men conduct legitimate businesses on the side and thus likewise seek to gain upper-class respectability. The leaders of "shady" society often have business affiliations with similar promoters in Detroit or New York, and they lavishly entertain visiting celebrities of the Negro stage and screen. In fact, this group is characterized by its conspicuous spending.

Negroes of the upper-middle class include the Pullman porters and dining-car waiters, most of the postal employees, the less successful businessmen, and professional men with small practices. They have to struggle hard to maintain good homes and keep up their dues in lodges and clubs. They appear to make greater efforts than do upper-class Negroes to achieve the standards of respectability, and they put great emphasis on thrift and industry. In some cases they are well satisfied with their status, but most of them strive to give their children good educational advantages. "Shadies" in the upper-middle class are usually ostentatious, vulgar spenders, and many have

[66] *Ibid.*, pp. 26–27.

prison records. Negroes in the middle classes make up the bulk of lodge members, and they have a general fondness for organized social clubs, improvement associations, and neighborhood civic societies. The "respectable" members of this class are usually Baptists or Methodists, although the socially ambitious of their number sometimes affiliate with the fashionable churches of the upper class. A light complexion is a decided social asset for middle-class women ambitious to improve their status.

In the lower-middle class are the Negroes who fill such jobs as tailors, bartenders, dressmakers, hairdressers and barbers, store clerks, low-salaried white-collar workers, skilled laborers, and well-paid servants. The less important racketeers are classified with this group. Whereas most "respectable" members of the upper class are conservative in their social outlook, Negroes in the two middle classes furnish most of the supporters for reform movements. They are less inclined to resent the upward striving of lower-class Negroes than are the people of the upper class. The family is usually dominated by the father, who is often aggressively determined to "rule the roost."

In the lower class, to which the great masses of Chicago Negroes belong, the family is virtually matriarchal or presided over by the mother. Since common-law marriage is frequent in this group, family life tends to be unstable. Children within a single family may have different fathers and, because of the family breakup, they are often brought up by their maternal grandparents. Within the "shady" lower class there is hardly any family life at all. Whereas many people of the older generation still emphasize religion, the young people tend to drop all church connections. Lower-class Negroes are quite inclined to attribute their personal inadequacies and economic difficulties to race prejudice, and they resent upper-class Negroes as disloyal to the race. Many express the conviction that something like a "race war" or "divine intervention" will be necessary some day to "vindicate the Negro."

For leisure-time activities people of this class go to poolhalls, hang out on street corners, loaf in numbers game or policy stations, go to the movies, or frequent dance halls and taverns. "Shadies" of the lower class live by their wits, boast of their ability to win at policy, and flatter both white and Negro superiors to wheedle money out of them. They are afraid of the law and definitely respect the police. Dream books, numerology, luck, and magic are persistent topics of their conversation.

Within the lower class there are few organized groups except street-corner gangs and church societies. Many of these people are on relief and report that they cannot have a social life in the crowded quarters where they have to live. There are some mixed cliques of young people who gather for delinquent sexual behavior, but social contacts of any kind are very limited. Few of them can afford to pay lodge dues. Their socio-economic condition is one of the most deplorable in Chicago; most of them are poverty stricken, bewildered individuals. In a land of plenty they lack the minimum essentials of decent living and, under present conditions, the barriers to their advancement seem to be almost insuperable.[67]

[67] Reprinted from *Color and Human Nature* by W. Lloyd Warner, B. H. Junker, and W. A. Adams, pp. 20–23, by permission of the American Council on Education. Copyright 1941 by the American Council on Education.

Frazier finds the social structure in Negro communities in the urban North more complex than in the border cities. Greater emphasis on occupational specialization, income, education, and public behavior, together with less attention to family, color, and morals, has resulted in new kinds of social distinctions. Three classes—upper, middle, and lower—are identified, but the lines between them are better defined than in southern and border cities. Frazier makes the important point that the Negro upper class "has its present status, primarily, because of its position in a segregated social world. If members of the Negro upper class were integrated into American society, their occupations and incomes would place them in the middle class."[68]

Later, Frazier examined the consequences to the Negro middle class in the United States of (1) cutting itself off from the Negro masses, and (2) being rejected by the white world. The "black bourgeoisie" has created a "world of make-believe" in which the social myth of the importance of Negro business occupies an important place. Negro "society" is a phase of the same world. Middle-class Negroes, Frazier says, have sought to compensate for their isolation by ostentatious spending. Money enables them to create for themselves a false impression of their place in American society. The failure of whites to take Negroes seriously and their attitude that Negro activities are unimportant encourage a spirit of irresponsibility and an attitude of "play" among middle-class Negroes. Frazier concludes that education, business, the professions, art, politics, and religion are not taken seriously by the majority of this class. Their main preoccupations are said to be sports, metaphysics, spiritualism, and games of chance.[69]

In a study of a middle-sized upstate New York community of 60,000 persons, of whom 3 percent were Negroes, Johnson divided the Negro group into five discrete strata on the basis of socioeconomic status: (1) the isolated "elites," (2) the "stable pillars," (3) the "steady industrious" migrants, (4) the working "floaters," and (5) the indigents, seniles, and "winoes." Later, using criteria of sex, age, status, and social participation, subgroupings were impressionistically placed in the community until approximately fifty subworlds were plotted, each "with its own style of behavior, physical locus, pattern of belief, and reference group."[70]

The most comprehensive analysis of the Negro social-class system in the urban North is presented in Drake and Cayton, *Black Metropolis* (see Figures 11.5 and 11.6).[71]

Another description of upper-, middle-, and lower-class Negroes is

[68] E. Franklin Frazier, *The Negro in the United States*, p. 291.
[69] E. Franklin Frazier, *Black Bourgeoisie*, The Free Press, 1957, chaps. 7–10.
[70] Robert Johnson, "Negro Reactions to Minority Group Status," in Milton L. Barron (ed.), *American Minorities*, Alfred A. Knopf, Inc., 1957, p. 199.
[71] Figures 11.5 and 11.6 are from St. Clair Drake and Horace Cayton, *Black Metropolis*, Harcourt, Brace & Company, 1945, pp. 522 and 525 respectively.

	Negro		Total	
Upper	5%		10%	
Middle	30%		40%	
Lower	65%		50%	

FIGURE 11.5. The Negro Class Structure. Comparison of class distribution of Negroes in Chicago with total population, using education, rental, and occupation as criteria.

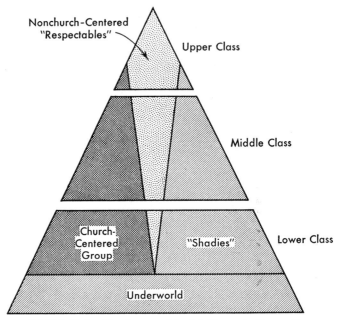

FIGURE 11.6. The System of Social Classes in Bronzeville.

given in Myrdal's monumental investigation of Negro-white relations in the United States. Communities are not treated regionally or according to an urban-rural breakdown, except incidentally. The Negro-white social structure is diagrammed in two ways (see Figure 11.7).[72]

Few studies of social classes within nationality groups in the United States are available. Table 11.1 correlating class and ethnic groups is taken from the Yankee City researches.[73]

[72] From Gunnar Myrdal, An American Dilemma, Harper & Brothers, 1944, pp. 692, 700–705.
[73] W. Lloyd Warner and Paul S. Lunt, op. cit., p. 225. The population of Yankee City was divided into ten groups: Native, or Yankee; Irish; French (French Canadians); Jewish; Italian; Armenian; Greek; Polish; Russian; and Negro. All groups except the first are called "ethnics." In this study "ethnic" does not mean simply foreign birth. "An individual was classified as belonging to a specific ethnic group if (1) he considered himself or was considered by the Yankee City community as a member of the group, and (2) if he participated in the activities of the group." Ibid., p. 211.

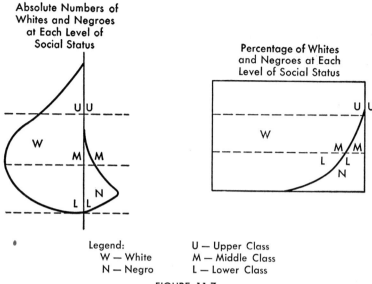

Absolute Numbers of
Whites and Negroes
at Each Level of
Social Status

Percentage of Whites
and Negroes at Each
Level of Social Status

Legend:
W — White   U — Upper Class
N — Negro   M — Middle Class
                   L — Lower Class

FIGURE 11.7.

Cliques

Cliques are in part subdivisions of classes, yet they are to some extent independent of social classes. They operate on the basis of close personal friendship and are comparable to the play groups or "gangs" of children in the intimacy of their primary group relationships. They may or may not be limited to persons of one sex, but the members usually fall within the same age range. Although cliques are constantly forming and reforming, it is not unusual for a clique's membership to continue relatively unchanged for many years. Clique members often share common occupational or recreational interests or have similar tastes along intellectual or artistic lines. A given person may belong to two or more cliques, but usually he will participate more frequently in one clique than in the others. Cliques are ranked and clique members are quite aware of the clique structure. The authors of *Deep South* found more than sixty cliques in the white society of Old City, and twenty-six cliques were identified in the colored society.[74] It is in the family and the clique that the child gets most of his indoctrination with respect to the customs and attitudes of his social class.[75] In the adult world these groups block individuals from participating in both informal and formal activities.

[74] Allison W. Davis, B. B. Gardner, and M. R. Gardner, *op. cit.*, pp. 138, 210.
[75] Allison W. Davis and John Dollard, *op. cit.*, pp. 261–262.

TABLE 11.1   Class and Ethnic Groups in Yankee City

	UU	LU	UM	LM	UL	LL	Total
	100.00	95.42	83.44	67.10	38.00	42.80	
Yankee	2.69	2.78	15.93	35.26	23.15	20.19	53.96
		4.58	15.69	32.78	61.49	56.57	
Total ethnic		0.16	3.55	20.39	44.33	31.57	45.58
		4.58	13.42	22.74	38.33	11.54	
Irish		0.31	5.89	27.52	53.75	12.53	23.43
			0.82	4.05	10.69	15.64	
French			0.96	13.15	40.29	45.60	8.72
			0.70	3.52	3.45	0.71	
Jewish			3.02	41.81	47.61	7.56	2.39
			0.06	0.83	2.18	2.95	
Italian			0.35	13.73	41.90	44.02	1.71
			0.17	0.93	2.28	1.75	
Armenian			1.22	17.89	50.81	30.08	1.48
			0.52	0.47	2.69	5.48	
Greek			2.20	5.37	35.85	56.58	2.46
				0.11	1.21	14.27	
Polish				0.74	9.78	89.48	4.06
				0.13	0.66	2.34	
Russian				4.26	25.53	70.21	0.85
						1.89	
Negro						100.00	0.48
			0.87	0.12	0.51	0.63	
Unknown			19.74	7.89	36.84	35.53	0.46
Total	1.45	1.57	10.30	28.36	32.88	25.44	

NOTE: The boldface numbers indicate in percentages the ethnic composition of the six social classes.

The Importance of Social Classes in the Study of Racial and Ethnic Groups

We believe it is more useful to think of social stratification in the United States in terms of social classes, which have varying aspects because of race, culture, and region, than to employ the concept of castes. But, as Warner says in a commentary previously cited, it is of little consequence which term is used if we understand that the status system organizes and powerfully influences our lives.

The significance of social classes in the study of racial and ethnic groups seems to be along the following lines:

1. Class standing has effects upon the development of personality of the members of racial and ethnic minorities. Relationships between race and personality were treated in an earlier chapter, but it may be mentioned here that various studies have shown that the social-class

standing of the "ethnic," both in the larger community and within the more or less separate racial or cultural "social world," has definite effects on personality formation.[76]

2. Class analysis contributes to an understanding of the institutions and behaviors of racial and cultural groups. A consideration of the distribution of Negroes and ethnics in the overall social structure of the community, as well as the social differentiation within the minority group, throws light on the social institutions of the at least partially segregated community and on the aggressive, fearful, withdrawn, compensatory, and other behaviors of its members. In fact, the life of these groups cannot be understood except in relation to their varying statuses in the class structure.

3. Class analysis is useful in predicting behavior in a given race-relations situation. Every social position carries with it a cluster of prerogatives and obligations. Although the "ideal" pattern for a position is seldom if ever perfectly reproduced in actual behavior, it unquestionably affects action.[77] One learns in childhood what the expectations of others in his culture and subcultures are for those who occupy the various social positions, including racial statuses. Conceptions of self and others develop as the child assumes in his play such positions as mother, father, baby, teacher, salesman, policeman, soldier, and so on, and sees himself through the eyes of others. The translation of a position's ideal pattern of rights and duties into concrete action in specific situations constitutes a role.[78] The variations in the manner in which a position is filled are seldom great enough to prevent the prediction with considerable accuracy, even by those who are not social psychologists, of the reactions of others in a given context. If this condition were not true, there could be no social order; human association would be literally a shambles.[79] In systematizing the prediction of human behavior, sociologists and social psychologists utilize the concept of role. We are particularly interested here in the prediction, professional and nonprofessional, of behavior in situations involving members of different racial and cultural groups. We are concerned, too, with the possibilities of changing behavior in such situations.

4. Class analysis aids in determining the extent to which racial and cultural minorities have been assimiliated into American life. Occupational differentiation, degree of participation in the life of the whole community, and amalgamation of racial and nationality groups have all

---

[76] See, for example, W. Lloyd Warner, B. H. Junker, and W. A. Adams, *op. cit.*, pp. 6–19; Allison W. Davis and John Dollard, *op. cit.*, p. 259.

[77] Ralph Linton, *op. cit.*, p. 102; Robert K. Merton, "Bureaucratic Structure and Personality," *Social Forces*, May, 1940, p. 3.

[78] Ralph Linton, *op. cit.*, p. 114; E. C. Hughes, "Institutional Office and the Person," *American Journal of Sociology*, November, 1937, pp. 404–405.

[79] Talcott Parsons, *The Structure of Social Action*, McGraw-Hill Book Company, 1937, pp. 582–583.

been associated with the emergence of socioeconomic classes in this country. The study of social stratification, as Frazier says, "provides a measure of the process of acculturation and integration of the Negro into the American community." This observation of course applies to groups other than the Negro.

5. Class analysis shows the differentials in social opportunities according to class standing. Although we shall not try—to use Gross's expression—"to demonstrate the ontological priority of social classes as a fundamental force in society,"[80] documentation will be provided to show that there are definite relationships between the class statuses of members of minority peoples and such matters as life expectancy, amount of education, community influence, economic security, contact with law-enforcement agencies, and recreational activities.

As we proceed to the study of the place of minorities in the institutional structures (economic, political, familial, religious, educational, and aesthetic), the importance of social stratification in affecting majority-minority relations, and as a reflection of those relations, will be demonstrated.

[80] Llewellyn Gross, op. cit., p. 415.

CHAPTER 12

Minorities in the Economy of the United States

Among the most important indications of the status and power of a group is its place in the economic structure. Nowhere are prejudice and discrimination more clearly shown than in the barriers to economic improvement that are thrown in the way of minority-group members. Job opportunities are important not only in the narrow economic sense, but also in terms of their influence on the whole style of life of individuals and on the institutional structure of groups. The political influence of a group, its family patterns, religious beliefs, educational ambitions and achievements, even the possibilities of good health and survival cannot be understood until the place of that group in the total economy is studied. The relationship is, of course, reciprocal; political, familial, religious, and other institutional patterns also affect the economic situation.

This analysis deals with the roles of minority groups in the American economy. The degree to which similar forces are involved in other societies may be seen by referring to some of the general principles discussed in Chapter 4. Since Negroes not only represent one of the largest minorities but are the group most affected by economic discrimination, we shall be largely concerned with their place in the economy.

The Negro Population in the South

Two major demographic changes have occurred in the South since 1930. The first change is the loss of three million population by migration, a figure equal to one-fourth or more of the South's natural increase; the second is the marked trend toward urbanization. Out-migration was considerably heavier for the Negro than the white population; and despite a high rate of natural increase, the proportion of Negroes in the southern population dropped from 26 to 23 percent between 1930 and 1950.[1] Migration and urbanization have so transformed the Negro population that a 1956 estimate places only 2,700,000 Negroes in the southern-farm category; 8,300,000 are classified as southern-non-farm, and the remaining 6,300,000 as urban in the North and the West.[2]

Negro Farmers

Despite the changes which have occurred since 1930, the poorest farm families in the United States are concentrated in the cotton region of the Old South. Everything about them testifies to their meager existence. The shacks which pass for houses, their unbalanced diet, their pathetically low incomes, their rudimentary farm equipment, their lack of medical care, their semiliteracy, and their political impotence mark them as a forlorn, low-status segment of the population. Many of these families are white, but the Negro families have a racial handicap in addition to the other disabilities of this occupational group.

Land tenure among Negroes in the South is still largely a matter of some type of tenancy, as can be seen in Table 12.1. A part owner is a farmer who owns part and rents part of the land he cultivates. Cash tenants are provided with land, a house, and fuel; in return they pay a fixed cash rental. A share tenant (crop-share) receives some fertilizer, in addition to the items provided the cash renter, and usually pays the landlord from one-fourth to one-third of the crop. Livestock-share tenants, a very small group, work on the same basis as the crop-share farmers. Sharecroppers are supplied everything: land, a cabin, farm equipment, fuel, and one-half of the fertilizer. In return they give the landlord one-half of the crop. In many cases in which the landlord has more than one kind of tenant on his land, the croppers are put on the best land, given relatively small tracts, and supervised closely. In addition to these categories of agricultural workers, there is an increasing number of "wage hands" or farm laborers.

While there was a net decrease in both white and nonwhite croppers in the South during World War II years, the rate of decrease was considerably greater in the white group. Street attributes this difference to the greater opportunity for nonfarm employment among the whites,

[1] B. U. Ratchford, "The Reorganization of the Southern Economy," in Jessie P. Guzman (ed.), *The New South and Higher Education*, Tuskegee Institute, 1954, p. 38. Ginzberg estimates that two million Negroes moved from the South to the North and the West in the decade 1940 to 1950. Eli Ginzberg, *The Negro Potential*, Columbia University Press, 1956, p. 37. In 1950, there were 2,600,000 Negroes who had been born in the South but were living in other sections of the country. *Ibid.*, p. 14.
[2] L. T. Hawley, "The Negro's New Economic Life," *Fortune*, September, 1956, p. 128.

TABLE 12.1. Number of Farms, by Color and Tenure of Operator, for the South, 1880-1954[3] (data for 1954 are based on reports for only a sample of farms).

Color and Tenure of Operator	No. of Farms					Increase or Decrease (−) (Number)		
	1954	1950	1940	1930	1900	1950–54	1945–50	1940–45
White, total	1,853,820	2,093,333	2,326,904	2,342,129	1,879,721	−239,513	−122,389	−111,182
Full owners	1,145,372	1,269,641	1,185,788	1,050,187	1,078,635	−124,269	−78,435	162,288
Part owners	300,280	274,135	185,246	183,469	105,171	26,145	108,780	−19,891
Managers	9,190	9,740	13,215	16,529	17,172	−550	−3,011	−464
All tenants	398,978	539,817	942,655	1,091,944	678,743	−140,839	−149,723	−253,115
Cash	60,634	80,293	189,667	140,112	187,088	−19,659	−78,799	−30,575
Share-cash	18,808	24,367	32,131	n.a.[a]		−5,559	8,818	−16,582
Crop-share	144,918	202,864 }	n.a.	n.a.	491,655	−57,946 }	44,280	−128,132
Livestock-share	13,327	14,285 }				−958 }		
Croppers	107,416	148,708	242,173	383,381		−41,292	27,552	−65,913
Other	23,810	19,361 }				4,449 }		
Unspecified	30,065	49,939 }	89,123	n.a.	n.a.	−19,874 }	−7,910	−11,913
Nonwhite, total	463,476	559,090	680,266	881,687	740,670	−95,614	−106,323	−14,853
Full owners	129,854	141,482	141,902	140,496	158,479	−11,628	−19,498	19,078
Part owners	50,736	51,864	31,361	41,523	28,197	−1,128	23,612	−3,109
Managers	381	239	365	829	1,593	142	−203	77
All tenants	282,505	365,505	506,638	698,839	552,401	−83,000	−110,234	−30,899
Cash	28,148	39,562	64,684	97,920	271,702	−11,414	−33,580	8,458
Share-cash	3,463	5,656	6,547	n.a.		−2,193	376	−1,267
Crop-share	69,235	95,461 }			280,699	−26,226 }	3,369	4,345
Livestock-share	1,506	1,736 }				−230 }		
Croppers	160,246	198,057	299,118	392,897		−37,811 }	−72,239	−28,882
Others	11,543	11,442 }	46,806	n.a.		101 }		
Unspecified	8,364	13,591 }				−5,227 }	−8,160	−13,613

[3] U.S. Census of Agriculture, 1954, General Report, vol. 2, pp. 954–955.
[a] n.a.—not available.

and possibly to a stronger preference of farm owners for Negro workers.[4] Changes in tenure status within the region varied during the war years. Every state showed a decrease in the number of white sharecroppers between 1940 and 1945, but five states showed an increase in nonwhite croppers by 1945. The main increases occurred in North Carolina, South Carolina, and Georgia, where in many cases more liberal tenure arrangements were offered. Similar arrangements in other states met with less success. Mississippi lost 8500 white and 20,000 Negro sharecroppers from 1940 to 1945, and another 1400 white and 21,000 Negro sharecroppers from 1945 to 1950. As Street points out, it is impossible to determine how many of these croppers left farming; undoubtedly some climbed the agricultural ladder, and others may have become wage laborers on farms.[5] The number of sharecroppers continued to decline in the postwar years, the decrease occurring in every state and at an accelerated rate. The decline in the number of Negro sharecroppers in these years was so great that the rate of decrease for the whole decade was nearly as great for them as for whites. From 1940 to 1950, the decrease in farms operated by croppers in the South was approximately 195,000, or 36 percent.[6]

Every study that was made of the rural South during the 1930's underlined the poverty of the Negro families. A sample of 646 plantations with five or more resident families, including the landlord, in the eastern cotton belt in 1934 showed that croppers had a net income of $312, share tenants of $417, cash renters $354, and wage hands $180.[7] Since this study was limited to medium- and large-sized plantations, incomes on the smaller, less efficient plantations were probably smaller. On the largest, most rationally operated cotton plantation in the South (Delta and Pine Land Company of Scott, Mississippi) the total income per cropper was $405 in 1933, $461 in 1934, $446 in 1935, and $525 in 1936.[8] While most tenants' incomes increased during the 1940's and 1950's, these gains were offset to a considerable degree by continued reductions in the purchasing power of the dollar.

Because of the low income levels, the economic year for many tenants is divided into four periods: one of about three months when they have a little cash, a similar period when they are receiving "advances" from the landlord or merchant, and two periods of destitution.

In years of low prices a tenant's money and his store of pork, meal, and sweet potatoes are usually exhausted by Christmas, or even before. He then

[4] James H. Street, *The New Revolution in the Cotton Economy*, University of North Carolina Press, 1957, p. 213.
    [5] *Ibid.*, p. 213.
    [6] *Ibid.*, p. 214.
    [7] T. J. Woofter, Jr., *Landlord and Tenant on the Cotton Plantation*, Works Progress Administration, 1936, p. xxxiii.
    [8] "Biggest Cotton Plantation," *Fortune*, March, 1937, p. 160.

faces a period of from two and one-half to three months (before advances begin in late March or April), when he has neither money, credit, nor stored food. A second period of destitution follows the stopping of advances in July, when he is again without money, credit, or stored food, and when the heat has withered the spring gardens. The months when most tenants have little or nothing to eat and no money, therefore, are the coldest months and the hottest months, namely, February, all or part of March, and all or part of July, August, and September. One of the landlords who defined these periods stated that, of the two, the summer was the period of more widespread destitution; practically all tenants were without money by July, whereas during the winter some few still had money from the sale of their cotton. In the summer, furthermore, pork and meal will not keep, the store of sweet potatoes has long since been exhausted, and gardens are withered.[9]

In arranging "the furnish," the landlord or merchant acquires a lien on the tenant's share of the crop. While the usual carrying charge is a flat 10 percent, the actual interest rate is from 35 to 50 percent because (1) most of the food and clothing are advanced to the tenant after March and the debt is settled in September, and (2) a special "credit" price is charged on goods consumed in the spring. This statement on actual interest rates assumes that the records of credit and of cotton are honestly kept, an assumption which is not always warranted, as we shall point out later. As Raper and Reid remark, the few hundred dollars of income which the tenant family has is actually worth much less than that in cash.[10]

The predominant type of tenant house is a two- or three-room unpainted shack built of a single thickness of rough boards, with no screening and with primitive sanitation. As Charles Johnson said, "The open well, the kerosene lamp, the fireplace, and the privy are standard equipment" in these homes. In representative counties, Raper and Reid found that one-third of the tenants' cabins had no window sash, one-half had no window panes, and nearly two-thirds had leaky roofs.

In former years, the credit system in the cotton region of the old South was such that it was difficult for a landlord to operate without cheating his tenants, and this situation has not changed entirely. In the Natchez, Mississippi, section, "a businessman . . . whose business furnished him with a close knowledge of the credit dealings of most landlords and tenants in the county, stated that 'practically all landlords' cheated their tenants in 'one way or another.' "[11] The actual words of several Negro tenants on this score are enlightening:

I don't care how good your cotton is, a colored man's cotton is always

[9] Allison W. Davis, B. B. Gardner, and M. R. Gardner, *Deep South*, University of Chicago Press, 1941, pp. 379–380.

[10] A. F. Raper and I. De A. Reid, *Sharecroppers All*, University of North Carolina Press, 1941, p. 22.

[11] Allison W. Davis, B. B. Gardner, and M. R. Gardner, *op. cit.*, p. 351.

second or third-grade cotton if a colored man sells it. The only way you can get first prices for it is to get some white man to sell it for you in his name. A white man sold mine once, and got market prices for it.[12]

I know we been beat out of money direct and indirect. You see, they got a chance to do it all right, 'cause they can overcharge us and I know it being done. I made three bales again last year. He said I owed $400 at the beginning of the year. Now you can't dispute his word. When I said "Suh?" he said, "Don't dispute my word; the book says so." When the book says so and so you better pay it, too, or they will say "So, I'm a liar, eh?" You better take to the bushes too if you dispute him, for he will string you up for that.[13]

So I looked at my cotton receipts and my debt and I said, "A. D., you's goin' to town; you had a good year, but you ain't got nothin' and you never will have nothin' as long as you stay here." So me and my old lady and the chillun jes' lef'. No suh, I ain't got nothin' but some kin folks here and I ain't found them yet, but I's through with farmin'. Through, Yes sir, through.[14]

The landlord's viewpoint has often been that tenants are lazy, inefficient, untrustworthy, and irresponsible. Some landlords have regarded themselves as philanthropists supporting improvident tenants. Their argument is that in the event of crop failure or a drastic reduction in the price of cotton, the landlord takes the principal loss and is compelled to make further advances to the tenants. They cite losses caused by tenants who moved away just at the time they were needed most in the cotton fields. They mention the tendency of tenants to burn fence rails, porch floor, or an outhouse for firewood rather than to cut wood in the timber. They say that tenants seldom make repairs on the buildings located on the farm and that often ténants steal from the landlord.

There are good reasons why many tenants do display some or all of these characteristics. They are not supposed to show any initiative, but to follow instructions. They receive little for their labor. Their diet is inadequate, and medical care is scarce. Their status in the community is unenviable. In view of these conditions, it is not surprising to find low vitality, little enthusiasm for their tasks, irresponsibility, improvidence, and destructiveness in the cotton tenant group.

There is no point in blaming landlords in general or tenants in general for the situation in the plantation region. Landlords and tenants are parts of a social structure which has in it many of the characteristics of the slavery regime. The tenant system sprang up in the period following the Civil War because landlords had to have cheap labor and the freedmen had to find work. For the most part, the members of neither group knew how to continue economically except to follow the old familiar

[12] Charles S. Johnson, *Shadow of the Plantation*, University of Chicago Press, 1934, p. 128.
[13] *Ibid*, p. 127.
[14] A. F. Raper and I. De A. Reid, *op. cit.*, p. 64.

paths. Tenancy was simply a modified kind of slavery, a *modus vivendi* which became a permanent system. In the 1870's and 1880's, large plantations set the ideological pattern and the customs for small plantations, and large planters dominated the economic and political life of the local areas. This is largely the case today.[15] County officials need the support of landlords. Landlords need credit and political favors. It is within this web of mutualism that the relatively wealthy but insecure owners, the small landowners, and the millions of landless and dependent tenants and wage hands must operate.

It is extremely difficult for a colored tenant to purchase land in the plantation area. Tenants who try to accumulate savings with which to buy land may be unable to get a farm for another year. Planters often combine to keep a "smart tenant" "in his place." Landlords are usually unwilling to sell land to tenants because the acquisition of land by such persons is a threat to the system of tenancy and the labor surplus. There is an exception, as the authors of *Deep South* point out. This is the practice of "selling" land to colored tenants in boom times without due process of law, and reclaiming it with the onset of hard times. This procedure yields several times the income that ordinary renting would bring. Under the racial system of the South, the colored mortgager can secure little or no legal protection in the courts—even in the case of fraud by the landlord.[16]

Some characteristics of the tenant seem to support the claim that he is an unimpressive human being who is not entitled to much more than he gets. He is ignorant, poor, ambitionless, inefficient, and he may upon occasion be dishonest and destructive. The point is that his behavior is closely related to his position in the social structure. He has been held down under the tenancy system, and his listlessness and the other qualities mentioned above are taken as evidence that his worth, and his children's worth, is small and not subject to change.

The worst types of exploitation which formerly characterized tenancy, and especially the sharecropper status, have been eliminated or greatly reduced. However, for Negro sharecroppers in the South considered as a group, Demerath's observation is too optimistic:

[15] As Rubin points out, parts of the plantation area of the Old South are in transition from feudal agrarianism to an industrial mass society. "If the traditional image of the society was based on the plantation owner's agrarian, paternalistic, white supremacy value systems, we now have a new image based on the merchant and industrialist with values centered in the town, rational economic qualifications for jobs, and money as a medium for the achievement of power and prestige. Economic crisis and scientific-education movements have forced the traditional plantation owner to convert to a rational operation that might be called a factory-in-the-field. The plantation house, domestic service, and other symbols of the old regime function for prestige and power only after the demands of rational economic institutions are met." Morton Rubin, "Social and Cultural Change in the Plantation Area," *Journal of Social Issues*, 1954, vol. 10, No. 1, pp. 34–35.

[16] Allison W. Davis, B. B. Gardner, and M. R. Gardner, *op. cit.*, p. 293.

. . . In the social relations of the economy, the South has today a new kind of farmer and sharecropper, white and Negro. Instead of being continuously in debt to the credit merchant or the plantation store, he rents from the finance company a thirty-five hundred automobile, a TV set, and a variety of kitchen and farm appliances his father never imagined. Out of cash, the county welfare will take him on or he can seek work in a nearby plant. He and his family are consumers in the new mass market in which newness is of the essence; and traditions, even in race, tend to go by the boards more rapidly than ever before, though not rapidly enough for those who feel their pinch or drag.[17]

When Bogue says that "instead of the ragged sharecroppers, we are becoming used to the skilled operators of tractors and complicated agricultural machinery—men who draw good wages and have more security because they are indispensable,"[18] it is clear that he is not referring to the generality of tenant farmers, and especially not to the remaining Negro sharecroppers. The majority of Negro farmers have not benefited from the important developments in southern agriculture (improved methods, bigger investments in capital and fertilizer, larger farm units, a shift from cotton and tobacco to diversified farming and cattle raising). Negro farmers have not had the education, capital, and credit to take advantage of these developments themselves, and very few Negroes have well-paid employment on the large scientific commercial farms.[19]

Anderson and Bowman point out that many whites who start as croppers are virtually apprentices to landlord fathers or other relatives (38 percent in South Carolina in 1950, 23 percent in North Carolina, 19 percent in Georgia, and 17 percent in Mississippi). Among Negroes the percentage of related croppers was less than 4. These authors doubt that many southern men of either race who are unrelated to their landlords rise to ownership on a scale involving control over cropper-operated farms. In their view, a more frequent shift is "from labor or cropper status to independent poverty outside the authoritarian hierarchy. The disappearance of that hierarchy awaits enlarged opportunities that give the submerged groups of both races a better bargaining position. In the last analysis, it is mobility out of agriculture that opens the door to mobility upward within agriculture."[20]

The development of huge managed estates, especially in Mississippi, has involved an increase of hired labor and a decrease in cropper farming.

[17] Nick J. Demerath, "Desegregation, Education, and the South's Future," *Phylon*, First Quarter, 1957, p. 44.
[18] Donald J. Bogue, "Population Distribution and Composition in the New South," in Jessie P. Guzman (ed.), *op. cit.*, p. 28.
[19] Eli Ginzberg, *op. cit.*, pp. 16–17.
[20] C. A. Anderson and M. J. Bowman, *Tenure Changes and the Agricultural Ladder in Southern Agriculture*, Bulletin 634, Kentucky Agricultural Experiment Station, 1955, p. 30.

Thus far this shift has been too small to affect the total situation greatly. If this trend should continue there is "at least the possibility that this system may come to provide channels of mobility upward within the employee structure that would be lacking where accumulation of capital was a prerequisite to advancement."[21]

In 1945, Negro farmers constituted one-fourth of all the farmers of the South but they operated less than one-twelfth of the acreage. According to Hawley, 86 percent of these farms were worth less than $3000. "Since 1945," he concludes, "the life of the Negro farmer has changed slowly—for the worse. The Negro lacks, in the best of times, even enough knowledge of the law to acquire sound title to his land; oral leases are legally permissible in every southern state. In a revolutionary time of mechanization, the Negro farmer is economically crippled. He lacks capital. He lacks credit. He lacks enough acreage to support mechanization. He lacks the technical skill to mechanize."[22]

In the past, the failure to diversify crops in the South was due to the fact that no crop could compare with cotton as a source of cash income. Landlords continued to plant cotton and to buy food and feed year after year as long as satisfactory profits were forthcoming. In a bad year when yields were small or the price was unusually low, the losses were heavy. The tendency was to plant cotton another year, or even for two or three years, in the hope of offsetting the losses with some really big money. Only if the prices remained low or the yields were poor for several years did the planters diversify their crops. Diversification came only when it was no longer possible to borrow money.

In recent years greater crop diversification has been stimulated in the cotton areas of the Old South by such factors as exhaustion of the land through continued use of the one-crop system; the ravages caused by the boll weevil; the programs of state and federal agricultural agencies; a growing interest in livestock, in the food and feed grains, and in other products which can be produced with less labor; the mechanization of cotton cultivation in the Southwest and California; and a decline in the share of the world's cotton supply which is produced in the United States.[23] Four-fifths of the world's cotton was produced in the United States in 1880, and four-fifths of this was grown in states east of the Mississippi River. "In 1938–1939 the United States produced only about two-fifths of the world supply and 55 percent of this came from west of the Mississippi."

In earlier years, the value of the cotton crop was approximately half of the total value of farm production in the South; now it is less than one-fourth.[24]

[21] *Ibid.*, p. 31.
[22] L. T. Hawley, *op. cit.*, pp. 252, 254.
[23] A. F. Raper and I. De A. Reid, *op. cit.*, p. 32.
[24] B. U. Ratchford, *op. cit.*, pp. 34–35.

The mechanization of cotton production has continued apace during the postwar period. The experimental models of only a few years ago have been replaced with more than 18,000 mechanical cotton harvesters of the spindle type, and 23,000 mechanical cotton strippers were in use in 1957.[25] In 1955 nearly three and a half million bales of cotton, constituting nearly one-fourth of the American crop, were harvested mechanically. Two-thirds of the California crop was harvested by machines. Almost as significant in its long-run effects as mechanical pickers and strippers is the bringing of other stages of cotton production under mechanical control. Much has been accomplished along these lines in the western sections of the cotton region, and the feasibility of completely mechanizing the crop in important localities has been established.[26]

The partial mechanization of cotton production has exerted pressure on portions of the rural population to leave the farms, and this pressure will continue.[27] When a plantation changes from horses and mules to tractors and mechanical cotton pickers, the acreage allotted to tenants is drastically reduced and the "day crop" is expanded.[28] Also, mechanized operations tend to augment the staff of management personnel. In 1941, fifty-eight white supervisory persons on one plantation managed the production operations of 2769 workers in tenant families and 256 day hands. Twelve years later there were seventy-five people on the white supervisory staff, 927 workers in the tenant families, and 400 regular day hands. Pedersen found that "the field hand has not been displaced as yet in the cotton-picking operation and is critically necessary for weed control."[29]

Street describes some interesting and significant changes in tenure arrangements which reflect the transitional stages of cotton mechanization in the South. Under the "through-and-through" or "across-and-across" plan each cropper family is assigned a specific crop acreage, but all the workers on the plantation tend the common fields under a gang system. Under a second set of arrangements the planter charges his croppers service fees for the operations performed with power equipment; other planters have shifted from the usual 50–50 to a 60–40 basis,

[25] James H. Street, op. cit., p. v.

[26] Ibid., pp. v–vi. Modern cultivation of cotton includes mechanization in disposal of plant residue from the preceding crop, application of the fertilizer, planting, thinning and weed control, insect control, defoliation, picking, and ginning.

[27] Street (ibid., p. 229) concludes that in only a few areas has the mechanization of cotton production been due directly to "a condition of actual labor unavailability in relation to customary cropping methods." The introduction of strippers into the High Plains area of Texas during World War II, and the postwar use of mechanical pickers in the Mississippi Delta and in California are cited as possible cases. For most other areas in the cotton belt, "total mechanization will have to push its way in against relatively abundant manpower resources."

[28] H. A. Pedersen, "Mechanized Agriculture and the Farm Laborer," Rural Sociology, June, 1954, pp. 147–148.

[29] Ibid., p. 147.

with the operator paying for all seed, fertilizer, and spray. In the latter arrangement, the operator receives 60 percent of the crops and 60 percent of the soil conservation and parity payments. A third arrangement, sometimes combined with the other two, divides the labor force into two parts. One consists of a crew assigned to weed control in ordinary seasons; this group is stabilized on the farm by being assured a sharecrop. The other group, constituting from half to two-thirds of the employees, is employed on a wage basis, the number fluctuating with the demands of the season and the year.[30] In areas where large-scale mechanization occurs, there will continue to be some demand for farm laborers. Those who are retained will be skilled and semiskilled workers who have acquired the skills necessary for mechanized operations.[31]

One of the interesting consequences of the changes in southern agriculture is the decreased dependence on child labor. In one county in Mississippi, the number of tractors increased five times between 1940 and 1950, and mechanical cotton pickers, introduced in 1943, numbered two hundred by the end of the decade. The school-age population in the county changed little during the ten years, but a large number of farm families moved to the principal town during this period. Urban school attendance increased markedly. "Negro children, who were six times as numerous as white children in the county, increased their average daily attendance by 41 percent in the urban schools during this period, and for the first time began to appear in grades above the eighth. Only a few years before most of these children were required to pick cotton from September through November and the teen-age boys spent the spring months plowing and cultivating. A change in the community attitude was reflected in the fact that beginning about 1950 the law against employment of children under sixteen years of age in the cotton fields was for the first time being enforced by local police."[32] Changes such as these are not due solely to the mechanization of agriculture—increased employment opportunities in urban areas have been important—but unquestionably it has had a strong effect. As Street points out, changes occasioned by mechanization can be painful at first, but over a period of time the effects may be beneficial. This may be true of race relations in general as well as for such specific matters as those mentioned above.

Employment of Urban Negroes

During the latter part of the nineteenth century, and in fact until World War I, the Negro population in both northern and southern cities was small. The usual occupations followed by colored people were

[30] James H. Street, op. cit., pp. 219–220.
[31] H. A. Pedersen, op. cit., p. 151.
[32] James H. Street, op. cit., pp. 249–250.

those of servant, porter, janitor, and, to a smaller extent, common laborer. Gradually, as labor disputes occurred, Negroes were brought in to break strikes and weaken labor unions. It was through strikebreaking that Negro workers obtained their first jobs in northern steel plants and in the meat-packing industry.

At the time of World War I, Negroes were brought into the great industrial centers of the North to overcome the shortage of unskilled workers. It was no mere trickle of workers who came, but hundreds of thousands of migrants. These people went into heavy industries, into domestic service, and into construction work. Within a few years Negroes had demonstrated that they were satisfactory workers in the urban environment.

When the industrial development of the South was accelerated in the years that followed World War I, Negro workers were already employed in the fertilizer, tobacco, turpentine, steel, and furniture manufacturing industries. The rapid expansion of industry, together with the increase in service industries and in hotel and restaurant operations, provided new job opportunities for the urban Negro. The bulk of the new jobs in domestic service also went to colored workers.

With the coming of the depression the northern Negro industrial worker lost much of the ground he had gained. He had very little seniority, he had not yet acquired much skilled status, and white workers were clamoring for such jobs as there were. Southern Negro workers experienced less unemployment and less occupational shifting, but the wage differentials based on race were continued. The trend whereby Negro artisans were displaced by whites in the building and hand trades was heightened in depression years. According to R. C. Weaver, "Almost a half of the skilled Negro males in the nation were displaced from their usual types of employment during the period 1930 to 1936; a third of those outside their usual occupations were in unskilled work, and over 17 percent were unemployed."[33] Drake and Cayton have provided data on unemployment among Chicago Negroes during the depression. "The first five years of the Depression had piled up a backlog of over 150,000 unemployed workers of whom 35,000 were Negroes. While Negroes made up only eight percent of the available workers, they constituted twenty-two percent of the unemployed. All along the line, Negroes had been displaced in a ratio of roughly three to one. Almost half of the Negro domestic servants, a third of the semi-skilled workers, and a fourth of the unskilled were unemployed in 1935."[34] The explanation of this overrepresentation of Negroes among the unemployed seems to be as follows: First, Negroes are concentrated in occupations (unskilled labor and domestic service) which almost immediately feel the effects of

[33] R. C. Weaver, Negro Labor, Harcourt, Brace & Company, 1946, p. 9.
[34] St. Clair Drake and Horace Cayton, Black Metropolis, Harcourt, Brace & Company, 1945, pp. 215, 217.

an economic slump; second, Negroes are likely to be dropped sooner than white workers; third, Negroes continued to come to Chicago because of the economic collapse of the cotton belt and discrimination in relief administration.[35]

MINORITIES AND EMPLOYMENT IN DEFENSE INDUSTRIES

The economic position of the Negro at the time the defense program was inaugurated in 1940 was discouraging. The proportion of Negroes in manufacturing (5.1 percent) was lower than it had been in 1910 (6.2 percent), and, with the exception of domestic service, similar losses had occurred in other kinds of employment. Also, the Negro was greatly underrepresented in the industries which are important in war production. In aircraft and parts, 0.1 percent of the workers were colored; in electrical machinery, 0.5 percent; other machinery, 1.0 percent; rubber products, 2.1 percent; apparel, 2.3 percent; nonferrous metals and their products, 2.4 percent; automobile equipment, 3.6 percent; iron and steel, 5.5 percent; ship and boat building, 6.4 percent. Negroes had not forgotten the dismissal, during the depression, of a high percentage of the colored workers brought into industry during boom years, and they campaigned for training, employment, and upgrading in all war industries.

During the years 1940–1944 a number of significant changes occurred in the Negro employment situation. The number of Negroes in skilled, single-skilled, and semiskilled jobs doubled. The percentage of Negro women employed as domestic servants decreased sharply, and Negroes were employed in industries and plants where few had held jobs before the war. More industrial and occupational diversification for Negroes occurred in four years during World War II than in the whole post-Civil War period. Colored workers had entered industrial work during World War I, but the traditional color line was drawn on jobs at that time. This was not the case during World War II; thousands of Negroes were able to demonstrate their abilities in types of work and in plants where colored men had not been employed previously. As Weaver has stated, "Most of the gains occurred after 1942. In the summer of that year, for example, it was estimated that only 3 percent of those in war industries were colored; by September 1944, the proportion was over 8 percent. Up-grading was, of course, a necessary, concurrent development in an economy where so many jobs required trained workers; and, with expansion of Negro employment, there came participa-

---

[35] *Ibid.*, p. 218. The concentration of Negroes in servant work is shown in this summary: "Over twenty-five out of every hundred employed Negro men and fifty-six out of every hundred Negro women were doing some kind of servant work on the eve of the Depression. This was at least four times their 'proportionate share,' for Negroes did over a third of all servant work performed by women, and a fourth of that done by men." *Ibid.*, p. 220.

tion in higher types of work. As a matter of fact, the entrance of a few Negroes into semi-skilled jobs was a preliminary step to greater numerical participation in most plants."[36] The percentage of Negroes in skilled jobs in industry increased from 4.4 percent in 1940 to 7.3 percent in 1944, and in the same period the percentage of Negroes in semi-skilled jobs increased from 13.0 percent to 22.4 percent. These statements must not be taken to mean that Negroes were enthusiastically welcomed into industry during World War II years. Even in times of full employment there is resistance to changes in the economic and occupational statuses of Negroes. The advances of colored people are often seen as a challenge to the existing racial system. Weaver's conclusion on this point well describes the obstacles to change: "To some, the changes represent a loss of Negro servants and laborers; by others they are interpreted as a threat to the white man's job in the post-war economy. Also, the higher earnings of the Negro make him an effective competitor for limited available supplies of housing, transportation, food, clothing, and other goods and services."[37]

By the fall of 1942, Negro women were being employed in increasing numbers as production workers in shipyards, ordnance plants, and aircraft factories. Charles S. Johnson stated that "sixty-four important war plants in eighteen states reported in October 1942 that they were employing Negro women as electricians, welders, sheet metal workers, assemblers, machine tool operators, lathe hands, drill press operators, power machine operators, aircraft production operators, explosive operators, rubber workers, and a number of other skilled and semi-skilled lines."[38]

NEGROES IN INDUSTRY IN THE POST-WORLD WAR II PERIOD

In 1947 there were 450,000 more Negro women in the labor force than in 1940, and the percentage of gainfully employed Negro women on farms had declined from 21 to 7 percent. The proportion of employed Negro women in domestic service decreased from approximately 70 percent in 1940 to less than 50 percent in 1947. During the same years the percentage of Negro women in semiskilled jobs more than doubled, and the proportion in clerical and sales positions nearly tripled. According to 1950 estimates, one-tenth of all workers on machine jobs were Negroes, although Negro males constituted 64 percent of male domestics and 25 percent of the common laborers. It is interesting to note that the proportion of Negro males in service occupations declined from 40 to 23 percent during the years 1940 to 1947. At the same time,

[36] R. C. Weaver, op. cit., p. 79.
[37] Ibid., p. 108.
[38] Charles S. Johnson, Into the Main Stream, University of North Carolina Press, 1948, p. 102.

Negro males in the skilled trades increased 25 percent; in semiskilled work the increase was 50 percent.[39]

Full employment in the postwar period has had little effect on the concentration of Negro job opportunities at the lowest levels of work. In the North the percentages of Negro men who are managers, officials, proprietors, or skilled workers are only slightly higher than in the South. The greatest advantage that northern Negroes have is a better opportunity to obtain clerical or sales work.[40] In the South the greatest occupational change for Negro men has been in the increase in the number of "operatives," but three-fourths of the men in this category are in the least desirable types of work—the dirtiest and heaviest jobs in factories, mills, refineries, etc.[41] In the southern labor market, direct personal competition between white and Negro workers is limited almost entirely to "isolated" jobs where the man works alone (truck-driving, gardening, janitoring, etc.). Since Negroes cannot advance to supervise whites or mixed crews, direct personal competition is restricted to the isolated jobs that are also dead-end jobs.[42] Because Negro and white workers do not usually work side by side at the same jobs in the South, the employer chooses between using white or Negro labor in a given set of jobs.[43] Dewey does not know of one cotton or rayon mill in the upper South that has upgraded a Negro work group since 1945, and among the 400,000 textile workers in Virginia, North Carolina, and South Carolina no Negroes are employed as weavers, spinners, or loom-fixers.[44] In tobacco, the South's second industry, the only permanent upgrading of Negro labor since 1940 has been restricted to twenty jobs in a North Carolina factory. Since the southern industrial employment pattern is not likely to change soon, the upgrading of Negroes will go ahead very slowly. In the face of this situation, and as the education and health of Negroes improve, migration to the North and the West will continue.[45]

---

[39] R. C. Weaver, "The Economic Status of the Negro in the United States," *Journal of Negro Education*, 1950, vol. 19, p. 239.

[40] Eli Ginzberg, *op. cit.*, p. 30.

[41] L. T. Hawley, *op. cit.*, p. 252.

[42] Donald Dewey, "Negro Employment in Southern Industry," *Journal of Political Economy*, August, 1952, p. 285.

[43] *Ibid.*, pp. 283, 285.

[44] *Ibid.*, pp. 285–286.

[45] The Lockheed Aircraft Corporation plant at Marietta, Georgia, employs 17,-350 workers, including 1350 Negroes. Of the 450 job classifications in this plant, Negroes are found in twenty. Opportunities for Negro promotion are extremely limited because Negroes are used only in the two all-Negro departments, and the majority of supervisors in these departments are white. This plant employs 2400 white women in electrical wiring and subassembly classifications; only seven Negro women are employed, and all of them are in janitorial and custodial positions. According to Hill, "When Negroes approach a seniority rating that would qualify them for a higher classification the Company often reclassifies the job or moves the operation completely out of the Negro work group." Herbert Hill, "Status of Negro Workers at Lockheed Aircraft Corporation," *The Crisis*, March, 1957, pp. 147–148.

Table 12.2 shows the occupational distribution of employed males by race and region for 1940 and 1950.

TABLE 12.2.   Occupational Distribution of Employed Males by Race and Region, 1940 and 1950[46]

| | 1950 | | | |
| | South | | Other Regions | |
	Negro	White	Negro	White
Professional, technical, and kindred workers	2.0%	7.0%	2.6%	8.3%
Managers, officials, and proprietors	1.4	11.5	3.0	11.7
Clerical and sales workers	2.4	12.9	7.8	14.2
Craftsmen, foremen, and kindred workers	6.4	18.5	10.8	20.4
Operatives and kindred workers	18.6	18.7	27.4	20.8
Service workers	11.2	3.7	21.4	5.8
Nonfarm laborers	23.6	5.8	24.9	7.0
Total nonfarm workers	65.6	78.1	97.9	88.2
Farmers and farm workers	34.4	21.9	2.1	11.8
Total	100.0	100.0	100.0	100.0

| | 1940 | | | |
| | South | | Other Regions | |
	Negro	White	Negro	White
Professional, technical, and kindred workers	1.6%	4.9%	3.1%	6.3%
Managers, officials, and proprietors	0.9	10.2	2.8	10.9
Clerical and sales workers	1.2	11.7	5.6	14.8
Craftsmen, foremen, and kindred workers	3.6	12.8	7.7	16.7
Operatives and kindred workers	10.9	16.0	19.6	20.0
Service workers	11.2	4.5	32.6	6.6
Nonfarm laborers	20.6	6.1	24.5	8.1
Total nonfarm workers	50.0	66.2	95.9	83.4
Farmers and farm workers	50.0	33.8	4.1	16.6
Total	100.0	100.0	100.0	100.0

Although the Negro continues to be highly disadvantaged in the urban economy, there are interesting developments. In pointing out that the proportion of northern Negroes in the upper-level occupations did not increase greatly between 1940 and 1950, Ginzberg notes that the cities of the North and West absorbed nearly two million new Negro residents during this period.[47] Most of these migrants from the South came in at the bottom. As can be seen in Table 12.2, there has been some increase in the proportion of Negroes employed at the higher job levels—from 7.3 percent to 12.2 percent in southern cities, and from 19.2 to 24.2 percent in the rest of the country.

[46] Eli Ginzberg, op. cit., p. 23.
[47] Ibid., p. 37.

In the South a number of employers have modified segregated employment procedures and have opened new opportunities for Negro
workers. Examples are found in Florida, North Carolina, Tennessee, and
Texas, and there are a few integrated plants in the deep South. One of
the leaders in providing new opportunities for Negroes is International
Harvester. This company's minority policy states that "there shall be
no discrimination against any person because of nationality, race, sex,
political or religious affiliation." Major plants are located at Evansville,
Indiana; Memphis, Tennessee; and Louisville, Kentucky. More than
half of the Negro workers in International Harvester's manufacturing
and raw-materials operations are in semiskilled jobs, about two-fifths
in unskilled work, and nearly 5 percent in clerical, technical, or managerial pursuits. Nearly one-fourth of the Negro employees were upgraded
during one year.[48] Some Negroes have been assigned to mixed production teams, and there are no differences in wages between white and
Negro employees performing the same task.

ETHNIC BACKGROUND AND INDUSTRIAL SPONSORSHIP

In considering recent changes in the types of work performed by
Negroes and members of other minorities, it is well to keep in mind
that ethnic background plays a part in job assignments. Embedded in
the industrial ideology of the western world is the belief in mobility,
that is, in ambition. Nevertheless, some managers

. . . speak with nostalgia of the unambitious first-generation of Poles,
French-Canadians or peasant-workers of other ethnic groups; people who
were content with their jobs, willing to work hard without hope of advancement. Of course, such people often had objectives outside industry to keep
them at work and content; notably, the desire to save money for buying
property. In spirit, they were not completely industrialized. A second or
later generation which insists on advancement within industry is compared
unfavorably with their fathers. The hostile reaction of many managers to
ambitious Negroes is too well-known to require documenting.[49]

Management, then, does not want all people, or certain kinds of people,
to be ambitious for promotion. Hughes reports that one large American
industrial concern has a breed known as the "Thank God for" people—
"the unambitious people who can be counted on to stay where they are,
and who keep things running while others are busy climbing the mobility ladder from one job to another."

[48] John Hope, II, "Negro Employment in Three Southern Plants of International
Harvester Company," in *Selected Studies of Negro Employment in the South*, National Planning Committee of the South (National Planning Association), 1953, pp.
16–17, 125–127.

[49] E. C. Hughes, "Queries Concerning Industry and Society Growing Out of
Study of Ethnic Relations in Industry," *American Sociological Review*, April, 1949,
p. 218.

Those in the higher levels of an industrial hierarchy have the power to keep their own ranks ethnically and racially exclusive. Through the mechanism of sponsorship, "promising young people are picked and encouraged in their mobility efforts by their superiors. In the course of their rise, they are not merely given a technical training, but also are initiated into the ways and sentiments of the managerial group and are judged by their internal acceptance of them. Ethnic, national and class loyalty are undoubtedly factors in the original choice of people to be sponsored and in their later rise."[50]

An interesting case of ethnic behavior in industry is presented by Orvis Collins, who found that in a New England factory the most important qualification after technical efficiency was ethnic identification. Ethnic qualification was necessary for holding certain jobs, with the result that a pattern of ethnic job expectations, sponsorship, and rejection has developed. Managerial jobs (president, vice-presidents, superintendents, personnel officials) are held by individuals of Yankee stock. Supervisory jobs are held almost exclusively by Irish; the "work level" jobs are held by other than Yankee or Irish.[51]

Negroes and Labor Unions

The role of labor organizations in discouraging or encouraging Negro members is an important part of the industrial experience of colored people. In earlier years the techniques used by labor unions to retard the employment of Negroes included "withholding membership from Negroes by means of constitutional provisions, by means of a provision of the ritual, or as an unwritten policy of the international or the local union; accepting Negro members but discriminating against them in referrals; hindering the up-grading of Negroes; championing the up-grading and employment of Negroes in plants in which the union has no bargaining agreements, while taking no action to correct discrimination in plants in which the union has an agreement."[52]

During the past twenty-five years there has been a sharp contrast between the racial policies of trade or craft unions on the one hand and industrial unions on the other. In general, the industrial unions have been much more favorable to the admission of Negroes than the trade unions. Exceptions to this generalization will be noted later.

American trade unions range from total exclusion of Negroes to full membership acceptance of them. Also, trade-union policies vary to some extent from community to community and from time to time according to circumstances. A union with liberal attitudes on race may force its rival to change its policies, and an exclusionist union may cause

[50] *Ibid.*, p. 219.
[51] Orvis Collins, "Ethnic Behavior in Industry: Sponsorship and Rejection in a New England Factory," *American Journal of Sociology*, January, 1946, pp. 293–295.
[52] R. C. Weaver, *Negro Labor*, p. 217.

a competitor to modify its principles in the hope of avoiding alienation of its predominantly white membership.

The exclusionary and discriminatory practices of trade unions have a long history, and most of the members of these unions favor them. The main reason for the prevailing trade-union attitudes seems to be the "scarcity consciousness" of craft workers. Skilled craft unionists have sought to restrict competition in order to obtain more work for themselves and higher wages. The fraternal and beneficial features of most of the railroad unions have been stumbling blocks to economic equalitarianism. The white members of these unions regard themselves as "the aristocrats of labor" in the skilled-semiskilled-unskilled hierarchy. They have refused to admit Negroes to their organizations because such a step would seem to imply that the colored man is a "social equal" (whatever that means), and thus far they have been unable to make such a concession.

A small number of trade unions do not officially and nationally exclude or restrict Negroes but do tolerate discrimination by the local branches through the organization of separate locals. Membership in a Negro auxiliary union usually means second-class union status. Auxiliary unions do not manage their own affairs, nor do they have any means of effectively influencing the supervising of white locals. The auxiliaries may be used to limit the number of colored workers, and they can be manipulated so that Negro workers are deprived of seniority rights. Grievance protection for the members of the auxiliary unions is frequently lacking in aggressiveness.[53]

The Congress of Industrial Organizations stated in its constitution that one of its main purposes was to "bring about the effective organization of the working men and women of America regardless of race, color, creed, or nationality." Most of the constituent unions of the CIO were of the industrial type; that is, they included all workers in a mass-production industry regardless of craft, skill, or lack of skill. No national CIO union barred Negroes or segregated colored members in an auxiliary. This did not mean that there was no discrimination in any of the CIO unions on either an individual or a local organization basis. On the whole, the CIO unions were much more active in facilitating the employment of Negroes than was the AFL. However, in many cases the CIO unions were slow in acting, and a number of work stoppages were caused by the introduction of colored workers into plants or occupations where they had not been employed previously. To reduce such incidents the national officers of the CIO issued strong statements on the subject of racial discrimination, some CIO unions had constitutional provisions prohibiting discrimination, and a number of

[53] Herbert Northrup, *Organized Labor and the Negro,* Harper & Brothers, 1944, p. 218.

these unions had special race-relations machinery to enforce their official policies. In addition, the CIO formed a National Committee to Abolish Racial Discrimination. This committee had a full-time director and established dozens of local, county, and state antidiscrimination committees.[54]

Brief accounts of the experience of Negroes in several important industries will illustrate the points made above. From its founding in 1890, the United Mine Workers has admitted all workers without regard to race, creed, or nationality. In the steel industry, the national officers of the United Steelworkers of America have stood for racial equality, and in general the same results among the workers have been found as in the coal industry. Negroes do not yet participate as fully as whites in union operations, but their participation is increasing. Negro activity in union matters is greater in Cleveland and Pittsburgh than in Birmingham.

The International Ladies' Garment Workers' Union has from its inception accepted workers regardless of race or color. It is an industrial union made up largely of immigrant workers who are strongly opposed to any kind of discrimination. In addition, the ILGWU has been characterized by strong interests in coöperative, humanitarian, and progressive enterprises. The general social philosophy of this union, in addition to its official policy, leaves little room for race prejudice.

The policies and philosophy of the Amalgamated Clothing Workers are similar in most respects to those of the ILGWU, but the number of Negro clothing workers included in its membership is much smaller than the 10,000 Negroes in the ILGWU. A colored organizer was engaged in 1919 to enroll the Negroes who had recently come into the industry. "Later, when Baltimore, Cincinnati and Richmond were organized, the Negroes, mainly pressers, were taken in as a matter of course. The same policy has been followed in the organization of cotton garment factories in recent years. A sizable portion of the southern cotton garment industry remains unorganized, as do the summer goods houses in New Orleans, where a fairly large proportion of Negroes are employed."[55]

In addition to (1) the "liberal" craft unions, (2) the unions which before the merger were members of the CIO, and (3) former AFL unions organized mainly on an industrial basis, that is, the Ladies' Garment Workers and the Hat, Cap, and Millinery Workers, the organizations which include workers engaged primarily in unskilled or semi-skilled labor, that is, the Hod Carriers, Building and Common Laborers, and the International Longshoremen's Association, usually offer membership on an equal basis to Negroes and whites.

[54] R. C. Weaver, *Negro Labor*, pp. 219–220.
[55] Herbert Northrup, *op. cit.*, p. 129.

The International Longshoremen's Association has always officially opposed racial discrimination. A large percentage of its members are Negroes, and in some years four of its fifteen vice-presidents have been colored. Race relations within the union vary from city to city, but in many cases they are amicable.

The Laundry Workers International Union admits Negroes without discrimination, and in the North Negroes are well represented in the various offices of the organization. This union has not made much headway in the South where the largest proportion of Negroes in the industry work, although there are a few locals in Galveston, Miami, Birmingham, and Tampa. Laundry workers in several cities, including New York, Detroit, and New Orleans, have been organized by the LWIU's rival, the Amalgamated Clothing Workers.[56] Members are referred by this union without reference to race, but employers may discriminate in the selection or retention of the workers. Negroes participate in the extensive educational and recreational activities of the Amalgamated at least as fully as whites.

In the tobacco industry, the Tobacco Workers International Union has forbidden racial or color discrimination since its founding in 1895, but it has usually organized Negroes in the South into segregated locals. Within the past decade the policies of this union have been liberalized to some extent. Local unions, Negro and white, have met together to discuss problems, and a policy of mixed unions "whenever possible" has been adopted. In general, though, the TWIU has not questioned the racial lines of the traditional job pattern in the tobacco industry. On the other hand, the United Cannery, Agricultural Packing and Allied Workers of America, which has had jurisdiction over tobacco workers since 1941, has made some attempts to modify the racial employment pattern. In 1943 it won bargaining rights for 12,000 white and Negro workers of the R. J. Reynolds Company in Winston-Salem, North Carolina. It remains to be seen whether unions composed of Negroes and whites, as well as of both sexes, can operate in the South. Northrup believes that a general change in employment opportunities is unlikely for some time, and he points out that the UCAPAWA in Winston-Salem has been compelled to deny that it is promoting "social equality." Also, white workers would undoubtedly protest any major changes in the job pattern, and colored workers would oppose the introduction of whites into stemmeries because of the loss of the limited employment opportunities which they now have. Northrup concludes, "It, therefore, does not seem probable that unionism will alter the racial-occupational segregation pattern in the tobacco industry in the near future."[57]

---

[56] *Ibid.*, p. 134.
[57] *Ibid.*, pp. 117–118.

The United Mine Workers of America has always been an industrial union admitting all workers "in and around the mines." The two races are mixed to a considerable degree in actual mining operations in the South, although there are differences in the racial distribution of types of jobs. Also, relationships within the southern locals have been worked out so that an adverse public opinion has not arisen. The number of Negro miners has declined sharply, and will probably continue to decrease, because of the competition of other fuels, more efficient utilization of fuels, and the greater use of loading machines. Negroes have been concentrated in hand loading operations, and thus far they have not received a proportionate share of machine loading jobs.[58]

Before World War II, Negroes were concentrated in unskilled work in the automobile industry, and such skilled occupations as they had were usually the most undesirable or hazardous. Most of this industry was organized by the United Automobile, Aircraft, and Agricultural Implement Workers of America between 1937 and 1941. The UAW has always admitted workers to membership regardless of race; but in spite of this policy, union organization had not made any great difference in the racial distribution of jobs prior to Pearl Harbor. In the war period the situation changed somewhat, with the hiring of Negroes in new types of jobs and the upgrading of many colored workers. An important agreement signed in July, 1957, by the UAW and the National Urban League calls for the elimination of racial discrimination in plants employing the union's one and a half million members. Approximately 20 percent of the union's members are Negroes. The agreement provides for coöperative action by the Urban League and the UAW's Fair Practices Committee in dealing with cases of discrimination. When the agreement was announced, Walter Reuther said: "Wage differentials on the basis of race, creed or color have been entirely eliminated. Except for isolated instances that occur from time to time, discrimination in the matter of promotions and transfers to more desirable jobs has been eliminated."[59]

The UAW local unions in the aircraft industry have never discriminated against Negroes, and in some plants they have pressed for the upgrading of colored workers. The UAW has organized as much of the aircraft industry as the Machinists, a discriminatory union.

The years since 1940 have brought a major change in policies in most of the important unions outside the South and, to some extent, even in the South.[60] Some unions still refuse to admit Negroes; others have

---

[58] *Ibid.*, pp. 160–167.

[59] Cleveland *Plain Dealer*, July 11, 1957, p. 4. L. T. Hawley (*op. cit.*, p. 258) points out that the UAW's skilled-trades department is effectively segregated. There are fewer than a dozen Negroes among all of General Motors' automotive tool-and-die personnel in the United States.

[60] Eli Ginzberg, *op. cit.*, p. 37.

changed their by-laws to eliminate discrimination, but Negroes have little chance of being accepted. As a rule, collective bargaining in the South operates to freeze whatever racial division of labor is established when a plant is first organized.[61] In 1952 no more than 5 percent of the organized workers in the South were Negro, and the larger firms (two hundred or more employees) that are of greatest interest to organizers are mostly in textiles and furniture manufacture—both predominantly white industries.[62] In some occupations the formidable obstacles to apprenticeship training are due in part to union policies. In the building trades, for example, unions have considerable control over the admission of apprentices, and this control is used frequently to exclude Negroes.[63]

International Harvester's minority policy was adopted before unions obtained bargaining rights in the Evansville, Memphis, and Louisville plants; but nearly all of the union locals, both CIO and AFL, which became representatives of the workers accepted the policy and included it in their contracts with management.[64] An outstanding effort to combat racial discrimination is found in the application of the national antidiscrimination program of the United Packinghouse Workers of America to its southern locals. All master contracts with the Big Four packers (Swift, Cudahy, Armour, and Wilson) contain nondiscrimination clauses outlawing discrimination against applicants or employees in plants over which it has jurisdiction. Among the southern cities where plant desegregation in the Cudahy and Armour companies is proceeding are Fort Worth, Atlanta, Birmingham, Albany, Tifton, and Moultrie (Georgia).[65] An important union development for Negroes occurred in the middle 1950's in the oil industry. The first changes came when the Sinclair and Shell refineries in the Houston area opened job categories which had been closed to Negroes. Later, after a bitter struggle with leaders of the white local, the Oil, Chemical and Atomic Workers signed a new contract with the Beaumont, Texas, refinery of Magnolia Petroleum (subsidiary of Socony Mobil) assuring new Negro job opportunities. Other oil companies have had to follow suit.[66] Hawley quotes a NAACP leader on the importance of these achievements: "What has mattered so much here has been the danger to the Negro of rapidly increasing mechanization. So long as he remained sealed in the lowest job categories, there was the gravest chance that he would soon be displaced by machines entirely, and so wholly driven from the industry itself."

[61] Donald Dewey, *op. cit.*, p. 289.
[62] *Ibid.*, p. 290.
[63] *Ibid.*, pp. 105–106.
[64] John Hope, II, *op. cit.*, pp. 125–126.
[65] John Hope, II, "Efforts to Eliminate Racial Discrimination in Industry—With Particular Reference to the South," *Journal of Negro Education*, Summer, 1954, pp. 263, 266.
[66] L. T. Hawley, *op. cit.*, p. 256.

Some progress against union discrimination has been made through state laws and FEP commissions. Eighteen states now prohibit discrimination in union membership because of race or religion. The New York State Commission Against Discrimination has persuaded several unions to eliminate racial restrictions from their by-laws, and a number of unions have suspended restricted provisions in FEPC states. The Connecticut Commission on Civil Rights ordered the electrical workers to cease discriminating against Negroes. Oregon ordered the Brotherhood of Railway Carmen to admit five Negroes. The California Supreme Court outlawed the segregated auxiliaries of the boilermakers, and the Kansas Supreme Court took the same action against railway carmen.[67] The Cleveland Community Relations Board (municipal FEP body) ordered the International Brotherhood of Electrical Workers, Local 38, to cease from denying a Negro electrical worker membership because of his race.[68]

The shift which tens of thousands of Negroes have made in the last few decades, both in the North and in the South, from personal and domestic service to industrial work has many economic and noneconomic consequences.[69] From an economic standpoint, it has meant higher pay and more regular work. But there are broader implications as well. The association of majority and minority workers in union meetings, picnics, picket lines, and elsewhere has sometimes affected "racial" attitudes. A colored shop chairman in a small plant said of the changed atmosphere in his concern: " 'Well, I'll tell you what the CIO has done. Before, everyone used to make remarks about 'that dirty Jew,' 'that stinkin' black bastard,' 'that lowlife Bohunk,' but you know I never hear that kind of stuff any more.' "[70]

Drake and Cayton found little evidence in Chicago that "the basic patterns of separate Negro and white family, clique, and associational relationships, other than union relationships, have been much affected by these developments." It is not suggested that the meeting of Negroes and whites in factories and in unions always results in greater understanding, but qualified observers believe that the organization of these and other "racial" groups has resolved many of the antagonisms which existed in the past. Another result of the greater participation of

[67] John A. Davis, "Negro Employment: A Progress Report," *Fortune*, July, 1952, pp. 161–162.
[68] *Race Relations Law Reporter*, October, 1956, p. 979.
[69] See C. A. Anderson and M. J. Bowman, "The Vanishing Servant and the Contemporary Status System of the American South," *American Journal of Sociology*, November, 1953, pp. 215–230. "The incidence of servants in the nation dropped from 20 to 15 per thousand during and after the first World War, and this new lower level was stabilized for another twenty years. Then came another drop to 9 servants per thousand persons in 1950, a decline for the decade 1940–50 twice as large as that in the period 1910–20. The larger shrinkage in the later period is attributable in part to the greater participation of the South in the change."
[70] St. Clair Drake and Horace Cayton, *op. cit.*, p. 326.

Negroes in industry has been an increase in self-respect. Also, changes in self-attitudes, plus increased pay and steadier work, have resulted in more stability in Negro family life.[71]

Kornhauser makes an interesting distinction between the roles of "trade unions" and of the "labor movement." The former is a highly organized service institution demanding specific changes in its members' terms of employment. The labor movement is a loosely organized social movement expressing new ideas concerning the worker's position in society. Race-relations programs are a part of the ideological conceptions of labor intellectuals and reformers. Such programs are marginal to the trade union as an interest group. When unions become involved in race-relations questions, they devise tactics to meet the situation rather than developing formal programs. If a union is confronted with competition for its Negro members from another union, dissatisfaction from those members, etc., it may sponsor a Negro for higher union office. In this way it hopes to gain the allegiance of Negro members. Thus the Negro's position in the union is improved when race relations bear directly upon the union's interest.[72]

Labor organization may have effects on race relations beyond the plant situation, but it cannot be assumed that the nondiscriminatory behavior of union members on the job will lead to the same kind of behavior in the community.[73] Union leaders who wish to influence neighborhood policies must be aware of the organizational structuring of the community and must be able to show that nondiscriminatory behavior will serve the individuals' interests better than discriminatory behavior.[74]

The question of school desegregation has affected labor organization in the South. A leader of Montgomery's typographical union said: "First we are white men—then union men." Some angry white union leaders in International Harvester's Memphis plant are quoted as saying: " 'We'll take segregation and leave you guys up in Detroit.' " The editor of the *Alabama Labor News* wrote: "If Walter Reuther and his left-wing civil-rights committee attempt to force upon us their theories,

[71] E. Franklin Frazier, *The Negro Family in the United States*, University of Chicago Press, 1939, p. 475.

[72] William Kornhauser, "Ideology and Interests," *Journal of Social Issues*, 1953, vol. 9, No. 1, pp. 49–50.

[73] A Chicago study of Negro-white interaction in three situations involving white industrial workers (the residential neighborhood, the industrial work situation, and neighborhood shopping centers) found that there was no evidence to support the common belief that persons who show a high degree of acceptance of Negroes on the job will necessarily show a low degree of rejection of Negroes in their home communities. J. D. Lohman and D. C. Reitzes, "Notes on Race Relations in Mass Society," *American Journal of Sociology*, November, 1952, p. 244.

[74] D. C. Reitzes, "The Role of Organizational Structures," *Journal of Social Issues*, 1953, vol. 9, No. 1, pp. 43–44. See also Arnold M. Rose, "The Influence of a Border City Union on the Race Attitudes of Its Members," *Journal of Social Issues*, 1953, vol. 9, No. 1, p. 23.

then and there you will see one of the damnedest rebellions you have ever witnessed." As Hawley points out, such threats may be largely bluff, but they have helped to slow down the AFL-CIO organizing campaign throughout the South.[75]

In summary, unionism has had and will continue to have important effects on the economic life of American minorities and on racial and ethnic relations in general. Most of the important unions in expanding industries, with the exception of the Machinists, the Electrical Workers, the Plumbers and Steamfitters, and the Railroad Trainmen, seem to favor the improvement of the economic position of the Negro. Labor unions have at least one and a quarter million Negro members. Weaver states that "organized labor, as a whole, has become an economic and political ally of the black worker."[76] Insofar as the merger of the CIO and the AFL has any effect on the question of racial discrimination, it should serve to extend nondiscriminatory policies.

MANAGEMENT AND THE MINORITY-GROUP WORKER

Management plays an important role in introducing minorities into new types of work. If management is convinced of the need for Negro or other minority workers, it can usually transmit its conviction to supervisors, foremen, and workers.[77] This point is illustrated by the change in management's attitude during World War II. In the early part of the war effort, management often said that white and colored labor would not work together. This reason for not using Negroes was given despite the fact that there was much evidence in the history of American industry to refute it. The records of the largest meat-packing plants, the tobacco industry, some automobile factories, northern and southern shipyards, iron and steel plants in both the North and the South, and a few other important branches of industry showed that racial groups could work together. The war years demonstrated more possibilities

---

[75] L. T. Hawley, op. cit., p. 256. On the threat of withdrawal by many local unions in protest against national AFL-CIO support of school desegregation, see Henry L. Trewhitt, "Southern Unions and the Integration Issue," The Reporter, October 4, 1956, pp. 25–28. A survey of more than 100 representative locals in Alabama, Florida, Georgia, North Carolina, South Carolina, Tennessee, Louisiana, and Mississippi, prepared for the AFL-CIO, showed that two-thirds of these locals have both Negro and white membership, and one-quarter have at least one Negro officer. None of these locals has disaffiliated because of the national organization's position on the Supreme Court's school decision. The survey warned that the race issue could seriously disrupt many southern local unions, and recommended a comprehensive program for assisting local union leaders in the South in coping with current racial problems. NAIRO Reporter, June, 1957, p. 4.

[76] R. C. Weaver, "The Economic Status of the Negro in the United States," p. 241.

[77] An interesting booklet was published during World War II on the integration of Negro workers in industry: John A. Davis, How Management Can Integrate Negroes in War Industries, New York State Committee on Discrimination in Employment, 1942.

along these lines. "During World War II American industry introduced scores of thousands of colored workers into new establishments and occupations in aircraft, ordnance, machinery, electrical goods, rubber, and ship-building. The fact that aircraft, which started out with a pronounced and announced color prejudice, had by the end of 1944 hired some 100,000 Negroes shows that management can successfully introduce and up-grade Negro workers."[78]

As Northrup points out, there are some industries, especially textile manufacturing, the printing trades, and clerical and white-collar pursuits, where Negroes are generally excluded by the decisions of management. "Undoubtedly, however, such decisions meet with the approval, if not the assistance of the majority of the white workers in these fields."[79]

EARNINGS OF NEGROES IN THE UNITED STATES

The average (median) income per family for whites in 1935–1936 was $1100 in southern rural communities, $1570 in southern cities of 2500 population and over, and $1720 in north central cities of 100,000 population and over. For Negroes in that year it was $480, $525, and $1095 respectively.[80] In 1945, the median family income for whites was $2718 and $1538 for Negroes. Urban white families had a median income of $3085 as compared with $2052 for urban Negro families; the figures for rural-farm families were $1602 and $559, respectively.[81] According to Myrdal, the one-tenth of the United States population which is Negro did not receive more than 4 percent of the national income, and the actual percentage was probably 3.[82]

Significant gains in earnings were made by the nonwhite population of the United States during the war years, but more than 40 percent of urban and rural nonwhite families earned less than $1500 in 1948 and 11 percent received under $500. In spite of the greater prosperity of farm families in the years immediately following World War II, more than half of the nonwhite rural families earned less than $1000 a year in 1948, and an additional one-sixth earned less than $1500. Concerning urban communities in the United States, Weaver reports:

 . . . Despite the economic privation of the lowest-paid third of the Negro population, about one-half of the residents have something approaching an adequate economic base, and there is a growing number of Negro families

---

[78] R. C. Weaver, *Negro Labor*, p. 194.

[79] Herbert Northrup, *op. cit.*, p. 6.

[80] Maurice R. Davie, *Negroes in American Society*, McGraw-Hill Book Company, 1949, p. 109; the source is the U.S. Resources Committee, *Consumer Incomes in the United States*, p. 28. For a discussion of family incomes, family expenditures, relief grants, and housing conditions see Richard Sterner, *The Negro's Share*, Harper & Brothers, 1943, chaps. 5–12. A. F. Raper and I. De A. Reid, *op. cit.*, pp. 99, 102, 240, discuss differential wages for Negroes, including the devices used in the industrial codes which were a part of the NRA program of the New Deal.

[81] Maurice R. Davie, *op. cit.*, p. 108.

[82] Gunnar Myrdal, *An American Dilemma*, Harper & Brothers, 1944, p. 307.

which can afford decent standards of living. This stands in striking contrast to the situation in 1935 when, in our larger metropolitan centers, less than five per cent of Negro families eaned $2,000 or more (as contrasted to about 25 per cent of white families) and in smaller cities the figure ranged from one to two per cent. Today, over 8 per cent of urban Negro families earn $5,000 a year or more.[83]

Weaver points out that the gap between the earnings of whites and Negroes is slowly being narrowed.

For the United States as a whole, median family income for whites in 1948 was estimated at $3,310. For non-whites (of whom 95 per cent were Negroes) the figure was $1,768. In urban areas corresponding figures were $3,694 for whites and $2,172 for non-whites; rural averages were $4,435 for whites and $942 for Negroes. Both extremes of the distribution are revealing. Only a tenth of urban white families earned less than $1,500 per year, almost a third non-whites did. Slightly less than a fourth of the white urban families earned from $1,500 to $2,999, while four-tenths of the non-whites fell in this interval. Four-tenths of urban white and one-fifth urban non-white families received from $3,000 to $4,999, and over a quarter of the white and a twelfth of the non-whites had $5,000 or over. Lowest earnings are in the South, and Negro agricultural workers earn, on the average, much less than other Negroes, but the number and proportion of Negro farm laborers has greatly declined in recent years.[84]

Table 12.3 compares the money incomes of white and nonwhite families in the United States in 1954.

TABLE 12.3.   Median Money Income of U.S. Families by Race, Region, and Residence, 1954[85]

	White	Nonwhite	Percent Nonwhite of White
Total U.S.	$4339	$2410	56
Total urban	4827	2876	60
South	4428	2425	56
Northeast	4837	3243	67
North Central	5059	3283	65
West	4812	n.a.	n.a.
Total rural-farm	2157	763	49
South	1516	742	49

Data are given here for all nonwhites together whenever such data are available from Census publications and when separate Negro data are not available. Since Negroes constitute 95 percent of the nonwhite population, data for nonwhites represent a close approximation of data for Negroes alone.

[83] Robert C. Weaver, "The Economic Status of the Negro in the United States," p. 242.
[84] *Ibid.*, p. 241.
[85] Eli Ginzberg, *op. cit.*, p. 16.

Two *Fortune* charts (Figure 12.1) compare the increases in the Negro urban population of the United States and in Negro cash income. Two other *Fortune* charts (Figure 12.2) compare the U.S. Negro's

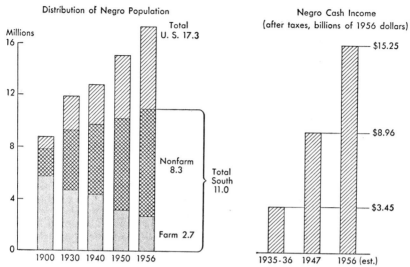

FIGURE 12.1. "The related rises in Negro urban population and Negro income is shown by the upward steps of these two charts, like matching stairs. In the last fifteen years (left) Negro nonfarm population (including nonfarm workers in rural areas) has risen from 8,500,000 to 14,600,000. Farm population has declined by 1,700,000. The cash income of Negroes, over the last twenty years, has soared almost 350 per cent (right). Their present income of $15.25 billion represents a sum almost as great as the value of all goods exported annually by the U.S."

income with the per capita income in four other countries and show the income of Negro and white family units in the United States.[86]

Minority Business Operations

Barriers faced by minority-group members in entering upon jobs in the business field, and obstacles to their success if they have gained an entrance, are even more difficult than those faced in jobs in industry. Fundamental questions of social power and status are involved in business occupations in a way that concerns some of the most basic aspects of our society. In general, where large-scale organizations have dominated a field, minorities have had small opportunities; in businesses where individual shops and isolated small establishments are feasible they have had more success.

[86] Figures 12.1 and 12.2 are from L. T. Hawley, "The Negro's New Economic Life," *Fortune*, September, 1956, © 1956 by Time Inc., pp. 128 and 129 respectively.

Negro Business

Negroes as a group are poor, but seventeen million people constitute a sizable market. Negro business enterprise, however, is concentrated in fields which are not subject to the full competition of white business. Pierce's study showed that more than 70 percent of Negro business

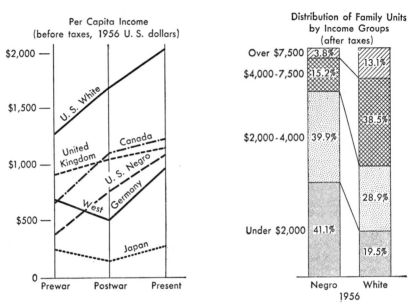

FIGURE 12.2.   (Left) "The rise in Negro per capita income, from a prewar $384 to a present $1,070, is dramatically highlighted by this comparison with other populations. The U.S. Negro's income today surpasses even that of the prosperous West German. Measured in percentage terms, the Negro's income has climbed from a prewar 30 per cent of U.S. white income to a present 53 per cent."

(Right) "The still remaining gap between Negro and U.S. white incomes is shown at right. Of all Negro families, 81 per cent—as against 48 per cent of white families —have incomes of less than $4,000. Despite Negroes' progress, 41 per cent of them are still in the category 'under $2,000.' "

establishments in twelve cities were in such personal service fields as beauty shops, barber shops, cleaning and pressing shops, shoe repair shops, undertaking establishments, taverns, and filling stations, and in food stores and eating and drinking places.[87]

Negro businesses are small businesses, as may be seen both in the volume of transactions and in the number of employees involved. Pierce's survey of 3866 retail stores, service establishments, and miscellaneous businesses showed that almost 70 percent of these concerns had

[87] J. A. Pierce, *Negro Business and Business Education*, Harper & Brothers, 1947. See also Robert Kinzer and Edward Sagarin, *The Negro in American Business*, Greenberg: Publisher, 1950.

a volume of less than $10,000. Actually, the proportion is probably higher because 17 percent of the businesses included in the study did not specify their volumes. Less than 5 percent of these establishments reported a volume of $25,000 or more.[88] The latter establishments fall in the miscellaneous business category, and specifically in life insurance companies and casket factories. The same study found that the average number of employees per retail store is 2.8, 2.3 for the service establishment, and 9.1 for the miscellaneous business.

Although it might seem that Negro business has a chance to monopolize the Negro market, the actual situation is that racial enterprises get but a small fraction of the money spent by colored people. For example, the whole Negro population spent only $24,000,000 in food stores operated by Negroes in 1939, or less than two dollars per person for the year.[89] In 1938 Negroes owned and operated 2600 businesses in Chicago, whereas whites had about 2800 enterprises within the black belt. According to Drake and Cayton, the Negro businesses did less than one-tenth of all the business in the Negro areas.[90] In Pierce's study of Negro businesses, 99 percent of the Negro consumers buy clothing and shoes from white businessmen. The percentage of Negroes who buy furniture, hardware, and other household supplies in Negro stores is only slightly higher. The grocery stores get 28 percent of the Negro trade, and the service establishments receive a much larger proportion of Negro business. For shoe repairs, cleaning and pressing, and tailoring, the percentages run between 75 and 80.[91]

In the Pierce survey, none of the operators said they have no Negro customers and only 3 percent said that less than half of their patrons are Negroes. Forty-four percent of the businesses in this sample have only Negro patronage, and 84 percent have clienteles which are 80 percent or more Negro.[92]

Despite the efforts of many Negro businessmen to capitalize on race, and the many appeals which are made to racial solidarity, loyalty, and pride, the chief reasons listed by Negro consumers for buying goods and services of all kinds are good quality, nearness to home, good styles, courteous service, and low prices.[93] There is no mention here of supporting businessmen because they are Negroes.

Negro businessmen often have to compete with Jews, Greeks, Italians, and other whites who seek Negro trade. These non-Negro business operators provide strong competition for these reasons: (1) they have available more capital and easier credit, (2) they may offer better serv-

[88] *Ibid.*, p. 70.
[89] *Ibid.*, p. 32.
[90] St. Clair Drake and Horace Cayton, *op. cit.*, p. 438.
[91] J. A. Pierce, *op. cit.*, pp. 52–53.
[92] *Ibid.*, p. 51.
[93] *Ibid.*, p. 53.

ice, (3) they can buy a wider variety of standard goods, (4) they frequently have had more training and experience, (5) they ingratiate themselves with their Negro customers by seeming to be much interested in their welfare; in addition, (6) the Negro businessmen are unable to obtain choice locations on the main business streets, (7) they lack sufficient patronage to enable them to acquire capital and to make improvements, (8) they cannot organize for coöperative action, and (9) many Negroes expect that Negro businessmen will deal with them on the basis of friendship rather than in a strictly business manner.[94]

A concept which is fairly closely related to the doctrine of a separate Negro economy is the attempt to find employment for Negroes in white businesses which serve Negro buyers. The slogan of this movement is "Don't Buy Where You Can't Work." If carried to its logical conclusion this campaign would mean the displacement of all white workers in these establishments. The advisability of trying to promote a "semiseparate Negro economy" has been strongly condemned by economists because of the probable boomerang effect of this type of boycott. As Abram Harris says, ". . . In final analysis it would be the hundreds of thousands of black workers in white industry who would have to bear the cost of the movement's success in obtaining a few thousand jobs for Negro clerks, salesmen, and managers. What would be more natural than a retaliatory movement of whites demanding that Negroes be employed only by those white capitalists whose income is mainly derived from Negro patronage?"[95]

An interesting and serious aspect of the separate Negro economy and the semiseparate economy is the prejudice they encourage against other groups, especially the Jewish people.

Denied equal competition with whites in the higher positions of the capitalist set-up and thwarted in its ambition to develop a miniature capitalism within its own segregated racial domain, the Negro middle class is being driven into a position of extreme racial chauvinism toward other minorities. It views these minorities, especially the Jew, as the source of its economic frustrations rather than as the mirror of the small man's common weaknesses and . . . aspirations. In Harlem . . . there is a growing feeling that the Jewish landlord and the Jewish shopkeeper are responsible for the high rents and prices of that Negro city. This exploitation is felt to be doubly oppressive because these Jewish business concerns afford employment to only a small number of Negroes. . . . With the exception of a few large concerns . . . the establishments owned by Jews in Harlem depend upon the immediate family for labor and therefore could not increase their employment of Negroes any more than can the approximately two hundred and sixty

[94] St. Clair Drake and Horace Cayton, op. cit., p. 437; J. A. Pierce, op. cit., p. 23.
[95] A. L. Harris, The Negro as Capitalist, American Academy of Political and Social Science, 1936, p. 181.

Negro stores in Harlem. While it may be true that the Jews constitute the largest group of business men from a single racial group and may, for this reason, be the chief beneficiaries of Harlem's high rents and prices, it is silly to see anything especially Jewish in the exploitation. If there is exploitation of the black masses in Harlem, the Negro business man participates in it as well as the Jew, while both the Jewish business man and the Negro are governed by higher forces that are beyond their control.[96]

Similar reports have come from Chicago, but in New Orleans the Italian merchants are the scapegoats.

In 1938, about three-fourths of the merchants in Bronzeville [the Negro community of Chicago] were Jewish. During that year an organized anti-Semitic drive arose in Bronzeville. A small newspaper, *Dynamite*, scurrilously attacked all Jews. Jewish philanthropists were accused of trying to dominate Negro institutions; Jewish merchants were dubbed exploiters. Suggestions were made that all Jews should be expelled from Bronzeville. Finally, after conferences between Negro and Jewish leaders as well as representatives of various labor unions, the editor of the paper was dissuaded from publishing further attacks. . . . As the most highly visible and most immediately available white persons in the community, Jewish merchants tend to become the symbol of the Negroes' verbal attack on all white businessmen, and anti-Semitic waves sometimes sweep through Bronzeville. In New Orleans, where Italian merchants predominate in Negro areas, "Dagoes" are the target of attack.[97]

The participation of Negroes in wholesaling and manufacturing has been extremely limited. In Pierce's study of Negro business, there were no wholesale firms and only nineteen manufacturing concerns in twelve cities. These manufacturing businesses were distributed as follows: cosmetics—eight; caskets—five; artificial flowers, cabinets, food, and hair—one each. The explanation of the Negro's failure to go more extensively into manufacture seems to be that (1) he has not been able to obtain the necessary experience for the successful operation of such concerns, and (2) he lacks capital and credit.[98]

---

[96] *Ibid.*, p. 183.

[97] St. Clair Drake and Horace Cayton, *op. cit.*, p. 432.

[98] J. A. Pierce, *op. cit.*, pp. 224–225. Writing in 1950 of trends in Negro-controlled enterprise after World War II, Robert C. Weaver said: "As in the post-World War I boom, the greatest advances are being made in those businesses, undertaking, insurance, publishing, beauty culture, and the like, which serve a segregated community. At the same time, a few individual Negroes are branching out into the larger economy, where they are manufacturing chemicals, medical supplies, constructing large buildings and roads and doing scores of other things. The tragedy in this situation is that in 1950, when the well-trained Negro is ready to compete effectively in most fields and is finding unexpected opportunities in governmental, education, and professional callings, the American economy is less receptive to the new enterpriser than it has ever been before. Much of the real business talent, therefore, is shunted off into shady enterprise as typified by policy." Robert C. Weaver, "The Economic Status of the Negro in the United States," p. 242. See St. Clair Drake and Horace Cayton, *op. cit.*, chap. 17, for a discussion of the policy racket.

In 1951, the fourteen banks owned and operated by Negroes had total assets amounting to $32,000,000 and total deposits of $29,000,000. With the exception of one bank in Philadelphia, another in Washington, D.C., and a third in Kansas City, Kansas, all of these banks were located in the South. These banks employed from three to fifteen persons.[99] In pointing out the insignificance of Negro banking, Myrdal states that "there were not even 1,000 Negro bankers, brokers, cashiers, and other white collar workers in banks in 1930, or less than one for every 600 white workers in such occupations."[100] Harris sees no economic justification for the Negro bank and considers that its continued existence is due to race prejudice on the part of whites and race pride from the standpoint of Negroes. According to Harris, the "Negro banker like the Negro business man is an uneconomic man, and the same circumstances that force the one to carry on his petty trade at the margin of gain, force the other to do likewise in the realm of small finance. Like the Negro business man, the Negro banker is a marginal man whose opportunities for profit are few." He concludes that the Negro masses have no real need of banking, and that their needs may be met best by the credit union, the industrial loan society, and the building and loan society.[101] Neither Myrdal nor Harris sees any real future for a segregated Negro financial system. The former regards Negro banks as a poor substitute for the employment of Negroes in white-owned financial institutions "and more consideration for them as insurance or credit seekers."[102] Harris advocates the transformation of Negro banks into actual subsidiaries of larger white banks.[103]

There are forty-four Negro insurance companies, and more progress has been made in this field than in banking. Some 9000 Negro officials and white-collar workers are in the insurance business, but they constitute only 2 percent of the national total. One white establishment is known to have more Negro business than all of the Negro-owned companies together.[104]

The 169 Negro newspapers in the United States (85 in the South, 66 in the North, 18 in the West; 162 weeklies, 5 semiweeklies, and 2 dailies) have an estimated total valuation of $10,000,000 and provide full-time or part-time employment for about 6000 persons.[105]

An important factor which has not yet been mentioned in this discussion of Negro business is the larger framework of American business within which Negro concerns must operate. Negro business rarely if ever exhibits such characteristics of "big business" as financial com-

---

[99] E. Franklin Frazier, *Black Bourgeoisie*, The Free Press, 1957, p. 57.
[100] Gunnar Myrdal, *op. cit.*, p. 314.
[101] A. L. Harris, *op. cit.*, pp. 175–176.
[102] Gunnar Myrdal, *op. cit.*, p. 318.
[103] A. L. Harris, *op. cit.*, p. 175.
[104] Gunnar Myrdal, *op. cit.*, p. 314. See also J. A. Pierce, *op. cit.*, chap. 4.
[105] E. Franklin Frazier, *Black Bourgeoisie*, pp. 57–58.

binations, mass production and marketing methods, complex organizations, industrial integration, etc. Those who advocate a separate Negro economy have not shown how Negro business, which is small business, can thrive in this context.[106] As Myrdal says, "The days have passed when there was much of a future for the small entrepreneur, whether Negro or White."[107]

For many years the members of the middle and upper classes in the Negro population have found themselves in a difficult ideological situation. Their dilemma is that the walls of the racial system limit their economic and social opportunities, but at the same time segregation protects and advances such interests as these classes already possess.[108]

During the late twenties and early thirties many Negro businessmen felt that the rank and file of Negroes could be convinced that it was their duty to patronize Negro stores and banks, even if they had to pay higher prices and absorb greater losses by this course of action. But as Harris writes, ". . . Even if the Negro masses had been constrained to adopt this policy as a matter of racial pride their economic poverty would have caused them, in the long run, to patronize cheaper concerns. Thus, with the penetration of the chain stores and some of the better organized independents into Negro neighborhoods, racial protectionism collapsed."[109]

Frazier writes of the social myth of Negro business, the belief that Negroes will own factories, banks, and stores in large numbers and that they will employ many Negroes. The "black bourgeoisie" dreams of gaining a monopoly of the Negro market, but it rejects identification with the masses. Identification with the white propertied classes is impossible, so the black bourgeoisie—living in a world of make-believe—attempts to maintain the style of living of wealthy whites. According to this analysis, most of the members of the "black bourgeoisie" fear competition with whites "partly because such competition would mean that whites were taking them seriously, and consequently they would have to assume a more serious and responsible attitude towards their work."[110]

Coöperatives among Negroes were inconsequential before the depression, and they are still not very numerous. Pierce believes, however, that in recent years coöperative enterprises have taken firm root

---

[106] A thoughtful summary of the main problems of Negro business operation, namely, "Growth and Expansion of Certain Lines of Business," "Capital and Credit," "Patronage," "Trained Personnel," "Accounting and Record Keeping," "Coöperation with Other Negro Business," and "Relations with Government," is given in J. A. Pierce, *op. cit.*, chap. 7. This author devotes chaps. 10 and 11 to a discussion of the present status and the future needs of Negro business education.

[107] See J. A. Pierce, *op. cit.*, chap. 1; Gunnar Myrdal, *op. cit.*, p. 314; and A. L. Harris, *op. cit.*, chaps. 8–9.

[108] Gunnar Myrdal, *op cit.*, p. 305.

[109] A. L. Harris, *op. cit.*, p. 178.

[110] E. Franklin Frazier, *Black Bourgeoisie*, pp. 216, 166, 168.

among Negroes and that they will increase in number and strength in the near future. He feels that for "Negroes, who are usually excluded from business ventures of more than very small local value, the prospect of finding employment in the large and growing co-operative movement offers a definite hope for the future."[111]

Two recent and possibly promising developments in the field of Negro commercial enterprises are the biracial economy and the integration of Negro business into the general American business structure. These trends include, or might include Negro-white partnerships which would create larger working capital and bring in customers from both races, white-owned and Negro-managed and Negro-staffed businesses operating in Negro neighborhoods, and Negro-managed chain stores. Pierce states that the complete realization of the objective of integration may require considerable time, but the process, if it continues, "will furnish wider employment opportunities, establish higher wage levels, and provide many of the types of business experience so badly needed by Negroes."

This trend is growing even in the Deep South. In Atlanta there is the example of a branch of a drug store chain where the soda-fountain restaurant is managed and staffed by Negroes and occupies over one-half of the floor space, whereas the drug department, operating on the other side of the store, is managed and staffed by whites. Other instances of infiltration are found in a hosiery chain's Negro-managed shops, chain laundry neighborhood stations, employment in white-owned five-and-ten-cent stores located in Negro communities, and employment in the soda-fountain restaurant in one of New Orleans' largest variety stores.[112]

The present status of Negro business is well summarized by Hawley:

> Real estate and insurance have always been favored: the first because it is in such demand and its sale requires little training, while the second largely reflects the persistence of traditional Negro concern with the rites of death. Even so, Negro insurance companies have written less than 0.4 per cent of the value of all U.S. life-insurance today in force. The total number of all other substantial Negro businesses in manufacturing or construction across the nation—e.g., a publishing company in Chicago, a cosmetics company in Atlantic City, a construction company in Atlanta—can almost be counted on one hand. Detroit, for all its huge Negro population, has developed few Negro businesses beyond the elementary service or retail outfits, relatively modest in size and limited to Negro patronage."[113]

JEWS IN INDUSTRY, BUSINESS, AND THE PROFESSIONS

The economics of the Jewish group in the United States is affected by several characteristics not found in any other minority group or in

[111] J. A. Pierce, op. cit., p. 178.
[112] Ibid., pp. 27–28.
[113] L. T. Hawley, op. cit., p. 254.

the composite American people. In the first place, Jews are predominantly urban. In the United States, more than four million of the five million Jews live in cities of 100,000 and over. About one-half of the Jewish population of the United States lives in New York and Chicago. Jews constitute 4 percent of the total population but 11 percent of the population of cities of more than 100,000. They make up a small fraction of 1 percent of the rural population but about 30 percent of the population of New York City. As Reich says, "Jews are thus not merely an urban, but to a large extent, a metropolitan people." The economic welfare of a large percentage of the Jews is therefore closely related to the economic welfare of large cities.[114] In the second place, Jews are concentrated in a relatively few occupations. They are no longer traders to the extent that they were at the opening of the nineteenth century, but their occupational specialization is still a significant matter. There are considerable differences between the occupational distribution of the New York City Jewish population, which includes 40 percent of the Jewish population of the United States, and the non-New York Jewry residing in other cities. In the latter (for example, Dallas, Texas; Detroit, Michigan; New London, Connecticut; Norwich, Connecticut; Passaic, New Jersey; Stamford, Connecticut; and Trenton, New Jersey) the percentage engaged in commerce is twice as large as in New York City, and the proportion of Jews in the professions is considerably higher than in New York. Recognizing these differences between New York City and other cities, Reich concludes that ". . . of one hundred Jews gainfully employed in the United States between thirty-five and forty draw their sustenance from commercial occupations; between fifteen and twenty from manufacturing industries; some ten or twelve are in the professions; and the remainder are scattered among personal services, transportation, construction trades and other occupations. The corresponding figures for the American population at large are: in trade 13.8 percent, in manufacturing industries 26.3 percent, and in professional services 6.8 percent."[115] In the occupational distribution of American Jews the trade group is three times as large as in the total population of the United States, the professional group is about twice as large, but the manufacturing group is below that for the composite population. Whereas 17.5 percent of the gainfully occupied in the total population are in agriculture, less than 2 percent of the Jewish population is so employed.[116]

The concentration of Jews in tertiary or servicing industries, such as commerce, transportation, the professions, personal service, and public service, may be accounted for in part by the general economic develop-

[114] Nathan Reich, "Economic Trends," in Oscar Janowsky (ed.), *The American Jew*, Harper & Brothers, 1942, p. 162.
[115] *Ibid.*, p. 165.
[116] *Ibid.*, p. 165.

ment which has occurred in the past century and a half. According to Reich, census reports indicate a sharp relative decline in the proportions of people employed in the primary industries (agriculture, fisheries, and forest products); an increase in the proportion of those employed in secondary or converting industries (manufacturing industries) during the early period of industrialization, followed later by a stabilization of that proportion; and a steady increase in the percentage of people engaged in servicing industries.[117] Thus, he regards the concentration of Jews in the tertiary group not as an abnormal manifestation but as a perfectly natural and obvious development. Reich observes that ". . . occupational trends began to manifest themselves at about the time when Jews were being gradually freed from the legal and political restraints. The Jews entered upon the modern world at the time when certain areas of economic activity began expanding at a faster rate than others. It was their good fortune that by tradition and experience Jews were excellently equipped precisely for those activities which were at the threshold of greatest expansion."[118]

An important part of the occupational concentration of Jews in the United States is the anti-Semitism of the past and present. Contrary to a widespread belief, Jews dominate in very few fields of American business and finance. The *Fortune* survey (*Jews in America*, 1936) clearly revealed the segments of the American economy in which Jewish participation is slight. Jewish influence is insignificant in both commercial and investment banking. Only thirty-three Jews were among the 420 directors of the nineteen members of the New York Clearing House in 1933, and outside New York City the influence of Jews in banking is even smaller. The *Fortune* survey found that "the absence of Jews in the insurance business is noteworthy." Jewish participation in heavy industry is virtually nonexistent. Jewish participation in advertising is from 1 to 3 percent of the total field. At that time, about the only magazines controlled by Jews were *The New Yorker*, *The American Mercury*, and *Esquire*. Jews are an important influence in book publishing, job and trade printing, and radio, television, and motion pictures. Their systematic exclusion from participation in the basic industries of the country, the industries that exercise a decisive control over the entire economy, would seem to be a more adequate explanation of the curious occupational distribution of Jews than the *Fortune* explanation in terms of "psychological traits—their clannishness, their tribal inclination."[119]

---

[117]Nathan Reich, "The Economic Structure of Modern Jewry," in Louis Finkelstein (ed.), *The Jews, Their History, Culture, and Religion*, Harper & Brothers, 1949, vol. 2, pp. 1256–1257.

[118] *Ibid.*, p. 1258.

[119] See Carey McWilliams, *A Mask for Privilege*, Little, Brown & Company, 1948, pp. 142–146.

Generally speaking, the businesses in which Jews are concentrated are those in which a large risk-factor is involved; businesses peripheral to the economy; businesses originally regarded as unimportant; new industries and businesses; and businesses which have traditionally carried a certain element of social stigma, such, for example, as the amusement industry and the liquor industry. Not being able to penetrate the key control industries, Jews have been compelled to occupy the interstitial, the marginal, positions in the American economy. In short, it is the qualitative rather than the quantitative aspect of their participation in industry and finance that most graphically delineates their position.[120]

The middle-class position, and the position of the Jews within the middle class, deserve special attention. Jews have risen faster than other ethnic groups,[121] and this rapid upward circulation has created hostility toward them on the part of both the non-Jewish "native" middle class and the immigrant groups which have been slower to develop a middle class. McWilliams sees this "in-between" position of the Jews as constituting "their particular peril in the United States."

As this concentration [of wealth and economic power] progresses, the amount of the national income left for the middle class, after monopoly has extracted its share, becomes the prize of an ever-fiercer struggle. The exposed economic position of the Jew is then subject to increased pressure from three directions: from above (monopoly); from below (the working class); and from within the middle class itself. . . . As Waldo Frank has so well said . . ."Whenever that class (middle class) flourished, the Jews, functioning in it, were tolerated by it. Now that it droops and its spoils dwindle, it turns—like a threatened beast—against its weaker neighbor."[122]

Jews face job discrimination in certain sectors of our private economy. They have the greatest difficulty in the fields that have traditionally been non-Jewish in ownership and management. Especially notable in this respect are clerical and office employment in insurance companies and private utilities. As McWilliams says, "The effect of this 'closed shop' attitude on the part of the industrial and financial giants is to intensify the pressure of Jewish applicants for jobs in those businesses which have always pursued a less systematic policy of exclusion, to become small enterprisers, or to enter the professions."[123]

In public employment Jews have met a minimum amount of discrimination. American democratic traditions and an effective civil service have combined to give them little cause for complaint in government employment. This is a new development in Jewish experience, for

---

[120] *Ibid.*, pp. 147–148.

[121] See, for example, W. Lloyd Warner and L. Srole, *The Social Systems of American Ethnic Groups*, Yale University Press, 1945, p. 61.

[122] Carey McWilliams, *op. cit.*, pp. 156–157.

[123] *Ibid.*, p. 158.

in other countries Jews have often been barred from public employment. In the United States, they have sought jobs in the public service because they are frequently refused work in private organizations.[124]

JAPANESE BUSINESS

Some economic aspects of Japanese-American life are discussed in a later chapter which deals with minority families, but we may say here that the "Little Tokyos" in west coast cities provided every kind of service to the Japanese residents. There were Japanese grocery stores, restaurants, rooming houses, bathhouses, barbershops, theaters, banks, newspapers, and insurance agencies. There were physicians, lawyers, and other professional persons. Such services, however, did not support the whole Japanese population, and it was necessary to cater to the non-Japanese population too. The Japanese were driven out of the steam laundry business many years ago simply by being refused boiler licenses. The dry-cleaning business was substituted for steam laundries because of the small capital investment and the ability of a family to operate a business without hiring employees. Bradford Smith has summed up the occupational distribution of the Japanese-Americans at the time of Pearl Harbor: "When war came in 1941, the service industries—principally domestic service, dry cleaning, and lodging houses—provided the only major source of income to the Japanese community outside of that based on agriculture. Lack of capital, boycott, discriminatory regulations, and consistent attack by anti-Oriental organizations and unions had kept the Japanese out of other fields. With its hand labor and domestic service, its small shops, its dependence on the farms, Nihonmachi (Little Tokyos) belonged to an earlier economic era, an age without industrial enterprise."[125]

After the relocation centers closed, Japanese-Americans did not regain all of the economic and occupational ground they had lost during World War II. According to Bloom and Riemer, the neatly articulated system of agricultural production and distribution had not been reëstablished by 1948. Japanese-American farmers had been able to establish claims to a relatively small percentage of their prewar holdings, and "wholesale produce dealers, with a smaller source of supply and fewer outlets, were less numerous, and retail producers had not been able to assert themselves in successful competition with chain stores."[126] The extremely difficult housing situation faced by Japanese-Americans on their return to Los Angeles provided a number of individuals with the

[124] Oscar Janowsky (ed.), op. cit., pp. 179–180.
[125] Bradford Smith, Americans from Japan, J. B. Lippincott Company, 1948, pp. 238–239. For an excellent analysis of the Japanese-Americans in agriculture, see Leonard Bloom and Ruth Riemer, Removal and Return: The Socio-Economic Effects of the War on Japanese Americans, University of California Press, 1949, chaps. 3 ("Agriculture and Produce Trade") and 4 ("Contract Gardening").
[126] Leonard Bloom and Ruth Riemer, op. cit., p. 64.

opportunity to establish boarding or rooming houses or hotels. One of the important prewar newspapers was being published daily in English and Japanese by the end of 1945. The displacement of Negroes from the shops and stores they had acquired during the war was rapid. By 1947, approximately forty restaurants and a number of grocery stores, barber-shops, and other personal service establishments had been reopened. Limitations on commercial and financial relations with Japan had prevented the reëstablishment of banking organizations and many of the Oriental and art-goods stores by 1948. Many of the lawyers, physicians, and dentists had returned to the community within three years of the closing of the centers.[127] Despite very considerable losses, the Japanese community in Los Angeles soon took on much of its prewar character.[128]

[127] *Ibid.*, p. 65.

[128] On the economic losses of Japanese-Americans after evacuation, see Bradford Smith, *op. cit.*, pp. 282–288, and Leonard Bloom and Ruth Riemer, *op. cit.*, chap. 5.

CHAPTER 13

Minorities in the Economy of the United States (continued)

Negroes in the Professions

THE MEDICAL FIELD

The Negro professional personnel in the medical field consists of approximately 4000 physicians, 1600 dentists, 9000 nurses, and 1400 pharmacists. The minimal standard of safety generally accepted is one physician to 1500 population. In 1942 the proportion of Negro physicians to the Negro population was one to 3377.[1] This statement does not give a completely accurate picture of the Negro medical care situation because (1) Negro doctors are concentrated in the cities, and (2) about two-fifths of the American Negroes who obtain medical care get it from white physicians.

Nearly all Negro physicians in the United States are general practitioners. Only a few Negroes have become specialists or have been seriously involved in medical research. Although the number of colored physicians who keep up with advances in medicine is small, this group is increasing in size. Among the younger men the proportion reading the medical journals and joining the medical societies is larger. In the group of older physicians few joined the medical organizations, and those who did remained largely within the Negro societies.[2]

[1] Florence Murray (ed.), *The Negro Handbook*, The Macmillan Company, 1949, p. 30. Fewer than 200 Negro doctors graduate each year. L. T. Hawley, "The Negro's New Economic Life," *Fortune*, September, 1956, p. 254.
[2] Charles S. Johnson, *The Negro College Graduate*, University of North Carolina, 1938, pp. 324–325. The Georgia Medical Association now allows county medical associations to grant full membership to Negro physicians. Some of the county associations have opened their membership to Negroes, but some of these have granted only qualified or "scientific" memberships. A "scientific" membership en-

It is difficult to give an accurate estimate of the proportion of Negro clients who go to white doctors. Some years ago Carter G. Woodson concluded that Negro physicians receive about three-fifths of the Negro trade.[3] The proportion in Richmond was 48 percent prior to 1929, but ten years later it was less. The reasons why a larger percentage of the Negro population does not use Negro physicians are interesting. White physicians have more training, prestige, and equipment, and these items are important to patients who are critically ill. When white employers in rural areas send Negro workers to a doctor, the Negroes may feel compelled to go to a white physician even though they are paying the bills themselves.[4] Also, a white man is a good reference in establishing credit with a white doctor, but such support would not be provided for treatment by Negro physicians. It has been suggested that jealousy of successful professional men in a disadvantaged group where it is difficult to get ahead economically is a factor in the unwillingness of many minority persons to patronize practitioners in their group. In the absence of convincing evidence on this allegation, it seems likely that as many minority persons are attracted to professional men within their own groups because of expected understanding and sympathy as are repelled by envy.

Negroes usually expect to get substandard care from white doctors, as they do in hospitals and other professional agencies. Johnson reports that in Richmond most of the white physicians prefer to call on the Negro patient at his home rather than to have him visit the office.[5] Complaints, at least in the rural areas, are restrained or withheld altogether because of the fear that worse treatment may be accorded later.

Most Negro physicians are limited to a Negro clientele. As Myrdal points out, white persons would not ordinarily consult a Negro doctor because of race prejudice or because of lack of confidence in his ability. There are exceptions in eastern, northern, and west coast cities, especially in the immigrant populations. In the South, the whites who go to Negro physicians usually, although not always, are trying to conceal venereal disease or pregnancy from their white relatives and friends. In some of the upland country of West Virginia, North Carolina, eastern Tennessee, and western Virginia some whites of low income go to Negro doctors because they have trouble in getting medical service from competent white physicians.[6]

---

titles the Negro doctor to participate in professional discussions but he cannot participate in social activities. See R. O. Johnson, "Desegregation of Public Education in Georgia—One Year Afterward," *Journal of Negro Education*, Summer, 1955, p. 235.

[3] C. G. Woodson, *The Negro Professional Man and the Community*, Association for the Study of Negro Life and History, Inc., 1934, p. 96.

[4] Charles S. Johnson, *Patterns of Negro Segregation*, Harper & Brothers, 1943, pp. 76–77.

[5] *Ibid.*, p. 77.

[6] Gunnar Myrdal, *An American Dilemma*, Harper & Brothers, 1944, p. 322.

Despite the preference of many Negroes for white physicians and the fact that most of their patients have low incomes, Negro doctors in many cities seem prosperous. A rather large proportion of the Negro physicians, however, obtain a substantial part of their income from sources other than medicine. According to Mydral, "Some of them work for Negro insurance companies and benevolent societies. Some have made fortunes in real estate. There are those who own drug stores. Others have their own private hospitals, benefiting from a monopoly arising from segregation in public health service. There are observers who characterize some of these business practices as exploitative. In addition they help to keep down the professional record of the Negro doctor."[7]

Very few hospitals in the United States maintain a system of complete equality for Negro and white doctors. Harlem Hospital and Sydenham Hospital in New York City have this arrangement. There was not a single Negro doctor in San Francisco who could treat patients in any accredited hospital until 1947, when one received courtesy privileges. In Chicago only one hospital in forty-two included a Negro physician on its attending staff, although two others extended courtesy privileges to two Negro doctors and varying privileges were given by hospitals not included in the forty-two investigated.

In many Northern hospitals which advertise that they freely admit patients without regard to race or color, there is an overt or implicit ban against Negro physicians and nurses. On the other hand, a Negro or two may be admitted to the staff of a hospital without a relaxation of strict limitations as to the number and location (within the building) of Negro patients accepted. Even though great strides toward integration were made in some cities during the recent war, few examples can be found of hospitals where the race of doctor or patient is not a vital factor; and institutions loud in their claims of interracial cooperation are subtly infected with quotas on personnel and patients.[8]

There are almost no hospital facilities for Negroes in the rural areas of the South, and those in the larger towns and cities are far below minimum standards. In Mississippi, where the proportion of Negroes in the population is higher than in any other state, there is 0.5 bed per 1000 Negroes as compared with 2.3 beds per 1000 whites. The Hill-Burton Hospital Construction Act sets the minimum standard at 4.5 general hospital beds for every 1000 persons.[9] Even when there are facilities for Negro patients, white physicians may care for the whites in one section and Negroes in the "colored wing." Until the Flint-Goodridge Hospital "was built in New Orleans with the assistance of the Rosenwald Fund

---

[7] Ibid., pp. 324–325.
[8] M. M. Davis and H. H. Smythe, "Providing Adequate Health Service to Negroes," Journal of Negro Education, July, 1949.
[9] Ibid.

and the General Education Board, there was not a single modern hospital in Louisiana where a Negro physician may take his patients. A corresponding situation prevails in most of the other southern states. North and South Carolina are an exception due mainly to the assistance of the Duke Endowment Fund."[10]

Many Negro physicians, especially in the South, doubt that they will be given a place in the expanded public health facilities of the future. If they are not included on something like a fair basis of representation, their situation will be serious because of the loss of most of their low-income patients. Actually, this would mean the loss of most of their clienteles. On the other hand, if they are brought into the public health programs there will be much more employment for them.

According to the editor of the *National Medical Association Journal*, industrial health benefits which extend protection to Negro workers "strike at the pride, pocketbook and solidarity of the Negro doctor, and that is why Negro doctors split on integration, even though many will not admit it."[11] Because company-union-negotiated health plans are administered by county medical societies, some Negro physicians have lost their practices. Dr. Cobb states that despite their exclusion from county medical societies, or from all but "scientific" activities in these societies, "many Negro doctors feel that a fully segregated clinic, where they have access to all positions, is better than some northern hospitals where only fringe positions are open to them."

The shortage of Negro dentists, nurses, pharmacists, and other trained medical personnel is even greater than is that of physicians. The recommendation of the Federal Security Administrator is one dentist to each 1650 persons. In 1945, the 1533 Negro dentists constituted a ratio of one to approximately 8800 Negroes in the population. Only 313 Negro dental students were in training in 1947.

The Negro dentist, like the Negro physician, may have some white patients. But many Negroes go to white dentists, even though they are segregated in the South in a separate chair and separate instruments are used on them. The fact that there are few Negro dentists in the rural areas forces many Negroes to turn to white dentists whether they want to or not.[12]

In 1940, 7191, or 2 percent of all the trained and student nurses in the United States were Negroes. It is interesting to note that 63 percent of the active Negro nurses in 1941 were in hospital and institutional work, 28 percent in public health, 6 percent in private practice, and 1 percent in industrial training.[13] Myrdal says that one might expect the limitations on opportunities for Negro professionals in the public health system to

[10] Gunnar Myrdal, *op. cit.*, p. 323.
[11] Cleveland *Plain Dealer*, August 6, 1957.
[12] Gunnar Myrdal, *op. cit.*, p. 325.
[13] Jessie P. Guzman (ed.), *Negro Year Book*, Tuskegee Institute, 1947, p. 334.

be somewhat less rigorous in the case of nurses, "since it would seem to be inconsistent with Southern ideas to let white women care for Negro male patients. But a solution to this delicate problem has been found other than that of letting the Negro nurse monopolize the work in the colored hospital wings. White nurses may treat Negro patients, but they are assisted by Negro maids who do most of the dirty work." Nevertheless, there has been a steady increase in the number of Negro public health nurses; in 1945 Negro nurses represented about 5 percent of all public health nurses.

During World War II, attempts were made to increase the number of graduate Negro nurses as well as to increase opportunities for them to assist in the war effort. Most of these nurses were trained in the United States Cadet Nurses Corps; in May, 1945, 4128 Negro student nurses were receiving free tuition in this program. Among the agencies which employed Negro nurses were the War Food Administration, the Veterans Administration, the American Red Cross, and a number of official and voluntary public health agencies. Three hundred and forty-three Negroes were serving with the Army Nurse Corps in February, 1945, some on overseas duty. After the Navy Department dropped its restriction in January, 1945, four Negro nurses served in this branch.[14]

THE LEGAL PROFESSION

In 1930, Negro lawyers constituted less than 1 percent of all the lawyers in the United States. Most Negro lawyers are graduates of northern law schools, and two-thirds of the 1200 Negro lawyers practice outside the South. Alabama had four Negro lawyers in 1930, as against 1600 white lawyers. Mississippi had six Negro lawyers and 1200 white lawyers.[15] The practice of Negro lawyers is limited largely to civil cases involving property or divorce and to the affairs connected with Negro churches and fraternal orders. In the past a Negro attorney had little chance of winning a case in a southern court where "protection by a 'respectable' white person usually counts more . . . for a Negro client than would even the best representation on the part of a Negro lawyer."[16] Johnson reported that the courts have improved in many cities in recent years, at least in the sense that Negro lawyers do not now have to give as much thought to dealing with racial factors as they do with law. Some younger lawyers who have moved to southern cities have found that a dignified and lucrative practice is now possible.[17]

The northern migration during World War I changed the legal pro-

---

[14] *Ibid.*, p. 334. Recent changes in the field of nursing which are favorable to Negroes are discussed in M. J. Ravitz, "Integration of Nurses," *Phylon*, Third Quarter, 1955, pp. 295–302.

[15] Gunnar Myrdal, *op. cit.*, pp. 325–326.

[16] *Ibid.*, p. 326.

[17] Charles S. Johnson, *The Negro College Graduate*, p. 337.

fession for the Negro from a "starvation" profession to one with considerable prestige. As a rule, it was formerly a disadvantage to be represented in court by a Negro. Johnson says that whereas northern Negro lawyers had formerly tried to build up a large practice among white people, the younger Negro lawyers began to open offices in the center of the Negro business districts and to devote all of their time to Negro practice.[18] A 50 percent sample of the two hundred lawyers in Chicago showed that 86 percent considered themselves civil lawyers. Although the socioeconomic position of most Negroes is such that they are more often in difficulty than in need of business advice, the Negro lawyer typically tries to "improve" his practice by building a clientele comprised mainly of persons considered socially desirable.[19]

THE TEACHING PROFESSION

Schoolteaching, as Myrdal and others have pointed out, is the principal Negro profession. Teachers and ministers constitute nearly two-thirds of all Negro professional workers. In 1866 there were only 2031 teachers for a population of 1,500,000 Negroes of school age, and only 458 of these teachers were Negroes.[20] By 1890 there were more than 15,000 teachers of Negro children. Despite the spectacular increase in the number of Negro teachers, Negroes have only half the representation in the teaching profession that they have in the total population.[21]

It is widely believed that too many Negroes wish to enter the teaching profession. In terms of attaining a balanced distribution of professional workers, this belief has some justification. But from the standpoint of the supply of teachers and teachers-in-preparation, there is still a serious shortage of Negro teachers. This situation results in a teaching load in the majority of segregated public schools that is considerably higher than it would be if national standards were observed.[22]

The development of a competent group of Negro teachers has been greatly complicated by the extremely low salaries offered and by racial wage discrimination. In the past there were "few major cases of racial wage discrimination so clear-cut and so pronounced as that found in the teaching profession in the South. In most other cases there is not so much direct wage discrimination as there is a tendency to let whites monopolize jobs in skilled occupations or in high-paying and expanding industries. Those having political power in the South have shown a firm determination to maintain these salary differentials in the Negro schools."[23] Teachers' salary differentials based on race alone were de-

[18] *Ibid.*, pp. 335–336.
[19] W. H. Hale, "The Negro Lawyer and His Clients," *Phylon*, First Quarter, 1952, pp. 57–63.
[20] Charles S. Johnson, *The Negro College Graduate*, p. 309.
[21] Gunnar Myrdal, *op. cit.*, pp. 318–319.
[22] Jessie P. Guzman (ed.), *op. cit.*, p. 142.
[23] Gunnar Myrdal, *op. cit.*, p. 320.

clared unconstitutional in 1940, but many school systems failed to eliminate them. However, as we indicate in Chapter 19, the trend in the
South is toward equalization of teachers' salaries.

Another factor of importance in the recruitment of Negro teachers is
that nearly all of them—from the isolated teacher in a one-room rural
school to the president of a Negro college—are appointed by white
leaders and they are constantly under the threat of losing their positions
if they become "troublesome."[24] Elementary schoolteachers in rural
areas are particularly subject to white control, and in some cases they are
used as disseminators of the expectations which white people have for
the Negro community. In their actual classroom work these teachers
may be able to exercise considerable independence because the white
superintendent and the white school board usually are relatively indifferent about what happens in a Negro school. In some counties the
superintendent has never visited the majority of his Negro schools. As
long as informants do not report that the teacher is giving the children
dangerous ideas, the rural Negro schoolteacher is usually ignored.[25] In
some communities, race sentiment encourages the selection of the poorest teacher available because of the fear that a new style of education
for Negroes would introduce disquieting questions.[26]

Negro teachers in the rural South must carefully observe the racial
etiquette but at the same time show enough self-respect to retain the
respect of the Negro community. Middle- and upper-class Negroes are
not as unanimous in their protest against segregation in education as
they are in protesting against exclusion in hotels, restaurants, theaters,
concerts, and transportation facilities. Negro schools provide employment for Negro teachers who in some instances have had a difficult
time finding positions in a desegregated system. Where segregated
schools exist, there is a tendency on the part of middle- and upper-
class Negroes to work for the improvement of the Negro schools and
for the equalization of teachers' salaries.[27] The effects of desegregation
on the jobs of Negro schoolteachers are discussed in Chapter 19.

City teachers have many advantages over teachers in rural areas. Buildings and equipment are considerably better, salaries are higher, and
status in the Negro community is much greater. In the state colleges for
Negroes, conditions are similar except that (1) faculty members have
still greater status in the Negro community and (2) the college is inclined to follow a life of its own. This tendency of the college to work
out its own destiny appreciably increases the independence of the teaching staff. The professors in the private colleges for Negroes are freest
from local white opinion within the limits of the campus. Myrdal re-

[24] *Ibid.*, p. 769.
[25] *Ibid.*, p. 880.
[26] Charles S. Johnson, *The Negro College Graduate*, p. 309.
[27] Gunnar Myrdal, *op. cit.*, p. 795.

ports that a friendly white churchman told Atlanta University students that their teachers enjoyed greater academic freedom than their white colleagues at the Georgia state universities. The policies and general atmosphere of the private Negro colleges in the South are affected by the northern philanthropists and church bodies who have contributed to these institutions, although this influence is often exerted through southern white liberals and interracialists and through prominent Negro leaders. But, as Myrdal observes, ". . . even this control is conservatively directed when compared with northern standards."[28]

The prestige of the teacher in the Negro community is said by a European observer to be comparable to that held by teachers in northern European countries. In general, the Negro teacher has a symbolic prestige from the importance of his profession. Since there are often few business opportunities in the Negro community, the teacher is also freer from competition for status. The exception to this situation is the teacher in the rural South. There the low standard of selection, the low income, the (frequently) inadequate teaching ability, and great dependence on white men combine to yield a fairly low standing in the rural Negro community. Even there, however, teachers of good education can attain higher status. In any event, "the [public-school] teacher and the school house are usually integrated into the Negro community, since the teacher's social life is bound up with that of the parents of her pupils, and the school house is usually used for community purposes."[29]

Social Work

In 1940 there were more than 4000 Negro social workers. More than half of these lived in the North despite the preponderance of Negroes in the South, partly because social work is largely an urban occupation. Negroes are now employed as case workers, and there are some Negro officials in housing projects and in farm and home extension work. Professional opportunities for Negroes have been enhanced by the programs of social work at Howard University and Atlanta University.[30]

The Ministry

The ministerial profession was the first to be established among Negroes, and for many years ministers were the principal leaders of the Negro race. In the past few decades this leadership has been taken over to a considerable extent by lawyers, physicians, dentists, social workers, teachers, and journalists.[31] Many of the men and women in the latter

[28] Ibid., pp. 880–881.
[29] Ibid., pp. 881, 885, 948.
[30] Ibid., p. 326.
[31] B. E. Mays and J. W. Nicholson, The Negro's Church, Institute of Social and Religious Research, 1933, pp. 38, 50.

professions have acquired more education than the ministry requires. Their incomes often exceed those of clergymen. The increasing trend of secularization of life, particularly in urban centers, has not failed to affect the Negro population. Nevertheless, the ministry continues to be an important profession in the Negro group, and clergymen are second in numbers only to teachers among Negro professional people.

The clienteles of Negro ministers, like those of Negro teachers and lawyers, are limited mainly to the Negro group. Negroes are over-churched, as we shall point out in Chapter 18, and the ministry is the only profession in which Negroes have greater representation than they have in the population of the United States. Many Negro clergymen are teachers, farmers, or laborers who devote only a small part of their time to the church. In some cases "ministers are offered free shares in business enterprises in return for using their influence in behalf of such economic ventures. Some Negro ministers are associated with morti-cians. Small gifts from benevolent whites also play a role in many Negro ministers' budgets."[32]

ENGINEERING AND RELATED PROFESSIONS

Before 1950 few jobs in engineering were open to Negroes and few Negroes were being trained in this field. The strong demand for engineering and related technical personnel following the outbreak of hostilities in Korea brought increased job opportunities to Negroes.[33] Since then the enrollment of Negro students in engineering has increased, but in 1955 only 150 of the 23,000 graduating engineers were Negroes.[34] Agencies seeking to broaden economic opportunities for Negroes recently have found more openings in engineering than there are professionally qualified Negroes to fill them.[35]

IMPORTANCE OF THE PROFESSIONS TO NEGROES

We may conclude this summary of the professions with a statement concerning the appeal which these occupational fields have for Negroes.

Professional employment has long been the goal of the vast majority of Negroes who manage to continue their education through college. The reasons for the concentration of Negroes in the professions are not difficult to discover. The segregated schools have afforded employment opportunities for the largest number of college-trained Negroes while the ministry, medicine, dentistry, law, and more recently, social service have attracted most of the remainder. Virtually all of these professions can be successfully practiced without sharp conflict with many prevailing racial patterns in most sections of the country. Aside from that, they provide a certain measure of social and

---

[32] Gunnar Myrdal, *op. cit.*, pp. 321–322.
[33] Eli Ginzberg, *The Negro Potential*, Columbia University Press, 1956, pp. 12–13.
[34] L. T. Hawley, *op. cit.*, p. 254.
[35] Eli Ginzberg, *op. cit.*, pp. 108–109.

community prestige not found in many other occupations. Moreover, there have been relatively few employment opportunities in commerce and industry for ambitious Negro college graduates.[36]

With an increase in the number of college students in the past few years, it appears that the professions will claim an increasing number of Negroes.

Negroes in Government Service

The Civil Service Act of 1883 ended half a century of the spoils system. Negroes had not been the recipients of many jobs under the spoils regime, and at the time of the creation of the Civil Service Commission only 620 Negroes were employed by the government in Washington.[37] In the years 1885 to 1889 the number of Negro federal employees increased to 2393. As the total number of government employees grew, there was an increase in Negro employees, but the number of Negroes in responsible jobs declined. In 1912 Negroes held more than 19,000 jobs in the federal service, including a number of important positions as collectors of customs, collectors of ports, postmasters, paymasters, and diplomats which had carried over from previous years.

During the administration of Woodrow Wilson, "humanitarian and citizen of the world," Negroes were completely eliminated from responsible government positions. A Negro auditor of the Navy and other officials were asked to resign, and Negro postmasters were ousted. This was no mere party action; these men were not replaced by other Negroes.

Segregation appeared in the Navy Department, the Treasury Department, the Post Office Department, and the Bureau of Engraving and Printing. The latter resulted from the personal action of the first Mrs. Woodrow Wilson. Monroe Trotter reported that the President himself said to a delegation protesting segregation in the Post Office and the Treasury Department that he was in favor of segregation as beneficial to both races.

The Navy Department set a precedent by placing Negroes behind screens where they could not be seen by white clerks and also ordered segregation in the use of lavatories. The Treasury followed suit in the segregation policy regarding the use of lavatories. In nearly every department and bureau of the Government, the Wilson administration succeeded in establishing segregation and discrimination in employment, lavatories and restaurants.[38]

Appointing officers during Wilson's administration used two personnel procedures to keep Negroes out of clerical and other desirable civil

---

[36] Jessie P. Guzman (ed.), op. cit., pp. 141–142.
[37] For the experience of the Negro in government service prior to World War II we rely on an excellent article by John A. Davis and Cornelius L. Golightly, "Negro Employment in the Federal Government," *Phylon*, Fourth Quarter, 1945, pp. 337–340.
[38] *Ibid.*, p. 338.

service jobs. The first method, the "rule of three," dated back to the early years of the civil service; it allowed the appointing officer to choose among the three highest eligibles. The second method was the requiring of a photograph. These two practices made it possible to avoid appointing most Negro applicants, and they were continued under Harding, Coolidge, and Hoover. The number of Negroes employed by the government steadily increased, but the jobs were mainly those of custodians.

During the depression the government had special problems of relief for Negroes. President Roosevelt and other white government officials attempted to get a fair share of employment for Negroes. However, most of the Negro appointees under Roosevelt in peacetime were not regular federal job-holders but advisers dealing exclusively with Negro problems. Thus the "black cabinet" held such positions as Director, Division of Negro Affairs of the NYA; Race Relations Adviser in the National Housing Agency; Racial Relations Officer in the Federal Works Agency; Civilian Aide to the Secretary of War; and Chief of Minorities Group Service, Bureau of Placement, War Manpower Commission. The rank and file of Negro workers in the federal government continued to be mainly in custodial categories. Hayes found that Negroes constituted 8.4 percent of a total of 115,552 federal employees in Washington in 1938. This percentage was low in view of the fact that the 1940 census showed 28.2 percent of all persons in Washington to be Negroes. In 1938, 82,000 Negroes, or 9.9 percent of the total 861,914 government employees, were listed in the annual report of the Civil Service Commission. For the District of Columbia, 90 percent of the Negro government employees were in custodial service; 9.5 percent were in the clerical, administrative, fiscal, or clerical-mechanical classifications; and 0.5 percent were subprofessional.[39]

President Roosevelt issued Executive Order 8802 on June 25, 1941, and the Committee on Fair Employment Practice was appointed. The President sent an intragovernment letter in September, 1941, in which he asked all heads of departments and independent establishments to examine "their personnel policies and practices to the end that they may be able to assure me that in the Federal service the doors of employment are open to all loyal and qualified workers regardless of creed, race, or national origin." This letter was followed by another in March, 1942, in which Mr. Roosevelt authorized the FEPC to obtain employment data from all government agencies and departments.[40] These actions brought quick results. By November, 1942, the number of Negro government workers in the District of Columbia had increased to 17 percent of all employees. On July 31, 1943, Negroes constituted 12 percent

[39] *Ibid.*, p. 340.
[40] *Ibid.*, pp. 340–341.

of all federal workers as compared with 9.9 percent in 1938; they made up 18 percent of all persons in departmental service (chiefly located in the District of Columbia).[41]

The war agencies in the federal government employed the greatest number of Negroes. According to Davis, 12 percent of their employees were Negroes, with colored workers forming 11.8 percent of the army employees and 14.6 percent of the navy employees. Most of the army and navy workers were not in the classified service, although the war agencies as a group showed the best classification distribution of Negro employees. "The highest utilization in terms of classifications and grades within these classifications came in the National War Labor Board, the Office of Price Administration, the War Manpower Commission, and the War Production Board, which were also noted for using Negroes in regular line administrative positions."[42]

That the gain made by Negroes in the federal service was qualitative as well as quantitative is shown in a comparison of workers in departmental service, mainly District of Columbia employees, in 1944 and Negro federal workers in the District in 1938. Whereas in the earlier year 90 percent of the federal employees in the District were in the Custodial classification, 9.5 in the Clerical, Administrative, and Fiscal classifications, and 0.5 percent in the Subprofessional or Professional, the percentages in the departmental service in 1944 were 39.6 in Crafts-Protective and Custodial; 9.9 in Clerical-Mechanical; 49 in Clerical-Administrative and Fiscal; and 1.1 in Professional and Subprofessional categories.[43]

During World War II the executive departments compared unfavorably with other agencies in the employment of Negroes. The Departments of Commerce, Interior, and Labor increased the numbers of Negroes employed and utilized them in more classifications during wartime. "The Treasury and the Post Office have usually hired large numbers of Negroes, but utilization has left much to be desired. On the whole, the records of Justice, State, and Agriculture have not been good, although some wartime improvement has been noted."[44]

The introduction of Negroes into better positions and their integration into government agencies required considerable personnel skill. Questions arose as to the use of toilets, cafeterias, and recreation facilities on an unsegregated basis. There were also such matters as the use of Negro secretaries and the right of Negroes to supervise white persons. As Davis points out, Negroes often approached the new jobs with fear

[41] John A. Davis, "Nondiscrimination in the Federal Services," *Annals of the American Academy of Political and Social Science*, March, 1946, p. 72.
[42] *Ibid.*, p. 72.
[43] *Ibid.*
[44] *Ibid.*, pp. 72–73.

and aggression. "Significant personnel work in regard to these problems of human behavior, caused by the American caste system, was achieved in OPA, WLB, FEA, WMC, TVA, Interior, War, and Navy."[45]

The rule concerning the submission of photographs with applications was abolished in December, 1940; but, as Myrdal remarks, an applicant's race can usually be ascertained. Ordinarily professional workers are interviewed by the official under whom they are to work. Formerly it was possible, when a newly appointed person proved to be a Negro, to find his work unsatisfactory and have him dismissed after a short time. It was also relatively easy to prevent Negroes from being upgraded. These procedures have been more difficult to invoke since the establishment of President Truman's Fair Employment Board of the Civil Service Commission in 1948 and President Eisenhower's committee against discrimination in federal employment in 1955. These agencies are treated more fully in the section on FEPC.

During President Eisenhower's first term, many Negroes were dismissed as a result of the personnel reductions and changes which go with the election of a new administration. Eventually the number of appointments given to Negroes equaled or exceeded those of the Truman administration. The highest appointment made was that as an Assistant Secretary of Labor. No Negroes were appointed in the so-called supergrades (Grades 17 and 18), and most of those appointed in Grades 14 and 15 were placed in staff or advisory positions as race-relations advisers.[46]

Over a twenty-year period, Negro employment at TVA has varied from 8 to 12 percent in a region whose population is about 10 percent Negro. Most of the Negro TVA employees are found in trades and labor jobs rather than in white-collar positions. It has been pointed out that Negroes are reluctant to apply for jobs traditionally held by whites in the South and that Negroes have had limited opportunity to secure training and experience. Daves claims that TVA has made as much if not more progress in the placement of Negroes in clerical, professional, and technical positions than any federal or private industry in the South. Recently TVA has begun a campaign of recruitment and placement, including the seeking of qualified applicants in Negro schools and colleges.[47]

Although it is not unusual for northern Negroes to hold positions in the system for administering justice, there are no Negroes in the South who share in directing or controlling judicial and penal institutions. In

[45] Ibid., p. 73.
[46] V. J. Browne, "Racial Desegregation in the Public Service, with Particular Reference to the U.S. Government," Journal of Negro Education, Summer, 1954, pp. 246–247.
[47] J. H. Daves, "TVA and Negro Employment," Journal of Negro Education, Winter, 1955, pp. 87–90.

1943 Charles Johnson found that the South had "no Negro judges, few Negro officers of the law, and no Negroes serving in minor clerical positions in official agencies. In the rural counties visited there were no reports of Negroes serving as jurymen; and a Negro lawyer is still an anomaly in the small towns."[48] As we point out in Chapter 15, approximately 1000 Negro police officials are now employed in the South.

The future of Negroes in government service is uncertain. Myrdal concluded that there is more hope for the Negro in public service than in most other work. This forecast was based on the probable expansion of government work, the fact that employment in the public service is susceptible to political pressure, and the new consciousness of the American creed which was stimulated by World War II. He acknowledged that it would be a long time before pro-Negro pressure on southern administrations would have any effect, but he felt that "Negroes have not yet exhausted their present possibilities of forcing the federal government and the Northern state governments to employ an increased number of Negro workers."[49] Northrup is not so hopeful about the Negro's chances for increased participation in federal agencies or federal-sponsored projects.

Agency after agency which has made an honest attempt to further Negro participation has been disbanded, has had its appropriations reduced, or has been forced to modify its policy to suit the working majority of recent Congresses, which have been composed of northern Republicans and southern Democrats. The United States Housing Authority, the Civilian Conservation Corps, the National Youth Administration, the Federal Works Agency, and the Domestic Branch, Office of War Information are all cases in point. Nathan Straus, former USHA Administrator, and John M. Carmody, former Federal Works Agency head, allegedly were both forced to resign to save their agencies from a Congress which they had displeased by their firm upholding of the rights of Negroes to a share of skilled jobs on building construction projects. The United States Employment Service was threatened by a House of Representatives committee with dismemberment if it abolished its Jim Crow setup in the nation's capital and consolidated white and colored offices. One has only to read the *Congressional Record* or examine published hearings of the House of Representatives Appropriations Committee for many other examples. Thus the opposition to a federal nondiscriminatory program is so strong that one must be pessimistic about its probable adoption.[50]

In the years since the above was written, it has been easier for Negroes to obtain better jobs in federal installations in the South than in private industry. In concluding that each year the opportunities of Negroes

---

[48] Charles S. Johnson, *Patterns of Negro Segregation*, p. 30.

[49] Gunnar Myrdal, *op. cit.*, pp. 328–329.

[50] Herbert Northrup, *Organized Labor and the Negro*, Harper & Brothers, 1944, p. 253.

in the Federal Civil Service will probably increase as further effort is made to put nondiscriminatory policies into effect, Ginzberg supports the predictions of Myrdal rather than those of Northrup.[51]

Fair Employment Practices Committees

An important recent development that may have strong effects on the place of minorities in the American economy is the federal wartime Fair Employment Practices order and the numerous state and municipal employment laws that have been passed in the last few years.

THE FEDERAL FEPC DURING WORLD WAR II

When Negroes continued to be greatly underrepresented in the defense industries in the months before Pearl Harbor, a march on Washington was organized by A. Philip Randolph, president of the Brotherhood of Sleeping Car Porters. Negotiations between the administration and Mr. Randolph resulted in the calling off of the march and the issuance by President Roosevelt on June 25, 1941, of Executive Order 8802. In part, this order stated: "I do hereby reaffirm the policy of the United States that there shall be no discrimination in the employment of workers in defense industries or government because of race, creed, color, or national origin, and I do hereby declare that it is the duty of employers and of labor organizations, in furtherance of said policy and of this order, to provide for the full and equitable participation of all workers in defense industries, without discrimination because of race, creed, color, or national origin." All departments and agencies of the government of the United States concerned with vocational and training programs for defense production were instructed to take special measures to assure the administration of such programs without discrimination. All contracting agencies of the government were to include provisions obligating the contractor not to discriminate against any worker because of race, creed, color, or national origin. The order also established in the Office of Production Management a Committee on Fair Employment Practice, which consisted of a chairman and four other members to be appointed by the President. The committee was empowered to receive and investigate complaints of discrimination and to take "appropriate steps to redress grievances which it finds to be valid." The committee was also asked to "recommend to the several departments and agencies of the Government of the United States and to the President all measures which may be deemed by it necessary or proper to effectuate the provisions of this order."

On May 27, 1943, Mr. Roosevelt issued Executive Order 9346, which amended Executive Order 8802 "by establishing a new committee on

---

[51] Eli Ginzberg, op. cit., p. 26.

fair employment practice and defining its powers and duties." The revised order established a Committee on Fair Employment Practice in the Office for Emergency Management of the Executive Office of the President. This committee was to consist of a full-time chairman and not more than six members to be appointed by the President. The committee was now authorized to utilize the services and facilities of other federal departments and agencies, as well as such voluntary and uncompensated services as might be needed. Provision was also made for the acceptance of the services of state and local authorities and officials.

A total of 14,000 complaints of discrimination were handled during the five years that the federal FEPC was in existence. Eighty percent of the appeals for protection against discrimination were from Negroes. Discrimination on the basis of creed constituted 6 percent of the total, and most of these complaints came from Jews. The other 14 percent appealed because of national origin, and nearly all of these workers were Mexican-Americans. There were almost no charges of discrimination filed by American Poles, Czechoslovakians, Italians, Germans, Lithuanians, and other national groups.[52] Malcolm Ross is correct in saying that this record does not enable us to say that four-fifths of American prejudice is directed against the colored race, but it does give a rough indication of the exploitation which other Americans have found profitable.

In five years FEPC satisfactorily settled nearly 5000 cases by peaceful negotiation, including forty strikes caused by racial differences. FEPC held fifteen public hearings and docketed a total of 3485 cases, settling 1191 of them, during the last year of the war. "These settlements were not publicized and generally escaped attention. The contrary impression, that FEPC normally met with unyielding opposition, was created by the comparatively few difficult cases which received emphasis through public hearings and public expressions of defiance by some recalcitrant employers and unions."[53]

The committee was not dominated by industry or by labor, by political party or by color. During the five years labor at one time or another was represented by William Green, Philip Murray, Frank Fenton, Boris Shishkin, John Brophy. The Negro members were Earl B. Dickerson, alderman of the city of Chicago; Milton P. Webster, international vice-president of the Brotherhood of Sleeping Car Porters; P. B. Young, editor of the Norfolk *Journal and Guide*; Charles H. Houston, Washington lawyer. Industry's representatives were David Sarnoff, president of the Radio Corporation of America; Miss Sara Southall, supervisor of employment and service, International Harvester Company; Samuel

---

[52] For an excellent account of all aspects of the federal FEPC, see Malcolm Ross, *All Manner of Men*, Reynal and Hitchcock, 1948.
[53] Fair Employment Practice Committee, *Final Report*, Government Printing Office, 1947, p. viii.

Zemurray, president of the United Fruit Company; Charles L. Horn, president of the Federal Cartridge Company. Monsignor Francis J. Haas was the first chairman; Mark F. Ethridge, the second; and Malcolm Ross, the third.

On the question of whether the committee was successful in achieving its twin goals of creating greater economic opportunities for minority-group members and of fully utilizing our resources of manpower in the war effort, it may be pointed out that minority-group workers rose from less than 3 percent in 1942 to more than 8 percent in 1944; i.e., there was an addition of a million and a half Negroes and Mexican-Americans at work in vital war industries. However, it cannot be said that FEPC was the only factor in opening the plants to workers who had been previously excluded.

Such firms as the National Smelting Company of Cleveland and the Western Electric Company of Chicago accepted Negro workers in all capacities on their own initiative. So did many others. Moreover, the War Manpower Commission, the War and Navy Departments, the Maritime Commission, the War Shipping Administration, the Civil Service and other agencies had many staff members working on discrimination, and, on the whole, they did the bulk of the work under the wartime injunction to keep all gates open.

FEPC was the specialist who took the cases which the other doctors along the row failed to analyze or cure. The healthy patients never entered its door.[54]

One might speculate, of course, on whether some of the "healthy" patients would have been so well if there had been no FEPC or no war.

We cannot present in any detail the summaries, findings, and directives of the public hearings of the FEPC, but an abbreviated account of hearings against seven prime war producers in St. Louis in 1945 is given here.

The FEPC at St. Louis heard seven war producers testify that they supported the national policy of nondiscrimination in general, but that the opposition of their white workers made its application impossible in their plants. Evidence showed that male Negro workers were hired only as janitors, porters and sweepers, and Negro women were refused work on production lines. In plants where Negro men were given semiskilled jobs, the quota system limited their numbers. The usual defense was that the customs of St. Louis forbade integration.

In its directive FEPC set forth the loss to war manpower resulting from keeping Negro males at jobs below their acquired skills and from refusing to tap the last unused reservoir of local labor, the 5,000 Negro women then registered at USES.

Prewar St. Louis had indeed kept Negroes mostly at common labor, but

[54] Malcolm Ross, op. cit., p. 48.

the citing of a "social pattern" as excuse to fix quotas was artificial and went no further back than the Defense period when it was invented.

Most of the seven producers made timid attempts at compliance, such as hiring a few Negro women for work in a segregated annex. Such token performance might have stood for the limit to which the St. Louis "social pattern" could be stretched, were it not for notable examples which disprove that contention.

The General Cable Corporation's St. Louis plant had all the problems with which other war producers in St. Louis were confronted. This employer, however, had laid an educational foundation for integrating Negroes. When a first attempt to utilize Negro women was met with threats of a strike, the Corporation's President flew from New York and spent 24 hours presenting to white employees the reasons why the company was going to follow through with the hiring of Negro women. The strike threats faded. Two months later Negro women were integrated into all production departments of the plant.

A similar success was achieved by the U. S. Cartridge Co. It had adopted the quota system and also had placed Negroes in a separate building. At the time of the FEPC hearings, both these factors were making it difficult to hire enough workers. The company's ammunition was desperately needed on both war fronts.

U. S. Cartridge accepted an FEPC directive and set about hiring more Negroes and integrating them in a building with white workers. Despite the defection of many rank and filers, the Union officials refused to retreat from a policy of nondiscrimination.

The reverse of the U. S. Cartridge Co. experience appears in the case of Western Cartridge Co. of East Alton, Ill. Western is the parent company of U. S. Cartridge, and is located across the river from St. Louis. FEPC held two hearings in East Alton, a town which has excluded Negroes for decades. Among the company's 10,000 ammunition workers there was not a single Negro.

Three hundred Western Cartridge brass mill workers struck for an afternoon and attended the FEPC hearings with demands to be heard against Negroes. Their union leaders threatened to strike if any Negroes were hired. The Western Cartridge management deplored this display of their workers' intolerance. Nevertheless, FEPC was unable to obtain any change of practice at the Western Cartridge plant.[55]

About 25 percent of the committee's total case load was made up of government cases. Davis' explanation of such a high percentage is that more people in government service complain because they feel more secure against retaliation. Also, government procedures necessary for the operation of the merit system make it harder to prove discrimination. For these reasons, cases from government sources constituted only 17.5 percent of satisfactory adjustments, whereas business, "against which 69.4 percent of the cases were docketed provided 81 percent of the

[55] Fair Employment Practice Committee, *Final Report*, pp. 18–19.

satisfactory adjustments."[56] The quantitative and qualitative gains in the federal service during the war years are summarized in the section on "Negroes in Government Service."

The opposition to FEPC came from many sources and was not limited to the South.

Outside the South, the reaction to changes in racial patterns was less violent but often extremely critical. Many local chambers of commerce were alarmed by the new "militancy" of the Negro and the government's "encouragement" of it. The non-discrimination executive orders were blasted, usually in confidential letters or memoranda. The Negro press was severely scored, and Negro leadership was accused of being interested chiefly in self-aggrandizement and monetary gains. Some representatives of management dogmatically stated that Negroes and whites could not work together and that governmental efforts to force them to do so would result in widespread violence and serious loss of production.[57]

To the South "FEPC was an unpatriotic plot, contrived by rats and moral lepers, concealing under hypocritical guise a hope to cause disaster to the South."[58] A Mississippi Democrat in a debate in the House called on his party to kill FEPC, saying, " 'I come to you as an American asking you as another American for God's sake to help us.' "[59]

At one hearing conducted by the House special committee on the rotary-hiring-list system of the War Shipping Administration in New York, three southern congressmen, one from Michigan, and the committee's counsel questioned two officials from the Recruitment and Manning Organization on the subject of "social equality" and intermarriage. Congressman Jennings finally asked: "You do feel, I take it, if a white man wanted to marry a colored woman, or a colored man wanted to marry a white woman and they mutually agreed on the union, it ought to be consummated, they ought to live together as man and wife. That is the ultimate end of social equality, is it not?" The witness protested that the term "social equality" meant different things to different people, and added: "I make a distinction in my own mind between economic opportunities and social opportunities. I believe that economic opportunities mean equality of opportunity. I believe that when it comes to mingling together, that is a matter of preference, and there, in my own thinking, the question is not so much a man's name or his race or his color, but I just happen to like some people, so I have a natural preference to deal with the people I like."[60] We cite this incident to show how very old sentiments, slogans, and prejudgments could

---

[56] John A. Davis and Cornelius L. Golightly, *op. cit.*, p. 342.
[57] R. C. Weaver, *Negro Labor*, Harcourt, Brace & Company, 1946, p. 239.
[58] Malcolm Ross, *op. cit.*, p. 116.
[59] *Ibid.*, p. 115.
[60] *Ibid.*, p. 112.

interfere with the practical problem of trying to find seamen to man ships during wartime.

The assertion that FEPC was trying to impose social equality on the South echoed and reëchoed throughout the South. Righteous men proclaimed that only the South really understands Negroes and that the Negro race had made great progress under the guidance of wise southern leaders. As Ross says, FEPC was thought of as a radical movement, designed to eradicate the traditions of the South. It was, of course, bound to "subject white women to great danger." No one mentioned the personal economic advantage of the existing occupational arrangements to upper- and middle-class white Southerners.

One honest speech would have brought the issue down to reality. The wives of my constituents, a candid senator might have said, object to better wages for Negroes. Maids who formerly could be had at four dollars a week are now getting twenty-five at war plants. Yard men are no longer to be had. All Negroes will be thoroughly spoiled unless they are made to understand that these ridiculous wages are merely a temporary expedient for war production and will be stopped instanter with the coming of peace. Furthermore, the white workers among my constituency will not permit Negroes to work at skilled trades nor join their unions.[61]

In addition to being harassed constantly by powerful economic and political forces opposed to its existence, the committee was badly handicapped by inadequate appropriations, insufficient staff, and excessive administrative controls. Also, FEPC was forced to produce immediate results. As a result, there was little opportunity for long-run planning and programming.

The most conspicuous example of such neglect was the failure of the committee to pursue fully the possibilities of getting the contracting agencies of the government to enforce the non-discrimination clauses in their contracts. Closely associated was the tendency of the committee to take over all governmental operations relative to the development of employment opportunities for minorities in war industries. This action succeeded in developing widespread support for FEPC among minorities and their friends, but it did not lead to the most effective and aggressive enforcement of Executive Order 8802.[62]

The committee had no authority to compel compliance with its directives. It had to rely on public censure. Some large and powerful corporations, such as Vultee Aircraft in California, Buick Aircraft in Chicago, and Wright Aeronautical in Paterson, New Jersey, were cited and compliance was secured. The same is true of the exposure and pressure upon the International Association of Machinists at the Los Angeles hearings

[61] Ibid., p. 36.
[62] R. C. Weaver, op. cit., pp. 137–138.

and the mechanical building craft unions at the Chicago hearings. All of these efforts did help to increase the employment of minorities; Negroes did enter new occupations, plants, and industries; Negroes and whites did work together.[63]

It is important to note, however, that persuasion is not sufficient to end discrimination. In the period 1941–1946, employers needed war workers, their patriotism was aroused, and they disliked exposure. These were strong factors in reducing discrimination; but discriminatory policies "seldom disappeared spontaneously. The intervention of a third party, with authority to act if necessary, was required to start the process in motion." FEPC found that persuasion has its limits in a number of important cases which it was never able to settle. "Relatively few in number, these employers and unions which successfully defied the national policy of nondiscrimination proved that persuasion must be backed by final authority if conformity with the policy is to be realized.[64]

Since FEPC is one of the major issues in race relations in the United States at mid-century, it seems worth while to consider some of the objections which are advanced against it both at the federal and at state levels. One widespread remark directed against FEPC is that prejudice cannot be removed by law. This is not, of course, the intent of legislation. The Fourteenth Amendment to the Constitution of the United States is concerned with the equal protection of the law, the Fifteenth Amendment with the right to vote. Neither was designed to eliminate prejudice; both sought to protect the rights of ex-slaves. Fair economic practices legislation does not eliminate prejudice. It can only remove the economic barriers created by prejudice and offer some economic protection against gross discrimination in hiring and upgrading. It is sometimes said that education should precede legislation. The antithesis "education versus legislation" appears to be a false one. Both would seem to be useful in modifying the racial occupational patterns. Malcolm Ross, chairman of FEPC during the last three years of its existence, stated that "in what FEPC has described as its difficult cases (Western Cartridge, Capital Transit, West Coast Shipyards, Southern Railroads, etc.), education alone could not end discrimination, yet education would be an invaluable aid to create the atmosphere in which authority could work out its solution peacefully." The proponents of FEPC maintain that campaigns for legislation are in themselves educational campaigns, and they point out that in New York State an educational program parallels the work of the FEPC. It is often asked: "Is there need for such a law?" It may be pointed out that immediately after

---

[63] *Ibid.*, pp. 137, 239.
[64] Fair Employment Practice Committee, *Final Report,* pp. viii–ix.

V-J Day many Negroes were dropped from government service; white industrial workers were retained disproportionately in higher-paid jobs; the United States Employment Service consistently referred Negro workers to low-paid jobs only; and newspapers, except in New York and New Jersey, carried "Gentile only" advertisements.

These questions are only a few of the more important ones which are asked, apparently with a view to preventing the passage of FEPC legislation or pulling the teeth of any proposed acts. Other questions which are raised include: Is such legislation constitutional? What is its effect on business? Does it reflect public opinion? Is it a good public investment? Is it a factor in public morale?[65] Would it not be better to let the matter be handled on the state level?

The chairman of the New York State Commission Against Discrimination makes the following comment about the effectiveness of a state FEP agency:

A state agency's power is in any case less effective than would be that of a Federal agency, since some interstate employers may be in the position to claim immunity from state controls, while others can hire labor in states where no restrictions against discrimination in employment exist. Federal policy has not risen to this challenge, despite the expansion of Federal power, the rising concentration of industry engaged in interstate operations, the growing size of labor unions, and the increased number of public and private enterprises dealing with the Federal government or benefitting from its aid. Though power to act exists with Congress, with the Executive, and to a certain extent with the Supreme Court, progress has been virtually halted on all three levels.[66]

Reference is made later in this chapter to the program of the President's Committee on Government Contracts.

Finally it is asked: Would such a law work? Unquestionably it would have opposition, but this has been true of all social legislation (eight-hour day, child labor, collective bargaining rights, social security, unfair trade practices, etc.). Ross believes that the storm "would eventually be calmed by a strict limitation of the law to the industrial and government-service fields."

At the end of World War II Congress failed to pass legislation establishing a permanent FEPC. The members of the committee resigned on June 28, 1946. When the bill was before Congress in January, 1946, southern senators conducted a typical filibuster. Senator George of Georgia said, "At a time when the very life of the nation is at stake, we are called upon to consider a bill to compel people in the field of human relationships to do what their judgment directs them not to do. We are

[65] On these points see American Council on Race Relations, *State FEPC—What the People Say*, April, 1945.

[66] Charles Abrams, "Civil Rights in 1956," *Commentary*, August, 1956, p. 107.

called upon to go Nazi. We are called upon to go totalitarian." Senator Eastland of Mississippi said that communists were the chief sponsors of the legislation. Jews and Negroes, he said, ought to oppose the measure because "if Congress can pass a bill against discrimination it can pass one in favor of discrimination. The Jew is the last person to want such a program because, as a class, he is richer than the gentiles."[67] Both the Republican party and the Democratic party adopted planks in their platforms for the 1944 and the 1948 campaigns calling for the establishment of a federal FEPC. Northern Republicans have coöperated with southern Democrats in avoiding the enactment of such legislation.

The last chairman of FEPC has suggested that a permanent FEPC, modeled after any one of several existing administrative agencies, should have these features:

1. A clear definition of equal job opportunity and of the duties of employers and unions in protecting it.
2. Publication of rules and regulations under which the Commission shall operate, with provision for their approval by Congress.
3. Reliance on informal negotiation to settle cases by persuasion in the first instance.
4. Protection of due process of law through notice of hearings, the right to produce witnesses and cross-examine, a written record, and all other safeguards as formulated by Congress itself last spring (1946) in the Administrative Procedure Act.
5. No jail sentences or fines to be imposed by the agency.
6. Issuance of cease and desist orders subject to judicial review and enforcement.
7. Final appeal to the Supreme Court.[68]

Within this framework it would seem advisable to provide that no employer of less than fifty workers would be subject to the law. Such legislation would not compel an employer to engage unqualified workers or to employ any particular qualified worker. Its purpose would be to reduce systematic, gross discrimination against whole groups of people merely because they happen to belong to a minority race, religion, or nationality group. In 1958 it seemed highly unlikely that a permanent federal FEP agency would be established in the foreseeable future.

FAIR EMPLOYMENT POLICIES IN THE FEDERAL GOVERNMENT AFTER 1948

On July 26, 1948, two years after the refusal of Congress to enact permanent federal fair employment practice legislation, President Truman issued Executive Order 9980 to provide machinery for implement-

[67] *Philadelphia Record*, January 19, 1946, pp. 1, 3.
[68] Malcolm Ross, "The Outlook for a New FEPC," *Commentary*, April, 1947, pp. 306–307.

ing fair employment policy and redressing the discrimination evident in the federal government.[69] According to this Executive Order:

1. The head of each department in the executive branch of the Government shall be personally responsible for an effective program to insure that fair employment policies are fully observed in all personnel actions within his department.

2. The head of each department shall designate an official thereof as Fair Employment Officer. . . . The Fair Employment Officer shall, among other things—

(a) Appraise the personnel actions of the department at regular intervals to determine their conformity to the fair-employment policy expressed in this order.

(b) Receive complaints or appeals concerning personnel actions taken in the department on grounds of alleged discrimination because of race, color, religion, or national origin.

(c) Appoint such control or regional deputies, committees, or hearing boards, from among the officers or employees of the department, as he may find necessary or desirable on a temporary or permanent basis to investigate, or to receive, complaints of discrimination.

(d) Take necessary corrective or disciplinary action, in consultation with, or on the basis of delegated authority from, the head of the department.

3. The findings or action of the Fair Employment Officer shall be subject to direct appeal to the head of the department. The decision of the head of the department on such appeal shall be subject to appeal to the Fair Employment Board of the Civil Service Commission. . . .

The Fair Employment Board of the Civil Service Commission is to consist of not less than seven persons who shall—

A. Have authority to review decisions made by the head of any department which are appealed pursuant to the provisions of this order (Executive Order 9980), or referred to the Board by the head of the department for advice, and to make recommendations to such head. In any instance in which the recommendations of the Board are not promptly and fully carried out the case shall be reported by the Board to the President, for such action as he finds necessary.

B. Make rules and regulations, in consultation with the Civil Service Commission, deemed necessary to carry out the Board's duties and responsibilities under this order.

C. Advise all departments on problems and policies relating to fair employment.

D. Disseminate information pertinent to fair-employment programs.

E. Coordinate the fair-employment policies and procedures of the several departments.

[69] In 1940 the Ramspeck Act revising our civil service procedures stated: "In carrying out the provision (of the Civil Service classification system), there shall be no discrimination against any person or with respect to the position held by any person on account of race, creed, or color." Public Law 1881, 76th Congress, 3rd Session, Title 2, Section 3 (E).

F. Make reports and submit recommendations to the Civil Service Commission for transmittal to the President from time to time, as may be necessary to the maintenance of the fair-employment program.

In January, 1955, President Eisenhower abolished the Fair Employment Board and established a five-man committee to carry out a nondiscrimination order. Instead of operating under the Civil Service Commission the new committee was asked to report directly to the President. This Executive Order stated that discrimination against any employee or applicant for employment in the federal government because of race, color, religion, or national origin was prohibited. The committee was empowered to conduct inquiries and advise the President concerning the compliance of federal agencies with the nondiscrimination policy.[70]

On August 13, 1953, President Eisenhower abolished the Committee on Government Contract Compliance which had been established in December, 1951, and formed the Committee on Government Contracts. The new committee was charged with obtaining compliance for equal employment opportunity from contractors or subcontractors doing business with or for the federal government. The procedures followed by this committee and its staff include compliance reviews; the preparation of a manual for the guidance of field personnel responsible for obtaining compliance; training programs for representatives of the federal contracting agencies; conferences with business and industrial organizations, leaders of labor unions, state and municipal antidiscrimination agencies; and the development of an educational program.[71] Abrams remarks that the President's Committee on Government Contracts has only fifteen employees and a budget of only $190,000.[72] The committee has tried to obtain compliance by seeking the coöperation of industry rather than resorting to cancellation or nonrenewal of contracts.[73]

STATE AND LOCAL FAIR EMPLOYMENT PRACTICE LAWS

Fifteen states—Colorado, Connecticut, Indiana, Kansas, Massachusetts, Michigan, Minnesota, New Jersey, New Mexico, New York, Oregon, Pennsylvania, Rhode Island, Washington, and Wisconsin—have passed fair employment practice legislation.[74] The weakest of these state laws is found in Indiana, where no provisions are made for enforcement. Bills have been introduced but defeated in many other states, including

[70] Cleveland *Plain Dealer*, January 20, 1955.
[71] President's Committee on Government Contracts, *Second Annual Report, 1954–55*, and *Third Annual Report, 1955–56*. Government Printing Office.
[72] Charles Abrams, *op. cit.*, p. 107.
[73] Eli Ginzberg, *op. cit.*, p. 130.
[74] Since 1941 fifteen states have enacted laws concerning the hiring of public or state employees. John H. Burma, "Race Relations and Antidiscriminatory Legislation," *American Journal of Sociology*, March, 1951, p. 418.

such important industrial states as Ohio and Illinois. These laws have been enacted because (1) a federal FEPC was lacking and (2) the state FEPC has certain areas of operation which cannot be covered by a national law. As Weaver points out, a shift is under way to employment in the service industries and the distributive trades. Also, the number of persons employed in public and semipublic utilities is increasing. These branches of industry would not be reached by a federal employment agency, which would be limited to firms engaged in interstate commerce.[75]

The New York FEPC was the first to be established. The Ives-Quinn Law became effective on July 1, 1945, and it has been the model for several of the other state laws. The law applies to employers, labor unions, and the advertisements and preëmployment inquiries of employers and employment agencies. Educational work of the commission is carried on through (1) the collaboration of the State Department of Education, (2) local or regional councils, and (3) the direct action of the commission. The New York commission first tries persuasion on a discriminating respondent. If persuasion fails, "we tell him frankly that he is breaking the law and point out the penalties for continuing to do so. To date, every respondent against whom a verified charge of discrimination was filed has modified his employment practices to make them legal."[76]

The record of the New York commission is impressive.

Since July 1, 1945, when the New York law became effective, we have received 1,407 complaints of discrimination in employment. We have initiated investigations of our own in 422 additional cases. Two hundred nineteen of the cases are still open. The remaining 1,610 cases—each of which involved anywhere from four employees or job-seekers or union members or students to 65,000—have been closed to the commission's satisfaction, which means either that no evidence of discrimination was found or, which was much more common, that the respondent stopped discriminating. *In every instance we were able to obtain compliance with the law by conciliation and persuasion without going to court.*[77]

[75] R. C. Weaver, *op. cit.*, p. 312.

[76] Caroline K. Simon, "Causes and Cure of Discrimination," New York *Times Magazine*, May 29, 1949, p. 35.

[77] *Ibid.*, p. 36. By 1952, state FEP commissions had investigated more than 5000 complaints, but only five public hearings against employers had been held. Limited court action was resorted to only four times. In one case, Railway Mail Association v. Corsi, the constitutionality of FEP legislation was upheld by the Supreme Court as an exercise of the police power of the state. See John A. Davis, "Negro Employment: A Progress Report," *Fortune*, 1952, p. 158. For an excellent examination of state FEP commissions, see Elmer Carter, "Policies and Practices of Discrimination Commissions," *Annals of the American Academy of Political and Social Science*, March, 1956, pp. 62–77. Carter (pp. 72–74) cites two interesting cases of discrimination by labor unions which were handled by state commissions against discrimination (Connecticut and New York).

As Miss Simon indicates, these figures deal only with lawbreakers or suspected lawbreakers. There is no way of determining how many organizations, under the impact of the law, have voluntarily revised their practices. Perhaps the number of job opportunities now open to all is a better test of the effects of the law than the number of complaints received. The application blanks of 4000 business firms have been reviewed, and all references to race, color, and religion are now omitted. Nearly all employment agencies have stopped asking for or forwarding such information. "Every union in the state which had a 'Caucasian' clause in its constitution or by-laws has either removed the clause, or made it inoperative in New York. With the exception of domestic help, all daily newspapers in New York State now omit discriminatory specifications from 'Help Wanted' and 'Position Wanted' classified ads. . . ." Three percent of all Negro women employees in New York City in 1940 had clerical or sales positions; by 1947 the figure was 13 percent. Sixteen percent of the employed Negro women in 1940 worked in semiskilled trades; the percentage had almost doubled (31 percent) by 1947. During the same period, Negro women employed as domestic servants dropped from 64 to 36 percent.[78]

From the beginning of the New York commission's work in mid 1945 until the end of 1955, a total of 3345 verified complaints were filed. Alleged discrimination because of color accounted for 71 percent of this number, creed for 15 percent, and national origin for 6 percent.

On July 1, 1952, the area of public accommodations, resorts, and amusements was brought under the jurisdiction of the New York State Commission Against Discrimination, and on July 1, 1955, public and publicly assisted housing were also included. Of the 398 complaints filed during 1955, 76 alleged discrimination in places of public accommodation, resort, or amusement.[79] The commission was given jurisdiction over FHA- and VA-aided housing on July 1, 1956; and in the following five months approximately one-fourth of the complaints related to housing. The commission anticipated that handling complaints in this area would be one of its main tasks from 1957 on.[80]

In 1956, the New York commission inaugurated a program of industry-wide investigations to change the policies of industries as a group, including both employers and unions. The industries included airlines,

[78] Caroline K. Simon, op. cit., p. 36.

[79] New York State Commission Against Discrimination, Report of Progress, 1955, p. 2. The laws in New Jersey, Connecticut, Rhode Island, and Massachusetts also have been amended to provide for the use of conciliation procedures, as developed in the field of employment, in cases involving discrimination in the areas of public accommodation and publicly assisted housing. See Elmer Carter, op. cit., p. 74.

[80] Address by Charles Abrams, Chairman of the New York State Commission Against Discrimination, at the Annual Meeting with Civic and Social Agencies, New York City, December 3, 1956, pp. 5–6.

baking, brewing, hotels, and railways.[81] The most important development resulted from negotiations with airlines and led to a joint statement in December, 1956, in which the airlines agreed to judge applicants in all categories of employment and upgrading on the basis of merit and without regard to race, creed, color, or national origin.[82]

Although full employment has been an important factor in the economic situation in the post-World War II period, there is general agreement that there has been a significant increase in opportunities for employment for Negroes in most of the FEP states and in many of the FEP cities. The evidence is not as clear, but it is believed that resistance to the employment of Jews has also steadily declined where state and municipal FEP legislation has been passed.[83] In a survey of employers, *Business Week* found:

1. Employers agree that FEPC laws haven't caused near the fuss that opponents predicted. Disgruntled job-seekers haven't swamped commissions with complaints. Personal friction hasn't been at all serious. Some employers still think there's no need for a law. But even those who opposed an FEPC aren't actively hostile now.

2. Commissions say that the laws have created no new problems for either a business or a community. They haven't interfered with any employer's basic right to choose the most competent man for a job, the commissions say. And the unanimous view is that minority groups are finding openings in places barred to them before.[84]

The same report said that a check of 79 major New Jersey employers by the state commission against discrimination showed: "(1) No new difficulties or problems in business policy; (2) no interference with their 'basic right to select the most competent workers for [their] operations'; and (3) 'as far as we know,' the law has been 'fairly and effectually administered.' The commission had had no complaints of FEPC-bred 'racial tensions' or of anyone's refusing or vacating a job 'because of minority group employment.' "[85]

Despite the accomplishments of state FEP programs, a number of shortcomings have been noted in the existing laws against discrimination and in the functioning of the commissions. The laws have been put on the statute books to satisfy minority groups, but legislators have opposed the granting of adequate power or funds.[86] In some states, the budgets of commissions against discrimination have been too small to provide for

---

[81] *Ibid.*, p. 2.
[82] *Race Relations Law Reporter*, December, 1956, p. 1148.
[83] Elmer Carter, *op. cit.*, p. 71.
[84] *Business Week*, February 25, 1950, p. 114.
[85] *Ibid.*, p. 115.
[86] See Charles Abrams, "Civil Rights in 1956," p. 107; and Gerhart Saenger, *The Social Psychology of Prejudice*, Harper & Brothers, 1953, pp. 267–268.

the dissemination of publicity concerning the law. Even in New York, the "massive educational effort" of SCAD during the first three years of the state program did not lead to a wide knowledge of the law.[87] Another finding concerning the state FEP programs is that knowledge of the law does not always lead to complaints. In 1948 only one-sixth of New York City's Jewish population and one-fourth of its Negro population believed that the law would be effective in combating discrimination.[88] Some have questioned whether Jews have benefited substantially from state FEP laws. Jewish discrimination is more likely to be a matter of quotas, or of token employment or segregation in certain departments, rather than total exclusion. Perhaps FEP commissions have tended to concentrate on Negro discrimination because it is more pressing and easier to handle. Maslow thinks that Jewish organizations may have been at fault in not trying to find out the facts about the changing Jewish job market and directing complaints to governmental agencies.[89]

More than forty cities, including Chicago, Philadelphia, Minneapolis, Cleveland, and Youngstown, have passed fair employment practice ordinances, in part because no state laws have been enacted in their states. The municipal ordinance is not "considered merely as a substitute for a state law, but as supplementing the state law just as the latter would complement the proposed federal law."[90]

It is difficult to predict the future of fair employment practice laws at the local, state, and federal levels. Northrup's conclusion in 1944 seems not to be fully justified in view of the passage of a number of state and municipal laws since 1945 and the issuance of Executive Order 9980 in 1948. Northrup wrote: "There is . . . almost no chance whatever that state laws forbidding discrimination will be adopted where they are needed most—namely, in the South. Nor are many northern states likely to pass effective legislation of that type. More important, however, is that after a start toward the policy advocated here [in his book], federal policy has recently veered in the opposite direction."[91]

The future employment opportunities of minority-group members are closely related to the degree of their political power. We turn now to an analysis of their part in the political and legal structure.

[87] Gerhart Saenger, op. cit., pp. 268–269.
[88] Ibid., p. 269.
[89] Will Maslow, "The Uses of Law in the Struggle for Equality," Social Research, Autumn Quarter, 1955, p. 303. Maslow states that the Chicago Bureau on Jewish Employment Problems, a voluntary organization, handled more complaints of discrimination against Jews than the ten state and the thirty municipal FEP agencies in existence in 1955 put together.
[90] Alex Elson and Leonard Schanfield, "Local Regulation of Discriminatory Employment Practices," Yale Law Journal, February, 1947, p. 454.
[91] Herbert Northrup, op. cit., p. 251.

CHAPTER 14

Minorities and the American Political and Legal Processes

As societies have become more complex, a larger and larger proportion of key decisions have been made through political processes, and law has come to occupy an increasingly influential place in our lives. Our study of the place of minority groups in the social structure, therefore, must give careful attention to the ways in which these groups influence and are influenced by political decisions and legal processes. Some of the political and legal aspects of American minority life are dealt with in other chapters. Fair employment practice legislation and the representation of minority groups in the Federal Civil Service have been considered in the preceding chapter on minorities in our economy. Recent decisions of the United States Supreme Court on educational questions, as well as fair educational practice legislation, are examined in later chapters on the education of racial and cultural minorities.

The Legal Status of the Negro Before 1900

We shall not consider in this chapter the legal status of indentured servants and slaves during the colonial and early national periods. Some reference to it was made earlier in the treatment of majority-minority relations and social stratification.

In the matter of voting, even free Negroes were disfranchised throughout the South and in most of the North and the West in 1860. New England, with the exception of Connecticut, permitted Negroes to vote. New York required Negroes who wished to vote to own a certain amount of property, a qualification which did not hold for whites. Wisconsin granted the suffrage to Negroes in 1849. Other northern and border states disfranchised them as follows: Delaware in 1792, Kentucky in 1799, Maryland in 1809, Connecticut in 1818, New Jersey in 1820, Virginia in 1830, Tennessee in 1834, North Carolina in 1835, and Pennsylvania in 1838. Other states in the South and West did not permit Negroes to vote.[1]

After the adoption in 1865 of the Thirteenth Amendment abolishing slavery and involuntary servitude, except as a punishment for crime after due conviction, special restrictive legislation was enacted in the southern states. These laws, which became known as the Black Codes, virtually reintroduced the slave codes. They covered apprenticeship, labor contracts, migration, vagrancy, civil and legal rights.[2] The passage of the Black Codes brought about the adoption of the Fourteenth Amendment containing the famous statement: "No State shall make or enforce any law which shall abridge the privileges or immunities of citizens of the United States; nor shall any State deprive any person of life, liberty, or property, without due process of law; nor deny to any person within its jurisdiction the equal protection of the laws." The Fifteenth Amendment—"The right of the citizens of the United States to vote shall not be denied or abridged by the United States or by any State on account of race, color, or previous condition of servitude" —was also a reaction to the Black Codes, as was the federal Civil Rights Act of 1875. This act was declared unconstitutional in 1883, and soon thereafter the southern states began to enact segregative legislation.[3]

One of the controversial aspects of the early years of the Reconstruction period was the program carried on by the Bureau of Refugees, Freedmen, and Abandoned Lands. The Freedmen's Bureau in the War Department was created by a bill passed in 1865 and was in operation until 1872. It was criticized for the tactlessness, ineptitude, and corruptness of some of its officials. On the other hand, especially in recent years, this agency has been acclaimed for its positive accomplishments. At the time it was abolished, it had 2600 day and night schools in operation, with 3300 teachers (most of them trained by the bureau). It established Howard, Fisk, Hampton, and St. Augustine Normal School. In many parts of the South it was responsible for setting up what later became tax-supported public schools. Institutions were founded to care for the aged, the crippled, and the mentally diseased. A medical-aid program for Negroes was set up, and hospitals were established. Orphans and the destitute were furnished aid, and some

[1] C. S. Mangum, Jr., *The Legal Status of the Negro*, University of North Carolina Press, 1940, pp. 371–372.
[2] See E. Franklin Frazier, *The Negro in the United States*, The Macmillan Company, 1949, pp. 126–127.
[3] Carey McWilliams, "Race Discrimination and the Law," *Science and Society*, Winter, 1945, p. 11.

30,000 displaced freedmen were returned to their former homes. The bureau was instructed by Congress to give every freedman forty acres and a mule. Some abandoned and confiscated land was distributed, but the bureau never had more than 800,000 acres to dispose of (only 2/10 of 1 percent of the land of the seceding states was ever held by the bureau). Even if all these lands had been available, less than one acre could have been given to every freedman. As McWilliams indicates, most of the lands were quickly repossessed by the former owners as a result of wholesale amnesties, and Negroes who had acquired small tracts were dispossessed.[4]

Many interesting developments occurred during the Reconstruction years. In 1869 a Georgia court declared invalid a prewar statute preventing anyone with one-eighth or more Negro ancestry from holding public office. An article of the Louisiana constitution requiring racial separation in the schools was suspended in 1868, and the South Carolina public schools were opened to both races in the same year. It is reported that the University of South Carolina admitted Negro students in the first Reconstruction years, and that Richard T. Greener, a Negro graduate of Harvard, was librarian. Negroes were elected to Congress for the first time during the forty-first session (1870–1871). H. K. Revels, of Mississippi, came to fill the Senate seat of Jefferson Davis; Jefferson F. Long was a representative from Georgia. From 1870 to 1901, twenty Negroes were seated as representatives and two as senators. The largest number elected for any one Congress during these thirty years was seven (1876–1877).[5]

There is no need for us to present a detailed account of the Reconstruction period. Such a record is available in the many works dealing with the period. Most readers are more or less familiar with the martial law; the arbitrariness of some military officers and officials of the Freedmen's Bureau; the New England schoolteachers who came south; the collaboration of some Negroes, carpetbaggers, and scalawags; the waste and corruption; the positive achievements such as the new state constitutions, new laws on voting, new schools, etc.; and the disappointment and resentment of southern leaders at the loss of the war and of their cause.

The famous "Bargain of 1876" restored "white supremacy" to the South. The Republicans agreed not to oppose the election of Democrats to state office in South Carolina, Louisiana, and Florida and to withdraw troops from these states; the Democrats agreed to hand Hayes the presidency which Tilden had won. The bargain carried with it the nullification of the Civil War amendments insofar as the Negro

---

[4] Carey McWilliams, *Brothers Under the Skin*, Little, Brown and Company, rev. ed., 1951, pp. 357–359.

[5] Charles S. Johnson, *Patterns of Negro Segregation*, Harper & Brothers, 1943, pp. 164, 342.

was concerned. From then on Negroes were to be "eliminated from politics."[6]

The important thing today, as Myrdal points out, is that the average white Southerner resists the thought that Negroes should vote in the same way white men do. He needs to believe that life was unbearable when the Negro voted. The myth of "the horrors of Reconstruction" thus enables the Southerner to reconcile his unwillingness to see the Negro vote on the same basis that whites do with his attachment to the Constitution.[7]

The Disfranchisement and Reënfranchisement of Negroes in the United States

To assure the permanent elimination of the Negro from political affairs in the South, various legal and nonlegal devices were invented. "Grandfather clauses" were included in a number of the disfranchising constitutions adopted by southern states in the 1890's. The Louisiana constitution of 1898 provided that one might register permanently before September 1, 1898, if he was entitled to vote in any state January 1, 1867, or if he was the son or grandson of a person so entitled and twenty-one years of age or over in 1898. North Carolina included a "grandfather clause" in her revised statutes of 1905.[8] These clauses excluded Negroes from voting while permitting white persons of all kinds to vote. The United States Supreme Court held these clauses to be unconstitutional in 1915.

Some southern states have disfranchised Negroes through educational qualifications for voting. Ostensibly these requirements are nondiscriminatory, and they are not limited to southern states. The Supreme Court declared in 1898 that these requirements do not violate the

---

[6] Carey McWilliams, *Brothers Under the Skin*, p. 265. For an excellent discussion of the Reconstruction period see Paul Lewinson, *Race, Class, and Party*, Oxford University Press, 1932, chaps. 2–5. See also Gunnar Myrdal, *An American Dilemma*, Harper & Brothers, 1944, chap. 20; and E. Franklin Frazier, *op. cit.*, pp. 114–139.

[7] Gunnar Myrdal, *op. cit.*, p. 448. Moon points out that "the freedmen had neither the political know-how nor the audacity to match the corrupt practices of Huey Long of Louisiana and Theodore (The man) Bilbo of Mississippi." According to Moon, "There is ample evidence that this propertyless class played a minor role in the corrupt practices of the post-war period in which there was nationwide relaxation of standards of political morality." More importantly, Negroes did not dominate the state governments of the South. " 'The majority of state executive offices and the most important were always filled by white men. The congressional delegations were composed of the same class of individuals. The leading men in both branches of every state legislature were representatives of the dominant race. . . .' " Every attempt was made by white Southerners to assure the failure of the Reconstruction governments; the participation of Negroes in the political process was unthinkable. See H. L. Moon, *Balance of Power: The Negro Vote*, Doubleday & Company, Inc., 1948, pp. 62–64.

[8] Charles S. Johnson, *op. cit.*, p. 165.

Fifteenth Amendment. In actual practice, they are seldom demanded of whites, but almost always of Negroes. White election officials, especially in the deep South, have often failed to find any educationally qualified Negro voters. In most cases the "educational" test consists of reading and writing a section of the federal or state constitution in such a way that the registrar is "satisfied." At the present time there are only two states, Mississippi and Louisiana, which require, in addition to reading and writing a section of the constitution, that the prospective voter "interpret" it to the "satisfaction" of the election official. These registrars have been hard to satisfy, and reports of extraordinary rulings on the meaning of the state and federal constitutions are numerous. Ralph Bunche cites a report of an Alabama registrar who asked a Negro to recite the Constituion. The Negro eloquently recited the Gettysburg Address, and the registrar exclaimed: "That's right. You can go ahead and register."[9]

Property requirements for voting are still in effect in Alabama, Georgia, and South Carolina, but they are invoked only if an applicant cannot meet the educational requirements. They call for the ownership of forty acres of land or personal property worth $300 to $500, and thus provide a way out for illiterate white people. The "character" requirement for voting exists now only in Louisiana and Georgia and is used both to disfranchise Negroes and to enable whites who cannot meet the property or educational requirements to register. Myrdal reports that actually the "character" qualification is used illegally elsewhere in the South where Negroes must be vouched for by whites.[10]

Between 1889 and 1908, ten southern states (Alabama, Arkansas, Florida, Louisiana, Mississippi, North Carolina, South Carolina, Tennessee, Texas, and Virginia) through constitutional provision or statutory law adopted a poll tax requirement for voting. The effectiveness of the poll tax as a device to regulate voting was considerably enhanced in Alabama, Mississippi, Louisiana, and Virginia by the provision that there would be no proceedings to collect the tax until it was three years overdue.

The effect of the new disfranchising constitutions is seen strikingly in Louisiana. The number of registered Negro voters in 1896 was 130,-344; in 1900 it was 5320. For one reason or another, the number of Negro registrants had dropped to 1772 in 1916. The following figures refer to (1) the twenty-one-year-old and literate Negro populations in certain states in 1920 and (2) the Negro voters at any time, 1920–1930, in those states: Alabama: 269,847 and 3500; Georgia: 369,511 and 10,000

[9] Ralph Bunche, "The Disfranchisement of the Negro," in Sterling A. Brown, Arthur P. Davis, and Ulysses Lee (eds.), The Negro Caravan, The Dryden Press, Inc., 1941, p. 930.
[10] Gunnar Myrdal, op. cit., pp. 483–484.

at most; Mississippi: 290,792 and 850; Virginia, 248,347 and 12,000 to 18,000.[11]

The poll tax has disfranchised millions of whites and seems, in some cases, to have been deliberately designed for that purpose.[12] The significance of the poll tax in reducing the white vote is seen in these percentages: "In 1940, Oklahoma . . . had 60 percent of its adult citizenry voting compared to 18 percent in Arkansas; North Carolina had 43 percent compared to 22 percent in Virginia; and Louisiana, which has been without the poll tax only since 1934, had 27 percent compared to 14 percent in Mississippi."[13] The tight control exerted by many southern politicians over their districts was indicated also in the estimates given on the floor of the House of Representatives on July 21, 1947. "In the Presidential elections of 1944, 10 percent of the potential voters voted in the seven poll-tax states, as against 49 percent in the free-vote states. In the congressional elections of 1946, the figures are 5 percent for the poll-tax states as compared with 33 percent for the free-voting states."[14]

The final device for disfranchising Negroes by the use of law was the "white primary." Since nomination in the Democratic primary is equivalent to election in the South, exclusion from the primary election meant the removal of Negroes from participation in the democratic process. In 1923 Texas passed the first "white primary" law, in which it was stated that "in no event shall a Negro be eligible to participate in a Democratic party primary election held in the state of Texas." This law was based on the Supreme Court's declaration in Newberry v. United States (256 U.S. 232, 1921) that Congressional primaries were not "elections" within the meaning of the Constitution. This statute came to the Supreme Court in 1927 in Nixon v. Herndon (273 U.S. 536), and the Court ruled that it violated the equal-protection clause of the Fourteenth Amendment. Governor Dan Moody of Texas announced that Texas would not permit Negroes to vote regardless of what the Supreme Court said. He then called a special meeting of the Texas legislature, and a new statute was passed empowering every political party in the state through its executive committee "to prescribe the qualifications of its own members" and permitting it to determine "who shall be qualified to vote or otherwise participate in such political party." The state executive committee quickly adopted a resolution which read, "All white Democrats who are qualified under the Constitution and laws of Texas and none others are to be allowed to participate in the primary elections." By a vote of five to four the Court

[11] Paul Lewinson, op. cit., pp. 214, 218, 219, 220.
[12] Ralph Bunche, "The Negro in the Political Life of the United States," Journal of Negro Education, July, 1941. Reprinted in Arnold M. Rose (ed.), Race Prejudice and Discrimination, Alfred A. Knopf, Inc., 1951, p. 226.
[13] Gunnar Myrdal, op. cit., p. 483.
[14] President's Committee on Civil Rights, To Secure These Rights, Simon and Schuster, Inc., 1947, p. 39.

held the second Texas law unconstitutional (Nixon v. Condon, 286 U.S. 73, 1932). Three weeks later the state Democratic convention, instead of the state executive committee, voted to exclude all but whites from the primary. In 1935, in Grovey v. Townsend (295 U.S. 45), the Supreme Court held that a vote of the state convention of a political party to restrict participation in the primary of that party did not violate the Fourteenth and Fifteenth amendments, provided the expenses of such primaries were paid by the party and not by the state. The Court took the position that this rule was simply the action of a private group acting on its right to determine its own membership and policies.[15]

If these tactics for the disfranchisement of Negroes seem surprising to some, it should be remembered that "the actual trickery, cheating, and intimidation necessary for the smooth operation of disfranchisement need be indulged in by only a small number of persons. Most people can avoid it. Their collaboration is necessary only to the extent of preserving a public sentiment upholding and supporting the system. In most cases, a resolute registrar can himself take care of the matter. And even he does not need to act openly when it has once become generally known among the Negroes in a community that they had better keep away from all politics."[16]

Violence or the threat of violence is still used from time to time in the South to keep the Negro out of politics. In 1948 a Negro, the father of six children, was shot and killed because he had insisted on voting in Georgia's Democratic primary election.[17] However, since the elimination of the Reconstruction government by 1877, the general tendency has been to abstain from violence and to use other means of disfranchisement. It has been "easier to buy, steal, or fail to count the Negro vote or to block the Negroes voting by intricate election laws and manipulation of the election machinery."[18]

Negro voters have often been intimidated by stares, insults, and such questions as "What do you want, nigger?" Economic sanctions have been reported; they include increases in taxes, loss of jobs, and "warnings" to ministers, teachers, and others. Still other techniques have been used—telling Negroes that the registration cards have "run out"; using tricky registration cards; giving assistance to white voters but none to Negro voters; waiving some of the usual requirements for the aged or for war veterans in the white group but not for Negroes; withholding the vote from Negroes who have been convicted of a crime,

---

[15] See R. E. Cushman, "The Laws of the Land," *Survey Graphic*, January, 1947, pp. 14–15; and Walter White, *A Man Called White*, The Viking Press, Inc., 1948, pp. 83–88.

[16] Gunnar Myrdal, *op. cit.*, p. 449.

[17] New York *Times*, September 12, 1948.

[18] Gunnar Myrdal, *op. cit.*, p. 450.

but overlooking this provision for whites; informing Negroes that they have to go elsewhere to vote; and saying that a registration cannot be accepted because all members of the board are not present.[19]

The following summaries, adapted from *The Reporter* and the New York *Times*, provide data on the recent use of illegal tactics, violence, and intimidation in Mississippi and Louisiana to eliminate Negro voters.

In 1954 there were thirteen of Mississippi's eighty-two counties in which no Negroes were registered at all, nine other counties in which six or less were registered, and twenty-nine others in which fewer than a hundred were registered.

In Lowndes County, where only fifty-two out of a possible 9,200 Negro voters were registered, Negroes received anonymous letters like the one sent to Caleb Lide: "Last warning. If you are tired of living, vote and die." In Forrest County, where only sixteen out of a possible thirteen thousand Negro voters were registered, the registrar disappeared when Negroes tried to register, told them to come back later, said the books weren't open to colored people that day, or simply said "No."

In Humphreys County Negroes were not even permitted to pay their poll tax until 1953. When seventeen Negroes finally brought suit against the sheriff, a Federal court ordered him to end this practice, and in 1953 485 Negroes succeeded in paying their poll tax. But these 485 soon found themselves the victims of a campaign of pressure and intimidation, and only two hundred of them actually registered. A year later the number was down to 126. The newly formed Citizens' Council began circulating lists of the registrants and still more withdrew. As the 1955 gubernatorial primary approached, Negro registration dropped to ninety-two. These few held firm until the shotguns came out.

On May 7, 1955, one of the county's Negro leaders, the Reverend George W. Lee, was shot in the face by a shotgun fired from a car passing close to the one he was driving. His murderers were never apprehended. The sheriff said that Lee probably had had a heart attack and was killed in the crash that followed, and that the lead pellets in his face were probably fillings from his teeth. With that statement the matter was considered closed. The Citizens' Council then told Gus Courts, president of the local unit of the National Association for the Advancement of Colored People, "We're not going to let Negroes in this county vote and we're not going to let the N.A.A.C.P. operate. You're leading the Negroes, trying to get them to register and vote; we're going to put you out of business." And they did. On November 25, 1955, Gus Courts, while working in his grocery store, was shot and seriously wounded by a shotgun fired, again, from a passing car. Gus Courts made up his mind. He packed up and left Mississippi.

No Negroes vote in Humphreys County today. They have given up for the time being and say they will not make another attempt until they are guaranteed Federal protection.

Another effective technique was that used in Jefferson Davis County. The

[19] *Ibid.*, pp. 485–486.

1954 registration survey indicated that 1,221 of the 3,900 Negroes of voting age in the county were registered. During the summer of 1956, the board of supervisors called for a reregistration and cleared the rolls. All the white voters reregistered without difficulty. The Negroes who tried to reregister found that they had to interpret portions of the Federal and state constitutions to the satisfaction of the registrar (an illegal procedure since in 1949 the Supreme Court held such provisions of state constitutions to violate the Fifteenth Amendment). Of the 1,221 Negroes previously registered in Jefferson Davis County, only sixty were able to overcome the technical obstacles put in their way and were allowed to register in 1956.[20]

The following, which describes some of the tactics that the administration's civil rights legislation was intended to stop, is taken from the Federal Bureau of Investigation's reports on incidents in five southern parishes in Louisiana in 1956. The Justice Department presented cases on the investigations to a federal grand jury in Louisiana early in 1957 but the all-white jury refused to return any indictments.

In each of the five parishes (counties) hundreds of qualified Negro voters were removed from the registration books just before the 1956 election.

In Caldwell Parish some 68 of the 450 registered Negroes were challenged by two private white citizens in May, 1956. The challenges were not verified, as required by Louisiana law. Nor were they published. Nevertheless, the Negroes were all prevented from voting at a city election in June.

In September the Caldwell registrar was summoned to a joint meeting of the local Citizens Council and the parish police jury and "admonished." Soon afterward he challenged 266 Negroes on the basis of alleged errors in registration cards that he had accepted. Those who tried to resist the challenge were told that they had to have three registered Negro voters from the same precinct as witnesses and had to be identified by a police officer. Only two Negroes of the group stayed on the voting rolls.

Some Negroes were disqualified because they had made an error of one day or more in stating their exact age in years, months and days. Others were dropped because, in filling out new applications to register, they could not swear that there had been no errors in an earlier application.

In De Soto Parish one Negro who had been challenged presented an affidavit signed by four white voters. These four men were approached thereafter by the president of the local Citizens Council, and two withdrew their names.[21]

The Reëntry of Negroes into Politics

Several developments in recent years have had the effect of increasing the number of Negro voters in the southern states. North Carolina eliminated the poll tax from her voting requirements in 1920, and dur-

[20] Edward Gamarekian, "A Report from the South on the Negro Voter," The Reporter, June 27, 1957, pp. 9–10.
[21] Anthony Lewis, "Negro Vote Curbs Exposed by F.B.I.," New York Times, August 4, 1957, p. 50.

ing the next three decades this qualification was removed by Florida, Louisiana, South Carolina, and Tennessee. The five states which retained the poll tax in 1957 were Alabama, Arkansas, Mississippi, Texas, and Virginia. A drive in Congress for a law which would forbid the use of a poll tax as a requirement for voting in federal elections has been unsuccessful. Three bills of this type have passed the House, but all have been filibustered to death by southern senators.

On April 3, 1944, the Supreme Court reversed its 1935 ruling on the white primary. The case involved Lonnie E. Smith, who contended that he was denied the right to vote in a 1940 primary by Houston, Texas, election judges because of his race. The majority opinion of the Court said the Democratic party in Texas is required to follow state legislative procedure in selecting party nominees in primary elections and thus the party becomes a state agency. It held that when primaries become a part of the machinery for choosing state and national officials, the same tests for discrimination apply to a primary as to a general election. The first reaction on the part of a number of southern senators, representatives, governors, and state committee chairmen was one of strong condemnation of the ruling and an expressed determination to find ways of preventing Negro participation in the Democratic primary. Senator John H. Overton of Louisiana asserted, "We're not going to submit to Negro voting in our elections. We don't need white primaries nor poll taxes. We can keep them out on educational qualifications." Senator Walter F. George of Georgia stated that "this decision seems essentially unrealistic and inevitably leads into a field into which the courts ought not to go." Herbert Holmes, chairman of the Democratic executive committee in Mississippi, declared, "We will have a few State's rights left, and one of our rights is to have Democratic primaries and say who shall vote in them. The Supreme Court or no one else can control a Democratic primary in Mississippi." Representative Nat Patton of Texas commented, "Let the Negroes form their own primaries if they like. I don't think many Negroes want to vote in the Texas white primaries. A few hotheads are stirring this thing up. I think the Southern white man is the best friend the Negroes have." In a message to the special session of the general assembly, the governor of South Carolina said: "After these statutes are repealed, in my opinion, we will have done everything within our power to guarantee white supremacy in our primaries and in our State insofar as legislation is concerned. Should this prove inadequate, we South Carolinians will use the necessary methods to retain white supremacy in our primaries and to safeguard the homes and happiness of our people. White supremacy will be maintained in our primaries; let the chips fall where they may." The governor of Texas talked of asking for a rehearing of the Court's ruling, and some southern political leaders considered legal moves to abolish the primary and return to a convention system of nominations. Democratic party leaders in Tennessee, North Carolina, and Virginia responded differently, saying that Negroes were not barred from voting in the primaries in those states.

In spite of the strong statements of many southern Democratic leaders at the time of the 1944 Supreme Court white primary decision (Smith v. Allwright case), large numbers of Negroes have voted in both primary and general elections since 1946. In several of the states, however, attempts were made immediately after the decision to minimize Negro voting. In 1945 Arkansas passed an act legalizing separate state and federal primaries, and this law was upheld by the Arkansas Supreme Court. Because of the expense of conducting separate primaries in state and federal elections, the legislature repealed the cumbersome measure.[22] Negroes voted in large numbers in the Arkansas primary election held during the summer of 1950, and a Negro candidate for alderman appeared for the first time on the ballot in Little Rock. On July 27, 1950, the Arkansas Gazette commented editorially that the one-party system, built to keep the Negro out of politics, does not serve that purpose today and therefore no longer makes sense. In South Carolina it was necessary to bring suit in the federal district court. Judge J. Waties Waring ruled in July, 1947, that Negroes must be permitted to vote in what had previously been the all-white Democratic primary. This decision was upheld in the United States Circuit Court of Appeals on December 30, 1947. The NAACP estimates that approximately 35,000 Negroes voted in the South Carolina Democratic primary election of 1948. Intimidation and violence were used in Mississippi to keep Negroes away from the polls in the first years after the 1944 white primary decision. In addition, the legislature passed two bills in March, 1947, which were intended to prevent Negroes from voting. One limited participation in the primaries to voters who subscribe to the party principles laid down by the Democratic executive committee. The other authorized county executive committees to purge the voting lists of those whose opinions were contrary to the welfare of the party. Neither of these laws proved to be effective in eliminating Negro voters, and a fair number of Negroes voted in the 1947 primaries, for the most part without intimidation. It is true, however, that in this primary some were asked to subscribe to such principles as the poll tax and opposition to an antilynching bill and to fair employment measures.[23] The Mississippi primary election of August, 1951, was interesting because Negroes were thought to represent the balance of power, and the frequently used "Negro issue" was conspic-

[22] Florence Murray (ed.), The Negro Handbook, The Macmillan Company, 1949, p. 52.

[23] Ibid., p. 51.

uously absent in the campaign oratory. It was estimated that Mississippi had at that time 20,000 Negroes registered as qualified voters, and Negro leaders claimed that at least three-fourths of them voted.

In 1947 Florida's state Democratic party established separate polling places for Negroes, but this procedure did not prevent Negroes from voting in unprecedented numbers. The separate voting booths were abolished in the 1948 state primary, and registered Negro Democrats voted in the same booths with whites.[24] Considerable difficulty was experienced by Negro voters in certain sections of Louisiana following the primary decision of 1944, but an important suit was won by Edwar Hall of New Orleans. Contending that he had been refused permission to register by being required to take tests not demanded of prospective white voters, Mr. Hall won the decision in the circuit court. Rose reports that Negro registration in Louisiana increased 400 percent in one year, and Negroes are said to have aided the new mayor to win his post and to have cast the deciding votes in the extension of the city limits of Baton Rouge.[25]

Alabama responded to the Supreme Court decision of 1944 by adopting the Boswell amendment to the state's constitution. This amendment required prospective voters to be able to read, write, understand, and explain any section of the Federal Constitution, the decision concerning their qualifications to rest with the registrars. A minister, E. J. Baxter of Birmingham, challenged this amendment in the courts in May, 1948. "Mr. Baxter claimed that the registrars had denied him permission to register on the grounds that he did not satisfactorily understand and explain a section of the United States Constitution, and contended that in so doing the board exercised 'arbitrary powers of discretion,' and had no visible standards by which to measure his qualifications to vote."[26] A federal court in Mobile ruled the Boswell amendment unconstitutional in January, 1949, stating that its intention was to discriminate against Negroes.

The Democrats in Georgia provided separate polling booths for Negroes in September, 1947. Some prospective voters were compelled to sign pledges in favor of a white primary and other measures opposed to the interests of Negroes, but this practice was abandoned when white as well as Negro voters protested against it. Some Negro voters were frightened away from the polls by Ku Klux Klan demonstrations. Nevertheless, it was estimated that 125,000 Negroes voted in the 1947 primaries.

In 1955, Alabama ratified a new version of the Boswell amendment by a margin of 369 votes in a state-wide referendum. A similar measure,

[24] *Ibid.*, p. 52.
[25] Arnold M. Rose, *The Negro's Morale,* University of Minnesota Press, 1949, pp. 119–120.
[26] Florence Murray (ed.), *op. cit.*, pp. 50–51.

rejected in 1952, was ratified in Mississippi in 1954. Georgia and South Carolina adopted other legal tactics for limiting the Negro vote, including pledges from voters in Democratic primaries that they opposed federal legislation for civil rights.[27] Although the new voting regulations caused some confusion among both Negro and white voters, especially in Georgia and Mississippi, the upward trend in Negro voting continued. The only exception was Mississippi, where economic reprisals, intimidation, and violence have reduced the already small Negro vote.[28]

A striking case of gerrymandering to reduce the Negro vote drastically occurred in Tuskegee, Alabama. Senator Sam Engelhardt's bill transferring all but ten of Tuskegee's 420 Negro voters out of the city limits became law in July, 1957, with a unanimous vote in both houses of the legislature but without Governor Folsom's signature. Passage of the law, which deprives virtually all of Tuskegee's voters of a voice in municipal affairs, produced a boycott of white merchants by the city's Negro population. Senator Engelhardt, who has watched the number of Negro voters grow (1053 Negro voters in Macon County's Negro population of 27,234, a county with 2600 voters among the county's 4703 whites), has stated that it may be necessary to abolish the county to prevent Negro control. Essentially, Engelhardt's plan to abolish the county follows: ". . . The county would be divided into five pieces, each slice going to an adjoining county—Bullock (already 74 percent Negro), Elmore (36 percent), Lee (40 percent), Montgomery (44 percent), and Tallapoosa (29 percent)."[29] The aim of the Engelhardt proposal is to dilute the Negro voting potential and weaken the Tuskegee Negro leadership. Such a bill would have to pass a state-wide referendum. Macon County's personal property would be sold and the proceeds distributed among the five counties, and the county's indebtedness would be handled in the same way. Real property and other taxes would be assessed on the basis of the new boundaries. Some state representatives from adjoining counties have expressed doubts about the merits of the plan, but a newspaper poll showed that most of the white people of Macon County favor it. Engelhardt has said that twelve other counties where Negroes outnumber whites might have to be abolished as well as Macon.

Negroes have encountered little difficulty in voting in Oklahoma, Kentucky, Tennessee, and Virginia in recent years. The main obstacle in Virginia has been the poll tax, but in some years Negroes in that state have voted in proportionately greater numbers than whites. In North Carolina, educational tests have been a stumbling block to mass Negro voting. Since the end of World War II there has been little organized opposition to Negro registration and voting in southern

[27] H. L. Moon, "The Southern Scene," *Phylon*, Fourth Quarter, 1955, p. 356.
[28] *Ibid.*, p. 357.
[29] *Southern School News*, August, 1957, p. 4.

cities with populations of 25,000 or more. In Atlanta, Memphis, Jacksonville, and New Orleans, Negroes may qualify as easily as in any northern city.[30]

Negro candidates have had less success in Florida than in several of the more "southern" states that have a larger Negro population. As in other southern states, Florida's one-party system is a major handicap to Negro voters. Shifting factionalism provides no fixed centers of power and makes balance-of-power politics impracticable. Concentration on the primary rather than the general election invites Negro-baiting and makes it more difficult for any candidate to appeal publicly for Negro support. This situation leads to private deals with Negro voting leagues and deprives Negro voters of the opportunity to make their own political choices.[31]

Table 14.1 shows the increase in Negro major-party registration in Florida in the period 1944–1956. During these years the difference be-

TABLE 14.1. Negro Major-Party Registration in Florida, 1944–1956[32]
(as of May in each year)

Year	Number of Negro Democrats	Number of Negro Republicans	Total Major-Party Negro Registration	Percentage of 1950 Adult Negro Population Registered
1944	0	20,000[a]	20,000	5.5
1946	32,280	15,877	48,157	13.1
1948	53,368	8,647	62,015	16.9
1950	106,420	9,725	116,145	31.7
1952	112,868	8,045	120,913	33.0
1954	119,975	8,354	128,329	35.0
1956	128,437	9,098	137,535	37.5

[a] Estimate.

tween the percentage of registered Negroes and of whites going to the polls has decreased greatly. In the gubernatorial primary of 1956, 70 percent of Jacksonville's registered Negro Democrats and 75 percent of the white Democrats voted. There is wide variation in Negro political participation in the main metropolitan counties of Florida, mainly because of differences in the interest shown by local white politicians in seeking Negro support. Jacksonville and Miami have the largest groups of Negro voters in the state, but Tampa and St. Petersburg maintain a municipal white primary system.[33]

[30] Charles C. Dawson in Jessie P. Guzman (ed.), *The Negro Year Book*, Tuskegee Institute, 1952, p. 313.
[31] H. D. Price, *The Negro and Southern Politics*, New York University Press, 1957, pp. 78–87.
[32] *Ibid.*, p. 33.
[33] *Ibid.*, pp. 77, 55.

There are some resemblances between the ethnic voting organizations which flourished in large eastern cities in past years and the Negro voting leagues in the South, but there are also major differences. The Irish, Italian, and Jewish immigrants were gradually absorbed into party organizations and were elected to state-wide offices. Racial prejudice in the South is much stronger than ethnic or religious prejudice, and the one-party system makes it difficult for a Negro voting league to attempt to elect its own members or to bargain for representation on a composite slate. Price sees the role of a Negro voting league as limited to that of a pressure group which seeks to reward its friends and defeat its enemies. The power of different leagues in a given city varies according to their reputation among Negro voters for getting concessions for the Negro community; their standing with white candidates depends upon the following they are believed to have among Negro voters.[34]

As the result of lack of long civic experience, most Negro voters in Florida go to the polls only when there is a contest that is of direct interest to them. The tendency of nearly half of the Negro voters to express a choice in only one or two contests which they regard as important is a serious limitation on the influence of Negro political par-

---

[34] *Ibid.*, 67–70. Price's observations on current political tactics of Negroes in some parts of the South are cogent: "For tactical reasons Negro political leagues have generally been organized as separate groups in the Negro community. The high degree of differentiation among Negro organizations has a sounder reason than merely to provide a large number of prestige positions. Most Negro communities find it advantageous to have a militant branch of the NAACP for legal action, a voters league for bargaining with local politicians, a civic welfare group to make nonpartisan appeals on behalf of the Negro community, and a number of 'accommodating' leaders who are fully trusted by the white community. In practice, of course, the active leadership and the bulk of the membership of several of the groups will overlap, but the proliferation allows different delegations to represent the Negro community for different purposes and in different circumstances. . . .

"The increased importance of the Negro's political activities has led to the development of a growing number of Negro specialists in political leadership. The Negro minister, the church organization, the fraternal orders, and the community morticians have generally declined in political influence, especially in the larger cities. The ministers, however, are still very important and quite willing to assume leadership; fresh evidence is provided by their role in the direction of the Montgomery and Tallahassee bus boycotts. In fact, the Negro church is still one of the most popular meeting places for political rallies. In the 1952 campaign in Miami, for instance, rallies were held at the Greater Bethel AME Church, Mt. Tabor Baptist Church, and St. Johns Church. The Reverend Theodore R. Gibson of Miami served as second vice-president of the Dade County Young Democratic Alliance, the most powerful of the Miami Negro voting leagues. In Jacksonville the Reverend A. B. Coleman of the Shiloh Baptist Church served for several years as chairman of the Duval County Voters' League. So long as the Negroes' very right to vote was at issue this reliance on ministerial leadership was not unnatural, but with growing acceptance of the Negro voter and competition between candidates for Negro support the need is no longer for a quasi-religious crusade but for hard-headed political bargaining and door-to-door organizing work. Although some Negro ministers are effective bargainers and have their church membership well organized for political purposes, the congregation is hardly the ideal unit for political organization." *Ibid.*, pp. 68–69.

ticipation.[35] Nevertheless, Florida's Negro voters, now constituting 10 percent of the state's electorate, play an important part in presidential and gubernatorial elections and are an accepted part of local politics in several counties.

Negro political activity in Atlanta has produced some results. Negro leaders have sought to acquaint voters with the issues and candidates, and "friendly" county and city administrations were elected in 1949 and 1953. According to Bacote:

> Negro policemen have been hired. Police brutality has been reduced to a minimum. Race-baiting groups such as the Klan and the Columbians have been suppressed. City officials have been more courteous and sensitive to the demands of Negroes. Courtroom decorum has improved. In city planning the city fathers began looking at the needs of all citizens regardless of color. Two Negro deputies have been added to the Fulton County Sheriff's office. Better streets, lights, sewers, water, and sidewalks have made Negro neighborhoods attractive. In addition, modern school buildings have been erected to accommodate the growing Negro population.[36]

In the November, 1956, election, Negro voters in the South shifted heavily to the Republican party. President Eisenhower carried predominantly Negro election districts in Baltimore, Richmond, Norfolk, Louisville, New Orleans, Baton Rouge, Atlanta, Greensboro, Birmingham, Mobile, Memphis, Nashville, Charleston, South Carolina, and many other southern cities.[37] In three of the five southern states won by president Eisenhower—Virginia, Tennessee, and Louisiana—the preference of Negro voters for the Republican party was an important if not the deciding factor in the final results.[38] Tennessee went Republican by 5000 votes. Perhaps four times that many Negro voters shifted from the Democratic to the Republican party in Memphis alone.[39] The shift of southern Negro votes has been attributed by some analysts primarily to school segregation-desegregation and other civil rights issues; others have concluded that these issues were secondary to the "peace and prosperity" appeal. A *Southern School News* survey found that in few sections did civil rights issues appear to have been the decisive factors in the Negro vote shift. The exceptions were Tennessee and Louisiana.[40]

At the time of the Supreme Court's white primary ruling in 1944, no Negroes held elective public offices south of the border states except in all-Negro towns such as Mound Bayou, Mississippi; in a few towns in North Carolina, they held the office of justice of the peace. Rufus E.

---

[35] *Ibid.*, p. 77.
[36] C. A. Bacote, "The Negro in Atlanta Politics," *Phylon*, Fourth Quarter, 1955, pp. 349–350.
[37] *The Crisis*, December, 1956, p. 615.
[38] *New York Times*, November 11, 1956, p. 60.
[39] *Ibid.*, July 21, 1957, p. 5 E.
[40] *Southern School News*, December, 1956, p. 1. See also *The Crisis*, December, 1956, pp. 614–615.

Clement, president of Atlanta University, was elected to the Atlanta Board of Education in a city-wide contest in 1953. Dr. Clement carried the majority of the predominantly white precincts as well as all of the Negro districts and won over the white incumbent by a vote of 22,200 to 13,900. He was reëlected in 1957. Many other southern Negroes have been elected to public office since 1944. Negroes have been elected to boards of education in San Antonio, Texas; Greensboro, North Carolina; Knoxville, Tennesess; and Augusta, Georgia. They have been elected to the governing bodies of Winston-Salem, Greensboro, Fayetteville, Durham, and Chapel Hill, North Carolina; Nashville, Tennessee; Richmond and Nansemond County, Virginia. Negro candidates in other communities have been serious contenders for elective offices.[41]

The southern Negro vote was estimated to be 70,000 in the 1920's, 250,000 in 1940, and 750,000 in 1946.[42] By 1952, 1,200,100 Negroes were registered to vote in thirteen southern states.[43] The estimated number of registered Negroes in eleven states (Alabama, Arkansas, Florida, Georgia, Louisiana, Mississippi, North Carolina, South Carolina, Tennessee, Texas, and Virginia) in 1956 was 1,238,000,[44] and it was 1,400,-000 for thirteen southern states in the same year. There are more than five million Negro citizens of voting age in the thirteen southern states. Educational and other qualifications will continue to be used to restrict Negro voting; but the Supreme Court's ruling on the white primary and new federal interest in civil rights legislation make it likely that from two to two and a half million southern Negroes will vote within a decade.

The Negro Vote in the North and West

More than 3,000,000 Negroes now vote in the North and West. In Chicago only a few prominent Negroes took an active part in politics before the Great Migration, and the Negro vote was not important until 1915. Although both the Republican and the Democratic machines sought control of the Negro vote, Chicago was strongly Republican throughout the twenties. Roosevelt received only an estimated 23 percent of the Negro vote in 1932. Hoover was not popular with Chicago Negroes, but they were doubtful about a candidate who had served in the Wilson administration and they did not want to take the chance that a man like Garner would succeed to the presidency in the event of Roosevelt's death. Opinion shifted in 1936 and 1940; 49

[41] H. L. Moon, "*The Southern Scene*," pp. 357–358.
[42] *Ibid.*, p. 352.
[43] Estimates of the number of Negroes registered to vote in the southern states in 1952 are as follows: Alabama, 30,000; Arkansas, 60,000; Florida, 120,900; Georgia, 146,200; Louisiana, 120,000; Mississippi, 23,000; North Carolina 100,000; Oklahoma, 55,000; South Carolina, 110,000; Tennessee, 135,000; Texas 205,000; Virginia 70,000; West Virginia, 35,000. *Ibid.*, pp. 353–354.
[44] New York *Times*, July 21, 1957, p. 5 E.

and 52 percent respectively of the Chicago Negro vote went to Roosevelt. Probably the WPA was an important factor in these changes. After Roosevelt's personal appearance in Chicago in November, 1944, where he mentioned the poll tax, the FEPC, and equal opportunity for all men, the Democratic ticket polled 65 percent of the Negro vote. Some shift back to the Republicans with the beginning of World War II was a convincing demonstration that Negroes, voting as a bloc whenever they feel they have vital interests at stake, may sometimes hold the actual balance of power.[45]

Negro political behavior differs little from white political behavior in the North. Negroes vote in about the same proportion as whites, they are not tied to one party, and they go along with the machines rather than with third parties and reformers. However, Negroes carefully appraise the attitudes of candidates and parties toward their group. Professional politicians quickly realized the potentialities in the Negro vote and went about organizing Negroes as they had formerly done with the Irish, the Germans, the Poles, and other newcomers to city life. In Chicago, Big Bill Thompson's rise to political power was coincident with the Great Migration. The Negro population in that city rose from 44,103 in 1910 to 109,458 in 1920 and 233,903 in 1940 and was concentrated in a few wards. Although Thompson was a clown and a corrupt politician, he treated Negroes more fairly than they had ever been treated before. With his blessing, Negroes developed their own ward machines and in return they demanded concessions for support.

Oscar DePriest quickly learned the ways of political machines and, during the first three decades of the century, built a powerful organization in Chicago. His precinct captains and ward committeemen "fixed" such matters as getting exceptions made to zoning ordinances, arranging for beds in the county hospital or the sanitarium, getting constituents "out of trouble" with the police, finding jobs, getting immediate relief, lending a hand to a church with mortgage problems, arranging for a club to use a public park for an outing, or straightening things

[45] St. Clair Drake and Horace Cayton, *Black Metropolis*, Harcourt, Brace & Company, 1945, pp. 109, 352–354, 359–360. The influence of the Negro population has been cut down in some instances by the practice of gerrymandering, that is, of arranging election district boundaries so that the Negro group's vote is submerged by the vote of the majority group. Gunnar Myrdal, *op. cit.*, pp. 492–493. Moon's report on this point is of interest here. "In addition to Representatives Dawson and Powell, there were Negro candidates for Congress in three other districts in 1946. Dawson and Powell ran against Negro candidates in predominantly Negro districts, whereas the others were in competition with white candidates in districts which are in a state of flux and which, if not gerrymandered, will be predominantly Negro within a few years. The defeated Negro candidates ran in Los Angeles (Fourteenth Congressional District, California); Philadelphia (Pennsylvania Fourth), and the Bronx, New York City (New York Twenty-fourth). Winning Negro candidates in these districts and others in Chicago, Detroit, and St. Louis will be sent to Congress within the next few elections as the districts, under pressure of the ghetto system, take on a progressively darker hue." H. L. Moon, *op. cit.*, p. 199.

out with the Bureau of Licenses. Payment for these services came in the form of votes or actual cash.[46] Similar developments have occurred in Detroit, Philadelphia, Cleveland, New York, and St. Louis.

Negroes have been most active politically in the North in Chicago and New York City. Chicago Negroes have been elected to both branches of the Illinois legislature and have held numerous municipal positions as judges, assistant prosecutors, councilmen, assistant corporation counselors, and lesser officials. Oscar DePriest was elected to Congress in 1928 as the Republican candidate of the First Congressional District of Illinois. He was succeeded in 1934 by Arthur W. Mitchell, a Negro Democrat; and in 1942 another Negro Democratic congressman, William L. Dawson, succeeded Mitchell. The first Negro congressman from New York, Adam Clayton Powell, was elected on the Democratic, Republican, and American Labor party tickets in 1944. Powell was reëlected in 1946 with the support of the Democratic and American Labor parties. His reëlection in 1948 and 1950 came with American Labor party support, but in 1952, 1954, and 1956 he was reëlected as a Democrat. With the exception of Chicago, New York has the largest number of Negro officeholders.

In the North and West, Negroes remained Democratic in the 1956 election, but with smaller margins. Although there was a definite trend away from the Democratic ticket, it was not strong enough to give President Eisenhower a majority in any major area of northern Negro registration. Harlem voted Democratic but by substantially reduced percentages; four assembly districts gave four-fifths of their votes to the Democrats in 1952 but only two-thirds in 1956. Only a slight shift was shown in the Chicago Negro vote. Mr. Stevenson's pluralities were a slightly smaller percentage than in 1952, but a large drop in registrations due to slum clearance projects and other factors had some effect on the voting. In the Detroit area in Michigan, neither party claimed any shift of Negro votes, but there was a slight shift from the Democrats to the Republicans in California. In Philadelphia and several other cities, the falling off of the vote in a number of Negro districts was interpreted as an indication of dissatisfaction with the performance of both major parties.[47] As in the case of the much greater shift in the South, the changes in Negro voting behavior in the North in the 1956 election may be attributed in part, but by no means entirely, to school segregation-desegregation and other civil rights issues.

[46] St. Clair Drake and Horace Cayton, op. cit., pp. 342, 348, 351, 362–364.
[47] New York Times, November 11, 1956, p. 60; The Crisis, December, 1956, pp. 614–615. A postelection poll made by the Survey Research Center of the University of Michigan and published in March, 1957, showed that the Republicans received 35 percent of the Negro vote in 1948 and 36 percent in 1956. A Gallup Poll release in January, 1957, showed that the Republicans received 39 percent of the Negro vote in 1956. David Lawrence, " 'Rights' Minimized as a Vote Getter," Washington Post and Times-Herald, July 21, 1957.

Mexican-American, American Indian, and Puerto Rican Voting

In 1948 Strong wrote that there was no comparison between the degree of Negro political sophistication and that of Mexican-Americans. At that time practically no group-conscious political leadership had developed among the latter.[48] It is difficult to explain the lack of leadership in the Mexican-American population, but one study suggests that the distinction between "real Spanish" and "Mexicans" which is often made by Anglo-Americans is one source of divisiveness. Because of their greater mastery of Anglo-American culture, there is more social acceptance of the "real Spanish" than of the "Mexicans" by the Anglo-Americans. As a result of the feeling between the relatively assimilated "leaders" and the other people of the community, "the hypothetical leaders are unwilling to lead and the hypothetical followers are unable to accept followership."[49]

The views of the 250,000 or more Mexican-Americans who served in the armed forces during World War II were broadened. Industrial workers and a slowly increasing middle class have shown more interest in political action. Mexican-Americans have been elected to city councils or other offices in Texas cities and in Denver and Los Angeles, and to the state legislature in Arizona. Unity Leagues stress voter education, and such organizations as the League of United Latin-American Citizens, the Latin-American Educational Foundation, and the Alianza Hispano-Americana are working to improve the status of Mexican-Americans. In recent years there has been some shift away from the mutual-aid and self-improvement approach to a more vigorous demand for equality and the elimination of discrimination. In 1954 the Alianza Hispano-Americana organized a Civil Liberties Department with a program dedicated to "education plus action." These and other developments indicate that the lack of political sophistication and the political inertia which have been characteristic of the Mexican-American group are decreasing.[50]

American Indian voting has lagged because of a lack of knowledge of issues and candidates, experience in the mechanics of voting, and effective organization. Largely because of the development and growth of their own organizations, tribal and intertribal, and of the Congress of American Indians, marked increases were recorded in registering and voting on many Indian reservations in 1956. Although the American Indian population is small, the Indian vote could be—and in some cases

[48] Donald S. Strong, "The Rise of Negro Voting in Texas," *American Political Science Review*, June, 1948, pp. 510–522.

[49] J. B. Watson and J. Samora, "Subordinate Leadership in a Bicultural Community," *American Sociological Review*, August, 1954, pp. 419–420.

[50] J. Milton Yinger and George E. Simpson, "The Integration of Americans of Mexican, Puerto Rican, and Oriental Descent," *Annals of the American Academy of Political and Social Science*, March, 1956, pp. 126–127.

has been—a decisive factor in Montana, Idaho, Colorado, Washington, Oregon, North Dakota, Utah, Minnesota, Nebraska, and Alaska.[51]

Approximately four-fifths of the half million mainland Puerto Ricans live in New York City, but only 10 percent of those qualified are registered and their vote is light.[52] Nevertheless, Puerto Ricans are important in a number of voting districts in New York City, and as they acquire greater knowledge and experience they are bound to play a larger political role there and in a number of other cities.

Political Appointments on the Basis of Race

The appointment of Negroes to positions in the federal government was considered in the preceding chapter. The first gains of any consequence were made between 1933 and 1940 when 103 Negroes were chosen by President Roosevelt. The most important of these organized an informal council, popularly known as the "Black Cabinet," to discuss common problems. Many of these positions were in temporary agencies, and all of the appointees were subordinated to the white heads of the respective bureaus. Although these appointments were sometimes criticized on the ground that they were made in an effort to keep Negroes satisfied, there were a number of important achievements and they represented the first significant step in recent years toward Negro participation in the work of the federal government.[53] During President Eisenhower's first term the number of Negro appointments to federal positions was at least as large as it had been during the Truman administration. With the exception of the appointment of a Negro as an Assistant Secretary of Labor, no Negroes were appointed to the two highest grades in the civil service. A very large proportion of the better positions held by Negroes continued to be staff or advisory positions, particularly in the category of race-relations advisers. Negroes at a fairly high level of appointment have rarely been a part of the ordinary line of command. In the past twenty-five years, the number of Negroes employed by federal agencies has steadily increased, and the trend has been to employ them in more diverse capacities. With better educational opportunities, the number of Negroes qualified for public service, especially in the higher grades, will increase.[54]

In the rural areas surveyed by Charles Johnson in the early forties, no Negroes were employed as mail carriers or clerks in any post office, although they were often engaged as janitors and there were Negro postal

[51] Helen L. Peterson, "American Indian Political Participation," Annals of the American Academy of Political and Social Science, May, 1957, pp. 123–124.

[52] J. Milton Yinger and George E. Simpson, op. cit., p. 129.

[53] Gunnar Myrdal, op. cit., p. 503.

[54] V. J. Browne, "Racial Desegregation in the Public Service, with Particular Reference to the U.S. Government," Journal of Negro Education, Summer, 1954, pp. 246–247.

carriers in several southern cities. A number of poll tax deputies, deputy constables, and deputy sheriffs have been appointed in Texas communities in recent years. One count showed that 718 Negro police officials were employed in 128 cities, towns, and counties in the South. Some local fire departments have employed Negroes. More than 6500 Negroes are employed by southern municipalities, approximately one-twelfth of this number being in professional and/or clerical capacities.[55]

As yet, the southern Negro has obtained little in the way of political patronage. In many parts of the South, the appointment of Negroes even to minor administrative posts produces strong protests. In Florida, Negroes have tried with little success to secure the appointment of members of their group to offices less important than the one regarded in other states as the minimum patronage appointment, the assistant district attorneyship. In Miami, a Negro municipal judge was appointed to deal with Negro offenders; but when Governor Collins appointed a Negro as assistant state attorney in Miami the matter became a major issue in the 1956 campaign. After an investigation of charges and counter charges, the new appointee was removed from office. This may be an indication that advances in desegregation in some parts of the South will come about only at the cost of temporary setbacks in political affairs.[56] Elsewhere in the South, a sizable Negro vote will bring recognition in the form of patronage, and more substantial personal rewards will encourage more strenuous political activity.[57]

With the political power which Negroes in Chicago had acquired by the early thirties, they were in a position to demand appointive positions for a few hundred individuals and fair treatment in the courts for the rank and file. In addition, they were able to check discrimination in the administration of the civil service laws. Chicago whites do not select Negroes to be their representatives, administrators, or judges, but they do not protest when an occasional Negro is appointed to a position of considerable prestige.[58] The experience of Negroes in other northern cities is not unlike that of the Negro group in Chicago.

Deviant Political Action and the Negro

Political belief and action are known to vary with class, occupation, residence, and other factors. In a study of minority groups, it is pertinent

[55] George S. Mitchell, "The Extension of Citizenship," in Jessie P. Guzman (ed.), *The New South and Higher Education*, Tuskegee Institute, 1954, p. 53.

[56] H. D. Price, *op. cit.*, pp. 80–81. According to Price: "In a radio broadcast intended to win greater cooperation with the authorities from Miami Negroes, the new assistant attorney allegedly stated that the office in which he worked had been integrated." This report was given wide publicity by an all-out segregation candidate for governor who claimed that this meant that Collins was in favor of race-mixing in the schools.

[57] H. L. Moon, "The Southern Scene," p. 358.

[58] St. Clair Drake and Horace Cayton, *op. cit.*, pp. 109–111.

to inquire how their status affects the likelihood of their taking part in deviant political behavior. We shall refer only to the Negro, but equally useful analyses can be made of other minorities.

The Socialist party has never included many Negroes. In New York City a few Negro intellectuals have advocated the Socialist point of view, but the mass of Negroes have been unaware of or unresponsive to the Socialist program. Even during depression years, Socialist activity among Negroes was limited to friendly declarations in the platforms prepared for national election campaigns and in party publications and speeches.[59]

From the beginning of its history in the United States, the Communist party has stressed "the Negro question." Special studies, special publications, and a very considerable amount of time and resources have been devoted to Negro causes. This extensive activity has enrolled only an inconsequential number of Negro members in the party. In 1928, Negro membership in the Communist party was estimated at 150 to 200 in a total membership of 14,000. In 1930 the party did not have more than 1000 Negro members. The membership doubled in the period 1935–1939, but it is doubtful if it was ever more than 8000 at one time.[60]

The position of the Negro worsened rapidly during the economic depression which began in the fall of 1929. Unemployment was more widespread among Negroes than in the white group, and in the early depression years relief agencies were unable to cope with the situation. In Chicago, and in other cities, the Communists attempted to capitalize on the misery of the Negro masses. A large volume of literature was distributed, frequent mass meetings and demonstrations were held, house-to-house canvasses were conducted, and strikes among Negro and white workers were promoted. Subsidiary organizations, including the Unemployed Councils, the League of Struggle for Negro Rights, the Young Communist League, the United Scottsboro Defense, the Pioneers, and the Trade Union Unity League, were formed. These strenuous efforts were rewarded with the recruitment of very few party members. At the end of a two-month period of intensive activity, it was announced that over a hundred new Negro Communist party members had been secured in Chicago. Not more than 500 ever joined the party in that city, and as the depression continued the numbers declined.[61] In Detroit, 3.2 percent of the Negro voters supported a party other than Democratic or Republican in 1930. This percentage was larger than the third-party vote of native whites, but it was less than that of Detroit foreign-born

[59] Wilson Record, The Negro and the Communist Party, University of North Carolina Press, 1951, p. 20; Harold F. Gosnell, Negro Politicians, University of Chicago Press, 1935, p. 322.

[60] Wilson Record, op. cit., pp. 25–26, 62, 183, 299.

[61] Harold F. Gosnell, op. cit., pp. 325, 327, 352.

groups. The percentage for third parties dropped to 1.5 in 1932, lower than that for foreign-born groups and equal to that of native whites. In Cleveland the Communist party had less than 200 Negro members at the peak of the depression.[62]

In the years 1928–1934 the Communist party pushed its program of "self-determination in the black belt." This campaign for a Negro republic in the southern states was based on Stalin's definition of a nation, and on figures for the 1930 census. According to Stalin, "A nation is an historically developed community of people with a common language, territory, economic life, and an historical tradition reflecting itself in a common culture."[63] The Communists pointed out that the census of 1930 showed that in 192 counties in the South Negroes constituted half or more of the population. In addition, there were 285 counties bordering on the counties of clear Negro majority in which Negroes constituted from 30 to 50 percent of each county taken singly. "In this more or less continuous stretch, comprising 477 counties, there are 13,744,424 inhabitants, of which 6,163,328 are Negroes, forming 44.8 percent of the total population in 1930."[64] Communist ideologists denied that "self-determination" was a mechanical application of the formula used in the Soviet Union to deal with linguistic and cultural minorities, but their explanations were unconvincing to non-Communist scholars. Stalin wrote that a common language is necessary for every nation, but "a different language is not necessary." Such a statement has no meaning, if a group constitutes a nation either with or without a distinct language. To those outside the Communist fold it did not appear that Negroes in the so-called "black belt" had either a common economic life or a common culture. Also, it was clear to non-Communists that every year brought about a not inconsiderable amount of spatial shifting of the Negro population. Both white and Negro intellectuals outside the party wondered about intensifying the separation between members of the two races, and some recalled the fiasco of reservations for American Indians. Apparently the Negro masses saw no connection between the self-determination slogan and their problems of daily life. In any event, their response to this appeal was negligible. It should be added that the party has always stood for "full equality" for Negroes outside the "black belt." At the end of 1934, the Communist International ordered its affiliates to support united-front movements in opposition to fascism, and the self-determination program in the United States was dropped. It was revived feebly in 1939, dropped in 1941, renounced completely

[62] Gunnar Myrdal, op. cit., p. 495.
[63] Harry Haywood, "The Theoretical Defenders of White Chauvinism in the Labor Movement," in The Communist Position on the Negro Question, p. 30. Reprinted from The Communist, June, 1931.
[64] James S. Allen, "The Black Belt: Area of Negro Majority," The Communist, June, 1934, pp. 581, 582–583.

after Teheran, and restored to a central place in the Communist program on the Negro question in 1945. The party's position on the Negro question is always closely tied in with the current Soviet foreign policy.[65]

The greatest participation of Negroes in Communist enterprises occurred in the Unemployed Councils which the party sponsored. Not all of the Negroes interested in these organizations were Communists, although attempts were made to bring them into the party. Party influence in the councils did not extend to the broader aims of the Communist movement but was limited largely to the immediate needs of Negro and white unemployed persons.

Communist activities among employed workers in the period 1928–1934 were carried on through the Trade Union Unity League. This labor arm of the party tried to develop unions in the meat-packing, electrical, steel, and other industries. The party line during these years was to establish its own trade unions and at the same time to organize opposition within the American Federation of Labor unions. The work of the TUUL in general was not very successful, and it never attained any real strength among Negroes.[66]

Another organization founded by the Communist party in the 1928–1934 period was the League of Struggle for Negro Rights, which hoped to unite a wide variety of Negro groups in a sweeping program working for full rights to trade-union membership, to relief, to relief work, to jobs in industry; the abolition of residential segregation; free, universal, and compulsory education without discrimination; banning of textbooks which presented a "distorted" version of the Negro; the right of Negroes to vote, hold office, and sit on juries; the abolition of segregation in the armed services; the abolition of all forms of Jim Crowism; the mass boycotting of newspapers, radio stations, and other agencies representing the Negro in a derogatory way; etc. The league failed almost completely; its membership never ran to more than a few hundred and practically all of these were already attached to the party in one way or another.[67]

During its united-front period (1935–1939) the Communist party relied on the National Negro Congress and the Southern Negro Youth Congress to look after its Negro program. The first organization was started as a broad, united-front Negro movement in 1936. It became Communist-dominated in 1940 and thereafter rapidly declined in numbers. Organized in 1937, the SNYC followed the Communist line. It remained small in size and was taken over completely by the party by 1939.[68]

According to Record, the International Labor Defense was the most effective Communist agency from 1928 to 1934. This organization was

[65] Wilson Record, *op. cit.*, pp. 60–63.
[66] *Ibid.*, pp. 116–117; Harold F. Gosnell, *op. cit.*, p. 117.
[67] Wilson Record, *op. cit.*, pp. 78–83, 117.
[68] *Ibid.*, pp. 153–165, 191–200.

not intended to attract large numbers of Negroes to a civil rights program. It was a propaganda and fund-raising operation which capitalized on the Scottsboro and Herndon cases. Although it reached a large Negro audience, the response was to the Scottsboro men and not to self-determination or any of the other Communist slogans.[69]

In November, 1938, the Southern Conference for Human Welfare was organized at Birmingham for the purpose of launching a program of political and economic action that would transform the whole region. After several years, the Communists were able to gain control of the SCHW and thus it lost the promise it originally offered.[70]

The Civil Rights Congress is the successor to the International Labor Defense and at mid-century was the most effective Communist instrument in the Negro field. Although it claims to be interested in constitutional liberties, in civil and human rights, it is clearly concerned with these issues only when Communist interests are to be served. The CRC has failed to enlist the support of liberal organizations, and it has no Negro following of any consequence.[71]

The intensive campaign which the Communists waged to transfer the Negro's allegiance to the Progressive party in 1948 was a failure. Of the two million votes received by Wallace and Taylor, considerably less than 10 percent came from Negroes.[72]

The Communist party has tried hard to capture the NAACP, but this attempt has been wholly unsuccessful. Presumably only if a prolonged depression brought despair and desperation to the Negro masses could the party gain control of this organization. Considerable organizational flexibility and stringent steps to prevent Communist infiltration make Communist domination unlikely.[73]

The most active anticommunist forces, at least in Chicago in the early thirties, were the churches, the police, and the New Deal. Although some church groups worked with a number of party-front organizations during the united-front period, Negro denominations have been suspicious of communism. The police, deputy bailiffs, and deputy sheriffs have been used to frustrate and break up the movement. Special "red squads" have been established in some cities, and spies and stool pigeons report regularly to the police. The relief, the reforms, and the feeling of confidence brought in by the Roosevelt administration gave Negroes new hope and weakened whatever appeal the party may have had for the unemployed and the hungry.[74]

A political movement based on colonization was organized by Marcus

[69] Ibid., pp. 86–91, 117.
[70] Ibid., pp. 165–171, 200–202.
[71] Ibid., pp. 253–263.
[72] Ibid., pp. 282–283.
[73] Ibid., p. 268.
[74] Harold F. Gosnell, op. cit., pp. 352–356.

Garvey, a Jamaican Negro, in 1918. Garvey's organization was known as the Universal Negro Improvement Association, and the founder's plan was to lead American Negroes back to Africa where a Negro nation and a Negro culture would be developed. Auxiliary organizations, including a steamship company, were formed, and negotiations were entered into with the Republic of Liberia. The Empire of Africa was announced in 1921, and Garvey was named Provisional President of Africa. Tried for using the mails to defraud, Garvey was sentenced to the Atlanta federal prison in 1925. In developing his grandiose scheme, he had appealed to the uneducated black masses and had ridiculed the well educated and those of mixed ancestry. This chauvinistic movement is of interest only because it is the only Negro movement thus far that has had mass support.[75]

In the middle thirties a number of political organizations sprang up which were anti-Negro, anti-Semitic, anti-Oriental, or antiforeign. One small group, led by Lawrence Dennis and known as the American Fascists, claimed not to be racist-minded. One of the present writers heard Dennis say in 1936 that racism was not inevitably a part of a fascist movement. Dennis' viewpoint was that the end is rapidly approaching for liberal democracy in the United States, that communism has no chance of acceptance, and that fascism is the wave of the future. His advice to Negroes was to get on the band wagon.[76]

A deviant political development which stemmed from Negro-white relations was the States' Rights movement. The "Dixiecrats" met in Birmingham, Alabama, in July, 1948, to denounce the civil rights stand adopted by the Democratic party in Philadelphia earlier that month. Plank 4 in the States' Rights platform read: "We stand for the segregation of the races and the racial integrity of each race; the constitutional right to choose one's associates; to accept private employment without government interference, and to earn one's living in any lawful way." The fifth plank stated: "We oppose and condemn the action of the Democratic covention in sponsoring a civil rights program calling for the elimination of segregation, social equality by federal fiat, regulation of private employment practices, voting and local law enforcement."[77] This party, which received only a few electoral votes in the national election of 1948, was defunct by 1956. Dissident southern Democrats preferred to form "Democrats for Eisenhower" clubs rather than to affiliate with the Republican party, for campaigning on the Republican ticket would mean political suicide. Vance says that conversations of conservative Democrats in the South usually end with the question:

[75] See E. D. Cronon, *Black Moses*, University of Wisconsin Press, 1955.
[76] It seems unlikely that racist appeals would be overlooked by any strong fascist movement which might develop in the United States. Racial doctrines are congenial to fascist thinking, and racism has a high propaganda value in fascist drives.
[77] Associated Press report, Cleveland *Plain Dealer*, July 18, 1948, pp. 1, 12.

"Why don't you join the Republican Party?"[78] Southern Democrats became increasingly unhappy during the Eisenhower administrations when the Supreme Court decisions of 1954 and 1955 were followed by the serious efforts of administration forces in 1957 to enact a meaningful civil rights law.

There is no possibility that Negroes will form a third party in the United States. Only by refusing to identify too closely with either of the major parties can Negroes use their bargaining power to advance their liberation. Other reasons for believing that a "Negro party" will not emerge follow: There could be no hope of ever coming to power, and such an aspiration is essential for party formation; Negroes know that the fear of "Negro domination" would defeat their chance of playing a significant role in American politics; small parties are not favored in the American political system; Negroes are interested in free participation in American life, and not in any kind of group exclusiveness.[79]

[78] Rupert B. Vance, "The South's Changing Political Leadership," *Journal of Social Issues*, 1954, vol. 10, no. 1, p. 15.

[79] R. M. MacIver, *The More Perfect Union*, The Macmillan Company, 1948, pp. 181–182; Gunnar Myrdal, *op. cit.*, p. 505. Record's concise comment on this point is pertinent here: "American Negro intellectuals will continue to follow with a great deal of interest and sympathy the efforts of colored peoples in the colonial areas to rid themselves of white control; and they will defend the right of these people to establish their own national states. They will not, however, attempt to duplicate such achievements here. They will take vicarious pride as Negroes in Africa, for example, demonstrate their capacity for self-government and challenge the dominant position of the whites; they will use such developments as a weapon against discrimination in the United States. But they are not likely ever to define the solution of their problems as members of a racial minority in terms of separation from the larger American society. Their stake in the latter is too great and the opportunities for full participation too promising." Wilson Record, "The Negro Intellectual and Negro Nationalism," *Social Forces*, October, 1954, p. 18.

CHAPTER 15

Minorities and the American Political and Legal Processes (continued)

The Civil Rights of Minorities

We have referred to the Supreme Court's decision declaring the Civil Rights Act of 1875 unconstitutional. This act, which provided that Negroes should have full equality in the use of theaters, hotels, and public conveyances, was part of the legislation designed to give the former slaves the status of free men. In 1896 the Court, in Plessy v. Ferguson (163 U.S. 537), confirmed a Louisiana law requiring racial segregation on common carriers. This ruling held that separate but equal accommodations did not violate the equal-protection clause of the Fourteenth Amendment. Later this principle was extended to cover schools, parks, playgrounds, hotels, places of amusement, restaurants, and all types of public transportation facilities.[1]

[1] R. E. Cushman, "The Laws of the Land," *Survey Graphic*, January, 1947, p. 18. Konvitz distinguishes political rights, such as the right to vote, from civil liberties (freedom of speech, freedom of the press, freedom of assembly, religious freedom, the right to bear arms, the right to security against unreasonable searches and seizures, security against double jeopardy and excessive bail, the right to trial by jury, security against self-incrimination, and other rights mentioned in the Bill of Rights) and civil rights. "In its more technical, limited sense, the term civil rights, as distinguished from political rights and civil liberties, refers to the rights of persons to employment, and to accommodations in hotels, restaurants, common carriers, and other places of public accommodation and resort. The term contemplates the rights enumerated in the federal Civil Rights Act of 1875 and the various acts against discrimination found on the statute books of eighteen states." Milton R. Konvitz, *The Constitution and Civil Rights*, Columbia University Press, 1946, p. vi. For specific court cases involving the civil liberties of Negroes in recent years, see Florence Murray (ed.), *The Negro Handbook*, The Macmillan Company, 1949 (peonage, pp. 82–84; extradition, pp. 82–84; criminal cases based on civil rights issues, pp. 78–81; and marriage cases, pp. 76–78). Alison Reppy discusses the constitutionality of the California miscegenation statute in *Civil Rights in the United States*, Central Book Company, 1951, pp. 183–186.

The "separate but equal" doctrine holds that the separation of Negroes and whites in public places prevents conflicts, insures better race
relations, and is therefore a proper exercise of the state's police power.
As Cushman notes, the northern states use their police powers through
civil rights laws to forbid the segregation which southern states require.
In several decisions the Court's interpretation of the Fourteenth
Amendment was that "mathematical" equality of treatment in the
treatment of segregated groups is not required, but only "substantial"
equality. In some cases very little equality was considered to be "substantial." In Cumming v. Board of Education (175 U.S. 528, 1899),
"the Court found that a Georgia county had not denied substantial
equality in failing to provide a high school for sixty qualified colored
children although it had a high school for white children. The Court
seemed entirely satisfied by the county's argument that it could not afford to maintain two high schools."[2] By 1914 the Court had begun to
tighten its definition of equality in segregation cases. In McCabe v.
Atchison, T. & S. F. Ry. Co. (235 U.S. 151), it decided that an Oklahoma law did not provide equal accommodations when railroads were
allowed to offer sleeping, dining, and chair cars for whites without furnishing them on demand for Negroes.[3] In June, 1946, the Supreme
Court ruled against segregation on interstate buses, and in September,
1946, a federal court of appeals for the District of Columbia held unconstitutional the segregation of interstate Negro passengers by a railroad
company. In the same year a United States district court of southern
California enjoined school authorities from establishing separate grade
schools for "Mexicans."[4] Of importance in defining the meaning of
equality under segregation is the ruling of the Circuit Court of Appeals
in 1940 in Allston v. School Board of the City of Norfolk (112 Fed.
2d 992). Here it was held that Negro and white teachers must be paid
the same salaries for the same work. By refusing to review the case the
Supreme Court affirmed the decision of the lower court.

In 1949 the Department of the Interior was challenged on its policy
of nonsegregation in Washington's public swimming pools. As a result
of violence by hoodlums, the Anacostia pool was closed for the remainder of the 1949 season. In preparation for the 1950 season, the National
Capital Parks conducted a training program for its personnel which
stressed their duty to follow the official policy of nonsegregation. In
September, 1950, the Washington *Post* carried the following editorial
comment: "The completion of the first full year of nonsegregated swimming at the six Washington pools controlled by the Interior Depart-

[2] R. E. Cushman, *op. cit.*, p. 18.
[3] *Ibid.*, p. 18.
[4] R. M. MacIver, *The More Perfect Union*, The Macmillan Company, 1948,
p. 172.

ment affords an appropriate opportunity for sober reexamination of what has been an overheated community issue. Total attendance at the six pools during the summer months of 1950 was 235,533; of this number, about 90,000 swimmers were colored and about 140,000 were white. No disturbance or unhappy incident of any kind occurred in the course of the season."[5] St. Louis' first efforts to integrate swimming pools also met with some violence, but, as in Washington, firmness on the part of public authorities resulted in the peaceful operation of the pools.[6] The Swope Park Swimming Pool in Kansas City was closed for a time, but it was opened to both Negroes and whites in 1954. The courts have consistently ruled that the Fourteenth Amendment requires publicly owned and operated pools to be operated without discrimination or segregation. Furthermore, the courts have not permitted alleged leases to dummy corporations to be used to evade the intent of the Fourteenth Amendment. The policy of the courts on publicly owned swimming pools was extended by the Pennsylvania courts to privately owned pools open to the public. Under the Pennsylvania Civil Rights Act, it was held in the case of Everett v. Harron that "a privately owned swimming pool soliciting patronage from the general public could not refuse admission to Negroes while admitting whites generally."[7] The court rejected a so-called "club" membership card as a device to exclude Negroes.

On June 8, 1953, the Supreme Court upheld an 1873 law which required District of Columbia restaurants to serve persons of any race provided they are well behaved. The 1873 law, unenforced for many years, came to the Supreme Court after the U.S. Court of Appeals had ruled it and a similar law of 1872 invalid. The Justice Department, in joining the District of Columbia in urging the Supreme Court to overrule the Court of Appeals, called attention to statements by President Eisenhower that he would "use whatever authority exists in the office of the President to end segregation in the District of Columbia, including the Federal government."[8] During 1953 the three main theaters in downtown Washington began to admit Negroes, and two legitimate theaters soon opened on a nonsegregated basis. Later, neighborhood theaters began to admit Negroes. Competition from television was an important factor in this desegregation.[9]

The public-school decision of the United States Supreme Court in 1954 opened the way for further legal attacks on segregated facilities.

[5] J. D. Lohman and D. C. Reitzes, "Notes on Race Relations in Mass Society," *American Journal of Sociology*, November, 1952, pp. 244–245.
[6] Sol Rabkin, "Racial Desegregation in Places of Public Accommodation," *Journal of Negro Education*, Summer, 1954, p. 260.
[7] *Ibid.*, p. 260.
[8] Associated Press release, June 9, 1953.
[9] Carl Rowan, *Go South to Sorrow*, Random House, Inc., 1957, p. 228.

On March 14, 1955, the U.S. Fourth Circuit Court of Appeals in Richmond, Virginia, reversed a decision of the federal district court at Baltimore which had held that segregation in public recreational facilities was permissible if both races were given equal facilities. The Circuit Court said that the May 17, 1954, decision of the Supreme Court "swept away" as well any basis for separating the races in public parks or playgrounds.[10] By 1955, several southern cities had opened their public libraries and museums on a nonsegregated basis.[11]

On February 12, 1956, Nashville's four public golf courses were desegregated;[12] and on February 20, 1957, a federal district court issued a permanent injunction against the city authorities of Fort Lauderdale, Florida, requiring the admission of persons to the municipal golf course without regard to race or color. The court held in the Fort Lauderdale case that financial loss to the city was not a reason for denying constitutional rights and ordered the admission of Negroes to the golf course on the same basis as whites.[13]

On July 14, 1955, the Circuit Court of Appeals in Richmond, Virginia, held in a Columbia, South Carolina, bus case that the Supreme Court decree outlawing public-school segregation "should be applied in cases involving transportation."[14] On June 5, 1956, a three-judge U.S. district court panel in Montgomery, Alabama, ruled segregation on Montgomery and Alabama public conveyances unconstitutional. The court traced the evolution of the law from the Plessy v. Ferguson doctrine of 1896 to the public-school decision in 1954, saying that the latter ruling had completely "destroyed" the "separate but equal" point of view. The court said: ". . . Statutes and ordinances requiring segregation of the white and colored races on . . . motor buses of a common carrier of passengers . . . violate the due process and equal protection of the law clauses of the . . . Constitution."[15] The U.S. Supreme Court upheld this ruling on November 13, 1956, and on December 17, 1956, it rejected pleas by Alabama and the city of Montgomery for reconsideration of this decision.[16] Attorney General Brownell called a conference of district attorneys from fourteen states to meet in Washington on December 10, 1956, for the purpose of outlining a campaign to end racial segregation in intrastate transportation. Mr. Brownell and others were well aware of the difficulty of proving criminal conspiracy

[10] Cleveland *Plain Dealer*, March 15, 1957.
[11] C. Vann Woodward, *The Strange Career of Jim Crow*, Oxford University Press, 1955, pp. 142–143. This was not true of Atlanta in 1955. In July of that year the Atlanta Public Library Board declined to open the main library to Negroes. Cleveland *Plain Dealer*, July 15, 1955.
[12] *Southern School News*, March, 1956, p. 15.
[13] *Race Relations Law Reporter*, April, 1957, p. 409.
[14] Cleveland *Plain Dealer*, July 15, 1955, p. 6.
[15] *Southern School News*, December, 1956, p. 13.
[16] Cleveland *Plain Dealer*, December 18, 1956, p. 35.

to deprive citizens of their rights and of the other legal problems which go with cases of this type.[17]

For several reasons the bus desegregation issue is interesting and important. Separation in transportation is less deeply rooted than public-school segregation. Most of the separate seating laws were passed around the turn of the century.[18] Unlike the public-school issue, bus integration does not involve complex administrative problems. No qualifications or special abilities are needed for boarding a bus. Of all forms of public-facility desegregation, bus integration has the widest appeal because it touches the daily lives of more Negroes than any other type of segregation. The intransigents among the whites, contending that bus integration would weaken the whole segregationist cause, have taken a "hold-the-line-at-all-costs" stand.[19] The theme of nonviolence introduced into the Montgomery, Alabama, campaign against bus segregation by the Reverend Martin Luther King, Jr., of Montgomery, is a noteworthy development in southern race relations.[20]

A district court decision on January 3, 1957, ruled that Miami and Florida bus segregation laws are illegal.[21] On January 7, 1957, the City Commission of Tallahassee, Florida, passed an ordinance providing for emergency powers to be exercised with respect to the seating of patrons on city buses. The ordinance provides for seating by the bus driver and makes refusal to obey the driver's directions a misdemeanor.[22] On March 12, 1957, the Birmingham, Alabama, City Commission passed an ordinance to "reaffirm, reenact and continue in full force and effect" a prior ordinance providing for racially segregated seating on city buses.[23] Although bus desegregation continued to be a highly controversial issue in many parts of the Old South, more than twenty cities—Little Rock, Pine Bluff, Fort Smith, and Hot Springs, Arkansas; Charlotte, Greensboro, Durham, and Winston-Salem, North Carolina; Richmond, Norfolk, Portsmouth, Newport News, Petersburg, Charlottesville, Freder-

[17] See Luther A. Huston, "Desegregation on Buses Presents Legal Problems," New York Times, November 25, 1956.

[18] Concerning segregation on trains Woodward writes: ". . . Their [Negroes] presence on trains was once regarded as normal, acceptable, and unobjectionable. . . . Later on . . . the partitions and Jim Crow cars became universal. And the new seating arrangements came to seem as normal, unchangeable, and inevitable as the old ways. And so it was with the soda fountains, eating places, bars, waiting rooms, street cars, and circuses. . . ." C. Vann Woodward, op. cit., pp. 91–92. Woodward shows that segregation in all aspects of life was not widespread in the South during slavery, or even during the Reconstruction period. Jim Crowism is relatively recent—since 1900—and perhaps reached its peak around 1940.

[19] John N. Popham, "Report on Bus Desegregation," New York Times, February 3, 1957, p. 8 E.

[20] For an excellent account of the Negro boycott of buses in Montgomery, see Carl Rowan, op. cit., chap. 6.

[21] Atlanta Constitution, January 4, 1957, p. 1.

[22] Race Relations Law Reporter, April, 1957, p. 459.

[23] Ibid., p. 457.

icksburg, Lynchburg, and Roanoke, Virginia; San Antonio, Corpus Christi, and Dallas, Texas; and Knoxville, Tennessee—had quietly ended bus segregation by the early part of 1957.[24]

Civil rights statutes have been enacted by twenty-two states and are now found in every state except Vermont, nine western states, and the seventeen southern or border states, not including Louisiana. In the latter state the law is contemptuously disregarded by its public officers.[25] Violation of these laws is a misdemeanor in ten states and is punishable by fine and imprisonment. Seven other states permit the aggrieved individual to sue for damages. One state provides for civil damages only, and in the other three states either civil damages or a criminal proceeding, but not both, is permitted. The minimum fines or minimum recoveries in civil suits provided by nine states are small, varying from $10 in New Hampshire to $100 in New York.

On the whole, these laws have not been effective, although there are some notable exceptions. Public prosecutors consider such offenses insignificant and are unwilling to prosecute unless provided with unquestionable cases. The injured individuals often prefer to ignore humiliation rather than spend the time and money necessary to carry through a lawsuit in view of the small minimum recovery allowed and the difficulty of demonstrating larger damages. Because jail sentences are seldom imposed and fines are small, most of those subject to the statutes regard the occasional fine as a business expense, try to avoid detection, and continue to discriminate. The only powerful sanction, the suspension or cancellation of license required to operate nearly all public places, is lacking in all of these laws except that of Louisiana.[26] Comment has already been made on the civil rights law of that state.

The President's Committee on Civil Rights recognized the weaknesses of the existing civil rights machinery: "The civil suit for damages and the misdemeanor penalty have proved to be inadequate sanctions

---

[24] *Ibid.*, p. 146.

[25] Will Maslow, "The Law and Race Relations," *Annals of the American Academy of Political and Social Science*, March, 1946, p. 76. Konvitz points out that two of these states should not be counted. "Maine and New Hampshire have acts which prohibit places of public accommodation from issuing advertising matter that suggests discrimination against persons of 'any religious sect, creed, class, denomination, or nationality' (as phrased in the Maine act) or against 'any religious sect, class or nationality' (as phrased in the New Hampshire act). There is no mention of discrimination on account of color or race in either statute, nor is the actual discrimination prohibited—the only thing prohibited is publicity that one is practicing discrimination." Milton R. Konvitz, *op. cit.*, p. 116. According to Konvitz (*ibid.*, chap. 8), twenty states have statutes compelling or allowing segregation or discrimination in varying degrees. Ten states leave the matter to private discretion. According to Burma, antidefamation laws which prohibit written or spoken material advocating hatred because of race, color, or religion were passed by six states in the period 1941–1950. John H. Burma, "Race Relations and Antidiscriminatory Legislation," *American Journal of Sociology*, March, 1951, p. 418.

[26] Will Maslow, *op. cit.*, p. 76.

to secure the observance of these laws. Additional means, such as the revocation of licenses, and the issuance of cease-and-desist orders by administrative agencies are needed to bring about wider compliance. We think that all of the states should enact such legislation, using the broadest possible definition of public accommodation."[27] The first two states to follow this recommendation were New Jersey and Connecticut. Each enacted laws in 1949 "giving administrative state agencies authority to handle charges of discrimination in places of public accommodation by persuasion and conciliation or, if such attempts at mediation fail, by cease-and-desist orders."[28] By 1955 New York, Rhode Island, and Massachusetts had passed similar laws.[29]

In addition to extending the administrative technique used in combating discrimination in employment to discrimination in places of public accommodation, Connecticut amended its definition of such places. The amendment deleted from the law the limited list of specific places which had been considered "places of public accommodation" and substituted this definition: "Any establishment . . . which caters or offers its services or facilities or goods to the general public. . . ." Another important part of the amendment was the specific statement, for the first time, that "segregation" and "separation" were discrimination within the meaning of the act and were therefore prohibited.[30] In 1956, thirty-eight complaints in the area of public accommodations were filed with the New York State Commission Against Discrimination. According to the chairman of the commission, "The effect of the law in this area has been notable, particularly in hotels, restaurants and other public places where, in contrast to the picture ten years ago, minorities can today obtain access to many accommodations theretofore barred to them."[31] Abrams mentions as another 1956 gain the opening of the Automobile Club of Buffalo to Negro membership through an agreement made between the commission and the club.

Extralegal techniques commonly used to circumvent state civil rights laws and discriminate against Negroes include finding that a "mistake" has been made in a hotel reservation; stating that all tables or all rooms are reserved; claiming that only "members" of an association or club are

[27] President's Committee on Civil Rights, *To Secure These Rights*, Simon and Schuster, Inc., 1947, p. 171.

[28] Arnold Forster, *A Measure of Freedom*, Doubleday & Company, Inc., 1950, pp. 206–207.

[29] Elmer Carter, "Policies and Practices of Discrimination Commissions," *Annals of the American Academy of Political and Social Science*, March, 1956, p. 74. The Massachusetts Commission Against Discrimination, which administers that state's Fair Employment Practice Laws and other antidiscrimination laws, published in May, 1955, a statement of the policies which would guide it in executing the laws. See *Race Relations Law Reporter*, April, 1957, pp. 531–535.

[30] Sol Rabkin, *op. cit.*, p. 252.

[31] Charles Abrams, statement at the Annual Meeting with Civic and Social Agencies, New York City, December 3, 1956, pp. 7–8.

admitted to some recreational facility; quoting differential prices on the basis of race; adulterating the food served to Negroes; ignoring Negro customers or waiting on them only after all whites have been served or after a long delay; humiliating Negroes by remarks or acts, such as breaking a glass after it has been used by a Negro; and ushering Negroes to a special section in a theater.

Maslow points out that while defenders of Negro rights have won many notable victories in the United States Supreme Court, litigation has been used very little as a means of protecting the Jewish community. The NAACP has attacked the discriminatory actions of governmental bodies—of school boards, state legislatures, jury commissioners, etc.; but "The anti-Semitism that vexes the Jew in the United States is . . . that of private groups, of personnel managers, resort owners, admissions committees, or rabble-rousers, almost entirely non-governmental and hence not subject to the majestic prohibitions of the Fifth or Fourteenth Amendments. Although these may be 'private governments' in the power they wield to deny employment or educational opportunities, their acts do not fall within the accepted categories of legal wrongs. Before these private groups can be sued, new laws have to be created making their conduct unlawful."[32] According to Maslow, the situation in one area, that of religious liberty, has begun to change. Recent developments include the challenging of released-time practices in the public schools, the protection of Jews denied unemployment compensation because they refused jobs requiring work on Saturday, the defense of Jewish shopkeepers arrested for violations of Sunday blue laws, prohibition of the distribution of the New Testament in the public schools, and legal representation in the courts for Jewish foster parents seeking to adopt non-Jewish children.[33]

The right of Negroes to serve on juries has been somewhat enhanced since 1935. In the second Scottsboro case (Norris v. Alabama, 294 U.S. 587, 1935), the Supreme Court ruled that a Negro was denied equal protection of the law if he was indicted and tried in a county where qualified Negroes resided but in which Negroes were never on a grand or trial jury panel. Five years after this decision, Mangum predicted that the white man in the South would not care to have Negroes serve on juries to any extent, and that he would make extensive use of various subterfuges, such as placing Negroes on jury lists and then excusing them for some reason.[34] In states where the law provides that jurymen must also be electors, Negroes may be kept off the panel by using such devices as the "understanding" clause. Those who qualify may usually

[32] Will Maslow, "The Uses of Law in the Struggle for Equality," *Social Research*, Autumn Quarter, 1955, p. 306.
[33] Ibid., p. 307.
[34] C. S. Mangum, Jr., *The Legal Status of the Negro*, University of North Carolina Press, 1940, pp. 333–334.

be eliminated by challenges, either peremptory or for cause. In 1945 in Adkins v. Texas (325 U.S. 398), the Supreme Court held that no race or group is entitled to proportional representation in the composition of juries, and that the facts did not show racial discrimination. In this case the jury commissioners had placed one Negro, a man over eighty, on the grand jury panel. He also served on the trial jury. Each jury commissioner frankly admitted, "I did not have any intention of placing more than one Negro on the panel."[35] It seems probable that the letter rather than the spirit of the Court's ruling in Norris v. Alabama will prevail in southern communities for some time to come. However, the South cannot completely disregard the decision without risking the reversal of every case in which a Negro has been convicted.

On May 3, 1954, the Supreme Court, applying the same reasoning it followed in the Scottsboro case, ruled unanimously in the Hernandez case that Jackson County, Texas, had been violating the Constitution by keeping Mexican-Americans off juries. The practice of excluding Mexican-Americans from juries had been prevalent in many counties in Texas and a number in New Mexico.[36]

Another aspect of the civil rights of minorities in the legal field is the recognition of an undeniable right to challenge a juror for race prejudice, "except that he may not be asked concerning his desire to live socially apart from the Negro. . . ." There is "a very thin line between social and legal prejudice," according to Mangum, "but this is probably the only criterion available under the circumstances, especially in the South where a more rigid rule would certainly disqualify most of the white candidates for jury duty."[37]

Many citizens of the United States are unaware of the existence of the Civil Rights Section, a unit of the Criminal Division of the Department of Justice. Some who do know about it mistakenly believe it to be a powerful branch of the government which effectively protects civil liberties. This is not the case, as the President's Committee on Civil Rights made clear. "It may easily be a direct result of the Civil Rights Section's subordinate position that the total picture of work derived from the staff survey is that of a sincere, hardworking, but perhaps overcautious agency. Its relative lack of prestige in the Department of Justice, the legal and constitutional difficulties which confront it, the problems caused by its administrative relation to the FBI, the hostility of some United States Attorneys, the force of local prejudice, and the size of its staff all combine to make the Section less effective and less self-assured than the challenge of its assignment demands."[38]

In July and August, 1957, the Republican administration, with the

[35] R. E. Cushman, op. cit., p. 98.
[36] Cleveland Plain Dealer, May 4, 1954.
[37] C. S. Mangum, Jr., op. cit., p. 342.
[38] President's Committee on Civil Rights, op. cit., p. 125.

support of northern Democrats, sought passage of a civil rights bill with the following main provisions:

1. Establishment of a special Civil Rights Division within the Department of Justice.

2. Creation of a Federal Civil Rights Commission armed with subpoena powers to compel witnesses to testify and produce records.

3. Authority for the Department of Justice to intervene, in the name of the United States, in behalf of individuals in instances of actual or threatened violations of civil rights—such as the right to vote or to attend an integrated school.

4. Federal prosecutors could obtain injunctions from Federal district judges against such real or threatened violations. Persons disobeying these injunctions could be fined or imprisoned for contempt by Federal judges, without jury trial.[39]

This bill, passed by the House, was weakened by amendments in the Senate. The two most important amendments limited Section 3 to cases involving the right to vote and provided for jury trials in all federal court criminal contempt cases. The final bill, the first civil rights legislation to come from Congress in eighty-two years, contained modifications of the jury trial proviso. The bill gives the federal government power to protect and enforce the right to vote with court orders. In cases of civil contempt (in which the judge is trying to compel obedience to his order) and in many cases of criminal contempt (in which the judge is punishing disobedience) the jury will be excluded. The bill provides that a judge may refuse to grant a jury trial, but that if he does so and subsequently assesses punishment above $300 in fines and 45 days' imprisonment the defendant can demand a jury to retry the action. The campaign for a new civil rights act has important political implications because of the increasing voting strength of Negroes. As we pointed out in the preceding chapter, northern Democrats are attempting to retain the Negro vote and the Republicans are trying to regain it. Striking evidence of the political power of Negroes was seen in the vote to make civil rights the business before the Senate. The border states—Maryland, West Virginia, Kentucky, Tennessee—and Texas, which have usually supported the South in previous struggles of this type, voted solidly with the North. Presumably the issue will continue to be a major one.

HOUSING

Residential segregation laws were declared illegal by the Supreme Court in 1917 when a Louisville, Kentucky, racial zoning ordinance was held to violate the Fourteenth Amendment. In 1925 the Court dismissed a New Orleans ordinance which sought to evade the pro-

[39] New York Times, July 21, 1957.

hibition on racial segregation by providing for written consent of the majority race inhabiting a block as a condition upon residence there by a member of the other race, by referring to its decision in the Louisville case.

Racial discrimination in housing has taken many forms since 1917. Urban Negroes usually pay more rent and higher purchase prices for poorer housing. They encounter difficulties in arranging mortgage loans and sometimes pay more than the usual interest rates. Building permits or the extension of utilities may be withheld. But the most common means for bringing about housing segregation has been the racial restrictive covenant. This is an agreement between parties to the sale of real property whereby the purchaser agrees not to rent or sell his property to members of specified races, nationalities, or religions. Examples of restrictive clauses in deeds are:

"And furthermore, no lot shall be sold or leased to, or occupied by, any person [not] of the Caucasian race."

"Provided further, that the grantee shall not sell to Negroes or permit use or occupation by them, except as domestic servants."

"Shall not permit occupation by Negroes, Hindus, Syrians, Greeks, or any corporations controlled by same."[40]

An analysis which covered subdivisions in Chicago, Kansas City, Cleveland, Boston, Louisville, Minneapolis, Baltimore, Detroit, Long Island, Oakland, Los Angeles, San Francisco, Seattle, and other cities found that racial restrictions were contained in forty of the eighty-four deeds examined. In all but two of these deeds the restrictive covenants were drawn up after 1920. The chairman of the Chicago Housing Authority stated that more than 80 percent of Chicago's residential area was covered by restrictive covenants.[41]

In the early forties the National Association of Real Estate Boards issued a booklet in Washington, D.C., which contained the following statement of policy: "No property in a white section should ever be sold, rented, advertised, or offered to colored people." The Real Estate Board's Code of Ethics included this statement:

When, for example, in any respectable neighborhood, a house is wanted for conversion to an objectionable use, no respectable broker will consent to represent the buyer.

The latter might be a bootlegger who would cause considerable annoyance to his neighbors, a "madam" who had a number of "call girls" on her string, a gangster who wanted a screen for his activities by living in a better neighborhood, a colored man of means . . . giving his children a college education and thought that they were entitled to live among the whites, but no matter what the motive or character of the would-be purchaser, if the deal

[40] Elmer Gertz, "American Ghettos," *Jewish Affairs*, February 1, 1947, p. 4.
[41] *Ibid.*, p. 12. All aspects of restrictive covenants are discussed in H. H. Long and C. S. Johnson, *People vs. Property*, Fisk University Press, 1947.

would instigate a form of blight, then certainly the well-meaning broker must work against its consummation.

Later the executive secretary of the National Association of Real Estate Boards disowned the statement and expressed regret that the publication had been circulated. He insisted that the statement did not represent the official attitude of the association toward the Negro.[42]

Restrictions on Negro housing, by whatever means they are achieved, have resulted in more and more overcrowding, and more squalor, as the Negro populations of urban centers have continued to increase. The main part of the Negro area in Chicago has a density of more than 75,000 persons per square mile, and the least congested sections have 50,000 persons per square mile. (The Chicago Plan Commission gives the average residential density desirable in new areas as 12,000 to 15,000 persons per square mile.) In Detroit, overcrowding in housing among Negroes has been twice as great as for whites, and 50 percent of the dwellings occupied by Negroes are substandard as compared to 14 percent for whites. One Harlem city block (141st Street, between Lenox and 7th avenues) has 3871 people, the highest dwelling density in any comparable area in the world.[43] The population density of the most crowded Harlem block could be equaled only if the entire U.S. population were packed into two-thirds of New York City. Philadelphia's Negro population is more than one-fifth of the city's total; but of the 60,000 new homes built in the metropolitan area during 1953–1955, only 400 (0.7 percent) were made available to Negroes.[44]

Innumerable further examples could be cited to show the enormous need of members of minority groups for housing accommodations. Housing in Puerto Rican sections of New York City is among the worst in the United States. The west side Mexican slum of 60,000 in San An-

[42] Charles Gomillion, "The Negro and Civil Rights," Negro Year Book, Tuskegee Institute, 1947, p. 292.

[43] Elmer Gertz, op. cit., pp. 7, 18. Robert C. Weaver points out that many whites fear that the coming of any Negro family will inevitably result in a mass movement of Negro residents, cause the moving out of whites, a decline in neighborhood standards, and considerable loss of property values. Weaver writes: "It is in areas contiguous to the Black Belt that overcrowding, physical deterioration, and decline of neighborhood standards have occurred as Negroes have expanded. All sound analyses of the problem indicate that the causes are economic and not racial. They are occasioned by the extreme overcrowding which occurs when any group of people lives in areas of inadequate size. This latter fact, in turn, is an inevitable result of hemmed-in, low-income families, regardless of race, into housing which is ill adapted to their needs and incomes. If there were an adequate supply of low-rent and low-cost housing available to all groups in the population, the probability of excessive overcrowding in any area incident to minority groups' occupancy would be greatly reduced." R. C. Weaver, "Housing in a Democracy," Annals of the American Academy of Political and Social Science, March, 1946, pp. 96–97. Weaver discusses occupancy standards, regardless of the racial group using the property, in ibid., p. 99. See also R. C. Weaver, The Negro Ghetto, Harcourt, Brace & Company, 1948.

[44] L. T. Hawley, "The Negro's New Economic Life," Fortune, September, 1956, p. 258.

tonio has been called the largest solid bloc of the underpossessed in the country. The Detroit area "still seethes" with racial feeling.[45] In Dearborn, a suburb of Detroit, Mayor Hubbard was elected and reëlected on the issue of keeping Negroes out of the city. Similar exclusion practices are found in Grosse Point, Bloomfield Hills, and Birmingham, which are also suburbs of Detroit. Other "closed cities" which keep out the "wrong kind of people" include Cicero and Berwyn, Illinois, the Levittowns (New York and Pennsylvania), and Fairless Hills, Pennsylvania.[46] Abrams points out that an increasing number of communities now tend to hire white labor exclusively, at least until the supply runs out, and to hire minority-group persons only when there are nearby cities in which they can live in large numbers. In this way countryside and suburbs are spared the effort or expense of providing homes for them.[47] Thus the Negro workers in the steel plants near Levittown and Fairless Hills have to find homes in Trenton, Camden, and Philadelphia. Negroes who work in the Ford plant in Dearborn have to crowd into Detroit.

During the summer of 1946 the New York office of the Anti-Trust Division of the United States Department of Justice filed suit against the Mortgage Conference of New York, accusing the members, including thirty-three of the nation's leading banks, trust companies, and insurance companies, of violating the Sherman Antitrust Act. The petition charged that the mortgage money market was monopolized; that the firms distributed maps of the city showing blocks in which Negro and Spanish-speaking people lived; that they refused to grant mortgage loans to property owners in such blocks; and that they influenced real-estate dealers to prevent Negroes and Spanish-speaking people from moving into certain sections. The decision went against the defendants in the U.S. District Court of the Southern District of New York on June 16, 1948, and they were ordered to dissolve the conference and to cease "all restrictive practices in New York City." The order specifically prohibited any mortgage lender from placing mortgages or competing for mortgages because "the property is owned or occupied by persons belonging to any particular racial or national group."[48]

---

[45] Charles Abrams, *Forbidden Neighbors*, Harper & Brothers, 1955, p. 99. The nonwhite population of Detroit grew from 150,790 in 1940 to 360,000 in 1957. In a number of sections of the city Negroes who seek to break the barrier of segregated private housing still face such obstacles as tacit neighborhood agreements against selling to them, difficulties in getting mortgages, unreasonable sale prices, and general hostility. The widely publicized case of Mrs. Ethel Watkins revealed that demonstrations, molestation, and threats were used in an attempt to drive her from the house she had purchased. New York *Times*, March 3, 1957, p. 66.

[46] Charles Abrams, *Forbidden Neighbors*, pp. 60–65, 51–55, 91–99, 101–102. The first Negro family moved into Levittown, Pennsylvania, in August, 1957. When neighbors protested, state troopers were called to prevent violence.

[47] Charles Abrams, "Civil Rights in 1956," *Commentary*, August, 1956, p. 106.

[48] Florence Murray (ed.), *op. cit.*, pp. 189–190.

Prior to 1948, racial restrictive covenants could be enforced in state courts. When a party to a restrictive covenant brought suit against a violator, the court could order the proscribed purchaser or tenant to give up possession of the property. In 1948 the Supreme Court held that restrictive covenants deny equal protection of the laws guaranteed by the Fourteenth Amendment. Advocates of restrictive covenants argued that the Fourteenth Amendment did not forbid court enforcement of such agreements because they were private agreements entered into by private persons respecting private property. They claimed that the amendment was involved only when the state attempted to discriminate on racial grounds. They contended also that Negroes were free to enter into such agreements against white persons. The court's position was that if a state court issued an injunction which prevented a person from occupying or buying property it was acting for the state. The ruling declared that the Fourteenth Amendment is not "ineffective simply because the particular pattern of discrimination, which the State has enforced, was defined initially by the terms of a private agreement. State action, as that phrase is understood for the purpose of the Fourteenth Amendment, refers to exertions of state power in all its forms." On the contention that Negroes have the same right to restrict the ownership and occupancy rights of white people, the Court said: "It is no answer . . . to say that the courts may deny white persons rights of ownership and occupancy on grounds of race or color. Equal protection of the laws is not achieved through indiscriminate imposition of inequalities." According to the Court, the rights to own, use, and enjoy property "are civil rights intended to be protected from discriminatory state action by the Fourteenth Amendment."[49]

The Court held that restrictive covenants standing alone do not violate the rights guaranteed by the Fourteenth Amendment. If the agreements are carried out by voluntary adherence to their terms, in the Court's view, there is no action by the state and hence no violation of the amendment. Unquestionably many property owners will continue to enter into racial restrictive covenants, but these agreements will be effective only so long as all parties and their successors abide by them. If an owner changes his mind, the cosigners can no longer obtain the court's help in forcing him to comply. It may be noted that the Department of Justice issued a statement saying that in its opinion the ruling of the Supreme Court in the racial restrictive covenant cases is "applicable with equal force to similar agreements based on creed."

New methods of racial and religious discrimination have been developed since the Supreme Court covenant decision. These include:

---

[49] Loren Miller, "Supreme Court Covenant Decision—An Analysis," The Crisis, September, 1948, p. 265.

1. A covenant which prevents the sale of property without the consent of the original owner of the tract of land.
2. Club membership, a device under which no one may buy property in a neighborhood unless acceptable to the board of the community club.
3. The leasehold system, a device by which the occupant leases the land for 99 years and may not sell without consent of the community's overseers. Before qualifying as a purchaser a person must live in the area for a year.
4. Urban redevelopment corporations, which are authorized by the laws of 15 states. This method was first used by the Metropolitan Life Insurance Company to construct Stuyvesant Town in New York City, a housing development which excludes Negroes.
5. The mortgage device, through which mortgage lenders agree not to make loans in an area in which racial infiltration has occurred or is threatened.
6. Brokers' agreements by which it is agreed that property will not be sold or rented to certain groups of persons.[50]

The effectiveness and the legality of such practices have not yet been tested; but as Abrams points out, the list is long enough (his list includes thirteen techniques) to effect exclusion if one or several of the devices are successfully attacked in the courts.[51] Some discriminatory tactics are inevitable if real-estate dealers and property owners are determined to use them, but the Court's ruling makes discrimination more difficult.

Despite the use of techniques to circumvent the Supreme Court's 1948 decision, the changed legal status of restrictive covenants brought some results. In Chicago, for example, the black belt began almost immediately to expand southward and westward.[52] Similar ghetto extensions occurred in Detroit and Washington; but, in addition, Negroes with high incomes have bought expensive property in neighborhoods where high selling prices seem to preclude appreciable nonwhite inundation for some time. Philadelphia has some racially mixed housing areas which appear to be stable.[53]

[50] Florence Murray (ed.), *op. cit.,* p. 56.
[51] Charles Abrams, *Forbidden Neighbors*, pp. 224–225.
[52] Gerald D. Bullock, "Chicago—Poignancy and Platitudes," *The Crisis*, May, 1957, pp. 262–263.
[53] R. C. Weaver, "Integration in Public and Private Housing," *Annals of the American Academy of Political and Social Science*, March, 1956, pp. 91–92. According to Sexton, the United States census shows that Negroes now live in all but thirty-seven tracts out of a total of 368 in Detroit. Brendan Sexton, "The Intervention of the Union in the Plant," *Journal of Social Issues*, 1953, vol. 9, p. 10. For a study of the attitudes of whites toward Negro neighbors in Minneapolis see Arnold M. Rose, F. J. Atelsek, and L. R. McDonald, "Neighborhood Reactions to Isolated Negro Residents: An Alternative to Invasion and Succession," *American Sociological Review*, October, 1953, pp. 497–507. A report on social interaction between white and Negro tenants in public housing projects in Connecticut, as well as the interracial attitudes of the tenants, is given in Henry G. Stetler, *Racial Integration in Public Housing Projects in Connecticut*, Connecticut Commission on Civil Rights, 1955, chap. 5.

The Supreme Court has never passed on the constitutionality of racial segregation in public housing projects. The Court refused in June, 1950, to review the appeal of three Negro war veterans from their exclusion as tenants from the Metropolitan Life Insurance Company's Stuyvesant Town housing project in New York City. This project houses more than 25,000 persons in 8759 apartments. The plaintiffs questioned the earlier ruling of the New York Court of Appeals that the discrimination against Negroes did not violate the equal-protection provision of the federal Constitution or a similar provision in the state constitution. They contended that the project was built under the development companies law of New York with "public aid and participation." They pointed out that a $50,000,000 tax exemption over a period of twenty-five years made limited rents possible, and that this was the result of the contribution of "all city taxpayers, Negroes as well as whites." The Metropolitan Life Insurance Company maintained that the basic question was whether a private corporation has a right as a landlord to select tenants of its own choice, and claimed that no public funds had been contributed to the enterprise. The company stated that decisions of this type were "business decisions" and mentioned that at Riverton, a similar rehabilitation project which was financed and is operated by a wholly owned subsidiary, Negroes are accepted as tenants. In 1954 the Supreme Court refused to review an appeal by the Housing Authority of San Francisco from a lower court ruling that the "neighborhood pattern" policy (filling the apartments of a project according to the racial pattern of the neighborhood) violated the "equal-protection" clause of the Fourteenth Amendment.[54] The Court has often said that refusal to review does not mean an affirmance.[55] There is disagreement as to whether the public-school decision of 1954 foreshadows a ruling on the "separate but equal" doctrine in public housing.

In October, 1955, a district court refused relief, under the separate-but-equal doctrine, to Negroes in Savannah, Georgia, who sought admission to a public housing project. The court found that public housing projects constructed for Negroes in Savannah were substantially equal, in quantity and quality, to those constructed for whites.[56] In December, 1955, a district court issued an injunction against the St. Louis Housing Authority restraining that body from refusing to rent public housing units solely on the basis of race. The court found that the Authority had discriminated, and, citing the school segregation cases, it held that such discrimination was unconstitutional.[57] In a simi-

[54] Lawrence E. Davies, "Housing 'Pattern' of Races Dropped," New York Times, May 30, 1954, p. 44.

[55] Charles Abrams, Forbidden Neighbors, p. 300.

[56] Race Relations Law Reporter, April, 1956, p. 347.

[57] Ibid., p. 353.

lar case against the Benton Harbor, Michigan, Housing Commission a district court on December 21, 1956, held that, under the school segregation decision, segregation in public housing on the basis of race is, per se, a denial of the equal protection of the laws.[58]

Despite the idealistic and "radical" tone of New Deal legislation, it is interesting to note that Negro housing became increasingly segregated from 1934 to 1948. From the beginning of the FHA until the Supreme Court ruled against racial covenants, FHA policies emphasized racial unity as a condition for the highest evaluations of neighborhoods and insisted that racial homogeneity was essential to a neighborhood's financial stability.[59]

As a result of pressure from civil rights groups and the attorney general, the FHA eventually ruled that it would no longer insure mortgages on properties having covenants that had been placed on them after February, 1950. It continued to insure properties on which covenants existed before that date.[60] In December, 1949, Solicitor General Philip B. Perlman, speaking with the approval of the President and the attorney general of the United States and the housing administrator, announced: "The Federal Housing Administration is amending its rules so as to refuse to aid the financing of any properties, the occupancy or use of which is restricted on the basis of race or creed or color." The limitations of this policy affected FHA financing guarantees for housing projects and one-unit dwellings, GI loans for veterans' housing, and slum clearance projects and land transactions by public agencies.

In 1949 a comprehensive housing bill passed by Congress provided for an urban redevelopment program. Title I included a write-down subsidy on land costs in slum or blighted areas, with two-thirds of the subsidy to be paid by the federal government and one-third by the municipality. The program was designed primarily for private developers, but public housing authorities could benefit from the subsidy.[61] The Housing Act of 1954 amended existing housing laws, putting major emphasis upon urban renewal.[62] Nondiscrimination applies to publicly assisted redevelopment and urban renewal programs in Connecticut, Minnesota, New Jersey, New York, Pennsylvania, and Wisconsin, as well as in Cincinnati, Cleveland, Los Angeles, and San Francisco. Adequate data on occupancy patterns under this program are not available, but its initiation has had adverse effects on the stability of interracial low-rent housing projects. According to Weaver:

[58] *Ibid.*, June, 1957, p. 611.
[59] L. T. Hawley, *op. cit.*, p. 258; and Charles Abrams, *Forbidden Neighbors*, pp. 161–162, 223, 231, 235.
[60] Charles Abrams, *Forbidden Neighbors*, p. 224.
[61] *Ibid.*, pp. 244–245.
[62] B. T. McGraw, "The Housing Act of 1954 and Implications for Minorities," *Phylon*, Second Quarter, 1955, p. 171.

About two-thirds of those displaced by redevelopment projects are non-whites and, as relocation families, usually have a priority on vacancies in public housing projects. Their admittance often upsets the racial balance in projects, hastening a development's becoming all or predominantly Negro. At the same time, displacement of large numbers of nonwhite families incident to slum clearance and public improvements places additional pressures on all transitional neighborhoods. The resulting immediate need for shelter on the part of a large number of colored families offers great economic incentives for doubling up and improvised conversions. Where there are not effective ordinances and occupancy standards, inundation of areas is inevitable and, in its course, racially integrated neighborhoods are threatened.[63]

Weaver presents data to show that local authorities (or states) participating in the federal public housing program may adopt open-occupancy policies and yet not effect compliance in some projects. A public housing development which is located in or is adjacent to an established nonwhite area usually becomes an all-nonwhite project. This happens because nonwhites try to get into the development, whereas whites tend not to enter and remain in a predominantly non-white community. It has been found that a racially integrated project is difficult to maintain if the proportion of nonwhite tenants exceeds 40 to 60 percent. By 1955 nine states had open-occupancy policies in public housing, and an additional eighteen states had one or more localities with such a policy. Housing integration varied in these states, with spatial integration in two southern communities (Rayne, Louisiana, and Crystal City, Texas) occurring on the basis of supply and demand.[64] According to Rutledge, tenants are selected without regard to race, creed, color, or national origin in less than one-fifth of the public housing projects in the United States.[65]

An important development in legislation against discrimination in housing was the extension of the definition of publicly assisted housing (the second Metcalf-Baker law) in New York to include FHA- and VA-insured construction. Connecticut's Commission on Civil Rights has interpreted FHA- and VA-insured construction as publicly assisted housing and therefore subject to the state's nondiscrimination and non-segregation law. New Jersey's laws have been amended to require that mortgages be made without regard to race, creed, or color of the borrower.[66] A New Jersey law of June, 1957, prohibits discrimination in

[63] R. C. Weaver, "Integration in Public and Private Housing," p. 90.

[64] Ibid., pp. 86–87.

[65] Edward Rutledge, "Site Selection, Costs and Interracial Housing," a paper prepared for the annual meeting of the National Association of Intergroup Relations Officials at Milwaukee, Wisconsin, December 2, 1955, p. 8. Rutledge shows the financial savings to be had through the construction of integrated versus biracial housing projects, and stresses the importance of site selection in planning integrated programs.

[66] R. C. Weaver, "Integration in Public and Private Housing," p. 92.

FHA-aided housing and vests jurisdiction in the state's Division Against Discrimination.[67]

On December 30, 1957, the first city ordinance in the United States forbidding discrimination in private housing was signed into law by Mayor Robert F. Wagner. Effective April 1, 1958, the law is designed to assist Negroes and members of other minority groups to move out of congested areas. The ordinance makes it illegal to refuse to rent or sell an apartment or multiple dwelling housing three or more families because of a prospective tenant's race, creed, or national origin. Unless they are part of housing developments of 10 or more, one- and two-family dwellings are exempt. It is estimated that the law will affect 1,787,000 apartments and more than five million residents of New York City. The original proposal provided for violators to be taken directly to court and subjected to fines up to $500. The final bill provides for conciliation and review before court action.

Several riots have occurred in connection with attempts by Negroes to move into "white" neighborhoods. A score of men were taken to the hospital, and more than a score to jail, in February, 1942, when Negroes attempted to enter their rented homes in the Sojourner Truth housing project in Detroit. This project for defense workers was built in a mixed white and Negro neighborhood. More than 500 police had to be assigned to quell a mob of thousands of white residents in November, 1946, when two Negro veterans were given homes in the Chicago Housing Authority's Airport Homes project. "From May, 1944, through July, 1946—a period of twenty-seven months—59 attacks were made on Negro residences in Chicago. About half were arson-bombings. There were 22 cases of stoning, three shootings, three house-wreckings, two stench-bombings. Three persons were killed and many were injured."[68] From July, 1949, to July, 1952, there were four race riots over housing situations in Chicago, and there were nine such riots from 1945 to 1954. In addition, from 1949 to July, 1951, there were "more than a hundred lesser incidents in the Chicago area: bombings, fires, or organized assaults against Negro families, one of these by a hit-and-run incendiary who started a fire that cost ten lives. . . ."[69] In July, 1951, a mob of several thousand, led by young hoodlums, rioted in Cicero, Illinois, in protest against the renting of an apartment to a Negro family. Martial law was declared by the governor of Illinois, and five companies of the National Guard were sent to Cicero. Twenty-three soldiers, policemen, and civilians were injured during the fighting, and sixty-four rioters were arrested, but only after the apartment house had been wrecked in days of rioting, with the police being indifferent. Instead of indicting the persons responsible for the vandalism and for

[67] *NAIRO Reporter*, June, 1957, p. 3.
[68] Elmer Gertz, *op. cit.*, pp. 9–10.
[69] Charles Abrams, *Forbidden Neighbors*, p. 106.

preventing Harvey C. Clark, Jr., from living where he chose, a grand jury investigation indicted the attorney who represented him. Also indicted were the owner, her lawyer, and her rental agent, all of whom were charged with conspiracy to injure property by causing "depreciation in the market selling price." After civic groups protested, the indictments were dropped and indictments were issued against the town president, the fire chief, the police chief, the town attorney, and three policemen. The police chief and two policemen paid a total fine of $2500.[70]

For more than three years after the first of several Negro families moved into the Trumbull Park low-rent housing project on the far South Side of Chicago on July 30, 1953, the neighborhood was marked by violence, rioting, beatings, vandalism, and racial clashes. At times as many as 1353 policemen were on duty to keep the peace at the 462-family development, and an average of 300 policemen were always on duty. Nearly 250 arrests were made during this period.[71] Since 1956 Trumbull Park has had comparative peace, and the twenty-eight Negro families are expected to stay.

Such protests against interracial housing have all occurred in situations in which official indifference and laxness or police connivance have been involved. In situations in which nonsegregated housing has been planned and the interracial policy has been backed by skillful and firm action, interracial housing not only has resulted in no conflict but has reduced prejudice.

It is of interest, in this regard, to consider the findings of a study of interracial housing directed by Robert K. Merton for the Lavanburg Foundation.

From three-quarters to nine-tenths of a cross-section of the American public has expressed itself as favoring residential segregation of Negroes. The great majority of Whites expressing this view in the North have not, of course, lived in the same neighborhoods with Negroes. In the absence of direct experience, they could only give voice to a deep-seated prejudice. That a considerable proportion of these would have different opinions is indicated by the Lavanburg Foundation study of Hilltown, an inter-racial housing community in Pittsburgh. Before moving into this project, only 4% of the whites expected race relations to turn out well, whereas 21% were convinced that it would involve nothing but conflict. Most of the remainder had their doubts. After a few years, fully 21% found that race relations had turned out better than they had anticipated. Only 6% felt that it was worse than their expectations. More importantly, 3 out of every 4 who had expected serious racial conflict found that their fears were unfounded. Direct experience had shown what general admonitions for tolerance would prob-

[70] *Ibid.*, pp. 105–106.
[71] New York *Times*, July 24, 1955, and February 24, 1957.

ably not have shown: that inter-racial fears and hostilities were exaggerated and distorted beyond all resemblance to the reality.[72]

Two interesting reactions on the issue of residential segregation have come from the South since the Supreme Court's public-school decision of 1954. The first response minimized the decision, saying that residential segregation would reduce or prevent change. The second view holds that proper housing in separate areas must be provided for non-whites to prevent school desegregation. Although the school decision is not universally accepted in the North, the resistance to it and to unsegregated living is less intense than in the South. Furthermore, the increasing political power of Negroes will enlarge the scope and the enforcement of northern housing legislation.[73]

Housing has lagged behind integration in other aspects of American life. Since unsegregated housing is crucial for school integration, many regard it as the outstanding problem in race relations.[74] In a period of change a number of developments stand out.

1. Relocation which goes with urban renewal programs will continue to create new slums as dislocated people are forced into already overcrowded areas, and it will upset the racial balance in some public housing projects. Where there are adequate protective legislation, effective compliance organization, and favorable public opinion, urban renewal ultimately will serve to disperse the nonwhite population.
2. Whites will continue to migrate to all-white suburbs, but this movement will be accompanied by certain countertendencies. Some cities will use the redevelopment program to bring some suburbs back into the central city. Nonwhites now have higher earnings, and some of them will move into neighborhoods partially vacated by whites who have moved into newly constructed housing. With effective legislation behind them, some major producers of new housing may establish open-occupancy developments in suburban areas.
3. The banning of racial discrimination in FHA- and VA-insured housing in several states will support and accelerate nondiscrimination in publicly assisted housing.

[72] Cited in R. M. MacIver, op. cit., p. 238. For intensive studies of conditions underlying behavioral and attitudinal consequences of interracial contact in public housing, see Morton Deutsch and Mary E. Collins, Interracial Housing, University of Minnesota Press, 1951; and D. M. Wilner, R. P. Walkley, and S. W. Cook, Human Relations in Interracial Housing, University of Minnesota Press, 1955.
[73] R. C. Weaver, "Integration in Public and Private Housing," pp. 93–94.
[74] A comprehensive housing program at the local, state, and national levels is suggested in Charles Abrams, Forbidden Neighbors, pp. 346–385.

Relief and Welfare Services

Negroes receive most consideration from federal agencies in the field of relief; public agencies supported by the state rank next in the amount of attention shown Negroes. Welfare institutions supported by local governments discriminate most on the basis of race, and aid to Negroes from private and semipublic agencies is often unsystematic charity rather than welfare assistance.

In southern cities Negro and white clients usually have separate waiting rooms, and Negroes report that white social workers fail to accord them fair and courteous treatment. In this connection it should be said that organized public and private relief is administered almost entirely by whites. Relief allowances for Negroes in the South are usually lower than those for white people.

The Importance of the Legal Pattern

A tendency has existed among both social scientists and lawyers to minimize the influence of the legal pattern and to emphasize the importance of the mores in race relations. Many sociologists, including W. G. Sumner, Robert E. Park, W. F. Ogburn, and Ellsworth Faris, have held this point of view, and it has been shared by a number of state courts and, until the middle thirties, by the Supreme Court.[75] In the past fifteen years Gunnar Myrdal, R. M. MacIver, Charles S. Johnson, Carey McWilliams, and others have vigorously challenged the thesis that legislation can do little about discrimination.

MacIver and McWilliams both go back to the civil rights cases of 1883 in tracing the ramifications of the doctrine that laws cannot overcome social prejudices. Justice Harlan, the sole dissenter in the Supreme Court's decision on this occasion, pointed out that the purpose of the Civil War amendments was to prevent racial discrimination. In the Plessy v. Ferguson case in 1896 involving racial segregation on common carriers, the Supreme Court said: "Legislation is powerless to eradicate racial instincts or to abolish distinctions based upon physical differences, and the attempt to do so can only result in accentuating the difficulties of the present situation. . . . If one race is inferior to the other socially, the Constitution of the United States cannot put them upon the same plane." In his dissent, Justice Harlan maintained that the Court had erred in basing the case on the issue that law cannot control social prejudice and then treating racial segregative attitudes as unchanging racial "instincts" which are beyond the power of law.[76]

Laws cannot compel "social acceptance." The purpose of civil rights

[75] Gunnar Myrdal, An American Dilemma, Harper & Brothers, 1944, pp. 19–20, 525, 580 n., 1048–1057.

[76] R. M. MacIver, op. cit., pp. 170–171, and Carey McWilliams, "Race Discrimination and the Law," Science and Society, Winter, 1945, pp. 10–12.

statutes, however, is not to force social intercourse upon unwilling persons but to prohibit legal discrimination. A *Columbia Law Review* statement is pertinent here. "Civil rights acts undoubtedly have the effect of coercing those persons who like to attend places of public accommodation and amusement into what is to some of them distasteful contact. But non-action on the part of a legislature is equivalent to sanctioning the existing state of affairs and deprives many of accommodations and facilities merely because of their race or religion, and, in addition, tends to engender racial and religious prejudice in people who otherwise would never feel it."[77] Burma makes the point that laws, of themselves, do not automatically eliminate the abuses they are intended to correct, but laws do establish criteria for judging actions. "Passage of civil rights legislation does establish the fact that certain behavior has been judged to be inimical to the public welfare and contrary to public policy, and such legislation does establish a frame of reference within which other necessary processes can be systematized and accelerated. These are the most significant long-term values to be derived from such legislation."[78]

Court decisions reflect the climate of opinion, and from 1868 until 1936 the rulings of the Supreme Court functioned to support the prevailing racial system. The narrow and legalistic interpretations of the Court during these years, as MacIver observes, had the effect of reducing to a minimum some of the liberties guaranteed by the Constitution. During this period the Court played an important part in "keeping the Negro in his place." However, Supreme Court decisions modify as well as reflect opinion, and the decisions since 1937 have greatly influenced public opinion and have prepared the way for legislative action.[79]

Segregation, Discrimination, and Integration in the Armed Services

On July 26, 1948, President Truman established, through Executive Order 9981, an advisory committee known as the President's Committee on Equality of Treatment and Opportunity in the Armed Services. This order declared it "to be the policy of the President that there shall be equality of treatment and opportunity for all persons in the armed services without regard to race, color, religion or national origin. This policy shall be put into effect as rapidly as possible, having due regard to the time required to effectuate any necessary changes without impair-

---

[77] "Legislative Attempts to Eliminate Racial and Religious Discrimination," *Columbia Law Review*, June, 1939, p. 1000. Quoted in Carey McWilliams, *op. cit.*, p. 17.

[78] John H. Burma, *op. cit.*, p. 423. See also Morroe Berger, *Equality by Statute*, Columbia University Press, 1952, chap. 5.

[79] Carey McWilliams, *Brothers Under the Skin*, Little, Brown & Company, rev. ed., 1951, p. 16. See also Morroe Berger, *op. cit.*, chaps. 2–3.

ing efficiency or morale." While the scope of the committee's work included persons in the armed services of all racial, religious, and nationality groups, no evidence was presented to the committee indicating formally defined service policies denying equality of treatment and opportunity except in the case of Negroes. Inequality of treatment and opportunity for Negroes had official sanction and was incorporated in regulations. Although the committee sought a formula which would be applicable to all minorities, its report is limited throughout to recommendations affecting Negroes.[80]

The two basic questions which have been faced by military staffs in considering the question of Negro utilization are: (1) Do Negroes have the mental and technical qualifications to be used in the full range of military jobs? and (2) Shall Negroes be utilized only in Negro units? The committee found that until quite recently the first question had been answered negatively and the second in the affirmative.

Negroes had served as enlisted men in the Navy's general service until the end of World War I, but Negro enlistments were stopped at that time. When enlistments were reopened in 1932, only the messman's branch recruited Negroes, and this situation continued until the middle of 1942. Partly because of the pressure of Negro organizations and partly because it could not make full utilization, in shore installations and harbor craft, of the technical skills of a large number of men after it began to receive its manpower through selective service, the Navy experimented in 1943 and 1944 (1) with two segregated ships and (2) with assigning Negroes to twenty-five auxiliary ships. In the latter case the Negroes were integrated completely with white crews, although no ship had more than 10 percent Negroes in its enlisted group. Since the second experiment proved to be more successful than the first, several changes in policy were made in 1945; and on February 27, 1946, the Navy ordered that ". . . all restrictions governing types of assignments for which Negro naval personnel are eligible are hereby lifted. Henceforth, they shall be eligible for all types of assignments in all ratings in all activities and all ships of the naval service. . . . In the utilization of housing, messing, and other facilities, no special or unusual provisions will be made for the accommodation of Negroes." The President's committee was impressed by the fact that within five years the Navy had changed from a policy of complete exclusion of Negroes from general service to a policy of complete integration in general service. The committee expressed concern over the small number of Negro officers and the relatively low percentage (2 percent) of Negroes in the total general service ratings in the Navy in 1950. Although by 1950 the

[80] President's Committee on Equality of Treatment and Opportunity in the Armed Services, *Freedom to Serve*, Government Printing Office, 1950, pp. 4–5. The members of this committee were Lester B. Granger, Dwight R. G. Palmer, John H. Sengstacke, William E. Stevenson, and Charles Fahy, chairman.

Navy had abolished segregation in the Marine Corps during basic training, some Negro marines were assigned to Negro units.

The racial policy of the Air Force during World War II was that of the Army—a 10 percent quota on enlisted men, segregated units, and severely limited job opportunities. By 1945 many officers of high rank were dissatisfied with these policies on the ground that segregation resulted in the loss of many skills. After the issuance of Executive Order 9981 in July, 1948, the Air Force began to develop a new policy. The new program, announced on May 11, 1949, provided that there be no strength quotas of minority groups on a troop basis; that qualified Negro personnel be assigned to any position vacancy; that all individuals, regardless of race, be given equal opportunity for appointment, advancement, professional improvement, promotion, and retention in all components of the Air Force. Among the conclusions of the President's committee on the experience of the Navy and the Air Force were these: The enlisted men were much more ready for integration than the officers had believed; segregation results in wastage and malassignment of manpower; integration, instead of presenting insurmountable difficulties, had brought a decrease in racial friction.[81]

The Army had had Negro units since the establishment of two infantry and two cavalry regiments in 1866. During World War I Negroes served in supply and supporting units, and also in two combat divisions. Despite the recommendations of several studies made by the Army War College between World War I and World War II that the Army never again form Negro units of divisional size, two Negro divisions were reactivated in World War II. According to the President's committee, the historical record proved that segregated units do not result in maximum efficient utilization. Instead the Army experienced "endless trouble" with them. The Gillem Board, a special board of general officers, was appointed in October, 1945, to study the question of utilizing Negro manpower. Although this board was impressed with the great improvement in education and industrial skill which Negroes had made in two decades, and although it became convinced that the Army had not given sufficient recognition to these changes, it concluded that segregation was necessary and recommended the retention of a Negro quota in proportion to the civilian population. The Gillem Board made five specific recommendations, but two of these were not approved by the Army, and nothing was done about one of the recommendations that was approved. The board's proposal to utilize Negroes in overhead units (post housekeeping detail which performs the duties connected with the administration of an Army base) was followed, but the committee found in 1949 that a large number of jobs in the whole field of Army occupations were still closed to Negroes. The same serious depri-

[81] *Ibid.*, p. 44.

vation existed with respect to the opportunity to attend Army schools. The committee recommended to the Army in May, 1949, a four-point program for the achievement of the objective in Executive Order 9981:

"1. Open up all Army jobs to qualified personnel without regard to race or color.

"2. Open up all Army schools to qualified personnel without regard to race or color.

"3. Rescind the policy restricting Negro assignments to racial units and overhead installations, and assign all Army personnel according to individual ability and Army need.

"4. Abolish the racial quota."[82]

Between September, 1949, and March, 1950, the four recommendations were accepted by the Army. In closing its report in May, 1950, the committee expressed the hope that with the acceptance of these recommendations Negro soldiers would shortly enjoy complete equality of treatment and opportunity in the Army.

Both in World War I and in World War II the initial reports concerning Negro soldiers were highly favorable. Later there were stories about Negro cowardice and the necessity for courts-martial. Reports were unavailable for investigation after World War I, and the witnesses were scattered after World War II. The pattern of reports was repeated after the outbreak of war in Korea. Thirty-six men convicted in court-martial cases sought the assistance of the NAACP. Permission was at first denied Thurgood Marshall, special counsel of that organization, to go to Tokyo, where the prisoners were. General MacArthur cabled that there was "not the slightest evidence here of discrimination as alleged" and added that there would be no objection to having the special counsel represent the accused in future courts-martial in Korea. Interest in the men already tried led to another exchange of cables and clearance was arranged for Mr. Marshall in January, 1951.[83] Investigation revealed many errors and many injustices, including these cases: a man who was able to prove that he was in an Army hospital during the time he was charged with not being on duty; four men who were convicted of misbehavior in the presence of the enemy although they were stationed miles behind the battle line and assigned to mess duty; and a sergeant, charged with refusing to obey an order, who had received a statement from the medical officer saying that he was on the verge of battle fatigue and should be returned to the rear. Trials were often of less than an hour's duration, desired counsel were usually not available, and there was almost no time for the counsel to prepare his case.[84]

[82] *Ibid.*, p. 61.
[83] Thurgood Marshall, "Summary Justice—The Negro GI in Korea," *The Crisis*, May, 1951, p. 298.
[84] Thurgood Marshall, *Report on Korea*, National Association for the Advancement of Colored People, 1951, pp. 10, 15.

There was evidence that many officers had openly announced that they despised Negro troops and told them they didn't know how to fight. According to Marshall, this attitude created a lack of confidence between the enlisted men and their assigned officers. Consequently, the casualty rates among the enlisted men and officers were disproportionately high. The high casualty rate among officers is considered by the investigator to be the cause of the large number of courts-martial. A scapegoat was needed and the Negro soldier was at hand.

The NAACP counsel found no large numbers of courts-martial in the mixed units of the Air Force and the Navy, and concluded that the Korean cases were "rooted in the Jim Crow policies still persisting in the Army." He attributed the responsibility for maintaining the color line in the Army in the Far East to General MacArthur, who "failed to implement the President's order for the elimination of segregation from the armed services. While there are a few mixed units in the Army in Korea, the general practice is one of rigid segregation."[85] The sequel to this investigation was the Army's announcement in July, 1951, that segregation was to be eliminated in the Far East Command. At that time the Army had not ended segregation in Europe and the United States.[86]

The performance of Negro soldiers in segregated units both in World War I and in World War II was less effective than that of whites. In World War II the quality of performance seemed to depend largely on the organization of the Negro troops. When they fought in platoons together with white soldiers, Negroes did well; most of those organized into larger units, such as companies, did less well.[87] The explanation of this difference is attributed to factors other than innate racial qualities. The great majority of the Negro soldiers were handicapped by inadequate schooling and by their home and community backgrounds. Their inferior status in American society had given them little understanding of the values for which the United States was fighting and little familiarity with the complex structure and technology of an organization such as the Army. Segregation in training and utilization had a depressing effect on morale, as did the shortage of competent officers, white and Negro. Many whites who became officers had strong prejudices concerning Negroes and their abilities. Some who were unprejudiced became impatient at the slow learning ability of many Negroes. Color made the Negro soldier who did a poor job highly conspicuous.[88] There were numerous exceptions to the general performance referred to above. The 99th Fighter Squadron and the 332nd Fighter Group

[85] Ibid., p. 17.
[86] News from N.A.A.C.P., August 2, 1951, p. 3.
[87] Eli Ginzberg, The Negro Potential, Columbia University Press, 1956, p. 76. Ginzberg presents a thorough review of the status of the Negro soldier during and following World War II.
[88] Ibid., pp. 76–86.

made outstanding records, the 2000 volunteer infantry replacements at Ardennes performed very well, and Negro troops gave strong support to combat units at Iwo Jima, Anzio, Okinawa, Salerno, and elsewhere.

Integration in the Army, begun in Europe in 1951, went ahead swiftly in 1952.[89] By the summer of that year, segregation in that command had virtually disappeared.[90] The Marine Corps was the last of the services to admit Negroes at all, but its last two all-Negro units were integrated by the summer of 1952.[91] In visiting seven military bases from coast to coast in 1953, Nichols found "that the wall of racial segregation was almost gone."[92] According to him:

> Gone were the complaints of wide-scale "melting-away" of Negro units that plagued many American commanders in two world wars and during the early months of the Korean War. Exhaustive studies rated America's Negro soldiers on close par with white fighting men *when serving in racially mixed units*. Far from the general predictions of ruined efficiency, wrecked morale, even bloody revolt, white units showed little reaction when Negroes were sprinkled among their ranks. Some officers even reported *heightened morale* among their once all-white units after Negroes were added.[93]

Although no all-Negro units remain in the major branches of the services, some exceptions are found in civilian components, mainly in a number of school and college Reserve Officers' Training Corps. Integration includes organization, training, assignment, billeting, mess, supervised recreation, and all other unit operations.[94]

	July 1, 1949	July 1, 1954
Army officers	1.8	2.97
Army enlisted men	12.4	13.7
Navy officers	0.0	0.1
Navy enlisted men	4.7	3.6
Air Force officers	0.6	1.1
Air Force enlisted men	5.1	8.6
Marine Corps officers	0.0	0.1
Marine Corps enlisted men	2.1	6.5

A comparison[95] of the percentage of Negroes in the personnel of the armed forces, by services, in 1949 and 1954 is of special interest because the Department of Defense has eliminated all racial statistics.

Since integration, Negroes have made considerable progress as non-

[89] Lee Nichols, *Breakthrough on the Color Front*, Random House, Inc., 1954, pp. 129–130.

[90] Eli Ginzberg, *op. cit.*, p. 87.

[91] Lee Nichols, *op. cit.*, p. 203.

[92] *Ibid.*, p. 143.

[93] *Ibid.*, p. 7.

[94] James C. Evans and David A. Lane, Jr., "Integration in the Armed Services," *Annals of the American Academy of Political and Social Science*, March, 1956, p. 81.

[95] *Ibid.*, p. 81.

commissioned officers in the Army. Toward the end of World War II, 18 percent of the Negro enlisted men, as compared with 31 percent of the whites, held the grade of sergeant or better. By the end of 1955, 28 percent of the Negro enlisted men were in the three highest non-commissioned grades, as compared with 26 percent of the white soldiers. The percentage of Negro officers in all branches of the services is low; but improvement in the general economic and educational status of American Negroes, as well as the broadening of opportunity within the forces, will change this situation. An increasing number of Army schools are admitting Negro enlisted men and there has been a substantial increase in the proportion of Negro enlisted strength in Army schools in recent years. Despite these gains, many Negro soldiers will continue to be handicapped to some extent by their educational and other environmental backgrounds. The important contribution of integration is that it insures that nonwhite men and women in the services will be utilized to their full capacities.[96] Many of the problems that remain stem from civilian personnel employment practices and from ROTC, National Guard, and other civilian component operations which are not under the control of the federal government. The latter operations will become more important as efforts to strengthen the reserve forces are made.[97]

To many, including a large number of officers in the services, the achievement of integration in the armed forces has been surprising. Most of the officers who asserted that the military establishment is not an agency of social reform have found that military efficiency has been improved by the elimination of racial segregation. It is somewhat ironical that one of the most conservative institutions should have demonstrated the remarkable ability of whites and Negroes to adjust satisfactorily to new racial relations. In addition to military integration itself, the armed forces have provided examples of integrated housing, transportation, religious services, education, recreation, and other aspects of life for service personnel and civilian employees and their families within their own communities, both in the United States and overseas. As Ginzberg says, through these achievements the armed services "have not only strengthened the nation by strengthening themselves, but have taken the leadership in showing the nation what good will and determination can accomplish."[98]

[96] Eli Ginzberg, op. cit., pp. 89–90.

[97] James C. Evans and David A. Lane, Jr., op. cit., p. 84. Since 1947 a number of states have passed laws against racial and religious discrimination and segregation in their state militias. These states include New Jersey, Connecticut, Wisconsin, Illinois, Massachusetts, New York, Pennsylvania, and California; and an executive order by the governor of Minnesota has had the same effect. Arnold Forster, op. cit., p. 209.

[98] Eli Ginzberg, op. cit., p. 91; see also James C. Evans and David A. Lane, Jr., op. cit., p. 84.

Criminal Justice and Minorities

Although gross crime rates are often higher among Negroes than the rates among whites for similar crimes, the differences in the rates cannot be attributed either to the innate characteristics of racial groups or to the proportion of Negroes in a community's population. Finding that the incidence of crime varies greatly among southern cities, Porterfield and Talbert say: "If we could determine carefully the relative opportunities of Negroes in different cities for achieving social status, economic security, and personality growth, we could have a more adequate explanation of its crime rates."[99]

The position of the Negro in the American social order is of great importance in Negro crime. Guy Johnson refers to this position in terms of "subordination, frustration, economic insecurity, and incomplete participation."[100] Regardless of specific laws on the statute books, conflict situations between white persons and Negroes may be defined as Negro crimes. "Forgetting to say 'Mister' to a white man, 'looking at' a white woman, entering the wrong waiting room, 'sassing' the landlord, disputing a white man's word, taking the wrong seat on a bus or street car, riding in a Pullman car—these are some of the things which may define a dangerous situation. If the Negro persists in being 'insolent' or aggressive, anything from abusive language to homicide may occur, but whatever occurs is likely to be to his own disadvantage."[101] It cannot be said at present how much of the behavior which is labeled "criminal" stems from violations of racial etiquette. Johnson believes that many of the cases booked as "creating a disturbance on a public vehicle," "resisting arrest," "assault," "felonious assault," "manslaughter," and "murder" actually are "violations of segregation laws." Relatively few offenses are listed under the latter heading.

The Negro's position, especially in the South, is such that he may be blamed for crimes committed by whites. Thus a white person may commit a crime in such a way that suspicion will fall upon some Negro (blackening his face prior to the crime is one way of achieving this end); a crime may be committed so that a particular Negro will appear to be guilty; a white woman may allege rape when discovered in sexual delinquency or when she considers some inconsequential action an insult or an "attack." In the latter instance, a man hunt follows and a Negro is "identified" and legally convicted or illegally harmed.[102]

---

[99] Austin L. Porterfield and Robert H. Talbert, "Crime in Southern Cities," in Rupert B. Vance and N. J. Demerath (eds.), *The Urban South*, University of North Carolina Press, 1954, p. 188.

[100] Guy B. Johnson, "The Negro and Crime," *Annals of the American Academy of Political and Social Science*, September, 1941, p. 104.

[101] *Ibid.*, pp. 95–96.

[102] *Ibid.*, p. 96.

One aspect of interest in the administration of criminal justice for Negroes in the South is the absence, in many communities, of any Negro officers, judges, lawyers, or jurymen. In such communities the Negro's only roles are those of defendant and witness, except in a few types of civil cases.[103] Of course, he does not participate in the lawmaking process. Approximately 1000 Negro police officials are now employed in about 150 cities and in twenty-two counties in the South. However, in most southern cities Negro officers are permitted to arrest only Negroes or offenders "on their beats." Their beats are in all-Negro areas.[104]

Crime rates for Negroes are highest in urban centers. Nine-tenths of the Negro population in the North and West live in cities, and nine-tenths of these live in or adjacent to disorganized slum areas. Poverty, overcrowding, vice, crime, and social disorder characterize these areas and are factors in Negro crime causation. In a study of 300 institutionalized delinquents—179 Negro, 121 white—Axelrad found that the courts commit on a differential basis. The Negro children had been committed younger, for less serious offenses, with fewer previous court appearances, and with less prior institutionalization. Also, there were differences in family pattern. The white delinquents tended to have lived more with biological parents, the Negro delinquents with mother and stepfather, with mother only, with other relatives, or in unrelated families. The mother was the only person employed in 5 percent of the white families, as compared with 26 percent of the Negro families.[105]

Class position within the Negro group, as within the white population, affects the treatment of offenders by the police and by the courts. Lower-class Negroes in the deep South are arrested more frequently for lower-court offenses than upper-class Negroes; the latter, however, are not immune to the same extent that upper-class whites are. The proceedings of the lower courts, especially the justice-of-the-peace courts, are similar in rural and urban areas. However, differences between Negro-white relations in the two types of areas influence the cases that come to court. In the deep South rural areas the planter exercises controls over his Negro tenants which are exercised in urban communities by the police and courts. It is not unknown for a rural justice "to advise planters to whip Negroes for theft rather than to bring them into court." Some planters settle fights and disputes among "their Negroes" and thus keep a certain number of cases out of the

---

[103] Allison W. Davis, B. B. Gardner, and M. R. Gardner, *Deep South*, University of Chicago Press, 1941, pp. 512–513.

[104] Carl Rowan, *How Far from Slavery*, Minneapolis Star and Tribune Company, 1951, chap. 6.

[105] Sidney Axelrad, "Negro and White Male Institutionalized Delinquents," *American Journal of Sociology*, May, 1952, pp. 573–574.

courts.[106] If a house servant or tenant is arrested, it is not uncommon for the employer or the landlord to provide assistance in the form of bail, a lawyer, influence, and payment of the fine.

An interesting aspect of the administration of criminal justice for Mexican-Americans is the absence of leaders who will lend assistance to lower-class Mexicans. The middle-class Mexican is still so insecure that his chief concern is to demonstrate his superiority to the Mexican masses. When presented with evidence of police injustice, the middle-class Mexican often finds it convenient to refer to the presumed incorrigibility of the Mexican lower class.[107]

In the United States there are really four categories of offenses from the standpoint of Negroes and whites: (1) Negro crimes against whites; (2) white crimes against whites; (3) Negro crimes against Negroes; and (4) white crimes against Negroes. Beginning with the last category of crimes, which are regarded as the least serious, it may be said that whites have little fear in the South that violence against Negroes will bring legal reprisal.

Any white man can strike or beat a Negro, steal or destroy his property, cheat him in a transaction and even take his life, without much fear of legal reprisal. The minor forms of violence—cheating and striking—are a matter of everyday occurrence, but the major ones are infrequent enough to be talked about. Negroes, of course, try to avoid situations in which such violence is likely to occur, and if Negroes do incur the displeasure of a white man, a mere command or threat is usually enough to control them without the use of actual violence. The Negro's economic dependence upon whites makes these verbal controls especially potent. But accidental insult, and sometimes nothing at all except the general insecurity or sadism of certain whites, can serve as occasion for violence. Of course, there are certain checks on violence: most Southerners do not want to be mean or dishonest toward Negroes directly. Public opinion in the South tends to frown upon any white man who acquires a reputation for being consistently mean or dishonest, and on rare occasions may even ostracize him socially or encourage the application of legal sanctions against him. But the general attitude is one of laissez faire; if a plantation owner cheats or beats his Negro tenants, "that's his business"; if a Negro is the victim of a sudden outburst of violence, "he must have done something to deserve it." Above all, the Negro must be kept in his "place."[108]

Incidents such as the following indicate the readiness to respond to rumor with violence: An armed band of white farmers shot a Negro field worker on the false rumor that he had kidnaped a white woman. Actually, the Negro, given a ride in the white woman's car, had carried her baby son to a physician's office after the car had been in a minor

[106] Allison W. Davis, B. B. Gardner, and M. R. Gardner, op. cit., pp. 511–512.
[107] Beatrice Griffith, American Me, Houghton Mifflin Company, 1948, p. 203.
[108] Gunnar Myrdal, op. cit., p. 559.

accident.[109] The Emmett Till case attracted nation-wide attention in 1955. Till, a fourteen-year-old Chicago Negro visiting relatives in a rural section of Mississippi, was killed for allegedly "wolf-whistling" at a white woman. Two white men, presumably his murderers, were acquitted by an all-white jury; later, an all-white grand jury refused to indict them for kidnapping.[110]

Negroes can do little to protect themselves against white aggression or cheating, even when they are in the majority. The police and the courts ordinarily give them no protection unless the whites involved are poor or are men of bad reputation. "The police usually discourage such actions [charges against whites]; and in trying such cases, the court protects the whites by technicalities and by attacking the truth of the Negro testimony. In one case, when Negro witnesses testified against whites, the judge was quite evidently annoyed, continually abused and found fault with the prosecuting witnesses, and finally threw the case out of court on technicalities."[111] If Negroes strike back, they can expect to meet violent retaliation to themselves and possibly to other Negroes. If they are not beaten up, tarred and feathered, or lynched, they may be put in jail for "attacking a white man," or they may be told to leave town and not to return.

Offenses by Negroes which involve actual or potential danger to whites are punished more severely than they would be if the offenders were white. The South makes free use of the death penalty, and Negro criminals are involved in more than their share of executions. In many instances Negroes who commit offenses against whites are punished extralegally either by an individual or by a mob.

Negro offenses against Negroes are treated generally in the South with undue leniency. A high percentage of Negro crime occurs within the Negro community, and most of it is found among lower-class Negroes. Lower-class Negroes bear the brunt of the racial stigma. Their lives are characterized by hopelessness and degradation. Their personalities and motives "are tied up with their roles as lower-class members of a subordinate race. They let off most of the 'steam' of their frustrated desires among their own group." As Guy Johnson also points out, community controls are not strong enough to offset the disorganizing influences. In fact, violence often becomes a virtue. Furthermore, the South, and to some extent the North, does not have a tradition of rendering strict justice to Negroes who have committed offenses against Negroes.[112] The white viewpoint on Negro immorality and lack of restraint combines with the low social value placed upon Negro life

[109] Associated Press report from Brundidge, Alabama, June 21, 1951.

[110] New York *Times*, October 30, 1955; Carl Rowan, *Go South to Sorrow*, chap. 3.

[111] Allison W. Davis, B. B. Gardner, and M. R. Gardner, *op. cit.*, p. 505; Gunnar Myrdal, *op. cit.*, p. 559.

[112] Guy B. Johnson, *op. cit.*, p. 103.

to reduce the punishment of Negroes as long as they control their relations with whites.[113] "Oh, they're just big laughing children and can't be held responsible," a McMinnville, Tennessee, judge explained as he gave only a warning to a Negro guilty of repeated offenses against other Negroes.

The bitterness arising from the general social position of the Negro is increased by the feeling that the law is unjust. We have referred to the release of hostile impulses within the Negro group, but the evidence of severe emotional strain is not limited to such attacks. Arson, burglarly, injury to livestock, petty thieving, and, perhaps, some of the sexual offenses of Negro men indicate revengeful behavior.[114]

The police in the South symbolize the law-enforcing machinery for Negroes. Most of the officers are recruited from the white lower middle class where racial prejudice is strong. These relatively uneducated, economically insecure officials, concerned with the "superiority" of white status, have the authority to administer punishment and death without fear of any serious reprisal. In southern rural areas white domination is so complete that the duties of the police are intermittent. In the cities racial separation is sharper and policing is a continuous and specialized task.[115]

One police practice is that of staging mass "roundups" of minority persons or arresting them on slight suspicion. Since lower- and even middle-class persons of minority status are often unable to protect themselves against abuses, the police generally feel free to use force in arresting, handling witnesses, and obtaining confessions. Some southern officers and magistrates bring Negroes in on trivial charges in order to earn fees.

A prevalent feeling in the South is that Negro suspects should be punished bodily. If they resist arrest, act "uppity" or surly, complain about their treatment, refuse to obey orders, or attempt to escape, they are likely to receive immediate, unofficial punishment. If, in the judgment of the police in the deep South, the courts fail to punish Negro offenders properly, the police may supplement the official punishment. In connection with the case of a Negro who had been dismissed when his wife refused to prosecute, a policeman said: "The next time he raises hell down there I am not going to arrest him but just 'work him over' myself. That is the only way we can handle some of these troublemakers because, if we don't see the fighting or trouble ourselves, the others will never prosecute."[116] Direct action by the police is justified on the ground that it reduces crime. Other "preventive"

---

[113] Allison W. Davis, B. B. Gardner, and M. R. Gardner, *op. cit.*, p. 520.
[114] Guy B. Johnson, *op. cit.*, pp. 102–103.
[115] Charles S. Johnson, *Patterns of Negro Segregation*, Harper & Brothers, 1943, pp. 32–33; Gunnar Myrdal, *op. cit.*, p. 538.
[116] Allison W. Davis, B. B. Gardner, and M. R. Gardner, *op. cit.*, pp. 500–501.

work includes ordering a strange Negro to leave town, ordering a Negro man and woman who are having trouble to separate, and picking up Negroes who are on the streets late at night.

In Philadelphia, more than half of the district patrolmen find it "necessary" to be more strict with Negro than with white offenders. However, neither length of service nor amount of contact with Negro policemen or offenders is correlated statistically with treatment of Negro offenders. Patrolmen who practice differential treatment are also the ones who have unfavorable opinions about Negro policemen, the implication being that the treatment of the Negro offender is not entirely a product of the latter's belligerence.[117]

It should be pointed out that there are notable exceptions to the types of police behavior cited above. The Chicago Park District in 1947 issued a manual called *The Police and Minority Groups*, and similar texts have been prepared elsewhere. Two months after the zoot-suit riots in Los Angeles Robert W. Kenny, then attorney general of California, called a conference to establish the Governor's Peace Officers Committee on Civil Disturbances. The result of this meeting was the Richmond Plan, a training conference for police officers, minority-group consultants, and specialists. Later a police-training bulletin was sent to other police and sheriffs' offices in the state.[118] Courses in the thirteen-week Cadet Training School operated by the police department of Los Angeles devote considerable attention to the composition of the city's population—racial, religious, economic, political, occupational, etc. Officers are acquainted with the department's policy of one standard of police treatment for all citizens. A Community Relations Detail in the Public Information Office seeks to establish and maintain communication between the police and the minority groups in the community. A similar detail operates through the Juvenile Division.[119]

Citing the effective action of police officers in Washington and Chicago, Lohman and Reitzes point out the importance of a clearly stated police policy and a definition of the professional role of the police in racial disturbances. The training of the police does not change personal attitudes and prejudices, nor is it designed to do so. However, "the performance of the police [after special training] showed marked differences in these varying collectively defined situations. And similarly, the public's conduct reflects the definition provided by authoritative and unambiguous statements of policy. . . . In modern mass society the group continues as the essential reality in human behavior, but the

[117] William M. Kephart, "The Negro Offender," *American Journal of Sociology,* July, 1954, pp. 46–50.

[118] Beatrice Griffith, *op. cit.,* pp. 213–214.

[119] W. H. Parker, "The Police Role in Community Relations," a paper presented to the Institute on Police-Community Relations sponsored by the National Conference of Christians and Jews at Michigan State University on May 19, 1955, pp. 12 ff.

relevant and controlling collectivities are, increasingly, deliberately organized interest groups."[120]

In addition to the police, the attitudes and procedures of juries and prosecutors have a bearing on minority crime. In general, the Negro's opportunity of obtaining bail and efficient legal counsel, of paying fines instead of going to jail, and of appealing his case, is much smaller than the opportunity of the white man. Everything about the courtroom is white from the judge to the guards, with the possible exception of some of the witnesses and spectators. In the lower courts of the South, both Negro witnesses and defendants may be the object of crude humor. A distinguished foreign social scientist was amazed to see how carelessly Negro defendants—and sometimes lower-class whites—were sentenced in these courts upon scanty evidence. He observed that the jury, for the most part, was more guilty of partiality than the judge and the prosecuting attorney.[121] These conditions, plus the double standard of justice maintained by the courts as well as the police, influence crime causation. Undue leniency encourages lawless persons and stimulates recidivism.[122]

Jails and prisons enter the picture of Negro crime causation because they are to some extent breeding places for crime. This is especially true in the South, where segregation invites discrimination in treatment. In many places there is a lack of special institutions for women and for juvenile Negro offenders. Negroes are assigned the least desirable work, and "accidents" happen almost exclusively to Negro prisoners. The white guards do not spare the lash or hesitate to shoot to kill. Negro prisoners come out, in a high proportion of cases, brutalized and embittered. Relatively more Negroes than whites get the treatment of the jail, chain gang, and prison because of their greater inability to pay fines.[123]

Discrimination in the system of criminal justice appears also in the matter of release from prison. Those who are not executed may die in prison, escape, serve out their sentences, or be pardoned or paroled. Most Negroes serve out their time, with certain deductions for good behavior. They do not receive their share of pardons because, as a rule, they lack the political influence which is often needed to obtain a par-

---

[120] J. D. Lohman and D. C. Reitzes, *op. cit.*, pp. 245–246.

[121] Gunnar Myrdal, *op. cit.*, pp. 551–553.

[122] Guy B. Johnson, *op. cit.*, pp. 97–98. Mangum believes that there is "very little discrimination on the basis of race alone in respect to the sentences imposed by the courts of the nations, even in the South." He feels that other things, including wealth, political power and influence, social prestige, and community feeling, influence a judge in sentencing a convicted criminal. He does not believe that racial discrimination in the courts is prevalent or at all common. He mentions that "oftentimes a judge will be lenient just because the culprit is a Negro," without seeming to realize that such leniency is actually a form of discrimination. C. S. Mangum, Jr., *op. cit.*, pp. 368, 370.

[123] Guy B. Johnson, *op. cit.*, p. 101.

don. There is some evidence to indicate that Negroes are discriminated against in getting paroles, and that the selection of those paroled is unfortunate both for the parolee and for society.

In recent years much has been written about "culture conflict" and crime. This type of analysis would be expected to show a high rate for the second-generation immigrant. However, Taft found that the "corrected" rate for the children of "old" immigration was about half that of the native born. The explanation here is their generally rural environment compared with the urban environment of second-generation south and east Europeans whose rate is higher. Both rates exceed those of the first generations. As the second generations have been assimilated into American life their criminality has become Americanized by a shift from predominantly violent crimes to predominantly predatory crimes. Wood concludes that minority groups are too differentiated to permit a general statement about their criminality. In his analysis, economic and religious factors, taken alone, cannot be regarded as direct causal factors in criminal behavior. He believes, however, that the available evidence strongly suggests "that cultural and social integration, sometimes influenced by economic conditions and persecution," is closely related to crime rates.

Cultural integration is indicated by the degree to which the folkways of a group enable people to attain their culturally defined ends. As frustration increases, demoralization sets in and crime becomes one of the methods of adjustment. Social integration, or the interaction and interstimulation of individuals, tends to fortify the group's mores through the threat of ostracism. When this is weakened, crime is also more common. Thus, economically disadvantaged and persecuted alien groups can maintain low crime rates when they are socially and culturally integrated. As they migrate from their minority-group communities or assimilate the democratic ideology of the American culture such conditions tend to maximize these rates. Subjectively felt "culture conflict" is only significant after the minority-group has identified itself with the prevailing culture.[124]

LYNCHING AND RIOTS

Lynching has usually been defined as mob action which deprives a person of his life without due process of law. According to NAACP records, there were 5112 lynchings in the period 1882–1937. Of this number, 3657 were Negroes; 1455 were whites. In recent years a strong sentiment against lynching has developed in the South, where most lynchings have occurred. Politicians, including governors, church organizations, white women's organizations, and other groups have taken

[124] Arthur L. Wood, "Minority-Group Criminality and Cultural Integration," *Journal of Criminal Law and Criminology*, March, 1947, pp. 498–510. Reprinted in Arnold M. Rose (ed.), *Race Prejudice and Discrimination*, Alfred A. Knopf, Inc., 1951, pp. 404–405.

firm stands against lynching. There are few open apologists for it anywhere today. In the past the rationalizations of lynching went along these lines: (1) The Negro is by nature criminally inclined, and periodic lynchings are necessary to keep him under control; (2) criminal justice is slow and unsure; and (3) particularly abhorrent crimes produce more or less spontaneous reactions on the part of an outraged citizenry. In connection with the last rationalization, it may be said that only 60 percent of those who have been lynched have even been accused of murder or rape. Approximately 10 percent of the lynched Negroes were charged with minor offenses, including some seventy Negroes who were lynched ostensibly for insulting white persons. Almost 300 Negroes were lynched because of charges of alleged robbery and theft.

Lynchings have decreased from nearly 200 annually in the 1890's to ten per year in the 1930's and four per year in the 1940's. In the decade 1936–1946 there were forty-three lynchings. In this ten-year period no person who participated in a lynching mob received the death penalty, and the majority of guilty persons were not prosecuted.[125] Since 1947, lynchings have ranged from none to three yearly.

Some "new techniques" in lynching have developed during recent years. Eight or ten unrecorded cases of lynchings were cited at a meeting of the executive committee of the Southern Regional Council in October, 1946. These mass murders had not been included in the record of lynchings because the numbers participating were smaller than the groups usually defined as mobs. The NAACP issued a statement in August, 1947, on new lynching techniques based on data provided by Daniel E. Byrd. These included "self-defense murders" in which white men had shot Negroes, sometimes in the back; the killings were labeled as justifiable homicides by all-white coroners or juries.[126] The President's Committee on Civil Rights felt that the large number of attempted lynchings since 1937 indicated, "even more than those which succeeded, the widespread readiness of many communities to resort to mob violence." More than 200 Negroes, according to the conservative estimates of Tuskegee Institute, were rescued from threatened lynchings in seven of the ten years between 1937 and 1946.[127]

A detailed analysis of lynching behavior will not be presented here, but some of the elements behind this behavior will be indicated. First, as a consequence of their economic, sexual, and other treatment of Negroes, white men project their own hostile feelings onto Negroes and

[125] President's Committee on Civil Rights, op. cit., p. 23.
[126] Florence Murray (ed.), op. cit., p. 91.
[127] President's Committee on Civil Rights, op. cit., p. 24. For an able discussion of lynching as a federal crime, see Milton R. Konvitz, op. cit., chap. 4. The anti-lynching bill introduced in the House of Representatives on January 6, 1943, is given in ibid., pp. 155–157.

then react with real fear. The anxiety thus generated leads to more hostility and so on around the cycle. Second, the white man unconsciously envies and is therefore hostile toward the Negro because of the latter's alleged freer impulse gratification.[128] Third, lynchings offer an opportunity for undistinguished whites to release pent-up emotions generated in their frustrated lives by deprivations (economic, political, sexual, egoistic) which have little or nothing to do with race per se. A study of the twenty-one lynchings which occurred in 1930 showed that the majority of the lynchers were young, propertyless, unemployed, irresponsible native whites, many of whom had court records.[129]

Myrdal makes an interesting distinction between "massacres" and "riots." He prefers to call the killing and beating of a large number of Negroes a massacre or mass lynching, and to reserve the term "riot" for "mass violence in which Negroes fight as unreservedly as Whites." Since Negroes fight back only when there is a chance to gain something, the riot is more characteristic of the North than of the South.[130]

[128] See I. D. MacCrone, *Race Attitudes in South Africa*, Oxford University Press, 1937, pp. 309–310; and Gunnar Myrdal, *op. cit.*, p. 562.

[129] Arthur Raper, *The Tragedy of Lynching*, University of North Carolina Press, 1933. For an excellent statement on the lynching mob, see Hadley Cantril, *The Psychology of Social Movements*, John Wiley & Sons, Inc., 1941, chap. 4.

[130] Gunnar Myrdal, *op. cit.*, pp. 566–567. For a comprehensive sociological study of race riots, see Alfred M. Lee and Norman D. Humphrey, *Race Riot*, The Dryden Press, Inc., 1943. This book presents a chronological account of the Detroit race riot of 1943 and compares that riot with the Harlem and Los Angeles riots.

CHAPTER 16

Family Patterns of Minorities

Sociologists and anthropologists have long stressed the importance of familial and kinship institutions in the life of a given tribal or national group. These institutions govern the biological reproduction of the society, and through them many of man's economic and emotional needs are met. It would be inappropriate here to present a generalized picture of the place of the family in American social life,[1] and full accounts of the family life of all racial and ethnic groups in the United States cannot be given. Much of the interaction in minority families parallels that in other American families. We are primarily concerned in this chapter with the ways in which minority status affects family life. As interesting examples of minority family life we shall consider the Negro family, the Italian family, the Mexican family, the Jewish family, the Chinese family, and the Japanese family. To these discussions we shall add, in Chapter 17, an analysis of intermarriage—interracial, interfaith, and internationality.

The Negro Family

During slavery the sexual impulses of American Negroes were no longer subject to control by African customs. In this situation, the range in types of mating was from purely physical contacts to permanent family associations based on strong affection between spouses and

---

[1] For sociological analyses of the family, see M. Nimkoff, *Marriage and the Family*; E. W. Burgess and H. Locke, *The Family*; J. Folsom, *The Family and Democratic Society*; R. E. Baber, *Marriage and the Family*; E. Groves, *The Contemporary American Family*; R. S. Cavan, *The Family*; W. Waller and R. Hill, *The Family*.

between parents and children.[2] There were cases, too, in which masters bred slaves as they bred their stock.

Differences in physical appearance, abilities, and work assignments on the plantations brought about differential assimilation into the world of the master race. Although some slaves closely approached the organization of family life characteristic of whites, it was always possible for the economic interests of the master group to disrupt familial bonds. As Frazier points out, the Negro mother was the most stable and important figure in the family. "Within this world the slave mother held a strategic position and played a dominant role in the family groupings. The tie between the mother and her younger children had to be respected not only because of the dependence of the child upon her for survival but often because of her fierce attachment to her brood. Some of the mothers undoubtedly were cold and indifferent to their offspring, but this appears to have been due to the attitude which the mother developed toward the unborn child during pregnancy as well as the burden of child care."[3] It should be remembered that, in addition to the children they bore to their spouses, some slave women bore children for the men of the master race, and that slave mothers were sometimes called upon to act as foster mothers to their masters' children.

Emancipation snapped the loose ties which had held many of the slave families together. Both men and women wandered about the country, although women with children usually settled in one place and assumed responsibility for their offspring. Powdermaker found in a Mississippi county seat that among both middle-class and lower-class Negroes the woman is usually the head of the household.

Even where husband and wife share responsibility for maintaining and directing the family, the woman is likely to contribute the larger share of the income and to assume the larger share of family responsibility. The economic disparity is most evident in town, where employment is so much more available to the women than to the men. The matriarchal nature of the family organization obtains equally on the plantations. In many cases the woman is the sole breadwinner. Often there is no man in the household at all. In a number of instances, elderly women in their seventies and their middle-aged daughters, with or without children and often without husbands, form one household with the old woman as the head.[4]

Thus maternal family organization has persisted to a considerable ex-

---

[2] The authoritative work on the Negro family is E. Franklin Frazier, *The Negro Family in the United States*, University of Chicago Press, 1939. This section relies heavily on that study.

[3] *Ibid.*, p. 481.

[4] Hortense Powdermaker, *After Freedom*, The Viking Press, Inc., 1939, pp. 145–146. Later (p. 197) Powdermaker points out why the fatherless household among lower-class Negroes is not as serious psychologically for the children as in certain fatherless white families.

tent as a part of the heritage of slavery, and the widespread illegitimacy still found in rural communities has helped to maintain it.

It should be said that there were slave fathers who became deeply attached to their spouses and children. Some of these men were able to buy their wives and children before emancipation. Approximately a half-million Negroes were free before the Civil War, and it was within this group that the family was first established on a firm basis. As time passed, these free families formed the nuclei of the higher classes in both the North and the South. They took over the manners of the white population, and they "placed an exaggerated valuation upon moral conduct and cultivated a puritanical restraint in opposition to the free and uncontrolled behavior of the larger Negro world."[5] From emancipation until the end of the nineteenth century quite a number of former slaves and their descendants acquired some education, bought homes, and created stable families in the rural communities. In some cases these families intermarried with families of free ancestry.

Since World War I at least a million Negroes have migrated from the rural South to the urban South, and more than that have come to the urban North. The migrants have included solitary, disorganized men and women, as well as illiterate or semiliterate impoverished Negro families. The children in these disorganized families have contributed more than their share of juvenile delinquency in the urban slums where their new homes are located. Illegitimacy, which was a relatively harmless matter in the country, has become an economic and social problem of some magnitude in the city.[6]

About 60 percent of the lower-class men and women in Chicago claim to be married, but this figure includes many common-law marriages. A majority of the unmarried women claim to have been married at some time. Most of them list themselves as "widowed," a designation used by lower-class women to include desertion. According to Drake and Cayton, only one woman in five listed herself as single, and they state that this term also probably includes some deserted wives.[7] Some couples "manage to stick it out and maintain a stable, unbroken home, but this is not the typical lower-class pattern. . . . In the study of the relatively stable West Side, for instance, over half the homes were broken, and in at least a third of the remaining families one partner had been previously married."[8]

The 1950 census showed that more than one-third of the Negro women who had ever been married, as compared with one-fifth of the white women, were no longer married or no longer living with their husbands. As both Frazier and Ginzberg point out, the absence of an

[5] E. Franklin Frazier, op. cit., p. 246.
[6] Ibid., p. 484.
[7] St. Clair Drake and Horace Cayton, Black Metropolis, Harcourt, Brace & Company, 1945, p. 584.
[8] Ibid., p. 587.

adult male model makes it difficult for the Negro boy to develop strong work motivation.[9] In addition, the father's absence means that the mother must work to support herself and her children. According to the 1950 census, approximately 35 percent of the Negro mothers under forty-five, as compared with 19 percent of the white mothers, were in the labor force.

Dollard found that the lower-class Negro family exercises less coercive control over children and liberates them earlier for productive activity.[10] He also found that "they are likely to be exposed vigorously to a knowledge of death, birth, parental sexual relations, and violence," and that these children, especially the girls, are more likely to have responsibility for younger siblings.[11]

Charles S. Johnson's studies of the rural Negro population show that sex is not an acute problem in this group. Greater freedom from traditional sex controls is part of a social structure which places more emphasis upon the economic than the romantic factor in family life. Johnson observes that "there is less formal marriage and greater freedom of separation. So important is this factor of flexibility in maintaining a balanced economic unit that it has, for this group, become a part of the survival technique itself. In this sense, freedom from the traditional controls of the larger society is an asset."[12] There are, of course, forms of sex control within this special organization of family life. According to Johnson, ". . . There is less incest than appears in some culturally isolated white groups, there is less homosexuality and other forms of perversion, and there are certain group sanctions which distinguish between types of sex behavior. But the fact remains that taboos relating to extramarital sex relations and sex play in children are less rigid in this group than in other groups of the Negro population."[13]

The same studies reveal that the sex attitudes of rural Negro youth are changing and that sex standards of Negro and white young people are approaching each other. Attitudes toward family life have also been undergoing change in the rural Negro group. Especially notable is the increasing opposition to common-law marriage and easy separation. Johnson reports that "rural Negro girls are no longer willing to suffer the disadvantages of rearing large families, of being the family's major wage earner, of working in the fields as a farm hand, of putting up with drunken and shiftless husbands."[14]

---

[9] E. Franklin Frazier, "Problems and Needs of Negro Children," *Journal of Negro Education*, Summer, 1950, pp. 269 ff.; Eli Ginzberg, *The Negro Potential*, Columbia University Press, 1956, p. 98.

[10] John Dollard, *Caste and Class in a Southern Town*, Yale University Press, 1937, pp. 412–413.

[11] *Ibid.*, p. 490.

[12] Charles S. Johnson, *Growing Up in the Black Belt*, American Council on Education, 1941, p. 225.

[13] *Ibid.*, p. 226.

[14] *Ibid.*, pp. 232, 239, 240, 241.

Lower-class Negro children are taught by their parents to conform to the prevailing mores with respect to Negro-white relations. They have learned "to do as we were told, be as courteous as possible to white people, don't talk back to them, and do your work as well as possible. They said 'niggers' that are liked by white people are those who don't give any trouble and don't ask for much." Some of these children are taught that " 'if you can act big enough monkey, you can get almost what you want.' " There is a tendency among these children to rebel against such instructions and to display considerable hostility toward white people, but, despite their revolt, lower-class children adopt the prevailing unfavorable stereotypes of the Negro and the techniques of "getting by" in the larger world. One mother said that she had never told her children anything about racial etiquette because she saw no reason for such advice. Frazier's comment is that apparently some members of the lower class regard existing race relations as so natural and inevitable that everyone will know how to act.[15]

The indoctrination which the lower-class Negro child receives in the home is supplemented in important ways by the neighborhood environment. As a result of studying lower-class children, Negro and white, in Chicago, Allison W. Davis concludes that gang life in the slum teaches the lower-class child to fear ". . . being 'taken in' by the teacher, . . . being a 'softie' with her. To study 'homework' seriously is literally a disgrace. Instead of boasting of good marks in school, one conceals them, if one ever receives any. The lower-class adolescent fears not to be thought a street-fighter; it is a suspicious and dangerous social trait. He fears not to curse. If he cannot claim early sex relations, his virility is seriously questioned."[16]

Some changes are occurring in the family life of lower-class urban Negroes. Many urban Negro workers must still find employment in personal and domestic service, but an increasing number are doing skilled and semiskilled work. The new body of black industrial workers has acquired an outlook on life which is based neither on an emulation of the behavior of the white group nor upon the ideals and standards of the brown middle class. According to Frazier, ". . . As the Negro worker becomes an industrial worker, he assumes responsibility for the support of his family and acquires a new authority in family relations.

[15] E. Franklin Frazier, *Negro Youth at the Crossways*, American Council on Education, 1940, pp. 42–44, 68.

[16] Allison W. Davis, "Child Rearing in the Class Structure of American Society," address delivered at the symposium on "Human Relations in Science and Practice," Community Service Society of New York, January 30, 1948, p. 8. The emphasis which is placed on fighting and violence by the lower-class child's family is discussed by E. Franklin Frazier, *Negro Youth at the Crossways*, pp. 52, 68, and by Allison W. Davis and John Dollard, *Children of Bondage*, American Council on Education, 1940, pp. 240, 267–268, 270. The whole issue of the *Journal of Negro Education* for July, 1950, is devoted to the subject, "The Negro Child in the American Social Order."

Moreover, as the isolation of the black worker is gradually broken down, his ideals and patterns of family life approximate those of the great body of industrial workers."[17]

The middle class in the Negro group as defined by Frazier includes the families whose incomes are derived from skilled and semiskilled occupations.[18] Children here are members of permanent family groups, and the father plays a much more important role both as breadwinner and as disciplinarian than the lower-class father. School attendance and school records are carefully watched, and the child is sent to Sunday school and church. Play is closely supervised and playmates and clique mates are directly or indirectly selected. Parents exert influence upon their children to avoid aggression at school, to inhibit sexual impulses, and to avoid poolrooms, gambling parlors, and cabarets. One of the most important pressures on the middle-class Negro child is that of staying away from lower-class children and also abstaining from behavior which might identify him with the lower class. He boasts about never having "any sort of trouble," meaning that the family has not been involved with the law. He is taught to "stand up for his rights" without entering into actual physical combat. Middle-class Negro parents are ambitious for their children, and they stress the value of "education" and "hard work" as the means of rising in the world. The goals set before the children are a high-school education, a skilled or white-collar job, and a "good" marriage.[19]

While the majority of middle-class Negro families in Frazier's study seemed to be accommodated to their status, they were not as reconciled to their station in life as lower-class parents and their children. The middle-class families are less likely, as we noted in Chapter 7, to encourage their children to act in a subservient manner toward white people. Although ". . . in some middle-class families the children have

[17] E. Franklin Frazier, *The Negro Family in the United States*, p. 475.
[18] E. Franklin Frazier, *Negro Youth at the Crossways*, p. 55.
[19] See Allison W. Davis and John Dollard, *op. cit.*, pp. 139, 265, 274–275; John Dollard, *op. cit.*, pp. 413, 489; E. Franklin Frazier, *Negro Youth at the Crossways*, pp. 57–58; St. Clair Drake and Horace Cayton, *op. cit.*, p. 666; Hortense Powdermaker, *op. cit.*, pp. 210–211. In a study of fifty Chicago mothers in each of four groups—white middle class, white lower class, Negro middle class, and Negro lower class—Davis and Havighurst found significant differences in child-rearing practices between the middle and lower classes. The differences between middle-class and lower-class Negroes are similar to those between middle- and lower-class whites. "Middle-class parents are more rigorous than lower-class parents in their training of children for feeding and cleanliness habits. They also expect their children to take responsibility for themselves earlier than lower-class parents do. Middle-class parents place their children under a stricter regimen, with more frustration of their impulses, than do lower-class parents." In addition to the social-class differences, these investigators found the following differences between Negroes and whites in child-rearing practices: "Negroes are more permissive than whites in the feeding and weaning of their children, but they are much more rigorous than whites in toilet-training." Allison W. Davis and Robert J. Havighurst, "Social Class and Color Differences in Child-Rearing," *American Sociological Review*, December, 1946, p. 710.

been told to avoid conflicts with whites and to use such techniques as 'jiving' or flattery in order to get along with them, one is likely to find that the children will not accept wholeheartedly such advice."[20]

Middle-class Negro children seem to be characterized by a greater awareness and sophistication about their racial status, and by more social and race consciousness, than lower-class Negro children. They have a more critical attitude toward the lacks in Negro life and a stronger resentment against the discrimination of the white group.[21]

. . . Race conscious members of middle-class status think that a self-respecting attitude should prevent people from going where they will be embarrassed. This is not mere rationalization on their part, since they have a sense of personal dignity which they attempt to instill in their children. Children of the middle class are better acquainted with the achievements of Negroes and have more knowledge of outstanding leaders. Their parents seek to cultivate respect for Negroes and the children feel that they should know more. One boy remarked, "I think we ought to know more about our folks, living and dead—what good is it to learn so much about white people and their great men?" Children of this class seem to have two different attitudes toward "passing" for white. In some cases their parents have taught them that it is disloyal to the Negro race to "pass," and in other cases that it is quite all right to "pass" in order to get what you want so long as you are not disloyal to Negroes. Thus loyalty to the Negro becomes a criterion of one's behavior.[22]

Upper-class Negro parents never inculcate servile attitudes toward white persons in their children. They may tell children to ignore disparaging epithets on the ground that only "white trash" use such terms, and they make it clear to their offspring that fighting is not becoming to persons of their status. As Frazier remarks, this causes many young Negroes to believe that only "poor whites" have race prejudice. Parents in this class go to great lengths to protect their children from embarrassing situations, but they cannot, of course, completely avoid all rebuffs. Sooner or later the youth come face to face with the appraisals, the mythology, and the discriminations of the white group.

The upper-class Negro family tends to be of the patriarchal type, with the man assuming the major economic responsibility and exercising the major authority. The family is usually smaller, although it may not be limited to parents and children. Supervision by parents is even more strict than in the middle-class family, and the child's friends are still more carefully chosen.[23]

Upper-class fathers are business and professional men who devote

[20] E. Franklin Frazier, *Negro Youth at the Crossways*, pp. 55–56, 68.

[21] *Ibid.*, p. 55.

[22] *Ibid.*, pp. 59–60.

[23] Allison W. Davis and John Dollard, *op. cit.*, p. 278; and Hortense Powdermaker, *op. cit.*, p. 148.

their lives to their careers, "restrained good times," and participation in community "uplift" and "racial advancement" causes. According to Drake and Cayton, half or more of the upper-class wives are either career women or women who are occasionally employed in white-collar work. The other wives are "society" women, with the exception of a number of "race women" who spend most of their time in race enterprises.[24]

Davis and Dollard found that the family rather than the racial system of the South was of primary importance in determining the basic attitudes of the child. "The actual caste behavior of the parents themselves appears to be more important in determining the child's type of accommodation to white people than does verbal instruction on this point. As in other forms of learning the child discovers what behavior *will be punished* and what *rewarded* by observing his parents and listening to their accounts of experiences with white people."[25] This is not to say, of course, that he does not learn much from contacts with white children. At adolescence the parental pressures on middle- and upper-class children increase because of the urgency of the issues related to sex and occupation.

Color is a problem in the Negro group both within the family and between families and social classes. Color differences within the family may cause sharp antagonisms, with the child of dark complexion developing hostilities toward his closest relatives and toward those outside the family. In a family which has considerable solidarity and possesses feelings of race consciousness, an attempt may be made to prevent the discussion of color differences on the ground that it is "very much out of place for colored people to be talking about color." Nevertheless, it is virtually impossible to suppress all mention of color.[26]

The instability of the Negro family will continue for some time, but the processes of assimilation and acculturation will reduce the differences between it and other families. There is no reason to suppose that the differences in family life within the Negro community will not persist and become even greater. The middle-class Negro family will continue to stress conventional behavior in the desire of its members to achieve respectability, and the number of middle-class families will in-

[24] St. Clair Drake and Horace Cayton, op. cit., p. 540.

[25] Allison W. Davis and John Dollard, op. cit., pp. 251–252; and John Dollard, op. cit., p. 489.

[26] E. Franklin Frazier, *Negro Youth at the Crossways*, pp. 51–52, 58–59. Davis and Dollard (op. cit., p. 254) report that several discussions of the color and hair of a prospective or newborn child were heard by the female interviewers in Old City and New Orleans. These upper-class and upper-middle-class parents and grandparents condoled each other if the child "was darker or had 'worse' hair than had been expected," and felicitated each other "if it was lighter or had 'better' hair than had been expected." Apparently most of these parents have such concerns, even if they are not verbalized. "It is a justifiable point of anxiety, certainly, since it is a vital factor in the child's class and caste opportunities."

crease. The small Negro upper class will tend to put still more emphasis upon conspicuous consumption. Families in both of these classes will limit the number of children and will use the family more and more for companionship and personal happiness. The racial system is not as potent in the urban community as it is in the rural section or the village. As Negroes and whites participate more in the same occupations they will come to associate more closely in other ways than they have in the past. The rate of assimilation, acculturation, and amalgamation will depend upon "the extent to which the Negro becomes integrated into the economic organization and participates in the life of the community."[27]

Concerning the general trend in American Negro family life, Frazier concludes: "The deviations in the character of the Negro family from the dominant American patterns have been owing chiefly to the social isolation and economic position of the Negro. As the Negro acquires education and enjoys greater economic opportunities and participates in all phases of American life, he is taking over the American patterns of behavior characteristics of different classes and regions. His family life increasingly conforms to the American pattern, which is becoming a part of his cultural heritage."[28]

The Italian Family

The closely knit family of southern Italian background is dominated by the father, but ideally this domination is regarded as benevolent rather than tyrannical. Authority over a child is held to be absolute until the latter's marriage, and includes such important decisions as choice of occupation and selection of a marriage partner. Even after marriage the control may be maintained to a high degree.

In a family of south Italians, children are expected to enter full-time work at an early age. Usually the child, regardless of his age, turns over all his earnings to his parents. Other characteristics found by Child include greater cohesion and a stronger feeling of mutual responsibility than in contemporary American families; a taboo on explicit hostility within the family; an even stronger taboo on overt physical display of affection except toward infants and small children; greater average size than in the American family; and a more uniform reticence about sexual matters, although crowded living conditions may make children more aware of the realities of sexual life than are children in other families.

Child classifies the responses of second-generation south Italians to this family pattern as the "in-group" reaction, the rebel reaction, and

[27] E. Franklin Frazier, *The Negro Family in the United States*, p. 488.

[28] E. Franklin Frazier, "Ethnic Family Patterns: The Negro Family in the United States," *American Journal of Sociology*, May, 1948, p. 438.

the apathetic reaction. The in-group informants' ideals about their own marriages showed much more adherence to Italian patterns than was the case among the "rebels." However, there was virtually no difference between the various groups of informants concerning the number of children they would like to have. Most of the second generation want fewer children than their parents had, and some informants stated that this desire came from an interest in attaining a higher standard of living than their parents had.

The rebels' break with Italian ideals is seen in the choice of a wife who is not of Italian descent or an Italian girl who is very much Americanized; emphasis upon a high standard of living and unlimited aspirations for their children; a determination on the man's part not to dominate his wife but to have an equalitarian relationship with her; the plan to give the children full information about sex; and the husband's desire to have his wife find some interests outside the home. In some cases ". . . the individual's desires for acceptance as an American, partly frustrated, may be clearly seen to be projected onto his children; this condition provides additional incentive for making his family life as American as possible in order that his children's opportunities for acceptance will be improved."[29]

The marriage ideals of those in the "apathetic reaction" group showed a tendency toward conformity with Italian ideals and were therefore similar to those of the in-groupers. They were influenced more by American culture than the in-groupers, but less than the rebel informants.

The stages of adjustment to American life through which the Italian family passes have been analyzed by Campisi as the initial-contact stage, the conflict stage, and the accommodation stage. The first stage covers the first few years of American life when the family is still highly integrated, although the different physical environment, new equipment, new types of work, attendance of children in public and parochial schools, recognition that the Italian way of life means low status, perhaps work outside the home for the wife, and pressure from American economic and political institutions mean that considerable modification has to be made in the peasant family pattern. The conflict stage begins about ten years after the family's arrival in the United States and when the children begin to acquire American ways while their parents attempt to enforce Old World patterns. During this stage there is much frustration and misunderstanding as the father loses his importance, the daughters acquire a "shocking" independence, and the parents give ground on accepting an American way of life. The accommodation stage is reached when parents and children realize that further hostility will bring about the complete deterioration of the family. This

[29] I. L. Child, *Italian or American*, Yale University Press, 1943, p. 110.

period begins when offspring reach adulthood and establish families of their own. The children are more tolerant of their parents, but they tend to work out their family destinies along the lines of the contemporary urban American family. Campisi says that the adjustment of the American-born parents to the American culture takes three forms:

(a) Complete abandonment of the Old World way of life. Individual changes his name, moves away from Italian neighborhood and has little to do with his parents and relatives. This type of family usually passes for an American family. A rare form. [Corresponds to Child's "rebel" reaction.]

(b) Strong desire to become Americanized and to pattern the family after the contemporary American family. Parental way of life not wholly repudiated, although there is some degree of rejection. Likely to move out of Italian neighborhood and to communicate less and less with first-generation Italians, but family ties are not completely broken. Relationships with parents and immigrant relatives are affectionate and understanding.

(c) Second-generation family oriented inward toward an Italian way of life. This type of family prefers to remain in the Italian neighborhood, close to the parental home. Interaction with the non-Italian world is at a minimum. [Corresponds to Child's "in-group" reaction.][30]

Campisi states that the second form, a marginal one, is most representative of the second-generation Italian family in the United States.

The Mexican Family

Although there are great variations in the background and social positions of the Mexican population in the United States, the majority of the Mexican families are concentrated in rural areas in the West and the Southwest where a high percentage of them earn livelihoods as migratory laborers. Although the marriage ceremony has been considered desirable, it has not always been observed because of its high cost. Large families are the rule, and the children work in the fields and orchards with their parents. In general, these low-paid, highly mobile families lack adequate housing, schooling, and recreation. Church and home are closely linked through the devotion of rural Mexicans to Catholicism, and religious rituals and instruction are prominent parts of family life. Godparents are often loved almost as much as the parents; in the event of the parents' death they are obligated to care for the child. As in rural Mexico, the family is dominated by the father, and this control extends over the grown children. At the same time, as Bogardus points out, the father views large numbers of children care-

[30] P. J. Campisi, "Ethnic Family Patterns: The Italian Family in the United States," *American Journal of Sociology*, May, 1948, p. 447.

lessly and may desert if they become too numerous and the burden of feeding them is too heavy. Women in these families are limited in their work largely to household activities, and divorce is almost unknown. If deserted, the mother stands by and provides as well as she can for her offspring. Conflict between mother and daughters is common when the latter reach adolescent and marriageable ages. The viewpoint of a young Mexican-American girl illustrates this conflict.

But for me there was just hell. My mother and dad got too many old-fashioned ideas. She's from another country. I'm from America, and I'm not like her. With Mexican girls they want you to sit in the house like moscas muertas, dead flies, like that. If you tell them what the teachers say, they say the teachers don't know, and what they tell us will only get us in trouble. They think they know what is good, not the American teachers. And even if we take our parents to school to explain them—our parents don't hear. They only know from Mexico.

I remember when me and my sister told my mother we wanted to dress neat and American they beat us and said no, to dress like they wanted us to, in old Mexico. So after a while it's no use. You can't have any fun, so you get your fun where you find it. Like little Cutdown said to the teacher when she asked why she drank, "It's the only fun I have, Miss," she told her, and it's true.[31]

Girls are chaperoned in Mexico, but the opposite rule prevails in the United States. Mexican mothers complain about "this terrible freedom in America" and try to be vigilant against possible elopements.[32]

In the city the Mexican peasant family undergoes considerable change. Low incomes necessitate the keeping of roomers, and the resulting overcrowding has a deteriorating effect on family life. The father's exercise of moral protection over the wife and children decreases as the structure of the family is modified. Prestige and authority no longer range from father to mother, son, and daughter. The oldest male child acts as mentor to the younger children and exercises authority over them and, in some situations, over his parents. His status in the family approximates that of the father and is above that of the mother.

The relationships between the school, the home, and the gang are extremely important in the life of the Mexican-American boy.

Discovering that his status approximates the second-rate school has the effect of instilling in the Mexican boy a resentment directed against the school, and all it stands for. At the same time, it robs him of a desire to turn back to his home. For the home which he knew prior to entering school no

[31] Beatrice Griffith, *American Me*, Houghton Mifflin Company, 1948, p. 151.
[32] See R. C. Jones, "Ethnic Family Patterns: The Mexican Family in the United States," *American Journal of Sociology*, May, 1948, pp. 450–452; Emory S. Bogardus, *The Mexican in the United States*, University of Southern California Press, 1943, chap. 3.

longer exists. All of the attitudes he has learned at school now poison his attitude toward the home. Turning away from home and school, the Mexican boy has only one place where he can find security and status. This is the gang made up of boys exactly like himself who live in the same neighborhood, and who are going through precisely the same distressing process at precisely the same time.[33]

In the urban environment the children speak English, attend church to please their parents but go irregularly, do not belong to any Mexican clubs, become competitive, give up holiday celebrations after marriage, and settle down as American working-class people.[34]

The Jewish Family

Throughout their history Jews have placed a high value upon the family. Together with the synagogue and the school, it has constituted the basis of Jewish life. The founding of a family has been regarded not merely as a social ideal but as a religious duty. "The Rabbis declared that the first affirmative precept in the Bible was the injunction 'Be fruitful and multiply,' and they invested marriage with the highest communal significance. They despised the bachelor and pitied the spinster. Only he who had founded a house in Israel was worthy to be considered a full-fledged member of the community; only she who had become a mother in Israel had realized her destiny."[35] Jewish tradition stressed chastity of both the man and the woman before marriage, matrimonial fidelity on both sides, desire for large families, respect of children for their parents, and unlimited love and devotion of parents for their children. Women were not to enter public life but to devote themselves to domestic duties or assist their husbands in their work. Daughters remained at home until marriage, usually before the age of twenty. The husband's authority over his wife and children rested upon tradition rather than force.[36] Goldstein points out that in the time when the woman occupied a lower status in law and in the ritual of religion than the man, she was highly esteemed and the equal of man in the Jewish home.[37] Despite this familial emphasis, and the large volume

---

[33] Carey McWilliams, North from Mexico, J. B. Lippincott Company, 1949, p. 240.

[34] See N. D. Humphrey, "The Changing Structure of the Detroit Mexican Family: An Index of Acculturation," American Sociological Review, December, 1944, pp. 622–623. See also John H. Burma, Spanish-Speaking Groups in the United States, Duke University Press, 1954, pp. 84 ff; and Sister Frances Jerome Woods, Cultural Values of American Ethnic Groups, Harper & Brothers, 1956, pp. 171–177.

[35] Israel Cohen, Jewish Life in Modern Times, Dodd, Mead & Co., Inc., 1914, p. 40.

[36] Arthur Ruppin, The Jews in the Modern World, The Macmillan Company, 1934, p. 277.

[37] S. E. Goldstein, Meaning of Marriage and Foundations of the Family: A Jewish Interpretation, Bloch Publishing Company, 1942, pp. 136–137.

and range of scholarly work produced by Jews, it is interesting to note that there are virtually no inductive studies of Jewish family life.[38]

Although there is some evidence to support the widespread belief that the Jewish family has more solidarity than other families,[39] the decline in the stability of the family generally has its counterpart in Jewish life. The reasons given for this weakening of Jewish family life are the growth of feminism, the transfer of home functions to other institutions, the declining birth rate, a decrease in parental and religious authority, and the large number of mixed marriages.[40] In Minneapolis, Gordon finds that the status of the Jewish woman has changed markedly from the European pattern. In that city "the patriarchal family that is traditionally associated with Jewish life has largely given way to the 'equalitarian' family."[41]

Second-generation Jews, like children in other immigrant groups, are frequently in disagreement with their elders' views and are likely to regard their foreign language and customs with some disfavor. As a rule, they know less and care less than their parents do about the traditional form of Jewish life, including the religious customs and ceremonies formerly observed in the home.

Although its distinctiveness is decreasing, the Jewish family is still a strong unifying force. It is possible that Jewish family solidarity tends to be strengthened by prejudice, whereas the effect of prejudice and discrimination on more economically disadvantaged groups without traditions of family solidarity is to weaken the family. In view of this possibility, it is interesting to note Wessel's observation: "The Jewish family is today subjected to all the strains which affect family life in general in a sick society, plus those which come from identification with victims of extermination or which arise from increasing discrimination. The Jewish family, relatively more united than the gentile family, seems to increase in cohesion as it offers an oasis of understanding. . . ."[42]

Although adequate supporting data are lacking, Wessel suggests that there seems to be a trend among Jews of upper socioeconomic levels to seek residence near one another. This tendency to improve and strengthen the ethnic community is said to be the result of a desire on the part of Jews to provide a healthy environment for the development of personality and for social participation. "These are Jews who erst-

---

[38] B. B. Wessel, "Ethnic Family Patterns: The American Jewish Family," *American Journal of Sociology*, May, 1948, p. 439. Goldstein's "preparation for marriage" book, mentioned above, is written from a Jewish viewpoint, but it cites no inductive studies of Jewish family life.

[39] S. R. Brav, *Jewish Family Solidarity: Myth or Fact?* quoted in M. Nimkoff, *op. cit.*, p. 268. See also Sister Frances Jerome Woods, *op. cit.*, pp. 180–183.

[40] *The Universal Jewish Encyclopedia*, vol. 4, p. 244.

[41] Albert I. Gordon, *Jews in Transition*, University of Minnesota Press, 1949, pp. 193, 200.

[42] B. B. Wessel, *op. cit.*, p. 442.

while escaped from areas of residential concentration. Is it that a close, warm community offers security for children and for families who have suffered from discriminatory conduct? 'We made a mistake bringing up our children in gentile communities, they have been hurt. The early friendships don't count. When returning from college, they do not know where to turn for friends.' "[43]

The Chinese Family

During the latter decades of the last century and the first quarter of the twentieth, it was common practice among the Chinese-Americans, where the sex ratio was high, to marry their daughters to middle-aged men of some financial standing.[44] The social distance between the marriage partners was frequently so great as to make life intolerable for the young bride.

Her husband was a cook, one of those old cooks you hear so much about, always grinning, the kind you hear Americans say you can't get again. He had worked for lots of the pioneer American families, and he began when he was about nine. He came from China when he was nine, and wanted to go to school and get an education. But he had just one hour of it. His father came into the school, grabbed him by the scruff of the neck, and said, "There's a lady out here who wants a little China boy to work, so come on!" That was before they had a law about going to school. He learned to cook in that family, but he was always sore. After awhile he was section boss in a lumber camp at Weed, Oregon, and married a wife fourteen years old. He had a horrible disposition, suspicious and jealous, and my sister's life was one long tragedy with him. . . .[45]

Another type of parental matchmaking in Chinese families during this period occurred when one parent was about to die. The daughters of marriageable age were married and went immediately into another family, thus assuring the departing parent that they would be well cared for.

One suitor was a distant cousin that I did not know very well, and had never suspected of any such feeling. My mother was in favor of him. My father was against him, but in favor of another man about 27 years old, who had been divorced from his wife, but my mother hated the thought of that. Divorce nearly always means something queer in China. . . . I was 17 years old, and I hated them both, and I stood out against them all. I finally said that I would pack my suitcase and go, if they did not stop this torture. It was bad enough, having parents do the matchmaking, but when they did

[43] *Ibid.*
[44] W. C. Smith, *Americans in Process*, Edwards Brothers, 1937, p. 229.
[45] "The Story of a Chinese Girl Student" (San Francisco), in Jitsuichi Masuoka and Charles S. Johnson, "Orientals and Their Problems of Cultural Adjustment," *Social Science Source Documents*, no. 4, Social Science Institute, Fisk University, 1946, pp. 15–16.

not even agree on the man, and began quarreling about it, as they often did, it was terrible.[46]

For more than three decades the younger generation in this country, and in China, has been increasingly in revolt against parental interference in mate selection.[47]

The selection of mates for the second generation is narrowed when clan and family exogamy must be observed strictly. ". . . The children whose parents belonged to either a four-clan association or a family association are considered 'cousins,' although no actual blood relationship is involved. . . . To solve the problem, Chinese-Americans are forced to follow one of three courses: (1) remain single and stay in the city of their birth; (2) find mates in other Chinatowns; or (3) permit parents to arrange a suitable marriage."[48] According to Lee, the second course is followed more extensively than the other two, with the result that the Chinese population has been undergoing redistribution to larger western and eastern Chinatowns where many clans reside.

Many members of the Chinese-American group, like those in other second-generation immigrant groups, have grown up in two worlds. The clash of cultures represented by home on the one hand and by school and community on the other has meant a conflict of loyalties. The confusion of these maturing persons has been heightened by a lack of understanding of them by both Occidentals and Orientals. The following statement by a college girl in Hawaii illustrates the situation:

At the end of my second year I went home for a vacation and there I met the problem of my life—the racial problem. I am afraid I will be called a hypocrite, but when you finish reading this you will understand. I am proud of what I am, but there is a constant conflict within me that I can't control. I am an American of Chinese parentage and I have been educated in American schools, lived with the Americans, and worked with them in social groups. Consequently I am Americanized. How much of the Chinese custom could I follow when I didn't even know enough of it to make myself sociable? I was lost in a crowd of Chinese-speaking people. I couldn't understand their ideas or customs, I could not speak Chinese except baby talk; every time I started to say something I was laughed at. The Chinese friends of my parents thought that my brother deserved an education more than I, in spite of what I was sacrificing to obtain it. Because I was unable to explain my point of view in Chinese, these people would take advantage of me by jeering at me in the presence of my brother. . . . Oh, I hated Chinese then. I wished I was something other than a Chinese. I thought I could never live with a Chinese unless he were thoroughly Americanized, although I admired them in their moral aspects. I loved to hear the tales and stories

[46] "The Story of a Chinese College Girl," in *ibid.*, pp. 3–4.
[47] Rose Hum Lee, "Research on the Chinese Family," *American Journal of Sociology*, May, 1949, p. 500.
[48] Rose Hum Lee, "The Decline of Chinatowns in the United States," *American Journal of Sociology*, March, 1949, p. 430.

of the great men of China, but I never had the notion of calling China my own and of being loyal to her.[49]

A number of influences have operated to occasion changes in the family life of Chinese-Americans. Wars and depressions have weakened the economic and social structures of the Chinatowns and have brought about a redistribution of their populations.[50] In some cities, among them Seattle and Vancouver, a number of Chinese-American families have moved outward from Chinatown. Hayner and Reynolds report that moving into a white middle-class residential area results in a marked speeding up of the westernizing process in the children.[51] The same investigators find that "the more conservative American-Chinese husbands are strikingly helpless in combating what they consider unfortunate tendencies on the part of their wives in the demand for education, freedom, self-expression and the right to appear in public, the revolt against drudgery, and the discard of traditional behavior in relations with other men."[52]

An important development in Chinese-American life was the arrival in the United States of 12,151 Chinese immigrant aliens (1314 males and 10,837 females) in the period 1945–1953. These immigrants came as a result of (1) the repeal of the Chinese Exclusion Act on December 17, 1943, and the establishment of an annual quota of 105 for persons of Chinese ancestry; (2) the amendment, in August, 1946, of the Immigration Act of 1924 admitting alien wives of citizens on a nonquota basis and giving alien wives and alien children of resident aliens preferential treatment within the quota limitations; and (3) the lifting, on July 22, 1947, for two years and a half, of the racial restrictions embodied in the "Brides Act." Under the latter action, 6000 men rushed to China, got married, and brought their wives back to this country. In some cases these "war wives" and their husbands have been congenial from the beginning; in other cases, these marriages have been characterized by discord, and in more than a dozen instances by divorce. Many of the husbands, wives, and teen-age children in the "separated" families have had some difficulties after being brought together in the United States, but the majority of these families are happy to be in this country and to have avoided living under the communist regime in China.[53]

Racial-cultural barriers cut many Chinese-American young people off

[49] W. C. Smith, op. cit., pp. 241–242.

[50] Rose Hum Lee, "The Decline of Chinatowns in the United States," pp. 430–431.

[51] Norman S. Hayner and Charles N. Reynolds, "Chinese Family Life in America," American Sociological Review, October, 1937, p. 634.

[52] Ibid.

[53] For details concerning this interesting development in the Chinese-American group, see Rose Hum Lee, "The Recent Immigrant Chinese Families of the San Francisco–Oakland Area," Marriage and Family Living, February, 1956, pp. 14–24.

from full membership in American society and throw them back upon their own group. In past years these barriers have served to revive and stimulate pride in Chinese culture.[54] However, the future of Chinese-Americans would seem to lie along the lines followed by other small minority groups which have become integral parts of American society. As the process of acculturation continues they will strive for higher status through education, enter professions, be employed in American industries, and become dispersed in the American population. "With acculturation and settlement among the members of the larger society, amalgamation will increase, and in time assimilation will be attained."[55]

The Japanese Family

After a period of welcome in the 1890's, agitation against the Japanese began in the early 1900's. This campaign resulted in the exclusion of further Japanese immigration in 1924, denial to Japanese of the privilege of naturalization, passage of state laws forbidding Japanese aliens to own land in the state and forbidding intermarriage between Japanese and Caucasians, and the legislated but never generally enforced bills to segregate Japanese children (most of whom were citizens) in the public schools of California. In addition there were social, occupational, and economic barriers which restricted the Japanese in their relations with white persons and which caused them to associate largely with other Japanese.[56]

Prior to World War II the Japanese-American population was rather sharply divided into a young group and an old group, with virtually no middle-aged representatives. The average age of the Nisei, the native-born American generation, was nineteen in 1939; of Issei, the original immigrant stock, fifty-eight; and the average period of residence was thirty years. To these two groups a third should be added: the Kibei.[57] This term refers to the Nisei who spent much or all of their lives in Japan and who returned to the United States. These persons were sent to Japan to be indoctrinated with Japanese ways as their parents sought to counteract American conditioning. It has been estimated that there were some 50,000 of them in Japan in 1937 and that in 1942 more than 25,000 United States citizens of Japanese parentage had been educated in schools in Japan.[58] The return of the Kibei created endless conflicts in Japanese-American families.

---

[54] Norman S. Hayner and Charles N. Reynolds, op. cit., p. 637.

[55] Rose Hum Lee, "The Decline of Chinatowns in the United States," p. 432.

[56] Bureau of Sociological Research, Colorado River War Relocation Center, "The Japanese Family in America," *Annals of the American Academy of Political and Social Science*, September, 1943, p. 153.

[57] F. J. Brown and J. S. Roucek (eds.), *One America*, Prentice-Hall, Inc., 1945, p. 329.

[58] *Ibid.*, p. 333.

They came back with manners that were Japanese—with the rather strained and tense sensitivity toward life, the earnestness, the quietness. The girls came back submissive and shy, the boys somewhat arrogant and expecting their superiority as males to be acknowledged. They came back from a Japan very different from that which their parents had left thirty or forty years before. The difference this made in them was a constant puzzle to their disappointed parents. For it was not that intellectual curiosity and ferment of the Meijo era which their parents had expected but the unreasoning jingoism of the age ironically called Enlightened Peace. Immediately they had trouble with their brothers and sisters. American-raised girls would not stand being treated like Japanese women, and Nisei brothers found the returned brother a pain in the neck with his puritanical notions about jazz and dancing and movies, with his unflattering comparisons of America and Japan. There was an unending battle in the family, and one more burden added to the cares of parents who saw another cherished plan—the return of the Japan-educated child to guide the other children by example—come a cropper.[59]

In addition to sending many Nisei to Japan, the Issei group established Japanese-language schools in such cities as San Francisco, Los Angeles, and Seattle in their attempt to retain some hold on their children. It is alleged that these schools were subsidized by the Japanese government and that the teachers were alien Japanese. There were 248 of these schools in California in 1941, teaching about 18,000 children the Japanese language and culture after public-school hours and on Saturday.[60] The position of the Issei, like that of other immigrant or of native Indian parents, was strengthened by the discrimination and enforced segregation which denied members of these minority groups full participation in American life. Assimilation is hindered when "economic and prestige rewards are minimized, and contacts with the majority group, which are the means whereby the new culture can be acquired, become punishing for the members of the minority." Under these circumstances, minority-group persons "tend to withdraw from such contacts back into association with members of their own group, where they do not meet with rebuff."[61]

Despite the obstacles created by the white population on the coast, the second generation made impressive headway in Americanization prior to World War II. As a result of this culturalization, much misunderstanding and conflict occurred between parents and children.

. . . Culturally the Nisei were much closer to the dominant groups than they were to their own parents. This cleavage was not only apparent: it was notorious. For years the vernacular newspapers had featured the split between

[59] Bradford Smith, *Americans from Japan*, J. B. Lippincott Company, 1948, p. 253.
[60] F. J. Brown and J. S. Roucek, *op. cit.*, pp. 333–334.
[61] Bureau of Sociological Research, Colorado River War Relocation Center, *op. cit.*, p. 150.

the two generations; for years Little Toyko had echoed with family discord and bickering. . . . It is amusing to note that while California reiterated the slogan "Once a Jap, Always a Jap," and persisted in the belief that the Japanese were the most clannish people on earth, the Japanese communities were echoing with internal dissension. . . . The rift was widened by the fact that the parents had been so intensely preoccupied with their stores and shops that they had neglected the children. In the eyes of these children, the Japanese home was not an overly attractive institution. They tended to shift for themselves; to live outside the world in which they slept. Lack of understanding was a constant irritant. "You wouldn't understand it, skip it," was a familiar Nisei rejoinder.[62]

Bradford Smith points out that "the real trouble was that the Nisei, having rejected the land and culture of their parents, had been rejected by their own land. Though far more American than Japanese, they were not entirely at home in either culture. As a result of numerous rejections they developed a marginal culture of their own. They were socially at ease only among themselves, lacking the etiquette for Japanese company and fearing always the intrusion of prejudice in an American setting. . . ."[63]

About 112,000 Japanese, or 88.5 percent of the total Japanese population in the United States, lived in the Pacific coast states at the time of Pearl Harbor. Between March 2 and June 8, 1942, 100,000 Japanese men, women, and children—two-thirds of whom were citizens—were moved from their homes into temporary assembly centers. Between June and November they were moved into ten relocation centers in western and southwestern states. This wholesale rejection of the Japanese by other Americans occurred at a time when German and Italian enemy aliens were being treated on an individual basis.[64]

The families were faced with wholly new conditions of life in the relocation centers. The barracks were crowded, eating and toilet facilities were shared in common, and there was almost no opportunity for family privacy. Parents gave up their roles of breadwinner and housewife. The disciplining of children became difficult in the presence of many people. It was frequently felt that family life was disintegrating,[65] and this feeling was deepened when the later government policy of getting

[62] Carey McWilliams, Prejudice—Japanese-Americans: Symbol of Racial Intolerance, Little, Brown & Company, 1944, pp. 97–98.

[63] Bradford Smith, op. cit., p. 252.

[64] See Carey McWilliams, Brothers Under the Skin, Little, Brown & Company, 1943, p. 172; and Bureau of Sociological Research, Colorado River War Relocation Center, op. cit., p. 150.

[65] The centers stimulated the Nisei's emancipation from the family by (1) granting economic independence and (2) strengthening peer groups against family groups. Leonard Broom and John I. Kituse, The Managed Casualty: The Japanese-American Family in World War II, University of California Press, 1956, p. 40. This monograph includes ten detailed case studies of evacuated families from the prewar period through the postwar situation.

as large a number of people as possible out of relocation centers split some families, for the older sons and daughters left while the first-generation parents and younger children remained behind. A very important dividing influence was the difference of opinion concerning one's orientation to America or Japan in the future. At the same time, the following factors operated to increase family unity: emotional reaction against evacuation and discrimination, the geographical isolation of the centers, and the drawing together of parents and younger children because of the departure of the older Americanized children.[66]

Several thousand Japanese-Americans left the relocation centers during the war, and the others have dispersed over the country since 1945. In four years, 1942–1945, these people lost much of the economic ground they had gained in the United States. Property holdings were greatly reduced, financial reserves were dissipated, and their occupational distribution was strongly modified. Within two years after the relocation centers were closed, Japanese-Americans "with great determination made substantial progress toward again making a stable place for themselves in the metropolitan area [of Los Angeles county]."[67] But as a result of the wartime policies, it seems unlikely that the Japanese population will ever be as concentrated on the Pacific coast as it was before World War II.

While the economic integration of Japanese-Americans steadily increases, as we indicated in Chapter 12, social assimilation is slow except for those whose education and broad interests make it possible for them to arrange their own contacts in the larger community. Presumably long-run influences will bring about the complete integration of the members of this group.[68]

Conclusion

A number of minority families have been briefly examined. All of them, as well as the minority families which have not been considered here, have much in common with other families in the United States. Although each minority family has certain features peculiar to it, several qualities seem to characterize nearly all minority families.

1. Minority families tend to be concentrated in the lower class and the lower middle class.

2. A minority family is part of a subculture and it is an important factor in perpetuating that subculture through the conditioning of children.

[66] Bureau of Sociological Research, Colorado River War Relocation Center, op. cit., p. 156.
[67] Leonard Bloom and Ruth Riemer, *Removal and Return: The Socio-Economic Effects of the War on Japanese Americans*, University of California Press, 1949, pp. 4, 67.
[68] Bradford Smith, op. cit.. p. 369.

3. There is often serious misunderstanding and conflict between parents and children in a minority group.

4. As they reach adulthood there is a strong tendency for minority children to establish more or less typical working-class, business-class, or professional-class American families.

The extent to which these new families approximate American family life in general would seem to depend upon several interrelated factors: amount of exposure to majority family patterns, urban or rural residence, region of the country, degree of alienation between the elders and the young married people, and social class (with related variables such as occupation, income, education, neighborhood, etc.).

CHAPTER 17

Intermarriage: Interracial, Interfaith, and Internationality

Intermarriage here will include interracial, interfaith, and internationality unions. Because of the extensive sexual association of majority and minority men and women outside of marriage, miscegenation and concubinage will also be considered.

Miscegenation and Concubinage During the Slavery Period[1]

Sexual association between whites and Negroes began with the introduction of Negroes into the colonies. Intercourse between the two races was not limited to white males and Negro females, and a considerable number of bastard children by Negro men were born to indentured white women. Marriages of Negroes and whites occurred frequently enough to cause laws against such unions to be enacted. Later in the colonial period, censure and penalties were imposed almost exclusively on the association of Negro men and white women.

The evolution of slavery as a social institution did not decrease the sexual association of Negroes and whites. The sale of mulatto women for prostitution became part of the slave trade in southern cities, and there were many casual relationships between white men and free Negro women. Where the associations became more or less permanent, as they did in Charleston, Mobile, and New Orleans, a system of concubinage

[1] This section is based largely on E. Franklin Frazier, *The Negro Family in the United States*, University of Chicago Press, 1939, chap. 4. See also Otto Klineberg (ed.), *Characteristics of the American Negro*, Harper & Brothers, 1944, pp. 263–268; and Gunnar Myrdal, *An American Dilemma*, Harper & Brothers, 1944, pp. 123–127.

developed. Intermixture of the races also occurred under various types of associations between the men of the master class and slave women on the plantations. At one end of the scale was physical compulsion and rape, with the Negro woman becoming separated from her mulatto child at an early date. At the other extreme was the slaveholding aristocrat who took a mulatto woman as concubine and lived with her and their children affectionately and permanently. Between these two extremes were all degrees of attachment and involvement. Some men of the master class sold their own mulatto children. Others quickly abandoned their mistresses. The prestige of the white race was a factor in bringing about compliance of black and mulatto women. In many cases certain advantages came to the Negro woman, including freedom from field labor, better food and clothing, special privileges for her half-white child and perhaps his eventual freedom.

A Contrasting Situation: Hawaii During the Early Years of Race Contact

During the first century of interracial contacts in Hawaii, 1778–1878, conditions existed which caused foreign men, mainly Chinese and white, · to desire Hawaiian wives. The most important factors were the lack of white women in Hawaii and a freedom from the control of their group mores antagonistic to out-marriage. In this situation large numbers of foreign men married Hawaiian women and a considerable group of people of mixed racial ancestry came into existence. The extensive intermarriage of foreign men and Hawaiian women and the presence of their descendants led to a special pattern of race relations. This code assumed racial equality, sanctioned intermarriage, and gave the children of such marriages a satisfactory social status. As the number of persons of mixed ancestry has increased the code has become more effective.[2] This brief reference to the situation in Hawaii is made to show that the rigid lines and the strong feeling of most of the people in the United States are not inevitable. Attitudes and practices with respect to intermarriage depend upon the total context within which contact occurs.

Negro-White Miscegenation and Concubinage in Recent Years

Emancipation brought profound social and personal disorganization to the former slaves. Promiscuity was common, and interracial sexual relations in the decades immediately following the Civil War were at least as frequent as they were during slavery. It is more difficult to ascertain early twentieth-century and present trends.[3] Most of the sociologi-

---

[2] For an excellent statement on the history of intermarriage in Hawaii see R. Adams, *Intermarriage in Hawaii*, The Macmillan Company, 1937, pp. 46–68.

[3] Gunnar Myrdal, *op. cit.*, pp. 127–128; and Otto Klineberg (ed.), *op. cit.*, pp. 276–300.

cal investigations of recent years have brought the conclusion that interracial sexual relations are decreasing,[4] although Dollard concludes that
"rising social pressure has brought people to exaggerate the actual decline" in miscegenation and concubinage since slavery days.[5] Also,
Charles Johnson finds that the practice of sex relations, including the
"keeping" of Negro "second wives," has been continued, particularly in
the rural areas of the South.[6] Powdermaker notes some changes in the
circumstances of interracial sex relations, including the fact that the
Negro woman today is in a position to refuse the advances of a white
man. This writer also mentions that currently most of the white men in
interracial sexual relationships are middle-aged, and that popular sentiment against Negro-white cohabitation is increasing in both groups.[7]
Her explanation of these changes in attitude is in (1) the increasing
irregularity of intrawhite relationships and (2) the increasing race pride
and demand for respect on the part of Negroes. The informants in one
study said that knowledge of interracial sexual association is limited, for
the most part, to the Negro community; and Johnson remarks that if
this information were generally known, "race relations" would be seriously disturbed.[8] This situation represents a marked change from the
slavery period, when extramarital relations, even of prominent men,
were well known.

The taboo on interracial sex relations seems to be as strong in the
border areas as in the South, although the penalties are not always so
severe.[9] The taboo continues in the North, although it is often violated.
There is more contact in this section than in other areas and a higher
proportion of associations between white women and Negro men. Some
interracial marriages occur and common-law alliances are more frequent.
According to Johnson, ". . . The associations, while much limited and
frowned upon in practice, are not as dangerously unnatural as in the
South or in border areas; and this applies especially to the Negro residence districts in northern cities."[10]

One aspect of interracial sexual association that is of interest is the
widespread belief among the white group, especially white men, that
Negro men are constantly planning attacks upon white women. We
examined this question in Chapter 3 and need to mention it only

[4] Charles S. Johnson, *Patterns of Negro Segregation*, Harper & Brothers, 1943,
pp. 147, 292; Hortense Powdermaker, *After Freedom*, The Viking Press, Inc., 1939,
p. 181; Gunnar Myrdal, *op. cit.*, p. 128.
 [5] John Dollard, *Caste and Class in a Southern Town*, Yale University Press, 1937,
p. 143.
 [6] Charles S. Johnson, *op. cit.*, p. 148.
 [7] Hortense Powdermaker, *op. cit.*, pp. 181, 195–196.
 [8] Charles S. Johnson, *op. cit.*, p. 147.
 [9] *Ibid.*, p. 291.
 [10] *Ibid.*, p. 150.

briefly here. There is in this belief a large amount of projection. Certainly more Negro women have been attacked or seduced by white men than has been the case with white women and Negro men. Despite the seeming lack of seriousness with which many white men have looked upon illicit relations with Negro women, these relations are accompanied by some feelings of guilt, anxiety, and fear of retaliation. Reuter, one of the first sociologists to analyze the South's fear of the Negro in these terms, says in his treatment of lynching:

> One source of this fear is the treatment that the Negro has received at the hands of the whites. The slavery of the Negro, his economic and industrial exploitation, his moral degradation, and other historic facts of the modern situation are fundamentally repugnant to civilized moral standards. The members of the dominant racial group are more or less conscious of the injustice that the Negro has suffered at their hands. There is in consequence an uneasy sense of moral guilt, as may be seen reflected in the rationalized justifications of the historic treatment and of the existing social situation as well as in the naive apologies for behavior not defensible on accepted moral standards. By a familiar psychological process, *sentiments and attitudes that non-socially trained persons imagine that they would have had they been subjected to similar treatment, are imputed to the Negro;* the Negro thereby becomes possessed of behavior tendencies menacing to the white man, to his domination of the social situation, and to the culture he represents. This fear complex . . . functions to create an external image which objectifies the psychological state; the Negro becomes the objective symbol of that subjective state rather than an objective reality.[11]

According to this interpretation, white men have often taken Negro women for sexual reasons, and they have often wondered what they would do if they were in the position of the defenseless men in the Negro group. What they have imagined has frightened them, and they have become convinced that their womenfolk are in constant danger of attack. In a situation involving a Negro man and a white woman it is never proper to suspect the woman. Negro men of all classes are acquainted with this attitude and, except in the North, carefully avoid all situations that would bring them in lone contact with white women.[12]

Regardless of whether interracial sexual relations are decreasing, the offspring from intermixture may be decreasing. As Myrdal points out, greater use of effective contraception has the same genetic effect as decreased interracial sexual relations. This investigator thinks it probable that there has been a decrease in the more stable type of sex associations—marriage and concubinage—and "these are the types of relations most productive of offspring." Prostitution is for the most part sterile,

[11] E. B. Reuter, *The American Race Problem*, Thomas Y. Crowell Company, 2nd ed., 1938, pp. 379–380. (Italics ours.)

[12] Charles S. Johnson, *op. cit.*, p. 286.

and the other types of casual relations may have made increasing use of contraceptives.[13]

One study in the rural South found that the white women who became involved in illicit sexual relations with Negro men are persons isolated from their own group. This condition did not hold for Negro men, most of whom continued to have normal social relations within their own group. Their behavior is seen as a rebellion against the racial system rather than as a symptom of personal maladjustment.[14]

The same investigation throws light on the stable type of union between a white man and a Negro woman in the deep South. Today such affairs tend to isolate the man, and they must be conducted discreetly if he does not wish to give up many of his relations within the white group. Even more important is the fact that outside the home the man is white, the woman and the children Negroes. Beyond the home the man and his mistress must behave according to the racial regulations. Hence they may not appear publicly as a family group or participate as a family in either racial community. Any relations of equality which the woman or children have are within the Negro group, and the same condition is true for the man within the white group. The relations of the woman and children to other whites are mainly subordinate occupational relations, whereas the relations of the man to others in the Negro group are those of a superordinate.[15]

The Negro man, at least in the South and the border areas, is helpless to prevent sexual relations between white men and Negro women, and his relations with Negro women are affected by his subordinate role in the racial system. "If he marries, his wife may at least sometimes compare him with that potential ideal, a white lover. If he seeks after the more attractive girls, or those educated or better dressed, he must compete with the white man who can offer money, prestige, and security. The hopelessness of the situation was shown in a story told by an upper-class Negro girl about a Negro boy who approached her in behalf of his white employer. When she berated him for his action, he replied: 'I'd like you for myself, yes indeed, I'd like you fo' myself, but I works for him.' "[16]

In "Old City" (Mississippi) the situation is quite different for the Negro woman. Her association with a member of the dominant race gives her more security than is the rule in her group. She has a protector in her relations with whites, and she is by no means isolated in the Negro community. ". . . The woman frequently has an active social life outside her home. The white man does not enter into this social

[13] Gunnar Myrdal, *op. cit.*, p. 128.

[14] Allison W. Davis, B. B. Gardner, and M. R. Gardner, *Deep South,* University of Chicago Press, 1941, p. 30.

[15] *Ibid.*, pp. 31, 35–36.

[16] *Ibid.*, p. 38.

life, however, nor does the woman entertain her friends when he is home. Otherwise the relationship imposes few restrictions. She may be active in Negro church and club affairs and may give generously of her time and money to their enterprises. In a few cases the woman may be a leader in clubs and social activities, with complete acceptance on the part of the Negro group."[17]

In interracial sexual relations, then, particularly in the South, white men have access both to white and to Negro women. The same situation obtains for Negro women with respect to Negro and white men, except that generally they are the objects rather than the choosers.[18]

As we noted in Chapter 8, it is interesting to inquire why, considering the derogatory attitudes that whites have toward Negroes, Negro women are still attractive sexually. Dollard says that the answer is too simple if it is phrased in terms of crude sexual motive alone, although straight sexual desire is a part of this situation.[19] Also to be taken into account, both in transitory and in permanent relations, are the element of mastery; the attempt to show the racial inferiority of the Negro by the wanton use of Negro women; an irresponsible relationship free of cares, threats, and duties; and the fact that Negro women cannot be protected by Negro men.[20]

A complementary question asks why Negro women are accessible to such sex relations with white men outside of marriage. The answer seems to lie in sexual pleasure wishes; money given to low-paid or low-income women; the prestige of the white man; the wish, often unconscious, for light children; an element of revenge on the domineering or conceited white woman; and the looseness of the marriage ties in the lower-class Negro group with its mother-centered family and the economic independence of the woman.[21]

Extensive miscegenation has an effect on the general relations between whites and Negroes. The feeling in Old City was that Negroes are not so strongly subordinated as they are elsewhere in the same state. One Negro gave the following explanation of the belief that miscegenation

[17] *Ibid.*, p. 36.
[18] John Dollard, *op. cit.*, p. 135.
[19] Using a psychoanalytic viewpoint, Dollard suggests that the idealization of white women in the South (even though actual behavior does not always correspond with the ideal) may have an effect on the sexual behavior of white men toward women in their own group. This idealization produces a feeling that white women are "untouchable, that sexual sentiments are unbecoming in relation to them, and that sexual behavior toward white women must take place, though, of course it does take place, only against a personal sense of guilt." On the other hand, the image of the Negro woman is the exact opposite, that is, it is "rather that of a seducing, accessible person dominated by sexual feeling. . . ." This split-image theory explains "the luxury of preserving the image of the untouchable white woman and at the same time having available on easy terms the Negro woman as a target for the withdrawn affect." *Ibid.*, pp. 136–138.
[20] *Ibid.*, pp. 143–145.
[21] *Ibid.*, p. 152.

softens the rigors of the racial rules: "I'll tell you why they get along well
here. It's easy to see why. So many of these white men got colored children and families. Why there are two white men who live with their
colored families. And there are gangs of them who live with colored
women or got colored children. That's why they don't start hurting
people. They don't know who they'd be hitting. They might hit some
of their own children."[22]

Incidence of Intermarriage in the United States

Racial intermarriage does not occur frequently in the United States.
Religious intermarriage is somewhat more common, and ethnic intermarriage (internationality marriage) occurs most often. The highest
known racial intermarriage rate in this country, recorded in Los Angeles
during the period 1924–1933, was 1.2 per 100 marriages. It is worth noting that this record rate, actually very low, occurred under the following
conditions favorable to intermarriage: First, a fairly high proportion (8
percent) of the total population consisted of Mexicans, Filipinos, and
American Indians, all of whom were then permitted by law, and to a
lesser extent by the mores, to intermarry with white persons. Second,
Los Angeles is less tradition-bound and has a less rigid social structure
than is the case in many American cities. Third, there was a marked
disparity in the ratio of the sexes of some minorities, especially in the
Filipino group. Fourth, cultural similarities existed between certain
racial minorities, as, for example, between the Mexicans and the people
of Latin culture from Central and South America. Despite these conditions, racial minorities in Los Angeles County in-married to a high
degree.[23]

A number of other recent studies reveal the incidence of different
types of intermarriage. A New Haven study was designed to discover
whether general intermarriage or stratified intermarriage is taking place,
that is, whether there is a single melting pot in the United States or
one "with two or more separate compartments, each producing a special
blend of its own." The main conclusions of this investigation follow:

The increasing intermarriage in New Haven is not general and indiscriminate but is channeled by religious barriers; and groups with the same religions
tend to intermarry. Thus, Irish, Italians, and Poles intermarry mostly among
themselves, and British-Americans, Germans, and Scandinavians do likewise,
while Jews seldom marry Gentiles.

When marriage crosses religious barriers, as it often does, religion still
plays a dominant role, especially among Catholics. The high frequency of
Catholic nuptials sanctioning the out-marriages of Irish, Italians, and Poles

[22] Allison W. Davis, B. B. Gardner, and M. R. Gardner, *op. cit.*, p. 39.
[23] Constantine Panunzio, "Intermarriage in Los Angeles," *American Journal of
Sociology*, March, 1942, pp. 690–701.

implies that their choice of spouses is determined largely by the willingness of their non-Catholic mates to be brought over to the church. Indeed, Catholic nuptials are increasing in marriages of Catholics with non-Catholics.

. . . Our main conclusion is . . . that assortative mating rather than random intermarriage has been occurring in New Haven since 1870 and that assimilation in this city is of a stratified character. The "melting-pot general-mixture" idea popularized by Zangwill and supported by others has failed to materialize in this particular community. Religious differences function as the chief basis of stratification.[24]

Hollingshead's study of five factors (race, age, ethnic origin, religion, and class) in the selection of marriage mates agrees with Kennedy's conclusions on the importance of religious barriers in New Haven inter-marriages. Hollingshead, investigating all marriages in that city in 1948, found that religion divided the white race into three pools. "Persons in the Jewish pool in 97.1 percent of the cases married within their own group; the percentage was 93.8 for Catholics and 74.4 for Protestants."[25]

A comprehensive study of the rate of intermarriage between Catholics and non-Catholics by John L. Thomas indicates that New Haven is not representative, even of Connecticut, in its intermarriage patterns. According to Kennedy, the percentages of Italians, Irish, and Poles inter-marrying with British-Americans, Scandinavians, Germans, and Jews were: 1870, 4.65 percent; 1900, 14.22 percent; 1930, 17.95 percent; and 1940, 16.29 percent. As we have noted, Hollingshead found that only 6.2 percent of the New Haven Catholics married outside their religious group. Thomas points out that the figures in the Kennedy and the Hollingshead studies refer to all intermarriages and not simply to those sanctioned by Catholic nuptials. In his study of interfaith marriages in Connecticut, Thomas discovered that "the rate for just the mixed marriages sanctioned by Catholic nuptials was 40.2 percent of all Catholic marriages in 1949." If the mixed marriages not sanctioned by Catholic nuptials were added, Thomas believes that the most conservative esti-mate would bring the total rate to more than 50 percent.[26] Thomas

---

[24] Ruby Jo Reeves Kennedy, "Single or Triple Melting-Pot? Intermarriage Trends in New Haven, 1870–1940," *American Journal of Sociology*, January, 1944, p. 339. A later report on intermarriage in New Haven resulted in approximately the same conclusions as the earlier study. In 1950, Italians and Poles were the only two large groups showing an increasing tendency toward intermarriage. Ruby Jo Reeves Kennedy, "Single or Triple Melting-Pot? Intermarriage in New Haven, 1870–1950," *American Journal of Sociology*, July, 1952, pp. 56–59.

[25] A. B. Hollingshead, "Cultural Factors in the Selection of Marriage Mates," *American Sociological Review*, October, 1950, p. 627.

[26] According to Thomas, there are no adequate data on the number of mixed marriages not sanctioned by Catholic nuptials. His study, which included all of the mixed marriages to be found in 132 parishes distributed throughout the East and Middle West, showed that 11,710 in 29,581 mixed marriages (39.6 percent) were not sanctioned by Catholic nuptials. He feels that this rate is fairly representative for the part of the country covered, but he does not predicate the same rate for other sections of the United States since his investigations show considerable sec-

concludes that three principal factors influence the intermarriage rates of Catholics: first, the relative percentage of Catholics in the total population (scarcity of prospective mates within the Catholic group occasions a high rate of intermarriage—provided that ethnic or other differences do not prevent contacts between Catholics and non-Catholics); second, the presence of cohesive ethnic groups within the community (loyalty to the group, social standing of the ethnic group, language, nationality prejudices, and religion combine to put a check on intermarriage); and third, the socioeconomic class of the Catholic population (in Thomas' study of the intermarriage patterns of 51,671 families distributed in thirty parishes of a large urban center the following percentages of mixed marriages in all Catholic marriages were found: lower rental area, 8.5; mixed lower and middle, 9.1; middle rental area, 12.0; mixed middle and upper, 16.3; upper rental area, 17.9; and suburban, 19.3). Thomas' investigations lead him to believe that there will be a gradual but steady increase in the number of marriages between Catholics and non-Catholics. His reasons are as follows: First, the decline in immigration, the horizontal and vertical mobility of our population, and the increased cultural contacts due to modern means of communication will reduce the influence of ethnic groups over individuals' choices of marriage partners; second, mixed marriages have a cumulative effect

---

tional differences. Thus he finds that mixed marriages sanctioned by Catholic nuptials constituted 70 percent of the Catholic marriages in the dioceses of Raleigh, Charleston, and Savannah-Atlanta, but that they were only 10 percent for the dioceses of El Paso, Corpus Christi, and Santa Fe. "During the decade 1940–1950, mixed marriages sanctioned by Catholic nuptials approximated 30 percent of all Catholic marriages in the United States. The rate . . . for 1950 is 26.2." About 30 percent of the 912,851 Catholic marriages in the United States during the thirties were mixed. John L. Thomas, "The Factor of Religion in the Selection of Marriage Mates," *American Sociological Review*, August, 1951, pp. 488, 489, 491. Loren E. Chancellor and Thomas P. Monahan ("Religious Preference and Interreligious Mixtures in Marriages and Divorces in Iowa," *American Journal of Sociology*, November, 1955, p. 237) report that state records in Iowa show that 42 percent of all marriages involving a Catholic in 1953 were mixed marriages. For "first" marriages the percentage was 35. If all civil marriages are eliminated, the percentages were 33 for the total and 29 for "first" marriages. (The *Catholic Directory* listed 30 percent of the marriages in Iowa in 1953 sanctioned by the Catholic Church as mixed.) For the years 1945 and 1955, Locke, Sabagh, and Thomas found high negative correlations between the interfaith marriage rates—at least for Catholics—and the percentage of Catholics in the population of the forty-eight states. Data on Catholics and Anglicans in Canada also support the hypothesis that the rate of interfaith marriage of a given religious group increases as the proportion of that group decreases in the population. Two additional hypotheses are stated: (1) that social distance may be one variable affecting the low intermarriage rates in some states in the United States (Catholics in Texas and New Mexico are predominantly Mexican-Americans, whereas a high percentage of Connecticut's Catholics are of Irish, Polish, or Italian origin), and (2) that the higher the economic status of a religious group, the higher the intermarriage rate (supporting data are cited from Arizona, where both income level and intermarriage rates of Catholics are higher than in Texas, and from two parishes in New Orleans). Harvey J. Locke, Georges Sabagh, and Mary Margaret Thomas, "Interfaith Marriages," *Social Problems*, April, 1957, pp. 329–333.

because the children of mixed marriages tend to marry outside their religious group more often than do the children of in-group marriages; third, the attitude of young people, both Catholic and Protestant, appears to be increasingly tolerant; and fourth, both the family and the church have less control over youth than in former years.

A study of internationality marriage in Burlington, Vermont, showed that the great majority of householders whose wives were living and whose families had been three generations or more in this country had married into the "American" group.

The extent of intermarriage among Americans, including both Old Americans and people of other ethnic origin who have been here for three generations, is interesting. Although 20 percent of 2,277 householders of this group married into a wider range of nationalities than did any other group, 80 percent of them are married to other Americans of the third generation or more. This indicates, at least, how marked the tendency is for people to marry among those who are at home in the American environment, rather than among people of the first or second generation who may be of the same ethnic stock but who are less at home in this country.[27]

The Negro-white intermarriage rates in New York City, New York State, Boston, and Los Angeles have been from 1 to 5 percent of all marriages in which Negroes participated. These intermarriages appear to be declining.[28]

Perhaps the fullest data on Negro-white intermarriages in the United States are for Boston. Stone found that there were 143 such intermarriages for the period 1900–1904, or an average of 28.6 per year. The rate per 100 Negro marriages was 13.6. Data secured from the Boston Registry Department by Wirth and Goldhamer for the period 1914–1938 are given in Table 17.1.[29]

The considerable decrease in Negro-white intermarriage in Boston cannot be explained by the hypothesis that the smaller the proportion of a minority race in the total population the higher will be the rate of intermarriage. The percentage of the Negro population in Boston was practically constant from 1900 to 1920 (1900, 2.1; 1910, 2.0; 1915, 2.1; 1920, 2.2). It was not markedly higher in 1930 (2.6). Wirth and Goldhamer attribute this decline mainly to two factors. First, though Boston was at one time a center of abolitionist agitation and was known for cordial relations between the races, it was not to be expected that this

[27] E. L. Anderson, *We Americans*, Harvard University Press, 1937, p. 190.

[28] According to *Ebony* (December, 1949, pp. 20–21), the Chicago marriage license bureau reported a record number of 200 Negro-white marriages in 1948. If this is correct, it represents the highest known number of Negro-white intermarriages for any city in the United States. No data on intermarriage rates or trends are available for Chicago. Milton L. Barron, *People Who Intermarry*, Syracuse University Press, 1948, p. 189.

[29] Louis Wirth and Herbert Goldhamer, "The Hybrid and the Problem of Miscegenation," in Otto Klineberg (ed.), *op. cit.*, p. 277.

situation could continue with the coming of a new population from Europe; and second, the migration of Negroes to the North during World War I brought southern Negroes whose economic and cultural status was unfavorable to interracial marriage.[30]

TABLE 17.1. Number of Negro-White Marriages and Percent Negro-White Marriages of All Marriages Involving Negroes and of All Marriages Involving Whites, Boston, 1914–1938

Year	Number of Negro-White Marriages	Percent Negro-White Marriages of All Marriages Involving Negroes	Percent Negro-White Marriages of All Marriages Involving Whites
1914–1918	89	5.2	0.18
1919–1923	47	3.1	0.10
1924–1928	53	3.6	0.12
1929–1933	40	3.6	0.11
1934–1938	47	3.7	0.12
Total	276	3.9	0.13

The Boston rate of Negro-white marriages in all Negro marriages in the period 1914–1938 was 3.9 as compared with 3.4 for New York urban areas exclusive of New York City in 1919–1937. The Boston rate changed little after 1919, whereas the New York rate, except during the period 1922–1924, dropped steadily. Whereas the former high rate of intermarriage in Boston was unique, the present Boston rate does not seem to be atypical.[31]

According to Barron, the "other colored" races in the United States, especially the Filipinos and American Indians, have had considerably higher intermarriage rates than the Negro. Also, there has been a greater variation in rate among the Chinese, Japanese, Indians, and Filipinos than among Negroes. In some places where these minority races have had very small numbers, intermarriage has exceeded in-marriage.[32]

Writing of the pre-Pearl Harbor days, Smith says that the number of marriages between American-born Japanese and other Americans was negligible, even though the Nisei had much in common with white youth. The Nisei on the coast had a strong prejudice against mixed marriages, although they resented the state laws that forbade them to marry Caucasians. These laws, which are referred to later in this chapter, do not prevent Negro-Oriental marriages, but this point is unimportant since the Nisei are opposed to such marriages.[33] The incidence of the out-marriage of Japanese in Hawaii is interesting.

[30] *Ibid.*, pp. 278–279.
[31] *Ibid.*, p. 280.
[32] Milton L. Barron, *op. cit.*, pp. 189–190.
[33] Bradford Smith, *Americans from Japan*, J. B. Lippincott Company, 1948, pp. 256–257.

According to Smith, 11 percent of all marriages in the territory were interracial in 1913, but only 1 percent of the Japanese out-married at that time. In 1932 the respective percentages had risen to 22 and 8, but in that year approximately one-fourth of the Chinese and Koreans intermarried. "The war accelerated outmarriages tremendously, especially among Nisei girls. In 1943–44 about twenty per cent of the grooms of Nisei brides were non-Japanese, and more than half of these were haole [white]."[34]

It is difficult, if not impossible, to determine the number of Jewish-gentile intermarriages in the United States. Persons who do not wish a religious ceremony are married by civil officials, and their marriages are not recorded by either Christian ministers or Jewish rabbis.[35]

Available data indicate the following rates of intermarriage per 100 marriages involving Jews in United States cities: New Haven, 1870, 0.00; New Haven, 1900, 1.18; New Haven, 1930, 2.99; New Haven, 1940, 5.68; Drachsler, New York City, 1908–1912, 2.27; Brickner, Cincinnati, 1916–1919, 3.6; Koenig, Stamford (study made in 1938; years of marriage varied), 7.16. Seidler and Ravitz state that while the statistics concerning the intermarriage of Jews in the United States are neither clear nor definite, there is no evidence to indicate that the rate is greater than 5 percent.[36] Known European rates vary from 0.39 in Lithuania in 1931 to 51.00 for Germany in 1915. The rate for Canada, excluding Quebec, for 1920–1931 was 6.52; for all of Canada in the years 1926–1931 it was 4.82.[37]

Some students of Jewish-gentile relations believe that there is a tendency to exaggerate the extent of intermarriage between members of these groups. According to them, it is highly probable that the rate of intermarriage was high in colonial days and during the pioneer period in the West. Single men predominated among the Jews in those areas at the time, and many of them married non-Jews and left the Jewish group.[38] This point of view questions whether Jewish-gentile intermarriage must progressively increase.

There does tend to be a hardening of Jewish communalism as the group is longer domiciled, and after the second generation has broken loose for a time, it tends to find its life more largely within its own cultural group. Indeed, there is evidence that a very large proportion of the intermarriage

[34] *Ibid.*, p. 164.
[35] C. E. Silcox and G. M. Fisher, *Catholics, Jews, and Protestants*, Harper & Brothers, 1934, p. 240.
[36] M. B. Seidler and M. J. Ravitz, "A Jewish Peer Group," *American Journal of Sociology*, July, 1955, p. 14.
[37] Milton L. Barron, "The Incidence of Jewish Intermarriage in Europe and America," *American Sociological Review*, February, 1946, p. 7. The New Haven rate for 1950 was 3.9 percent. Ruby Jo Reeves Kennedy, "Single or Triple Melting-Pot? Intermarriage in New Haven, 1870–1950," p. 57.
[38] C. E. Silcox and G. M. Fisher, *op. cit.*, p. 264.

which takes place concerns Orthodox Jews; as the Jew becomes successful, he is apt to attach himself to the liberal synagogue and find there a social status more acceptable than he may discover outside of Judaism or in Orthodox Judaism. He then finds his friends and his mates in that circle.[39]

Two interesting points are given in an explanation of the low intermarriage rates of Jews in Derby, Connecticut. There are 110 Jewish families in this city of 10,000 population. Members of the Greek Orthodox and the Greek Catholic faiths also constitute small groups in Derby, but both have high intermarriage rates. The Jews are concentrated in the merchant and professional economic classes; the Greek Orthodox and Greek Catholics are recent immigrants who work as unskilled and semiskilled laborers. The higher economic status of the Jews enables them to circulate freely in the larger neighboring Jewish communities and thereby overcome the handicap of small numbers. Also, their longer existence as a minority group and their more varied experience in migration have contributed to the development of attitudes and techniques of resisting intermarriage.[40]

There would seem to be no reason for believing that Jewish-gentile intermarriage necessarily adheres to a pattern of increasing incidence or decreasing incidence. As Barron says, "It varies in time and place according to the fluctuations of social conditions."[41]

There is a general tendency for the men of a racial, religious, or ethnic minority to out-marry to a greater extent than the women. Although the sexes in the Jewish group in Canada are almost equally divided, the number of Jewish men who marry non-Jews is regularly larger than the number of Jewish women who marry non-Jewish men.[42] Likewise, Jewish women in Europe have been more conservative than Jewish men in intermarrying.[43] In Koenig's Stamford, Connecticut, study the overwhelming majority of the Jewish partners in Jewish-gentile marriages (forty out of fifty-nine) were male.[44] Bloom's study of "Buna" (Akron, Ohio) also found that Jewish males are more likely to intermarry than Jewish females, although "in the higher income brackets and among the

[39] *Ibid.*, p. 263.
[40] Milton L. Barron, "The Incidence of Jewish Intermarriage in Europe and America," p. 13.
[41] *Ibid.* Barron points out that in Europe "Jews have intermarried more in prosperous times than in times of economic depression and social oppression." Also, "generally, in western European countries where Jews have been numerically few and 'emancipated' in the sense of enjoying full civil rights and of practicing a relatively diluted form of Judaism, they have intermarried more and at a faster rate than Jews elsewhere in Europe." In Canada, "intermarriage rates have been low, more so in Quebec because of French Catholic cooperation with Orthodox Jews in aversion to intermarriage and stringency of regulation." *Ibid.*, pp. 9–10.
[42] C. E. Silcox and G. M. Fisher, *op. cit.*, p. 266.
[43] Milton L. Barron, "The Incidence of Jewish Intermarriage in Europe and America," p. 9.
[44] *Ibid.*, p. 12.

Reformed Jews, the number of Jewish women entering intermarriage was proportionately higher."[45] In Minneapolis, Gordon found that in nearly all cases of intermarriage, "it is the Jewish youth who marries the non-Jewish girl . . . in most instances the Jewish youth is financially better off than the girl he marries."[46]

The most common type of Negro-white intermarriage is that of Negro men and white women.[47] The majority of intermarriages in which the "other colored" races in the United States participate are between non-white males and white females.[48]

After California's antimiscegenation law was nullified by a state court in 1948, the intermarriage rate was not high. During a thirty-month period (November, 1948, to April 30, 1951), 78,266 licenses were issued in Los Angeles County, of which 445 were between persons of the white and some other race (Mexicans are considered white). This rate of 56 per 10,000 marriages is slightly more than one-half of 1 percent of all marriages. Of the marriages between whites and other races, 41 percent involved Filipino men; 20.5 percent, Negro men; 20.4 percent, Anglo men (because Mexicans are legally "white," the term "Anglo" is used to denote whites of non-Mexican descent); 7.6 percent, Chinese men; 5.3 percent, Mexican men; and 4.5 percent, Japanese men. For the women, 44.4 percent involved Anglo women; 29.2 percent, Mexican women; 7.4 percent, Negro women; 7.4 percent, Japanese women; 5.9 percent, Filipino women; and 3.9 percent, Chinese women. The rates of intermarriage according to race or nationality are shown in Table 17.2.

The study did not record separately interracial marriages not including whites, but the estimate of the total rate of intermarriage if these are included is 65 per 10,000 marriages. The sample seems to indicate that in the marriages of whites to whites about 3.5 percent are between Anglos and Mexican-Americans, with marriages of Anglo males to Mexican-American females constituting about four-fifths of this total. The sample of 1000 marriages indicates that of the marriage licenses issued in Los Angeles County, about 75 percent are Anglo-Anglo, approximately 11 percent are Mexican-Mexican, almost 10 percent are Negro-Negro, and the other 4 percent are intraracial marriages involving other racial groups or interracial marriages. Since Los Angeles has a relatively large number of minority groups and of intermarriages, it should not be concluded that it is a typical city in the matter of intermarriage.[49]

[45] *Ibid.*

[46] Albert I. Gordon, *Jews in Transition,* University of Minnesota Press, 1950, pp. 206–207.

[47] Milton L. Barron, *People Who Intermarry,* p. 189.

[48] *Ibid.,* pp. 189–190.

[49] John H. Burma, "Research Note on the Measurement of Interracial Marriage," *American Journal of Sociology,* May, 1952, p. 587.

A study of all interracial marriages in Washington, D.C., for the years 1940–1947 disclosed 373 such marriages. The distribution of these

TABLE 17.2. Rates per 1000 Marriage Licenses Issued to Mixed Couples of White and Nonwhite Races in Los Angeles County, November 1, 1948, to April 30, 1951, by Race or Nationality

Filipino-Anglo[a]	217
Filipino-Mexican	193
Negro-Anglo	146
Anglo-Japanese	67
Anglo-Negro	58
Negro-Mexican	59
Chinese-Anglo	54
Anglo-Chinese	34
Anglo-Filipino	34
Japanese-Anglo	27
Mexican-Filipino	25
Chinese-Mexican	22
Japanese-Mexican	18
Mexican-Negro	16
Anglo-Korean	11
Mexican-Japanese	7
Mexican-Chinese	5
Other mixtures	7
Total	1000

[a] Male listed first in all cases.

TABLE 17.3. Interracial Marriages in Washington, D.C., 1940–1947, by Sex and Race

Groom	Brides							Total Grooms
	Filipino	Chinese	White	Negro	Indian	Other Races[b]	Japanese	
Filipino	...	...	209	9	...	...	...	218
Chinese	...	...	48	6	...	...	...	54
White	3	8	...	7	10	3	13	44
Negro	...	...	19	...	1	...	...	20
Indian	...	...	12	3	...	...	...	15
Other races[a]	...	...	13	1	...	...	...	14
Japanese	...	...	8	...	...	...	...	8
Total brides	3	8	309	26	11	3	13	373

[a] Guamian, 2; Hindu, 1; Hawaiian, 5; Siamese, 3; East Indian, 3.
[b] Hawaiian, 1; Korean, 2.

marriages by sex and race is shown in Table 17.3. According to this study, there were 43 Negro-white marriages in the period 1923–1927 as compared with 23 such marriages in 1943–1947.[50]

[50] Sister M. Annella, "Some Aspects of Interracial Marriage in Washington, D.C.," *Journal of Negro Education*, Fall, 1956, pp. 380–391.

One notable exception to the generalization on the out-marriage of minority men and women is found in the case of the Catholic women of Canada. In every province, including Quebec, the number of Catholic women who out-marry is greater than the number of Catholic men who do so. The reasons given are: Protestant men will accept the conditions of marriage imposed by the Catholic Church more readily than will Protestant women; Catholic women may prefer to marry Protestant men because their economic status tends to be higher than that of Catholic men; the average Catholic girl is educated beyond the level of the average Catholic boy; the somewhat rigid attitude of the church with reference to some aspects of the sex relation may cause some Catholic women to prefer Protestant husbands.[51]

The factors responsible for the usual tendency of the men in a minority racial, religious, or ethnic group to out-marry more than the women do may be summarized as follows:

1. The women in these groups have fewer opportunities for meeting the men in other groups than the minority men have for meeting women outside their own group.

2. Religious and other institutional controls of behavior may exert a stronger influence on minority women than on minority men.

3. Men take the initiative in dating and courtship.

4. Marrying a woman in the majority group, or a woman in the minority group whose appearance and manners closely approximate those of majority-group women, is a symbol of success, of prestige, of being accepted in the larger community. In the case of the Negro in the United States, it may also mean the realization of a wish, perhaps an unconscious wish, to have children who will be nearer to the ideal physical type of this country. Majority women who intermarry typically are of lower socioeconomic status than the minority men they marry. They exchange majority prestige for higher socioeconomic standing. The woman in the minority group who is least visible from the standpoint of minority status has many competitors for marriage among majority women. Within the minority group she has marked advantages maritally.

In summary, we may say that people in the United States and elsewhere have been predominantly endogamous with respect to race, religion, and ethnic group. Of these three types of intermarriage, racial intermarriage has usually been the least common and ethnic intermarriage the most frequent. Time, place, and conditions have affected the incidence of each type of intermarriage. There is no single pattern in the trend of intermarriage incidence.[52]

[51] C. E. Silcox and G. M. Fisher, *op. cit.*, p. 255.
[52] Milton L. Barron, *People Who Intermarry*, pp. 188–189.

The Legal Aspects of Intermarriage

The legal history of intermarriage in the United States is fascinating and fantastic.[53] We begin a brief summary of this subject by mentioning that Mississippi has a criminal statute providing for the punishment of anyone who publishes, prints, or circulates any literature in favor of or urges interracial marriage or social equality, and that the Texas court upheld an ordinance enacted by Fort Worth that it is unlawful for whites and Negroes to have sexual intercourse with one another within the city limits.[54]

There has been so much intermixture in Louisiana that it is said that a marriage license would be refused only in cases where mixture is obvious from the appearance of the person making the application. Ordinarily the marriages of white persons to individuals with a small amount of Negro ancestry are questioned only by those interested in property succession, and the courts have dealt leniently with children of mixed ancestry. Despite these conditions, it is certain that any attempt to modify the laws of Louisiana would meet the strongest opposition.

California's antimiscegenation law was declared unconstitutional by a state court in 1948. Two Catholics, one Negro and one white, declared that their religious freedom was hampered by the law; the sacrament of marriage was being unconstitutionally denied them by the law.[55] The United States Supreme Court has never ruled on the

[53] This summary is based largely on C. S. Mangum, Jr., *The Legal Status of the Negro*, University of North Carolina Press, 1940, chap. 10. See also Otto Klineberg (ed.), *op. cit.*, pp. 358–364; Charles S. Johnson, *op. cit.*, pp. 162, 163, 169; and Milton L. Barron, *People Who Intermarry*, pp. 50–58.

[54] ". . . The legislatures of quite a number of southern and western states have found it expedient to enact statutes expressly punishing members of different races and sexes for living in a state of concubinage or for indulging in acts of sexual intercourse with one another, whether it be fornication or adultery. Illicit interracial sexual relationships are also punishable under ordinary statutes prohibiting unlawful cohabitation generally. Louisiana has even gone to the extent of enacting a statute which specifically penalizes cohabitation between a Negro and an Indian. Texas punishes the continuance of a cohabitation between a white person and a Negro after a marriage either in or out of the state, but the marriage is an essential element of the offense and must be averred and proved. There is no other general cohabitation statute in Texas which specifically affects interracial relations, but one of the cities of the state was allowed to put an ordinance of this kind into effect." C. S. Mangum, Jr., *op. cit.*, pp. 256–257.

The evidence which is admissible in trying to establish the race of anyone accused of miscegenation or of his or her accomplice is extremely interesting. Certain types of testimony have been held to be acceptable, including bringing either the defendant or his or her paramour into court for the jury to view and to ascertain whether or not this individual is a Negro. The same may be done with respect to "the immediate direct or collateral kindred of the person involved." It has even been considered as proof, with or without photographs, of Negro ancestry if "one of the party's none-too-distant ancestors had kinky hair and other racial characteristics of the Negro." *Ibid.*, pp. 262–263.

[55] John H. Burma, *op. cit.*, p. 587.

constitutionality of state laws forbidding intermarriage, but lower courts have held that such statutes do not violate the Fourteenth Amendment. A case in which a Chinese and a white person left Virginia for North Carolina to be married in that state, in order to avoid the Virginia statute prohibiting marriage between persons of those races, recently came before a Virginia court in a suit for annulment of the marriage. The Virginia court annulled the marriage, and, on appeal, the Supreme Court of Appeals of Virginia held that the marriage was void by virtue of the Virginia miscegenation statute. On appeal the United States Supreme Court held that the constitutional issue of the validity of the Virginia statute was not squarely before it and remanded the case for clarification of the issues of the relationship of the parties to the state of Virginia at the time of the marriage. On January 18, 1956, the Supreme Court of Appeals of Virginia stated that there was no provision in Virginia practice to reopen the case in the trial court and adhered to its prior opinion.[56]

Laws barring intermarriage were on and off the statute books of at least six southern states during the nineteenth century. Louisiana seems to have been the first state to enact such a law (1810), North Carolina followed in 1830, Arkansas in 1838, and Mississippi and South Carolina in 1865. These laws were repealed for longer or shorter periods of time during Reconstruction, but all had reappeared by 1894.

States differ with respect to the amount of Negro ancestry which will prevent a person from entering a valid marriage with a white person. Mulattoes are specifically mentioned in the statutes of Arkansas, Delaware, Idaho, Kentucky, Mississippi, South Carolina, Tennessee, and Wyoming, but in most cases there is no reference to the amount of Negro ancestry which is considered to come within the law. Three states (Maryland, North Carolina, and Tennessee) prohibit the marriage of whites to persons of Negro "blood" to the third generation inclusive. This is equivalent to making it illegal for a white person to marry an individual whose ancestry is one-eight Negro. Six states (Indiana, Mississippi, Missouri, Nebraska, North Dakota, and South Carolina) have the same provision, but the language of the statutes is in terms of the marriage of whites with persons of one-eighth or more Negro "blood." Florida has contradictory rules, the constitution prohibiting marriage to the fourth generation inclusive (one-sixteenth Negro ancestry), whereas the definition of Negro in the statutory law prohibiting intermarriage is a person of one-eighth or more "Negro blood." Oregon makes the prohibited proportion of Negro ancestry one-fourth or more. Seven states (Alabama, Arizona, Georgia, Montana, Oklahoma, Texas, and Virginia) prohibit marriages of whites with

[56] *Race Relations Law Reporter*, April, 1956, p. 404.

persons who have any Negro ancestry. In two states (Utah and West Virginia) the statutes do not indicate what amount of Negro ancestry will make a person ineligible to marry a white person. Altogether, twenty-seven states now prohibit, through constitutional provision or statutory law or both, the marriage of white persons and those who are defined in these varying ways as "Negro." Two states, South Dakota and Colorado, repealed their miscegenation statutes in 1957.[57] California's anti-intermarriage law was nullified by a state court in 1948. Thirteen states have laws which expressly or impliedly prohibit the marriage of Caucasians and Mongolians, eight states do likewise for whites and Malays, and five prohibit the marriage of whites and Indians.[58] Louisiana and Oklahoma prohibit unions of Indians and Negroes, and North Carolina has placed a ban on the marriage of Cherokee Indians in Robeson County with persons of Negro ancestry to the third generation inclusive. Although statistically the chances of marriages between Malays and Negroes would not seem to be great in Maryland, that state takes no chances and forbids them.

Since most of the original laws against intermarriage go back many years, it is impossible to determine recent feeling against Negro-white marriages by indicating the number of states enacting laws against them. However, it appears from revisions of the original laws that the trend is toward increasing severity. States that formerly forbade marriage between whites and persons whose ancestry was one-fourth, one-eight, or one-sixteenth Negro have tended to reduce the amount of Negro ancestry that will make marriage with whites illegal. In this connection, it is interesting that Georgia (1927) and Virginia (1930) have race registration acts requiring every person in the state to give racial data on his forebears. Wirth and Goldhamer point out that while legal barriers to Negro-white marriages are at least as severe as in earlier years,

[57] *Ibid.*, April, 1957, p. 479, and June, 1957, p. 707.

[58] The states which forbid Caucasian-Mongolian marriages are Arizona, Georgia, Idaho, Mississippi (one-eighth or more), Missouri, Montana, Nebraska (one-eighth or more), Nevada, Oregon (one-fourth or more Chinese), South Carolina (white woman permitted to marry white man only), Utah, Virginia, Wyoming.

The states prohibiting white-Malay marriages are Arizona, Georgia, Maryland, Nevada, Oregon (one-fourth or more Kanaka), South Carolina, Virginia, Wyoming. A California act, invalid since 1948, was passed in 1933 forbidding white-Malay intermarriage after the decision of the California court that a Filipino was not a "Mongolian" within the marriage statute. (Other states have interpreted their laws in such a way that Filipinos are included among the "colored" peoples whom whites may not marry. Milton L. Barron, *People Who Intermarry*, p. 55.)

Those banning white-Indian marriages are Arizona, Georgia (including West Indian), North Carolina (to third generation), Oregon (more than one-half), South Carolina (mestizo included). Washington formerly had such a law. Such a marriage is illegal in a state which prohibits it even if the ceremony took place on an Indian reservation.

In addition to the interdictions just given, Arizona forbids white-Hindu marriages, and Georgia and Virginia prohibit marriages with Asiatic Indians. C. S. Mangum, Jr., *op. cit.*, p. 253.

a larger proportion of the Negro population now resides in states where there are no laws against intermarriage.[59]

There is much doubt concerning the effectiveness of racial inter-marriage laws. One authority says that the California law of 1933 (nullified in 1948) prohibiting Filipino-white intermarriage was not successful in preventing such unions. Filipinos continued to inter-marry with whites in California and they went to states which had no laws forbidding such intermarriages (Oregon, New Mexico, Utah, and Idaho).[60] Another writer expresses the belief that laws prohibiting racial intermarriage are effective only if they coincide with the mores of the community, and that such laws probably have no effect upon the rate of racial intermixture.[61]

Additional evidence of the inutility of the racial intermarriage laws is seen in the low rates of intermarriage in states where the practice is legal. Details on these rates are given in the preceding section of this chapter, but we may point out here that in New York State in 1929 only 2.7 percent of the Negro grooms and 0.8 percent of its Negro brides married whites. Also, in 4885 marriages by Negroes in Los Angeles during the decade 1924–1933, 989 per 1000 were racial in-marriages and only 11 per 1000 were racial intermarriages.[62]

Important court decisions have been made recently concerning the children of intermarriages. In a Texas case involving the section of the Roman Catholic Ante-Nuptial Contract and Promises which states that all children born of a "mixed" union shall be baptized and edu-cated solely in the Catholic faith, the court held that the promises are not valid in law; they are only binding in "good faith."[63] The New Jersey Court of Errors and Appeals held that a Jewish mother who had divorced her Roman Catholic husband had the right to rear her two children in the religion she saw fit. The father had contended that the right to control religious training is vested exclusively in the father. The court rejected this argument, pointing out that according to the state law each parent has an equal right in the matter and noting that in this case the custody of the children had been awarded to the mother.[64] Following a divorce of a Negro man and a white woman, the

[59] Louis Wirth and Herbert Goldhamer, op. cit., p. 364.
[60] B. T. Catupusan, "Filipino Intermarriage Problems in the United States," Sociology and Social Research, January–February, 1938, p. 266. Quoted in Milton L. Barron, People Who Intermarry, pp. 57–58.
[61] E. B. Reuter, Race Mixture, McGraw-Hill Book Company, 1931, p. 103, and The American Race Problem, p. 134. Quoted in Milton L. Barron, People Who Intermarry, p. 58. In the latter reference Reuter points out that in the colonial period the intermarriage laws prevented intermarriage but they could not check mis-cegenation.
[62] Milton L. Barron, People Who Intermarry, p. 58.
[63] Milton L. Barron, "Research on Intermarriage: A Survey of Accomplishments and Prospects," American Journal of Sociology, November, 1951, p. 253.
[64] Ibid., p. 253.

custody of their two children was awarded to the father. Later, the former wife petitioned an Illinois state court for award of custody of the children. Although the court found that custody could be awarded to either the mother or father, it ordered the custody to remain in the father on the ground that the children had predominantly Negro characteristics. On appeal the Illinois Appellate Court reversed this decision, holding that the trial court had abused its discretion in considering the children's racial characteristics to be determinative of the award of custody.[65]

Barron among others has pointed out the inconsistency in the conservative attitudes toward intermarriage held by many Americans and their activities in creating social and cultural conditions favoring intermarriage. The reference here is to public-school attendance, children being sent to colleges away from home, the campaigns against discrimination in employment and housing, and participation in interfaith activities. Inevitably an increase in intergroup contacts will lead to some intermarriages.[66]

Minority-group persons oppose anti-intermarriage laws not because they desire intermarriage, but because such laws (1) indicate inferior status, (2) leave minority women unprotected, and (3) limit freedom of choice in marriage.

Rationalization of the Opposition to Intermarriage

The taboo against intermarriage varies from section to section in its complexity and in the sanctions that enforce it. In the South's racial system such unions are unthinkable, and southern sentiments, attitudes, myths, dogmas, customs, and laws work to prevent them. As Charles Johnson points out, "In this culture area the proscription involves not merely a 'climate of opinion' but a total ideology incorporating moral perspectives." To illustrate, Johnson quotes a Georgia city minister: "The white race has never recognized the propriety of intermarriage. It's a sin to marry a Negro or to mix with them, just as it's a sin to peddle dope instead of teaching school. Such a man throws away his opportunities and debases himself by failing to use his opportunity as a white man and sinks to a lower standard. He allows his creative capacity, his traditions, his descendants to be corrupted. He pronounces a curse on all his descendants. He no longer has pure white blood in his veins. He has produced a mule in the human family."[67]

The widespread opposition to Negro-white intermarriage finds expression, especially in the South, in the slogan of "no social equality."

[65] *Race Relations Law Reporter*, April, 1957, p. 435.
[66] Milton L. Barron, "Research on Intermarriage: A Survey of Accomplishments and Prospects," p. 255.
[67] Charles S. Johnson, *op. cit.*, p. 222.

The term is vague; at times it covers and justifies all types of segregation and discrimination, whereas at other times it seems to be limited to intimate personal and social relations and intermarriage. Any questioning about the doctrine will bring a stout insistence on preventing amalgamation and "preserving the purity of the white race." The ban on intermarriage is concentrated on white women, and it covers both formal marriage and illicit sexual relations. When the possibility of intermarriage is used to defend the whole caste system, "it is assumed both that Negro men have a strong desire for 'intermarriage,' and that white women would be open to proposals from Negro men, *if* they are not guarded from even meeting them on an equal plane. . . . The conclusion follows that the whole system of segregation and discrimination is justified. Every single measure is defended as necessary to block 'social equality' which in its turn is defended as necessary to prevent 'intermarriage.' "[68]

Myrdal tentatively concludes that the doctrine of "no social equality" is a rationalization of social segregation and discrimination which enables white people to avoid making "an open demand for difference in social status between the two groups for its own sake." In other words, *"what white people really want is to keep Negroes in a lower status."*[69]

An interesting example of this position is the case of Davis Knight of Ellisville, Mississippi, who was sentenced in 1949 to five years in prison for violating the state's miscegenation laws. Knight does not have Negroid physical characteristics, nor has he lived in the Negro community. For seventy years his family has been considered white. Rumors spread about his ancestry, and he was brought to trial charged with marrying a white woman. Knight appealed the case on the ground that the alleged nonwhite "blood" in his ancestry was Indian rather than Negro.[70]

Determined opposition to intermarriage occurs occasionally in states where such alliances are legal, as is seen in a situation which developed in southern Ohio in 1949. Mrs. Lee Reynolds and her seven children were driven at night from the house the family occupied near Tupper Plains by a mob of seven or eight men. The mob cursed her, shot pistols into the air, burned a cross in the yard, and threatened harm to the family unless they went away. Mr. Reynolds, a white man, was in Clarksburg, West Virginia, attending a watchmakers' school. The Reynoldses had been married fifteen years, and their children ranged in age from ten months to fourteen years. Mrs. Reynolds went to her nearest neighbor's home, one-quarter of a mile away, and summoned the sheriff. When he arrived two hours later, the cross was still burning. The

[68] Gunnar Myrdal, *op. cit.*, p. 587.
[69] *Ibid.*, p. 591.
[70] R. L. Gillespie, "Community Relations," Cleveland *Plain Dealer*, January 9, 1949.

sheriff refused to protect the family for the rest of the night and made no attempt to investigate the attack. His advice to Mrs. Reynolds was to get out. Finally, he took the family in his car to Belpre Heights, Ohio, and from there the mother and her children walked eight miles into Belpre where Mrs. Reynolds' grandmother lives. One day later they went to Marietta, then to Columbus. Mrs. Reynolds believes that the reason for the attack was fear on the part of some Tupper Plains people that the children would intermarry with white families in the community.[71]

Gross exaggeration of the likelihood of intermarriage can be utilized as a device for keeping the Negro "in his place." It can be utilized as the justification for not hiring Negro men in certain jobs, or as an excuse for separation in places of public accommodation, separate schools, or residential segregation. As Drake and Cayton say, "The ultimate appeal for the maintenance of the color-line is always the simple, though usually irrelevant question, 'Would you want your daughter to marry a Negro?' To many white persons this is the core of the entire race problem."[72]

"Social Types" Who Intermarry

Little is known about the "social types" who intermarry. In Chicago most of the married couples seem to fall into four broad groups: (1) the intellectuals and "Bohemians," (2) the religious and political radicals, (3) the "sporting world," and (4) the stable middle class. In 1945 there were fewer than a dozen couples in the last category. The religious radicals are members of the Bahai movement. If the white spouse in a Negro-white marriage does not belong to one of these groups, he is likely to be a foreign-born person who is incompletely assimilated into American life and does not fully realize what intermarriage means, or did not at the time of marriage. Typically in Chicago, intermarried couples become acquainted through occupational contacts, or as neighbors living in the same district, or through a common friend. Few of these marriages were the result of school, political, or religious contacts. Ordinarily a Negro professional man, businessman, or politician would not risk losing his position of leadership by marrying a white woman, no matter what her status might be.[73]

[71] Cleveland *Call and Post*, February 17, 1949, p. 1.
[72] St. Clair Drake and Horace Cayton, *Black Metropolis*, Harcourt, Brace & Company, 1945, p. 129.
[73] *Ibid.*, pp. 138, 139, 148. In 1933 Resnik suggested a fourfold classification of social psychological types of Jews who intermarry. Later, Slotkin added four types to Resnik's original four. The latter list included (1) the emancipated person, (2) the rebellious person, (3) the detached person, (4) the adventurous person, (5) the unorganized or demoralized person, (6) the promiscuous person, (7) the marginal person, (8) the acculturated person. See R. B. Resnik, "Some Sociological Aspects

Problems of the Intermarried

The intermarried, especially the racially intermarried, in the United States face certain trials at the middle of the twentieth century.[74] First, there is the matter of keeping a job. It is often necessary for both partners to keep their marriage a secret. Those who seem least vulnerable to economic reprisals are civil service employees, independent business people, Negro physicians (in some northern communities), and labor leaders (in some unions). Second, it is often difficult to find a place to live. If the Negro partner is not light enough to pass, it will be necessary in most cases for the couple to live in the Negro community. There may be trouble within the Negro community since many of the most desirable hotels and apartment houses hesitate to rent to intermarried couples on the ground that they may not really be married and therefore are not "respectable." Third, the intermarried couple will have to face the social ostracism of society in general and perhaps of their friends and relatives in particular. A Japanese man reported concerning his marriage to a white woman: "I was married to a white woman at one time but my married life was not very happy and ended in a divorce. . . . I guess it is very hard for an American girl to marry a Japanese and be happy unless she is content to find all her happiness in her home. She is considered outcaste by most Americans and that is hard. Street car conductors make remarks that are not nice and neighbors say to my wife, 'If you like Japanese so well why don't you go down into the Japanese section to live where there are more of them?' "[75] The white spouse may commit "sociological suicide" and bury himself in the Negro community. In any case it is difficult for the white partner "to maintain steady friendships with other white people." Fourth, children of an intermarriage create problems. "One of these [problems] is the attitude of the parents and relatives of the white partner. To them, the Negro spouse is a difficult enough problem to adjust to, but

---

of Intermarriage of Jew and Non-Jew," *Social Forces*, 1933, vol. 12, pp. 94–102; and J. S. Slotkin, "Jewish-Gentile Intermarriage in Chicago," *American Sociological Review*, February, 1942, pp. 34–39. The present writers agree with Barron that "these concepts and types appear to have little value because they overlap considerably. Furthermore, they are nebulous to the extent that they may be used in classifying almost any individual, whether he inmarries or intermarries, in one or more types." They do not follow Barron in his failure "to see where any patterns or types of intermarrying individuals exist, either among Jews or any other groups." See Milton L. Barron, "The Incidence of Jewish Intermarriage in Europe and America," pp. 12–13.

[74] This discussion is based in part on St. Clair Drake and Horace Cayton, *op. cit.*, pp. 140–144, 155. For an interesting discussion of the problems involved in Negro-white marriage, see Anonymous, "My Daughter Married a Negro," *Harper's Magazine*, July, 1951, pp. 36–40.

[75] Jitsuichi Masuoka and Charles S. Johnson, "Orientals and Their Problems of Cultural Adjustment," *Social Science Source Documents*, no. 4, Social Science Institute, Fisk University, 1946, p. 77.

still is not a blood relative. The child of the intermarriage, however, is a blood relative, and must be either accepted or rejected. This can be a real emotional crisis. Some couples reported that they had not informed white relatives of the existence of children for this reason."[76]

Some interracial couples have refrained from having children because of possible difficulties or embarrassments, but they seem to have been the exceptions. Most of the Negro-white couples in Chicago have children, but they are Negro children. According to Drake and Cayton, good adjustment for the children of interracial marriages is difficult but not impossible. Such persons are usually not accepted by the white community unless they pass, but, in Chicago at least, the stigma of having a white parent is not very strong and the community may forget the interracial background completely. If the child of an interracial marriage wishes to pass but cannot do so, he may become seriously maladjusted. In Chicago such "in-betweens" constitute a small percentage of the children of mixed parentage. Most make a successful adjustment to life in the Negro community; a few pass completely over into the white group.[77]

In New York City, where half of the marriages of Issei males have been with white women, there is a Eurasian population of fair size. In Eurasian-white marriages virtually all trace of Japanese influence disappears. The Eurasians are said to be more thoroughly integrated into American life than are the Nisei.[78]

Passing

One of the results of marital and extramarital miscegenation is the appearance of a number of persons who cannot be distinguished physically from members of the majority group. Such individuals may or may not "pass" for whites. This question was discussed in Chapter 7 in connection with the avoidance type of adjustment of minority-group members.

There are no accurate figures on the extent of passing which occurs in the United States. Estimates of those who leave the Negro group permanently and are absorbed by white society vary from a few thousands to tens of thousands annually.[79] It is impossible to estimate the

[76] St. Clair Drake and Horace Cayton, op. cit., p. 155.
[77] Ibid., pp. 154, 158.
[78] Carey McWilliams, Prejudice—Japanese-Americans, Little, Brown & Company, 1944, p. 169.
[79] St. Clair Drake and Horace Cayton, op. cit., p. 160. See pp. 159–171 of this work for an excellent discussion of passing, and pp. 171–173 for a statement on the "black baby" bugaboo. See also Otto Klineberg (ed.), op. cit., pp. 301–319. Concerning the probable decline in "passing" by Negroes, Rose writes: "Using the census-vital statistics method, Hornell Hart estimated that during the decade 1900–10, 25,000 Negroes passed each year. Using almost the same method for the decade 1930–40, Eckard found that less than 2,000 Negroes a year were passing. Whether these figures are nearly accurate or not, the trend they indicate is in accord with

number of Negroes who pass only temporarily or occasionally. Some Negroes pass unintentionally as they go to theaters and restaurants where Negroes are not welcomed or obtain jobs because they are mistaken for whites without their realizing it. Probably most of those who "cross to the other side" remain in the white group, but thousands have returned after a trial period has shown that life for them in the Negro community is more enjoyable and more comfortable.

The several degrees of passing are:

1. Passing unintentionally.

2. Passing for convenience in patronizing beauty parlors, buying theater tickets, etc.

3. Passing for fun. "This behavior, too, can be engaged in without any feeling of guilt or disloyalty to the race; it is looked upon as having fun at the white folks' expense. Couples, and sometimes parties, will go to white cabarets and exclusive dancing places just to see what they are like and to get a thrill."[80]

4. Passing for economic necessity or advantage. Girls pass in order to obtain jobs as stenographers, clerks, receptionists, etc., which would be closed to them as Negroes. Men pass usually to get technical positions. "Usually the individual returns to the Negro community for all of his social contacts and uses his light skin color simply as a method of circumventing economic discrimination. Friendships with whites are generally avoided, as they would lead to complications."[81]

5. Final stage—permanent passing. "For a Negro to pass socially means sociological death and rebirth. It is extremely difficult, as one loses in the process his educational standing (if he has gone to a Negro school), intimate friends, family, and work references. People well established in the Negro world and older people seldom pass socially and completely. There is too much to lose and too little to be gained."[82]

Social Effects of Intermarriage

As Adams points out, if some members of the dominant racial or ethnic group marry members of a subordinate group, they will be inclined to give their children the advantages which are supposed to be reserved for the more privileged group. They will want property, education, political rights, and social status for their offspring. A large number of persons of mixed ancestry will gradually come into existence who will be indistinguishable from the members of the dominant group. Miscegenation then tends to increase, and finally the boundary becomes so

---

expert Negro opinion—namely, that passing has declined markedly since the period of low Negro morale from 1890 to 1910. Certainly there are few Negroes who are beginning to pass knowingly today." Arnold M. Rose, *The Negro's Morale*, University of Minnesota Press, 1949, pp. 113–114.

[80] St. Clair Drake and Horace Cayton, *op. cit.*, p. 162.

[81] *Ibid.*, pp. 162–163.

[82] *Ibid.*, p. 163.

indistinct that discriminatory regulations cannot be enforced. It is for this reason that the dominant group, if it is to remain dominant, "must prohibit by law and sentiment" the marriage of its members to members of the dominated group, and such illegitimate children of mixed ancestry as may be born must be denied the status of the "race" of superior privilege.[83]

Factors Which Facilitate Intermarriage

A number of factors seem to facilitate intermarriage. One is the attitudes of individuals toward intermarriage. The nature and the effectiveness of these attitudes are determined by the marriage mores (types of marriage mores: nineteenth-century Boston, Los Angeles in 1924–1933, Chicago in 1948, the southern and border states) and the other influencing factors to be mentioned shortly. In his study of intermarriage in Derby, Connecticut, Barron found that attitudes alone are not responsible for intermarriage patterns.[84] There were general similarities between intermarriage attitudes and practices, but the attitudes were more liberal than the practices.

The second group of factors are demographic, and include the sex ratio and the numerical size of minority groups. A marked disparity in the distribution of the sexes, as is the case with the Filipinos in the United States, favors intermarriage. The Chinese in New York City are also a case in point.

The Chinese community of New York City . . . has functioned throughout its history as an economic outpost to which the natives in certain districts in eastern Kwantung province come to work for a period of years, send remittances home (one in three of the men has a wife in China), accumulate capital, and then return to live in comfort. In such circumstances, the general sex ratio must, of course, be high (8:1 in 1930), while the ratio between males and females of reproductive age is naturally very much higher—14:1 in 1930. Therefore, there were in 1930 fewer than 500 complete conjugal families in New York City's population of about 10,000 Chinese. . . . Such an abnormal sex ratio increases pressures favorable to out-group marriage. In fact, intergroup marriages exceeded intragroup marriages during the most abnormal years, but it is interesting to note the reassertion of the endogamous tendency as the number of Chinese women increased.[85]

Generally speaking, intermarriage varies indirectly and breadth of selection varies directly with the relative size of the minority group.

[83] R. Adams, op. cit., pp. 51–52.
[84] Milton L. Barron, *People Who Intermarry*, p. 326. Our treatment of the factors which facilitate intermarriage is an adaptation and extension of Barron's analysis of why people intermarry.
[85] Shepard Schwartz, "Chinese Marriages in New York City, 1931–38," in *Race and Racialism* (a symposium from a seminar on Race Problems conducted by Cedric Dover in the Graduate Faculty of Political and Social Science, New School for Social Research, Fall Term, 1948), p. 29.

The third set of factors which affect intermarriage rates are the propinquous factors. They include place of residence, place of work, place of recreation, place of education, etc. These factors were mentioned previously in connection with Drake and Cayton's study of Negro-white intermarriage in Chicago. Segregated minority groups tend to in-marry, whereas dispersed minorities tend to intermarry. (One should not infer a causal connection here. It may be that dispersed minorities intermarry more for the same reason that they are dispersed, namely, a lower prejudice against them.)

The fourth category of factors influencing the incidence of intermarriage consists of cultural similarities. Included here are similarity of European background, length of residence in the United States, occupational and economic class, amount and type of education, church affiliation or lack of it, and linguistic similarity. We referred ealier to the importance of cultural similarities in intermarriage in Los Angeles and to the practice of most of the men in Burlington, Vermont, whose families have been here for three or more generations, of taking wives of the third generation or more. The New Haven study shows the importance of similar religious backgrounds in intermarriage in that city. Barron concludes that those who do not recreate in organizations affiliated with their own churches or nationalities or who "belong to and recreate at secular and non-ethnic organizations" tend to intermarry. We mentioned the tendency of majority women to marry minority men whose socioeconomic status exceeded theirs; Drake and Cayton stress the importance of occupational similarities.

To these rather specific factors we might add the general social conditions of "political emancipation, intermingling of culture, and the spread of tolerance and growth of fellowship" in modern times.[86] Barron suggests several hypotheses which need to be tested by empirical studies: (1) that postadolescence and the premarital years constitute an age of rebellion against the parents and are conducive to intermarriage, (2) that the "romantic complex" of American culture is a factor in the individualistic choice of a marriage partner; (3) that self-hatred among many members of minority groups plays a role in intermarriage, and (4) that the drive toward upward social mobility may find expression in out-marriage.[87]

Factors That Retard Intermarriage

Most of the parents of persons considering intermarriage use their influence to prevent it. There are no laws in the United States for-

[86] S. E. Goldstein, *The Meaning of Marriage and the Foundations of the Family,* Bloch Publishing Company, 1942, p. 161.

[87] Milton L. Barron, "Research on Intermarriage: A Survey of Accomplishments and Prospects," p. 251.

bidding interfaith or internationality marriages, but twenty-seven states prohibit Negro-white intermarriage and a number of states ban other kinds of interracial marriage. We indicated earlier in this chapter that such laws are rather ineffective if the mores do not support them. With the exception of certain subcultures in the United States, the mores contain a strong taboo against interracial marriages and to a lesser degree against interfaith marriages.

Some religious faiths, through teaching and the personal influence of clergymen, have always tried to discourage intermarriage.[88] According to the *Catholic Encyclopaedia*, the Catholic Church was particularly opposed to Catholic-Jewish intermarriages " 'owing to the intense Jewish hatred for the sacred name of Christ.' " Even today it is more difficult to obtain dispensations for such marriages than for marriages of Catholics with "heretical" Christians.[89]

Most Jews have long opposed intermarriage on two grounds: first, because of the importance that the home has in religious life, and second, because there is no other way to preserve the Jewish community. On the first point Finkelstein says: "Because of the special place that the home occupies in Judaism as a center of religious life and worship, almost co-ordinate with the synagogue itself, Judaism holds it essential that both parties to a Jewish marriage be members of the Jewish faith. There is, of course, no objection to marriage with a sincere convert to Judaism. But it is not possible for the home to function in the manner prescribed by Jewish law unless both husband and wife are of the Jewish faith."[90] The second point is well summed up by Ruppin:

The restriction of marriage to co-religionists formed the strongest bond between the Jews until far into the nineteenth century, making them into a homogeneous unit, able to show a unique power of resistance against the assimilating forces of Christianity and Islam. Even Jews who have become indifferent to their religion often remain averse to marrying outside their community; this is perhaps the last remnant of their national consciousness.

[88] For a detailed statement on Roman Catholic, Jewish, Protestant, and Greek Orthodox regulation of religious intermarriage, see Milton L. Barron, *People Who Intermarry*, pp. 22–47.

[89] J. F. Doherty states the position of the Catholic Church on interracial marriage as follows: "1. The Roman Catholic Church in no wise forbids interracial marriage as such. 2. The natural right to marry includes also the natural right to marry the person of one's own choice, to marry this person regardless of race. 3. The exercise of this right involves great benefits to the individual and to society regardless of the undesirable concomitants in many sections of this country. The parties to an interracial marriage may justifiably enter such a marriage to secure these benefits despite the undesirable consequences they may suffer. 4. The entrance upon an interracial marriage is in itself, a morally good act." J. F. Doherty, *Moral Problems of Interracial Marriage*, Catholic University of America Press, 1949, p. 154; quoted in Sister M. Annella, *op. cit.*, p. 384.

[90] Louis Finkelstein (ed.), *The Jews, Their History, Culture and Religion*, Harper & Brothers, 1950, vol. 2, p. 1329.

They feel that, although they have dropped the Jewish ritual, they will remain Jews so long as they and their children intermarry with Jews, and that only a mixed marriage would finally separate them from their people. Indeed, intermarriage, as soon as it appears on a large scale, marks the end of Judaism.[91]

Intermarriage is opposed by some Jews even when the non-Jew joins the Jewish group because "an alien element is introduced." According to Goldstein, the feeling that this alien element is "a source of weakness and danger" has become stronger in recent years owing to the spread of a nationalistic spirit among the Jewish people.[92]

Gordon notes that there has been considerable change in the attitudes of Jews in Minneapolis toward intermarriage. He points out that traditionally intermarriage was considered calamitous and that the early Jewish residents in Minneapolis felt sick when they heard about it. "When it occurred among the children of Orthodox Jews, parents 'sat Shiva'—they observed the traditional seven-day period of mourning as if the child had died. Parents were distraught and ashamed to face their friends."[93] Now, despite disapproval, the out-marriage of Jews takes place in ever increasing numbers. According to Gordon, nearly all those who intermarry remain in the Jewish group. "They join synagogues and temples, the golf club, and other organizations. They usually go to the Reform or Conservative synagogues, feeling, correctly, that their wives will be more readily accepted than at Orthodox ones. Even when the wife has not been formally converted to Judaism, she is permitted to join the women's organization of several of the synagogues and occasionally even plays a role of some prominence in its affairs."[94]

As far as Negro-white marriage is concerned, many white people will continue

. . . to exploit the fear of intermarriage as a means of retaining economic dominance, and as a devastating question to be raised in connection with any concessions, no matter how small, which the Negro community requests. A few intermarriages will no doubt continue to take place, as well as clandestine "affairs," but "crossing the line" is not uppermost in the minds of the Negroes. Relaxation of the taboos against intermarriage is something

[91] Arthur Ruppin, *The Jewish Fate and Future*, The Macmillan Company, 1940, p. 106.

[92] S. E. Goldstein, *op. cit.*, pp. 161–162. Goldstein states that forty years ago the Central Conference of American Rabbis passed a resolution declaring that " 'mixed marriages are contrary to the tradition of the Jewish religion, and should, therefore, be discouraged by the American rabbinate.' " In the Burlington, Vermont, study, fifty-three of the fifty-seven Jewish persons interviewed believed that Jews should not intermarry for these reasons: the dangers of assimilation, family conflict, and child disorganization. E. L. Anderson, *op. cit.*, p. 188.

[93] Albert I. Gordon, *op. cit.*, pp. 205–206.

[94] *Ibid.*, pp. 206, 207.

white people are most reluctant to grant. It is also the "concession" which Negroes, as a group, are least likely to request. That it looms so large in the white mind is the irony of race relations in Midwest Metropolis [Chicago].[95]

The Success or Failure of Intermarriage

Evidence concerning the success or failure of intermarriage is not extensive. Intermarriage—like in-marriage—does not always turn out well. Statistics on divorces for interracial couples are not available, but some students believe that the divorce rate is no higher, and may not be as high, for the interracial marriages as for intraracial marriages.[96] In the event of marital difficulty, it may be difficult to discover whether the racial factor is directly or indirectly involved.

In a study of 325 mixed marriages in New York City (48 cases of interracial marriage, 118 cases of internationality marriage, and 159 cases of interfaith marriage), Baber found that the happy marriages outnumbered the unhappy ones by three to one. However, his sample was small, and, as he points out, there were at least two possible sources of error. First, there may have been some unconscious selection of cases through a neglect of divorce cases; and second, it is possible that outside observers rated a couple's happiness too high. For the groups in his study, "the degree of happiness varied inversely with the degree of difference in culture or color."[97]

By 1936, 8000 of the original 10,000 marriages of American soldiers and French women after World War I had ended in divorce.[98] Such intermarriages are fraught with more and greater difficulties than marriages between native-born persons of different nationality backgrounds, and they are probably less likely to succeed than intermarriages involving foreign-born men and native-born women.

Comparative data on marital adjustment in intermarriage are found in studies made in Panama and Britain. Among other findings, Biesanz and Smith report that the marriage of a Panamanian woman to an American man has a greater chance of success than the marriage of an American woman to Panamanian man.[99] Collins shows that white women in Britain who marry colored men from British West Africa and the West Indies play an important role as intermediary between the wife's family and the white community, seeking to gain concessions from the privi-

[95] St. Clair Drake and Horace Cayton, op. cit., p. 173.
[96] Ibid., pp. 153–154.
[97] R. E. Baber, "A Study of 325 Mixed Marriages," American Sociological Review, October, 1937, p. 716.
[98] E. M. Duval and Reuben Hill, When You Marry, D. C. Heath and Company, 1945, p. 117.
[99] John Biesanz and Luke M. Smith, "Adjustment of Interethnic Marriages on the Isthmus of Panama," American Sociological Review, December, 1951, pp. 819–822.

leged group.[100] Little points out that disapproval and ostracism of white friends and acquaintances lead the white wife to identify with the colored group, but when the child leaves school he may find it difficult to develop friendships with white persons at work without giving up the colored friends of his earlier years.[101]

Considering the fact that the people in fifty Negro-white intermarriages in Philadelphia married later than the general population, and that a sizable proportion of them had had previous marital experience, Golden concluded that these marriages probably had a good chance to survive.[102]

An exploratory study of twenty American-Japanese couples did not confirm the belief that such marriages would have a high rate of failure because of the assumption that they were hasty and involved sharp cultural conflict. "The serviceman's stay in Japan averaged about two years. Severe cultural conflict was not found in in-group and out-group relationships; husbands identified themselves with their wives' circles; there were no regrets and no serious in-law problems. Coöperation and adaptation were common, wives learning English, and there were no religious conflicts. A study of age at marriage, educational attainment, residence separate from in-laws, first marriage, and average number of children all indicated stability rather than conflict."[103]

In Slotkin's investigation of 183 Jewish-gentile marriages, 57 percent of the intermarried people were either partially or entirely accepted by both families. Sixteen percent of the gentiles were not accepted by their own families, and 27 percent were not accepted by the family of the spouse. The nonacceptance by the Jewish families was higher, with 20 percent of the Jews not being accepted by their own families and 23 percent not being accepted by the family of the spouse.[104]

With respect to the question of success in the Jewish-gentile mar-

[100] Sydney F. Collins, "The Social Position of White and 'Half-Caste' Women in Colored Groupings in Britain," *American Sociological Review*, December, 1951, pp. 796–802.

[101] Kenneth Little, "The Position of Colored People in Britain," *Phylon*, First Quarter, 1954, p. 62.

[102] Joseph Golden, "Patterns of Negro-White Intermarriage," *American Sociological Review*, April, 1954, p. 147. See also his "Characteristics of the Negro-White Intermarried in Philadelphia," in *ibid.*, April, 1953, pp. 177–183.

[103] G. J. Schnepp and A. M. Yui, "Cultural and Marital Adjustment of Japanese War Brides," *American Journal of Sociology*, July, 1955, pp. 48–50. According to Schnepp and Yui, the International Institute estimates that there are from 40 to 50 Japanese war brides in the St. Louis area, and the Chicago Resettlers Committee estimates that between 2000 and 2500 reside in the Chicago area. Of the 15,500 marriages which went through the American consulates in Japan between 1945 and 1954, at least two-thirds are estimated to have been American-Japanese war marriages. *Ibid.*, p. 48.

[104] J. S. Slotkin, "Adjustment in Jewish-Gentile Intermarriages," *Social Forces*, December, 1942, pp. 226–230.

riages in Minneapolis, Gordon remarks that the number of divorces between intermarried couples does not appear to be high. He adds that if another measure of success or failure in marriage is considered, the number of intermarried couples who "do not get along" seems to him to be rather high.[105]

A study of 4108 mixed and nonmixed marriages among the parents of college students in Michigan showed that 4.4 percent of the marriages ended in divorce when both parents were Catholic, 5.2 percent if both were Jewish, 6.0 percent if both were Protestant, 14.1 percent in mixed Catholic-Protestant marriages, and 17.9 percent if neither parent was religious. Marriages between Catholic men and Protestant women had the highest divorce rate of all, 20.6 percent.[106] In an analysis of the marital status of 6548 families of public and parochial school children in Spokane, Washington, Weeks found a divorce rate of 3.8 percent among Catholics, 10.0 for Protestants, 17.4 in mixed marriages, and 23.9 if there was no religion.[107] Bell found in studying 13,528 families of mixed and nonmixed Maryland marriages that the divorce rate among Jews was 4.6 percent, among Catholics 6.4 percent, among Protestants 6.8 percent, 15.2 percent in mixed marriages, and 16.7 percent if there was no religion.[108]

A higher percentage of those who intermarry than of those who in-marry may be unconventional persons. Since studies of success or failure in marriage have shown that unconventional individuals are poorer marital risks than conventional persons, the marital difficulties of some of the intermarried may lie more in their personality tendencies than in their intermarriage. At least this hypothesis is worth testing empirically.

When husbands and wives in the Burgess and Cottrell study were classified in the broad religious categories of Catholic, Jewish, and Protestant, no differences of statistical importance appeared between the happiness of couples of the same and of different religious beliefs. This study covers only the early years of marriage; as these authors suggest, the real test would come after the sixth year of marriage when conflict typically arises over the religious rearing of the child.[109]

Conclusion

Our conclusions on intermarriage may be stated briefly as follows:
1. From a statistical standpoint, the chances for success in marriage

---

[105] Albert I. Gordon, op. cit., p. 208.

[106] J. T. Landis and M. G. Landis, Building a Successful Marriage, Prentice-Hall, Inc., 1948, p. 139.

[107] H. Ashley Weeks, "Differential Divorce Rates by Occupation," Social Forces, March, 1943, p. 336.

[108] H. M. Bell, Youth Tell Their Story, American Council on Education, 1938, p. 21.

[109] E. W. Burgess and L. Cottrell, Predicting Success or Failure in Marriage, Prentice-Hall, Inc., 1939, pp. 87–88.

may be somewhat less for intermarriage than for in-marriage in the United States at mid-century.

2. The legality of intermarriage is an important aspect of equal civil rights.

3. Race mixture is not biologically inadvisable.

4. Intermarriage on a large scale would produce a relatively homogeneous population, physically and culturally. The elimination of intergroup conflicts based on race and culture would have societal advantages, although some would lament the passing of cultural pluralism.

5. A great increase in intermarriage rates in the United States in the foreseeable future is highly unlikely.

CHAPTER 18

Minorities and Religion

One of the most sensitive indexes of the majority-minority situation in a society is to be found in the religious patterns. It is well established in the sociology of religion that the religious beliefs and institutional structures of a group not only show intrinsic religious aspects but reflect its secular position and the secular problems it faces. Our discussion in this chapter will be primarily concerned with some of the ways in which religious practices—of both dominant and minority groups—reflect and affect intergroup relations.

Negro Churches

Negro churches are of many varieties, indicating the wide differences among Negroes in all of the forces that affect religious life—occupation, residence, education, secular group membership, and the like. Approximately half of the Negro population of the United States are members of some Christian church, perhaps 7,500,000 of them being Protestants and about 500,000 being Catholics. Most of the Negro Protestants and about two-thirds of the Negro Roman Catholics are in segregated churches.[1] As we shall see below, this pattern is beginning to change, but quantitatively the shift is not yet important.

[1] See John LaFarge, *The Catholic Viewpoint on Race Relations*, Doubleday & Company, Inc., 1956, p. 22; see also Liston Pope, "Caste in the Church," *Survey Graphic*, January, 1947, p. 59. Loescher's estimate of Negro Protestants is 8,000,000. F. S. Loescher, *The Protestant Church and the Negro*, Association Press, 1948, p. 76. *The Negro Handbook* (Florence Murray, ed., The Macmillan Company, 1949, pp. 288–289) lists 7,160,889 members of nine all-Negro Baptist denominations, 1,794,577 members of six all-Negro Methodist denominations, 85,000 members of three all-Negro Presbyterian denominations, and 11,521 members of the Negro Mission of the Lutheran Synodical Conference of North America.

Urban Negro Churches

A more or less typical distribution of Negro churchgoers in the urban North is shown in the data on Chicago. This city's 200,000 Negro church members are distributed among nearly 500 churches in more than thirty denominations. The two Negro National Baptist Conventions include almost half of the churches and more than two-thirds of the members. Neither the Negro Baptist congregations nor the ministers have contacts of any consequence with white Baptists. Other denominations in Chicago include three Methodist denominations, the colored Holiness, Spiritualist, and Community churches. In addition, there are a number of local denominations and "such all-Negro 'cults' as the African Orthodox Church, the Christian Catholics, the Temple of Moorish Science, and numerous fly-by-night groups organized around enterprising and untrained preachers."[2] More than fifty Negro churches in Chicago seat between 500 and 2000 persons, but three-fourths of the Negro churches are "store-front" or house churches which average fewer than twenty-five members. There were "missions" in the black belt before the big migration from the South began, but the large number of store-front churches now in existence seems to be the result of a lack of buildings at the beginning of the northward trek.

In Chicago, 10 percent of the Negro churches, but less than 10 percent of the church members, are affiliated with "white" denominations— Methodist Episcopal, Episcopal, Presbyterian, Congregational, Roman Catholic, Lutheran, Christian Scientist, Seventh-Day Adventist, and Disciples of Christ. Negroes are not welcomed in many of the white congregations of these churches, nor do they have much influence in the national organizations of these denominations. A number of "white" churches have educational or welfare projects for Negroes throughout the country.

An interesting study of forty Negro churches in Chicago resulted in a classification of four types of worshipers: (1) the ecstatic cults, or the crowd that dances; (2) semidemonstrative groups, or the groups which indulge in demonstrative assent; (3) deliberative churches, or the congregations which prefer sermon-centered services; and (4) liturgical denominations, or churches with formal liturgy. Daniel classifies the ritual elements of the four types of services under the headings: Equipment; Liturgy and Sacerdotalism; Hymn Themes; Prayer Themes; and Sermon Topics. In addition, elements of Emotional Lay Participation are cited for the first two types; Special Aspects of Cult Rituals, and Testimony Stereotypes are given for the ecstatic cults; Invitation and Reception of New Members, and Offerings and Usher Services for

[2] St. Clair Drake and Horace Cayton, *Black Metropolis*, Harcourt, Brace & Company, 1945, p. 413.

the semidemonstrative services. The elements of the Sermon Topics are given here to illustrate this analysis.

SERMON TOPICS IN FOUR TYPES OF URBAN NEGRO CHURCHES

I. The Ecstatic Cults	Some conventional sermons and themes, but usually the sermons are simply pastoral expositions of scripture passages read by members of the congregation, a verse at a time. The principal emphases are sexual sins and their consequences; healing by fasting and prayer; God helps the poor.
II. Semidemonstrative Cults	"Wisdom"; "The Ten Virgins"; "The Peril of Knowing Too Much"; "Spiritual Mountain Climbing"; "A Great Experience"; "The Value of Knowing, Believing, Trusting the Living God"; "An Invitation and Its Refusal"; "Love"; "None Given"; "The Folly of Our Excuses."
III. Deliberative Churches	"The Triumphal Entry"; "Evidences of Life"; "Knowing God"; "Prayer"; "What Kind of Gospel Does Today Need?"; "Building a New World for God"; "The Miracle of Christ"; "Replenishment"; "Transfiguration"; "Dead Folks Walking Around"; "The Failure of the Church"; "Man"; "God's House"; "The Work of a Son."
IV. Liturgical Denominations	"The Church and Fiery Trials"; "The Great Supper"; "The Holy Catholic Church"; "The Prayer of Consecration"; "Easter Day"; etc.[3]

Many lower-class Negroes are members of Baptist, Pentecostal, and Spiritualist churches, and some are Catholics. However, the usual lower-class religious group is an emotional, store-front cult. Persons of lower-middle-class status in Chicago's black belt support the semidemonstrative churches. Those with the smallest incomes in the lower middle class tend to affiliate with the smaller Baptist and Methodist churches; the others join the larger churches. These devotees are profound believers in the power of the supernatural, but there are both respectable and nonrespectable lower-middle-class people who regard strong religious devotion as a symbol of lower-class status. For them religion is something sponsored by the upper classes as a means of controlling the unsuspect-

---

[3] V. E. Daniel, "Ritual and Stratification in Chicago Negro Churches," *American Sociological Review*, June, 1942, pp. 352–358.

ing, and they maintain an indifferent or resentful attitude toward all religious activities. The colored upper middle class shares the general sentiments and ambitions and follows the behavior patterns of the middle class. Religiously this group shows the greatest variation of all the social classes in the Negro community. The Congregational, Episcopal, and Presbyterian churches are most popular, but some upper-middle-class people belong to Methodist and Baptist churches. Ritual and ceremony are much like those found in upper-class white churches. The most important activities of the Negro upper class are not found in church-centered affairs. Unless members of this class are identified with lower- or middle-class churches for business or professional reasons, they tend to be affiliated with such ritualistic or deliberative churches as the Episcopal, Presbyterian, and Congregational.[4]

Father Divine's Cult. Father Divine's cult is perhaps the most interesting, and certainly it is the most influential, of the urban Negro cults. It is impossible to obtain an accurate estimate of the size of his following. There are tens of thousands of public devotees, mainly Negro but not exclusively so. These are mainly lower- or lower-middle-class people, but there are numerous exceptions. Father Divine has established dozens of missions or "heavens" in the United States and in other countries, and in them dwell one class of public members (angels).

He [the angel] has renounced the things of this world completely. He no longer plans his own life, but lives it completely in accordance with the instruction of Father Divine. If he is the possessor of worldly goods, he disposes of them in a manner agreed upon between him and the leader. He does not choose his own vocation or business, but places himself at the disposition of the Father, making himself completely subject to Father Divine's suggestion, instruction, or command. Literally everything which such a member receives, the bread he eats, the raiment he wears, his lodging and work, whatever personal remuneration he may receive, comes through the direction of Father Divine.[5]

The other category of public followers consists of persons who subscribe to the beliefs and practices of the cult but otherwise live as ordinary citizens in the community. In addition to these two classes of believers there are thousands of "secret" followers who are influenced by the true devotees of Father Divine although they have no first-hand

---

[4] *Ibid.*, pp. 359–360.

[5] A. H. Fauset, *Black Gods of the Metropolis*, University of Pennsylvania Press, 1944, pp. 59–60. This book contains the best account of urban Negro cults yet published. An interesting account of a banquet in one of the "heavens" and reports on Father Divine's speeches and publications are given in Hadley Cantril, *The Psychology of Social Movements*, John Wiley & Sons, Inc., 1941, pp. 132–133. Sherif and Cantril explain the maintenance of unity within the kingdom by "the almost complete break most of the children have made with the outer world." *Ibid.*, pp. 128–129. Cases are cited to illustrate "the complete incompatibility of Father's microcosm and the world of reality." *Ibid.*, pp. 137–138.

contact with him. No one in the Father Divine Peace Mission Movement questions the fact that Father Divine is God.

RURAL NEGRO CHURCHES

Religious gatherings were the first forms of association permitted under the slave system, and the first leaders of Negroes were religious teachers. The other-worldliness doctrine provided a needed emotional escape from slavery and later from economic poverty and cultural isolation. Many of the patterns of religious belief in the rural Negro church were based upon the practices of lower-class whites. Some of the borrowed religious sentiments were at odds with existing social values.

The rural church is often regarded as the outstanding social institution in the Negro community and the only one which provides an effective organization of the Negro group. Charles Johnson distinguishes the plantation church from the church outside the plantation area. The plantation church is small and neglected, with a congregation consisting of 75 or 100 hard-working sharecroppers and a few struggling owners and their children. The average preacher is skilled in histrionic devices and "acts out" the journey to heaven and other favorite themes. His sermons are long and repetitious, and the congregation responds frequently with shouts of approval. Usually several persons experience hysterical seizures during which they testify to being saved or bemoan a hard life or some unjust treatment.

The rural church in the nonplantation areas has been more strongly influenced by the towns and cities. It provides a more intelligent ministry and a type of Sunday school that is more subject to innovations and is characterized by greater participation by young people in the religious program. "The sermon is still directed to the older people, the church is still dominated by the deacons and other elders, emphasis is still on 'old time religion,' and many forms of innocent recreation are still banned; occasionally, however, there is a disposition to provide within the church a substitute for wordly pleasures denied, and at the same time there is, as a result of an improved cultural level, a more serious emphasis upon a code of conduct consistent with the standards of the larger culture."[6]

TWO INTERPRETATIONS OF THE RELIGIOSITY OF THE NEGRO MASSES

What aspects of the past experience and the contemporary situation of Negro Americans are important in influencing their religious life?

---

[6] Charles S. Johnson, *Growing Up in the Black Belt*, American Council on Education, 1941, p. 146. See also the same author's *Shadow of the Plantation*, University of Chicago Press, 1934, chap. 5. Interesting accounts of revival meetings in rural Negro churches are given in Hortense Powdermaker, *After Freedom*, The Viking Press, Inc., 1939, pp. 253–256; and in John Dollard, *Caste and Class in a Southern Town*, Yale University Press, 1937, pp. 226–230, 231–232.

Two different answers have been given to this question. Although they contradict each other to some degree, they can also be combined in a helpful way.

The Influence of African Cultures. According to M. J. Herskovits, the strong interest which Negroes have shown in religion, and the style of their religious patterns, cannot be attributed to "racial" characteristics, nor can they be explained entirely by "a quasi-Freudian interpretation of the socio-economic situation of the Negro."[7] Herskovits attributes part of the ordinary American Negro's concern about religion to ancient African traditions which have persisted in the New World.[8] The West Indian hybrid cults are seen as the central link in the cultural chain stretching from Africa to the United States.[9]

Herskovits points out that everywhere in Negro societies the supernatural is a "major focus of interest."

The tenability of this position is apparent when it is considered how, in an age marked by skepticism, the Negro has held fast to belief. Religion is vital, meaningful, and understandable to the Negroes of this country because, as in the West Indies and West Africa, it is not removed from life, but has been deeply integrated into the daily round. It is because of this, indeed, that everywhere compensation in terms of the supernatural is so immediately acceptable to this underprivileged folk—and causes them, in contrast to other underprivileged groups elsewhere in the world, to turn to religion rather than to political action or other outlets for their frustration. It must therefore be assumed that not only in particular aspects of Negro religious life . . . but in the very foundations of Negro religion, the African past plays a full part. And we must hold this in mind as we turn to a review of those manifestations of Negro religion which, like its fundamental sanctions, can be traced to a pre-American past.[10]

A clear example of the persistence of an African religious trait in the New World is the association of water, especially of rivers, with sacred ceremonies. Herskovits refers to the invariable visits to the river or ocean among the Yoruba and the Ashanti, and in Dahomey; and he mentions river rituals observed in Dutch Guiana and Haiti. One of the present writers has called attention to the many references to water in the *vodun* cult of northern Haiti. The capital of the *Zanges* (*vodun* gods) is said to be "under the water"; the favorite abodes of many *Zanges* are near springs, rivers, or ponds, or under bridges; and visits are made

[7] He uses the terms "bent" and "drive," but it is clear that he is not referring to innate biological phenomena. M. J. Herskovits, *The Myth of the Negro Past,* Harper & Brothers, 1941, p. 207.

[8] E. Franklin Frazier, G. B. Johnson, and several other students, as well as A. H. Fauset, do not share this interpretation. See *ibid.,* pp. 3–6.

[9] *Ibid.,* p. 224.

[10] *Ibid.,* p. 207. This is the outstanding work on Africanisms in the New World. It should be read in entirety by all who are interested in American Negro life. Chapter 7, "The Contemporary Scene: Africanisms in Religious Life," is the most important chapter as far as the present subject is concerned.

during some ceremonies to sacred places near some body of water.[11] As Herskovits indicates, the water rituals of Negro Baptists in the United States are those of baptism, and the concept of crossing the river Jordan at the time of death is a concept which any African would understand.

The abundance of beliefs concerning snakes, both in Africa and in the New World, is another example of Negro religious continuities. Rainbow serpents are prominent in the Dahoman religion, and they have their counterparts in Dutch Guiana and Haiti. While doing field work in the Plaisance region, one of the present writers was told that he should never throw a stone at a snake lest the snake "eat" him. Since there are no poisonous snakes in Haiti, this reverence for the snake appears to be an Africanism. The Haitian peasant rationalization of this taboo on injuring a snake is that it may be a *Zange* (god) in disguise. Herskovits concludes that the wealth of Negro beliefs concerning snakes in the southern United States indicates a preoccupation that is significant.

Pouring liquor and tossing morsels of food on the ground for the gods is a West African religious custom which is found in one form or another in Haiti, Trinidad, Guiana, and New Orleans.[12]

The importance of the crossroads in West African belief has carried over to Haiti, Guiana, Trinidad, and the United States. The guardian of the crossroads (Legba in Dahomey, Elegbara in Yoruba belief) is found both in peasant religious ceremonies in parts of the New World and in the practice of magic. His United States counterpart, the Devil, must be propitiated at the crossroads.

As Herskovits points out, ghosts, witches, and vampires are known in Africa as in Europe, and the problem becomes one of specifying the African aspects of these beings. The same methods of discovering, holding, and punishing witches and vampires are found in Nigeria, Dahomey, among the Ashanti, and in Jamaica, Haiti, Guiana, Barbados, and Trinidad. For example, sprinkling red pepper in the discarded skin of a witch while the witch is going about the countryside performing evil deeds is a technique of witch-killing common to West Africa, many southern states, the Sea Islands, the Bahamas, and Haiti.

Herskovits' interpretation of the phenomena of sanctification and possession in the Negro cults of the United States differs, then, from

---

[11] George E. Simpson, "*The Belief System of Haitian Vodun*," American Anthropologist, January–March, 1945, pp. 35 ff.; "Haitian Magic," *Social Forces*, October, 1940, pp. 95 ff.; "The Vodun Service in Northern Haiti," *American Anthropologist*, April–June, 1940, pp. 236 ff.; "Two Vodun-Related Ceremonies," *Journal of American Folklore*, January–March, 1948, pp. 49–52.

[12] M. J. Herskovits, *op. cit.*, p. 236; and George E. Simpson, "The Vodun Service in Northern Haiti," p. 240. The following sentence appears in the latter reference: "The priest then offers libations to the gods, throws white flour and pours liqueur on the ground, and tosses fried corn in the air."

that given by Fauset. The former sees a correspondence in the relationship between the "sanctified" and their God in such cults and the relationship between cult initiates in Dahomey and their deities. Possession by a god is the outstanding manifestation of West African religion. The motor behavior of Dahomans and North American Negroes during spirit possession links the two areas in a manner which cannot be questioned.

Herskovits has done more than anyone else to fill in the steps by which the worship of the African gods, with drums, rattles, and songs, was transformed into the forms of religious practice found today in the Negro cults in the United States.[13] The following summary illustrates the type of analysis which his work provides.

In the coastal area of Guiana, the behavior of the drummers and singers who accompany the possessed dancers is almost identical with that witnessed in West Africa. The same relaxed movements of the fingers as the drummers sometimes even play rhythms identical with West African beats on the drumheads, the same swaying of the bodies by the singers that makes of their singing itself a dance, and the same cupped hands with which the clapping is done, all testify to the manner in which these descendants of Africa are but repeating motor habits current in the homeland of their ancestors. There is likewise little difference between the two regions—or, for that matter, between these two and what is found in the United States "shouting" churches—in the meaning of such a rite for the participants.[14]

The Functional Interpretation of Negro Religious Tendencies. In addition and to some degree in opposition to the emphasis on African influences, the functional approach to religious movements is more concerned with the contemporary situation to which Negroes are responding. From this point of view, religious practices and beliefs are efforts to make a difficult situation more meaningful and bearable and, more recently in urban areas, to help oppose that situation. According to Fauset, members of the urban Negro cults feel that they are moving up spiritually when they become attached to an esoteric church. To be converted to an evangelical faith is only the first step; one must then be sanctified; and finally, one must be filled with the Holy Spirit. The third step may involve evidence of an ability to speak in tongues, a miraculous healing, the sound of a heavenly voice, or a special dream or vision. To be one of the elect, it is necessary to have taken all three steps. By this series of exacting demands, disprivileged persons struggle with the meaninglessness and harshness of their situation.

In addition to aiding the specifically religious quest for salvation, Negro churches perform a number of social functions. These are not different in kind from the functions found in the churches of other

[13] M. J. Herskovits, op. cit., pp. 218–221.
[14] Ibid., p. 219.

minority peoples or of the white majority population. However, they are of special importance in Negro churches because of the Negro group's social isolation. The most noteworthy functions are self-expression, entertainment and recreation, adjustment to life crises, economic and other-world compensations.[15] These functions have had adjustive value for individual Negroes and adaptive (survival) value for the Negro group. For the most part, Negro churches have contributed to the perpetuation of the American racial system through their reinforcement of the extant mores. Only a relatively small number of urban churches have sponsored programs designed to overcome current discriminatory practices.

The stress which the Negro population generally puts upon the religious sphere appears to be directly related to the "comparatively meager participation of Negroes in other institutional forms of American culture, such as business, politics, and industry, a condition which is bound up intimately with the prevailing custom of racial dichotomy which restricts the normal participation of Negroes in many avenues of American life."[16] Although there has been some decrease in self-expression through the Negro church in recent years, the masses still have more opportunities to express themselves in this enterprise than in any other. In the church the rank and file of the Negro population finds "release from the restraint, strain, and restriction of the daily grind." If the Negro expresses himself more emotionally in his religious services than the white man does, it is not because he is more emotional by nature but because of the restrictive environment in which he lives. Even in the realm of religion, he knows and feels that in most white churches ". . . he is not desired, even though a sign on the outside of the church may read 'Welcome to All.' He understands perfectly well that the welcome does not include him. He comprehends clearly that in many of them he would be ushered to the rear or to the gallery, or be refused admission altogether; and in some other instances he would be patronized and tolerated."[17] On the other hand, he can be "somebody" in the Negro church. The recognition which has been obtainable in the Negro church has enabled many Negroes to face life situations that otherwise would have been almost intolerable.

A truck driver of average or more than ordinary qualities becomes the chairman of the Deacon Board. A hotel man of some ability is the superintendent of the Sunday church school of a rather important church. A woman

[15] In their analysis of Father Divine's Kingdom, Muzafer Sherif and Hadley Cantril give three reasons for the existence of this microcosm: (1) escape from material hardships, (2) the giving of meaning to the environment in which the "children" live, and (3) raising the status of the followers. Hadley Cantril, op. cit., pp. 139–142.

[16] A. H. Fauset, op. cit., p. 107.

[17] B. E. Mays and J. W. Nicholson, The Negro's Church, Institute of Social and Religious Research, 1933, pp. 282–283.

who would be hardly noticed, socially or otherwise, becomes a leading woman in the missionary society. A girl of little training and less opportunity for training gets the chance to become the leading soprano in the choir of a great church. These people receive little or no recognition on their daily job. There is nothing to make them feel that they are "somebody." Frequently their souls are crushed and their personalities disregarded. Often they do not feel "at home" in the more sophisticated Negro group. But in the church on X street, *she* is Mrs. Johnson, the Church Clerk; and *he* is Mr. Jones, the chairman of the Deacon Board.[18]

Not only does the Negro have an opportunity for self-expression within his own church, but he can display political leadership in the affairs of the county, state, and national conventions in the Baptist churches and in the local district, state, and quadrennial conferences of the Methodist churches. The conventions and conferences are substitutes for Democratic and Republican conventions, legislatures, and Congress.[19] If the Negro had had greater freedom in the social, economic, and political spheres, fewer Negroes would have been "called" to preach and there would have been fewer Negro churches.[20] Drake and Cayton regard the chance for self-expression which the Negro church provides as it main attraction. "It gives [opportunity] for large masses of people to function in an organized group, to compete for prestige, to be elected to office, to exercise power and control, to win applause and acclaim. Even church fights, although dubbed 'unchristian,' are interesting."[21]

From the beginning of their history in this country, Negroes have had to supply themselves with recreational opportunities. Negro churches have long been centers of activity, and in both city and country they have served as quasi community centers. In the smaller, lower-status churches there is singing and praying; in the larger ones, club meetings, plays, concerts, movies, socials, and mass meetings. The church building is usually available to labor unions, American Legion posts, and other community groups if the church itself has nothing scheduled that night.[22]

The church is still the dominant factor in the social life of rural southern Negro youth. Although these young people "may not 'get saved,' or believe in the sermons, or take the pastor seriously, and although they frequently look down upon the shouting, the church still provides them with most of their social contacts and approved entertainment."[23]

The church services themselves have an entertainment-recreation function. Many people give no "religious" reasons at all for attending church. They say they go because they like "good speaking" and "good singing"

[18] *Ibid.*, p. 281.
[19] *Ibid.*, p. 9.
[20] *Ibid.*, p. 11.
[21] St. Clair Drake and Horace Cayton, *op. cit.*, p. 424.
[22] See *ibid.*, p. 417; and B. E. Mays and J. W. Nicholson, *op. cit.*, p. 285.
[23] Charles S. Johnson, *Growing Up in the Black Belt*, p. 156.

or because they find the services "restful and beautiful." "Bronzeville's churches are centers of entertainment as well as places of worship. Popular preachers and a wide variety of musical offerings draw large crowds both on Sundays and on week nights. It is not unusual to find a total of over 10,000 people attending Sunday evening musicales in the four largest churches, and an equal number distributed among the smaller churches. The most popular pastors in the Black Belt are excellent showmen. Their sermons are replete with humor and apt illustration, as well as pithy epigram, good jokes, and rousing flights of oratory."[24]

In the rural South the Negro church contributes to the adjustment of its members to difficult life conditions. The emotional release and relief from tension were expressed by one woman in the statement: "It just seem like I can stand my worries better when I go to church."[25] Dollard suggests that the highly emotionalized services of lower-class Negroes may provide the release from internal pressures which gives them the "often-observed poise and freedom . . . in the ordinary doings of life." Religious institutions, according to this viewpoint, "play exactly the opposite role from that usually ascribed to them in a Puritanical society; instead of stressing self-control and bringing pressure toward impulse renunciation, they aid the individual in increasing his daily satisfaction in life by the ceremonials which relieve his guilt."[26]

In the North the most important "adjustment-to-life-crises" function of the Negro church is that of assisting the newcomer to accustom himself to urban life. "The erstwhile southern Negro [is] embarrassed by the presence of thousands of 'sophisticated' Negroes who want no reminders of 'back-home' ways, but the infinitely more baffling problem of making a new adjustment to life as a relatively free man, and consequently having to meet free competition (instead of the paternalistic regard so commonly manifested towards Negroes by white people in the South) are more than this type of Negro is able to cope with easily, after the experience of many years in the South."[27] The types of behavior which are permitted and encouraged in the ecstatic sects enable the believer to live temporarily in a world devoid of the hardships and humiliations of everyday life. Enhancing the morale of the most recently transplanted southern Negroes is not, however, the only aspect of this social function of the Negro church. Daniel has shown that "the congenial informality of the semi-demonstrative church group affords fellowship, personal recognition, and tension release, so consoling to the former ruralite in the urban situation." For Negroes who have adjusted to city life there are the deliberative and liturgical churches which emphasize

[24] St. Clair Drake and Horace Cayton, op. cit., p. 423.
[25] Charles S. Johnson, Growing Up in the Black Belt, p. 169. See also Hortense Powdermaker, op. cit., p. 284.
[26] John Dollard, op. cit., p. 249.
[27] A. H. Fauset, op. cit., p. 80.

meeting the issues of the day rather than seeking escape through emotional release.[28]

No thoroughgoing study of the economic functions of the Negro church is available. We have referred previously to the support which Negro ministers give to Negro business and professional men. Drake and Cayton say that in Chicago "Negro Baptists think of their organization as a 'Race Church,' and their leaders concern themselves with such matters as fighting the Job Ceiling and demanding equal economic opportunity as well as 'serving the Lord.' "[29]

The most spectacular economic function of the Father Divine movement lies in its real-estate holdings. The scores of "extensions" or "heavens" are actually hotels. This is an important phenomenon, for, as Fauset says, "Quite apart from the item of expense in which these hotels are distinguished by the amazingly low cost of services rendered (usually two dollars a week room rent, and fifteen cents a meal with no tips allowed), the significant fact lies in this: here we have a functional transformation with regard to a very vital need of American Negroes growing out of the general practice of American hostelries to refuse to receive them."[30]

During the depression years of the 1930's the doctrines of the Negro church in the rural South incorporated the idea that their own thriftlessness and sinfulness rather than the agricultural economy were responsible for the widespread destitution of tenants. In Natchez, "no preacher in either the rural or urban county was ever heard to complain in his pulpit against the plantation system. The dogma concerning economic behavior was always that the members should be hard and faithful workers."[31]

The other-world compensation function of the Negro church has had great adjustment value for individual Negroes. Slavery, segregation, and discrimination have all been conducive to developing other-worldliness "in which the righteousness of God would be vindicated and this suffering people delivered. Seeing little or no hope in this world, the Negro has done what other people have done, he has projected his hopes in a heaven above."[32]

Powdermaker mentions a sermon by a leading southern Negro minister on the poor-rich and the rich-poor theme which might be considered a very indirect attack against the white type of Christianity, although the term "white" was not used. It is ". . . the story of a rich woman who lived in a big house and had not time for God. When she

[28] V. E. Daniel, op. cit., pp. 352, 361.

[29] St. Clair Drake and Horace Cayton, op. cit., p. 413.

[30] A. H. Fauset, op. cit., p. 92.

[31] Allison W. Davis, B. B. Gardner, and M. R. Gardner, Deep South, University of Chicago Press, 1941, pp. 416–417.

[32] B. E. Mays and J. W. Nicholson, op. cit., p. 93.

went to heaven she was given an old shanty in which to live and she exclaimed: 'Why, that's the shanty my cook used to live in!' The cook, who on earth had given all her time to God, was now living in a big house in heaven, very much like the one in which her former mistress used to live."[33] In spite of its implicit criticism of the powerful, this sermon supports the racial system by telling the Negroes that their reward will come in heaven. The poor may be rich in their poverty if they are also holy. Such messages provide considerable comfort to economically depressed sharecroppers and domestic servants.

The emphasis on the importance of the other world decreases as Negroes acquire more education and a firmer economic hold. Mays and Nicholson expect that an increasing number of Negro ministers will seek primarily to relate religion to the affairs of this world.

Finally, the Negro church, especially in the rural South, has functioned to reinforce and perpetuate the segregation system in general. Davis, Gardner, and Gardner refer to its functions of "integrating the lower caste" and "increasing intercaste solidarity." Their analysis of a large number of sermons in the rural section near Natchez, Mississippi, showed "great emphasis upon the necessity for effective organization and complete solidarity of the church as a social group." Evidence of the rural Negro church as an agency reinforcing the interracial situation was found in the fact that the "travels" or "visions" of all converts placed the highest value upon whiteness. "In all of them the sinner had been convinced of the authenticity of his conversion and of his 'state of grace' only when he had 'seen' a white man, woman, or child, a white house, a white horse, or some other white object." Presumably the white persons or objects symbolized the powerful white individual (the landlord) and gave him an ultimate and supernatural authority. The analogy between God and the white landlord was often used in Rural County, with the preacher saying: " 'Ain't no use in goin' tuh de office unless you done made you' crop.' "[34]

The conservative influence of the rural Negro church is seen in the observations of Dollard's informants. One man said the planters have always welcomed plantation churches but have shown much less enthusiasm for schools. The church is looked upon by the planters as supporting the status quo by offering an illusory consolation to the Negroes; the school constitutes a threat by giving every human being ideas of personal dignity which menace the racial system. Another informant remarked that religion centers the attention of the Negro on a future life while negating the value of this one or the importance of effort here and now that is designed to better conditions.[35]

Any attempt at functional analysis must include the concepts of

[33] Hortense Powdermaker, op. cit., p. 243.
[34] Allison W. Davis, B. B. Gardner, and M. R. Gardner, op. cit., pp. 414–416. See also Liston Pope, op. cit., p. 101.
[35] John Dollard, op. cit., p. 248.

functional alternatives, or functional equivalents, or functional substitutes. Merton advances the theorem that "just as the same item may have multiple functions, so may the same function be diversely fulfilled by alternative items." Functional needs are seen as "permissive, rather than determinant, of specific social structures. . . . There is a range of variation in the structures which fulfill the function in question." Religion meets certain needs of many Negroes, but it is neither universal nor indispensable.[36] For some Negroes as for some white persons, other institutions and other organizations meet the same needs. We have in mind here such interest fields as art, science, politics, club life, and so on.

Functional analysis does not stop with a consideration of the positive functions (defined here as the contributions which a given activity makes to the perpetuation of the existing social structures) of social forms.[37] There may be dysfunctional consequences from the religions of Negroes, or of other minority groups. Donald Young observes that, under certain conditions, religions have served to provoke rebellion; and Max Weber has shown that religions "have served to motivate or to canalize the behavior of great numbers of men and women toward the modification of social structures."[38]

Insofar as separatism in religions reinforces group prejudice, it has dysfunctions for the majority individual, as we showed in the discussion of the costs of prejudice (Chapter 8). The dysfunctions of Negro religious cults, from the standpoint of some individual members, are revealed by the Sherif and Cantril study. Father Divine's command that the "children" think constantly of him makes it difficult for persons in responsible positions to perform efficiently. Forbidding followers to receive any medical or dental attention, or to use any drugs, may have serious results. For some married followers the taboo on talking to one's spouse and having sexual relations with the spouse creates loneliness and unhappiness. The fear of the Father which pervades the Kingdom "may partially account for some of the psychopaths taken from the kingdoms to the Bellevue Hospital."[39]

Our conclusion concerning the great interest which the Negro in this country has shown in religion in the past is that it is based upon (1) the strength of the African traditions,[40] and (2) his social and economic condition in the United States.

[36] Robert K. Merton, *Social Theory and Social Structure*, The Free Press, 1949, pp. 35–36.

[37] See *ibid.*, pp. 37 ff.

[38] Cited in *ibid.*, pp. 45–46.

[39] Hadley Cantril, *op. cit.*, pp. 135–137.

[40] The present writers have not had opportunities to make first-hand observations of African religious behavior, but one of them has had field experience in Haiti and has collected data there on the *vodum* cult. He has also witnessed Pocomania rites in Jamaica. His field observations support Herskovits' interpretations with respect to African "retentions." See George E. Simpson, "Jamaican Revivalist Cults," *Social and Economic Studies* (whole issue), December, 1956, especially chaps. 4, 7, 8. It should be emphasized that the Africanisms mentioned are not meaningless,

The relative importance of the church in Negro life, especially urban life, has been declining for several decades. Fifty years ago, church news was prominently displayed in the Negro press. In recent years club news has occupied more space than church news, and it usually takes some kind of scandal to get stories about churches or preachers on the front page. The church is the oldest and the wealthiest institution in the Negro community, and it is still an important part of urban Negro life. However, it is not the central agency that it was prior to World War I or that it still is in the small towns of the South.[41]

THE ROLE OF THE NEGRO MINISTER

Consideration has been given in the chapters on "Minorities in the Economy of the United States" to some phases of the ministerial profession, but several additional points relative to the Negro minister are pertinent here. Historically the ministry was the first profession to gain recognition, and Negro preachers became the principal race leaders. Even today Negro ministers, especially in the North, have the greatest freedom of any Negro leaders. They answer to no one except their congregations and they are expected to be real "race men."

They can say what they please about current affairs and race relations; there are no church superiors to discipline them and no white people to take economic reprisals. . . . Preachers are subjected to continuous community criticism, and to retain the allegiance of their followers they are forced to concern themselves with a wide range of secular activities—political action, protest against discrimination, advice on securing jobs and legal aid, and the encouragement of Negro business enterprises.[42]

If the Negro pastor sees fit to condemn from his pulpit practices with respect to low wages, long hours, the working of children in industry, the unfair treatment of women in factories, the denying to the worker the right to organize, and the injustices of an economic system built on competition, self-interest, and profit—he is more likely not to be censured, and less likely to lose his position than his white brother who preaches in the same city. It is more than likely that no committee will wait on him advising him to go slow. No leading financier will walk out of the church threatening never to return. To the contrary, it is highly possible that the Negro minister would receive many congratulations and "Amens" from his congregation if he were to preach such a gospel.[43]

---

quaint "survivals." They are cultural characteristics which have been unwittingly transmitted through tradition—not through genes. They are found in unsophisticated, lower-class Negroes along a frequency continuum running from Dutch Guiana (high) to instances among recent migrants from southern states to northern cities (low). The meaning of some of the elements has no doubt changed, but they are a part of a total religious complex that, in the main, is highly functional.

[41] St. Clair Drake and Horace Cayton, *op. cit.*, p. 418; and Liston Pope, *op. cit.*, p. 101.

[42] St. Clair Drake and Horace Cayton, *op. cit.*, pp. 427–428.

[43] B. E. Mays and J. W. Nicholson, *op. cit.*, p. 291.

The influence of the Negro minister is waning. Lawyers, physicians, teachers, journalists, social workers, dentists, and businessmen are assuming much of the leadership formerly provided by the clergy. Experts in these secular fields often have more academic training than the ministers, and they render many services formerly performed only by the preachers. There is an increasing tendency among Negroes to evaluate ministers upon the basis of their personal characteristics rather than to accord respect to all who claim that they have been "called" to preach.[44]

Negro Overchurching

There can be no question that the Negro population of the United States is overchurched; that is, there are more churches than can be adequately supported by available funds. Not only is the membership of the average Negro church small, but less than half of the members can be depended upon to contribute regularly. Many Negro churches are heavily in debt.

There seem to be two principal reasons for this state of affairs. First, denominational rivalry is such that a given denomination feels it must take care of its folk lest they join some other church. "In a small Georgia community where a Baptist and Methodist church exist with only sixty members each, including children, and where both churches were in very poor physical condition, the investigators asked one of the officials what were the possibilities of merging the two. The officer simply replied that it would take God to do that. This case could be multiplied scores of times in the sixteen centers comprising the rural and urban study."[45] The second reason for Negro overchurching is the survival value which a multiplicity of churches has had for a group so largely excluded from participation in the life of the larger community, or, as Mays and Nicholson put it, from "a civilization that has developed primarily to meet the needs of the majority." We discussed earlier in this chapter the attractions and the social functions of the Negro church. Apparently, some of the emotional needs of disadvantaged people can be met as well or better in small churches where "consciousness of kind" is high, and where opportunities for self-expression and social recognition are abundant, than in churches which have large memberships drawn from a wider social-class range.

Segregation and the Churches

Most Negro Americans attend segregated churches. This pattern is beginning to change, however, and the change goes far beyond the official pronouncements against discrimination of a decade ago. In our

[44] *Ibid.*, p. 50.
[45] *Ibid.*, p. 12.

judgment, the trend toward integrated churches will continue at an accelerating pace, supported by and supporting the general process of desegregation. As we explore the facts of segregation in churches, therefore, we must be equally alert to the small but growing number of situations in which religious organizations have been integrated.

Segregation can occur both on the state or national organizational level and on the congregational level. Although there are changes almost every year, more than 90 percent of Negro Protestants are still in separate denominational structures.[46] Thousands of sermons and Sunday school lessons and hundreds of forums and study groups have dealt in rather abstract and artificial ways with "better understanding" among all peoples. But, as Pope says, "there has been very little effort to bring the groups face-to-face so that they could use their 'understanding' and practice their 'good-will.'" Generally speaking, churches have seemed to be more concerned with the Negro's secular disadvantages than with his separation from his white coreligionists in the churches themselves.[47]

Loescher found that

. . . from the local church through the regional organizations to the national assemblies over 93 per cent of the Negroes are without association in work and worship with Christians of other races except in interdenominational organizations which involve a few of their leaders. The remaining 500,000 Negro Protestants—about 6 per cent—are in predominately white denominations, and of these 500,000 Negroes in "white" churches, at least 99 per cent, judging by the surveys of six denominations, are in segregated congregations. They are in association with their white denominational brothers only in national assemblies and, in some denominations, in regional, state, or more local jurisdictional meetings. There remains a handful of Negro members in local "white" churches. How many? Call it one-tenth of one per cent of all the Negro Protestant Christians in the United States—8,000 souls—the figure is probably much too large. Whatever the figure actually is, the number of white and Negro persons who ever gather together for worship under the auspices of Protestant Christianity is almost microscopic. And where interracial worship does occur, it is, for the most part, in communities where there are only a few Negro families and where, therefore, only a few Negro individuals are available to "white" churches.[48]

Of interest is Loescher's finding that no "white" church in his study of 18,000 churches in six denominations had an "open" or mixed membership in an area undergoing transition. Only when Negroes are in the majority is membership open in transition areas. The usual pattern in

[46] F. S. Loescher, "Racism in Northern City Churches," *Christian Century*, February 8, 1956, p. 175.

[47] Liston Pope, op. cit., p. 102.

[48] F. S. Loescher, *The Protestant Church and the Negro*, pp. 76–77.

Protestantism is initial resistance to the coming of Negroes; but when the transition has occurred, the property is sold to a Negro group. Since an individual congregation in the Episcopalian and the Catholic groups does not own the equity, the diocese or other organization can meet the situation more gracefully by assigning the property for use as a Negro Episcopal or Catholic church.[49]

As Loescher points out, an important factor in the lack of stated racial policies among the Protestant churches is their highly decentralized type of organization. The structure of the Friends, Disciples, and Baptists approaches anarchy, and even in the Protestant Episcopal, Lutheran, and Methodist denominations there is a large degree of local church autonomy. National bodies have no authority over the local church in the matter of Negro membership. The practices of local churches seem to be influenced more by community situations than by national policies. "Where there is a small Negro population, integration sometimes occurs, and the church reflects it. Where there is a larger Negro population, segregation is the rule and the church reflects that, too. There are a few exceptions and a few rather courageous local experiments which have had, however, little assistance from national church bodies." It is overwhelmingly true that the question of Negro membership in white Protestant churches is still in the talking stage.[50]

Hospitals, colleges, theological seminaries, restaurants, and welfare agencies of various kinds which are under denominational control segregate more than the churches themselves. "Protestant hospitals seldom surpass secular hospitals in admitting Negro patients without discrimination or in employing Negro medical personnel. Church colleges appear to lag behind state universities, on the whole, in their proportion of Negro students, and they have had almost no Negro faculty members."[51]

To what degree has this situation changed in the ten years since Loescher wrote? A list of some of the changes on the national and local levels may give an indication of the trend, although we can scarcely speak in precise quantitative terms. In 1952, the Presbyterian Church in the U.S. (southern) "voted to abolish its Negro synod and absorb the Negro congregations into the regional synods."[52] In 1952 the Methodist Church began and in 1956 took a longer step toward the abolition of its segregated Central Jurisdiction for Negro churches. Its General Conference recommended "that discrimination or segregation by any method

[49] Ibid., p. 79.
[50] Ibid., pp. 82, 88–89.
[51] Ibid., pp. 60, 101.
[52] W. A. Visser 'T Hooft, The Ecumenical Movement and the Racial Problem, UNESCO, 1954, p. 28.

or practice whether by conference structure or otherwise in The Methodist Church be abolished with reasonable speed."[53] The influence of the large southern membership in the Methodist Church is shown in the phrase "reasonable speed" (reminiscent of the terminology of the Supreme Court in its 1954 school decision). In 1956, the United Presbyterian Church of North America voted for "complete integration of all churches, agencies, and institutions."[54] The state Council of Churches in Virginia, North Carolina, and Georgia, and many local councils have been formed on an interracial basis in the last few years.

Such changes in the larger organizational structures have been matched by desegregation of local congregations. We cannot speak with precision concerning the extent of this change, although it still represents a small minority of Protestant churches in the United States. The following items may indicate, however, that segregation is no longer the virtually universal rule: In a study of 13,597 churches (United Lutheran, Congregational-Christian, and Presbyterian Church in the U.S.A.) Kramer found that 1331, or nearly 10 percent, reported racially integrated congregations. Most of the integrated churches had only a few nonwhites (83 percent reported fewer than five).[55]

In a survey of four of the city's boroughs, the Protestant Council of the City of New York found that about half of the city's Protestant churches have at least some interracial aspects. Questionnaires filled out by 315 of the 1500 Protestant churches showed that 51 percent were segregated (that is, had membership all of one race, or only a tiny minority from another race), 25 percent were nonsegregated ("a reasonable percentage of persons from minority groups in membership, in church attendance, and/or in the church school and other organizations"), and 24 percent were integrated (persons from minority groups were serving as officers, on boards and committees "to a degree that indicates minority groups are participating in the leadership and activities of the church").[56] Most of the segregated churches were in segregated neighborhoods. The majority indicated that they would welcome members from other races. Further research by the Protestant Council may disclose the degree to which the 315 churches are representative of the city's Protestant churches. In 1956, the Disciples of Christ reported that out of 7000 congregations studied, 464 local groups in forty states were racially mixed to some degree.[57] Loth and Fleming in their survey of desegregation received reports of 130 churches which in the

---

[53] Quoted by B. E. Mays, *Seeking to Be Christian in Race Relations*, Friendship Press, 1957, pp. 51–52.

[54] *Ibid.*

[55] Alfred S. Kramer, "Patterns of Racial Inclusion Among the Churches of Three Protestant Denominations," *Phylon*, Third Quarter, 1955, pp. 283–294.

[56] New York *Times*, February 10, 1957.

[57] J. Oscar Lee, "The Churches and Race Relations—A Survey," *Christianity and Crisis*, February 4, 1957, p. 4.

two years, May, 1954, to May, 1956, had included Negroes for the first time as members, worshipers, or program participants.[58]

Although most American Negroes are Protestants, the number of Negro Catholics now approaches half a million. In recent years the Catholic Church has taken a greater interest in Negroes; her activities with regard to desegregation, therefore, are of growing importance. Now, in addition to the 300,000 Negro Catholics who belong to segregated churches, there are thousands who attend racially mixed churches. For many years the Catholics had only a few Negro priests and their work was limited largely to segregated parishes.[59] In 1949 approximately 570 Catholic priests, 30 brothers, and 2000 sisters were devoting themselves entirely to the work of the Catholic Church among American Negroes in churches, schools, hospitals, clinics, and orphanages. In that year there were 26 Negro priests in the United States, and seven other American Negroes were doing foreign missionary work in Africa and the British West Indies. About 150 Negro seminarians were preparing for the priesthood in various Catholic seminaries in the United States. It is expected that there will be 1000 colored priests by 1960.[60] According to the 1949 data, there were in this country four communities of Negro nuns totaling 571 members, and a number of Negro sisters who were members of other communities of nuns. At that time there were 292 Catholic grade schools for Negroes, 79 high schools, 17 boarding schools, a nurses' training school, a college, and a theological seminary. Together these educational enterprises enrolled 65,000 students.[61]

Many Catholic schools and colleges have admitted Negroes since a precedent was established several years ago by the Manhattanville College of the Sacred Heart in New York City. "At present, the Catholic institution outside of the South which excludes the Negro is the exception rather than the rule. The same applies to nursing schools and other agencies."[62] Although Catholic schools in the deep South have not yet been desegregated, integration is the goal of the church leaders.

Most of the Negro priests serve Negro parishes, but in a few instances colored clergy have been appointed to serve congregations that are largely white. "They hear confessions, visit the sick, and bury the dead—all without any racial reference or distinctions whatever." The

[58] See David Loth and Harold Fleming, *Integration North and South*, The Fund for the Republic, 1956, pp. 37–44, 91–96; see also Elsa Kruuse, "The Churches Act on Integration," *National Council Outlook*, March, 1957, pp. 6–8; Lee Nichols and Louis Cassels, "The Churches Repent," *Harper's Magazine*, October, 1955, pp. 53–57; S. Garry Oniki, "Interracial Churches in American Protestantism," *Social Action*, January 15, 1950, pp. 4–22.

[59] John LaFarge, "The Roman Catholic Experience," *Survey Graphic*, January, 1947, p. 105.

[60] Yves M.-J. Congar, *The Catholic Church and the Race Question*, UNESCO, 1953, p. 49.

[61] Florence Murray (ed.), *op. cit.*, p. 291.

[62] John LaFarge, "The Roman Catholic Experience," p. 106.

church has organized an interracial educational program through interracial councils established in New York, Philadelphia, Brooklyn, Washington, Los Angeles, St. Louis, Chicago, Detroit, and other cities. LaFarge believes that "full and complete integration of the Negro in the Catholic Church in the United States is a future certainty. The interracial movement that has been started will not, and cannot, be reversed. It is characteristic of the Catholic Church to move slowly, but not to reverse its path once it is in motion."[63]

The difference between the Catholic and Protestant churches with reference to the Negro is due, according to Alexander, to "the fact that, in most cases, a Protestant church is to some extent a social organization as well as a place of worship; the Catholic church, with its emphasis on worship, is more nearly an altar before which all men are equal."[64]

THE CHURCHES' INTEREST IN THE DESEGREGATION OF OTHER INSTITUTIONS

When we examine the evidence concerning the role of the churches in promoting an integrated society, we find the same mixed picture that we found in the church situation itself: support of segregation or indifference on the one hand, and the beginnings of vigorous efforts to promote integration on the other.

Although the churches stress (1) the dignity and worth of the individual and (2) the brotherhood of man, the racial behavior patterns of most church members have not been substantially affected by these principles. With the exception of the financial support which white churches contributed to Negro secondary schools and colleges, they have until recently given very little attention to the American racial situation. They have issued pronouncements, passed resolutions, conducted "interracial Sunday" once a year, held occasional conferences, sponsored summer camps and work camps with an interracial aspect, published a number of pamphlets, and used racial or interracial themes in study groups.

In the twenty-year period before the depression, the Protestant churches were almost completely silent on the subject of race relations. The number of resolutions increased during the thirties, but these pronouncements were quite general and dealt mainly with the gross aspects of the disabilities and injustices which Negroes experience. "The majority of the statements focus on the most obvious evil—lynching— and scarcely a word is uttered on the more controversial and more basic issue of economic discrimination. Indeed, discrimination is rarely men-

---

[63] *Ibid.*, pp. 104–106. See also this author's *The Race Question and the Negro*, Longmans, Green & Co., Inc., 1943; and his *The Catholic Viewpoint on Race Relations.*

[64] W. W. Alexander, quoted in F. S. Loescher, *The Protestant Church and the Negro*, pp. 81–82.

tioned. And there is only a single use of the word segregation."[65] During the first half of the 1940's a flood of pronouncements on race relations materialized. In March, 1946, the Federal Council of Churches of Christ in America declared that it renounced ". . . the pattern of segregation in race relations as unnecessary and undesirable and a violation of the Gospel of love and human brotherhood. Having taken this action, the Federal Council requests its constituent communions to do likewise. As proof of their sincerity in this renunciation they will work for a non-segregated Church and a non-segregated society." Subsequently, four denominations adopted the statement as their own, and three other denominations, without adopting the council statement, have recommended that their churches welcome Negroes.[66]

These pronouncements have certain limitations. They are verbal acts, and in many cases they represent minority opinion. There is little evidence that the rank-and-file membership of Protestant denominations is greatly influenced by these official actions. Concerning the Protestant Church and the Negro, Loescher says:

> If one were to write a history of Protestantism's relations to Negroes the balance sheet would be heavily on the debit side. Protestantism arose in the time of European exploitation of non-white peoples. It blessed slavery. It sanctioned a caste system with its stamp of inferiority on a whole race. But there were exceptions. Individuals and some groups became sensitive to the incompatibility of the Christian ethic and the slave system. Some dedicated their lives to teaching the freedmen.
> Latterly this number of concerned individuals has grown and we find many church members devotedly working for "a non-segregated Church and a non-segregated society."[67]

Alexander points out that "so long as the church is a segregated institution, segregation in secular life has a great moral sanction. Until the church becomes a non-segregated institution in its worship, membership, and patterns of action, it can have little influence in getting rid of segregation in employment, housing, and public services."[68] This conclusion is relevant regardless of whether the racial-cultural minorities involved are Negroes, Japanese, or others.

Have the churches been drawn into the current activity and debate over desegregation? Their interest and their work have undoubtedly increased, but the improvement of race relations is still scarcely a major part of their programs. At the top organizational level there has been almost unanimous approval of the Supreme Court decision calling

---

[65] *Ibid.*, p. 31.
[66] *Ibid.*, p. 42.
[67] *Ibid.*, p. 117.
[68] W. W. Alexander, *Racial Segregation in the American Protestant Church*, Friendship Press, 1946, p. 14.

for desegregation of the schools. "Every major Protestant denomination in the South has made public pronouncements commending the decision."[69] Catholic leaders and the National Council of Churches have repeatedly declared that discrimination and segregation are evil. Ministers in New York, Cleveland, and elsewhere have worked for better housing for Negroes. Many ministers in Virginia were among the leaders in the opposition to the Gray plan to prevent school desegregation. The Nashville Association of Churches and the Nashville Ministers Association have supported the school board's plan for gradual desegregation, beginning in the fall of 1957. Negro clergymen led the Montgomery, Alabama, bus boycott. At least ten white ministers in the South have been forced to resign because of their support of school desegregation. These items will give an indication of the growing concern over racial discrimination among many churchmen.

The shift, however, has not been a major one. Loescher asks: "How much do all the Protestant denominations spend in a year to develop an integrated church and an integrated society? Less than $250,000. How many people with major responsibilities for race relations are employed in all the Protestant denominations? Less than a dozen."[70]

Waldo Beach, referring primarily to the South, puts the matter even more strongly:

It is precisely in the most heavily "churched" section of the nation, by all counts, the most self-consciously "Christian" region, that the churches are the most segregated and have the least impact on public policy. The failure of churches is not a regional peculiarity, of course, but the gap is the more glaring where the piety is so conspicuous. Quantitatively measured, the churches enjoy a phenomenal prestige, but qualitatively they fail so lamentably to be the consciences of the communities in which they stand that their dismissal by social scientists as "functions of culture" seems amply justified by the evidence.[71]

Some persons are using religion to defend racism; others have joined the struggle against segregation on religious grounds. But as Beach says, "By far the great majority of the churches are in the middle, maintaining a troubled, uncertain silence."

To the student of the sociology of religion, this range of attitudes is scarcely surprising. The religious life of man is not something aloof from the rest of his experience; it is intimately tied to the whole of life, with its tensions and errors as well as its sublime moments. Churches will move toward desegregation as the rest of society moves, affecting and being affected by all the other forces at work.

[69] John Hope, II, "Trends in Patterns of Race Relations in the South Since May 17, 1954," *Phylon*, Second Quarter, 1956, p. 107.

[70] F. S. Loescher, "Racism in Northern City Churches," p. 176.

[71] Waldo Beach, "Storm Warnings from the South," *Christianity and Crisis*, March 19, 1956, p. 30.

ATTITUDES OF NEGROES TOWARD SEGREGATED CHURCHES

It is useful to distinguish between the attitudes of rural and urban Negroes toward the Negro church. The older generation of rural Negro church members is relatively uncritical of the church and ministers. There is a more critical attitude toward both among rural Negro youth. For many of them religion belongs to the past, and they are impatient with "shouting" and religious frenzy.[72] However, the great majority of rural Negro youth are not antagonistic to religion or opposed to the church as a social or a religious institution. Nearly four-fifths of the young people in Charles Johnson's study "were critical of the ministers; half of them registered a belief that the main interest of the ministers was to get all the money they can from the people; a third objected to what seemed to them to be a bickering emphasis on church politics and on inconsequential, sectarian disputes; and half of the number made a distinction between churches, some of which they classified as all right and others as 'all bunk.' "[73] The criticisms of Negro youth in the Johnson study are directed more at the illiterate preachers of the isolated plantation areas than at those in communities which have been influenced by a city of some size. The seventeen-year-old daughter of a Tennessee sharecropper said, "I think a preacher out here ought to preach today about things of today. He ought to give the people advice and help them out of their troubles by talking about things that happen today. I don't think a preacher ought to try to preach you into heaven." An eighteen-year-old Alabama boy said, "Some of the preachers get drunk and treat their wives dirty; they go out with other women. All they is after is money."[74]

The young people in the plantation areas have more education than their elders, and they are more mobile and less docile. When the church has taken their needs into account it seems to have retained their interest and respect.

Many urban Negroes, of both the older and the younger generations, hold critical attitudes toward their churches. Drake and Cayton list the following criticisms by their Chicago informants:

1. The church is a "racket."
2. There are too many churches.
3. The churches are too emotional.
4. There's no real religion among the members.
5. Churches are a waste of time and money.
6. Ministers don't practice what they preach.
7. Ministers don't preach against "sin."

[72] Hortense Powdermaker, op. cit., pp. 269–270.
[73] Charles S. Johnson, Growing Up in the Black Belt, pp. 150–151.
[74] Ibid., pp. 148–149.

8. The church places too much emphasis upon money.

9. Negroes are too religious.[75]

It is expected that Negro ministers will encourage Negro business, but in giving this encouragement they risk being accused of "racketeering."

. . . Most of the larger churches advertise Negro-owned businesses on the theory that successful colored businessmen are "advancing The Race." They try to throw business toward certain Negro undertakers, physicians, and retail stores. Church newspapers carry ads of colored enterprises in Bronzeville and of white stores that employ Negroes. Sometimes a pastor will appoint special agents or representatives within his church to plug specific stores or products. Naturally, the community assumes that the ministers get "kickbacks" and special considerations from these businessmen.[76]

Frazier found that in many cases urban Negro youth had broken away from the church. Their "worldly-wise" behavior and attitudes reflected the secularizing influence of the city. One seventeen-year-old youth said, "I'd rather like church, but I get tired of the same old baloney. I think the church should give an interpretation of the Bible in keeping with modern times. The same sort of tripe that was taught in churches forty years ago is out of date just like schools were forty years ago. The church seems to refuse to become modern."[77] Frazier too found that not all of the Negro youth he investigated were skeptical about the church. "In those relatively few cases where churches show some intelligent understanding of the outlook and problems of Negro youth and set up organizations to this end, the response on their part is, on the whole, favorable."[78]

Despite increasing criticism, especially in the cities and among young people, the Negro church seems destined to be important so long as segregation in general and in the churches in particular continues. Pope concludes, "With the system of segregation as it is, most Negroes seem to prefer to worship separately and to control their own churches; but they are opposed to the system, and they probably would not prefer their own church to equal status in a color-blind church and denomination."

The Religions of Mexican-Americans

The majority of Spanish-speaking persons in the United States belong to the Catholic faith, but the number of Protestants among them is

[75] St. Clair Drake and Horace Cayton, op. cit., p. 419.

[76] Ibid., p. 428.

[77] E. Franklin Frazier, Negro Youth at the Crossways, American Council on Education, 1940, pp. 114, 124.

[78] Ibid., p. 133.

growing. One estimate of the number of Protestant Mexicans in Chicago is one in thirty, as compared with the usual estimate of one in 200 in Mexico. Another estimate places the national figure at about 50,000 Spanish-speaking Protestants—served by 500 churches.[79]

Usually Mexican-American mothers are more zealous about getting their children to take part in the life of the Catholic Church than the fathers are. "The average father will have his children baptized and confirmed, but is apt to believe that 'religion is for the women,' and his own observances will be nominal. One brickyard worker in Los Angeles said, 'I am a Catholic, but not a fanatic. I haven't gone to church since I have been here, nor have I had time to pray, for my work hasn't allowed me to do that, but I have baptized my children and have tried to see that they, especially my daughters, should lean towards the Catholic faith—but I am not a fanatic.' "[80]

The indoctrination of Mexican-American children in Catholic dogma involves problems which are not encountered in training Catholic children of immigrant European families. The latter have Catholic doctrines presented to them in a way they can understand, and they are fairly well prepared in the teachings of the church by confirmation time. Few Mexican-American children go to parochial schools because of the tuition fees. What they learn of the church doctrines is acquired in catechism classes before first communion and later on at confirmation. At the same time that instruction in the catechism is being received in English from Catholic officials, their mothers tell them folk tales in Spanish and provide interpretations of religious occurrences.

Teen-age Spanish-speaking Americans tend to judge the Catholic Church in their community by the priest. His interest in the needs of young people is more important to them than the number of persons attending Mass or the number of confessions he hears. " 'What we need,' say the boys and girls in the Mexican communities, 'are priests who want to help us—you know, how to get jobs and better houses, real men in Los Angeles . . . not just priests hidden in the church. There's a world around us and he should be in it like we are, if he's going to really help us.' "[81]

Not infrequently the Spanish-speaking priest has difficulty adjusting to the American community. He himself may have felt the prejudice of Anglo-Americans, both Catholics and Protestants. Most of the older Mexican priests do not understand the behavioral changes in many Mexican immigrants. "They are not the same submissive Mexicans as in

[79] Beatrice Griffith, *American Me*, Houghton Mifflin Company, 1948, p. 190. The first estimate was given by Robert Jones, of the Pan American Union; the second by Vernon McCombs, superintendent of the Latin-American Mission for the Methodist Church in Los Angeles.

[80] *Ibid.*, p. 184.

[81] *Ibid.*, pp. 184, 186.

old Mexico, and this is disturbing as well as frustrating to some priests who prefer the ignorance of bondage. They say of the local Mexicans, 'They are ill bred. They have acquired all the bad habits of these gringoes.' To these reactionary priests Protestantism and Yankeeism are synonymous, so they seldom if ever work with the Protestant leaders, the public-school authorities, or civic leaders in their towns." Such priests retreat into the old pattern of parish life and thought. They refuse to become American citizens, and they discourage their parishioners' taking out citizenship. In short, they miss their chance to bridge the gap between the Mexican and American communities.[82]

Although the status of the average Mexican priest has declined, the position of the Catholic Church in the community remains strong. It continues to be the meeting place for the CYO and numerous lay organizations for men and women. "Community organizations can often reach Mexicans who would not otherwise be reached through these groups, for instance with T.B. and X-ray drives, diphtheria inoculations, war-bond drives."

It has already been mentioned that Protestantism is on the increase among Mexican-Americans. However, segregation is widely practiced. "Not only are there 'Keep Out—For Whites Only' signs on churches in Texas, but in Anaheim, Cucamonga, Azusa, Fullerton, Santa Ana, Orange, Pomona, Chino, Riverside, Corona, Ventura, San Luis Obispo, San Jose, and elsewhere in California Protestant churchgoers leave their brotherhood of man and Christ's teachings at the Church door-step." Discrimination on the part of these white Protestant church members is justified in elaborate ways. "They are Catholics, and not our concern. They are a subnormal race, mostly Indian; they can't learn our American way of living and don't want to; they are just greasers and could never be anything anyway. The crimes of this town come from these people— we're already paying out more for their health and charity than for any group. They cause all the trouble in the community."[83] The effect of such rationalizations, and of guilt feelings, is often "even more stringent methods of repression, more subtle ways of showing prejudice."

Funds are given for home missions and for missionary work outside the United States, but ministers are cautious about pressing for changes in race relations in their home communities. Even in the places where there is no open discrimination the Protestant church has done little to integrate Mexicans into the American community. Ignacio Lopez, California editor and former OWI official, told a Methodist convention in 1945 that the Mexican Protestant church " 'has done very little to raise the economic level of its members; it has not co-operated with groups trying to get through legislative measures such as FEPC (State and Federal), full employment, or other progressive social legislation; there

[82] *Ibid.*, pp. 186–187.
[83] *Ibid.*, p. 191.

has been no positive attitude toward the problems of the Pachucos and delinquency in general, and there has been no active participation in political and civic movements, of which these churches and their leaders should be the spearheads.' "[84]

Changes in traditional religious behavior probably will occur more slowly among Mexicans than in some minorities, for example, the Japanese, Jewish, and Italian groups. From present indications, the Mexican Protestant church will continue to grow but the Catholic Church will play the major religious role in the lives of Mexican-Americans, especially in the rural areas and the small communities, for many years.

The Religions of Japanese-Americans

Of chief interest here is the rivalry between Christianity and Buddhism which has existed in the Japanese-American population of the United States. On the whole, Christianity seems to have had a stronger and Buddhism a weaker influence on the west coast than in Hawaii. The Buddhists had no organization on the mainland until a youth association was established in San Francisco in 1898. By 1940 there were forty-eight temples, with estimates on adherents varying from 55,000 to 80,000, depending upon the definition of adherent. A census of religious belief taken in relocation centers showed that 55 percent preferred Buddhism, 31 percent were for Christianity (mostly Protestant), and less than ½ of 1 percent were for Shinto.[85]

According to Smith, most Japanese agree that Christianity has oriented them to American life and has helped bridge the gap between Japan and this country. Buddhism has oriented its followers toward Japan. Nevertheless, language and prejudice have caused the establishment of separate churches in the Protestant denominations. The first Presbyterian congregation was formed in 1885, the first Methodist church in 1886. "The Methodists soon had a whole string of missions on the West Coast, separately administered almost as if they were foreign missions. Other sects followed suit. So Christianity, which began by directing its adherents toward America, ended by keeping them in segregated churches and helping to calcify the shell which surrounded them."[86]

Despite the segregated nature of Christianity, these churches were prompt in meeting many of the needs of the people and they became an important part of the Japanese-American community organization. Most of the children got their first schooling in Methodist or Baptist kindergartens, and the Protestant churches provided guidance and social outlets not available elsewhere for Japanese women. Even among the

[84] *Ibid.*, p. 192.
[85] Bradford Smith, *Americans from Japan*, J. B. Lippincott Company, 1948, pp. 228–229.
[86] *Ibid.*, p. 228.

adherents of Buddhism there were many who also attended the Christian church.[87]

Buddhism has failed to attract the Nisei in spite of strenuous efforts and such features as Sunday schools, the observance of American holidays, hymn singing, choirs, and robes. Less than half of the American-born Japanese have remained in the Buddhist fold. The Buddhist sects have been forced to remain Japanese to retain the support of the first generation. The members of the second generation regard themselves as Americans, and they have revolted against the attempts of Buddhism to provide a bridge between cultures and generations. Young Christian Japanese-Americans see Buddhism as a target, as a "symbol of their hated difference from other Americans." They find "that a gap exists between themselves and their Buddhist contemporaries who seem to them, for the most part, a little withdrawn from American life, a little 'Japanesey.' "[88] After the Pearl Harbor attack the Buddhist mission urged its member temples to buy bonds, join the Red Cross, hold services in English, and Americanize their programs, but these moves had little effect upon the attitudes of the Nisei.

During the relocation period of World War II the Christian churches helped Japanese-Americans maintain contacts with the outside world. "The residents had their own ministers, and to make them most fully available the centers were divided into parishes with all Protestant denominations united. Church folk from nearby towns came visiting and invited evacuees to their churches in return. A Minidoka choir gave concerts in surrounding towns. District young people's meetings gave the Nisei a chance to re-enter American life. Through the efforts of the churches thousands of toys were sent in to take some of the sting out of an imprisoned Christmas."[89] At the time of resettlement, the Christian Church encouraged its members to leave and helped them find jobs and homes. The Buddhist sects had no fostering organization outside; many of their priests were interned, and others could not or did not want to resettle. Buddhism therefore encouraged its members to stay in the centers.

One conclusion seems clear. Buddhism is fighting a losing battle with Christianity for the support of Japanese-Americans. The question of segregation within the Christian Church is part of the larger issue of biracialism versus integration.

The Jewish Religion

The Jewish religion in its traditional form, more than language, tradition, or secular culture, distinguished European Jews from their Chris-

[87] *Ibid.*, pp. 224, 225.
[88] *Ibid.*, p. 229.
[89] *Ibid.*, p. 300.

tian neighbors through the Middle Ages and into the nineteenth century. Through these centuries, and until the present time, Judaism has provided the basis for group solidarity among the Jews. But, according to Arthur Ruppin, "the influence of Jewish religion on the life of the Jews is now incomparably weaker than in former times."[90]

From the period of heavy Jewish immigration, 1880–1915, until the mid-1930's, Judaism was rapidly changed by the new American setting. Religion continued to be an extremely important part of life for most Jewish Americans, but practices and beliefs that were functionally connected with life in different societies, in eastern Europe for example, seemed awkward or irrelevant in the United States. It was difficult for Judaism to withstand the influences toward assimilation which prevailed in small communities, and the result was that the intermarried abandoned the Jewish faith in appreciable numbers. Also, the concentration of Jews in urban centers made it easy for those who wished to avoid the synagogue to do so. Not that the Jewish population ceased to maintain a variety of Jewish communal agencies, but more and more the direction of the Jewish organizations

. . . is vested in the hands of the un-synagogued. For example, the community welfare funds and the federations of charity, which have become almost exclusively secular, are conducted in many instances by social workers who happen to be Jews by birth and work for Jews, but who do not work as Jews. The character of the Jewish community is being determined in large and increasing measure by individuals and by organizations virtually independent of the synagogue, while the synagogue is playing a subsidiary part in the totality of organized Jewish life.[91]

In the large American cities some Jews have come to admire liberal Christian preachers and have joined Unitarian or other liberal churches. A few have become members of the Christian Science Church. Still others are "nonreligious" or "antireligious."

Despite these trends, the predominant fact is the continuing strength of the sense of identity with Judaism. Indeed, since about 1933 the pressures toward assimilation have been countered to an important degree by forces that have renewed the Jewish community in the United States. What we observe today, therefore, is the paradox of the continuing "Americanization" of Judaism at the same time that the feeling of a distinctive identity with Judaism persists and perhaps even grows among its members.

We can only suggest some of the factors involved in this development. In part, it shares in the general "return to religion" so much re-

[90] Arthur Ruppin, *The Jews in the Modern World*, The Macmillan Company, 1934, pp. 274–275.
[91] David de Sola Pool, "Judaism and the Synagogue," chap. 2 in O. I. Janowsky (ed.), *The American Jew*, Harper & Brothers, 1942, p. 52.

marked on the contemporary scene. The religions to which Protestants, Catholics, and Jews are returning in substantial numbers seem to many observers to be glossy, secularized attempts to establish "confident living." They are efforts to overcome the sense of anomie, to escape the loneliness of the crowd, by close identity with a religious group. Jews can now do this as Jews more readily than they could a generation ago, for they are less insecure, less "foreign." The American pattern of freedom of religion and the separation of church and state allows religion to be the carrier of this attempt to find a place. The continuing identity with Judaism was also reinforced by the rise of Nazism. If such vicious anti-Semitism could appear in Germany, where Jews were as fully assimilated as anywhere in the world, the whole idea of assimilation must be thought through again. Biculturalism of an eastern European model was certainly unattractive to most American Jews; but a more vigorous emphasis on cultural pluralism—attention to their religious and to some degree their cultural distinctiveness as well as to their ties to American society—became common.[92]

In any religious group whose members differ widely in background, level of education, occupation, and social class, denominations with different types of belief and practice tend to appear. Although there has been a blurring of the lines of distinction in recent years, one can readily distinguish the Orthodox, the Conservative, and the Reform branches of Judaism in America. Reform Judaism bears somewhat the same relationship to Orthodoxy that Protestantism does to Catholicism. The Reform group is less mystical, its ceremonies are less elaborate, and it makes fewer demands on its members. It represents the influence of modern urban life, the improvement of status, the sharp reduction of disprivilege, the increased secularization that many Jews experienced, first in western Europe and then in the United States. A sociologist's comment on the Reform group in an American industrial city is of interest:

As to doctrine, the Reformed group, of course, has made the most complete compromises. Protestants who visit the Temple say they recognize little difference between its services and those which they attend in their own churches. Only the brief recitations in Hebrew, the letters on the windows, are there to remind them that the very pew in which they sit bridges a cultural gap. Here no hats are worn, the men and women sit together, there is an organ loft and a choir, and the ghetto seems very far away. The mild Sunday-morning exhortation of Rabbi Golder is equivalent to that of the Methodist minister across the way. Indeed, Rabbi Golder calls himself "ambassador to the Christians." They understand him well, for he is cut out

[92] See Marshall Sklare, *Conservative Judaism*, The Free Press, 1955; Marshall Sklare and Marc Vosk, *The Riverton Study. How Jews Look at Themselves and Their Neighbors*, American Jewish Committee, 1957; Will Herberg, *Protestant-Catholic-Jew*, Doubleday & Company, Inc., 1955.

of the same cloth as their clergy. He visits in their pulpits and is a leader in the social work of the city. His congregation is proud that its leader is so universally a respected and an important factor in the larger community. In his hands Judaism is no vital, compulsive force, but a mannerly social practice in the best Gentile taste. The Orthodox part of the community frankly distrusts him.[93]

Conservative Judaism is traditional in its outlook, although in some respects it is closer to Reform Judaism than to Orthodoxy. In contrast to Reform Judaism, Orthodox and Conservative Jews have avoided the formulation of a general Jewish creed. The two latter groups try to arrange public services on weekdays as well as on the Sabbaths and holidays. Also, in both, the men pray with covered heads. Many Conservative congregations have these characteristics in common with Reform Jews: abolition of the separation of the sexes in the synagogue, admission of women to the choir, the synagogues being spoken of as temples, and the expectation that the Messianic age will come about through the efforts of many thinkers and teachers.[94] Conservative Judaism is essentially an American denomination. Its programs and doctrines can be seen as an effort to preserve what is believed to be essential in Judaism while at the same time encouraging practices and beliefs harmonious with the American environment. Sklare describes its development in functional terms:

The greatest contribution of the German Reform movement may be said to be its function as the provider of a cushion for the disintegrative effects of emancipation. It helped to indicate a *modus vivendi* between assimilation and a no-longer acceptable Orthodoxy. In the same tradition, American Conservatism has cushioned the effects of the dissolution of Judaism as an integrated and highly traditional sacred system. It too has offered a *modus vivendi* for the alienated. . . . The signal contribution of Conservatism would seem to be that of offering an acceptable pattern of adjustment to the American environment for many East-European-derived Jews.[95]

For many years Orthodox Judaism reflected eastern European life. It was maintained largely by a fairly steady stream of European immigrants. The virtual cutting off of European immigration does not necessarily mean that Orthodoxy will die out in the United States. According to Rabbi Pool, Orthodox Judaism has shown that it is adapting itself to the American environment, and he cites such innovations as the late Friday evening service, the removal of the women's gallery, the confirmation of girls, and the community *seder* (celebration on Passover eve). The goal of some Orthodox Jews is to harmonize unquestioning

[93] Leonard Bloom, "The Jews of Buna," in Isacque Graeber and S. H. Britt (eds.), *Jews in a Gentile World*, The Macmillan Company, 1942, p. 186.
[94] Louis Finkelstein (ed.), *The Jews, Their History, Culture, and Religion*, Harper & Brothers, 1949, vol. 2, chap. 35.
[95] Marshall Sklare, op. cit., p. 249.

faith with modern living.[96] The unprecedented persecution of Jews in Europe during the Nazi regime increased the strength of Orthodoxy by intensifying the consciousness of the Jewish heritage.

The many elements of Judaism have resisted the organization of a denominational group, and it seems unlikely that this independence will give way in the foreseeable future. In spite of the differences between the Orthodox and the Reform groups, however, each regards the other as a part of Judaism.

It is possible for them to do so, because of the principle that even an unobservant or a heretical Jew does not cease to be a member of the covenant made between God and Israel at the time of the Revelation. Only actual rejection of Judaism, by affiliation with another faith, is recognized as separating one from the Jewish community. So long as a follower of the Jewish faith has not by overt act or word and of his own free will declared himself a member of another religion, other Jews are bound to regard him as one of their own faith, and to seek his return to its practice and beliefs.[97]

In the absence of any central organization or authority, the only bond which unites the Jewish people is a "consciousness of a *Keneset Yisrael* (the congregation of Israel) which Solomon Schechter translated into 'Catholic Israel.' "[98]

There is no exact knowledge as to the numbers of Jews who belong to the three denominations. Sklare believes that they are of about equal size, although there are considerably more Orthodox congregations. In any event, it is well to remember that to a substantial degree what is one generation's reform is the next generation's orthodoxy. There seems to be a tendency for the Conservative movement to emerge as the dominant one among American Jews, but even as it does so, it continues to change. Although we cannot generalize from the "Riverton" data to all American communities, the trends that Sklare and Vosk describe are doubtless indicative of changes elsewhere:[99]

	Grandparents	Parents	Children
Orthodox	81%	16%	9%
Conservative	11	43	42
Reform	5	30	31
Nonreligious	2	4	8
Don't know, it depends, or no answer	1	7	10
	100%	100%	100%

Only 23 percent of the children in Orthodox families intend to remain Orthodox; half of them plan to turn Conservative.

We can get a picture of some of the influences at work on Judaism in

[96] David de Sola Pool, *op. cit.*, pp. 53–54.
[97] Louis Finkelstein (ed.), *op. cit.*, pp. 1333, 1352.
[98] *Ibid.*, pp. 1352–1353.
[99] Marshall Sklare and Marc Vosk, *op. cit.*, p. 16.

the United States by examining A. I. Gordon's study of the Jewish community in Minneapolis. His review of some of the changes which have occurred in that city indicates the extent and depth of recent modifications in Jewish religious patterns.[100] The ritual changes in the east European Jewry of Minneapolis have been more marked than those of the early German Jewish settlers because the latter never favored the perpetuation of "the minutiae of Jewish ritual and ceremony" in their homes. Changes in the degree of ritual observance have been accompanied in the second and third generations by a considerable transformation in the basic beliefs of Judaism pertaining to God, immortality, belief in a life hereafter, and prayer. The Sabbath has become as much, or even more, a day of recreation as it is a day of worship and rest. "Children use the day for parties, movie-going, shopping, dancing, music, and other special lessons, eating out, and in general having a good time. Mothers in ever-increasing numbers do their shopping, attend theaters and parties and the like. Fathers go out to the golf clubs, attend football games, indulge in a friendly game of cards, or take the family on an outing."[101] The main feast and fast days vary in importance in the lives of Minneapolis Jews, but the high holy days are still widely observed. The Sabbath and the minor fast days are diminishing in importance. There is an increasing tendency for children to forget their Hebrew names, and this is strongest among the families of the Reform temple. Circumcision is still considered a religious must, but more and more of these operations are performed by Jewish doctors rather than by the mohels. The modern rabbi's duties have undergone significant changes. Formerly he was solely a preacher and teacher; today he is also an administrator, a member of boards in both the Jewish community and the general community, and a personal counselor. Finally, the traditional definition of "the good Jew" seems to have been revised.

There is less emphasis upon ritual and observance, less concern for the theological concepts and basic beliefs. The good Jew is generally regarded as the man who is charitable, who has a sense of social sympathy which prompts him to look upon all men as his brothers. The good Jew is one who has a highly developed ethical and moral sense, who practices these virtues in his home and in the market place, as well as in the synagogue. Finally, the good Jew is one who despite any personal denominational predilections works with and for a united Jewish community.[102]

---

[100] It may be pointed out that Minneapolis is not too typical of cities where a large number of Jews reside. Half of the Jewish population lives in New York City, and cultural isolation and rigidity are strong in many neighborhoods. It is entirely possible that this discussion gives the impression that there has been more change in the Jewish group than has actually been the case.

[101] Albert I. Gordon, Jews in Transition, University of Minnesota Press, 1949, p. 97.

[102] Ibid., p. 82. Citations for items mentioned in the preceding summary are pp. 74, 80, 97, 120, 125, 122, 170, 171.

Parts of a life history which Gordon includes in his study indicate clearly the general trend of change in the Minneapolis Jewish community during a period of three generations.

People growing up in this country are living more American lives. The old folks are dying off. This generation isn't any worse from the point of view of the way it lives than the earlier generation. Today they go to schools and universities and they just know more. Children do what they think is right when their parents die.

I think that the old type of synagogue, the Orthodox synagogue as I knew it, just isn't good for young people. They need the newer type of modern synagogue. Otherwise they just won't come at all. Not so many years ago we wouldn't think of kindling the lights in our home on Shabbas because it was against Jewish law. We used to have a Gentile turn off the lights for us. Today the whole world has changed and everybody, I think, thinks nothing of turning on lights on Shabbas.

Another thing that has changed is the establishment of Talmud Torahs. Maybe it's better that there are such modern institutions. Time will tell if our young people are better Jews because of them. I think that it's a good thing that there are Sunday schools for our children today. The synagogue should be what I tried to make the Kenesseth Israel Synagogue, the second home for the people.

There are ever so many changes in the lives of this generation from the way it was in the past. Formerly everybody spoke Yiddish. Today our children certainly don't speak it as a regular thing. They have almost forgotten it. In the early days in this community, many women wore sheitels (wigs) in accordance with the practice of shaving off the bride's hair before marriage. Today no one wears such a thing. Formerly everyone prayed every day, or at least most people did when I first came here. Today they just don't. I remember that when one of my sons was attending university, I found out that he hadn't been praying in the mornings, and I slapped him because of it. We used to call our children by their Hebrew and Yiddish names. That stopped when the teachers in the public schools actually gave our children American names. In early days here we used to make the motzi (grace before meals) at every meal. My children don't practice that. Another change I can think of is that when there was a circumcision ceremony, we would have the mohel (a Jewish person skilled in the rite of circumcision) perform the ceremony. Today I think that most people have regular doctors. People used to come to shule in early days to give their daughters and sons names in the presence of the congregation. I think that few people do these things today.

I can think of other changes too. In our early days here funeral services were conducted for practically all but the very finest, pious people in their homes. A eulogy was never delivered except for the very righteous. Today everyone gets a eulogy and some very unworthy people are even brought into synagogues for their funeral services. Maybe, though, it's better this way.

Yahrtzeiten (observances of the anniversary of death of members of one's family) were always observed. Everyone observed it. Today ever so many people either forget it or have someone else say kaddish for them. There used to be no embalming. Today practically all bodies are embalmed, even though it's against Jewish law. And they bring flowers to funerals today, another custom that was forbidden. Today every young Jew seems to like sports. In the early days that certainly wasn't true. In fact we got rid of a rabbi here because he used to like to ice skate and ride horseback. People weren't used to those things in their rabbis, although there was really nothing wrong. We used to have study groups in the synagogues of 50 or 60 people right here in Minneapolis. Tell me where they are today.

Not so many years ago children listened to their parents. There was real discipline. Today parents are relegated to an inferior position by their children. In the early days people entertained by visiting with their friends or playing a friendly game of cards. Today they spend so much for entertainment, and they don't enjoy the same kind of entertainment we did. I don't think that many people keep kashrus (the dietary laws) today the way we used to in the early days.

Of course there were freethinkers in those early days as well as today. They were the people who came over from Europe trying to rid themselves of their Jewishness as quickly as possible. But they were only a small group.

I think that most of the differences of which I am talking are due to the influence of American schools. The children would go to school, listen to the teacher, and then wonder why the home wasn't like the teacher said. First they would wonder, then they would try to make it that way.

Despite all these changes, I do not think that Judaism is dying in America. I think that Orthodoxy is losing ground very quickly, but I think that the Conservative movement is helping to keep Jewish life up very nicely.

Of course, my children are all grown. Practically all of them are married and have their own families and homes. They do things differently from the way my wife and I did them. But I think that they're not such bad Jews, everything considered. They're also good Americans.[103]

The "institutional synagogue" is regarded by some religious Jews as "one of the most promising features in American Jewish life."

The synagogue center has come to stay, despite fears that Judaism might be diluted by the secular attractions of the gymnasium, the swimming pool and similar extension activities. The house of worship, whether orthodox, conservative or reform, is gradually being transformed into a center of social life in the Jewish community. The week-end synagogue is again assuming the character of the beth hakneseth of older times, the seven day a week rallying center of Jewish life. The synagogue center attempts to embrace the totality of Judaism—worship first and foremost, but, along with it, forums and institutes for the study of the Hebrew language, Jewish history and literature, a Jewish library, family celebrations such as bar mitzvah or confirmation and weddings within the synagogue. The synagogue is tending to

[103] Reprinted from Jews in Transition by Albert I. Gordon, pp. 224–227, by permission of the University of Minnesota Press. Copyright 1949 by the University of Minnesota Press.

become once more a focus for Jewish needs and causes. In this lies a strong hope of a Jewish life once more reintegrated in and around the synagogue.[104]

Gordon concludes that, in spite of the departure from detailed observance of traditional ritual, there is still a regard among Minneapolis Jews for ritual *per se*. In his implicitly functional analysis, the choice of ritual practices in the future will depend on the contribution which these practices can make to the survival of the Jews as a people rather than on divinely ordained law. "His desire to accommodate his religious and cultural life to the culture of the majority while avoiding complete assimilation—that is, loss of identity—will make his task difficult."[105]

The impact of the "Enlightenment," which began in France in the second half of the eighteenth century and spread to the educated classes of the rest of the European Jewish population, was powerful. Ruppin points out that the process of giving up the Jewish religion was gradual and that it usually took three or four generations for its completion. In the first generation there was a more lax observance of ritual; in the second generation religion was eliminated from daily life and relegated to Sabbath and feast days; the third generation was characterized by a religious indifference which remembered only the high holidays and by occasional conversions; and in the fourth generation conversions became quite common.[106]

The recency and the severity of anti-Jewish policies in Nazi Germany have made many Jews in the United States dubious about complete assimilation. We have also suggested that the desire to find personal identity in a complicated society has supported allegiance to one's traditional religious community. But whether or not the current revival of Judaism is a long-run trend, or a short-run reversal of a dominant trend toward assimilation, is not entirely clear. It is our guess that we shall see a paradoxical result: continuing identity with Judaism for most Jews, but at the same time a reduction in the elements that differentiate it from other religions in the American environment. This does not mean that only Judaism will change. It means that all alike, as they struggle with religious problems in the fundamentally new context of a mobile industrial society, will revise many aspects of religious traditions that developed in vastly different settings.

[104] David de Sola Pool, *op. cit.*, p. 54.
[105] Albert I. Gordon, *op. cit.*, p. 309.
[106] Arthur Ruppin, *op. cit.*, pp. 274–275.

CHAPTER 19

The Education of Racial and Cultural Minorities in the United States

The Education of Minorities and the Social Order

The education of racial and cultural minorities cannot be treated exhaustively in a work which attempts to cover many aspects of majority-minority relations in the United States. Instead of examining the educational status of all minority peoples, we shall concentrate mainly on educational policies for Negroes as the most severely handicapped group. Some attention is given to Mexican-American, Puerto Rican, and American Indian children because of the linguistic, economic, and residential factors which affect their education. Consideration is given also to a matter of some importance to Jews, namely, admission to colleges and professional schools. In analyzing this phase of intergroup relations, it is well to keep in mind the political, economic, and social importance of education in a free society.

We shall give no detailed account of the education of the Negro prior to World War I. The Negro's educational experiences in the ante-bellum period, during the Reconstruction years, in the late nineteenth and early twentieth centuries are admirably set forth in the works of H. M. Bond, E. F. Frazier, and M. R. Davie.[1]

Public-school systems are responsive to the dominant social influences of the communities of which they are parts; their operations cannot be understood unless this point is grasped. State commissions of education, as well as county, city, and town boards of education, exercise control

[1] H. M. Bond, *The Education of the Negro in the American Social Order*, Prentice-Hall, Inc., 1934; E. Franklin Frazier, *The Negro in the United States*, The Macmillan Company, 2nd ed., 1957, chaps. 17–18; and Maurice R. Davie, *Negroes in American Society*, McGraw-Hill Book Company, 1949, chap. 6.

over educational policies. All of these agencies are subject to political forces, and inevitably they vary in competence and in social attitudes. The policies of principals and teachers are limited by the authority of superintendents and assistant superintendents, and often the latter are not well qualified in the field of intergroup relations.[2]

During Reconstruction years both conservatives and radicals in the South seemed to feel that proposals for Negro education were based on the assumption that the Negro population was to acquire the same general social standing and stratification as the white population had. The development of the sharecropping type of tenancy nullified much of the earlier discussion of Negro education. Bond points out that under such an exploitative system an educated labor force would be a liability rather than an asset. There was no reason for "spoiling a good plow-hand" or letting the Negro "get ahead of himself." In the Alabama constitutional convention of 1910 a planter "said that there was no fear of the illiterate Negro, but of 'the upper branches of Negro society, the educated, the man who after ascertaining his political rights forced the way to assert them.'"[3]

The Negro was well regarded in the Old South at the end of the nineteenth century as long as he remained "in his place." This "place" was that of a humble laborer. The fear that education would disturb the status system of this period is shown in the following "Letter to the Editor."

Editor, *Advertiser:*

The "new South" humiliation having made itself nauseous to the dwellers in our benighted section, we are next to be begrimed with the hogwash of the hopeful "nigger" and his prospects here in the South. Reasonable speculation and study of the questions as to what is to come of it if the negro gets strong enough to have a controlling influence in legislation, not to say in social arrangements, in a white civilization, is all well enough and proper. If the inquiry were put to a genuine Yankee whether it would advance the cause of liberty, personal morals, individual and national greatness, and general universal loveliness, to flood this country (not with niggers, but) with free Patagonians, or Feegians, or Hottentots, or even the "Heathen Chinee," or Cossacks, or Turks, or the freedom loving followers of the Mahdi, he could and would answer you most promptly, No.

. . . He would say to you that these people are not of us nor like us in any kind or degree; that physiologically, psychologically, constitutionally, they differ from us; that to absorb them would be to mongrelize and debase to a lower level the masses of our own. . . . He would tell you that education, whatsoever else it might do, will not bring forth the fruits with those races that it does with us.

[2] R. M. MacIver, *The More Perfect Union,* The Macmillan Company, 1948, pp. 208–209.

[3] H. M. Bond, *Negro Education in Alabama, A Study in Cotton and Steel,* The Associated Publishers, 1939, pp. 141–142.

. . . In our dismay . . . we turn tail and fly to education. "Wo! Is me, Alabama!" Well, of course, let education go on. It serves our purpose: it appeases, a little, political masters and religious cranks. But it is a stupendous farce and a snare.

. . . When sycophants of the Tom's Cabin sort and slobbering milksops, who mistake themselves for philanthropists, would mislead the mind of the Southern youth with that fallacy of fallacies that education can make the Negro their equal, we should denounce the false teaching, as wicked as false.

Old South[4]

For several decades after Reconstruction a debate raged over "industrial education" for Negroes. This term had varying meanings for different white people. Some believed that such education was "practical" and the only kind of public education worth stressing. Others thought that advocacy of "industrial" training was the only politically feasible way of improving Negro education. A good many advocated the formula as a means of rationalizing discrimination and keeping appropriations low for Negro schools.[5]

Booker T. Washington's influence in the industrial-school movement was strong and channeled philanthropy into the industrial school. "Riding on the Washington band wagon, the word 'Industrial' found its way into the names of schools of many types. The opposition of white persons to high schools for Negroes was mollified by calling these establishments 'Industrial Schools' when they were neither 'Industrial' nor 'High.' . . . The South was willing to embrace the suggestion of 'industrialized' schools when it was unwilling to tolerate the idea of secondary schools for Negroes."[6]

Actually, the industrial training for Negroes given in the public schools never was effective except in cooking and menial service. The South has not been willing to supply the expensive equipment and teaching necessary for real education in the industrial field. "Vocational" education for Negroes has been little more than a slogan to cover poor, cheap, and ineffective Negro education. The movement has died down in recent years for several reasons: the great reduction of illiteracy among Negroes; the realization on the part of public agencies, philanthropic foundations, and Negroes themselves that Negroes need the same varieties of education as others; the decline in importance of the issue of the educability of the Negro; and the fact that acculturation has been faster than had been anticipated.[7]

The ineffective educational programs for Negroes fitted in well with the developing industrialization of certain parts of the South. It helped

---

[4] *Ibid.*, pp. 142–143.

[5] Gunnar Myrdal, *An American Dilemma*, Harper & Brothers, 1944, p. 897.

[6] S. J. Wright, "Hampton-Tuskegee Pattern," *Phylon*, 1949, vol. 10, p. 340.

[7] Gunnar Myrdal, *op. cit.*, pp. 897–899; and S. J. Wright, *op. cit.*, pp. 340–342.

to keep Negro labor cheap and presumably it would provide insurance against labor troubles. An early Alabama industrialist stressed this point of view.

About 40 per cent of the total city population of Birmingham is Negro. About 90 per cent of the labor employed by all the furnaces, near Birmingham, is Negro.

Besides the Negro furnace labor, much of the labor employed by the city manufacturing industries in iron, such as the rolling mills, foundries, etc. is Negro. Increasing relative employment of it is the rule with all the hard labor enterprises.

The manifest result of the presence of the Negro labor here is that we have a more intelligent and orderly white laboring population than otherwise might be anticipated. The Negro of Birmingham fills the industrial position which elsewhere in great manufacturing towns is filled by a low class of whites. The Negro here is satisfied and contented; the low whites elsewhere are dissatisfied and turbulent. The white laboring classes here are separated from the Negroes, working all day side by side with them, by an innate consciousness of race superiority. This sentiment dignifies the character of white labor. It excites a sentiment of sympathy and equality on their part with the classes above them, and in this way becomes a wholesome social leaven.[8]

Industrial promoters and school superintendents held the viewpoint that Negroes were incapable of skilled mechanical work and relegated them as a race to the pool of common labor. The highly skilled work of Negro artisans on the plantations in the period before the Civil War was overlooked as the dominant men in the white group assured themselves that the needs of industry coincided with Negro capacity.[9]

The earlier attitudes and policies of southern industry were modified somewhat in the early 1900's by the coming of new concentrations of capital. In Alabama the larger industrial concerns, especially those in coal and iron, decided to elevate Negroes slightly in the socioeconomic scale. H. M. Bond shows the educational implications of this change in the self-conscious planning of the Tennessee Coal and Iron Company.

The principal labor in the mines was formerly furnished by Negro convicts, farmed out to private companies by the State of Alabama. With no "decent houses, no decent schools," the situation was described as "terrible" for George Crawford, installed as managing president, "who had a complicated metallurgical and developing problem thrust upon him and who needed steady, trustworthy labor if he was to succeed." The large industrial corporations were also faced with the problem of labor trouble. . . .

The Tennessee Company began at once to build up complete industrial and housing units, fitted with hospitals, welfare centers, and schools, by which means it was frankly hoped to regularize the uncertain Negro labor. It was officially stated that this was not a philanthropic movement: "The

---

[8] H. M. Bond, *Negro Education in Alabama*, p. 145.
[9] *Ibid.*, pp. 146–147.

Steel Corporation is not an eleemosynary institution," and its first object was "to make money for its stockholders."[10]

It is apparent that during the development of industrial centers like Birmingham Negro education was adjusted to the needs of the dominant members of the white group.

A close relationship has existed also between rural Negro schools and the agricultural system of the Old South. The dates for the opening and closing of school in the cotton belt were not set in advance but were determined by the landlords watching the crop. "In the spring and fall the internal school program is changed to accommodate the farming system. Chapel exercises, lunch hours, and recreational periods are either shortened or eliminated entirely in order that school may close at an earlier hour, to let children get away to the farms."[11]

The net result of the financial, political, and social forces playing upon education for Negroes is well pointed up in the report of the President's Commission on Higher Education.

According to the U.S. Bureau of the Census, data for 1940 revealed that Negro adults 25 years and over completed on the average only 5.7 years of schooling while the average for native white adults was 8.8 years and for foreign-born white adults was 7.3 years. While 92.5 percent of the native whites and 71.0 percent of the foreign-born whites had completed at least 5 years of grade school, only 58.0 percent of the Negroes had done so. While 82.7 percent of the native whites and 56.3 percent of the foreign-born whites had completed seventh grade, only 36.1 percent of the Negroes had accomplished as much. High school data are even more significant: 7.3 percent of the Negroes completed 4 years of high school; this contrasts with 28.8 percent of the native whites and 11.6 percent of the foreign-born whites. In higher education only 1.3 percent of the Negroes in contrast to the 5.4 percent of the native whites and 2.4 percent of the foreign-born whites completed a 4-year college course.[12]

Several relationships may be discerned between the social order of the South and Negro schools. First, the lower classes have not exerted much influence on public-school legislation and educational policies. Negroes have been virtually disfranchised since Reconstruction days, and, for the most part, the white working population has been politically impotent. Second, Negro public education has been keyed to the interests of those in the white group who have been in control of legislation and finance at a given time. Third, better provision for Negro education appears to have been made in (1) urbanized industrialized communities than in rural areas and in (2) counties with a small Negro population

[10] *Ibid.*, p. 240.

[11] Charles S. Johnson, *Patterns of Negro Segregation*, Harper & Brothers, 1943, p. 21.

[12] President's Commission on Higher Education, *Higher Education for American Democracy*, Government Printing Office, 1947, vol. 2, p. 30.

than where a larger population would require a greater expenditure.[13] In connection with these points, Myrdal's observation is pertinent: ". . . *The Southern whites have never had the nerve to make of Negro educa- tion an accomplished instrument to keep the Negroes in their caste status.* . . . The Southern whites' caste policy has been halfhearted all through. . . . The interest of educating the Negroes to become faithful helots has been obvious, but the Southern whites have not even at- tempted to make it effective in practice. Instead, they have merely kept Negro education poor and bad."[14]

Negroes in the Public Schools

A number of indexes are used to ascertain the availability and quality of educational opportunity. On the financial side, an important measure is instructional expenditures. These expenditures are calculated to have been 43 percent equalized between white and Negro schools in the South in 1940, and 75 percent in 1952.[15] The disparity between current expenditures per pupil in white and Negro schools is considerably greater in rural than in metropolitan areas. As Table 19.1 shows, in some

TABLE 19.1. Current Expenditures per Pupil in White and Negro Schools of Metropolitan and Rural Districts in the South, 1952[16]

	Metropolitan Districts		Rural Districts		Negro as Percent of White	
	White	Negro	White	Negro	Metro- politan	Rural
Seven states	$166.32	$126.45	$138.24	$ 85.10	76%	62%
Alabama	147.20	105.40	122.14	96.41	72	79
Arkansas	135.74	111.58	97.71	67.24	82	69
Florida	204.58	179.54	189.51	119.22	88	63
Georgia	184.57	132.66	147.34	89.79	72	61
Mississippi	152.30	78.11	82.73	27.05	51	33
North Carolina	169.64	161.14	148.98	117.23	95	79
South Carolina	170.21	116.75	179.31	78.77	69	44

[13] H. M. Bond, *Negro Education in Alabama*, pp. 290–291.

[14] Gunnar Myrdal, *op. cit.*, p. 896.

[15] T. M. Pierce, J. B. Kincheloe, R. E. Moore, G. N. Drewry, and B. E. Carmi- chael, *White and Negro Schools in the South*, Prentice-Hall, Inc., 1955, pp. 177–178. In 1929–1930, the seven states of Alabama, Arkansas, Florida, Georgia, Louisiana, North Carolina, and South Carolina averaged $43.50 current expenditure for each white pupil enrolled and $11.26 for each Negro pupil enrolled. See Alethea H. Wash- ington, "Availability of Education for Negroes in the Elementary School," *Journal of Negro Education*, 1947, vol. 16, pp. 446–447. The figures for the average current ex- penditure per white pupil and per Negro pupil in Mississippi in 1943–1944 were $71.65 and $11.96. See R. M. MacIver, *op. cit.*, pp. 37–38.

[16] Harry S. Ashmore, *The Negro and the Schools*, University of North Carolina Press, 1954, p. 155. These figures do not include transportation costs. The 1952 figures for North Carolina are for the 1950–1951 school year. (This and Table 19.2 are derived from data gathered by the SSCPEA staff from records and reports of state

states expenditures for Negro children in metropolitan areas exceed expenditures for white children in rural areas.

Another measure of financial differentials between white and Negro schools is capital outlay. Some progress has been made in reducing this difference, but the gap is still substantial. Table 19.2 indicates the trend from 1940 to 1952.

TABLE 19.2.   Capital Outlays per Pupil for White and Negro Schools in the South, 1940 and 1952[17]

| | 1940 | | 1952 | | Negro as Percent of White | |
	White	Negro	White	Negro	1940	1952
Eight states	$4.37	$ .99	$36.25	$29.58	23	82
Alabama	6.68	.62	14.19	8.55	10	60
Arkansas	3.20	.70	5.48	3.24	22	59
Florida	6.39	.80	74.03	79.18	13	107
Georgia	2.14	.23	26.80	14.28	17	53
Mississippi	n.a.	n.a.	25.48	35.23	. . .	138
North Carolina	6.04	1.84	59.10	54.90	30	93
Oklahoma	1.49	3.86	n.a.	n.a.	259	. . .
South Carolina	6.25	.66	24.70	11.45	11	46

n.a.—not available.

In the period 1940–1952, some interesting changes occurred in the value of public-school property for Negroes and for whites in southern states (Alabama, Arkansas, Florida, Georgia, Louisiana, North Carolina, South Carolina, and Virginia). In these states, Negro school property increased by 280 percent per child, as compared with an increase of 127 percent per white child. This change reduced the 4-to-1 ratio in favor of white children to 2.39 in 1952. Pierce and his collaborators point out, however, that "the dollar increase was much larger in white schools than in Negro schools, amounting to $254 per white pupil as compared to $140 per Negro pupil. . . . While $150.00 per Negro pupil would have been necessary for absolute dollar equalization in 1940, $264.00 per Negro pupil would have been required in 1952."[18]

An important item in school expenditures is teachers' salaries. The tradition in the South of paying higher salaries to white teachers than to Negro teachers with equivalent training and experience has gradually broken down. Since 1940, the salaries of Negro teachers have increased more than the salaries of white teachers, but in 1952 the average for white teachers was still $352 a year more. Teachers' salaries for whites

departments of education.) See *ibid.*, p. 154, for an explanation of the manner of compiling these figures.
    [17] *Ibid.*, p. 156.
    [18] T. M. Pierce et al., *op. cit.*, pp. 218–219, 237.

and Negroes varied from state to state, with the greatest difference in 1952 ($982) occurring in Mississippi. Negro teachers in North Carolina, Oklahoma, Tennessee, and Virginia averaged slightly higher salaries than white teachers in 1952. In these states the average training of Negro teachers is slightly higher than that of white teachers, and the Negro population is concentrated in urban areas, where salaries exceed those in rural areas.[19]

By 1951–1952, near equality had been achieved in teacher training; the average college experience for Negro teachers was 3.5 years, as compared with 3.8 for white teachers.[20]

The length of the school year has been almost completely equalized for white and Negro pupils. Such differences as remain are found in rural areas and, of course, favor white children.[21]

Pupil-teacher ratio is another index of educational effectiveness. In 1929–1930, white teachers in seventeen southern states averaged 33 pupils, whereas the average load for Negro teachers was 45. Fifteen years later white teachers in the segregated states had 32 pupils, and Negro teachers averaged 36. By 1951–1952, the pupil-teacher ratio was 23.6 for white schools and 25.6 for Negro.[22]

Supplemental services provide another index of the availability of education, and it is in these services that Negro children have fared worst. The number of school library books available per Negro pupil is less than half the number per white pupil, and the percentage of pupils eating in federally-aided school lunchrooms has been twice as great for whites as Negroes.[23] Complete transportation data for the separate school states for 1929–1930 are not available, but in five of these states (Georgia, Louisiana, Maryland, North Carolina, and Texas) 17.39 percent of the white pupils were transported to school, as compared with 0.55 percent of the Negro pupils. By 1944–1945, 37.94 percent of the white and 11.0 percent of the Negro pupils in these states were transported.[24] In 1952, 45.5 percent of the white children and 31.6 percent of the Negro children enrolled in the public schools of seven southern states (Alabama, Arkansas, Louisiana, North Carolina, Oklahoma, South Carolina, and Virginia) were being transported.[25]

Although substantial improvements have been made in Negro education in the South, the differential between white and Negro education remains large. Several supplementary points need to be added to this general conclusion. First, the shift of Negroes to metropolitan counties, where expenditures are higher, and the large increase in Negro secondary

[19] *Ibid.*, pp. 205–206.
[20] Harry S. Ashmore, *op. cit.*, p. 64.
[21] T. M. Pierce *et al.*, *op. cit.*, p. 238.
[22] Harry S. Ashmore, *op. cit.*, p. 64.
[23] *Ibid.*, p. 64.
[24] Alethea H. Washington, *op. cit.*, pp. 444–445.
[25] T. M. Pierce *et al.*, *op. cit.*, p. 231.

enrollment have made the relationship between the percentage of Negro population and the degree of equalization of expenditures much less significant.[26] Second, educational inequality varies widely within states and between states in the South. Anderson found that race differentiation in schooling "as measured by a 'discrimination index' ranges, among the subpopulations of the South, from a high of 85 to a low of 16 on a scale of 100."[27] Third, substantial additional school revenues are available without imposing an undue tax burden.[28] In some districts additional funds will be used to improve schools that for various reasons will remain all-Negro or preponderantly Negro; in other districts the increased monies will be invested in integrated education.[29]

ATTITUDES OF NEGROES TOWARD SEGREGATED EDUCATION

Few Negroes advocate segregated education. Those who do give the following reasons for supporting separate schools: (1) Mixed schools are concerned only with the needs of the white group; (2) the social discrimination which Negro children face in mixed schools has detrimental personality effects; (3) segregated schools provide an increased number of administrative and teaching positions for Negroes; and (4) segregated schools, completely controlled by Negroes, are better than mixed schools in which Negroes have no influence at all.[30] Those who argue along the lines of (1) and (2)—and their number includes some white people as well as Negroes—feel that the Negro child will get more "inspiration" or more "social participation" in the segregated school than he will in the mixed school. They say that a mean, indifferent, or obtuse white teacher can hurt a Negro child knowingly or unknowingly. As Reddick remarks, it is hard to measure the effect of this kind of teacher-pupil relationship. Assigning Negro pupils to all-Negro schools with Negro

[26] Ibid., pp. 177–178.

[27] C. A. Anderson, "Inequalities in Schooling in the South," American Journal of Sociology, May, 1955, p. 547.

[28] T. M. Pierce et al., op. cit., p. 150. Estimates of the price and the South's ability to pay the costs of (1) equalizing expenditures for public education between the races in the South, (2) the elimination of the capital deficit (the amount needed to bring the existing plant and equipment up to a minimum standard and to provide adequate space for the existing school population), (3) the increase in current expenditures and transportation to meet the yearly growth in average daily attendance, and (4) the increase in plant and equipment outlay to accommodate the growth in enrollment, are given in Ernst W. Swanson and John A. Griffin (eds.), Public Education in the South Today and Tomorrow, University of North Carolina Press, 1955, chaps. 8–9.

[29] For several years prior to the Supreme Court's decision on May 17, 1954, most of the southern states were engaged in a "billion-dollar effort" to provide "separate but equal" facilities for white and Negro students. Much of this effort has been continued since the decision. Mississippi has launched a $120,000,000 program for physical equalization of Negro public schools with those of the whites to discourage integration efforts. The first phase—consolidation of about 1000 local taxing districts into an estimated 150 in the 82 counties—was completed July 1, 1957. See Southern School News, June, 1957, p. 8.

[30] Charles S. Johnson, op. cit., pp. 23–24.

teachers does not insure fair and enlightened treatment. Negro pupils "are too often exposed to mean, indifferent, and obtuse Negro teachers, especially when the pupils are lower class and the teachers middle or upper class." Alternatives to the separate school include the assignment of teachers who have some knowledge and skills in intergroup relations and the organization of curricular and extracurricular activities as nearly as possible on the basis of full participation for all pupils.[31] In reply to (3), those who oppose the separate school feel that the question of administrative and teaching positions for Negroes should be thought of as part and parcel of the problem of full and fair employment.[32] On (4) the opponents of the separate school say that Negroes have no real control of Negro schools in a segregated system. According to this point of view, a dual system consists not of separate but autonomous units. Rather it has "the effect of a dominant system and a wardship, for Negro parents have little voice in determining or administering school policies for their children. The Negro school public is impotent, without authority and without responsibility."[33]

Most Negroes fight segregation if there is any chance of success. Even among those who are seemingly resigned to the force of race prejudice, there is strong resentment against segregation and discrimination.[34] The principal grounds for opposing segregation are that (1) in the past separate schools invariably have meant inferior schools for Negroes and (2) Negroes cannot participate fully in American life as long as they are compelled to live separately.[35] As we indicated earlier in this chapter, there has been abundant evidence over the years to support the first point. With regard to the second, it may be noted that until 1949 it was the policy of the National Association for the Advancement of Colored People to base its lawsuits on the ground that colored schools were not "substantially equal" to the corresponding white schools and that Negro children were therefore the victims of discrimination. The more recent program of the association is based on the contention that segregation itself violates the Fourteenth Amendment to the Constitution.

The Supreme Court's Decisions of May 17, 1954, and May 31, 1955

The decisions of the United States Supreme Court in the public-school cases in 1954 and 1955 were not sudden legal developments.

[31] L. D. Reddick, "The Education of Negroes in States Where Separate Schools Are Not Legal," *Journal of Negro Education*, 1947, vol. 16, p. 297.
[32] *Ibid.*, p. 298.
[33] Charles S. Johnson, *op. cit.*, pp. 12–13.
[34] Donald Young, *American Minority Peoples*, Harper & Brothers, 1932, pp. 497–498.
[35] Charles S. Johnson, *op. cit.*, p. 24.

These decisions affecting education were preceded by the Murray case of 1936, the Gaines case of 1938, and the Sweatt and McLaurin decisions of 1950 (see Chapter 20). Notable decisions in other areas included the ruling on the white primary in 1944, the racial restrictive covenants decision of 1948, and the banning of segregated interstate travel in 1946.

On May 17, 1954, the Supreme Court, consolidating cases arising in Delaware, Kansas, South Carolina, and Virginia, ruled unanimously that the separate-but-equal doctrine (Plessy v. Ferguson) which had been used to exclude Negro children from public schools maintained for white children was unconstitutional. The Court held that the plaintiffs, by being required on the basis of race to attend separate schools, were deprived of the equal protection of the laws assured by the Fourteenth Amendment. In a related case, the Supreme Court ruled on the same day that the separate-but-equal doctrine, when applied to exclude Negro children from admission to the public schools of the District of Columbia, violates the due-process clause of the Fifth Amendment.[36]

The Court pointed out that the Plessy case, long used to justify separate schools, was concerned with transportation rather than education. In none of the previous education cases had the Court actually decided that the Plessy doctrine applied to education. Since separate but equal facilities existed in the South Carolina and Virginia cases, the 1954 decisions could be based only on this ground. The Court found that education today is not merely "social" as in 1896 but "is perhaps the most important function of state and local governments" and "is a principal instrument in awakening the child to cultural values, in preparing him for later professional training, and in helping him to adjust normally to his environment." The Court concluded that racially separate schools have "a tendency to retard the educational and mental development of Negro children and to deprive them of some of the benefits they would receive in a racially integrated school system." Whereas the Plessy opinion held that segregation does not necessarily imply a badge of inferiority, the 1954 decision said that to separate grade- and high-school children from others solely because of race "generates a feeling of inferiority as to their status in the community that may affect their hearts and minds in a way unlikely ever to be undone."

In the District of Columbia case, the Court held that "segregation in public education is not reasonably related to any proper governmental

[36] Race Relations Law Reporter, February, 1956, pp. 5, 9. Because of the volume of court decisions, new legislation, and policy changes by school boards, any discussion of the desegregation process is soon outdated. In this section we attempt to summarize developments at the local, state, and national levels in the three years following the May 17, 1954, decision. Students of this crucial aspect of race relations in the United States will find the following publications indispensable in keeping abreast of current changes: Southern School News (monthly), Race Relations Law Reporter (quarterly), and Journal of Negro Education (quarterly).

objective. . . ." Pointing out that the Fourteenth Amendment contains a due-process clause in the same language as the Fifth Amendment, Hill and Greenberg conclude that "from now on all segregation by state as well as federal governments will have to pass the apparently unpassable test of 'reasonable relationship.' "[37]

Recognizing the complexity of implementing its far-reaching decrees of May 17, 1954, the Supreme Court postponed arguments on how the ruling should be carried out. The attorneys general of the separate-school states were invited to submit proposals in the fall of 1954 for accommodating their school systems to the new legal principle. The Court's second unanimous decision, handed down on May 31, 1955, stated: "All provisions of federal, state or local law requiring or permitting such discrimination must yield to this [the May 17, 1954] principle." Trial courts that had originally heard the cases were instructed to order a "prompt and reasonable" start toward desegregation with a view to "good faith compliance at the earliest practicable date." No deadline was set for the desegregation of the public schools, but the Court said it should be carried out "with all deliberate speed."

The Supreme Court did not require immediate compliance with its two decisions because it recognized that local conditions vary and that time must be allowed for administrative changes. Legitimate grounds for delay included "problems related to administration, arising from the physical condition of the school plant, the school transportation system, personnel, revision of school districts and attendance areas into compact units to achieve a system of determining admission to the public schools on a non-racial basis, and revision of local laws and regulations which may be necessary in solving the foregoing problems."

WHAT DO THE 1954 DECISIONS MEAN?

In the simplest terms, the historical decisions of 1954 mean that the rigid and arbitrary separation of the races in the public schools solely on the basis of race is no longer legal. An explanation of the Court's decisions was given in Judge Bryan's memorandum in the Arlington school cases. He wrote:

It must be remembered that the decisions of the Supreme Court of the United States in Brown v. Board of Education, 1954 and 1955, 347 United States 483 and 349 United States 294, do not compel the mixing of the different races in the public schools. No general reshuffling of the pupils in any school system has been commanded. The order of that court is simply that no child shall be denied admission to a school on the basis of race or color. Indeed, just so a child is not through any form of compulsion or

[37] Herbert Hill and Jack Greenberg, *Citizen's Guide to Desegregation*, The Beacon Press, 1955, p. 120.

pressure required to stay in a certain school, because of his race or color, the school heads may allow the pupil, whether white or Negro, to go to the same school as he would have attended in the absence of the ruling of the Supreme Court.[38]

In Houston, Texas, in May, 1957, U.S. District Judge Ben Connally made the same point in distinguishing between racial desegregation and "forced integration."[39] In actual practice, as later discussions in this section will indicate, many school districts have gone considerably beyond the minimum policy changes called for by the Court's decisions.

ACCEPTANCE OF AND RESISTANCE TO THE DECISIONS OF THE SUPREME COURT

The public-school decisions were welcomed enthusiastically by supporters of civil liberties, "liberal" political leaders in both major parties, and spokesmen for minority-group organizations. Within four months of the decisions, public-school desegregation had been started in four large cities (Baltimore, St. Louis, Washington, and Wilmington) and in more than forty smaller cities and towns. By the end of 1954, twenty-five of West Virginia's forty-four counties had begun or completed desegregation. Separate schools in Arizona were practically eliminated by the Court's decisions. Within less than a year, nine of the twelve cities in Kansas which were authorized by local option to have segregated schools had started to integrate. In Missouri, Negro children were admitted to previously all-white schools in 110 school districts.[40] Kansas and Missouri did not argue questions of implementation in the Court in May, 1955, and other states asked only for recognition of their plans for desegregation and for time for their completion.

Pro-segregationists criticized the decisions and the justices of the Supreme Court. Senator Russell remarked that the Court had substituted psychology for law, and Senator Eastland said that the South "will not abide by or obey this legislative decision by a political court." M. D. Collins, Georgia's State Superintendent of Schools, said he was "not certain" the ruling applied to Georgia. Senator Byrd called the decisions "the most serious blow that has yet been struck against the rights of the states in a matter affecting their authority and welfare," and Representative Thomas B. Abernathy of Mississippi stated: "The white and Negro children of my state are not going to school together despite the Constitution." In the spring of 1956, nineteen senators and eighty-two representatives from eleven states signed a manifesto denouncing the Supreme Court's decisions on school segregation. In addition, this state-

[38] *Southern School News*, September, 1956, p. 8.
[39] *Ibid.*, June, 1957, p. 2.
[40] Herbert Hill and Jack Greenberg, *op. cit.*, pp. 130–131.

ment commended "the motives of those states which have declared the intention to resist forced integration by any lawful means."[41]

On the official political level, opposition to the school segregation decisions has taken many forms: legislative acts and resolutions, amendments to state constitutions, and decisions by state supreme courts.[42] By November, 1957, the legislatures in eleven states had adopted a total of 142 pieces of pro-segregation legislation. A number of southern states have endorsed the doctrine of "interposition."[43] Several states have established "watch-dog" (state sovereignty) commissions to implement their resolutions of interposition.

Mississippi and South Carolina have amended their constitutions to permit abolition of public schools by legislatures, counties, or school districts, and similar amendments have been proposed in other states.[44] Devices to implement the proposed abolition of public schools include grants-in-aid to private schools, direct grants to pupils, and the right of school trustees to sell or lease school property. In Georgia it is a felony for any state, municipal, or county school official to spend tax money for public schools in which the races are mixed, punishment being two years in the penitentiary in addition to liability for the money expended.[45] Georgia's State Board of Education has abandoned two resolutions previously adopted which provided for revocation of the teaching license of any teacher who held membership in the National Association for the Advancement of Colored People or who approved or agreed to teach racially mixed classes, but it requires teachers to sign an oath to "uphold, support, and defend the constitution and law" of Georgia.[46]

---

[41] *Southern School News*, April, 1956, p. 1. Doubtless political forces, and not simply agreement with the manifesto, played some part in the signatures.

[42] *Ibid.*, May, 1957, p. 1.

[43] According to Professor Wylie H. Davis, of the law school of the University of Texas, " 'Interposition' is a label for the doctrine that any one of the American states has the legal right to 'interpose' its sovereignty against an exercise of national governmental power deemed by that state to violate the federal Constitution, and specifically deemed to violate it by usurping powers not delegated to the national government but reserved to the states or to the people. The idea is that the state's sovereign, protective right of resistance is 'placed between' the national government's act and the state's citizens." Davis calls "interposition" a euphemism for nullification; and in his opinion, "as anything more than a formal and official protest against federal action, the doctrine is a legal absurdity." *Ibid.*, March, 1956, pp. 1–2.

[44] J. M. Nabrit, Jr., "Legal Inventions and the Desegregation Process," *Annals of the American Academy of Political and Social Science*, March, 1956, pp. 41–42. Nabrit points out that these proposals are similar to the action taken in South Carolina to circumvent the ruling against the white primary. According to Nabrit, "South Carolina repealed all its statutes and constitutional provisions relating to primary elections. In an action brought in federal district court to enjoin officials of the South Carolina Democratic party from refusing primary ballots to Negroes, the officials contended that the party was a private organization free from all state control. . . ." The Circuit Court of Appeals held that the party officials were subject to the limitations of the Fourteenth and Fifteenth Amendments.

[45] *Ibid.*, p. 38.

[46] *Ibid.*, p. 40.

Louisiana and Mississippi have amended their constitutions to provide for separate schools as an exercise of the state police power "to promote and protect health, morals, better education and the peace and good order of the state and not because of race."[47]

A procedure which has been favored by those seeking continuance of segregated public schools is the pupil placement law. This type of legislation, adopted by Alabama, Arkansas, Florida, Louisiana, North Carolina, Tennessee, and Virginia, provides for the assignment of students to specific schools on grounds other than race.[48] Reassignments are made by school officials for a variety of reasons, including residence, possession of birth certificate, and economic and psychological factors. Opponents of segregation say these laws are designed to create administrative obstacles to legal action. They claim the phrasing of the laws makes it hard to separate pseudoadministrative difficulties from actual ones. It has been pointed out also that when it is necessary to sue each school board or superintendent, the impact of any adverse legal decision is weakened.[49] Virginia's pupil assignment law has been held unconstitutional "on its face" by a federal judge, and a federal court handed down a similar ruling on Louisiana's segregation statutes.[50] An interesting and important development occurred on June 17, 1957, when the United States Supreme Court approved, without comment, a lower court order to desegregate New Orleans public schools, an order which also invalidated the state's pupil assignment act.[51]

Of major importance in the conflict between the pro-segregation and pro-desegregation forces, and a development which has implications for the civil liberties of the whole population, is the effort to destroy or to frustrate the NAACP. Since the decision of May 17, 1954, eleven states (Alabama, Arkansas, Florida, Georgia, Louisiana, Mississippi, North Carolina, South Carolina, Tennessee, Texas, and Virginia) have used legislative or court actions to restrict or to halt the program of this organization.[52] In Alabama, the NAACP was banned by court order on July 25, 1956, and fined $100,000 for contempt because it refused to turn

[47] *Ibid.*, p. 39. Port Arthur, Galveston, and other communities in Texas dropped plans for desegregating their schools in the fall of 1957 because of a new state law which provided penalties, including loss of state aid, for districts which desegregate without a popular vote. Districts which had integrated schools in 1956–1957 could continue their programs without holding an election. *Southern School News*, August, 1957, pp. 1, 8.

[48] *Ibid.*, February, 1957, p. 1.

[49] J. M. Nabrit, Jr., *op. cit.*, p. 36.

[50] *Southern School News*, February, 1957, p. 1. In July, 1957, the U.S. Fourth Circuit Court of Appeals upheld the district court's ruling on Virginia's pupil placement act. Desegregation in Norfolk and Newport News, and in Arlington and Charlottesville, will depend upon the action taken by the Supreme Court in the appeal. *Ibid.*, August, 1957, p. 16.

[51] *Ibid.*, July, 1957, p. 7.

[52] See Joseph B. Robison, Benjamin Mintz, and Spencer Rich, *Assault upon Freedom of Association*, American Jewish Congress, 1957, pp. 10–29.

over a list of its members to the state's attorney general.[53] Other states, including Louisiana and Texas, have also issued injunctions against the NAACP. The Alabama case, upheld by the Alabama Supreme Court, has been appealed to the U.S. Supreme Court. Statutes passed in 1957 in Georgia, South Carolina, and Tennessee defining the crime of barratry (the fomenting or inciting of litigation)[54] are aimed mainly at the NAACP.

In many parts of the South, White Citizens' Councils have been organized to intimidate Negroes who support desegregation. Negroes who sign petitions to admit their children to nonsegregated schools often lose their jobs and have little or no opportunity for other employment. In addition to other types of economic pressure such as the stopping of credit, loans, and supplies, some of the councils have discouraged Negroes from voting and from belonging to the NAACP. Although the membership and leadership of the councils vary considerably, many of the leaders are persons of some standing in their community and state.[55] The original leaders, six citizens of Sunflower County, Mississippi, agreed that violence should not be a part of the movement. Apparently actual threats of physical violence usually come from unofficial sources, but the Clinton, Tennessee, incidents and the attack on Nat King Cole indicate the steps which some councils are prepared to take.[56] One speaker at an organizing meeting in Dallas County, Alabama, explained the principle of economic coercion in this way: "The white population in this county controls the money, and this is an advantage that the council will use in a fight to legally maintain complete segregation of the races. We intend to make it difficult, if not impossible, for any Negro who advocates desegregation to find and hold a job, get credit or renew a mortgage."[57] After the condemnation which this widely publicized statement received in the South and elsewhere, some White Citizens' Council leaders minimized or disclaimed organizational responsibility for economic sanctions. Harold C. Fleming points out that regardless of the degree of direct responsibility attributed to the councils, both economic and social reprisals have been used extensively against

[53] "Alabama Ban," The Crisis, May, 1957, p. 297.

[54] Race Relations Law Reporter, April, 1957, pp. 501–503.

[55] F. B. Routh and P. Anthony, "Southern Resistance Forces," Phylon, First Quarter, 1957, pp. 50–52, estimate a membership of 325,000 and a combined treasury of $2,000,000 for the resistance movement. They give as the four chief "planks" in the movement's platform: (1) political activity (gaining support of state governments, commissions, and political leaders; legislation and court action against the NAACP; resolutions on interposition; legislation to maintain segregation; etc.); (2) large grass-roots membership; (3) mobilization of public opinion (editorials and columns in southern newspapers; articles in United States News and World Report, in Harper's Magazine, and in other publications with national circulation; and television programs); (4) social and economic pressure. See also J. M. Nabrit, Jr., "Desegregation and Reason," Phylon, Third Quarter, 1956, pp. 287 ff.

[56] F. B. Routh and P. Anthony, op. cit., pp. 51–52.

[57] Montgomery Advertiser, December 1, 1954.

those who favor desegregation.[58] It should be added that white citizens who advocate compliance are subject to economic and social pressures, and that the councils have threatened to screen all candidates for local, state, and national offices for pro-Negro sentiments.[59]

STATUS OF PUBLIC-SCHOOL DESEGREGATION IN 1957

Many school systems in the United States did not wait for the Supreme Court decision of 1954 before beginning the desegregation process. Among other reasons for the changes instituted by school boards and officials in the early 1950's were the Court's rulings in the Sweatt and McLaurin cases of 1950, the economies to be effected by integration, and the campaigns carried on by the NAACP and other organizations. In one study of twenty-four communities in six states bordering the South (desegregation was required by law in Illinois, Indiana, New Jersey, and Ohio; in Arizona and New Mexico it was permitted but not required), only two communities had made no attempts at desegregation before May 17, 1954.[60]

On February 1, 1954, Defense Secretary Charles E. Wilson ordered the Army, Navy, and Air Force to end segregation in all military post schools by September 1, 1955. This order affected the separate schools, operated by local school agencies with funds provided by the federal government, on twenty-one bases. The order stated that if the local agencies would not, or because of state laws could not, maintain integrated schools on the bases, the United States Office of Education had agreed to operate the schools.[61]

By November 15, 1957, 761 biracial districts in the seventeen southern and border states, plus the District of Columbia, had begun or accomplished the desegregation process. Still entirely segregated were 2247 biracial districts. With the exception of ten districts in Arkansas, three in North Carolina, and three in Tennessee, all of the 761 desegregated districts are in the border states and Washington, D.C.[62] There were 1,953,898 white pupils and 375,195 Negro pupils in "integrated situations." No public-school desegregation below the college level had

[58] Harold C. Fleming, "Resistance Movements and Racial Desegregation," *Annals of the American Academy of Political and Social Science*, March, 1956, p. 49.

[59] Hodding Carter, "A Wave of Terror Threatens the South," *Look*, March 22, 1955, p. 34.

[60] Robin Williams, Jr., and Margaret W. Ryan (eds.), *Schools in Transition: Community Experiences in Desegregation*, University of North Carolina Press, 1954, p. 19.

[61] Cleveland *Plain Dealer*, February 1, 1954.

[62] Three North Carolina cities—Charlotte, Greensboro, and Winston-Salem—accepted a dozen Negro pupils into formerly all-white schools "in the eight-state Southeast and Deep South area where resistance to the U.S. Supreme Court decisions has been strongest." *Southern School News*, August, 1957, p. 1. For details of three cities in Arkansas (Little Rock, North Little Rock, and Fort Smith) where integration began in the fall of 1957, see New York *Times*, July 21, 1957. Desegregation began also at Van Buren, Arkansas, by court order.

TABLE 19.3. Enrollment Data for November, 1957.[63] (Includes 1957–1958 estimates where available, 1956–1957 enrollments where current estimates not available)

Enrollment in public schools	12,353,575
White	9,431,004
Negro	2,922,571
Percentage Negro	23.65%
Number of school districts	8,832
Number having Negroes	3,008
Number of teachers	438,372
White	346,566
Negro	91,806

Status of Desegregation, Public Schools

	School Districts			Estimated Enrollment, 1957			Students in Integrated Situations	
	Total	Bi-racial	Deseg.	White	Negro	Avg. % of Total	White	Negro
Alabama	111	111	0	475,500	279,300	37.0	0	0
Arkansas	423	228	9	316,709	102,000	24.3	16,609	1,929
Delaware	102	61	18	56,913	12,429	17.8	25,706	5,145
District of Columbia	1	1	1	33,000	77,000	70.0	33,000	77,000
Florida	67	67	0	703,800	196,200	21.8	0	0
Georgia	200	196	0	649,800	300,200	31.6	0	0
Kentucky	217	170	114	551,771	38,358	6.5	218,615	23,500
Louisiana	67	67	0	390,625	234,375	37.5	0	0
Maryland	24	23	21	417,214	116,275	21.6	387,938	106,930
Mississippi	151	151	0	276,276	269,724	49.4	0	0
Missouri	3,600	244	209	675,000	77,000	10.0	—	60,000
North Carolina	172	172	3	755,000	322,000	29.8	44,353	23,787
Oklahoma	1,469	271	214	495,664	36,390	6.8	247,541	24,817
South Carolina	107	107	0	337,000	253,000	42.8	0	0
Tennessee	152	141	3	657,560	133,740	16.9	18,020	1,644
Texas	1,800	841	123	1,627,307	258,333	13.7	560,000	24,600
Virginia	114	114	0	584,285	190,413	24.5	0	0
West Virginia	55	43	46	428,300	25,834	5.4	402,116	25,834
Total	8,832	3,008	761	9,431,004	2,922,571	23.65	1,953,898	375,195

[63] Data provided by Southern Education Reporting Service, December, 1957.

occurred in the states of Alabama, Florida, Georgia, Louisiana, Mississippi, North Carolina, South Carolina, and Virginia.[64]

There was no change in the status of the Clarendon County, South Carolina, case, one of the five cases involved in the Supreme Court's decision of 1954. Although that case is on the docket with orders for "prompt and reasonable" compliance, the schools of the Summerton district are still segregated. In another of the five original cases, a U.S. district court, in refusing to set a deadline for desegregation in the Prince Edward, Virginia, case, said that public opinion in the county was unfavorable to desegregation and the possibility that schools would be closed required it to defer entering an order in the case.[65]

LOWER COURT DECISIONS OF 1956 AND 1957

Among the important court decisions and orders of 1956 and 1957 are the following:

A United States District Court denied an injunction .n an action brought against the school officials of Little Rock, Arkansas, to prevent the enforcement of Arkansas' constitutional and statutory provisions requiring segregation in the public schools. The defendants, conceding the invalidity of the constitutional and statutory provisions, presented the court a plan for the gradual integration of the schools. That plan called for integration to begin at the high school level in the fall of 1957 and to be extended throughout the system in approximately six years. The plan was approved as constituting a "prompt and reasonable start" toward full integration, but the court retained jurisdiction of the case.[66]

On July 31, 1956, a U.S. district court found that the plaintiffs in the Arlington, Virginia, public school case had effectively exhausted available state administrative remedies and granted an injunction to the plaintiffs. The injunction provided for the admission of pupils to the elementary schools without regard to race on January 31, 1957, and to junior and senior high schools in September, 1957. Jurisdiction was retained to supervise the enforcement of the injunction.[67]

No desegregation occurred in January, 1957. The United States Supreme Court refused to review the Arlington County and Charlottesville desegregation orders.[68]

A federal court approved integration by the Hoxie, Arkansas, District and granted an injunction against interference by pro-segregationists.[69]

A district court ordered the public schools of Norfolk and Newport News to desegregate.[70]

The Court of Appeals for the Fifth Circuit upheld the decision of a

[64] *Southern School News*, June 1957, p. 1.
[65] *Race Relations Law Reporter*, April, 1957, p. 295.
[66] *Ibid.*, October 1956, p. 851.
[67] *Ibid.*, p. 890.
[68] *Southern School News*, June, 1957, p. 4.
[69] *Ibid.*, June, 1957, p. 8.
[70] *Ibid.*, p. 4.

federal district court requiring the admission of children to public schools in Orleans Parish, Louisiana, without racial discrimination.[71]

A U.S. district court declined to issue a permanent injunction requiring the admission of Negro children on a racially nondiscriminatory basis to the public schools of Hopkins County, Kentucky, but it held that the plan of voluntary integration which would have begun with the first grade and integrated one grade each year could not be regarded as meeting the requirements of "all deliberate speed." At a later hearing (February 8, 1957), the school officials submitted a substitute plan, calling for the completion of integration over a period of four years. The District Judge did not approve the amended plan and ordered that integration of the schools be completed by September, 1957.[72]

A federal district judge ordered the admission of four Negroes to a white high school in Earlsboro, Oklahoma, for the spring semester of 1957, and advised the district to provide for full integration in 1957–1958.[73]

The United States Circuit Court of Appeals ordered Dallas, Texas, to desegregate its schools, reversing a decision by a district judge. No time limit was set, but the court ordered that the schools be integrated "with all deliberate speed."[74]

Under federal court order, the Nashville, Tennessee, school board decided to begin desegregation in the first grade in September, 1957.[75]

In a suit filed by Negro school children in Clayton, Delaware (one of eight such suits brought in the federal district court in that state), the school district officials moved to dismiss the action on the grounds that the complaint failed to allege that no administrative impediments existed to school desegregation. The court held that administrative impediments to the opening of public schools without regard to race were not matters to be alleged by persons seeking admission. Such questions, the court held, were matters of mitigation which might be shown by school officials in indicating their good faith compliance with the mandate of the Supreme Court. After granting a motion by the plaintiffs for a summary judgment, the court directed the school board to present to the State Board of Education, within thirty days, a plan for integrating the schools and ordered the state board to submit its plan to the court within sixty days.[76]

Thus the action of the lower courts has consistently supported the desegregation decision.

DESEGREGATION IN LEXINGTON AND LOUISVILLE, KENTUCKY

Most of the desegregated school districts in Kentucky have adopted the voluntary or free-choice plan. Lexington was the first large city in the state to desegregate (1955); but of some 2750 Negro pupils, only 25 chose to enroll in formerly all-white schools in 1955, and only 35

[71] Race Relations Law Reporter, April, 1957, p. 295.
[72] Ibid., p. 305.
[73] Southern School News, June, 1957, p. 5.
[74] Cleveland Plain Dealer, July 24, 1957.
[75] Southern School News, June, 1957, p. 5.
[76] Race Relations Law Reporter, April, 1957, p. 301.

in 1956. The initial enrollment decreased by five at the end of each year. The white enrollment is 5705.[77]

On February 6, 1956, the Louisville, Kentucky, Board of Education approved a plan for redistricting "without regard to race" its fifty-six elementary schools, and top-to-bottom (kindergarten through twelfth grade) desegregation was put into effect in September, 1956. A flexible, free-choice transfer provision permitted pupils to transfer to other schools if they preferred to be in one predominantly of their own race. Most Louisville parents did not request transfers from the schools to which their children were originally assigned. In the case of children assigned to schools in which their race would have been greatly outnumbered, 85 percent of the white parents and 45 percent of the Negro parents asked for (and in nearly all cases received) their children's transfers to schools which had a majority of pupils of their own race. Louisville's enrollment in the fall of 1956 consisted of 33,831 white and 12,010 Negro pupils; 73.6 percent of the total of 45,841 were in racially mixed classes. In the six senior high schools there were 5832 students, with 20.3 percent in one all-Negro school; none in all-white schools; and 79.7 percent in mixed schools. In thirteen junior high schools with a combined enrollment of 8004, 8.4 percent were in three all-Negro schools, 17.8 percent in one all-white school, and 73.8 percent in nine mixed schools. In fifty-six elementary schools with an enrollment of 19,917, 10.7 percent were in five all-Negro schools, 17.3 percent were in ten all-white schools, and 72 percent in 51 mixed schools.[78]

DESEGREGATION IN WASHINGTON, D.C.

One week after the May 17, 1954, decision of the Supreme Court, the board of education in Washington, D.C., adopted a desegregation policy. When the schools opened in September, 116 (73 percent) of them had mixed student bodies. Thirty-eight faculties were integrated. Children were given the option of staying where they were enrolled until graduation or asking for a transfer. Several thousand pupils were granted transfers, most of the transfers being from Negro to white schools.[79] New school boundaries were drawn, and provision was made for all who wished to attend school on the basis of the desegregated boundary lines to do so, beginning in 1955. Newly enrolled children were assigned according to the new map.

Integration proceeded smoothly until a student strike began early in

---

[77] *Southern School News*, June, 1957, p. 12.

[78] *Ibid.*, February, 1956, p. 7; March, 1956, p. 7; September, 1956, p. 5; November, 1956, p. 11. Louisville and its county, Jefferson, announced that there would be no integration of faculties in desegregated schools "for the time being." *Ibid.*, August, 1957, p. 1.

[79] Irene Osborne and Richard K. Bennett, "Eliminating Educational Segregation in the Nation's Capital, 1951–1955," *Annals of the American Academy of Political and Social Science*, March, 1956, p. 102.

October, 1954. The strike lasted one week, with 2500 junior and senior high-school students out of school at its peak. More than 100,000 pupils continued in classes that were not affected by the strike.

By September, 1955, school administrators claimed that the dual school system had been eliminated. While not every school had both white and Negro students, no child was denied admission to any school because of race.[80]

Two-thirds of the public-school pupils in Washington, D.C., were Negroes in November, 1956. According to Superintendent Corning, the percentage of white enrollment has dropped each year since 1945, when 56 percent of the public-school population was white and 44 percent Negro. Migration to the suburbs, a continuing process over a period of years, "was probably stepped up somewhat due to integration," but the drop in white enrollment is not attributed to integration alone.[81]

Desegregation in the Baltimore, Maryland, Schools

The Baltimore superintendent, administrative staff, and school board proceeded on the assumption that talking in advance about integration would only focus attention on presumed problems and give the impression that difficulties were expected. The superintendent gave a talk to the teachers, but there was no special preparation for handling mixed classes. Enrollment figures at the end of the first month of desegregation showed that only 1576 colored pupils (3 percent of the Negro school population) had entered formerly all-white schools; 55,488 Negro students had entered or remained in Negro schools.

Most residential areas in Baltimore are all-white or all-Negro, and the schools in those areas remained all-white or all-Negro. In the few neighborhoods that are racially mixed, the schools became racially mixed.

At the end of September, picketing and demonstrations were begun by pupils or parents in about a dozen of the forty-eight schools that included white and Negro students. More than 97 percent of all the pupils remained in their classes during the demonstrations, and no estimate can be given as to how many of the remaining 3 percent were actually in sympathy with the protesters.[82]

Desegregation in Little Rock, Arkansas, in 1957

By September, 1957, ten school districts in Arkansas had desegregated or had made arrangements to desegregate to some degree. The Little Rock plan for gradual desegregation over a period of seven years, beginning with the high school, had been approved by the federal district

---

[80] *Southern School News*, March, 1957, p. 9.

[81] *Ibid.*, December, 1956, p. 16.

[82] Maryland Commission on Interracial Problems and Relations and the Baltimore Commission on Human Relations, *Desegregation in the Baltimore City Schools*, July, 1955, pp. 16–23.

court and was due to go into effect in September, 1957. On the night before nine Negro students were to enter Central High School, formerly an all-white school, Governor Faubus called out a National Guard unit of 150 men. The governor stated that the people of Little Rock were ready to riot, that caravans of white citizens from all over the state were moving toward Little Rock, and that stores were running out of knives. According to Governor Faubus, the Guard was called out only to preserve peace and prevent violence. A check by the city police had found no indication of trouble. The mayor of Little Rock said that the National Guard had been called out to put down trouble when none existed. Faubus' political opponents and some journalists asserted that the governor planned to run for a third term and needed some emotional issue to build himself up. Others suggested that Governor Faubus, who had once been regarded as relatively liberal on the race question, had joined with some of the strongest segregationists in the South to see how far they could go in devising ways for a state to defy the orders of a federal court. In any case, Governor Faubus directed the Guard to "place off limits to white students those schools for colored students and to place off limits to colored students those schools heretofore operated and recently set up for white students." United States District Judge Ronald Davies ordered the Little Rock school board to go ahead with its plan for integration and asked the Federal Bureau of Investigation to obtain facts concerning Governor Faubus' allegations and his defiance of the orders of a federal court. As a result of the furor, the Little Rock school board asked for a postponement of integration, but Judge Davies denied its request. The governor asked for a conference with President Eisenhower and a meeting was arranged for September 13. Apparently little was accomplished at this session. Mr. Faubus stated that the people of Arkansas would obey "valid court orders" and that in doing so they would have his support. On September 20, 1957, Judge Davies granted a preliminary injunction against Governor Faubus and the commanding officers of the Arkansas National Guard, enjoining them from obstructing or preventing by using the Guard or other means the attendance of Negro students at Central High School under the plan of integration approved in the federal court. The National Guard was withdrawn that night, and the following day President Eisenhower issued two statements approving the withdrawal.

Little Rock police were stationed at the school on September 23. The Negro students entered the school but disturbances during the day caused them to be withdrawn. On that day, President Eisenhower issued a statement saying that he would "use the full power of the United States, including whatever force may be necessary to prevent any obstruction of the law and to carry out the orders of the federal court." That evening the President issued a proclamation commanding all persons engaged in obstruction of justice at Little Rock to "cease and desist."

Such obstruction of justice, the President said, constituted a denial of the equal protection of the laws secured by the Constitution of the United States and impeded the course of justice under these laws. On September 24, the Army flew 500 regular paratroopers into Little Rock (the number was increased later to 1000), and the President federalized the Arkansas National Guard. The nine Negro students, guarded by paratroopers within the school, attended classes the next day. On September 28, President Eisenhower said that if Arkansas had used its police powers to support the orders of the court, "the ensuing violence and open disrespect for the law and for the federal judiciary never would have occurred."

The Conference of Southern Governors asked President Eisenhower to meet with a committee of its members to discuss the Little Rock situation. A meeting was held and a statement drawn up providing for the withdrawal of federal troops, the defederalization of the Arkansas National Guard, and the protection of the Negro students at Central High School. In making the statement public, Governor Faubus added two words which so modified the agreement reached between the President and the committee from the Conference of Southern Governors that it was unacceptable to Mr. Eisenhower.

Nationally, the Little Rock school situation is important because of its state-federal relationships. As President Eisenhower put the issue in his telegram to Senator Russell on September 28, "The police powers of the state of Arkansas" have "been utilized . . . to frustrate the order of the court." By early November, 1957, the number of federal troops in Little Rock had been cut in half and a majority of the members of the Arkansas National Guard were no longer under federal orders. Later, the number of paratroopers was reduced to 225 and all had been withdrawn by November 27. At that time, only 900 of the 10,500 Guardsmen were still federalized. Only a few soldiers were on duty at the high school each day.

Internationally, the Little Rock situation is important because of the unfavorable impressions it has given of the United States. One photograph in a Russian newspaper showed Vice President Nixon with his arm around a Negro; another photograph showed National Guardsmen with rifles raised to prevent a Negro student from entering Central High School. Japan's leading pictorial magazine published two pages of Little Rock pictures under the caption "America's Incurable Disease." President Eisenhower has said: "Our enemies are gloating over this incident and using it everywhere to misrepresent our nation." Kenneth Holland, president of the Institute of International Education, wrote from Poland on September 30: "The events in Little Rock during the last few weeks have done more to lower the prestige of the United States in the eyes of foreigners than anything that has happened in recent years."

Common Apprehensions About Desegregation

The problems usually feared in school desegregation concern health, behavior, social contact, and the lowering of academic standards. After a year's experience with integration, Baltimore found the first three of these fears without foundation and the fourth open to some questions. The Baltimore report states:

> As for academic problems, Baltimore had none in the first year as far as white children suffering from integration was concerned. Academic standards were not lowered or classwork slowed down to accommodate the colored children. There were some top Negro pupils, some middling ones, and some who learned very little, as was the case with white children. But in some elementary schools, where most of the mixing took place, it was noted that the proportion of slow learners among the colored children was greater than among the white. The difference was not apparent in the kindergarten and first grade, where Negro children made fine progress, but showed up in the upper grades.
>
> The explanations were obvious ones: The colored children had come by and large from overcrowded colored schools, with less individual attention, and from overcrowded homes with less opportunity to study in quiet and with less adult emphasis on educational values. And behind all that was the fact that Negroes have had fewer opportunities to obtain the jobs that are the supposed rewards of higher education and hence have had less incentive to learn. The native ability of colored children to learn was plain enough in those mixed classes where they entered as beginners, but among the older children who had transferred from segregated classes, it was equally plain that native abilities had not always been fully developed.[83]

Soldan High School in St. Louis, Missouri, previously an underpopulated all-white school, increased in size from 900 to 1400 in one year, and its Negro student population constituted one-third of the total. Desegregation was accomplished without any identifiable incidents or racial friction. Integration is complete, including seven Negro teachers among the faculty of eighty-three. Some faculty members have shown concern that "a too-rapid rise in the Negro student population, reflecting a heavier concentration than that which prevails in the surrounding community, could accelerate the exodus of white families"; and "the presence of students with varied and uneven elementary school training" has created some problems. Faculty members report a "general tendency of Negro students (with individual exceptions) to be tardier to school, tardier to class, more prone to skip an afternoon's classes, more inclined to absenteeism. Without reference to racial prejudice, and attributing the facts solely to differences in cultural, social or economic background, teachers say there is a definitely larger incidence of slackness, irresponsibility and intellectual laziness among the Negroes than among whites."

[83] *Ibid.*, pp. 28–29.

Because of their background and inferior grade-school training, Negroes as a group in Soldan High School rank lower in academic aptitude and achievement than whites. Since integration the teacher's job has become more difficult, but the general attitude on the part of the faculty is that "the problems of integration simply have to be faced and eventually solved."[84]

After three years of experience with racial integration, the staff of John Pitman School in Kirkwood, Missouri, believes that some progress has been achieved. They say that the third year was easier than the second, especially in the lower grades in which Negroes had had their entire school experience in a mixed school.[85]

The attitudes of Negro teachers in the South toward desegregation are of interest. A South Carolina study showed that half of the 150 subjects would prefer to teach in a desegregated school system, the other half would prefer segregated schools.[86] The economic aspect of desegregation is a major concern for many Negro teachers, although other considerations and justifications for the continuance of segregation are involved.

Many, perhaps most, of the 462 Negro teachers in the border states who were dismissed from their jobs because of school desegregation have been placed in other teaching jobs, in some cases at higher salaries. Oklahoma, where the bulk of teacher displacement occurred during the first two years of desegregation, may have been an exception. Approximately one-sixth of the 1697 Negro teachers employed in that state in 1954 were displaced when 112 Negro schools were abolished.[87] One study finds that the danger of Negro teachers' losing their jobs because of desegregation is not as great as many in the profession who favor segregation have believed. Negro teachers in large cities apparently fare best, those in very small or rural schools seem likely to lose out, and those in middle-sized districts appear to have the greatest doubts and conflicts. Despite the fact that the present teacher shortage will ease the situation of many Negro teachers, a sizable number of the 100,000 Negro teachers in public segregated schools are apprehensive concerning their jobs and other losses which they think may result from desegregation.[88]

EVALUATION OF PUBLIC-SCHOOL DESEGRATION, 1954–1957, AND FUTURE PROSPECTS

The results of the Supreme Court decisions of May 17, 1954, and May 31, 1955, are difficult to assess. It was pointed out earlier that

[84] *Southern School News*, February, 1956, p. 3.

[85] *Ibid.*, July, 1957, p. 6.

[86] H. H. Doddy and G. F. Edwards, "Apprehensions of Negro Teachers Concerning Desegregation in South Carolina," *Journal of Negro Education*, Winter, 1955, p. 42.

[87] *Southern School News*, November, 1956, p. 1.

[88] Jonas O. Rosenthal, "Negro Teachers' Attitudes Toward Desegregation," *Journal of Negro Education*, Winter, 1957, p. 70.

three years after the first decision virtually all of the desegregated schools were in the border states, and that more than four-fifths of the 3700 school districts in seventeen southern and border states had not begun desegregation. Apparently most of those who favor and those who oppose desegregation agree that (1) resistance to desegregation increased during 1955, 1956, and 1957; (2) there will be much litigation over the decisions for at least a decade; and (3) residential segregation will cause three-fourths or more of the Negro pupils in the South to attend separate schools for a decade or more. A fourth point that would not be conceded by many opponents holds that desegregation will proceed slowly in most parts of the South but is inevitable in the sense that eventually no child will be denied admission to any public school because of race.

Let us examine some of the reasons for these conclusions. Concerning the first point—increased resistance to desegregation in 1955–1957—the necessity of delaying the ruling on implementation until May, 1955, seems to have been of some importance. The doubling of the expected time span between the two decisions gave opponents of desegregation an opportunity to organize and develop support and strategies.[89] The failure for more than three years of President Eisenhower and his attorney general to speak out on the issue of enforcement may have been a factor in the reluctance of some districts to comply.[90] Attachment to

---

[89] In a few communities desegregation was marked by violence. In August, 1956, Clinton, Tennessee, experienced several days of mob activity, school picketing, and several arrests when twelve Negroes enrolled in the high school. The antidesegregation campaign in Clinton was directed by Frederick John Kasper, executive secretary of the Seaboard White Citizens Council of Washington, D.C. Six hundred National Guardsmen and one hundred Highway Patrolmen were sent to Clinton to quell the disturbances. The first year of desegregation ended quietly on May 17, 1957, with the graduation of the high school's first Negro student. At the end of the school year six of the original twelve students, including the graduating senior, remained in school. See Southern School News, September, 1956, p. 3; October, 1956, p. 15; June, 1957, p. 15.

[90] Attorney General Herbert Brownell urged the Supreme Court to remand the cases to the District Courts for enforcement under its supervision, and in the closing statement of his brief promised executive support. He said: "The responsibility for achieving compliance with the court's decision in these cases does not rest on the judiciary alone. Every officer and agency of the government, federal, state and local is likewise charged with the duty of enforcing the Constitution and the rights guaranteed under it." Charles Abrams, "Civil Rights in 1956," Commentary, August, 1956, p. 108. Abrams says it was always assumed that the President would back the Court with his prestige, his economic power, his vast influence in Congress and throughout the country, and, if necessary, his patronage powers. Instead, the impression was allowed to develop that the Supreme Court is responsible for all enforcement.

On September 24, 1957, the Executive Office of the President of the United States issued a statement concerning the duties and responsibilities of the executive branch of the federal government in school desegregation cases. The main points of the statement follow:

"1. The executive branch of the Federal Government does not participate in the formulation of plans effecting desegregation. . . . Although the Federal Government has no responsibility to initiate action to desegregate public schools or to formulate any plans for desegregation, the courts have made it clear that the De-

"southern traditions" and the reiteration of those traditions by the militant and articulate spokesmen for segregation have made it difficult for many Southerners to accept desegregation. The "southern way of life" has separated Negroes and whites in nearly every sphere of life and has given whites ascendancy in the social structure. According to a study by a group of southern educators, "The typical Southerner finds it very difficult to substitute the more radical doctrine of placing Negroes and whites in the same school for the doctrine he only recently accepted of providing equal educational programs for the two races."[91] They point out that the Court's decision creates turmoil in the average Southerner, for he has not yet found a way to reconcile his value commitments as an American with the race situation.

On the second point—the probable litigation—unquestionably there will be enough interest on the part of parents of Negro school children, and enough zeal on the part of attorneys general and "state sovereignty" commissions in southern states, to result in a large volume of litigation for several years to come. (Approximately 150 court cases dealing with segregation-desegregation questions were handled by the state and federal courts between May 17, 1954, and November 15, 1957.)

The third point concerns the influence of residential segregation on school desegregation in the near future. Probably more than three-fourths of the South's urban, small-town, village, and rural-nonfarm Negroes live in residentially segregated areas. Most of the pupils in these separate communities will find the nearby schools convenient and congenial, and efforts will be made to improve rather than abolish them.

---

partment of Justice, at the invitation of the Court, must participate in litigation involving high school desegregation for the purpose of assisting the Court.

"2. The period of time within which any such plan should be put into effect likewise must be proposed by the local authorities and approved by the courts. . . . The executive branch of the Government does not play a part in these local deliberations or, under existing law, in the court proceedings when such plans are considered.

"3. A final order of a Federal court giving effect to a desegregation public school plan must be obeyed by state authorities and all citizens as the law of the land. . . . It is the duty of the state authorities to give full aid to the enforcement of a desegregation plan once it is finally ordered by the Court. This obligation is not open to any doubt. It is also a required responsibility of good citizenship that every person in the community respect the law and its processes. Such observance of law is fundamental to our existence as a nation of free people under constitutional government.

"4. Powers of a State Governor may not be used to defeat a valid order of a Federal court. . . . The Governors of the respective states have the primary responsibility for maintaining domestic order. However, under a pretext of maintaining order a Governor may not interpose military force or permit mob violence to occur so as to prevent the final order of a Federal court from being carried out. When an obstruction of justice has been interposed or mob violence is permitted to exist so that it is impracticable to enforce the laws by the ordinary course of judicial proceedings, the obligation of the President under the Constitution and laws is inescapable. He is obliged to use whatever means may be required by the particular situation." NAIRO Reporter, December, 1957, p. 3.

[91] T. M. Pierce, et al., op. cit., p. 305.

In mixed or marginal residential areas there will be some mixed schools, and a small but increasing number of outstanding Negro students will request admission to "white" schools because of courses available there but not in the Negro schools. Guy B. Johnson predicts that "not more than ten percent of the total of Negro and white pupils will be attending school together in the cities of the South for a long time to come."[92]

Although there is no official segregation in northern cities, there are segregated schools. In New York City approximately twenty-five junior high schools and seventy-five elementary schools are "de facto segregated"—with almost totally colored enrollments. Under a plan started in the fall of 1957, school districts were rezoned where practicable to embrace racially diversified sectors, some Negro students were transported to white districts and vice versa, new schools were to be located so as to serve mixed populations, and attempts were made to equalize the quality of faculties in prosperous and poor neighborhoods. Inducements were offered for teachers to transfer to the "hardship" schools. The objective of the plan, according to the deputy superintendent of schools, "is to raise the achievement level of all pupils, with particular emphasis on Negro and Puerto Rican children."[93]

The fourth point mentioned above is that widespread integration in the public schools of the South will not occur in the next decade, but that desegregation will increase gradually and that the principle of not denying any child admission to any public school merely because of race will be generally if not universally accepted. A number of factors in present-day southern life seem to point to this conclusion. The marked drop in the Negro population in the rural areas will cause a large reduction in school attendance, and the economic problem of maintaining separate Negro schools for a steadily declining enrollment will be a serious one.[94] One estimate of the effect of the financial burden of trying to provide separate but equal schools is that within twenty to twenty-five years half of the rural school units in the South may consist of mixed student bodies.[95] Undoubtedly, the savings to be effected by desegregating urban schools will not be overlooked by some cities. A *Southern School News* questionnaire sent to the fifty-five county school superintendents in West Virginia indicates that considerable amounts of money have been saved and the teacher shortage somewhat eased by

[92] Guy B. Johnson, "A Sociologist Looks at Racial Desegregation in the South," *Social Forces*, October, 1954, p. 8.

[93] George W. Cornell (A.P.), Cleveland *Plain Dealer*, March 4, 1957. In 1957, about 75 percent of New York's public-school children attended elementary and junior high schools which are virtually on a segregated basis. In these schools 90 percent or more of all the pupils were either white, Puerto Rican, or Negro. See Benjamin Fine, "Education in Review," New York *Times*, July 21, 1957, p. E 7.

[94] See H. S. Ashmore, *op. cit.*, p. 60.

[95] Guy B. Johnson, *op. cit.*, p. 8.

eliminating separate school facilities for Negro and white children. The savings range from $250,000 annually in Kanawha County to a few hundred dollars in Lewis County.[96] Before desegregation in the Washington, D.C., school system, the continuing effort to maintain a rigidly segregated school system in the face of a rapidly shifting residential pattern produced crises, financial and otherwise. Commissioner F. Joseph Donohue estimated the financial cost of maintaining segregation in 1952 as between seven and eight million dollars—more than one-fourth of the total school budget.[97] In some areas with a heavy Negro concentration, however, there are factors that make it more costly to establish integrated schools. Where the expenditure per pupil in the Negro schools has been considerably below that for white pupils, an integrated situation that maintained the previous all-white expenditure rate would increase the cost of schools. This economic problem is greatest in precisely the areas least likely to desegregate because of other reasons.

Since there seems to be no possibility that the Supreme Court will take any position other than the one it took in the May 17, 1954, decision, we can expect that the final outcome of all future litigation concerning the exclusion of children from public schools solely on the basis of race will end with the finding that such exclusion is illegal. Because basic civil liberties questions are involved, it is highly improbable that the southern attack on the NAACP will succeed in preventing that organization from carrying on its program. Recent increases in the size of the Negro vote in the South, and further increases as a result of new civil rights legislation, will strengthen the political position of the Negro and will cause his voice to be listened to in education as well as in other matters. The continued industrialization of the South will tend to further desegregation in the schools. An indication of an awareness that racial peace must be maintained is seen in a speech made by Governor LeRoy Collins of Florida during the primary campaign of 1956. Like all candidates, Governor Collins came out for continued segregation, but he said:

> Believe me when I say Florida cannot afford an orgy of race conflict and discord. I have talked to many here and in other regions of the United States now poised preparatory to making substantial investments in Florida. One of the most effective appeals has been that we can offer soundness, stability, and security. Nothing will turn these investors away quicker than the prospect of finding here communities hepped up by demagogery and seething under the tension and turmoil of race hatred.[98]

Much has been said and written about the dire consequences of desegregating the public schools. The experiences of the schools which

[96] *Southern School News*, June, 1957, p. 3.

[97] H. S. Ashmore, *op. cit.*, p. 92.

[98] *Southern School News*, March, 1956, p. 13. In its year-end summary on Florida (June 1957, p. 11), this publication stated that Florida had "shifted from 'gradual-

desegregated during the first three years after the decision of May 17, 1954, do not bear out these predictions, but neither do these experiences show that integration is without its problems. For the South as a whole, the change will be gradual, but "gradual" in this context does not mean "never."[99] Desegregation is under way and it is unlikely that legislation, litigation, or activity on the part of White Citizens' Councils will reverse the process. Developments in the school situation are part of the vast changes in almost every aspect of American society in the last quarter of a century. Urbanization, political realignments, a shift toward more skilled jobs, and international developments are among the factors in the situation within which school desegregation is proceeding. It supports and is supported by the changes in other parts of the social structure, in all of which desegregation is the dominant process.

Mexican-American, Puerto Rican, and American Indian Children in the Public Schools

The large increase in the Mexican-American population in the southwestern states since 1900, together with a number of social factors—peasant background, low income, inadequate housing, linguistic differences, parent-child conflict, and antagonism from majority-group persons—has occasioned numerous tensions and problems in the public schools. There are now about two and a half million persons of Mexican descent in the United States, half of them in Texas.

The education of Mexican-American children has been notable for the low rate of school attendance. There are numerous reasons for the failure of these children to enroll in school. The parents of many of them are migratory laborers whose swing through the cotton-growing areas continues until December or January. Half a year's schooling is lost in this way. Although many of these children enroll for the second semester, they are placed, year after year, in the same grades because of the time they have lost. Some areas have crop schools, but these schools have not been successful. Other reasons related to the economic situation of these families include illness of the child or of some member of the family who needs attention; the inability to dress like other children, or to take lunches from home that can be eaten without embarrassment in the presence of the other children; and the economic need for each grown member of the family to be self-supporting or to help support the family—a strong pressure in many families during the adoles-

---

ism' to adamant opposition to integration and now seemed moving in the direction of its original position." In his second inaugural message, Governor Collins said that integration is inevitable, but that the pupil assignment law would prevent mixed schools in the foreseeable future. *Ibid.*, p. 11.

[99] See Herbert Hill and Jack Greenberg, *op. cit.*, pp. 153, 160; Harry S. Ashmore, *op. cit.*, pp. 79–80; and J. M. Nabrit, "Desegregation and Reason," p. 289.

cent's last two years in high school. Another reason for the nonattendance at school of many Mexican-American children is the attitude of the Anglo-American children or teachers. The word "Mexican" is sometimes used as a term of opprobrium, and children from Spanish-speaking homes are made to feel that they are not wanted. An additional factor is the attitude of parents toward education. Since many Mexican-American parents, whether they grew up in Mexico or in this country, have had very little schooling, they do not regard education for their children as important. Finally, the compulsory school attendance laws are often laxly enforced.

The practice of segregating Mexican-American children has been followed in many southwestern communities. Where these pupils are segregated, the usual pattern of discrimination is found. Overcrowded buildings, inferior equipment, less competent teachers, and shorter school terms are the rule in such schools. Griffith summed up the meaning of education to many Mexican-American children in segregated situations.

> To children required to live in segregated areas, the insecurity and sense of inferiority that comes early in childhood is intensified by school segregation. Throughout the Southwest, many Mexican-American children see the big school bus going through the streets of their town picking up the "Americans," one by one, to take them blocks away to the big school, with its auditorium, cafeteria, and play equipment. The "Mexican" youngsters often walk down the long road to the small school where "specially trained" teachers teach them about that almost unknown world that is America.[100]

This pattern, however, has been significantly changed. The Delgado case in Texas in 1948 established the illegality of segregating Mexican-American children in the schools. Following this decision the Texas State Board of Education issued a policy statement in harmony with the ruling, and instructions were sent to the local school districts to eliminate segregation of Mexican-American children.[101] The court permitted separate classes at the first-grade level only for those who, after scientific tests of language proficiency, do not know English, whatever the national or cultural background. In 1946–1947 the courts ruled in the Mendez case in California that segregation of Spanish-speaking children was illegal. Judge McCormick's ruling anticipated some of the arguments of the Supreme Court decision of 1954 in its emphasis on the harm done by segregation, with its inevitable implication of inferiority. In Driscoll, Texas, an action was brought in the federal district court stating that placing children of Mexican descent in separate classes

[100] Beatrice Griffith, *American Me*, Houghton Mifflin Company, 1948, p. 153.
[101] See George I. Sanchez, *Concerning Segregation of Spanish-Speaking Children in the Public Schools*, University of Texas, 1951.

for the first and second grades of school and requiring their attendance in these two grades for a period of four years was in deprivation of their rights under the Fourteenth Amendment as being discrimination on the basis of ancestry. On January 11, 1957, the court found that grouping pupils on the basis of ancestry was arbitrary and unreasonable and ordered that, beginning with the 1957–1958 school term, pupils should be grouped only on the basis of individual ability to speak and understand the English language.[102]

There is some disagreement concerning the degree to which these court decisions, and other influences, have brought about the desegregation of Mexican-American children in the schools of the Southwest. Most observers agree that substantial progress in the direction of desegregation has been made. A growing number of educators have concluded that the best way to teach English to a Spanish-speaking child is to place him in a class where many of his fellow pupils speak English as their first language.[103] This conclusion has eliminated one of the rationalizations for segregation on a language basis that easily carried over into segregation on the basis of Spanish name and nationality background. The lack of any legal basis for the segregation of Mexican-American children in the schools has accelerated the process of integration. Some segregation still exists because of gerrymandering and the free choice of school principle.[104] The economic status of most Mexican-Americans imposes barriers to school integration. With only a few months of schooling in the fall and spring, the children of migrant workers often fall behind their classmates, and many of them drop out of school at an early age. Legal desegregation does not eliminate barriers to full integration based on economic disadvantage.[105]

In 1957, Puerto Ricans comprised 14.0 percent of the public-school pupils in New York City (Manhattan, 32.0 percent Puerto Rican; Bronx, 19.3 percent; Brooklyn, 10.7 percent; Queens, 1.4 percent; and Richmond, 1.2 percent).[106] In the Puerto Rican group, 38.3 percent of the children were non-English-speaking. Seventy-five schools in Manhattan

---

[102] *Race Relations Law Reporter*, April, 1957, p. 329.

[103] There is no inconsistency between this point of view and the increasing attention being given to the special needs of Mexican-American children. See *Teachers' Guide to the Education of Spanish-Speaking Children*, Bulletin of the California State Department of Education, October, 1952; and *Teaching Children Who Move with the Crops*, Fresno County Public Schools, September, 1955.

[104] A four-year campaign against gerrymandering in the elementary schools of El Centro, California, was ended in December, 1955, when officials of Imperial County agreed to eliminate the protested practices. A suit had been filed in the United States District Court in February, 1955, and a retrial was pending when the settlement was reached. See New York *Times*, December 4, 1955, p. 64.

[105] J. Milton Yinger and George E. Simpson, "The Integration of Americans of Mexican, Puerto Rican, and Oriental Descent," *Annals of the American Academy of Political and Social Science*, March, 1956, p. 125.

[106] New York *Times*, July 21, 1957, p. E 7.

have had some concentration of Puerto Ricans, and these children have constituted 50 percent or more of the pupils in eight schools.[107]

Efforts to avoid the segregation of Spanish-speaking children in New York City schools have included special "vestibule" classes under a Spanish-speaking teacher who teaches pupils some English and some orientation to school and community life; substitute auxiliary teachers who speak Spanish and are assigned to orient Puerto Rican pupils and their families; individual help from teachers or from English-speaking students designated as "big brothers" and "big sisters"; and encouraging English-speaking and Spanish-speaking children to play games together and to go on sightseeing trips together.[108]

Separate federal schools for Indians were established primarily as a result of the treaties entered into by Indian tribes and the federal government. In the early 1880's the government gave subsidies to schools established by missionaries, and these responsibilities were expanded in accordance with provisions in treaties made up to 1880 and in some cases when treaties made no provision for education. Following church-state separation discussions around 1870, the government gradually withdrew its support of mission schools and began to increase the number of federal schools. When citizenship was given to all Indians residing in the country in 1924, education became a state responsibility. Laws enacted by Congress since 1936 have provided financial aid to states and local districts and have increased the public-school enrollment of Indian children.[109] Many public schools which Indian children attend are all-Indian. Nevada's supervisor has found that the situation is most satisfactory when Indian students constitute a minority of the total school enrollment and that results are less satisfactory when public schools are located on a reservation and the enrollment is entirely Indian.[110] Certainly attitudes have changed since 1928, when a state superintendent of public instruction wrote that the Indian "will never develop into

[107] Sophia M. Robison, "Social and Welfare Statistics on the New York Puerto Rican Population," in A. J. Jaffe (ed.), Puerto Rican Population of New York City, Bureau of Applied Social Research, Columbia University, 1954, p. 50.

[108] Since 1949, special steps have been taken by the Board of Education to deal with the problems of Puerto Rican education, including the establishment of workshops in the teaching of bilingual pupils and courses on educational programs for Puerto Rican children; the publication of a seventy-six-page booklet, Teaching Children of Puerto Rican Background; and "The Puerto Rican Study" (financed by the Fund for the Advancement of Education). The professional teachers' journals of New York City have carried numerous articles in recent years on the education of Puerto Ricans.

[109] See E. P. Dozier, George E. Simpson, and J. Milton Yinger, "The Integration of Americans of Indian Descent," Annals of the American Academy of Political and Social Science, May, 1957, p. 163. For an excellent review of past and present policies on the education of American Indians, see Hildegard Thompson, "Education Among American Indians: Institutional Aspects," Annals of the American Academy of Political and Social Science, May, 1957, pp. 95–105.

[110] Statement provided by E. A. Haglund on September 19, 1955.

much more than a mediocre American citizen," Indian children should be segregated from white children, and these children should be taught only the use of simple tools, the basic elements of farming, cattle raising, gardening, washing, ironing, cooking, sewing, etc.[111]

[111] State of Nevada, *Biennial Report of the Superintendent of Public Instruction,* 1927–28, p. 37.

CHAPTER 20

The Education of Racial and Cultural Minorities in the United States (continued)

Minorities in Higher Education

UNDERGRADUATE INSTRUCTION IN THE NEGRO COLLEGE

Despite the trend toward desegregation, a substantial majority of Negro college students (over three-quarters) attend segregated institutions.

There were thirteen Negro colleges in the United States in 1880, twenty-two in 1890, and thirty in 1900. College enrollment increased slowly because of the lack of qualified matriculants. Only three schools had more than 100 college students in 1900, and some had as few as six. Work for these students was not standardized, and the schools were not accredited.[1]

Approximately one-third of the Negro institutions (38 of 106) are publicly controlled, and half of these public colleges are land-grant institutions largely supported by the federal government.[2] All but seven of the private colleges are church-affiliated. For the most part, the private colleges are located in the seventeen southern or border states or the District of Columbia.[3]

In 1930 there were slightly more than 10,000 Negro students enrolled in Negro colleges. The number had increased to more than 29,000 by

---

[1] Charles S. Johnson, *The Negro College Graduate*, University of North Carolina Press, 1938, p. 281.

[2] G. N. Redd, "Present Status of Negro Higher and Professional Education: A Critical Summary," *Journal of Negro Education*, 1948, vol. 17, p. 401; Gunnar Myrdal, *An American Dilemma*, Harper & Brothers, 1944, p. 951.

[3] R. E. Clement, "The Present and Future Role of Private Colleges for Negroes," *Phylon*, 1949, vol. 10, pp. 323–324.

1940, to 58,000 in 1946, to 73,174 in 1947,[4] and to 90,000 in 1955.[5] During this period the number of Negro colleges remained fairly constant. Of the 5201 earned degrees granted by Negro colleges in 1940, 97 percent were bachelor's degrees, 3 percent were master's, and none were doctorates. The percentages for all other institutions in the same year were: bachelor's, eighty-six; master's, twelve; and doctorates, two.[6]

Negro colleges have gone through four periods of development. In the period 1864–1903 the schools which have become today's Negro colleges were founded through missionary effort and personal philanthropy. From 1903 to 1916 higher education for Negroes assumed a definite pattern, and considerable physical development occurred as a result of grants from large philanthropic foundations. In the third period, 1916–1930, increased appropriations from public funds and additional foundation subventions gave rise to more adequate physical plants and stimulated educational planning. The fourth period, from 1930 to the present, has been characterized by rapid development, both quantitatively and qualitatively, much of it stimulated by the decision of regional and national bodies to accredit Negro institutions according to established standards.[7]

In the first accrediting of Negro institutions by the Southern Association of Colleges and Secondary Schools in 1930, only two colleges were placed on the approved list. Both were private colleges; one received an "A" rating, the other a "B" rating. "In 1947–48, the names of sixty-two Negro colleges, located in eleven of the seventeen states with separate schools, appeared on the approved list of the Association. In addition, six Negro colleges in five states and the District of Columbia, which lie outside the area of the Southern Association of Colleges and Secondary Schools, are on the approved list of their respective regional associations. Three of these institutions are approved by the Association of Colleges and Secondary Schools of the Middle States and Maryland; and three by the North Central Association of Colleges and Secondary Schools."[8] The number of Negro institutions receiving national recognition through accreditation by the Association of American Universities increased from one in 1933 to seven (Fisk, Howard, Talledega, North Carolina College, Atlanta, Morehouse, and Spelman) in 1947–1948. With one exception, these are private institu-

[4] G. N. Redd, op. cit., p. 401.

[5] W. C. Eells, "The Higher Education of Negroes in the United States," *Journal of Negro Education*, Fall, 1955, p. 432. The enrollment of Negroes in institutions of higher learning per million Negro population (6000) is higher than the higher education enrollment per million population in Canada (4927), Japan (4639), France (3267), Sweden (2390), Western Germany (2278), Great Britain (2086), Mexico (1381), India (1042), Brazil (533), and many other countries. *Ibid.*, p. 432.

[6] President's Commission on Higher Education, *Higher Education for American Democracy*, Government Printing Office, 1947, vol. 2, p. 31.

[7] G. N. Redd, op. cit., p. 400.

[8] *Ibid.*, pp. 405–406.

tions. Accreditation by the regional and national agencies indicates improvement in faculty, library facilities, finance, etc. It should be noted, however, that these improvements do not compare favorably with those that have been taking place in white institutions.[9]

The increased demand by Negroes for college and professional education has been met predominantly through existing institutions rather than through the admission of Negroes to white colleges and universities or the development of new segregated institutions. As a result of this practice, "new curriculums have been added to the state institutions whenever an emergency arose. The typical land-grant college is now a mosaic of every kind of curriculum demanded by Negroes; and it has become everything but what its name signifies, for it serves simultaneously as an agriculture and mechanical college, a liberal arts college, a teachers' college, a professional school, a graduate school; or more generally as the Negro state university."[10]

An interesting aspect of the rapid growth of Negro higher education has been the tendency for the segregated colleges to become increasingly Negro in control. The proportion of Negro faculty members has increased and a number of the larger institutions have elected Negro presidents. The growing tendency to staff Negro colleges with Negro teachers is due largely to the need for vocational opportunities on the part of the well-qualified graduates of these same colleges. Many of these colleges feel obliged to give preference to a Negro if he is as well trained as a white applicant.[11]

A problem in the administration of colleges for Negroes, especially public colleges, that has impressed a New York University educator is that the board of control is usually entirely or largely white. Most of these colleges are located in the South and are closely related to the political and social structure of the respective states.

The president must carry out the policies of his board, regardless of how unpalatable they may be on the campus. It seemed to me that in the Negro colleges there was even less in common, and less communication between the board, on the one hand, and faculty and students on the other, than is usual in other institutions. All too often even the president is treated as a person who cannot be trusted with administrative responsibility. Sometimes a white man employed by the board stands between the president and the board and exercises veto power over most of the administrator's decisions. In at least one instance I found that this representative remained completely aloof from the college, yet insisted upon deciding what requisitions could be approved, who could be appointed, whose salaries increased, and so on.[12]

[9] *Ibid.*, p. 406.
[10] *Ibid.*, p. 403.
[11] Charles S. Johnson, *op. cit.*, pp. 297–298.
[12] Alonzo F. Myers, "The Colleges for Negroes," *Survey*, May, 1950, p. 235. Myers visited a number of Negro colleges during 1949–1950.

Myers concluded that in many of the publicly supported colleges for Negroes

. . . it is difficult for a man of integrity to continue for any length of time as the administrative head. . . . Only if the president is willing to forget professional ethics and professional standards can he count on long tenure. But in order to do this he must rule the college with an iron hand, ruthlessly suppressing whatever ideas and actions on the part of faculty and students do not meet with the approval of the most bigoted elements in the community. Of course, if he behaves in this manner he can serve no useful educational purpose. In making this observation, I am not referring to crusaders against segregation—none of them would ever receive such an appointment.[13]

The solution, Myers believes, must come through the Southern Association of Colleges and Secondary Schools, the regional accrediting agency. Unless some change occurs, "most of the public colleges for Negroes must continue to be places where no honest and able Negro educator can afford to remain, either as administrator or as teacher."[14]

Public funds for Negro higher education are provided by federal, state, and local governments. Federal aid to state educational programs began in 1862 with the first Morrill Act. Funds allotted by the federal government to seventeen southern states increased from $5,000,000 in 1922–1923 to $10,000,000 in 1934–1935 and $16,000,000 in 1935–1936. However, discrimination against Negroes was continuous during this period. Negroes constituted one-fourth of the population between the ages of eighteen and twenty-one inclusive of the seventeen states receiving $16,000,000 in 1935–1936, but they received only 5.4 percent of the total federal allotments.[15]

Great increases have been made in annual appropriations to public and private institutions for Negroes since the depression years, but increases in the appropriations for white colleges and universities have been larger. The gap between expenditures for Negro higher and professional education and expenditures for white students continues to be as great as, if not greater than, it was in the early and middle thirties.[16] Negro students constituted about 10 percent of the total college enrollment of the southern region in 1943–1944. Negro institutions in the South spent 8.2 percent of the total expenditures for higher education in that year. On a per student basis, these expenditures represented roughly four-fifths as much money expended on Negro as on

[13] *Ibid.*, pp. 235–236.

[14] *Ibid.*, p. 236. One important difference between the public and the private colleges for Negroes is that in most of the latter the faculty member is free to oppose segregated education while working within it. In most of the public colleges he must give up the freedom to oppose segregation.

[15] Charles S. Johnson, *Patterns of Negro Segregation*, Harper & Brothers, 1943, p. 13.

[16] G. N. Redd, *op. cit.*, p. 406.

white students. However, when the total population of the area is used as a base, the disparity is much greater. Expenditures per white person in the total population were $2.43 for the public institutions and $4.28 for the public and private institutions combined. Expenditures per Negro in the total population were 56 cents for the public institutions and $1.43 for the public and private institutions combined.[17]

Students of Negro higher education have concluded that Negro colleges do not have the faculties and the school facilities to provide an adequate education.[18] The situation is complicated by the fact that very few southern Negroes attend northern universities, but a large number of northern Negroes attend southern Negro colleges. In 1938–1939, 3000 of the 4000 northern Negroes attending Negro colleges were enrolled in colleges in the South. A report of the U.S. Office of Education concluded, "Thus it appears that institutions located in those States which have the least wealth are providing educational facilities for Negro residents from more economically favored regions."[19]

In a comprehensive study of graduates of northern and Negro colleges, Charles S. Johnson found that the great bulk of Negro college graduates (approximately three-fourths) have gone into the professional field. Roughly half in this field are in teaching and one-fourth in medicine and dentistry. Law and ministry have each accounted for about 4 percent of the graduates. The vocational schools have sent more of their graduates into professional fields than into industry; most of these professionals have gone into elementary teaching, and a large proportion of them have been teachers of manual training. As Johnson remarks, "The industrial departments of the Negro colleges seem never to have been seriously intended to produce craftsmen." Agriculture received less than 1 percent of the graduates of either the colleges or the vocational schools.[20]

Most colleges for Negroes are in small towns or rural areas where the setting is wholly different in nature and either actively or potentially hostile. Typically there is limited access to the meager resources of the community for the intellectual or leisure-time activities of students and faculty members. The tendency to confine all types of activity to the campus creates morale problems that affect human relations in the college community as well as the educational process. Learning and working in the separate college come to be regarded as a tour of duty during which one looks forward to the periodic "return to civilization" in a metropolitan center. Newer teachers and administrators feel the

[17] M. D. Jenkins, "The Availability of Higher Education for Negroes in the Southern States," *Journal of Negro Education*, 1948, vol. 17, pp. 467–468.

[18] Gunnar Mydral, *op. cit.*, p. 95.

[19] U.S. Office of Education, *The National Survey of the Higher Education of Negroes*, 1942. Quoted in President's Commission on Higher Education, *op. cit.*, p. 32.

[20] Charles S. Johnson, *The Negro College Graduate*, pp. 113, 124, 125.

greatest pressure because their high expectations of recognition and congenial association can rarely be satisfied in the isolated Negro college. Anxieties and frustrations develop, faculty-administration clashes arise, and morale sinks. The lack of productivity and of enthusiasm in teaching are rationalized as the individual makes an uneasy peace with a "tough" situation. Under these circumstances, "it is probably harder for him (the Negro student) to learn in a college for Negroes; or better, teacher and student have to work harder in order for him to get what he wants."[21] Alonzo F. Myers was troubled because at several colleges for Negroes he observed an even greater "social distance" between faculty and students than is the case on most campuses. This situation may be related to the frequently rather great differences in social, economic, and cultural backgrounds of faculty and students. As Myers points out, the short-changing of so many Negro children in their basic schooling results in many students' coming to college with such serious deficiencies that it is difficult for them to pursue college work. Myers was concerned about the lack of confidence in the students on the part of the faculty, the harsh and repressive regulations, and the absence of cordial faculty-student relationships. These observations do not apply to all Negro colleges, and the same things are found—although in Myers' opinion in less pronounced form—in white colleges.[22]

One critical evaluation of the "black bourgeoisie" holds that many Negro teachers refuse to identify with the Negro masses and regard teaching mainly as a source of income. According to Frazier, "In many cases they have nothing but contempt for their Negro pupils. Moreover, they have no real interest in education and genuine culture and spend their leisure in frivolities and in activities designed to win a place in Negro 'society.' "[23] Frazier says that the present generation of Negro college students think of education mainly in terms of the money it will enable them to earn as professional and business men.[24] In view of the history of Negro-white relations in the United States, such attitudes on the part of Negro teachers and students at this time are not surprising. Increasingly desegregation will reduce the isolation of Negro scholars and Negro students and modify their outlook on the academic enterprise.

Those persons, Negro and white, who oppose segregation in higher education agree with the conclusion reached by the President's Committee on Civil Rights: "The separate but equal doctrine stands convicted on three grounds. It contravenes the equalitarian spirit of the American heritage. It has failed to operate, for history shows that in-

[21] Hylan Lewis, " 'Tough' Aspects of Higher Education," *Phylon*, 1949, vol. 10, pp. 359–361.

[22] Alonzo F. Myers, *op. cit.*, pp. 234, 236.

[23] E. Franklin Frazier, *Black Bourgeoisie*, The Free Press, 1957, pp. 235–236.

[24] *Ibid.*, pp. 84–85.

equality of service has been the omnipresent consequence of separation. It has institutionalized segregation and kept groups apart despite indisputable evidence that normal contacts among these groups tend to promote social harmony."[25] They feel that to contribute to or favor the improvement of Negro colleges is to help vested interests of both racial groups entrench themselves and thus make it more difficult ever to abolish segregation.

The position of the advocates of the separate college is that it is needed for the Negro population still residing in the states where segregation is in force. The majority of these people, it is said, do not have the resources to attend institutions in other parts of the country where racial segregation is not operative. The situation is viewed as a choice between no higher education for tens of thousands of Negroes or the utilization of separate colleges.[26] It is pointed out that although some 2000 Negro students at the graduate level had been admitted by 1956 to universities formerly open only to white students, the situation at the undergraduate level has not changed significantly.[27] The closing of the Negro colleges is not seen as the answer, since the southern states have given no indication that they plan quickly to abolish segregation below the graduate level. There is the further contention that the best institutions for the higher education of Negroes have been the privately supported colleges. This school of thought denies that Negro colleges constitute an endorsement of segregation and insists that they will disappear when physical characteristics cease to be used as criteria in deciding admissions policies. When segregation laws disappear, these colleges will be centers for the training of all qualified students who wish to enroll, without reference to race or creed.[28] According to Charles S. Johnson,

The distinction will simply shift from white and Negro colleges to good and bad colleges. It would probably not harm the cause of higher education if some of the poorer Negro colleges combined with other weak institutions for a stronger institution with higher standards. It would, indeed, not harm the cause of Southern education if some of the less adequate institutions abandoned their roles entirely. . . . The problem is not encompassed with Negro students trying to enter Southern white universities. There should be Negro universities good enough in their own right to attract as many students of other races as they might lose to the other colleges."[29]

[25] Quoted in the President's Commission on Higher Education, op. cit., p. 31.
[26] R. E. Clement, op. cit., p. 325.
[27] Letter to the Editor, by W. J. Trent, Jr., executive director of the United Negro College Fund, New York Times, November 12, 1950; Southern School News, October, 1956, p. 1.
[28] R. E. Clement, op. cit., p. 327.
[29] Charles S. Johnson, "Some Significant Social and Educational Implications of the U.S. Supreme Court's Decision," Journal of Negro Education, Summer, 1954, pp. 368–369.

RACIAL AND RELIGIOUS FACTORS IN ADMISSION TO NONSEGREGATED
UNDERGRADUATE COLLEGES

Jewish students make up 9 percent of the total enrollment in American and Canadian schools of higher learning.[30] More than half of all Jewish students attend schools in New York City. This fact reflects the large population of Jews in that city, which contains approximately four-tenths of all the Jews in the United States.[31] Other factors in the concentration of Jewish students in that area include New York City's system of free city colleges, discrimination in admission policies elsewhere, and the lack of interest Jewish students have in many small institutions—schools which are located, for the most part, in sections of the country where few Jews live.

Following New York City in the number of Jewish college students enrolled are the Middle Atlantic states, with 14.5 percent of all Jewish college students; the East North Central states, with 13.3 percent; the New England states, with 5.5 percent; the Pacific states with 4.8 percent; and the South Atlantic states with 4.5 percent. The remaining areas in the United States, Canada, and the territories account for 7.2 percent of the Jewish college students. Fifty institutions enroll 77 percent of all Jewish students in the United States and Canada, and nearly all of these are large schools located in or near metropolitan areas. Whereas 21.5 percent of all college students go to schools with a registration of 1000 or less, only 6.1 percent of the Jewish students attend these schools. A 1947 study found that 426 schools out of 1533 from which returns were received had no Jewish students. Publicly supported schools enroll 53.1 percent of the total number of American and Canadian college students and account for 55.3 percent of the Jewish students. Private nondenominational schools account for 26.2 percent of all students and 39.4 percent of Jewish students. The denominational schools include 20.7 percent of all students and 5.3 percent of Jewish students. The last figure includes 0.6 percent in Jewish theological schools.[32]

Jewish students constitute 8.8 percent of all graduate students, about

[30] Since Jews constitute less than 4 percent of the total population of the United States, it may be asked why discrimination is considered to exist when Jewish students make up 9 percent of the total college enrollment in this country and Canada. Interest in obtaining a college education is related to urban residence, social class, and desire to enter a profession. A higher percentage of Jews than of other groups happen to be middle-class urban residents interested in the professions. Our viewpoint is that placing restrictions on admission to undergraduate work or to professional courses not on the basis of qualifications and interest, but on religious, nationality, or racial grounds constitutes discrimination. As we point out later, there has never been an assumption in this country that each ethnic and religious group should be economically and professionally self-sufficient.

[31] M. F. Baer, "Counting the Jewish College Students," *National Jewish Monthly*, October, 1947, p. 70.

[32] *Ibid.*, pp. 70–71.

the same proportion as the percentage of Jewish students in the total enrollment. Of all graduate students in New York City, 50.5 percent are Jewish.[33]

A study by Elmo Roper for the Committee on a Study of Discriminations in College Admissions of the American Council on Education throws much light on the religious factor in the admission of students to undergraduate schools.[34] The data in this study were gathered by personal interviews with high-school seniors who were members of 1947 graduating classes and who were first interviewed in May, 1947. One group of 10,000 students constituted a representative sample of white high-school seniors throughout the country; a second group was made up of high-school seniors in large cities only. The conclusions of this comprehensive study which are of most interest here may be summarized as follows:

1. "Par for the course" on applications made by the total national sample is 72% . . . approximately 72% of all applications made by white high school students in the United States in 1947 were accepted. (p. xxxii)

2. An outstanding fact in the study is the great difference in application success rate between those who apply from the Northeast area and those who come from other parts of the country. Only 58% of the Northeast applications are accepted as against 80% for the Midwest, 84% for the Far West, and 81% for the South. . . . When the selection is as severe as it is in the Northeast it may well be that all the characteristics and qualifications of applicants get weighted differently there, and that such items as an extra-curricular leadership record or a particular religious affiliation have a different effect on admissions officers than they would . . . in the West. (p. xxxii)

3. It is easier for a boy or girl to get into a public institution than it is to be admitted to a private college. Seventy-seven percent of all the applications from both sexes to publicly supported institutions of higher education are successful as compared with 65% of those made to private colleges and universities. (p. xxxv)

4. The average individual Jewish application in the country as a whole has a considerably smaller chance of being accepted than an application from a Catholic or Protestant. But while the ratio of success, on a national basis, is 77% for Protestants, 67% for Catholics, 56% for Jews, these figures, taken by themselves, would be seriously misleading. The information on *application* success must be set alongside the results. . . . On *applicant* success . . . Jewish applicants *get into some college or other* 87% of the time, Protestants 88%, and Catholics 81%. . . . They [individual Jews] succeed ultimately in getting a chance at some kind of college education as often as Protestants do but they try more colleges in order to do it. (p. xxxvii)

5. The Jews succeed less often in getting into the college of their first or

[33] *Ibid.*, p. 71.
[34] A report by Elmo Roper for the Committee on a Study of Discriminations in College Admissions, *Factors Affecting the Admission of High School Seniors to College*, American Council on Education, 1949.

second preference: 82% of the applications by Protestants were accepted at institutions with first choice rating, 71% of the applications by Catholics were so accepted, and 63% of the applications by Jews were so accepted. (pp. xxxvii-xxxix)

6. Application figures refer to the country as a whole. . . . Both because the admission pressure is so much greater in the Northeast than elsewhere and because 80% of the Jewish applicants come from that area, it is necessary to treat the Northeast separate from the rest of the country so far as religious breakdowns on admissions rates are concerned. . . . In the Midwest, Far West, and South combined the success rates for applications are 82% for Protestants, 78% for Catholics, and 76% for Jews but in the Northeast they are 61% for Protestants, 59% for Catholics and 54% for Jews. (p. xxxviii)

7. The Jewish applicant in the Northeast has a better chance (86%) of getting at least one of his applications accepted than has either Protestant (80%) or Catholic (75%). The disparity between the two sets of Northeast figures (applications and applicants) is . . . due to the fact that the individual Jew makes more different applications. . . . Jews in the Northeast file an average of 2.4 applications per applicant as against 1.7 for Protestants and 1.6 for Catholics. (p. xxxviii)

8. . . . The more favorably circumstanced socio-economically the Jewish senior is the more discrimination there is against him. . . . A Jewish first quintile senior whose father is a college graduate has a 60% chance of getting an application accepted, as against a 74% chance for a Protestant with these same attributes. And a Jewish first quintile son or daughter of a professional or executive parent rates a 59% chance as compared with 75% and 72% respectively for similarly situated Catholics and Protestants. . . . It is possible that they are the ones who have the "temerity" to apply to the colleges who do discriminate, and thus acquire a low batting average, while the Jews with less qualifications content themselves with applying to colleges where discrimination does not take place. (pp. xliii-xliv, xlvi, xlviii)

9. . . . A Jew who applies to a college in his home city has as good a chance as any one of his own quintile rating. But . . . when a Jewish boy or girl of top quintile standing seeks to go outside his place of residence for a college education he or she is at a disadvantage as against first quintile Protestants and Catholics who apply outside their home town or state. (p. xliv)

10. The study indicates clearly that Jews are a definitely disadvantaged group when it comes to getting into college, but the situation is complex, and cannot be described in the simple terms of general, across-the-board, discrimination. (pp. xlviii-l)

11. The typical city university in the Northeast, especially if it is supported by public funds, tends to take applicants pretty much in accordance with evidence of scholastic aptitude, modified somewhat, perhaps, by extracurricular activity record or family tradition, but not influenced very much (except possibly at Catholic colleges) by the applicant's religion. . . . The private college outside the city in the Northeast accepts not only a smaller absolute number of Jewish applications than non-Jewish, but also a smaller proportion of Jewish applications than non-Jewish. (p. lii)

12. The frequent charge made against the colleges that they discriminate against Jewish students seems . . . to be proven, but only in part and perhaps not nearly to the extent which is frequently charged. (p. liv)

The New York State Education Department and the Board of Regents sought to ascertain by a repeat study in 1949 what effect, if any, the Quinn-Olliffe law had had upon college entrance practices. This study was based upon a sampling of the opinions of high-school principals and of the experiences of the high-school seniors in seeking admission to college. All of the conclusions of the study cannot be presented here, but we shall list three. First, on the basis of opinions of high-school principals, there was a definite decrease in discriminatory practices in general on the part of the colleges in New York State between 1946 and 1949. Second, Jewish, Catholic, and Protestant applications from New York City graduates are rejected with almost the same frequency. Jewish graduates of upstate high schools, however, are rejected about twice as frequently as Catholic or Protestant graduates. Third, Jewish graduates in the first and second quarters have greater difficulty in gaining admission to upstate colleges than do non-Jewish applicants of equal academic rank.[35]

The application form is perhaps the chief medium through which colleges and professional schools obtain information that may be used as the basis for racial or religious discrimination. Approximately 90 percent of all colleges and universities in the United States require a statement of the student's religion or "religious preference" in their application blanks. As a rule, candidates are also asked to provide data on racial origin, nationality, father's birthplace, etc., and to include a photograph. Other means of acquiring information concerning the race or religion of applicants include the preliminary application questionnaire, letters of recommendation, and personal interviews. As the President's Commission on Higher Education remarks, "It can almost be said that the request for certain information on application forms constitutes an all but prima facie case that such information is likely to be used for discriminatory purposes." The commission adds that although many facts about ancestry, religious affiliation, and so forth are useful to the college or university, information of this type can readily be obtained *after* the student has been admitted rather than before. On this ground the commission recommended the removal from application forms of all questions pertaining to religion, color, and national or racial origin and endorsed the type of state legislation which leads to the elimination of questions along these lines.[36]

The attitudes of college students toward racial and religious minori-

[35] Theodore Bienenstok and Warren W. Coxe, *Progress Toward Equality of Opportunity in New York State Colleges*, University of the State of New York, 1950, pp. 18–19.
[36] President's Commission on Higher Education, *op. cit.*, p. 38.

ties are of interest in connection with the question of admission policies. The most extensive study thus far of such sentiment was made
by Elmo Roper in the early fall of 1949. Interviews were held with
1000 college freshmen and 1000 college seniors on fifty different campuses in the United States, with allocations so arranged as to constitute
a representative sample of college freshmen and seniors in the four-
year institutions.[37]

The responses made by college seniors indicate that the majority
wish to set no limits, short of intermarriage, to their association with
the named minorities (Negroes, Mexicans, Chinese, Filipinos, Jews,
Italians, Catholics). The social-distance attitudes of non-Jewish college
seniors in the Roper study is shown in Table 20.1.

TABLE 20.1.   Social-Distance Attitudes of Non-Jewish College Seniors[38]

	Would Prefer Not to Work with if They Had an Equal Position to Mine and Worked Beside Me	Would Prefer Not to Have as Guest in Home	Would Prefer Not to Have Move into My Neighborhood to Live	Would Prefer Not to Have Marry a Close Relative of Mine
Negroes	15%	26%	45%	75%
Mexicans	7	9	22	38
Chinese	2	6	12	43
Filipinos	4	7	15	39
Jews	5	3	10	25
Italians	2	2	5	10
Catholics	1	0	0	12
Protestants	0	0	0	3
No difference	78	68	47	19
Not answered	3	5	4	5

Roper found that 20 percent of the Jewish seniors would prefer not to
see intermarriage between one of their close relatives and a Catholic
or a Protestant. While only one-fifth of the non-Jewish seniors said
that it made no difference to them if a relative married a minority-
group member, a number of others qualified their statement that they
preferred not to have a close relative marry a Negro, a Filipino, a Jew,
etc., by saying, "But of course it's really up to him (or her) to decide
whom to marry."[39]

College seniors are overwhelmingly opposed to excluding Jews from
colleges or applying some restrictive quota to them. Nine-tenths of the

[37] Elmo Roper, "A Study of Anti-Minority Sentiment in Colleges," unpublished,
1949. This study is summarized in Arnold Forster, A Measure of Freedom, Doubleday & Company, Inc., 1950, chap. 8, "Prejudice on the Campus."
[38] Arnold Forster, op. cit., p. 150.
[39] Ibid., p. 151.

students said they would prefer a child of theirs to go to a college which admits the best students who apply whether they are Jewish or not; 5 percent favored a college which admits Jewish students in the same proportion as there are Jews in that region; 3 percent preferred a college which admits Jews only if they are especially outstanding; and a college which admits no Jews at all appealed to 2 percent of the seniors.[40]

On the question of admitting Jews to fraternities and sororities, considerably more prejudice was found than on the question of admitting Jews to the student body. Of the non-Jewish fraternity and sorority seniors in the study, 31 percent preferred an organization completely restricted to gentiles; 23 percent favored one that admitted Jews occasionally but was always at least 90 percent gentile; and 44 percent preferred one that freely admitted both Jews and gentiles and that usually contained a considerable number of each. Fraternity and sorority members tended to be more anti-Semitic than nonmembers on the same campuses. Forster suggests that the nature of the fraternity or sorority as an exclusive social grouping probably tends to make its members more suggestible to current anti-Semitic prejudices, and remarks that it is surprising that fraternity and sorority members are as little more prejudiced than the nonmembers as they are.[41] Lee found that among both fraternity and nonfraternity students in all sections of the country the number wishing to retain restrictions within the college community constitute a steadily diminishing minority.[42] Since admissions quotas have virtually disappeared from many leading American colleges and universities, discriminatory policies on the part of student organizations toward Jews, Negroes, and members of other groups is of concern to the college. As Lee points out, the problem becomes one of whether the college or the national fraternity is going to determine the chapter's criteria for membership.[43]

Student attitudes toward minorities were also revealed in the aforementioned study by Elmo Roper in questions about extracurricular activities. About six out of ten non-Jewish seniors said that they would have no preference as between Jewish and non-Jewish candidates for the editorial board of the college newspaper, even though a Jew's election gave his religious group a board majority. Two out of ten said they would be

---

[40] *Ibid.*

[41] *Ibid.*, pp. 151, 152, 160.

[42] Alfred M. Lee, *Fraternities Without Brotherhood*, The Beacon Press, 1955, pp. 52–53.

[43] *Ibid.*, p. 128. This study provides a full discussion of discriminatory practices in college fraternities as well as recent proposed and actual changes. (A few decades ago, a large majority of the sixty-one national fraternities included in the National Interfraternity Conference had restrictive clauses in their constitutions. Forty-five retained such provisions in 1948, but by 1955 this number had dropped to ten social fraternities. Anti-Defamation League, *Rights*, April-May, 1957, p. 14.)

willing to see the Jewish candidate elected if that did not mean a Jewish majority on the board. There were 17 percent among the non-Jewish seniors who would oppose the election of a Jewish student as a board member in any case. When a question was put concerning a hypothetical situation in which the six best players on the varsity football team were Jews or Negroes, the overwhelming majority of the non-Jewish seniors favored fielding its best team, regardless of what racial or ethnic group contributed a majority of the members.[44]

Interesting regional differences appeared in this study of student attitudes. The far-western students were less anti-Semitic as measured by the questions in these interviews than the students of other regions. Although other studies have produced contrary results, this representative survey indicates that in the South students are apt to be more anti-Semitic. Since Jewish students are not numerous either in the South or in the Far West, the greater anti-Semitism of the southern students is interpreted as a reflection to a considerable degree of the differing regional cultural patterns.

Southern students as a group seem to be more concerned about keeping social distance between themselves and Jews, which may be a reflection of the traditional attitude of the "Old South." Many more of them profess to be worried about the economic and political power that the Jews are allegedly acquiring. But the anti-Semitism of Southern students is only a pale imitation of their anti-Negro prejudice. Almost three times as many would prefer not to see six Negroes on the football team as would object to six Jews on it and, whereas only 3 percent would not like to entertain a Jew in their home, 45 percent say they would not want to play host to a Negro.[45]

The arguments of the advocates and the critics of the use of more or less definite ratios for racial and religious minorities fall into about eight categories.[46] We refer here mainly to the private institutions.

1. If the colleges do not conform to the prejudices of the students and the faculty, the morale of the campus community will be seriously damaged.

The data obtained in the Elmo Roper study above referred to, as well as some of the other reports which are available, contradict this assertion. The evidence from these sources seems to indicate that such statements are policy makers' rationalizations.

2. If quotas are not maintained, the colleges will be swamped by persons from minority groups. Other students will stay away from a

[44] Arnold Forster, op. cit., pp. 153–154. Ninety percent of these seniors favored fielding the best team if a majority of the players were Jewish; 83 percent, if a majority were Negroes.

[45] Ibid., pp. 157, 160.

[46] Much of the following summary is based on the discussion of this subject in Arnold Forster, op. cit., pp. 117–120. See also D. W. Dodson, "College Quotas and American Democracy," American Scholar, Summer, 1946, pp. 8–12.

college which has a disproportionate number of minority-group persons.

If all colleges, or even most of them, dropped discriminatory barriers, minority-group students would disappear into the national collegiate body. Also, American youth is considerably less prejudiced than the individuals in charge of the schools.

3. It is reasonable and just to have quotas equaling the percentage of racial and religious groups in the total population.

Those opposed to quotas say that this argument violates the tradition that the individual stands on his own merits. Redfield says: "It has never been assumed that this country should be composed of self-sufficient ethnic or religious groups, each providing all the services required of that sub-community from among its own members."[47]

4. Quotas reduce antiminority prejudice.

Opponents of quotas point out that no noticeable prejudice has developed in the colleges where minority representatives constitute a substantial part of the student body. Another point is that discriminatory quotas themselves create antiminority feelings because the minority-group members who are admitted are much more rigorously selected than those coming from the majority group; the consequence is that the average majority student may be outshone by a few minority-group students and come to resent them on this account.

5. Geographical quotas are necessary if a college wishes to become a national institution. Most colleges limit the number of Northeasterners accepted.

The announced objective of obtaining a representative student body may be used as a subterfuge to discriminate against minority groups. There is no objection to a geographical quota as such.

6. The colleges must not get too far out of line with community prejudices in the proportion of minority-group persons admitted or they will lose status and their students will have difficulty obtaining jobs after graduation. College and university officials sometimes state that it is unfair to an applicant to admit him to a professional school if that student will find later that it is impossible for him to serve his apprenticeship and be placed within his chosen profession.

Opponents of quotas contend that the university should not practice discrimination because of pressure from without. Dodson says: "The schools are not the custodians of the forces of darkness, of ignorance, of bias, bigotry and hate. The schools cannot afford, not if they are to serve as centers of enlightenment, passively to accept the ill-founded prejudices of our society, to say nothing of actively abetting them." In addition to their moral force, the schools are in a position to meet society in this way: "Either you accept these Negro and Jewish engi-

---

[47] Robert Redfield, "Race and Religion in Selective Admission," *Journal of the American Association of Collegiate Registrars*, July, 1947, p. 10.

neers, doctors, lawyers, who are among the best we can produce, or do without. We can no longer compromise with bigotry without compromising ourselves."[48] Forster observes that "our institutions of higher learning must seek to elevate the community, rather than permit the bad customs of our society to degrade our academic leadership."[49]

7. Because of parental objections, it is "sound business" to bar Jews or other minority students. This reason was frankly stated by Marshall H. Nye, principal of the Admiral Billard Academy, New London, Connecticut, when he wrote to an applicant: "We are returning your application for admission and check herein since we do not have any Jewish boys at Billard. The Academy itself is without prejudice in the matter of accepting students of any faith. However, our parental group has indicated a desire to have us restrict the enrollment. From a purely commercial point of view we are following the desires of our present clientele. Since about 75 percent of our new enrollments come through recommendations on the part of previous graduates and their parents, we find it sound business to follow their desires."[50]

8. Restriction of enrollment is necessary to preserve a certain quality of the college community: the college must remain "Christian" or "nonurban" or "the kind of college it has always been."

The reply to this viewpoint is that it should not be accepted without question that every college and university ought to remain what it always has been. Institutions may find that they may be able to do a better job of education if they widen their ethnic and cultural representation.[51]

Graduate and Professional Training for Negroes

It was mentioned previously that no Ph.D.'s are given by Negro colleges, and that only 3 percent of the degrees awarded by these colleges in 1940 were master's. In the same year, 12 percent of the degrees granted by all other institutions were master's and 2 percent were doctorates. In 1946–1947, some 40,000 advanced degrees were granted in the United States. Negro colleges and universities gave 481 of these, all of them master's degrees. In unsegregated institutions, eight Negroes were awarded the Ph.D. degree, while 3775 doctorates were received by non-Negro students.

Educational opportunities for Negroes are greatly restricted in medicine, dentistry, and nursing. Twenty of the nation's seventy-seven medical schools are located in the South and do not admit Negroes. Only one-third of the fifty-five presumably nonsegregated schools actually

[48] D. W. Dodson, *op. cit.*, p. 11.
[49] Arnold Forster, *op. cit.*, p. 120.
[50] D. W. Dodson, "Religious Prejudice in Colleges," *American Mercury*, July, 1946, pp. 5–6.
[51] Robert Redfield, *op. cit.*, p. 11.

admit Negro students. In 1938, the last year when Negro and white students were separately reported by the American Medical Association, only 372 Negroes were enrolled in all medical schools; forty of these were enrolled in seventeen of the fifty-five nonsegregated schools. In 1946, 507 of the 592 Negro medical students were enrolled in Meharry Medical College and Howard University; eighty-five were enrolled in twenty nonsegregated schools. The two Negro medical schools can train only a fraction of those who desire and are qualified for careers in medicine. The freshman class at Howard University Medical School was limited to sixty students in prewar years. By overtaxing its facilities the number had been increased in 1947 to seventy-five. The principal limiting factor in the training of Negro physicians is the barring of Negro students from clinical facilities, even in tax-supported hospitals. Internship, an essential part of medical training, is another discriminatory area. With very few exceptions, Negro students train only in Negro hospitals, and only fourteen of the 112 Negro hospitals are approved for the training of interns.[52]

Dentistry is even more restricted for Negroes. Discrimination places most of the responsibility for training Negro dentists on Howard University and Meharry Medical College.[53]

In the training of nurses, 1214 schools in the United States are for whites only; thirty-eight admit Negroes and whites, and twenty-eight admit Negroes only.[54]

Before 1937 only five Negro institutions in the country offered instruction on the graduate level. After the United States Supreme Court declared in the Gaines case in 1938 that a state must offer equal educational opportunities to Negroes, several southern states forced poorly equipped public Negro colleges to establish graduate work.[55] Ten years later, however, there were seven southern states where no graduate instruction whatever was offered in Negro institutions—Arkansas, Delaware, Kentucky, Maryland, Mississippi, Oklahoma, and Louisiana. A variety of professional and graduate work is available to white citizens in all of the southern states, and the opportunities for such work are provided for more than two-thirds of the students in these fields through public funds. Master's work can be taken by whites in each of the seventeen southern states, and there is at least one graduate school in each of thirteen states which offers work leading to the doctorate. In professional training the southern states in 1948 provided for whites: fifteen medical schools, sixteen law schools, seventeen schools of engineering, fourteen schools of pharmacy, eleven schools of library science, four schools of dentistry, and nine schools of social work. In contrast to

[52] President's Commission on Higher Education, *op. cit.*, pp. 33–34.
[53] *Ibid.*, p. 34.
[54] *Ibid.*
[55] Gunnar Myrdal, *op. cit.*, p. 951.

these arrangements, no Negro institution offers work for the Ph.D. or its equivalent, and a limited amount of graduate work for the master's degree is given in ten schools in eight southern states. In 1948 there were six law schools and one school of library science for Negroes.[56]

A landmark in the history of Negro education in the United States is the case of Lloyd L. Gaines v. University of Missouri. Gaines, who had an A.B. degree from Lincoln University, contended that he was denied admission to the law school of the University of Missouri solely because he was a Negro. The University of Missouri said that the admission of a Negro would be contrary to the constitution, laws, and public policy of the state. The university stated that the Missouri legislature had provided that Lincoln University, until it developed a law school for Negroes, should pay the tuition at the university of any adjacent state for Missouri Negroes wishing to study law. Gaines did not apply for a scholarship to study elsewhere, but sought a writ of mandamus to compel the curators of the University of Missouri to admit him. The circuit court denied his petition and was upheld by the state supreme court. The case was then taken to the Supreme Court of the United States on a writ of certiorari, which denied the university the right to exclude Gaines, saying that what would otherwise be an unconstitutional discrimination within the state could not be justified by providing opportunities elsewhere through scholarship aid. "The Court held further that, although the curators of Lincoln University had a discretionary obligation to reorganize that institution so that it would afford Negroes of the state an opportunity for training equal in standards to that of the University of Missouri, such an obligation was not sufficiently mandatory to relieve the state of the charges of illegal discrimination in the opportunities provided for the legal education of Negroes."[57]

The Gaines case had an interesting precedent in Maryland in the University v. Murray case of 1936. Donald Murray, an Amherst College graduate, was refused admission to the law school of the University of Maryland because he was a Negro. He applied to the court for a writ of mandamus to force the Board of Regents to admit him to the law school on the ground that exclusion on the basis of race was unconstitutional. The court issued a writ ordering the university to admit Murray. The Regents appealed to the court of appeals, the highest tribunal in the state, which decided that the writ of mandamus had been properly issued by the trial court. The court of appeals held that

---

[56] G. N. Redd, op. cit., pp. 404, 407; C. H. Thompson, "Negro Higher and Professional Education in the United States," *Journal of Negro Education*, 1948, vol. 17, pp. 222–223.

[57] Charles S. Johnson, *Patterns of Negro Segregation*, pp. 181–182; Walter White, *A Man Called White*, The Viking Press, Inc., 1948, p. 143; Associated Press report in *Evening Public Ledger* (Philadelphia), December 12, 1938.

the state must provide equal educational facilities if it separated the races, and said that a scholarship to another state would not only mean additional expense for Murray but would deprive him of the opportunity of specializing in Maryland law.[58]

The University of Maryland admitted Murray to its law school after the decision of the court of appeals. A few threats of violence were made against Murray, mostly by persons who had no connection with the university, and there was much tension in the institution on Murray's first day on the campus. One faculty member suggested to Murray's NAACP advisers that he sit in the rear of the classroom to show that he was not "forcing himself" upon the other students. Instead he took a seat that was neither conspicuous nor inconspicuous and which would permit his fellow students to sit as near him or as far away from him as the size of the room would allow. The tension disappeared when a white student, who came from a town on the Eastern Shore of Maryland where a Negro had been lynched a short time before, and who was the most popular man in the class, came over to Murray, shook hands with him, and sat down beside him. Murray experienced no trouble in the law school and graduated with an excellent record.[59]

In addition to offering out-of-state scholarships to Negroes who will accept them in spite of the ruling in the Gaines case, some of the southern states have used other expedients in trying to comply with the United States Supreme Court's decision. Graduate work has been added in existing Negro state colleges, separate professional and graduate schools for Negroes have been established, and white state university faculty members have been used on a part-time basis.[60]

The establishment of makeshift graduate and professional courses for Negroes deserves special mention. Eighteen Negro institutions (Florida A. and M. College, South Carolina A. and M. College, Fort Valley State College, Meharry Medical College, Howard University, Fisk University, Hampton Institute, Atlanta University, Xavier University, Virginia State College, Prairie View A. and M. College, North Carolina State College, North Carolina A. and T. College, Lincoln University [Missouri], Alabama State Teachers College, Tennessee A. and I. State College, Tuskegee Institute, and Texas State University) in ten states (Alabama, Florida, Georgia, Louisiana, North Carolina, South Carolina, Tennessee, Texas, Virginia, and Missouri) and the District of Columbia now offer graduate and professional work of some kind for Negroes. Questionnaires returned by sixteen of the Negro graduate institutions showed that 970 graduate students were enrolled during the year 1947–1948, and when summer-school attendance was included the

[58] Charles S. Johnson, *Patterns of Negro Segregation*, p. 182.
[59] Walter White, *op. cit.*, pp. 160–161.
[60] Charles S. Johnson, *Patterns of Negro Segregation*, p. 19.

figure reached 3301. These figures do not include Negro graduate students who were enrolled outside the South.[61]

The rapid development of much of this instruction has been accompanied by low salaries, heavy teaching loads, a shortage of qualified instructors, a lack of funds and facilities for research, and a certain amount of cynicism due to frustration and professional isolation.[62] "In spite of the strivings of all of these schools toward a degree of excellence there remains much to be desired. . . . The graduate schools conducted for white people in the South, as inept and lacking in educational breadth and vision as they are, offer to their students courses of instruction that are much richer and more extensive."[63] It is significant that in 1948 only three of the eighteen Negro institutions which offered graduate work were approved by the Association of American Universities as having undergraduate curriculums of sufficient quality to prepare students for graduate study.[64]

With the exception of training for the teaching profession, most professional education for Negroes in the South was carried on, prior to 1950, in private institutions. Education in law was provided at Howard University, in medicine and dentistry at Howard and Meharry, in pharmacy at Howard and Xavier, in social work at Howard and Atlanta, in theology at Johnson C. Smith and Atlanta, in nursing at Meharry, and in library science at Atlanta. During the first decade after the Gaines decision state law schools were established in Missouri, North Carolina, South Carolina, Texas, Oklahoma, and Louisiana.[65] In these years one school of journalism and one school of library science for Negroes were opened.

One of the segregated law schools was established in 1939 as a part of Lincoln University. Originally located in two rooms of a St. Louis basement, it was later housed in a building large enough to accommodate 600 or 700 students. The new location is in the heart of the Negro district of St. Louis. Thirty-four students enrolled the first year; the attendance in 1943 had dropped, in part owing to the war, to seven. At that time the all-Negro staff consisted of three full-time instructors, one part-time instructor, a librarian, clerks, and secretaries. The library consists of 31,000 volumes and was one of the three largest law-school libraries in the South in 1945. It has been approved by the Missouri Board of Bar Examiners and by the Association of American Law Schools. The school's instructors are competent, and its graduates have

[61] J. M. Bond, "Some Aspects of Graduate and Professional Education for Negroes," *Phylon*, 1949, vol. 10, p. 395.
[62] L. H. Evans, "The Magnificent Purpose," *Phylon*, 1949, vol. 10, pp. 319–320.
[63] J. M. Bond, *op. cit.*, p. 395.
[64] G. N. Redd, *op. cit.*, pp. 406–407.
[65] *Ibid.*, p. 407.

been readily admitted to the bar.[66] The original funds appropriated by the state legislature to establish this law school totaled more than half a million dollars.[67] In 1950–1951, fifty-three full-time students were enrolled and there were seven full-time faculty members.[68]

Missouri's school of journalism for Negroes is located on the Lincoln University campus at Jefferson City and was created in response to a ruling of the state court in 1940 that Lucille Bluford would have to be admitted to the University of Missouri School of Journalism or provided with equal educational facilities within the state. According to McWilliams, "The school is housed in an attractive building; it has a workable library; it receives a large number of newspapers; it has a good print shop; the faculty is excellent; and the students get practical experience in editing a newspaper."[69] This school also was established at considerable expense to the taxpayers of Missouri, especially so in view of its small enrollment—twelve students in 1945, twenty in 1950–1951. Technical compliance with the court's decision in the case of either a medical school or a school of mines would involve an expenditure of several million dollars.[70]

A case of importance in the period between the Gaines decision and the Sweatt and McLaurin cases was that of Ada Sipuel. Suit was filed in her behalf on April 6, 1946, after the University of Oklahoma Law School had refused to admit her because of race. The lower court ordered the state to admit Miss Sipuel or to provide a "substantially equal" law school for Negroes. It was almost two years before the case reached the Supreme Court of the United States, during which time Oklahoma did nothing to comply with the court's mandate. On January 12, 1948, the U.S. Supreme Court unanimously ordered Oklahoma to supply forthwith a legal education to Miss Sipuel. The Court avoided giving a specific ruling on the issue of segregation, but the forthwith order appeared to mean admitting Miss Sipuel to the existing law school, since a separate school could not be created overnight. The Board of Regents voted seven to one to admit Miss Sipuel and all other qualified Negroes to professional work at the university which was not offered at the State College for Negroes at Langston. The state attorney general then issued an opinion implying that Oklahoma laws prohibiting white and Negro students from attending the same school took precedence over the mandate of the United States Supreme Court. On January 17, 1948, the Supreme Court of Oklahoma ordered the Board of Regents "to afford the plaintiff, and all others

[66] Carey McWilliams, "The World's Smallest Law School," *Negro Digest*, April, 1947, pp. 15–16. Condensed from *The Nation*, February 24, 1945.

[67] Walter White, *op. cit.*, p. 162.

[68] Communication from the Registrar, Lincoln University, September 13, 1951.

[69] Carey McWilliams, *op. cit.*, p. 16.

[70] *Ibid.*, pp. 16, 18.

similarly situated, an opportunity to commence the study of law at a state institution as soon as citizens of other groups are afforded such opportunity." Five days later, the District Court of Cleveland County of Oklahoma directed the Oklahoma State Regents for Higher Education to enroll plaintiff or not enroll "any applicant of any group in said class (first-year class of the School of Law of the University of Oklahoma) until said separate school is established and ready to function." The Board of Regents hastily roped off a space in the state capitol as a "law school" for Miss Sipuel "and all others similarly situated" and assigned three instructors to the school. Since this arrangement fell far short of the minimum requirements of the American Bar Association and the Association of American Law Schools, Miss Sipuel refused to enroll.[71] Subsequently the U.S. Supreme Court refused by a seven-to-two vote the petition for a writ of mandamus filed in behalf of Miss Sipuel, but the case was finally resolved after the Sweatt and McLaurin decisions of June, 1950, by her admission to the law school without segregation.

Before turning to the highly important United States Supreme Court decisions of 1950, note should be made of the first developments in the education of Negroes on the graduate level in several southern "white" institutions. West Virginia University was the first segregated state university to admit Negroes to graduate classes after the ruling in the Gaines case.[72] The University of Delaware announced during 1947–1948 that henceforth it would admit Negro students to its graduate schools. The University of Arkansas was the first institution in the deep South to admit Negro students to regular classes in its graduate schools, and the step was taken without court action. As soon as the United States issued its opinion in the first University of Oklahoma case (the Ada Sipuel case) in January, 1948, the University of Arkansas admitted a Negro student to its law school. At first the student was segregated in the classroom, but this policy was abandoned after a few months.[73] On August 24, 1948, it announced that the freshman medical class would include a young Negro woman, and the university's vice-president in charge of medical education stated that Miss Irby "will be a part of her class, just like any other member—without segregation."[74] In publicizing her admission, university officials stated that the applicant was twenty-eighth in an aptitude test given to determine the ninety students who would make up the freshman class. Of interest in this connection is the statement of the National Association for the Advancement of Colored People, whose legal staff, in coöperation with local attorneys, took all of the racial discrimination cases, beginning

[71] Walter White, op. cit., pp. 144–148.
[72] Roy Wilkins, Letter to the Editor, New York Times, September 10, 1950.
[73] Ibid.
[74] The Crisis, September, 1948, p. 264.

with the Gaines case, through the courts. Commenting editorially on Miss Irby's admission, *The Crisis* said, "Give the Negroes the same tests, rate them fairly as others are rated, and take the ones that can make the grade. The Negro applicant asks no special favors; he asks only a chance to compete on equal terms."[75] This is an important statement in view of the possibility that the admission, deliberately or otherwise, of some unqualified Negroes to graduate study in southern universities may be disillusioning to some members of both racial groups.

In addition to the developments in state universities in Maryland, West Virginia, Delaware, and Arkansas, a number of private "white" schools in Maryland, Missouri, North Carolina, and the District of Columbia admitted Negro students in some or all departments prior to 1950.[76] One of these institutions, St. Louis University, decided in the spring of 1944 to open all of its courses to Negroes, and the following year seventy-seven Negroes were in attendance.[77]

Ranking in importance with the Gaines case are the Hemon Sweatt and the G. W. McLaurin cases ruled on by the U.S. Supreme Court on June 5, 1950. Mr. Sweatt began action on May 15, 1946, after being denied admission to the University of Texas Law School. One month after the suit was started, the One Hundred and Twenty-Sixth District Court of Travis County, Texas, granted the writ of mandamus against the Board of Regents. Issuance of the writ was stayed for six months to enable Texas to establish a "separate law school for Negroes substantially equal to the one at the University of Texas." When no other law school of any kind had been established six months later, another petition for mandamus was filed. A "law school" was then set up in the basement of a building in Houston, but Sweatt refused to enroll in it. The petition for mandamus was dismissed and an appeal was taken to the Texas Court of Civil Appeals. On the basis of the appeal, the lower court was ordered on March 5, 1947, to rehear the case. The case was reheard and was then reargued in the Court of Civil Appeals early in 1948. On the latter occasion the higher court again affirmed the trial court's refusal to order the Regents to admit Sweatt to the law school.

[75] *Ibid.*

[76] G. N. Redd, *op. cit.*, p. 407.

[77] Carey McWilliams, *op. cit.*, p. 17. In 1950–1951 St. Louis University had sixty-two full-time Negro students and 182 part-time night-school students in arts and sciences; thirteen full-time day-school Negro students and sixty-four full-time night-school students in commerce and finance; thirteen full-time Negro students in nursing; five full-time Negro students in the Institute of Technology; in the schools of law, dentistry, and medicine there were seven full-time Negro students; and in the graduate school from one-fourth to one-third of the total of 102 full-time students were Negroes. In addition, a number of Negro graduate students were enrolled for courses on a part-time basis. These figures do not include summer-school students. Information provided by Mr. P. T. McDonald, registrar, in letter of July 17, 1951.

In the June 5, 1950, unanimous decision of the U.S. Supreme Court, Chief Justice Vinson said that the Court could not agree with Texas that the fifty-four-year-old precedent that "separate but equal" facilities for Negroes do not violate the equal protection clause of the Fourteenth Amendment should be affirmed.[78] He noted the reluctance of the Supreme Court to deal with constitutional issues except "in the particular case before it" and added that the Court did not "need" to rule on Mr. Sweatt's contention that the old ruling should be reëxamined and abandoned. Mr. Vinson compared the faculties and the libraries of the school at Austin and the new Houston school. The law faculty at Austin had nineteen members and a library of 65,000 volumes. The plans for the Houston school called for no independent faculty or library. The teaching was to be carried on by four professors from the University of Texas Law School, and few of the 10,000 volumes scheduled for Houston had actually arrived. He pointed out too that since the trial of this case had begun, a law school had been added at the Texas State University for Negroes and is "apparently on the road to accreditation" with five teachers and a library of 16,500 books. The Chief Justice wrote, "Whether the University of Texas Law School is compared with the original or the new law school for Negroes, we cannot find substantial equality in the educational opportunities offered white and Negro law students in the state." He said further that the University of Texas Law School "possesses to a far greater degree those qualities which are incapable of objective measurement but which make for greatness in a law school." Included here are "reputation of the faculty, experience of the administration, position and influence of the alumni, standing in the community, tradition and prestige." To these remarks a new point in cases of this type was added: the fact that the Negro law school "excludes" 85 percent of the population of Texas, and most of the lawyers, witnesses, jurors, judges, and others with whom Mr. Sweatt would deal when he became a member of the Texas bar. "With such a substantial and significant segment of society excluded," the decision said, "we cannot conclude that the education offered is substantially equal to that which he would receive if admitted to the University of Texas Law School." In his final conclusion Mr. Vinson held that legal education equivalent to that offered by the

---

[78] The "separate but equal" dictum has a long and interesting Supreme Court history. "In 1868 a Negro woman, Catherine Brown, tried to board a 'white' railroad car from Alexandria, Va., to Washington. When she was ejected, she brought suit. The Supreme Court ruled in 1873 that separate accommodations, even if identical, were not equal under the Constitution, and that the railroad had violated the law. However, in 1896 the court took a different view of segregation in Plessy versus Ferguson. The issue was whether a Louisiana provision for separate railroad accommodations denied equal protection. The court held that the segregation did not stamp Negroes 'with a badge of inferiority' and that segregation was justified under the 'separate but equal' ruling." Benjamin Fine, "Education in Review," New York Times, June 4, 1951.

state to students of other races was not available to Mr. Sweatt in a separate law school as offered by the state, and that the equal-protection clause of the Fourteenth Amendment required that he be admitted to the University of Texas Law School.[79]

G. W. McLaurin, a retired Negro teacher in his early fifties and holder of a master's degree, applied for admission to the University of Oklahoma in 1948 to seek the degree of Doctor of Education. Originally he was denied admission because of race, but the Oklahoma legislature amended the state laws to allow admission on a segregated basis. This decision, also unanimous and written by Chief Justice Vinson, said that Mr. McLaurin was required first to sit in an anteroom to a classroom, at a special desk on the mezzanine floor of the library, and to eat at a different time from other students in the cafeteria. Later the arrangements were modified, and he was seated in a place railed off, and with a sign "Reserved for colored." After other changes he was, at the time of the trial, assigned to a classroom set apart for colored students, assigned to a table on the main library floor, and allowed to use the cafeteria at the same time as other students, though at a designated table. Mr. Vinson held that such restrictions "set McLaurin apart" from other students and handicapped him in pursuing his graduate instruction effectively. "Such restrictions impair and inhibit his ability to study, to engage in discussions and exchange views with other students, and in general, to learn his profession." The ruling went on to say that it could be argued that Mr. McLaurin, even with restrictions removed, might still be set apart by his fellow students. This argument is irrelevant, according to the Court, because of the vast difference— a constitutional difference—between restrictions imposed by the state which prohibit the commingling of students and the refusal of individuals to associate where the state raises no such bar. Finally, the opinion said, the restrictions deprive Mr. McLaurin of his right to equal protection of the laws. "We hold that under these circumstances, the Fourteenth Amendment precludes differences in treatment by the state based upon race. [He] having been admitted to a state supported Graduate School, must receive the same treatment at the hands of the state as students of other races."[80]

Two days after the Sweatt decision the University of Texas admitted Mr. Sweatt and two other Negro students. The University of Kentucky had admitted thirty Negro students before the Sweatt case ruling. The University of Louisville dropped its racial barriers in the graduate and professional schools in the fall of 1950 and admitted forty Negro students. The abolition of the Louisville Municipal College, segregated liberal arts school, in June, 1951, eliminated remaining racial admission

[79] Lewis Wood, "Supreme Court Rulings Bar Segregation in Two Colleges," New York Times, June 6, 1950, pp. 1, 18.

[80] Ibid., p. 18.

barriers at the university. A three-judge federal court ordered the University of Virginia in September, 1950, to admit Gregory Swanson, a Negro lawyer who had applied for admission to do graduate work. Two Negroes entered the university that fall. In November, 1950, Louisiana State University opened its law-school classes to a Negro for the first time, after a federal court ordered the university to accept him and "other qualified Negroes." The first court ruling affecting instruction on the undergraduate level came in Delaware, when a state court ruled that the University of Delaware must accept qualified Negro applicants. This decision was followed by a federal district court ruling ordering the Paducah, Kentucky, Junior College, a municipal school, to admit qualified Negro students. A state court in Maryland held that the University of Maryland must admit a Negro student to the graduate school for the study of sociology.[81] On April 4, 1951, the trustees of the University of North Carolina voted to admit qualified Negroes to professional and graduate schools. It was announced that this action would affect only university schools offering courses not provided in the state's Negro colleges.[82] This announcement is of interest because later in the same week the Fourth United States Circuit Court of Appeals held that four Negro applicants for admission to the University of North Carolina Law School were entitled to enter, if otherwise qualified. The state based its case on the "separate but equal" doctrine and pointed out that its separate Negro law school had been in operation at Durham for a decade. This school had twenty-eight law students and a library of 30,000 volumes, and was served by two white professors. The state argued that since Negro lawyers have only Negro clients, graduates of the segregated school would not be handicapped by associating only with members of their own race in law school. The appellate court held that "these arguments do not reach the complainants' case or the deficiencies which it discloses." Some of the deficiencies cited by the court were physical, but the main issue was segregation, per se. The court held that it is "a definite handicap to the colored student to confine his association in law school to people of his own class."[83]

Within three years after the admission of the first Negro student to graduate study at the University of Arkansas, 200 Negroes were enrolled on the graduate level. The year 1950–1951 saw nearly a hundred Negro graduate students at the University of Oklahoma, and the total number of Negro students on "white" campuses, public and private, in the South was well over 1000 (or over 2000 if summer schools are included).

[81] National Association for the Advancement of Colored People, Civil Rights at Mid-Century, Annual Report, 1950, p. 25.

[82] Josephine Savoca, "Racial Segregation Loses Ground," New York Herald Tribune, January 7, 1951; New York Times editorial, September 10, 1950; Associated Press reports in Cleveland Plain Dealer, December 5, 1950, and April 5, 1951.

[83] New York Times editorial, "Carolina's Decisive Case," April 8, 1951.

DESEGREGATION IN COLLEGES AND UNIVERSITIES SINCE THE SUPREME COURT DECISION OF MAY 17, 1954

Of the 208 tax-supported colleges and universities in the South, 110 now admit Negroes. In Kentucky, Maryland, Missouri, Oklahoma, and West Virginia, all institutions of higher learning maintain nonsegregation policies, but in several schools no Negroes have applied for admission. Florida, Georgia, Mississippi, and South Carolina have admitted no Negroes to "white" public colleges or universities, and the one Negro student admitted to the University of Alabama was later expelled. Mississippi had no applications from Negroes for admission to any of its white public colleges in 1956–1957; Alabama received two applications, as did South Carolina's Clemson Agriculture and Mechanical College. Refusal by both the University of Florida and the University of Georgia to admit Negro applicants to their law schools has resulted in court actions. Whereas there were approximately 1000 Negro students enrolled in both public and private colleges and universities in the South at the time of the Court's decision, two years later approximately 2000 Negroes were attending these colleges during the regular terms and about the same number were enrolled in summer sessions.[84] Examples of desegregation follow.

Arkansas—Eight formerly all-white colleges have from 50 to 100 Negro graduates and undergraduates combined. One all-Negro college remains.

Delaware—The University of Delaware has admitted Negro students for several years, but no estimate is available of the number attending. The state still maintains one all-Negro school.

Kentucky—All eight of the formerly white public colleges now admit Negroes. Twenty-nine colleges and universities, public and private, enroll Negroes. More than 550 Negroes were attending previously all-white schools in 1956, with the University of Louisville having "several hundred" Negroes. The Negro enrollment at the University of Kentucky has been in the eighties. One predominantly Negro college is still maintained by the state.

Maryland—All 10 of the formerly white tax-supported colleges and universities now have non-segregation policies. The state maintains three all-Negro institutions.

Missouri—Negro students are enrolled at 10 of the 15 formerly all-white colleges and universities. Enrollments vary from "a few" at Central State College to 200 at Harris Teachers College. Predominantly Negro Lincoln University had 10 to 20 white students in 1955–56.

North Carolina—In eleven publicly-supported colleges mainly for whites, North Carolina had 19 Negroes enrolled in four divisions of the consolidated university system. Chapel Hill had seven Negro graduate students and four undergraduates; the other eight Negro students were undergradu-

[84] *Southern School News*, October, 1956, p. 1. State-by-state figures on Negro enrollments in southern colleges is given each year in the October issue of this periodical.

ates at North Carolina State College, the Woman's College, and Gaston Technical Institute.

Oklahoma—All 22 publicly-supported colleges and universities operate on an unsegregated basis, including Langston University which is predominantly Negro. No estimates are available of the total number of Negro students or of the number of schools which actually have Negro students on campus.

Tennessee—Six of the seven public colleges and universities operate under non-segregation policies at the graduate level and the senior level in the undergraduate divisions. The University of Tennessee accepts Negroes at the graduate level only. No Negro applicants for the senior class have been received at any of the state white schools, although the court-approved gradual desegregation plan extended to that level for 1956–57.

Texas—Five senior colleges and 14 junior colleges of the 46 predominantly white public colleges and universities accepted Negroes in 1956–57. Estimates of Negroes enrolled were 125 in senior colleges (including 100 at the University of Texas) and 150 in junior colleges.

Virginia—Negroes were enrolled in four of the 10 publicly-supported colleges and universities in 1956–57—University of Virginia, 18; Medical College of Virginia, 11; Richmond Professional Institute, 5; and Virginia Polytechnic Institute, 4.

West Virginia—Negroes attend seven of the eight formerly all-white public colleges and universities. An estimated 150 Negro students were enrolled in predominantly white schools in 1955–56, and about 460 white students were enrolled in predominantly Negro schools.[85]

The situation in Louisiana during 1956–1957 was especially interesting. Laws enacted in that state in 1956 included these provisions: (1) Registrants must have "good character" certificates from their high-school principals and parish school board superintendents; (2) the signing of a "good character" certificate for a Negro applying for admission to a previously all-white college constitutes an act supporting integration; and (3) such an act is sufficient to cause the discharge of the principal or superintendent. Although Louisiana State University had been opened to Negro undergraduates by federal court order, none applied for admission for the 1956–1957 year. The new legislation discouraged Negro students who could have stayed at least another term in previously all-white colleges. LSU, with 121 Negro graduate students at the end of the term in June, 1956, reënrolled only 61, and the total Negro enrollment at the state university plus that at McNeese College, Southwestern Louisiana Institute, and Southeastern Louisiana College dropped from approximately 400 to less than 200.[86] In a decision handed down April 15, 1957, by Federal Judges J. Skelly Wright and Herbert Christenberry in a combined case against four state colleges fighting integration, Acts 15 and 249 of the 1956 legislature were held to be

[85] Ibid., pp. 1–2.
[86] Ibid., p. 5.

"integrally related" and a "transparent device" to avoid the equal-protection clause of the Fourteenth Amendment, and therefore unconstitutional. The decision also imposed injunctions on the four integrated state colleges seeking to oust Negroes. About 100 Negroes had enrolled in these colleges for the spring semester under protection of a temporary restraining order.[87]

Another important case in the legal conflict over the admission of Negroes to institutions of higher learning involves the law school of the University of Florida. Prior to the U.S. Supreme Court decision of May 17, 1954, the Supreme Court of Florida dismissed the action of a Negro who sought admission to the University of Florida law school. After the first ruling in the school segregation cases, the U.S. Supreme Court reversed this decision and remanded the case. On the remand, the Supreme Court of Florida continued the case pending questions of capacity, plant, and other "conditions that now prevail" at the College of Law. When the Negro applicant asked the U.S Supreme Court to review this action, the Court refused the review but, after vacating its prior order, entered a new order. The new order "makes it clear that, while the principle of the initial decision in the School Segregation Cases is applicable to *all levels of public education* [italics added], the factors of possible delay in the public schools recognized in the second 'implementation' decision in those cases are not involved in graduate professional schools."[88] Subsequently the Supreme Court of Florida refused to order the admission of a Negro to the law school at that time on the ground that such an admission would result in "violence in university communities and a critical disruption of the University system."[89]

Miss Autherine Lucy's admission to the University of Alabama precipitated a three-day demonstration during the first week of February, 1956, which led university officials to exclude her from classes indefinitely.[90] U.S. District Judge H. Hobart Grooms ruled on February 29 that the university must readmit Miss Lucy before March 5, 1956. Several hours later the University of Alabama's board of trustees "permanently expelled" Miss Lucy for her "outrageous, false and baseless accusations" in alleging that the university had "conspired" in the demonstrations which led to her temporary suspension on February 6.[91] Miss Lucy brought suit in a federal district court to compel university authorities to allow her to continue her studies, but the court refused

[87] *Ibid.*, May, 1957, p. 13; February, 1957, p. 16.

[88] *Race Relations Law Reporter*, April, 1956, p. 297.

[89] *Ibid.*, April, 1957, p. 295.

[90] *Southern School News*, March, 1956, pp. 6–7. For a vivid account of this case, see Carl Rowan, *Go South to Sorrow*, Random House, Inc., 1957, chap. 8.

[91] *Southern School News*, April, 1956, p. 5.

to hold university officials in contempt for having expelled her, saying that the university was justified in its action for her unproven charges that the university conspired in the riots which drove her from the campus in February, 1956[92]

An important judicial action came on May 20, 1957, when the Supreme Court refused to review a lower court's ruling that Memphis State College had no right to limit admissions on the basis of color or race. In effect, the Court rejected the state-promulgated "stair-step" program for integration beginning with the senior year.[93]

With the exception of the rioting produced by the admission of Miss Lucy to the University of Alabama, Negro students seem to have fared rather well on previously all-white campuses. Many of the first Negroes admitted to these colleges turned out to be good legal, social, and academic risks. Guy B. Johnson found that "they were very much aware of their importance as pioneers in a new pattern of race relations. They were mostly graduate and professional students, and they were serious, studious, cautious, very eager to succeed and to reflect credit on their group. Most of them played the pioneer role successfully, and there can be little doubt that they did much to elicit favorable attitudes and to establish an expectation of good performance."[94]

Although most white students seem to have been either indifferent or sympathetic in their reactions to the presence of Negro students, two separate social worlds have been maintained. According to Johnson:

A few years ago most southern white people would have shuddered at the thought that their sons and daughters might have to share their classrooms, dining halls, and dormitories with Negroes. Such "social" contacts have had a heavily loaded symbolic value and they still have a certain amount of it even on the campuses, but the students have quickly learned these new patterns of social interaction even to the point of having interracial banquets, picnics, etc., without feeling any undue threat to their sense of social or personal privacy. At the same time, it cannot be denied that there exists on the campuses a strong undercurrent of anxiety among the white group on the matter of "social mingling" as a potential threat, and that among the Negro students there is a constant malaise which centers around the conflict between their desire for complete acceptance and the white people's touchiness on the question of "social equality." As matters stand, such equal-status contacts as interracial dating, dancing, and fraternity membership have been so thoroughly understood as being taboo that they have scarcely been mentioned, let alone practiced. We believe that this social dualism which has been carried over from the larger society to the southern campus constitutes

---

[92] Race Relations Law Reporter, April, 1957, p. 295; Southern School News, June, 1957, p. 13.

[93] John N. Popham, New York Times, May 26, 1957.

[94] Guy B. Johnson, "Racial Integration in Southern Higher Education," Social Forces, May, 1956, pp. 310–311.

a crucial accommodative factor in the relatively peaceful transition from segregation to integration in southern higher education.[95]

The off-campus community (movies, eating places, etc., on the fringe of the campus) is still a bulwark of legal segregation.

We referred above to the attempts made in Louisiana during 1956 to eliminate such integration in publicly supported colleges and universities as had taken place. At the same time, Louisiana State University's board of supervisors revealed a new student segregation policy designed to steer a course through conflicting state and federal laws. This policy sought to keep educational activities integrated and social affairs segregated. Negroes at the university "are eligible for honor societies but may not attend their banquets. They may live in campus dormitories but not share rooms with whites. Negroes may eat in desegrated dining halls, attend desegregated religious services, and march with whites in graduation ceremonies. Seating at scholastic ceremonies may be nondiscriminatory, but seating at athletic events may not. Out of bounds to Negroes are campus-wide dances and the swimming pool. The LSU athletic department was ordered not to schedule any out-of-state athletic games with schools who use Negro athletes."[96]

In their classrooms, faculty members have encountered no unpleasantness with Negro students. There have been some problems because Negroes are handicapped by their generally inferior educational background. Ashmore found that very few faculty members suggest that this situation is due to racial traits; most face the fact that few southern Negroes have had the prior schooling which would make it possible for them to compete on equal terms with whites.[97]

When an Associated Press reporter inquired about the first Negro undergraduates at the end of their first semester at the University of North Carolina, he found that "not even startled expressions" greeted them on the campus. The first-semester grades of the three boys "were about average, a scattering of C's and B's." These students were admitted in the fall of 1955 on orders of a federal district court.[98]

As in the case of desegregation in primary and secondary schools, it is difficult to assess the results of integration in higher education. In general, it has been easier to desegregate at the graduate and professional level than at the undergraduate level; but, as was mentioned previously, Florida, Georgia, Mississippi, and South Carolina have admitted no Negroes at any level (including the public elementary and secondary

[95] *Ibid.*, p. 312.
[96] *Southern School News,* October, 1956, p. 5.
[97] Harry S. Ashmore, *The Negro and the Schools,* University of North Carolina Press, 1954, p. 43.
[98] *Southern School News,* March, 1956, p. 16.

schools) and the one Negro student admitted to the University of Alabama was later expelled. In the University of Florida law school case, the United States Supreme Court made it clear that its initial decision on desegregation includes all levels of public education and that the factors of possible delay in the public schools recognized in its May 31, 1955, decision do not hold for graduate professional schools. Appeals, reviews, and lawsuits to compel compliance with the Court's decisions, and lawsuits over the constitutionality of new legislation intended to provide means of circumventing those decisions, and physical and other kinds of intimidation will delay but cannot prevent further integration. It is likely that within a decade after the Supreme Court's decisions there will be a sharp increase in desegregation in publicly supported colleges and universities in many parts of the South.

RESTRICTION ON ADMISSION OF JEWS TO PROFESSIONAL SCHOOLS

The investigation of discrimination in the admission of students to medical schools on the basis of religion or race has been hampered in some cases by the disappearance of the records. The Special Investigating Committee of the Council of the City of New York found that both the Cornell University Medical School and the College of Physicians and Surgeons of Columbia University had destroyed all of the applications made in years prior to the investigation, with the exception of those for the class admitted the previous year. These records were burned despite the fact that for at least a decade colleges and professional schools had been charged in legislative bills, lawsuits, newspaper articles, and elsewhere with discrimination against applicants because of their religion or racial origin.[99] Under the circumstances the destruction of the evidence was regarded in some quarters with suspicion.

One nation-wide survey found that although the number of applications for admission to medical schools by Jewish Americans had not declined, the number of Jewish students in these schools decreased by approximately 50 percent in the twenty-year period 1925–1945. At the end of this period the medical colleges were receiving between 35,000 and 40,000 applications each year from about 14,000 individuals. Medical officials estimated that from 5000 to 7000 of the applicants were Jewish. Some 6000 of the non-Jewish students were accepted annually, as compared with 500 Jewish applicants. The ratios of acceptance at this time therefore ran about three out of every four for non-Jews and one out of thirteen for Jewish students. During the second decade of this period the total number of medical students increased slightly, but the number of Jewish students declined rapidly in spite of an increase in

---

[99] W. R. Hart, "Anti-Semitism in New York Medical Schools," *American Mercury,* July, 1947, pp. 54–55.

Jewish applicants. The class of 1937 included 794 Jewish students, the class of 1940 only 477.[100]

A study of the acceptance of graduates of City College, New York City, who applied for admission to medical schools showed a steady decline from 1925 to 1943. In 1925, 58.4 percent of the City College graduates applying to medical schools were accepted; in 1943, 15 percent were accepted. The same general trend was evident for Brooklyn College, Queens College, and other institutions which had a high percentage of Jewish, Italian, and other minority-group students. At the College of Physicians and Surgeons of Columbia University the enrollment of Jewish students dropped from 46.92 percent in 1920 to 6.4 percent in 1940. The Jewish enrollment in the Medical College at Long Island University declined from 42.24 percent in 1932 to 14.14 percent in 1940. At Syracuse University Medical School the percentage of Jewish students dropped from 19.44 in 1936 to 6 in 1942. The decline at Cornell University was from 40 percent after World War I to 5 percent at the time of our entrance into World War II. New York University was one of the few major medical schools in the United States, perhaps the only one, which continued to disregard the quota system during the period cited. From 40 to 50 percent of its medical students were Jewish in those years.[101] Another study indicates that in each of the medical schools in New York City a significant decrease occurred in the number of graduates of New York City colleges admitted in the forties as compared with the number admitted in 1920. In some years none of the graduates of the city colleges succeeded in gaining admission to some of the medical schools.[102] Data obtained by B'nai B'rith from the same fifty-seven of the seventy-nine medical schools for 1935 and 1946 showed an absolute loss of 408 Jewish students, although the enrollment in these schools increased by 557. The decline of Jewish students in total number of students was from 16.1 percent in 1935 to 13.3 percent in 1946.[103]

A list of some of the medical schools which maintained a rigid quota system in 1945 despite denials to the contrary included Yale, Johns Hopkins, Harvard, Dartmouth, Columbia, Cornell, Rochester, Duke, Wake Forest, Virginia, Northwestern, Syracuse, and Baylor. Schools with a policy of discrimination but less rigid in its application included Chicago, Maryland, Boston, Wayne, Washington University, Cincinnati, California, Jefferson, Temple, and Pennsylvania. In the middle forties the most important examples of medical schools with a nonquota policy were those of New York University and the University of Illinois. The

[100] Frank Kingdom, "Discrimination in Medical Colleges," *American Mercury*, October, 1945, pp. 392–393.

[101] *Ibid.*, pp. 394–395.

[102] W. R. Hart, *op. cit.*, pp. 56–57.

[103] President's Commission on Higher Education, *op. cit.*, p. 39.

schools not included in the above lists are largely state universities or sectional schools in the Middle West or the South. They operated on a strict quota system, although their acceptances were said to be based on geographical distribution rather than on religion or race.[104]

In the middle forties nearly all medical colleges asked the applicant for his race or religion or both. Some asked whether he had ever changed his name. Changes in the application forms of the professional schools in New York City were studied by the special investigating committee appointed by the New York City Council. Before 1920 an applicant was asked to give the following information: name, address, age, place of birth, name of secondary school or college, scholastic record, and recommendations. Later many institutions required data concerning his religion and the place of birth of his father and mother. Then he was requested to provide a photograph. Some of the schools substituted a question on "racial origin" for the one concerning religion, or they asked an applicant to state his "mother's maiden name." The committee concluded that the institutions were "extremely anxious . . . to ascertain the racial origins, religion, and color of the various applicants for a purpose other than judging their qualifications for admission."[105]

The B'nai B'rith study referred to above revealed that the same twenty-eight out of forty dental schools showed an increase of 175 in total enrollment but a decrease of 486 in Jewish enrollment from 1935 to 1946. The percentage decrease in this eleven-year period was from 28.5 to 19.7.[106] In this connection, it may be mentioned that a survey conducted by Horner in 1944 recommended that dental colleges along the eastern seaboard bring their student population more in line with the ethnic composition of the nation.[107]

In most of the professions other than medicine and dentistry the proportion of Jewish students also dropped between 1935 and 1946. In 77 out of 160 law schools the percentage of Jewish students fell from 25.8 to 11.1. The enrollment in these 77 schools increased from 22,809 to 25,796, but Jewish enrollment decreased from 5884 to 2862. The total enrollment of the 46 private schools in the 77 declined 600, but they had 2800 fewer Jewish students. The Jewish proportion dropped by the following percentages in schools of these professions: architecture, from 8.5 to 4.4; social work, 13.6 to 11.1; commerce, 16.7 to 10.7; fine arts, 15.5 to 8.4; and engineering, 6.5 to 5.6. In journalism the Jewish proportion remained at 10.4 percent. It rose from 0.8 to 2.6 in nursing; from 3.1 to 4.7 in education; and from 9.1 to 20.3 in osteopathy. The last-mentioned increase was due mainly to the barriers in medicine. The Report of the President's Commission on Higher Education points

[104] Frank Kingdon, op. cit., pp. 398–399.
[105] President's Commission on Higher Education, op. cit., p. 37.
[106] Ibid., p. 39.
[107] D. W. Dodson, "College Quotas and American Democracy," p. 5.

out that the figures of professional-school enrollments given in the B'nai B'rith study include data for years in the middle forties when rejections of all types of candidates tended to be much higher than acceptances, and that the figures presented in that report have to be regarded as indicative rather than as absolutely conclusive testimony.[108]

Recent Developments and Proposals for the Education of Minorities

REGIONAL COMPACTS

In February, 1948, fourteen southern states entered into a "regional compact" for the announced objective of arranging to pool their educational facilities so as to insure that students receive the best possible education. In June, 1949, eleven state legislatures created an organization known as the Board of Control for Southern Regional Education to investigate the possibilities of regional education. The governor and three citizens of each state, appointed by the governor, constitute the board. The board's duties are, first, to administer service programs already approved by the state legislatures and, second, to conduct continuous long-range studies of regional educational needs and to develop coöperative arrangements among institutions and states to meet these needs.[109]

The first method of regional education which has been employed is the "contract for services." In the first round of contracts, fourteen institutions arranged to provide instruction in three fields: veterinary medicine, medicine, and dentistry. In veterinary medicine four schools (Alabama Polytechnic Institute, Tuskegee Institute, the University of Georgia, and Oklahoma A. and M. College) agreed to accept a total of 101 first-year students, and they were to receive $1000 for each student. Seven institutions (Duke, Emory, Louisiana State, Meharry Medical College, Tennessee, Tulane, and Vanderbilt) were to receive 173 students in medicine at $1500 per student. Dental training was arranged at six institutions (Emory, Loyola of Louisiana, Maryland, Medical College of Virginia, Meharry, and Tennessee) for 114 students at a cost of $1500 per student. All of these contracts provided for state quotas and for the selection of students according to the admission policies of each school. Students are certified as eligible for admission on the basis of any criteria the states wish to establish. These arrangements were scheduled to provide for 207 white students and 181 Negro students during 1949–1950 at a cost of approximately $1,500,000.[110]

The Board of Control for Southern Regional Education has studied

---

[108] President's Commission on Higher Education, *op. cit.*, p. 38.
[109] John E. Ivey, Jr., "Regional Education," *Phylon*, 1949, vol. 10, pp. 381–384.
[110] *Ibid.*, pp. 385–386.

such additional fields as graduate studies, social work, architecture, forestry, phases of engineering, agriculture, and professional education. Also, it has investigated methods of regional coöperation besides the contractual arrangements to exchange students and funds among the states. Other methods which are being contemplated include joint use of research facilities, the movement of students from one institution to another for training purposes, the exchange of faculty members, joint research projects, and voluntary specialization in curricular offerings.[111]

The Board of Control takes the position that its regional program does not affect segregation one way or another, since admissions to the service institutions are decided by the schools and the states themselves. John E. Ivey says that the contracts do not designate the type of students to be admitted but merely the state from which they come.[112]

Regional education would be opposed by very few Negroes if it were arranged on a completely nonsegregated basis. Negroes are opposed, however, to segregated regionalism because (1) they do not believe that equal educational opportunity can be provided under the "separate but equal" doctrine, (2) current public opinion makes segregated graduate and professional education unnecessary, (3) even if "separate but equal" educational opportunity were theoretically possible, it would be uneconomical and actually unattainable in practice, and (4) evidence obtained during the forties has convinced Negroes that, as far as graduate study is concerned, the old cliché of "half a loaf is better than no bread," is fallacious.

Negroes are skeptical about the possibility of "separate but equal" education because they believe that southern whites want better education for whites than for Negroes, and they fail to see how inequality would be abolished by pooling resources. The Regional College Plan has not been tested directly in the Supreme Court, but an attempt was made during 1949–1950 to use it in support of segregation. Miss Esther McCready was denied admission to the School of Nursing at the University of Maryland, but the state offered to send her to the Meharry Nursing School in Nashville, Tennessee, pursuant to an agreement with the Board of Control for Southern Regional Education. The Baltimore City Court accepted the defense of the state, but its decision was overruled by the Maryland Court of Appeals.[113] The United States Supreme Court refused to review the case, a development which was not surprising considering the decisions of that body in the Gaines and the Sweatt cases. It is interesting to note that the Board of Control for Southern Regional Education intervened in the McCready case with the statement: "The Board's position is that it shall make regional arrangements to supplement educational facilities within States. It is

[111] Ibid., pp. 386–387.
[112] Ibid., p. 387.
[113] NAACP, op. cit., pp. 25–26.

not the purpose of the Board that the Regional compact and the contracts for educational service thereunder shall serve any State as a legal defense for avoiding responsibilities established or defined under the existing state and federal laws and court decisions." The board points out that the McCready case does not concern the legality of the compact itself, and it does not consider that regional arrangements can properly be used in place of facilities required by law for all groups if provided for any one group.[114]

Ashmore states that it is clear that the regional education program has not served as a legal device to preserve segregation.[115] He points out that between 1949 and 1953 twenty previously segregated public institutions admitted Negroes. A number of Negro leaders have continued to criticize the plan and probably will continue to do so unless the Southern Regional Council of Education advocates nonsegregated regional education.[116] It may be added that the President's Commission on Higher Education supported regional education but only on a nonsegregated basis.[117]

FAIR EDUCATIONAL PRACTICES LEGISLATION

Along with the recent important court decisions regarding education for minorities, several state laws have been passed aimed at eliminating discrimination. The first fair educational practices law (Quinn-Olliffe Law) was passed in New York State in April, 1948. Schools above the secondary level are prohibited from excluding or limiting or otherwise discriminating against applicants for admission because of race, religion, creed, color, or national origin. The law permits religious and denominational schools to select students exclusively or primarily from members of their religious faith, but a denominational school may not exclude a student because of his race.[118] The New York law is enforced by the commissioner of education and the Board of Regents. The commissioner of education is authorized to investigate charges of religious or racial discrimination and to seek the elimination of such practice informally through persuasion, conciliation, or mediation. If these procedures are unsuccessful, the commissioner may refer the matter to the Board of Regents for a formal hearing. The Board of Regents may order the com-

---

[114] John E. Ivey, Jr., op. cit., p. 388.

[115] Harry S. Ashmore, op. cit., p. 37.

[116] B. E. Mays, "Segregation in Higher Education," Phylon, 1949, vol. 10, p. 404.

[117] President's Commission on Higher Education, op. cit., p. 36.

[118] As of June, 1949, twenty-nine of these institutions filed certificates as Roman Catholic institutions, ten as Protestant, one as Russian Orthodox, and two as Jewish. In addition, two Roman Catholic and three Protestant junior colleges asked to be considered as religious or denominational institutions. The enrollment of these forty-seven institutions constitutes about 15 percent of the total enrollment in colleges and universities in the state. The University of the State of New York, The State Education Department, Education Practices Administration, Annual Report, August 16, 1948—June 30, 1949.

plaint dismissed or direct the defendant to cease and desist from the unfair practice. An order from the board is enforceable through court action.

New Jersey and Massachusetts adopted fair educational practices acts in 1949. The New Jersey law is an amendment to the fair employment law of that state, and one agency is charged with the enforcement of all the provisions in the Law Against Discrimination. The Massachusetts law has no connection with that state's fair employment legislation; enforcement is in the hands of the state Board of Education.

Certain differences appear in these three laws. Originally, the New York law covered only schools above the secondary level, but vocational and trade schools were added by legislative amendment in 1951. Legislation in the other two states includes kindergartens, elementary and high schools, trade schools, undergraduate and graduate colleges, and professional schools. New Jersey and Massachusetts exempt from their coverage schools which are "distinctly private" in character.[119]

The term "distinctly private" is not clear-cut, and determination of what is meant by it may at times prove difficult. "The fact that an educational institution is not a public school in the sense of a school maintained and controlled by public authorities does not make it a school 'in its nature distinctly private.' To fall within the description 'distinctly private' such institutions must limit themselves to a very narrow group of persons. An ultra-exclusive private finishing school for girls would be an example. A private institution that accepts applications from the public generally would certainly remain outside the definition, as would an institution appealing to the public for funds."[120]

The New York law contains no stipulation concerning "distinctly private" schools, but it is limited to institutions "subject to visitation, examination or inspection" by the Regents or the commissioner of education. The University of the State of New York, an organization whose history goes back to the post-Revolutionary War period, is a holding corporation that is in general charge of education in the state, both higher and below that level, and both public and private. Even the so-called private colleges and universities in New York are incorporated as subsidiary corporations within the framework of the University of the State of New York. The State University of New York consists of the collection of institutions under public support. This latter organization has its own board of trustees and is subject to the supervision of the Board of Regents. The provisions of the fair educational practices act are applicable both to public and to private institutions.

Massachusetts follows the New York law in the matter of religious and denominational schools, but the New Jersey law exempts such

---

[119] Arnold Forster, op. cit., pp. 138–141. A model bill on fair educational practices has been prepared by the Anti-Defamation League. The text is given in ibid., p. 217.

[120] Ibid., pp. 139–140.

schools altogether. In the latter state a denominational school may not be held for discriminating against applicants because of race or national origin. The Massachusetts law is limited in its scope to citizens of the United States and thus fails to make any provision for aliens.

Another difference in these laws is the provision in New Jersey against discrimination in the use of recreational, social, and other campus facilities after students have been admitted to educational institutions. The New York and Massachusetts laws are limited to prohibiting discrimination in admission. A final difference in these laws is the provision in Massachusetts that it is unlawful, except for religious inquiries in the case of denominational schools, "to cause to be made any written or oral inquiry concerning the race, religion, color or national origin of a person seeking admission." The New York law does not forbid questions pertaining to race, religion, or national origin on the application forms, but the Education Practices Administration conducted a survey during 1949–1950 of the controversial questions on the application blanks of all post-secondary institutions in the state for the purpose of securing the elimination of these items. By the end of that year "direct questions on race, color, religion and national origin had almost completely disappeared from the application blanks on file from 123 denominational and nondenominational colleges, universities and junior colleges, only one nondenominational unit an optional question on religion, one unit a question on nationality and one unit a question on race. A total of 673 controversial questions had been eliminated to date."[121] By September, 1951, 952 of these questions had been eliminated.

Disagreement exists concerning the effectiveness of fair educational practices laws. Those who favor the legislation believe that the statutes have called attention to the problem of discrimination and that the educational work carried on by the commissioners is valuable. There have been fewer formal complaints than anticipated, but the commissioners have used their conciliatory powers to encourage a review of institutional policies on admission. A study by the New York Department of Education showed that 45 percent of three different classes in the nine medical schools in the state were Jews. The percentage of Jews in Cornell's medical school was 28, and in Columbia's 40. Jewish enrollment in these schools is estimated to have doubled during the first six years of the law's operation.[122]

---

[121] The University of the State of New York, *op. cit.*, July 1, 1949—June 30, 1950, p. 1.

[122] Will Maslow, "The Uses of Law in the Struggle for Equality," *Social Research*, Autumn Quarter, 1955, pp. 303–304. Maslow points out that very few complaints have been filed by students or by organizations acting on their behalf, and that the administrators of the law have initiated no investigations of their own. Research studies have been published by the State Department of Education and by Jewish agencies. That scrutiny, plus the establishment of two new state medical schools, may account for the very considerable increase in Jewish students.

Legislation probably can play a part in reducing discrimination in college admissions, but the question cannot be solved through legislation alone. Morroe Berger observes: "As a means of combating educational discrimination, legislation becomes increasingly unnecessary as the colleges grow more mindful of their democratic responsibility to all the people."[123]

FEDERAL SUBSIDIES AND THE EDUCATION OF MINORITIES

A survey of higher education reveals that the American people are favorably disposed toward the subsidization by the federal government of qualified high-school students who otherwise could not afford to go to college. The percentages in this poll were: those who favored the plan, 56; those who opposed the plan, 32; those who expressed no opinion, 12.[124] The G.I. Bill of Rights provided opportunities for many veterans of World War II who could not have afforded further education, and presumably similar arrangements will be made for future veterans. The private colleges face ever increasing deficits and many of them will require federal assistance sooner or later if they are to continue. States with meager resources probably will need outside funds to maintain publicly supported institutions of higher learning. From the standpoint of the education of minorities, it is advisable that any proposed federal legislation include an antidiscrimination condition. The President's Commission on Higher Education recommended that "all such legislation should clearly specify that there may be no discrimination in the channeling of such funds, either as regards possible individual beneficiaries under student grants-in-aid and fellowships, or as to institutions for white students as compared to institutions for Negroes only."[125]

Attempts have been made annually for the last thirty-five years to pass bills in Congress providing for federal assistance to the public schools of the nation. The moving spirit behind these proposals has been the National Education Association, and the strongest opposition has come from the Chamber of Commerce on the grounds of federal control and expense. The Roosevelt, Truman, and Eisenhower administrations have all advocated passage of a federal aid bill. A large part of the federal funds would go to the southern states. Several reasons are given for the failure to pass such a bill: (1) the religious issue, in which

[123] Morroe Berger, "Fair Educational Practices Legislation," *Annals of the American Academy of Political and Social Science,* May, 1951, pp. 45–46.

[124] Elmo Roper, "Higher Education," *Fortune,* September, 1949, p. 4.

[125] President's Commission on Higher Education, *op. cit.,* p. 36. The Report of this commission points out that such provisions have not always been made in federal legislation and cites the Smith-Hughes Act as an example. On the subject of special federally aided educational programs and services (vocational education, agricultural and home economics extension services, agricultural research, vocational rehabilitation of the physically handicapped, etc.) see Doxey Wilkerson, *Special Problems of Negro Education,* Government Printing Office, 1939, chap. 5, and the *Journal of Negro Education,* Summer, 1947.

one group wanted to compel the states to use federal funds to pay for the transportation of parochial-school children, and others desired to prohibit the states from doing so; (2) the issue of the possibility of federal control over local school systems; (3) the desegregation issue; (4) the economy issue, in which emphasis was placed on the current deficit budget. Those who have emphasized the last point wished to see the states make a greater effort to improve their schools without help from the federal government, or they favored granting money only to the needy states.[126] As in higher education, it is important, from the standpoint of minorities, that absence of discrimination be made a condition of any federal aid program which is established for the elementary and high schools.[127] As of 1957, no program of federal subsidies had been adopted.

The Importance of Education to Minorities

Education seems to be the principal factor in the stratification of the Negro community. Those in the professions constitute a large part of the Negro upper classes, and educational levels indicate differences in the middle and lower classes. In addition, as Myrdal observes, education has a special and symbolic significance for Negroes; "the educated Negro has, in one important respect, become equal to the better class of whites."[128] This point was borne out in the study of the Chicago Negro community, where education has a heavier weighting than occupation on the Negro social-status scale.[129] Informants there maintained that social position was not correlated with the type of work one did. A physician said that many of his fraternity brothers took jobs as Pullman porters or dining-car waiters or in the big hotels after they left school. "With a very narrow occupational spread, education is used to mark off social divisions within the same general occupational level. Persons who wish to circulate near the 'top,' whatever they may lack in money or job, must have enough education to avoid grammatical blunders, and to allow them to converse intelligently. Ignorant 'breaks' and inability to cite evidence of education—formal or informal—can bar a person permanently from the top."[130] Traditionally the professions have had the most prestige among the occupations. Other distinctions are based

[126] See Benjamin Fine, "Education in Review," New York Times, March 19, 1950.
[127] Gunnar Myrdal raises the question of preserving local financial responsibility when the federal government steps in. "If the federal government undertakes further financial responsibility for education, it will be up against a problem which has been bothering the philanthropic foundations for a long time. . . . How is it possible to aid without decreasing local responsibility?" Op. cit., p. 905.
[128] Ibid., p. 879.
[129] St. Clair Drake and Horace Cayton, Black Metropolis, Harcourt, Brace & Company, 1945, p. 515.
[130] Ibid.

on attendance at high-ranking northern universities and those of lesser standing, earned higher degrees and "honorary" degrees, and membership or the lack of it in honorary societies. In 1940 some 4000 Negro adults in Chicago had graduated from college, and 6000 more had attended college. At that time they made up 2 percent of the adult Negro population. For most of Chicago's Negro population high-school graduation is regarded as a "great step upward." For many girls it means a greater chance of avoiding domestic service and factory work and more possibility of "marrying up." Education, then, "is an important measure of the man (or woman)."[131]

Several factors appear to have some bearing on the strong interest which Jews show in education. The tradition of learning has been strong among Jews for centuries. Jews are concentrated in the middle class and in urban centers, and there are close relationships between these variables and a high value on education. The professional fields appeal to a higher percentage of Jews than of members of other groups, and professional licensing and practice require extensive training. On the basis of present evidence it is inadvisable to attempt to establish a definite relationship between the minority status of Jews and efforts to validate the self and the Jewish group through scholastic achievement. There is a fairly widespread feeling among Jews, however, that discrimination necessitates exceptional attainments in a half-friendly, competitive society.

Chinese-Americans and Japanese-Americans have shown considerable interest in high-school and college education. Other minorities in the population of the United States, in addition to the Negro group, have been underrepresented in the enrollments of secondary schools, colleges, and universities. Among these groups are the Mexican-Americans, the Filipinos, the American Indians, and the southern and eastern Europeans. Economic condition, linguistic handicap, stage of acculturation, group traditions, and dominant-group hostility have been among the factors affecting the progress of children in these groups beyond the elementary school. However, the number of people in each of these groups who continue their schooling is increasing, and these persons provide a disproportionate share of the leaders in their groups.

Minorities as a group have more difficulties than the majority in obtaining adequate and equal educational opportunities. If training is completed, placement and advancement offer more problems than is the case with majority-group persons. But because education affords prestige and is advantageous in a competitive specialized society, it has great importance for members of minority groups—especially to those who aspire to and those who wish to retain middle- or upper-class standing.

[131] *Ibid.*, pp. 515–516.

CHAPTER 21

Minorities and Art

The Art of Minorities

Art produced by and about minority-group members constitutes an important part of American art as art, and in reflecting the life of the social classes in given periods it provides insights concerning majority-minority relations. Our discussion centers primarily on Negro materials as illustrative of the influences at work on this art.

ARTISTIC ACHIEVEMENTS OF NEGROES

Twenty-five years ago Donald Young wrote concerning the "extravagant praise of ordinary accomplishments" in art produced by Negroes. Specifically mentioned was the poetry of Paul Lawrence Dunbar, James Weldon Johnson, Countee Cullen, Claude McKay, Jean Toomer, and Langston Hughes; the fiction of Jessie Fauset, Charles W. Chesnutt, Walter White, Nella Larsen, and W. E. B. DuBois. He spoke of "prejudiced overpraise" and "racial treason" in connection with the appraisal of the works of these average, or above average but not distinguished, authors. This lack of outstanding literary work on the part of Negroes in the United States was attributed not to any kind of racial incapacity but to the limitations imposed by prejudice and socioeconomic conditions.

Recent criticism of Negro authors dwells upon the small volume, in absolute or comparative terms, of writing done by Negroes and upon the need for a mastery of craftsmanship.[1] In the drama there has never been notable achievement by Negroes, and the situation has changed

---

[1] Blyden Jackson, "An Essay in Criticism," *Phylon*, Fourth Quarter, 1950, p. 338; Thomas D. Jarrett, "Towards Unfettered Creativity: A Note on the Negro Novelist's Coming of Age," *ibid.*, p. 315; Nick A. Ford, "A Blueprint for Negro Authors,"

little in the last few years. The most significant of the later plays have been the stage version of *Native Son*, Langston Hughes' adaptation of *Mulatto* (*The Barrier*), Owen Dodson's *Divine Comedy* and *Bayou Legend*[2] and Louis Peterson's *Take a Giant Step*.

In the pictorial and plastic arts there have been few American Negroes of outstanding merit (Henry O. Tanner, Richmond Barthe, Aaron Douglas, Augusta Savage).[3] Alain Locke points out that Afro-Americans were cut off from the African art traditions and skills by slavery, and that "stripped of all else, the Negro's own body became his prime and only artistic instrument, so that dance, pantomime and song became the only gateways for his creative expression." In this way the American Negro was "forced away from the craft arts and the old ancestral skills to the emotional arts of song and dance. . . . No comment on the Negro in the plastic and pictorial arts would be sound without this historical perspective."[4]

In the field of the dance, the work of Katherine Dunham and of Pearl Primus has been notable. Both have attained a high level of artistic achievement in the adaptation of folk dances of the Caribbean, the United States, and Africa, and in the modern dance field. Outstanding concert artists in the United States in recent years have included Marian Anderson, Dorothy Maynor, Roland Hayes, Paul Robeson, Todd Duncan, and Carol Brice.[5] Among American actors of high rank the Negro group

---

ibid., p. 374; Blyden Jackson, "The Blythe Newcomers," *Phylon*, First Quarter, 1955, p. 9; Blyden Jackson, "The Continuing Strain: Résumé of Negro Literature in 1955," *Phylon*, First Quarter, 1956, p. 35; John Lash, "A Long, Hard Look at the Ghetto," *Phylon*, First Quarter, 1957, p. 8.

[2] Charles H. Nichols, Jr., "The Forties: A Decade of Growth," *Phylon*, Fourth Quarter, 1950, p. 379; Nick A. Ford, *op. cit.*, p. 374. See F. W. Bond, *The Negro and the Drama*, The Associated Publishers, 1940, for a survey of this field. See also Sterling A. Brown, *Negro Poetry and Drama*, Associates in Negro Folk Education, 1937, Part II.

[3] Gunnar Myrdal, *An American Dilemma*, Harper & Brothers, 1944, p. 989.

[4] Alain Locke, *The Negro in Art: A Pictorial Record of the Negro Artist and of the Negro Theme in Art*, Associates in Negro Folk Education, 1940, p. 8. Locke states that there is ". . . a prevalent impression that the fine arts, with their more formalized techniques, are a less characteristic and less congenial mode of expression for the Negro's admitted artistic genius than the more spontaneous arts of music, dance, drama, or poetry. Such views ignore the fact that, although the interpretive, emotional arts have been the Negro's special forte in America, his dominant arts in the African homeland were the decorative and craft arts. These—sculpture in wood, bone, and ivory, metal-working, weaving, pottery—combined with skillful surface decoration in line and color, involve every skill in the category of the European fine arts, even if not in specific terms of the European traditions of easel painting, marble sculpture, engraving and etching. The Western world knows today, belatedly, that the Negro was a master artist in the idioms of his original culture, and that the characteristic African virtuosity was in decoration and design." *Ibid.*, p. 8. See also James A. Porter's survey of painting and sculpture produced by Negroes in the United States, *Modern Negro Art*, The Dryden Press, Inc., 1943.

[5] A list of Negro concert artists, conductors, educator-artists, and arranger-composers is given in *The Negro Yearbook*, Tuskegee Institute, 1947, pp. 422 ff., and in *ibid.*, 1952, pp. 52–64.

has had Bert Williams, Charles Gilpin, Richard Harrison, Ethel Waters, and Canada Lee. Competently written short stories have been produced by Langston Hughes, Chester Himes, and Richard Wright.[6] More books of poetry have been published by Negroes than any other type of writing. In 1941, the editors of *The Negro Caravan* observed that "writing poetry is still popular among Negroes, but it is largely occasional verse, derivative, and escapist."[7] Many interesting novels have been written by Negroes, but none of first-rate distinction until the last fifteen years.[8]

Critics have noted constant improvement in the writings by American Negroes. The best work of Gwendolyn Brooks, Margaret Walker, Owen Dodson, M. Carl Holman, and M. B. Tolson shows extraordinary mastery of craftsmanship and gives them a high place among contemporary poets.[9] Such novelists as Richard Wright, J. Saunders Redding, Willard Motley, Ann Petry, Chester Himes, and Ralph Ellison are held to be superior to their predecessors in writing ability. Speaking of the work of the later writers of fiction, *The Negro Caravan* editors comment that

. . . as various as their purposes and techniques may be, fiction by Negroes may be said to have come of age. The literary inbreeding that caused too many Negro novelists to repeat the stock characters and situations is disappearing. The awareness of and apprenticeship to the masters of the craft of fiction, American, English, or Continental European; the increasing contact with white writers of good will toward Negro fellow-craftsmen; the recognition that dramatic presentation can convey ideas and protest better than lecturing; the frank recognition of weaknesses among Negroes, and the refusal to show only Negro victims and white villains; an audience losing its hypersensitivity and growing in its respect for the artist; all of these may mean a genuine advance in the fiction by Negro authors.[10]

The role of literary criticism has been important in the improvement of writings by Negroes. Among the first interpreters of Negro art was Alain Locke, whose guidance of the Negro renaissance in the 1920's and whose articles and annual reviews in *Opportunity*, *Phylon*, and other journals

---

[6] *The Negro Caravan* (The Dryden Press, Inc., 1941), edited by Sterling A. Brown, Arthur P. Davis, and Ulysses Lee, an anthology of writings by American Negroes, includes short stories, novels (selections), poetry, drama, folk literature, biography, and essays. See also V. F. Calverton, *Anthology of American Negro Literature*, Modern Library, Inc., 1929.

[7] Sterling A. Brown, Arthur P. Davis, and Ulysses Lee (eds.), *op. cit.*, p. 282. For collections of American Negro poetry in addition to *The Negro Caravan* and the *Anthology of American Negro Literature* see J. W. Johnson (ed.), *The Book of American Negro Poetry*, Harcourt, Brace & Company, 1922; Countee Cullen, *Caroling Dusk*, Harper & Brothers, 1927; and Langston Hughes and A. Bontemps, *The Poetry of the Negro*, Doubleday & Company, Inc., 1949.

[8] Nick A. Ford, *op. cit.*, p. 374.

[9] Charles H. Nichols, Jr., *op. cit.*, p. 378; Arthur P. Davis, "Integration and Race Literature," *Phylon*, Second Quarter, 1956, pp. 144–145.

[10] Sterling A. Brown, Arthur P. Davis, and Ulysses Lee (eds.), *op. cit.*, p. 144.

are widely known.[11] The evaluations of Sterling Brown and his associates, of J. Saunders Redding, of Hugh M. Gloster, and the issues of *Phylon* devoted to literary criticism are laudable.[12]

NEGRO FOLK ART

The folk songs, dances, and stories of the American Negro have had important effects upon life in the United States. Among popular dances which appear to have a Negro background are the Lindy Hop, the Big Apple, the Cakewalk tradition (". . . the urbanization of the plantation folk-dances, incorporating in the whole such separate figures as the Black Annie, the Pas Mala, the Strut, the Palmer House, and later Walkin' the Dog, Ballin' the Jack, and other individual expressions"), and the Charleston.[13] The Uncle Remus stories about Brer Rabbit and other animals, the tall tales of John Henry, and other folk stories have amused young and old, black and white, for generations. But, as Donald Young remarks, the Negro's folk music is his supreme folk gift. Like all folk music, the authors are unknown. The songs have grown out of the Negro's experience as an American peasant. This art of untutored slaves came from cotton and tobacco plantations, the slave marts and slave quarters, camp meetings, factories, and forests. The titles of the spirituals are poetic—"Swing Low, Sweet Chariot"; "Sometimes I Feel Like a Motherless Child"; "Steal Away"; "Death's Goin' to Lay His Cold, Icy Hand on Me"; "We Shall Walk Through the Valley in Peace"; "Ride on King Jesus"; "He Never Said a Mumbaling Word"; "Go Down, Moses"; "Singing with a Sword in My Hand"; "No More Auction Block"; "Deep River"; "I Been Rebuked and I Been Scorned."[14] These songs, molded by the hardships and suffering of folk Negroes, brought release from trouble and pain. But, as Zora Neale Hurston insists, they were not just "Sorrow Songs." There was, and there still is, much vitality and zest in the singing of these songs by folk singers.[15] Today groups closer to the people than college choirs carry modified spirituals throughout the country. The Golden Gates, the Silver Echoes, the Coleman Brothers, and others, together with soloists like Mahalia Jackson, Marie

[11] Alain Locke, *The New Negro*, Albert and Charles Boni, 1925.

[12] Sterling A. Brown, Arthur P. Davis, and Ulysses Lee (eds.), *op. cit.*; Sterling Brown, *The Negro in American Fiction*, Associates in Negro Folk Education, 1937, and his *Negro Poetry and Drama*; J. Saunders Redding, *To Make a Poet Black*, University of North Carolina Press, 1939; Hugh M. Gloster, *Negro Voices in American Fiction*, University of North Carolina Press, 1948; *Phylon*, Fourth Quarter, 1950; and annual reviews of Negro literature, *Phylon*, First Quarter, 1955, 1956, 1957.

[13] Katherine Dunham, "The Negro Dance," in Sterling A. Brown, Arthur P. Davis, and Ulysses Lee (eds.), *op. cit.*, pp. 997–999.

[14] J. W. Johnson, *The Book of American Negro Spirituals*, The Viking Press, Inc., 1947; Sterling A. Brown, Arthur P. Davis, and Ulysses Lee (eds.), *op. cit.*, pp. 434–446.

[15] Sterling A. Brown, Arthur P. Davis, and Ulysses Lee (eds.), *op. cit.*, p. 420.

Knight, and Sister Rosetta Tharpe, sing the spirituals in churches and concert halls, and on records. Tambourines, cymbals, trumpets, trombones, and bass fiddles are used in some churches as the spirituals are given a more pronounced rhythm and a jazz quality. The Gospel songs, sung "out of the book," are crowding out the spirituals. These songs put an even greater emphasis on jazz and blues effects. Evaluating these new songs, Sterling Brown says: "Many lovers of the older spirituals disdain the Gospel Songs as cheap and obvious. But this new urban religious folk music should not be dismissed too lightly. It is vigorously alive with its own musical values. . . . To hear some fervent congregations sing 'Just a Closer Walk with Thee,' 'He Knows How Much You Can Bear,' and 'We Sure Do Need Him Now' can be unforgettable musical experiences. In sincerity, musical manner, and spirit, they are probably not so remote from the old prayer songs in the brush arbors."[16]

Among the secular songs of folk Negroes, the blues are the most popular. Among the best known of the adaptations of the blues, which probably go back to slavery, are W. C. Handy's "St. Louis Blues" and "Memphis Blues," and Ma Rainey's "Li'l Low Mamma Blues." Subject matter of the blues includes a woman's longing for her "man"; bewailing tornadoes, high water, hard times in farming; and the need for traveling, for leaving this cold-hearted town.[17] Less well-known seculars are the work songs, social songs, ballads, and satires, but they too have had an important place in Negro life. In the rural South, better roads and more motor vehicles, radio, and television, the phonograph and juke box, movies, churches, schools, and the Negro press combine in reducing isolation. Although Negro folk culture is breaking up, it has by no means disappeared.[18] The possible influence of the impressive body of Negro folk song on Negro-white relations is considered in a later section of this chapter.

AFRICAN RETENTIONS

Since the principal concern of this book is intergroup relations rather than cultural analysis, only brief reference is made here to the question of the retention of Africanisms in the arts. While there is no complete African culture in the New World, Herskovits' point is that a considerable number of African culture traits have been retained. According to his analysis, there is a continuum for such traits with Dutch Guiana at one end, the southern states (with the smallest number) at the other, and Haiti, Brazil, Cuba, the Dominican Republic, and the islands of the

---

[16] Sterling A. Brown, "Negro Folk Expression," *Phylon*, First Quarter, 1953, p. 50.
[17] See Sterling A. Brown, Arthur P. Davis, and Ulysses Lee (eds.), *op. cit.*, Part IV; Sterling A. Brown, *Negro Poetry and Drama*, chap. 2; H. W. Odum and G. B. Johnson, *The Negro and His Songs*, University of North Carolina Press, 1925, pp. 148–268. For an excellent statement on the blues, see Sterling A. Brown, "The Blues," *Phylon*, Fourth Quarter, 1952, pp. 286–292.
[18] Sterling A. Brown, "Negro Folk Expression," p. 60.

British, Dutch, and (sometime) Danish West Indies between the two extremes.[19]

Although a number of Negro intellectuals are interested in African politics, customs, and art, it is true today, as it was twenty-five years ago, that "the ordinary Negro knows little and cares less about African ways of life."[20] Nevertheless, it is of interest here to note certain evidence concerning African influences upon Negro music and dance in the United States. When a musicologist, Dr. M. Kolinski, analyzed the songs appearing in several volumes of spirituals, "thirty-six were found to have the same scales (tonal structures) as specific songs in the West African collection, while identical correspondences in melodic line were even found in a few instances. Thirty-four spirituals had the same rhythmic structure as some of the West African melodies, while the formal structure of fifty spirituals—their phrasing and time—were found to have African counterparts."[21] Motion pictures of some of the ceremonial dances taken by Herskovits in West Africa show a remarkable resemblance to the Charleston of the 1920's. Katherine Dunham writes concerning the Charleston: ". . . In Haiti, I found the Charleston in the dance La Martinique; and in terms of the retention of choreographic forms through transition periods, I would say that such a dance must have been known during the North American folk period. I have certainly seen possessed devotees in 'store-front' churches propelling themselves up and down the aisles with a practically pure Charleston step. It is not so surprising, then, that at one point the Charleston should have become such a popular and general expression of American culture."[22]

THE USE OF RACIAL THEMES IN ART PRODUCED BY NEGROES

In the ante-bellum period most of the literary expression of Negroes was along antislavery lines. This was true of speeches, many letters, pamphlets, poems, and a few items of fiction. Writing was thought of as a part of the struggle for freedom. After emancipation, Negroes wrote to advance the struggle for the rights and responsibilities of citizenship; and in the twentieth century, creative and social literature continued to

[19] This question was discussed in Chapter 18 in connection with our examination of the retention of African religious traits in the New World. See M. J. Herskovits, *The Myth of the Negro Past*, Harper & Brothers, 1941, p. 16. A different viewpoint is found in E. Franklin Frazier, *The Negro in the United States*, The Macmillan Company, 1949, pp. 3–21.

[20] Donald Young, *American Minority Peoples*, Harper & Brothers, 1932, pp. 561–562. The former head of the Art Department of Hampton Institute writes: "During this period (1940–1945) I have not found one student who showed the desire to study African art. However, almost as a rule I found the students rather ashamed or uneasy when confronted with the 'primitivity' of African art." Viktor Lowenfeld, "Negro Art Expression in America," *Madison Quarterly*, January, 1945, p. 5.

[21] M. J. Herskovits, *op. cit.*, p. 268. See Herskovits' remarks on the intangibles of singing techniques and motor habit accompanying song (pp. 265–267).

[22] Katherine Dunham, *op. cit.*, pp. 999–1000.

be used as instruments of protest against racial discrimination.[23] Propaganda, racial defense, and racial advertisement, then, were characteristic, at least until the 1920's, of most of the art produced by Negroes in the United States.[24]

A subject of some importance in considering racial themes in the writings of Negroes is the use of dialect. The first Negro poet to use dialect consistently was James Edwin Campbell, who wrote at the end of the nineteenth century. Campbell's dialect more closely reproduced plantation Negro speech than that of any other writer. Writing at about the same time, Paul Lawrence Dunbar, the best known of the Negro dialect poets, fashioned a synthetic dialect which was "modeled closer upon James Whitcomb Riley's colloquial language than upon the speech it was supposed to represent." Redding illustrates the difference between the two dialects by citing a stanza from a poem by each. From Campbell's "My Merlindy Brown":

> O, de light-bugs glimmer down de lane,
>   Merlindy! Merlindy!
> O, de whip-will callin' notes ur pain—
>   Merlindy! Merlindy!
> O, honey lub, my turkle dub,
>   Doan you hyah my bawjer ringin',
> While de night-dew falls an' de bo'n owl calls
>   By de ol bo'n gate Ise singin'.

From Dunbar's "When Malindy Sings":

> Fiddlin' man jes' stop his fiddlin'
>   Lay his fiddle on de she'f;
> Mockin' bird quit try'n to whistle
>   'Cause he jes' so shamed hisse'f
> Folks a-layin' on de banjo
>   Draps dey fingahs on de strings—
> Bless yo' soul—fergits to move 'em,
>   When Malindy sings.[25]

Dunbar's synthetic dialect could be read easily and with pleasure by northern whites "to whom dialect meant only an amusing burlesque of Yankee English," but it is impossible, as Redding remarks, "to speak the whole heart of a people . . . through such a bastard medium." Dunbar's dialect form limited him to the humorous and the pathetic.[26]

---

[23] Sterling A. Brown, Arthur P. Davis, and Ulysses Lee (eds.), *op. cit.*, p. 6.
[24] Hugh M. Gloster, *op. cit.*, p. 252.
[25] J. Saunders Redding, *op. cit.*, pp. 51–52.
[26] *Ibid.*, p. 63. Of the dialect written by Joel Chandler Harris, a white author, Redding says: ". . . [It] is skillful and effective misrepresentation, a made language in every sense of the word, conveying the general type of impression of untaught imagination, ignorance, and low cunning with which he believed the Negro endowed" (p. 52).

It may be said that Dunbar himself wished to achieve recognition as a writer of pure English, and that he devoted himself assiduously to such writing. However, the minstrel tradition was so strong that his dialect poetry received far more attention than his poetry, novels, and short stories in the pure tongue.[27]

Some of the Negro writers who followed Dunbar, especially Sterling Brown, have made effective use of dialect, but of a very different form of dialect. Commenting on Brown's work, James Weldon Johnson said, ". . . He has made more than mere transcriptions of folk poetry, and he has done more than bring to it mere artistry; he has deepened its meaning and multiplied its implications. He has actually absorbed the spirit of his material, made it his own; and without diluting its primitive frankness and raciness, truly re-expressed it with artistry and magnified power. In a word, he has taken this raw material and worked it into original and authentic poetry."[28] Some notion of Brown's dialect form may be gained from the poem "Southern Road":

> Swing dat hammer—hunh—
> Steady bo';
> Swing dat hammer—hunh—
> Steady, bo';
> Ain't no rush, bebby,
> Long ways to go.
>
>   . . . . .
> Doubleshackled—hunh—
> Guard behin';
> Doubleshackled—hunh—
> Guard behin';
> Ball an' chain, bebby,
> On my min'.[29]

Our point here is that, while dialect has constituted an important aspect of the racial theme in the writings by Negroes, there are great differences between Campbell's reproductions of plantation dialect, the synthetic dialect of Dunbar, and the "reëxpressed" dialect of Brown. Reproduced, spurious, and bastard dialects tend to reinforce unfavorable racial stereotypes. For some, dialect poetry of the Sterling Brown type may also reinforce stereotypes, but for the initiated it provides valuable insights into folk Negro life.

A new approach to the Negro character in fiction was introduced by Charles W. Chesnutt at the turn of the century. Chesnutt wrote objectively, utilizing southern folk material, the situation of near-whites in

---

[27] *Ibid.*, pp. 56–64.

[28] J. W. Johnson, Introduction to Sterling A. Brown, *Southern Road*, Harcourt, Brace & Company, 1932, pp. xiv–xv.

[29] Sterling A. Brown, *Southern Road*, pp. 46–47. Reprinted from *Southern Road* by Sterling Brown, by permission of Harcourt, Brace & Company. Copyright 1932 by Harcourt, Brace & Company.

Cleveland, and the results of miscegenation (*The Conjure Woman, The Wife of His Youth, The House Behind the Cedars*). In his later novels (*The Marrow of Tradition* and *The Colonel's Dream*), Chesnutt became propagandistic, but Negro creative literature had been advanced by his exposure of the Negro to critical analysis in the early part of his career.[30]

In the years of confusion following World War I, much of the writing produced by Negroes, like that of white authors, was literature of escape.[31] Spokesmen for the New Negro made extensive use of the racial theme, but they wrote mainly for a white audience and most of their critics were white. Rich whites underwrote Negro poets; and Negro poetry, regarded as "the prattle of a gifted child," became a fad. This period was called the "Negro renaissance," but the viewpoint of Negro writers during the twenties was limited by their isolation from the literary life of whites and by the general pattern of racial segregation.[32] In spite of that, the devotion to racial defense and praise so characteristic of the prewar years was replaced to some extent by

. . . a wider range of creative activity, a greater diversity of techniques and ideologies, and a keener appreciation for universal values. Realistic portraiture was done of Southern folk life, the Mid-Western small town, Harlem, and West Indian peasant experience. Analysis was made of the problems of color and caste among the bourgeoisie of the metropolitan North. Agitation for racial justice was conducted on an international as well as a national or sectional basis. Attention was directed to the primitivistic and exotic aspects of Negro life in Harlem. Rollicking satire was employed to attack the American race problem.[33]

This is the period of Langston Hughes' *The Weary Blues*, Claude McKay's *Harlem Shadows*, Countee Cullen's *Color* and *Copper Sun*, Jean Toomer's *Cane*, Jessie Fauset's *There Is Confusion*, Wallace Thurman's *The Blacker the Berry*, James Weldon Johnson's *God's Trombones*, and George Schuyler's *Black No More*.

Consideration of the Negro writer's audience throws further light on the importance of the racial theme. The Negro writer has lacked a helpful audience, that is, one that is both sympathetic and critical.[34] The predicament of the short-story writer illustrates the situation. He cannot solve his audience problem merely by producing the type of story which it is interested in because (1) he faces two audiences, and (2) he must try to maintain his own integrity. One of his audiences is composed of white readers conditioned by popular white writers like Octavus Roy Cohen, Julia Peterkin, and Roark Bradford; the other audience is made

---

[30] J. Saunders Redding, *op. cit.*, pp. 68–76.
[31] *Ibid.*, p. 119.
[32] Margaret Walker, "New Poets," *Phylon*, Fourth Quarter, 1950, pp. 345–346.
[33] Hugh M. Gloster, *op. cit.*, pp. 253–254.
[34] Blyden Jackson, "An Essay in Criticism," p. 338.

up of similarly conditioned Negro readers who like the same fare but who at the same time expect Negro writers to portray Negro life in a more complimentary manner. It is almost impossible to satisfy both audiences, and the result is that short stories by Negroes are limited in range and appeal. The large number of short stories written by Negroes tend to fall into two classes: those produced for Negro magazines and those intended for general circulation. Style and subject matter for these two magazine types differ, and each places certain restrictions upon the writer. The Negro magazine does not welcome "satirical, humorous, and closely critical stories," and the general magazine is uninterested in "polemical narratives."[35] The dilemma, as far as the short-story writer is concerned, is perhaps not as great today as it was when the *Opportunity-Crisis* story type followed the lynching-passing-praising pattern.[36] *Opportunity* is no longer published, and *The Crisis*, *Ebony*, and *Jet* do not publish short stories. This is true also of the scholarly publications (*Phylon*, *Journal of Negro History*, *Journal of Negro Education*). At the present time Negro newspapers, *Tan Confessions*, and general magazines are the principal outlets for the publication of short stories by Negro authors.

To Negroes who were creative writers, the Federal Writers' Project of the WPA meant the removal of some of the barriers which had isolated them from other writers. In northern cities no color line was drawn in the projects and a new school of Negro and white writers quickly sprang up. This association seems to have been an important factor, especially in the case of the Negro poets, in shifting the emphasis from narrower racial themes to broader social protest subjects and the universal point of view.[37]

With the passing of time, Negro writers have developed greater skill in handling racial themes. In Langston Hughes' *The Ways of White Folks*:

. . . The realities of Negro life swim into the consciousness of the reader, making him realize that there is a greater depth in Negro-white relationships of the most casual sort than other writers have suggested. Without truculence, Hughes counterpoises realized Negro characters and white types, disclosing to view several gradations of white attitudes. The result is a revelation of the breadth of unexplored areas available to Negro writers. Even when dealing with the tradition-bound problems of "passing" and miscegenation, Hughes is able to emphasize a phase of the subject that has generally escaped notice. This is because he accepts the fact of the situation as one which, readily understandable in itself, needs no explanation. It is the effect of the fact that interests him.[38]

[35] Sterling A. Brown, Arthur P. Davis, Ulysses Lee (eds.), *op. cit.*, pp. 11–12.
[36] *Ibid.*, pp. 12–13. *The Negro Caravan* was published in 1941.
[37] Margaret Walker, *op. cit.*, p. 346.
[38] Sterling A. Brown, Arthur P. Davis, and Ulysses Lee (eds.), *op. cit.*, p. 16.

The same critics regard all of the stories in Richard Wright's *Uncle Tom's Children* (1938) as "worthy of study as a clinical case illustrating the extremes to which the unhealthy race relations of the plantation South can lead men, black and white alike."[39]

Additional insights on race are provided by Hughes through a comic figure, Mr. Jesse B. Semple—or just Simple—in *Simple Speaks His Mind* (1950) and *Simple Takes a Wife* (1953). According to Davis, the Negro reader finds in Simple "all of the slightly mixed-up racial thinking, all of the 'twofold loyalties,' and all of the laughable inconsistencies which the segregation pattern produces in us. The pressure of jim crow living is so uniform that even though Simple is an uneducated worker his responses to this pressure ring true for all classes."[40]

The racial theme, then, has been predominant in the writing by American Negroes. This writing has reflected the life and thought of the Negro people from slavery through the Great Migration, the depression, two world wars, and the prosperity and the anxieties of recent years. The prominence of this theme has not resulted in a distinctive artistic pattern. Adopting literary traditions that were useful for their purposes, Negro writers have been influenced "by Puritan didacticism, sentimental humanitarianism, local color, regionalism, realism, naturalism, and experimentalism."[41] Even though it seems likely that Negro writers will give increasing attention to situations which have universal significance, there is no reason to suppose that racial themes will be abandoned. Many phases of Negro life have not yet been explored, and the possibilities for the Negro writer to present these areas from within appear to be unlimited.[42]

THE JEWISH THEME IN ART PRODUCED BY JEWS

As a whole, the art produced by Jewish artists in the United States deals as often, or more often, with universal as with Jewish themes. This question does not arise in connection with Hebrew or Yiddish literature; regardless of the subjects treated, this literature is considered critically as "Jewish."[43] Jewish artists of high rank are found in contemporary

---

[39] *Ibid.*

[40] Arthur P. Davis, "Jesse B. Semple: Negro American," *Phylon*, First Quarter, 1954, pp. 21–28.

[41] Sterling A. Brown, Arthur P. Davis, and Ulysses Lee (eds.), *op. cit.*, p. 6.

[42] *Ibid.*, pp. 144–145.

[43] Marie Syrkin, "The Cultural Scene: Literary Expression," in Oscar Janowsky (ed.), *The American Jew*, Harper & Brothers, 1942, chap. 4. According to Miss Syrkin, every literary mode in the United States (realism, expressionism, imagism, free verse, "proletarian" writing, and traditionalism) has its Yiddish practitioners. "One cannot escape the conclusion that the literary output of Yiddish writers in the United States has reached greater heights than that attained by American Jewish writers, except possibly in the field of drama. Whether this is due to a longer cultural tradition, a profounder rooting in Jewish history and Jewish folkways, is a speculation that is worth advancing." *Ibid.*, pp. 119, 120.

music, painting, sculpture, architecture, and the dance, but in these fields Ernest Bloch is virtually alone in feeling that "racial consciousness is absolutely necessary in music even though nationalism is not. . . . I am a Jew. I aspire to write Jewish music not for the sake of self-advertisement but because it is the only way in which I can create music of ability."[44] Artistic achievements of American Jews have been greatest in the drama, but Jewish life as such is seldom presented. "Dreamy Jewish tailors, hilarious Hollywood producers, noble Jewish scientists, smart-alecky Jews and helpless, idealistic souls march across the stage in a considerable number of productions, but rarely is Jewish life or a Jewish problem the dominant explicit theme."[45] American Jewish poets utilize Jewish subjects only occasionally. "Curiously enough, the agony of modern Jewry has found little adequate lyric expression, considering the vastness of the tragedy. There has been no general literary reaction to the Nazi persecutions equaling in scale that aroused by Emma Lazarus after 1881. The specifically Anglo-Jewish poets, who devote themselves energetically to hymning Jewish pain and disaster, are for the most part negligible as literary figures."[46]

Jewish consciousness is seen most intensely in the novel. Mary Antin's *The Promised Land* (1912) proclaimed the delight of the persecuted immigrant from central Europe in being in America and expressed a desire to renounce her European past. The New York East Side furnished material for novels by Abe Cahan (*The Rise of David Levinsky*, 1917), Anzia Yezierska, and Fannie Hurst (*Humoresque*). Edna Ferber's *So Big* and *Cimarron* are "purely American in subject matter," but *Fanny Herself* (1917) traces the development of the native-born American Jew.

Fanny Herself is a literary milestone in the integration of the American Jew with his country. Many brilliant Jewish boys and girls over the land, growing up in the years before the first World War, were to find achievement limited only by their capacities, but the proud conviction of Mary Antin is gone. A cloud appears on the apparently unbounded horizon. Hitler is still twenty years in the future, but the realization of a Jewish problem has come. There is as yet no awareness of anti-Semitism, but a rankling consciousness of prejudice, painful rather than tragic in its effects. Fanny meditates on the problem. "Antagonism here isn't religious. It's personal almost. . . . They don't object to us as a sect, or as a race, but as a type."[47]

In the negative writings of Jerome Weidman (*I Can Get It for You Wholesale*, 1937, and *What's In It for Me?*, 1938), in the character

---

[44] Quoted in *ibid.*, pp. 120–121.

[45] *Ibid.*, pp. 109–110. Exceptions are Arthur Kober, Clifford Odets, and Irwin Shaw. Among the outstanding Jewish playwrights Miss Syrkin mentions Elmer Rice, John Howard Lawson, Ben Hecht, George S. Kaufman, Sidney Kingsley, Clifford Odets, Irwin Shaw, Lillian Hellman, S. N. Behrman.

[46] *Ibid.*, pp. 114, 115.

[47] *Ibid.*, pp. 99–100.

studies of Budd Schulberg (*What Makes Sammy Run?*), and in the novels of the "proletarian" writers—Henry Roth (*Call It Sleep*, 1934), Albert Halper (*Union Square* and *The Foundry*), and Michael Gold (*Jews Without Money*, 1930)—there was an increasing awareness, implicit or explicit, of a Jewish problem in the United States. The uncritical "melting pot" and "promised land" viewpoints and the denial of the past were discarded. The outstanding Jewish author of this school was Ludwig Lewisohn (*Upstream* and *The Island Within*).

Upstream tells directly the story of the failure of assimilation which Lewisohn was to retell in subsequent novels. The realization that though his "psychical life was Aryan through and through," the fact of Jewish birth was an obstacle to complete acceptance by the American Gentile world, leads him to the poetic formulation: "So long as there is discrimination, there is exile." In *Upstream* Lewisohn already expresses the dominant theme of all his later writing: "The friend of the Republic, the lover of those values which alone make life endurable, must bid the German and the Jew, the Latin and the Slav, preserve his cultural tradition and beware of the encroachments of the Neo-Puritan barbarism—beware of becoming merely another dweller on endless Main Street."[48]

The Social Protest of the 1930's

The protest against unemployment, poverty, slum living, and prejudice caused the depression decade to be called the socially-conscious thirties. Negro writers, especially the poets, joined their white confreres in producing "socially significant" books.[49] Sterling Brown's poem "Old Lem" exemplifies the mood of these years.

> I talked to old Lem
> And old Lem said:
> "They weigh the cotton
> They store the corn
>   We only good enough
>   To work the rows;
> They run the commissary
> They keep the books
>   We gotta be grateful
>   For being cheated;
> Whippersnapper clerks
> Call us out of our name
>   We got to say mister
>   To spindling boys
> They make our figgers
> Turn somersets

[48] *Ibid.*, pp. 104, 105–106.

[49] The mood of disillusionment, prevalent during the twenties, and the "social consciousness" movement of the thirties are reflected in the work of Jewish novelists. We have referred above to the fiction produced by Roth, Halper, and Gold.

> We buck in the middle
> Say, 'Thankyuh, sah.'
>> They don't come by ones
>> They don't come by twos
>> But they come by tens."[50]

The coming of World War II did not immediately affect the mood of the thirties, and Negroes continued to publish books of poetry in the social protest vein until the middle forties. The contrast between the poetry of the New Negro period (roughly 1920–1935) and that of the early forties is striking. An example of the latter is seen in Robert Hayden's poem, "Speech."

> Hear me, white brothers
> Black brothers, hear me:
> I have seen the hand
> Holding the blowtorch
> To the dark, anguish-twisted body;
> I have seen the hand
> Giving the high-sign
> To fire on the white pickets;
> And it was the same hand,
> Brothers, listen to me,
> It was the same hand.[51]

The same point of view is shown also in Margaret Walker's poem, "For My People."

> For my people standing staring trying to fashion a better way from confusion, from hypocrisy and misunderstanding, trying to fashion a world that will hold all the people, all the Adams and Eves and their countless generations;
> Let a new earth rise. Let another world be born. Let a bloody peace be written in the sky. Let a second generation full of courage issue forth; let a people loving freedom come to grow. Let a beauty full of healing and a strength of final clenching be the pulsing in our spirits and our blood. Let the martial songs be written, let the dirges disappear. Let a race of men now rise and take control.[52]

Melvin Tolson's poem "Dark Symphony" is another illustration of this temper.

> Out of abysses of Illiteracy
> Through labyrinths of Lies,
> Across wastelands of Disease . . .
> We advance!
> Out of dead-ends of Poverty,

---

[50] Reprinted by permission of Sterling Brown. Copyright 1939 by Sterling Brown.
[51] Robert E. Hayden, *Heart-Shape in the Dust*, Falcon Press, 1940.
[52] Reprinted from *For My People* by Margaret Walker, by permission of Yale University Press. Copyright 1942 by Yale University Press.

> Through wildernesses of Superstition,
> Across barricades of Jim Crowism . . .
> We advance!
> With the peoples of the World . . .
> We advance![53]

The lowering of racial barriers in recent years and the possibility of considerable integration in the foreseeable future have tended to destroy the protest element in Negro writing. Although the lives of most Negroes have been affected hardly at all by integration, a change of climate has come about and the Negro writer has been looking for new themes. According to Davis, he has retained Negro characters and backgrounds but has shifted his emphasis from protests against racial discrimination to problems and conflicts within the Negro group. In 1943, Chester Himes wrote *If He Hollers*; his *Third Generation* (1953) dealt with school life in the deep South and the conflicts which color differences caused within a Negro family. Written recently, Owen Dodson's *Boy at the Window* and Gwendolyn Brooks' *Maud Martha* portray Negro middle-class life. William Demby's *Beetlecreek* reversed the protest theme by showing the cruelty of a Negro to a white man. The main character in Richard Wright's *The Outsider* is a Negro, but this philosophical novel is concerned with the problems of living rather than with racial protest. Although all the characters in Langston Hughes' *Sweet Flypaper of Life* are Negroes, there is no trace of protest based on race in this novel. William Gardner Smith's *Anger at Innocence*, Ann Petry's *Country Place*, Richard Wright's *Savage Holiday*, and Willard Motley's *Knock on Any Door* have either no Negro characters or no main Negro characters. With the exception of Motley's novel, all the others are second novels and follow successful first works which stressed racial protest. Davis cites the work of M. B. Tolson (*Rendezvous with America* as compared with his later *Libretto for the Republic of Liberia*), of Gwendolyn Brooks (*A Street in Bronzeville* and the more recent *Annie Allen*), and of others to illustrate the same tendency among Negro poets.[54] (An exception to the trend away from protest themes is found in Ralph Ellison's *The Invisible Man*, a novel showing why a normal life is almost impossible for Negroes in the United States.)[55] In Negro writings in 1954 and 1955, Jackson notes a trend away from the bitter and broken hero, or the hero who is just picturesque, to heroic heroes of a modest kind.[56]

[53] Reprinted by permission of Dodd, Mead & Company from *Rendezvous with America* by Marvin Tolson. Copyright 1944 by Dodd, Mead & Company, Inc.
[54] Arthur P. Davis, "Integration and Race Literature," pp. 141–146.
[55] Nick A. Ford, "Four Popular Negro Novelists," *Phylon*, First Quarter, 1954, p. 34.
[56] Blyden Jackson, "The Blythe Newcomers," pp. 9–10.

Universal Appeal in Art Produced by Minorities

The general trend in the writings by Negroes has passed from the exoticism and racial exhibitionism of the twenties, through the social protest period of the thirties, to the universal point of view of more recent years.

In *Native Son* (1940) Richard Wright makes it clear that Bigger Thomas is a Negro, but he makes it equally as clear that he could be "white." His experiences might well have been those of a white youth in the ghettoes of Chicago. The struggle of Lutie Johnson for a better way of life for herself and her son in Ann Petry's *The Street* (1946), despite what would seem to be occasional excessive sermonizing on the plight of Negroes, has undeniable universal appeal. In *Knock on Any Door* (1947), a work in which Willard Motley evinces a superb handling of sustained and meaningful imagery, Nick Romano, a victim of the ulcerous maladies of the city and the slums, might well have been a Negro, although for Motley's purposes he is Italian.[57]

The career of Frank Yerby is of interest in considering the trend toward writing with universal appeal. His first work, *Health Card* (1944), was entirely devoted to a racial theme, but such later works as *The Foxes of Harrow* (1946) and *The Vixens* (1947) completely abandoned racial material. A racial symbol, the symbol of rejection, is substituted in all of his nonracial novels.

He finds in the social rebels of the white race, in men and women who because of birth, or manner of livelihood, or disregard of social and moral proprieties have become pariahs among their own people, an archetype of racial rejection. But these white rejectees fight back. They build industrial empires, or pile up huge mountains of illicit wealth, or become swashbuckling pirates who defy the laws of the smug and the respectable. Thus, symbolically the white rejectees get their revenge on a proud and haughty society, and through them the rejected Negro can feel a sense of vicarious triumph.[58]

[57] Thomas D. Jarrett, *op. cit.*, pp. 315–316. In a later paper ("Recent Fiction by Negroes," *College English*, November, 1954, p. 87), Jarrett says that it is ". . . the general tendency of Negro fictionists today not only to move away from the racial problem *per se*, but also to treat more complex themes, and to strive for universality in the handling of them."

[58] Nick A. Ford, "A Blueprint for Negro Authors," p. 377. Later Yerby is quoted as saying that the novelist "hasn't any right to inflict on the public his private ideas on politics, religion or race. If he wants to preach he should go to the pulpit." Nick A. Ford, "Four Popular Negro Novelists," p. 38. Blyden Jackson's point of view is that Yerby has race consciousness but kept it under control until he built up a large following. Jackson says: "In *Benton's Row* . . . he makes . . . the most heretical and blood-curdling comments about southern religion, southern womanhood, the Old Southern Mansion, planter culture . . . , the southern defense of lynching, and even southern cooking. . . ." Blyden Jackson, "The Continuing Strain: Résumé of Negro Literature in 1955," pp. 38–39.

Three books of poetry which appeared during the forties reveal a decided shift from social protest to the universal viewpoint. These are *From the Shaken Tower* (1944) by Bruce McWright, *The Lion and the Archer* (1948) by Robert Hayden and Myron O'Higgins, and *Annie Allen* (1949) by Gwendolyn Brooks. According to Margaret Walker: "Each one of these books is less preoccupied with the theme of race as such. Race is rather used as a point of departure toward a global point of view than as the central theme of one obsessed by race. . . . *Annie Allen* is a fine delineation of the character of a young Negro woman from childhood through adolescence to complete maturity, but with slight racial exceptions, it could apply to any female of a certain class and society."

It is not suggested that writings by Negroes have reached maturity. The works of many Negro writers are still narrow in scope, and much hypersensitivity remains.[59] Some critics assert that, on the whole, the artistic expression of Negroes has become sounder, more objective, and less racialistic in the chauvinistic sense. They believe that this work has become more racial in the sense of being "more deeply felt and projected," and this achievement is regarded as desirable from the standpoint of universal acceptance.[60]

Finally, it may be pointed out that in the United States minorities wish to be identified as closely as possible with the majority. They wish to be accepted and to participate in the life of the larger community. The separatism that is so common in Europe, and that manifests itself in attempts to preserve national or ethnic customs and institutions is almost altogether absent in America.[61] As things stand now, the Negro will probably continue, for the most part, to express himself artistically on the things he knows best, namely, what it means to be a Negro in America.[62] The hope of some critics is that minority artists will exploit their heritage for a contribution to the larger culture. In doing this they will be free to consider all life. Any other viewpoint would mean the acceptance of "the principle that racial experience is the only natural

[59] Thomas D. Jarrett, *op. cit.*, pp. 313–314. Four years later Jarrett wrote that it might be argued that the Negro novelist ". . . has now entered into the mainstream of American fiction. He has a higher regard for literary values, and he evinces a growing social consciousness and a universality in the treatment of a greater variety of themes. The utilization of self-pity and oratory moralizing is noticeably on the wane. Yet he must still overcome barriers that prohibit a full, objective treatment which leads to great fiction. There is, I believe, some danger in his striving too hard and too self-consciously to approach universality; but he must go through this period of writing and face the danger, until he achieves an approach that is natural." Further artistic development on the part of the Negro novelist ". . . will come as an inevitable by-product of his growing awareness that he is not writing for *an* audience but *all* audiences." Thomas D. Jarrett, "Recent Fiction by Negroes," p. 91.
[60] Alain Locke, "Self-Criticism: The Third Dimension in Culture," *Phylon*, Fourth Quarter, 1950, p. 392.
[61] Ulysses Lee, "Criticism at Mid-Century," *Phylon*, Fourth Quarter, 1950, p. 329.
[62] Sterling A. Brown, Arthur P. Davis, and Ulysses Lee (eds.), *op. cit.*, p. 282.

province of the Negro writer" and would approve "an artistic double standard that is just as confining and demoralizing in American literature as is segregation in American life."[63]

Minority Themes in the Art of Dominant-Group Members

Racial themes are important not only in the work of minority artists but also among some members of the dominant group. They are often handled in a stereotyped, unimaginative way by persons of majority status.

RACIAL AND CULTURAL STEREOTYPES AND COUNTER-STEREOTYPES IN ART

The first song-and-dance act impersonating a Negro was given about 1830, and the first minstrel show was staged in 1843. These shows reached their peak between 1850 and 1870; in 1880 there were thirty companies, but in 1919 only three first-class organizations were playing.[64] According to Adams, the standard minstrel portrait of the plantation Negro "emphasized traits suggested by the adjectives lazy, shiftless, improvident, superstitious, stupid, ignorant, and slow, and those reflected in a fondness for watermelons, chickens, gin, crap games, razors, and big words."

Immigrants have been a poor second to Negroes in the amount of comical material they have provided for the American stage. Neither immigrants in general nor any particular nationality group has been the inspiration for a theatrical production comparable to the minstrel show. Germans, Jews, the Irish, and many others have been presented, along with numerous other "character" types, in comedies, farces, and revues; even more frequently they have been caricatured in burlesque, variety, and vaudeville sketches.

The Irish stand next to the Negro in the volume of comical material furnished the stage. It is interesting to note that the early Irish plays (roughly 1828–1840) were Irish in scene and very romantic in theme, but that during the years of heaviest Irish immigration (1840–1860) sentimentalism was transformed to hostility and ridicule. The standard English low-comedy characters have been eccentrics even when played by English actors. In the 1860's Sothern presented a caricature of the foppish Englishman in *Our American Cousin*, and in the early twentieth century a long long of English low comediennes with cockneyisms, outlandish dress, and other exaggerations regaled American audiences.

---

[63] Hugh M. Gloster, "Race and the Negro Writer," *Phylon*, Fourth Quarter, 1950, p. 371.

[64] This summary of stage caricaturing of minorities is based on Harold E. Adams, "Minority Caricatures on the American Stage," in G. P. Murdock (ed.), *Studies in the Science of Society*, Yale University Press, 1937, pp. 1–26.

Adams observes: "The stage Englishman is never a hero, and in his role of comedian he is laughed at with brutal scorn. To the average red-blooded he-American his tea-drinking is evidence of racial decay, and so are the cut of his clothes, his broad a, and his occasional use of such highly un-American locutions as 'jolly,' 'awfully' and 'ripping.' " Chinese types were displayed in *A Trip to Chinatown*, which began a long run in 1891; Weber and Fields distorted Chinese, German, and Irish types in their 1896 burlesque, *The Geezer*. Chinese characters were popular in the 1920's and later in movie murder mysteries and in mystery stories. Occasionally an Italian organ grinder and accordion player appears in comic sketches and the movies.

Stage devices like a red nose, a monocle, green clothing, and a black face assisted an audience in identifying the type being portrayed. "An actor using a foreign accent and jumble of American words is immediately classified by the audience as a Jew, Italian, Irishman, etc., although in some cases the identification must be aided materially by other symbols, such as a low-crowned derby, a beard, or an immigrant name, e.g., Fritz, Abie, or Tony."

Adams concludes that one may assume that theatergoers accepted these characters as typical of their nationalities, and that the stereotyped picture of the Negro presented in the minstrel show conformed closely to the conception which many white people have at the present time.

The stereotyping of Negro character has occurred, and still occurs, in the works of both well-intentioned and prejudiced white writers. Although this has been the rule, there have been exceptions to the numerous literary interpretations which justify the exploitation of the Negro, and these exceptions are becoming more common. The most incisive analyses of the white stereotyping of the Negro have been done by Sterling Brown.[65]

In the ante-bellum period the Negro was often represented as a natural slave. In J. P. Kennedy's *Swallow Barn* (1832) Negro children are shown "basking on the sunny sides of cabins [like] terrapins luxuriating on the logs of a mill-pond." One character says: "I never meet a Negro man—unless he is quite old—that he is not whistling; and the women sing from morning to night." The complement of the *contented slave* was the *comic Negro* of the minstrel shows. Later variations of the latter type are found in Octavus Roy Cohen's pseudo-Negro dialect stories in the *Saturday Evening Post* and in the "Amos 'n' Andy" radio and tele-

[65] Sterling A. Brown, "Negro Character as Seen by White Authors," *Journal of Negro Education*, January, 1933, pp. 180–201. Excerpts of this article are reprinted in Alain Locke and B. J. Stern (eds.), *When Peoples Meet*, Hinds, Hayden and Eldredge, Inc., rev. ed., 1946, pp. 327–349. See also Sterling A. Brown, *The Negro in American Fiction*, and Sterling A. Brown, Arthur P. Davis, and Ulysses Lee (eds.), *op. cit.*, pp. 2–5. Our discussion is based mainly on Brown's work. The stereotyping of Negro character, with specific reference to prejudice, is discussed in chap. 5.

vision programs. The *wretched freedman* stereotype is illustrated in Mrs. M. J. McIntosh's *The Lofty and the Lowly, or Good in All and None All-Good* (1854). Daddy Cato is given his freedom, of which he is not proud, late in life. After following his family to Boston, he is insulted when approached by abolitionists. "Make me free! how can I free any more? Dem da nonsense people, and what dem want take me from Miss Alice for? . . . I wonder if I been sick and couldn't do any ting, ef dem would nuss me and take care o' me liken Miss Alice . . . I tink dem crazy 'bout free. Free bery good ting, but free ent all; when you sick, free won't make you well, free won't gib you clo's, no hom'ny, let 'lone meat." The rebellious, the ironic, the abused Negro failed to appear in the plantation tradition books. Miscegenation is absent from these stories, although it was commonplace; slavery was presented as a charitable institution.

The *brute Negro* stereotype was a specialty of Thomas Nelson Page in *Ole Virginia* (1887), *The Negro: The Southerner's Problem* (1904), *Red Rock* (1898), and *Pastime Stories* (1894). This stereotype was further developed by the Reverend Thomas Dixon in *The Leopard's Spots* (1902) and *The Clansmen* (1905). In *The Leopard's Spots*, "Dick, an imbecile, crushes with a rock the head of a white child and then attacks her. The assaulted child and the burning of the Negro are described with gusto. Drunk Negro soldiers drag white brides from their homes; criminal Negroes rove the countryside, forcing whites to take to the cities."[66] The brute Negro has not disappeared from the pages of modern fiction.

The *tragic mulatto* was the principal stereotype produced by the writers of antislavery fiction; others were "the victim," "the noble savage," and "the perfect Christian." Antislavery novels concentrated on the abuses of slavery: whippings, the slave market, domestic slave breeding, slave hunts, persecuted freedmen, etc. The tragic mulatto received his share in the treatment of these situations. He appeared in Harriet Beecher Stowe's *Uncle Tom's Cabin* (1851) and *Dred, A Tale of the Dismal Swamp* (1856). In Richard Hildreth's *Archy Moore, or The White Slave*, and in Boucicault's *The Octoroon*, Negroes of mixed ancestry play leading roles. George Washington Cable, a Confederate officer who later went to Massachusetts to live, made use of the tragic mulatto in *Old Creole Days* (1879) and in *The Grandissimes* (1880). However, Cable did not overidealize the Negro, and unlike Page and Harris he did not use his material to support old traditions. The tragic mulatto was often portrayed by prejudiced writers as a human being of divided inheritance, divided loyalties, and conflicting impulses. This

[66] Sterling A. Brown, *The Negro in American Fiction*, p. 94. In *The Negro Caravan* the editors say, "In Reconstruction the wretched freedman became the brute, swaggering about, insulting, and assaulting, and it must be added, wanting to vote" (pp. 3–4).

theme has persisted through the years in such works as *A Black Drop*, *Madame Margot*, *White Girl*, *The No-Nation Girl*, *A Study in Bronze*, *Gulf Stream*, and *Dark Lustre*. The woes of these mixed-ancestry characters, mostly female and the majority octoroons, are many.

One of the favorite stereotypes of the twentieth century is that of the *exotic primitive*. In the reaction against Puritanism and Babbitry after World War I, the stereotyped primitivity of the Negro was very appealing. Those who were once shackled in slavery became the symbol of escape from a drab industrial civilization. White authors rushed to Harlem cabarets and the river fronts to see the unmoral, flamboyant, carefree children of nature. Their books portrayed what they regarded as the Negro's savage inheritance: hot jungle nights, tom-toms, esoteric rites, violence, and frankness. This is the formula of Carl Van Vechten's *Nigger Heaven* (1925), T. Bowyer Campbell's *Black Sadie* (1928), Sherwood Anderson's *Dark Laughter* (1925), and many others.

As we have indicated earlier, not all white authors have stereotyped the Negro. Herman Melville (*Mardi*, 1849), George Washington Cable (*Old Creole Days*, 1879, and *The Grandissimes*, 1880), Mark Twain (*Huckleberry Finn*, 1884), Albion Tourgée (*One of the Fools*, 1879, and *Bricks Without Straw*, 1880), Upton Sinclair (*The Jungle*, 1905), Gertude Stein ("Melanctha" in *Three Lives*, 1909). T. S. Stribling (*Birthright*, 1922, *The Forge*, 1931, *The Store*, 1933, *Unfinished Cathedral*, 1934), DuBose Heyward (*Porgy*, 1925, and *Mamba's Daughters*, 1925), E. C. L. Adams (*Congaree Sketches*, 1927, and *Nigger to Nigger*), Lyle Saxon (*Children of Strangers*, 1937), Paul Green (*In Abraham's Bosom*, 1924, *The House of Connelly*, 1932, and a number of short stories), Hamilton Basso (*Relics and Angels*, 1929, *Cinnamon Seed*, 1934, *Courthouse Square*, 1936), Erskine Caldwell (*We Are the Living*, 1933, *Kneel to the Rising Sun*, 1935, *Trouble in July*, 1940), Evelyn Scott (*Migrations*, 1927, *The Wave*, 1929, *A Calendar of Sin*, 1931, William March (*Come In at the Door*, 1934), Carson McCullers (*The Heart Is a Lonely Hunter*, 1940), Lillian Smith (*Strange Fruit*, 1944), and Bucklin Moon (*Without Magnolias*, 1949) are among the writers who have portrayed Negroes as many-sided persons rather than as caricatures of human beings. But for the most part Negro life and character in American literature have been presented in ways which give support to prevailing social policies toward the Negro.

With the exception of the considerable use of the exotic primitive during the "roaring twenties" and the occasional appearance of the tragic mulatto, the favorite Negro stereotypes of white authors do not appear frequently in the writings of Negroes. More often the Negro writer has produced counterstereotypes; that is, he has attributed ideal characteristics to his Negro characters. The Negro fictionists of the nineteenth century and of the first two decades of the twentieth felt called upon to meet propaganda with counterpropaganda, and in doing so they employed stereotyped situations and characters just as one-sided as those of the Negrophobe writers. Their stock in trade was the virtuous Negro and the vicious white man.[67] Gloster lists twenty-five of these writers in the years between 1853 (William Wells Brown's *Clotel, or The President's Daughter: A Narrative of Slave Life in the United States*) and 1918 (Sarah Fleming's *Hope's Highway*).[68]

One critic says that the characters of Negro novelists "usually become walking, talking propaganda, rather than completely rounded individuals. The Negro writer hesitates, perhaps unconsciously, to temper the goodness of his Negro characters with the dialectical 'evil.' Fearful of reenforcing stereotypes in the white reader's mind, he often goes to the other extreme, idealizing his characters, making them flat rather than many-sided." Or, according to this critic, in his desire to show that he is not idealizing his Negro characters the Negro writer may go to the other extreme and portray the American Negro "as an exaggerated Bigger Thomas, with all the stereotyped characteristics emphasized three times over."[69] In any event, Negro authors give a picture of Negro life which differs considerably from the simplified version so often presented in American literature.

Many types of Negroes have never been placed in books. Themes and characterizations have been repressed, consciously or unconsciously, by Negro writers because of the fear of being accused of "misrepresentation" and group disloyalty. A critic asks, "Why . . . this protective silence about the ambivalences of the Negro upper classes, about the dilemmas of intra-group prejudice and rivalry, about the dramatic inner paradoxes of mixed heritage, both biological and cultural, or the tragic breach between the Negro elite and the Negro masses, or the conflict between integration and vested-interest separatism in the present-day life of the Negro?"[70] These omissions doubtless represent the impact of minority position on artistic work.

In painting, as in literature, the Negro was until quite recently presented in stereotypes. In this medium the main caricatures have been the humble retainer, the sentimental character, and the comic. According to Alain Locke, the plantation formula had its widest currency during the Reconstruction. "A plague of low-genre interest multiplied the superficial types of uncles, aunties and pickaninnies almost endlessly, echoing even today in the minstrel and the vaudeville stereotypes of a Negro half-clown, half-troubadour."[71]

[67] Hugh M. Gloster, *Negro Voices in American Fiction*, pp. 253–254.
[68] *Ibid.*, pp. 25–98.
[69] William G. Smith, "The Negro Writer: Pitfalls and Compensations," *Phylon*, Fourth Quarter, 1950, p. 298.
[70] Alain Locke, "Self-Criticism: The Third Dimension in Culture," pp. 393–394.
[71] Alain Locke, *The Negro in Art*, p. 139. Realism, local color, and a general change of style and viewpoint in American painting have done much to replace this stereotyping with "a fresh and more vital version of Negro life." In the work of

The present writers know of no systematic study of the stereotyping of Jewish characters by Jewish or non-Jewish authors. Marie Syrkin refers briefly to a number of stereotypes presented by Jewish fictionists, including the sentimental pictures of the Jewish East Side mother (Anzia Yezierska and Fannie Hurst), the comic types in Montague Glass's *Potash and Perlmutter* series, and the stereotype of "the rapacious, Jewish go-getter, without qualm or decency of any kind." Harry Bogen (Jerome Weidman, *I Can Get It for You Wholesale* and *What's In It for Me?*), "crooked and cruel in every relationship, is a monster who could have been lifted straight from Goebbels' propaganda sheets. . . . Harry Bogen . . . bears only the most superficial resemblance to reality of any kind."[72] Similar stereotypes appear in the work of some non-Jewish novelists.

ART AND RACIAL PROPAGANDA

The racial propaganda incorporated in literature and other forms of art in the United States has come, for the most part, from the initiative of artists as individuals. Certainly artistic creation has not been officially organized and supervised by the state.

It is generally accepted in western Europe and America that the artist is concerned with truth as he sees it. In the case of the novelist, that truth is revealed through the emotions and thoughts of the characters, but it is "controlled and molded by an artistic process. . . ." Because of an almost inevitable strain of bitterness, the Negro writer is often driven to write a tract rather than a work of art. The deliberate inclusion of the didactic element decreases the effectiveness of his artistic work as art. It may also defeat his purpose as propagandist.[73]

The situation is quite different in those places where artistic life is controlled by the state. In the Soviet Union the "social assignment" (the complex of themes to be taken up by authors, artists, or scientists) is an extremely important social institution.

These subjects are the same in the whole Union. Thus, for instance, in the first period of the Revolution, all Soviet writers were given the assignment of writing about the Revolution which they, of course, accepted. In this connection we may recall that the first great novel about the French

---

the new regional realists, ". . . humor has the tang of folk pride, and sometimes the irony of social criticism; there is no coddling of the sentimental fictions of Southern tradition; there is little, if any, covering up of the social facts, even such unpleasant ones as lynching and sharecropper poverty and disillusionment, and the double standard of human values has almost been driven out of the picture." *Ibid.*, pp. 139–140.

[72] Marie Syrkin, *op. cit.*, pp. 98, 103. Miss Syrkin points out that well-rounded portraits of Jewish life are found in the writings of Ludwig Lewisohn and Irving Fineman and in such historical novels as Milton Steinberg's *As a Driven Leaf* and Harry Sackler's *Festival at Meron*. *Ibid.*, p. 107.

[73] See William G. Smith, *op. cit.*, p. 298; and Thomas D. Jarrett, "Towards Unfettered Creativity: A Note on the Negro Novelist's Coming of Age," p. 314.

Revolution, by Victor Hugo, came many decades after the event, and Anatole France's *The Gods Are Thirsty* was written about a century after the Revolution. In Russia such novels appeared together with their subjects. During the period of the Five Year Plan, all authors were given the assignment of writing about the great process of industrialization and collectivization. Now, during the war, all authors are writing on patriotic subjects only.[74]

AGENCIES OF MASS COMMUNICATION AND MINORITIES

The agencies of mass communication—the motion picture, the radio, the newspaper, television, the magazine, and the play—provide most of the "educational" stimuli which the great majority of the people receive after the completion of their formal schooling. Presumably these art and quasi-art mediums exert some influence on racial and religious attitudes.

Until World War II years no consistent effort was made by American motion-picture companies to dispel group prejudice through films. Minority-group characters were, in fact, generally treated in a stereotyped way. The industry's Production Code of Ethics, the only set of rules for Hollywood film-making, refers to "race" only once—in forbidding the depiction of "miscegenation (sex relationship between the white and black races)." The code forbids the portrayal of ministers as "comic characters or as villains" and the ridicule of any religious faith. Concerning "national feelings" the rules require that "the history, institutions, prominent people and citizenry of other nations shall be represented fairly." Apparently these sections of the code were drawn up and have been interpreted in terms of safeguarding the industry from the wrath of influential groups rather than in the interests of "spiritual and moral progress . . . and correct thinking," as stated in the preamble.[75]

From 1942 to 1945 Hollywood made a conscious effort to promote better understanding among the racial, religious, and national groups in the United States and among the nations and races allied with us in the war. A number of films dramatizing and condemning Nazi anti-Semitism were produced, including *The Mortal Storm, Escape, Address Unknown, This Land Is Mine, The Hitler Gang, None Shall Escape,* and *Tomorrow the World.* Other films, such as *Pride of the Marines, Air Force, Winged Victory, Objective Burma,* and *The Purple Heart* portrayed Jewish characters as comrades in arms. During these years film audiences were introduced to many new Negro actors, musicians, and dancers; among them were Bill Robinson, Hazel Scott, Lena Horne, Duke Ellington, the late Fats Waller, Katherine Dunham, Paul Robeson,

[74] Jacob Robinson, in R. M. MacIver (ed.), *Group Relationships and Group Antagonisms,* Harper & Brothers, 1944, pp. 193–194.
[75] J. T. McManus and Louis Kronenberger, "Motion Pictures, the Theater, and Race Relations," *Annals of the American Academy of Political and Social Science,* March, 1946, p. 152.

Teddy Wilson, and Kenneth Spencer. Nearly all of these artists were presented either in an all-Negro film or in a segregated sequence. The film *In This Our Life* had one scene showing a young Negro law student in association with a white family. This scene, booed when the film was shown in the southern states, eventually disappeared from most versions. Memphis and other southern cities banned the showing of *Brewster's Millions* because Eddie ("Rochester") Anderson's role in the film placed him in charge of the office staff during the boss's absence.[76]

While there have been some protests by white Southerners concerning the appearance of Negro actors on television programs (for example, Negro entertainers on the Ed Sullivan show, and the use of an allegedly interracial couple in the principal parts of a TV Playhouse presentation in which Sidney Poitier, a Negro actor, and Hilda Simms, a Negro actress, were starred),[77] there has been no substantial disapproval by southern audiences or viewers of programs in which Negroes were cast in roles other than stereotyped, submissive ones.[78]

Films which portrayed Negroes in a favorable light in the war years were *Bataan*, *Sahara*, and *The Curse of the Cat People*. The outstanding attempt to combat prejudice through the motion picture was the Army's *The Negro Soldier*, shown both in commercial theaters and by those using nontheatrical film libraries. The motion-picture industry did far less during World War II in trying to assist in the elimination of anti-Negro prejudice and in advocating the integration of the Negro in the nation's life, than it did in attempting to combat anti-Semitism. The explanation of this difference, given by competent critics, is that Hollywood seldom crusades, and the films dealing with anti-Semitism were merely in step with, and not in advance of, national sentiment and

---

[76] Most of the Jim Crow theaters are in the South, and it is in the southern area that films showing nonstereotyped characters and situations are banned. McManus and Kronenberger attribute the wary policy on treatment of the Negro in motion pictures to the white, southern film audience. The part of this audience which is prejudiced against the Negro constitutes less than one-eighth of the total American film audience. The prejudices of this fraction of motion-picture patrons are a strong influence in the way Negroes are portrayed in films for audiences in this country and in the rest of the world. *Ibid.*, pp. 156–157. Atlanta's film censor refuses permits, or demands cuts, because films invite the breaking of Georgia laws or because they might tend to incite the audience to violence. These two rules give the censor rather large room for action. *Lost Boundaries*, *Imitation of Life*, and *Birth of a Nation* have been banned by the present censor, but the last two films have played in Atlanta in the past. *Intruder in the Dust*, *Pinky*, and *Home of the Brave* have been shown in Atlanta, with only the first uncut. Films dealing with the problem of race hatred as a minor theme, including *Red Ball Express* and *Bright Victory*, have also played. *The Well* has had a commercial run, and *The Quiet One* has been shown noncommercially by both white and Negro groups. Gerald Weales, "Pro-Negro Films in Atlanta," *Phylon*, Third Quarter, 1952, pp. 299–300.

[77] Carl T. Rowan, *Go South to Sorrow*, Random House, Inc., 1957, pp. 193–196.

[78] Elmer Carter, "Policies and Practices of Discrimination Commissions," *Annals of the American Academy of Political and Social Science*, March, 1956, p. 71.

custom.[79] It is interesting to note that two years after the war the motion-picture executive who was responsible for *Crossfire*, a film attacking anti-Semitism, wrote, "It [*Crossfire*] says something. It says in no uncertain terms that bigotry and hatred are evil and must be rooted out if our world is to know and enjoy peace. . . . It is time that our subjects became significant of our times and honestly reflect our changing society. . . ."[80]

In his Atlanta interviews, Weales found that a number of Negroes felt that the incidents around which Negro "problem" films are built are too specialized and, often, too melodramatic to have much influence. While violence in the form of a murder or a race riot is frequently an element in film plots, the Negro's problem, especially in the South, is seen not so much as one of potential violence but rather as the cumulative effect of assaults on human dignity in a climate of prejudice. Some critics suggest abandoning the racial picture, contending that treating the Negro as a "problem" forces him into a new kind of stereotype. The films best liked by Atlanta Negroes were those like *Lifeboat* and *The Oxbow Incident* in which the Negro takes part in the action as a man, not only as a Negro.[81] Following his outstanding success as a Hollywood actor, Harry Belafonte said that *Island in the Sun* is a "stinking" picture and that he is "through with problem pictures about interracial relations." Turning down roles in *Porgy and Bess* and *The Emperor Jones*, Belafonte said of the first: "The music is great, but I wouldn't want to do it as the Dubose Heyward script was written. All that crap shooting and razors and lust and cocaine is the old conception of the Negro." The second, he said, "is an even worse conception of the Negro. I wouldn't consider it."[82]

There is evidence that the use of the usual Negro stereotypes fell off sharply in films produced after 1942. Some "shockers" are of recent vintage, and some Negro actors who are themselves stereotypes (Willie Best, Butterfly McQueen, and occasionally Rochester) are still performing. But much of the standard stereotyping of former years has disappeared. The year 1949 saw a number of important films on Negro-white relations. The movie version of William Faulkner's *Intruder in the Dust* was widely acclaimed, as were the films adapted

[79] J. T. McManus and Louis Kronenberger, *op. cit.*, pp. 152–155.

[80] Dore Schary, "The Screen and Society," *National Jewish Monthly*, October, 1947, p. 60.

[81] Gerald Weales, *op. cit.*, pp. 303–304.

[82] Bob Thomas, "Power Is Difference to Richer Belafonte," *Cleveland Plain Dealer*, August 11, 1957, p. 10. H. Belafonte's view of *Porgy and Bess* was not shared by Brooks Atkinson, dramatic critic of the New York *Times*. When criticisms arose in 1952 over the State Department's sponsorship of a *Porgy and Bess* company in Vienna and Berlin, Atkinson wrote that Europeans "do not have to be convinced that the decisive factor in any genuine work of art is less the material than the spirit of the authors and composers." Brooks Atkinson, "Negro Folk Drama," New York *Times*, September 9, 1952.

from Broadway plays: *Home of the Brave, Lost Boundaries, Pinky,* and *The Quiet One.* Concerning these films Alain Locke says, "That they simultaneously register new seriousness and dignity in Negro characterization and new moral dimensions in theme makes for unprecedented progress. . . . It may be that suddenly and unexpectedly Hollywood has been converted, and the American film brought nearer to moral and artistic maturity."[83]

According to Jefferson, dozens of capable Negro actors have been waiting unsuccessfully for roles of some substance in major dramas, musical comedies, and revues. Without radio and television, especially the latter, the Negro actor would have had great difficulty earning a living professionally. Even in radio and television, most of the roles offered Negroes have been inconsequential.[84] At the request of the Coordinating Council for Negro Performers, the New York State Commission Against Discrimination called a conference of representatives of large advertising agencies and the television and radio networks for the purpose of examining employment conditions within the industry. These business representatives "conceded that without violating artistic standards it would be possible to cast Negroes in a number of acts which would not carry the connotation of Negro roles."[85]

Broadway, the leader of the commercial theater, has virtually eliminated Jewish stereotypes. Negro stereotypes remain, principally the comic servant.[86] As McManus and Kronenberger point out, the comic servant in itself is a stereotype, regardless of racial or national identity. However, the Negro servant predominates, "and there is frequently an element of condescension in the comedy he provides." On the positive side, such plays as *Native Son, Deep Are the Roots,* and *Strange Fruit* made frontal attacks on race prejudice. "*Native Son* made a less illuminating play than book . . . but [it] did have social impact. . . . And both *Deep Are the Roots* and *Strange Fruit,* whatever their artistic shortcomings may be, go straight to the point, show what segregation, prejudice, and conscious injustice have done, and are doing, in the South."[87]

Negro actors have been little used on Broadway in recent years. During the 1954–1955 season only two new productions consisted largely of Negro actors; in the others their services were employed in the ensemble

[83] Alain Locke, "Wisdom de Profundis: The Literature of the Negro, 1949," *Phylon,* First Quarter, 1950, pp. 10–11.

[84] Miles Jefferson, "The Negro on Broadway, 1954–1955," *Phylon,* Third Quarter, 1955, p. 303.

[85] Elmer Carter, *op. cit.,* pp. 70–71.

[86] For an account of the campaign for better roles for Negroes in Broadway plays, see Florence Murray (ed.), *The Negro Handbook, 1946–47,* Current Books, 1947, pp. 262–263. A list of interracial dramas and musical shows with all-Negro or racially mixed casts on Broadway is given in Florence Murray (ed.), *The Negro Handbook,* The Macmillan Company, 1949, p. 327. See also *The Negro Yearbook,* Tuskegee Institute, 1947, pp. 443–444; *ibid.,* 1952, pp. 89–90.

[87] J. T. McManus and Louis Kronenberger, *op. cit.,* p. 157.

or in bit parts. More Negro actors were employed in 1955–1956 than in the previous season, but the assignments were unimportant—good parts in poor plays or minor parts in successful shows. The only play in which a Negro had a major part which approached the outstanding class was *Mister Johnson*.[88]

Many radio networks and stations have issued instructions for staff and sponsors which contain statements similar to those made by the Mutual Broadcasting System: "Because America is made up of peoples of all races, colors and nationalities, Mutual accepts no program which misrepresents, ridicules, or attacks any of them. References to religious faiths, tenets, or customs must be respectful and in good taste, free of bias and ridicule."[89]

The directors of radio networks have learned that dull programs representing worthy causes receive indifferent attention. They know too that a listener who tunes out a program does not return to the same station for several programs. Now a program to fulfill a public responsibility is not put on unless it is of high quality. Bryson and Rowden consider it unfeasible to attempt a listing of the numerous radio programs specifically intended to promote intergroup understanding. If such a list were drawn up, it would present an inadequate picture of radio's influence in this field because of the omission of programs which present group relations by indirection. The latter programs may be more effective than the former in lessening tensions.[90]

Some efforts have been made to eradicate stereotypes from radio programs.[91] The Writers' War Board sought to convince radio writers of the disservice caused by stereotypes. A member of the board, Robert J. Landry, supervisor of writing for the Columbia Broadcasting System, prepared a memorandum which concluded, "In sum, the use of a little ingenuity in devising new types of characters for minor roles, and the eschewing of the cut-and-dried minority group types, will not only save you from the serious offense of fostering group prejudice; it will also benefit your writing."[92] Many popular programs still feature stereotypes of racial, religious, and nationality groups. Two approaches have been suggested by persons interested in eliminating such stereotypes. One is a long task of education to improve taste and promote tolerance, a task to be shared by radio, educators, social scientists, and others who

[88] Miles Jefferson, "The Negro on Broadway, 1954–1955," *Phylon*, Third Quarter, 1955, p. 303; Miles Jefferson, "The Negro on Broadway, 1955–1956," *Phylon*, Third Quarter, 1956, pp. 227–228.

[89] Lyman Bryson and Dorothy Rowden, "Radio as an Agency of National Unity," *Annals of the American Academy of Political and Social Science*, March, 1946, p. 137.

[90] *Ibid.*, pp. 138, 140.

[91] For a discussion of "The Negro on Radio Programs," see John S. Brown's article in *The Negro Yearbook*, 1947, pp. 446–451.

[92] Lyman Bryson and Dorothy Rowden, *op. cit.*, pp. 142–143.

are concerned about unity and understanding.[93] The other is an active campaign of protest against the use of stereotypes. The latter approach is seen in the efforts made during 1951 by the National Association for the Advancement of Colored People to bring about the discontinuance of the "Amos 'n' Andy" television show. Labor, church, and liberal groups joined the NAACP in protesting this program, the first result of which was the removal of the show by WTMJ-TV in Milwaukee, the home city of the sponsor.[94]

Every study of the Negro's treatment in the "white" newspapers of the United States, regardless of period or region, has shown "a heavy concentration upon crime news and only slight attention to achievement." The chief change is a "tendency less pronounced today than formerly, to handle Negro items with a light or humorous touch."[95] In the main, the Negro press, consisting of weekly newspapers, is "sensational." It plays up crime news, especially reports of crime within the Negro community and the crimes of whites against Negroes. It hammers the Negro protest in every issue. Typically "an additional newspaper," it stresses "society" and "personal" news of the Negro community. Like the foreign-language newspapers which flourished during the nineteenth and early twentieth centuries, this press appeals to group pride and helps to give its readers feelings of confidence and importance.[96]

Approximately a hundred Jewish periodicals, with a circulation of 250,000, are published regularly in sixty communities in the United States. According to Marie Syrkin, the general intellectual and literary

[93] *Ibid.*, p. 143.

[94] News from NAACP, July 19, 1951, and August 2, 1951. In a bulletin issued on August 15, 1951, the National Association for the Advancement of Colored People listed twelve reasons "Why the 'Amos 'n' Andy' TV Show Should Be Taken Off the Air." The following were among these reasons: "1. It tends to strengthen the conclusion among uninformed and prejudiced people that Negroes are inferior, lazy, dumb and dishonest. 2. Every character in this one and only TV show with an all-Negro cast is either a clown or a crook. 3. Negro doctors are shown as quacks and thieves. 4. Negro lawyers are shown as slippery cowards, ignorant of their profession and without ethics. 5. Negro women are shown as cackling, screaming shrews, in big-mouth close-ups, using street slang, just short of vulgarity. 6. All Negroes are shown as dodging work of any kind. 7. Millions of white Americans see this 'Amos 'n' Andy' picture of Negroes and think the entire race is the same. . . ."

[95] L. D. Reddick, "Educational Programs for the Improvement of Race Relations: Motion Pictures, Radio, Press, and Libraries," *Journal of Negro Education*, 1944, vol. 13, p. 386.

[96] For an excellent analysis of the Negro press see Gunnar Myrdal, op. cit., pp. 915–924. See also J. A. Bayton and E. Bell, "An Exploratory Study of the Role of the Negro Press," *Journal of Negro Education*, 1951, vol. 20, pp. 8–15. In May, 1951, the foreign-language press in the United States consisted of 914 publications— eighty-four dailies, the others weeklies, semiweeklies, etc. The 1940 population by mother tongue for the several groups (Spanish, German, Italian, Yiddish, Polish, Hungarian, Czech, Lithuanian, French, Swedish, Slovak, Norwegian, Ukrainian, Greek, Portuguese, Russian, Hebrew, Armenian, Finnish, Chinese, Danish, Japanese, Slovene, Arabic, Carpatho-Russian, Croatian, Dutch, Latvian, Flemish, Welsh, etc.) taken together was 22,292,473. From a bulletin of the Common Council for American Unity, "Foreign Language Press in the United States," May, 1951.

level of this press has not been high. Since the work of the ablest Jewish journalists is readily accepted in general American periodicals, the English-Jewish papers, until the period of Hitler and World War II, concerned themselves mainly with local community affairs. A greater awareness of Jewish issues during the past two decades has improved their content and style. Jewish ideologies and the reactions of American Jews to current problems are reflected in these journals. The circulation of the Yiddish press in the United States is about 400,000. Its general level is said to be "infinitely higher than that of the Anglo-Jewish press" owing to the fact that it receives contributions from the ablest Yiddish writers.[97]

The treatment of minorities in magazine fiction is clearly revealed in a study by Bernard Berelson and Patricia Salter.[98] In nearly 200 stories containing 900 identifiable characters, only sixteen Negroes and ten Jews appeared. For the most part these characters played background roles, and typically only one of them was included in a single story. Although minorities constitute 40 percent of the population, they made up only 10 percent of the population of the stories. The "Americans," and those of Anglo-Saxon or Nordic stock, provided almost all of the heroes and heroines. The "Americans" appeared in the major roles much more frequently than did those of Anglo-Saxon or Nordic stock and The Others. Similar differences occurred in terms of the approval or disapproval attached to the story roles.

The approved characters were likeable, personable, wise, desirable, respectable, honest, upright; the disapproved characters were the opposite. In such "light" fiction as these magazine stories—which are entertaining and pleasant rather than "realistic" or "serious"—the large majority of the characters are approved. This was true, in this sample, for all three groups—but not equally true. Here THE AMERICANS and THE AS&NS were approved more often than THE OTHERS. Incidentally, the heavy appearance of neutral characters among the minority and foreign groups reflects the colorless roles to which they were assigned.[99]

Representatives of foreign and minority groups were usually portrayed in accordance with prevailing stereotypes. "Of all the stories including one or more minority or foreign characters, familiar and usually disparaging stereotypic descriptions were employed in fully three-fourths."[100] These stories gave no sanction to interlove and intermarriage: 85 percent of the love or marriage partners were American-American, 5 percent were American-AS&NS, 4 percent were American-Others, 3 percent

[97] Marie Syrkin, op. cit., pp. 117, 119–120.

[98] Bernard Berelson and Patricia Salter, "Majority and Minority Americans: An Analysis of American Magazine Fiction," Public Opinion Quarterly, Summer, 1946, p. 168–190.

[99] Ibid., p. 177.

[100] Ibid., p. 179.

were AS&NS-AS&NS, 2 percent were Others-Others. "In these stories, the world belonged to them [the Americans], and they ran it. . . . The rules seem to be that the character receives better treatment the closer he is to the norm of THE AMERICAN, i.e., white, Protestant, English-speaking, Anglo-Saxon. . . . Of all the distinguishable groups of characters in magazine fiction, the Negroes and the Jews were depicted least favorably. . . ."[101]

The findings of the Writers' War Board on the agencies of mass communication in 1945 have been summarized as follows:

The stage is the most liberal of all the media in presenting minority characters sympathetically and honestly.

The novel is, like the theater, in the forefront of liberalism.

The motion picture has continued to make disparaging presentation of minorities, but there has been some improvement.

The radio ranges from innocuous to sympathetic, despite some invidious stereotypes.

The comic cartoon has accorded the greatest recognition and credit to the Negro fighter.

The press in the North is, with some notorious exceptions, generally fair. About sixty percent of the southern press is considered anti-Negro despite all disclaimers.

Advertising copy is openly and self-admittedly addicted to the Anglo-Saxon myth because of reliance on "snob appeal."

The short story uses the most stereotypes, and is the worst offender.[102]

Art and Intergroup Relations

Art never corresponds with reality. Few themes, if fully explored, can be confined to a thousand-page novel or to a single piece of canvas. Complete reality, if it could be portrayed, would be so detailed that it would be inexpressibly dull. The artist selects and interprets a segment, or a few segments, from his total experience. Aspects of the "real" world are filtered through his sensitive nervous system, but his interpretation of them must not be too far removed from the experiences of others or it will lack meaning for everyone except himself.

Art themes lack homogeneity in the United States, for, as we have already pointed out, the state does not impose "social assignments" on artists. Art production depends upon the conditioning, including the art training, which the individual artist has undergone. In this environment works of art have thousands of themes and angles.

One factor which has had some influence on the kind of art produced by minority artists is marketability. The public of Negro artists is mostly white, and it is no secret that the exotic element in Negro art is responsi-

---

[101] *Ibid.*, p. 186.
[102] Florence Murray (ed.), *The Negro Handbook, 1946–47*, pp. 259–260.

ble for much of the white man's interest.[103] This factor is perhaps less important now than it was in the twenties because of the somewhat greater integration of the Negro into American life in recent years.

A factor exerting an influence in the opposite direction in the case of the Negro artist has been the assumption that "the Negro author will use his literary gifts to good ends. If his work does not improve race relations, it is assumed that it should not harm them." Thus, some criticized Richard Wright's *Native Son* not on artistic grounds, but for the reason that it might reinforce unfavorable attitudes about Negroes. Likewise, *Black Boy* was attacked by some because it failed to include such characteristics as kindness and gentleness, widely regarded as important parts of Negro life.[104] On this point Lee says, "The arts and the artists have been viewed generally as ambassadors of good will. The artist is not only interpreter of one people to another through universal media. He is also a prime exhibit of achievement and of racial potentialities."[105]

Minority status itself influences the kind of art produced by Negroes. The almost inevitable bitterness generated by prejudice and discrimination has been referred to previously, as has the likelihood that for some time to come the Negro will continue, for the most part, to express himself artistically on what it means to be a Negro in America. Viktor Lowenfeld has advanced the hypothesis that modern Negro expression has the same psychological characteristics as modern expressionist art. In both, the significance and the importance of the self are strongly emphasized. This emotional relationship to the world, the subjective world of experiences, stands in sharp contrast to the impressionist world, the world of appearances, the world of the senses.

The modern Negro through his minority status and the restrictions resulting from it necessarily must be self-centered. He . . . places the self in value relationship to environment. . . . Thus New Negro Art is not the art of visually minded people who feel as spectators. It is the art of people who feel involved in their own struggle. . . . The narrower, the more restricted, three-dimensional space on the space of the psychological experiences is, the more importance is assigned to the self. . . . In visual space, the space of appearances, distance is expressed by an increasing *diminution* of distant objects. The longing for freedom, however, *grows* with its remoteness.[106]

An interesting question relates to the possible influence of Negro folk songs on Negro-white relations. Certainly the editors of *The Negro Caravan* are correct in saying that from the "folk expressions of slavery to contemporary blues and worksongs, the folk Negro has revealed himself to be much more than contented slave, comic buffoon, and

[103] Donald Young, *op. cit.*, pp. 560–561.
[104] Ulysses Lee, *op. cit.*, p. 328.
[105] *Ibid.*, pp. 329–330.
[106] Viktor Lowenfeld, *op. cit.*, p. 7.

wretched freedman."[107] However, the important thing from the standpoint of group relations is not what the objective situation is but rather what people think it is. It is still true that "while such folk music may be viewed by the select few as a contribution to culture worthy of the highest respect, the masses tend to look on it as something growing out of and appealing to man's grosser nature, a heritage of savagery which should be suppressed by civilized society or indulged in only with apologies."[108]

The effect of the films produced by Hollywood during World War II denouncing anti-Semitism cannot be accurately estimated. Two of them carried scenes which provided anti-Semitic elements the opportunity deliberately to create disturbances in theaters. A scene in *None Shall Escape* showed a Polish rabbi and his congregation being mowed down by a Nazi machine gun when they broke out of a cattle car which was to transport them to a concentration camp. In *The Hitler Gang*, Adolf Hitler shouted anti-Semitic remarks (translated into script English) before a workers' meeting in Munich. Both scenes invited anti-Semitic demonstrations, but the influence of the films, and others of the same type listed earlier in this chapter, cannot be discounted because of the disturbances. These films against anti-Semitism made millions of people, who would not have been reached through newspapers and magazines, aware of the existence and injustice of anti-Semitism.[109] However, the assertion by McManus and Kronenberger that the film medium has a "residue value" which "survives longer than momentary misgivings on seeing the film" has not been clearly demonstrated.

A number of studies have analyzed propaganda intended to confirm or evoke prejudice, but few have dealt with procedures which are effective in reducing prejudice. It has been shown that the film *The Birth of a Nation* had a marked effect on a group of high-school students, increasing their prejudice against Negroes. Films presenting the "outgroup" favorably are less conclusive since in most cases the "out-group" that was shown was not the one toward which the students had given any indication of prejudice. MacIver does not conclude that "favorable presentation in motion pictures of a group subject to prejudice is of no avail. Quite the contrary. The moral is rather that, where prejudice already exists, sustained and repeated impacts are needed to weaken it whereas a single thrust may suffice to strengthen it."[110]

The Federal Theater Project, with its concern for social values, its nation-wide coverage, and its development of documentary techniques, had the potentialities of becoming a potent agency for dispelling group

---

[107] Sterling A. Brown, Arthur P. Davis, and Ulysses Lee (eds.), *op. cit.*, p. 5.
[108] Donald Young, *op. cit.*, p. 546.
[109] J. T. McManus and Louis Kronenberger, *op. cit.*, p. 153.
[110] R. M. MacIver, *The More Perfect Union*, The Macmillan Company, 1948, p. 218. For further discussion of the effects of propagandistic films see chap. 22.

prejudice. It was on the way to providing a series of effective dramas concerning the conflicts of labor, migratory workers, immigrants, Negroes, and Jews.[111] McManus and Kronenberger conclude: "The FTP reached people who had never been inside a theater before, preached to people who were more often ill informed than ill disposed. Killing it off was a tragedy, not least for the propagandist and educational role it could have played."[112]

In considering the relationships between art and intergroup relations it seems advisable to separate the work by minority-group persons about minority experience from the work by members of the majority group dealing with minority subjects. The editors of *The Negro Caravan* believe that the writings by Negro authors about Negro experience are significant as literature and because they throw light upon "a social reality."[113] Undoubtedly these writings do illuminate interpersonal and intergroup relations which have been only imperfectly understood by both majority- and minority-group members. An important question, though, is how many persons in the Negro and the white groups are acquainted with these writings and with the work produced by Negroes in other mediums. We suspect that the audience is not large. Moreover, majority-group artists who present stereotyped minority characters and situations help to reinforce the attitudes of those already prejudiced in the majority group. In addition, such art drives these prejudices into the minds of minority persons. The members of one minority group tend to look down upon those of another, and there is evidence that the stereotypes which the majority uses to characterize a minority have been accepted by the members of that minority as applying to themselves.[114] In this respect art has played the ironic role of assimilating American minorities to the traditional pattern of prejudices.

In the main, the members of a public select artistic and quasi-artistic products which present points of view along the lines of their own sentiments. When some prejudiced persons read all or part of *Native Son*, their anti-Negro feelings were intensified. Many nonprejudiced readers felt the book gave them much insight into lower-class life in general and lower-class urban Negro life in particular. In other words, art does not speak for itself. What one gets from a book or other

[111] In the previously cited study of magazine fiction, Berelson and Salter say, "One of this country's favorite ideologies claims equality for the diverse national, racial, and religious strains which make up the United States. In one sense, it is 'immoral' to suggest that inequality actually exists or, if that is acknowledged, that it cannot be attributed to biological factors or individual inadequacies. This ideology is not challenged in these stories. Minority differences are regularly recognized but the minorities are not overtly depreciated. Of our sample of 185 stories, only four contained a direct reference of any kind to this problem area in American life." Bernard Berelson and Patricia Salter, *op. cit.*, p. 189.

[112] J. T. McManus and Louis Kronenberger, *op. cit.*, p. 157.

[113] Sterling A. Brown, Arthur P. Davis, and Ulysses Lee (eds.), *op. cit.*, p. 7.

[114] Donald Young, *op. cit.*, p. 576.

artistic product, if one gets to it at all, depends to a considerable extent on what one takes to it.

The relationship between art and society is interactive, but art and quasi art doubtless reflect more than they affect their times.[115] On a continuum of influence, presumably abstract music and abstract painting would stand at one extreme (least influence), and the motion picture and other mass agencies of communication at the other (greatest influence).

The social functions of art may be looked at from the standpoints of the minority artist, the members of a minority group, and majority-group members. For the minority artist, the creative process provides emotional release, social recognition, and perhaps some financial return. For minority persons, art by or about the members of the group provides entertainment and may inspire feelings of confidence and pride. For those in the majority group, such art affords amusement and tends to strengthen existing attitudes, whatever they may be, toward persons of minority status.[116] Some prejudice against minorities may be undermined by works of art and by the mass agencies of communication, but adequate data are lacking on this point.

[115] For a stimulating examination of theories of the relationship of literature and society, see M. C. Albrecht, "The Relationship of Literature and Society," *American Journal of Sociology*, March, 1954, pp. 425–436.

[116] The "presumable effects" of reading magazine fiction dealing with majority and minority Americans are discussed by Berelson and Salter. "These stories are probably offered and accepted purely as entertainment. Their typical effect upon readers is a respite effect; that is, they normally provide a satisfying and enjoyable vacation from daily routines and daily cares. That may be the typical effect, but it is certainly not the only one. Many communications have other than their intended effects upon readers or listeners and this is probably such a case. In all likelihood, the consistent deprivation of The AS&NS [Anglo-Saxon and Nordic Stock] and especially The Others in these stories, over a long period of time, serves to activate the predispositions of a hostile or even an indifferent audience. Readers with latent tendencies to assign the usual stereotypic descriptions to groups whom they do not know, or toward whom they are unsympathetic, or with whom they do not come in personal contact, can find support for their convenient tags, labels, and aggressions in such magazine fiction. And this is all the more striking as a result of the implicit comparison with The Americans. Thus the condition and behavior of fictional characters can readily be used to 'prove' that the Negroes are lazy or ignorant, the Jews sly, the Irish superstitious, the Italians criminal, and so on." Bernard Berelson and Patricia Salter, *op. cit.*, p. 188.

PART III

Prejudice, Discrimination,
and Democratic Values

CHAPTER 22

The Reduction of Prejudice and Discrimination: Changing the Prejudiced Person

In the first two parts of this volume we have followed the tangled patterns of relationship that develop between dominant groups and minority groups. We have examined the causes of prejudice and discrimination and described their results, for the individuals involved and for the social structure. We have seen that to some degree the institutional patterns of the minority groups can be understood only by reference to their statuses. Throughout this analysis, we have attempted to maintain an objective approach. Our own value stand has not been disguised, but we have tried to prevent it from distorting the picture.

In turning to the analysis of strategies that are effective in reducing prejudice and discrimination, our value stand becomes more explicit. We believe that the categorical judgment and treatment of human groups not only is evil in itself but brings with it a host of other evils. Having stated that premise, we shall attempt to analyze strategies on a thoroughly objective basis. The surgeon cannot afford to be sentimental.

Even in this section our concern is not simply with social-action programs—although we shall hope to contribute to them. One of the most effective ways of learning about the nature of intergroup hostility is to study the techniques that are effective, and those that are ineffective, in reducing it; for such a study, to be valid, must be concerned with the causes and functions of that hostility.

In recent years, as we have seen, there have been important changes in many aspects of majority-minority relations. Vicious genocide and new waves of imperialism have arisen; but significant gains have also been made. Since 1940 there has been dramatic improvement in the status of the Negro in the United States, although many barriers to his full participation in society still stand. The problems associated with the integration of many immigrant groups into America are being reduced; but the lot of the migrant from Mexico and Puerto Rico is still difficult. Americans of Japanese ancestry were treated with great injustice during World War II; but, perhaps as a reaction to that injustice, their status is now improved. Altogether, Americans cannot afford to feel at all complacent about the changes, both because there is still so much discrimination within this country and also because some of the internal gains are only a function of the rise of international tension. During times of crisis dominant groups often court their minorities quite fervently, hoping to win added support for the external struggle. The measure of the success comes when the gains are recorded in less hectic times. All the gains are not likely to be lost, but their preservation cannot be assumed.

Variables to Consider in the Development of Strategies

Effective strategy is based on a precise knowledge of the goals one wants to achieve and on a thorough understanding of the obstacles in the way. We need to consider:

1. Types of goals for which different groups are striving.

2. Types of persons to be affected, in terms of their relation to prejudice and discrimination.

3. Types of situations, in time and place, to which strategy must adjust.

TYPES OF GOALS

Those who are seeking to reduce prejudice and discrimination do not all agree on the immediate or long-run objectives. Some believe that peaceful coexistence is most desirable. Others are willing to accept and work for economic and political equality and integration but are opposed to "social" equality (there is a vague and shifting line separating economic and political from social). Still others are working for complete integration, for a situation where each individual will be judged and treated as an individual and not in any way as a member of a *supposed* or functionless group. Functional group membership will continue to be important—it would be foolish to treat physicians as if they were engineers. Prejudice and discrimination, however, are characterized precisely by the fact that they disregard function; they treat the Negro physician and engineer and farm laborer and machine operator and teacher and unskilled worker as if they were all alike, although they share nothing in common as Negroes but a few physical traits—and these have a wide range of variation. That is why we call them a functionless group, just as "white" people are.

The present authors believe in the third goal mentioned above—complete equality and integration. This goal is harmonious with peaceful coexistence or pluralism, provided that the pluralism is chosen by individuals of the minority group as a matter of right and not enforced on them by the majority as a categorical requirement. Plural rights are limited, of course, by the legitimate needs for security and integration of the whole society. One of the great problems of modern society is the determination of differences that are allowable and are harmonious with the principle of the greatest good to the greatest number. We believe these differences can be very broad—broader than most societies, in this day of crisis, are permitting. Differences in language, in religion, in belief in the best methods for achieving life's values—these are not only permissible but necessary for a society that is eager to find better ways to solve its problems.[1] *Active allegiance* to a system of law that opposes the democratic method for settling disputes is doubtless beyond the range of differences that an integrated society may permit. Advocacy of such a system is less dangerous to democracy than its suppression; but active programs may well represent "a clear and present danger." Unfortunately, in the difficult and important task of separating advocacy from active programs, a legitimate and necessary pluralism has been weakened. Opposition to those who are working for an undemocratic state has been extended, by some, to opposition to those who have different ideas, believe different religious doctrines, have different conceptions of the proper extent of governmental activity, and trace descent from different ancestors. Thus reaction and prejudice have frequently been joined in our society. We believe that America can prosper only by encouraging the integration of all groups while permitting a wide and diversified pluralism.

The goal we are describing is also harmonious, in the short run, with the goal of those who favor economic and political equality but oppose social equality. "In the short run" is a key phrase in that sentence. It implies a consideration of strategy but not a change of principle. It seems unwise to try to establish social equality first, when minority groups lack political power and are of unequal economic status. Social equality may well come as a *result* of other changes. The long-run goal of complete integration certainly implies social equality—no person is to be judged on any grounds simply as a member of a functionless group. This is in the nature of a first premise, a moral consideration. Short-run goals, however, involve strategic considerations, questions of method

[1] See J. Milton Yinger, "Civil Liberties in Crisis," *Common Ground*, Winter, 1949, pp. 3–9.

that must vary in time and place. In some times and places, working for economic and political equality is most likely to serve ultimate integration.

TYPES OF PERSONS

Those who declare that *the* way to eliminate prejudice is "education" or "law" or "more contact between peoples," or those who, oppositely, declare that prejudice cannot be eliminated because *the* prejudiced person is torn by a deep-seated anxiety that is basic to his ego, both make the mistake of failing to distinguish among the many different types of persons who show intergroup hostility. The reduction of prejudice and discrimination demands that we make such distinctions, for a different strategy will be effective for each of the different types of persons.

Robert Merton has devised a useful classification of four types of persons for each of whom a different group of strategies is appropriate.

1. The unprejudiced nondiscriminator, or all-weather liberal; the person who accepts the "American creed" in both belief and action. Such a person must be the spearhead of any effective campaign to reduce prejudice and discrimination; but his force is reduced by several errors. There is the "fallacy of group soliloquies." "Ethnic liberals are busily engaged in talking to themselves. Repeatedly, the same groups of like-minded liberals seek each other out, hold periodic meetings in which they engage in mutual exhortation, and thus lend social and psychological support to one another."[2] This activity does not appreciably spread the creed for which they are working. The fallacy of group soliloquies produces the illusion that there is consensus on the issue in the community at large and thus leads to the "fallacy of unanimity." The all-weather liberal mistakes discussion in like-minded groups for effective action and overestimates the support for his position. His isolation from other points of view also produces the "fallacy of privatized solutions."

The ethnic liberal, precisely because he is at one with the American creed, may rest content with his own individual behavior and thus see no need to do anything about the problem at large. Since his own spiritual house is in order, he is not motivated by guilt or shame to work on a collective problem. The very freedom of the liberal from guilt thus prompts him to secede from any *collective* effort to set the national house in order. He essays a *private* solution to a *social* problem. He assumes that numerous individual adjustments will serve in place of a collective adjustment. His outlook, compounded of good moral philosophy but poor sociology, holds that each individual must put his own house in order and fails to recognize that privatized solutions cannot be effected for problems which are essentially social in na-

[2] Robert K. Merton, in R. M. MacIver (ed.), *Discrimination and National Welfare*, Institute for Religious and Social Studies (distributed by Harper & Brothers), 1949, p. 104.

ture. For clearly, if each person were motivated to abide by the American creed, the problem would not be likely to arise in the first place.[3]

These fallacies lead to the paradox of the passive liberal's contributing, to some degree, to the persistence of prejudice and discrimination by his very inaction. They may be overcome by having the liberal enter groups that are not composed solely of fellow liberals (giving up the gratifications of consistent group support); by realization that discrimination brings rewards—or seems to—and that exhortation, therefore, is not enough if the social environment is not changed at the same time; and by action on the part of the militant liberal to show the passive liberal how he contributes to prejudice and discrimination by his inaction.

2. The unprejudiced discriminator, or fair-weather liberal. This is the person who, despite his own lack of prejudice, supports discrimination if it is easier or profitable. He may show the expediency of silence or timidity, or discriminate to seize an advantage. He may refuse to hire Negroes because it "might hurt business." The fair-weather liberal suffers from some degree of guilt and is therefore a strategic person for the all-weather liberal to work on. The need is to bring him into groups of all-weather liberals, where he will find rewards for abiding by his own beliefs.

3. The prejudiced nondiscriminator, or fair-weather illiberal. This is the reluctant conformist, the employer who discriminates until a fair employment practices law puts the fear of punishment and loss into him, the trade-union official who, though prejudiced himself, abolishes Jim Crow because the rank and file of his membership demands it, the bigoted businessman who profits from the trade of minority-group members. Like the fair-weather liberal, he is a person of expediency, but this disguises a basic difference. "Whereas the timid bigot is under strain when he conforms to the creed, the timid liberal is under strain when he deviates."[4] Adequate strategy must recognize this difference. The fair-weather illiberal can be kept from discrimination only by an environment that makes discrimination costly and painful, not by appeal to his value creed. Legal controls, strictly administered, may at first increase his prejudice—or at least his verbalization of it—but they will reduce his discrimination.

4. The prejudiced discriminator, or all-weather illiberal. He is consistent in belief and practice. He believes that differential treatment of minority groups is not discrimination, but discriminating. Strategy in dealing with such persons must vary from region to region. In some subcultures of the United States the all-weather illiberal is a conformist, supported by the group norms; if he were to change, he would be alien-

---

[3] *Ibid.*, p. 105.
[4] *Ibid.*, p. 108.

ated from the people important to him. In other subcultures he is isolated, and a change in his attitudes and behavior would help to bring integration with people significant to him. He can be moved toward type three. Change of the illiberal who is supported by group norms requires legal and administrative controls and large-scale changes in the economic supports to prejudice.

It is important to understand the distribution of these various types and to realize the kinds of strategies that are effective with each. To try to appeal to all of them in the same way, or to assume that a given proportion of each type is found, when they are in fact very differently distributed, is to make serious strategic errors. Merton, to illustrate this point, makes a guess of the possible distribution of types in two communities:[5]

	A Deep South Community
Types	Local Cultural Clichés Identifying Types
I	—"Nigger lover"
II	—(Clandestine liberal conformist)
III	—(This type virtually non-existent here)
IV	—"Any white man's better than any nigger."

	A New England Community
I	—"All men are created equal . . ."
II	—"Some of my good friends are Negroes."
III	—"A Negro's dollar's as good as a white's."
IV	—"They're all right in their place."

This is, of course, a hypothetical profile of proportions, not a measured distribution. We need to note that such a classification has little reference to the intensity dimension; two all-weather illiberals, for example, may have very different patterns of behavior because prejudice and discrimination occupy an important place in the personality organization of one and an unimportant place for the other. One cannot assume, moreover, that the same distribution would be true for each minority. In a given community one might find discrimination against both an Indian and a Negro group, but most of the white population may be fair-weather liberals toward the Indians and all-weather illiberals toward the Negroes.

Levinson draws a valuable distinction between the openly antidemocratic individual and the pseudodemocratic individual. The former is nearly the equivalent of Merton's all-weather illiberal, except that Levinson emphasizes the deep-seated irrational sources (a specialized causal

[5] *Ibid.*, p. 122; for this whole discussion by Merton, see *ibid.*, pp. 99–126.

explanation that Merton might not share entirely). The pseudodemocratic person is somewhat similar to the fair-weather liberal; but Levinson places a useful emphasis on the ambivalence of such a person's feelings: he discriminates but has some sense of guilt about it; he is prejudiced but also believes in democratic values. This is probably a widespread type of individual in the United States; hence development of an adequate strategy in reducing his prejudice and discrimination is an important task. Levinson says:

An idea may be considered openly antidemocratic when it refers to active hatred, or to violence which has the direct aim of wiping out a minority group or of putting it in a permanently subordinate position. A pseudodemocratic idea, on the other hand, is one in which hostility toward a group is somewhat tempered and disguised by means of a compromise with democratic ideals. Pseudodemocratic statements about Jews are often introduced by qualifying phrases which deny hostility or which attempt to demonstrate the democratic attitude of the speaker, e.g., "It's not that I'm prejudiced, but . . ."; "Jews have their rights, but. . . ."[6]

The author notes the strategic importance of recognizing the ambivalence of the pseudodemocratic person. Such an individual is relatively unaffected by current literature which attacks prejudice as "un-American" or "un-Christian," for he has disguised his prejudice from himself by a group of rationalizations that seem to square his behavior with his value creed. Strategy must find a way not simply of exposing his rationalizations (for the problem is not essentially a rational one with the individual), but of lowering the need for prejudice while strengthening the belief in democratic values.

It is probably an error to regard the pseudodemocratic compromise as a mere surface disguise used deliberately and skillfully by prejudiced people to camouflage their actual, conscious antidemocracy. . . . The concern with democratic values, and the resistance to antidemocratic ones, must be considered as psychologically and socially important facts in any attempt to understand prejudice, American variety. Undoubtedly very many people who are now pseudodemocratic are potentially antidemocratic, that is, are capable in a social crisis of supporting or committing acts of violence against minority groups. Nevertheless, it is important to understand the attempted compromise with democratic values: because it may reveal a democratic potential which might, if supported and strengthened, ultimately gain the upper hand; because it colors the whole fabric of pseudodemocratic social thinking; and, since this compromise reflects the prevalent forms of overt discrimination in this country—quotas, segregation, exclusion, denial of opportunities—to understand the former may help to combat the latter.[7]

[6] T. W. Adorno, Else Frenkel-Brunswik, D. J. Levinson, and R. N. Sanford, *The Authoritarian Personality*, Harper & Brothers, 1950, p. 60.
[7] *Ibid.*, p. 61.

Many of us are pseudodemocratic. Our actions may seem to others to be discriminatory, but if they tell us so, it is easy to say, "Who, me? Why I believe in democracy, an equal chance for everyone. But why should I pay those Mexicans higher wages to buy more liquor with? They're just as happy the way they are. Why should I put in a bathtub for my Negro tenants? They'd just fill it with coal. Why should we let the Japs buy California land? They're not loyal to the government."

The human mind has an enormous capacity for holding mutually contradictory ideas without any feeling of discomfort. The pseudodemocratic individual will not become thoroughly democratic until the personal and group functions and the traditional supports of prejudice and discrimination are sharply reduced.

The strategic problem of distinguishing types of persons is also indirectly involved in Isidor Chein's discussion of "dimensions of prejudice." A person in whom one dimension is largest will respond to a different approach than the person in whom another dimension is largest. There is the "informational" dimension—for example, the holding of stereotyped beliefs—for which education is an important strategy. The "conformity" dimension represents a need on the part of the prejudiced person to conform to the prevailing patterns. Legal measures proscribing discrimination will affect him. The "status" dimension is the desire for ego satisfaction, for a position of superiority. Reduction of this factor in prejudice requires the equalization of opportunities and rights—giving ego motives less to thrive on. The "emotional" dimension involves attitudes of actual hatred and hostility toward minorities. The need here is for the minimization of frustration.[8]

A definitive classification of the types of persons involved in prejudice and discrimination would have to be far more complicated than those we have discussed. When so many variables are involved, a few types cannot cover the range of empirical combinations. Nevertheless, the distinctions drawn by Merton, Levinson, and Chein can be of great value in strategic considerations.

Types of Situations

When one has distinguished the types of goals and types of persons involved, he has a great deal of information about a situation in which prejudice and discrimination are found. But other factors must also be considered if his strategy is to be effective. What is the legal pattern? Does it support discrimination or condemn it? Does the law condemn it ideologically but fail to provide enforcement techniques? To try the same strategy in a situation where one can count on legal support as he

---

[8] See Isidor Chein, "Some Considerations in Combating Intergroup Prejudice," *Journal of Educational Sociology*, March, 1946, pp. 412–419.

tries in a situation where the law is weak or actually supports discrimination is to be ineffective.

Is the situation one that requires immediate action, or is there time for more deliberate analysis? What is called for in one would be foolish in the other. Schermerhorn distinguishes between emergency problems and tractable problems.

Emergency problems are those in which a crisis arises, where a tangle of circumstances forces an immediate decision on responsible administrators. At this stage it is too late to alter the conditions that gave rise to the emergency. In a lynching, a riot, gang warfare, or violence of any kind between groups, it is useless at the moment to ask what preventive measures would have checked the trouble at the source. . . .

Tractable problems are those in which the need for immediate action is less urgent. Haste gives way to deliberation, and coercion to more strategic considerations. Time permits research, the marshaling of evidence, and comparison of alternative methods.[9]

Strategic errors have been made in both directions. In a time of critical hostility a community may "appoint a committee" when what is most needed is training for their police in how to disperse a mob with the least violence. Or, oppositely, a group may "call in the cops," may throw down the gauntlet to discriminators when what is most needed is the careful analysis of causes, the skillful rallying of allies, and the creation of a more favorable environment for change. No easy formula can separate emergency problems from tractable problems, but to neglect to take account of their differences is to invite failure.

Is the discrimination supported mainly by lower-class members of the "dominant" group, themselves insecure and hoping to climb a little higher on the backs of minority-group members? Or is the pattern primarily set by powerful groups who are exploiting prejudice to maintain their authority? Or, more accurately, how are these two supports interrelated? Is the strategy to be aimed at a large group of people or only a few? What will work for a small neighborhood, with an intimacy factor involved, will be ineffective in a large city, a state, or a nation, either because the principles involved may be different or simply because what is feasible for a few may be impossible for many (one could not take a nation of 150 millions on tour.)[10] Are the cultural differences between the majority and minority large or small? The most effective strategies for improving the treatment of first-generation immigrants from peasant villages in the Ukraine are different from those that will reduce discrimination against thoroughly urbanized Negroes, for example.

[9] R. A. Schermerhorn, *These Our People*, D. C. Heath and Company, 1949, p. 519.
[10] See David Krech and Richard Crutchfield, *Theory and Problems of Social Psychology*, McGraw-Hill Book Company, 1948, pp. 500–501.

Mapping Out a Program

Having defined his goals and analyzed the kinds of persons and situational factors to be dealt with, the strategist is in a position to plan his antihostility program. Unfortunately, planning and testing are not common. It is only in the last few years that systematic attempts to test the effectiveness of programs for reducing prejudice and discrimination have been made. Williams says:

> It is clear that organized attempts to improve intergroup relations are numerous and significant. Considering the seriousness of the problems, the possibly dangerous results of inappropriate action, and the very great amount of time and money involved, it might be anticipated that these agencies of social engineering would systematically check the effectiveness of their efforts by appropriate research. With only a few exceptions, however, this has not been done until very recently. Such agencies as the Commission on Community Interrelations have begun to operate on the principle, "no action without research, no research without action." Over most of the field it remains true, however, that the administrator, student, or interested citizen who wishes to gauge the comparative effectiveness of given programs or techniques can find little scientific evidence to guide him.[11]

Well-intentioned but unguided programs can be useless or even harmful. When they fail, many people may conclude, as Williams points out, that intergroup hostility is inevitable. Others may decide that such hostility is so deeply embedded in our society that only a major institutional change can produce results. Assumptions of these kinds can be tested only by action that is guided by research. The effects of such action "should be to develop realistic confidence and to stabilize expectations in such a way as to reduce the dangers of unchecked utopianism on the one hand and fatalistic disillusionment on the other."[12]

One of the functions of research is to discover the points at which prejudice and discrimination can be attacked most successfully. Myrdal refers to the white man's "rank order of discriminations" toward the Negro, with particular reference to the South. He believes the white man is most willing (although not necessarily very willing) to grant economic and political gains to Negroes and is least willing to grant what he calls "social" equality. The Negro, on the other hand, is primarily concerned with just the "concessions" the white man will make most readily. This seems to carry the obvious strategic implication that action programs should center upon economic and political discriminations. MacIver also states that the "economic front" is a weak point in

---

[11] Robin Williams, Jr., *The Reduction of Intergroup Tensions*, Social Science Research Council, 1947, p. 8.

[12] *Ibid.*, p. 10.

the defenses of the discriminator. Advances in this area do not encounter the emotional block that guards questions of segregation in
social contact. If this assumption is borne out by careful study, it can
help to guide strategy.

No formula, however, can declare in advance what will be most effective in a particular situation. And every change will carry some "calculated risk," for every gain is likely to entail some losses. It is the total
result that must be measured. In the pages to follow we shall examine
many types of strategies. We shall see that weak points must be determined for each situation, on the basis of knowledge of the kinds of
persons and the social forces involved and the resources available.

Strategies with Major Emphasis on Changing the Personality

It has frequently been noted that attempts to reduce intergroup
hostility can focus either on the prejudiced individual or on those aspects of the situation which allow and encourage discrimination. The
former strategies try to change the values, the attitudes, the needs of
individuals. They are sometimes based on the oversimplified theory
that majority-minority conflict is "fundamentally" based on personality
factors. But they are sometimes consciously chosen specialties that are
used in full awareness of the value and necessity of other approaches.
As Chein notes, "Many a program has been roundly condemned as inadequate or useless, the critics thinking in terms of one dimension of
prejudice and failing to apprehend the suitability of the program for
other dimensions. Many a program has been hailed as a panacea, its
proponents failing to realize that it may be effective for only one dimension. Prejudice is multidimensional and the war against it must be
carried on multidimensionally."[13]

We shall describe and evaluate five kinds of approaches that emphasize the need for changing the persons who show prejudice and discrimination: exhortation, propaganda, contact, education, and personal
therapy. These are not analytically precise and mutually exclusive categories, but one can draw useful distinctions among them. It is particularly difficult to distinguish clearly among the first four, because of
differences in the use of terms. Many people contend that any discussion about values or in controversial areas is "propaganda," or, since
they usually disparage such activities, "only propaganda." Other writers
believe that any symbolic activity to change people's attitudes is "educational." This kind of conceptual poverty blocks understanding. Symbolic communication is of many varieties and we would do well to have
that fact reflected in our vocabularies.

[13] Isidor Chein, *op. cit.*, p. 419.

It is perhaps helpful to think, not of a dichotomy (propaganda or education), but of a continuum:

Propaganda  Education

Particular activities can be located along this continuum on the basis of several criteria:

1. The degree to which the controversial nature of a topic is recognized or disguised.

2. The degree to which emotional appeals are used.

3. The degree to which all the relevant facts and evidence are brought to bear.

4. The degree to which the sources and motives of the person seeking influence are hidden or revealed.

The use of other criteria would make for a sharper distinction, but perhaps these four are sufficient to enable us to classify the various activities aimed at reducing prejudice and discrimination. Propaganda, then, is the manipulation of symbols on a controversial topic when the controversial element is disguised, emotional appeals are used, some or all of the relevant facts are left out or distorted, and the motives of the propagandist and/or the sources of the propaganda are hidden. Education is the transmission of noncontroversial information (it may or may not be true, but it is generally regarded as true in the society involved); or it is the handling of controversial topics by recognizing them as controversial, using an objective approach, bringing all relevant facts to bear, and noting clearly the sources and motives of the educator. No empirical act will be simply propaganda or education. We are describing "pure types" that may never be found. Each event can be placed along the continuum on the basis of the criteria used. If we get rid of "pigeonhole" thinking, we will not say that because a given educator has a few things in common with the propagandist he is "nothing but" a propagandist; we will say that he is 94 or 87 or 51 percent "pure." Nor will we say, when a propagandist uses a few facts, that he is an educator.

Exhortation seems ordinarily to be at about the midpoint between propaganda and education. It often minimizes the controversial nature of the topics with which it deals and uses emotional appeals; but it frequently marshals a great many facts and makes no effort to disguise its motives or its sources. Efforts to encourage contact between minority- and majority-group members are also near the midpoint, although perhaps somewhat more educational than propagandistic, as we have defined those terms. They are partially propagandistic because they frequently distort the facts in the guise of studying facts, for the contacts are selected on the basis of their ability to change attitudes, not according to their typicality.

EXHORTATION

Exhortation is perhaps the most frequently used method in trying to reduce intergroup hostility. Appeal to men's better selves; revivify belief in their value creed; change their hearts and they will change their ways. Despite the frequency with which this approach is used, its value has not been tested in any way that permits one to speak with confidence about the degree of its effectiveness. Myrdal's famous work has brought a strong emphasis on the importance of the "American creed" as an ideological weakness of the prejudiced person. There is a moral struggle going on *within* most Americans, says Myrdal, that prevents race relations from being worse than they are and makes an ideological approach to their improvement feasible. "The American Negro problem is a problem in the heart of the American." Because he believes in democracy, in the rights of the common man, in the rightness of free enterprise (no barriers to freedom of economic activity), the American cannot believe, without some mental gymnastics, that prejudice and discrimination are justified. The strategy of exhortation tries to bring this contradiction to the forefront of our attention, to revitalize the creed.

In the context of other changes, exhortation may help to reduce prejudice—particularly by increasing the enthusiasm of those who are already convinced. It may also inhibit the discriminations, although it may not affect the prejudices, of many fair-weather illiberals who do not want to violate the community standards openly. It is easy, however, to exaggerate the influence of exhortation. As MacIver points out, the charge of inconsistency doesn't reach most men; they can easily get along on compromises. "It is well to expose their rationalizations but nevertheless they have great capacity for finding new ones. They may have some uneasiness on this score, but often it is not potent enough to make them change their ways."[14] This uneasiness, in fact, may lead to stronger intolerance, for it may raise one's guilt feelings, which are then allayed by a blinder defensiveness, by new discriminations which actually furnish new justifications for the prejudices.

The American creed, moreover, is not of equal importance among all individuals or in all times and places. Merton writes, "In so far as it is a 'sacred' part of American culture, hallowed by tradition, it is largely immune to direct attack. But it may be honored simply in the breach. It is often evaded, and the evasions themselves become institutionalized, giving rise to what I may call the 'institutionalized evasion of institutional norms.' Where the creed is at odds with local beliefs and practices, it may persist as an empty cultural form partly because it is so flexible."[15] Persons who deviate from the creed can justify their actions

---

[14] R. M. MacIver, *The More Perfect Union,* The Macmillan Company, 1948, pp. 88–89.

[15] Robert K. Merton, *op. cit.,* p. 101.

by declaring that they are conforming with the spirit of the creed, not with the "sterile letter." Beyond that, one must recognize a contrary creed—a moral code that justifies prejudice and discrimination.

Effective strategy seems to indicate that exhortation can play only a modest role in the total efforts to reduce prejudice and discrimination. The moral premises which it rests upon are not universally shared and are alloyed with countervalues; most of us are skilled at compartmentalizing our professions of belief and our other actions, overlooking any contradictions; and those who are most likely to show hostility to minority-group members are probably those who are least often reached by exhortation.

Propaganda

The "propaganda menace" has received so much attention in recent years that many people have come to regard it as almost all-powerful. The success of the mass campaigns of persuasion by modern nations and the skill with which commercial propaganda (advertising) has converted cigarettes and chewing gum into necessities make us believe that a tremendously powerful instrument for controlling human behavior has been created. Why not turn this instrument to the purpose of reducing intergroup hostility?

Before examining attempts to use propaganda to control intergroup behavior, it may be wise to state briefly the contemporary answer to the question, How effective is propaganda? As we have learned more and more about the problem, we have seen that there is no *general* answer. The question must be more complicated: How effective is a specific propaganda campaign with a stated group of people in a particular situation? Gradually it has become apparent that far more limits are imposed on the power of propaganda than was generally believed to be true a few years ago.

Modern societies, to be sure, are more susceptible to propaganda than stable "sacred" societies. The entrance of more and more questions into the area of controversy, because of the breakup of traditional answers; concomitant personal insecurities that make many people eager for some simple answer to life's problems; the spread of mass media of communication, capable of bringing simultaneous stimuli to millions of people; and even the rise of the sciences of man—these and other factors have made propaganda more likely and more powerful than before.

Propaganda is limited, however, even under such favorable conditions. It is limited by knowledge of the facts on the part of propagandees; it is limited by a counterpropaganda; and above all, it is limited by the already existing values, needs, and hopes of the persons to whom it attempts to appeal. To put this point oppositely: Propaganda is most effective when it is dealing with a poorly informed public, when it has a monopoly in the field of communication (censorship), and when it either is working in an area in which the values and needs of the public are diffuse and poorly structured or ties its appeals closely to well-structured needs and values.

Political propaganda in the United States, for example, that hopes to win support from people who ordinarily give their allegiance to another party, is usually unsuccessful. The propagandees, even if they can be persuaded to listen or read, are usually in possession of evidence from their own party, they are strongly influenced by counterpropaganda, and they believe themselves tied by interest to their original party. The main effects of political propaganda have been found to be the strengthening of the convictions of those who are already convinced, the activation of latent political attitudes that might otherwise remain unexpressed, and perhaps the swaying of a few marginal voters.[16] These may be important and decisive political effects, but they do not reveal an all-powerful propaganda influence.

The propagandist has the difficult job of persuading those who disagree with him to listen to him or read his material in the first place. If he succeeds in reaching some of the "unconverted," he has to try to get them to make the "right" response and then persuade them to act upon their new convictions. Leonard Doob shows how the responses of two persons to the same propaganda may vary. An orator makes a flourishing reference to the "American home" (of which he is in favor):[17]

Individual A	Individual B
1. This man is talking about the American home.	1. This man is talking about the American home.
2. I like my home.	2. I like my home.
3. This man is going to protect my home.	3. My house requires new shingles on the roof.
4. Therefore I like what he is saying.	4. I wonder whether I can afford new shingles right now.
5. I also like him—now what is he saying?	5. I don't think so—now what is that man saying?

Propaganda may have wholly unexpected and unintended effects, for ultimately it is interpreted by specific individuals whose own values and needs are brought to bear.

The story is told of a missionary who pointed to a table and repeatedly said "table" until his audience of non-literates could repeat the word. After some time, he was dismayed to learn that some non-literates referred to a tree as "table," because both were brown. Others called dogs "tables" since both had four legs. In short, each listener had selected some aspect of the

[16] See Paul Lazarsfeld, Bernard Berelson, and Hazel Gaudet, *The People's Choice*, Duell, Sloan & Pearce, 1944.
[17] See Leonard Doob, *Public Opinion and Propaganda*, Henry Holt & Company, Inc., 1948, p. 336.

complex object, which for the missionary was so well designated as a whole by the word "table." In the same way, it is instructive to see how often the effects of propaganda can be totally unexpected.[18]

Unintended or "boomerang" effects of propaganda are particularly likely to occur when one tries to influence a heterogeneous group. A morale program, broadcast shortly after Pearl Harbor, had two dominant themes: the power and potentialities of the United Nations, to combat defeatism, and the strength of the enemy, to combat complacency. But what if the complacent heard only theme number one, and the defeatist heard only theme number two, the opposite arguments being disregarded? "To judge from interview materials, this is evidently what happened." The propaganda had the opposite effect from what was intended.[19]

Propaganda to Reduce Intergroup Hostility. On the basis of this brief discussion of some contemporary concepts employed by students of propaganda, we can perhaps evaluate more accurately the usefulness of propaganda as a strategy in the reduction of prejudice and discrimination. Literally millions of leaflets, pamphlets, cartoons, comic books, articles, and movies have been issued in the struggle against intergroup hostility. How effective are they? Flowerman suggests that this question can be answered only when we have the following information: To what degree do pro-tolerance groups control the media of communication? What is the level of saturation—the proportion of a population who are reached by the appeals? What is the attention level? (Modern radio, with its aim of something for everybody, has developed a "radio deafness," a casualness toward the flow of stimuli. The intensity of attention varies with the specificity of the audience, the cruciality of the situation, and other factors.) How do the propagandees reinterpret the message? Does the propaganda conform to group standards? (If it does not, it can have little effect. And those standards may include prejudice.) What is the sponsorship? Is it held in high esteem?[20]

The evidence seems to suggest that on many of these counts antiprejudice propaganda has not been very effective. For the most part it reaches those who already agree with it. Radio programs of "intercultural education" that describe the culture and history of the Italians, Yugoslavians, and Greeks are listened to, respectively, by Italians, Yugoslavians, and Greeks. Each group may be made to feel better, more secure, more important, but they are scarcely informed about the others.

In some instances individuals have been confronted with antipreju-

[18] Robert K. Merton, *Social Theory and Social Structure*, The Free Press, 1949, pp. 273–274.
[19] See *ibid.*, p. 276.
[20] See S. H. Flowerman, "Mass Propaganda in the War Against Bigotry," *Journal of Abnormal and Social Psychology*, October, 1947, pp. 429–433.

dice propaganda involuntarily. Some fight it, openly or covertly; a few may accept it; but many evade it by managing to misunderstand its message. A number of studies have been made of the effects of a "Mr. Biggott" series of cartoons, designed to show an absurd man exhibiting ridiculous prejudices. "In each of them, Mr. Biggott, the central character, is shown as a cantankerous and unattractive man of middle age and moderate income. In each of them he displays the anti-minority attitudes from which he earns his name."[21] Three cartoons are used in the study by Kendall and Wolf. One shows Mr. Biggott glowering at an "honor roll" billboard on which the community war heroes are listed. He says, "Berkowitz, Fabrizio, Ginsberg, Kelly—disgraceful!" In another cartoon Mr. Biggott, lying sick in bed, says to a somewhat startled doctor, "In case I should need a transfusion, doctor, I want to make certain I don't get anything but blue, sixth-generation American blood!" In an "Indian" cartoon Mr. Biggott says to a humble American Indian, "I'm sorry, Mr. Eaglefeather, but out company's policy is to employ 100 per cent Americans only."

The assumption behind the cartoons was that the picturing of an absurd man exhibiting absurd ideas would lead one to reject his own prejudices. Cooper and Jahoda found, however, that prejudiced persons created many mechanisms of evasion. Understanding may be "derailed" by avoiding identification with Mr. Biggott (despite the sharing of prejudice). Mr. X, on seeing the "blood transfusion" cartoon, looked upon Mr. Biggott as an inferior *parvenu*: "I'm eighth generation myself. . . . He may not be the best blood either." Then Mr. X leads off into other subjects. Having understood the cartoon at first ("He don't want anything but sixth-generation American blood! Ha! That's pretty good."), he then felt it necessary to disidentify.[22]

A prejudiced person may accept a cartoon on the surface but make it invalid for him by declaring that one is entitled to his prejudices or by stating that the situation is not real. He may change the whole frame of reference of the cartoon to make it conform to his own views. One cartoon of a series that shows a congressman with native fascist, anti-minority views has the congressman interviewing a man in his office. The man has produced a letter of recommendation that indicates he has been in jail, started race riots, smashed windows. "Of course I can use you in my new party," says the congressman. One respondent said, "It might be anything crooked . . . might be a new labor party." In response to another cartoon in this series one person declared, "It's a Jewish party that would help Jews get more power." Thus prejudiced

<hr/>

[21] Patricia Kendall and Katherine Wolf, in Paul Lazarsfeld and Frank Stanton (eds.), *Communications Research, 1948–49*, Harper & Brothers, 1949, p. 158.
[22] See Eunice Cooper and Marie Jahoda, "The Evasion of Propaganda: How Prejudiced People Respond to Anti-Prejudice Propaganda," *Journal of Psychology*, January, 1947, p. 17.

persons were able to reinterpret the cartoon to identify the congressman with whatever seemed bad to them.[23] In some instances prejudiced persons evaded the meaning of the cartoons by finding the message too difficult; they seemed simply not to understand what it meant.

Because of the difficulties of reaching the audience for whom the propaganda would be most useful and because of the ease with which its points can be evaded, we cannot rely heavily on propaganda as a strategy. To be sure, a cartoon series is a brief stimulus. We do not know what the effects of an intensive, long-run propaganda campaign would be. A movie is a stronger stimulus, on the effects of which we have some information. There have been many studies to test the effects of movies on attitudes; and, partly on the basis of the results obtained, in recent years several movies (some propagandistically and others educationally inclined) have aimed at the reduction of prejudice. Our knowledge of the total long-run effects of movies, however, is still far from adequate because of several methodological weaknesses. Sampling problems have not been given much attention (school populations are so readily available to the researcher); the distortions in evidence produced by the "before-after" type of experiment (the kind that has been most often used) have not been adequately explored; and the relation between pencil-and-paper responses and other kinds of behavior has usually not been studied.

Despite these weaknesses it seems fair to say that many movies do have a measurable effect on attitudes as recorded in verbal tests. L. L. Thurstone and his associates made the first extensive studies in this field. For example, The Birth of a Nation, which pictured Negroes in a very unfavorable light, was shown to 434 students, grades six to twelve, in a small Illinois town containing no Negroes. The students were tested for their attitudes toward Negroes both before and after seeing the film. In the latter test they were, on the average, 1.48 scale points (on an eleven-point scale) more unfavorable to the Negro. After five months they were retested, and it was found that 62 percent of the change that had been attributed to the film remained.[24] We do not know if the nonverbal behavior of the children was affected, whether the new attitudes actually reshaped later experiences, whether giving them a test before the picture "sensitzed" them to prejudice so that the movie was a different experience from what it would have been had they not been pretested. We do not know if the test five months after the movie was a stimulus that renewed memory associations with the movie and

[23] Ibid., pp. 19–20.
[24] See Ruth C. Peterson and L. L. Thurstone, Motion Pictures and the Social Attitudes of Children, The Macmillan Company, 1933, pp. 35–38. Merton has made a pointed criticism of the weaknesses of this kind of measurement in "Fact and Factitiousness in Ethnic Opinionnaires," American Sociological Review, February, 1940, pp. 13–28.

the earlier test—and so was inevitably highly correlated with that test. Tentatively, however, we may say that movies do seem to influence attitudes of prejudice.

Some of the studies of the Thurstone group measured the effects of antiprejudice movies. The pro-Chinese film *Son of the Gods* was shown to 182 children, and their average attitude shift in the direction favorable to Chinese was 1.22 points (a statistically significant shift).

Raths and Trager studied the effects of the movie *Crossfire* on the attitudes of high-school students in a middle-sized Ohio city. The film describes the murder of a Jew and the tracking down and killing of the murderer, and points up strongly the evils of prejudice. One day before seeing the film and two days afterward, the students were given a questionnaire asking what proportion of their friends they believed disliked various groups. (By asking opinions about their friends' prejudices, Raths and Trager hoped that the students would express themselves more freely, without having to worry about guilt feelings, and yet would reveal their own attitudes. This correlation has been demonstrated in other studies.) These were the estimates of the proportions who disliked:

	Before	After
Members of other religions	24	15
Negroes	34	21
Jews	20	15

The differences were not large, but they were consistent and in the expected direction. No "backfire" effects were noted.[25]

Within the limits set by the present evidence it seems unwise to say either that antiprejudice propaganda is powerless or that it can, by itself, effect extensive changes. Flowerman points out these minimum requirements if it is to have any influence: The propaganda must be received under favorable conditions, so that it will be looked at or heard; it must attract and hold the attention of the propagandee; it must be enjoyed, not bring pain; it must be understood, not evaded by misunderstanding.[26] None of these is easy to accomplish. Propaganda is usually seen only by the already converted; if prejudiced persons happen to see it, they usually turn away; if they don't turn away, they often find it painful (because of guilt feelings or a sense of hostility); and if they don't find it painful, they frequently misunderstand its point. It is with the mildly prejudiced and the neutral, particularly with children, that these disadvantages are at a minimum.

Williams summarizes a number of principles that help one to understand the effectiveness of antiprejudice propaganda:

[25] Louis E. Raths and Frank N. Trager, "Public Opinion and *Crossfire*," *Journal of Educational Sociology*, February, 1948, pp. 345–368.
[26] S. H. Flowerman, *op. cit.*, pp. 434–435.

In intergroup relations, as in many others, word-of-mouth propaganda, especially that which appears spontaneous and informal, is more effective than visual or formal propaganda in influencing attitudes and behavior. . . .

In intergroup relations, as in many others, propaganda which makes an "emotional" (value-oriented) appeal is likely to be more effective than that which is restricted to factual appeal.

But this plausible assertion may be countered with the view that such appeals arouse relatively uncontrolled emotions which are not likely to lead to tolerant or humane behavior. It certainly appears that there are sufficient dangers in strongly emotional propaganda to warrant careful testing with different types of audiences. . . .

In intergroup relations, as in many others, the "propaganda of the deed" is especially likely to have effects upon attitudes and behavior. . . .

Propaganda which appeals to minority rights on the basis of the group's achievements tends beyond a certain point to arouse insecurity-hostility in the dominant group by stressing group differences and competitive success.

This hypothesis implies that appeals which suggest a status-threat to prejudiced groups are to be avoided. . . .

It is dangerous technique to employ mass propaganda emphasizing "rising tides of prejudice" as a means intended to mobilize defenders of minority rights and good intergroup relations. Such propaganda is likely to have a boomerang effect upon slightly prejudiced or wavering elements: it creates the presumption of group support for hostile actions.[27]

How Should Prejudiced Propaganda Be Handled? Wise strategy needs to understand not only the possible uses of propaganda but also the techniques that are most effective in counteracting prejudiced propaganda. In recent years there has been a vigorous debate, and sharp differences in action, between those who believed that "hatemongers" should be exposed, ridiculed, and made to stand in the glare of public attention and those who contended that they should be disregarded and offset by positive action. Experience with the problem of counteracting rumors during World War II added strength to the arguments of those who held that hate propaganda should often be ignored, so far as a direct response is concerned. By "ignored" we do not mean "overlooked." One must pay careful attention to destructive rumors or propaganda against minorities; but they should usually be opposed indirectly, by positive action, not directly, by exposing them and pointing out their errors. If one tries to prove a rumor wrong by repeating it and then describing the truth, many of his listeners may hear only the rumor, if that is all they want to hear. Thus one does the opposite of what he intends. If one ignores the rumor but supplies truthful information, those who have not heard the rumor may to some degree be "vaccinated" against it. When the British movie production of *Oliver Twist*

---

[27] Robin Williams, Jr., *op. cit.*, pp. 66–67.

was brought to the United States, several groups opposed its release because one of the "villains" of the story is a Jew. They thought seeing the movie might increase anti-Semitism. Their opposition made it more likely that the movie would be widely attended and that those with mild or latent anti-Semitism would be sensitized to the unfavorable Jewish character. Such people would not, however, have read or understood the arguments of those who opposed the characterization. Violent anti-Semites, moreover, were given the rare opportunity of parading as defenders of civil liberties—upholding free speech and opposing censorship.

There is a danger that proponents of the "silent" treatment of hate propaganda will drift into a position of no treatment. If one ignores not only the hatemonger but the problem he represents, the silent strategy will fail completely. McWilliams draws a distinction "between unorganized and organized defamation; between individual slander and conspiracies to violate the rights of citizens of the United States."[28] Organized conspiracy against the rights of a minority requires vigorous positive action. This may spotlight the conspirators; but they should be spotlighted as slanderers, vandals, and murderers—if that is what they are. They would usually not be portrayed as attackers of particular minorities and their strength should not be exaggerated by well-meaning opponents who want to arouse their neighbors to action. If they are shown to be very powerful, some individuals who feel a need to be identified with power and are filled with free-floating hostility may be drawn to the movement. ". . . Making a group appear weaker or more hated than it actually is, is an incitement to sadism. For every sympathizer gained by the defensive propaganda of ill-advised apologists ten harpies are stimulated to attack it and a dozen average people are inclined to despise it."[29]

Those who oppose giving publicity to the hatemonger and those who support it both give illustrations to demonstrate the effectiveness of their approach. The need is to see that there are very different ways of bringing public attention to an issue. Many professional haters are sensationalists who thrive best on exposure if it brings them into a conflict situation where they can pose as martyrs and heroes to their followers and potential followers. Fineberg describes the reception of a rabble rouser, whom he calls "the Kodfish," in a situation where he was noisily opposed:

In Boston on July 13, 1947, he spoke in the morning at a church to an audience of less than forty people. Such a weak showing must certainly have

---

[28] Carey McWilliams, A Mask for Privilege: Anti-Semitism in America, Little, Brown & Company, 1948, p. 251.
[29] S. A. Fineberg, Punishment Without Crime, Doubleday & Company, Inc., 1949, p. 120.

pained the Kodfish and disappointed his followers. That afternoon he was scheduled to hold a meeting in Old Town Hall where, had the event gone unpublicized, his followers would certainly have been lost in a sea of empty seats. In this instance, however, the Kodfish had the help of enthusiastic alarm criers. A group of leftists, including officials of the Communist party of Massachusetts, arranged a counterdemonstration for the afternoon occasion. The hall was packed by leftists, fellow travelers, silly young people, and downright fools. They kept up a clamor that prevented the Kodfish from being heard. The police sided with the Kodfish, since it was the opposition that was out of order. It was not they but the Kodfish who had rented the hall. The Kodfish enjoyed it immensely. He hugged an American flag for the benefit of press photographers and cheered the crowd on with "Louder, you dopes!" The net result of this whole misbegotten adventure was that the Kodfish got a hundred thousand dollars of free publicity throughout the nation. . . .

You cannot educate the public by massing crowds at a rabble-rouser's meeting any more than you can end illiteracy by demonstrating at the doors of illiterates. To pass out at his door handbills denouncing the demagogue to the persons who enter his hall is like standing at the door of a synagogue and handing anti-Semitic literature to the worshippers.[30]

Such publicity was clearly unwise antiprejudice strategy. Exposure of the hatemonger, however, need not be of this awkward variety. Negative opposition that emphasizes a conflict situation and arouses emotions is likely to be ineffective, but McWilliams cites another variety that had different results:

Obviously some types of opposition are catnip to a man like [Gerald L. K.] Smith, but he certainly does not relish all types of opposition. On July 20, 1945, ten thousand citizens of Los Angeles attended a rally at the Olympic Auditorium to protest Smith's activities in Southern California. The meeting was called for the same evening on which Smith was scheduled to address a rally at the Shrine Auditorium. With a miserable attendance at his meeting, Smith spent most of the evening denouncing the individuals who had organized the counterdemonstration. Obviously this was one type of opposition he did not relish.[31]

The Los Angeles rally did not interfere with Smith directly; it did not make him the center of attention, it publicized the problem but not the man; it did not confuse the issue by opposing his right to speak. In this question of strategy, as in all others, a flexible policy is necessary, a policy that varies with the situations and persons involved. These rules may help to guide one's decisions:

1. Do not overlook the importance of hate propaganda.

2. Where possible, deal with it indirectly, by furnishing true information, by developing people immune to prejudice, not by direct attack.

[30] *Ibid.*, pp. 130–131.
[31] Carey McWilliams, *op. cit.*, p. 258.

3. Do not exaggerate the extent of the rabble-rouser's following or the strength of his influence.

4. Stress the injury his actions bring to the whole society, not to some "poor, oppressed minority."

CONTACT

In recent years, in developing strategies for changing prejudiced persons, no factor has received more attention than the effects of contact between members of different groups. It is often said, "If there were only more contact, if people only knew each other better, there would be less prejudice." Yet it is also known that prejudice frequently seems most intense in areas where there is most contact. How effective is contact with members of a minority group in changing attitudes and behavior toward that group? This question requires careful study, for there are many factors that affect the results. It is related to broader questions of international relations, where it is also frequently assumed that contact *per se* will improve understanding.

In interviews with nineteen Indian and other Asian students in the United States, Lambert and Bressler discovered that contact—even when it was courteous and helpful—did not automatically create favorable attitudes. The effects depended not so much on the personalities of the individuals involved as on the total structure of the situation, especially the status conceptions of the two countries. Whenever the Indian students encountered certain "sensitive areas" that involved implications of low status for their country—even if the Americans involved were disagreeing with the implications—they tended to respond negatively. Ideas that Indians are basically inferior, that India is an undesirable place to live, that India's social structure is undemocratic, inhumane, unenlightened, and the like, created negative responses when they were discussed. From the results of their interviews, Lambert and Bressler formulate several tentative propositions concerning the effects of contact with a foreign society:

1. Attitude formation differs significantly as between nationals from countries of "high status" and of "low status.". . .

2. Visitors with low status form their attitudes toward the United States largely as the end product of a "looking-glass" process based on the visitor's perceptions of American attitudes to his country and by extension to him.

3. In normal social interaction Americans will inadvertently allude to certain national status-rooted "sensitive areas," the mere mention of which even in a neutral or favorable context will cause the visitor to perceive hostility, a condition which will in turn evoke reactive hostility.

4. The identification of personal and experiential variables associated with desirable attitude formation but not specific to culture is likely to be of little diagnostic value for visitors of low status. Individual variation will be restricted by a historically and culturally imposed set of perceptions;

carefully manipulated circumscribed experiences will nevertheless include some abrasion of sensitive areas.[32]

It is not known how widely these same principles may apply to contacts between persons of different status from the same society; but evidence from some of the studies discussed below suggests that they may have wide applicability. At the least, it supports the proposition that contact does not necessarily lead to improved understanding. The task is to discover the conditions under which attitude change does take place. Converging evidence from the sociology of knowledge and the psychology of perception shows that experience is situational; what we see or hear, what we believe, how we think are all dependent upon the total situation in which these actions occur and upon our total mental context. We never see an isolated unit of human behavior; we see behavior in a larger situation through the perspectives we have acquired. Most of us can look a "fact" squarely in the face and, if we already have a frame of reference that involves it, turn it completely around. In a study of the rumor process, Allport and Postman described to various persons a picture containing a Negro and a white man with a razor in his hand. After the description, each person was asked to tell all he could about the picture to a third person, the third to a fourth, and the fourth to a fifth. In over half of the experiments, the razor was reported to be in the Negro's hand; and in several the Negro was threatening the white man with it.[33]

The ambiguity of many aspects of human behavior makes it possible to perceive that behavior in a way which harmonizes with an already established belief. When a person greets you warmly, it is possible that he is a true friend, but it is also possible that he is busily engaged in opposing you behind your back and wants to prevent you from suspecting it. If you already "know" which is true, you will interpret his behavior in that light.

A strong prejudice can have an almost paralyzing effect on observation and rational judgment. Whatever the behavior involved, it can be "explained" by the prejudice. Even opposite kinds of behavior are used as "proof" of a supposed trait, as is well illustrated in the statement of General J. L. DeWitt concerning the evacuation of the Japanese from the west coast in 1942:

In the war in which we are now engaged racial affinities are not severed by migration. The Japanese race is an enemy race and while many second and third generation Japanese born on United States soil, possessed of United States citizenship, have become "Americanized," the racial strains

---

[32] Richard D. Lambert and Marvin Bressler, "The Sensitive-Area Complex: A Contribution to the Theory of Guided Culture Contact," *American Journal of Sociology*, May, 1955, p. 584.

[33] See Theodore M. Newcomb and E. L. Hartley (eds.), *Readings in Social Psychology*, Henry Holt and Company, 1947, pp. 547–558.

are undiluted. . . . That Japan is allied with Germany and Italy in this struggle is no ground for assuming that any Japanese, barred from assimilation by convention as he is, though born and raised in the United States, will not turn against this nation when the final test of loyalty comes. It, therefore, follows that along the vital Pacific Coast over 112,000 potential enemies of Japanese extraction, are at large today. There are indications that these are organized and ready for concerted action at a favorable opportunity. The very fact that no sabotage has taken place to date is a disturbing and confirming indication that such action will be taken.[34]

The conclusion, the attitude, is found in the first part of this statement. The last sentence shows how any fact, even one that to the naïve observer must seem to be an exact refutation of the conclusion, can be made to seem to support it. Contact with the members of a minority group can scarcely weaken a prejudice that is so impervious to experience. Behavior that does not harmonize with the prejudice may not be seen at all; our perceptions are made selective and partial by the prejudice itself, which thus becomes self-confirmatory. Or if the behavior is seen, it is treated as an "exception": "Some of my best friends are Jews," but—they're not typical. Marrow and French showed that factory experience with "old" (over thirty!) women workers who showed high production records and low rates of absenteeism did not change the stereotypes of management and foreladies that the "old" workers were liabilities.[35] Human beings have an enormous ability to resist the meaning of facts that contradict their already established beliefs.

Contact with the members of a minority group may, of course, be of an unpleasant variety. This is sometimes held to be a cause of prejudice—the attitude is simply a generalization from a few unfortunate experiences. Allport and Kramer found that individuals who were most prejudiced against Negroes and Jews also had the most unfavorable memories of contact with them. These memories may indeed help to explain not the prejudice itself, but why it is stronger than the average. Unpleasant experience with individual members of a minority group, however, can scarcely be the cause of prejudice, because that experience would not be generalized to the whole minority group unless the prejudice were already there. Moreover, only 20.5 percent of the respondents in the Allport-Kramer study who were in the quartile showing most prejudice to the Negro reported any unpleasant memories. The prejudice of the other 79.5 percent in this top quartile of prejudiced persons cannot be accounted for by nonexistent contacts. Finally, we cannot be certain that persons who report more unpleasant memories

---

[34] From United States Army Western Defense Command and Fourth Army, *Japanese in the United States, Final Report: Japanese Evacuation from the West Coast*, Government Printing Office, 1943, pp. 33–34.

[35] See A. J. Marrow and J. R. P. French, "Changing a Stereotype in Industry," *Journal of Social Issues*, December, 1945, pp. 33–37.

of contact with members of minority groups have actually had more such contacts. Memory is selective; they may remember (or invent) such contacts *because* they already have a stronger than average prejudice.[36]

Thus we find that prejudice is sometimes explained as a result of the *lack* of contact with members of a minority group and sometimes explained as the result of the *presence* of such contact. Both theories explain only surface relationships. Hartley found that a prejudiced person would exclude the nonexistent Danireans because "I don't know anything about them." The nonprejudiced person would accept them for the same reason. As Newcomb points out, Turks are strangers to most Americans, Negroes are not, yet both occupy positions low on the scale of social distance. Newcomb found, in a study of attitudes toward Spain, that pro-Loyalist Bennington College students and pro-Franco Catholic University students were equally well supplied with "facts," and those with the more intense attitudes had the best information, even on such neutral facts as names and dates. People with attitudes tend to acquire information in their service.[37]

Such observations do not mean, however, that one's experiences with individual members of a minority group have no effect on his attitudes toward that group. Prejudice does not entirely precede and coerce the interpretation of experience. Unpleasant contacts probably increase the strength of prejudice. Oppositely, *certain kinds of contact* are effective in reducing the strength of a tradition of prejudice. We are learning to examine contact against a background of knowledge of the total personality of the individuals involved, the leadership, the power structure, the place of one attitude in a total value system.[38]

Allport has prepared a valuable outline of the variables that we must have in mind in any analysis of the effects of contact between members of different groups.

Quantitative aspects of contact:
   a. Frequency
   b. Duration
   c. Number of persons involved
   d. Variety
Status aspects of contact:
   a. Minority member has inferior status.
   b. Minority member has equal status.

[36] See Gordon Allport and B. M. Kramer, "Some Roots of Prejudice," *Journal of Psychology,* July, 1946, pp. 17–18.

[37] Theodore M. Newcomb, "Autistic Hostility and Social Reality," *Human Relations,* 1947, vol. 1, pp. 69–86; and Theodore M. Newcomb, "The Influence of Attitude Climate upon Some Determinants of Information," *Journal of Abnormal and Social Psychology,* July, 1946, pp. 291–302.

[38] See Ronald Lippitt and Marian Radke, "New Trends in the Investigation of Prejudice," *Annals of the American Academy of Political and Social Science,* March, 1946, pp. 167–176.

c. Minority member has superior status.

d. Not only may the individuals encountered vary thus in status; but the group as a whole may have relatively high status (e.g., Jews) or relatively low status (e.g., Negroes).

Role aspects of contact:

a. Is the relationship one of competitive or cooperative activity?

b. Is there a superordinate or subordinate role relation involved; e.g., master-servant, employer-employee, teacher-pupil?

Social atmosphere surrounding the contact:

a. Is segregation prevalent, or is egalitarianism expected?

b. Is the contact voluntary or involuntary?

c. Is the contact "real" or "artificial"?

d. Is the contact perceived in terms of intergroup relations or not perceived as such?

e. Is the contact regarded as "typical" or as "exceptional"?

f. Is the contact regarded as important and intimate, or as trivial and transient?

Personality of the individual experiencing the contact:

a. Is his initial prejudice level high, low, medium?

b. Is his prejudice of a surface, conforming type, or is it deeply rooted in his character structure?

c. Has he basic security in his own life, or is he fearful and suspicious?

d. What is his previous experience with the group in question, and what is the strength of his present stereotypes?

e. What are his age and general education level?

f. Many other personality factors may influence the effect of contact.

Areas of contact:

a. Casual

b. Residential

c. Occupational

d. Recreational

e. Religious

f. Civic and fraternal

g. Political

h. Goodwill intergroup activities

Even this list of variables that enter into the problem of contact is not exhaustive. It does, however, indicate the complexity of the problem we face.[39]

Effects of Equal-Status Contact. The influence that has been most carefully explored in recent research is the degree of status equality or status difference among the participants in intergroup relations. Allport and Kramer contend that close, involuntary, tension-laden contact is likely to increase prejudice, but that contacts between individuals having the same or a nearly equal social and economic status reduce prejudice. They found that persons who were less prejudiced against Jews and Negroes reported having had more "equal-status" contacts

[39] Gordon Allport, *The Nature of Prejudice*, Addison-Wesley, Reading, Mass., 1954, pp. 262–263.

with them than did the more prejudiced persons. Of 69 people who said they knew no Negro with an educational status equal to theirs, 61 were in the more prejudiced half. Those authors believe that "equal-status" contacts help to prevent or weaken stereotypes; one is less suggestible to the "lazy and shiftless" picture of the Negro if he knows Negroes who contradict that stereotype.[40] It can scarcely be said that they have confirmed their hypothesis. We noted above how resistant stereotypes are to evidence; and equal-status contacts are perhaps more likely to involve competition (as they themselves note, when they indicate that contact between persons of equally *deprived* status increases prejudice). In his study of an interracial adolescent group, Irwin Katz found that, despite its liberal and friendly atmosphere, there was the danger that competition for leadership and the other inevitable group tensions—having nothing to do with race—would be seen as racial in origin and meaning.[41] This is especially likely to happen when the surrounding environment in which the equal-status contact occurs does not support the implications of equality. We should note, moreover, that it is impossible to tell from the evidence of the Allport-Kramer study whether the relationship they observe is a cause or an effect; it may be that persons with less prejudice both look for more equal-status contacts and interpret what contacts they do have in that way more often.

Nevertheless, Allport and Kramer's attempt to differentiate the kinds of contact that are more likely to reduce prejudice is very useful. Some other studies have concluded that what might be called "stereotype-breaking contacts" reduce prejudice. MacKenzie found that among university students, when several variables that might influence the results were controlled, knowing professional Negroes and having a variety of contacts with Negroes produced statistically significantly more favorable attitudes.[42]

A somewhat unusual kind of stereotype-breaking contact was experienced by many soldiers of the United States Army in Europe during the winter and spring of 1945. In March and April, 1945, several Negro rifle platoons were attached to white companies. Two months later, the Information and Education Division of the Army Service Forces conducted a survey to discover the response of white officers and men to this change. Five trained interviewers asked all available white company grade officers and a representative sample of platoon sergeants in twenty-four companies that contained Negro platoons:

[40] Gordon Allport and B. M. Kramer, *op. cit.*, pp. 22–25.

[41] Irwin Katz, *Conflict and Harmony in an Adolescent Interracial Group*, New York University Press, 1955.

[42] Barbara K. MacKenzie, "The Importance of Contact in Determining Attitudes Toward Negroes," *Journal of Abnormal and Social Psychology*, October, 1948, pp. 417–441.

"Has your feeling changed since having served in the same unit with colored soldiers?"

Response	White Officers (Percent)	White Noncoms (Percent)
No, my feeling is the same.	16	21
Yes, have become more favorable.	77	77
No answer.	7	2

Eighty-four percent of the white officers and 81 percent of the white noncoms answered "Very well" (the most favorable answer on a four-point scale) to the question, "How well did the colored soldiers in this company perform in combat?"[43]

In a survey of 1710 enlisted men on the same subject, the Information and Education Division discovered results that may well support the hypothesis that prejudice is reduced by contact. The men were asked, "Some Army divisions have companies which include Negro and white platoons. How would you feel about it if your outfit was set up something like that?"[44]

	Percentage of white enlisted men answering: "Would dislike it very much."
Cross section of field force units which do not have colored platoons in white companies (1450 cases)	62
Men in same division, but not in same regiment as colored troops (112 cases)	24
Men in same regiment, but not in same company as colored troops (68 cases)	20
Men in company with a Negro platoon (80 cases)	7

There may have been a slight selectivity involved among the Negro troops in these platoons. They were all volunteers; 22 percent, as contrasted with 18 percent for all Negro troops in the ETO, were high-school graduates; and there were other slight differences. These certainly do not account, however, for the marked differences in attitude between white soldiers who had served in mixed units and those who had not.

Several years ago F. T. Smith carried out an interesting study of the effects of contact on prejudice. He invited 354 students at Teachers College, Columbia, to spend two week ends in tours of Harlem. Forty-six accepted the invitation. Previous to that he had given all of them a group of tests to measure their attitudes toward Negroes. He found

[43] "Opinions About Negro Infantry Platoons in White Companies of Seven Divisions," by the Information and Education Division, United States War Department, reprinted in Theodore M. Newcomb and E. L. Hartley (eds.), *op. cit.*, pp. 542–546.

[44] *Ibid.*, p. 545. It is interesting to note that the Army decided not to publish these data during the war, "feeling that this experiment was not representative and fearing possible unfortunate repercussions. . . ." See President's Committee on Equality of Treatment and Opportunity in the Armed Services, *Freedom to Serve*, Government Printing Office, 1950, p. 53.

that the forty-six who volunteered for the tours had a wide range of attitudes. His control group was another forty-six from the original number who had been matched with the volunteers for attitude scores, age, sex, and geographical origin. The experimental group spent two week ends visiting with Negroes, seeing a great deal of the community, and hearing lectures. Their program was well planned and enjoyable. Ten days later the original 354 students were retested, and it was found that the control group had not changed but that the experimental group had much more favorable attitudes toward Negroes (the standard error was 7.36). A comparison was also made between the forty-six who took the tours and twenty-three who had originally volunteered to go but had been unable to join the group. This comparison was an attempt to test the question of selectivity. If the forty-six volunteers were persons already predisposed to adopt more favorable attitudes, then one may not conclude that the experiences of friendly and pleasant contact with Negroes and a Negro community produced the observed result. The twenty-three who had volunteered to go and then were unable to go, however, showed no change in attitude on the second test. Smith concluded that this ruled out the likelihood of selectivity. Several months later a majority of the experimental group were retested, and most of them continued to show significantly more favorable attitudes.[45]

This study tends to support the hypothesis that pleasant, sterotype-breaking contacts reduce prejudice. Two methodological difficulties, however, prevent it from being definitive. We have a measure of only the changes in responses to verbal tests, not of other behavioral changes; and the problem of self-selection is not entirely solved. To be sure, twenty-three persons who had originally volunteered to join the tours, but who for various reasons were unable to go, did not change; but their "inability" to go in itself may have represented more rigid attitudes in some instances. They may have found reasons for not being able to go because as the time approached they felt unwilling to subject their prejudices to such a test. In a survey type of design, one never knows whether such a spurious variable might not have affected the results.

There are other studies which more nearly solve the problems of self-selection and limitation to verbal behavior. Deutsch and Collins report the interesting results of different patterns of interracial housing. In two housing projects Negro and white families were assigned to apartment buildings regardless of race (the integrated pattern); in two other projects different buildings or different parts of the project were used for Negroes and whites (the segregated biracial pattern). Inter-

[45] F. T. Smith, *An Experiment in Modifying Attitudes Toward the Negro*, Teachers College, Columbia University, 1943.

views with the housewives in these situations revealed that the integrated pattern reduced prejudice much more sharply.

TABLE 22.1.   Nature of Housewives' Relations with Negro People in the Project[46]

	Integrated		Segregated	
	Koaltown	Sacktown	Bakerville	Frankville
Friendly relations	60%	69%	6%	4%
Accommodative relations	24	14	5	1
Mixed relations	7	11	2	3
No relations	5	0	87	88
Bad relations	4	6	0	4
Total cases	102	90	100	101

In the integrated projects only one-third as many women spontaneously expressed prejudice in the interviews as in the segregated projects (13 percent and 10 percent compared with 36 percent and 31 percent). About two housewives want to be friendly for one who wants to avoid contact with Negroes in the integrated arrangement; but in the segregated situation there are ten who want to avoid contact for one who wishes to be friendly. It is particularly interesting to know that 67 percent and 71 percent of the women in the integrated projects have positive attitudes toward the interracial aspects of their communities, many having come to like it more; but in the segregated projects most of the women liked the interracial aspects less than they did before they moved into the community.[47]

The effects of such types of contact would not be the same, of course, on persons whose prejudices were so strong that they would not join an interracial community; but among families who did accept housing on a biracial basis persons assigned (without regard to their original attitudes, for the type of arrangement was an administrative decision, not an individual choice) to integrated patterns discovered that their prejudices were very inadequate modes of adjustment. Those in the segregated projects had no such opportunity for revising their attitudes.

In a follow-up study of the effects of interracial housing, Wilner, Walkley, and Cook derived evidence that supports many of the findings of Deutsch and Collins, but also introduces some qualifications. In interracial neighborhoods, "the assumption that segregation is right and inevitable is challenged" by the authority of the community project; and the white resident is confronted with the problem of reconciling the evidence concerning the behavior of actual minority-group members with his stereotypes. Thus contact weakens the supports of prejudice. There are, however, a number of complicating factors:

[46] Morton Deutsch and Mary E. Collins, *Interracial Housing*, University of Minnesota Press, 1951, p. 79.
[47] *Ibid.*, chap. 11.

the relation between *proximity and contact*, and the relation of each to
attitude change; the influence of initial attitude on the outcome of the
contact experience; the influence of social pressures—or social climate
regarding intergroup association—on the outcome of the contact experience, and the ways in which the social climate is established and manifested;
the effect that different proportions of minority group members has on the
experience associated with proximity or contact; and the dimensions of
attitude which undergo change.[48]

The four housing projects studied by Wilner, Walkley, and Cook had
a small proportion of Negro residents; none had more than 10 percent.
In all four projects, the extent of contact with Negroes was closely
tied to proximity. The contacts that occurred were not simply un-
planned conversation, but neighborly activities of various kinds—borrowing and lending, helping during sickness, visiting. The white women
who lived near Negroes perceived, more often than those living farther
away, that the opinions of other white women in the project were
favorable to interracial contact. They also held Negroes in higher esteem
and were more likely to believe that the races were equal in such things
as cleanliness, manners, intelligence, ambition. Although the attitudes
toward Negroes which the white women had when they entered the
project affected their responses, they were less important than proximity
in the project. "Whether we consider the initially more favorable or
initially less favorable respondents, those who live near Negroes in a
project are more likely than those living farther away to report neighborly
contact, to anticipate that white friends in the project will approve of
such contact, to have high esteem for the Negroes in the project, to
approve of the biracial aspect of the project, and to have a favorable
attitude toward Negroes in general."[49]

Without discussing various refinements in the two studies of interracial housing, we can perhaps indicate their major finding by means
of Table 22.2.

TABLE 22.2.   Percentage Sharing at Least One Kind of Neighborly Activity[50]

Two Integrated Projects of the Deutsch and Collins Study (192)	Integrated Projects of the Wilner, Walkley, and Cook Study (91)	Two Segregated Projects of the Deutsch and Collins Study (201)	Segregated Areas of the Wilner, Walkley and Cook Study (234)
54%	50%	3%	· 5%

We cannot conclude from such data that a decrease in prejudice is
the inevitable result of equal-status contact. There is still need for a

[48] Daniel M. Wilner, Rosabelle Price Walkley, Stuart W. Cook, *Human Relations
in Interracial Housing: A Study of the Contact Hypothesis*, copyright 1955, University
of Minnesota, p. 6.

[49] *Ibid.*, p. 95.

[50] *Ibid.*, p. 143.

great deal of research to explore the effects of specific conditions. For example, when are there too few members of the minority to break stereotypes (a few can be regarded as "exceptions"), and when are there so many that a sense of threat to status develops? What is the impact of personal insecurity in response to equal-status contact? In a study of 106 white boys from New York, most of them from the lower class, who attended a four-week interracial camp, Mussen found that 28 boys became significantly less prejudiced against Negroes, but 27 boys became significantly more prejudiced. Those whose prejudice increased were those who had more aggressive feelings and needs and greater need to defy authority, felt themselves victims of aggression, felt that others were not kind and helpful, were more dissatisfied with the camp.[51] This might not have been the result had there been a different proportion of Negro campers (they made up about half the group), had the camp lasted longer, or had various other conditions prevailed. The study points up clearly, however, the need for careful attention to the complexity of the results of equal-status contact.

One can perhaps sum up the present knowledge about the effects of contact on prejudice in these four related propositions:

1. Incidental, involuntary, tension-laden contact is likely to increase prejudice.

2. Pleasant, equal-status contact that makes it unnecessary for the individuals to cross barriers of class, occupational, and educational differences as well as differences in symbolic (nonfunctional) group membership represented by such symbols as "race" is likely to reduce prejudice.

3. Stereotype-breaking contacts that show minority-group members in roles not usually associated with them reduce prejudice. It must be added, however, that many people have little capacity for experiencing the members of minority groups as individuals; their stereotypes easily persist in the face of contrary evidence.

4. Contacts that bring people of minority and majority groups together in functionally important activities reduce prejudice. This is largely an illustration of point 3. When white soldiers find Negroes fighting side by side with them, they are more likely to see them as fellow soldiers, less likely to see them as "Negroes." When white seamen shipped with Negroes, their prejudice declined, even though mixed crews were compulsory union policy, not freely chosen situations.

EDUCATION

Most Americans have a good deal of faith in the power of education (often accompanied by an anti-intellectualism that exalts the "practical"

---

[51] Paul H. Mussen, "Some Personality and Social Factors Related to Changes in Children's Attitudes Toward Negroes," *Journal of Abnormal and Social Psychology*, July, 1950, pp. 423–441.

man, the man of "action," and disdains the expert and intellectual).
It is frequently declared that education (empirically shading off into
programs of contact, exhortation, and propaganda) could reduce prejudice sharply. Discussion of the value of education frequently fails to
distinguish two levels of argument. One proposition might state: *If we
were able to have* a scientifically adequate and nation-wide program of
education in majority-minority relations, prejudice would be reduced.
But the more frequent declaration is simply: Education can reduce
prejudice.

The latter statement pays no attention to the obstacles in the way of
getting an adequate program of education in intergroup relations. There
is no likelihood that schools, communities, adult education programs,
and the like will suddenly develop adequate and widespread studies
of prejudice, for they are part of the total society, largely reflecting its
traditions and power structure—and its prejudices. Merton writes:

> The appeal to "education" as cure-all for the most varied social problems
> is rooted deep in the mores of America. Yet it is nonetheless illusory for all
> that. For how would this program of racial education proceed? Who is to do
> the educating? The teachers in our communities? But, in some measure
> like many other Americans, the teachers share the same prejudices they are
> urged to combat. And when they don't, aren't they being asked to serve
> as conscientious martyrs in the cause of educational utopianism? How long
> the tenure of an elementary school teacher in Alabama or Mississippi or
> Georgia who attempted meticulously to disabuse his young pupils of the
> racial beliefs they acquired at home? Education may serve as an operational
> adjunct but not as the chief basis for any but excruciatingly slow change in
> the prevailing patterns of race relations.[52]

Effective strategy demands that we distinguish these two problems
in developing a program of education to reduce prejudice and discrimination:

What are the barriers to setting up such a program? Who will oppose
it, and how may their opposition be reduced? Who will finance it?

After one has set up the program, what techniques are most effective
in changing the attitudes of different groups of people?

We perhaps know more about the second problem than about the
first. One is justified in a modest optimism that when a program has
been set in motion, particularly with children, it can be fairly effective
in preventing or reducing prejudices. But under what circumstances will
an educational program be set in motion? The school system is perhaps
the area of least resistance. Despite the close connection between formal
education and the rest of society, there is a measure of autonomy in the
school system. This autonomy is easy to exaggerate, but it is a strategic
error to dismiss it too lightly, as Merton perhaps does in the quotation

[52] Robert Merton, *Social Theory and Social Structure*, p. 183.

above. Those professionally connected with education, because of their functional role in society, are somewhat more concerned with the pursuit of truth, a little less likely to be provincial. In our society they are also inclined to be somewhat more liberal than the average, although some are timid and others are emotionally identified with the upper classes. Those who control the school systems, moreover (the school boards and trustees), are not inclined to determine every action of the teacher, because they are to some degree dependent on him as the conserver and pursuer of knowledge, as the expert and trainer of experts, who, despite the disdain in which he is held by the "practical" man, is indispensable to our society. An ideology of freedom for the teacher is also involved. The result is that the teacher has some autonomy, some power to attack prejudice if he wants to—and some teachers want to.

This modest resource has been only slightly used, although efforts to increase intergroup education have been greatly expanded in recent years. Educational institutions themselves still contain a great deal of discrimination. Few teachers are trained specifically in the analysis of majority-minority relations; seldom is a teacher chosen from a minority group; and few courses treat their material in a way designed to reduce prejudice.

In the last several years some labor unions have proved to be organizations in which the barriers to educational programs concerned with reducing prejudice have not been too high. The efforts of such unions as the United Automobile Workers and the National Maritime Union show that progressive leadership can take advantage of the functional unity of the members of various minorities and the majority to reduce prejudice.

What Kind of Education?   The first job of strategy, in making use of education, is to determine the areas—such as schools and unions— where programs are most likely to be adopted. But that is only half the job. Having cleared the ground, one must decide how to proceed. Is it a matter simply of transferring information, for knowledge leads to action? Or are the ways in which the knowledge is acquired, the total situation of learning, as crucial as the facts themselves? More and more we see that the latter is the case. How one learns an idea is important to his mastery of it, to his acceptance of the idea as valid, and to the likelihood of his acting upon it. The total personality is involved in the learning process. One type of situation may stimulate a personality "set" that makes a person unable to acquire new knowledge. Or knowledge may be "learned" on a symbolic level but be so compartmentalized that it does not affect other ideas or overt behavior.

Education and reëducation must be guided by the fact that prejudice is frequently "used" by the person; it is functional (not necessarily effective, be it noted). It will be "unlearned" only when the entanglements with the total personality are loosened by the nature of the learning situation, by the reduction of tension and the elimination of any threats to one's ego. At the very least, when one gives up a prejudice he admits an error—and most of us are reluctant to do this. Fineberg illustrates the way in which sensitivity to the feelings of the prejudiced person contributes to reëducation:

Mrs. Tenney, a brilliant young woman active in community relations work, had remained silent at a dinner party when a woman whom she and her husband were meeting for the first time spoke of members of another race as mentally inferior to white people. It was an incidental remark. The conversation quickly drifted to something else.

Driving home, Mr. Tenney said to his wife, "I was watching you when Mrs. Hammond put in that nasty crack about colored people. Why didn't you speak up?"

"And spoil the chance of ever changing her mind?" asked Mrs. Tenney. "Had I spoken up, Mrs. Hammond would have defended her opinion. If I had won the argument, it would have been to my satisfaction but not to hers. She would have disliked me for embarrassing her among her new acquaintances. She looks like a sincere, capable person. I think we can change her views on several things. When she made that quip about racial inferiority, I put it down in my little mental notebook. And what do you think I did while we were getting our wraps?"

Mr. Tenney smiled. "Knowing you as I do, I'd say you made a date with Mrs. Hammond."

"Right! When we know each other better, I'll introduce Mrs. Hammond to Dr. Sanford and to Mrs. Taylor, who are as intelligent as any white person she ever met. One of these days Mrs. Hammond will be working for our Interracial Commission. That's not a promise, John, but I'll try hard."

In less than two months Mrs. Hammond had abandoned the notion of racial inferiority without having been forced to recant, apologize, or even to recall the invidious remark. Her mentor, Mrs. Tenney, is one of the few—there are altogether too few—who is concerned enough about racial and religious prejudice and astute enough to undertake the re-education of mildly prejudiced individuals.[53]

Kurt Lewin was undoubtedly the leader in "action research"—the analysis of the conditions under which change in human relations takes place and the study of the processes by which it occurs. Out of his studies has come the emphasis on the involvement of the total personality in the educative process. This has led to the development of several principles: Create an informal situation; see education as a group process, not simply an individual process; maximize the individual's sense of participation in getting new ideas. Some of these principles are developed in the following quotation from Lewin:

[53] S. A. Fineberg, op. cit., pp. 183–184.

Only by anchoring his own conduct in something as large, substantial, and superindividual as the culture of a group can the individual stabilize his new beliefs sufficiently to keep them immune from the day-by-day fluctuations of moods and influences to which he, as an individual, is subject. . . .

Changes in sentiments do not necessarily follow changes in cognitive structure. . . . The sentiments of the individual toward a group are determined less by his knowledge about that group than by the sentiments prevalent in the social atmosphere which surrounds him. . . .

Re-education is frequently in danger of reaching only the official system of values, the level of verbal expression and not of conduct; it may result in merely heightening the discrepancy between the super-ego (the way I ought to feel) and the ego (the way I really feel), and thus give the individual a bad conscience. Such a discrepancy leads to a state of high emotional tension but seldom to correct conduct. It may postpone transgressions but is likely to make transgressions more violent when they occur. . . .

Much stress is laid on the creation, as part of the re-educative process, of an atmosphere of freedom and spontaneity. Voluntary attendance, informality of meetings, freedom of expression in voicing grievances, emotional security, and avoidance of pressure, all include this element.

. . . If re-education means the establishment of a new super-ego, it necessarily follows that the objective sought will not be reached so long as the new set of values is not experienced by the individual as something freely chosen.

One of the outstanding means used today for bringing about acceptance in re-education . . . is the establishment of what is called an "in-group," i.e., a group in which the members feel belongingness. . . . Allport formulates this point as a general principle of teaching people when he says, "It is an axiom that people cannot be taught who feel that they are at the same time being attacked." . . .

When re-education involves the relinquishment of standards which are contrary to the standards of society at large (as in the case of delinquency, minority prejudices, alcoholism), the feeling of group belongingness seems to be greatly heightened if the members feel free to express openly the very sentiments which are to be dislodged through re-education. . . . Expression of prejudice against minorities or the breaking of rules of parliamentary procedures may in themselves be contrary to the desired goal. Yet a feeling of complete freedom and a heightened group identification are frequently more important at a particular stage of re-education than learning not to break specific rules.

This principle of in-grouping makes understandable why complete acceptance of previously rejected facts can be achieved best through the discovery of these facts by the group members themselves. Then, and frequently only then, do the facts become really *their* facts (as against other people's facts). An individual will believe facts he himself has discovered in the same way he believes in himself or in his group.[54]

[54] Kurt Lewin, *Resolving Social Conflicts*, Harper & Brothers, 1948, pp. 59–68.

We are not expounding a general theory of education. We are concerned with the learning process in an area where emotional attitudes and stereotypes affect observation and the acceptance of evidence. The degree to which different principles are involved in different learning situations is a problem that cannot be examined here.

Several recent developments in the use of education to reduce prejudice have shown an awareness of the two problems discussed above—the obstacles to setting up an educational program and the analysis of the kinds of program that are most effective. We can mention only four briefly: school programs, community self-surveys, workcamps, and workshops.

Intergroup Education in the Schools. Discussions of the meaning and value of democracy were greatly stimulated by World War II and by the publication of such works as Gunnar Myrdal's An American Dilemma. One of the consequences of this soul searching was the rapid development of courses in intergroup education. Elementary schools, high schools, teachers' colleges, and liberal arts colleges gave increasing attention to the study of interracial, intercultural, interfaith, and international questions. The merits of various approaches to intergroup relations were examined. Among these are (1) the "incidental" approach, which makes use of a specific, immediate interest to provide a point of departure for intercultural teaching; (2) the "pervasive" approach, which emphasizes human relations throughout the social studies and, to some extent, in other fields; and (3) the "specific units of study" approach, which focuses attention on significant topics, issues, or problems.[55]

Many of the larger public-school systems of the United States prepared courses of study in intergroup relations. Among the cities which have introduced such programs are Pittsburgh; San Francisco; Chicago; Detroit; Springfield, Massachusetts; Lansing, Michigan; Santa Barbara, California; and Atlantic City. Teachers and administrators are aided in their efforts by advice and guidance from specialized national agencies such as the Department of Supervision and Curriculum Development of the National Education Association, and the Commission on the Defense of Democracy of the NEA.[56] These organizations make recom-

[55] Hilda Taba and William Van Til, Democratic Human Relations: Promising Practices in Intergroup and Intercultural Education, National Education Association, 1945, p. 87.

[56] Among the volumes published in the Bureau for Intercultural Education Series are William Vickery and S. G. Cole, Intercultural Education in American Schools, Harper & Brothers, 1944; Hortense Powdermaker, Probing Our Prejudices, Harper & Brothers, 1944; Spencer Brown, They See for Themselves, Harper & Brothers, 1945; Theodore Brameld, Minority Problems in the Public Schools, Harper & Brothers, 1946. Included in the publications sponsored by the NEA are Hilda Taba and William Van Til, op. cit.; We, The Children, 1945; and More—than Tolerance, 1946. Both the Bureau for Intercultural Education and the American Council on Race Relations, which formerly produced materials in this field, have been discontinued. Research and instruction in intergroup education are currently sponsored by

mendations on such matters as the proper training of teachers, the establishment of coöperative relations between the school and the community, the construction of a curriculum, and textbooks and reports.[57] On the college level, important studies, reports, and reprints have been provided by such organizations as the American Council on Education and the Anti-Defamation League of B'nai B'rith.[58]

Variations in intergroup education programs are numerous. Subjects dealt with include the nature of prejudice, the people (racial and ethnic groups) in a city or state, the fundamental concepts of democracy, the strengths and weaknesses of democracy, the contributions of various nationalities to the development of the United States, discrimination in employment, the program of the United Nations, etc. Pedagogical techniques include fact-finding, discussions, documentary plays, lectures, motion pictures, etc. In some cities, notably Springfield, Massachusetts, the program has been extended to the community. The purposes of the Springfield adult program are to interpret the public-school effort to parents and to the adult community, to develop an interest on the part of adults in communal affairs, and to initiate action toward correcting some of the existing undemocratic community practices. Attempts to achieve these purposes are being made through the use of newspapers and radio to arouse interest in the program; public forums on controversial subjects; film forums dealing with such subjects as housing, municipal government, racial, religious, and economic minorities; nonpartisan political meetings in public-school buildings; the investigation, with the coöperation of the Council of Social Agencies, of the conditions of domestic workers; the investigation of the social and economic conditions of the Negro population in Springfield; the use of the School Placement Bureau to break down discrimination in employment; realistic discussions of social, economic, and political problems in adult evening classes.[59]

Several obstacles and weaknesses have become apparent in the short history of deliberately planned intergroup education. One fault on the part of many administrators is the segregation of teachers on racial or ethnic lines. Intergroup instruction is distorted if minority groups are not represented on the teaching staff. There have, however, been some

---

the following, and other, institutions: University of Chicago (Committee on Education, Training, and Research in Race Relations); Teachers College, Columbia University (Intergroup Relations Program); Fisk University (Race Relations Department); New York University (Research Center for Human Relations); University of Pennsylvania (Albert Greenfield Institute of Human Relations).

[57] R. M. MacIver, op. cit., p. 211.

[58] Lloyd A. Cook (ed.), College Programs in Intergroup Relations, American Council on Education, 1950; Arnold Forster, A Measure of Freedom (An Anti-Defamation League Report), Doubleday & Company, Inc., 1950; Lloyd A. Cook and Elaine Cook, Intergroup Education, McGraw-Hill Book Company, 1954.

[59] Alice L. Halligan, "A Community's Total War Against Prejudice," Journal of Educational Sociology, February, 1943.

notable changes in recent years. Hundreds of Negro teachers in the North and border areas now teach interracial classes; and, in higher education, over a hundred Negroes are regular members of so-called "white" faculties.

A second type of difficulty in the new field of intergroup education lies in the attitudes of teachers. Intergroup education has no possibility of being effective unless those who are charged with carrying it out are competent and sympathetic. Routine performance of an assigned program accomplishes little or nothing. Subtle or obviously prejudiced remarks or acts on the part of the teacher outside the program itself may more than offset that which is included in formal instruction. Many pupils come from homes where prejudice is strong. If the teacher also harbors prejudice, the results of intergroup education are likely to be negligible. A few school systems, of which Springfield, Massachusetts, is an example, now include interest and skill in intergroup relations among the criteria used in the selection of new teachers.

Recent studies indicate that the imparting of specific information about minority groups does not materially alter attitudes toward members of those groups. This is not to say that transmitting such information has no value, but simply that its usefulness in producing more favorable attitudes toward "out-groups" is less great than many professional educators have believed. About all that can be claimed for purely factual instruction is that "it tends to mitigate some of the more extreme expressions of prejudice and that, where there is any readiness to receive it, it provides some protection against the mob-raising appeals to which ignorance is exposed. . . . Greater knowledge may not seriously change our evaluations, since the latter are so dependent on our prior indoctrinations and since our interests as well as our indoctrinations are constantly at work suggesting appropriate imputations of motive such as will reconcile them with whatever facts we may recognize or admit."[60] The alert and sympathetic teacher's task, as MacIver points out, is to dispel the sense of cultural barriers between group and group. "The exclusiveness of the group must be broken by an educational process that integrates it within a more inclusive group. Prejudice is the expression of alienation and only the experience of the greater community can establish the bond of membership above the division of groups. The prejudiced person must learn to feel that the object of his prejudice also 'belongs.' "[61]

In short, knowledge may be helpful but its acquisition does not automatically produce understanding and appreciation. For effective action the main attack must be made on basic and often emotionally held attitudes rather than on opinions.

[60] R. M. MacIver, op. cit., pp. 222, 223. Chap. 5 of this work, "The Educational Front," is excellent.
[61] Ibid., p. 224.

MacIver's cogent conclusions on the nature and consequences of prejudice and discrimination and the purposes of intergroup education may be summarized as follows:

1. The acquisition of prejudice begins at an early age, and therefore the counteracting of prejudice should begin with very young children.

2. Since the impact of social prejudice is continuous, counterindoctrination cannot be limited to any age period.

3. Counterindoctrination calls for great skill and persistence. "Education should be concerned not so much to show the contributions and the qualities of particular groups as to impart a sense of the greater common heritage, the transcending common interest, so that the concept of what is 'ours' becomes inclusive, not divisive."

4. Accurate information about minority groups is not very effective. Intergroup education must relate the facts to the values and interests of all groups alike.

5. The type of prejudice which is derived more from the frustrations or maladjustments suffered by individuals early in life than from general social conditioning yields, if at all, to more specialized treatment. For the second type, effective counterindoctrination is indicated.[62]

We cannot analyze further the many school programs concerned with questions of prejudice but will summarize some of the general principles that guide their development.[63] These principles are well stated by Krech and Crutchfield: (1) "The over-all content of the child's education must be carefully synchronized with the objective of teaching for democracy." One course, three times a week, is not enough. What readings are used in literature courses? How are minorities handled in studies of history? (2) "The educational program must be carried out under appropriate general conditions." Nonprejudice can be taught only with difficulty in a school that exhibits prejudice—that practices segregation or employs no teachers from minority groups or turns intergroup education over to teachers who are themselves prejudiced. (3) "A school program, insofar as possible, must enlist the support of the children's parents." This is often a precondition for setting up a program; but even more, it is a necessity for effective work. An adult education program and the use of parents in planning the work in the school can reduce the likelihood that the child will have undone at home what is being done at school. (4) "Specific 'intercultural' education must avoid emphasizing or creating differences." To have each child do something supposedly typical of his group may strengthen stereotypes and encourage the im-

[62] Ibid., pp. 263–265.

[63] See, in addition to the works already mentioned, C. L. Chatto and Alice L. Halligan, Story of the Springfield Plan, Barnes & Noble, Inc., 1945; N. D. Myers, Education for Cultural Unity, California Elementary School Principals' Association, 1946; G. M. Wiley, Education for Unity, State Education Department of New York, 1947; Committee on the Study of Teaching Materials in Intergroup Relations, Intergroup Relations in Teaching Materials, American Council on Education, 1949.

pression that other groups are "queer." ". . . To ask a Mexican child to report on the culture of the Chinese and a Protestant child on the religious practices of the Jews would be more effective and more genuine 'intercultural' education than to ask the Mexican child to come dressed to school in *his* quaint dress or to ask the Chinese child to tell the other children how to prepare 'bird's nest soup.'" (5) "Education for democracy must include training in the techniques of democracy." The ability to work with others, to practice group decision-making and other democratic processes is essential to the reduction of intergroup hostility.[64]

Most of these principles apply to education on the college level; but there has been little study of the degree to which college experiences harmonize with them. Many general college programs are concerned with studying the democratic tradition and strengthening belief in the democratic heritage, but few have the specific aim of reducing prejudice, nor have they used techniques appropriate to that end. There are, of course, hundreds of courses in departments of sociology, anthropology, and social psychology concerned with minorities and prejudice. These are usually elective courses, dealing with self-selected students; and they therefore face different problems in reducing prejudice. The changing of attitudes, if it is recognized at all, is only one aim, although that hope probably lies behind most of the courses. Since the reducing of prejudice is not explicitly sought—and methods appropriate to that aim are not adopted—one does not judge the effectiveness of a course by measuring changes in attitude. Nevertheless, many such measurements have been made, and they reveal that one of the results—perhaps a by-product—of the study of minorities and prejudice may be an increase in tolerance. The results, however, are far from definite. About a third of the studies have found that the course of study produced no change of attitude.[65] The studies vary widely, moreover, in the degree to which they have controlled variables and eliminated the effects of self-selection which so often distort the analysis of human behavior. But their total weight gives some support to the hypothesis that knowledge may reduce prejudice. It can undermine the rationalizations of prejudiced persons and make their attitudes seem less respectable. But the ambiguity of the results prevents any easy optimism. Courses that are not concerned with the functions of prejudice to the individual and are not designed to deal with them are unlikely to be very effective. Although facts may be stubborn things to the scientist, to most people they are extremely pliable compared with the stubborn quality of their stereotypes.

[64] David Krech and Richard Crutchfield, *op. cit.*, pp. 519–523.
[65] A summary of the results of many of these studies is found in Arnold M. Rose and Caroline Rose, *America Divided: Minority Group Relations in the United States*, Alfred A. Knopf, Inc., 1948, p. 282.

Related to the question of the efficacy of intergroup education as such is the question of the general influence of college education on antiminority sentiment. Some light is thrown on this problem by one of the Elmo Roper studies. Differences in the attitudes of freshmen and seniors do not indicate that the college exerts a clear-cut liberalizing influence in the matter of religious prejudice specifically.[66] The differences are small and are not always in the same direction. There seems to be a slight tendency toward lesser prejudice by seniors on a majority of the questions, but not on the fraternity issue and the college admissions question. The differences on such social-distance questions as "Would prefer not to work side by side with Jews," "Would prefer not to have Jews as guests in my home," "Would prefer not to have Jews move into my neighborhood" are small, but "college students in general have so little resistance to associating with Jews (except for intermarriage) that there is not much left to be done by the colleges in this respect."[67]

If the differences in attitudes between college freshmen and seniors are not marked, the same cannot be said for college seniors and adults. College seniors differ greatly both from adults generally and from adults with a college education. The seniors are less anti-Semitic on all questions, and the differences are so large that they can hardly be accounted for by any changes that may gave occurred in the total population in the period between the two studies (1948 to 1949). There is some question about the interpretation of the differences. If there is a definite trend in the direction of less anti-Semitism among college students, it may be due more either to modern primary and secondary education or to general culture factors outside the school.[68]

A final citation on the subject of instruction in intergroup relations in the colleges is a question asked in the *Fortune* survey of higher education. The question and the answers were:[69]

Should colleges have classes that take up the subject of racial and religious prejudice or should racial and religious prejudice be discussed in classes only when students ask about it, or would it be better not to discuss it at all?

	Total	Protestants	Catholics	Jews
Have classes	38%	38%	34%	56%
Discuss only when students ask	22	24	22	14
Have no discussion at all	23	22	28	22
Express no opinion	17	16	16	8

Altogether, we can speak only tentatively about the strategic value of intergroup education in our schools; but the evidence at hand seems

[66] Elmo Roper, "A Study of Anti-Minority Sentiment in Colleges," unpublished, 1949. See Arnold Forster, *op. cit.*, pp. 161–165.

[67] Arnold Forster, *op. cit.*, p. 161.

[68] Elmo Roper, *op. cit.* See Arnold Forster, *op. cit.*, pp. 164–165.

[69] See Elmo Roper, "The Fortune Survey on Higher Education," *Fortune*, September, 1949, p. 9.

to indicate that well-designed educational plans, when integrated with other programs, can occupy an important, if not fundamental, place in the campaign to reduce prejudice. Present uncertainty concerning the efficacy of programs of intergroup education makes it important that serious efforts be made to check the results. So far little has been done in this direction. High praise, strong sponsorship, and adequate finances are not sufficient. If such experiments do not have continuous skilled appraisal, they may be futile or actually detrimental to the end they seek to achieve.[70]

Community Self-Surveys. Surveys of majority-minority relations within a community are not new. For example, in 1922 the Chicago Commission on Race Relations published the famous volume, *The Negro in Chicago*, which was an extensive survey of all phases of Negro life in Chicago. Information of this kind may be gathered primarily for scientific and academic purposes, or the sponsors may hope that it will furnish the basis for effective community action in improving intergroup relations. Seldom has the latter goal been realized. Few people have seen the studies; those who are most prejudiced have been least likely to see them; and even if they are acquainted with their findings, they have shown little concern for changing their actions. Extensive surveys by "outsiders" may be of scientific value and of some indirect use in improving the situation, but they have not proved to be effective strategy.

In recent years a different type of survey has been developed (by Charles S. Johnson, Ronald Lippitt, Marian Radke, Isidor Chein, and others) that is concerned specifically with questions of strategy. How can the process of finding out about majority-minority relations in a community be carried on in such a way as to make action most likely? The community self-survey is offered as an answer to this question. It is based on many of the principles of learning that we have discussed— the maximization of participation in getting the facts, the creation of a group learning situation, and others.

A self-survey is initiated by a group of people who are eager to reduce prejudice and discrimination in a community; but they seek to bring in as sponsors a wide circle of other people whose opinions and recommendations carry weight in the community. Too often, the findings of surveys are dismissed as the ideas of "crackpots" or at best of "outsiders." Self-surveys prevent this charge. They may have among their sponsors persons who are themselves prejudiced or discriminatory, persons who have been drawn in by a desire to be civic-minded, or by the accident of group representation, or even by a desire to keep unpleasant facts from appearing or seeing that the survey doesn't "get out of hand." The project brings people of different racial, national, and religious groups together. The fact that they are working together on a common task

[70] R. M. MacIver, *op. cit.*, p. 231.

affects their attitudes. They are more likely to accept data which they themselves have gathered, for the facts become *their* facts; their unity as a functional group obscures the ethnic lines that divide them; and the group factor—the development of in-group support to new ideas and feelings—also makes for acceptance.

Community self-surveys take every precaution to insure accuracy of the total picture. They usually avoid, however, singling out specific individuals, organizations, or businesses for unfavorable publicity. This is not a strategy of force but one of persuasion. The findings of the survey are thoroughly discussed by all the participants, and a report is prepared to describe the results to the community. As John Haring points out, even prejudiced persons or those who would like to deny the facts of discrimination can scarcely oppose the data that they have helped to gather in a group to which they belong. With their information in hand, the participants in the self-survey work for appropriate community action to eliminate the discrimination they have revealed.[71]

The basic hypothesis of this kind of educational strategy is that a situation in which facts are discovered by the participants is more likely to lead to action than a situation where those who must change have been in no way involved in discovering the facts. Self-surveys rest upon the premise that belief in the American creed is widely shared but that its violation has often been overlooked because many people did not believe that discrimination existed, or they felt no sense of personal responsibility, or they saw no way in which they could take effective action.[72] If belief in equality of treatment is weak or if many people have consciously chosen discrimination because it is profitable, self-surveys are unlikely to be effective.

The value of the community self-survey has perhaps been exaggerated by some of its proponents. They still face the difficult problems of getting the coöperation of the very people who are most likely to be prejudiced and of following study with action. The evidence seems to show, however, that important changes can be brought about, at least in communities where discrimination results more from inertia than from functional importance. Such changes as a city ordinance for fair employment practices, the employment of Negroes as police, teachers, salesclerks, and nurses, the admission of Negro doctors and patients to community hospitals, the breaking of the segregation line in unions, and other changes have followed self-surveys.[73]

[71] John Haring, "Some Basic Principles of Self-Surveys," *Journal of Social Issues,* Spring, 1949, pp. 21–29.
[72] *Ibid.*
[73] See Claire Selltiz and Margot Haas Wormser (issue eds.), "Community Self-Surveys: An Approach to Social Change," *Journal of Social Issues,* Spring, 1949 (whole issue); R. C. Weaver, *Community Relations Manual,* American Council on Race Relations, 1945; A. Zander, *Centerville Studies Itself,* University of Michigan Press, 1941.

Workcamps. There are many intergroup educational aspects to the workcamps sponsored by the American Friends Service Committee and other groups. These bring together young people from many racial, religious, and national groups around a task that is not primarily concerned with majority-minority relations but often influences them indirectly in a marked way. The workcampers make a voluntary contribution to the program or facilities of some disadvantaged group. They help to build a new rural schoolhouse, or repair housing in a slum area, or add to the facilities of an agency serving minority groups. The actual physical work is intensive and continuous (often through a summer or more), but it is largely unskilled, so that the effects of the workcamp are small if measured in terms of the physical construction accomplished. The educational effects, however, are often strong. Three groups of people are affected by the workcamp: the campers themselves, the residents of the disadvantaged community in which they work, and the members of the dominant group in the area.

Workcampers are self-selected for a difficult job and so are likely to seem quite free of prejudice to begin with. Those who belong to the dominant group are frequently only superficially aware, however, of the depth of the problems that minority-group members have to deal with. By working with them around a common task, by living in their communities, by becoming acquainted with their leaders, the campers' knowledge is deepened. One college girl, engaged during the first day of a workcamp in helping to landscape the grounds of a Negro social service agency, crossed a class line quickly, in her understanding. She had probably never held a shovel before and the day was hot. After about an hour of ambitious if somewhat ineffective "shoveling," she leaned wearily upon her shovel and declared: "Those WPA jokes aren't funny any more!" She will probably never again be so ignorant of the life of the "common laborer" and of the work of most minority-group members.

The minority-group community in which the workcamp is located is also educated by its program. Reciprocal prejudices against the dominant group, the categorical judgments often made about all members of the majority are weakened by the work of people who are willing to give a good deal of time and energy (without pay—in fact, paying their own expenses) to assist in the improvement of some facility or program.

The interest of many members of the dominant community is frequently aroused by the activities of the workcamp. No one tells them that they have been indifferent, or perhaps active contributors, to an important problem in their city; but when they see or hear about the program of the workcamp, they often tell themselves that. In a middle-western city a few years ago the manager of a large department store was going out to the store's warehouse on some item of business. Across the street from the warehouse he saw a group of college-age young people—men and women, white and colored—cleaning the mortar from old bricks. His curiosity was aroused. He talked with them and discovered that they were members of an American Friends Service Committee workcamp that was assisting in the preparations for a new building for the city's Negro social service agency. He became interested in the program, and as a small contribution he invited the men to use the warehouse shower room after the day's work. He instructed the custodian of the warehouse to let them in each day and to get them soap— billing his personal account for its cost. By some mistake, the cost of the soap was included on the store's ledger; and at the next meeting of the store's directors, as the accounts were being studied, there appeared among the tens of thousands of dollars for this item and hundreds of dollars for that item the innocently conspicuous entry: "50¢ for soap, for Quakers." This incident, involving the interest of the manager in the workcamp, aroused the curiosity of other store officials and other leaders of the dominant community. Several became both active supporters of the work of the agency and concerned with problems of discrimination in their city.

Workcamps are modest programs reaching only a few people, but those who come in contact with them are likely, through the vivid knowledge they obtain, to be strongly influenced toward less prejudice and discrimination.[74]

Workshops. Since the end of World War II an increasing number of summer workshops in intergroup relations have been held. In April and May, 1957, the *Nairo Reporter* listed 66 workshops in twenty-five states for the summer of that year. Most of them were held on the campuses of colleges and universities, with the coöperation of the National Conference of Christians and Jews or the Anti-Defamation League. Among other sponsors were city community relations boards, the American Jewish Committee, the American Jewish Congress, and a number of colleges and universities.

The topics considered in summer workshops vary, but include such subjects as intergroup education, the social psychology of prejudice, problems of minority groups, sociometry and sociodrama, intergroup agencies, use of community resources, social scientific concepts of human relations, and the like. Perhaps the following statement from the workshop at Central Michigan College is representative of the range of interests:

The workshop is concerned with the elements of harmonious relations between racial, religious, nationality, and other groups, as well as with the means for developing such relations. The focus of attention is upon the problems of human relations peculiar to local situations, in the school or

[74] See J. Milton Yinger, "Breaking the Vicious Circle," *Common Ground*, Autumn, 1946, pp. 3–8.

the community, and upon programs for dealing with them. Principles of inter-cultural education and intergroup relations are applied to practical problems in teaching and community relationships.[75]

Workshops have averaged between thirty and forty students, with a range from seventeen to 150, and have varied in length from one day to a summer term of six weeks or more. Typically students from diverse racial and cultural groups are included in a workshop, and frequently several parts of the country are represented. Among the students are those who are seeking a general background of intercultural and intergroup education and those who need assistance on projects and activities in particular school and classroom situations. National organizations, such as those mentioned above, frequently contribute scholarships, offer staff personnel, supply films and pamphlets, and assist in arranging the programs. Graduate credit for participation in these workshops is given by colleges and universities according to the time involved.[76]

A different type of workshop was held in Washington, D.C., during July, 1951, under the auspices of CORE (Congress of Racial Equality) and the Fellowship of Reconciliation. Thirteen college students, living in the Annex of Inspiration House, stated their purpose as twofold: "(1) to do what we can to eliminate racial segregation and discrimination in Washington, D.C.; and (2) to study and apply the techniques of non-violent direct action for our own enlightenment and for use in our own communities in challenging existing racial or religious prejudices."[77] During their four weeks in Washington these students investigated segregation and discrimination in the Gem Theater, several restaurants, Hoover playground, and the Chickland Club in Capitol Heights, Maryland. Nonviolent action was employed in the group's attempts to bring about changes in racial policy. A permanent workshop operates along these lines in Washington during the year.

The effectiveness of workshops is seldom tested. Full measurement would require attention to changes in skill and desire to work in intergroup relations on the part of the participants, not simply to changes in attitude. Changes in skill and motivation are exceedingly difficult to measure, but there is at least a strong impression among participants and leaders of workshops that members return to their communities equipped with new ideas and techniques and with renewed enthusiasm for improving intergroup relations. Changes in attitudes are somewhat more readily measured. Levinson and Schermerhorn, for example, tested the 32 participants at the beginning and again at the end of a six-week workshop. Most of the members were low in prejudice to begin with, as measured by the E and F scales of the Berkeley studies. Nevertheless,

[75] *Nairo Reporter*, April, 1957, p. 2.
[76] "Summer Workshops for Teachers in Intergroup and Intercultural Education," Anti-Defamation League, 1950, mimeographed.
[77] "Summer Interracial Workshop Bulletin," July 6, 1951, p. 1, mimeographed.

there was a significant reduction in prejudice, especially among those who had relatively higher scores at the beginning.[78]

Workshops, as attempts to bridge the gap between knowledge and action, deserve careful study by the strategist. Their emphasis on participation in fact gathering and their own intergroup make-up help to create a strong influence on the members. Their greatest problems are to reach a wider group and to avoid the "fallacy of group soliloquies."

Personal Therapy

If prejudice and discrimination are frequently manifestations of personal insecurities or of a basic personality instability, then an effective program of strategy must be concerned with the reduction of emotional disturbances. The prevention and treatment of personality disorganization is a very large area which we can only touch upon; but we need to examine some of the general principles involved, as they refer to our problem. We need to avoid, as some specialists fail to do, exaggerating the effectiveness of personal therapy as a strategy. The authors of *The Authoritarian Personality* write, "The major emphasis should be placed, it seems, not upon discrimination against particular minority groups, but upon such phenomena as stereotypy, emotional coldness, identification with power, and general destructiveness."[79] Such a statement is the result of an inadequate theory of the causes of prejudice and discrimination. There are some situations, in the view of the present authors, in which personality factors are relatively unimportant, others in which they loom large; but more often the several factors are closely interlocked, and none should be chosen for "major emphasis."

Personal therapy is frequently most effective when the reduction of prejudice is simply a by-product of the larger goal of a stable personality. In this field, as in so many others, prevention is far more effective than cure. The creation of a society and interpersonal situations that make possible the maximum satisfactions of needs will reduce the likelihood of intergroup hostility. There is the danger in this strategy, as in education, of our adopting a "bootstrap" kind of thinking—asking unstable persons living in a prejudice-prone society to devise situations in which personal stability and tolerance prevail more widely. We have here no cure-all, but simply one approach, among many, that may contribute to the reduction of hostility. With this limitation in mind, we may say that anyone who contributes to the development of "an economy of abundance," to a political situation that gives each individual some sense of control over his government, to a satisfying recreational program, to the growth of less restrictive and frustrating personal relations, particu-

---

[78] D. J. Levinson and R. A. Schermerhorn, "Emotional-Attitudinal Effects of an Intergroup Relations Workshop on Its Members," *Journal of Psychology*, 1951, vol. 31, pp. 243–256.

[79] T. W. Adorno, et al., *op. cit.*, p. 973.

larly between parents and children—such a person is assisting, directly or indirectly, in the reduction of prejudice.[80]

Even an extensive program of prevention, however, would be inadequate. For a long time to come we need to be equally concerned with a program of cure—of treatment for insecure persons who use prejudice and discrimination as modes of adjustment to their insecurities. Techniques of therapy may concentrate primarily on the tendencies of the individual or on the situations which are activating those tendencies. The latter approach is too often disregarded by psychiatrists and others concerned with personality reorganization; yet to treat "society as the patient" is frequently a more effective approach than the intensive analysis of each individual (who, in any case, can be understood only by examining the situational factors as well as individual tendencies).[81]

In the treatment of "problem children" particularly—children who may exhibit prejudice among other manifestations of insecurity—a change in the situation around them is often far more effective than direct attention to their problems. Often, in fact, the child can be disregarded completely. James Plant reports the case of a rebellious, truculent boy, the second son in a professional family of insistent ambition. The boy had much less native ability than his brother, was having a difficult time in school, and seemed badly "maladjusted"—the kind of person who could develop vigorous prejudices. At home, the parents frequently make invidious comparisons of the younger boy with the older. When the problem was brought to a school clinic, the doctor might have made complete psychiatric examinations of both the parents and the children. Actually, he scarcely saw them; he examined the situation. The younger brother, and four other boys who were having academic difficulties, were given special school work. They did their geography by reporting about ships that had docked, their civics by visiting city hall. The boy's rebellion disappeared; he was now the one who had the interesting stories to tell at meals and became the subject of his father's anecdotes. A whole constellation of family problems disappeared as a result of an interesting outlet for the boy in school. "One is tempted to compare this sort of therapy where the psychiatrist did not see the boy until he was gaily moving along both at home and in school a year later, with the approach which would have crystallized all his defeat and resentments in order that he and the psychiatrist might laboriously, but finally in triumph, erode away the last vestige of the difficulty."[82]

When personal insecurities are more deeply set, the situational approach is less likely to be effective. The responses of the individual may

[80] See Scudder Mekeel, "Race Relations. Cultural Aids to Constructive Race Relations," *Mental Hygiene*, April, 1945, pp. 177–189.

[81] See L. K. Frank, *Society as the Patient*, Rutgers University Press, 1948.

[82] James Plant, *Personality and the Culture Pattern*, The Commonwealth Fund, 1937, pp. 37–38.

take on a rigidity that coerces the interpretation of every situation into the same mold. Alongside the therapeutic approaches that seek to modify the tension-laden situations, therefore, we need the direct treatment of unstable persons. This treatment can range from friendly counseling (simply listening, frequently) to intensive psychoanalysis.[83] Techniques that help an individual to face the causes of his hostility help to reduce its sharpness. Dorothy Baruch reports the case of a girl, Marjorie, who showed deep prejudice against Negro fellow students. Before a counselor, Marjorie unfolded the story of her life, exposing the causes of her insecurities and hostilities. Her father had died when she was a young girl. Her mother had been very domineering, but the girl had never admitted to herself that her mother was anything but perfect. The mother frustrated her at every turn, interfered with her love affairs, tried to make every decision for her. Once this came out to the counselor, Marjorie began to lose the need to be "mad at her teachers" all the while and the compulsion to hate Negroes. She fell in love. Even her relationships with her mother became less tense, for Marjorie understood her mother better and felt no need for a forced love.[84]

Group Therapy

Individual therapy is certainly a strategy that any complete program must use, particularly in the treatment of persons with deep-seated prejudices. It suffers, however, from two disadvantages. It is costly in time and energy; "we cannot psychoanalyze everybody." And it is inadequate to cut the supports of prejudice that derive from groups.

Group therapy tries to overcome these disadvantages. It is an attempt to produce changes in the personality by using the knowledge of the effects of groups on attitudes and behavior. The activities of therapeutic groups may range all the way from doing simple rhythmic actions together—a major step for some isolated schizophrenics—to enacting a plot that contains the anxiety-laden problem, to discussions in which fellow "patients" get insight into their own problems by studying those of another. Group therapy has a long implicit history in religion, in drama, in other group practices; but as an explicit method of treatment for disorganized persons it is quite new, and as a strategy in the reduction of prejudice it is even newer.

The underlying theory is that the feeling of belongingness of group members breaks down their feelings of isolation, facilitates interaction among them, encourages role-taking and self-knowledge. The sharing of

---

[83] There is a vast literature on problems of therapy, much of it relevant to the reduction of prejudice, even though it does not directly deal with it. See, for example, Fritz Redl and David Wineman, *Children Who Hate*, The Free Press, 1951; and Bruno Bettleheim, *Truants from Life*, The Free Press, 1955.

[84] See Dorothy W. Baruch, *The Glass House of Prejudice*, William Morrow & Co., Inc., 1946, pp. 160–165.

symptoms and problems with others brings a sense of security and a lowering of guilt tensions—"I'm not the only one who faces this difficulty." The therapist attempts to create a situation that is thoroughly permissive and informal. Individuals are allowed to express their feelings of hostility freely, for self-discovery can scarcely occur in situations that require inhibition and concealment.

Group therapy is closely related to the approach to education that we have discussed above. It is based on the same conception of change as a group process. The sense of participation makes the problem one's own problem. Lewin describes a number of studies which examine this underlying principle that group decision is effective in social change. In one study the comparative effectiveness of lecture and discussion methods in persuading mothers to use more milk for their children was tested. Three groups (from six to nine members) were lectured to, three groups discussed the question. They all had the same leader and received the same information. The discussion process achieved far greater results; about three times as many mothers increased the use of milk (as measured one week, two weeks, and four weeks later).[85]

Ronald Lippitt and his associates, in a series of studies, compared the effects of democratic and autocratic leadership on the behavior of ten- and eleven-year-old children. In the autocratic group, the children were told what to do, they were given no overall perspective of what they were doing (making masks), and the praise and criticism of the leader were given arbitrarily, with no objective reasons. In the democratic group all policies were determined by the members, the whole process was explained and technical help offered, alternatives were suggested, members chose freely what to do and with whom to work, praise and criticism were objective. These differences in group atmosphere had very different effects on the interaction of the children and on their relations with the adult leader. There was far more hostile domination of one child over another in the autocratic group, more demands for attention, more hostile criticism. On the other hand, the children were more submissive toward the leader in the autocratic group. Since there was no chance of becoming a leader, they expressed far less individuality. A scapegoat situation developed, in which the children, unable to resist the demands of the adult, attacked one of the other children.[86]

The kind of principle of group process represented by the two studies just mentioned is basic to the attempts to reduce intergroup hostility by group therapy. Morris and Natalie Haimowitz report the effects of about thirty-five hours of group therapy in small groups with twenty-

[85] See Kurt Lewin, "Group Decision and Social Change," in Theodore M. Newcomb and E. L. Hartley (eds.), op. cit., pp. 330–344.

[86] For a summary of several papers on this question, see Ronald Lippitt and Ralph H. White, "An Experimental Study of Leadership and Group Life," in Theodore M. Newcomb and E. L. Hartley (eds.), op. cit., pp. 315–330.

four persons. The individuals involved were from twenty-five to sixty years of age; they had a master's degree or its equivalent in psychology and three years of experience. Before and after the six-week period they were given the Bogardus social-distance test, the group being divided into "friendly" and "hostile" in their attitudes toward nineteen minorities on the basis of their willingness or unwillingness to admit members of the minorities to their clubs and neighborhoods (steps two and three on the scale), even if not to marriage (step one). The scores after the group therapy were significantly (at the 1 percent level) different from the scores before the therapy:

	Before	After
Friendly	7	13
Hostile	17	11

It is interesting to note that it was the mildly hostile, not the strongly hostile, who were most likely to change. Six of them moved into the friendly group, but only one strongly hostile person (out of nine) became mildly hostile. Four strongly hostile persons (and one mildly hostile) actually increased in prejudice during the sessions, apparently having been made more defensive about their attitudes by the experience.

The study gives tentative support, at least for the kind of people involved in the therapy, to the conclusion of the authors that

. . . with improved adjustment, hostility to minority groups declines. As the individual feels less threatened, he is less hostile in his reactions to the world. He becomes more able to cope with the source of his frustrations directly and effectively. There is less hostility to be canalized, and less displacement in the expression of whatever tensions do arise. . . . The experience of releasing feelings about their own personal problems, and developing ways of constructively dealing with the problems of life, resulted in a decrease in the amount of ethnic hostility with which they came to the therapy experience.[87]

One may wonder whether a social-distance scale is a valid measure of "ethnic hostility" and whether the changes in attitude persisted, but the study suggests an approach that a complete strategic plan will contain.

In an eight-hour course in race relations that he was giving to forty public officials in an eastern city, Gordon Allport employed some of the principles of group therapy with effective results. The course was compulsory for the officials and there was some resentment. The first several hours were filled with aggressive, hostile talk, aimed at minorities, the instructor, the press, parents, intellectuals, and others. One purpose

[87] Morris Haimowitz and Natalie Haimowitz, "Reducing Ethnic Hostility Through Psychotherapy," *Journal of Social Psychology*, May, 1950, pp. 235, 238.

of this talk seemed to be to test the teacher. It was thought that he might look down his nose at the group. There were attempts to protect status: Why do we need this course? We've never had any trouble with minorities. There was some guilt projection involved.

The permissive atmosphere of the group contributed to the effectiveness of the course. Allport believed that there may have been a "complacency shock"—having gone on uninhibitedly, one gets himself out on a limb, sees his own injustice and one-sidedness. There was satiation or fatigue—they became bored with complaining and were ready to listen to new ideas. Because of the completely free atmosphere of the group there was no need to rehearse covertly and to defend their old ideas. In the "griping" process some were able to restructure their old attitudes without loss of face.[88]

In sum, as we examine the strategies that seek to reduce prejudice and discrimination primarily by changing attitudes, we find an increasingly effective approach which, in conjunction with other strategies, can help to reduce intergroup hostility.

[88] See Gordon Allport, "Catharsis and the Reduction of Prejudice," *Journal of Social Issues*, December, 1945, pp. 3–10. See also S. R. Slavson, *An Introduction to Group Therapy*, The Commonwealth Fund, 1943; and Virginia M. Axline, "Play Therapy and Race Conflict in Young Children," *Journal of Abnormal and Social Psychology*, July, 1948, pp. 300–310.

CHAPTER 23

The Reduction of Prejudice and Discrimination: Strategies with Major Emphasis on Changing Situations

Because the causes of hostility between majority and minority groups are complex, only a multiple strategy can be effective. Programs that limit themselves solely to the effort to change the attitudes of prejudiced persons may find themselves with an ever recurring job because the situations which are producing the prejudices—or giving them opportunity to be translated into discriminations—persist. Strategies that are primarily concerned with changing the social institutions or the practices that encourage discrimination must also be employed. We are learning that it is frequently possible to prevent conflict or discrimination despite the existence of prejudices, and that such prevention helps to create a situation which, in the long run, will reduce prejudice.

In recent years, in fact, strategic efforts to improve intergroup relations have increasingly given attention to discrimination. Some students in the field have suggested that individual prejudice has little to do with intergroup relations, that these vary with changes in the social structure, not with changes in individual attitudes.[1] Although this is a valuable corrective to the overemphasis on the reduction of prejudice that characterized work in this field for so long (perhaps a manifestation of the individualistic and laissez-faire atmosphere in which the concepts were developed), it may swing the pendulum too far in the other direction. There are some situations in which attention to individual attitudes may be the most strategic approach. In general, these would be situa-

[1] See, for example, Arnold M. Rose, "Intergroup Relations vs. Prejudice," *Social Problems*, October, 1956, pp. 173–176.

tions where the effort to improve the status of disprivileged persons has little community backing, where law, tradition, and the stratification patterns firmly support discrimination. Even under more favorable circumstances, it is a mistake to disregard individual prejudices entirely. Major attention should often be given to discrimination, but to overlook hostile attitudes is to be blind to a possible stumbling block.

Nevertheless, the recent shift in emphasis is based on sound observation and theory. Many studies show that individual behavior can be modified by changes in the situation, independently of personality structure. Or, to put this in terms that we believe are theoretically more adequate, a very high proportion of persons have tendencies toward nondiscrimination that may be called out by strategic situational changes even though such tendencies normally are dormant. There are, in Merton's terms, many fair-weather liberals and illiberals. Group supports, legal sanctions, economic pressures, firm action on the part of leaders can create the kind of climate in which their nondiscriminatory tendencies bloom.

This statement concerning the influence of the situation in interaction with personal tendency is only illustrative of a principle that has far wider application than the field of intergroup relations. A long series of studies, many of them influenced by the concepts of Kurt Lewin, have shown that the way that workers will respond to changes in technology, housewives to appeals to change feeding practices with their children, boys to different leadership patterns in their clubs, and many other actions, can be predicted at useful levels of probability without any attention being given to individual personality make-up. Modes of communication, group process, status relationships are the focus of attention in this kind of research.

This principle is applied to intergroup relations in several of the propositions outlined by Dean and Rosen in their recent summary. For example: "Proposition 7: Conformity with the practices of segregation and discrimination is often quite unrelated to the intensity of prejudice in the individuals who conform." Southerners who come to New York use a variety of nonsegregated facilities because they are the established practices and are accepted by other users. "Proposition 8: Within wide limits, prejudiced persons will accept and participate in a thoroughly mixed and integrated setting if integrated patterns are established and accepted by other participants in that situation."[2]

Compromise Versus Contention

Does this emphasis on discrimination mean that the extent of opposition is unimportant in strategic considerations? In our judgment

[2] John P. Dean and Alex Rosen, A Manual of Intergroup Relations, University of Chicago Press, 1955, pp. 58–60.

it does not. It is an emphasis appropriate to the contemporary American scene, but not necessarily to all other situations. In facing problems of discrimination against members of minority groups, the wise strategist will try to decide to what degree the practices should be opposed directly and immediately, and to what degree they should be attacked indirectly by eroding away their supports. Enthusiastic supporters sometimes defend a particular approach as *the* strategy, as if a willingness to compromise or a flat refusal to compromise with discriminatory practices were wise in every situation. A skilled general knows when to retreat, when to consolidate, and when to advance. In intergroup relations, the problem is to determine when a vigorous program is likely to be successful *despite* the opposition it will arouse in some people, and when compromise is required *despite* the short-run sacrifice of some aspects of one's ultimate goal. It is scarcely necessary to note that the latter is more necessary when one has few allies, when prejudices are widespread, when the discriminatory practices are deeply embedded in the social structure. Sixty years ago Booker T. Washington became a great Negro leader by accepting the idea of segregation and yet insisting upon the larger unity of the whole community. We can be, he said to the whites, as separate as the fingers, but as united as the hand. Some opposed his strategy then, and many more oppose it today, perhaps forgetting the different circumstances in which he worked. Washington concentrated on self-improvement because he thought the lack of skills and self-discipline of many Negroes to be a major cause of their difficulties. By such tactics he certainly made no touchdowns; but perhaps he succeeded in holding the ball at a time when the opposition, had they been on the offensive, could have made many points. He helped to make interracial work respectable. His was a strategy of compromise, not of contention, in dealing with segregation.

When discriminatory practices are deeply entrenched, an attack, particularly from those who may be labeled "outsiders," may strengthen the hand of those who profit by the discrimination. Many a southern politician has proudly waved the criticisms of him that have come from the North and then asked his listeners whether they or the damyankees were going to elect their representatives. This illustration does not mean that all opposition must be indigenous, but only that some kinds of opposition from the outside are ineffective. It needs to be noted, of course, that who is an outsider depends on one's point of view. In a very real sense the whole nation—and the world—is directly concerned with an act of discrimination anywhere. Moreover, the claims that "outside" interference only makes matters worse are frequently belied by the facts. The public spotlight in court trials, for example, has led to greater justice for Negroes in the South. Unfortunately, the decision whether to oppose discrimination directly or to compromise in favor of modest gains is frequently based not on careful analysis of the strategic problems involved, but on temperamental factors. Since most people like to avoid trouble and prefer to accept an undesirable situation rather than arouse hostility in an attempt to change it, there is a far greater likelihood that too much compromise will be made than that too little will be offered.

When, during World War II, the New York Stage Door Canteen accepted all servicemen on an equal basis, the directors were often told that their policy would not work, that it would increase interracial friction and prejudice rather than reducing it. But in whom, asks Margaret Halsey, do we see this increase? Certainly the anger, hostility, and resentment of Negroes toward white people are reduced. The attitudes of strongly prejudiced people are probably not increased—although they may be made more articulate. And mildly prejudiced people—or the indifferent—may well be favorably affected by an interracial program in action. The New York canteen refused to compromise —and it worked. As Halsey says:

> Reluctance to stir up the emotions of the Negro-phobes is certainly a natural feeling and one that can readily be sympathized with. But a democracy has the right to maintain itself as a democracy, and a nation sometimes has to discipline its citizens as a parent does a child, and for the same reason. Few parents or educators would maintain that when a child throws soup in his father's face, he must not be reprimanded or punished because that would only increase his desire to throw soup. Reprimanding or punishment will certainly provoke the young one into screaming that he is going to throw soup whenever he wants to. But a wise parent—however much he understands childish aggressions and sympathizes with childish difficulties in adjusting to the grown-up world—realizes that the child has to live in a world where the use of soup as a projectile is not well thought of.
>
> Giving full rein to a youngster's desire to fling soup not only impairs the quality of the family meals, but it is not, in the last analysis, a competent or effective way of preparing the child to be a happy adult. However formidable the screams and outcries of the strongly prejudiced, it does not seem—taking the long view—that we do either them or ourselves any service by permitting them to continue utterly undisturbed in their immature courses.[3]

The strategist must decide not only the degree of contention and the degree of compromise that he will use, but also the way in which his program will be carried on. There can be compromise that represents almost complete capitulation ("We mustn't raise that issue, for it will arouse too much hostility; we need a program of education"); and there can be compromise that keeps long-run goals clearly in mind while making necessary day-by-day adjustments. There can be contention that effectively prevents the very thing it is trying to do, by arous-

---

[3] Margaret Halsey, *Color Blind*, Simon and Schuster, Inc., 1946, pp. 78–79.

ing hostile opposition; and there can be contention that destroys a discriminatory pattern. Ineffective contention is often the kind that attacks individuals, that blames them for their discriminations, rather than trying to understand them. It is usually necessary to secure the coöperation of the discriminator in changing an unhappy situation. This is not likely to be accomplished by exposing him to ridicule, attacking him as a person, and generally threatening his security. Opposition to discriminators is very different from opposition to discrimination. Fineberg illustrates the point well:

In a suburban town the young secretary of an organization established to create better relationships between racial and religious groups discovered that a local Y.M.C.A. did not admit Negroes to membership. Although Negroes were not denied use of the facilities of the institution, it had been customary to enroll only white members. The zealous, well-intentioned but inexperienced young woman called upon officials of the Y.M.C.A. and demanded that they abandon the discriminatory practice. Finding them unwilling to do so, she threatened to picket the building. When friends warned her to be more tactful, she called them "appeasers" and insisted on being "militant."

Her threats angered the Y.M.C.A. leaders, who thereupon became entirely hostile toward her organization. In addition she lost the co-operation of many who thereafter referred to her associates as a "radical bunch that believes in strong-arm methods."

What if that young woman had analyzed the situation and asked, "What is the underlying fault in the relationship of this institution toward Negroes?" She might well have decided that there was an attitude of benevolence on a basis of charity rather than equality. Her task then would have been to change that concept of the relationship. That change could be brought about much more readily by constructive, positive steps than by arguments of a vitriolic nature. Had Negro neighbors asked permission to donate a picture of George Washington Carver or some other outstanding Negro to the Y., that gift could hardly have been refused. The picture could have been hung in an appropriate place and the effect would have been the inclusion of a Negro among those whom the institution honored. Negroes could well, with little expense, have presented athletic equipment to the institution and in other ways gained recognition as benefactors rather than beneficiaries. After such steps as these, a request for membership would have been much more likely to receive favorable reception.[4]

A different approach from that of the young lady just described was taken by a group of students who were studying international relations in a summer seminar in Arizona. The group was made up of many nationalities and races and included one American Negro. One day they told the owner of a public dance hall that they would like to attend. He at first said yes; but at noon of the day selected he called to say that

[4] S. A. Fineberg, *Punishment Without Crime*, Doubleday & Company, Inc., 1949, pp. 45–46.

some of his best customers had told him they would never dance again if a Negro danced—and that there might be violence. The director of the group, the Negro, and two other students then went to see the owner. They reassured him that they respected his rights and did not want to injure his business. They asked him if there was anything he could suggest to solve the problem. Out of their discussion, it was decided that the seminar group could hire the hall one Saturday night. They advertised an interracial, international dance, with pictures of persons of all races on posters around the area. The charge was the same as usual. The crowd was the largest the owner had ever had and there were no incidents. The owner told the seminar that they were welcome, thereafter, at any time.

THE STRATEGY OF DESEGREGATION

The current desegregation process in the United States is essentially a strategy of contention. It challenges the institutional structures of segregation directly, and as we saw throughout Part II, there have been substantial results. There are a great many strategic lessons to be learned from a careful study of the desegregation controversy. Two related questions arise: What kinds of situations make pressure for desegregation wise strategy? Once a decision in favor of desegregation has been made, what specific steps will contribute to its accomplishment?

With regard to the first question, we believe that to make desegregation the primary focus of attention in all situations is unwise. We doubt that this would have been wise strategy in the United States in 1910 or that it is the way to attack apartheid in South Africa today. This is not to say that constant pressure for desegregation should not be a part of every strategic plan; but it is to suggest that it can be the major effort only under certain conditions. Without certain fundamental supporting processes in society, the effort to desegregate is likely to be ineffective. Perhaps this point can be illustrated by an examination of the important changes taking place in the southern region of the United States.

Ralph McGill has said that desegregation, insofar as it is a southern process, began with the boll weevil. Lest we give the little devil too much credit, it should be remarked that his attack on cotton was most intense at the same time that a major depression was attacking the economy. Between the two, the one-crop system was dealt a serious blow. The federal government began to give greater encouragement to crop diversification, the mechanization of agriculture increased rapidly, an accelerated movement to urban areas was set in motion, and the pace of industrialization was quickened. Many an ardent segregationist, in fact, was a strong supporter of moves to encourage the location of industry in the South. Had he been an equally ardent student of social organization, he might have been curious about some of the unintended consequences. Urbanization, the beginning of unionization, the up-grading of some Negro workers, the migration of Yankees, the development of an urban middle class, the growing integration with the national economy—all of these factors disturbed the existing patterns. Although the South is still less urban than most other areas of the country—43 percent compared with 59 percent for the whole country in 1950 (47 and 64 percent according to the new census definition)—it has been urbanizing more than twice as rapidly as the rest of the nation since 1900, the comparative rates of growth of the urban populations being 436 percent and 190 percent. One half of the Negroes in the South now live in urban areas; the rural South lost a million Negro residents in the 1940–1950 decade alone, many having migrated to the North and West, but a large number to southern cities as well.

The move to the cities has been accompanied by a rapid increase in industrial employment. On common indexes of industrial production, the South, since 1930, has increased at a rate about one-third faster than the rest of the nation. This increase, to be sure, is from a lower base; but the gap is being closed. Per capita income in the South was less than half the national average in 1929, but by 1952 it was two-thirds.

What is the significance of these population and income data for the question of desegregation? Hylan Lewis puts the issue well: "The normal economic, political, and social imperatives of urban life are such that the Negro in the cities of the South gets an automatic increment in his struggle for status and power merely by the fact of being there. The urban premium on freedom, impersonality, efficiency and profits, voluntary organizations, and participation by representation provides for Negroes and whites a new frontier for the shaping of a common destiny."[5]

Even the Old South, the black belt itself, is feeling the impact of important changes, not only in the surrounding areas with which it has contact, but in its own internal structure. If patterns of segregation were an integral part of the plantation one-crop economy, we would expect, on the basis of contemporary sociological theory, to find those patterns changing as the system in which they were embedded changes. That indeed is the case. In an interesting application of Parsons' concept of the "pattern variables," Morton Rubin describes the gradual transformation of some of the plantation area. The dependence of Negro tenants on the plantation owner in almost every facet of life is slowly giving way in the face of public welfare services, hourly pay rates, increased need for semiskilled and skilled workers on the job, increased shopping in town stores. There is some decrease in the ascription of status, and some increase in achievement of status. It is difficult to assign a Negro cow-

[5] Hylan Lewis, "Innovations and Trends in the Contemporary Southern Negro Community," *Journal of Social Issues*, 1954, vol. 10, No. 1, p. 24.

boy or skilled cotton-picking machine operator to a traditional status. Vocational programs in the schools, extension programs for veterans and other adults are beginning to train the workers that the new economy requires. As Alison Davis has observed, the values of free enterprise and private property have long restricted the full application of "caste" in the South. Now an increasing number of white merchants, real-estate agents, and industrial employers ". . . for rational economic reasons have subordinated white supremacy values to economic gain."[6] The merchant is caught in much sharper cross-pressures than those that affect the plantation owner. He may believe in segregation, but he also believes in customers. As a result, even in the Deep South, Negroes are beginning to get a minimum of business-oriented courtesy in the use of titles, more nonsegregated service in stores, the right to try on clothing, and the like.[7]

If this way of looking at desegregation is helpful, we must be careful not to give our sole attention to the dramatic legal changes of the last decade without full regard for the quiet revolution that is slowly weakening the foundation of the structure of segregation. The multiple forces at work—demographic, economic, international, religious, and many others—are drastically changing the context in which the legal developments take place.

The desegregation process is not automatic or inevitable, once the changes we have described begin to transform a society. The speed with which it will occur, the degree of conflict, the extent to which attitudes will also be transformed all vary, depending upon the skill of the various contending parties. Without articulate and determined opposition the structure of segregation can remain for generations despite a favorable setting for integration. It is clear from the experience of the last several years that strong community leaders who act without hesitation can frequently accomplish the desegregation of a community facility under circumstances where timid leadership would fail. Desegregation proceeds most readily when official leaders are backed by a wide variety of private agencies. Quiet preparation for a change, by training school personnel, by discussing the process with interested groups, by planning the agenda of change with full regard for the strength of the opposition at various sectors, can contribute to the success of desegregation.[8]

The Place of Law and Administration in the Desegregation Process. The dogma that law is impotent to enforce interracial justice has been sharply challenged by contemporary social science. In this challenge,

---

[6] Morton Rubin, "Social and Cultural Change in the Plantation Area," *Journal of Social Issues*, 1954, vol. 10, No. 1, p. 34.

[7] See *ibid.*, pp. 34–35.

[8] See Robin Williams, Jr., and Margaret W. Ryan (eds.), *Schools in Transition*, University of North Carolina Press, 1954; and Omer Carmichael, "The Louisville Story," New York *Times Magazine*, October 7, 1956, p. 12 ff.

there has sometimes been a failure to seek out the conditions under which law is most likely to be effective. Some observers, looking at the problem from the perspective of the United States in mid-twentieth century, a setting in which the legal approach is effective, have simply reversed the earlier dogma to affirm that law is the crucial weapon in the fight to improve intergroup relations. The task is to describe the factors involved in the variation in the effectiveness of an approach through law. In our judgment it can best be described as a "middle strategy." It is unnecessary to wait until everybody in a society is ready for a change before it can be incorporated into law, as the extensive emphasis on the situational approach that we have given throughout this volume makes clear. On the other hand, to pass a law that has little support in other institutional patterns is a relatively ineffective move, although it may not be entirely meaningless. The fate of efforts in the United Nations to protect minorities shows that it is too early to hope to reduce discrimination substantially by international legal action. This does not mean that the efforts are not worth while; but it means that far more preparation by way of economic strength for minorities, shared values, the reduction of stereotypes and traditional prejudices, the relaxation of fear of war, and the like, is necessary before international legal action to protect minorities can be particularly helpful.

Within the United States and many other societies, however, the necessary preparation for improving intergroup relations through the organized political community has been accomplished. Indeed, the analyses of social scientists concerning the nature and consequences of segregation are among the preparations. The Supreme Court and other judicial bodies and, more obscurely, the legislative branches of government have relied on the knowledge of social science for some aspects of their decisions.

It is wise to make some distinction between enforcing a neglected law and passing a new law, although the distinction is by no means sharp. Proponents of civil rights legislation contend that it is simply a process of securing ways to enforce legal patterns that are already in our Constitution. Opponents contend that such legislation is a drastic new departure from the established law. On a local scene, however, there is less likely to be such ambiguity. The task is sometimes to enforce a law, sometimes to get a new law. Either task can be a valuable part of the strategy of intergroup relations in contemporary America.

The bus boycott in Montgomery, Alabama, in 1955–1956 illustrates the situation in which a national legal pattern favors the desegregation process and the local legal pattern enforces segregation. Several factors combined to make the use of economic and legal sanctions effective in that setting. The supremacy of the Constitution in the American legal system left no doubt what the ultimate court decision would be.

The interdependent economy of the city meant that white supporters of desegregation were ambivalent. The bus company needed Negro riders; and white women, many of them working for seventy-five dollars a week, needed their Negro maids, whom they paid twenty dollars. The quiet technique of the Reverend Martin Luther King and his co-workers was ideally suited to win the support of moderates and weaken the opposition, who were put in the position of extremists. In these circumstances, the restrained but insistent demand for equal services by the use of legal processes was effective.

In other circumstances there is no doubt about the law, but enforcement has been lax. Effective strategy for the improvement of intergroup relations may require a clear-cut challenge to violations of the law. This need not imply court litigation. Several states have given their commissions against discrimination jurisdiction over discriminatory treatment in places of public accommodation and public housing. They have emphasized the technique of conciliation. Legal action, with or without court litigation, is also the approach in some private efforts—for example, in the dozen or more suits that were brought simultaneously against downtown restaurants in Columbus, Ohio, for failure to serve Negroes. The suits were based on a state civil rights statute and resulted in a change of practice by the restaurants. Or one may follow the plan of the Committee on Racial Equality (CORE) of the Fellowship of Reconciliation. This is a nonviolent program much influenced by the work of Gandhi. An interracial group will ask for service in a restaurant or a recreational center. They treat everyone with respect and courtesy, and absorb any violence that may occur without retaliation. If they are served without incident, they are careful to thank the management for its courtesy; if they are discriminated against, they try to discuss the matter with the management. Failing that, they adopt some nonviolent protest—passing out copies of the state law against discrimination to other customers or perhaps just sitting quietly, even the white members, who may have been served, refusing to touch their food or drink. Frequently the management decides—often after some hours' delay—to serve them.

These are only brief illustrations of some of the possible strategies in dealing with discrimination. They may indicate the need for a variety of approaches. Myrdal points out, with reference to discrimination against Negroes, that one unified organization is unlikely to be successful. It could not appeal to the great majority of Negroes and still draw in any but a handful of whites. The need is for specialized groups, with specific aims and an appeal for different groups. They need the support of white people because of the relative poverty of Negroes and their lack of power. Thus there is room for a militant National Association for the Advancement of Colored People, taking its stand on the Constitution; for an Urban League, concerned with the economic placement of skilled and professional Negroes or with general social service; for a more compromising group in the South, such as the Southern Regional Council. Myrdal suggests that further specialization, not unification, is the need. There would be value in an organization specifically designed to integrate minorities into the labor movement, another with skills specialized for achieving political influence, and other groups concerned particularly with additional questions of discrimination.[9] The programs of such diverse groups must be in harmony with one another, of course —suggesting the need for a coördinating council on local and national levels. In the next section we shall describe the programs of some of the groups that are working in the United States today.

Organizations Opposing Discrimination

One of the most significant developments in recent years has been the growth of the profession of intergroup relations and the increase in the number of organizations whose programs, wholly or in part, are dedicated to the reduction of prejudice and discrimination. Two forces are involved in this development. Minority-group members have established a vast variety of organizations whose aim is the elimination of their own disprivileges and those of other minorities; and out of the total community have come other groups, public and private, concerned with the full realization of democratic values. These two sources are, of course, not distinct.

Protest organizations and movements have a long history in the United States. Negro opposition to slavery, the abolition movement, immigrant protective associations were important in the nineteenth century. Requisites for effective organization, however, were often lacking. Literacy, trained leadership, some economic power in the hands of the minorities, and a growing awareness of the costs of discrimination in the dominant group create a situation in which opposition to disprivilege can be much more effective. By the twentieth century these influences had grown; and by 1940, in particular, an environment favorable to a massive attack on discrimination had been created.

This situation is reflected in the rapid growth in the number and power of organizations concerned with intergroup relations and in the concomitant increase in professional staffs. According to McWilliams, over 500 local, state, and national organizations are working in the field of intergroup relations; more than half of them have been established since 1943.[10] As more and more people have been drawn into the field, it has gone through the process of "professionalization" as an occupa-

[9] See Gunnar Myrdal, An American Dilemma, Harper & Brothers, 1944, pp. 852–857.

[10] Carey McWilliams, Brothers Under the Skin, Little, Brown & Company, rev. ed., 1951, p. 20.

tion; there have developed a body of principles to guide their work, a program of training for staff members, coördinating organizations for the exchange of experience, and professional publications for research and information. This process is by no means complete. It will doubtless be some time before we have graduate schools of "intergroup relations" to match our medical schools (or more probably, departments of intergroup relations in professional schools of "social engineering"). But steps in this direction have been taken at several universities and it seems highly probable that further development along this line will take place.

Probably the focal point of this professionalization is the National Association of Intergroup Relations Officials (NAIRO), an organization which describes itself as: "A national organization of individuals primarily engaged in intergroup relations. An association to improve intergroup relations and aid in the attainment of equality of opportunity for all persons regardless of race, religion, national origin or ancestry. An organization which seeks to improve standards of work in the field of intergroup relations and to advance professional and technical knowledge." A picture of the range of its membership in terms of organizational connections, and also of the variety of groups now involved in the efforts to reduce prejudice and discrimination, is provided by a listing of the professional connections of the officers and directors of NAIRO in a recent year:

> Michigan Fair Employment Practices Commission
> American Friends Service Committee
> National Conference of Christians and Jews
> Commission on Community Relations, Detroit
> Commission on Community Relations, Pittsburgh
> National Community Relations Advisory Council
> Urban League of Pittsburgh
> Mayor's Friendly Relations Committee, Cincinnati
> American Jewish Committee
> Bureau of Unemployment Compensation, Cleveland
> Commission on Intergroup Relations, New York
> National Committee Against Discrimination in Housing
> Race Relations Department, Fisk University
> Commission on Human Relations, Chicago
> Anti-Defamation League of B'nai B'rith
> Southern Regional Council
> Commission on Community Relations, Detroit
> National Association for the Advancement of Colored People
> Commission on Human Relations, Philadelphia
> Los Angeles County Committee on Human Relations
> Jewish Community Relations Bureau, Kansas City
> University of Miami

PUBLIC AND QUASI-PUBLIC AGENCIES IN INTERGROUP RELATIONS

We cannot begin even to list the numerous agencies and departments of various organizations now concerned with intergroup relations. Among public agencies there are the staffs of fair employment and fair educational practices commissions, administrators of public housing, school officers, and advisers in various branches of the federal government and in the armed services. We discussed some aspects of their work in earlier chapters. On the local level there has been an extensive development of "community relations boards" or "mayor's committees," as they are frequently named. Some of these may be called quasi-public, for they are primarily advisory and have no official status. But many have been established by community ordinance and have professional staffs (with membership from 1 to 24) financed out of public funds.

The municipal agencies have several handicaps and weaknesses as forces in the movement to reduce discriminaiion, but they also have some significant strengths and accomplishments. Most of them work on small budgets. In 1954, only five municipal groups had budgets over $20,000 and only seven employed more than one professional staff person.[11] They are often affected by the local political situation. This can be an advantage insofar as minority groups are in a balance-of-power position. More often, however, it is a disadvantage, because those seeking to hold or gain political power will give only token support to the agency if powerful interests in the community oppose the agency's recommendations on housing, recreation, or job opportunities. This is not to criticize the skill of the various mayor's committees, but only to suggest that they work within the framework of an often difficult political structure. Matching difficulties are found on the national level, of course, as any student of Congress and its activities with regard to fair employment practices, civil rights, antilynching bills, housing regulations, school aid bills, and the like, will recognize.

Partly because of policy and partly because of budget limitations, mayor's committees usually work closely with the schools, with private agencies, with other municipal organizations. Again, this is a source of both strength and weakness. The agency gains in strength if it can get the support and employ the facilities of other groups. Wide community sponsorship may thus be secured for a project that could not be sustained by the community relations board itself. But the need to rely on other groups for implementation can also be a source of weakness. As every professional staff person knows, the best of plans may be seriously weakened as they are passed from group to group, from community relations board to coördinating committee to city council.

[11] *Nairo Reporter*, January, 1954.

Despite the obstacles faced by local civic unity groups, they have, in the brief period of fifteen years since they began to develop, made important contributions to intergroup relations in many cities. They have countered violence and the threat of violence with firmness, with facts and open discussion.[12] They have helped to reduce discrimination in city employment, particularly by increasing the employment of Negroes in police departments, schools, and public transportation. They have worked closely with city administrations, school officials, and fair employment practices commissions (which in some instances—Cleveland, Gary, Youngstown, Philadelphia—are part of the same agency). A few community relations boards have been assigned responsibilities in connection with public housing, and most of the boards are concerned with housing problems. There is little doubt that these agencies occupy a strategically important place in the efforts to reduce discrimination in American cities.

PRIVATE ORGANIZATIONS IN THE FIELD OF RACE RELATIONS

In the preparation of a handbook of agencies in the field of race relations at the beginning of the post-World War II period, it was found that there were 123 national organizations whose work justified including them in the volume. If the church organizations, the agencies concerned primarily with international relations and oppressed peoples in foreign countries, individual labor unions, and a few agencies established to promote particular legislation such as the abolition of the poll tax are omitted, the list contains seventy-five national organizations dealing specifically with problems of intergroup relations. Federal agencies are excluded, although a number of them are of considerable importance in this field. Charles S. Johnson has classified these seventy-five organizations according to their major interests as follows:

13 of them are primarily concerned with problems of Negroes or Negro-white relations in America.
5 with the foreign-born.
4 with persons of Oriental descent.
1 with American Indians.
2 with Latin-Americans.
7 with Jewish problems.
8 with general problems of interracial, intercultural, and interfaith relations.
7 with the effective functioning of democracy.
7 with youth and recreation.
5 with labor.
2 with civil liberties.
7 with education in schools and institutions.

[12] See Hannah Lees, "How Philadelphia Stopped a Race Riot," *The Reporter,* June 2, 1955, pp. 26–29.

3 with adult education.
1 with art.
1 with housing.
1 with veterans.
1 with conditions in agriculture.

When these seventy-five organizations were classified on the basis of strategies and techniques, the following distribution was obtained: Fifteen agencies are involved to some extent in action programs and community organization; thirteen are interested in education in the schools; thirty-seven are concerned with some type of adult education program; ten engage in cultural and recreational activities; five work through the courts; eleven carry on research of a substantial character; and seven work primarily to secure legislative action.[13] We shall describe a few of these agencies briefly to give a picture of the variety and extent of their work.

National Association for the Advancement of Colored People. The NAACP, founded in 1909, works for the elimination of segregation and discrimination against Negro and other Americans because of race, creed, or color. For the most part, it seeks its objectives through court and legislative action. Campaigns for equality of opportunity and equality of rights have been waged in the fields of housing, employment, education, recreation, law, travel, the armed forces, voting, and officeholding. Efforts have also been made to ban residential segregation, to secure passage of antilynching laws, and to bring about coöperation between religious organizations and the NAACP. The Research Department has compiled a large quantity of material on race relations and civil rights, and the national office has published a monthly journal, *The Crisis*, since 1910.

The NAACP is a militant organization but one which operates within the framework of the democratic ideology and the democratic society. It is regarded by many whites, especially in the South, and by some upper-class Negroes, as a radical organization; actually it has adopted various measures to exclude communists from its membership. The leadership realizes that communist infiltration would lead to the same results which occurred in the National Negro Congress and the Southern Negro Youth Congress.

Since the salaried staff in the national office is not large, and since its funds are quite limited, the NAACP must select its cases for their strategic importance. At the local level it serves as a legal aid society; but in fighting for the Negro's rights at the national level the best strategy requires that cases be undertaken only where there is good chance of

---

[13] Charles S. Johnson, "National Organizations in the Field of Race Relations," *Annals of the American Academy of Political and Social Science*, March, 1946, pp. 117–118.

success. Lawyers of national reputation, who may or may not be members of the organization's legal staff, coöperate with local attorneys in arguing a case of key importance. Frequently it is expected that the decision will be adverse in the lower courts, but cases are prepared with extreme care so that they will stand up in the higher courts. In Chapter 15 we discussed some of the outstanding cases which the NAACP has taken to the Supreme Court of the United States. Among these are the white primary, residential segregation by municipal ordinance, private residential restrictive covenants, and the admission of Negroes to schools, colleges, and graduate training supported by state funds. By early 1950 the NAACP had won twenty-seven of the thirty cases it had taken before the Supreme Court.

The NAACP is an interracial organization, but its membership is preponderantly Negro. As its strength has grown and as the number of trained Negroes has increased, the influence of white members and officers has declined at the national level.[14] It is more effective on the national than on the local level, where, according to Bunche, the normal condition is inactivity. The major part of the work of the typical local chapter is carried on by a few active members; occasional flurries of activity are stimulated by some leader or event. Although there are 600 or 700 branches, youth councils, and college chapters, the total membership is less than 100,000. The leadership and a rather high percentage of NAACP members belong to the middle class; perhaps the chief weakness of the organization is its relatively small membership. However, a recent survey by Elmo Roper shows that "the position of the NAACP on political matters is held in high respect by at least forty-five percent of Negroes."[15]

In spite of the criticisms which have been directed at the NAACP from time to time during its existence, the present writers agree with Myrdal that this organization has been unusually effective in the fields of civil liberties and civil rights.

The National Urban League. Operating as an interracial social work agency, the National Urban League devotes a large part of its program to extending economic opportunities for Negroes and integrating them into industry, business, and the professions. This objective is sought through discussions and conferences with business executives, industrialists, and labor-union officials. Many Urban Leagues now provide clients with expert testing and counseling services in the professional, technical, clerical, skilled, and semiskilled job categories. Other activities

[14] Wilson Record, "Negro Intellectual Leadership in the NAACP," *Phylon*, Fourth Quarter, 1956, pp. 375–388.

[15] *News from NAACP*, June 19, 1952, p. 30. For the Bunche-Myrdal summary and critique of the NAACP, see Gunnar Myrdal, *op. cit.*, pp. 819–836. An interesting account of the organization's activities and cases, and the roles of Walter White, Charles Houston, Thurgood Marshall, and others in them, is given in Walter White, *A Man Called White*, The Viking Press, Inc., 1948.

include providing information about Negroes, serving as adviser to governmental agencies and industry on health, welfare, and employment matters affecting Negroes, developing programs to provide for the adjustment and social needs of in-migrant Negro workers, and assisting in the interracial planning of social services and community projects. Fifty-eight affiliates of the national organization are located in twenty-nine states, northern and southern, and the District of Columbia. For twenty-six years the National Urban League published *Opportunity: Journal of Negro Life*, and it has issued many well-prepared pamphlets on such subjects as housing and employment. Like the NAACP, it has been criticized by some members of both races for being too "radical" and by others for being too "timid." Myrdal believes that it is a tactical blunder to assume that there should be only one unified Negro movement and concludes that the National Urban League fills "an unquestionable and eminently useful community need."[16]

Jewish Organizations in the Field of Intergroup Relations. The leading Jewish organizations in the intergroup relations field are the American Jewish Congress, the Anti-Defamation League of B'nai B'rith, and the American Jewish Committee. According to Robison:

The first of these is best known for activities designed to invoke legal sanctions against discrimination, including drafting legislation and participating in litigation affecting constitutional and legislative rights. It also engages in research on intergroup tension, investigates and publicizes the existence of discrimination, provides assistance in the handling of tension situations, and organizes community action in support of its objectives. While the Anti-Defamation League and the American Jewish Committee engage in these activities to some degree, their major emphasis has been on changing unfavorable community attitudes through the extensive use of the mass media of communication. They also investigate and expose anti-Semitic groups. Supplementary activities are carried on by the Jewish War Veterans and the Jewish Labor Committee.[17]

The Anti-Defamation League has 26 regional offices that work in coördination with other agencies on programs to reduce discrimination in communities. On the national level the League has sponsored scores of workshops, published a great deal of antiprejudice material, and developed an interest in most phases of intergroup relations. The American Jewish Committee has emphasized educational work and is particularly prominent for its encouragement and sponsorship of research.

A number of the Jewish agencies have joined together to form the National Community Relations Advisory Council in order better to co-

---

[16] See Gunnar Myrdal, *op. cit.*, pp. 837–842; Charles S. Johnson, *op. cit.*, pp. 118–119; National Urban League, *And the Pursuit of Happiness* (40th Anniversary Year Book), 1950; *Cleveland Urban League* (a brochure prepared by the Public Education Department of the Cleveland Urban League).

[17] Joseph B. Robison, "Organizations Promoting Civil Rights and Liberties," *Annals of the American Academy of Political and Social Science*, May, 1951, p. 21.

ordinate their various programs and to undertake some common projects. The Council is composed of the American Jewish Congress, the Jewish Labor Committee, the Jewish War Veterans, the Union of American Hebrew Congregations, the Union of Orthodox Hebrew Congregations, the United Synagogue of America, and 35 state and local organizations. "The purposes of the Jewish community relations field have been defined as the protection and enhancement of equal rights and equal opportunities and the fostering of conditions that contribute toward the vitality of Jewish living."[18] The range of activities of the members of NCRAC is suggested by the program guides: American policy in the Middle East, desegregation, equal educational opportunities, revised immigration laws, civil liberties, international relations (alertness to communist dangers), religious liberty and interreligious relationships, politics, and population movements.[19] Various members of the NCRAC specialize on particular aspects of this total program. Indeed, there is some disagreement in emphasis, some competition for particular types of programs, for which various groups claim priority or special facilities. The American Jewish Committee and the Anti-Defamation League withdrew from the NCRAC in disagreement with the "MacIver Report" recommendations for closer coördination and specialization among the member agencies.[20] Those who supported the recommendations believed that a great deal was to be gained by the elimination of duplication and the development of special skills; those who opposed them believed that problems are often not specialized but reach into many phases of community life, so that an agency with broad interests is in a better position to deal with them. We cannot explore that controversy here. It is important to realize, however, that despite such disagreements, the various groups contribute to common goals and coöperation continues on specific activities. The Jewish agencies have regarded the problem of discrimination as indivisible and have participated in cases involving other minorities as well as those affecting Jews.[21]

The National Conference of Christians and Jews. Although the National Conference of Christians and Jews has been, from its founding in 1928, primarily concerned with the promotion of harmonious relations among members of different religious faiths, it has also been interested in other aspects of intergroup relations. It has worked on the community level through its 62 regional offices, and on the national level by promoting seminars, providing advanced training in intergroup relations, sponsoring Brotherhood Week, and encouraging research. The

[18] National Community Relations Advisory Council, *Joint Program Plan for Jewish Community Relations 1956–57*, 1956, p. 2.

[19] *Ibid.*, pp. 4–16.

[20] See R. M. MacIver, *Report on the Jewish Community Relations Agencies*, National Community Relations Advisory Council, 1951.

[21] See Joseph B. Robison, *op. cit.*, pp. 20–23.

Conference is strictly an interfaith agency, with the aim of developing understanding, tolerance, and coöperation, but with no desire to eliminate differences among the faiths. Its methods, broadly speaking, are educational, with more attention given to the use of the mass media than perhaps is true of any other agency concerned with intergroup relations.[22]

The effectiveness of educational programs is difficult to judge, especially when they are aimed at wide and diverse audiences. The problem of self-selection, the likelihood that only those who already share the message of brotherhood will be reached, looms large. This is not always the case, however. In Louisville, for example, the regional office of the NCCJ in coöperation with the superintendent of schools sponsored a series of Human Relations Institutes. One of these, involving 800 teachers, brought forty groups, all of them interracial, into careful discussion of the problems of desegregation. Such education was part of the preparation which made effective desegregation in Louisville possible.[23]

Common Council for American Unity. The Common Council, created in New York City in 1939, has carried forward the work which the Foreign Language Information Service did for twenty-two years. The organization has not limited itself to the foreign-born but has sought to promote unity and mutual understanding among Americans of all national and racial origins. Publication has been suspended on *Common Ground*, a periodical published by the Common Council for a decade. Charles S. Johnson observes: "Probably the special usefulness of the Common Council for American Unity in the field of race relations is that, through its weekly releases and radio program service for the foreign language press and radio broadcasters, it carries an adult education program in the field of intergroup understanding to foreign language groups which are often an easy prey to ideas of intolerance."[24]

Southern Organizations in the Field of Intergroup Relations. One of the first organizations in the South to concern itself with race relations was the University Commission on Race Questions. This association was supported by the Phelps-Stokes Fund from the time of its inception in 1912 until it was discontinued in 1925. Its activities consisted mainly of holding conferences, issuing a series of open letters which analyzed various problems of the South, and stimulating the introduction of race relations courses in southern colleges and universities. Another race relations organization which originated in the South was the Commission

---

[22] See James Pitt, *Adventures in Brotherhood*, Farrar, Straus and Company, 1955; and Everett R. Clinchy, *The Growth of Good Will: A Sketch of Protestant-Catholic-Jewish Relations*, National Conference of Christians and Jews, 1953.

[23] Omer Carmichael, *op. cit.*

[24] Charles S. Johnson, *op. cit.*, p. 121. See Louis Adamic, "This Crisis Is an Opportunity," *Common Ground*, Autumn, 1940.

on Interracial Cooperation, whose life span ran from 1919 to 1944. The CIC was formed for the purpose of reducing tensions in Negro-white relations in the period immediately after World War I. Interracial committees were organized in some 800 counties, state committees were formed, and a headquarters for these organizations was established in Atlanta. The CIC's liberal-humanitarian, gradualistic program of securing better employment opportunities and increase school, recreational, and health facilities was carried on within the traditional framework of race relations in the South. This program was criticized by young Negroes for being too slow, by the Communist party for being too mild, and by southern conservatives for being too radical. Research studies on such subjects as lynching and tenancy were conducted by staff members, and many pamphlets and publicity releases were issued. The organization was interracial, although whites outnumbered Negroes two to one on the governing commission and no Negroes were employed in the Atlanta office.[25] The CIC was succeeded by the Southern Regional Council, a biracial association interested in the improvement of social, civic, economic, and racial conditions in the South. According to Davie:

> It is not exclusively a race-relations organization. It believes that it is a mistake to regard the problems of the South purely in terms of race. "Friction between the races," it states in one of its pamphlets, "can best be combated by bringing the entire population of the South abreast of modern standards in health, education, employment, farming, and culture. To work toward the goal of a higher standard of well-being for all the South's citizens is to work for equal opportunity for members of all races." Its functions include coordination of the work of agencies concerned with Southern problems; research and surveys; educational activities through its monthly bulletin, the New South, and through pamphlets, press, radio, conferences, and personal contacts; consultative services; and promotion of specific programs of action through its staff and membership. Its program calls for the assurance of the civil rights of all the people of the South, abolition of the poll tax, equitable law enforcement, extension of the practice of employing Negro policemen, jury service for all, employment of all persons on the basis of ability, equalization of educational opportunity and facilities and of pay for teachers, extension of publicly financed low-cost housing, increased publicly financed medical and dental care available to both races on an equal basis, and equal accommodations for Negroes on all public transportation facilities.[26]

The Southern Regional Council has recently been reorganized and now stands as "the hub of a twelve-state network of human relations councils." Its major effort is both to keep open and to extend the channels of communication between Negroes and whites in order to

---

[25] Gunnar Myrdal, op. cit., pp. 842–846; Maurice R. Davie, Negroes in American Society, McGraw-Hill Book Company, 1949, pp. 479–480.

[26] Maurice R. Davie, op. cit., p. 481.

reduce conflict and promote equality of opportunity. It has established a panel of social scientists and professional human relations workers to assist the affiliated agencies in their programs.[27]

Church Organizations and Intergroup Relations. A recent study cites the positions taken by various church organizations on such questions as civil rights, fair employment practices, the poll tax, displaced persons, and federal aid to education.[28] The Department of Race Relations of the Federal Council of Churches of Christ in America (now the National Council . . .), created in 1921, conducts conferences, surveys, and clinics in race relations. The Race Relations Division of the American Missionary Association, established in 1942, sponsors annual institutes of race relations and subsidizes research studies in this field. The American Friends Race Relations Committee has established a placement service to find positions for Negroes which they have not held heretofore, visiting lectureships for Negro scholars in white schools and colleges, interracial workcamps and seminars. Interracial councils have been set up in many cities by the Roman Catholic Church; we discussed above the programs of research and action sponsored by Jewish organizations.

Congress of Racial Equality. Some CORE groups are affiliated with the Fellowship of Reconciliation, but not all. This organization, which does not plan to enroll large memberships, has branches in a dozen or so cities and is committed to direct but nonviolent action. All groups are interracial and must submit to careful training and planning. The techniques employed include negotiation, distributing leaflets, picketing, talking to patrons of firms which maintain policies of racial discrimination, sit-down strikes, and appeals to law in the states which have civil rights statutes.[29]

Other Agencies and Coördinating Groups. With these brief references we have only given examples of the hundreds of groups now concerned with intergroup relations. Interested students will want to explore their programs with care and investigate the work of such other agencies as the American Association on Indian Affairs, the Alianza Hispano-Americana, and the Japanese-American Defense League. Each of these is primarily concerned with the reduction of discrimination against a particular minority group. We should note also that there are a number of organizations whose programs do not primarily concern intergroup relations, but who carry on work of great importance in this field. The Congress of Industrial Organizations adopted a policy of no

[27] See John Hope II, "Trends in Patterns of Race Relations in the South Since May 17, 1954," *Phylon*, Second Quarter, 1956, p. 109.

[28] Luke Ebersole, *Church Lobbying in the United States*, The Macmillan Company, 1951. Chapter 18 of the present work contains a discussion of the pronouncements of church bodies on intergroup relations.

[29] Helen Buckler, "The CORE Way," *Survey Graphic*, February, 1946, pp. 50–51, 60. See also pamphlet of same title issued by CORE in November, 1947.

discrimination and established the Committee to Abolish Discrimination to enforce it within the CIO. The same policy has been continued, at least on the national level, since the AFL-CIO merger late in 1955. The American Civil Liberties Union is actively engaged in legal actions to protect the civil liberties, as guaranteed in the Bill of Rights, of all groups and individuals in the United States. Americans for Democratic Action and other associations have as their objective the achievement of democracy for all people.

In recent years attempts have been made to coördinate the activities of intergroup organizations working for the same or similar goals. National and state committees have been formed to support specific legislation; examples are the National Committee to Abolish the Poll Tax and the National Council for a Permanent FEPC. Committees to advocate state fair employment legislation have had the support of a large number of specialized intergroup organizations, as well as many mass organizations. In 1949 the Emergency Civil Rights Mobilization was formed under the leadership of the NAACP, and 4000 delegates from 100 organizations were sent to Washington in January, 1950, in a strong but unsuccessful attempt to persuade Congress to enact the fair employment practices bill. Robison reports that "agreement was achieved not only on a single objective but also on strategy, such as the decision to obtain consideration of the bill in the House of Representatives before the Senate."[30]

In a complex society a large share of effective social action must, inevitably, stem from organized groups, such as the ones we have mentioned here. Only well-planned groups can support the research, plan the strategies, and focus the power necessary for significant institutional changes. Many of the economic and political changes discussed in Chapters 12 to 15, the growth of fair employment practices, the increase in minority-group participation in politics, and other developments, have been strongly encouraged by the activities of many organizations. They are beginning to demonstrate that direct action on the "economic front" and the "political front" can reduce discrimination and help to create an environment in which prejudice will decline. The strengthening of these organizations—the further development of both coördination and specialization—is among the primary strategic tasks.[31]

Changing the Minority-Group Member

We have seen at several points that the responses of minority-group members to prejudice and discrimination frequently lend support to

---

[30] Joseph B. Robison, op. cit., p. 23.

[31] For excellent suggestions on strategy in general and on the economic front and the political front, see R. M. MacIver, *The More Perfect Union*, The Macmillan Company, 1948, chaps. 6, 7, 9.

further hostility. One line of approach that strategy may take, therefore, is to discover ways of changing some of the responses of the minorities. Many comfortable people—including the relatively more comfortable members of the minorities themselves—too often emphasize this as *the* solution. Let the Negro improve himself, they say, and prejudice will disappear. When the Jew stops being Jewish, there will be no discrimination against him. If the immigrant will adopt American ways, no one will oppose him. This approach suffers from the double error of "bootstrap" thinking (demanding that minorities change many characteristics that are the *results* of prejudice *before* the prejudice can be reduced) and a limited monocultural, homogeneous view of society that is probably not harmonious with the realities of the modern, complex world. There is, however, a small way in which this approach is useful, as part of a total strategy. To the prejudiced person, the characteristics and the responses of minority-group members are part of the total situation that seems to him to justify his action. If they can be changed, or his conception of them changed, he will perceive the situation differently.

Under most circumstances, any program that will make it more difficult to perceive minorities as different—culturally, racially, economically, educationally, and so on—will reduce prejudice. An improved school, a job barrier eliminated, better morale and motivation among minority-group members, improved newspaper reporting practices—in general, the kinds of changes that the strategies we have been discussing seek to achieve—will have a cumulative effect. They will change not only the minorities but the actions of the majority which in turn will change the minority.

Such changes will in the first instance be more an effect than a cause of the reduction of prejudice and discrimination, although once set in motion they will also be causes. We are interested, in this section, not only in such general changes but also in the specific responses of minority-group members to incidents of discrimination. Should they disregard them to concentrate on self-improvement, leaving it to friends among the dominant group to lead the opposition? Should they protest directly and vigorously? Or should they express their opposition by quiet contention?

The emphasis on self-improvement is greeted with derision by some minority-group members because it seems to place the responsibility for prejudice on the oppressed people. In our view "responsibility" for hostility, if one wants to use that term, must be located in the nature of man; but effective strategy may require attention to the best responses by members of the minorities. Aptheker objects strongly to Myrdal's "insulting and petty reformist" advice to Negroes to cultivate honesty and Oswald Garrison Villard's recommendation "in which he said that the most important message he had for them, after his fifty years of service, was—to be courteous!"[32] Although Aptheker gives a one-sided and inaccurate picture of the full range of the views of Myrdal and Villard, we must certainly agree that there is a strategic danger in emphasizing minority self-improvement as the way to reduce prejudice and discrimination.

Nevertheless, attention by minority-group members to the effects of their characteristics and their responses to hostility, *however caused*, can be of value. Fineberg describes a situation in which thoughtfulness rather than anger governed the response of a Jewish merchant to an anti-Jewish tirade:

"An aged woman returned a sweater which she had bought a month before. The garment had been torn, evidently by a knife or on a nail.

"I told her I was sorry that I could not refund the purchase price, since the sweater had been worn for a month and there had been no flaw in the material or workmanship. The woman turned red with anger.

" 'That's just what I deserve,' she said, 'for dealing with Jews.'

"She went on pouring out the vilest insults about Jews. And somehow, while she was carrying on, I kept cool instead of getting angry. When she was out of breath, I answered her very quietly and in a friendly tone.

" 'It isn't the two dollars,' I explained patiently. 'If you came in here and told me you're a poor woman in need of two dollars I'd give it to you at once. But there must be some rules in managing a business. If the article is used and injury is done to it which is not our fault at all, we don't owe the customer anything. I don't owe you a refund just because a sweater you bought here was torn on a sharp instrument.

" 'If I give you two dollars now, it won't be a refund. It will be charity. And you don't look to me like a woman who wants charity. Here then is my suggestion. You give me the name of your church. I'll make out a check for two dollars as a donation to the church.'

"The woman gave me the name of her church. I made out the check. It was cashed by the church. That woman has come back again as a customer and has brought her friends."

Evidently this merchant does not assume that every person hurling epithets and invectives against the Jews is on the point of starting a pogrom. To him the woman appeared as someone in a bad mood who might have spoken as contemptuously and insultingly of her own husband when in that mood, even though she would not divorce him for half the world.[33]

Some people look upon this kind of response as spineless compromise, the loss of an opportunity to show the woman her errors. But Fineberg is simply asking: What is most likely to be effective? He agrees that it may sometimes be necessary for a "Victimian" to oppose prejudice much more directly, but points out that self-control and concern for the total community are always necessary.

[32] Herbert Aptheker, *The Negro People in America*, International Publishers, 1946, p. 26.
[33] S. A. Fineberg, *Overcoming Anti-Semitism*, Harper & Brothers, 1943, pp. 93–95.

An editorial in the Norfolk, Virginia, *Journal and Guide*, a leading Negro newspaper, makes much the same point.

WE SHOULD QUIT SINGIN' THE BLUES

Though we are confronted with many obstacles in our struggle upward, all of our handicaps are not imposed upon us by our white neighbors as one would be led to think by the nature of some complaints.

A few illustrations will doubtless suffice to drive this thought home.

For example, the white people are not preventing us from reducing our large number of debt-overburdened churches to a smaller number of better built, more attractive, and debt-free institutions.

They are not preventing us from demanding and having a smaller number of better educated and better paid clergymen.

There is no record, legal or otherwise, that white people are stopping us from efficiently managing our fraternal organizations.

We have yet to hear of any white people preventing us from organizing cooperative consumers' leagues and producers' associates which would offer some jobs and hope to the thousands who come out of school each year wondering what they are going to do with their education.

As we went to press, we heard of no white people forcing Negroes to waste their money on bad liquor, needless dances, unnecessary and costly conventions, and the numbers game.

There is no evidence that the dominant group has handed down an order that colored business places must be ramshackle, dirty, indifferent as to service, and uninviting on the whole.

The Whites have not decreed that colored citizens should be inefficient, lack discipline and solidarity, and disregard the laws of sanitation and hygiene.

White people, it is true, are guilty of discrimination, segregation, and disfranchisement, but they are not guilty of the ends mentioned above, which are just as bad.

Of course, we need to continue intelligent agitation for full social equality in the broad sense of that term. Nevertheless, we should concentrate on some of the evils surrounding us and for which we are primarily responsible and place ourselves in a better condition to solve our other problems.[34]

The editorial greatly oversimplifies the causes of the difficulties it deplores—disregarding the importance of discrimination itself—but it points out that the problems can be reduced in part by changes initiated by Negroes themselves. Such an emphasis is far more likely to be effective when it comes from a member of a minority group than when it is offered as gratuitous advice by a member of the dominant group (who is often encouraged, thereby, to disregard his own involvement in the circle of interaction).

Williams well summarizes a number of the principles involved when he writes:

[34] Reprinted in Maurice R. Davie, *op. cit.*, pp. 473–474.

A vulnerable minority can itself help to reduce hostility and conflict insofar as there is group control over individual members, by:

(a) educating its members to an understanding of the dominant group's reaction to the minority's values and behavior

(b) careful study of the behaviors of its own members which are regarded as objectionable by other groups

(c) minimizing conspicuous display of traits of marked negative-symbol value

(d) participation as individuals in wider community activities which are widely regarded as necessary in the common welfare.[35]

Conclusion

Throughout this analysis we have emphasized the interactive and cumulative nature of the forces influencing intergroup relations. For purposes of discussion, it has frequently been necessary to isolate one aspect of the total pattern; but it would be a costly error to forget the total empirical scene, for that is what, in the last analysis, we want to understand and to control. The interlocking of the many factors that affect majority-minority relations greatly complicates the work of the student and of the social engineer. We have all too often tried to untangle this complexity by oversimplified theories and strategies. Williams emphasizes this point strongly:

. . . The known facts create a strong presumption that a main source of the persistence of intergroup hostility is precisely the interlocking and mutual reinforcement of cultural differences, other visible differences, realistic interests, deflected aggression, and other factors. In short, the most important questions may concern not the influence of particular factors but the way in which mutual reinforcement operates, and determination of the strategic factors in a plan for shifting the resultant pattern. In this connection, there is a definite possibility that the factors which are most important in producing hostility and conflict are by no means the same as those which are most important for control purposes. Thus, the roots of intergroup hostility may lie in the early socialization of children in the home. But this process is so inaccessible to direct external control that other, even seemingly far removed approaches may be more promising for immediate action.[36]

The problem can perhaps be illustrated by an analogy. What causes tuberculosis? It seems to be the interaction and accumulation of several factors: perhaps a hereditary predisposition, early environmental conditions (diet and living quarters), general physical health, specific occupational hazards, contact with infected persons, and so on. To say that tuberculosis is "caused" by a hereditary predisposition or by poor general

---

[35] Robin Williams, Jr., *The Reduction of Intergroup Tensions*, Social Science Research Council, 1947, p. 77.

[36] *Ibid.*, pp. 41–42.

physical condition or some other factor is equivalent to saying that prejudice and discrimination are caused by personal insecurity or economic competition or some other one factor.

The analogy might also apply to the question of prevention or cure. Hereditary predisposition might be important in many cases of tuberculosis, but at the present time that is completely beyond our control. An effective campaign must be directed at the most vulnerable factors— perhaps the isolation of infected persons or the removal of specific occupational hazards, or a school program of examination and dietary supplements that greatly reduces the problem of persuading fifty million families to improve their diets or have regular examinations.

This distinction between the causal factors and the factors most vulnerable to strategic attack applies equally well to intergroup hostility. Some of the (frequently brilliant) analyses of the personality elements in prejudice leap too easily to strategic conclusions. As MacIver says:

> Since policy measures can hardly hope to change the basic drives of human beings whereas they have some potency over social institutions and economic conditions the concentration of effort should be directed to the latter rather than to the former aspects of the discrimination complex. We doubt, for example, whether any serious gain can be made by high-lighting the "scapegoat" element in discriminatory treatment. It need by no means be left out of the reckoning, but any advantage to be derived from the exposure of it will be at best quite subsidiary to a strategy the main assault of which must be delivered against less elusive and more controllable factors.[37]

Williams suggests that four principles must guide research and the planning of programs of action in intergroup relations: (1) the principles of multiple causation and the interdependence of variables, (2) the theorem of cumulation in social change, (3) the principle of limits in social change (the recognition of obstacles and the eschewing of utopianism), (4) the principle of indirection in plans for social change.[38] These prevent any easy optimism, but they provide a sound basis upon which to build effective programs for the reduction of prejudice and discrimination.

The Need for Research. A great deal of time and energy are now being spent in trying to improve intergroup relations. Only a small proportion of this time and energy, however, is devoted to research—to analysis of the effectiveness of specific programs and to the study of the total causal complex; hence much of the work may be inefficient or even harmful. In many areas of modern life, extensive research is considered indispensable. In industry, in medicine, in the development of military weapons, no important program is adopted before vast sums have been

---

[37] R. M. MacIver, *The More Perfect Union*, p. 81.
[38] Robin Williams, Jr., *op. cit.*, p. 43.

spent to develop the most efficient means. This approach is only beginning to be used in the analysis and control of human behavior. It is only in a partial sense that this is a "scientific age." A great many people, faced by the confusion and anxiety of modern life, have developed a prideful antiscientism when it comes to understanding human beings. The qualifications that science demands, the painstaking research, the refusal to declare unqualifiedly that this or that is true, regardless of conditions—these aspects of the scientific frame of mind seem to increase the anxiety of many people for they prevent the acceptance of easy, comforting answers to life's problems. We experience a "failure of nerve" when it comes to analyzing ourselves; we seek a way to "escape from freedom."

But the present authors firmly believe (this is a premise, not a conclusion) that the turning back to old formulas—traditional answers, unqualified nationalism, the seemingly self-confident declarations of the "practical" man—can only deepen our problems. In the field with which we are concerned we must demand of every proposition its methodological credentials: What is the evidence? What variables are involved? How were they controlled? How does this harmonize with, or contradict, existing theoretical positions? It may seem like tedious business to some —to others it is exciting adventure—but there is no easier way to understanding and control.

Of the research that we do have in the area of intergroup relations a high proportion has been concerned with the causes of prejudice and discrimination, relatively little with the strategies that are effective, in specific situations, in reducing them. There is great need for more of the latter. A large number of the studies have been of the pencil-and-paper variety; these must be supplemented by more studies of other kinds of behavior and of the relation between verbal and nonverbal responses in intergroup relations.

Science and Values. It is sometimes said that science cannot contribute to the solution of such moral problems as prejudice because its predictions are of the "if and when" variety; they tell us only what will happen when certain specified variables are controlled, not what will occur in a particular situation. True, science cannot make concrete predictions; it must state its predictions for specific situations in terms of probability limits, depending upon the degree to which certain variables are operative. Nevertheless, as we isolate more and more of the influencing factors and learn more about their interaction, we can greatly narrow the probability limits. We can classify situations into more and more homogeneous types on the basis of the variables involved, and thus come nearer to understanding specific situations.

The discouraging aspects of the concepts of interaction, of the vicious circle and the self-fulfilling prophecy, have led some to believe that science, in describing these processes, has deepened our pessimism and injured the will to action. But science does not say that these things are inevitable; it says they will occur if certain variables do not change.

The self-fulfilling prophecy, whereby fears are translated into reality, operates only in the absence of deliberate institutional controls. And it is only with the rejection of social fatalism implied in the notion of unchangeable human nature that the tragic circle of fear, social disaster, reinforced fear can be broken. . . .

Nor can widespread, even typical, failures in planning human relations between ethnic groups be cited as evidence for pessimism. In the world laboratory of the sociologist, as in the more secluded laboratories of the physicist and chemist, it is the successful experiment which is decisive and not the thousand-and-one failures which preceded it. More is learned from the single success than from the multiple failures. A single success proves it can be done. Thereafter, it is necessary only to learn what made it work.[39]

It is often said that social science is deterministic in the sense that it makes any human effort useless. Man behaves the way he does because of what he is. He is a product of heredity and environment; since his nature cannot be changed, nothing can be done. If this view is taken, one gives up or becomes either a cynic or a theologian.

This is not the sense, however, in which science is deterministic. Science does state that events have a natural pattern and that man is part of the natural world, a creature of law. If certain forces are operative, these will be the results. But it may well be (and it is at this point that science is deterministic, but not predeterministic) that an understanding of the nature of events is a new variable that changes the results. Natural laws indicate that if I eat certain kinds of food in excess and fail to brush my teeth, I am liable to tooth decay. *Knowledge of those facts is a new variable that may prevent that result.* The laws are still true—*if.* Knowledge can help to free us; it does not bind us to the inevitable *application* of the natural laws. It will not work fast. Parents may know, intellectually, the best way to deal with their children, yet be unable to apply it. Some specific acts are more subject to rational control—institutional processes that do not involve the emotions of individuals, for example. These can improve the second generation, which, in turn, can bring knowledge and action more closely into line; it can change a little more, creating a better situation for the next generation. Those who demand the millennium day after tomorrow will be frustrated by this slow process. But many may find in the promise of this difficult road a quiet confidence that modern man sorely needs.

[39] Robert K. Merton, *Social Theory and Social Structure*, The Free Press, 1949, pp. 194–195.

APPENDIXES

APPENDIX A

Some Data on the Size of Minority Groups in the United States and Elsewhere

NOTE: Precise data on the size of minority groups are frequently lacking. Difficulties of definition or the failure of official counts to secure information on group membership may make a definitive statement impossible. What is the race of a "Mexican"? Who is to be listed as a Jew? These questions may be answered in a variety of ways.

Keeping in mind the inadequacies of the data, we might list the major minorities in the United States in 1957 in the following round numbers:

Negroes	17,300,000
Other nonwhites	700,000
Mexicans	2,500,000
Foreign-born whites	10,200,000
Jews	5,500,000

This list does not add up to 36,200,000, because the categories are not mutually exclusive; the foreign-born group includes some of the Jews and Mexicans. Altogether, over thirty million Americans—one-fifth of the nation's population—belong to one or another of these major minority groups. This is a smaller percentage than that of 1910, when the foreign-born and the Negro groups alone made up over 25 percent of the population. The trend in the last several decades has been for the United States population gradually to become more homogeneous. There is, of course, a large "second-generation" population in the United States, made up of persons one or both of whose parents were foreign-born. In 1950, over twenty-three millions were of "foreign or mixed parentage." A high proportion of the "second-generation" population are among those who experience the impact of minority status. When they are added to the list above, we find over fifty million Americans, one-third of the nation, belonging to minority groups.

The following data indicate some of the demographic trends.

TABLE 1.   United States Population by Race[1]

	White (in 000)	Negro (in 000)	Negro (% of Total)	Indian (in 000)	Chinese (in 000)	Japanese (in 000)	Others (in 000)
1790	3,172	757	19.3				
1800	4,306	1,002	18.9				
1810	5,862	1,378	19.0				
1820	7,867	1,772	18.4				
1830	10,537	2,329	18.1				
1840	14,196	2,874	16.8				
1850	19,553	3,639	15.7				
1860	26,923	4,442	14.1		35		
1870	33,589	4,880	13.5		63		
1880	43,403	6,581	13.1		105		
1890	55,101	7,489	11.9	248	107	2	
1900	66,809	8,834	11.6	237	90	24	
1910	81,732	9,828	10.7	266	72	72	3
1920	94,821	10,463	9.9	244	62	111	9
1930	110,281	11,891	9.7	332	75	138	51
1940	118,215	12,866	9.8	334	78	127	50
1950	134,942	15,042	10.0	(other nonwhites, total, 1950, 713)			

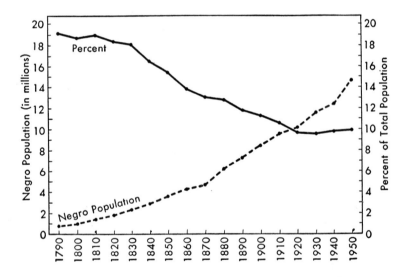

FIGURE 1.   Growth of the Negro Population in the United States.

[1] Bureau of the Census, *Statistical Abstract of the United States,* Government Printing Office, 1956.

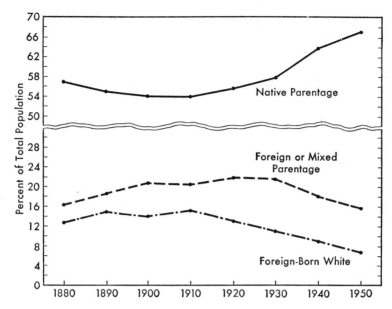

FIGURE 2.   White Population of the United States, by Nativity and Parentage, 1880–1950.

TABLE 2.   White Population of the United States, 1880–1950[2]

	Native Parentage Number (in 000)	Percent	Foreign or Mixed Parentage Number (in 000)	Percent	Foreign-Born White Number (in 000)	Percent
1880	28,568	57.0	8,275	16.5	6,560	13.1
1890	34,476	54.8	11,504	18.3	9,122	14.5
1900	40,949	53.9	15,646	20.6	10,214	13.4
1910	49,489	53.8	18,898	20.5	13,346	14.5
1920	58,422	55.3	22,686	21.5	13,713	13.0
1930	70,401	57.3	25,902	21.1	13,983	11.4
1940	84,125	63.7	23,158	17.5	11,419	8.6
1950	101,191	67.1	23,589	15.7	10,161	6.7

Note that the proportion of the population that is foreign-born has been declining since 1910 and the actual number of foreign-born has been declining since 1930.

TABLE 3.   Immigration into the United States, by Decades, 1820–1955 (in 000)[3]

1820–1830	152	1891–1900	3,688
1831–1840	599	1901–1910	8,795
1841–1850	1,713	1911–1920	5,736
1851–1860	2,598	1921–1930	4,107
1861–1870	2,315	1931–1940	528
1871–1880	2,812	1941–1950	1,035
1881–1890	5,247	1951–1955	1,088

[2] Ibid.
[3] Ibid.

TABLE 4. National Origin of the Foreign-Born Whites in the
United States, 1940 and 1950[4]

	Number (000)		Percent of Foreign-Born White	
	1940	1950	1940	1950
Italy	1,624	1,427	14.2	14.0
Germany	1,238	984	10.8	9.7
Canada	1,066	995	9.3	9.8
Russia	1,041	895	9.1	8.8
Poland	993	861	8.7	8.5
England and Wales	657	585	5.8	5.8
Eire	572	505	5.0	5.0
Austria	480	409	4.2	4.0
Sweden	445	325	3.9	3.2
Mexico	377	451	3.3	4.4
Czechoslovakia	320	278	2.8	2.7
Hungary	290	268	2.5	2.6
Scotland	279	244	2.4	2.4
Norway	262	202	2.3	2.0
Lithuania	166	148	1.5	1.5
Greece	163	169	1.4	1.7
Yugoslavia	161	144	1.4	1.4
Asia	154	180	1.3	1.8
Denmark	138	108	1.2	1.1
Finland	117	96	1.0	0.9
Rumania	116	85	1.0	0.8
Netherlands	111	102	1.0	1.0
Northern Ireland	106	15	0.9	0.1
France	103	108	0.9	1.1
All others	440	577	3.9	5.7
Total	11,419	10,161	100.0	100.0

TABLE 5. Composition of the Population of the United States, by Region, 1950
(in Percentage)[5]

	Northeast	North Central	South	West
Native white	81.7	89.1	76.6	87.2
Foreign-born white	13.2	5.9	1.6	8.0
Negro	5.0	4.8	21.6	2.9
Other races	0.1	0.2	0.2	1.8

Although slightly over half of the foreign-born whites are still found in
the Northeast, they have tended to become more widely dispersed in recent
years, at the same time that the total number of foreign-born was dropping.
The Negro group is also becoming more widely dispersed. In 1860, over
90 percent of the Negroes lived in the South. The figure still stood at 89

[4] *Ibid.*
[5] Bureau of the Census, "General Characteristics of the Population, by Regions,
April 1, 1950," preliminary report released April 30, 1951.

percent in 1910; but by 1950 it had fallen to less than 69 percent. Between 1940 and 1950, Negroes in the West increased by 237 percent.

TABLE 6. Location of the Negro Population, by Region, 1790–1950[6]

| | North[a] | | South | | West | |
	Number	Percent	Number	Percent	Number	Percent
1790	67,424	8.9	689,784	91.1		
1860	340,240	7.7	4,097,111	92.2	4,479	0.1
1910	1,027,674	10.5	8,749,427	89.0	50,662	0.5
1940	2,790,293	21.7	9,904,619	77.0	170,706	1.3
1950[b]	4,109,000	27.6	10,208,000	68.5	576,000	3.9

[a] Includes Northeast and North Central.
[b] Estimated.

TABLE 7. Some Population Data for Three Multiracial Societies

Racial Composition of the Union of South Africa[7]

| | European | | Native (Bantu) | | Coloured | | Asiatic | |
	Number (in 000)	Per-cent	Number (in 000)	Per-cent	Number (in 000)	Per-cent	Number (in 000)	Per-cent
1904	1,117	21.6	3,411	67.4	445	8.6	123	2.4
1921	1,519	21.9	4,698	67.8	546	7.9	166	2.4
1946	2,373	20.9	7,832	68.6	928	8.1	285	2.5

Racial Composition of Hawaii[8]

| | Hawaiian | | Part-Hawaiian | | Caucasian | | Chinese | |
	Number (in 000)	Per-cent	Number (in 000)	Per-cent	Number (in 000)	Per-cent	Number (in 000)	Per-cent
1910	26	13.6	13	6.5	44	23.0	22	11.3
1920	24	9.3	18	7.0	55	21.4	24	9.2
1930	23	6.1	28	7.7	80	21.8	27	7.4
1940	14	3.4	50	11.8	104	24.5	29	6.8
1950	13	2.8	77	16.5	82	17.5	31	6.5

| | Filipino | | Japanese | | Other | | Total |
	Number (in 000)	Per-cent	Number (in 000)	Per-cent	Number (in 000)	Per-cent	(in 000)
1910	2	1.2	78	41.5	6	2.9	192
1920	21	8.2	109	42.7	6	2.2	256
1930	63	17.1	140	37.9	7	2.0	368
1940	53	12.4	158	37.3	16	3.8	423
1950	61	13.1	185	39.5	19	4.1	468

[6] Bureau of the Census, *Historical Statistics*, Government Printing Office, 1949; and Bureau of the Census, "General Characteristics of the Population, by Regions, April 1, 1950," preliminary report released April 30, 1951.

[7] Census and Statistics Office of the Union of South Africa, *Official Yearbook of the Union*, number 24, Government Printer, Pretoria, 1948, p. 1079.

[8] Bureau of the Census, *Sixteenth Census of the United States*, 1940, *Population*, Second Series, "Characteristics of the Population: Hawaii"; and "Official Release of the Bureau of Health Statistics," July 1, 1950.

Racial Composition of Brazil[9]

The Brazilian government makes no official census count by race, and the estimates vary, partly because of different schemes of classification. Two estimates are given here:

White	71.1%	White	51%
Negro and mulatto	28.8	White and Negro	22
Oriental	1.0	Negro	14
		White and Indian	11
		Indian	2

[9] For the estimate on the left, *Brazil, 1946*, Department of Information and Statistics, Rio de Janeiro, 1946; for the estimate on the right, James G. Leyburn, "World Minority Problems," *Public Affairs Pamphlet*, No. 132, 1947, p. 24.

APPENDIX B

Bibliography

Abrams, Charles, *Forbidden Neighbors*, Harper & Brothers, 1955.

Abrams, Charles, "Civil Rights in 1956," *Commentary*, August, 1956, pp. 107 ff.

Abrams, Charles (Chairman of the New York State Commission Against Discrimination), Address at the Annual Meeting with Civic and Social Agencies, December 3, 1956, New York City.

Ackerman, Nathan, and Jahoda, Marie, *Anti-Semitism and Emotional Disorder*, Harper & Brothers, 1950.

Adamic, Louis, *From Many Lands*, Harper & Brothers, 1939.

Adams, Harold E., "Minority Caricatures on the American Stage," in G. P. Murdock (ed.), *Studies in the Science of Society*, Yale University Press, 1937.

Adams, R., *Intermarriage in Hawaii*, The Macmillan Company, 1937.

Adler, Cyrus, and Margolith, Aaron M., *With Firmness in the Right, American Diplomatic Action Affecting Jews, 1840–1945*, American Jewish Committee, 1945.

Adorno, T. W., Frenkel-Brunswik, Else, Levinson, D. J., and Sanford, R. N., *The Authoritarian Personality*, Harper & Brothers, 1950.

Albrecht, M. C., "The Relationship of Literature and Society," *American Journal of Sociology*, March, 1954, pp. 425–436.

Alexander, W. W., *Racial Segregation in the American Protestant Church*, Friendship Press, 1946.

Allen, James S., "The Black Belt: Area of Negro Majority," *The Communist*, June, 1934, pp. 581–599.

Allen, James S., *Reconstruction, the Battle for Democracy*, International Publishers, 1937.

Allport, Gordon, "The Bigot in Our Midst," *Commonweal*, October 6, 1944, pp. 582–586.

Allport, Gordon, "Catharsis and the Reduction of Prejudice," *Journal of Social Issues*, December, 1945, pp. 3–10.

Allport, Gordon, "Prejudice: A Problem in Psychological and Social Causation," *Journal of Social Issues*, Supplement Series, November, 1950.

Allport, Gordon, *The Nature of Prejudice*, Addison-Wesley Publishing Company, Inc., 1954.

Allport, Gordon, and Kramer, B. M., "Some Roots of Prejudice," *Journal of Psychology*, July, 1946, pp. 9–39.

American Council on Education, Committee on the Study of Teaching Materials in Intergoup Relations, *Intergroup Relations in Teaching Materials*, American Council on Education, 1949.

Anderson, C. A., "Economic Status Differentials Within Southern Agriculture," *Rural Sociology*, March, 1954, pp. 50–67.

Anderson, C. A., "Inequalities in Schooling in the South," *American Journal of Sociology*, May, 1955, pp. 547–561.

Anderson, C. A., and Bowman, M. J., "The Vanishing Servant and the Contemporary Status System of the American South," *American Journal of Sociology*, November, 1953, pp. 215–230.

Anderson, C. A., and Bowman, M. J., *Tenure Changes and the Agricultural Ladder in Southern Agriculture*, Bulletin 634, Kentucky Agricultural Experiment Station, 1955.

Anderson, E. L., *We Americans*, Harvard University Press, 1937.

Annella, Sister M., "Some Aspects of Interracial Marriage in Washington, D.C.," *Journal of Negro Education*, Fall, 1956, pp. 380–391.

Anonymous, "My Daughter Married a Negro," *Harper's Magazine*, July, 1951, pp. 36–40.

Antonovsky, Aaron, "Toward a Refinement of the 'Marginal Man' Concept," *Social Forces*, October, 1956, pp. 57–62.

Aptheker, Herbert (introduction by Doxey A. Wilkerson), *The Negro People in America*, International Publishers, 1946.

Ashmore, Harry S., *The Negro and the Schools*, University of North Carolina Press, 1954.

Atkinson, Brooks, "Negro Folk Drama," *New York Times*, September 9, 1952.

Atwood, J. H., Wyatt, D. W., Davis, V. J., and Walker, I. D., *Thus Be Their Destiny*, American Council on Education, 1941.

Axelrad, Sidney, "Negro and White Male Institutionalized Delinquents," *American Journal of Sociology*, May, 1952, pp. 569–574.

Axline, Virginia M., "Play Therapy and Race Conflict in Young Children," *Journal of Abnormal and Social Psychology*, July, 1948, pp. 300–310.

Baber, Ray E., "A Study of 325 Mixed Marriages," *American Sociological Review*, October, 1937, pp. 705–716.

Bachrach, Arthur J., and Blackwell, Gordon W. (eds.), "Human Problems in the Changing South," *Journal of Social Issues*, 1954, vol. 10, No. 1, whole issue.

Bacote, C. A., "The Negro in Atlanta Politics," *Phylon*, Fourth Quarter, 1955, pp. 333–350.

Baer, M. F., "Counting the Jewish College Students," *National Jewish Monthly*, October, 1947, pp. 70–71.

Banks, W. S. M., II, "The Rank Order of Sensitivity to Discrimination of

Negroes in Columbus, Ohio," *American Sociological Review*, August, 1950, pp. 529–534.

Barron, Milton L., "The Incidence of Jewish Intermarriage in Europe and America," *American Sociological Review*, February, 1946, pp. 6–13.

Barron, Milton L., *People Who Intermarry*, Syracuse University Press, 1948.

Barron, Milton L., "Research on Intermarriage: A Survey of Accomplishments and Prospects," *American Journal of Sociology*, November, 1951, pp. 249–255.

Baruch, Dorothy W., *The Glass House of Prejudice*, William Morrow & Co., Inc., 1946.

Bass, Bernard M., "Authoritarianism or Acquiescence," *Journal of Abnormal and Social Psychology*, November, 1955, pp. 616–623.

Bayton, J. A., "The Racial Stereotypes of Negro College Students," *Journal of Abnormal and Social Psychology*, January, 1941, pp. 97–102.

Bayton, J. A., and Bell, E., "An Exploratory Study of the Role of the Negro Press," *Journal of Negro Education*, 1951, vol. 20, pp. 8–15.

Beach, Waldo, "Storm Warnings from the South," *Christianity and Chrisis*, March 19, 1956, pp. 27–30.

Beals, Ralph, "Indian-Mestizo-White Relations in Spanish America," chap. 18 in Lind, A. W. (ed.), *Race Relations in World Perspective*, University of Hawaii Press, 1955.

Bell, Daniel, and Lipset, Seymour M. (eds.), "Trade Unions and Minority Problems," *Journal of Social Issues*, 1953, vol. 9, No. 1.

Bell, H. M., *Youth Tell Their Story*, American Council on Education, 1938.

Benedict, Ruth, *Race: Science and Politics*, Modern Age Books, 1940.

Bennett, J. W., and Tumin, M. M., *Social Life: Structure and Function*, Alfred A. Knopf, Inc., 1948.

Berelson, Bernard, and Salter, Patricia, "Majority and Minority Americans: An Analysis of American Magazine Fiction," *Public Opinion Quarterly*, Summer, 1946, pp. 168–190.

Berger, Morroe, "Fair Educational Practices Legislation," *Annals of the American Academy of Political and Social Science*, May, 1951, pp. 45 ff.

Berger, Morroe, *Equality by Statute*, Columbia University Press, 1952.

Bernard, Jessie, "The Conceptualization of Intergroup Relations, with Special Reference to Conflict," *Social Forces*, December, 1950, pp. 243–251.

Berry, Brewton, *Race Relations*, Houghton Mifflin Company, 1951.

Bettleheim, Bruno, and Janowitz, Morris, *Dynamics of Prejudice. A Psychological and Sociological Study of Veterans*, Harper & Brothers, 1950.

Biesanz, John, and Smith, Luke M., "Adjustment of Interethnic Marriages on the Isthmus of Panama," *American Sociological Review*, December, 1951, pp. 819–822.

Birnie, Cassandra M., "Race and Politics in Georgia and South Carolina," *Phylon*, Third Quarter, 1952, pp. 236 ff.

Blalock, H. M., "Economic Discrimination and Negro Increase," *American Sociological Review*, October, 1956, pp. 584–588.

Bloom, Leonard, and Riemer, Ruth, *Removal and Return: the Socio-Eco-*

nomic Effects of the War on Japanese Americans, University of California Press, 1949.

Blumer, Herbert, "Social Science and the Desegregation Process," *Annals of the American Academy of Political and Social Science*, March, 1956, pp. 137–143.

Boas, Franz, *Anthropology and Modern Life*, W. W. Norton & Company, Inc., 1928.

Boas, Franz, *General Anthropology*, D. C. Heath and Company, 1938.

Bogardus, Emory S., *Immigration and Race Attitudes*, D. C. Heath and Company, 1928.

Bogardus, Emory S., *The Mexican in the United States*, University of Southern California Press, 1943.

Bogue, Donald J., "Population Distribution and Composition in the New South," in Jessie P. Guzman (ed.), *The New South and Higher Education*, Tuskegee Institute, 1954, pp. 3–25.

Bond, F. W., *The Negro and the Drama*, The Associated Publishers, 1940.

Bond, H. M., *The Education of the Negro in the American Social Order*, Prentice-Hall, Inc., 1934.

Bond, H. M., *Negro Education in Alabama, A Study in Cotton and Steel*, The Associated Publishers, 1939.

Bond, J. M., "Some Aspects of Graduate and Professional Education for Negroes," *Phylon*, 1949, vol. 10, pp. 393–394.

Boyd, George F., "The Levels of Aspiration of White and Negro Children in a Non-Segregated Elementary School," *Journal of Social Psychology*, November, 1952, pp. 191–196.

Boyd, William C., *Genetics and the Races of Man*, Little, Brown & Company, 1950.

Brameld, Theodore, *Minority Problems in the Public Schools*, Harper & Brothers, 1946.

Brookover, Wilbur, and Holland, John, "An Inquiry into the Meaning of Minority Group Attitude Expressions," *American Sociological Review*, April, 1952, pp. 196–202.

Broom, Leonard, and Kituse, John I., "The Validation of Acculturation: A Condition to Ethnic Assimilation," *American Anthropologist*, February, 1955, pp. 44–48.

Broom, Leonard, and Kituse, John I., *The Managed Casualty: The Japanese-American Family in World War II*, University of California Press, 1956.

Broom, Leonard, and Shevky, Eshref, "Mexicans in the United States, a Problem in Social Differentiation," *Sociology and Social Research*, January–February, 1952, pp. 150–158.

Brown, F. J., and Roucek, J. S. (eds.), *One America*, Prentice-Hall, Inc., 1945.

Brown, J. F., *Psychology and the Social Order*, McGraw-Hill Book Company, 1936.

Brown, Roger W., "A Determinant of the Relationship Between Rigidity and Authoritarianism," *Journal of Abnormal and Social Psychology*, October, 1953, pp. 469–476.

Brown, Spencer, *They See for Themselves*, Harper & Brothers, 1945.

Brown, Sterling A., *Southern Road*, Harcourt, Brace & Company, 1932.

Brown, Sterling A., "Negro Character as Seen by White Authors," *Journal of Negro Education*, January, 1933, pp. 180–201.

Brown, Sterling A., *The Negro in American Fiction*, Associates in Negro Folk Education, 1937.

Brown, Sterling A., *Negro Poetry and Drama*, Associates in Negro Folk Education, 1937.

Brown, Sterling A., "The Blues," *Phylon*, Fourth Quarter, 1952, pp. 286–292.

Brown, Sterling A., "Negro Folk Expression," *Phylon*, First Quarter, 1953, pp. 50–60.

Brown, Sterling A., Davis, Arthur P., and Lee, Ulysses (eds.), *The Negro Caravan*, The Dryden Press, Inc., 1941.

Browne, V. J., "Racial Desegregation in the Public Service, with Particular Reference to the U.S. Government," *Journal of Negro Education*, Summer, 1954, pp. 246 ff.

Bryson, Lyman, and Rowden, Dorothy, "Radio as an Agency of National Unity," *Annals of the American Academy of Political and Social Science*, March, 1946, pp. 137–143.

Bullock, Gerald D., "Chicago—Poignancy and Platitudes," *The Crisis*, May, 1957, pp. 262–263.

Bunche, Ralph, "The Negro in the Political Life of the United States," *Journal of Negro Education*, July, 1941.

Bureau of Sociological Research, Colorado River War Relocation Center, "The Japanese Family in America," *Annals of the American Academy of Political and Social Science*, September, 1943, pp. 150–156.

Burgess, E. W., and Cottrell, L., *Predicting Success or Failure in Marriage*, Prentice-Hall, Inc., 1939.

Burma, John H., "Humor as a Technique in Race Conflict," *American Sociological Review*, December, 1946, pp. 710–715.

Burma, John H., "Race Relations and Antidiscriminatory Legislation," *American Journal of Sociology*, March, 1951, pp. 416–423.

Burma, John H., "Research Note on the Measurement of Interracial Marriage," *American Journal of Sociology*, May, 1952, pp. 587–589.

Burma, John H., *Spanish-Speaking Groups in the United States*, Duke University Press, 1954.

California State Department of Education, *Teachers' Guide to the Education of Spanish-Speaking Children*, October, 1952.

Calverton, V. F., *Anthology of American Negro Literature*, Modern Library, Inc., 1929.

Campisi, P. J., "Ethnic Family Patterns: The Italian Family in the United States," *American Journal of Sociology*, May, 1948, pp. 443–449.

Cantril, Hadley, *The Psychology of Social Movements*, John Wiley & Sons, Inc., 1941.

Carter, Elmer, "Policies and Practices of Discrimination Commissions," *Annals of the American Academy of Political and Social Science*, March, 1956, pp. 62–77.

Carter, Hodding, "A Wave of Terror Threatens the South," *Look*, March 22, 1955, pp. 34 ff.

Carter, R. L., and Marshall, Thurgood, "The Meaning and Significance of the Supreme Court Decree," *Journal of Negro Education*, Summer, 1955, pp. 397–404.

Catapusan, B. T., "Filipino Intermarriage Problems in the United States," *Sociology and Social Research*, January–February, 1938, pp. 265–272.

Caudill, William, and DeVos, George, "Achievement, Culture and Personality: The Case of the Japanese Americans," *American Anthropologist*, December, 1956, pp. 1102–1126.

Cayton, Horace R., and Mitchell, G. S., *Black Workers and the New Unions*, University of North Carolina Press, 1939.

Chancellor, Loren E., and Monahan, Thomas P., "Religious Preference and Interreligious Mixtures in Marriages and Divorces in Iowa," *American Journal of Sociology*, November, 1955, pp. 233–239.

Chapman, Loren J., and Campbell, Donald T., "Response Set in the F Scale," *Journal of Abnormal and Social Psychology*, January, 1957, pp. 129–132.

Chapple, E. D., and Coon, C. S., *Principles of Anthropology*, Henry Holt Company, Inc., 1942.

Chatto, C. L., and Halligan, Alice L., *Story of the Springfield Plan*, Barnes & Noble, Inc., 1945.

Chein, Isidor, "Some Considerations in Combating Intergroup Prejudice," *Journal of Educational Sociology*, March, 1946, pp. 412–419.

Ch'Eng-K'un Cheng, "Assimilation in Hawaii and the Bid for Statehood," *Social Forces*, October, 1951, pp. 16–29.

Child, I. L., *Italian or American*, Yale University Press, 1943.

Christie, Richard, and Garcia, John, "Subcultural Variation in Authoritarian Personality," *Journal of Abnormal and Social Psychology*, October, 1951, pp. 457–469.

Christie, Richard, and Jahoda, Marie (eds.), *Studies in the Scope and Method of "The Authoritarian Personality,"* The Free Press, 1954.

Citron, A. F., and Harding, John, "An Experiment in Training Volunteers to Answer Anti-Minority Remarks," *Journal of Abnormal and Social Psychology*, April, 1950, pp. 310–328.

Citron, A. F., Chein, Isidor, and Harding, John, "Anti-Minority Remarks: A Problem for Action Research," *Journal of Abnormal and Social Psychology*, January, 1950, pp. 99–126.

Clark, Kenneth B. (ed.), "Desegregation: An Appraisal of the Evidence," *Journal of Social Issues*, 1953, vol. 9, no. 4.

Clark, Kenneth B., *Prejudice and Your Child*, The Beacon Press, 1955.

Claude, Inis L., Jr., *National Minorities*, Harvard University Press, 1955.

Clement, R. E., "The Present and Future Role of Private Colleges for Negroes," *Phylon*, 1949, vol. 10, pp. 323–327.

Clinchy, Everett R., *The Growth of Good Will: A Sketch of Protestant-Catholic-Jewish Relations*, National Conference of Christians and Jews, 1953.

Cohen, Israel, *Jewish Life in Modern Times*, Dodd, Mead & Co., Inc., 1914.

Collins, Orvis, "Ethnic Behavior in Industry: Sponsorship and Rejection in a New England Factory," *American Journal of Sociology*, January, 1946, pp. 293–298.

Collins, Sidney F., "The Social Position of White and 'Half-Caste' Women in Colored Groupings in Britain," *American Sociological Review*, December, 1951, pp. 796–802.

Congar, Yves M.-J., *The Catholic Church and the Race Questions*, UNESCO, 1953.

Cook, Lloyd A. (ed.), *College Programs in Intergroup Relations*, American Council on Education, 1950.

Cook, Lloyd A., and Cook, Elaine, *Intergroup Education*, McGraw-Hill Book Company, 1954.

Coon, Carleton S., *The Races of Europe*, The Macmillan Company, 1939.

Cooper, Eunice, and Jahoda, Marie, "The Evasion of Propaganda: How Prejudiced People Respond to Anti-Prejudice Propaganda," *Journal of Psychology*, January, 1947, pp. 15–25.

Cooper, R. L., "The Frustrations of Being a Member of a Minority Group: What Does It Do to the Individual and to His Relationships with Other People," *Mental Hygiene*, April, 1945, pp. 189–195.

Coughlin, Richard J., "The Chinese in Bangkok: A Commercial-Oriented Minority," *American Sociological Review*, June, 1955, pp. 311–316.

Coutu, Walter, *Emergent Human Nature*, Alfred A. Knopf, Inc., 1949.

Cowgill, Donald D., "Trends in Residential Segregation of Non-whites in American Cities, 1940–1950," *American Sociological Review*, February, 1956, pp. 43–47.

Cox, Oliver C., *Caste, Class and Race*, Doubleday & Company, Inc., 1948.

Cox, Oliver C., "Max Weber on Social Stratification: A Critique," *American Sociological Review*, April, 1950, pp. 223–227.

Criswell, Joan H., "Racial Cleavage in Negro-White Groups," *Sociometry*, 1937, vol. 1, pp. 81–89.

Cronon, E. D., *Black Moses*, University of Wisconsin Press, 1955.

Cuber, John F., and Kenkel, William F., *Social Stratification in the United States*, Appleton-Century-Crofts, 1954.

Cullen, Countee, *Caroling Dusk*, Harper & Brothers, 1927.

Culver, Dwight W., *Negro Segregation in the Methodist Church*, Yale University Press, 1953.

Current, G. B., "Segregated Schools—On Trial in East St. Louis," *The Crisis*, March, 1949, pp. 77–79.

Cushman, R. E., "The Laws of the Land," *Survey Graphic*, January, 1947, pp. 14–18, 97–99.

Dahlberg, Gunnar, *Race, Reason and Rubbish*, Columbia University Press, 1942.

Daniel, V. E., "Ritual and Stratification in Chicago Negro Churches," *American Sociological Review*, June, 1942, pp. 353–358.

Daniel, Warren, "Availability of Education for Negroes in the Secondary School," *Journal of Negro Education*, 1947, vol. 16, pp. 457 ff.

Daves, J. H., "TVA and Negro Employment," *Journal of Negro Education*, Winter, 1955, pp. 87–90.

Davie, Maurice R., *Refugees in America*, Harper & Brothers, 1947.

Davie, Maurice R., *Negroes in American Society*, McGraw-Hill Book Company, 1949.

Davies, Lawrence E., "Housing 'Pattern' of Races Dropped," *New York Times*, May 30, 1954, p. 44.

Davis, Allison W., "Child Rearing in the Class Structure of American Society," in *The Family in a Democratic Society*, Columbia University Press, 1949, pp. 56–69.

Davis, Allison W., and Dollard, John, *Children of Bondage*, American Council on Education, 1940.

Davis, Allison W., and Havighurst, Robert J., "Social Class and Color Differences in Child-Rearing," *American Sociological Review*, December, 1946, pp. 710 ff.

Davis, Allison W., and Havighurst, Robert J., *Father of the Man. How Your Child Gets His Personality*, Houghton Mifflin Company, 1947.

Davis, Allison W., Gardner, B. B., and Gardner, M. R., *Deep South*, University of Chicago Press, 1941.

Davis, Arthur P., "Jesse B. Semple: Negro American," *Phylon*, First Quarter, 1954, pp. 21–28.

Davis, Arthur P., "Integration and Race Literature," *Phylon*, Second Quarter, 1956, pp. 141–146.

Davis, John A., *How Management Can Integrate Negroes in War Industries*, New York State Committee on Discrimination in Employment, 1942.

Davis, John A., "Nondiscrimination in the Federal Services," *Annals of the American Academy of Political and Social Science*, March, 1946, pp. 65–74.

Davis, John A., "Negro Employment: A Progress Report," *Fortune*, July, 1952, pp. 161 ff.

Davis, John A., and Golightly, Cornelius L., "Negro Employment in the Federal Government," *Phylon*, Fourth Quarter, 1945, pp. 337–340.

Davis, Kingsley, "A Conceptual Analysis of Stratification," *American Sociological Review*, June, 1942, pp. 309–321.

Davis, M. M., and Smythe, H. H., "Providing Adequate Health Service to Negroes," *Journal of Negro Education*, July, 1949.

Dawson, Charles C., "Voting," in Guzman, Jessie P. (ed.), *The Negro Yearbook*, Tuskegee Institute, 1952.

Dean, John P., and Rosen, Alex, *A Manual of Intergroup Relations*, University of Chicago Press, 1955.

Demerath, Nick J., "Desegregation, Education, and the South's Future," *Phylon*, First Quarter, 1957, pp. 43–49.

Deutsch, Morton, and Collins, Mary E., *Interracial Housing*, University of Minnesota Press, 1951.

Dewey, Donald, "Negro Employment in Southern Industry," *Journal of Political Economy*, August, 1952, pp. 285 ff.

Divine, Robert A., *American Immigration Policy, 1924–1952*, Yale University Press, 1957.

Doddy, H. H., and Edwards, G. F., "Apprehensions of Negro Teachers Concerning Desegregation in South Carolina," *Journal of Negro Education*, Winter, 1955, pp. 26–43.

Dodson, D. W., "College Quotas and American Democracy," *American Scholar*, Summer, 1946, pp. 3–12.

Dodson, D. W., "Religious Prejudice in Colleges," *American Mercury*, July, 1946, pp. 5–13.

Doherty, J. F., *Moral Problems of Interracial Marriage*, Catholic University of America Press, 1949.

Dollard, John, *Caste and Class in a Southern Town*, Yale University Press, 1937.

Dollard, John, "Hostility and Fear in Social Life," *Social Forces*, October, 1938, pp. 15–26.

Dollard, John, Miller, Neal, Doob, Leonard, Mowrer, O. H., and Sears, R. R., *Frustration and Aggression*, Yale University Press, 1939.

Donne, John, *Devotions upon Emergent Occasions*, Cambridge University Press, 1923.

Doob, Leonard, *Public Opinion and Propaganda*, Henry Holt & Company, Inc., 1948.

Doyle, Bertram, *The Etiquette of Race Relations in the South*, University of Chicago Press, 1937.

Dozier, E. P., Simpson, George E., and Yinger, J. Milton, "The Integration of Americans of Indian Descent," *Annals of the American Academy of Political and Social Science*, May, 1957, pp. 158–165.

Drake, St. Clair, and Cayton, Horace, *Black Metropolis*, Harcourt, Brace & Company, 1945.

DuBois, Rachel D., *Neighbors in Action*, Harper & Brothers, 1950.

Dunn, L. C., and Dobzhansky, T., *Heredity, Race, and Society*, Penguin Books, Inc., 1946.

Duval, E. M., and Hill, Reuben, *When You Marry*, D. C. Heath and Company, 1945.

Edmunds, Edwin R., "The Myrdalian Hypothesis: Rank Order of Discrimination," *Phylon*, Third Quarter, 1954, pp. 297–303.

Eells, W. C., "The Higher Education of Negroes in the United States," *Journal of Negro Education*, Fall, 1955, pp. 426–434.

Elson, Alex, and Schanfield, Leonard, "Local Regulation of Discriminatory Employment Practices," *Yale Law Journal*, February, 1947, pp. 454 ff.

Evans, James C., and Lane, David A., Jr., "Integration in the Armed Services," *Annals of the American Academy of Political and Social Science*, March, 1956, pp. 78–85.

Evans, L. H., "The Magnificent Purpose," *Phylon*, 1949, vol. 10, pp. 319–320.

Fair Employment Practice Commission, *Final Report*, Government Printing Office, 1947.

Fauset, A. H., *Black Gods of the Metropolis*, University of Pennsylvania Press, 1944.

Fensterheim, Herbert, and Birch, H. G., "A Case Study of Group Ideology and Individual Adjustment," *Journal of Abnormal and Social Psychology*, October, 1950, pp. 710–720.

Festinger, Leon, and Kelley, Harold H., *Changing Attitudes Through Social Contact*, Research Center for Group Dynamics, Institute for Social Research, University of Michigan, September, 1951.

Fineberg, S. A., *Overcoming Anti-Semitism*, Harper & Brothers, 1943.

Fineberg, S. A., *Punishment Without Crime*, Doubleday & Company, Inc., 1949.

Finkelstein, Louis (ed.), *The Jews, Their History, Culture, and Religion,* Harper & Brothers, 1949, 2 vols.

Fishman, Joshua A., "An Examination of the Process and Function of Social Stereotyping," *Journal of Social Psychology,* February, 1956, pp. 27–64.

Fleming, Harold C., "Resistance Movements and Racial Desegregation," *Annals of the American Academy of Political and Social Science,* March, 1956, pp. 44–52.

Flowerman, S. H., "Mass Propaganda in the War Against Bigotry," *Journal of Abnormal and Social Psychology,* October, 1947, pp. 429–439.

Ford, Nick A., "A Blueprint for Negro Authors," *Phylon,* Fourth Quarter, 1950, pp. 374–377.

Ford, Nick A., "Four Popular Novelists," *Phylon,* First Quarter, 1954, pp. 38 ff.

Foreman, Paul B., "The Implications of Project Clear," *Phylon,* Third Quarter, 1955, pp. 263–274.

Forster, Arnold, *A Measure of Freedom,* Doubleday & Company, Inc., 1950.

Forster, Arnold, and Epstein, Benjamin R., *Cross-Currents,* Doubleday & Company, Inc., 1956.

Forster, Nora C., Vinacke, W. E., and Digman, J. M., "Flexibility and Rigidity in a Variety of Problem Situations," *Journal of Abnormal and Social Psychology,* March, 1955, pp. 211–216.

Fortune, "Biggest Cotton Plantation," March, 1937, pp. 125–132.

Francis, E. K., "Variables in the Formation of So-Called 'Minority Groups,'" *American Journal of Sociology,* July, 1954.

Frank, L. K., *Society as the Patient,* Rutgers University Press, 1948.

Franklin, John Hope, *From Slavery to Freedom,* Alfred A. Knopf, Inc., 1948.

Frazier, E. Franklin, "The Negro in the American Social Order," *Journal of Negro Education,* July, 1935, pp. 294 ff.

Frazier, E. Franklin, *Negro Youth at the Crossways,* American Council on Education, 1940.

Frazier, E. Franklin, "Sociological Theory and Race Relations," *American Sociological Review,* June, 1947, pp. 265–271.

Frazier, E. Franklin, *The Negro Family in the United States,* The Citadel Press, rev. ed., 1948.

Frazier, E. Franklin, "Ethnic Family Patterns: The Negro Family in the United States," *American Journal of Sociology,* May, 1948, pp. 432–438.

Frazier, E. Franklin, *The Negro in the United States,* The Macmillan Company, 1949.

Frazier, E. Franklin, "Problems and Needs of Negro Children," *Journal of Negro Education,* Summer, 1950, pp. 269 ff.

Frazier, E. Franklin, *Black Bourgeoisie,* The Free Press, 1957.

Frazier, E. Franklin, *Race and Culture Contacts in the Modern World,* Alfred A. Knopf, Inc., 1957.

Freedman, Maurice (ed.), *A Minority in Britain. Social Studies of the Anglo-Jewish Community,* Vallentine, Mitchell and Company, Ltd., 1955.

Frenkel-Brunswik, Else, "Studies of Social Discrimination in Children," *American Psychologist*, October, 1946, p. 456.

Frenkel-Brunswik, Else, "A Study of Prejudice in Children," *Human Relations*, 1948, vol. 1, pp. 295–306.

Frenkel-Brunswik, Else, and Sanford, R. N., "Some Personality Factors in Anti-Semitism," *Journal of Psychology*, October, 1945, pp. 271–291.

Fresno County Public Schools, *Teaching Children Who Move with the Crops*, Fresno, California, September, 1955.

Fuchs, Lawrence H., *The Political Behavior of American Jews*, The Free Press, 1956.

Gallagher, Buell, *American Caste and the Negro College*, Columbia University Press, 1938.

Gallagher, Buell, *Color and Conscience*, Harper & Brothers, 1946.

Gamarekian, Edward, "A Report from the South on the Negro Voter," *The Reporter*, June 27, 1957, pp. 9–10.

Gans, H. J., "American Jewry: Present and Future," *Commentary*, May, 1956, pp. 422–430.

Gans, H. J., "The Future of American Jewry," *Commentary*, June, 1956, pp. 555–563.

Garn, S. M., and Coon, C. S., "On the Number of Races of Mankind," *American Anthropologist*, October, 1955, pp. 996–1001.

Gerth, Hans H., "The Nazi Party: Its Leadership and Composition," *American Journal of Sociology*, January, 1940, pp. 517–541.

Gerth, Hans H., and Mills, C. W., *From Max Weber: Essays in Sociology*, Oxford University Press, 1946.

Gertz, Elmer, "American Ghettos," *Jewish Affairs*, February 1, 1947.

Gilbert, G. M., "Stereotype Persistence and Change Among College Students," *Journal of Abnormal and Social Psychology*, April, 1951, pp. 245–254.

Gillin, John, *The Ways of Men*, Appleton-Century-Crofts, 1948.

Ginzberg, Eli, *The Negro Potential*, Columbia University Press, 1956.

Ginzburg, Benjamin, "Anti-Semitism," *Encyclopædia of the Social Sciences*, The Macmillan Company, 1930, vol. 2, pp. 119–125.

Gist, Noel P., "Caste Differentials in India," *American Sociological Review*, April, 1954, pp. 126–137.

Gist, Noel P., "Caste in Transition: South India," *Phylon*, Second Quarter, 1954, pp. 155–164.

Gittler, Joseph B. (ed.), *Understanding Minority Groups*, John Wiley & Sons, Inc., 1956.

Glazer, Nathan, "The Jewish Revival in America," *Commentary*, December, 1955, pp. 493–499, and January, 1956, pp. 17–24.

Glick, C. E., "Collective Behavior in Race Relations," *American Sociological Review*, June, 1948, pp. 287–294.

Gloster, Hugh M., *Negro Voices in American Fiction*, University of North Carolina Press, 1948.

Gloster, Hugh M., "Race and the Negro Writer," *Phylon*, Fourth Quarter, 1950, pp. 369–371.

Gobineau, Arthur de (trans. by Adrian Collins), *The Inequality of Human Races*, G. P. Putnam's Sons, 1915.

Golden, Joseph, "Characteristics of the Negro-White Intermarried in Philadelphia," American Sociological Review, April, 1953, pp. 177–183.

Golden, Joseph, "Patterns of Negro-White Intermarriage," American Sociological Review, April, 1954, pp. 144–147.

Goldenweiser, Alexander, Anthropology, Appleton-Century-Crofts, 1937.

Golding, Louis, The Jewish Problem, Penguin Books, Inc., 1938.

Goldschmidt, Walter, "Social Class in America—A Critical Review," American Anthropologist, October–December, 1950, pp. 483–498.

Goldstein, M. S., Demographic and Bodily Changes, University of Texas Press, 1943.

Goldstein, S. E., The Meaning of Marriage and Foundations of the Family: A Jewish Interpretation, Bloch Publishing Company, 1942.

Golightly, Cornelius L., "Race, Values, and Guilt," Social Forces, December, 1947, pp. 125–139.

Golovensky, David I., "The Marginal Man Concept: An Analysis and Critique," Social Forces, March, 1952, pp. 333–339.

Goodman, Mary Ellen, Race Awareness in Young Children, Addison-Wesley Press, 1952.

Cordon, Albert I., Jews in Transition, University of Minnesota Press, 1949.

Gordon, Milton M., "Social Class in American Sociology," American Journal of Sociology, November, 1949, pp. 262–268.

Gosnell, Harold F., Negro Politicians, University of Chicago Press, 1935.

Gough, Harrison G., "Studies of Social Intolerance," Journal of Social Psychology, May, 1951, pp. 237–269.

Graeber, Isacque, and Britt, S. H. (eds.), Jews in a Gentile World, The Macmillan Company, 1942.

Greenberg, Herbert, Chase, A. L., and Cannon, T. M., Jr., "Attitudes of White and Negro High School Students in a West Texas Town Toward School Integration," Journal of Applied Psychology, February, 1957, pp. 27–31.

Griffith, Beatrice, American Me, Houghton Mifflin Company, 1948.

Grodzins, Morton, Americans Betrayed, University of Chicago Press, 1949.

Grodzins, Morton, "Making Un-Americans," American Journal of Sociology, May, 1955, pp. 570–582.

Grodzins, Morton, The Loyal and the Disloyal, University of Chicago Press, 1956.

Gross, Llewelyn, "The Use of Class Concepts in Sociological Research," American Journal of Sociology, March, 1949, pp. 409–421.

Grossack, Martin M., "Group Belongingness Among Negroes," Journal of Social Psychology, February, 1956, pp. 167–180.

Group for the Advancement of Psychiatry, Psychiatric Aspects of School Desegregation, Report No. 37, 1957.

Guilford, J. P., "Racial Preferences of a Thousand American University Students," Journal of Social Psychology, May, 1931, pp. 179–204.

Hacker, Helen Mayer, "Women as a Minority Group," Social Forces, October, 1951, pp. 60–69.

Hager, Don J., Glock, Charles Y., and Chein, Isidor (eds.), "Religious Conflict in the United States," Journal of Social Issues, 1956, vol. 12, No. 3, whole issue.

Haimowitz, Morris, and Haimowitz, Natalie, "Reducing Ethnic Hostility Through Psychotherapy," *Journal of Social Psychology*, May, 1950, pp. 231–241.

Hale, W. H., "The Negro Lawyer and His Clients," *Phylon*, First Quater, 1952, pp. 57–62.

Halligan, Alice L., "A Community's Total War Against Prejudice," *Journal of Educational Sociology*, February, 1943.

Halsey, Margaret, *Color Blind*, Simon and Schuster, Inc., 1946.

Handlin, Oscar, *The Uprooted*, Little, Brown & Company, 1951.

Handlin, Oscar, *Race and Nationality in American Life*, Little, Brown & Company, Boston, 1957.

Harding, John, Citron, A. F., and King, Estelle, "An Experimental Study of Answers to Anti-Negro Remarks," *Journal of Social Psychology*, February, 1953, pp. 3–17.

Haring, John, "Some Basic Principles of Self-Surveys," *Journal of Social Issues*, Spring, 1949, pp. 21–29.

Harlan, Howard H., "Some Factors Affecting Attitude Toward Jews," *American Sociological Review*, December, 1942, pp. 816–827.

Harris, A. L., *The Negro as Capitalist*, American Academy of Political and Social Science, 1936.

Hart, W. R., "Anti-Semitism in New York Medical Schools," *American Mercury*, July, 1947, pp. 53–65.

Hartley, Eugene, *Problems in Prejudice*, King's Crown Press, 1946.

Hatt, Paul K., "Stratification in the Mass Society," *American Sociological Review*, April, 1950, pp. 216–222.

Hauser, Philip M., "The Labor Force as a Field of Interest for the Sociologist," *American Sociological Review*, August, 1951, pp. 530–538.

Havighurst, R. J., and Neugarten, Bernice L., *American Indian and White Children. A Socio-Psychological Investigation*, University of Chicago Press, 1954.

Havighurst, R. J., and Taba, Hilda, *Adolescent Character and Personality*, John Wiley & Sons, Inc., 1949.

Hawley, L. T., "The Negro's New Economic Life," *Fortune*, September, 1956, pp. 128, 252, 254, 256, 258.

Hayden, Robert E., *Heart-Shape in the Dust*, Falcon Press, 1940.

Hayner, Norman S., and Reynolds, Charles N., "Chinese Family Life in America," *American Sociological Review*, October, 1937, pp. 630–637.

Haywood, Harry, "The Theoretical Defenders of White Chauvinism in the Labor Movement," in *The Communist Position on the Negro Question*, pp. 30 ff., reprinted from *The Communist*, June, 1931.

Herberg, Will, *Protestant-Catholic-Jew*, Doubleday & Company, Inc., 1955.

Herskovits, M. J., *The Myth of the Negro Past*, Harper & Brothers, 1941.

Hill, Herbert, "Status of Negro Workers at Lockheed Aircraft Corporation," *The Crisis*, March, 1957, pp. 147–148.

Hill, Herbert, and Greenberg, Jack, *Citizen's Guide to Desegregation*, The Beacon Press, 1955.

Himelhoch, Jerome, "Tolerance and Personality Needs: A Study of the Liberalization of Ethnic Attitudes Among Minority Group College Students," *American Sociological Review*, February, 1950, pp. 79–88.

Hirsh, Selma, *The Fears Men Live By*, Harper & Brothers, 1955.

Hitler, Adolf, *Mein Kampf*, Reynal and Hitchcock, 1940.

Hoebel, E. D., *Man in the Primitive World*, McGraw-Hill Book Company, 1949.

Hollingshead, A. B., "Selected Characteristics of Classes in a Middle Western Community," *American Sociological Review*, August, 1947, pp. 385–395.

Hollingshead, A. B., *Elmtown's Youth*, John Wiley & Sons, Inc., 1949.

Hollingshead, A. B., "Cultural Factors in the Selection of Marriage Mates," *American Sociological Review*, October, 1950, pp. 619–627.

Hooft, W. A. Visser 'T, *The Ecumenical Movement and the Racial Problem*, UNESCO, 1954.

Hooton, E. A., *Up from the Ape*, The Macmillan Company, rev. ed., 1946.

Hope, John, II, "Negro Employment in Three Southern Plants of International Harvester Company," *Selected Studies of Negro Employment in the South*, Case Study No. 1, National Planning Association, 1953.

Hope, John, II, "The Self-Survey of the Packinghouse Union," *Journal of Social Issues*, September, 1953, pp. 36 ff.

Hope, John, II, "Efforts to Eliminate Racial Discrimination in Industry—With Particular Reference to the South," *Journal of Negro Education*, Summer, 1954, pp. 263 ff.

Hope, John, II, "Trends in Patterns of Race Relations in the South Since May 17, 1954," *Phylon*, Second Quarter, 1956, pp. 103–118.

Horney, Karen, *The Neurotic Personality of Our Time*, W. W. Norton & Company, Inc., 1937.

Horowitz, Eugene L., "Development of Attitude Toward Negroes," *Archives of Psychology*, No. 194, 1936.

Horowitz, Ruth, "Racial Aspects of Self-Identification in Nursery School Children," *Journal of Psychology*, January, 1939, pp. 91–99.

Hourwich, Isaac A., *Immigration and Labor*, G. P. Putnam's Sons, 1912.

Hughes, E. C., "Institutional Office and the Person," *American Journal of Sociology*, November, 1937, pp. 404–413.

Hughes, E. C., *French Canada in Transition*, University of Chicago Press, 1943.

Hughes, E. C., "Queries Concerning Industry and Society Growing Out of Study of Ethnic Relations in Industry," *American Sociological Review*, April, 1949, pp. 211–220.

Hughes, E. C., and Hughes, Helen, *Where People Meet: Ethnic and Racial Frontiers*, The Free Press, 1952.

Hughes, Emmet John, "The Negro's New Economic Life," *Fortune*, September, 1956, pp. 127–131 ff.

Hughes, Langston, and Bontemps, A., *The Poetry of the Negro*, Doubleday & Company, Inc., 1949.

Humphrey, N. D.,"The Changing Structure of the Detroit Mexican Family: An Index of Acculturation," *American Sociological Review*, December, 1944, pp. 622–626.

Huston, Luther A., "Desegregation on Buses Presents Legal Problems," *New York Times*, November 25, 1956.

Huxley, Julian, *Evolution, The Modern Synthesis*, Harper & Brothers, 1942.

Ivey, John E., Jr., "Regional Education," *Phylon*, 1949, vol. 10, pp. 381–384.

Jackson, Blyden, "An Essay in Criticism," *Phylon*, Fourth Quarter, 1950, pp. 338–343.

Jackson, Blyden, "The Blythe Newcomers: A Résumé of Negro Literature in 1954," *Phylon*, First Quarter, 1955, pp. 5–12.

Jackson, Blyden, "The Continuing Strain: Résumé of Negro Literature in 1955," *Phylon*, First Quarter, 1956, pp. 35–40.

Jackson, D. N., Messick, S. J., and Solley, C. M., "How 'Rigid' Is the 'Authoritarian,'" *Journal of Abnormal and Social Psychology*, January, 1957, pp. 137–140.

Jacobson, Alan, and Rainwater, Lee, "A Study of Management Representative Evaluations of Nisei Workers," *Social Forces*, October, 1953, pp. 35–41.

Janowitz, Morris, and Marvick, Dwaine, "Authoritarianism and Political Behavior," *Public Opinion Quarterly*, Summer, 1953, pp. 185–201.

Janowsky, Oscar (ed.), *The American Jew*, Harper & Brothers, 1942.

Janowsky, Oscar, *Nationalities and National Minorities*, The Macmillan Company, 1945.

Jarrett, Thomas D., "Towards Unfettered Creativity: A Note on the Negro Novelist's Coming of Age," *Phylon*, Fourth Quarter, 1950, pp. 313–317.

Jarrett, Thomas D., "Recent Fiction by Negroes," *College English*, November, 1954.

Jefferson, Miles, "The Negro on Broadway, 1954–1955," *Phylon*, Third Quarter, 1955, pp. 303–312.

Jefferson, Miles, "The Negro on Broadway, 1955–56," *Phylon*, Third Qaurter, 1956, pp. 227–237.

Jenkins, M. D., "The Availability of Higher Education for Negroes in the Southern States," *Journal of Negro Education*, 1948, vol. 17, pp. 467–468.

Jennings, H. S., et al., *Scientific Aspects of the Race Problem*, Longmans, Green & Co., Inc., 1941.

Johnson, Charles S., *Shadow of the Plantation*, University of Chicago Press, 1934.

Johnson, Charles S., *The Negro College Graduate*, University of North Carolina Press, 1938.

Johnson, Charles S., *Growing Up in the Black Belt*, American Council on Education, 1941.

Johnson, Charles S., *Patterns of Negro Segregation*, Harper & Brothers, 1943.

Johnson, Charles S., *Into the Main Stream*, University of North Carolina Press, 1946.

Johnson, Charles S., "National Organizations in the Field of Race Relations," *Annals of the American Academy of Political and Social Science*, March, 1946, pp. 117–127.

Johnson, Charles S., "Some Significant Social and Educational Implications of the U.S. Supreme Court's Decision," *Journal of Negro Education*, Summer, 1954, pp. 368–369.

Johnson, Charles S., Embree, E. R., and Alexander, W. W., *The Collapse of Cotton Tenancy*, University of North Carolina Press, 1935.

Johnson, Guy B., "Personality in a White-Indian-Negro Community," *American Sociological Review*, August, 1939, pp. 516–523.

Johnson, Guy B., "The Negro and Crime," *Annals of the American Academy of Political and Social Science*, September, 1941, pp. 93–104.

Johnson, Guy B., "A Sociologist Looks at Racial Desegregation in the South," *Social Forces*, October, 1954, pp. 1–10.

Johnson, Guy B., "Racial Integration in Southern Higher Education," *Social Forces*, May, 1956, pp. 309–312.

Johnson, J. W. (ed.), *The Book of American Negro Poetry*, Harcourt, Brace & Company, 1922.

Johnson, J. W., *The Book of American Negro Spirituals*, The Viking Press, Inc., 1947.

Johnson, R. O., "Desegregation of Public Education in Georgia—One Year Afterward," *Journal of Negro Education*, Summer, 1955, pp. 235 ff.

Johnson, Robert, "Negro Reactions to Minority Group Status," in Barron, Milton L. (ed.), *American Minorities*, Alfred A. Knopf, Inc., 1957, pp. 192–214.

Jones, R. C., "Ethnic Family Patterns: The Mexican Family in the United States," *American Journal of Sociology*, May, 1948, pp. 450–452.

Journal of Educational Sociology, "The Negro College—Its Place in Democracy," April, 1946.

Kahl, Joseph A., *The American Class Structure*, Rinehart & Co., 1957.

Kallen, Horace M., *Cultural Pluralism and the American Idea*, University of Pennsylvania Press, 1956.

Kane, John J., *Catholic-Protestant Conflicts in America*, Henry Regnery Co., 1955.

Kaplan, Bernice, "Environment and Human Plasticity," *American Anthropologist*, October, 1954, pp. 780–800.

Kardiner, Abram, and Ovesey, Lionel, *The Mark of Oppression*, W. W. Norton & Company, Inc., 1951.

Katz, David, and Braly, Kenneth, "Racial Stereotypes of One Hundred College Students," *Journal of Abnormal and Social Psychology*, October–December, 1933, pp. 280–290.

Katz, Irwin, *Conflict and Harmony in an Adolescent Interracial Group*, New York University Press, 1955.

Kennedy, Ruby Jo Reeves, "Single or Triple Melting-Pot? Intermarriage Trends in New Haven, 1870–1940," *American Journal of Sociology*, January, 1944, pp. 331–339.

Kennedy, Ruby Jo Reeves, "Single or Triple Melting-Pot? Intermarriage in New Haven, 1870–1950," *American Journal of Sociology*, July, 1952, pp. 56–59.

Kephart, William, "The Negro Offender," *American Journal of Sociology*, July, 1954, pp. 46–50.

Kephart, William, and Monahan, Thomas P., "Desertion and Divorce in Philadelphia," *American Sociological Review*, December, 1952, pp. 719–727.

Kibbe, Pauline R., *Latin Americans in Texas*, University of New Mexico Press, 1946.

Killian, Lewis M., "The Effects of Southern White Workers on Race Relations in Northern Plants," *American Sociological Review*, June, 1952, pp. 327–331.

Killian, Lewis M., "The Adjustment of Southern White Migrants to Northern Urban Norms," *Social Forces*, October, 1953, pp. 66–69.

King, Charles E., "The Process of Social Stratification Among an Urban Southern Minority Population," *Social Forces*, May, 1953, pp. 352–354.

King, Martin Luther, Jr., "Facing the Challenge of a New Age," *Phylon*, First Quarter, 1957, pp. 25–34.

Kingdon, Frank, "Discrimination in Medical Colleges," *American Mercury*, October, 1945, pp. 391–399.

Kinzer, Robert, and Sagarin, Edward, *The Negro in American Business*, Greenberg: Publisher, 1950.

Kiser, Clyde V., "Cultural Pluralism," *Annals of the American Academy of Political and Social Science*, March, 1949, pp. 117–130.

Klineberg, Otto, *Negro Intelligence and Selective Migration*, Columbia University Press, 1935.

Klineberg, Otto, *Race Differences*, Harper & Brothers, 1935.

Klineberg, Otto, *Social Psychology*, Henry Holt & Company, Inc., 1940.

Klineberg, Otto (ed.), *Characteristics of the American Negro*, Harper & Brothers, 1944.

Klineberg, Otto, *Tensions Affecting International Understanding*, Social Science Research Council, 1950.

Kluckhohn, Clyde, "Physical Anthropology," *American Anthropologist*, December, 1955, pp. 1280–1295.

Kogan, Nathan, "Authoritarianism and Repression," *Journal of Abnormal and Social Psychology*, July, 1956, pp. 34–37.

Kohn, M. L., and Williams, Robin, Jr., "Situational Patterning in Intergroup Relations," *American Sociological Review*, April, 1956, pp. 164–174.

Konvitz, Milton R., *The Constitution and Civil Rights*, Columbia University Press, 1946.

Kornhauser, Arthur, "Public Opinion and Social Class," *American Journal of Sociology*, January, 1950, pp. 333–345.

Kornhauser, William, "The Negro Union Official," *American Journal of Sociology*, March, 1952, pp. 443–452.

Kornhauser, William, "Ideology and Interests," *Journal of Social Issues*, 1953, vol. 9, No. 1, pp. 49–60.

Kramer, Alfred S., "Patterns of Racial Inclusion Among the Churches of Three Protestant Denominations," *Phylon*, Third Quarter, 1955, pp. 283–294.

Kramer, Bernard M., "Dimensions of Prejudice," *Journal of Psychology*, April, 1949, pp. 389–451.

Krech, David, and Crutchfield, Richard, *Theory and Problems of Social Psychology*, McGraw-Hill Book Company, 1948.

Kroeber, A. L., *Anthropology*, Harcourt, Brace & Company, rev. ed., 1948.

Kruuse, Elsa, "The Churches Act on Integration," *National Council Outlook*, March, 1957, pp. 6–8.

Kuper, Leo, "The Control of Social Change: A South African Experiment," *Social Forces*, October, 1954, pp. 19–29.

Kuppuswamy, B., "A Statistical Study of Attitude to the Caste System in South India," *Journal of Psychology*, October, 1956, pp. 169–206.

Kutner, Bernard, Wilkins, Carol, and Yarrow, P. R., "Verbal Attitudes and Overt Behavior Involving Racial Prejudice," *Journal of Abnormal and Social Psychology*, July, 1952, pp. 649–652.

LaFarge, John, "The Roman Catholic Experience," *Survey Graphic*, January, 1947, pp. 61–62, 104–106.

LaFarge, John, *The Catholic Viewpoint on Race Relations*, Doubleday & Company, Inc., 1956.

Lambert, Richard D., and Bressler, Marvin, "The Sensitive-Area Complex: A Contribution to the Theory of Guided Culture Contact," *American Journal of Sociology*, May, 1955, pp. 583–592.

Landis, J. T., and Landis, M. G., *Building a Successful Marriage*, Prentice-Hall, Inc., 1948.

LaPiere, R. T., "Attitudes vs. Actions," *Social Forces*, December, 1934, pp. 230–237.

Lash, John, "A Long, Hard Look at the Ghetto: A Critical Summary of Literature by and About Negroes in 1956," *Phylon*, First Quarter, 1957, pp. 7–24.

Lasker, Bruno, *Race Attitudes in Children*, Henry Holt & Company, Inc., 1929.

Lasker, Gabriel W., "Ethnic Identification in an Indian Mestizo Community," *Phylon*, Second Quarter, 1953, pp. 187–190.

Lawrence, David, " 'Rights' Minimized as a Vote Getter," *Washington Post and Times-Herald*, July 21, 1957.

Lazarsfeld, Paul, and Stanton, Frank (eds.), *Communications Research, 1948–49*, Harper & Brothers, 1949.

Lee, Alfred M., *Fraternities Without Brotherhood*, The Beacon Press, 1955.

Lee, Alfred M., and Humphrey, Norman D., *Race Riot*, The Dryden Press, Inc., 1943.

Lee, Alfred M., and Lee, E. B., *Social Problems in America*, Henry Holt & Company, Inc., 1949.

Lee, Everett S., "Negro Intelligence and Selective Migration: A Philadelphia Test of the Klineberg Hypothesis," *American Sociological Review*, April, 1951, pp. 227–233.

Lee, J. Oscar, "The Churches and Race Relations—A Survey," *Christianity and Crisis*, February 4, 1957, pp. 4–7.

Lee, Rose Hum, "The Decline of Chinatowns in the United States," *American Journal of Sociology*, March, 1949, pp. 422–432.

Lee, Rose Hum, "Research on the Chinese Family," *American Journal of Sociology*, May, 1949, pp. 497–504.

Lee, Rose Hum, "The Recent Immigrant Chinese Families of the San Francisco–Oakland Area," *Marriage and Family Living*, February, 1956, pp. 14–24.

Lee, Ulysses, "Criticism at Mid-Century," *Phylon*, Fourth Quarter, 1950, pp. 328–337.

Leighton, Alexander, *The Governing of Men*, Princeton University Press, 1945.

Lenski, Gerald E., "American Social Classes: Statistical Strata or Social Groups?" *American Journal of Sociology*, September, 1952, pp. 139–144.

Levinger, Lee J., *Anti-Semitism, Yesterday and Tomorrow*, The Macmillan Company, 1936.

Levinson, D. J., and Schermerhorn, R. A., "Emotional-Attitudinal Effects of an Intergroup Workshop on Its Members," *Journal of Psychology*, 1951, vol. 31, pp. 243–256.

Levitt, E. E., and Zelen, S. L., "The Validity of the Einstellung Test as a Measure of Rigidity," *Journal of Abnormal and Social Psychology*, October, 1953, pp. 573–580.

Lewin, Kurt, and Grabbe, Paul, "Conduct, Knowledge, and Acceptance of New Values," *Journal of Social Issues*, December, 1945, pp. 53–64.

Lewin, Kurt, *Resolving Social Conflicts*, Harper & Brothers, 1948.

Lewinson, Paul, *Race, Class, and Party*, Oxford University Press, 1932.

Lewis, Anthony, "Negro Vote Curbs Exposed by F.B.I.," *New York Times*, August 4, 1957, p. 50.

Lewis Hylan, " 'Tough' Aspects of Higher Education," *Phylon*, 1949, vol. 10, pp. 359–361.

Lewis, Hylan, "Innovations and Trends in the Contemporary Southern Negro Community," *Journal of Social Issues*, 1954, vol. 10, No. 1, pp. 19–27.

Lewis, Hylan, *Blackways of Kent*, University of North Carolina Press, 1955.

Lewis, J. L., *The Biology of the Negro*, University of Chicago Press, 1942.

Lind, A. W. (ed.), *Race Relations in World Perspective*, University of Hawaii Press, 1955.

Lindsey, Quentin W., *Farm Tenure: The Framework for Long-Run Adjustments in Southeastern Agriculture*, Publication No. 13, Southeast Land Tenure Research Committee, August, 1954.

Lindzey, Gardner, "An Experimental Examination of the Scapegoat Theory of Prejudice," *Journal of Abnormal and Social Psychology*, April, 1950, pp. 296–309.

Linton, Ralph, *The Study of Man*, Appleton-Century-Crofts, 1936.

Linton, Ralph (ed.), *Acculturation in Seven American Indian Tribes*, Appleton-Century-Crofts, 1940.

Linton, Ralph (ed.), *The Science of Man in the World Crisis*, Columbia University Press, 1945.

Lippitt, Ronald, and Radke, Marian, "New Trends in the Investigation of Prejudice," *Annals of the American Academy of Political and Social Science*, March, 1946, pp. 167–176.

Little, Kenneth, "The Position of Colored People in Britain," *Phylon*, First Quarter, 1954, pp. 58–64.

Little, Wilson, *Spanish-Speaking Children in Texas*, University of Texas Press, 1944.

Locke, Alain, *The New Negro*, Albert and Charles Boni, 1925.

Locke, Alain, *The Negro in Art: A Pictorial Record of the Negro Artist and of the Negro Theme in Art*, Associates in Negro Folk Education, 1940.

Locke, Alain, "Wisdom de Profundis: The Literature of the Negro, 1949," *Phylon*, First Quarter, 1950, pp. 10–11.

Locke, Alain, "Self-Criticism: The Third Dimension in Culture," *Phylon*, Fourth Quarter, 1950, pp. 391–394.

Locke, Alain, "The High Price of Integration," *Phylon*, First Quarter, 1952, pp. 9 ff.

Locke, Alain, "From Native Son to Invisible Man," *Phylon*, First Quarter, 1953, pp. 34 ff.

Locke, Alain, and Stern, B. J. (eds.), *When Peoples Meet*, Hinds, Hayden and Eldredge, Inc., rev. ed., 1946.

Locke, Harvey J., Sabagh, Georges, and Thomas, Mary Margaret, "Interfaith Marriages," *Social Problems*, April, 1957, pp. 329–333.

Loescher, F. S., *The Protestant Church and the Negro*, Association Press, 1948.

Loescher, F. S., "Racism in Northern City Churches," *Christian Century*, February 8, 1956, pp. 174–176.

Logan, Rayford W., *The Negro in American Life and Thought. The Nadir: 1877–1901*, Dial Press, Inc., 1954.

Lohman, J. D., and Reitzes, D. C., "Note on Race Relations in Mass Society," *American Journal of Sociology*, November, 1952, pp. 240–246.

Lohman, J. D., and Reitzes, D. C., "Deliberately Organized Groups and Racial Behavior," *American Sociological Review*, June, 1954, pp. 342–344.

Long, H. H., and Johnson, C. S., *People vs. Property*, Fisk University Press, 1947.

Loth, David, and Fleming, Harold, *Integration North and South*, The Fund for the Republic, 1956.

Lowenfeld, Viktor, "Negro Art Expression in America," *Madison Quarterly*, January, 1945, pp. 3–8.

Lowenthal, Leo, and Guterman, Norbert, *Prophets of Deceit. A Study in the Techniques of the American Agitator*, Harper & Brothers, 1949.

Lowie, R. H., *The German People*, Farrar and Rinehart, 1945.

Lowie, R. H., *Social Organization*, Rinehart & Co., 1948.

Luchins, Abraham S., "Personality and Prejudice: A Critique," *Journal of Social Psychology*, August, 1950, pp. 79–94.

Lundberg, George A., and Dickson, Lenore, "Selective Association Among Ethnic Groups in a High School Population," *American Sociological Review*, February, 1952, pp. 23–35.

Macartney, C. A., *National States and National Minorities*, Oxford University Press, 1934.

McBride, G. M., "Plantation," *Encyclopædia of the Social Sciences*, The Macmillan Company, 1934, vol. 12, pp. 148–153.

MacCrone, I. D., *Race Attitudes in South Africa*, Oxford University Press, 1937.

MacCrone, I. D., "Reactions to Domination in a Colour-Caste Society: A Preliminary Study of the Race Attitudes of a Dominated Group," *Journal of Social Psychology*, August, 1947, pp. 69–98.

McGraw, B. T., "The Housing Act of 1954 and Implications for Minorities," *Phylon*, Second Quarter, 1955, pp. 171–182.

MacGregor, Gordon, Warriors Without Weapons, University of Chicago Press, 1946.

MacIver, R. M. (ed.), Group Relationships and Group Antagonisms, Harper & Brothers, 1944.

MacIver, R. M., The More Perfect Union, The Macmillan Company, 1948.

MacIver, R. M. (ed.), Discrimination and National Welfare, Institute for Religious and Social Studies, 1949.

MacIver, R. M., Report on the Jewish Community Relations Agencies, National Community Relations Advisory Council, 1951.

MacKenzie, Barbara K., "The Importance of Contact in Determining Attitudes Toward Negroes," Journal of Abnormal and Social Psychology, October, 1948, pp. 417–441.

MacKinnon, William J., and Centers, Richard, "Authoritarianism and Urban Stratification," American Journal of Sociology, May, 1956, pp. 610–620.

McManus, J. T., and Kronenberger, Louis, "Motion Pictures, the Theatre, and Race Relations," Annals of the American Academy of Political and Social Science, March, 1946, pp. 152–158.

McMillan, Robert T., "Effects of Mechanization on American Agriculture," Scientific Monthly, July, 1949, pp. 23–28.

McWilliams, Carey, Prejudice—Japanese-Americans: Symbol of Racial Intolerance, Little, Brown & Company, 1944.

McWilliams, Carey, "Race Discrimination and the Law," Science and Society, Winter, 1945.

McWilliams, Carey, A Mask for Privilege: Anti-Semitism in America, Little, Brown & Company, 1948.

McWilliams, Carey, North from Mexico, J. B. Lippincott Company, 1949.

McWilliams, Carey, Brothers Under the Skin, Little, Brown & Company, rev. ed., 1951.

Malinowski, Bronislaw, Myth in Primitive Psychology, W. W. Norton & Company, Inc., 1926.

Mangum, C. S., Jr., The Legal Status of the Negro, University of North Carolina Press, 1940.

Maritain, Jacques, A Christian Looks at the Jewish Question, Longmans, Green & Co., Inc., 1939.

Marrow, A. J., Living Without Hate, Harper & Brothers, 1951.

Marrow, A. J., and French, J. R. P., "Changing a Stereotype in Industry," Journal of Social Issues, December, 1945, pp. 33–37.

Marshall, Thurgood, Report on Korea, National Association for the Advancement of Colored People, 1951.

Marshall, Thurgood, "Summary Justice—The Negro GI in Korea," The Crisis, May, 1951, pp. 297–304, 350–355.

Maryland Commission on Interracial Problems and Relations and the Baltimore Commission on Human Relations, Desegregation in the Baltimore City Schools, July, 1955.

Masling, Joseph M., "How Neurotic Is the Authoritarian?" Journal of Abnormal and Social Psychology, April, 1954, pp. 316–318.

Maslow, Will, "The Law and Race Relations," *Annals of the American Academy of Political and Social Science*, March, 1946, pp. 75–81.

Maslow, Will, "The Uses of Law in the Struggle for Equality," *Social Research*, Autumn Quarter, 1955, pp. 297–314.

Massing, Paul W., *Rehearsal for Destruction. A Study of Political Anti-Semitism in Imperial Germany*, Harper & Brothers, 1949.

Masuoka, Jitsuichi, and Johnson, Charles S., "Orientals and Their Problems of Cultural Adjustment," *Social Science Source Documents*, No. 4, Social Science Institute, Fisk University, 1946.

Mays, B. E., "Segregation in Higher Education," *Phylon*, 1949, vol. 10, pp. 403–404.

Mays, B. E., *Seeking To Be Christian in Race Relations*, Friendship Press, 1957.

Mays, B. E., and Nicholson, J. W., *The Negro's Church*, Institute of Social and Religious Research, 1933.

Mekeel, Scudder, "Race Relations. Cultural Aids to Constructive Race Relations," *Mental Hygiene*, April, 1945, pp. 177–189.

Merton, Robert K., "Fact and Factitiousness in Ethnic Opinionnaires," *American Sociological Review*, February, 1940, pp. 13–28.

Merton, Robert K., *Social Theory and Social Structure*, The Free Press, 1949, rev. ed., 1957.

Miller, Loren, "Supreme Court Covenant Decision—An Analysis," *The Crisis*, September, 1948, pp. 265–266.

Mills, C. W., Senior, Clarence, and Goldsen, R. K., *The Puerto Rican Journey*, Harper & Brothers, 1950.

Milner, Esther, "Some Hypotheses Concerning the Influence of Segregation on Negro Personality Development," *Psychiatry*, August, 1953, pp. 291–297.

Mitchell, George S., "The Extension of Citizenship," in Jessie P. Guzman (ed.), *The New South and Higher Education*, Tuskegee Institute, 1954, pp. 50–55.

Monahan, T. P., and Kephart, W. M., "Divorce and Desertion by Religious and Mixed-Religious Groups," *American Journal of Sociology*, March, 1954, pp. 454–465.

Montagu, M. F. Ashley, *Man's Most Dangerous Myth: The Fallacy of Race*, Columbia University Press, 2nd ed., 1945.

Montagu, M. F. Ashley, *Statement on Race*, Henry Schuman, Inc., 1951.

Moon, Bucklin, *The High Cost of Prejudice*, Julian Messner, Inc., 1947.

Moon, H. L., *Balance of Power: The Negro Vote*, Doubleday & Company, Inc., 1948.

Moon, H. L., "The Southern Scene," *Phylon*, Fourth Quarter, 1955, pp. 351–358.

Moore, W. E., "Slave Law and the Social Structure," *Journal of Negro History*, April, 1941, pp. 172–184.

Moore, W. E., and Williams, R. M., "Stratification in the Ante-Bellum South," *American Sociological Review*, June, 1942, pp. 343–351.

Moreno, J. L., *Who Shall Survive*, The Beacon House, 1934.

Morse, Nancy C., and Allport, F. H., "The Causation of Anti-Semitism: An Investigation of Seven Hypotheses," *Journal of Psychology*, October, 1952, pp. 197–233.

Morsh, J. E., and Smith, M. E., "Judgment of Prejudice Before, During and After World War II," *Journal of Social Psychology*, August, 1953, pp. 375–379.

Moses, Earl R., "Differentials in Crime Rates Between Negroes and Whites, Based on Comparisons of Four Socio-Economically Equated Areas," *American Sociological Review*, August, 1947, pp. 411–420.

Motheral, Joe R., Metzler, William H., and Ducoff, Louis J., *Cotton and Manpower: Texas High Plains*, Texas Agricultural and Mechanical College System, Bulletin 762, May, 1953.

Murphy, Gardner, *Personality*, Harper & Brothers, 1947.

Murphy, Gardner, *In the Minds of Men*, Basic Books, 1953.

Murray, Florence (ed.), *The Negro Handbook*, The Macmillan Company, 1949.

Mussen, Paul H., "Some Personality and Social Factors Related to Changes in Children's Attitudes Toward Negroes," *Journal of Abnormal and Social Psychology*, July, 1950, pp. 423–441.

Myers, Alonzo F., "The Colleges for Negroes," *Survey*, May, 1950, pp. 233–239.

Myers, Henry J., and Yochelson, Leon, "Color Denial in the Negro," *Psychiatry*, February, 1948, pp. 39–46.

Myers, N. D., *Education for Cultural Unity*, California Elementary School Principals' Association, 1946.

Myrdal, Gunnar, *An American Dilemma*, Harper & Brothers, 1944, 2 vols.

Nabrit, J. M., Jr., "Legal Inventions and the Desegregation Process," *Annals of the American Academy of Political and Social Science*, March, 1956, pp. 35–43.

Nabrit, J. M., Jr., "Desegregation and Reason," *Phylon*, Third Quarter, 1956, pp. 286–290.

Newcomb, Theodore M., "The Influence of Attitude Climate upon Some Determinants of Information," *Journal of Abnormal and Social Psychology*, July, 1946, pp. 291–302.

Newcomb, Theodore M., "Autistic Hostility and Social Reality," *Human Relations*, 1947, vol. 1, pp. 69–86.

Newcomb, Theodore M., and Hartley, E. L. (eds.), *Readings in Social Psychology*, Henry Holt & Company, Inc., 1947.

New York State Commission Against Discrimination, *Report of Progress, 1955*, and *Report of Progress, 1956*.

Nichols, Charles H., Jr., "The Forties: A Decade of Growth," *Phylon*, Fourth Quarter, 1950, pp. 377–380.

Nichols, Lee, *Breakthrough on the Color Front*, Random House, Inc., 1954.

Nichols, Lee, and Cassels, Louis, "The Churches Repent," *Harper's Magazine*, October, 1955, pp. 53–57.

Noland, E. William, "Industry Comes of Age in the South," *Social Forces*, October, 1953, pp. 33 ff.

Northrup, Herbert, *Organized Labor and the Negro*, Harper & Brothers, 1944.

Odum, H. W., and Johnson, G. B., *The Negro and His Songs*, University of North Carolina Press, 1925.

Ogburn, William F., and Grigg, Charles M., "Factors Related to the Virginia Vote on Segregation," *Social Forces*, May, 1956, pp. 301–308.

Oniki, S. Garry, "Interracial Churches in American Protestantism," *Social Action*, January 15, 1950, pp. 4–22.

Opler, Morris Edward, "The Bio-social Basis of Thought in the Third Reich," *American Sociological Review*, December, 1945, pp. 776–786.

O'Reilly, Charles T., and O'Reilly, Edward J., "Religious Beliefs of Catholic College Students and Their Attitudes Toward Minorities," *Journal of Abnormal and Social Psychology*, July, 1954, pp. 378–380.

Osborne, Irene, and Bennett, Richard K., "Eliminating Educational Segregation in the Nation's Capital, 1951–1955," *Annals of the American Academy of Political and Social Science*, March, 1956, pp. 98–108.

Ottley, Roi, *New World A-Coming*, Houghton Mifflin Company, 1943.

Overstreet, Harry A., "Racial Attitudes of the 'Liberal' North," *Saturday Review of Literature*, March, 1945, pp. 7–8.

Panunzio, Constantine, "Intermarriage in Los Angeles," *American Journal of Sociology*, March, 1942, pp. 690–701.

Park, Robert, and Burgess, Ernest, *Introduction to the Science of Sociology*, University of Chicago Press, 2nd ed., 1924.

Parker, W. H., "The Police Role in Community Relations," a paper presented to the Institute on Police-Community Relations sponsored by the National Conference of Christians and Jews, at Michigan State University on May 19, 1955 (mimeo.).

Parkes, James W., *The Jewish Problem in the Modern World*, Thornton Butterworth, 1939.

Parkes, James W., *An Enemy of the People: Antisemitism*, Penguin Books, Inc., 1946.

Parsons, Talcott, *The Structure of Social Action*, McGraw-Hill Book Company, 1937.

Pearl, David, "Psychotherapy and Ethnocentrism," *Journal of Abnormal and Social Psychology*, March, 1955, pp. 227–229.

Pedersen, H. A., "Mechanized Agriculture and the Farm Laborer," *Rural Sociology*, June, 1954, pp. 147 ff.

Perlmutter, Howard V., "Correlates of Two Types of Xenophilic Orientation," *Journal of Abnormal and Social Psychology*, January, 1956, pp. 130–135.

Peterson, Helen L., "American Indian Political Participation," *Annals of the American Academy of Political and Social Science*, May, 1957, pp. 116–126.

Peterson, Ruth C., and Thurstone, L. L., *Motion Pictures and the Social Attitudes of Children*, The Macmillan Company, 1933.

Pettigrew, T. F., "Desegregation and Its Chances for Success: Northern and Southern Views," *Social Forces*, May, 1957, pp. 339–344.

Pfautz, Harold W., and Duncan, O. D., "A Critical Evaluation of Warner's Work in Community Stratification," *American Sociological Review*, April, 1950, pp. 205–215.

Phillips, U. B., "Slavery—United States," *Encyclopædia of the Social Sciences*, The Macmillan Company, 1934, vol. 14, pp. 84–90.

Phillips, U. B., *Life and Labor in the Old South*, Little, Brown & Company, 1939.

Pierce, J. A., *Negro Business and Business Education*, Harper & Brothers, 1947.

Pierce, T. M., Kincheloe, J. B., Moore, R. E., Drewry, G. N., and Carmichael, B. E., *White and Negro Schools in the South*, Prentice-Hall, Inc., 1955.

Pierson, Donald, *Negroes in Brazil*, University of Chicago Press, 1942.

Pierson, Donald, "Race Relations in Portuguese America," chap. 19 in Lind, A. W. (ed.), *Race Relations in World Perspective*, University of Hawaii Press, 1955.

Pinson, K. S. (ed.), *Essays on Antisemitism*, Conference on Jewish Relations, 1946.

Pitt, James, *Adventures in Brotherhood*, Farrar, Straus and Company, 1955.

Plant, James S., *Personality and the Culture Pattern*, The Commonwealth Fund, 1937.

Pope, Liston, "Caste in the Church," *Survey Graphic*, January, 1947, pp. 59–60, 101–104.

Popham, John N., "Report on Bus Desegregation," New York *Times*, February 3, 1957.

Porter, James A., *Modern Negro Art*, The Dryden Press, Inc., 1943.

Porterfield, Austin L., and Talbert, Robert H., "Crime in Southern Cities," chap. 9 in Vance, Rupert B., and Demerath, N. J. (eds.), *The Urban South*, University of North Carolina Press, 1954.

Powdermaker, Hortense, *After Freedom. A Cultural Study in the Deep South*, The Viking Press, Inc., 1939.

Powdermaker, Hortense, "The Channeling of Negro Aggression by the Cultural Process," *American Journal of Sociology*, May, 1943, pp. 750–758.

Powdermaker, Hortense, *Probing Our Prejudices*, Harper & Brothers, 1944.

President's Commission on Higher Education, *Higher Education for American Democracy*, Government Printing Office, 1947.

President's Committee on Civil Rights, *To Secure These Rights*, Simon and Schuster, Inc., 1947.

President's Committee on Equality of Treatment and Opportunity in the Armed Services, *Freedom to Serve*, Government Printing Office, 1950.

President's Committee on Government Contracts, *Second Annual Report, 1954–55*, and *Third Annual Report, 1955–56*, Government Printing Office.

Price, H. D., *The Negro and Southern Politics*, New York University Press, 1957.

Prothro, E. T., "Ethnocentrism and Anti-Negro Attitudes in the Deep South," *Journal of Abnormal and Social Psychology*, January, 1952, pp. 105–108.

Prothro, E. T., "Social Psychology of the South: Challenge Without Response," *Journal of Social Issues*, 1954, vol. 10, No. 1, pp. 36–43.

Prothro, E. T., and Jensen, J. A., "Comparison of Some Ethnic and Religious Attitudes of Negro and White College Students in the Deep South," *Social Forces*, May, 1952, pp. 426–428.

Prothro, E. T., and Miles, O. K., "Comparison of Ethnic Attitudes of College Students and Middle Class Adults from the Same State," *Journal of Social Psychology*, August, 1952, pp. 53–58.

Rabkin, Sol, "Racial Desegregation in Places of Public Accommodation," *Journal of Negro Education*, Summer, 1954, pp. 249–261.

Radke-Yarrow, Marian, and Lande, Bernard, "Personality Correlates of Differential Reaction to Minority Group Belonging," *Journal of Social Psychology*, November, 1953, pp. 253–272.

Raper, A. F., *The Tragedy of Lynching*, University of North Carolina Press, 1933.

Raper, A. F., *Preface to Peasantry*, University of North Carolina Press, 1936.

Raper, A. F., "The Role of Agricultural Technology in Southern Social Change," *Social Forces*, 1946–1947, vol. 25, pp. 21–30.

Raper, A. F., and Reid, I. De A., *Sharecroppers All*, University of North Carolina Press, 1941.

Ratchford, R. U., "The Reorganization of the Southern Economy," in Jessie P. Guzman (ed.), *The New South and Higher Education*, Tuskegee Institute, 1954, pp. 31–39.

Raths, Louis E., and Trager, Frank N., "Public Opinion and Crossfire," *Journal of Educational Sociology*, February, 1948, pp. 345–368.

Ravitz, M. J., "Integration of Nurses," *Phylon*, Third Quarter, 1955, pp. 295–302.

Razran, Gregory, "Ethnic Dislikes and Stereotypes: A Laboratory Study," *Journal of Abnormal and Social Psychology*, January, 1950, pp. 7–27.

Record, Wilson, *The Negro and the Communist Party*, University of North Carolina Press, 1951.

Record, Wilson, "Intellectuals in Social and Racial Movements," *Phylon*, Third Quarter, 1954, pp. 231–242.

Record, Wilson, "The Negro Intellectual and Negro Nationalism," *Social Forces*, October, 1954, pp. 10–18.

Redd, G. N., "Present Status of Negro Higher and Professional Education: A Critical Summary," *Journal of Negro Education*, 1948, vol. 17, pp. 401 ff.

Reddick, L. D., "Educational Programs for the Improvement of Race Relations: Motion Pictures, Radio, Press, and Libraries," *Journal of Negro Education*, 1944, vol. 13, pp. 386 ff.

Reddick, L. D., "The Education of Negroes in States Where Separate Schools Are Not Legal," *Journal of Negro Education*, 1947, vol. 16, pp. 297 ff.

Redding, J. Saunders, *To Make a Poet Black*, University of North Carolina Press, 1939.

Redfield, Robert, "Race and Religion in Selective Admission," *Journal of the American Association of Collegiate Registrars*, July, 1947.

Reid, Ira De A. (ed.), "Racial Desegregation and Integration," *Annals of the American Academy of Political and Social Science*, March, 1956 (16 articles).

Reitzes, D. C., "The Role of Organizational Structures, *Journal of Social Issues*, 1953, vol. 9, No. 1, pp. 45–48.

Reppy, Alison, *Civil Rights in the United States*, Central Book Company, 1951.

Resnik, R. B., "Some Sociological Aspects of Intermarriage of Jew and Non-Jew," *Social Forces*, 1933, vol. 12, pp. 94–102.

Reuter, E. B., *Race Mixture*, McGraw-Hill Book Company, 1931.

Reuter, E. B., *The American Race Problem*, Thomas Y. Crowell Company, 1938.

Reuter, E. B., "Racial Theory," *American Journal of Sociology*, May, 1945, pp. 452–461.

Richmond, Anthony H., *Colour Prejudice in Britain: A Study of West Indian Workers in Liverpool, 1941–1951*, Routledge and Kegan Paul, 1951.

Roberts, A. H., and Rokeach, Milton, "Anomie, Authoritarianism, and Prejudice: A Replication," *American Journal of Sociology*, January, 1956, pp. 355–358.

Robison, Joseph B., "Organizations Promoting Civil Rights and Liberties," *Annals of the American Academy of Political and Social Science*, May, 1951, pp. 20–23.

Robison, Joseph B., Mintz, Benjamin, and Rich, Spencer, *Assault upon Freedom of Association*, American Jewish Congress, 1957.

Robison, Sophia M., "Social and Welfare Statistics on the New York Puerto Rican Population," in Jaffe, A. J. (ed.), *Puerto Rican Population of New York City*, Bureau of Applied Social Research, Columbia University, 1954.

Rokeach, Milton, "Generalized Mental Rigidity as a Factor in Ethnocentrism," *Journal of Abnormal and Social Psychology*, July, 1948, pp. 259–278.

Roper, Elmo, *Factors Affecting the Admission of High School Seniors to College*, American Council on Education, 1949.

Roper, Elmo, "Higher Education," *Fortune*, September, 1949, pp. 1–16.

Rose, Arnold M., *Studies in the Reduction of Prejudice*, American Council on Race Relations, 1947.

Rose, Arnold M., *The Negro's Morale*, University of Minnesota Press, 1949.

Rose, Arnold M. (ed.), *Race Prejudice and Discrimination*, Alfred A. Knopf, Inc., 1951.

Rose, Arnold, "The Influence of a Border City Union on the Race Attitudes of Its Members," *Journal of Social Issues*, 1953, vol. 9, No. 1, pp. 23 ff.

Rose, Arnold M., "Intergroup Relations vs. Prejudice," *Social Problems*, October, 1956, pp. 173–176.

Rose, Arnold M., and Rose, Caroline, *America Divided: Minority Group Relations in the United States*, Alfred A. Knopf, Inc., 1948.

Rose, Arnold M., Atelsek, F. J., and McDonald, L. R., "Neighborhood Reactions to Isolated Negro Residents: An Alternative to Invasion and Succession," *American Sociological Review*, October, 1953, pp. 497–507.

Rosenblith, Judy F., "A Replication of 'Some Roots of Prejudice,'" *Journal of Abnormal and Social Psychology*, October, 1949, pp. 470–489.

Rosenthal, Jonas O., "Negro Teachers' Attitudes Toward Desegregation," *Journal of Negro Education*, Winter, 1957, pp. 63–71.

Ross, Malcolm, "The Outlook for a New FEPC," *Commentary*, April, 1947, pp. 301–308.

Ross, Malcolm, *All Manner of Men*, Reynal and Hitchcock, 1948.

Rostow, E. V., "Our Worst Wartime Mistake," *Harper's Magazine*, September, 1945, pp. 193–201.

Routh, F. B., and Anthony, P., "Southern Resistance Forces," *Phylon*, First Quarter, 1957, pp. 50–58.

Rowan, Carl, *How Far from Slavery*, The Minneapolis Star and Tribune Company, 1951.

Rowan, Carl, *Go South to Sorrow*, Random House, Inc., 1957.

Rubin, Morton, *Plantation County*, University of North Carolina Press, 1951.

Rubin, Morton, "Social and Cultural Change in the Plantation Area," *Journal of Social Issues*, 1954, vol. 10, No. 1, pp. 28–35.

Ruppin, Arthur, *The Jews in the Modern World*, The Macmillan Company, 1934.

Ruppin, Arthur, *The Jewish Fate and Future*, The Macmillan Company, 1940.

Rutledge, Edward, "Site Selection, Costs and Interracial Housing," a paper presented to the annual meeting of the National Association of Intergroup Relations Officials, at Milwaukee, Wisconsin, December 2, 1955.

Saenger, Gerhart, *The Social Psychology of Prejudice*, Harper & Brothers, 1953.

Saenger, Gerhart, and Gordon, Norma S., "The Influence of Discrimination on Minority Group Members in Its Relation to Attempts to Combat Discrimination," *Journal of Social Psychology*, February, 1950, pp. 95–120.

Samuel, Maurice, *The Great Hatred*, Alfred A. Knopf, Inc., 1940.

Sanchez, George I., *Concerning Segregation of Spanish-Speaking Children in the Public Schools*, University of Texas, 1951.

Sanford, Nevitt, "Recent Developments in Connection with the Investigation of the Authoritarian Personality," *Sociological Review*, July, 1954, pp. 11–33.

Sartre, Jean-Paul, "Portrait of the Antisemite," *Partisan Review*, Spring, 1946, pp. 163–178.

Schermerhorn, R. A., *These Our People*, D. C. Heath and Company, 1949.

Schermerhorn, R. A., "Power as a Primary Concept in the Study of Minorities," *Social Forces*, October, 1956, pp. 53–56.

Schnepp, G. J., and Yui, A. M., "Cultural and Marital Adjustment of Japanese War Brides," *American Journal of Sociology*, July, 1955, pp. 48–50.

Schreike, B., *Alien Americans*, The Viking Press, Inc., 1936.

Schwartz, Shepard, "Chinese Marriages in New York City, 1931–38," *Race and Racialism*, New School for Social Research, 1948, pp. 29 ff.

Schwarz, Solomon M., *The Jews in the Soviet Union*, Syracuse University Press, 1951.

Scodel, Alvin, and Freedman, Maria Livia, "Additional Observations on the Social Perceptions of Authoritarians and Nonauthoritarians," *Journal of Abnormal and Social Psychology*, January, 1956, pp. 92–95.

Scodel, Alvin, and Mussen, Paul, "Social Perceptions of Authoritarians and Nonauthoritarians," *Journal of Abnormal and Social Psychology*, April, 1953, pp. 181–184.

Seeman, Melvin, "Intellectual Perspective and Adjustment to Minority Status," *Social Problems*, January, 1956, pp. 142–153.

Seidler, M. B., and Ravitz, M. J., "A Jewish Peer Group," *American Journal of Sociology*, July, 1955, pp. 11–15.

Selltiz, Clair, and Wormser, Margot Haas (issue eds.), "Community Self-Surveys: An Approach to Social Change," *Journal of Social Issues*, Spring, 1949.

Sexton, Brendan, "The Intervention of the Union in the Plant," *Journal of Social Issues*, 1953, vol. 9, No. 1, pp. 7–10.

Shapiro, H. L., *Migration and Environment*, Oxford University Press, 1939.

Sherif, Muzafer, *An Outline of Social Psychology*, Harper & Brothers, 1948.

Sherif, Muzafer, and Sherif, Carolyn, *Groups in Harmony and Tension*, Harper & Brothers, 1953.

Shevky, Eshref, and Bell, Wendell, *Social Area Analysis*, Stanford University Press, 1955.

Silcox, C. E., and Fisher, G. M., *Catholics, Jews, and Protestants*, Harper & Brothers, 1934.

Simon, Caroline K., "Causes and Cure of Discrimination," *New York Times Magazine*, May 29, 1949, pp. 10, 34–36.

Simpson, George E., *The Negro in the Philadelphia Press*, University of Pennsylvania Press, 1936.

Simpson, George E., "The Vodun Service in Northern Haiti," *American Anthropologist*, April–June, 1940, pp. 236–254.

Simpson, George E., "Haitian Magic," *Social Forces*, October, 1940, pp. 95–100.

Simpson, George E., "The Belief System of Haitian Vodun," *American Anthropologist*, January–March, 1945, pp. 35–59.

Simpson, George E., "Two Vodun-Related Ceremonies," *Journal of American Folklore*, January–March, 1948, pp. 49–52.

Simpson, George E., "Jamaican Revivalist Cults," *Social and Economic Studies*, December, 1956 (whole issue).

Simpson, George E., and Yinger, J. Milton (eds.), "American Indians and American Life," *Annals of the American Academy of Political and Social Science*, May, 1957 (16 articles).

Sklare, Marshall, *Conservative Judaism: An American Religious Movement*, The Free Press, 1955.

Sklare, Marshall, and Vosk, Marc, *The Riverton Study. How Jews Look at Themselves and Their Neighbors*, American Jewish Committee, 1957.

Slavson, S. R., *An Introduction to Group Therapy*, The Commonwealth Fund, 943.

Slotkin, J. S., "Jewish-Gentile Intermarriage in Chicago," *American Sociological Review*, February, 1942, pp. 34–39.

Slotkin, J. S., "Adjustment in Jewish-Gentile Intermarriages," *Social Forces*, December, 1942, pp. 226–230.

Smith, Bradford, *Americans from Japan*, J. B. Lippincott Company, 1948.

Smith, Charles U., and Prothro, James W., "Ethnic Differences in Authoritarian Personality," *Social Forces*, May, 1957, pp. 334–338.

Smith, F. T., *An Experiment in Modifying Attitudes Toward the Negro*, Teachers College, Columbia University, 1943.

Smith, Lillian, *Killers of the Dream*, W. W. Norton & Company, Inc., 1949.

Smith, Lillian, *Now is the Time*, The Viking Press, Inc., 1955.

Smith, W. C., *Americans in Process*, Edwards Brothers, 1937.

Smith, William G., "The Negro Writer: Pitfalls and Compensations," *Phylon*, Fourth Quarter, 1950, pp. 297–303.

Smythe, Hugh H., "Note on the Racial Ideas of the Japanese," *Social Forces*, March, 1953, pp. 258–260.

Smythe, Hugh H., and Pine, Jerry J., "The Jew in America Since World War II," *Phylon*, First Quarter, 1955, pp. 65–70.

Solomon, Barbara Miller, *Ancestors and Immigrants*, Harvard University Press, 1956.

Sperling, A. P., "A Comparison Between Jews and Non-Jews with Respect to Several Traits of Personality," *Journal of Applied Psychology*, December, 1942, pp. 828–840.

Spero, S. D., and Harris, A. L., *The Black Worker*, Columbia University Press, 1931.

Srole, Leo, "Social Integration and Certain Corollaries: An Exploratory Study," *American Sociological Review*, December, 1956, pp. 709–716.

Starke, Juanita G., "Symbolism and the Negro College," *Phylon*, Fourth Quarter, 1956, pp. 365–373.

Steele, H. Ellsworth, "Jobs for Negroes: Some North-South Plant Studies," *Social Forces*, December, 1953, pp. 152–162.

Stephan, A. Stephen, "Population Ratios, Racial Attitudes, and Desegregation," *Journal of Negro Education*, Winter, 1957, pp. 22–29.

Stephens, Oren, "Revolt on the Delta," *Harper's Magazine*, November, 1941, pp. 656–664.

Sterner, Richard, *The Negro's Share*, Harper & Brothers, 1943.

Stetler, Henry G., *Racial Integration in Public Housing Projects in Connecticut*, Connecticut Commission on Civil Rights, 1955.

Stoddard, Lothrop, *The Rising Tide of Color Against White World-Supremacy*, Charles Scribner's Sons, 1920.

Stonequist, Everett V., *The Marginal Man. A Study in Personality and Culture Conflict*, Charles Scribner's Sons, 1937.

Stouffer, Samuel, Suchman, Edward, DeVinney, Leland, Star, Shirley, and Williams, Robin, Jr., *The American Soldier: Adjustment During Army Life*, Princeton University Press, 1949, vol. 1, pp. 486–599.

Street, James H., *The New Revolution in the Cotton Economy*, University of North Carolina Press, 1957.

Strong, Donald S., *Organized Anti-Semitism in America*, American Council on Public Affairs, 1941.

Strong, Donald S., "The Rise of Negro Voting in Texas," *American Political Science Review*, June, 1948, pp. 510–522.

Sullivan, Patrick L., and Adelson, Joseph, "Ethnocentrism and Misanthropy," *Journal of Abnormal and Social Psychology*, April, 1954, pp. 246–250.

Sussman, M. B., and Yeager, H. C., "Mate Selection Among Negro and

White College Students," *Sociology and Social Research*, September, 1950, pp. 46–49.

Sutherland, Robert L., *Color, Class, and Personality*, American Council on Education, 1942.

Sutker, Solomon, "The Jewish Organizational Elite of Atlanta, Georgia," *Social Forces*, 1952, vol. 31, No. 2, pp. 136–143.

Swanson, Ernst W., and Griffin, John A. (eds.), *Public Education in the South Today and Tomorrow*, University of North Carolina Press, 1955.

Sward, Keith, and Friedman, Meyer, "Jewish Temperament," *Journal of Applied Psychology*, February, 1935, pp. 70–84.

Taba, Hilda, and Van Til, William, *Democratic Human Relations: Promising Practices in Intergroup and Intercultural Education*, National Education Association, 1945.

Taft, Donald R., and Robbins, Richard, *International Migrations*, The Ronald Press Company, 1955.

Talbert, Robert H., *Spanish-Name People in the Southwest and West Fort Worth*, Texas Christian University, Leo Potishman Foundation, 1955.

tenBroek, Jacobus, Barnhart, Edward N., and Matson, Floyd W., *Prejudice, War, and the Constitution*, University of California Press, 1954.

Thomas, Dorothy S., *The Salvage*, University of California Press, 1952.

Thomas, Dorothy S., and Nishimoto, Richard S., *The Spoilage*, University of California Press, 1946.

Thomas, John L., "The Factor of Religion in the Selection of Marriage Mates," *American Sociological Review*, August, 1951, pp. 487–491.

Thomas, W. I., and Znaniecki, Florian, *The Polish Peasant in Europe and America*, Alfred A. Knopf, Inc., 1927, 2 vols.

Thompson, C. H., "Negro Higher and Professional Education in the United States," *Journal of Negro Education*, 1948, vol. 17, pp. 222 ff.

Thompson, E. T. (ed.), *Race Relations and the Race Problem*, Duke University Press, 1939.

Thompson, Hildegard, "Education Among American Indians: Institutional Aspects," *Annals of the American Academy of Political and Social Science*, May, 1957, pp. 95–105.

Tietze, C., and Lewit, S., "Patterns of Family Limitation in a Rural Negro Community," *American Sociological Review*, October, 1953, pp. 563–564.

Tomăsić, D., "The Structure of Balkan Society," *American Journal of Sociology*, September, 1946, pp. 132–140.

Toynbee, Arnold J., *A Study of History*, Oxford University Press, 1934, vol. 1.

Trager, Helen G., and Yarrow, Marian R., *They Learn What They Live: Prejudice in Young Children*, Harper & Brothers, 1952.

Trewhitt, Henry L., "Southern Unions and the Integration Issue," *The Reporter*, October 4, 1956, pp. 25–28.

Tuck, Ruth D., *Not with the Fist*, Harcourt, Brace & Company, 1946.

Turman, James A., and Holtzman, Wayne H., "Attitudes of White and Negro Teachers Toward Non-Segregation in the Classroom," *Journal of Social Psychology*, August, 1955, pp. 61–70.

Turner, Henry C., "Tolerance in Industry: The Record," New York *Times Magazine*, August 24, 1947, pp. 14, 38–39.

Turner, Ralph H., "Relative Position of the Negro Male in the Labor Force of Large American Cities," *American Sociological Review*, August, 1951, pp. 524–529.

Turner, Ralph H., "Foci of Discrimination in the Employment of Non-Whites," *American Journal of Sociology*, November, 1952, pp. 247–256.

Turner, Ralph H., "Negro Job Status and Education," *Social Forces*, October, 1953, pp. 51 ff.

Turner, Ralph H., "Occupational Patterns of Inequality," *American Journal of Sociology*, March, 1954, pp. 437–447.

United States Army Western Defense Command and Fourth Army, *Japanese in the United States, Final Report: Japanese Evacuation from the West Coast*, Government Printing Office, 1943.

Universal Jewish Encyclopedia (Isaac Landman, ed.), 1939, vol. 1, pp. 341–409, "Anti-Semitism."

Valentin, Hugo (trans. by A. G. Chater), *Anti-Semitism Historically and Critically Examined*, The Viking Press, Inc., 1936.

Vance, Rupert B., "The South's Changing Political Leadership," *Journal of Social Issues*, 1954, vol. 10, No. 1, pp. 15–18.

Vickery, William, and Cole, S. G., *Intercultural Education in American Schools*, Harper & Brothers, 1944.

Vickery, William, and Opler, Morris, "A Redefinition of Prejudice for Purposes of Social Science Research," *Human Relations*, 1948, vol. 1, pp. 419–428.

Vinacke, W. Edgar, "Explorations in the Dynamic Processes of Stereotyping," *Journal of Social Psychology*, February, 1956, pp. 105–132.

Voget, Fred, "The American Indian in Transition: Reformation and Status Innovations," *American Journal of Sociology*, January, 1957, pp. 369–378.

Wagley, Charles (ed.), *Race and Class in Rural Brazil*, UNESCO, 1952.

Walker, Margaret, "New Poets," *Phylon*, Fourth Quarter, 1950, pp. 345–346.

Warner, W. Lloyd, "American Caste and Class," *American Journal of Sociology*, September, 1936, pp. 234–237.

Warner, W. Lloyd, Junker, B. H., and Adams, W. A., *Color and Human Nature, Negro Personality Development in a Northern City*, American Council on Education, 1941.

Warner, W. Lloyd, and Lunt, Paul S., *The Social Life of a Modern Community*, Yale University Press, 1941.

Warner, W. Lloyd, and Srole, L., *The Social Systems of American Ethnic Groups*, Yale University Press, 1945.

Washington, Alethea H., "Availability of Education for Negroes in the Elementary School," *Journal of Negro Education*, 1947, vol. 16, pp. 440 ff.

Watson, Goodwin, *Action for Unity*, Harper & Brothers, 1947.

Watson, J. B., and Samora, J., "Subordinate Leadership in a Bicultural Community," *American Sociological Review*, August, 1954, pp. 413–421.

Weales, Gerald, "Pro-Negro Films in Atlanta," *Phylon*, Third Quarter, 1952, pp. 299–300.

Weatherford, W. D., and Johnson, Charles S., *Race Relations*, D. C. Heath and Company, 1934.

Weaver, R. C., *Negro Labor*, Harcourt, Brace & Company, 1946.

Weaver, R. C., "The Economic Status of the Negro in the United States," *Journal of Negro Education*, 1950, vol. 19, pp. 239 ff.

Weaver, R. C., "Recent Developments in Urban Housing and Their Implications for Minorities," *Phylon*, Third Quarter, 1955, pp. 275–282.

Weaver, R. C., "Integration in Public and Private Housing," *Annals of the American Academy of Political and Social Science*, March, 1956, pp. 86–97.

Weeks, H. Ashley, "Differential Divorce Rates by Occupation," *Social Forces*, March, 1943, pp. 334–337.

Weintraub, Ruth G., *How Secure These Rights*, Doubleday & Company, Inc., 1949.

Wells, W. D., Chiaravallo, Gene, and Goldman, Seymour, "Brothers Under the Skin: A Validity Test of the F-Scale," *Journal of Social Psychology*, February, 1957, pp. 35–40.

Wessel, B. B., "Ethnic Family Patterns: The American Jewish Family," *American Journal of Sociology*, May, 1948, pp. 439–442.

West, James, *Plainville, U.S.A.*, Columbia University Press, 1945.

Westie, Frank R., "Negro-White Status Differentials and Social Distance," *American Sociological Review*, October, 1952, pp. 550–558.

Westie, Frank R., "A Technique for the Measurement of Race Attitudes," *American Sociological Review*, February, 1953, pp. 73–78.

White, Walter, *A Man Called White*, The Viking Press, Inc., 1948.

White, Walter, *How Far the Promised Land*, The Viking Press, Inc., 1955.

Wiley, G. M., *Education for Unity*, State Education Department of New York, 1947.

Wilkerson, Doxey, *Special Problems of Negro Education*, Government Printing Office, 1939.

Williams, Robin, Jr., *The Reduction of Intergroup Tensions*, Social Science Research Council, 1947.

Williams, Robin, Jr., and Ryan, Margaret W. (eds.), *Schools in Transition: Community Experiences in Desegregation*, University of North Carolina Press, 1954.

Williams, Robin, Jr., Fisher, Burton R., and Janis, Irving L., "Educational Desegregation as a Context for Basic Social Science Research," *American Sociological Review*, October, 1956, pp. 577–583.

Wilner, D. M., Walkley, R. P., and Cook, S. W., *Human Relations in Interracial Housing*, University of Minnesota Press, 1955.

Winder, Alvin, "White Attitudes Toward Negro-White Interaction in a Number of Community Situations," *Journal of Social Psychology*, August, 1956, pp. 15–32.

Wirth, Louis, *The Ghetto*, University of Chicago Press, 1928.

Wirth, Louis, "Race and Public Policy," *Scientific Monthly*, April, 1944, pp. 302–312.

Wirth, Louis, "The Problem of Minority Groups," in Ralph Linton (ed.),

The Science of Man in the World Crisis, Columbia University Press, 1945, pp. 347–372.

Wish, Harvey, "George Fitzhugh, Conservative of the Old South," *Southern Sketches,* No. 11, 1st series, 1938, pp. 15 ff.

Wood, Arthur L., "Minority-Group Criminality and Cultural Integration," *Journal of Criminal Law and Criminology,* March, 1947, pp. 498–510.

Woods, Sister Frances Jerome, *Cultural Values of American Ethnic Groups,* Harper & Brothers, 1956.

Woodson, C. G., *The Negro Professional Man and the Community,* Association for the Study of Negro Life and History, Inc., 1934.

Woofter, T. J., Jr., *Landlord and Tenant on the Cotton Plantation,* Works Progress Administration, 1936.

Woodward, C. Vann, *The Strange Career of Jim Crow,* Oxford University Press, 1955.

Wright, Richard, *Black Boy,* Harper & Brothers, 1937.

Wright, S. J., "Hampton-Tuskegee Pattern," *Phylon,* 1949, vol. 10, pp. 334–342.

Yinger, J. Milton, "Breaking the Vicious Circle," *Common Ground,* Autumn, 1946, pp. 3–8.

Yinger, J. Milton, *Religion in the Struggle for Power,* Duke University Press, 1946.

Yinger, J. Milton, "Civil Liberties in Crisis," *Common Ground,* Winter, 1949, pp. 3–9.

Yinger, J. Milton, *Religion, Society, and the Individual,* The Macmillan Company, 1957.

Yinger, J. Milton, and Simpson, George E., "The Integration of Americans of Mexican, Puerto Rican, and Oriental Descent," *Annals of the American Academy of Political and Social Science,* March, 1956, pp. 124–131.

Young, Donald, *American Minority Peoples,* Harper & Brothers, 1932.

Young, Donald, *Research Memorandum on Minority Groups in the Depression,* Social Science Research Council, 1937.

Young, Kimball, *Social Psychology,* Appleton-Century-Crofts, 2nd ed., 1944.

Zawadski, Bohdan, "Limitations of the Scapegoat Theory of Prejudice," *Journal of Abnormal and Social Psychology,* April, 1948, pp. 127–141.

Zeligs, R., and Hendrickson, G., "Racial Attitudes of 200 Sixth-Grade Children," *Sociology and Social Research,* September–October, 1933, pp. 26–36.

A great many periodicals carry articles on topics relevant to the subject matter of this book. Among those which most frequently publish valuable papers are the following:

American Anthropologist
American Journal of Sociology
American Sociological Review
Annals of the American Academy of Political and Social Science
Commentary

Crisis
Human Relations
Journal of Abnormal and Social Psychology
Journal of Applied Psychology
Journal of Educational Sociology
Journal of Negro Education
Journal of Negro History
Journal of Psychology
Journal of Social Issues
Journal of Social Psychology
Nairo Reporter
National Jewish Monthly
News from the National Association for the Advancement of Colored People
Phylon
Race Relations Law Reporter
Rights
Social Forces
Social Problems
Sociology and Social Research
Sociometry
Southern School News
Survey (formerly Survey Graphic and Survey Midmonthly)

Indexes

INDEX OF NAMES

INDEX OF SUBJECTS

Civil rights—(*Continued*)
  right of Negroes to serve on juries, 486–487
  right to challenge a juror for race prejudice, 487
  section in the Department of Justice, 487
  statutes, 484–485
  violation of, of Jews, 486
    See also Discrimination; Fair employment practice; Segregation; Supreme Court
Civil Rights Congress and Communist party, 476
Civil service, Act of 1883, 431
  experience of Negroes in, 431–436
Class conflict, use of prejudice in, 119–121
Colleges, and fair educational practices laws, 682–685
  application forms of, 656
  attitudes of students in, toward racial and religious minorities, 656–659
  desegregation of, since May 17, 1954, 672–677
  discrimination in admission policies of, 653–656
  effects of, on prejudice, 767–768
  extracurricular activities in, 658–659
  intergroup education in, 766–768
  Negro, 646–652
  New York City, 678
  regional compacts of southern, 680–682
    See also Education; Negro education; Universities
Colonialism, 138–139
  changes in, 10, 11
Columbia University, College of Physicians and Surgeons, 677, 678, 684
Commerce, Jewish students in, 679
Commission on Interracial Cooperation, 797–798
Common Council for American Unity, 797
Communism, 343
  among Negroes, 281
  imperialism of, 10
  in Germany, 311
Communist party, attempts to recruit Negroes, 281, 473–476
  forces opposing, 476
  Negro membership in, 473
  organizations founded by, 473–476
  "self-determination in the black belt" policy of, 474
Community self-surveys, 768–769
Compromise versus contention in strategies to reduce discrimination, 780–784

Concubinage, 540–546
Congregational denomination and Negroes, 575
Congress of Industrial Organization, Committee to Abolish Discrimination, 799–800
  racial policies of unions in, 399–400, 403, 406
"Consciousness of kind" as source of prejudice, 153
Contact with minority-group members, effects on minorities of, 747–748
  effects on prejudice of, 747–757
  variables controlling influence of, 750–751
CORE (Congress of Racial Equality), 772, 788, 799
Cornell University Medical School, 677, 678, 684
Costs of prejudice, economic, 273–277
  ignorance, 265–267
  international relations, 282–287
  moral ambivalence, 268–273
  political, 277–282
Credit system of the cotton plantation area, 384–385
Crime, and criminal justice for minorities, 508–515
  and "culture conflict," 515
  and police practice, 510–514
  of Mexican-Americans, 510
  of Negroes, 508–513
Crop diversification, 389
Cults, Negro, 575, 576, 577, 581
    See also Negro churches
Culture, influence of, on aggression, 239–241
  prejudice as part of, 71–72, 150–182, 340
"Culture conflict" and crime, 515
Czechoslovakia, minorities policy of, 32, 313–314

Dahomey, 579, 580, 581
Dentists, Negro, 425
  professional training, of Jewish, 679; of Negro, 425, 661, 662, 665
Desegregation, acceptance of and resistance to public school, 623–627
  bus, 483
  churches' interest in, of other institutions, 594–596
  common apprehensions about, 635–636
  cost of opposition to, 274
  evaluation of public school, 636–641
  in Baltimore public schools, 632
  in Catholic churches, 593–594